THE NEW TESTAMENT

GOD'S MESSAGE OF GOODNESS, EASE AND WELL-BEING
WHICH BRINGS
GOD'S GIFTS OF HIS SPIRIT, HIS LIFE, HIS GRACE,
HIS POWER, HIS FAIRNESS,
HIS PEACE AND HIS LOVE

AN EXPANDED AND AMPLIFIED TRANSLATION
CONTAINING MULTIPLE RENDERINGS,
ALTERNATE DEFINITIONS OF GREEK WORDS,
CONTRASTING MANUSCRIPT READINGS,
AND OCCASIONAL
NOTES AND COMMENTS
2019 EDITION

D1288128

BY

JONATHAN PAUL MITCHELL, MA

TABLE OF CONTENTS

Introduction

Acknowledgements

Textual Apparatus

ISBN 978-1-4507-0505-9

INTRODUCTION

[2019 EDITION]

Throughout this version, I have adopted the philosophy of Kenneth Wuest, who said that in his translation he would use as many English words as it takes to give the Greek meaning.

Special Features of the Jonathan Mitchell New Testament

This translation of the Greek New Testament offers:

- multiple renderings of Greek words, presented parenthetically in lightface type, or as a conflation;
- contrasting readings from other New Testament manuscripts are presented, in addition to readings from different eclectic Greek texts and early individual NT manuscripts that present a significant change in the meaning of the text;
- multiple renderings of clauses, phrases and verses, where the optional readings all make sense to the context, with expansions and amplifications presented parenthetically;
- expanded renderings of Greek verbs to show the meanings of their individual tense characteristics;
- auxiliary adverbs are added which indicate the durative, lineal character of verbs in the present tense, the imperfect tense and the future tense. Examples of these explanatory words are: "continuously; constantly; repeatedly; habitually; progressively," accordingly as the contexts suggest. Other examples are: "keep on; continue; one-after-another;"
- rendering the aorist tense (punctiliar action) as either, or both, a simple past tense, or as a simple present tense – a tense that simply presents the fact of the action, apart from whether the action was/is completer or incomplete; as a sudden, or point in time, or snapshot, of the whole action; as indefinite as to kind of action (whether ongoing or completed) – depending on the context;
- rendering the perfect tense as a completed action of the past which continues in effect on into the present time of the writing of the text;
- rendering each verse in boldface, for one complete translation of the verse;
- inserting other well-attested manuscript readings, in brackets;
- a translation that is on the literal side of the literal-to-paraphrase spectrum;
- offering an additional, interpretive paraphrase where the literal rendering of the Greek text seems awkward, or uncertain;
- for continuity of the Hebrew and Christian Scriptures, inserting "[= Yahweh]" into OT quotes, where that Name was in the Hebrew texts;
- rendering many Greek terms by their linguistic elements (morphemes) to present the linguistic ideas behind the roots/stem and prefixes from which the words were built;
- supplies optional functioning of noun and adjective cases, where the context supports these options;
- offering multiple prepositions for the potential functions of noun cases, in prepositional phrase where there is no expressed preposition in the text; example: "to, for, by, in/among; with" before a noun in the dative case; or, with the genitive/ablative case, offering readings that indicate a possessive noun, a kind of relationship with the noun, the noun indicating a source, or, apposition (definition). Examples are: "the Word of God; God's Word; the Word relating to or pertaining to God; the Word from God; the Word, which is God." All of these options are possible from a single spelling of a noun in the genitive/ablative case, or in the dative case;
- this translation offers the reader the opportunity to participate with the Spirit in the various potential readings of a word, a phrase, a clause, a verse – so long as they make sense to the immediate and greater contexts.

On one occasion of multiplying "the loaves and the fishes," after the meal Jesus told His disciples to "gather up the fragments, so that nothing will be lost." This version presents to you many "fragments" of meaning of the Greek text that have often been lost to the reader of the common translations, or of "thought translations," or of translations that present "dynamic equivalents."

This is a work that seeks to give the reader some involvement in the process of translating by presenting a range of semantic meanings of significant Greek words in the midst of the text. Expansions or amplifications, and optional renderings, are placed in parentheses, in lightface font, and normally come after the word "or," followed by a colon. 1 Corinthians 7:19 provides an example:

> **The circumcision is nothing, and the uncircumcision is nothing – but to the contrary [what matters is the] observing and keeping of the goals implanted from God** (or: of the impartation of the finished product within, which is God; or: God's inward directives to [His] end).

Readings from other manuscripts (MSS) that differ from the eclectic texts (texts that are a compilation of what are considered by textual scholars to be the best readings from the many available manuscripts) are normally enclosed in lightface brackets, but are sometimes conflated (i.e., joined together) into my version. Also enclosed in brackets are words that I have added to make the English rendering sensible (see above example), as well as occasional notes, comments and suggested possible meanings of the text.

May I suggest that in reading a passage, read each verse first in the bold type without the additional meanings or alternate readings. Then read it with those other word meanings, or in the alternate rendering. Prayerfully consider the possible meanings of the verse, and let the Holy Spirit (or: set-apart Breath-effect) give you understanding, insights and revelation.

Koine Greek is an inflected language. The functions of nouns, adjectives, etc., are indicated by their spelling – which also determines the case for each use. However, the cases – especially the genitive and the dative – have a variety of functions. The translator must determine which function the author intended. This is normally determined by the sense of the context in which the word is used. Sometimes the function is clear, but many times it is not. To allow the reader to have some freedom from the translator's bias or personal choice, I have parenthetically included the other options. While reading the text, be aware that these other options exist. A classic example, presented in W.E. Chamberlain's *An Exegetical Grammar of the Greek New Testament*, is Romans 8:24. Here is a prepositional phrase with no expressed preposition, but only the word "expectation (or: expectant hope)" in the dative case. The question is, which function of the dative is appropriate to the context: the instrumental, the locative, or other functions? The following rendering of this verse is my solution (showing the optional prepositions underlined, for this example):

> 24. **For <u>in</u> the expectation and <u>with</u> hope we are suddenly made whole and healthy** (or: You see, <u>by</u> the expectation we are delivered and saved; or: For we were at one point rescued <u>to</u> expectation; or: To be sure, we were kept safe <u>for</u> this expectation)! **Now expectation** (or: expectant hope) **being continuously seen or observed is not expectation or hope, for who continues hoping in expectation for what he also constantly sees or observes?**

Often all the options can be used, thus amplifying and expanding the understanding of a particular phrase. This verse also gives the different meanings of the Greek word *sōdzō*, which can mean "made whole and healthy, delivered, saved or rescued," as given in the alternate renderings above, as well as "to keep safe; to restore to the original condition."

The function of the genitive case can be to show possession, indicate source, describe qualities or characteristics, state relationship, give reference or concern, or presents definition or identity (also called "apposition"). I have often presented this last function using the construction "which is," rather than "of." And example of this is found in John 2:21:

> **Yet that One** (= He) **had been laying [things] out concerning, and speaking about,**

the Sanctuary <u>which is</u> His body (or: the Divine habitation of the body belonging to, and <u>which is</u>, Him; the inner Temple pertaining to His whole corporeal and material substance).

This gives the correct meaning of what John said. I have also put this as a possible translation of the genitive in such cases as John 1:29:

God's Lamb (or: the Lamb from God; the Lamb having the character and qualities of God; or, in apposition: the Lamb <u>which is</u> God).

As well as giving expanded meanings, in places I have also conflated my text by simply giving more than one meaning of a Greek word, joined by the word "and." For example, the Greek word *dunamis* means equally "power" and "ability." To aid in readability I often render this word "**power and ability**."

The Greek word *pas* (all) is both masculine and neuter in some of its forms. With many translations you will only find the neuter rendered, for example with a plural, "all things." This version gives renderings of both the neuter and the masculine, when such is the case, translating the masculine as "all people; all humanity; or all mankind." An example of this is found in 1 Corinthians, chapter 13,

7. **[Love] continuously covers all mankind; it is habitually loyal to all humanity; it constantly has an expectation for all mankind; it is continuously remaining under and giving support to all people.**
(or, since "all" can also be neuter: It progressively puts a protecting roof over all things; it is habitually trusting in, and believing for, all things; it is continually hoping in or for all things; it keeps on patiently enduring all things.)

The Greek word *aiōn* has been rendered "age" or "eon," or "an indefinite period of time," and its adjective form *aionios* is rendered "eonian," following the lead of the Concordant Version, together with parenthetical expansions such as "having the character and qualities of the Age [of Messiah]," or "of and for the ages," following Weymouth's original work. An example is John 17:

3. **"Now THIS is** (or: exists being) **eonian life** (life of and for the ages; life pertaining to the Age [of Messiah])**: namely, that they may progressively come to intimately and experientially know You, the only true and real** (genuine) **God – and Jesus Christ, Whom You send forth as an Emissary** (or: as well as Jesus [as the] Anointed One, whom You sent off as a Representative).

When an individual manuscript (MS), or a group of manuscripts (MSS), has a reading that is different from the eclectic texts which I am using, at times I conflate the readings, since this is a practice found in some of the manuscripts and is done in creating an eclectic text. The Greek texts that I have used are: Nestle-Aland, 27th Ed.; Westcott and Hort; Tasker; Panin; Griesbach; and the Concordant Greek Text. My understanding of Koine Greek has been influenced by many scholars, beyond my initial course of study at Arizona State College, Flagstaff, in 1962. Especially influential have been A.T. Robertson, Kenneth Wuest, William Barclay, Marvin Vincent, and the scholars of the Concordant Publishing Concern. The lexicons which I used were those by Liddell and Scott; J.H. Thayer; E.W. Bullinger; Baur, Arnt and Gingrich; and by Timothy Friberg, Barbara Friberg and Neva Miller. The *Theological Dictionary of the New Testament*, along with the works of James Strong, Robert Young, Ray Summers, Dana and Mantey, W.D. Chamberlain, Ronald Ward, and R.C. Trench should also be mentioned. Some words I researched through their usage in the Greek translation of the Old Testament, commonly called *The Septuagint* (LXX). Others I have rendered based upon the meanings of their Greek elements (or, morphemes: the smallest unit of meaning in a language).

It is impossible to translate without some amount of interpretation and latent personal bias. I have endeavored to produce what I believe is an honest translation, and have tried to overcome any personal bias via the use of multiple renderings. Where possible, I have stayed close to the literal side of the translating spectrum. I have occasionally moved to the paraphrase side, but I put these in parentheses, following an "=" symbol. These paraphrases are only one suggested possible idiomatic rendering, and by their very nature include a certain amount of interpretation. They should be considered only as a potentially viable idea, to assist in understanding the literal.

An example of my use of auxiliary words is to insert "continuously, keep on, habitually, repeatedly, normally, presently, constantly or progressively" with the Greek imperfect, present and future tenses, which are durative, and describes continued, repeated or progressive action (also called "lineal action"). Thus readers will know, for example, what the writer meant when choosing the present tense rather than the aorist.

There are divided opinions among scholars regarding the aorist tense, which is not really a verb "tense" at all, e.g., in comparison to English verbs. This is a "fact" tense which gives no indication of the kind of action of the verb. Many translate this as a simple past tense; others as a simple present tense. I have presented both options, e.g., "do (or: did)." In some cases I have also followed scholars who greatly emphasized the punctiliar (or: point) aspect of this tense by adding such descriptive words as "at once," or "suddenly," or "at some point," according to what I perceive that the context calls.

This work has been a labor of love... a love for the Word, for the Truth and for people. It began as a quest to better know the Scriptures, but it has become a journey into the heart of our Father. What started as a personal challenge grew into a desire to share the wonders that I found in this inexhaustible Word. This is by no means a finished work, but continues to be an ongoing and unfolding revelation. My prayer is that the One who makes all things real, the "set-apart Breath-effect," will breathe these words into each and every heart that reads them. May God use this work to bring blessings to each reader, and to bring His reign into every heart.

For God's glory alone,
Jonathan Paul Mitchell
Surprise, AZ
2019

ACKNOWLEDGEMENTS

I first and foremost want to thank my wife, Lynda, for her love, prayer, patience, selflessness, longsuffering and kindness to me as I spent countless hours of our life engaged in study, research, the translation and ongoing minor revisions of this version, and for her help in proof reading and with the final production. I want to thank my father, Harper Brown Mitchell, for his introduction of Koine Greek to me when I was a child, for his inspiration to study Greek words, and for his copy of A Manual Grammar of the Greek New Testament, (Macmillan, 1955) by Dana and Mantey, which I began studying as a teen. I wish to thank my grandfather, Scott Anderson, for his worn copy of The Emphatic Diaglott. These two books were central roots of this work.

I wish to acknowledge certain scholars who, over the years, have enriched, guided and empowered me through their works. I pay tribute to Kenneth Wuest, and to The Amplified Bible by describing my version as "Expanded and Amplified," for these had a lasting impact on my life and my study of the Greek New Testament. The works of A.T. Robertson, Robert Young, William Barclay, R.C. Trench, Marvin Vincent, E.W. Bullinger, A.E. Knoch and the scholars who produced the Concordant Literal New Testament are high on my list of those who have taught me Koine Greek, since I took Beginning NT Greek at Arizona State College, Flagstaff, AZ, in 1962.

I want to acknowledge Rudolf Bultmann (Theology of the New Testament, Scribner, 1955) for the idea to re-introduce the Old English word "rightwised" (turned in the right direction) and its cognates, for the Greek dikaiosunē and its cognates; to recognize William Douglass Chamberlain (An Exegetical Grammar of the Greek New Testament, Macmillan, 1958) for the inspiration to expand my rendering of this word as "in accord with the Way pointed out." Douglas A. Campbell (The Deliverance of God: An Apocalyptic Rereading of Justification in Paul, Eerdmans, 2009) informed my decision to include the meaning, "eschatological deliverance" for Paul's use of this word. Ronald A. Ward, Hidden Meaning in the New Testament (F.H. Revell, 1969), has enriched this work. The suggested dating at the end of each book and letter is based on John A.T. Robinson, Redating the New Testament (The Westminster Press, 1976). My collection of translations, over the past fifty-five years, has consciously, and not doubt subconsciously, influenced this work. Further examples are: Rotherham's The Emphasized Bible; Young's Literal Translation; Charles Williams' A Translation in the Language of the People; Stern's Jewish New Testament; and more recently, Ann Nyland's The Source New Testament – these as well as the common versions and lesser-known translations were often sought as a reference when dealing with difficult verses. Dr. Nyland's work occasionally spurred further research on specific words. My friend Mike Davenport's research enlightened many Greek words. I have given occasional renderings gleaned from Paul Tillich's 3-Vol., Systematic Theology and A Complete History of Christian Thought, and cited short quotes from Bruce Chilton's Rabbi Jesus, Doubleday, 2000. I am grateful to Kenneth E. Bailey (Jesus Through Middle Eastern Eyes: Cultural Studies in the Gospels, IVP, 2008), to Walter Wink's works, and to Dallas Willard's, The Divine Conspiracy.

I am grateful for my friend Don Luther, for the idea of using **boldface** type, for technical support, for proofing on the first edition, and for years of encouragement. My friend Eddie Browne, a Greek scholar and fellow translator, helped me to think outside the "box" when approaching a word or passage; his influence frequently appears here. I am grateful for my sister, Rebecca Mitchell, for encouragement and proof reading, as well as for my son Joshua Mitchell for his feedback on my renderings, his technical support in the final phases of this production, and for being our webmaster. I want to recognize my friend Kenneth Greatorex for proof-reading my first draft, and also my friend, the theologian and teacher, John Gavazzoni for insightful input into the work. I thank T. Everett Denton for Hebrews Fulfilled, From Flawed to Flawless, (2011) with its studied insights, and for its being a catalyst for my recent honing of the renderings in the book of Hebrews. We give thanks for Petrus Vermaak for his creations of ebooks of all of our works.

Jonathan Mitchell, 2019

ABBREVIATIONS and TEXTUAL APPARATUS

ABBREVIATIONS:

MS: manuscript; MSS: manuscripts
LXX: The Septuagint – Greek version of the Old Testament
Gen., Ex., Mat., Rom., etc.: commonly accepted indicators of the books of the Bible
Aleph, A, B, C, D, Ψ, etc., indicate an individual codex or MS
p: signifies that the MS is a papyrus MS
Q: a reference to a Dead Sea Scroll text or fragment (e.g., 4Q521)
it: all or the majority of the Old Latin witnesses
TR: *Textus Receptus* (the "Received Text;" the "Majority Text")
cf: confer and compare
JM: translations of the LXX by the author
TDNT: *Theological Dictionary of the New Testament*

APPARATUS:

Brackets, [ ]'s, have been used for the following situations:
    to give a reading based upon other MSS.
    to insert notes or comments into the text
    to insert words to aid in the reading of the English version
    to indicate the reference of a quote from the Old Testament
    to insert explanations

Parentheses, ( )'s, have been used for the following situations:
    to give other possible meanings of a Greek word
    to give alternate renderings of phrases or verses
    to give a potential idiomatic translations

"=" has been placed before words for the following situations:
    to signifies that the following is a potential idiomatic translation, or paraphrase
    to give another spelling of a name or a suggested equivalent name
    to give a Hebrew equivalent of a word or name
    to give an explanatory note

OTHER PUBLISHED WORKS BY THE AUTHOR

PETER, PAUL & JACOB, Comments on First Peter, Philippians, Colossians, First Thessalonians, Second Thessalonians, First Timothy, Second Timothy, Titus, Jacob (James) [Paperback/Kindle/Nook]

JOHN, JUDAH, PAUL & ?, Comments on First John, Second John, Third John, Judah (Jude), Hebrews, Galatians [Paperback/Kindle/Nook]

JUST PAUL, Comments on Romans [Paperback/Kindle/Nook]

PETER'S ENCORE & LATER PAUL, Comments on Second Peter & Ephesians [Paperback/Kindle/Nook]

THE END of the OLD & THE BEGINNING of the NEW, Comments On REVELATION [Paperback]

Available from Harper Brown Publishing, www.jonathanmitchellnewtestament.com
Select works above created in Kindle & Nook editions, courtesy of Petrus Vermaak

MATTHEW

1. **A scroll of a lineage and birth** (or: genesis; origin; genealogy) **of Jesus Christ** (or: Jesus [the] Anointed One; = Yashua [the] Messiah) **– son of David; son of Abraham.** [note: the term "son" can mean "a descendant," or, "one having the qualities and characteristics of"]

2. **Abraham generated and became the father of Isaac; then Isaac produces Jacob, and then Jacob produced Judah and his brothers.**
3. **Now Judah produced Perez and Zerah from out of Tamar, then Perez produced Hezron, and Hezron begat Aram** (= Ram).
4. **Then Aram** (Ram) **produced Amminadab, Amminadab sired Nahshon, and Nahshon effected Salmon's birth.**
5. **Later Salmon generated Boaz from out of Rahab, then Boaz produced Obed from out of Ruth and Obed begat Jesse.**
6. **Now [it was] Jesse [who] effected the birth of David, the king.**

And then David caused the birth of Solomon from out of the woman (= wife) **[that had] belonged to Uriah.**
7. **Later Solomon fathered Rehoboam, next Rehoboam begat Abijah, and Abijah generated Asa.**
8. **Now Asa effected the birth of Jehoshaphat** (or: Joshaphat), **then Jehoshaphat produced Jehoram and Jehoram caused the birth of Uzziah.**
9. **Later Uzziah produced Jotham, next Jotham begat Ahaz, then Ahaz generated Hezekiah.**
10. **Now Hezekiah produced Manasseh, Manasseh produced Amos** (or: Amon), **and Amos** (Amon) **begat Josiah.**
11. **Then Josiah generated Jechoniah and his brothers upon the [occasion of] the change of abode** (= deportation and exile) **to Babylon.**

12. **Now after the change of abode** (deportation; exile) **to Babylon, Jechoniah begat Shealtiel, then Shealtiel produced Zerubbabel,**
13. **Zerubbabel generated Abiud** (or: Abihud), **Abiud produced Eliakim, and Eliakim sired Azor.**
14. **Then Azor begets Zadok, Zadok produces Achim, and Achim fathers Eliud.**
15. **Later Eliud causes the birth of Eleazar, then Eleazar generates Matthan, and Matthan produces Jacob.**
16. **Now [it was] Jacob [who] fathered Joseph, the husband of Mary – from out of whom Jesus, the One being normally called Christ** (or: termed Anointed [= Messiah]), **was given birth.**
17. **Consequently, all the generation from Abraham until David [were] fourteen generations, and from David until the change of abode** (the deportation and exile) **to Babylon [were] fourteen generations, and from the change of abode to Babylon until the Christ [were] fourteen generations.**

18. **Now the birth** (genesis; origin) **of Jesus Christ was in this way: During her being engaged and pledged** (contracted; espoused) **in marriage to Joseph, before the [situation for] them to come together, Mary – His mother – was found continuing in holding One** (as presently having [Him]) **within [her] womb** (= was discovered to be pregnant) **from out of a Set-apart Breath-effect** (or: from out of the midst of [the] Holy Spirit; or: from a Sacred Breath).
19. **However Joseph, her husband, continuing in being a fair person** (a just and humane man who lived in accord with the Way pointed out, with fairness to do the right thing), **and not purposing, intending or wanting** (or: being unwilling) **to make a public show, exhibit or**

example of her, was disposed with a desire and a resolve to secretly (covertly; i.e., without witnesses or need of giving proof) **loose her away** (or: release and dismiss her; divorce her).

20. **Yet during his inward passion about these things** (his reflection on his strong emotions and in heated pondering of the situation; or: his anger, disappointment and frustration about these [developments]) – **note and consider this! – an agent of [the] Lord** [= Yahweh's messenger], **down from and in the sphere of** (or: in accord with; in correspondence to; = in) **a dream, was set in clear light and made to appear to him, then saying, "Joseph, son of David** (= descendent of, or one with the qualities of, David), **you should not be afraid** (or: be caused to fear; be wary) **to at once take to your side, accept and receive Mary** [other MSS: Mariam], **your wife! You see, the One within the midst of her, being generated and produced from out of Breath-effect** (or: [the] Spirit) **exists being** (or: is) **Set-apart and Holy** (or: the One being brought to birth within her continues being forth from the midst of a Sacred Breath as His origin). 21. **"Now she will proceed giving birth to** (or: will be bringing forth) **a Son, and you will proceed calling His name Jesus** [= Yeshua/Yahshua, or Joshua; in Hebrew: the Savior is Yahweh], **for he will progressively restore His people to health and wholeness** (will salvage, rescue, save and deliver His people and return them to their original state and condition), **away from their failures to hit the target** (from their mistakes, errors, deviations and sins).**"

. 22. **Now this whole [occurrence; situation] has happened and has come into existence to the end that the thing, or situation, being spoken by [the] LORD** [= Yahweh] **through the prophet would** (or: could) **be fulfilled, [which] continues saying,**
23. **"Look and consider! The Virgin will proceed holding** (having) **one within the womb** (= The young woman of marriageable age will become pregnant) **and then will proceed giving birth to a Son, and they will repeatedly call His name 'Emmanuel,'"** [Isa. 7:14] **which is normally being translated and interpreted, "God [is] with us."** (or: "God Himself {literally: The God} [is present] with us.")

24. **Then Joseph, upon being awakened from sound sleep, did as the Lord's agent** (= the messenger of Yahweh) **had directed** (or: arranged toward) **him: he took his wife to his side** (or: he accepted and received his wife; = married her and took her home), 25. **and yet he continued having no intimate experience [with] or [sexual] knowing [of] her until [the situation] where she gave birth to a** [other MSS: her firstborn] **Son and he called His name Jesus** [= Joshua: Yahweh is the Deliverer; the Healer-Restorer-Savior is Yahweh].

CHAPTER 2

1. **Now pertaining to Jesus – being born within [the town of] Bethlehem, of the Judean [district], during the days of Herod the king – note and consider this: Great ones** (magi: from the Persian *magus* = great ones, who were often Persian, of the Zoroastrian priestly caste; interpreters of dreams; astrologers; royal spiritual advisors; or: magicians) **from eastern regions birthed their presence into Jerusalem** [Hebrew: City or Occupation of Peace and Wholeness]. 2. **They kept on saying, "Where is He being the one born 'King of the Judeans'? You see, we saw His star** (or: luminous heavenly body; meteor; flame of light) **in [its] rising** (or: within the East, the place of rising; or: we, [being] in the east, saw His star), **and we come** (or: came) **to do obeisance** (or: to kiss toward, fall down and give reverence, worship and pay homage) **to Him."** 3. **Now, upon hearing [of it], King Herod was shaken** (disturbed; unsettled; agitated; irritated with anxiety; stirred up) **– as well as all Jerusalem, along with him!** 4. **Then on gathering together all the chief** (or: ranking) **priests and scribes** (theologians; experts in the Law and Torah) **of the People** [= those of the Jewish culture and religion], **he, one after another, repeatedly investigated from them, ascertaining beside them where the Christ** (the Anointed One; = the Messiah) **is, by tradition, being born.** 5. **So they said to him, "Within Bethlehem** [Hebrew: House of Bread], **of the Judean [district], for thus it stands written through the prophet,** 6. **'And you, Bethlehem, [in the] land of Judah, are by no means least among the leaders** (= leading cities) **of Judah, for from out of you will proceed coming forth a**

Leader and Mentor, which very One will shepherd (= guide, nourish, care for and protect) **My People, Israel.'"** [Mic. 5:1]

7. **Thereupon Herod, at that time, secretly and covertly calling the "great ones"** (the magi), **ascertained accurately** (exactly) **from them the time** (= the date) **of the star's continued appearing and shining** (or: of the appearing star; = How long has the star been appearing since its rising in the East? [Vincent's rendering is similar]).

8. **So then, sending them into Bethlehem, he said, "As you are going on your way, you men make a diligent search for [him] and inquire exactly concerning the little boy, while examining [the situation]. Now whenever** (or: as soon as) **you may find [him], report back to me so that, upon coming, I also can myself do it obeisance** (or: pay homage to him)."

9. **Now they, upon hearing from the king, journeyed on their way and – note and consider this! – the star which they saw in [its] rising** (or: within the East, the place of rising; or: perceived [when being] in the East) **was still leading the way ahead of them** (or: began preceding them and kept on in front of them) **until coming above where the young Boy was, [and] it was caused to stand** (or: to take a stand; = made to stop; or: was established).

10. **Now upon seeing the star, they experienced joy – great joy.**

11. **Then, when coming into the house, they saw the little Boy with Mary, His mother, and at once falling down, they did obeisance, so as to pay homage and worship Him. And upon opening up their treasure-chests, they brought to Him their offerings** (approach-presents)**: gold; frankincense; myrrh.**

12. **However, upon being communicated useful and needed advice** (or: an oracle; a divine warning and message; a response to someone who consults) **– down from** (or: as a result of; in correspondence to) **a dream – not to return** (to not bend [their path] back) **toward Herod, they withdrew from the region** (vacated the area) **and returned into their country through another road** (path; way).

13. **Now, upon their withdrawing from the region [of Bethlehem?] and returning into their country, – note and consider this! – an agent from [the] LORD** [= Yahweh's messenger] **progressively makes himself visible** (or: as was the custom, is again made to appear) **down from** (or: in association with) **a dream to** (or: in) **Joseph, proceeding in saying, "Upon being roused, and getting up, take along the young Boy – as well as His mother – and progressively flee into Egypt. Then continue being** (or: existing) **there until I can** (or: should) **speak to you, for Herod proceeds about to be continuously seeking the young Boy, his purpose being to destroy Him!"**

14. **So, upon being aroused and getting up, he took along the young Boy and His mother – by night – and withdrew from the area, into Egypt.**

15. **And He continued being there until the termination** (or: the finishing act) **of Herod, to the end that the [oracle; prophecy] being spoken by [the] LORD** [= Yahweh] **could be fulfilled, [which] continues saying,**

"**I call** (or: summon; called) **My Son from out of the midst of Egypt.**" [Hos. 11:1]

16. **Then Herod, seeing** (= realizing) **that he was played as a fool** (duped; tricked; treated with scorn) **by the great ones** (magi; interpreters of dreams; astrologers; royal spiritual advisors), **was extremely furious** (was caused to breathe violently in a heat of passion; was enraged), **so, dispatching [soldiers]** (or: sending off agents), **he took up** (= put to death) **all the boys within Bethlehem and in all its boundaries** (= districts; surrounding areas) **– those from two years and under** (or: younger), **corresponding to the time which he had accurately ascertained from those great ones** (magi).

17. **At that time the [oracle; prophecy] being spoken through Jeremiah the prophet, [which] continues saying,**

18. "**A sound** (or: voice) **is heard within Ramah: shrieking, weeping** (sobbing, lamenting and mourning) **as well as much wailing** (loud expression of anguish);

Rachel continuously weeping [for; over] her children [= the descendents of Joseph and Benjamin], **and she continued refusing to be called alongside to receive comfort and consolation, because they are not** (do not continue existing)."
[Jer. 31:15]

19. **Now upon Herod's coming to his end** (finishing his course), **– note and consider this! – an agent of [the] LORD** [= Yahweh's messenger] **progressively makes himself visible** (or: as was the custom, is again made to appear) **down from a dream to Joseph** (or: in association with a dream in Joseph), **within Egypt,**
20. **proceeding in saying, "Upon being roused, and getting up, take along the young Boy – as well as His mother – and proceed on your way into the land of Israel, for the ones habitually seeking the soul** (conscious life) **of the young Boy have experienced the extinction of life, and are dead."**
21. **So he, being roused and getting up, takes along the young Boy and His mother, and enters into the land of Israel.**
22. **Yet, upon hearing that Archelaus is now reigning as king of Judea in the place of his father Herod, he was made to fear** (or: became afraid; was made wary) **to go off to that place. And then, being communicated useful and needed advice** (or: an oracle; a divine warning or message) **– down from** (or: in correspondence to; as a result of; in association with) **a dream – he withdrew from the region and departed into the districts of Galilee,**
23. **and coming into a city being normally called** (or: termed) **Nazareth, he settled down in a home – so that the [oracle; prophecy] being spoken through the prophets could** (or: would; should) **be fulfilled, that "He will habitually be called a Nazarene [Hebrew: a sprout; a shoot]."**

CHAPTER 3

1. **Now in those days** [i.e., years later, when Jesus would have come to be known as a Nazarene], **John, the Immerser** (or: Baptist; the one who immerses), **is repeatedly coming to be at the side, progressively birthing himself** (= making an appearance) **in the midst of the wilderness** (within the uninhabited area; in the desert) **of the Judean [district], continually making public proclamation as a herald,** [* cf Rom. 12:2]
2. **habitually saying, "You folks be continuously and progressively changing your thinking – change your perceptions, frame of mind, mode of thought and state of consciousness*, and turn back [to God, in a new direction], because the reign and dominion of the heavens**
      (the expression and effect of kingdom rule which has its source in the atmospheres; the activity of exercising the sovereignty which exists being 'the heavens'; the reigning [of the King] which pertains to the heavens; the kingdom which belongs to and comes from the atmosphere; the influence of the sovereignty which is 'the heavens') **has approached and is now near at hand and is close enough to touch** (= has arrived and is now accessible)!"
3. **You see, this is the man being spoken [of]** (or: this is the one [= declaration, or, prophecy] being spoken) **through Isaiah the prophet, continuing in saying,**
      "A voice! One repeatedly crying out (shouting; exulting; exclaiming; imploring): **'Within the midst of the wilderness** (desert; desolate place; abandoned and uninhabited region) **you folks prepare and make ready the road of [the] LORD** (or: the path whose source is [Yahweh]; the Way whose character is that of, and which pertains to, [the] Owner [= Yahweh])! **Be progressively constructing** (making) **His highway well-placed and straight.'"** [Isa. 40:3] (or: "A sound! One is continuously crying out within the midst of the desert: you folks prepare the road… His thoroughfare…")

4. **Now John himself was in the habit of having his clothing of woven camel's hair with a leather belt** (or: a girdle made of an animal skin) **around his waist and loins, and his nourishment continued being locusts and wild honey.**
5. **At that time [folks from] Jerusalem, all the Judean [area], and the region around the Jordan [River] were traveling out to** (or: toward) **him in a steady stream,**

6. **and they were one after another being immersed** (baptized) **by him in the Jordan River, while in turn openly confessing** (speaking out in agreement with) **their failures** (their mistakes, sins, deviations and failures to hit the target).

7. **Now upon seeing many of the Pharisees and Sadducees** [two religious and political sects of the Jewish culture] **repeatedly or in turn coming upon the immersion** (baptism) **[event], he said to them, "O offspring** (progeny; brood) **of vipers** (poisonous snakes)**! Who secretly pointed out to you people** (gave you a private, confidential suggestion) **to flee, so as to escape, away from the impending inherent fervor** (the internal swelling that gives rise to an impulse and mental bent which may be expressed in strong emotion, such as anger or wrath; a vigorous upsurge of [God's, or human,] nature) **which is now progressively about to occur?**
8. **"Produce, then, fruit which has a corresponding value to, and is appropriate of, a change in thinking, attitude and state of consciousness, as well as a turn [toward God].**
9. **"Furthermore, do not presume to be habitually saying among yourselves, 'We continue having Abraham [as] a father,' for I am now saying to you that God continues able** (or: constantly has power) **to at once raise up** (or: awaken) **children to Abraham** (or: for Abraham; in Abraham) **from out of these stones!**
10. **"Now you see, the axe is already continuing lying [being focused] toward** (or: facing toward) **the root of the trees. Therefore, every tree not habitually** (repeatedly; = seasonally) **producing beautiful** (ideal; fine) **fruit is customarily being cut out [of the orchard or garden], and is normally thrown into a fire.** [comment: to be used for fuel; also: prefigures AD 70]
11. **"I myself, on the one hand, continue immersing you folks in water, [which proceeds] into the midst of a change in thinking** (a change of perception, attitude, frame of mind, way of thinking, mode of thought, in state of consciousness, as well as a turning back [to Yahweh]). **On the other hand, the One progressively coming close after me is** (exists being) **stronger than I, Whose sandals I am not competent** (or: adequate) **to lift up and carry off. He, Himself, will proceed immersing** (baptizing) **you folks within the midst of a set-apart Breath-effect and Fire** (or: will repeatedly submerge you to the point of saturation, in union with [the] Holy Spirit, even to the permeation of a Sacred Attitude, as well as with [the] Fire) –
12. **"Whose winnowing fork** (or: shovel) **[is] within His hand, and He will proceed thoroughly cleaning up** (clearing, scouring and cleansing) **His threshing floor and then will progressively gather** (bring together) **His grain into the storehouse** (granary; barn), **yet the chaff** (straw and husks) **He will continue completely burning, in an inextinguishable Fire."**
> [cf Ezk. 36:26-27; 37:14; 39:29; Isa. 44:3; Joel 2:28; comment: a prophecy aimed at the Judean leadership; chaff, a figure of the old covenant and the first Adam (1 Cor. 15:45), is the part of the plant that bore the Grain, but is no longer useful, as food]

13. **At that time Jesus progressively births Himself** (or: emerges) **from the Galilee [province; region], coming to be at the side at the Jordan [River], [and coming] toward John for the purpose of being immersed by him** (or: in order to be baptized under him).
14. **Now John kept on trying to completely dissuade and prevent Him, repeatedly saying, "I, myself, continue having a need to be immersed** (baptized) **by, and under, You! And yet** *You* **are now coming to** *me***?!"**
15. **But, decidedly responding, Jesus said to him, "Let this situation flow its course and send [Me] off, right now** (at present), **for it is in this way proper and fitting for us to fulfill all that accords with eschatological deliverance in the Way pointed out, making full 'being turned in the right direction,' righting covenantal relationship." Then he let the moment flow on, and proceeded to allow Him** (or: At that point [John] yields, and sends Him forth).
16. **Now upon being immersed** (baptized), **Jesus, set for goodness** (placed for well-being), **immediately stepped back up from the water – and now look and consider! – the heavens at once opened back up again!** [or, with other MSS: the atmospheres were opened up to Him!] **Then He saw God's Spirit** (Breath-effect, which is God; a Breath from God) **– as if it were a dove steadily descending – progressively coming upon Him.** [cf Gen. 1:2]
17. **And then – look and consider! – a Voice** (or: sound) **from out of the midst of the atmospheres** (or: the skies and the heavens), **repeatedly saying, "This is My Son, the Beloved One in Whom I take pleasure and imagine thoughts of well-being** (or: This One exists being My dearly loved and esteemed Son, in Whom I approve)**!"**

CHAPTER 4

1. **Thereupon Jesus was led up into the wilderness by the Breath-effect** (or: was at once brought {or: guided} back again, under the Spirit, into the lonely, desolate and uninhabited region) **to be examined, tested, tried, put to the proof, and put through an ordeal under and by the one who thrusts [something] through [folks]** (or: the *devil*; the prejudiced adversary; the slanderous opponent; the backbiting false accuser; or: by that which was cast through [Him]).
2. **And after fasting forty days and forty nights, He subsequently experienced hunger** (or: felt famished).
3. **Then, upon approaching and facing [Him], the examiner** (the one continuously testing and bringing ordeals) **said to Him, "Since You are God's Son** (or: If you continue existing being a son of, and from, God), **speak so that these stones can become** (or: should come to be) **loaves of bread."**
4. **Yet He, making a discerning reply, said, "It has been written,**
    'Mankind (or: The human) **will not be habitually living on bread, alone, but rather on every utterance** (gush-effect; result of a saying; effect of a flow; declaration; spoken word) **which is constantly going forth** (or: proceeding out) **through God's [=** Yahweh's] **mouth.'"** [Deut. 8:3]

5. **At that time, the adversary** (the one who thrusts [something] through folks; the *devil*) **proceeds in taking Him along into the set-apart** (holy) **City, and then sets** (or: placed; stationed; stands) **Him upon the little wing of the Temple complex** (or: court; grounds),
6. **and it proceeds saying to Him, "Since You are God's Son** (or: If you exist being a son of, and from, God), **hurl** (fling; cast) **Yourself down, for it has been written,**
    'He will constantly give inner direction (or: progressively impart the goal, an inner-purposed aim and a united, centered destiny) **to His agents** (or: messengers) **about** (concerning) **You,' and, 'They will repeatedly lift You up** (or: = catch You) **on [their] hands** (or: = so as to carry You) **so that You would never strike Your foot against a stone** (or: = so that you can at no time stumble or hurt Yourself).'"** [Ps. 91:11-12]
7. **Jesus affirmed to it, "Again, it has been written,**
    'You will not continue putting [the] LORD [= Yahweh], **your God, to the test** (or: You will not repeatedly attempt to set Yahweh out on trial or check out some proof about Him).'"** [Deut. 6:16]

8. **Again the opponent** (adversary; one thrusting-through into [Him]; *devil*) **is progressively taking Him along – into an extremely high mountain range** (or: a very high mountain), **and successively points out for Him all the world's kingdoms** (or: progressively shows to Him all the reigns of the controlling ordered-system of secular society), **as well as their glory** (splendor and manifestations which call forth praise; reputations; assumed appearances).
9. **Then it said to Him, "I will give all these things to You, if – falling prostrate – You would pay homage to me** (worship me; do obeisance to me)."
10. **At this [saying], Jesus then says to it, "Bring [it] under control, adversary** (or: Subject [yourself], *satan*; Sink down below, adversary; Carry [this] off below, hateful accuser; or: Go away, *satan*)! **You see, it has been written,**
    'You will constantly pay homage to (do obeisance to; worship; fall down and kiss the feet of) **[the] LORD [=** Yahweh] **your God, and to Him alone you will repeatedly render hired service** (or: sacred service).'"** [Deut. 6:13]
11. **At that point, the opponent** (the adversary; the one who had been thrusting [Him] through) **progressively flowed away from Him** (or: proceeded to divorce Him; presently abandoned Him) **– and, note and consider this! – agents** (messengers) **approached** (came forward) **and began giving attending service to** (or: continued rendering ministering service and provision for) **Him.**

12. **Now [later], upon hearing that John was handed over** (delivered up; = arrested and put in prison), **He withdrew from the area and returned into the Galilee [province].**
13. **So after leaving Nazareth and coming into Capernaum-by-the-sea, He settled down** (took up residence) **[there] – within the midst of the territories of Zebulun and Naphtali,**

14. **to the end that the [prophecy; oracle] spoken** (declared) **through Isaiah the prophet would** (could; should) **be fulfilled [which] continues saying,**

15. **"O land of Zebulun and land of Naphtali: a pathway associated with [the] Lake** (or: Sea), **on the other side of the Jordan [River], Galilee-of-the-multitudes** (ethnic groups; nations; non-Israelites; pagans; *Goyim*) –

16. **The people continuously sitting within the midst of darkness** (the gloomy dimness of the shadow that lacked the light of the Day) **saw a great Light. And on** (or: to; for; in) **those constantly sitting within [the] province** (or: region) **and shadow of death, Light arises on** (or: rose to and among; dawned for or in) **them."** [Isa. 8:23-9:1; *cf* Jn. 1:4-5]

17. **From that time on, Jesus began to be repeatedly making loud public proclamations** (performing as a herald), **and to be continually saying, "You folks be progressively changing your thinking** (change your frame of mind, mode of thought, perceptions, understanding and state of consciousness, and then turn your focus to [Yahweh]), **because the sovereign reign, dominion and activity of exercising the sovereignty of the heavens** (or: kingdom from the skies and the atmospheres) **has drawn near and now continues being at hand and is close enough to touch** (= has arrived and is now accessible)." [*cf* Rom. 12:2]

18. **Now while proceeding in walking along Lake Galilee** (or: the Sea of Galilee), **He saw two brothers, Simon – the one commonly called Peter – and Andrew, his brother, repeatedly casting a purse net into the lake** (or: sea). **You see, they were by habit fishermen [for earning a livelihood].**

19. **So He proceeds to say to them, "Come here, back behind** (or: after) **Me! I will also make you men fishers of humans** (of people; of mankind)!"

20. **Now, set for goodness, at once abandoning their nets, they followed Him.**

21. **Then going on from there He saw two other brothers, Jacob** (or: James), **the [son] of Zebedee, and John, his brother – within the boat with Zebedee, their father, continuing in thoroughly adjusting, mending and preparing their nets – and He called them.**

22. **Now, set for goodness, at once abandoning the boat and their father, they followed Him.**

23. **Later, Jesus continued leading [them] around** (or: about) **within [the] whole of Galilee, continuously teaching** (or: progressively giving instruction) **within their synagogues and repeatedly making loud public proclamations about the good news** (the message of goodness, ease and wellness) **which pertains to the Kingdom** (or: which has its source in the Reign; which characterizes and belongs to the influence of Sovereignty; which is the Reign; or: the Kingdom's glad tidings) **– as well as continuing in curing** (or: giving attentive care and prescribing therapy or ongoing treatment for) **every chronic disease and every occasional illness** (sickness; delicate condition) **among the people.**

24. **So His reputation and the report concerning Him went off into the whole [region] of Syria. And people brought to Him all those having it badly** (those in poor conditions; = having an illness), **[those] with various diseases, and those being continuously gripped by pain** (or: confined in testing situations), **as well as those being habitually affected by demons** [note: a Hellenistic concept and term that denoted animistic influences], **and those being repeatedly affected by the moon** (either = lunatics, or, epileptics) **and paralytics – and He cured or gave attentive care or prescribed therapy or instigated ongoing treatment for them!**

25. **Consequently many and huge crowds followed Him – from the Galilee [province] and Decapolis** (the Ten Cities; a league of cities east of the Jordan) **and Jerusalem and Judea, as well as [from] the other side of the Jordan [River]** (or: Transjordan).

CHAPTER 5

1. **Now seeing the crowds, He climbed up into the mountain. Then, upon His sitting down, His disciples** (students; apprentices) **approached** (came toward) **Him.**

2. **So opening His mouth, He began teaching them, progressively saying** (laying it out),

3. **"The destitute folks [are] happy in spirit and attitude, because the reign and dominion of the heavens is continually belonging to, and made up of, them**
> (or: Blessed [are] those dependent for support on the Spirit, for the kingdom from the skies and the atmospheres is continuing to pertain to them; The people who need to beg for sustenance [are made] happy by the Breath-effect because the effect of the sovereignty of the heavens is being a source in and for them; The financially poor folks [exist being] happy with an attitude that the sovereign influence and activity from the atmospheres continuously exists with reference to them)!

4. **"Those constantly grieving and mourning [are] happy and blessed because** [other MSS: now that] **they, themselves, will habitually be called alongside to receive relief, help, aid, encouragement and comfort** (will continue receiving the services of the Paraclete)!

5. **"'The kind, considerate, gentle, mild-tempered, egoless and nonviolent folks** (people who do not use force)' **[are] happy and blessed because they, themselves, 'will proceed to be inheriting the Land** (or: be receiving and enjoying the earth as an allotment)!' [Ps. 37:11]

6. **"The people being habitually hungry and constantly thirsty for the eschatological deliverance of fairness, equity, right relationship and justice which characterize a rightwised state of being or situation within the Way pointed out** (or: the right direction of justice, in covenantal inclusion) **[are] happy and blessed, because they themselves will continue feeding and drinking [of these things] until they are filled and satisfied!**

7. **"The folks who are merciers** (who give and show mercy) **[are] happy and blessed, because they, themselves, will repeatedly be given and shown mercy!**

8. **"Those who are clean** (clear of admixture; pure; consistent) **in the heart [are] happy and blessed, because they, themselves, will progressively see God!**
> (or: = The folks that have had the core of their beings made clean [are] happy people, in that they will continue to see the Ground of Being [in everything]!)

9. **"The ones who make peace and create joining [are] happy and blessed because they, themselves, will continue being called God's sons** (or: termed 'sons of, and from, God')!

10. **"Those being ones having been pressed forward, chased or persecuted in the cause of right, and for the sake of fairness, equity, [covenant] relationships or justice which comes from the Way pointed out** (or: because of [God's] eschatological deliverance) **[are] happy and blessed because the reign of the heavens continually belongs to them**
> (or: for the kingdom of the heavens is continuing to pertain to them; because the reign and sovereign activities from the atmosphere and sky is being a source in and for them)!

11. **"You folks are and continue to be happy and blessed people!**
Now whenever people may denounce, reproach, heap insults on and persecute or chase you folks, and while continuously lying, may even say every bad thing (spreading malicious gossip; [other MSS: every misery-gushed utterance]) **down against you – for the sake of Me,**

12. **be continuously rejoicing and repeatedly express extreme exultation, because your wage** (compensation; reward) **[is] much** (large; great)**, within the heavens** (or: atmospheres [that surround you])**! You see, they persecuted the prophets before you in the same way.**

13. **"You people, yourselves, exist being** (are) **the salt of the Land** (or: territory; earth)**. Now if the salt should ever be made dull or tasteless** (literally: foolish; nonsensical)**, in what way will it continue being salted** (or: made salty)**? It still continues giving strength into nothing** (= it still cannot provide seasoning)**, except being thrown outside, to be repeatedly** (or: continuously) **trampled down by people** (or: tread down under the humans).

14. **"You folks, yourselves, exist being** (are) **the Light of the ordered System** (the world of culture, religion, politics, government, and secular society; = the human sociological realm; or: the aggregate of humanity)**. A city located up on a mountain** (or: situated on top of a mountain range) **continues unable to be hidden or concealed.**

15. **"Likewise, people are not normally lighting a lamp and then placing it under the measuring bowl** (or: a one-peck grain-measuring basket)**, but rather upon the lampstand – and it continues shining and giving light for all those within the house.**

16. **"In this way, let the Light, which you folks possess** (or: which has a source in you folks; or: which you people are)**, shine in front of the People** (before the humans)**, so that people can see your fine works** (or: the beautiful works that you are; the ideal acts which come from

you folks) **and they can give glory to** (or: and [these deeds; or: these works of beauty] will bring a good reputation to, and a manifestation which incites praise for) **your Father – the One in union with the atmospheres [that surround you folks]** (or: within the midst of the heavens)!

17. **"You folks should not infer from customary presumption or from established supposition that I came to loosen-down or demolish the Law** (or: Torah) **or the Prophets. I did not come to loosen-down or demolish, but to the contrary, to fulfill** (or: fill up; make full; bring fullness),

18. **"for assuredly** (or: amen; it is so), **I am here saying to you people, until the heaven and the earth** (or: the sky and the Land) **could ever go by and pass away, one iota** (the smallest Greek letter) **or one horn-like projection** (diacritical mark, such as an accent or breathing mark, or part of a Heb. letter; a serif; = the smallest detail) **can by any means pass away from the Law** [= Torah] **– UNTIL all things can birth themselves** (or: should occur; may happen)!

19. **"Whoever, then, should loosen [even] one of the least of these, the implanted goals** (impartations of the finished product within; inward directives) **– and should teach the People** (humans) **to that effect – he will repeatedly be called "least"** (or: a least one; = insignificant) **within the reign of the heavens** (or: the kingdom which pertains to the atmospheres; the sovereign influence and activities from the skies). **Yet, whoever may practice** (or: should perform and do) **as well as teach – this person will continue being called "great" within the reign of the heavens** (the kingdom, dominion or royal influence from these atmospheres).

20. **"You see, I am here saying to YOU people that if your covenantal fairness** (uprightness; justice, rightwisedness, and right relationships which conform to the Way pointed out) **should not habitually exceed and abound more than [that] of the scribes** (experts in the Law; scholars; theologians) **and Pharisees, in no way can YOU folks enter into the reign of the heavens** (or: the kingdom which is, and pertains to, the heavens; the sovereign rule of the atmospheres)!

[comment: here Jesus evaluates the "uprightness" of the scribe / Pharisees as below par]

21. **"YOU folks heard that it was said to the original People** (or: for the Beginning Folks; among those of the beginning period [of Israel]),

'You folks will not continue murdering.' [Ex. 20:13] **Yet whoever may commit murder will continue being held within the decision** (= held under the control of the crisis or the judging).

22. **"However, I Myself am now saying to YOU people that everyone, who – from internal swelling or agitated emotions of his natural disposition, or from the fruition of his mental bent – is habitually being randomly impulsive to, or without cause repeatedly intensely angry with, his brother** (= fellow member of this society) **will continue being held within the decision** (= under control of the judging of the local court). **Now whoever may at some point say to his brother, 'Raca** (an Aramaic word of verbal abuse: contemptible imbecile; worthless good-for-nothing; senseless empty-head; brainless idiot; blockhead)!' **will continue being held within** (= accountable to) **the Sanhedrin** (the ruling Jewish council). **Yet whoever may at some point say, 'Inept moron** (Stupid scoundrel; Despicable fool; Perverse idiot)!' **will continue being held within** (= accountable to) **[placement] into the [part of] the Valley of Hinnom which pertains to the fire** (i.e., the incinerator for refuse in the dump outside of Jerusalem).

[note: Dallas Willard, in his book *The Divine Conspiracy*, HarperSanFrancisco, 1998, p. 151-2, points out that *raca* was a word of contempt, and contempt, he says, is "a studied degradation of another," or, it is meant to "mark [someone] out" as being "contemptible." He further shows that using expressions of contempt "breaks the social bond" and excludes, pushes a person away, and leaves him isolated. Willard cites Prov. 14:16; 18:2 and 26:11 as Biblical definitions of a "fool;" he states that this word "is a combination of stupid perversity and rebellion against God"]

23. **"So if you folks should happen to be in the process of offering your gift** (or: bearing forward your gift [to be placed]) **upon the altar, and there you should be reminded that your brother continues holding something against you** (or: continues to have something [written] down pertaining to you, or possesses [evidence] that could bring you down),

24. **"at once abandon your gift – there, in front of the altar – and proceed on your way to bring things under control: first be reconciled with your brother** (or: have the situation thoroughly changed by your brother), **and then coming, continue offering** (bearing forward) **your gift.** [comment: an example of *anathema*: placing the offering up upon a receptacle]

[note: beginning with vs. 22, above, Jesus uses the word *brother* in its wider semantic range, in His teaching, to indicate the sense of solidarity, membership of a group, or fellow human being; other NT writers do the same – it often means "fellow believer," or "member of God's family, but here would likely mean "fellow countryman"]

25. **"Be in the habit of quickly having continued thoughts of wellness toward your opponent in a lawsuit** (or: of being quickly well-disposed and kind-minded with your plaintiff; or: Be quickly having your mind progressively at ease in relation to the person setting himself to resist or oppose you in matters of daily living) **settling matters while you continue being with him on the road [to court]** (or: while being with him within the Way – the Path [of this Life]), **lest at some time the plaintiff** (person having a complaint against you in some legal matter) **may hand you over** (or: transfer or commit you) **to the judge, and then the judge to the court officer, and next you may be thrown into prison** (jail; a guardhouse).

26. **"Truly I am now saying to you** (or: = Pay attention to Me), **you may not come out from the midst of there until you can give back** (repay) **the last small copper coin** (a quadrans; = the final dime or penny of the amount judged against you).

27. **"YOU folks hear** (or: heard) **that it was declared,**
    'YOU will not continue committing adultery!' [Ex. 20:13]
28. **"Yet I, Myself, am now saying to YOU people that every man who is continuing in, or, repeatedly looking at and observing** (constantly watching or leering at; = fantasizing over) **a [married] woman, with a view toward the [situation, or, condition] to crave her** (to experience strong passion for her, or, to desire to rush in a heat of emotion upon her), **has already committed adultery with her, within his heart!**
29. **"So if YOUR right eye is habitually a bait-stick which entraps you, immediately tear it out and throw it away from you! You see, it constantly brings things together for benefit and advantage in** (for; to) **YOU folks that one of your members should loose itself away** (may destroy itself; could come to be lost), **so that your whole body should not be thrown into the Valley of Hinnom** (Greek: Gehenna – the city dump [= to dishonor you by giving no burial; to treat you as a criminal]). [*cf* Jer. 31:38-40]
30. **"Also, if YOUR right hand is habitually a bait-stick which entraps you, at once cut it off and throw it away from you! You see, it constantly brings things together for benefit and advantage in** (for; to) **you folks that one of your members should loose itself away** (may destroy itself; could come to be lost), **so that your whole body should not go off into the Valley of Hinnom** (Gehenna – the city dump outside Jerusalem).
    [comment: vs. 29-30 are hyperbole; they also show the absurdity of trying to fulfill the law through works, when in fact it is a matter of the heart; observe the 1sr century context]

31. **"Now it was declared,**
    'Whoever should dismiss (loose-away; = divorce) **his wife, let him give a certificate of divorce** (or: a divorce; a standing-off and away) **to her.'**
    [Deut. 24:1; note: separation equaled a legal divorce; the document would pertain to property, child custody, and/or return of the dowry; it would also protect her from a charge of committing adultery if she was with another unmarried man]
32. **"Yet I, Myself, am now saying to you folks that every man proceeding in dismissing** (loosing-away) **his wife – outside of a case of infidelity** (fornication; prostitution; sexual misconduct) **– proceeds in making her a subject of adultery.**
    [comment: this would annul their then current practice for a man to be able to divorce his wife just for whatever reason he might choose; this statement by Jesus was a great advance toward cultural equality of the sexes]
33. **"Again, you folks hear** (or: heard) **that is was declared to the original People** (or: for the Beginning Folks; among those of the beginning period [of Israel]),
    'YOU will not repeatedly break an oath (swear without performing; swear falsely; commit perjury),**'** **and further, 'YOU will habitually give back** (repay) **to the LORD [=** Yahweh] **your oaths.'** [Lev. 19:12]
34. **"Yet I, Myself, am now saying to you folks to absolutely** (altogether) **not grab hold of a sacred object or make reference to a sacred sphere, so as to affirm an oath or swear**

confirmation – neither within the heaven (the atmosphere), **because it is God's throne** (seat of rule);

35. **"nor within the earth, because it is a footstool for His feet** [Isa. 66:1]; **nor** [referencing] **unto Jerusalem, because it is 'a city belonging to and having reference to the great King.'** [Ps. 48:2]

36. **"Neither within your head should you [mentally] touch something sacred so as to affirm an oath, because you continue having no power** (or: ability) **to make one hair shining white** (to have the character of bright light) **or black.**

37. **"So let your word** (or: thought) **habitually be 'Yes,' [and mean] yes; [or] 'No,' [and let] 'no' [end the matter]. Now the thing [which is] in excess of these is** (or: exists being) **forth from out of the midst of the bad condition [of mankind]** (the situation of hard labor, pain and misery-gush; or: the evil, malevolent and wicked [thought]; or: the worthless person).

38. **"YOU hear** (or: heard) **that it was declared,**
> **'An eye in substitution for** (instead of; in place of) **an eye,' and, 'A tooth in substitution for** (instead of; in place of) **a tooth.'** [Ex. 21:24]

39. **"Yet I, Myself, am now telling you folks not to at any point actively set yourself against, or take a counteractive or aggressive stand in opposition to, the bad situation**
> (or: = participate in armed resistance against the miserable condition; = mirror the painful, insulting or laborious situation; or: = 'render evil for evil' in opposition to the evil or wicked person; = rebel or be part of an insurrection; = stand off an enemy). **On the contrary,**
[to] whomever is repeatedly cuffing or habitually slapping into your right cheek (or: jaw), **turn to him the other one, also!**
> [note: In his book, *Engaging the Powers*, Walter Wink has pointed out that this act of slapping someone on the right cheek referred to a person in a superior position of that society "backhanding" someone in an inferior position. It was meant to either insult the person, or to put the person in "their place," or to "admonish" him. Wink suggests that turning the other cheek "… robs the oppressor of the power to humiliate." (p. 176)]

40. **"And further, to the person continuing in desiring** (wanting; purposing) **for you to be judged** (or: sued; or: presently intending to litigate with you) **and even to take your inner garment** (tunic; = shirt), **at once send off to him your outer garment** (cloak; coat) **as well!**
> [note: Under the Law the cloak was to be returned at each sundown (Ex. 22:25-27). Sending a creditor a cloak as collateral would say to folks that the creditor was taking everything from him and leaving him naked and destitute. It would show that this person was being inhumane. Wink says "indebtedness was endemic" in this land and time.]

41. **"Also, [for] whoever will** [other MSS: may] **proceed in pressing you into service** (conscript, requisition or commandeer you) **[for] one mile, continue submissively leading the way with him [for] two [miles].**
> [note: This impressed service refers to the Roman rule (*anagareia*) that allowed the occupation troops to compel someone to carry their soldier's pack or baggage for one mile – a rule often abused. Wink suggests that vss. 39-41 are non-violent, creative initiatives against social injustice. I suggest that they also demonstrate a heart of love and an acknowledging of brotherhood even with oppressors.]

42. **"Give at once to the person presently, or repeatedly, asking of you, and you should not be turned away from the one continuously wanting** (or: purposing) **to borrow money from you.**

43. **"YOU folks hear** (or: heard) **that it was declared,**
> **'You will habitually love** (accept) **the one near to you** (your neighbor or associate)' [Lev. 19:18] **– and yet you will constantly regard your enemy with ill will** (hate the one hostile to you; radically detach from the object of your hate or alienation).

44. **"Yet I, Myself, am now saying to you folks: Be constantly loving your enemies** (urging toward reunion with, and accepting as persons standing on the same ground, those folks hostile to you; [comment: this could have applied to the Romans, as well as to personal enemies]), **and be habitually praying goodness over the people continuously persecuting you** (constantly thinking and speaking on behalf of the folks repeatedly pursuing you to have ease and well-being)

45. **"so that** (or: By this manner; This is how) **you folks can be birthed** (may and would come to be) **sons of your Father – the One within [the] atmospheres and in union with [the] heavens – because He is repeatedly making His sun to rise back up again upon bad** (evil; wicked; worthless) **folks as well as [upon] good** (virtuous) **folks, and He is habitually sending rain upon fair and equitable people** (those in right relationship; those within the Way pointed out; just ones; rightwised ones) **as well as [upon] unfair and inequitable people** (those not in right relationship; those not in the Way pointed out; unjust folks).

46. **"You see, if you should happen to love, accept, give yourself to, and participate with the ones constantly loving you folks, what wage or reward do you continue holding** (or: having)**? Are not also the tax collectors constantly doing the very same thing?**

> [note: tax collectors worked for the state (for either one of the provinces, or for the Empire) and were thus despised and considered outcasts of the local society, being perceived as both collaborating with the Romans and as getting money dishonestly through their business AS a "tax-farmer," (someone who purchased from the state the right to collect official taxes, tolls, customs and dues: they made their money by adding on a percentage to the tax which they collected for the state), or by working FOR a "tax-farmer"]

47. **"And further, if you folks should only greet and welcomely embrace your brothers, what are you continuing to do [that is] excessive or extraordinary? Are not also the folks of the ethnic multitudes** (the nations; the pagans; the non-Israelites) **constantly doing the very same thing?**

48. **"Therefore, you folks will continuously exist being ones that have reached the purposed and destined goal: finished and completed ones; mature and perfected ones – in the same way as your heavenly Father** (or: your Father which has the qualities of, and is characterized by, the atmosphere) **constantly exists being One that is the goal and destiny: finished, complete, mature, perfect!**

CHAPTER 6

1. **"Now you folks make it a habit to hold to close attentiveness [so as] not to be doing, performing or practicing your fairness, equity or rightwised behavior – all which comprise the Way pointed out – in front of people, in order to be observed by them, otherwise you do not continue holding wages** (or: having a reward or a recompense) **alongside of** (from beside; = from the presence of) **your Father – the One in the atmosphere and the firmament, that is: in union with, centered in, and within the midst of the heavens.**

2. **"Therefore, whenever, as is your custom you may be making gifts of mercy** (be performing acts of mercy; be doing alms or practicing charity), **you should not blow a trumpet in front of you** (= toot your own horn ahead of your actions) **– even as the overly judging and critical folks**

> (*hupokrites*; or: those who put texts under close inspection to sift and separate and then give an answer, an interpretation, an opinion; or: those who live by separating things yet who under-discern; or: those who make judgments from a low view; or: those who under-estimate reality; or: perverse scholars who focus on tiny distinctions) **are constantly doing in the synagogues and on the narrow urban streets and alleys, so that they can receive a reputation from people** (be recognized, lauded and glorified by the humans). **I am saying to you truly: They are presently holding their full payment** (recompense)!

3. **"So during your customary making gifts of mercy, do not let your left hand become aware of what your right hand continues doing,**

4. **"so that your gift of mercy can continue existing within the hidden [realm; place]** (or: may be in hiding), **and then your Father – the One continuously looking within the hidden [realm; place]** (or: observing amidst the concealed) **– will continue giving back to you!**

5. **"And further, whenever you folks may by habit be thinking or speaking toward having goodness, ease and well-being** (or: praying), **you will not be as the overly judging and critical folks** (*hupokrites*: see vs. 2, above), **because they are constantly liking to be habitually speaking toward having goodness, ease and well-being** (or: praying) **while standing in the midst of the synagogues and on the corners of the broad streets and city**

squares – so that they can be visible to the people (or: be manifested and caused to shine for these humans). **I am saying to you truly: They are presently holding their full payment!**

6. **"Now as for you, individually, whenever you may by habit be thinking or speaking toward having goodness, ease and well-being** (or: praying), **enter into your storeroom** (or: barn; granary; chamber) **and, upon shutting** (locking; barring) **your door** (or: gate), **pray** (speak or think toward having goodness) **to your Father – the One within the hidden, concealed [realm; place]. So then your Father – the One continuously seeing within the hidden, concealed [realm; place] – will continue giving back to and in you** (or: = giving in answer for your expectation; or: will habitually be paying or rewarding you).

7. **"Now during speaking toward having goodness** (praying), **you folks should not babble** (or: make repetitious utterances; stack up meaningless phrases; or: stutter; speak without thinking; use empty words) **– even as those of the ethnic multitudes** (pagans; nations). **You see, they habitually imagine and continuously suppose that in their much speaking** (or: using many words; or: saying the same thing many times) **they will be fully heard and really listened to.**

8. **"So then, you folks should not be like, or made to resemble, them, for it follows that before the occasion for you to ask Him** [D & h read: to open the mouth], **God, your Father, has seen and thus knows** (is aware) **of what things you continue having need.**

9. **"Therefore, be continuously thinking and speaking toward having goodness, ease and well-being** (or: praying) **in this way:**

   'O our Father – the One within and in union with the heavens! (or: in the midst of the atmosphere and firmament!)

   Make Your Name to be set-apart and kept holy (or: treated as sacred).

10. **Make Your reign and kingdom come. Make Your will** (the effect of Your intent and purpose) **come into existence** (happen; come to be; be birthed) **– as within heaven** (or: [the] atmosphere), **so also upon earth.**

11. **Give to us** (Provide for us) **today our bread necessary for existence** (or: unto added being; or: the full-existence food) **that does not run out** [*Old Syriac* – Kenneth E. Bailey].

12. **And then, send away the results of our debts for us** (let the effects of our obligations flow away in us; cancel the condition of our indebtedness), **as we also dismiss and send away for, and give release to, those who owe us** (let flow away for those in obligation to us; cancel the situations and conditions of our debtors).

13. **Also, would** (or: may) **You not bring** (or: carry) **us into an ordeal, harassment, or a putting to the proof – neither by trial, nor by temptation, nor by examination. But to the contrary, rescue us** (drag us out of danger) **away from the bad situation** (the wicked person; the miserable condition; the painful labor; the unprofitable endeavor; the malicious man). [later MSS add: because Yours is the reign (kingdom) and the ability (power) and the manifestation which calls forth praise (the reputation; the glory), on into the ages. It is true (Make it so; Amen).]'

14. **"You see, if you folks can** (or: could; should; would) **send away** (let flow off; forgive; dismiss) **for** (or: from) **the people** (or: humans) **the effects of their falling to the side [of the Way; of the Path pointed out]** (or: their trespasses; their false steps and offenses; their goof-ups and blunders), **your heavenly Father** (or: your Father Who inhabits, and can be compared to, the atmosphere) **will continue sending away, dismissing, forgiving and letting [things;** some MSS add: the effects of your falling to the side] **flow off for** (or: in) **you, as well.**

15. **"Yet if you folks can** (would) **not send away for** (or: dismiss from) **the people the effects of their falling to the side, neither will your Father continue sending away** (dismissing; forgiving; letting flow away) **the effects of your falling to the side, offending or goofing.**

16. **"Now whenever you may periodically fast, do not proceed to become sad-faced or stern, gloomy people – as the overly judging and critical folks** [see vs. 2, above] **for they habitually remove the light from** (or: disguise or distort) **their faces so that they can continue to be visible to people** (or: be manifested for mankind and appear) **[as] ones in the process of fasting. I continue saying to you, truly: They are presently holding their full payment!**

17. "So YOU folks, during fasting anoint, rub and massage your head, then wash your face (= groom yourself),
18. "so that you would not appear to the people (or: may not be visible for mankind) **[to be] in the midst of fasting, but rather, to** (or: for) **your Father – the One within the hidden [sphere; place]. And your Father – the One continuously seeing within the hidden [sphere; place; situation] – will continue giving [something] back to** (for; in) **you!**

19. "Stop (or: Do not continue) **accumulating and storing up treasures for yourselves upon the earth** (or: on the Land) **– where moth and corrosion** (an eating action) **progressively causes [things] to disappear, and where thieves constantly dig** (or: tunnel; excavate) **through** (i.e., as to break in through a wall) **and then proceed in stealing.**
20. "So you folks be continuously accumulating and storing up for yourselves treasures within heaven (or: [your] atmosphere) **– where neither moth nor corrosion causes [things] to disappear, and where thieves do not constantly dig through** (or: penetrate) **nor are they repeatedly stealing.**
21. "You see, where your treasure is, there also will be your heart (= the core of your being).

22. "The eye is the lamp of the body. If, then, your eye may continue being single-fold (or: clear, simple and uncompounded; perhaps: single-focused, suggesting being straightforward; may = healthy; may suggest generosity), **your whole body will continue being** (will continuously exist being) **illuminated** (enlightened; or: lustrous; luminous; radiant; shining).
23. "Yet if your eye should continue being in a bad condition (useless; unsound; gushed with misery and labor; or: wicked; perhaps = diseased or clouded; may suggest stinginess or being grudging), **your whole body will continue being** (will continuously exist being) **dark** (or: in the dark; full of darkness). **If, then, the light [which is] within the midst of you is darkness** (or: continually exists being dimness and lack of Light), **how thick [is] the darkness** (or: how great and extensive [will be] the obscurity and gloom of that area of shadows)!

24. "No one continues being able (has habitual power) **to continue being, or performing as, a slave for two owners** (lords; masters). **You see, he will either proceed in hating** (or: inwardly detaching from or: regarding with ill will) **the one and will continue loving the different one, or he will continue holding firmly to and having instead the one, and will proceed despising** (having a negative attitude and disposition toward) **the different one. You folks are not able** (still have no power) **to continue being, or performing as, slaves for God and at the same time for money and riches** (*mammon*; or: you can't be enslaved to both God and wealth)!

25. "On this account I continue saying to you: Do not constantly take anxious care, worry or undue concern for your soul-lives (the consciousness or being which you are) **– what you can or should eat, or what you folks should or may habitually be drinking; nor, for your body – with what you folks should clothe yourselves. Is not the soul-life** (a person's inner being, life and consciousness) **more than nourishment, and the body [more than] clothing?**
26. "Make an intent observation into the birds of the sky (or: atmosphere), **so as to carefully consider them. [See within their situation]** that they are not constantly sowing seeds (planting), **neither are they periodically reaping** (harvesting) **nor gathering [food] together into storehouses** (or: barns), **and yet your heavenly Father** (or: your Father Who inhabits, and can be compared to, the atmosphere) **constantly feeds and nourishes them. Are you folks not exceedingly carrying-through more, so as to be of more consequence, than they** (= Are you not worth much more than they are)?
27. "Now who of you folks, while habitually taking anxious care, undue concern, worry or by fretting, is normally able (progresses in power) **to add to his stature one cubit** (eighteen inches) **or to provide one more arm's reach to his life-span?**
28. "And so why are you folks constantly worrying or fretting about clothing? Fully learn about, and from, the lilies of the field – how they are progressively growing (or: Learn thoroughly and consider well how the wild anemones continue growing and increasing). **They are not constantly working hard or becoming weary from struggle, nor are they habitually spinning to make thread for cloth,**

29. "yet I am now saying to (or: I continue laying it out for) **you that not even Solomon, in all his splendor and glory, clothed or arrayed himself as** (or: like) **one of these [flowers]!**
30. "**So now, if God thus continually dresses and adorns** (or: invests) **the vegetation of the field** (or: countryside) – **being in existence today, and tomorrow is being normally thrown into a furnace** (or: oven; stove) – **[will He] not much more readily and to a greater extent [take care of] you folks who have small faith and little trust?**
31. "**Therefore, you folks should not fret, be anxious, be full of care or be worrying, constantly saying, 'What can we eat?' or, 'What can we drink?' or, 'What can we put on ourselves to wear?'**
32. "**You see, the ethnic multitudes** (the nations; the Gentile people groups) **are habitually in eager pursuit of these things – spending all of their energy in seeking them! After all, your heavenly Father** (or: your Father Who inhabits, and can be compared to, the atmosphere) **has seen and knows that you folks repeatedly have need for all of these things.**

33. "**So you people be habitually and constantly seeking God's reign** (or: sovereign activity and influence; kingdom) **and the eschatological deliverance of fairness and equity from Him, as well as the His justice and rightwised behavior in the Way, which He has pointed out in covenant participation that has been set right – and all these things will be added to you!**
34. "**Therefore, you folks should not fret, be anxious, be full of care or be worrying [with a fixation] into the next day, for the next day will be concerned about itself** (or: will have anxiety of its own). **Sufficient and adequate for** (or: to; in) **the day [is] its own situation as it ought not to be** (bad quality and worthless condition).

CHAPTER 7

1. "**Stop separating, dividing-out and making distinctions** (or: Do not have a habit of sifting, evaluating and deciding, or judging) – **so that you folks would** (or: should; can; may) **not be sifted, separated-off, evaluated, decided about, or judged.**
2. "**You see, within and with whatever aspect of sifting to separate** (effect of evaluation; result of a discrimination decision; produce of deciding a judgment) **you folks are habitually or normally separating, dividing-out, discriminating, evaluating and judging, you will continue being judged** (sifted, decided about, etc.). **And further, within and with whatever measure or standard you folks are continuously using or applying, it will be constantly used to measure you, and that standard will be repeatedly applied to you** (or: = you will receive in the same proportion and manner that you give).
3. "**So why are you constantly or repeatedly looking at the speck** (splinter of shriveled wood; small piece of straw) – **the one in your brother's eye** (= the small thing hindering the ability of your friend or fellow to see)! – **and yet you are not continuing to fully consider and carefully think about the rafter** (beam of wood; shaft of timber) **in your own eye?**
4. "**Or how will you folks proceed in declaring to your brother, 'Allow [me], I can extract the speck** (splinter) **from your eye' – and now consider as you look! – the rafter** (log; beam) **[is] within the midst of your own eye?**
5. "**O hyper-critical one [**cf 6:2, above**]! First extract** (cast out) **the rafter** (log; plank) **from out of your own eye, and then you will proceed to be seeing clearly to extract** (cast out) **the speck** (splinter) **from out of your brother's eye.**

6. "**You folks should not give the set-apart** (holy; sacred) **things to the dogs, neither should you throw your pearls in front of the pigs** (hogs; swine), **lest at some time they will step on them and trample them down with their feet – and then, upon turning around, they might break forth on you folks and rip you up** (tear you in pieces).

7. "**Be habitually requesting** (or: Keep on asking), **and it** (or: He) **will proceed being given to** (or: for; in) **you people. Be habitually seeking** (or: Keep on searching and trying to find), **and you folks will repeatedly find. Be repeatedly** (or: Keep on) **knocking, and it** (or: He) **will habitually be opened up to** (or: for; in) **you.**

8. "You see, everyone habitually requesting is repeatedly receiving. He who keeps on seeking and searching is constantly finding. And to (in; for) the person repeatedly knocking it will be opened up.

9. "Well then, what person [is there] from among you folks from whom his son will request a loaf of bread – he will not proceed to be handing a stone to him, will he?

10. "Or, perhaps he will ask for a fish – he will not proceed to be handing a snake (serpent) to him, will he?

11. "Since, then (or: If, therefore), you folks – being miserable, bad and useless as you are – have seen [in life] and now know to be habitually giving good gifts (or: the results of virtue and excellence) to your own children, how much more will your Father – the One within and in union with the heavens and within the midst of the atmospheres – continue giving good, excellent things as well as virtues to those continuing in requesting from Him (or: asking Him)?

12. "Therefore, all things – as many as YOU folks may continue wanting or should by habit be purposing – that the People (or: these humans) should, or would, be habitually doing to or performing for YOU folks, thus also (or: so likewise), YOU folks, yourselves, be repeatedly doing to, and continuously performing for and among, THEM (or: = Treat others in the way that you yourselves would like to be treated). You see, THIS is (or: exists being; = is the meaning of) the Law and the Prophets (= this sums up the message of the Scriptures)!

13. "You folks enter at once through this (or: the) narrow, restrictive and cramping Gate – because wide [is] the gate and spacious (roomy, having the characteristics of free, open country) [is] the roadway habitually leading off into the loosing-away of loss, ruin and destruction (or: demolition), and many are the folks continuously (or: one after another in a steady stream) entering through, and by means of, it –

14. "for this (or: the) Gate is narrow, cramping and restrictive which is habitually leading off into the Life – and this (or: the) Path has been compressed and squeezed [to where the traveler is being pressed and encumbered] – and the folks presently (or: one after another, in a continuous procession) finding it are few.

15. "Constantly apply yourselves to holding off the false prophets – whatsoever ones that are habitually coming to you folks in clothing belonging to sheep (= disguised as sheep; pretending to have the covering or appearance of sheep), yet inside they are ravenous, savage wolves.

16. "You will come to be recognizing and fully knowing them from their fruits. People are not normally picking or gathering clusters of grapes from thorn bushes (prickly plants), nor ripe figs from thistles or briers.

17. "Likewise every good (or: = healthy) tree constantly produces fine, beautiful (choice; ideal) fruit, but the decaying and rotten tree repeatedly bears bad and worthless (= inedible) fruit.

18. "A good, healthy tree normally has no power or ability to bear bad and worthless fruit, neither [is] a rotten tree [able] to continue producing fine, beautiful fruit.

19. "Every tree not habitually producing choice, ideal fruit is normally being cut out [of the orchard] – and is normally being thrown into a fire (= used for fire wood).

20. "Consequently, you folks will recognize and come to accurately know them from their fruits (= from what their lives produce).

21. "Not everyone constantly saying to Me, 'O Lord! Lord!' will proceed to be entering into the reign (or: sovereign rule; kingdom; dominion, realm of action and activities) of the heavens (or: which has the character of, and emanates from, the atmospheres) but rather, the one habitually performing the result or progressively producing the effect of the will, intent and purpose of My Father – the One within and in union with the heavens, and in the midst of the atmospheres – [will proceed entering].

22. "Within (or: On) That Day many will repeatedly say to Me, 'Lord! O Lord! Do (or: did) we not prophesy in (or: by) Your Name? And do (or: did) we not cast out demons (Hellenistic

concept and term: = animistic influences) **in** (or: by) **Your Name? And do** (or: did) **we not perform many works of power and ability in** (or: by) **Your Name?**

23. **"And at that time I will repeatedly confess assuredly to them, 'I never came to know or became acquainted with you folks** (or: I not even once had intimate, experiential knowledge of you). **Those people habitually working** (performing; or: making a trade of; making a living in) **the lawlessness are now to go off to a space** (or: territory) **away, and proceed in giving way to Me and making room for Me.'** [Ps. 6:9]

24. **"Everyone, then, who continues obediently hearing these words** (thoughts; ideas; messages) **of Mine, and habitually does them** (or: acts on them), **will progressively be made to be and to become like an intelligent, considerate, thoughtful, prudent and sensible adult male, who builds** (or: built) **his house upon the rock-mass.**

25. **"And when the rain descended** (or: falls) **and the rivers came** (or: come) **[flooding] and the winds blew** (or: blow) **and lunged** (or: fall toward; lash against) **that house, it did** (or: does) **not fall, for it had been provided with a foundation and continued being established upon the rock-mass.**

26. **"And by contrast, everyone who continues hearing the words** (thoughts; ideas; messages) **of Mine and yet is not continuing in doing them** (or: acting on them) **will progressively be made to be and to become like a stupid, senseless adult male** (= an ignorant and careless builder) **who built** (or: builds) **his house upon the sand.**

27. **"And when the rain descended** (or: falls) **and the rivers came** (or: come) **[flooding] and the winds blew** (or: blow) **and lunged** (or: fall toward; lash against) **that house, it fell** (or: falls), **and its fall** (collapse) **was great."** [Isa. 28:14-18. Lu.6:46-49]

28. **And so it happened that when Jesus finished these discourses** (thoughts; ideas), **the crowds began to be amazed and astounded at what He taught and His way** (manner) **of teaching,**

29. **for He was continuing in teaching and instructing them as one holding authority** (or: having the right out of Being) **– and not as their scribes** (theologians; experts in the Law; scholars) **[taught]**.

CHAPTER 8

1. **Now upon His walking down from the mountain, large crowds followed after Him.**

2. **And then – look and consider! – a leper approaching began doing obeisance to** (paying homage to; worshiping) **Him, repeatedly saying, "O Lord** (Master), **if you should want to, You are able and continue having power to at once cleanse me!"**

3. **So, stretching out His hand, He touched him, while saying, "I am habitually wanting to: Be cleansed at once!" And, set for well-being, his leprosy was immediately cleansed!**

4. **Then Jesus continues saying to him, "See here. You may not tell [this] to even one person, but rather, proceed to depart, leading [yourself] under [this word]. [Then] show yourself to the priest and offer the gift which Moses arranged with a view to a witness for and among them, and provides evidence to** [J. Dominic Crossan suggests: = against them]**."**

5. **Now upon His entering into Capernaum, a centurion** (a commander of one hundred men in the Roman army) **approached Him, calling Him alongside and pleading with Him** (requesting Him to function as a paraclete), **and then saying,**

6. **"Sir, my orderly** (manservant; servant boy) **has been struck down with paralysis and is bedridden** (has been laid up) **within the house, constantly being dreadfully pained and grievously tested with this affliction."**

7. **So Jesus then says to him, "I, Myself, upon coming, will proceed to serve and cure him, then restore him to health."** (as a question: "Shall I, Myself, on coming, be serving and giving him attentive care or prescribing therapy or ongoing treatment that will restore him to health?")

8. **Now the centurion, giving a considered response, said, "O Sir, I am not fit or important enough to the end that you should enter under my roof. But rather, only say a word** (speak a message) **and my orderly** (manservant) **will proceed to be healed and made whole.**

9. **"You see, I too am myself** (or: even I, myself, am) **a person** (a man) **being set in a continued arrangement under authority – continuing in holding** (having) **soldiers under me – and I normally say to this one, 'Go your way,' and he proceeds going his way; and to another one, 'Proceed coming,' and he proceeds coming, and to my slave, 'Do this,' and by habit he is doing [it]."**

10. **Now at hearing [that], Jesus was astounded** (was amazed; marvels) **and said to those following after Him, "Truly** (Amen; It is so) **I am saying to you folks, with no one in Israel do I find so much faith, trust and loyalty [as this]!** (or: I did not find such great trust and confidence at the side of even one person within the midst of Israel!).

11. **"Now I further say to you that many people from eastern lands, as well as western regions, will continue arriving. And they will one-after-another be made to recline [and dine] with Abraham and Isaac and Jacob, within the reign and sovereign rule of the heavens** (or: the kingdom of the atmospheres).

12. **"Yet the 'sons of the kingdom** (or: reign; = those who were in line to inherit the kingdom; or: = those who were supposed to manifest its reign and dominion)' **will be progressively thrown out into the external darkness** (external obscurity of the shadows). **There** [= outside the banqueting building] **it will continue being 'the weeping and the grinding of teeth'** (or: The crying and the gnashing of teeth will continue being in that [outdoor] place, or situation)."

    [note: grinding/gnashing of teeth = either regret, or anger]

13. **So Jesus said to the centurion, "Go! In the same way that you trusted, let it come to be for you** (or: Just as you believe, let it be birthed and happen with you)!" **And so the orderly** (manservant; servant boy) **was healed and made whole in that hour.**

14. **Later, Jesus, upon coming into Peter's house, saw his mother-in-law having been thrown [out of good health] and now being bedridden and burning with a fever.**

15. **And so He touched her hand, and the fever flowed away from her. Then she got up** (arose) **and began giving attending service to, and dispensing [what was needed] for, Him.**

16. **Now with it becoming evening, people brought many folks being habitually affected by demons** [a Hellenistic word and concept: = animistic influences] **and He cast out the spirits** (breath-effects; attitudes) **with a word** (by a message; in a thought), **and He served, cured and restored to health** (or: gave attentive care or prescribed therapy or instigated ongoing treatment for) **all those continuously having it badly** (= those habitually with illness).

17. **In this way the things spoken through Isaiah the prophet would be fulfilled, [which] continue saying,**

    "He Himself took our incapacities (weaknesses; infirmities; sicknesses) **and then lifted up and bore away** (or: endured; supplied support with) **the diseases."** [Isa. 53:4]

18. **But then, upon seeing a crowd around Him, Jesus gave the order** (command) **to go off into the other side [of the lake].**

19. **Later, one scribe** (scholar; theologian; Law expert) **approaching [Him] said to Him, "Teacher, I will follow you wherever you may be now departing** (or: are about to go off)!"

20. **So Jesus then says to him, "The foxes continue having dens** (burrows), **and the birds of the sky** (or: atmosphere) **[have] roosts** (or: nests; lodging places), **yet the Son of the Man** (or: humanity's son; = the son of Adam; or: the eschatological messianic figure) **continues having nowhere He** (or: it) **can incline the head** (or: Head; = lay down the head for sleep)."

21. **Now a different one, from among the disciples** (students), **said to Him, "Master** (Sir; Lord), **permit me first to go off and to bury my father."**

22. **But Jesus says to him, "You continue following Me, and abandon** (divorce; leave behind; or: let; allow) **the dead folks to bury their own dead ones."**

23. **And so, with Him stepping into a boat, His disciples at once followed Him.**

24. **Later – look and consider! – a great quaking occurred** (an earthquake happened) **in the midst of the lake** (or: sea) **so that the boat was being repeatedly covered – to the point of being hidden and swamped – by the waves. Yet He kept on sleeping** (or: continued being fast asleep).

25. **So, approaching, they aroused Him, repeatedly saying, "O Lord** (Master)! **Rescue [us]** (Save [us]) **at once! We are progressively being destroyed and are perishing!"**

26. **And so He then says to them, "Why are you men frightened and lacking in courage? [You are] men with little trust and small faith!" At that point being aroused and getting up, He gave a respectful directive to** (or: spoke a value-based command upon) **the winds and the lake** (sea), **and a great calm was birthed** (or: it came to be utterly still).

27. **So the men were astounded with puzzled amazement, and one after another kept saying, "What kind** (or: sort) **of Person is this Man, that even the winds and the lake** (or: sea) **are in the habit of being obedient to Him** (or: are now submissively listening and paying compliant attention to Him)**?"**

28. **Then, upon His coming into the other side [of the lake] – into the country of the Gadarenes** [other MSS: Gergesenes] **– two men, affected or controlled by demons** [Hellenistic concept and term: = animistic influences, or, negative spirits], **met Him on their way coming out from among the memorial tombs** (the burial caves; graveyard). **[They were] extremely rugged men who were usually fierce to the point of being violent, savage, or hard to deal with, so that no one was normally strong enough to pass by through that way or along that road.**

29. **So look and consider! They cried out, repeatedly saying, "What [does this mean] for us and for You, O Son of God? Do** (or: Did) **You come here to test us or to cause us pain or distress before the appointed season** (or: before the right situation; before the fertile moment)**?"**

30. **Now there was a domestic herd of many pigs** (hogs; swine) **being habitually grazed some distance away from them,**

31. **so the demons** [Hellenistic concept and term: = animistic influences; violent spirits] **began calling Him to their side for help, and kept on pleading and bargaining with Him, saying, "Since** (or: If) **You are now in the process of casting us out, send us off on a mission** (or: as emissaries or representatives) **into that domestic herd of pigs!"**

32. **Accordingly He said to them, "Be proceeding on your way and bring things under control!" Now upon coming out, they went off into the pigs, and – now look and consider! – the entire herd at once stampeded down the steep slope** (or: precipice) **into the lake** (or: sea) **– and they died within the waters!"**

33. **Now the men habitually grazing** (the herdsmen normally tending and feeding [the pigs] at pasture) **ran off** (fled) **and, upon going** (or: coming) **away into the city, reported everything – as well as the situation and affairs pertaining to the men affected and controlled by the demons** [Hellenistic concept and term: = animistic influences].

34. **And now look and consider! The entire city came out to meet with Jesus. Then, upon seeing Him, they asked Him for help in the situation** (as a paraclete) **and, in bargaining, they earnestly urged Him so that He would change His steps and transfer Himself away from their boundaries** (territories; districts).

CHAPTER 9

1. **And so, upon stepping into** (or: boarding) **a boat, He passed right across through** (traversed, piercing through) **[the lake] and came into His own city.**

2. **Again look and consider! – People began bearing to Him upon a bed** (or: pallet; couch) **a paralytic, a man having been struck down [with paralysis] so as to be bedridden. And upon seeing their faith, trust and loyalty, Jesus said to the paralytic, "Be increasingly receiving courage and confidence, O child** (born one)**! Your failures and mistakes** (your times of missing the target; your errors and sins) **are being caused to progressively flow away** (or: are constantly being sent away and are habitually being forgiven)**!"**

3. **Now see what happens! – Certain ones of the scribes** (the scholars and theologians of the Law) **said among themselves, "This fellow is now blaspheming** (speaking impiously, villainously and inappropriately on matters of their religion)**!"**

4. **And having seen and thus perceiving** (knowing) **their inner emotions** (the rushing of thoughts and sentiments within them), **Jesus said, "To what end or purpose? You men are**

constantly having inward rushings of bad thoughts and angry, unprofitable sentiments within the midst of your hearts.

5. "For think about it, which is easier: to say, 'Your failures and mistakes are constantly being sent away and your sins are habitually forgiven,' or, to say, 'Proceed to rouse yourself and get up, and then continue walking around?'

6. "Yet now, so that you folks can see and know that the Son of the Man (the son of this humanity; mankind's Son; = Adam's son; or: = the eschatological messianic figure) constantly has (holds) authority from Being, and right upon the earth (or: Land) to habitually send away (make to flow off; forgive) sins and failures (mistakes and errors)" – He then continues saying to the paralytic, "Proceed to rouse yourself and get up. At once pick up your bed (or: pallet) and then, bringing yourself under control, be going into your home (or: house)!"

7. So upon being raised up, he went off unto his home (house).

8. Yet the crowds, seeing [what just happened], were struck with fear (or: became awestruck) and gave the glory to God (enhanced the reputation pertaining to God; formed opinions, made assumptions, and experienced impressions, about God) – the One giving such authority, from out of Being, to and for the human beings (or: people).

9. Then Jesus, continuing in leading [the group] along from there, saw a man called Matthew, who was presently sitting upon [the revenue receipts station at] the tax (customs; collections; tribute) office (or: at the toll booth), and He then says to him, "Be continuously following Me." And so, standing up, he at once followed Him.

10. Later, during His reclining [at a meal] within the house – now look and think about this! – it occurred [that] many tax collectors (customs and tribute agents; tax-farmers) and "sinners"

> (folks that the religious people considered "worldly" and by way of life ceremonially unclean and thus separated from the religious community: outcasts of society who failed to measure up to religious and cultural standards; irreligious folks) were coming and

began reclining back together with Jesus and His disciples [participating in their meal].

11. Well, upon seeing [this], the Pharisees began saying to His disciples, "Why or through what situation or arrangement does your teacher continue eating with the tax collectors and outcasts ('sinners')?"

12. Now He, upon hearing [this], said, "The strong and healthy folks are not normally having a need of a healer (a physician), but to the contrary those having it badly (= the sick; the ill) constantly do.

13. "Now, upon going your way, learn and become a disciple of what [this] is and means,
> 'I am presently desiring, habitually intending and progressively purposing mercy, and not a sacrifice!' [Hos. 6:6]

You see, I am not (or: did not) come to call 'righteous folks' (people who were supposedly in right relationship with God and community and who were convinced that they walked upright, in accord with the path pointed out), but on the contrary, outcasts ('sinners' who knew that they were neither connected nor in right relationship, nor approved in their way of life: failures)."

14. Then at one point the disciples of John proceeded in coming to Him, and proceeded in saying, "Why and through what situation or arrangement are we and the Pharisees constantly fasting, and yet Your disciples are not in the habit of fasting?"

15. So Jesus said to them, "The sons of the bridal chamber (or: attendants at a wedding hall; = the wedding guests and friends of the bridegroom; = those either at a wedding celebration or exemplifying that atmosphere) continue unable to mourn or be sad and lamenting upon the situation of however long (or: so long as) the bridegroom is with them. And yet days will continue coming when the bridegroom should be lifted up and withdrawn away from them, and at that time they will proceed to be fasting.

16. "Now nobody normally puts a patch of unshrunk cloth upon an old outer garment. You see, its filling-effect (i.e., the pre-shrunken patch which fills in the hole) is progressively pulling up away from the outer garment, and the split-effect (tear; rip; rent) progressively becomes worse.

17. **"Neither are people normally draining fresh, recently made, new wine into old skin-bags** (bottles), **otherwise the skin-bags are constantly bursting** (being torn open), **and then the wine is constantly being spilled out and the skin-bags continue being destroyed** (ruined). **To the contrary, people normally drain fresh, just-made, new wine into skin-bags having a new character and quality – and both continue being preserved.**

18. **During His speaking these things to them – look and consider! – one** (= a certain) **ruler was approaching [and] began bowing down in obeisance and worship to Him, proceeding in saying, "My daughter just now came to her end and died. But still, upon coming, at once put** (or: place) **Your hand upon her, and she will commence to be living!"**
19. **And so, being roused and getting up, Jesus and His disciples began following him.**
20. **Now look and consider this! – A woman [who was] constantly hemorrhaging** (bleeding) **for twelve years** [thus, being ceremonially unclean, and so, required to keep away from others so as not to contaminate them], **suddenly approaching, crept up from behind [and] touched the fringe** (or: tassels) **on the border of His cloak** (outer garment),
21. **you see, she had been saying within herself, "If only I can touch His cloak** (or: outer garment), **I will be healed and made whole!"**
22. **Now Jesus, being turned and seeing her, said, "Be increasingly receiving courage and confidence, daughter. Your faith, confidence and trust have healed you and you are now made whole!" And the woman was restored to health** (rescued; saved; delivered) **from that hour.**

23. **And so Jesus, coming into the ruler's house and seeing the flute players and the crowd continuing in being disturbed and thus making a commotion,**
24. **He began saying, "Withdraw and make room again! You see, the maiden** (little girl) **did not die, but rather she continues fast asleep." And so they began laughing at and ridiculing Him.**
25. **Now when the crowd had been forced out** (ejected), **He, upon entering, took a firm hold of her hand – and the maiden** (little girl) **was roused and raised up** (or: she got up)!
26. **Of course, the story of this – like the fame of the utterance of an oracle – spread out into [the] whole of that land** (or: territory).

27. **Now later, as Jesus continues leading [the crowd] in passing along from that place, two blind men followed Him [who] kept on crying out, repeatedly saying, "Mercy us** (Give mercy to us), **O Son of David** (this phrase may = "O descendant of David who also displays David's qualities and reminds us of the king of Israel;" or, it may be a phrase = "Messiah")!**"**
28. **So upon His coming into the house** (may = went indoors; or = arrived home), **the blind men came forward to** (or: approached) **Him, and Jesus then says to them, "Do you men continue having faith and are you believing that I am able and continue having power to do this?" They are [both] then saying, "Yes, O Lord** (or: Yes, Master; or: Yes, sir)."
29. **At that moment He touched their eyes, while saying, "Corresponding to your faith, confidence and trust, let it at once be birthed in you men** (or: let it come to be for, and happen to you)."
30. **And their eyes were instantly opened up! Jesus further, being deeply moved to the point of snorting with emotion for them, is then saying, "You are now continuing to see! Not even one person is to come to know, or continue with insight [about this]."**
31. **Yet they, upon going out, thoroughly spread the news about Him within that whole land** (or: territory).

32. **So in the midst of their going out** (leaving) **– look and consider this! – people brought to Him a person affected by a demon** (= a spiritual, or inner, influence) **with the result that he was unable to speak.**
33. **And then, upon the demon** [Hellenistic concept and term: = animistic influence] **being thrown out, the "mute man" spoke! And the crowds were amazed and filled with wonder, one after another saying, "Never was it thus seen** (or: was it shown in light to be made visible in this way) **within Israel!"**

34. **Yet the Pharisees began saying, "Within the [authority or power of], or in union with, or centered in, the ruler** (or: chief) **of the demons is he now expelling the demons."**

[comment: the Pharisees here give validity to the Hellenistic concept of demons, and to the pagan dualism which supposed that demons were beings which had a ruler. In the LXX, Isa. 65:3 spoke of Israel, saying "They repeatedly sacrifice in the gardens, and burn incense on the tiles, to the demons – which things do not exist!"]

35. **Next, Jesus began leading the way around all the cities and villages, habitually teaching within their synagogues and, as a herald, repeatedly making public proclamation of, and about, the good news** (the message of goodness, ease and well-being) **which pertains to and has its source in the "reign"** (of the sovereign influence which comprises the kingdom) – **as well as continuing in curing** (or: giving attentive care or prescribing therapy or ongoing treatment for) **every disease and all incapacities** (weaknesses; infirmities; sicknesses).

36. **Now upon seeing the crowds, He felt deep feelings, tender affection and compassion about them** (was affected in the inward parts of His body, encircling them with His emotions), **because they were** (they continued being) **folks having been skinned** (or: flayed and lacerated; and so: harried and troubled) **and hurled down or tossed out – as if [being] sheep not having a shepherd.**

37. **At that point He then says to His disciples** (students; apprentices), **"The harvest** (matured crop) **[is] indeed vast** (much; huge), **and yet the workers** (= the harvesters) **[are] few.**

38. **"Therefore, urgently ask – even beg – the Owner** (or: Master; Lord) **of the harvest so that He would thrust out workers into His harvest."**

CHAPTER 10

1. **And at one point, upon summoning His twelve disciples** (apprentices; students) **to Himself, He gave to them authority** (the right and privilege from out of Being) **pertaining to unclean spirits** (uncleansed attitudes; unpruned breath-effects), **to be habitually casting them out, as well as to be constantly curing** (or: treating and caring for) **every disease and all incapacities** (weaknesses; infirmities; sicknesses).

2. **Now these are the names of the twelve men sent forth with a mission** (emissaries; envoys; representatives): **First, Simon, the one called Peter, and then Andrew, his brother. Next, Jacob (James) the [son] of Zebedee, and his brother John.**

3. **And then [there are] Philip and Bartholomew, Thomas and Matthew – the tax collector** (or: tax-farmer), **Jacob the [son] of Alphaeus and Thaddaeus,**

4. **Simon the Cananaean** [other MSS: Cananite; possibly = a nationalist political party], **and then Judah (Judas) the one of Iscariot – the one transferring, commending and committing Him** (or: giving Him along; handing Him over; turning Him in [to the authorities]).

5. **Jesus commissioned and sent off these, the twelve, upon passing on announcements and instructions to them, continuing in saying, "You men should not go off into the roads or paths of ethnic multitudes** ([the] nations; the non-Israelite Gentiles; or: pagan ways), **and you should not enter into a Samaritan city.**

6. **"But, instead, continue on your way toward the lost and destroyed sheep that belong to, and are from, 'the house** (or: household) **of Israel.'**

7. **"Now as you are traveling on your way, be constantly performing the work of a herald, repeatedly saying publicly that the reigning and activity of exercising the sovereignty of the heavens** (or: kingdom of the atmospheres) **has drawn near and is close enough to touch** (= has arrived and is now accessible)!

8. **"Be constantly serving, curing and restoring to health** (or: giving attentive care to and treatment for) **those who are habitually weak, feeble and inadequate. Habitually be rousing and raising up dead people. Be continually cleansing lepers** (scabby folks). **Make it a habit to cast out demons** [Hellenistic concept and term: = animistic influences]. **You folks receive** (or: received) **freely** (as a gift; = without cost), **[so] give freely** (as a gift; = without charge).

9. **"You should not be procuring or acquiring gold, nor yet silver, nor even copper** [i.e., no pocket money] **into your belts or girdle purses.**

22

10. **"[Take] no beggar's pouch** (or: food bag; or: traveling knapsack) **into the road, nor two undergarments** (tunics) **or sandals nor yet a staff or club. You see, the worker [is] worthy of his nourishment** (or: is of corresponding value for his food, keep and support).

      [comment: be barefoot priests: the Land is holy; the villages are temples – Bruce Chilton]

11. **"Now, into whichever city or village you men may enter, search out who within it is suitable** (of corresponding values to your own; worthy), **[then] remain lodging there until you should leave** (go out of the midst [of the town]).

12. **"So, when entering in the house, greet, express good wishes and embrace the household,**

13. **"And if, indeed, the house should be suitable and worthy, you men let your peace** (the joining from and which is you folks; [= shalom]) **come upon it – yet if it may not be suitable or worthy, let your peace** (this joining from you) **be returned back upon yourselves.**

14. **"Also, whoever may not welcome and receive you men, nor even listen to your words or hear your message, as you are going outside, from out of the house or that city, shake the dust off your feet.**

      [note: Hospitality in those times and countries involved having a servant wash the feet of their guests; further: Jews did this when they left a Gentile country, so this would indicate that this town was being regarded as polluted and unholy, and in the same category as the Gentiles; comment: this could be a metaphor to shake off that incident, so as not to let their "humanity" cling to them]

15. **"Assuredly – I now say to you folks – it will proceed being more endurable in the land of Sodom and Gomorrah, in a day of separating and deciding, than in that city** (or: it will be more supportable for the land of Sodom and Gomorrah, in a day of judging, than for that town)!

16. **"Now look, and really see this situation: I, Myself, am now sending YOU folks off – being emissaries on a mission – as sheep within the midst of [a pack of] wolves! Therefore, habitually come to be thoughtful, prudent, cautious and discreet** (or: = wary and on the alert; = observant, decisive and timely) – **as the snakes [are]; and yet [still] unmixed** (pure; unblended; guileless; = without negative characteristics added) – **as the doves [are].**

17. **"So constantly hold your attention toward protecting yourself from the People** (or: the humans). **You see, they will periodically be giving YOU folks over** (commit you) **unto [their] local city councils and courts, and then they will proceed scourging YOU with lashes and whips.**

18. **"Yet YOU men will also, on My account, be from time to time led** (or: brought) **before** (or: on [the stand to speak to]) **governors and kings, with a view to being a witness to them and providing evidence for them – as well as to and for and among the ethnic multitudes** (the nations; the non-Israelite Gentiles; or: = the pagans).

19. **"However, whenever they may hand YOU folks over** (commit you), **you should not be anxious or overly concerned about how or what you should be speaking, for, what you should say will continue being given to you men – within that hour!**

20. **"You see, YOU, yourselves, are not the ones then speaking, but rather, [it is] the Spirit** (Breath-effect; Attitude) **of YOUR Father repeatedly speaking within you.**

21. **"So brother will continue giving over** (committing) **brother unto death – and a father, a child – and children will continue standing up upon** (or: rising up against or attacking) **parents and will from time to time murder them, or cause them to be put to death.**

22. **"And further, YOU folks will continue being hated, detached and regarded with ill-will by everyone – because of My Name. Yet the one remaining under [these conditions] to give support, and patiently enduring into a conclusion** (or: into an ending [of these events]; unto completion and [the] final act of the goal) – **this one will repeatedly be rescued** (delivered; saved; restored to health and wholeness).

23. **"Now whenever they may continue chasing YOU or be repeatedly persecuting YOU in this [particular] city, proceed taking flight** (escaping) **into a different one, for, truly – I now say to YOU folks – you can under no circumstances complete the circuit of** (or: finish [visiting]) **the cities** (or: towns) **of Israel until the Son of the Man** (humanity's son; = Adam's son; or: = the awaited Messianic figure) **should go** (or: comes; can come and then go).

24. **"A student** (or: disciple; apprentice) **is not over or above the teacher, nor [is] a slave over or above his owner** (or: master; lord).

25. **"[It is] sufficient and enough for the student** (or: disciple) **that he can come to be as his teacher, and the slave as his owner. Since** (or: If) **people call and surname the Sovereign** (Master and Sole Owner) **of the house** (or: the Householder) **'Beelzeboul'** [spellings vary; = lord of the flies, a Philistine deity], **how much rather** (or: more so) **those of His household.**

26. **"So then, you men should not be made to fear them. You see, there is nothing being veiled or covered which will not proceed having its covering taken away and be revealed, and hidden which will not be habitually made known and familiar.**

27. **"What I am now saying to YOU folks within the darkness** (the shaded areas of obscurity; = being within the system and religion of the dim shadows) **YOU say within the light** (= the light of the coming Day). **And what you are now hearing whispered into the ear, YOU people, as heralds, publicly proclaim upon the housetops** (= make it publicly known in the communities).

28. **"Stop being** (or: Do not continue being [other MSS: You should not be]) **made to fear from the one normally killing the body** [e.g., an enemy; a murderer], **and yet continuing unable** (powerless) **to be killing the soul** (interior life; consciousness; or: = one's honor and reputation). **But rather, be habitually fearing** (or: continue wary of, with a healthy respect for) **the person** [e.g., a ruler] **being constantly able and continuing with power to loose-away and destroy** (or: to cause to be lost) **both soul** (the interior life; [note: may refer to the person's reputation in regard to character and other personal qualities]) **as well as body within the Valley of Hinnom**
     (Greek: Gehenna; Jerusalem's garbage dump: the place where criminals and folks with disgraced lives, and thus considered unfit for proper burial, were cast away; the disgraced end of an outcast or criminal).

29. **"Are not two sparrows normally sold for a penny** (Roman copper coin of the smallest value)? **And yet not one from among them will proceed falling upon the ground without** (or: apart from) **your Father!** [comment: immanence; union of God with creation]

30. **"Now even the hairs of you head are all ones having been counted and numbered!**

31. **"Therefore, stop fearing** (or: Then do not continue fearing or being afraid). **You folks continuously carry on through so as to excel and be of more consequence than** (be superior to and thus of more value than) **whole flocks of sparrows!**

32. **"Everyone, then, that will keep on acknowledging union with Me and speaking in accord with Me in front of** (before and in the presence of) **the People** (the humans), **I, Myself, also will continue to acknowledge union with him and will keep on speaking of him in the same way** (saying the same thing of him) **in front of** (before and in the presence of) **My Father – the One within and in union with the heavens** (or: in the midst of the atmospheres).

33. **"Yet, whoever may at some point say, 'No' to, or contradict, Me** (or: would decline Me; or: can deny or disown Me), **in front of the People** (the humans), **I, Myself, also will proceed to say, 'No' to, or contradict, him** (or: will continue to decline, disown or deny him), **in front of My Father – the One within and in union with the heavens** (or: in the midst of the atmospheres).

34. **"YOU folks should not assume from custom or infer from the Law that I come** (or: go; came) **to throw peace** (a joining) **upon the Land** (or: earth). **I do** (or: did) **not come to throw** (impose) **peace or joining, but to the contrary, a sword** (a curved weapon for close combat)!

35. **"You see, I come** (or: came; go) **to disunite** (to make to be two and then pit):
     'a man against his father, and a daughter against her mother, and a bride against her mother-in-law,'

36. **"And so,**
     'a person's enemies [are/will be] those of his own household.' [Micah 7:6]

37. **"The person habitually having fondness and affection for father and mother over and above for Me is not suitable for Me** (or: worthy or of equal value with regards to Me). **Likewise the person continuing in having fondness and affection for a son or daughter over and above for Me is not suitable for Me** (worthy of Me). [comment: figures for Law and customs?]

38. **"Furthermore, he who is not habitually taking his cross** (execution-stake; hanging-pole) **and then constantly following after** (behind) **Me, is not suitable for Me** (worthy of Me).

39. **"The person who is searching and then finding his own soul** (his own will, intellect, emotions and self-life as his goals; or: the identity and consciousness that he is; or: the life from

him), **will be repeatedly losing it. And yet the person loosing-away or destroying his soul** (the consciousness which is him; his own will, self-focused life of a self-seeking, self-possessed persona and identity; or: his emotions, his plans and goals) – **on account of Me – will be progressively finding and discovering it** [i.e., his true self, identity, purpose & consciousness].

40. **"The person habitually receiving, welcoming and embracing YOU folks continually receives, welcomes and embraces Me; and the person that continues receiving, welcoming and embracing Me continuously receives, welcomes and embraces the ONE sending Me off as a representative with a mission** (as an emissary).
41. **"The person who by habit receives, welcomes and embraces a prophet, unto [regard or a function] that pertains to a prophet's reputation and vocation** (or: name), **will repeatedly receive a prophet's wage and reward. Likewise the person who by habit receives, welcomes and embraces a fair and just person** (one who maintains right relationships with God and mankind, and who has been rightwised into the path of the Way pointed out) **unto [regard or function] that pertains to a fair and just person's reputation and way of life** (or: with a view to [his or her having] a name, which is: 'a rightwised person'), **will habitually receive a wage and reward that pertains to a rightwised and equitable person.**
42. **"And further, whoever should give only a cup of cold water to drink to one of these little ones, only unto [regard or function] that pertains to the reputation and vocation of a disciple** (or: = solely with a view to his or her being named an apprentice), **assuredly** (amen), **I now say to** (lay it out for) **YOU folks, he can by no means lose his wage or reward.**

CHAPTER 11

1. **And so it came to be – when Jesus finished making thorough arrangements and completed the process of instruction for His twelve students** (or: disciples) **– [that] He redirected His steps and passed on from out of that place so as to continue teaching and making public proclamation within their cities and towns.**

2. **Now John, hearing in the prison** (or: jail) **[about] the works and acts of the Christ [and] sending by means of his disciples,**
3. **said to Him, "Are You the One progressively coming** (or: the ongoingly coming One), **or are we – or should we be – constantly projecting an opinion, an assumption or an anticipation into the future about a different one?"**
4. **And so, giving a considered response, Jesus said to them, "After traveling on your way, report back to John what you men are continuing to hear, and are repeatedly seeing:**
5. **"The blind folks again continue seeing, and the lame and crippled folks are continually walking about. The lepers are one-after-another being cleansed, and deaf people are constantly hearing.** [Isa. 35:5-6] **Even dead people are one-by-one being awakened and raised up** [Isa. 26:14] **– and the poor folks, the destitute ones, are continually having the good news of ease and well-being announced to them.** [Isa. 61:1]
6. **"And further, whoever is not caught by setting-off the trap-spring, and thus finding himself in a snare [of offence or antagonism] withn Me, continues being a happy person!"**

7. **Now with these men going their way, Jesus started saying to the crowds, concerning John, "What did you people go out into the wilderness to gaze** (or: gawk) **at and watch? A reed being constantly shaken** (cause to move to and fro) **by a wind?**
8. **"But further, what did you folks go out to see and perceive? A person having been clothed in soft, delicate garments? Think about it! Those normally wearing soft and delicate garments are in the houses that belong to kings.**
9. **"But to the contrary, why did you come** (or: go) **out? To see or perceive a prophet** (one with light ahead of time)**? Yes, I now say to you, even exceedingly more than a prophet.**
10. **"This person is he concerning whom it has been written,**

> **'Look and consider! I, Myself, am repeatedly sending forth My messenger, as an emissary on a mission – before Your face** (or: ahead of Your personal presence) **– who will progressively make Your road** (or: path) **useable by constructing or**

repairing and preparing it in front of You (or: who will prepare Your way before You).' [Mal. 3:1]

11. **"Truly, I am now saying to you folks, among those born of women there has not been raised up a person greater than John the Immerser** (the baptizer; the Baptist). **Yet the one of lesser importance** (or: the least; the smaller) **within, and in union with, the reign of the heavens** (or: kingdom of the atmospheres) **constantly exists being greater than he.**

12. **"Now from the days of John the Immerser until right now, the reign and dominion of the heavens** (or: sovereign influence and activities of the kingdom of the atmospheres) **is itself continuously pressing** (or: is progressively pressing and forcing itself) **forward with urgency, and those urging and pressing forward [toward the goal] are one after another grasping it and then drawing it up [to themselves].**

> [note: I have rendered *biazetai* (pressing and forcing itself) as a middle; it can also be rendered as a passive]

13. **"For you see, all the Prophets and the Law prophesy** (showed light ahead of time) **until** (to the point of time up to; till the time of) **John.**

14. **"And so, if you now desire and continue purposing to welcome, embrace and accept [it] or receive [Him], the One presently being at the point of being at [His] periodical coming and going is Himself** (or: the person currently being about to be presently and progressively coming: this very one exists being) **Elijah.**

15. **"Let the person now having ears to continue hearing, continue listening and hearing** (or: = pay attention)!

16. **"Now to what or with whom shall I compare, or say is like, this generation? It exists being like little boys and girls, habitually sitting in the marketplaces, who – constantly shouting to different people –**

17. **"are repeatedly saying,**

> **'We play the flute and pipe for you folks, and you are not dancing. We lament, wail and sing funeral songs, and yet you folks are not beating your chests or wailing.'**

18. **"You see, John came neither habitually eating nor constantly drinking, and people are continually saying, 'He continues having and holding a demon** [Hellenistic concept and term: = an animistic influence].'

19. **"The Son of the Man** (the son of mankind; humanity's son; = the son of Adam; or: the Human Being) **comes regularly eating and continuously drinking, and people are repeatedly saying, 'Look, see a person [who is] a glutton** (or: = a euphemism for those not keeping dietary rules; -- R. Eisenman) **and a drunkard** (one who habitually drinks too much wine), **a friend of tax collectors** (customs and tribute agents; or: tax farmers) **and outcasts**

> (sinners; folks that the religious people considered "worldly" and by way of life ceremonially unclean and thus separated from the religious community: outcasts of society who failed to measure up to religious and cultural standards; irreligious people)!'

Well, Wisdom was set and deemed in right relationship with fairness and equity in the Way pointed out – from its deeds (works and actions)!"

20. **At that point He started to censure and reproach the character and reputation of the cities within which most** (or: the majority) **of His powers and abilities** (or: expressions of power and deeds of ability) **happened** (were birthed), **because they did not change their minds to a new state of consciousness and way of thinking, and thus return to God:**

21. **"Tragic will be your fate, Chorazin! Tragic will be your fate, Bethsaida! Because if the powers and abilities being birthed and happening within you had taken place in Tyre and Sidon, long ago THEY would in sackcloth and ashes** (= humility and regretful sorrow) **have changed their minds, consciousness and way of thinking, and would have turned to God.**

22. **"What is more, I now say to you folks, it will consequently be more endurable in, and for, Tyre and Sidon, in a day of evaluation and decision** (judging), **than for you folks!**

23. **"And as for you, Capernaum! Will you proceed to be 'exalted as far as heaven** (or: the sky)'? **No!**

> **'You will be brought down and "mounted"** (as a female by a male) **as far as the Unseen** (*Hades*; = *Sheol*; the grave; the abode of the dead; = death)!' [Isa. 14:13, 15]

Because if the powers and abilities, being birthed and happening within you, had taken place in Sodom, it (= those people) **would have remained in place unto today.**

24. **"What is more, I now say to you folks, that it will consequently be more endurable in [the] land of Sodom** (= for Sodom's people), **in a day of evaluation and decision** (or: judging) **than for you folks!"**

25. **Speaking from a discerning and decided perception within that fitting situation** (or: during that particular season [of ministry]; or: at that strategic moment), **Jesus said, "I continue outwardly and joyfully acclaiming My concurrence with You, publicly admitting the same idea and reason as You, O Father – Owner, Lord and Master of the heaven and of the earth** (or: of the sky and atmosphere, as well as of the land) **– that You hide** (or: because You hid) **these things from 'wise folks'** (or: 'clever people') **and 'understanding, intelligent, intellectuals,' and You unveil** (or: revealed; disclosed) **them to infants** (babes who are not yet able to speak; = untutored, untaught, ordinary folks).
26. **"Yes Father, because in this way goodwill is birthed in front of You** (or: because thus does Your thought, imagination and presuming of ease and well-being come into existence in Your presence)**!"**

27. **"All humanity was transferred, given over** (or: All things were delivered and committed) **to Me by, and under, My Father, and yet no one is by habit completely or accurately knowing the Son in an intimate and personal way – except the Father – nor does anyone continue having an intimate experiential full-knowledge of the Father – except the Son, as well as to, or in, whomever the Son would continue desiring** (or: determining) **to unveil or reveal [Him].**
28. **"So everyone come here, toward Me! – all those constantly weary and exhausted from toil and labor, as well as folks having been caused to carry a load, and continuing burdened down – and I, Myself, will continue refreshing you and causing you folks to rest.**
29. **"You folks at once lift up My crossbeam** (or: the yoke which is Me; the balance beam that comes from and pertains to Me) **upon you, and instantly learn from Me, because I am** (or: I continuously exist being) **mild-tempered** (gentle; kind; considerate) **and humble** (low) **in the heart, and 'you folks will continue finding refreshment and discovering rest in and for your souls** (= consciousness and whole inner person; the mind, emotions and responses).' [Jer. 6:16]
30. **"You see, My crossbeam** (or: the yoke which is Me; the balance beam that comes from and pertains to Me) **is useful, well-fitting and kindly obliging, and My load** (the burden that is Me and which pertains to Me) **continues being light** (not heavy)**."**

CHAPTER 12

1. **In that particular situation** (or: On that occasion; or: Within that season [= the ripening of the grain, just prior to harvest]) **Jesus went His way through the fields of sown grain, on [one of] the sabbaths.**
Now His disciples were hungry, and they began to repeatedly pluck (or: pick; strip) **heads of grain and to continue eating [them].**
2. **So, seeing [this happening], the Pharisees said to Him, "Look! Your disciples continue doing what [is] not right or permitted to be doing during a sabbath, from [our] existence!"**

3. **But He said to them, "Do** (or: Did) **you folks not read what David – as well as those with him – did when he got hungry:**
4. **"how he entered into God's house** (home) **and they ate the loaves** (= the consecrated bread) **of the presentation** (the placing-before [God's presence]) **– which, from [our] existence [as God's People], was not normally being right or permitted for him to be eating, nor for those with him, except [by] the priests only?**
5. **"Or, do** (or: did) **you folks not read within the Law** [= the Torah] **that on the sabbaths the priest in the Temple courts** (grounds) **habitually profane** (= violate the sacredness of) **the sabbath, and continue being guiltless** (blameless; faultless; innocent)**?**
6. **"Now I am saying to you folks that there is now here** (in this place) **something greater** (or: = more important) **than the Temple courts and grounds!**
7. **"But, if you had come to personally** (or: by intimate experience or insight) **know what [this] is** (or: = means),

'I am habitually wanting (desiring), **repeatedly intending and continuously purposing mercy, and not sacrifice,'** [Hos. 6:6] **you folks would not ever oppose fairness, equity and justice, while you degrade the way pointed out in condemning the guiltless ones** (the blameless and innocent folks) [cf vs. 5, above: = the priests of the new order].

8. **"You see, the Son of the Man** (the son of the human; = the son of Adam; = a human being) **continues being a lord** (master; or: [the] Lord and Owner) **of the sabbath."**

9. **And so, re-directing His steps from out of that place, He went into their synagogue,**
10. **and – Look, and consider! – a man having a withered** (dried-up) **hand [was there]. So they put a question to Him – to the end that they could accuse** (bring charges against and discredit) **Him – by asking if it is right and permitted, from [their] existence [as God's People], to habitually serve, heal, cure or give medical treatment on the sabbaths.**
11. **So He now said to them, "Who from you folks will proceed to be a person** (or: What man of you people will there continue being) **who will continue having one sheep, and if this one should fall into a pit** (a hole in the ground; a well; a cistern) **on or during the sabbaths, will not proceed to be firmly grabbing hold of it and raising [it] up?**
12. **"Of how much more does a human habitually carry through to be of greater consequence or worth – than a sheep? It is always right and permitted, from [our] existence [as God's People], to habitually do ideally** (finely; beautifully) **on the sabbaths."**
13. **At that time, He is then speaking to the man, "At once stretch out** (or: forth) **your hand!" So he at once stretched [it] out, and it was at once restored to be sound and healthy, just as the other one [or: hand].**

14. **Now upon going outside, the Pharisees took deliberation together and resolved a jointly-considered purpose down against Him, so that they could loose Him away** (or: destroy Him; make Him to be lost-away from [them]; = to get rid of Him).
15. **Yet Jesus, aware [of this], withdrew from that place, and many people followed Him, and He served, attentively cared for, treated, prescribed therapies for, instigated ongoing procedures for, cured and, or, healed them all.**
16. **Following this, He respectfully gave them admonition, apprising them of the situation and His wishes, to the end that they would not draw attention to Him, making Him a visible public figure, nor disclose His identity.**
17. **[This was] so that the [prophecy; oracle] declared through Isaiah the prophet would** (or: could) **be fulfilled, [that] continues saying,**
18.   **"Look, and consider! My Boy** (or: My Servant; My personal attendant; My servant-boy) **Whom I select** (or: chose) **– My Beloved, [of] Whom My soul** (consciousness; inner life) **assumes ease and wellness** (or: [in] Whom My self takes pleasure; Whom My soul considers good and thinks well of)! **I will proceed putting** (placing) **My Spirit** (the effect of My breath; My Attitude) **upon Him, and He will continue sending-off a message regarding separating, evaluating, and a deciding FOR the ethnic multitudes**
            (or: will repeatedly announce a judging and bring a report of justice in the nations; will continue plainly declaring what justice and discrimination is to non-Jews; will continuously announce a deciding, among the Gentiles [= foreigners]).
19.   **He will neither proceed to quarrel** (strive; debate; be contentious) **nor will He continue shouting** (screaming or making outcry; causing clamoring; behaving loud-mouthed), **nor yet will anyone continue hearing His voice** [above the ambient noises] **in the town squares or broad streets.**
20.   **He will not proceed to break down a reed that has been bruised** (or: break in pieces a reed that has been crushed), **and He will not proceed to extinguish a flax lamp-wick that is continuing in being wrapped in smoke and made to smolder – until He can thrust-forth [the] separation-and-evaluating-derived deciding into a victory** (or: would cast-out judging – unto Victory)!
21.   **And then, the ethnic multitudes** (nations; pagans; foreigners; Gentiles) **will proceed to be continuously placing [their] expectations in His Name** (= on His character,

reputation and authority)!" [Isa. 42:1-4; comment: this passage describes a Person who is gentle and non-violent in character]

22. At that time people brought to Him a man continuously affected and controlled by a demon [a Hellenistic concept and term; = an animistic influence] **– blind and mute** (incapable of speaking). **And so He treated and cured him, so that the mute man [began] to be repeatedly speaking and continuously seeing.**

23. **Well, all the crowds began being set out of place** (or: being made to stand out of themselves) **in amazement, and began saying, "Is not this one perhaps 'the son of David'?"**

24. **Now upon hearing, the Pharisees said, "This person is not casting** (or: throwing) **out the demons except in union with Beelzebub** [other MSS: Beelzebul; Beezeboul], **the ruler** (or: chief; originator) **of the demons** [Hellenistic concept and term: = animistic influences]."

> [comment: Beelzebub, is the NT spelling for *Baal-zebub*, a Philistine deity (2 King 1:2). So here we have the Pharisees validating the existence of a pagan god! And yet, we are told in Ps. 96:5 (Heb.) that "all the gods of the peoples (= people groups) are mere idols (nobodies; things of naught)." The LXX (Greek OT) renders this: "all the gods of the ethnic multitudes (nations; non-Israelites) {are} demons." But Isaiah says in 65:3 (LXX), "This is a people that … offer{s} sacrifices in gardens, and burn{s} incense on bricks to the demons – which things DO NOT EXIST!" – JM]

25. **So, having seen and now knowing** (perceiving) **their inner impulses, emotions, sentiments and reflections, He said to them, "Every reign of a king** (kingdom; = government) **being parted** (divided and separated into parts) **down against itself is being progressively turned into a desert** (made desolate, waste and depopulated), **and every city or household being parted down against itself will not continue standing** (= be surviving).

26. **"So if '*Satan*' continues casting** (or: driving) **out '*Satan*,' he is parted** (divided and separated into parts) **upon himself. How, then, will his 'reign** (kingship; royal influence; governmental activities)' **continue standing** (= be surviving)?** [note: He equates the concept of "*satan*" (literally: an adversary) with their pagan deity "Beelzebub" – an idol that does not exist]

27. **"And if I, Myself, 'in union with Beelzebub' continue casting** (or: driving) **out the demons, in union with whom are your sons habitually casting and driving [them] out? Through this** (or: Therefore; For this reason), **they, themselves, will continue being your judges** (or: decision makers pertaining to you folks). [note: i.e., judging them as idolaters and false accusers]

28. **"Yet if I, Myself, in union with God's Spirit** ([being] within the midst of the effect of God's Breath; in an attitude which is God) **am constantly driving** (or: casting) **out the demons** [the animistic influences [a Hellenistic term] **God's reign** (the kingdom from God; the sovereign rule which is God, and the influence of God) **has consequently preceded and come beforehand upon you people** (or: has really overtaken you folks and is now arrived and settled upon you).

29. **"Or, how does anyone have power or ability to enter into the house belonging to a strong person and to seize** (snatch up and plunder) **his movable goods** (equipment; utensils; gear; belongings; possessions), **unless he can** (or: should) **first bind** (tie up) **the strong person? After that he will proceed in completely plundering** (thoroughly looting) **his house.**

30. **"The person not continually being with Me** (= on My side) **continues being against Me, and the person not habitually gathering** (or: leading together) **with Me is constantly scattering.**

31. **"For this reason, I continue saying to you folks, Every failure** (mistake; error; failure to attain the goal or hit the target; sin) **and blasphemy** (vilifying, abusive and slanderous speech; light-hindrance) **will be caused to flow away from** (will be divorced and sent off for; will be pardoned and forgiven) **the People** (humans). **Yet, the blasphemy of, or pertaining to** (vilifying, abusive, slanderous speech about), **the Spirit** (the Breath-effect; the Attitude) **will not be caused to flow away** (not be divorced and sent off; not be pardoned or forgiven) **the People.**

32. **"And further, whoever may say a word** (should speak a thought or message) **[directed] down against the Son of the Man** (the son of humanity; = Adam's son), **it will continue caused to flow away for him** (will be progressively divorced and sent off in him; or: he will continue pardoned and forgiven by Him). **Yet [for] whoever may speak down against the Set-apart**

Spirit (the Breath-effect of the Holy One; the Sacred Attitude), **it will not proceed to be caused to flow away from him** (or: he will not continue pardoned and forgiven by Him; it will not progress to be released and sent off in him) – **neither within this age, nor within the one being about to be** (the impending one).

33. **"[So first of all,] you folks either make the Tree ideal** (beautiful), **and thus its fruit [will be] ideal** (beautiful), **or make the Tree rotten, and its fruit [will be] rotten**

> (or: either grow and produce the Tree [that is] fine, and then its fruit [will be] fine, or else grow and produce the Tree [that is] decaying, and its fruit [will be] decaying; or: = either assume {judge; decide} that the Tree [is] healthy and sound, and assume {conclude} its fruit [will be] healthy and sound, or decide and consider that this Tree [is] unhealthy and rotten, and thus its fruit [will be] unhealthy and rotten, and tell us). **You see, the Tree is habitually being known and experienced from out of the [or: its] fruit.** [cf 3:10; cf Gen. 2:9]

34. **"Offspring** ([You] effects of the births) **of poisonous snakes** (vipers; serpents; [comment: perhaps equating them to satan])**! How are you able to habitually say good and virtuous things, being inherently good-for-nothing and useless folks** (being worthless and knavish; being folks in a sorry plight and oppressed by grievous toils; existing being base and wicked; continuously being ones characterized by evil)**? You see, from out of the midst of the effect of the excess from the heart's surrounding abundance, the mouth is continually speaking.**

35. **"The good and virtuous person is habitually extracting and spurting out good and virtuous things from out of the midst of the Good and Virtuous Treasure-house. And yet the good-for-nothing and useless person is continuously extracting and spurting out worthless, oppressive, knavish, base, wicked and evil things from out of the mist of the worthless treasure-house.** [comment: treasure-house = the heart, vs. 34; cf 13:52, below]

36. **"Now I continue saying to you folks that [for] every ineffective and unproductive** (idle and unemployed; thus: unprofitable) **effect of a gush or result of some flow** (or: thing spoken; saying; declaration) **which the People** (or: humans) **will be speaking, they will continue giving back** (rendering) **an account** (a word; a thought; an idea; = an explanation) **concerning it, within a day of separating, evaluating and deciding** (or: judging).

37. **"For you see, from out of your words** (or: verbal expressions; ideas and thoughts) **you [individually] will be progressively rightwised and brought into right relationships** (turned in the right direction, set right and made fair) **within the Way pointed out; and from out of your words** (expressed thoughts, messages and ideas) **you [individually] will continue being correspondingly bound to what is right by the Way pointed out** (or: accordingly opposed by justice and right relationships; or: convicted with an adverse sentence)**."**

38. **At that point some of the scribes** (scholars; theologians; experts of the Law) **and the Pharisees gave a calculated response to Him, one after another, saying, "Teacher, we continue wanting to see a sign from you!"**

39. **So He, making a decided reply, said to them, "A good-for-nothing, worthless, base, knavish, grievously oppressive and wicked – even adulterous** (unfaithful and immoral) – **generation repeatedly seeks intently for a sign! And yet a sign will not proceed to be given to it – except the sign of Jonah the prophet.**

40. **"You see, just as Jonah was within the midst of the belly of the huge fish** (or: sea monster) **[for] three days and three nights** [Jonah 1:17], **thus in this way will the Son of the Man** (humanity's son; = Adam's son) **continue being within the heart of the earth [for] three days and three nights.** [comment: then the message went to the Gentiles, vs. 41]

41. **"Adult males – Ninevites – will stand back up again with this generation, in the separating and deciding** (the judging), **and they will progressively make a corresponding decision about** (or: condemn) **it, because they changed their way of thinking and state of consciousness into the message publicly proclaimed by Jonah – and take note of this, something more than Jonah [is] here!** [Rom. 12:2; comment: they accepted the messafe]

42. **"[The] queen of [the] south will proceed to be aroused and raised up in the separating and deciding** (the judging) **with this generation, and she will progressively make a corresponding decision about** (or: condemn) **it, because she came from out of the extremities of the land to hear the wisdom of Solomon – and take note of this, something more than Solomon [is] here!**

43. "Now whenever **the unclean spirit** (or: unpruned attitude; unpurged breath-effect; foul wind) **should come forth** (or: go out) **away from the person** (or: human)**, it normally passes through waterless places, continuously seeking a resting place** (or: rest; a ceasing from activity) **– and it continues finding none.**

44. "**At that point, it proceeds to say, 'I will proceed turning back into my house from where I came** (or: moved) **out.' And, upon coming, it is then finding [it] continuing being unoccupied** (being unemployed, and thus, at leisure) **and having been swept clean with a broom – even having been put in orderly arrangement and decorated** (or: furnished)**!**

45. "**At that time it continues journeying on its way, and then proceeds taking along with itself seven different spirits** (attitudes; breath-effects; winds) **more good-for-nothing and useless** (base, wicked, knavish, grievously oppressive and evil) **than itself, and upon entering, it settles down and continues dwelling there in the house. So the last [circumstances] of that person becomes progressively worse than the first ones. Thus in this way will it also proceed being with** (or: for; in; to) **this good-for-nothing and wicked generation.**"

46. **While He was yet speaking to the crowds – look, and take note! – His mother and brothers** (= siblings) **had taken a position and now stood outside, persistently seeking to speak to Him.**

47. **Now someone said to Him, "Look – Your mother and Your brothers have taken a stand, and continue standing outside, persistently seeking to speak to You."**

48. **Yet He, making a considered response, said to the person then speaking to Him, "Who is My mother, and which ones are My brothers?"**

49. **Then, stretching out His hand upon [the assembly of] His disciples, He said, "Look at, and consider – My mother and My brothers!**

50. "**You see, whoever may be doing the will, intent, purpose and desire of My Father – the One within and in union with [the] heavens** (or: in the midst of [the] atmospheres) **– that very person is My brother and sister and mother!**"

CHAPTER 13

1. **On that day** (= That same day)**, after coming out of the house, Jesus had spent some time sitting on the shore, beside the lake** (or: sea).

2. **And so great was the concourse of people that were gathered together toward Him, that He was stepping into a small boat to continue sitting down – and the entire crowd stood on the beach.**

3. **And so he spoke many things to them, continuing in gathering thoughts and laying them in order, in parables**

> (things cast down at the side for comparison; illustrations; [note: used for Hebrew *masal* in the LXX, so = a variety of figures of speech: riddle; proverb; ethical maxim; by-word; allegory; fable; enigmatic saying that is meant to stimulate intense thinking)**:**

4. "**Look and consider! The sower comes out** (or: went out) **to be progressively sowing** (scattering seed [in a field])**. Now in the midst of his continued sowing, some [seeds] on the one hand fell alongside the path – and with the birds coming, they ate them down** (devoured them).

5. **On the other hand, other [seeds] fell upon the rocky places** (or: shallow soil where layers of rock lie near the surface)**, where it continues having not much soil, and immediately, set for success, it shoots forth again, back up – because of the [situation of] not having a depth of soil.**

6. **Yet upon a rising back up again of [the] sun, it was scorched – and thus, because of the [situation of] not having [sufficient] root, it was dried up and withered.**

7. **Now others fell upon the thornbushes** (or: prickly weeds)**, and the thornbushes came up and choked them off** (smothered them).

8. **But others fell upon the ideal soil, and it began and kept on yielding fruit – this one, on the one hand, a hundred; that one, on the other hand, sixty; yet some, thirty.**

9.   Let the person possessing ears continue listening, hearing and paying attention."

10. Then, approaching, the disciples said to Him, "Why (Through what [purpose; motive]) are you continuing to speak to them in parables (here: = illustrative riddles; = Hebrew *masal*)?"

11. So giving a decided response, He said to them, "To (or: For; With) you folks it has been given to intimately experience and insightfully know the secrets (mysteries) of the reign and dominion of the heavens (or: the kingdom which is the heavens; the royal rule, influences and activities which pertains to and has its origin in the heavens, and which emanates from the atmospheres), yet it has not been given to those people.

12. "You see, whoever continues possessing (presently and habitually holds [understanding]; repeatedly has [something]), to him it (or: something; or: [understanding]) will continue being given and he will habitually be made to superabound (or: have more than enough); yet whoever does not continue possessing (habitually holding; repeatedly having), even what he does have will be progressively taken away from him.

13. "Therefore I continue speaking in parables (with illustrations) to them, because while seeing (or: observing) they continue not seeing, and during listening (or: hearing) they are not hearing (or: listening) – neither are they comprehending or understanding (having things flow together so as to get the picture or see the relationships).

14. "And so the prophecy of Isaiah is progressively being filled up in (or: for; by) them – the one continuing in saying,

'In listening you folks will keep on hearing, and yet you can by no means have things flow together so as to get the picture or see the relationships (or: comprehend or understand), and while constantly looking, you will continue observing, and yet you can by no means see so as to perceive.

15.   'For the heart of this People was made thick and fat, and thus has become impervious, dull and insensitive, and with the ears they hear heavily, and are thus hard of hearing, and they shut (or: closed) their eyes (or: they squint their eyes), lest at some time they might see with [their] eyes and should then be listening and hearing with [their] ears, and with the heart they could make things flow together so as to comprehend – and they might turn about! And so, I will progressively cure and heal them!' [Isa. 6:9-10]

(or: ... and they squint their eyes! At some point should they not see with [their] eyes, and continue listening so as to hear with [their] ears, and thus understand in the heart? And then they can turn around, and I will continue healing them!')

16. "However, your eyes [are] happy (blessed and prosperous, and thus, privileged), because they continue seeing – as well as your ears, for they are presently and habitually hearing.

17. "You see I am now telling you frankly and truly that many prophets and rightwised folks (upright, fair and just people) passionately desired to see [the] things which you folks are now habitually seeing (or: looking at) – and yet they did not see; and to hear things which you are continuously hearing – and yet they did not hear.

18. "Therefore, you folks listen to, and be hearing, the parable (illustration cast by your side) of the sower (or: the scattering of seed).

19. "Concerning everyone constantly listening to and hearing the Word of the sovereign reign and activities (or: the thought, idea and message of the kingdom) and yet continuing in not understanding (being unable to have things flow together unto comprehension): the worthless person or the disadvantageous circumstance (or: the one who brings pain and misery through hard labor; the malevolent and wicked man; the evil one; or: the difficult and wearisome situation) is repeatedly coming and is habitually snatching up what has been sown (scattered as seed) within his heart – this is the one sown alongside the path or road.

20. "Now [as to] the one being sown (scattered) upon the rocky places, this one is the person continuing in hearing the Word (thought; idea; message), and at once, set for success, progressively receiving it with joy!

21. "However, he is not continuing to have a root within himself, but is instead existing for [only] a season (is temporary, or lasts only for that particular situation or occasion), so with an

occurring (happening; birthing) **of pressure** (tribulation; distress) **or pursuit and persecution – because of the message** (the Word; the idea) **– though set for success, he is at once caught in a trap, as though these circumstances were a trap-stick, and so he is made to stumble, being offended.**

22. **"Now [as to] the one being sown** (scattered) **into the midst of the thorns, this one is the person continuing in hearing the Word** (message; thought; idea), **and yet the anxiety** (care; worry; concern; distraction) **of the age** [other MSS: this age], **and the seductiveness and deception of the riches and wealth [involved], together progressively choke the Word** (or: message; idea) **and it** (or: he) **progresses to become unfruitful.**

23. **"As for the one sown** (scattered) **upon the ideal soil** (earth), **this is the person continuing in hearing the Word** (or: message; idea) **and progressively allowing things to flow together unto comprehension and understanding – who in reality does progressively bear fruit, and is continuing producing: this one, on the one hand, a hundred, that one, on the other hand, sixty, yet another one thirty [times what was sown]."**

24. **He placed** (or: put; set) **another parable** (illustration) **beside [the previous one] for them, proceeding in saying,**

> **"The reign and sovereignty activities of the heavens** (or: kingdom dominion of the atmospheres) **is likened and compared to a person** (human) **sowing** (scattering) **fine, ideal seed within his field.**

25. > **"Now during the continued sleeping of the people, his enemy** (the one hostile to him) **came and oversowed weed seeds** (scattered-on darnel [= a wild grass, or, bastard wheat]; i.e., plants that would compete with the main crop, and that would cause extra work at harvest time) **again, through the midst of the wheat** (or: grain), **and then went away.**

26. > **"So when the blade sprouted and put forth leaves, and then produced fruit** (a crop), **at that time the weeds** (darnel: indistinguishable from wheat stalks until close to harvest time) **also became apparent** (visible and evident).

27. > **"And so the slaves, upon approaching the householder, said to him, 'Master** (Lord; Sir), **did you not sow fine, ideal seed within your field? From where, then, is it now having weeds** (darnel)?'

28. > **"So the man affirmed to them, 'A person [who is] an enemy did this!'**
> **Now they continue in saying to him, 'Are you now, therefore, desiring [that] we, upon going off, should gather them** [i.e., the weeds] **together** (= cull them out)?'

29. > **"But he affirms, 'No, otherwise** (or: lest at some point) **during collecting together the weeds you men might at the same time uproot the wheat** (or: grain) **along with them.**

30. > 'Allow (or: Leave) **both to continue growing side by side until the harvest, and within the season of the harvest I will proceed to be telling the reapers, First gather the weeds together and bind them into bundles for the purpose of burning them down. But progressively gather the wheat** (or: grain) **into my barn** (storehouse).'"

31. **He placed** (or: put; set) **another parable** (illustration) **beside [the previous one] for them, proceeding in saying,**

> **"The reign and sovereignty of the heavens** (or: kingdom dominion of the sky and atmosphere) **exists being** (or: is) **like seed of a mustard plant – which, upon taking, a man** (a person) **sowed within his field –**

32. > **"which on the one hand is smaller than all the seeds, yet on the other hand, whenever it might grow, is greater than the vegetables** (= is the largest of the garden plants and herbs) **and progressively comes to be a [veritable] tree [in size and form], so that the birds of the sky** (or: atmosphere; heaven) **come and periodically roost within its branches."**

33. **He spoke another parable** (illustration) **to them:**

> **"The reign** (kingdom; sovereignty; dominion) **of the heavens and atmospheres exists being** (is) **like leaven** (or: yeast) **which a woman, upon getting** (taking; receiving) **[it], hides within** (= mixes in) **three large measures** (1.5 pecks, or 12 quarts, per measure)

of wheat flour, or meal, until [the] whole [batch] is leavened to thus be fermented, risen [and teeming with life]!"

34. Jesus spoke all these things in parables to the crowds, and apart from parables He was, and continued, speaking nothing to them,

35. so that the [prophecy; oracle] being declared through the prophet would (or: could) be fulfilled, [which] continues saying,

"I will repeatedly open My mouth in parables (illustrations); I will constantly disgorge and spew out things having been hidden from [the; a] casting-down

(a laying of a foundation; or, metaphorically: a conception [as used in Heb. 11:11, "a casting-down of seed"]) [other MSS add: of {the} organized System (or: world; cosmos; universe; or: the world of culture and religion)]." [Ps. 78:2]

36. At that time, after leaving (or: dismissing) the crowds, He went into the house. And then His disciples approached Him, one after another saying, "Make the parable (illustration) of the weeds (darnel) of the field thoroughly clear and distinct for (or: to) us (= explain it so that we can plainly understand it)."

37. So He, setting forth a reply giving discernment, said, "The person habitually sowing the fine, ideal seed is the Son of the Man (or: mankind's son; = the son of Adam; = the human).

38. "Now the field is the organized System (the ordered arrangement; the world of religion, economy, culture and government; = the realm of society; or: the aggregate of humanity). As for the fine, ideal seed, these are the sons of the reign (= the produce and resulting situation which have the kingdom as their source and origin; the offspring who are the reign; = those things having the character and quality of the kingdom and are associated with its reign). Yet the weeds (darnel) are the sons of the worthless person or the disadvantageous circumstance

(or: the sons whose source and origin is the one who brings pain and misery through hard labor; the produce whose character and quality are malevolent and wicked; the sons of the evil one; or: offspring of the difficult and wearisome situation [the predicament of mankind?]; the bad environment; may = the result of the work of a worthless person [perhaps: the words of a religious person]).

39. "And now the enemy (the hostile person) – the person sowing them – is the adversary (the person who will thrust something through you; or: the "devil"). And then [the] harvest is [the] bringing of the parts together to one destined end (or: a combined final act; a purposed consummation; a putting together of the final product; a joining of all aspects into the fruition of the goal) of an age, but the harvesters (reapers) are agents (messengers; folks with the message).

40. "Therefore, just as the weeds (darnel) are periodically collected together and are normally burned down (or: up) in a fire, thus will it be within the conclusion (the combined final act; the joining of all parts and aspects to one end and goal) of the age [other MSS: this age].

41. "The Son of the Man will progressively send off His agents (messengers; folks with the message) as emissaries, and they will continue gathering together out of His kingdom (collect and cull out of His reign) all the snares and things which entrap, as well as the folks habitually producing (or: doing; constructing; practicing; creating) the lawlessness.

42. "Next they will continue throwing them into the furnace (oven; kiln) of The Fire [note: a figure of being dealt with in, and by, God]: 'the weeping (crying and lamentation) and the grinding of teeth' will continue being in that situation (or: place).

43. "At that time, the fair and equitable (upright) folks – who live in the pointed-out Way of right relationships, rightwised behavior and justice – will be progressively giving out Light, as from lamps (or: will shine forth from out of the midst), in the same way as the sun, in union with the reign, and within the kingdom, of their Father. Let the person having ears to hear continue listening and be constantly hearing!

44.   "The reign (or: kingdom; sovereignty; dominion) of the heavens and atmospheres exists being (or: is) like a treasure – having been hidden (or: being concealed) within the midst of a field – which, upon finding, a person hid (concealed) [again] and

then, from the joy he has, he proceeds leaving [it] and one after another sells as many things as he is then possessing and is proceeding in purchasing that field.

45. "Again, the reign (or: kingdom; sovereignty; dominion) of the heavens and atmospheres exists being (or: is) like a human being – a traveling business man (or: merchant), constantly trying to find beautiful, ideal pearls.

46. "Now upon finding one very valuable pearl, after at once going away, he has exported for sale and disposed of everything – as much as he was holding (possessing) – and he buys it at the market place.

47. "Again, the reign (or: kingdom; sovereign influence) of the heavens and atmospheres exists being (or: is) like a dragnet (a seine) being cast into the lake (or: sea) and gathering together [some] of every species [of marine life, into the net],

48. "from which – when it was filled up, after hauling it up upon the beach and sitting down – they gathered together the ideal ones into containers (buckets, crocks or baskets). Yet the decayed and rotten ones they threw outside.

49. "It will be the same way within the destined conclusion (the combined final act; the joining of all parts and aspects to one purposed end and goal) of the (or: this) age: the agents (messengers; folks with the message) will be constantly going forth and will be progressively marking off boundaries for (limiting off, thus separating) the worthless and disadvantageous folks or circumstances (those people or situations who/which bring pain and misery through hard works; the wicked people or evil conditions) from out of the midst of the fair and equitable folks or situations (those having been placed within the Way of right relationships, rightwised behavior and justice)

50. "and then will continue casting them into the furnace (oven; kiln) of The Fire [= God's dealings]: the weeping (crying and lamentation) and 'the grinding of the teeth' will continue being in that situation or place. [cf vs. 8:12; 22:13; 24:51; 25:30; Lu. 13:28; Ps. 112:10]

51. "Do you folks understand all these things? Were you able to make them all flow together?" They were then saying to Him, "Yes (or, a tentative: Uh-huh; -- R.F. Capon)."

52. So He said to them, "In that the case (For this reason; Well then), every scribe (well-trained writer; scholar; expert and instructor in the Torah), being one taught, schooled and made a disciple by the reign and sovereign influence from the atmospheres (or: in the dominion of the skies; for the kingdom of the heavens) exists being (or: is) like a person (a human) – a master of a house (or: home owner or manager) – who is habitually extracting and spurting out from the midst of his store of treasures things different, innovative and new in kind, character and quality, as well as old, well-worn, age-mellowed and even obsolete things." [cf vs. 44; 12:35, above; comment: = drawing Truth from both covenants]

53. And then it happened (occurred), when Jesus finished these parables (illustrations), [that] He went across country (transferred Himself) from that place.

54. So later, upon coming into His fatherland (= His native land and home territory), He began, and continued, teaching them within their synagogue, with the result for them to be constantly moved from out of their positions and be overwhelmed with astonishment, even to be periodically saying, "From where [comes] this wisdom and the expressions (demonstrations; effects; works) of power and ability by (or: in; to; for) this person?

55. "Is this man not the builder's (carpenter's/stoneworker's; skilled craftsman's; journeyman's) son? Is not his mother the one normally being called Mary (or: Miriam) – and his brothers Jacob (James), Joseph, Simon and Judah (or: Judas)?

56. "And are not his sisters with us? From where, then, [come] all these things to (or: in; with; by) this person?"

57. And thus, they began being offended at Him, and continued stumbled, snared and entrapped by this trap-stick inherent in (or: in the midst of) Him.
So Jesus said to them, "A prophet is not un-honored or without value, except in the midst of his own fatherland (home territory) and within his own household."

58. And therefore He did not do (or: perform) many demonstrations (exhibitions; works; effects) of power in that place – through (or: on account of; with a view to) their lack of trust and absence of faith, confidence and loyalty.

CHAPTER 14

1. **Within that season Herod, the tetrarch** (the district ruler; regional or tribal governor), **heard the rumor** (news; fame) **concerning Jesus,**
2. **and said to his court servants and attendants, "This person is John, the immerser** (the one baptizing) – **he was raised from the dead ones, and through this the powerful works** (exhibitions and deeds of power; or: 'the powers') **are constantly operating within him!"**
3. **You see, on arresting John and keeping him in custody, Herod bound and put [him] away in prison** (or: jail) **because of Herodias, his brother Philip's wife,**
4. **for John kept on saying to him, "It is not right or permitted, from [our] existence, for you to continue possessing** (having and holding) **her!"**
5. **However, although constantly wanting and intending to at once kill him, he was made afraid by the crowd, because they continued holding** (= regarding) **him as a prophet.**

6. **Now during the occurring of Herod's birthday celebration, the daughter of Herodias danced within the midst – and thus, she captivated and gave pleasure to Herod,**
7. **because of which, with an oath, he made a binding statement – to at once give** (grant) **to her whatever she would request** (ask; demand)**!**
8. **So she, under her mother's advanced prompting** (or: by the pushing and inciting of her mother), **is then saying, "Give to me here, upon a platter** (or: a pine board), **the head of John the immerser** (baptist)**!"**
9. **And though being sorry and grieved** (or: distressed), **the king – because of the oaths and the people continuing in reclining at table with [him] – commanded** (ordered) **[it] to be given** (granted).
10. **And thus sending [the directive], he beheaded John within the prison** (or: jail).
11. **Then his head was brought** (or: carried) **upon a platter** (or: pine board) **and was given to the girl, and she brought** (or: carried) **[it] to her mother.**

12. **Later, upon approaching, his disciples removed his corpse and buried** (or: entombed) **it** (or: him), **and then coming, they reported to Jesus what had happened.**
13. **Now upon hearing [this], Jesus withdrew back from that place, in a small boat, into an isolated** (or: uninhabited; wilderness; lonely) **place – in accord with what was His own** (or: corresponding to His own [thoughts and feelings]; or: privately). **And yet, upon hearing [of His departure], the crowds followed Him on foot, away from the cities.**
14. **And then, upon going out from [His secluded location], He saw [the] large crowd – and He felt compassion upon** (was moved in His gut over) **them – so He tended, attentively served, gave treatment to, began therapy with, prescribed ongoing treatment for, or cured and healed the folks among them who were sick, ailing or without strength.**
15. **Now with evening approaching, the disciples approached Him, saying in turn, "The place** (or: This area) **is desolate and uninhabited** (or: is a wilderness), **and the hour is already advanced** (= it is already late in the day). **Release** (or: Dismiss) **the crowds so that, after going away into the villages, they can buy food for themselves in the market places."**
16. **However, Jesus said to them, "They are not having any need to go away. You men, yourselves, give them [something] to eat!"**
17. **Yet they, in turn, were saying to Him, "At present we have nothing here! – except five loaves of bread, and two fishes."**
18. **So He said, "Proceed in bringing them here, to Me."**

19. **And then, after directing the crowds to lie back** (or: recline) **upon the grass and vegetation, upon taking** (or: receiving) **the five loaves of bread and the two fishes, while looking up into heaven** (or: the atmosphere; the sky) **He spoke words of wellness and blessing. And then, braking [them] in pieces, He gave the loaves** (or: cakes) **of bread to the disciples, and the disciples [gave them] to the crowds.**

20. **So they all ate, and were satisfied** (like cattle or sheep being fed in a pasture until full). **Then they took up the surplus** (the excess; the leftovers) **of the broken pieces: twelve wicker hand-baskets full!**

> [note: the disciples now had provisions for themselves – for meals the following days? – beyond the original five loaves, where before they considered themselves to "have nothing"]

21. **Now those eating were about five thousand adult males – apart from women and little children.**

22. **And then, without delay, He compelled His disciples to board** (step into) **the little boat and to be progressively preceding** (going ahead of) **Him unto the other side – while He would be dismissing and dispersing the crowds.**

23. **And so, upon dismissing and dispersing the crowds, He went back up into the mountain** (or: hill country) **– in accord with what was His own** (or: corresponding to His own [thoughts and feelings]; or: privately) **– to be praying** (speaking or thinking toward having ease, goodness and well-being). **So then, it coming to be late in the evening, He was there alone.**

24. **Now the little boat, already many hundreds of yards** (i.e., many *stadia*) **away from land, was continuing distant in the midst of the lake** (or: sea), **continuously being tried – as with a touchstone to test its metal** (and thus, its mettle) **– [thus, pounded] by and under the waves, for the wind was continuing against [them]** (i.e., it was adverse and contrary).

25. **Yet during the fourth watch period of the night** (about three o'clock in the morning), **He came toward** (or: to) **them – continuing in walking upon the lake** (or: sea).

26. **But the disciples, upon seeing Him progressively walking about – upon the lake** (sea), **were at once shaken and troubled, one after another saying, "It's a ghost** (or: a phantom; or: an apparition; or: the effect of something being made visible)!**" – then they cried out from fear.**

27. **Yet Jesus at once spoke to them, proceeding in saying, "Continue in confidence and courage: I AM** (or: I am Being; I am continuous Existence; or: = Take heart and continue courageous, it is I – It's ME)! **Do not continue being afraid."**

28. **Now in a considered and discerning response, Peter said to Him, "Lord** (or: O Master), **since You are** (or: if You are You; = if it's really You), **direct** (or: order) **me to at once come** (or: go) **toward You upon** (= on the surface of) **the waters!"**

29. **So He said, "Come at once!"** (or: "Go [for it]!") **Then, upon stepping down from the little boat, Peter at once walked about upon the waters and came toward Jesus.**

30. **Yet while continuing in looking at [the effects of] the strong wind, he was made to fear** (or: became afraid). **And then beginning to progressively sink down, he cried out, saying, "O Lord** (Master), **save me now** (rescue me quickly)!**"**

31. **So immediately, and set for well-being, Jesus, stretching out [His] hand, got a hold upon him, then is saying to him, "O man of little trust** (or: confidence) **and small faith! Into what two places do you mentally stand** (= Why do you waver and hesitate)?**"**

32. **Then, at their stepping down into the little boat, the wind grew weary and died down.**

33. **Now the men within the little boat paid Him homage by kneeling down and with obeisance kissing toward Him – some reverently kissing His feet – while one after another was saying, "Truly, You are God's Son** (or: In reality You exist being a son of God; You really are [the] Son, whose origin, quality and character is God)!**"**

34. **Later, upon cutting right through [the waters] and traversing across [the lake], they came upon land, [entering] into Gennesaret.**

35. **Then, upon recognizing Him, the adult males of that place** (or: location) **sent off into that whole surrounding country** (or: area), **and were bringing to Him all the folks continually having it badly** (= everyone who was ill or needed help in some way).

36. **And they began calling Him to their side, and kept on begging and entreating Him** (asking Him to be a paraclete) **– with the purpose that they themselves might only touch the ritual fringe** (or: tassel) **of His cloak – and as many as touched [it] were thoroughly healed, restored to health, and made whole, through and through** (or: were completely rescued; or: were brought safely through [their illness]; were thoroughly saved)!

CHAPTER 15

1. **At that time, Pharisees and scribes** (scholars and theologians of the Law) **from Jerusalem progressively made an approach to Jesus, [and as a group] were saying,**
2. **"Why** (= Through what reason or situation) **are your disciples habitually side-stepping** (thus, deviating from) **the tradition of the Elders? For example, they are not regularly washing [their] hands [to make them ritually clean] whenever they may be periodically eating bread** (= a meal)**."**

3. **So He, giving a decided reply, said to them, "Why** (or: Through what situation or reasoning) **are you people habitually side-stepping and deviating from God's implanted goals** (impartation of the finished product within; inward directives) **through your tradition?**
4. **"For God said,**

> **'Be habitually honoring and expressing value for the father and the mother,'** [Ex. 20:12]

and,

> **'The person habitually saying a bad, ugly or worthless word or message to or concerning** (= verbally abusing) **father or mother, let him progressively come to fruition** (or: reach his end; be finished) **in** (or: by) **death.'** [Ex. 21:17]

5. **"Yet you, yourselves, are habitually maintaining, 'Whoever may at some point say to the father or the mother, "Whatever from me should have benefited or helped you [is now] a 'gift'** (an 'approach present' [to God])**,"'**

> [cf "Corban," Mark 7:11; meaning: a gift to God; i.e., it is consecrated for God's use, and can at any time be claimed for Temple use, and is thus unusable for any other purpose],

6. **"by no means will he [in this] continue honoring his father** (or: he will in no way [by this] be valuing his father; or: = will he still, in any way, be rid of the duty to honor his parents?)**! And thus you People at once invalidate** (make useless and void of authority; cancel and make of no effect) **God's idea, word and message** (or: the *Logos* from God) **through your tradition!**
7. **"[You] perverse scholars who in micro-scrutinizing make decisions from a low position** [see ch. 6:2]**! Isaiah beautifully and aptly prophesies about** (or: concerning) **you folks, continually saying,**
8. > **'This People habitually honor Me with [their] lips, yet it constantly holds their heart far away from Me** (or: yet their heart continuously holds [itself] off, distant from Me).
9. > **'So they habitually revere Me and commit acts of devotion to Me in vain** (to no profit; fruitlessly), **repeatedly giving instruction concerning teachings [that are] directions coming from humans** (or: constantly teaching for "[the] teachings" [the] results of inner goals and commands of people {or: man-made rules}).**'"** [Isa. 29:13]

10. **With that, upon calling the crowd forward, to Himself, He said to them, "Be constantly listening, so as to hear. And let things flow together, so as to understand:**
11. **"The things normally and habitually entering into the mouth do not repeatedly make the person unclean** (common; contaminated; defiled; polluted)**. To the contrary, [it is] the things habitually emerging and flowing forth from out of the mouth – this is constantly making the person contaminated** (unclean; common)**!"**

12. **At that point, after approaching, the disciples proceed saying to Him, "Did You see, or are You aware, that the Pharisees were caused to trip the bait stick and stumble into [their own] trap** (or: were snared and offended; perhaps: were horrified) **at hearing that thought and idea** (or: the word; the message; this reason; or: = that remark)**?"**
13. **Yet He, giving a decided reply, said, "Every plant, which My Father – the heavenly One** (or: the One Who inhabits, and can be compared to, the atmosphere) **– did not plant, will be one-after-another pulled out by the roots.**
14. **"Abandon them at once!** (other choices: Divorce them; Let them flow away; Leave them; Leave them [alone]; Send them away; Let them go; Forgive them) **They exist being blind**

guides of the Path (or: blind leaders of the Way). **Now if a blind person should ever lead or guide [another] blind person, both people will proceed to be falling into a pit!"**

15. Now Peter, after trying to separate the elements of the discourse and to discern the meaning of what He had spoken, said to Him, "Expound the parable in distinct terms and explain the meaning to (or: for) **us** (or: Tell us plainly the interpretation of the illustration)."

16. So Jesus said, "At this point in time, do you folks, as well, continue being unable to let things flow together, and are you without comprehension?

17. "Are you not habitually using your minds and your intelligence to carefully think, and grasp, that everything normally and habitually flowing into the mouth is progressively moving on into the stomach and then the intestines, and later is periodically discharged (or: thrust out) **into a toilet or a sewer?**

18. "Yet the things constantly emerging and flowing forth out of the mouth are continually coming forth from out of the midst of the heart

> (the core of the individual; the self as a whole, at its deepest level, which is the individual's animating and driving force [note: I owe these last phrases to Marcus Borg, *The Heart of Christianity*]) **– and those things continually make the person contaminated, defiled, ceremonially unclean and common.**

19. "For example, from out of the heart (the core of our being) **habitually come forth worthless reasonings** (wicked designs; considerations having a bad quality; miserable and laborious dialogues and arguments), **murders, adulteries, fornications and prostitutions, sexual immoralities** (fornications; prostitutions), **thefts, false testimonies** (or: perjuries; false presentations of evidence), **blasphemies** (malicious slanders; abusive misrepresentations).

20. "*These* continue being the things that are making the person contaminated (unclean; defiled; common) **– yet to eat a meal with unwashed hands does not make the person common, contaminated or unclean!"**

21. So next, upon going out from that place, Jesus withdrew back into the parts (= districts) **of Tyre and Sidon.**

22. And then – look and consider! – a Canaanite (= Phoenician) **woman from the boundaries of those regions, upon coming out [to Him], cried out, repeatedly saying, "O Lord** (Master) **– Son of David – mercy me right now** (or: extend the effects of compassion to me quickly)! **My daughter is being repeatedly affected in an ugly way by demons** (or: is incessantly badly-demonized [Hellenistic term, concept and belief: = affected by animism])!"

23. But He did not give a word of decision or reply to her. Then His disciples, upon approaching, began making a request to Him, saying, "Set her free, and then dismiss her, because she keeps on crying out behind us."

24. Yet He, making a discerning reply, said, "I was not commissioned and sent off as an emissary – except into the midst of those sheep having been destroyed, the ones that belong to [the] house of Israel. (or: Am I not sent away as a representative, if not unto the lost sheep from Israel's house?; or: I am not separated off for a purpose, except into the midst of those lost and destroyed sheep, which are a house of Israel)"

25. Yet (or: So) **she, upon coming, continued paying Him homage by kneeling down and with obeisance kissing toward Him, even reverently kissing His feet, repeatedly saying, "O Lord** (or: Master; Sir), **be now running to my aid and continue to give help to me!"**

26. Now He, responding from a discerning decision, said, "It is not proper or ideal (thus, it is not an act of beauty) **to take the children's bread and to throw it to the little dogs!"**

27. So the [woman] said, "Yes, sir. And yet... you see... the little dogs and puppies habitually eat from the little crumbs and bits which are constantly falling from their owner's (or: master's) **table!"**

28. At that point Jesus, in making a decided reply, said to her, "O woman (or: O dear lady), **your trust, faith, confidence and loyalty [are] great! Let it at once come to be and happen to, for and in you just as you continue intending and desiring." And so, from that hour, her daughter was cured and healed.**

29. **Next, re-directing His steps from out of that place, Jesus went along the Lake** (or: Sea) **of the Galilee. Then, after walking up into the mountain** (or: hill country), **He sat down and was continuing sitting there.**

30. **Then many crowds came toward Him, [they] having with them, or continuing in holding, lame and crippled folks, blind people, maimed and deformed ones or those with crooked [bodies], mute folks, as well as many [people with] different [maladies], and they deposited** (as it were, tossed) **them near His feet – and He tended, attentively served, gave treatment to, began therapy with, prescribed ongoing treatment for, or cured and healed them,**

31. **so that the crowd marveled with rapture and amazement – consecutively seeing mute ones speaking, the deformed** (crooked; maimed) **sound** (healthy), **and lame ones walking around, then blind folks now seeing – and they gave credit to** (formed opinions, made assumptions, and experienced impressions, about) **the God of Israel, adding to His reputation.**

32. **Now Jesus, upon calling His disciples to Himself, said, "I am being progressively moved with compassion** (in my gut) **upon the crowd, because they are yet continuing in staying with Me and keeping their focus toward Me three days already, and they are still not having something that they can be eating – and I am not intending** (or: wanting) **to release them and send them off fasting** (= being without food and hungry), **lest at some point they are caused to faint** (would be undone out of exhaustion) **in the path** (or: on the road)."

33. **And so the disciples are as a group saying to Him, "From where [are there] so many loaves of bread in an uninhabited region so as to feed and satisfy a crowd of this size?"**

34. **Then Jesus proceeds saying to them, "How many loaves of bread do you men still have?" And they replied, "Seven, and a few little fishes."**

35. **So, after directing the crowd to recline back upon the ground,**

36. **He took the seven loaves of bread and the fishes and, expressing the goodness of grace and offering thanks for the favor of the wellness in the gift, He broke [them] and began distributing to the disciples, and then the disciples [gave them] to the crowds.**

37. **And so everyone ate and all were fed until satisfied. Then folks picked up the surplus of the broken pieces [of food] – seven large provision baskets** (or: woven hampers) **filled full [of leftovers]!**

38. **Now those participating in the eating were four thousand adult males – apart from [counting] women and young children.**

39. **At last, after dismissing and releasing away the crowds, He stepped on into the little boat, and they went into the boundary regions of Magadan** [other MSS: Magdala].

CHAPTER 16

1. **Here, upon approaching, the Pharisees and Sadducees – after repeatedly examining and testing [Him] – laid a request upon Him to exhibit to them or demonstrate for them a sign from the midst of heaven** (or: from the atmosphere; out of the sky).

2. **So, giving a decided response, He said to them, "**[note: from here through vs. 3 is omitted by Aleph, B and others] **Upon the coming of evening, you folks are customarily saying, '[It will be] fair weather** (or: good weather; a fine day), **you see, the sky continues being fiery-red;'**

3. **"and early in the morning, [you say], 'Today [it will be] stormy** (or: rainy; or: wintry weather), **for the sky continues being fiery-red [and] is progressively being gloomy-looking.' On the one hand you, by experience and familiarity, habitually know how to read and discern** (thoroughly interpret, judge and decide about) **the face and appearance of the sky, yet on the other hand, you continue unable and without power [to discern and interpret] the signs of the appointed seasons and fitting situations** (or: fertile moments)!

4. **"A worthless, wicked and adulterous** (or: immoral; [note: an OT word and figure for Israel's idolatry, e.g. Ezk. 16:32]) **generation is habitually searching for and thoroughly seeking a sign, and yet a sign will not proceed in being given to it, except the sign of Jonah!" Then He went away, leaving them down behind** (or, perhaps: = Then turning His back on them, He walked away). [comment: Jonah was sent to a Gentile nation]

5. **At another time, when the disciples were coming into the other side** (= other shore), **[the state of their provisions] went unnoticed, and thus, they completely forgot to take loaves of bread.**

6. **Now on this occasion, Jesus said to them, "You men be constantly seeing, and be then attentive in holding [yourselves] away from the leaven** (yeast) **which comes from, characterizes, [and puffs up or permeates] the Pharisees and Sadducees."**

7. **So they began dialoguing and kept on reasoning among themselves, "We did not get or take loaves of bread."**

8. **Now Jesus, being aware [of their conversations] and knowing [what they were saying], said, "Why do you folks keep on discussing and reasoning among yourselves, O men of little trust and small faith? [Is it] because you are not presently having loaves of bread?**

9. **"Are you still not making it a habit to use your minds and intellects** (think carefully, conceive and consider, so as to apprehend, and get the point)? **Are you folks neither remembering the five loaves of bread pertaining to the five thousand people – and how many wicker hand-baskets you got** (or: took [up])?

10. **"Nor the seven loaves of the [situation with the] four thousand – and how many large provision baskets you received?**

11. **"How [is it that] you men are not using your heads to understand that I did not speak to you about** (or: concerning) **loaves of bread? Now continue holding your focus and be attentive to keep away from the leaven** (yeast) **which belongs to, comes from and characterizes the Pharisees and Sadducees!"**

12. **At that time they made things flow together and comprehended that He did not say to hold their focus and be attentive to keep away from the leaven of the loaves of bread, but rather, from the teaching which belongs to, comes from and characterizes the Pharisees and Sadducees.**

13. **Now later, upon coming into the parts** (= districts) **of Caesarea Philippi, Jesus began putting a question to His disciples, proceeding in saying, "Whom are the People** (the humans) **customarily saying the Son of the Man** (the son of the human; = the son of Adam; or: = a symbolic reference to the anticipated messiah) **is to be?"**

14. **So they said, "Well some, on the one hand, [say] John the Immerser** (Baptist), **yet other folks [say] Elijah. But then, different people [are saying] Jeremiah, or one of the prophets."**

15. **He is then saying to them, "But [how about] you men, who are you folks normally saying** (laying out) **Me to be** (or: what do you now make reference [of] Me being)?"

16. **Now Simon Peter, making a discerning and decided reply, said, "You, Yourself, continue being the Anointed One** (the Christ; = the Messiah), **the living God's Son!"**

17. **So Jesus, making a considered response, said to him, "You continue being a happy and blessed person, Simon, son of Jonah, because 'flesh and blood'** (= the human nature or intellect; or: = people; or: = the old covenant system) **did not uncover [this] for you, nor disclose [this] so as to reveal [it] to you** (or: = you did not come up with this revelation yourself, nor uncover it in yourself, nor disclose it by or for yourself). **To the contrary, [it was] My Father – the One within the heavens** (or: centered in the atmospheres)!

18. **"And now I, Myself, am saying to** (or: progressively laying it out for) **you that you are Peter** (or: that you continue being an isolated stone). **And you see, [it is] upon this, this rock-mass** (or: the bedrock), **[that] I will progressively be constructing and building up My House – the called-out, covenant community. And even gates of [the] Unseen**

> (or: double-winged doors of an unseen place; the openings or orifices which are unseen {e.g., entrance of a womb}; gateways or entrances from the Unseen; [= boulders on the entrances of graves; = {the prison} gates of the 'house of death'; or: = the bars enclosing the realm of the dead])

will not continue bringing strength down against it (or: will not proceed to be coming to their full strength in relation to it; or: will not continue overpowering it or prevail in resisting it).

19. **"I will continue giving to you the keys** [note: = means of locking or unlocking] **which have their origin and source in the reign and activities of the heavens**

(or: which pertain to and have the characteristics of the kingdom of the heavens; or: which belong to the sovereignty from the atmospheres; or, as a genitive of apposition: the keys which are the sovereign influences of the heavens). **And so, whatever you can** (or: may; should; would) **bind upon the earth will continue being [something] having been bound, and still remaining bound, within the midst of the heavens** (or: in union with the atmospheres). **Also, whatever you can** (or: may; should; would) **loose upon the earth will continue being [something] having been loosed** (unbound; untied), **and remaining free of bonds, within the midst of the heavens** (or: in union with the atmospheres)."

20. **At that point He gave respectful caution and admonition to the disciples, to the end that they would say to no one that He, Himself, exists being** (or: is) **the Anointed One** (the Christ; = the Messiah).

21. **From that time on, Jesus** [other MSS: Jesus Christ] **began to progressively point out, exhibit and demonstrate to, for and among His disciples that it is necessary [for] Him – even continues being binding [on] Him – to go away into Jerusalem, and to experience and suffer many things from the elders and chief** (or: ranking) **priests, as well as the scribes** (scholars and theologians of the Law), **and then to be killed off – but also to be aroused and raised up on** (or: during) **the third day.**

22. **And so Peter, taking Him to himself, began to then be respectfully admonishing Him, expressing increased value of Him, repeatedly saying, "Merciful covering on You** (or: [Be] kind and merciful to Yourself; [There is] favorable shelter for You; or: = [Heaven be] propitiously merciful to You; = May God spare You), **O Lord** (Master)! **By no means will this be for You!"**

23. **Now, being turned, He said to Peter, "Proceed leading the way** (or: bringing things under control) **behind Me, O adversary. You are My bait-stick, ensnaring and leading Me into a trap, because you are not in the habit of setting your mind on or having the attitude pertaining to the things of God, but instead, [you continually have opinions which align with] the things of the People** (or: humans)."

24. **At that point Jesus said to His disciples, "If anyone continues intending** (purposing; willing; wanting) **to come on behind Me, let him at once completely say, 'No,' to, deny and disown himself, and then in one move lift up his execution stake** (pole for suspending a corpse; cross), **and after that proceed to be by habit continuously following after Me!**

25. **"You see, whoever may intend** (or: should purpose; might set his will; happens to want) **to keep his soul-life safe** (rescue himself; preserve the conscious life that he is living) **will continue loosing-it-away and destroying it. Yet whoever can loose-away and even destroy his soul-life** (the consciousness of self) **on My account, he will continue finding it!** [cf 26:38]

26. **"For what will a person** (or: mankind) **proceed being benefited, or in what will he** (or: it) **continue helped or augmented, if he** (it) **can or would advantageously procure and gain the whole ordered system of society: government, economy, culture, religion – even the whole universe, yet would be undergoing the loss of, receive damage to, or be made to forfeit, his soul-life** (the consciousness which he is; or: its interior self [in its reality])? **Or what will a person** (or: mankind) **proceed giving as a result of a change-instead** (or: in exchange) **pertaining to his** (or: its) **soul** (or: as an effect corresponding to transformation of the consciousness of, or which is, himself/itself which makes him/it other than he/it is)?

27. **"You see, the Son of the Man** (or: mankind's son; or: = the Son of Adam; or: [the eschatological Messianic figure]; or: the Human Being) **is presently about to continue progressively coming** (or: repeatedly passing from place to place) **within the glory** (the manifestation which calls forth praise; the assumed appearance) **of His Father, with His agents** (messengers; folks with the message). **And at that time, He will proceed giving back** (or: repaying; recompensing) **to each one in corresponding accord with his practice, behavior and operation of business.**

28. **"It is so** (or: In fact; Amen), **I am now telling** (laying it out for) **you men, that there are some** (or: certain ones) **of the folks presently standing here who under no circumstances can** (or: may) **taste** (= partake of, or, experience) **death, until they can** (or: should) **perceive and see the Son of the Man** (mankind's son; = the eschatological Messianic figure; = Adam's Son) **progressively coming** (or: continuously coming and going; repeatedly passing from place to place) **in His reign** (or: within His kingdom; joined to His sovereign activities)."

CHAPTER 17

1. Then after six days, Jesus proceeds to take along (or: at His side) Peter, Jacob (James) and John, his brother, and progressively leads them up into a high mountain, privately, and to be in accord with what was His own.
2. And then, all of a sudden, He was transformed (transfigured; changed in external form and appearance) and His face radiated light, like a lamp, and shone like the sun. His outer garments also turned white – bright as the light! [cf 2 Cor. 3:18]
3. Next – consider this! – Moses and Elijah, continuing in a discussion and conferring together with Him, were seen by them [i.e., the disciples].

4. Now Peter, making a considered response, said to Jesus, "O Lord (Master), it is beautiful, fine and ideal [for] us to continue being (or: existing) here in this place. If You continue intending [to] (or: If You now will [it to be so]; If You desire [me to]), I will proceed erecting three tents (or: will progressively make three tabernacles; will be constructing three temporary shelters) here: one for You, one for Moses, and one for Elijah."
5. Now consider this! While he was still speaking, a cloud composed of light (or: a cloud full of light; a cloud radiating light; a luminous cloud; an illuminated cloud) suddenly brought shade upon them (or: cast a shadow over them; overshadowed, or enveloped them). And think of this! A Voice – from out of the midst of the cloud – progressively saying, "This Man continues existing being My Son! The Beloved One (or: The One exemplifying and expressing My love) within Whom I think good thoughts (or: in Whom I imagine thoughts of wellness and ease; in Whom I appear well; in Whom I approve and of Whom I have a good opinion). Make it a habit to listen, to continue paying attention, and then to [really] hear Him (= understand His words; implies: obey Him)!" [cf Ex. 24:16]

6. At once, upon hearing [this], the disciples fell (= flung themselves) upon their faces and then were made extremely afraid (or: became terrified).
7. So Jesus approached and, upon touching – and as it were kindling – them, said, "Be aroused, get up and stop being made afraid!"
8. Now, upon lifting up their eyes, they saw no one (or: not even one person) except Him – only Jesus (or: Jesus, alone).

9. Later, during their progressively walking down out of the mountain, Jesus gave an implanted goal (impartation of the finished product within; inward directive), while saying, "You men should speak of the results of what was seen (or: tell the vision; speak of the sight) to no one until [the situation] where the Son of the Man (mankind's son; = Adam's Son; or: = the eschatological Messianic figure) could (or: should; would) be aroused and raised up out from among dead folks."
10. At this, the disciples questioned Him, in saying, "Why, in light of this (or: therefore), are the scribes (the scholars; the experts in the sacred Scriptures) constantly saying that it is binding (necessary) for Elijah to come first?"   [Acts 3:21]
11. So He, giving a decided answer, said, "Elijah is indeed progressively (or: repeatedly) coming, and then He will progressively move and reintegrate all humanity away from where they have been placed (or: put) down, and from what has been firmly established.
12. "Yet, I am continuing in telling you men that Elijah already comes and they do not recognize (or: fully know) Him. But even more, they perform on Him as many things as they wish and intend. (or: Elijah already came, and they did not recognize him, but rather, they did in him as much as they wanted.) In this way (or: Thus), also, the Son of the Man (= Adam's Son; mankind's son; the Human Being; or: = the eschatological Messianic figure) is progressively about to continue experiencing [things] by them, even suffering under them."
13. At that point, the disciples put it together that He spoke to them about John the Immerser (or: baptist).

14. **Then, upon coming toward the crowd, a man came toward Him, proceeding to fall to his knees [before] Him, and then saying,**
15. **"O Lord** (Master), **mercy** (perform mercy on, or express mercy in) **my son, because he continues being moon-struck** (= a lunatic; perhaps = an epileptic) **and habitually has it badly** (= has an ugly time being ill). **You see, many times he has the habit of falling into the fire, and often into the water.**
16. **"So I brought him to Your disciples** (students; apprentices), **and yet they had no power** (were unable) **to cure or heal him."**

17. **Now Jesus, giving a discerning reply, said, "O faithless generation that is void of trust, as well as being one that has been thoroughly twisted and distorted! Until what time** (Till when; = How long) **will I continue being with you folks? Until what time will I, Myself, continue holding you people up? You folks proceed to bring him here, to Me."**
18. **Then Jesus dispensed further value and honor to him** ([i.e., the boy]; or: Jesus spoke respectful admonition to it [i.e., the demon]), **and "the demon"** [Hellenistic concept and term: = animistic influence] **went out and away from him. And so the boy was cured and healed from that hour.**
19. **At that point the disciples, coming to Jesus privately, down in His own spot, said, "Why and through what situation were we without power and unable to cast it out** (or: expel it)**?"**
20. **So Jesus proceeds saying to them, "Because of your little trust and small faith-confidence. For truly** (amen) **I am now saying to you people, if you can progressively hold trust, habitually have faith and continue possessing fidelity** (faithfulness) **– as a mustard seed** (grain of mustard), **you folks will be saying to this mountain, 'Transfer** (Move in step with, and after) **from this place [to] there!' and it will be progressively transferring** (moving). **And so, nothing will continue being impossible for** (or: to; in; with; among) **you."**
[21.] [the earlier MSS omit this verse: "Yet this kind does not normally go out, except within prayer and fasting."]

22. **Now during their being progressively twisted together [as strands of a single rope]** (or: being habitually turned together [as, toward one another; = experiencing increasing solidarity]; perhaps = coming together in a gathering; [with other MSS: turning back again together; may = going about together, wandering about]) **within the Galilee [district],** **Jesus said to them, "The Son of the Man** (= the son of Adam; = the eschatological messianic figure; or: the Human Being) **is progressively about to be passed along unto [the] hands of people** (or: delivered, committed and transferred, over into hands [= control] of humans),
23. **"and then they will kill Him off, and later, on** (or: in; during) **the third day, He will be aroused and raised up." Consequently, they were extremely pained, distressed and saddened with grief.**

24. **Now upon their coming into Capernaum, the men normally taking** (receiving; = collecting) **the two-drachma coin** [a yearly tax levied on individuals for the upkeep of the Temple] **approached Peter and said, "Is not your teacher in the habit of settling [the account; = paying] the two-drachma [dues]?"**
25. **He then says, "Yes** (= Sure; Of course; -- Robert F. Capon)**." However, upon coming into the house, Jesus anticipates and gets ahead of him by saying, "What do you normally think or suppose** (or: What is your usual opinion), **Simon? From which people are the kings of the land** (or: earth) **normally taking** (or: receiving; = collecting) **payment of duties** (taxes; customs; tributes) **or a census tax** (or: poll tax) **– from their sons** (= family; perhaps = their own tribe or people; perhaps idiomatically = their own citizens), **or from the aliens** (strangers; those belonging to another group, perhaps a conquered country)**?"**   [cf Rom. 8:21b]
26. **Now at [his] saying, "From the aliens** (strangers; those not belonging to their families, tribes or people; = those of subject territories),**" Jesus affirms, "Consequently then, the sons** (= family; or: = people; or: = citizens) **exist being** (are) **FREE** (in a state of freedom; unrestricted).
27. **"Yet, so that we would not be, as it were, bait on a trap-spring and thus snare them or cause them to stumble in regard to us, after going on your way unto the lake** (or: sea), **cast**

a fishhook [into the lake/sea], and pick up the first fish coming up. Then, upon opening up its mouth, you will find a stater (a silver coin worth four drachmas). **Taking [it], give that to them on behalf of Me, as well as you."** [note: *cf* "Son/sons" in vss. 5, 12, 22, 25, 26, above]

CHAPTER 18

1. **Now within that hour the disciples approached Jesus, [as a group] saying, "Who, consequently, exists being greater** (= most important) **within the heavens' reign** (or: the kingdom of the atmospheres)**?"**
2. **Then, after calling a little child to Himself, He placed** (set; stood) **it** [Greek is neuter: = a boy or a girl] **within their midst,**
3. **and said, "Truly** (or: Depend on it; Amen) **I am now saying to you men, If you folks are not turned around** [from going in this direction, or reverse your present trend of thinking] **and may birth yourselves** (or: become) **like little children, you can** (or: may; would) **by no means enter into the heavens' reign** (or: the kingdom of the atmospheres; or: heavens' sovereignty).
4. **"Therefore, whoever will be progressively bringing himself low in attitude, situation and condition, so as to be humble, insignificant and unimportant in his own eyes, like this young child – this person is the greater** (= more important) **with the heavens' reign** (or: the kingdom emanating from the atmospheres);
5. **"And whoever would take in his arms and welcomingly receive one such little child – on [the basis and premises involved in] My Name** (signifies: character, authority; identity) **– proceeds to take Me in his arms and continues welcomingly receiving Me.**
6. **"Yet, whoever may be the bait on the stick which springs the trap and ensnares one of these little folks that are habitually trusting Me and placing their faith into Me, it continues bringing [situations] and bearing [things] together by, and to, him** (or: with, for, or in, him), **so that a millstone – such as an ass may be used to turn – could** (or: may; should) **be hung around his neck, and then he could** (or: may; should) **be sunk down within the midst of the open sea!**
7. **"What tragedy [exists] in the System** (or: to and for the controlling world of culture, religion, economics and government; by the domination system; or: Alas for the aggregate of humanity; Woe to the cosmos) **[arising] from bait-laden traps and snares** (or: stumbling blocks or occasions of faltering). **You see, it continues being a compulsory necessity for the traps with their bait and snares to come, nevertheless, [it is] a tragedy for** (or: to; in) **the person through whom the traps and snares continue coming** [= the one constantly setting the traps].
8. **"So if your hand or your foot keeps on snaring you through hitting the trap-stick or going for the bait, cut it off at once, and throw [it] away from you! Is it [more] ideal for you to enter into the Life [being] maimed or lame, or, continuing having two hands or two feet, to be thrown into the fire that lasts for an indefinite period of time** (or: the eonian, or age-related, fire; or: the fire that comes with the Age [of the Messiah])**?**
9. **"Likewise if your eye keeps on snaring you through hitting the trap-stick or going for the bait, tear it out at once, and throw [it] away from you! Is it [more] ideal for you to enter into the Life [being] one-eyed, or, continuing having two eyes, to be thrown into the Valley of Hinnom** (Greek: Gehenna – the city dump where refuse, criminals and rebels are incinerated), **which is characterized by, and is a source of, that fire?**

10. **"You men be constantly seeing [to it]** (= be perceptive so as to take care) **[that] you should not even once think down on** (have a condescending attitude toward; think of low importance; despise; disdain; or: bring attitudes of thinking contemptuously of) **one of these little folks, for you see, I am now saying to you people that their agents within [the] heavens** (or: messengers centered in [the] atmospheres) **are throughout every situation continually observing the face** (= the presence; = expressed feeling and attitude) **of the Father – the One centered within [the] heavens** (or: in the midst of, and in union with, [the] atmospheres).
[11.] [this verse omitted by the earlier MSS, Origen and Eusebius, but is found in D, L's margin, W, θc and TR: "You see, the Son of the Man comes to rescue and make whole (to save and deliver) the person having been destroyed and lost."]

12. **"What do you men normally think or suppose** (or: How does [it] usually seem to you)**? If it should come to be with any person [having] one hundred sheep, [that] even one of them should be led astray and caused to wander** (thus: be deceived), **will he not leave** (or: let go; abandon; send-away) **the ninety-nine sheep on the hillside** (or: mountain) **and, going from place to place, continue trying to find the one continuing in being led astray?**
13. **"And if he should happen to find it, certainly** (amen; it is so; depend on it) **– I am now telling you – he continues expressing joy upon it, rather than upon those ninety-nine that have not been being led astray and have not been caused to wander.** [Lu. 15:4-7, 8-10]
14. **"In the same way it continues not being the will** (the effect of the desire, intent or purpose) **of My Father – the One within [the] heavens and within the midst of the atmospheres – that one of these little folks would destroy himself or should become lost.**

15. **"Now if your brother should make a mistake** (or: = your fellow believer may fail to hit the target for which he is aiming; or: your group member should be erring or sinning) [later MSS add: unto you; (= do you wrong)], **humbly go [to him and] test it** (or: bring convincing proof about it, laying the matter bare) **between you and him alone. If he can listen and should be hearing you, you made gain and profit for your brother.**
16. **"Yet should he not listen [to you], take still one or two [others] along with you, so that 'upon [the] mouth of two or three witnesses** (folks providing evidence) **everything that is said** (every gush-effect; each result of the flow [of conversation or outbreak]) **can be established and made to stand.'** [Deut. 19:15]
17. **"Now if he should put his hearing aside from** (= disregard and refuse to hear) **them, speak to the called-out community. Yet, if he should also put his hearing aside from** (or: disregard) **the called-out community, let him continue being with you** (or: among you folks), **just as** (in the same manner as) **the person of the ethnic multitudes** (or: nations; pagans) **and the tax collector [continue with you].**

> [comment: consider the behavior of Jesus with "sinners" and tax collectors; recall that these get into the kingdom before the religious; consider the place of the ethnic multitudes in relation to the good news]

18. **"It is true** (or: Truly; or: Make it so; or: Now listen), **I now say to you folks, Whatsoever things you can at some point bind or should tie upon the earth** (or: the Land) **will continue being things having already been tied or bound within heaven** (or: in [your] atmosphere). **Also, as many things [as] you would loose** (untie) **upon the earth** (Land) **will continue being things having already been loosed and untied within heaven** (or: in [your] atmosphere).
19. **"Again, truly, I continue saying** (laying it out) **to you folks that, if ever two from your group can utter sounds together that are harmonious and in symphony** (or: should voice together in agreement) **upon the earth** (or: Land) **concerning every effect of what is practiced** (or: every transaction of business; every result of the execution of operations or other matters) **– regarding which they may be requesting – it will progressively come to be** (be birthed into existence; happen) **for them** (in them; to them; with them) **at the side** (or: from the side [= presence]) **of My Father – the One within heavens and in union with atmospheres.**
20. **"You see, where there are two or three people that have been led and gathered together into My Name, I am there** (in that place) **within the midst of and among them."**

21. **Then, approaching, Peter said to Him, "Master** (or: Lord), **how many times will my brother habitually be wronging me** (or: failing to do or perform unto me as he rightfully should; committing a sin [which penetrates] into me [like being hit with an arrow]), **and I shall continue to let it pass away for him** (or: let it go off from him; forgive him)**? Until seven times?"**
22. **Jesus is then saying to him, "I don't normally say 'Till seven times,' but rather, 'Until seventy times seven!'**
23. **"Because of this [situation and reason], the heavens' reign** (or: the kingdom of the heavens and the sovereignty emanating from the atmospheres) **is likened to a man – a king – who willed and intended to settle** (to take up and reckon) **accounts with his slaves.**
24. **"Now at his beginning to proceed settling, one person was led toward him: a debtor [owing] ten thousand talents**

(probably = millions of dollars; [ten thousand was the highest number used in calculating; a talent was the largest denomination of currency, = sixty million denarii; therefore this was a staggering amount of debt – Jesus is obviously using hyperbole, as no slave could owe that much]).

25. **"So, at his not having [the means] to pay [it] back, the owner** (or: master) **gave orders for him to be immediately sold, as well as the wife, the children and everything – as many things as he is presently having – and then for payment to be made.**

26. **"Therefore, upon falling down, the slave was repeatedly doing obeisance to him, repeatedly saying, 'Be long-enduring in you strong emotions and put anger far away so as to be patient with me, and I will progressively pay back everything to you!'**

27. **"So, being moved with compassion in the pit of his stomach, the owner** (master) **of that slave released him and canceled** (let flow away; divorced; forgave) **the debt for him.**

28. **"Yet, upon going out, that slave found one of his fellow slaves who was owing** (or: who continued being indebted to) **him one hundred denarii, and, grabbing him, he began to choke [him], saying, 'Pay back the debt, since you continue owing me something!'**

29. **"Therefore, upon falling down, his fellow slave kept on calling upon him for help, even entreating and continuing to beg him, repeatedly saying, 'Be long-enduring in you strong emotions so as to be patient with me, and I will progressively pay [it] back to you!'**

30. **"However, he continued being unwilling, and furthermore, upon going off, he had him thrown into prison** (or: jail), **until he could** (or: should; would) **pay back what was continuing to be owed.**

31. **"Then, upon seeing the things that were happening, his fellow slaves experienced tremendous pain and were filled with extreme grief, and so after coming, they made it thoroughly clear and gave a distinct picture to their owner about all the things that were happening.**

32. **"At that point, after calling him** [i.e., the first slave] **to himself, the owner** (master) **proceeds saying to him, 'O worthless and wicked slave! I cancelled** (let flow away; divorced; forgave) **that entire debt for you, since you begged and entreated me.**

33. **"'Was it not of necessity binding [on; for] you, also, to dispense mercy to your fellow slave, just as I myself also dispensed mercy to you?'** [cf Col. 3:13; Eph. 4:32; 5:2]

34. **"So, internally swelling with indignation and anger, his owner handed him over** (committed him) **to 'the people who to test folks'** (literally: those who apply the touchstone to determine the grade, and to show the quality, of fine metals) **until where [the occasion or situation develops that] he could** (or: would) **pay back all that continued being owed.**

35. **"My heavenly Father** (or: My Father, Who inhabits, and can be compared to, the atmosphere) **will be progressively dealing with you folks in this same way** (or: will continue doing to you men in like manner), **too, if each person does not release and forgive his brother** (and let things flow away for him), **from your hearts."** [cf 5:7; 6:12, above; Eccl. 28:2ff]

CHAPTER 19

1. **And then it occurred, when Jesus finished these words** (or: sayings; discourses), **[that] He picked up and changed locations away from the Galilee [district] and went into the frontiers** (or: boundary areas) **of the Judean [district] on the other side of the Jordan [River].**

2. **Crowds of many people also followed Him, so He tended, attentively served, gave treatment to, began therapy with, prescribed ongoing treatment for, or cured and healed them there.**

3. **Later, Pharisees came to Him, examining, testing and trying to put Him to the proof, and then proceeding in asking if [a man] is normally right or permitted, from [their] existence** (out of being [God's people]), **to loose-away** (dismiss; divorce) **his wife in correspondence to every cause** (= for any sort of grounds or reason).

> [note: "every cause" was a technical term from current Jewish law that had been introduced by Rabbi Hillel; it allowed a man to divorce his wife if she did anything he disliked – even, e.g., for burning his food while cooking it]

4. **So He, giving a discerning reply, said, "Do** (or: Did) **you men not read that the Creator** (the Framer and Founder; [other MSS: the Maker]) **'makes** (or: made) **them male and female,' from [the] beginning?** [Gen. 1:27; 5:2]

5. **"Further on it said,**

> **'For this reason a man** (person; human) **will completely leave behind the father and the mother, and he will be glued to** [other MSS: welded toward and facing] **and joined in and with his wife, and so the two will be progressively existing into the midst of one flesh'?** [Gen. 2:24]

6. **"Consequently, they no longer exist being two, but rather [are] one flesh. Therefore, what God yokes together** (or: coupled together with a yoke), **let no human proceed to be splitting apart or separating."**

7. **They proceeded saying to Him, "Why, then, did Moses impart the directive whose end in view was to give a little scroll of divorce** (a standing-away; apostasy; defection) **and to release her** (or: loose her away)**?"** [Deut. 24:1, 3]

8. **Jesus then answers them, "Moses, facing** (or: with a view toward) **your hardheartedness, completely turned directions and made concession to you people, allowing you to divorce your wives. Yet from [the] beginning it had not happened in this way.**

9. **"Now I am saying to you that whoever may loose-away or divorce his wife** (or: woman) – **[when it is] not upon [the case of] infidelity** (fornication; sexual misconduct) – **and then should marry another woman, he is continuing in committing adultery. Also, the man involved in marrying a woman having been divorced proceeds in committing adultery."**

> [comment: Jesus here sides with Rabbi Shammai who held the earlier interpretation of Deut. 24:1-4 that marital unfaithfulness was the only cause for divorce]

10. **The disciples are, one after another, saying to Him, "Since** (or: If) **the situation** (or: predicament; case; or: cause for accusation) **of the person** (human) **with the wife continues being thus, [then] to marry does not continue to bring things together for advantage or profit!"**

> [comment: the disciples are apparently shocked that Jesus rejects the "every cause" form of divorce from the Hillel school]

11. **Yet He said to them, "Not all people are proceeding to give way and spread themselves to make room for this message** (word; idea; reason; thought; saying; = This does not apply to everyone), **but only those in, and to, whom it has been given, and so they now possess it.**

12. **"You see, there are eunuchs** (men in charge of a bedroom, usually having been castrated) **who were born thus out of [their] mother's womb, and there are eunuchs who were made eunuchs** (were gelded, emasculated) **by people, and then there are eunuchs who made themselves eunuchs** (emasculated themselves) **because of the reign of the heavens** (or: the kingdom of the atmospheres). **Let the person continuing having power and ability to give way, spread themselves and make room, continue to be making room."**

> [comment: Jesus is here rejecting the custom that all Jewish males are required to marry – a foreshadow of the impending new age – and then indicated that this is for those able to accept it]

13. **At that point, young children were brought toward Him so that He would lay** (or: could place) **[His] hands upon them and would** (or: might) **pray [for them]. Yet the disciples gave to them a respectful but discouraging admonition.**

14. **However, Jesus said, "Let this event flow on! Stop preventing them and allow the young children to come toward Me, for you see, the reign and kingdom of the heavens** (or: = the sovereignty of this atmosphere) **belongs to and is comprised of such folks as these!"**

15. **So then, after placing [His] hands on them, He journeyed on His way from that place.**

16. **And now, consider this: One person, after approaching Him, said, "Teacher, what good shall I proceed doing** (or, as a subjunctive: what virtuous act or excellent and worthwhile deed can I perform) **to the end that I can hold and possess eonian life** (life with the character of, and qualities from, the Age [of Messiah]; an age-lasting life; Age-related life)**?"**

17. **So He said to him, "Why are you now proceeding in asking Me about the Good? One continuously exists being** (or: is) **the Good.** (or: What do you now inquire of Me concerning 'goodness and virtue'? The Excellence {Intrinsic value; Quality; Good; Virtue} is one {or: unity; oneness}.) **Yet, if you continue desiring and intending to enter into the Life, continue habitually observing, guarding and keeping the implanted goals** (impartation of the finished product within; inward directives)."

18. **He then responds to Him, "Which ones** (or: Which sort [of inward directives])**?"**
So Jesus affirms, "These:
    'You will not continue committing murder.'
    'You will not continue committing adultery,'
    'You will not continue stealing.'
    'You will not continue bearing a false witness or giving a false testimony.' [Ex. 20:13]

19.   **'You will continue honoring and expressing value to the father and the mother.'** [Ex. 20:12] **'You will continue loving the one near you** (your neighbor and associate) **as he were yourself,'"** [Lev. 19:18]

20. **The young man then replies to Him, "I keep watch over and maintain all these. What yet am I habitually lacking; where am I still deficient and falling behind?"**

21. **Jesus affirmed to him, "Since** (of: If) **you continue desiring and intending to be mature and perfect** (= if you are serious about reaching the goal), **humbly proceed going your way, at once sell the things of your subsistence** (those things supporting you from your beginning and giving you authority; or: your possessions and belongings; or: the things currently at your disposal), **and give [the proceeds] to the poor and destitute folks. Then you will continue holding and possessing treasure within the midst of [the] heavens** (or: in [your] atmospheres). **After that, come here and be habitually following Me."**

22. **Now upon listening and hearing this message** (word; idea; saying), **the young man went away, progressively grieving and experiencing pain, for you see, he had been existing constantly having many acquisitions of possessions and properties** (the results of many acquisitions). [comment: the text does not indicate whether or not he did as Jesus instructed]

23. **So Jesus said to His disciples, "It is so** (or: Truly; Count on it), **I am now saying to you men, it is with things that are disagreeable and difficult for those who are hard to please that a rich and wealthy person will progressively enter into the reign of the heavens** (or: the heavens' kingdom; or: the sovereign rule pertaining to the atmospheres).

24. **"Now again** (or: Furthermore), **I continue saying to you folks, it is easier for a camel to squeeze through a needle's eye** (hole) **than for a rich, wealthy person to enter into God's reign** (or: kingdom influence and sovereign activities)." [comment: a cruciform life is required]

25. **Now upon listening and hearing [this], the disciples continued for a while being exceedingly struck out of themselves** (= surprised and astonished so as to be knocked out of their normal perceptions and assessments of life), **one after another saying, "Who, consequently, is normally able** (or: So is any one [of them] with power) **to be kept safe or rescued** (delivered or saved)**?"**

26. **So Jesus, gazing at and seeing within [the group], says to them, "With humans** (Alongside people) **this continues being impossible. But with God** (or: at God's side) **all things [are] possible."**

27. **At that time Peter, making a considered response, said to Him, "Look at our [situation]. We, ourselves, abandoned all, letting everything flow away, and we follow You. What will there consequently** (or: actually) **continue being for us?"**

28. **So Jesus said to them, "It is true** (or: Truly; Amen) **– I am now laying it out and saying to you men – in** (in union with) **the Rebirth** (Birth-back-again; Return-birth) **when the Son of the Man** (or: = the eschatological messianic figure; or: the Human Being) **would** (or: should; can) **sit upon the throne of His glory** (or: of his reputation and manifestation which calls forth praise; which is His assumed Appearance), **you yourselves – the folks following Me – you also will be habitually sitting down upon twelve thrones** (or: seats) **repeatedly separating-out**

[issues], evaluating and making decisions for, or administering justice to, the twelve tribes of Israel. [*cf* Tit. 3:5; Jn. 3:3, 7; 2 Cor. 5:17]

29. "And further, everyone – whoever, on account of My Name, abandons or lets flow away houses or brothers or sisters or father or mother or children or fields – will continually receive many times more [other MSS: a hundred times as much], and he will be progressively inheriting, and enjoying an allotment of, eonian life (life from, and with the quality of, the Age [of the Messiah]; or: life of, for and related to the ages). [Mk. 10:30; Lu. 18:30]

30. "Now many folks [being] first ones will proceed being last ones – and [many] last ones [will be] first ones.

CHAPTER 20

1. "So you see, the reign of the heavens (the heavens' kingdom; or: the sovereign rule and activities pertaining to the atmospheres) exists being like a person (human) – a householder – who went out at the usual time, early in the morning (or: at daybreak), to hire for himself workers [to send] into his vineyard.

2. "Now upon voicing together [and coming] out with an agreement with the workers – a denarius [for] the day [note: a normal day's wage] – he sent them off into his vineyard.

3. "Then, upon going out about [the] third hour [of the day; = about nine in the morning], he saw other folks having taken their place standing idle and unemployed, within the market place.

4. "And so he says to those folks, 'You people, also, lead the way under [my word and direction] into the vineyard, and whatever may be fair and equitable (just and in accord with the way pointed out; or: = the going rate) I will proceed in giving to you.'

5. "So they went off. Now again, upon going out about [the] sixth hour (= around noon), and later [at the] ninth hour (= about three in the afternoon), he did similarly (or: in just the same way; likewise).

6. "Now about the eleventh hour (= around five o'clock), after going out, he found other folks having taken their place standing, and he is proceeding to say to them, 'Why have you taken your place and are still standing here idle and unemployed the whole day?'

7. "They are, as a group, responding to him, 'Because nobody hired us.' He then replies to them, 'You people, also, lead the way under [my word and direction] into the vineyard.'

8. "Now when it was becoming evening, the owner of the vineyard proceeds saying to his foreman (or: manager; supervisor), 'Call the workers and pay the wages, starting from the last ones, [and proceeding] until the first ones.'

9. "So those coming about the eleventh hour received a denarius apiece.

10. "And then, when the first ones were coming, they concluded from inference to custom that they will receive more, and yet they, themselves, also received a denarius apiece.

11. "Now, upon receiving [the pay], they began muttering complaints and in low voices uttering discontent against the householder,

12. "one after another saying, 'These last folks do one hour, and you make them equal to us – the ones who were bearing the burden and intense heat of the day!'

13. "So, giving a decisive reply to one of them, he said, 'My friend, I am not doing wrong or acting unjustly to you. Did you not voice agreement with me for a denarius?

14. "'Take up what is yours and humbly go away. However, I, myself, continue wanting, and intending, to give to this last person just as [I] also [gave] to you.

15. "'Is it not right or permitted, from [our] existence [as His People], for me to do that which I continue wanting and intending, in [regard] to my own things? Or does your eye continue being worthless (= is your way of viewing things knavish, base, unsound and in a poor condition, or even malicious and degenerate) because I, myself, continue being good (virtuous; = having generous and benevolent qualities)?'

16. "It is in this way that the last folks will be first and the first folks [will be] last."

[comment: this parable shows the equity of kingdom life: all receive the same; first and last have no significance – it is an illustration of additional folks being added into the sovereign activities of the heavens, and being equal to regular workers; it further shows the care of the Householder for the needs of the "unemployed," i.e., those not at that time being a part of His sovereign reign, and how He repeatedly goes, even in the heat of the day, to search for those in need, pointing to outreach beyond the House]

17. **Now Jesus, being progressively about to be walking up in Jerusalem, took aside the twelve disciples down to a spot which corresponded to what is His own, privately, and in the midst of the path** (or: on the way) **said to them,**

18. **"Look at this, and consider. We are progressively walking up into Jerusalem, and later, the Son of the Man** (= Adam's son; the human; or: = the eschatological messiah figure) **will proceed being transferred** (turned over, delivered and committed) **to the chief** (or: ranking) **priests and scribes** (scholars and experts in the Law), **then they will according to pattern proceed judging** (condemning) **Him to** (for; with) **death.**

19. **"Next, they will proceed turning Him over to the ethnic multitudes** (the nations; = foreigners) – **into [a situation] to ridicule, make fun of and mock, and then scourge [Him] with a whip, and finally to suspend and execute [Him] on a torture stake** (or: to crucify [Him]). **Later, on** (or: in; during) **the third day, He will proceed being aroused and raised up."**

20. **Then the mother of the sons of Zebedee – with her sons – came up to Him, repeatedly bowing down in obeisance and homage, while making a request of something from Him.**

21. **So He said to her, "What are you continuing in wanting** (or: = What's you purpose)**?"** **She then replies to Him, "Say that these – my two sons – can** (or: should; would) **sit, one at Your right** (the place of power and authority) **and one on Your left** (the place of honor with a good name), **within the reign of Your kingdom."**

22. **But Jesus, giving a discerning reply, said, "You have not seen, so you are not aware of what you are now requesting for yourselves. Are you folks now able, and do you continue having power, to drink at once the cup which I, Myself, am continuing about to be progressively drinking?" They are presently insisting to Him, "We are now able and continue having the power."**

23. **He is then saying to them, "You will indeed be progressively drinking My cup. Yet to sit at My right and on [My] left is not Mine to give, but rather [it belongs] to those for whom it has been prepared and made ready by My Father."**

24. **And then, upon hearing [of it], the ten became indignant, annoyed, irate and resentful concerning the two brothers.**

25. **So Jesus, after calling them to His side, said, "The rulers and chiefs of the ethnic multitudes** (the nations or people groups; the pagans) **habitually lord it over them, bringing their ownership to bear down on them, while the 'great ones' are constantly wielding authority upon them, even tyrannizing them.**

26. **"It is not this way among you folks; but to the contrary, whoever may be now wanting or should continue intending to become great** (or: = to make himself to be important) **among you, he will continue** (or: proceed in) **being your attending servant.**

27. **"And whoever may now be wanting or should continue intending to be first** (or: foremost; = prominent) **among you folks, he will continue** (or: proceed in) **being your slave.**

28. **"Just as the Son of the Man** (= Adam's son; the eschatological human) **did not come to be taken care of by attending service and dispensing, but to the contrary, to give attending service and to dispense – even to give His soul-life** (consciousness; = Himself): **a corresponding ransom, a price paid for liberation** (or: a loosener), **in the place of many, to effect their release."**

29. **And now, as they are proceeding on their way out from [the town of] Jericho, a large crowd followed Him.**

30. **Then – look, and consider! – two blind men sitting beside the road, upon hearing that Jesus is presently passing by, cried out, repeatedly saying, "Lord, Master, Son of David, mercy us** (extend mercy into us at once)**!"**

31. **Now the crowd expressed respectful admonition to them, so that they would be silent** (keep quiet). **Yet they cried out even louder, continuing in saying, "O Lord, Master, mercy us at once, Son of David!"**

32. **Then standing, Jesus voiced a response to them and said, "What are you men wanting Me to do for you?"**

33. **They went on saying to Him, "O Lord** (Master), **[something] so that our eyes can be opened up!"**

34. **So Jesus, feeling compassion, touches and thus kindles the outer portion of their eyes, and immediately, set for goodness and well-being, they regained their sight** (or: saw again), **and then followed Him.**

CHAPTER 21

1. **Later, when they got close to [the] Jerusalem [area], after they went into Bethphage, [then on] into the Mount of Olives, Jesus at that time sent off two disciples on a mission,**

2. **while saying to them, "Be proceeding on your way into the village – the one opposite [us], down within your [view] – and immediately, set for success, you will be finding an ass: one having been tied, as well as a colt with her. Upon loosing [them], lead [them] to Me.**

3. **"And if anyone may say anything to you, you will say that the Lord** (Master; owner [?]; = Yahweh [?]) **is presently having a need of them, so he, set for goodness, will at once proceed to be sending them off** (or: ... and so He, positioned for success, will proceed sending them off [= back here] right away)."

4. **Now this whole event has happened** (or: come to be) **to the end that the [prophecy; oracle] spoken through the prophet would** (could; should; may) **be fulfilled – the one continuing in saying,**

5.   **"Say to** (or: Tell) **the daughter of Zion, 'Look and consider – your King is progressively coming to you folks with a mild, gentle, egoless and friendly disposition, and [He is] mounted upon an ass, even upon a colt, the male offspring of a yoked beast of burden." [Zech. 9:9]**

6. **So, upon going their way and doing according as Jesus had arranged and placed in order together with, and for, them, the [two] disciples**

7. **led the ass and the colt, and then put** (or: placed) **[their] cloaks upon them. Then He sat on top of them.** [note: when kings came in peace they came riding upon an ass – Barclay]

8. **Now most of the crowd spread out their cloaks and scattered their outer garments on** (= carpeted) **the path** (way; road), **yet others began cutting branches from trees and continued spreading and scattering [them] on** (i.e., carpeting) **the road.** [cf Lev. 23:40; 2 Kings 9:13]

9. **By now the crowds who were proceeding – progressively leading ahead of Him – as well as those who were continuing in following, kept on crying out, repeatedly saying, "O save us now by** (or: Hosanna to) **the Son of David! The One progressively coming in [the] Lord's** [= Yahweh's] **Name is One having been blessed with words of ease and well-being. O save us, among the highest ones** (or: Hosanna within the midst of the highest places)!" [Ps. 118:25-26]

10. **And then, at His entering into Jerusalem, all the city was shaken** (set in commotion [as in an earthquake]; caused to tremble), **one after another saying, "Who** (or: What) **is this?"**

11. **So the crowds kept on saying, "This is the prophet Jesus, the one from Nazareth of the Galilee [district]."**

12. **Next, Jesus entered into the Temple courts and threw out all the folks habitually selling [things], as well as those continuing in buying – as in a marketplace – within the Temple courts** (or: = and chased out all the vendors and shoppers from inside the Temple grounds), **and then He turned upside down the tables of the money-exchangers, along with the chairs and benches of the people continually selling the doves and pigeons.**

13. **And He proceeds saying to them, "It has been written,**
      'My house will continue being called a house of prayer (speaking, thinking or acting,
      with a view toward having goodness and well-being),' [Isa. 56:7; *cf Targum* Zech. 14:21]
yet you folks habitually make it a den of bandits (or: a highwaymen's cave)!" [Jer. 7:11-15]
      [note: here he implicitly invokes Jeremiah's prophecy of destruction]
14. **Later, blind folks and lame people came to Him within the Temple grounds** (or: courts),
and He cured them.

15. **Now the ranking priests and the scribes** (scholars; theologians of the Law), **at seeing and
perceiving the remarkable and wonderful marvels which He performed** (or: did), **and the
young children repeatedly exclaiming** (perhaps: shouting-out approval; cheering) **within the
Temple courts, and continually saying, "O save us now, by the son of David** (or: Hosanna to
the Son of David)," [Ps. 118:25] **they grew displeased, indignant and resentful.**
16. **And so they said to Him, "Are you listening and hearing what these people are
repeatedly saying?"**
So Jesus is then saying to them, "Yes! Did you men never read that,
      **'From out of the mouth of babes, and infants still nursing at the breast, You
      completely harmonize – by thoroughly arranging, adjusting and knitting together –
      praise for Yourself'?"** [Ps. 8:3]
17. **And then, leaving them behind, He went out – outside of the city – into Bethany, and
lodged there, spending the night in a court yard** (or: camped there in a sheepfold).

18. **Now, while leading [them] back in return into the city early in the morning, He got
hungry.**
19. **And then, upon seeing one [specific] fig tree upon the way** (or: on the path; = by the
road), **He came up on it and found nothing within it except leaves** (or: foliage). **So He is
then saying to it, "Fruit can under no condition any longer come into existence** (= be
produced) **from out of you, on into the Age." And later** (or: And so; And then) **– to the side of
resultant usefulness** (with regard to effecting need; or: without delay) **– the fig tree was
caused to dry up and wither.**
20. **Then, in perceiving** (or: at seeing [this]), **the disciples kept on expressing astonishment:
"How is** (or: was) **the fig tree to the side of resultant usefulness** (or: instantly) **caused to dry
up and wither?"**
21. **So Jesus, giving a decided reply, said to them, "Truly** (It is so; Depend on it; Amen), **I am
now saying and laying it out for you, if you can continuously hold trust** (or: if you folks
should constantly have faith) **and would not be affected by some separating factor passing
through your act of discerning or judging, leading you to hesitate, doubt, or completely
question your decision, [then] not only will you men do [what I did] to the fig tree, but
further, you can also say to this mountain range** (or: hill country; mountain), **'Be uplifted, and
then be flung** (cast) **into the midst of the lake** (or: sea)!' **It will progressively come to pass**
(It will proceed in birthing itself and happening).
      [comment: in prophetic language a mountain was a figure for a kingdom, and the sea
      represented the masses of humanity]
22. **"And so, you will progressively take to yourselves and receive all things – whatever,
as much or as many as you folks ever could** (or: may; would) **request in thoughts or words
toward having things go well** (or: centered in union with prayer), **while continuously trusting
and 'faithing'** (= expressing, living in, and being joined to faith, belief and loyal allegiance)!"

23. **Later, after His coming into the Temple courts and grounds, the chief and ranking
priests – as well as the elders** (or: older men) **of the People – came up to Him while [He was]
in the process of teaching. They, one after another, proceeded saying, "In what kind of
authority** (or: In association with what sort of right, from existing privilege) **are you continuing to
do these things?" And then, "Who gave this authority** (right; existing privilege) **to you?"**
24. **So Jesus, making a discerning response, says to them, "I, Myself, will proceed also
asking you one question** (thought; word; = thing), **which, if you folks can** (or: should; would)

tell Me, then I also will continue in telling you in what kind of authority (or: in association with what sort of right, from existing privilege) **I am constantly doing these things:**

25. **"The immersion** (baptism; = ceremonial washing) **which pertained to and was done by John – from what source or origin was it being; from out of heaven** (or: from [the] Atmosphere), **or from out of the midst of humans** (people)**?" Now they began reasoning and discussing among themselves, one after another saying, "If we should say, 'From out of heaven,' he will say to us, 'Why** (Through what cause or situation) **did you not trust or put faith in him?'**

26. **"Yet if we should say, 'From out of humans,' we continue fearing about the crowd** (= are afraid of how the crowd might react), **for they all are in the habit of holding John as a prophet."**

27. **And so, giving a determined reply to Jesus, they said, "We have not seen and so we do not know** (or: We are not aware)**." He also affirms to them, "Neither am I, Myself, laying it out or saying to you folks within what kind of authority** (right, from existing privilege,) **I continue to do or perform these things.**

28. **"But how is it normally seeming to you men** (= What are you now thinking of this situation; What is your opinion)**?**

> **A man had two children. Upon coming to the first one, he said, 'Child, be going** (or: lead the way) **under [my directive] today, and continue working in the vineyard.**

29. > **"Now he, giving a determined reply, said, 'I am neither wanting nor intending [to]** (or: I will not)**!' – yet afterward, changing his thoughts and interests** (or: regretting his behavior), **he went off.**

30. > **"So, upon going to the different one, he said similarly. Now, giving a considered reply, he said, 'I [go], sir,' – and yet, he did not go off.**

31. **"Which of the two did the will of the father?" They [as a group] are saying, "The first one."**

> [other MSS read vs. 29-31 thus: "Now he, giving a considered reply, said,' I {go}, sir,' and yet he did not go off. So, upon approaching the second one, he said likewise. Yet he, giving a determined reply, said, 'I will not! 'Subsequently, he thought better of it {and} went forth. Which of {these} two fulfilled the desire of {his} father?" They are saying, "The latter one."]

Jesus said, "That's right (You got it; Amen)**! I am now saying and laying it out for you that the tax** (or: tribute; toll) **collectors** (or: tax farmers; businessmen who bought the contract to collect taxes for the government) **and the prostitutes are constantly preceding you men into God's reign** (or: the kingdom of God; the sovereign activity of God)**!**

32. **"You see, John came toward you men within the path** (or: on the road) **of fairness and equity, in accord with the way pointed out, and in the right relationship which pertains to justice – and you men did not trust him or put your faith in him** (or: you did not believe him)**. However, the tax collectors and the prostitutes trusted him** (put their faith in him; believed him), **yet you men – upon seeing [this] – still did not change your thoughts or interests** (or: regret your behavior and think better of it) **[so as] to trust in him** (put faith in and believe him)**.**

33. **"Listen, and hear another illustration** (parable)**: There was a man** (human), **a householder, who planted a vineyard. Then he put a fence** (or: wall; hedge) **around it and excavated a trough-shaped receptacle as a winepress. Next he erected a viewing tower, then he leased [the vineyard] out to farmers who would cultivate and dress the vines. With that, he left his home country and traveled abroad.**

34. **"Now when the season of the fruits drew near, he sent off his slaves to the farmers** (= tenant-cultivators) **for the purpose of receiving and taking his [share of] the fruits.**

35. **"And then the farmers** (vinedressers; husbandmen), **upon taking hold of his slaves, thrashed one, killed another, and stoned another.**

36. **"So again, he sent off other slaves – more than the first ones – and they did the same to them!** [note: Palestine was a troubled land and absentee landlords were numerous – Barclay]

37. **"Lastly, he dispatched his son to them, saying, 'They will proceed being turned back on themselves in shame, and thus show respect for and reverence my son.'**

38. "Yet the vinedressers (farmers; cultivators) – upon seeing the son – said among themselves, 'This one is the heir! Come now! We should (or: can) kill him and then we can have his inheritance!'
39. "And so, upon taking hold of him, they threw him out – outside of the vineyard – and then they killed [him].
40. "Therefore, whenever the owner of the vineyard may come, what will he proceed to be doing to those farmers (vinedressers; husbandmen)?"

41. They, as a group, say to Him, "Worthless men (Evil, bad, ugly and malicious fellows)! He will proceed to destroy them in an ugly and vicious way! And then, he will proceed to lease out the vineyard to other vinedressers (farmers; cultivators), who will be habitually giving away (rendering) to him his due share of the fruits, in their proper seasons."

42. Jesus is then saying to them, "Did you never read in the Scriptures,
    'A stone which the builders rejected as the result of a test – this one is birthed into (or: comes to be for) a head of a corner (= a keystone; a capstone; a cornerstone).
    This [head] was birthed (came into existence) from [the] LORD's [=Yahweh's] side (or: presence), and it is wonderful and marvelous in our eyes'? [Ps. 118:22-23]
43. "Because of this, I am now saying to you men that God's reign (or: the kingdom of God; the influence and activity of God's sovereignty) will be progressively lifted up away from you folks, and it will proceed being given to an ethnic multitude (or: nation; people group; swarm of people) consistently producing its fruit!
44. "Further, the person at some point falling upon this Stone will continue jointly-bruised (or: be progressively shattered-together [with It], or completely dashed into pieces). Yet upon whom It may likely fall, It will be progressively winnowing him and scattering his chaff."

45. And so, upon hearing His illustrations (parables), the chief and ranking priests – as well as the Pharisees – knew by this experience that He had been speaking about them,
46. and although still seeking to seize Him, they were fearful about the crowd (= were afraid of how the crowd might react), since they had been holding Him into [the position of] (or: for; [other MSS: as]) a prophet.

CHAPTER 22

1. And further, giving decided response, Jesus again spoke in illustrations (parables) to them [i.e., the ranking priests and Pharisees], continuing in laying it out by saying,
2.   "The reign and sovereign activities of the heavens (or: The heavens' dominion and rule in the atmospheres) is compared to and considered like (or: made like) a person, a king (or: secular ruler), who made arrangements and prepared wedding festivities (things associated with a celebration, feast or banquet) for his son.
3.   "And then he sent off his slaves with the mission to call the folks having been invited unto the marriage festivities – and yet, they continued unwilling to go (or: kept on, one after another, not intending or desiring to come; = not wanting to attend).
4.   "So again he sent off other slaves, now saying, 'Tell the folks having been invited, "Consider, please! I have made my meal ready (or: finished the preparations for my afternoon dinner) – my bulls and grain-fattened animals having been slaughtered, and everything [is] set and ready! Come unto the wedding festivities.'"
5.   "But they, being unconcerned, lacking interest and not caring about it, went away – one, indeed, into his own field, yet another upon his commercial business (or: his trade),
6.   "but the rest [of them], forcibly taking hold of his slaves, insolently violated their human rights, and then killed [them]. So the king inwardly swelled with emotion and was made to teem with the passion of his natural disposition, and mental bent (or: in indignation and impulsive anger).

7.   **– Later, sending his soldiers** (troops), **he destroyed those murderers and set their city in flames –** [note: Barclay suggests that vss. 6-7 "somehow strayed in" to this context; perhaps a post-AD 70 addition]

8.   **"Thereupon, he is saying to his slaves, 'The wedding feast indeed continues being ready, yet those having been invited were not worthy folks** (folks of corresponding value; or: worthy of the honor).

9.   **"'Therefore, be progressively journeying on your way – on the thoroughfares, both the main roads exiting the city as well as the side roads passing through, and the intersections – and call as many people as you might happen to find unto the wedding festivities** (or: marriage feast).'

10.   **"And so, upon going out into the streets and alleys, the paths and roads, those slaves gathered and led together all whom they found – both worthless** (or: misery-gushed; bad; of poor character; wicked) **folks and good** (virtuous) **ones – and so the wedding hall was filled with folks presently reclining [at the tables].**

11.   **"Now, upon entering to view and watch those engaged in reclining [at the tables], the king noticed a person there who had not put on wedding apparel** (= not dressed appropriately for a wedding feast),

12.   **"And so he then says to him, 'My good sir** (or: Friend; Comrade; Dear fellow), **how are you entered here having no wedding apparel** (= how is it that you came into this place without dressing appropriately for a marriage feast)?' **But the man was muzzled** (rendered speechless; [note: this word was also used to mean "silenced by a spell"]).

13.   **"At that point, the king said to the servants, 'Upon binding his feet and hands, you men throw him out into the darkness** (dim obscurity) **which is farther outside. In that place there will continue being the weeping** (or: lamenting) **and the grinding of the teeth.'**

       [comment: compare the binding of feet in Hos. 11:1-4, LXX:

       1. Because Israel [is] a young child, I Myself also love him, and I once called his children together from out of Egypt.

       2. The more I called them [to Me], the more they distanced themselves and kept away from My face (or: immediate presence). They sacrificed to the Baals, and then burned incense to the carved and chiseled images (= idols).

       3. And so I, Myself tied the feet of Ephraim together (i.e., restrained him; = hobbled him to keep him from wandering) [then] I took him up upon My arm – and yet they did not realize (or: know) that I had healed them.

       4. In the thorough ruin and destruction of humans I stretch out to them and lay [My hand] on them in binding ties (or: bonds) of My love.

       And so I will be to them as a person slapping (or: striking) [someone] on his cheek, then I will look upon him (= either: keep an eye on him; or: give respect to him). I will prevail with him and then give ability and power to him. (JM)]

14. **"Now you see, many folks continue existing being called and invited ones, yet a few people [are also] chosen ones** (selected and picked out folks)!"

       [comment: notice the ironic inversion of this closing statement of the parable: here there were two sorts of people that were invited, the first group, then the second – which actually came to the feast; in this story, the one that was picked out (chosen and focused on) was also kicked out]

15. **At that time the Pharisees, after going their way, took counsel together so that they could lay a snare in a verbal expression** (thought; idea; word) **and would trap Him.**

16. **And so, they sent off their disciples with the Herodians** (supporters and members of the political associates of Herod) **on a mission to Him, as a group, saying, "Teacher, we have seen and now know that you are genuine and honest** (truthful; trustworthy; dependable; true), **and further, you habitually teach God's way** (path; road) **in truth and reality. Furthermore, it is not normally a concern or worry to you about anyone, for you are not constantly looking into peoples' faces [to see their reaction] or observing their outward appearance [to take into account their social position].**

17. **"Tell us, then, how it normally seeming to you** (= what are you now thinking of this situation; What is your opinion): **Is it normally right or permitted, from [our] existence [as God's People] to give** (= pay) **a poll** (or: census) **tax to Caesar** (the Roman emperor), **or not?"**
18. **But Jesus, knowing by intimate experience their worthlessness** (their poor character and wicked intent), **says, "Why are you men constantly examining and testing Me, you people who make close inspection of the writings so as to be opinionated and hyper-critical, having all the answers** [note: see 6:2, above, for *hupokritēs*]?
19. **"Show** (Exhibit to) **Me the coin used for the poll tax." So they brought a denarius** (silver coin) **to Him,**
20. **and He is then saying to them, "Whose [is] this image, and the inscription?"**
21. **They are then answering, "Caesar's." At that point He proceeds in response to them, "Give back, then, Caesar's things** (or: the things pertaining to Caesar, or from Caesar) **to Caesar – and God's things** (or: the things pertaining to God, or from God) **to God."**
22. **Well, upon hearing [that], [some] felt admiration [while others] were simply amazed, [then some] were dumbfounded. And so, letting Him alone to continue on** (or: rejecting and abandoning Him), **they went off.**

23. **During that day, [some] Sadducees – folks normally saying [that] there is to be no resurrection – came to Him and inquired of Him, proceeding to lay out this proposition:**
24. **"Teacher, Moses says, 'If anyone should die off while still not having children, his brother shall in addition marry his** [i.e., the brother's] **wife, and shall make seed** (= offspring) **to stand up for his brother.'** [Deut. 25:5-6; *cf* Acts 23:8]
25. **"Now there were seven brothers among us. And the first one, having married, came to [his] end** (or: finished [his] life) **and so – not having seed** (= offspring) **– leaves behind his wife to** (or: for) **his brother.**
26. **"In the same way, also, the second one, and then the third one – on until [all] seven.**
27. **"Now subsequently to all of them, the woman died.**
28. **"Therefore, within the resurrection, of which one of the seven will she proceed in being a wife – for you see, they all had her?"** [*cf* Jn. 11:25; 2 Cor. 5:17]

29. **Now Jesus, giving a discerning response, says to them, "You men are repeatedly being deceived and are continually caused to wander astray** (or: off track) **[from] not having seen the Scriptures with perception, nor yet knowing or being acquainted with God's power and ability.**
30. **"You see, within the resurrection folks are neither repeatedly marrying, nor are they constantly being given in marriage. To the contrary, they constantly exist as agents** (or: messengers) **– centered within the atmosphere** (or: in union with the heaven).
31. **"Yet concerning the resurrection of the dead ones, did you not read the thing spoken to, and for, you folks by God, continually saying,**
32.   **"'I, Myself, am** (continuously exist being) **the God of Abraham, and the God of Isaac, and the God of Jacob'?** [Ex. 3:6; *cf* 1 Cor. 15:40-54]
He is not the God of dead folks, but rather of continuously living people."
33. **Then the crowds began being struck out of themselves from amazement** (were being driven out of their composure with astonishment) **upon hearing His teaching.**

34. **Now, after hearing that He had muzzled** (put to silence; rendered speechless) **the Sadducees, the Pharisees were gathered together on the same [issue/place/purpose].**
35. **Then one of them – a legal expert** (or: one versed in the Mosaic Law; proficient in the Torah) **– asked a question, testing Him,**
36. **"Teacher, what kind of implanted goal** (impartation of the finished product within; inward directive) **[is] great** (or: which [is the] most important precept) **within the Law** (= Torah)?"
37. **So He affirms to him,**
     "' You will continue loving (fully giving yourself to; urging toward reunion with) **[the] LORD** [= Yahweh], **your God, in union with your whole heart – and within the midst of the core of your being, and in union with your whole soul – and within the midst of your entire soul-life** (consciousness), **and in union with your whole intellectual**

capacity – and within the midst of your whole thinking process and comprehension.' [Deut. 6:5]

38. **"This continuously exists being the great and foremost** (or: first) **implanted goal** (impartation of the finished product within; inward directive).

39. **"Yet [the] second one [is] like it:**
'**You will continue loving your associate** (or: overcoming existential separation from your neighbor; participating with the one close to you) **as he were yourself.'** [Lev. 19:18]

40. **"In the midst of** (or: In union with; Within) **these two imparted, goal-oriented directives the whole Law – as well as the Prophets – is continuously being hung!"**

41. **Now during the Pharisees' having been gathered together, Jesus inquired of them, laying out the question,**

42. **"How does it normally seem to you** (or: What do you folks now think and what is your view) **concerning the Anointed One** (the Christ; = the Messiah): **Whose Son** (or: Descendant) **is He?" They, as a group, are replying to Him, "David's."**

43. **He then says to them, "How, then, is David – within and in union with [the] Spirit** (or: in spirit; in the effect of [His] Breath; in attitude) – **normally calling Him 'Lord'** (Master)**?, saying,**

44. **"'[The] LORD** (= Yahweh) **said to my Lord** (Master), **"Be continuously sitting from out of** (or: at) **My right-hand [parts] until I should place** (or: put) **Your alienated ones** (or: folks filled with hate and hostility; enemies) **down under Your feet"'?** [Ps. 110:1]

45. **"Since** (or: If), **therefore, David is normally calling Him, 'Lord'** (Master), **how does He exist being His 'Son'?"**

46. **No one had power or ability to give a word or thought in considered response to Him, neither did anyone – from that day – dare** (or: have courage) **to any longer put a question to Him.**

CHAPTER 23

1. **At that time, Jesus speaks to the crowds – as well as to His disciples – then saying,**

2. **"The scribes** (scholars; theologians; experts in the Law [Torah]) **and the Pharisees sit upon Moses' seat.**

3. **"Therefore, you people be constantly doing and keeping** (observing; maintaining) **everything – as many things as they should tell you. But do not continue doing or performing according to their works or actions, for you see, they are habitually 'saying,' and yet they are not doing or performing** (= they are 'all talk and no action').

4. **"So they habitually tie up and bind heavy loads** (or: burdensome cargos), **and then constantly place [these] as an addition upon the shoulders of the People** (or: belonging to persons) **– yet they, themselves, are not willing to budge or put them in motion with their finger** (or: = to 'lift a finger' to help carry them)!

5. **"Still, they are habitually doing all their works** (or: performing all their acts) **for the purpose of being viewed and gazed at by people** (= their conduct is to attract public attention). **You see, they habitually make their phylacteries** (protective amulets: small boxes worn on themselves which encase certain Scripture verses; used to safeguard themselves) **broad, and are normally enlarging the hems and borders [of their garments], as well as lengthening the fringe or corner tassels [as a reminder to keep the commandments].**

6. **"Now they like the most prominent places of reclining during the evening meals** (or: = the places of honor at banquets) **and the front seats in the synagogues,**

7. **"as well as the formal salutations within the marketplaces, and [just love] to be called 'Rabbi'** (Heb. = my master, or, great one; used for teachers; equivalent to our 'Dr.') **by people.**

8. **"But you folks should not be called 'Rabbi,' because One is your Teacher! Now you people all exist being brothers,**

9. **"and you folks should not call [anyone] on the earth your 'father,' because you see, One is your Father: the heavenly One** (the One having the character and qualities of the atmosphere and heaven)!

10. **"Neither should you people be called 'leaders' or 'guides,' because One exists being your Leader and Guide: the Anointed One** (the Christ; = the Messiah; or: the Anointing)!

11. **"Now the greatest** (= most prominent or highest ranking) **among you will continue being your attending servant, and a dispenser [to, or for, peoples' needs].**
12. **"So, whoever shall exalt** (= promote) **himself will be progressively humbled and brought low, and whoever shall humble himself** (bring or make himself low; = demote and make himself of little significance) **will continue being lifted up and exalted** (= promoted).
13. **"And so, tragic will be the fate for you, scribes** (scholars; theologians; Law experts) **and Pharisees – [you] overly critical and perverse folks who make decisions from a low point of view** [see: 6:2, above]! **– because you consistently shut and lock up the reign of the heavens in front of the People** (humans)
> (or: the sovereign rule of the atmospheres, which is in the presence of people; or: the activity and influence of the realm of the sky and heaven which is resident within, and moves toward, the humans; or: the kingdom moving from within the midst and face to face with people). **For you, yourselves habitually do not enter, nor yet are you by practice allowing** (or: letting flow on) **those repeatedly coming into [your realm of influence] to continue to go in.**

[14.] [This vs. is omitted by Nestle-Aland, W&H, Tasker, and Panin; Griesbach makes it vs. 13, and brackets, as 14, vs. 13, above; it is absent in the early codices; it is included in the Byzantine/Majority text (TR), based only upon later MSS:
> **"It will be a tragic fate for you, scribes and Pharisees –** *hupokrites* (see 6:2, above)! **For you constantly consume** (eat down; devour; swallow up) **the houses belonging to widows** (or: the households of widows), **and then continue praying a long [time], for a disguise** (as a pretext). **Because of this you will receive a more abundant effect of a decision and judgment.**]

15. **"It will be a tragic fate for you, scribes and Pharisees – perverse scholars who live by separation and have all the answers** [see 6:2, above]! **Because you habitually go around the sea and dry [land] to make one convert** (proselyte), **and whenever he may become** (should be birthed) **[one], you proceed making him a son of the valley of Hinnom** (= a person having the character and qualities of a city dump, or a part of a refuse depository [Greek: Gehenna]) **twice as much as yourselves.**
16. **"It will be a tragic fate for you, blind guides of the way and leaders on the path, folks who are constantly saying, 'Whoever should lay hold of a sacred object in the Temple** (or: swear within, or in union with, the sanctuary), **it is nothing** (= it does not matter). **Yet whoever should lay hold of the gold of the Temple, as a sacred object** (or: swear an oath pertaining to a connection with the gold of the Temple), **he continues indebted and is owing [it].'**
17. **"[You are] senseless morons** (stupid folks), **as well as blind ones! For which is greater: the gold, or the Temple sanctuary which is setting apart and consecrating the gold?**
18. **"Further, [you say], 'Whoever grabs hold of the altar as a sacred object** (or: Whoever may swear an oath in connection with the altar), **it means nothing. Yet, whoever should lay hold of the gift** (or: may swear an oath in connection with the offering) **which is on top of it, he continues indebted and is owing [it].'**
19. **"Senseless morons and blind ones! You see, which one [is] more important** (greater): **the gift** (offering), **or the altar which is constantly setting the gift** (the offering) **apart and consecrating [it]?**
20. **"Therefore, the person laying hold of the altar for a religious purpose** (or: swearing an oath in conjunction with the altar), **continues holding onto it** (or: swearing in relation to it) **as well as in union with all the things which are on top of it.**
21. **"Also, the person holding onto something in the Temple sanctuary, or swearing in union with it, continues to hold onto it – or swearing in its midst – and also to, and in union with, the one making His home down in** (dwelling in; inhabiting) **it.**
22. **"Further, the one taking hold of something within the heaven** (or: in union with the atmosphere, sky or outer space), **or swearing in its midst, continues to hold onto, and is**

swearing in the presence of, God's throne, as well as the One constantly sitting on top of it. [comment: the term heaven refers figuratively to the Temple; the ark was "God's throne"]

23. "O the tragic fate by (or: for; with) you folks – scholars (theologians and experts in the Scriptures) and Pharisees – [you] under-discerning folks who live by close inspection of minor details [see 6:3, above]: [it is] that you habitually give away a tenth (or: tithe back) from the mint and the dill and the cummin, and yet you abandon and let flow away the weightier (= more important) matters of the Law [= Torah]: the justice (equity; fairly evaluated decisions), the mercy, and the trust (the faith; the faithfulness and the fidelity; the reliance and the reliability; the confidence). Now these things it continued being binding and necessary [for you] to do and perform – and not to abandon (neglect; set aside) those others!
24. "Blind 'guides and leaders' of the way: constantly filtering and straining [out] the gnat, yet habitually gulping (drinking; swallowing) down a camel!

25. "How tragic is the fate in you people – scribes (scholars, etc.) and Pharisees: overly-critical interpreters [see 6:2, above]! For you folks are habitually cleansing the outside of the cup and of the fine side dish – yet inside they continuously contain a full load from snatching (plunder; pillage; = the fruits of forceful greed) and lack of strength (or: self-indulgence; dissipation; immoderateness; dissoluteness).
26. "Blind Pharisee, first cleanse the inside of the cup and of the fine side dish – so that its outside can also come to be (be birthed) clean!

27. "Tragic will be the fate of you Law scholars and Pharisees – you who recite a front of your own opinions and answers (or: overly-critical folks; [see 6:2, above])! [It will be] because you continue closely resembling whitewashed (i.e., smeared or plastered with lime) tombs (sepulchers; grave sites), which indeed, from outside, continue being made to appear in the prime of beauty, for a time – yet inside they contain a full load of bones of dead folks, as well as every uncleanness.
28. "In this way you, yourselves, also on the one hand are continually made to outwardly appear to the People [to be] just (fair, righteous, in right relationships, and in accord with the way pointed out) – yet inside you continuously exist being men glutted and distended, full of opinionated answers (or: perverse detail-oriented scholarship; hyper-criticism and judgmentalism; well-sifted wicked interpretations) and lawlessness (= practice which is contrary to the Law [Torah]).

29. "It will be a tragic fate for you, theologians (scholars of the Law) and Pharisees [who are also] overly judging and critical [see 6:2, above]. Because, [you see], you are repeatedly building the tombs (sepulchers) of the prophets, and are constantly adorning and decorating the memorial grave monuments of just and rightwised folks,
30. "and you are habitually saying, 'If we had been existing in the days of our fathers (= ancestors), we would not have been participants (partners; ones who shared in common and took part) in [spilling] the blood of the prophets.'
31. "As a result, you are continually giving evidence in yourselves (testifying to and for yourselves) that you exist being sons of those that were murdering the prophets,
32. "And so, you, yourselves... Fill full the measure of your fathers!

33. "[You] snakes! [You] offspring (brood) of vipers (poisonous serpents)! How can you flee and escape from the judging which has the qualities, character and significance of the valley of Hinnom (= the sentence to the city dump [Greek: Gehenna; = the Valley of Hinnom]; the deciding which pertains to the waste depository of the city)? [cf Jer. 19:1-15]
34. "Because of this – look and consider! – I, Myself, am continuing in commissioning and sending off to you people prophets, wise people and scholars (scribes; theologians of the Law). Of them, [some] you folks will proceed to be killing, and [some] you will proceed to crucify (hang and put to death on stakes). Further, of them [some] you people will continue severely whipping (scourge; lash) within your synagogues, and then you, yourselves, will continue pursuing and persecuting [them] from city to city (or: town to town),

35. **"with the result that upon you, yourselves, can** (or: would; should) **come all [the] just** (equitable; rightwised) **blood being continuously poured out** (or: spilled) **upon the** (or: this) **Land – from the blood of rightwised** (just; fair; in-right-relationship; upright) **Abel, until the blood of Zechariah, the son of Barachiah** (or: Baruch), **whom you people murdered between the Temple and the altar.**
36. **"Assuredly** (Amen; Count on it), **I am now saying to you people, it will progressively move toward this point, and then arrive – all these things! – upon THIS generation!** ....

37. **"O Jerusalem, Jerusalem! The one repeatedly killing the prophets, and habitually stoning the people sent off with a mission to her. How many times** (or: How often) **I wanted** (intended; purposed; longed) **to progressively gather your children together upon [Myself] in the manner in which a hen normally gathers her chicks together under [her] wings – and you did not want [it]** (or: you do not intend [it]). [cf Ruth 2:12; Ps. 17:6; 36:7; 57:1]
38. **"Look, and think about this! 'Your House is progressively left [to be] a wilderness** (desert; desolate place) **for you people** [other MSS: is now abandoned to you]**.'** [Jer. 22:5]
39. **"You see, I now say to you, you should by no means perceive** (or: see) **Me from this time on, until you folks should at some point say,**
> **'The One periodically coming in [the] LORD's** [= Yahweh's] **Name is One having been given – and still having – words of ease and well-being** (or: having been given the Blessing and having the Blueprint of Goodness)!'"** [Ps. 118:26]

CHAPTER 24

1. **Later, upon going out from the Temple courts, Jesus was proceeding on His way, and then His disciples approached to additionally point out and show to Him the buildings of the Temple complex.**
2. **Yet He, giving a decided response, says to them, "You are not looking at all these things, are you** (or: Do you not observe all this)**? Truly** (or: Count on it; or: Assuredly), **I am now saying to you folks, there can under no circumstances be a stone left or allowed to be upon [another] stone which will not be progressively loosed down to bring utter destruction."**

3. **Now later, during His continued sitting on the Mount of Olives, His disciples approached Him, privately** (in accord with His being in His own space and place), **saying in turn, "Tell us, when will these things proceed in being, and what [is] the sign pertaining to Your presence, as well as** (or: even) **the combination of parts to one end** (or: the bringing to one end together; the combined consummation; the joint, final act) **of the** (or: this) **Age?"**
4. **Then making a discerning reply, Jesus says to them, "You men be constantly looking, seeing, and staying alert, [so that] nothing and no one can mislead or should deceive you folks and then cause you to go astray** (= stray from the Path).
5. **"You see, many people will be coming, upon [association with; the basis of, or, the supposed authority of; on the reference to] My Name, one after another saying, 'I, myself, am the anointed one** (or: the Christ),**' and they will be leading astray and deceiving many people.**
6. **"Now, you men** [= the disciples who had come to Him privately] **will be at the point to be repeatedly hearing [the noise of] battles and wars, as well as news of battles and reports or rumors of wars – each time see to it that you men are not disturbed, thrown into disorder, or terrified by the commotion, outcries or uproar. You see, it remains necessary for such to be birthed and to occur. However, it is not yet the destined end – the closing act of the goal** (the consummation; the final fruition, completion and perfection [of the plan]).
7. **"For you see, [one] ethnic group** (or: a nation) **will be caused to progressively rise up upon [another] ethnic group** (or: a nation) **– even [one] kingdom upon [another] kingdom** (or: a reign upon a reign) **– and there will continue being famines** [later MSS add: plagues (or: troublesome times)] **and earthquakes down in [various] places** (or: districts).
8. **"Yet all these things [are but] a beginning of birth pangs** [note: = travail to birth something {new}; also: = a time of distress].

9. "At that time people will be repeatedly handing you men over into pressure (squeezing; tribulation; affliction), and then, they will, one after another, kill you. Further, you will continue being men that were detached [by society], repeatedly treated with ill-will, and constantly hated by all the ethnic multitudes (or: the nations) – because of My Name.

10. "Also at that time, many people will be repeatedly trapped by taking the bait of the snare, or tripping over the trap-stick, and so, they will proceed in turning one another over [to the authorities or enemies] and committing or commending each other, as well as hating or radically detaching from one another, or treating each other with ill-will.

11. "Also, many false prophets will proceed in being raised up and they will be progressively leading many folks astray, deceiving them and causing them to wander.

12. "Then further, because the lawlessness is to be multiplied and increased, the majority of the people's love (or: the love of many folks; = acceptance from the masses) will be progressively caused to blow cold (or: will continue cooling off from the Breath blowing on it).

13. "Now [as to] the person remaining under [all this] and enduring unto [the] purposed goal (or: into a final, destined act), this one will be repeatedly rescued and delivered (or: continuously kept safe).

14. "Furthermore, this good news which pertains to the reign (or: this message of goodness, ease and well-being which belongs to and comes from sovereign action and influence of the kingdom) will be progressively publicly proclaimed within the whole inhabited area (or: the Hellenistic world, as opposed to barbarian lands; or: = the Roman Empire) – [leading] into a witness and evidence for all the ethnic multitudes (or: unto a testimony among all the nations), and at that point the purposed goal will proceed having arrived and continue here (or: and at that time the final act will have progressively come, and its product will continue being here; or: and so then the destined end will be progressively arriving).

15. "Therefore, whenever you men can see (or: may perceive) 'the effect of the loathing and nauseating [event; condition; thing; situation] from the desolation

> (or: the result from the abhorring abomination associated with, or which causes, the devastation and abandonment; or: the resulting effect of the desecration, which is an act of ruining, forsaking and leaving uninhabited like a desert),' that was being spoken

through Daniel the prophet, standing 'within the midst of a set-apart place (or: [the] holy place)' [Dan. 9:27; 11:31; 12:11] – let the person presently reading continue to use his mind and intellect for the comprehension [of this] (= figure out what this means!) –

16. "at that time, let the people within the midst of Judea progressively escape (flee; take flight) into the hills and mountains.

17. "Let the person upon the housetop (roof) not descend (= go downstairs) to pick up or carry away the things (= his possessions) from out of his house,

18. "and let not the one in the midst of the field turn back behind to pick up his cloak (= to get a coat or outer garment).

19. "Now it will progressively be a difficult or tragic time for the pregnant women and nursing mothers in those days!

20. "So you folks be progressively taking thought toward having ease, speaking for well-being and take action to have goodness (or: be praying) – to the end that your escape (flight) may not happen (occur) in a winter or rainy season, nor yet on a sabbath.

21. "You see, 'at that time there will be great pressure (squeezing; compression; affliction; tribulation) of the sort that has not happened (occurred; been birthed; come to be) from [the] beginning of [this] ordered arrangement (system; adorned order; systematic disposition; world) until now – neither under any circumstances could it have occurred (happened; come to be).' [Joel 2:2; Dan. 12:1]

22. "Furthermore, if those days were not curtailed (or: except those days be cut short), no flesh (= people) [at] all would likely be rescued (delivered; kept safe). Yet, because of the picked out and chosen folks, those days will proceed being curtailed (cut short).

23. **"At that time, if anyone should say to you folks, 'Look! Here [is] the Anointed One** (or: the anointing; or: the Christ; or: = the Messiah)!' **Or, 'There [He/it is]!' – you folks should not trust or believe [it].**

24. **"For you see, false christs** (or: false anointings; phony anointed ones; = counterfeit messiahs) **and false prophets will one after another be raised up, and they will continue giving** (presenting; = performing) **great signs and miracles** (amazing things; wonders) **so as to continuously mislead** (deceive; cause to wander; lead astray) **– if able** (if in [their] power; or: since [it is] possible) **– even the picked out and chosen folks.**

25. **"Look and remember – I have already said [this] before to you folks** (or: Look, and consider – I have told you beforehand, in advance, and have forewarned you people).

26. **"Therefore, if they should say to you folks, 'Look! He is within the desert** (wilderness; desolate place),' **you should not go out, [or], 'Look! [He is] within the inner chambers** (interior rooms; storehouses; barns; closets),' **you should not put your trust in [it] or believe [them].**

27. **"You see, just as the brightness** (the brilliant beam; the bright shining) **is habitually and progressively coming forth from [the] rising in the eastern parts** [= a figure of the sunrise] **and then is progressively and habitually shining and giving light as far as [the] western parts** (or: until the [recurring] settings), **in this way will proceed being the presence of the Son of the Man** (the Son from humanity; = Adam's son; or: = the eschatological Messianic figure; the Human Being).

28. **"Wherever the carcass** (corpse) **may be, the vultures** (or: eagles) **will be progressively led together and gathered.**

29. **"Now immediately after the pressure** (constriction; tribulation) **of those [particular] days, 'the sun will be progressively made dark and the moon will not continue giving its** (or: her) **diffused radiance,'** [Isa. 13:10; Ezk. 32:7; Joel 2:10] **and then the stars will, one after another, be falling from the sky** (or: heaven) **– 'and so, the powers and abilities of the heavens will be progressively shaken** (agitated; stirred up; made to rock so as to be ready to fall).' [Isa. 34:4; Hag. 2:6, 21]

30. **"And at that time, the 'sign' which is the Son of the Man** (the Human Being; = the expected Messianic figure) **will be made progressively visible in union with heaven** (or: And then, He will be brought to light and made to shine: the Sign which is the Son with the Human qualities, centered within the midst of [the] atmosphere). **And at that point 'all the tribes of the Land** (or: earth; or: this territory) **will continue beating themselves** (= a figure of striking one's breast in grief and remorse; or: as when grain is being threshed; or: give themselves to wearisome toil; or: cut themselves off, as when harvesting grain),' [Zech. 12:10, 14] **and they will proceed in seeing for themselves 'the Son of the Man progressively coming and going, upon the clouds of the atmosphere** (or: sky),' [Dan. 7:13-14], **with power and ability, as well as much glory** (or: an assumed appearance with many manifestations which call forth praise).

31. **"And then He will continue sending His agents** (messengers; folks with the message) **off on a mission 'with a great trumpet** (or: = a loud trumpet blast; [note: a figure of a publicly proclaimed message or instruction]),' [Isa. 27:13] **and they will progressively be fully** (or: additionally) **gathering together His picked out and chosen folks from out of the four winds – from [the] heavens'** (or: atmospheres') **extremities: until their farthest points** (= from the four quarters of the land, from one end of the sky to the other)!

32. **"Now learn the [point of the] illustration** (parable) **from the fig tree: Whenever its branch may already come to be tender** (= in bud), **and the leaves can progressively produce and sprout out, you normally know by experience that the summer [is] near.**

33. **"You folks, yourselves, in this way – whenever you men may see and can perceive all these [aforementioned] things – be also then knowing that it is near, upon [the] gates [of the City]** (or: He continues being at hand, close enough to touch, accessible at [the] doors)!

34. **"It is true** (Amen; Truly; Count on it), **I now say to you folks, that THIS generation can by no means pass by until all these things can happen** (should occur; may come to be).

35. **"The heaven and the earth** (i.e.: This Atmosphere and this Territory) **WILL progressively pass on by. Now in contrast, My thoughts and words** (or: messages; patterned declarations; transfers and conveyances of Meaning-bearing Blueprints) **can by no means pass on by.**

36. **"Now concerning that day and hour, no one has seen or known – neither the folks with the message from the heavens** (or: agents of the atmospheres; messengers who pertain to, or which are, the heavens), **nor even the Son – only the Father [being] the exception.**

37. **"For you see, even as [it was in] the days of Noah, thus** (in this same way) **will continue being the presence of the Son of the Man** (= Adam's son; = the son who is human; = the eschatological Messianic figure).

38. **"For as people kept on being** (or: habitually were) **within those days – the ones before the down-wash** (the deluge; the flood; the cataclysm) **– habitually eating and drinking; by custom marrying and by habit giving** (or: taking) **in marriage, up to the day in which Noah entered into the ark;**

39. **"and they did not know** (were not aware; took no note of the situation) **until the down-wash** (deluge; flood; cataclysm) **came and washed [the] whole population away** (or: picked up all [the] people to sweep [them] away) **– thus** (in this same way) **will continue being the presence of the Son of the Man!**

40. **"At that time two folks will continue being within the midst of the field: one man is being taken in hand** (seized) **and drawn to the side, and yet one man is repeatedly left alone to flow on his way** (or: continues on pardoned [with his debts] forgiven; or: is being sent away, allowed to continue relaxing while permitted to depart).

41. **"Two women are continuing to grind grain into meal and flour, within the mill** (or: in the midst [of working] the millstone)**: one woman is being taken in hand** (seized) **and drawn to the side, and yet one woman is repeatedly left alone to continue [in her work]** (or: pardoned; sent away; forgiven; etc., as in vs. 40).

42. **"Therefore, you folks stay constantly awake, be ever alert, and continue watchful, because you have not seen, nor do you thus know, in what sort of day your Owner** (Lord) **is in the habit of coming** (or: for what kind of day your Master repeatedly comes).

43. **"Yet you are progressively coming to know that by experience** (or, as an imperative: Now be personally knowing that, through normal experience), **because if the householder had seen and known in what sort of watch** (= which of the watches) **[of the night] the thief is normally coming, he would have kept awake, remained alert and kept watchful, and then he would not let** (permit) **his house to be dug** (or: tunneled) **through.**

44. **"Because of this, you yourselves progressively come to be ready and prepared as well, because at an hour for** (= about) **which you are not normally thinking** (imagining; supposing; = expecting), **the Son of the Man** (= the eschatological Messiah figure; humanity's son) **is normally** (or: repeatedly) **coming.**

45. **"Who, consequently** (or: really), **is the faithful** (trustworthy; loyal) **and thoughtful** (prudent; sensible; discreet; considerate) **slave whom the owner** (lord; master) **set down upon** (or: = places in full control over) **his household servants** (domestics) **[with the directive] to give to them nourishment within a fitting situation** (or: sustenance at the proper time; food in season)**?**

46. **"That slave is happy and blessed whom his owner** (lord; master), **upon at some point coming, will proceed in finding [him or her] habitually doing thus.**

47. **"Truly** (Amen; It is so), **I am now saying to you folks, that he will proceed in setting him down upon** (or: = place him in full control over) **all his possessions and things by which he normally subsists.**

48. **"But if that worthless** (ugly; bad quality) **slave should say within his heart, 'My owner** (master; lord) **continually delays and fails [to come] for a long time,'**

49. **"and then should start to repeatedly beat his fellow slaves, and may be eating and drinking with the people regularly getting drunk,**

50. **"the owner** (lord; master) **of that slave will be arriving on a day in which he is not normally anticipating, and within an hour which he is not usually knowing,**

51. **"and so he will proceed to be cutting him in two** [hyperbole for: severely punish; or, metaphor: cut him off from employment] **and then he will proceed putting** (placing; setting) **his part with the perverse, opinionated scholars who have all the answers and are hyper-**

critical and overly judgmental [*hupokrites*; see 6:2, above]. **The weeping, moaning and the grinding of the teeth will continue being in that place and situation.**

CHAPTER 25

1. **"At that time, the reign of the heavens** (or: the heavens' kingdom; the sovereign rule and influence from the atmospheres) **will continue being considered like** (or: caused to resemble; or: compared to) **ten virgins** (unmarried girls) **who, upon taking** (getting) **their lamps** (or: torches), **went out into the bridegroom's** [D and other MSS add: and the bride's] **meeting.**
2. **"Now five of them were foolish** (stupid; mentally dull), **and five [were] thoughtful and prudent.**
3. **"You see, the foolish and stupid maidens, in taking their lamps** (or: torches), **did not take oil with them,**
4. **"whereas the thoughtful and prudent ladies** (or: girls) **did take oil within the flasks** (or: crocks; receptacles) **with their personal lamps** (or: torches).
5. **"Now with the continued passing of time during [the; a] delaying of the bridegroom, they all became drowsy, nodded off, and then continued fast asleep.**
6. **"So, in the middle of [the] night, a shout had occurred, 'Look! The bridegroom! Be proceeding to now go forth into [the] meeting** (a moving from one place to participate in a face-to-face encounter with someone; [other MSS: unto his away-meeting])!'
7. **"At that point all those virgins** (girls) **were awakened and then at once put their lamps in order** (serviced their lamps; or: trimmed and adjusted their torches).
8. **"Now the foolish maidens said to the prudent ladies, 'Give us some of your oil, because our lamps** (torches) **are being progressively run dry and extinguished** (put out)!'
9. **"But the thoughtful and prudent ladies gave a discerning and decided reply, [each] saying, 'Not at this time. There would in no way be enough for [both] us and you folks as well. Instead, be going now on your way to the merchants** (the folks normally selling [oil]) **and at once buy for yourselves [at the market].'**
10. **"So, during their going off to make a purchase** (to buy), **the bridegroom came, and the ladies who were prepared and ready entered in with him into the wedding festivities** (or: marriage feast), **and then the gate was shut and barred** (or: the door was closed and locked).

11. **"Now subsequently the rest** (remainder) **of the virgins are finally coming as well, [as a group] saying, 'O sir! Sir!** (or: Master! Master!) **Open up at once to** (or: for) **us!'**
12. **"But the person [answering the door], making a discerning reply, said, 'I now say in truth to you folks, I have not seen you nor am I presently acquainted with you people.'**

13. **"Therefore, stay awake and be constantly alert and watchful, because you people have not seen or known [either] the day, nor yet the hour!**

14. **"You know, [it is] just as a person [who is] periodically** (or: presently about to be) **traveling abroad calls** (or: summoned) **his own slaves and turns over to them his possessions** (or: and then gave over to them [control of] the goods and committed to them property normally being his subsistence).
15. **"He also, on the one hand, gave to one five talents** [= thirty thousand silver coins (denarii); = one hundred years' wages], **yet to another, two [talents], and then to another, one** [talent; = six thousand denarii] – **to each one according to his own ability. And then he traveled abroad.**

16. **"Now the one receiving the five talents, immediately proceeding on his way, puts them to work in trading and gains** (or: made a profit of) **another five talents** (= doubled his investments).
17. **"And similarly, the person [being given] the two, further gains** (or: made a profit of) **another two.**
18. **"Yet the one receiving the one [talent], upon going off** (or: coming away), **digs a hole in the ground and hides his owner's silver [coins].**

19. "Now after much time [had passed], the owner (master; lord) of those slaves proceeds in coming, and then takes up a joint discussion with them, proceeding to settle the accounting.

20. "And thus, upon approaching, the person receiving the five talents brought to [him] five other talents, then saying, 'Master, you turned over (committed) to me five talents. Look! I gained five other talents by them!'

21. "The owner affirms to him, 'Well [done] (or: Excellent)! [You are] a good and trustworthy (loyal; faithful) slave. You were faithful and trustworthy (or: full of faith and trust) upon [the matter of] a few things; I will proceed to place you (set you down; appoint you) upon (= with responsibility for) many things. Enter at once into your owner's (master's) joy (or: into the state of the joy of your lord; = Come to my celebration)!'

22. "Now also coming forward, the person receiving the two talents said, 'Master, you turned over (committed) to me two talents. Look! I gained two other talents by them!'

23. "The owner affirms to him, 'Excellent (Well [done])! [You are] a good and trusting (or: loyal; faithful) slave. You were full of faith and trust (or: faithful and trustworthy) upon [the matter of] a few things; I will proceed to place you (set you down; appoint you) upon (= give you responsibility for) many things. Enter at once into your owner's joy!'

24. "Now also approaching, the one having received the one talent said, 'O master, I knew by experience that you are a hard (rough; = tough and stern) man, constantly harvesting (habitually reaping) where you do (or: did) not sow seed, and repeatedly collecting and gathering together from places where you do (or: did) not fully scatter and disperse [the chaff] (= winnow).

25. "'And so, being fearful (or: made afraid), upon going off I hid your talent (= silver) within the ground (earth; or: the Land). Look! You continue having what is yours!'

26. "Yet, giving a decisive reply, his owner said to him, '[You] worthless (incompetent) and hesitating (slothful; sluggish) slave! Had you seen, so as to be aware, that I am constantly harvesting where I do not sow, and repeatedly collecting and gathering together from places where I do not fully scatter (= winnow)?

27. "'It was therefore binding (necessary) for you to at once deposit my silver (= money) with the bankers (or: money-changers!) – and then upon coming I, myself, could likely recover that which is my own together with offspring (a birthed yield; = interest).

28. "'Therefore, you men at once take the talent away from him, and then give [it] to the one now holding (presently having) the ten talents.'

29. "– You see, to everyone habitually possessing (having and holding), it will continue being given, and, he will continue being made to superabound (be surrounded with excess); yet from the person not habitually possessing (having or holding), even that which he is currently holding will proceed in being taken away from him –

30. "'And now, you men at once throw the useless slave out into the darkness (dim obscurity and gloominess) which is farther outside. In that place there will continue being the weeping (or: lamenting) and the grinding of the teeth.' [cf 8:12; 22:13; 24:51, above]

31. "Now whenever the Son of the Man (= Adam's son; = the eschatological messianic figure; = the representative human) may come within His manifestation which calls forth praise (or: glory; assumed appearance) – as well as all the [other MSS add: set-apart] agents (folks with the message; messengers) with Him – at that time He will continue sitting down upon a throne which has the quality and character of His praise-inducing manifestation (or: which is His glory; or: of His good reputation; from the glory of His assumed appearance).

32. "And thus all the ethnic multitudes (or: nations; people groups) will continue being collected and gathered together in front of Him, and so He will continue marking off boundaries and separating them from one another, just as the shepherd is habitually separating [as in separate pens or groups] the sheep away from the kids (the immature goats).
     [note: this is something habitually done; both groups are clean animals, were used in sacrifices, and are a part of the shepherd's herd]

33. **"And so He will continue making the sheep, on the one hand, to stand at [places to] His right** [note: the place of power and receiving], **yet on the other hand, the kids** (immature goats) **at [places to His] left** (or: from a good name; idiomatically: = out of misfortune).

34. **"At that time** (or: point), **the King** (or: Reigning One) **will proceed saying to the folks at [the places to] His right, 'Come here, you folks having received words of ease and well-being from** (or: having been spoken well of by; or: having received the blessing of; or: bearing thoughts, ideas, expressions and the Word of goodness from) **My Father! At once come into possession of the inheritance of, and enjoy the allotment of,** [the place of, or realm of] **the reign** (or: kingdom; influence and activity of sovereignty) **having been prepared and made ready from a founding** (a casting down [as of a foundation; or: of seed]) **of a system** (or: of an aggregate of humanity; of an arranged order; of a world of government, religion and society).

35. **"You see, I was hungry** (or: I hunger) **and you folks gave** (or: give) **to Me [something] to eat; I was thirsty** (or: I thirst), **and you folks gave [something for]** (or: cause) **Me to drink; I was existing being a foreigner** (or: stranger), **and you people gathered Me together [with you]** (= showed Me hospitality and oneness with your group);

36. **"[I was/am] naked, and you people clothed** (or: clothe) **Me; I fell sick** (or: become weak), **and you folks carefully looked upon** (or: = visit and look out for; took oversight of) **Me; [I was/am] in prison** (or: jail), **and you came to Me** (or: come and set your face on Me).

37. **"At that point, the fair, just and rightwised folks who live in right relationship within the Way pointed out will proceed giving a considered response to Him, [together] saying, 'O Lord** (Master), **when did we see You continuing hungry, and we nourished [You], or continuing thirsty, and we gave [something for]** (or: caused) **[You] to drink?**

38. **"'And when did we see You a foreigner** (or: stranger) **and we gathered [You] and showed [You] hospitality, or naked and we clothed [You]?**

39. **"'Now when did we see You continuing sick and weak or in prison** (or: jail), **and we came to** (or: face-to-face with) **You?'**

40. **"And then, giving a decided reply, the King will proceed saying to them, 'I am truly now saying to** (or: It is true, I now tell) **you folks, Upon such an amount** (or: = To the extent) **that you did** (or: do) **and perform(ed) [it] to** (or: for) **one of these belonging to the least of My brothers** (the folks from the same womb as Me; used collectively: = the members of My family; or: = those of My group or brotherhood), **you did and perform [it] to and for Me!'**

41. **"At that point, He will also proceed saying to those at [the places] on [His] left** (or: from a good name; or: = out of misfortune), **'[You] folks having been brought under the curse, continue proceeding on your way** (keep journeying), **away from Me, on into the eonian fire** (or: the fire for an undetermined period of time; the fire which comes with the Age [of Messiah]; the fire pertaining to and having its source in the Age; the age-lasting fire; the fire having the quality and characteristics of the Age) **– the one having been prepared and made ready by** (or: in; with; for) **the person who thrusts [something] through [folks]** (the adversary; one who casts [something] through the midst and causes division; traditionally: the 'devil') **as well as by** (or: in; with; for) **his agents** (messengers).

42. **"'You see, I was hungry** (or: I hunger) **and you folks did** (or: do) **not give to Me [something] to eat; I was thirsty** (or: I thirst), **and you folks did not give [something for]** (or: do not cause) **Me to drink.**

43. **"'I was existing being a foreigner** (or: continued being stranger), **and you people did not gather Me together [with you]** (or: do not "synagogue" Me; or: = showed Me hospitality and oneness with your group); **[I was/am] naked, and you did** (or: do) **not clothe Me; [I was/am] sick, weak and in prison** (or: jail), **and you folks did** (or: do) **not carefully look upon** (or: = visit and look out for or take oversight of) **Me.'**

44. **"At that point they will also proceed giving a considered response, one after another saying, 'O Lord** (Master), **when did we see you continuing hungry or thirsty, or a foreigner** (a stranger) **or naked, or weak and sick, or in prison** (or: jail), **and did not give You attending service** (minister or dispense to Your needs)**?'**

45. **"At that time, He will continue making a decisive reply, continuing in saying to** (laying it out for) **them, 'Truly** (or: It is True; Amen), **I now say to you folks, Upon such an amount** (or: = To the extent) **that you did** (or: do) **[it] not to** (or: for) **one of these least folks, neither did** (or: do) **you do [it] to** (or: for) **Me.'**
46. **"And so, these folks will continue going off** (or: coming away) **into an eonian pruning** (a lopping-off which lasts for an undetermined length of time; an age-lasting correction and rehabilitation; a pruning which brings better fruit and which has its source and character in the Age; a cutting off for an age, or during the ages), **yet the fair, just and rightwised folks who are in right relationship with people and are in accord with the Way pointed out [continue going off or coming away] into eonian Life** (life which has its source and character in the Age [of the Messiah]; life pertaining to the Age; age-lasting life; or: the life of and for the ages). [cf Acts 4:21; 2 Pet. 2:9; Jn. 15:1-2]

CHAPTER 26

1. **And so, when Jesus finished** (concluded) **all these sayings** (expressed thoughts; words; messages; discourses; patterned Blueprints), **it occurred [that] He said to His disciples,**
2. **"You folks have observed and so know that after two days** (= two days from now) **the Passover is happening** (or: is progressing in occurrence), **and so the Son of the Man** (= Adam's Son; = the eschatological messianic figure; the representative human) **is presently going through the process of being transferred and committed unto** (or: handed over into) **the [situation for Him] to be put to death upon an execution stake** (or: crucified; suspended from a pole)."

3. **About that time the chief** (or: ranking) **priests and the elders** (or: the older [Judean] men [at least some being council members of the Sanhedrin, in Jerusalem]) **of the People [of Israel, the Jews] had been gathered together into the courtyard of the high** (chief; ranking) **priest – the one being usually called Caiaphas.**
4. **And so they consulted together** (jointly deliberated with a view to a consensus) **to the end that with bait** (or: by a contrivance for entrapping) **they could at once forcibly lay hold of and arrest Jesus, and then kill Him off.**
5. **However, one after another, they kept on saying, "Not during the festival** (Feast), **so that no riot** (or: unrest; uproar; outcry) **may happen among the People!"**

6. **Now when Jesus was happening to be in Bethany, within [the] house of Simon the leper,**
7. **there came to Him a woman holding an alabaster jar** (or: vase; flask) **of very expensive perfumed oil** (aromatic juices distilled from trees), **and she suddenly poured it down upon His head while [He] continued reclining [at a meal].**
8. **Now on seeing [this], the disciples became annoyed** (or: resentful; indignant; angry), **[various ones] saying, in turn, "Why** (or: Unto what [purpose is]) **this waste** (or: loss; destruction; ruin)**?**
9. **"For this was able to be sold for a lot [of money] and then given to the destitute folks and beggars!"**
10. **So Jesus, coming to know [their feelings and point of view], says to them, "Why are you men continuing to present this woman with a [verbal and emotional] beating** (or: make wearisome trouble for and abuse the woman)**? You see, she performed a beautiful act unto Me** (or: she worked an ideal deed into Me).
11. **"For you folks continue always having the poor with yourselves, yet you are not always continuing to have Me.**
12. **"After all, by spilling this perfumed oil upon My body, she, herself, did [it] with a view toward the preparation of Me for burial** (or: she of herself performs the preparation [leading] towards My burial).
13. **"Truly, I now am saying to you folks, wherever this good news** (this message of ease, goodness and well-being) **may be publicly proclaimed within the whole ordered, domination System** (world; arranged order of both the religious and the secular; aggregate of humanity), **that**

which she (or: this woman) **did will also be repeatedly spoken into a memorial relating to her** (or: will also continue being told in memory of her)."

14. **At about that time, one of the twelve – the person normally called Judah** (or: Judas) **of Iscariot – was going on his way to the chief** (or: ranking) **priests.**
15. **He said, "What are you presently willing to give to me? – and I, myself, will proceed in transferring and committing Him by turning Him over** (or: delivering Him) **to you men!"**
> "So they stacked up for him thirty silver coins [= the going price for a slave; some MSS read instead: thirty staters (an Attic silver coin, equal in value to the Jewish shekel, or four denarii's)]." [Zech. 11:12]

16. **And so, from that point on, he kept on seeking a good opportunity for the purpose of committing and transferring Him** (or: a suitable situation so that he could hand Him over).

17. **Now on the first [day] of the [Feast; festival] of The Unleavened** (unfermented) **Bread** (or: flat cakes; matzah), **the disciples came to Jesus, [as a group] asking, "Where** (or: What place) **are you presently desiring and intending [that] we should be preparing and making ready for You to eat 'the Passover'?"**
18. **So He said, "Under [these instructions] lead the way and go into the city to so-and-so** [note: this may have been a person whose name He did not want to mention], **and say to him, 'The Teacher is now saying, "My season** (My fitting situation; My appointed encounter; My fertile moment; My 'fullness of time') **is at hand** (= close enough to touch). **I, with My disciples, am in the process of doing** (= celebrating; observing) **The Passover with My face toward you** (= at your place).""**
19. **And so, the disciples did as Jesus had co-arranged and placed together in order, and they prepared and made ready The Passover.**

20. **So late in the day with it coming to be evening, He was reclining [at a meal] with the twelve disciples** (students; learners; apprentices).
21. **And during the process of their eating [the meal], He said, "Truly** (Count on it; Amen), **I am now saying to you folks, that one from among you will proceed transferring and committing Me, that is, turning Me in** (or: handing Me over and commending Me)."
22. **And then, continuing being tremendously pained, caused to be distressed and filled with sorrow, each one commenced to be saying to Him, in turn** [or, with p45, D, the Magdalen fragments, and others: each of them, joining in and speaking at once, were saying], **"I, myself, am not the one who You mean, am I, Master** (Lord)?"
23. **So, giving a decided reply, He said, "The person dipping [his] hand with Me in the bowl – THIS MAN will proceed committing Me by handing Me over** (or: turning Me in).
24. **"On the one hand, the Son of the Man** (= Adam's son; = the representative human; = the eschatological messianic figure) **is progressively leading the way under** (or: is now going away) **– just as** (correspondingly as) **it has been written about and concerning Him. Yet tragic will be the fate for THAT MAN through whom the Son of the Man is in the process of being transferred, committed and turned in** (or: delivered; handed over). **It was continuing being beautiful for HIM** [i.e., for the Son of the Man] (or: It was being ideal to Him; It was existing fine with Him) **– if THAT MAN was not brought to birth** (or: had [just] not been born)!"

25. **So Judah** (or: Judas) **– the one in process of transferring, committing and turning Him in** (delivering and handing Him over) **– making a discerning response, said, "I, myself, am not the one who You mean, am I, Rabbi?** (or: No way is it I, myself, Teacher!)" **Jesus then says to him** (or: continues laying it out for him), **"You, yourself, are saying [it]."**

26. **Now during the progression of their eating [the meal], upon taking the loaf of [unleavened?] bread and saying words of ease and well-being** (or: speaking blessing [to them?]), **Jesus broke [it in pieces]. And then at giving [them] to the disciples, He said, "You folks take [it]** (or: receive [this]). **Eat [it] at once. This is My body** (or: This is the body which is Me)."

27. **Next, upon taking a** [other MSS: the] **cup and speaking words about grace and expressing gratitude, He gave [it] to them, while saying, "All you men drink from out of it,**
28. **"for you see, this is My blood** (or: the blood which is Me) – **which pertains to the covenant** [with other MSS: this is The Blood – which is My new, different arrangement that is innovative in character, kind and quality] – **the [Blood] around** (or: encompassing and pertaining to) **many people** (or: peoples), **[the Blood] continuously** (or: presently) **being poured out and progressively diffused into a divorce from failures, a forgiveness for mistakes, a dismissal of errors, a release from deviations, and a flowing away of sins!**
29. **"Yet, I am now saying to you folks that from the present moment I can by no means** (or: under no circumstances) **drink from out of this product** (yield; offspring) **of the grapevine, until that day I can habitually drink with you folks in union with My Father's reign** (or: within the kingdom of My Father) – **whenever it [will be] new in kind, quality and character!"** [note: the word "it," being neuter, would refer back to the "product," i.e. covenant, of the grapevine]
30. **Later, after singing a hymn** [= the *Hallel*: a psalm, or, psalms of praise and thanksgiving], **they went out into the Mount of Olives.**
31. **At that time, Jesus went on saying to them, "All you folks will proceed being caught in the snare in union with Me, and will continue being caused to stumble, within this night. You see, it has been written,**

> **'I will proceed smiting** (or: striking down) **the shepherd and the sheep of the flock will proceed being thoroughly scattered and dispersed.'** [Zech. 13:7]

32. **"Yet after the [situation or occasion for] Me to be aroused and raised up** (= My resurrection), **I will proceed leading the way before you** (or: be preceding you folks) **into the Galilee [district]."**

33. **Now Peter, making a determined response, says to Him, "Even if everyone [else] will proceed being caught in the snare in union with You, and will continue being caused to stumble, I myself will never** (not even once) **proceed being ensnared or cause to stumble!"**
34. **And so Jesus affirmed to him, "Of a truth** (or: Really; Count on it; Amen), **I now am saying to you that within this night – before a rooster crows** (or: is to crow; other MSS: the crowing of the cock), **you will proceed to completely disown and renounce Me** (say, 'No,' in regard to Me) **three times."**
35. **Peter is then saying to Him, "Even if it should continue necessary for me to die together with You, under no circumstances could** (or: would; as a future: will) **I completely disown, renounce, or say, 'No,' concerning, You." And all the disciples spoke similarly** (or: said likewise).

36. **At that time Jesus continues going with them into a spot** (or: place; estate; literally: a freehold – piece of ground not subject to allotment, which could be bought and sold) **normally being called Gethsemane, and He then is saying to His disciples, "Sit down here, while upon going off there in that place, I can focus toward having ease and well-being** (pray)."
37. **And then, taking Peter and the two sons of Zebedee along, He began to be progressively pained, distressed and filled with grief – and to continue deeply troubled, depressed and dejected.**
38. **At that point He lays it out for them, saying, "My soul** (conscious being) **continues being surrounded by pain and exists encompassed by sorrow and grief – unto the point of death.** [*cf* 16:25-26, above] **You men remain here and continue being awake and watchful** (alert) **with Me."**

39. **And so, after going forward a little way** [other MSS: in approaching (or: moving toward) {a certain spot}], **He fell upon His face, continuously praying** (thinking and/or speaking toward having ease and well-being) **and** (or: even) **repeatedly saying, "My Father, if it is possible, let this cup pass** (or: since there is power and ability, cause this cup to go on by, or to the side,) **away from Me! Nevertheless, more than this, [let it be; it is] not as I continue willing** (wanting; intending), **but to the contrary, as You [will and intend]."**

40. **Then He proceeds coming toward the disciples, and He is presently finding them continuing fast asleep. So He then says to Peter, "So** (or: Thus [is the case]), **you folks have no strength to stay awake and watch with Me [for] one hour.**

41. **"You folks continue awake and keep on watching. And continue praying** (focusing toward having ease and well-being) **to the end that you folks may not enter into a test** (a trial; a putting to the proof). **On the one hand the spirit [is] eager** (the attitude [can be] the first to rush forward with passion); **on the other hand the flesh** (= the estranged human nature; the alienated self that is not yet reflecting God's image; the person who has been molded and dominated by the System) **[is] without strength** (weak and infirm)."

42. **Again, a second time, going off He prayed, repeatedly saying, "My Father, if this continues impossible** (unable) **to pass on by, from Me, if I should not** (or: unless I would) **drink it, let Your will and purpose be birthed and come to be!"**

43. **Then, going again, He found them continuing fast asleep, for their eyes were ones having been made heavy and continuing weighed down as with a burden.**

44. **And so, leaving them [and] again going away, He prayed** (focused on ease and well-being) **a third time saying the same word** (or: thought; idea) **again.**

45. **At that point, He proceeds again coming to the disciples and is then saying to them, "Are you folks continuing sleeping and resting the remaining time? Look! The hour has drawn near and is now close enough to touch – and the Son of the Man** (= Adam's son; the representative human) **is in the process of being transferred and committed** (or: delivered; handed over) **into hands of folks who deviate and make mistakes** (or: fall short of the goal; fail to hit the target; are in error; or: hands from sinners).

46. **"Be roused and awakened – get up – let us be going! Look! The person transferring and committing Me** (or: handing Me over) **has drawn near and is close enough to touch."**

47. **And while He was yet speaking – look and consider – Judah** (or: Judas), **one of the twelve, came, and with him a large crowd wielding swords and wooden implements** (clubs; staffs; etc.), **[sent] from the chief** (ranking) **priests and elders** (old men) **of the people.**

48. **Now the person in process of transferring and giving Him over gave a sign to them in saying, "Whomsoever I should kiss – it is He; you men immediately seize and arrest Him."**

49. **And so, set for success, upon immediately coming to Jesus, he says, "Continue rejoicing** (= Greetings; Hello), **Rabbi," and then he gave Him an intense** (or: prolonged, exaggerated) **kiss.**

50. **So Jesus said to him, "My good fellow** (or: O comrade!; Dear friend), **upon what [purpose; errand] are you now being present here beside [Me]** (= why do you cause this *parousia*)?" **At that point, upon approaching, they laid [their] hands upon Jesus and seized Him.**

51. **And then – look and consider! – one of the men with Jesus, in stretching forth [his] hand, drew away his large knife** (or: short sword) **and, striking the slave of the high** (chief; ranking) **priest, took off his ear.**

52. **At that point Jesus is saying to him, "Turn away** (= Return) **your knife** (or: sword) **into its place. You see, all those taking [up] a knife** (or: a sword) **will proceed in destroying themselves in union with a knife** (or: continue losing themselves [being] centered in a sword).

53. **"Or, are you continually imagining or supposing that I am not constantly able** (or: that I do not habitually have power) **to at once call My Father to My side for assistance, and He will right now place by Me** (or: furnish for Me; put at My disposal) **more than twelve legions** [= regiments; a legion was 6000 foot soldiers plus 120 on horse, plus auxiliaries] **of agents?**

54. **"How then could** (or: would) **the Scriptures** (or: writings) **be fulfilled that in this way it continues binding and necessary to happen** (take place; come to be; occur)?"

55. **In that hour Jesus said to the crowds, "You folks come out as upon a robber** (or: = social bandit or outlaw; or: highwayman) **or an insurrectionist – with knives, swords, staffs and clubs – to jointly seize** (or: apprehend) **Me. Daily I used to habitually sit facing you men**

within the Temple grounds, constantly teaching, and you did not take hold of Me (= lift a hand against Me or attempt to arrest Me).

56. **"Yet this whole [affair] has come to be** (has happened) **so that the Scriptures** (or: writings) **of the prophets would** (or: could) **be fulfilled."**
At this point His disciples – everyone abandoning Him – **took flight** (or: fled; made escape).

57. **Now those having a strong grip on Jesus led Him away to Caiaphas, the high** (chief; ranking) **priest, where the scribes** (theologians and scholars of the Law) **and the elders had been gathered together in assembly.**

58. **Yet Peter kept on following Him from a far distance, until [coming to] the courtyard of the high** (ruling; chief; ranking) **priest. Then upon entering within, he continued sitting with the subordinates** (Temple guards, attendants and servants – folks under orders of others) **to see the outcome** (or: the end [of the matter]; the final act; [His] destiny).

59. **Now the chief** (ranking) **priests and the whole Sanhedrin** (the ruling council of the Judean nation) **had been seeking false evidence** (testimony from false witnesses) **[to bring] down against Jesus so that they could put Him to death.**

60. **However, they found nothing – although many false witnesses were coming forward** (or: And yet they could not find many false witnesses [that were] coming forward). **Yet, subsequently, two false witnesses** (perjurers), **upon approaching, said,**

61. **"This man affirmed, 'I am able to demolish** (loose-down) **God's inner sanctuary of the Temple** (= the holy place and the holy of holies; God's divine habitation), **and – through** (or: during [the period of]; or: by means of) **three days – to build the house."**

62. **And then, upon standing up, the high** (ruling) **priest said to Him, "Are you continuing answering nothing** (or: Do you continue making no decided response of even one thing) **to what are these men presently testifying against you?"**

63. **Yet Jesus continued silent. And so the high** (ruling; ranking) **priest said to Him, "I now bind you to speak out an oath in accord with the living God** (or: Down from the living God, I am now exorcising you; or: I now bind you by oath in correspondence with the living God) **that you should say to us if you, yourself, are the Christ** (the Anointed one; = the Messiah) – **God's son** (= the one having the same relationship to God and to the people as did Israel as a nation, or Israel's king)!"

64. **Jesus is then saying to him, "You yourself are saying [it]** (or: are [so] saying)! **Moreover, I am now saying to you people, from now** (this present moment) **on you folks will continue seeing 'the Son of the Man** (= Adam's son; the eschatological Messiah figure; the representative human) **continuously sitting at the right [hand]' of the Power, and 'progressively coming** (or: repeatedly coming and going) **upon the clouds of the atmosphere** (or: sky; heaven).'"** [Dan. 7:13; Ps. 110:1]

65. **At that point the high** (ruling ranking) **priest tore and ripped his outer garments** (= his vestments?), **saying, "He blasphemes! What need are we still having of witnesses? See! You now** (at this moment) **heard his blasphemy** (villainous, defaming speech; harm-averment)!

66. **"What does [this] now seem to you men – what is your opinion?"**
So they, giving a decided response, said, **"He now is held within and under the control of death."**

67. **At that point they spit into His face and hit** (or: punched) **Him with their fists. Yet some men slapped Him, one after another saying,**

68. **"Prophesy to** (or: for) **us, O Christ** (or: O 'anointed one') – **who is the one striking you?"**

69. **Now Peter was sitting outside within the courtyard. And one servant girl came toward him, then is saying, "You, too, were with Jesus the Galilean."**

70. **But he contradicted [her], denied [it], and disowned [it] in front of them all, by saying, "I am not aware of what you are now saying** (or: I don't know what you are talking about)!"

71. **Now upon going out into the entry by the gate, another girl saw him and then proceeds saying to the folks in that place, "This fellow was with Jesus the Nazarene."**

72. **And again he contradicted, denied and disowned [it]** (or: said, "NO!," **with an oath: "I have not seen nor do I know the man!"**

73. **Now after a little while, upon approaching, the men standing [around] said to Peter, "Truly you also belong to them** (= are one of them), **for even your speech** (= dialect, or, the way you talk) **continues making you plainly evident** (or: conspicuous)."

74. **At that point Peter started to repeatedly lay down curses and confirm them with oaths** (or: continue swearing), **that, "I have not seen nor do I know the man!" And immediately a rooster crowed.**

75. **Then Peter remembered the saying of** (effect of the flow [of the discourse] from) **Jesus – He having said, "Before a rooster is to crow, you will proceed in denying and renouncing Me three times."**
And so, after going outside, he wept and lamented bitterly.

CHAPTER 27

1. **Now with the coming of morning** (or: at morning birthing itself), **the chief** (or: ranking) **priests and the elders of the people took counsel together, deliberating plans against Jesus to bring Him down, even so as to put Him to death.**

2. **And thus, upon binding Him, they led [Him] off and then handed** (or: committed; transferred) **[Him] over to Pilate, the governor.**

3. **At that time, upon seeing that He was correspondingly judged against** (or: condemned), **Judah** (or: Judas) **– the person transferring and committing Him – after changing his judgment and concern on the matter so as to be regretting and caring differently, returned the thirty silver [coins]** (or: pieces of silver) **to the chief** (ranking) **priests and elders,**

4. **while saying, "I made a grave mistake** (erred; failed to hit the target; sinned; fail to attain the goal) **in transferring, committing and giving-over just and innocent** (rightwised) **blood."**
But those men said, "What [does this mean] to us? You, yourself, will proceed seeing!"

5. **And so, upon hurling the silver [coins; pieces] into the inner Temple** (shrine; = the holy place), **he withdrew, and then going off, he at one point hugged, embraced and, as it were, compressed himself away [as in grief]** (or: suddenly squeezed or choked himself off; or, perhaps: strangled or hanged himself [note: only here in NT; only once in OT]). [cf Acts 1:18]

6. **Now the chief** (ranking) **priests, upon taking in hand the silver [coins], said, "It is not right or permitted, from [our] existence [as] being [God's People], to throw them into the temple treasury** (the gift receptacle; the corban), **since it is the price of blood."**

7. **After consulting together, they bought with them the Field of the Potter to serve as a burial ground for the strangers and foreigners** (= non-local folks).

8. **For this reason that field has been called "[The] Field of Blood" until today.**

9. **At that point the [oracle; prophesy] spoken through Jeremiah the prophet was fulfilled, continuing in saying,**
>   **"And so they took the thirty silver [coins; pieces] – the value and price of the Honored** (Valued; Respected) **One – Whom they valued from [the] sons of Israel** (or: the worth of a person being evaluated – for whom they set a value {or: price} from among [the people] of Israel),

10.   **And then they gave them for the Field of the Potter, just as the LORD** [= Yahweh] **jointly arranged with** (or: by; for; to) **me."** [Zech. 11:12-13]

11. **So now Jesus was positioned and stood in front of the [Roman] governor. Then the governor put a question to Him, by saying, "Are you, yourself, 'the king of the Judeans'?" So then Jesus affirms, "You, yourself, are now saying [so; it]."**

12. **And then, during the [situation] for Him to be repeatedly accused by the chief** (ranking) **priests and elders, in public assembly, He gave back no reply of judgment on even one thing** (or: He answered nothing; = He made no comment on the charges and gave no rebuttal).

13. **At that point, Pilate speaks up, saying, "Are you not hearing or listening to how many [charges] they continue testifying against, and bringing evidence down on, you?"**

14. **And yet He gave no decided reply to him – not even to one, single saying** (= charge; or: with not even one declaration), **so that the governor continues very astonished** (or: baffled) **and progressively fills with wonder** (or: amazement).

15. **Now corresponding to [the] Feast** (or: festival), **the governor had normally been accustomed to release one prisoner to the crowd – whomever they had been wanting** (desiring);
16. **and they had been holding at that time a notorious** (or: well-known) **prisoner normally called Jesus** [other MSS omit: Jesus] **Barabbas** (or: Bar-Abbas; = son of [the] father).
17. **Therefore, after their having been gathered together, Pilate said to them** [i.e., the crowd], **"Whom** (or: Which one) **are you people now wanting** (desiring) **that I should release to** (or: for) **you: Jesus** [other MSS omit: Jesus] **Bar-Abbas, or Jesus, the one now being call 'Christ** (Anointed; = Messiah)**'?"**
18. **You see, he had seen and was now aware that they transferred and committed Him** (or: handed Him over; surrendered Him; delivered Him up) **because of envy.**
19. **Now during his continued sitting upon the public elevated place** (a step, platform or place ascended by steps to speak in public assembly; dais; = an official bench of a judge or public official), **his wife sent off [a message] to him [which was] saying, "[Let there be] nothing [between, or, pertaining to] you and that just** (innocent; righteous; rightwised) **man, for I experienced many things today down from a dream** (or: in association with a trance) **because of him!"**
20. **But the chief** (ranking) **priests and elders persuaded the crowds, to the end that they, themselves, would ask for Bar-Abbas – and so they would destroy Jesus.**
21. **Now in giving a calculated response, the governor said to them, "Whom are you people now wanting, from the two, [that] I should release to** (or: for) **you?"**
So they, themselves, said, "Bar-Abbas!"
22. **Pilate continues saying to them, "What, then, shall I proceed doing [with] Jesus – the one being repeatedly termed, or called, 'Christ** (or: Anointed; = Messiah)**'?"**
They are all saying, "Let him be at once put to death on a stake (or: pole-hung; crucified)!"
23. **So the governor affirms, "For what? Did he do something bad, worthless or ugly?"**
But they kept on crying out (or: shouted) all the more, and louder, repeatedly saying, "Let him be at once put to death on a stake (or: suspended from a pole; crucified)!"
24. **Now, seeing that it continues benefiting nothing, but to the contrary, an uproar was progressively developing into a riot, Pilate, taking water, washes off his hands down in the presence of and facing the crowd, while saying, I am** (or: continue being) **without penalty** (guiltless; immune; not liable to punishment or responsible) **from this man's blood. You people will proceed seeing** (or: You folks see [to it])**!"**
25. **Then, giving a decided reply, all the people said, "His blood [is] upon us** (or: [be splattered] on us; = the responsibility for his death falls on us), **and upon our children!"**
26. **At that point he released Bar-Abbas to them, yet, upon scourging** (severely whipping and beating) **Jesus, he gave Him over** (transferred Him; delivered Him) **with the purpose that He would be put to death on a stake** (hung on a pole; crucified).

27. **So at that time the governor's soldiers, upon taking Jesus along into the Praetorium** (the governor's residence and headquarters), **gathered together upon Him the whole company of troops** (a tenth part of a legion, normally 600 troops).
28. **Then after disrobing** (stripping; [with other MSS: upon clothing]) **Him, they put a scarlet** (or: crimson; red) **cloak around Him.**
29. **Next, after weaving** (or: braiding) **a wreath out of thorns** (or: a thorn bush), **they put [it] upon His head, as well as a reed in His right [hand]. Then, while falling on [their] knees in front of Him, they mocked and ridiculed Him, repeatedly saying, "Be constantly filled with joy**

> (or: Rejoice continuously; = a common greeting which is a wish for well-being; = Greetings, Welcome, Hello, Hail; probably equivalent to the soldier's salute, 'Ave Caesar'), **O king of the Judeans!"**

30. **And then after spitting in [His face], and into** (= on) **Him, they took the reed [from Him] and kept on striking blows into His head.**
31. **Next – when they had finished making fun of Him – they stripped the cloak off Him and clothed Him with His own outer garments, then they led Him off into the [place and situation] to put [Him] to death on a stake** (to attach [Him] to a pole; to crucify [Him]).

32. **Now while proceeding out, they came across a Cyrenian man – named Simon – [and] they pressed** (conscripted; = forced) **this person into service to the end that he would lift up and carry His execution stake** (cross).
33. **And so, upon coming into [the] place normally being called "Golgotha," which is [also] often called a** (or: [the]) **"Place of a Skull"** [note: = a mound shaped like a skull; = "Skull Mound"],
34. **they gave to Him wine** (other MSS: vinegar, or, sharp wine vinegar) **having been blended with bile** (fluid of the gall bladder) **to drink. And yet, upon tasting [it], He was not willing to drink [it].**

35. **Now, after attaching Him to the execution stake** (hanging Him on a pole), **they divided His outer garments among themselves by repeatedly casting a lot** (= throwing dice).
36. **And while continuing sitting, they continued guarding and keeping watch over Him there.**
37. **They also posted above His head the written legal charge against** (or: pertaining to) **Him:**

THIS IS JESUS – THE KING OF (or: FROM AMONG) **THE JUDEANS**

38. **At that time two rebels** (or: robbers; social bandits; outlaws; highwaymen; insurrectionists; *cf* Lu. 23:32) **were in the process of being suspended and put to death on a stake** (were being progressively crucified) **together with Him – one on [His] right and one on [His] left.**
39. **Now as people are continuing passing by, they kept on speaking abusively, hurling insults at Him, "while repeatedly shaking** (or: wagging) **their heads,"** [Ps. 22:8]
40. **and one after another saying, "You, the person in process of dismantling** (demolishing; loosing-down) **the inner sanctuary of the Temple** (the holy place and the holy of holies) **and then proceeding in building the House within three days, save yourself now! – since** (or: if) **you are God's son** (or: a son of God), **descend from the stake** (or: climb down off the cross; come down off this pole that is used to suspend corpses)**!"**
41. **In like manner also, the chief** (or: ranking) **priests with the scribes** (scholars; theologians) **and elders – repeatedly ridiculing and making fun – kept on saying,**
42. **"He saved** (rescued; delivered; kept safe) **other folks – he continues unable** (he has no power) **to save himself! He is a king** (or: [the] king) **of Israel! – let him climb down** (descend) **now from the execution stake** (or: off the cross; away from the pole used for suspending corpses), **and then we will proceed putting our trust upon him** (or: shall be believing on him).
43. **'He has put his trust upon God! Let Him now guard him and drag** (pull) **him out of danger – if He wants him!'** [Ps. 22:9] **You know he said, 'I am God's son.'"**
44. **So in the same way and about the same thing, the rebels** (insurrectionists; or: robbers) **– those being crucified on execution stakes together with Him – also began and kept on bringing verbal abuse and unjustifiable reproach.**

45. **Now from [the] sixth hour** (noon) **until the ninth hour** (three in the afternoon) **darkness** (shadowy gloom; dimness) **came to be** (birthed itself) **upon the entire Land** (all the territory).
46. **But about the ninth hour Jesus loudly called out** (exclaimed; shouted) **at the top of [His] voice** (or: in a great voice), **saying, "*Eli! Eli!*** [other MSS: *Eloi, Eloi!*] ***Lema sabachthani!*** [note: George Lamsa translates the Peshitta (Aramaic Version) of these two words as: for this was I spared; or: this was my destiny] **– This is it! O My God, My God, for this certain purpose You have left Me as a remnant, down within the midst!"** [Ps. 22:1, LXX]
> (or: "My God – O God – this exists being for a specific end and destiny that You leave Me fully in union with!"

or: "My God. O God, do You leave from down within the midst of Me so that this certain end exists?"

or: that is, "O My God, My God, to what end and for what purpose do You at once completely abandon Me in [this situation]?")

[note: Scholars consider this a quote of Ps. 22:1, where the last phrase is the identical Greek in the LXX. However, in the Hebrew, the word often translated "forsake" (*azab*) has these three meanings: (1) to loose bands; to let go {a beast} from its bonds; (2) to leave {a person; a place}; to leave {anyone; or: a place}; to desert; (3) to leave off; to cease from {anything}]

47. **Now certain** (or: some) **folks standing there, upon hearing [this], began saying, "This fellow is now summoning** (or: calling out to, or for) **Elijah!"**

48. **So, set for success, immediately one of them, upon running and getting a sponge – and after filling it with "vinegar** (or: sour wine)**" and attaching [it] around a reed – "offered" Him "a drink."** [Ps. 69:22]

49. **But the rest of them said, "Hold off! We should see if Elijah is presently coming [and] will proceed to be saving** (rescuing) **him!"**

– Now later, another person, at one point taking a spear head, stabbed His side, so then water and blood came out – [note: this last sentence is included in Aleph, B, C & others MSS, but omitted by A & other MSS, along with the Majority Text, Nestle-Aland, Tasker, Panin, Griesbach, & bracketed by WH]

50. **Now Jesus, again at one point loudly crying out with a loud** (or: great) **voice** (or: sound), **dismissed the Spirit** (or: lets the breath-effect flow away; divorced [His] spirit; lets [His] breath go; abandoned the Spirit; or: set aside and rejected this attitude).

51. **And then – look and consider! – the curtain of the inner sanctuary of the Temple** [veil of the holy of holies] **was torn and split from above unto below** (= from top to bottom)**: into two – and the ground was caused to shake** (or: the earth quaked) **and rock masses were split.**

52. **Later, the memorial tombs** (graves) **were opened up, and many of the bodies of the set-apart** (holy; sacred) **People – of the folks who had fallen asleep and continued sleeping – were aroused** (awakened) **and raised up!**

53. **Then, upon going forth out of the memorial tombs – after His arousal and resurrection – they entered into the set-apart** (holy) **city and they were made visible in the midst of many people** (or: were made to inwardly shine to many folks; or: were made to appear in association with many).

54. **Now the centurion** (a Roman commander who normally is in charge of one hundred soldiers) **and those with him [who were] guarding and watching over Jesus, upon seeing the shaking** (= earthquake) **and the things occurring** (happening; being birthed), **were made extremely afraid, one to another saying, "Truly** (or: Really; Certainly) **this man was God's son."**

55. **But in addition, many women were there, continuing in viewing and watching from a distance – those who followed Jesus from the Galilee [district], constantly giving attending service to, and materially providing for, Him –**

56. **among whom was Mary Magdalene, and Mary the mother of Jacob** (or: James) **and Joseph** [other MSS: Joses] **– as well as the mother of the sons of Zebedee.**

57. **Now with evening coming on, there came a rich man from Arimathea, named Joseph, who himself also was discipled** (trained and instructed) **by Jesus.**

58. **This man, upon coming to Pilate, made a request for the body of Jesus. At that point Pilate gives orders for the body to be given over** (transferred back; awarded) **[to him].**

59. **And so, after taking the body, Joseph rolled and enwrapped it in clean fine linen,**

60. **then placed it within his new, unused memorial tomb which he had cut and quarried in the rock-mass. Next, after rolling a large stone to the door** (entry) **of the memorial tomb, he went away.**

61. **Now Mary Magdalene was there – as well as the other Mary – continuing in sitting off in an opposite position which faced the grave.**

62. **So on the arrival of the next day, which is after the preparation** [note: the preparation is from 3:00 p.m. to 6:00 p.m. on the day before a sabbath], **the chief** (ranking) **priests and the Pharisees were gathered together to Pilate,**
63. **as a group then saying, "Lord** (or: Sir; Excellency), **we are reminded that that straying** (or: wandering; vagabond) **deceiver said – while yet living, 'After three days I proceed being progressively aroused and raised up.'**
64. **"Therefore, command at once to have the grave made secure until the third day, lest at some time his disciples, upon coming, might steal him and then could** (or: might) **say to the people, 'He was aroused and raised up away from the dead ones,' and the last deception will be worse than the first."**
65. **So Pilate affirmed to them, "You men continue having** (holding) **a detachment of soldiers as a guard. Go and proceed bringing things under control. At once make things secure – just as you see and know [to do]."**
66. **Now they, after going their way with the detachment of guards, made the grave secure, sealing the stone. Now [it was] a late hour of** (or: an evening from, or among) **[the] sabbaths.**

CHAPTER 28

1. **During the progressive commencing of the light** (= at the approaching of the dawn) **[leading] into the midst of one of the sabbaths, Mary Magdalene and the other Mary came** (or: went) **to view and watch the grave.**
2. **And – notice, and consider! – a great** (= strong) **earthquake suddenly occurred, for you see, an Agent of [the] LORD** (= Yahweh's messenger; agent from [Yahweh]) **– upon stepping down** (or: descending) **from out of the midst of [the] atmosphere** (or: heaven; [the] sky) **and approaching – rolled away the stone from the door and was then sitting on top of it.**
3. **Now his outward appearance was, and continued being, as lightning** (or: a bright beam radiating from a lamp) **– and his clothing bright-white, as snow.**
4. **And so – from the fear of him – the men guarding and keeping watch over [the situation] were made to tremble, and came to be as dead men.**
5. **Yet the Agent, giving a decisive response, said to the women, "As for you, yourselves, do not continue being made afraid** (= stop being fearful), **for I have seen and thus know that you continue seeking** (looking for) **Jesus – the One having been put to death on the execution stake** (or: the One having been and still continuing having been crucified).
6. **"He is not here, for you see, He was aroused and raised up – just as He said. Come here, see the place where He [other MSS: the Lord] was lying.**
7. **"And so, upon quickly going your way, at once say to His disciples that He was aroused and raised up away from the dead folks. Further – consider and take note! – He progressively leads the way before you folks into the Galilee [district]. You folks will repeatedly see Him there. Now look and consider, I tell you** (or: Take note, I told you)!**"**

8. **So, quickly going away from the memorial tomb while experiencing apprehension mingled with overwhelming** (or: great) **joy, they ran to report back to His disciples.**
9. **And then – look and consider! – Jesus came suddenly and met them [i.e., the women] face to face, at that time saying, "Be constantly rejoicing!"** [note: also used as a greeting, can = Continuous joy to you; Shalom; Hi; Hello; Greetings]
Now they, upon approaching, took hold of His feet and, being prostrate, immediately gave homage and worship to Him.
10. **At that point Jesus continues to say to them, "Stop fearing** (or: Do not continue being made to fear). **Continue leading the way and bring things under control as you go. Immediately report back to My brothers** (folks from the same womb; = family) **so that they would go off unto the Galilee [district] – and there** (in that area) **they will repeatedly see Me."**

11. **Now – take note and consider! – some of the detachment of guards, proceeding on their way, after coming into the city reported back to the chief** (or: ranking) **priests all the events that were happening.**

12. **Then, being gathered together and taking joint counsel, they gave enough** (sufficient; adequate) **silver [coins] to the soldiers,**

13. **laying out [the situation] and saying, "Say that his disciples, upon coming by night, stole him during our continued sleeping.**

14. **"And then, if this [tale] should be brought to a hearing** (or: be heard) **on the governor's [agenda; or: ears], we ourselves will be progressively persuasive – and we will continue making you men free from care or worry.**

15. **So they, after taking the silver [coins], did as they were instructed. And thus, this idea** (saying; patterned message) **was rumored throughout and spread abroad among and by the Judeans** (or: the Jewish culture and religion) **until this very day.**

16. **Now the eleven disciples went on their way into the Galilee [district] – unto the mountain where Jesus had arranged for them.**

17. **And then, upon seeing Him, they prostrated themselves, giving homage** (and perhaps: worship) **– even though they** [perhaps: = some] **had divided thoughts** (or: wavered; hesitated; had doubts).

18. **And so, after approaching, Jesus,** [breaking the silence], **suddenly spoke to them, by saying, "All authority** (or: Every right and privilege from out of Being) **is** (or: was) **given to Me within heaven and upon the earth** (or: in sky and atmosphere, as well as on land)**!**

19. **"Therefore, while going on your way, instruct and make disciples** (at some point enlist students and apprentices) **of all the ethnic multitudes** (the pagans; the Gentiles; the nations; the non-Israelites), **habitually immersing them** [i.e., the people (masculine pronoun)] (or: one-after-another [B & D read: at some point] baptizing them to the point of infusion and saturation) **into the Name which has reference to, belongs to, has its origin and character in, and which represents, the Father and the Son, as well as the Set-apart Breath-effect**

> (or: the Name from the Father, as well as from the Son, and even which is the Holy Spirit;
> or: the Name of the Father and of the Son – even of the Holy Spirit;
> or: the Father's Name, even the Son's, and which pertains to the Sacred Breath;
> or: the Name belonging to the Father and the Son, and which is the Sacred Attitude;
> or: the Name of the Father, and then of the Son, and which comes from the set-apart Spirit;
> or: the Name which represents the Father, the Son and the Holy Spirit;
> or: the Name which comes from the Father, belongs to the Son, and corresponds to the Holy result of the Breath),
> [note: Eusebius gives this as "Go and make disciples of all the nations in my name." – *Eusebius: The History of the Church from Christ to Constantine*, translated by G. A. Williamson, Barnes & Noble Books, 1995, p 111. Williamson footnotes: "Matt. 28:19, in a simpler, perhaps a more primitive form." Comment: this may have been a paraphrase; it may come from a lost MS tradition; it may represent an interpretation of this verse in the early AD 300's; *cf* Acts 2:38; 8:16; 10:48; 19:5]

20. **"constantly teaching and progressively training them to habitually watch over, guard, keep and maintain everything** (or: all things) **– as many things as I Myself implanted as goals** (imparted as the finished product within; gave as interior, destiny-laden directives; set as the union-centered, purposed aim) **within, among and for you folks. And now – look and consider this! – I Myself continuously am** (exist being) **with you folks all the days, on until the joint-goal** (or: the conjunction; the end [of all] brought together; the conclusion, consummation and fruition; the combined finished product and actualization) **of the age** (or: which is that Age [= the Age of the Messiah]; or: as far as the attending and associated end of this age; or: until the consummation brought by the Age [of Messiah])**."**

[written circa A.D. 40-60 – Based on the critical analysis of John A.T. Robinson]

MARK

CHAPTER 1

1. **A beginning of the good news, which is Jesus Christ, God's Son** (or: [The] beginning of the message of goodness, ease and well-being which pertains to Jesus Christ – Son of God; or: A starting point from the evangel of [the] Anointed Jesus [= Messiah Yahshua], a son from God).
2. **In accord with what has been written in Isaiah the prophet** [other MSS: in the prophets]**:**
    "Look and consider! I, Myself, am periodically sending forth My agent (messenger) **on a mission – before Your face – who will progressively construct Your road** (or: make ready, furnish and equip the Way from You; build the Path which is You). [Mal. 3:1]
3.   **"A voice! One repeatedly crying out** (shouting; exulting; exclaiming; imploring aid)**:** 'Within the midst of the wilderness** (desert; desolate place; abandoned and uninhabited region) **you folks at once prepare and make ready the road of [the] Lord** (the path whose source is [Yahweh]; the Way whose character is that of, and which pertains to, [the] Owner [= Yahweh])**! Be progressively constructing** (or: Make it a habit of making and creating; Continue forming and producing) **His highways** (thoroughfares) **well-placed and straight.'"**
    (or: "A sound of a person constantly calling out within the midst of the desert: Prepare... ")
    [Isa. 40:3; cf Ex. 23:20]

4. **John – the one habitually baptizing** (immersing; dipping) **– came into the scene within the wilderness** (or: came to be in the uninhabited area of the desert), **repeatedly heralding the proclamation of an immersion** (a baptism) **which signifies, is connected to, and has the characteristics of, a change of thinking** [= recognition of being headed in the wrong direction]
    (or: from a change of perception, frame of mind and mode of thought; which is a change of understanding and a new attitude which is a new state of consciousness), **and thus, a turning [to Yahweh, which leads] into a letting-flow-away of, and divorcing from, failures**
    (a sending-away of errors; a letting-go of sins; a release from deviations; a dismissal of mistakes; an abandoning of situations where the target was missed). [cf Ezk. 36:25]
5. **And all the Judean territory** (province; region; country) **– even all the people of Jerusalem – kept on traveling out to him in a steady stream, [to be] face to face with him, and were one by one being immersed** (baptized) **by him within the midst of the Jordan River, while they were continuing in openly confessing-out and acknowledging their failures** (mistakes; errors; sins; deviations; times of being out of line and falling short of the goal). [cf Josh. 3:15-4:11]

6. **Now John was by habit being one who had dressed himself in a garment woven of camel's hair with a leather belt** (or: a girdle made of an animal skin) **around his waist and loins, and was customarily eating locusts** (or: [dried] grasshoppers) **and wild honey [as his food].** [cf 2 Ki. 1:8]
7. **And he had kept on making a loud public proclamation, as a herald, repeatedly saying, "Behind me the One** (or: the Man) **stronger than me is progressively approaching** (steadily coming) **– of Whom I am not** (do not exist being) **of adequate size or sufficient strength to be competent to, while stooping down, loose and unfasten the strap** (thong; lace) **of His sandals.**
8. **"I myself, indeed, immerse** (or: baptized) **you folks within water, yet He Himself will proceed immersing and saturating** (or: baptizing) **you in a set-apart spirit** (or: in union with Holy Spirit; [with other MSS: by an Uncommon Wind; for a consecrated Breath-effect; with a sacred attitude])."**

9. **And within the course of those days it occurred [that] Jesus came from Nazareth, of the Galilee [district], and was immersed into** (baptized in) **the Jordan, by** (or: under) **John.**
10. **Then immediately, while stepping back up straight from out of the water, He saw** (perceived and became aware of) **the atmosphere and sky** (or: the heavens) **being**

progressively split and torn apart, so as to be divided, and the Breath-effect (the Spirit; the Wind; the Attitude) – as a dove (or: pigeon) – progressively descending into the midst of Him! [with other MSS: progressively stepping down and continuously remaining upon Him.]

11. Then a Voice was birthed (or: a sound occurred) from out of the midst of the heavens (or: [torn] atmospheres; or: = the sky and outer space; or = the realms of God's presence; or = the holy places of the realms of spirit): "You Yourself are (or: continue being; habitually exist being) My Son – the Beloved and Accepted One! I seem at ease and appear well and prosperous in union with, and within the midst of, You (or: I delight in You; I think and imagine ease and wellness centered within You; I am well-pleased and approve in You)!"

12. Then the Breath-effect (the Spirit; the Attitude) progressively impels Him forth – set for goodness, ease and well-being (or: a straight, direct, upright and true One; or, as adverb: immediately) – into the midst of the wilderness (the uninhabited, desolate desert),

13. and He continued being within the midst of the wilderness forty days and was constantly being with the little (small) wild animals, being repeatedly (or: constantly) examined and put to the proof by [various] attempts in tests, ordeals and trials by (under [the influence of]) the adversary (satan). And yet agents (messengers) had kept on giving attending service and support for, as well as dispensing provision to, and in, Him.

14. Now, after the [occasion for] John to be given over and committed (or: to be delivered-up [i.e., arrested and imprisoned]), Jesus came (or: went) into the Galilee [district], continuously heralding God's good news (or: the message of goodness, ease and well-being from God, which is God, and which pertains to God) in a loud, public proclamation,

15. and constantly saying, "The season and appointed situation has been fulfilled (The fertile moment has been filled up and now continues full and is now ripe) and God's kingdom (the reigning and ruling of God as King; God's activity of exercising sovereignty) has approached and is now near at hand and is close enough to touch (= has arrived and is now accessible)! You folks be progressively and continuously changing your thinking* – change your perceptions, frame of mind, mode of thought, state of consciousness, your direction, and thus turn back [toward God] – and be progressively loyal and believing, while constantly placing your trust in the good news (the message of goodness, ease and well-being)!" [* cf Rom. 12:2]

16. And while passing along beside (= walking alongside) the Sea of (or: Lake) Galilee, He saw and perceived Simon and Andrew, the brother of Simon, repeatedly envelope-casting [their] purse net (a large, circular fishing net) in the sea, for they were fishermen (those who earned their living by catching fish).

17. Then Jesus said to them, "Hither, you [two] come on behind Me (= follow after Me and join Me), and I will proceed making you to become fishers of human beings (of people)!"

18. So at once (or: And so, set for goodness, ease and well-being), after abandoning the fishing nets, they followed Him (walked the same path with Him).

19. Next, upon stepping forward a little, he saw Jacob (= James), the [son] of Zebedee, and John, his brother, and perceived them while [at work] within the boat, putting the nets in order (i.e., mending, adjusting, cleaning and folding them – making ready for the next use in fishing),

20. so at once (or: so, set for goodness,) He called out to them ([i.e., presuming that the boat was off in the water]; or: Then He suddenly invited them). And after abandoning their father, Zebedee, within the boat with the hired men, they went off behind (= followed after) Him.

21. Later they continued traveling on and entered into Capernaum.

Later, on [one of] the sabbaths, set for goodness, ease and well-being (or, as adverb: immediately) upon entering into the synagogue, He, as was His habit, began teaching.

22. Now they became increasingly astounded and continued being progressively bewildered, so as to be completely amazed – even lost in admiration – at His content and manner of teaching, for He was progressively teaching them as one continuously possessing authority (holding and having the right from out of Being; = from out of Who He was) – and not as the scribes (scholars; experts in the Law; = ordained theologians).

23. **Also, within their synagogue there continued being a man – set on well-being and ease – [but] centered in an unclean spirit** (or: within the midst of an impure mood and a foul, unpruned attitude; in the sphere of influence of a contaminated breath, or an unpurged blowing), **and he momentarily shouts** (or: cried out), [note: vss. 23-27 "spirits" = "demons" in vss. 32, 34]

24. **in saying, "Ah! What [is there] for us and for you** (or: What [is there] in us and in you; What [is] with us, and with you), **Jesus, O Nazarene? You come to lose us and to ruin us away** (or: Did you come to destroy us?). **I have seen to know** (recognize; [other MSS: We now know]) **you – who you are: God's set-apart one** (or: the Holy One of God; the set-apart one, from God; or, as a genitive of apposition: the Holy One who is God)!"

25. **And Jesus spoke seriously but respectfully to him, adding value and worth**
    (or: Jesus respectfully charged it; or: Jesus appraised him and assessed a penalty, assigning a punishment upon him; or: Jesus strongly speaks to him in reproof {censure, reprimand, or strict enjoining}), **in saying, "Be muzzled** (= Be silent) **and go** (or: come) **forth from out of the midst of him at once!"**

26. **So momentarily convulsing him** (pulling him to and fro), **the unclean spirit** (or: mood; attitude) **– also uttering a great sound** (exclaiming or screaming in a loud voice) **– at once went forth from out of the midst of him.**

27. **Now everyone was startled and amazed** (or: suddenly filled with fearful astonishment; or: = at once swept over with admiration), **so as to keep on inquiring of one another** (discussing [the incident] among themselves), **repeatedly saying, "What is this? Fresh and effective teaching that is new in kind and character, corresponding to authority** (or: in the sphere of privilege from within the Being)! **He is even proceeding to assign a place upon** (set an arrangement upon) **the unclean spirits, and they are continuing to submissively hear and obey him."**
    (or: "This is some strange, new and novel teaching! In accord with authority, and backed up by the right to, he now gives orders to the impure motives, moods and attitudes – and in submission they proceed to obey him!")

28. **And so His report** (or: the rumor about Him) **– set for goodness and well-being – went forth everywhere** (in all places) **into the whole country around the Galilee [district; region].**

29. **Then, upon coming out of the synagogue, with Jacob** (James) **and John, they went directly, set on goodness, unto the house** (home) **of Simon and Andrew.**

30. **Now Simon's mother-in-law had for some time been bedridden and was still lying down continuing sick with a burning fever, and so, set on well-being and ease, they at once began telling Him about her.**

31. **So upon approaching and facing her, He, taking a strong hold on her hand, raised her up, and the fever suddenly flowed away and abandoned** (or: left) **her, and she began giving attending service to them.**

32. **Now with evening's arriving** (coming to birth), **when the sun set, they began and kept on in a steady stream bringing and carrying to Him all those continuing to hold badly** (= having an illness; = possessing a poor quality of life and a worthless condition) **– even those** (or: as well as those) **being habitually affected by demons** [note: a Hellenistic word and concept; = animistic influences; it represents a Greek world view, as assimilated by 2nd Temple Judaism] –

33. **and the whole city was eventually there, having gathered together right at, and facing, the door.**

34. **So He tended, attentively served, gave treatment to, began therapy with, prescribed ongoing treatment for, or cured and healed many folks who were continuing to hold badly** (= having a poor condition) **with** (or: in; by) **various kinds of sicknesses and diseases, and He threw** (or: cast; drove) **many demons** [= what was attributed to animistic influences] **from out of the midst, and He kept on refusing the demons** (= influences) **permission to continue speaking, because** (or: in that) **the folks** (or: they) **had come to see, and perceive, Him to be Christ** (or: anointed; [other MSS omit "to be Christ," so read: they had seen and knew Him]).

35. **And early one morning, rising very early while it was still dark, He came forth [outside] and went away into a desolate, out-of-the-way place, and there He began and continued praying** (thinking with a view toward having goodness and well-being; or: = talking to God).

36. **However, Simon and those with him tracked Him down** (hunted Him out)

37. **and found Him, and then proceed saying to Him, "Everyone is now trying to find You** (or: They all continue seeking You)**."**
38. **So He is then saying to them, "We should keep on going somewhere else** (or: Let us continue leading on elsewhere), **into the next adjoining and nearby** (or: neighboring) **unwalled country towns and villages, so that I can herald and publicly proclaim the message there also, for into this [mission and purpose] I am gone forth** (or: I came out)**."**
39. **And He came** (or: went) **into their synagogues – into [the] whole [region of] the Galilee [area] – constantly heralding** (loudly publicly announcing) **as well as repeatedly throwing out the demons** [Hellenistic concept and term: = animistic influences].

40. **There also is progressively coming toward Him, [to be] face-to-face with Him, a leper** (one who has some variety of various skin diseases), **repeatedly entreating** (imploring) **Him to come to his side to give him aid and encouragement, and then proceeding to kneel down, is repeatedly saying to Him, "If you should will it – and would from reason continue intending – you continue able and have the power to cleanse and make me clean."**
41. **Now Jesus, being instantly moved with compassion in His inward being** [other MSS: emotionally swelling internally from His natural disposition and movement of soul; or: filled with warm indignation], **instantly stretching out His hand, touches him, even as He continues in saying to him, "I continually will it and am habitually intending to! Be at once cleansed and made clean!"**
42. **And thus set for well-being, the leprosy** (skin disease) **at once went off and away from him, and he was at once cleansed and made clean.**
43. **And then, inwardly snorting** (possibly: = muttering) **at him with powerful emotion, He at once escorted him forth from out of the midst, set for ease and well-being,**
44. **and continues by saying to him, "See [the situation]. You should tell nothing to anyone [at all], but rather, begin to withdraw, then continuing to go off, show** (display; exhibit) **yourself to the priest, and bear forward the offering of the things which Moses set forth in order** (arranged and gave forth instruction; directed) **– concerning your cleansing – [directed] into a testimony among and witness to** (or: for; or: = against [J.D. Crossan]) **them."**
45. **Yet after going out, the man started** (began) **to repeatedly proclaim and loudly herald a great deal in public and to spread abroad the account, with the result that [it was] no longer possible [for] Him to continue to enter openly into a town, but to the contrary He continued being outside, upon desolate** (uninhabited and unfrequented) **places. And yet, people kept on coming to Him from all sides** (or: all parts; everywhere)**.**

CHAPTER 2

1. **And so, upon entering back into Capernaum after the ensuing days, it was heard** (or: And again entering into Capernaum, after some days it was heard) **that He is currently within [the] house** (or: = at home)**.**
2. **Consequently many folks were gathered together [there], resulting in there being no longer any room, not even [outside] facing the door, and so He was continuing in chatting and making conversation, then began speaking the message** (the Word; the *Logos*; the thought and idea; the patterned information) **to them.**
3. **[While He was speaking], folks are progressively coming, bringing toward Him a paralytic who, having been picked up, is being carried by four men.**
4. **But not being able to bring [him]** [other MSS: to come near] **to Him** (or: to carry [him] to a place before Him) **because of the crowd, they removed the surface of the roof** (unroofed the roof) **where He was, and after digging it out, they gradually lowered the matted pallet** (a poor person's bed) **whereon the paralytic was still lying down.**
5. **And Jesus, seeing their trust, faith and loyalty, proceeds to say to the paralytic, "Dear child, your failures** (mistakes; deviations; errors; deviations; mis-shots toward the target; sins) **are now being caused to abandon you**

    (are in process of being divorced from you; are progressively being let go off from you; are habitually being forgiven; [other MSS read perfect tense: have been caused to abandon you; have been divorced from you; have been released and let go off from you; have been forgiven for you])."

6. **Now there were some of the scribes** (or: certain men from the [group of] experts in the Law; = ordained theologians and scholars) **presently continuing to be sitting there, and they progressively reasoned to conclusions, thoroughly and critically deliberating and dialoguing in their hearts,**

7. **"Why does this fellow continue to speak in this way** (thus; in this manner)**? He continues blaspheming** (speaking slander; speaking insultingly [in regard to God])**! Who is able** (now has power) **to release and send away** (dismiss; forgive) **failures** (sins; errors; deviations; mistakes in trying to hit the target), **except One: God?"**

8. **And so, set on uprightness and for goodness, Jesus immediately experiencing full knowledge and added awareness in His spirit** (or: by the Spirit, which is Him; with His attitude) **that they are continuing to reason, deliberate and dialogue within themselves in this way** (to this conclusion) **then says to them, "Why are you men continuing to reason critically and to thoroughly dialogue about these things within your hearts?**

9. **"Which [of the two] is easier labor: to say to the paralytic, 'Your failures** (mistakes; sins; errors; mis-shots; deviations) **are now being cause to progressively abandon you**

> (are being in process of being divorced from you; are habitually forgiven for you; [other MSS: have been divorced and sent away so as to abandon you and you now exist being forgiven])**,' or to say, 'Get up** (Progressively raise yourself up) **and at once lift up and carry away your matted pallet, and start continually walking around'?**

10. **"Yet so that you men can see and thus know with understanding that the Son of Man** (or: mankind's adult son; or: the Son who is human; or: = a human being) **continuously holds authority** (or: from out of his being possesses [the] right) **to repeatedly send away** (to habitually release and dismiss; to constantly forgive) **mistakes** (failures to hit the target; errors; sins) **upon the earth..." – He then says to the paralytic,**

11. **"I am saying to you** (laying this out for you), **Get up** (Progressively rise up) **at once [then] lift up and carry away your matted pallet and be going away unto your house** (or: home)."

12. **And so he was aroused and caused to rise up, and set for goodness, ease and well-being, after lifting up the matted pallet, he went out – in front of everyone** (all) **– so that everyone** (all) **continued to be beside themselves** (standing out of their places in amazement) **and to continuously give glory to God** (increasing the reputation of God) **repeatedly saying, "We never** (not at any time) **saw anything like this** (or: in this manner)!"

13. **Later He went out again along** (beside) **the seashore, and crowd after crowd all kept on coming to Him, and in turn He was teaching them** (or: and from all sides, the crowd was progressively flocking toward Him, and He kept on progressively instructing them).

14. **Then while passing along, He saw Levi** [probably = Matthew], **the [son] of Alphaeus, as he continued sitting at the custom's station** (tax collector's desk; toll gate; revenue office), **and He is then saying to him, "Keep on following with Me** (or: Start following and continue coming after Me, walking the same road with Me)**!" So, after standing up, he [quit his business and] follows** (or: at once followed) **with Him.**

15. **Later, He happened to be lying down** (or: reclining) **in the midst of eating a meal in his** [note: probably refers to Levi's; see Lu. 5:29 for the parallel account] **house, and many tax collectors** (customs, revenue and tribute officials; or: tax contractors) **and outcasts**

> (or: sinners; failures; = those who on account of their way of life were shunned not only by Pharisees, but also by Law-abiding, "respectable folks" of the Jewish culture; also, = bad characters, irreligious and disreputable folks, and those who practiced vice and crime) **were participating in lying back and eating the meal together with Jesus and His disciples** (learners; apprentices; = pupils of a Rabbi) **– for there were many [such] folks, and they were continuing to follow with Him.**

16. **Now the scribes of [the sect of]** (or: professors and theologians of the Law, from) **the Pharisees, seeing and perceiving that He continues to eat with bad company** (the outcasts: failures and sinners who deviate from the Law) **and those working for the occupying government** (tax farmers [i.e., government sub-contractors] and customs officials who collected

money for Rome or Herod), **began saying** (or: repeatedly were saying) **to His disciples, "Does he regularly eat** [or, with other MSS: Why is it that he is now eating] **with the government workers** (tax men; tax farmers) **and riff-raff** (outcasts; sinners; = ceremonially unclean people)**?"**
17. **And Jesus, hearing [this], then says to them: "Those being habitually strong** (= people in good health) **normally have no need of a physician** (healer; doctor), **but rather, those continuing to have it badly** (= those who are ill and in a poor condition). **I did not** (or: am not) **come to call just ones** (the upright folks; righteous ones; those living in accord with the Way pointed out; or: = those who are part of the establishment and do all the right things; may = people who "think" they have no faults), **but to the contrary, outcasts**
>   (failures; deviants; sinners; those who fail to hit the target and make mistakes; riff-raff and ceremonially unclean folks – even criminals; also = those who did not observe the Law as defined by the scribes)**!"**

18. **Now the disciples of John and the Pharisees were folks who by habit are periodically fasting** [note: a ritual of abstaining from food from 6:00 a.m. to 6:00 p.m., after which normal food could be eaten]. **So these kept on coming to Him, saying, "Why** (Through what [reason of circumstance]) **are the disciples of John and the disciples of the Pharisees habitually fasting** (or: currently observing a fast), **yet your disciples are not habitually** (or: currently) **fasting?"**
19. **Consequently, Jesus said to them, "Is it now possible for the sons of the wedding hall** (= the bridegroom's friends and guests) **to be fasting in the [situation] in which** (or: = while) **the bridegroom continues being with them? No, they continue unable to start or to continue fasting** (or: there can be no fasting) **so long as** (or: for whatever time) **they continue having the bridegroom with them!** [comment: thus, the Messianic Banquet was in process]
20. **"Yet days will be coming when the bridegroom may be taken away from them, and then – in that day – they will proceed in fasting.** [comment: that celebration would soon end]

21. **"No one usually sews a patch of an unshrunk shred of cloth upon an old and worn out cloak** (coat; outer garment). **Yet, if [he does], is not the filling-result** (the [patch] that fills up [the hole]) **progressively lifting up away from it – the new, unused one from the old one – and a worse split-effect** (or: tear; rip) **is gradually happening?**
22. **"Further, no one normally pours freshly-made, new wine into old and worn out leather bottles** (wineskins). **Yet, if [he does], will not the wine proceed in bursting and ripping the leather bottles** (wineskins), **and the wine be progressively lost – as well as the wineskins** (bottles)**? To the contrary, new** (= newly made) **wine [is put] into new** (different, just beginning to be used) **wineskins** (leather bottles).**"**

23. **Now on one of the sabbaths it happened for Him to be progressively passing along [on a path] through some standing fields of grain, and His disciples started to gradually make [their] way, while repeatedly picking** (plucking off) **the heads of grain.**
24. **So the Pharisees began and kept on saying to Him, "Look** (See; Observe)**! What they are continuing to do is not – from [our] existence! – allowed on the sabbaths!"**
25. **And so He then says to them, "Did you men never once read what David did when he had need and was hungry – he and those with him?**
26. **"How he entered into the house** (= the Tabernacle) **of God – during the period of Abiathar, the high** (chief) **priest – and he ate some of the Loaves of the Presentation** (or: of the Preplacement; of the advanced setting; = the Bread of the Presence; [Ex. 25:30, LXX]) **which, from [the time of Israel's] existence, it is not allowed to eat – except for the priests – and he also gave [some] to those being there together with him?"**
27. **And He went on to say to them, "The sabbath came into being** (was birthed) **because of and for the sake of humanity** (or: the human; mankind) **– and not humanity** (or: the human; mankind) **because of and for the sake of the sabbath.** [cf 2 Bauch 14:18]
28. **"So then, the Son of Man is also Lord** (or: the son of the Human also continuously exists being master and owner; or: = the human continues being sovereign) **even** (or: then) **of the sabbath."**

CHAPTER 3

1. **So once again He entered into a [other MSS: the] synagogue, and there was a man there with a continuing condition of having a hand that had been dried-up and remained being withered and shriveled.**

2. **Now they** [= the Pharisees and Herodians, of vs. 6] **began narrowly watching and, at the side, kept on closely observing Him – [to see] if He will proceed tending, attentively serving, giving treatment to, beginning therapy with, prescribing ongoing treatment for, or curing and healing him on** (= during) **one of the sabbaths – so that they could accuse and bring charges against** (down on) **Him by a haranguing speech in a public assembly.**

3. **Then He begins saying to the man having the dried-up and withered hand, "Proceed to rise up, into the midst [of us]."**

4. **So he continues saying to them** [either the entire group, or perhaps, the Pharisees], **"On the sabbaths, is it allowed, from [our] existing, to do good** (or: to create or make something virtuous; to form inner harmonious perfection; to do an admirable act), **or to do something harmful or worthless** (to make something of bad quality; to do an evil act) **– to heal** (save; restore to health and its original condition; rescue) **a soul** (or: a breathing being), **or to kill?"** Yet, they kept on being silent (remained quiet).

5. **Then glancing around at them with swelling emotion from His natural disposition** (or: with indignation), **being increasingly grieved and experiencing pain and sorrow with [them] at the petrifying of their [collective] heart** (also: the covering-over of their heart with a hard, thick layer of flesh), **He next says to the man, "Stretch out your hand!" So he stretched [it] out, and his hand was at once restored to its former condition.**

6. **At that, on going out, the Pharisees immediately were offering** [other MSS: made, or, did a] **joint-counsel and design with the Herodians** (the supporters and adherents of Herod Antipas) **in reference to and against Him, so that they could** (or: might) **destroy Him.**

7. **Then Jesus, accompanied by His disciples, withdrew back toward a place at the sea** (lake) **and a vast multitude [of people] from the Galilee [district], as well as from the Judean [area], followed after Him.**

8. **– In fact, folks from Jerusalem and from Idumea** (= the Edom of the Old Testament) **and from [the] other side of the Jordan [River]** (= Transjordan, or, Perea/Peraea) **and even around Tyre and Sidon** (in the Roman province of Syria): **an immense crowd, constantly and repeatedly hearing how much He continues to be doing, [at one time or another] came to Him –**

9. **So He spoke to His disciples to the effect that a little boat should be continuously engaged** (or: constantly attending; persistently standing by) **for Him because of the crowd, so that they would not continue to press against or restrict Him.**

10. **This was because He tended, attentively served, gave treatment to, began therapy with, prescribed ongoing treatment for, or cured and healed many people – with the result that as many as had been having scourging diseases** (distressing illnesses) **kept on falling upon Him in trying to just touch Him!**

11. **Even the unclean breath-effects** (impure or foul spirits; indecent an unpruned attitudes) **– whenever they kept on gazing at and contemplating** (continued being a spectator of) **Him – were repeatedly falling toward Him so as to be prostrate to Him and kept on exclaiming** (calling or crying out in a loud voice), **saying, "You Yourself are** (continuously exist being) **God's Son** (or: the Son of God; as a genitive of apposition: the Son who is God)!**"**

> [comment: this action was being taken by people, but Mark identifies these folks with their condition – they were inwardly unclean, but still convicted by His presence and character, which they recognized]

12. **So, many times He was having to speak seriously, but respectfully, to them** (or: charge them with stern admonitions) **so that they would not make Him displayed in the light** (manifest; apparent and conspicuous; clearly seen).

13. **And later, He by habit is progressively walking back up into the mountain** (or: the hill country) **and is proceeding to be calling to Himself** (summoning for Himself) **those whom He**

Himself had been intending (purposing; wanting and desiring), **and they came away toward** (or: to) **Him.**

14. **Then He made [a group of] twelve** (or: He formed twelve) – **those whom He also named "sent-forth ones"** [comment: = a figure of the 12 tribes of Israel; cf Mat. 19:28; Lu. 22:30]
> (or: named "ones sent off as commissioned agents;" or: designated as emissaries or missionaries; [this phrase not in some MSS, and is omitted from the texts of Griesbach, Bover, Tasker and edition 24 of Nestle-Aland, but included in MSS Aleph, B and others, and in the texts of Panin, W&H, and Nestle-Aland edition # 27]) – **so that they could** (or: would) **constantly be with Him, and to the end that He could send them off with a mission to be repeatedly heralding and publicly proclaiming in loud voices,**

15. **and to continuously hold [the] right** (or: have authority from out of Being; [A, C2, D and others add: to habitually tend, attentively serve, give treatment to, begin therapy with, prescribe ongoing treatment for, or cure and heal sicknesses and diseases, and]) **to be constantly** (or: repeatedly) **throwing the demons** [Hellenistic concept and term: = animistic influences] **from out of the midst.**

16. **So He made** (formed; produced) **the twelve.** [cf Sirach 48:10b] **And then He put upon** (= added on) **Simon [the] name "Peter";**

17. **and [with] Jacob** (James), **the [son] of Zebedee, and John, the brother of Jacob** (James), **He also put upon** (= added on) **them [the] name "Boanerges" – which is** (= means) **"Sons of Thunder."**

18. **And [the others included were] Andrew and Philip and Bartholomew** (Bar-Tholomaeus; [may = Nathaniel]) **and Matthew and Thomas and Jacob** (James), **the [son] of Alphaeus, and Thaddaeus** [may = Lebbaeus] **and Simon the Cananite** [man from Cana; other MSS read: Cananaean; = the Zealot or the Enthusiast, a political party member; cf Lu. 6:15; Acts 1:13]

19. **and then, Judah** (Judas) **Iscariot** (= a Sicarii?) **the one who also** (later; eventually) **transferred, committed and delivered Him up** (or: gave Him over; handed Him along).

20. **Later, they are** [other MSS: He is] **then coming unto a house, and once again the crowd progressively flocks** (or: comes) **together, with the result that they were not able even to eat bread** (= they could not so much as take a meal),

21. **and so, upon hearing [this], those with** (or: beside) **Him went out to be firm and hold it** (i.e., to control the situation; or: to secure Him), **for some began saying that it** [i.e., the crowd] **was continuing confused and out of control** (or: it was out of place; or: that it was being beside itself, or out of its mind).

22. **Then later, the scribes** (men learned in the Scriptures; = Jewish theologians) – **those coming down** (descending) **from Jerusalem – had kept on saying that He possesses** (constantly has and holds) **Beelzeboul**
> [= an unclean spirit: see vs. 30; other MSS: Beezeboul; Vulgate & Syriac: Beelzebub; in Lu. 11:15 Jews identify this title as the "prince (ruler) of the demons"; Jesus, in vs. 23, understands them to be speaking of their concept of satan; see comment, Matt. 12:24],

and that in union with the prince (ruler; chief; Archon;) **of the demons** [a dualistic, Hellenist concept and term: = animistic influences] **He is repeatedly throwing** (casting) **out the demons.**

23. **So, calling them to** (or: toward) **Himself, He began in parables** (illustrations from things cast or placed alongside for comparison) **saying to them, "How is a satan continuing able to be constantly throwing out a satan** (or: How is an adversary repeatedly having power to continue casting out [that same] adversary [= itself])**?**

24. **"Also, if a kingdom should ever be divided or parted upon itself, that kingdom does not continue able** (constantly has no power) **to stand.**

25. **"And if a house** (= household) **should ever be divided or parted upon itself, that house** (household) **does not continue able** (constantly has no power) **to stand.**

26. **"So if the adversary** (satan) **rose upon** (or: stands up against) **himself** (or: itself) **and was divided** (or: is parted), **he/it continues unable** (constantly has no power) **to stand, but to the contrary, he/it progressively has an end** (continues to hold termination).

27. **"Furthermore, no one, upon entering into a strong man's house, continues able** (ever has power) **to completely plunder his gear** (or: thoroughly ransack his equipment, vessels,

utensils or moveable goods), **unless he should first bind the strong man – and then he will proceed in thoroughly plundering his house!** [notice the parallelism in vss. 24-27]

28. **"Assuredly** (Count on it; Amen) **I am now saying to you folks that all things** (everything) **will be progressively sent away** (caused to depart; divorced; forgiven) **for** (in; in regard to; by; with) **the sons of the humans: the effects and results of the failures** (errors; sins; times of missing the target; deviations) **and the slanders** (the hindering of the Light; the injurious things said; the malicious misrepresentations; the insults; the blasphemies) **– whatsoever** (or: however so many) **they may slander** (blaspheme; defame).

29. **"Yet whoever may speak injuriously into** (blaspheme unto; defame with a false image and vilify by abusive slander to; speak light-hindering words into the midst of) **the Set-apart Breath-effect** (the Holy Spirit; the Sacred Attitude) **continues not having a release** (not holding a deliverance or a divorce; not possessing a forgiveness) **– on into the midst of the Age. But rather, he continues existing being one caught within an eonian effect of a mistake and held, centered in the effects of an error that will last for an indefinite period of time**

> (or: within a result of having missed the target in the eonian realm; in the midst of an age-lasting result of a sin or of error; in union with an effect of failure with respect to things which pertain to [the realm of] the Age; in the midst of the result of a deviation with regard to the [Messianic] eon)."

30. **– [He said this] because they kept on saying, "He continues possessing** (having; holding) **an unclean spirit** (a defiled breath-effect; an impure attitude)."

31. **Now later, His mother and His brothers are proceeding to come. Then, continuing standing outside [the house, or the gathering], they sent off** (dispatched) **[a message] to Him, continuing to call** (or: summon) **Him,**

32. **for a crowd had been sitting down in a circle around Him. So one after another are saying to Him, "Look** (Take note), **Your mother and Your brothers** (= siblings) **continue seeking You** (= Your attention) **outside [the house, or the group]."**

33. **So after considering, He then says to them, "Who is** (exists being) **My mother – and [who are] My brothers?"**

34. **Then, glancing around at those still sitting in a circle around Him, He proceeds to say, "Look and take note of** (or: See and consider) **My mother and my brothers** (= siblings)!

35. **"Whoever may do** (perform) **the will, intent and purpose of God** (or: should construct what God wants and desires) **– this one is** (exists being) **My brother and sister and mother!"**

CHAPTER 4

1. **Once again He starts to continue teaching, beside the sea** (or: along the lake-side). **And a very great** (most numerous) **crowd is being progressively gathered toward Him, so that He, stepping into a little boat, takes a seat and continues sitting on the sea** (lake; = just off shore) **– and the crowd, facing toward the sea** (lake), **were all upon the land** (= the shore).

2. **Then He was continuing to teach them many things in parables**

> (illustrations by comparison; [note: used for Hebrew *masal* in the LXX, so = a variety of figures of speech: riddle; proverb; ethical maxim; by-word; allegory; fable; enigmatic saying that is meant to stimulate intense thinking]) **and was saying to them in the course of His teaching,**

3. **"You folks listen, and be hearing. Look and take notice** (See and consider). **The one habitually sowing** (The sower) **went out to continue sowing** (scattering seed).

4. **"And it happened, within the midst of the continued sowing, [that] some [seed] actually fell beside the path** (or: alongside the road), **and so the birds came and ate it down** (devoured it).

5. **"Then other [seed] fell upon the rocky place** (or: an area of ground that is like stone; = hardpan; or: a rock shelf) **– or, where it was not having** (or: holding) **much soil – and it at once** (straightway; or: = set intended for a good crop) **sprouted and shot up** (rose and stood up out), **because of the situation of not having a depth of soil.**

6. **"So when the sun rose back up again, it was burned** (scorched), **and because of the situation of not continuing to have a root** (= because it cannot strike root), **it was dried out and caused to wither.**

7. **"Still other [seed] fell into the thorns** (thistles; prickly weeds), **and the thorns ascended** (mounted upward) **and together choked** (overwhelmed and crowded) **it, and so it gave** (yielded) **no fruit.**

8. **"But still other [seeds] fell into the ideal soil – and, progressively ascending and being caused to continually grow and increase, it was continuing to give** (yield) **fruit** (= a crop), **and it kept on bearing into thirty-, in sixty-, even in one hundred-[fold]** [other MSS: it was continuing to bear: one, thirty; one sixty; and one a hundred-{times}].**"**

9. **Then He continued saying, "The one continually in possession of** (habitually having) **ears to continue hearing, let him continue to listen and be hearing!"**

10. **Now when He came to be in a more private situation** (in accord with ones [who are] alone [though with others]), **those [sticking close] around Him – together with the twelve – began questioning Him on the parables** (here: obscure illustrations).

11. **So He began saying to them, "The secret** (mystery; [J. Jeremias: singular, = its present irruption]) **of God's kingdom** (or: of the sovereign reign of God as King) **has been given and so stands as a gift to** (or: for; in) **you folks; yet to** (for; in) **those outside, everything** (all things; the whole) **continues to come to be birthed in parables** (= are in obscure, illustrative riddles),

12. **"to the end that,**

> **'continuously looking** (observing), **they may continually look** (observe) **and yet can** (may; should; would) **not see so as to perceive, and constantly** (or: repeatedly) **hearing, they may continually hear, and yet can** (may; should; would) **not make things flow together so as to comprehend or understand, nor can they at some point turn about** (or: unless they turn upon [their path]) **and the results** (effects) **of [their] sins and mistakes should be sent away** (set aside; divorced; forgiven) **for** (or: in) **them.'"** [Isa. 6:9-10; note: this reading follows synagogue paraphrase, as witnessed in the Peshitta and the Targum, while differing from the Hebrew and LXX – J. Jeremias]

13. **He further says to them, "Have you not seen, so as to know and perceive, this parable** (obscure illustrative comparison)**?** (or: You folks have not seen this parable [= Heb. *masal*: dark saying; riddle].) **So how will you folks come to personally know** (have intimate and experiential understanding of) **all the parables** (illustrations, or, riddles)**?**

14. **"The one habitually sowing** (The sower) **is continually sowing the Word** (the *Logos*; the idea; the thought; the meaning and reason; the message; the patterned or blueprint Information).

15. **"Now these beside the path** (road) **are existing** (or: are they [who are]) **where the Word** (thought; idea; message) **is being repeatedly sown, yet whenever they may hear, though set for goodness and well-being, immediately the adversary** (opponent; adversarial situation; *satan*) **is repeatedly coming and habitually takes away the Word** (*Logos*; thought; idea; message; patterned blueprint Information) **having been sown into them.**

> [comment: the parallel passage in Matt. 13 pictures birds (vs. 4) and the explanation of these as "the worthless person or disadvantageous circumstance" (vs. 19) as that which takes away the seed/Word]

16. **"And likewise these being repeatedly sown upon the rocky place are the ones who – whenever they may hear the Word** (message; thought; information; pattern-forming meaning and reason) **– at once** (or: set toward goodness,) **they are continuing to receive it with joy,**

17. **"and yet they are not continuing to have** (possess) **a root within themselves, but rather, continue existing being ones oriented toward the season or the opportune situation** (or: are folks focused on the temporary). **Then, at the next situation of pressure** (tribulation; affliction; squeezing) **or persecution occurring** (coming into being; happening) **because of the message** (Word; thought; idea; information), **they, [being] set for ease and well-being, immediately are caused to progressively** (or: to one-by-one) **stumble or falter from the bait or trap stick of the snare.**

18. **"Now there are others [who are] those being repeatedly sown into the thorns. These are those once hearing the Word** (message; thought; idea; pattern-bearing information),

19. **"and then the anxieties** (worries; cares; concerns; distractions) **of the age, as well as the deceptive seduction of the wealth** (from the riches) **and the over-desires** (or: full-rushing passions) **concerning the rest – progressively making their way into [their lives and situations] – together progressively choke the Word** (the thought, idea, message and information), **and it comes to be increasingly unfruitful.**
20. **"Finally, the ones being sown upon the ideal soil are those who continue listening so as to be constantly hearing the Word** (thought; idea; message; information) **and are habitually accepting it to their sides** (= warmly welcoming it), **they also are progressively producing a crop** (continuously bearing fruit) **– in [volumes or multiples of] thirty, in sixty, and in one hundred."** [*cf* Isa. 6:13b]

21. **And He went on to say to them, "The Lamp is not normally** (or: progressively) **coming so that it can** (or: may; should) **be placed** (or: set) **under the basket for measuring grain** (a peck measure) **or under the bed** (or: couch), **is it? [Is it] not so that it can** (or: may; should) **be placed** (or: set) **upon the lampstand?** [comment: Christ on the cross]
22. **"Just so, there is not anything hidden except for the purpose that it should be set in clear light and manifested. Neither did it come to be hidden away except for the end that it should** (or: could) **come into a lighted condition** (or: into a visible place where it is clearly seen and manifest). [*cf* Rom. 8:19; comment: this points to unveiling and revelation from the Day]
23. **"If anyone continues possessing** (or: proceeds in having) **ears to continue hearing, let him continue listening so as to progressively hear!"**
24. **He was further saying to them, "Habitually observe and take note of** (face, look at and regard; pay attention to) **what you folks are habitually listening to and hearing** (or: are presently hearing).
With what measure, rule, or standard [comment: a figure of the Law?] **you folks habitually measure** (or: In the measure by which you repeatedly measure [people; situations; things] or measure out [to people]), **it will habitually be measured in or for you** (or: measured out to you); **in fact, it will continue being placed toward you folks – or even added to and in you – or more** (or: extra) **will progressively be provided for you** (or: added for you [to do]),
25. **"for it follows that it will continue being given to** (or: for; in) **him who habitually possesses** (has and holds); **and yet from him who is not habitually possessing** (having and holding), **even what he normally possesses** [comment: a reference to the old covenant, or the kingdom? *Cf* Mat. 21:43] **will also** (or: next) **proceed being lifted up and taken away."**

26. **He was further continuing to say, "In this way and manner** (or: Thus) **is God's kingdom** (or: the sovereign reign, influence and activity of God as King)**: [it is] as a person** (man; human) **[who] may cast** (or: throw) **the seed upon the soil** (or: the Land).
27. **"Then he would repeatedly be successively sleeping and then waking up to arise – night and day – and the seed could be progressively sprouting** (germinating) **and then continuing to lengthen** (= to grow)**; just how, he has not seen so does not know.**
28. **"Spontaneously** (Furiously, eagerly and with purpose in itself; Automatically and with self-excitement) **the ground** (soil; earth; or: Land) **progressively bears fruit and produces a crop: first a sprout** (or: [the] blade of grass; shoot; herbage), **then a stalk head** (ear) **and finally a full grain within the stalk head** (ear).
29. **"Now at the time when the fruit may give from its side** (or: whenever the crop should transfer, commend, hand over, and deliver up [the grain]; = be ripe), **he, set for [its] goodness, at once progressively sends forth the sickle, because the harvest has stood at hand and provides itself** (or: the reaping has taken its place at the side; or: the harvest is present and stands ready)." [comment: the first to be harvested is the Firstfruit of the crop]

30. **And He went on to say, "How should we compare** (or: In what manner can we be likening) **God's kingdom** (the reign and action of God as King), **or within what parable** (illustrative comparison) **can** (or: should) **we place it?**
31. **"As to a seed** (kernel; grain) **of a mustard plant, which, whenever it may be sown upon the ground** (soil; earth; Land) **is existing being smaller than all the seeds of those upon the earth** (or: the Land; the soil). [comment: i.e., of those normally planted for a crop]

32. **"But whenever it should be sown, it progressively ascends** (grows up) **and comes to be** (is birthed to be) **greater than all of the herbs and vegetables of the garden** (things grown in a place that has been dug) **and progressively produces** (constructs) **great branches, so that the birds of the heaven** (or: sky; atmosphere) **continue able to from time to time settle down as in a tent** (= to roost or nest) **under its shadow** (or: shade)."

33. **So by means of many parables** (illustrative comparisons) **of this kind He continued speaking the message** (Word; *Logos*) **to them** (or: kept on conveying a flow of the information for them and progressively declared the Thought and Idea among them) **– according as they continued able to continue hearing** (or: continued having power to be repeatedly listening).

34. **Now apart from a parable** (illustrative comparison) **He was not normally** (in the habit of) **speaking to, or among, them. Yet privately and in accord to a person's own [ability] He was routinely loosening all things upon** (or: habitually releasing all for; so: explaining and interpreting everything to) **His own disciples** (students; learners; apprentices).

35. **Then with it coming to be late on that day** (= in the latter part of that day), **He then says to them, "We should pass on through unto the other side** (= the opposite shore)."

36. **So, abandoning** (or: releasing; leaving behind; dismissing) **the crowd, they proceed taking Him along – as He was within the boat, and other boats were there with Him.**

37. **Later a very great windstorm, fierce like a hurricane or whirlwind, progressively births itself** (occurs; develops) **and kept on dashing upon and breaking over into the boat, so that the boat is already starting to be filled up.**

38. **Now He was in the stern, continuing fast asleep upon the cushion** [Jonah 1:5]. **So they progressively arouse and awaken Him, and continue saying to Him, "Teacher! Is it not a care or concern to You that we are in the process of being destroyed and are perishing?"**

39. **When being thoroughly awakened, He at once spoke authoritatively yet respectfully to the wind, and said to the sea** (lake), **"Be progressively quiet and continue silent! Be as one having been muzzled, and remain so!"** [*cf* Ex. 14:21]
And so the wind instantly abated (ceased its labor and became exhausted) **and a great calm was birthed** (occurred; came to be; emerged).

40. **Then He said to them, "Why are you men continuing to be timid and filled with dread in this way? Are you not yet continuing to possess trust** (or: have faith and hold confidence)**?"**

41. **And they suddenly became reverently afraid – gripped [with] a great fear** (deferential awe) **– and began saying to one another, "Who, really** (or: then), **is this Man, that even the wind and the sea** (lake) **pay attention, obey and continue obedient to Him?"**

CHAPTER 5

1. **And so they came unto the other side of the sea** (lake) **into the territory** (region; district; country; countryside) **of the Gerasenes** [other MSS: Gedarenes].

2. **Then on His coming out of the boat, immediately out from among the memorial tombs there came a person set for ease and well-being to confront Him** (or: went out to present himself and to meet Him)**: a man in union with an unclean spirit** (or: within the midst of an uncleansed attitude; centered in a culturally-unpruned breath-effect),

3. **who was habitually having a permanent dwelling** (a settled home, where he lived) **within and among the memorial tombs – and as of yet, no one was continuing able** (was up to then having power) **to bind him: not even with a chain** (or: by handcuffs; in something that was unable to be loosened),

4. **because many times he was to have been bound with fetters and chains, and yet the chains had been burst-through and torn to pieces by him and the fetters** (or: shackles) **had come to be rubbed together so as to be shattered and crushed – so no one continued strong [so as] to subdue and tame him.**

5. **Thus, through every night and day he was being among the memorial tombs and within the mountains** (or: hill country) **– repeatedly crying out** (screaming; shrieking) **and constantly gashing down on himself with stones.**

6. **So upon catching sight of and perceiving Jesus from a distance** (or: from far away), **he runs** (or: rushed forward) **and does** (or: did) **Him reverence, homage and worship by kissing toward Him, bowing down and prostrating himself.**

7. **Then crying out in a loud voice, he is saying, "What [is there] for/with me and for/with You** (or: What [is there] in me and in You), **Jesus, Son of the Most High God? I continue adjuring You** (I am now solemnly appealing to You as with an oath; or: I proceed to put You under oath) **[to; by] God: may You not distress me or give me pain by examining me or putting me to the test with the touchstone** [the *lapis Lydius* which was applied to metals, especially gold, to test purity or quality]**!"**

8. **– for He had been saying to it, "You** [note: singular] **come** (or: go) **forth from out of the midst of the man, unclean spirit** (or: culturally-unpruned attitude; impure breath-effect)**." –**

9. **And so He was asking him** [i.e., the man: the pronoun is masculine], **"What [is] your name?" And he then says to Him, "My name is Legion, because we are** (we exist being) **many."**

10. **And he kept on entreating Him, asking Him to be a paraclete** (calling Him to his side for aid, assistance and comfort), **many [times], so that He would** (or: should) **not at once send it** [other MSS: them] **away, outside of the country** (rural area; region; territory; field; literally: space between two limits).

11. **Now a great** (large; numerous) **herd of young swine** (pigs; hogs) **continued being there, [moving] toward the hillside** (or: facing toward the mountain; or: on the hill country), **habitually feeding** (being grazed).

12. **So they** [other MSS: all the demons] **called Him to their side for help, assistance and comfort** (to be [their] paraclete), **repeatedly saying, "Send us into the young swine** (pigs; hogs), **so that we can** (may) **enter into them."**

13. **And, set for goodness, ease and well-being, Jesus immediately gave permission to them. So coming** (or: going) **out, the unclean spirits** (ceremonially impure breath-effects; culturally-unpruned attitudes) **entered into the young swine, and the herd immediately stampeded** (rushed headlong) **down the steep slope** (bank; cliff; precipice) **into the sea** (or: lake) **– about two thousand [of them] – and they began being choked** (or: were being choked, one after another), **within the sea** (lake). [note: unclean spirits/animals now gone]

14. **So those grazing** (feeding) **them fled and reported back** (or: brought away the news) **into the city and into the fields** (farms; countryside). **Then folks came to see what the situation is that had come to be** (or: what it was that had occurred).

15. **And they are progressively** (or: one after another) **coming toward Jesus, and continue intently looking at the "demoniac"** (the one that [had been] constantly affected or tormented by an animistic influence, or "demons") **– the one that had been having** (holding; possessing) **"the legion** [a Roman regiment of 4,000 to 6,000 troops]**" – now continuing sitting clothed and being continuously sensible, orderly and cooperative** (sane and of sound mind). **And they became afraid.**

16. **Then those having seen [it] thoroughly related to them how it happened to the "demoniac," and about the young swine** (hogs).

17. **So they at once began to be repeatedly entreating Him** (calling Him alongside to assist as a paraclete:) **to go off, away from their districts** (bounded areas or regions).

18. **And now, during His stepping into the boat, the "demoniac" kept on entreating Him** (requesting Him to be a paraclete), **at His side, to the end that he might continue being with Him.**

19. **But He did not let him** (or: did not release him from [his area]; did not allow him; or: And He did not abandon him). **Instead** (or: Nevertheless) **He is then saying to him, "Be going away** (or: Progressively lead the way) **into your home** (your house, or, household), **toward those of your area and association, and fully report back to them** (or: thoroughly tell them the news and the story of) **how much the Lord** [= Christ, or, Yahweh; D reads: God] **has performed for, done to and produced in, you; and He mercied you** (acted in merciful compassion to you)**."**

20. **So he went away and started** (or: goes off and begins) **to repeatedly herald a public proclamation within the Decapolis** [a league of ten cities] **how much** (or: as many things as)

Jesus did to (performed for; produced in) **him, and everyone continued being amazed** (or: all began expressing wonder and astonishment).

21. **After Jesus' passing through [the sea/lake], within the boat, into [the area] on the other side, a great crowd was gathered together upon Him** (= to Him upon His arrival) **as He was still beside the sea** (lake).

22. **Then** [other MSS add: – take note! –] **one of the presiding** (ruling; = leading) **officials of the synagogue – Jairus by name – is progressively coming, and seeing** (perceiving) **Him, he proceeds to fall toward His feet,**

23. **and is repeatedly entreating Him to be his paraclete** (or: begging for assistance) **many times, continually saying, "My little daughter is now having [her] last [moments]** (or: continues holding-on in a way that seems final; = is at the point of death)... **Please!** (O that!) **In coming You can** (or: might; would) **'place the hands' on her, to the end that she can be restored to health** (be saved; be rescued) **and can live** (or: will continue living)!**"**

24. **So Jesus went off** (away) **with him. And [the] great crowd kept on following Him, even repeatedly pressing together on, and crowding, Him.**

25. **Now a woman, continuously being in [a condition of] a flowing of blood** (being with a hemorrhage) **[for] twelve years**

26. **– even experiencing and suffering many things by** (or: under [the care of]) **many "healers" and physicians, and thus spending so as to use up all the things at her disposal, and yet was by nothing being helped or benefited, but to the contrary, was coming into the worse [condition]** (= had gone from bad to worse) **–**

27. **upon hearing the things about Jesus, she, coming within the midst of the crowd from behind, made contact with** (touched) **His cloak,**

28. **for she kept saying, "If I can just touch even His clothes, I will proceed being restored to health** (or: will be progressively healed, saved; and be rescued [from this condition])!**"**

29. **And set toward well-being, the fountain** (or: spring) **of her blood was immediately dried up, and she intimately knew by experience, in [her] body, that she had been healed and remained cured from the grievous illness** (or: disorder) **which had been like being scourged with a whip.**

30. **So, set for goodness and well-being and immediately becoming fully aware of the experience within Himself – the power from out of the midst of Him proceeding forth – Jesus, being turned about within the midst of the crowd, began saying, "Who touched** (made contact with) **My clothes** (outer garments)**?"**

31. **Then His disciples were saying to Him, "You are now looking at and continue seeing the crowd continuously pressing together on You and crowding You, and You are saying, 'Who touched Me?'"**

32. **Yet He continued looking around to see** (or: perceive) **the woman who was** (or: had been) **doing** (performing) **this.**

33. **Now the woman – being afraid and trembling – having seen and now knowing what had happened to her** (what had occurred in her; what had been birthed for her), **came and fell down toward Him, and told Him the entire truth** (all the reality).

34. **Yet He said to her, "Daughter, your faith and trust has restored you to health** (has saved and healed you; has rescued you [from your condition]). **Be progressively going your way into peace of the joining** [or: = shalom], **and continue being healthy and sound, away from the grievous illness** (or: disorder) **which pertained to you."**

35. **While He is still speaking, there are some men now coming from [the household] of the presiding officer** (ruler) **of the synagogue, proceeding to say [to him], "Your daughter died. Why continue to bother the teacher any further?"**

36. **Yet Jesus, set toward goodness and well-being, upon overhearing yet disregarding** (ignoring) **the message being then spoken, proceeds saying to the synagogue ruler, "Stop being caused to fear; only continue trusting** (or: progressively believe; keep on holding faith).**"**

37. **Now He did not allow anyone to follow together with Him, except Peter, Jacob** (James) **and John, the brother of Jacob.**

38. **So they are proceeding to come into the house** (home) **of the synagogue official, and He continues gazing upon** (watching and contemplating) **a confused uproar** (a tumultuous commotion) **– even many folks continuously weeping** (crying; lamenting) **and repeatedly screaming** (or: wailing loudly; similar to: making war cries).

39. **On entering, He then says to them, "Why are you people being caused to continue with [this] confused uproar** (tumultuous commotion) **and being caused to constantly weep and lament? The child** (or: little girl) **did not die away, but to the contrary, she continues fast asleep."**

40. **And they began laughing at Him and kept on ridiculing and scornfully mocking Him. But He, upon putting** (or: casting; throwing; = forcing) **everyone out, proceeds to take along the father and mother of the little girl – and those with Him** (= His companions) **– and continues making His way into where the little girl was reclining** (lying back).

41. **Then, taking a strong grip of the little girl's hand, He proceeds to say to her, "Talitha coumi** (or: koum)**," which is normally being translated and interpreted, "Little girl** (or: Maiden; = Young lady), **I am saying to you, wake up and proceed to arise** (or: get up)."

42. **And, set to wellness, the little girl at once arose and stood up, and began walking around – for she was about twelve years old. And immediately, placed in this goodness, they were** [D adds: all] **beside themselves in great ecstasy and amazement – being put out of their normal stance.**

43. **Then He made a determination and fully arranged many things for them, so that no one would know this, and said something should be given to her to eat.**

CHAPTER 6

1. **Then He went out** (left; departed) **from that place and continued going into His fatherland** (His own native country or territory), **and His disciples continued following Him.**

2. **Later, when it came to be a sabbath, He began to continue teaching within the synagogue. And then the majority of those hearing [Him] and continuing to listen began to be puzzled, then astounded and amazed, [one after another] in turn saying, "From where [are] these things in** (or: by) **this one? And what wisdom that [is] being given by** (or: in) **this man!** (or: And why [is] this wisdom being given to this fellow?) **– and such powers** (or: abilities) **repeatedly coming into being through** (or: happening by means of) **his hands!**

3. **"Is not this man the carpenter/stoneworker** (or: tradesman; craftsman; master artisan; journeyman), **the son of Mary** [p45 and others read: the son of the carpenter and of Mary] **and the brother of Jacob** (James) **and Joseph** [other MSS: Joses] **and Judah** (or: Judas) **and Simon? And are not his sisters here** (in this place) **with us?"**
So they began to be increasingly snared in (tripped or caught by the bait stick of the trap, so, caused to stumble in; = took offense at) **Him.**

4. **But Jesus continued, saying to them, "A prophet is not without honor** (or: does not continue being without value or worth), **except within his own country** (or: fatherland) **and among his relatives** (those of common birth and origin) **and even within the midst of his house** (or: home; household)."

5. **So He continued being unable** (having no power or ability) **to do even one ability** (or: make even one power; or: perform [a work] of even one power or ability) **there, except for placing [His] hands upon a few ailing folks** (sickly ones who had no strength or firmness) **[during which] He tended, attentively served, gave treatment to, began therapy with, prescribed ongoing treatment for, or cured and healed [them].**

6. **And He kept on finding it remarkable** [other MSS, aorist, thus: He marvelled and was astonished] **because of their lack of trust and faith** (or: their unbelief; or: their disloyalty and lack of allegiance).
So He kept on going around the villages, in a circuit, continually (or: repeatedly) **teaching.**

7. **[One day] He proceeded to call the twelve to Himself and began to be sending them off, two by two, and continued giving authority** (or: permission; rights; potentials from out of being with freedom to act) **pertaining to the unclean spirits** (impure breath-effects [= ways of living?]; perhaps: unpruned attitudes) **[as He sent them].**

8. **He also passed on instructions and announcements to them, to the end that they should not pick up or carry anything onto the road** (or: for the path) **– except a staff, only; no bread** (= food), **no bag** (sack; pack; food pouch; or: begging-bag), **[putting] no copper money into the belt** (girdle; = take no pocket money).

9. **Still further, having bound sandals under [the soles of their feet], [they were] not to clothe themselves with** (not to wear) **two undergarments** (tunics).

10. **He then continued saying to them, "Wherever you men may enter into a house, continue remaining** (dwelling; abiding) **there [as a guest] until you should be going forth from out of that place** (or: area; = leave that locality).

11. **"But whatever place may not welcome** (receive and embrace) **you folks nor should even listen to you or hear what you folks possess, on progressively journeying from out of that place, shake out** (or: off) **the dust from underneath your feet – into [it being] a witness to them**

> (a testimony for them; evidence in them) [see note in Matt. 10:14; A and other MSS add: It is true (Count on it; Amen), I am now saying to you, it will be more endurable (bearable; tolerable) for Sodom or Gomorrah within a day of sifting and decision (a separating in judging) than for that city]."

12. **So, going out, they publicly proclaimed the message so that people could change their mind, perception, way of thinking, attitude and state of consciousness [due to this added knowledge], and thus would turn back [to Yahweh's reign, in trusting obedience].**

13. **And they kept on casting many demons** [Hellenistic concept and term: = animistic influences] **forth from out of the midst, and were repeatedly anointing** (or: rubbing) **many weak and sickly folks with olive oil, and continued tending, attentively serving, giving treatment to, beginning therapy with, prescribing ongoing treatment for, or curing and healing [them].**

14. **Now Herod [Antipas], the king, heard – for His Name came to light and became apparent and recognized** (manifest and evident) **– and folks** [other MSS: he] **kept on saying, "John, the Baptist** (or: immerser), **had been awakened and raised up from out of the midst of dead ones, and through** (or: because of) **this the powers and abilities have been internally working** (operating) **and continue active and effective within Him."**

15. **Yet others kept on saying, "It is Elijah." Still others kept on saying, "He is a prophet, as** (or: like) **one of the prophets [of the past]."**

16. **Yet Herod, upon hearing [it], kept on saying, "This John, whom I myself beheaded, was raised up."**

17. **You see, Herod himself, sending [agents] off** (dispatching [men]), **seized and arrested John and bound him in prison** (within the midst of a jail) **because of Herodias, the wife of Philip, his brother, because [Herod] married her.**

18. **Thus John was repeatedly saying to** (or: in regard to) **Herod, "It is not permissible, from [Israel's] existence, for you to continue having** (holding; possessing) **your brother's wife."**

19. **Now Herodias was habitually nursing a grudge against him** (or: constantly had it in for him; kept on resenting him and hemming him in; was repeatedly entangling him) **and was constantly intending** (designing; willing; resolving; purposing; wanting) **to kill him off, and yet she continued powerless and unable,**

20. **for you see, Herod continued fearing** (perhaps: reverencing) **John, having seen and thus knowing him [to be] a fair** (equitable; in accord with the way pointed out; a just) **and set-apart** (holy) **man, so he continued with a consorted effort to watch over and guard him** (keep him safe and sound).

And after hearing many things in regard to him (or: So, often hearing from him), **he became perplexed and continued hesitating, at a loss to decide. And yet, he gladly continued hearing of him** (or: from him; = what he had to say; [or, with A C D & other MSS: And upon hearing him, he continued doing many things and hearing him with pleasure]).

21. **And so an opportune** (convenient; strategic) **day was happening** (coming to be), **when Herod, for his birthday celebration, made a formal dinner** (banquet) **for his great men** (= nobles; lords; courtiers; high dignitaries; top-ranking officials), **the military tribunes** (commanders of a thousand men) **and the foremost people** (= leading citizens) **of the Galilee [district].**

22. **And then at the entering of the daughter of this same Herodias, and upon [her] dancing, she charmed and gave pleasure to Herod and to those lying back [at dinner] with him. So now the king said to the young maiden** (girl; young woman), **"Request of me at once whatever you may presently be wanting** (could normally be desiring; should habitually be intending; can continue resolving with design and purpose), **and I will proceed giving [it] to you."**

23. **Then he earnestly** (or: vehemently) **swore an oath** (put himself under oath) – **as one touching some sacred object** – **to her, "Whatever you may ask** (request of) **me, I will give [it] to you** – **up to half of my kingdom!"**

24. **So, on coming out, she said to her mother, "What should I request** (demand; ask; perhaps = claim) **for myself?" The woman replied, "The head of John, the one constantly baptizing** (immersing)**."**

25. **And so, on entering** – **at once, and with haste for good placing toward the king** – **she made request** (demanded; asked) **for herself, saying, "I am presently desiring** (wanting) **that you here and now should instantly give to me the head of John, the one who baptizes** (immerses), **upon a plank** (board; or: plate; platter)**."**

26. **And the king, becoming engulfed with grief** (sorrow-stricken), **did not want** (desire; purpose) **to displace her** (to upset her; to set her aside; to thwart, reject, refuse or repudiate her; perhaps = disappoint or disregard her) **because of the oaths and those still reclining** (lying back) **[while dining with him].**

(or: And the king becoming greatly pained because of the vows...)

27. **So, for a good [political; social] positioning, the king immediately issued the order, sending off a [soldier of his personal] guard** (one who also acted as a sentinel, a spy or an executioner) **to bring his head.**

28. **And going off, he beheaded him within the prison** (or: jail) **then brought his head upon a plank** (board; plate; platter) **and gave it to the maiden** (young woman), **and then the young maiden gave it to her mother.**

29. **Then his disciples, upon hearing of it, came, lifted up and carried away his corpse, then placed it within a memorial tomb.**

30. **Later, those sent off on the mission** (the representatives) **were in turn gathered together to Jesus and reported back to Him everything** (or: all things) – **as many things as they did** (or: performed; produced), **and whatever they taught** (or: instructed).

31. **Now because of the many people constantly coming and going, [there was] not yet even a good opportunity or situation to eat. So He then says to them, "You men yourselves, come on, privately, into a place where we can be alone** (an uninhabited, isolated, desolate place) **and rest up a little** (briefly soothe and refresh yourselves)**."**

32. **And so they went away, in the boat, into an isolated and uninhabited place** (or: a place in the wilderness), **privately.**

33. **But people saw them going away, and many folks learned** (came to know) **of it and ran together there, on foot** – **from all of the towns** (or: cities) – **and went ahead, [some arriving] before them.**

34. **Upon getting out [of the boat], Jesus saw a large crowd and was at once moved in His inner being** (intestines and internal organs) **and compassion was extended upon them, because they were** (continued being) **"like sheep not having a shepherd," so He at once began** (started) **to continue teaching them many things.** [cf Nu. 27:17-20]

35. **Now it was happening that much of the day was already passed when His disciples, coming toward Him, began saying, "The place is isolated and desolate, and the hour [is] already late.**

36. "Release and dismiss them [i.e., the crowd] so that, upon going off (away) into the fields (= small farms) and villages round about, they can buy something for themselves [and] can eat."

37. Now, upon considering, He said to them, "You, yourselves, give them [something] to eat." And so they are then saying to Him, "[Then] going off, we should buy two hundred denarii [worth] of bread (= 200 day's pay for a laborer), and then we will proceed giving [it] to them to eat!"

38. But He now says to them, "How many loaves of bread do you folks presently have? Go and see." And so, coming to know (= when they found out), they are then saying, "Five, plus two fishes."

39. So He gave instructions to them, arranging for everyone to recline (lie back) upon the green grass, in groups for [eating and] drinking together (or: mess-party by mess-party; company by company). [cf Ps. 23]

40. And so they fell back (= laid back or reclined) plot by plot (or: similar to garden beds) [in groups] by hundreds and by fifties. [comment: = an organized mass of people]

41. Then receiving and taking the five loaves of bread and the two fishes, He, while looking up into the heaven (or: the sky and atmosphere), He spoke words of wellness and ease (or: He blessed) and broke down the loaves (or: cakes) into pieces and began giving [them] to the [other: MSS: His] disciples so that they could place [them] beside the people. And the two fishes He parted and divided to all (or: for and among everyone).

42. So they all ate and were fed (literally: pastured) until satisfied (or: gorged).

43. Then they [i.e., the disciples] picked up [the] fragments ([left over] results of the breaking the loaves into pieces) – twelve wicker food baskets filled full – as well as from the fishes.

44. Now those then eating the loaves of bread were (= numbered) five thousand males (or: men). [cf 2 Ki. 4:42-44]

45. Then, set for goodness and well-being (or: without delay), He compelled His disciples to step into the boat and to get under way in proceeding (going on ahead) unto the other side (= the opposite shore), toward Bethsaida, while He Himself continues to release and dismiss the crowd.

46. And upon making arrangements and saying good-bye to them, He went off into the mountain (or: the hill country) to pray (think or speak toward having goodness and well-being).

47. By now it was becoming evening, [and] the boat was still in the middle of the sea (or: lake) – yet He continued being alone, upon the land.

48. And seeing them being continuously tested (having the touchstone applied; being distressed; or, as a middle: = exerting themselves) within the midst of the constant driving [of the storm] and the need to be continuously rowing – for the wind continued being hostile and contrary, blowing in the opposite direction against them – He proceeded to come towards them, at about [the] fourth watch of the night (between three and six A.M.), progressively walking along upon the sea (or: lake). Now He had been intending to go past them (or: to pass them by; to go by alongside of them), [cf Ex. 33:19-22]

49. yet those having seen Him continuously walking around upon the sea (or: lake) suppose that it is the effect of an apparition (or: presume that He is a phantom or a ghost; thought that it is the result of something being made visible) and they cry out loud (or: let out a shriek) because they all saw Him and were shaken (troubled; disturbed; unsettled; agitated).

50. So, set for ease, He immediately speaks (or: spoke) with them, and continues saying to them, "Take courage, and continue being bold and confident! I am (or: I am Being; I am continuous Existence; or: = It is I)! Stop being afraid (or: Do not continue to be fearful)."

51. Then He stepped up toward them and climbed into the boat – and the wind at once subsided (grew weary and abated; suffered exhaustion and flagged). At this, within and among themselves, they became extremely astounded [other MSS add: from the extraordinary situation] and continued, as it were, standing outside themselves in amazement and kept on marveling with admiration.

52. You see, they had not put the pieces together on the [situation of] the loaves of bread, so as to understand or grasp the meaning, but to the contrary, their heart (= the core

condition of the group) **was continuing being in the condition of having been petrified** (made to be a stony concretion; or: made thick and hardened like calloused skin; or: = [their minds] were closed).

53. **And upon piercing and driving right through [the sea] and passing across onto the land, they came into Genneesaret then were anchored** (or: moored) **nearby** (= near the shore). [note: the Dead Sea scroll Mark fragment 7Q5 omits "onto the land"]

54. **Then after their disembarking from the boat, the people, at once recognizing Him [and being] set for goodness and well-being,**

55. **hurried** (ran) **around** (or: about) **that whole area** (district; region) **and started** (began) **to progressively carry about on cots** (mats; pallets) **those folks having [it] badly** (= having an illness or ailment) **[to] where they had been hearing that He at present is** (= was at that time).

56. **So wherever He kept on going His way and entering into villages, or into cities, or into farming districts, they kept on placing the sick** (weak; infirm; feeble) **folks in the midst of the marketplaces, and they repeatedly called Him to their sides for help so that they could touch [Him] – even if just the ritual fringe of His cloak** (or: robe). **And as many as did touch** [other MSS: were touching] **it** (or: that pertaining to Him; or, as an adverb: in that very place) **were proceeding to be healed** (or: kept on, one by one, being delivered, made whole, saved and restored to their original condition and state of being).

CHAPTER 7

1. **Now [one day] the Pharisees and some of the scribes** (men learned in the Scriptures; Torah-teachers; theologians), **upon coming from Jerusalem, are proceeding in being gathered together, facing toward Him.**

2. **And at seeing** (perceiving; noticing) **that some of His disciples are in the midst of eating the loaves** (bread; = their meal) **with ritually unclean** (defiled or contaminated from common use) **– that is, unwashed – hands, they found fault** (or: complained).

3. **For you see, the Pharisees and all the Jews** (or: the Judeans as a whole; [i.e., those who adhere to the practices of the Jewish culture]) **are not in the habit of eating, unless they can** (or: would) **ceremonially wash [their] hands up to the wrist** (or, perhaps: up to the elbow with a fistful of water; [Aleph & other MSS instead read: frequently]) **– continuing to keep a strong hold on the traditions of the elders** (also = the men of former times).

4. **Even when returning from a marketplace, they are not in the habit of eating unless they can** (or: should; would) **ritually sprinkle or dip** (= wash; baptize) **themselves – and there are many other similar things which they accepted and take to their sides to be constantly holding fast: immersions** (baptisms; = washings; ritual sprinklings) **of cups and pitchers and copper vessels** (or: bronze utensils), **and of couches** (beds; mats).

5. **So both the Pharisees and the scribes continued with a question to Him: "Why are your disciples not continuing to walk** (= conduct themselves; order their manner of living) **in accord with and corresponding to the tradition of the Elders** (the older men; the men of former times), **but to the contrary they continue to eat the bread** (= the meal) **with ritually unclean** (unwashed; common) **hands?"**

6. **Yet He insightfully and decidedly said to them, "Isaiah beautifully** (aptly; ideally) **prophesies** (or: prophesied) **about** (or: concerning) **you the overly judging and critical folks** (*hupokrites*; or: those who put texts under close inspection to sift and separate and then give an answer, an interpretation, an opinion; or: those who live by separating things yet who under-discern; or: those who make judgments from a low view; or: those who under-estimate reality; or: perverse scholars who focus on tiny distinctions), **as it has been written** [D reads: and said]:

> **'This people continues honoring Me with [their] lips, yet their heart is habitually distant** (continues holding [itself] far) **from Me.**

7. > **'But they habitually venerate Me** (show Me adoration and reverence in worship and pious deeds) **futilely** (uselessly; ineffectually; fruitlessly; in vain), **repeatedly teaching the results of men's directions** (or: the effects of human commands, ordinances, precepts and implanted goals) **for "teaching".'** [Isa. 29:13]

97

8. **"Abandoning** (Sending off; Divorcing; Letting go) **the implanted goal** (impartation of the finished product within; inward directive) **of and from God, you folks continuously keep a strong hold on the traditions of men** (things given along or transmitted from people)."
[some MSS add: – baptisms (= ceremonial washings) of pots (pitchers, jugs) and cups, and you are constantly doing many other similar things of this sort]

9. **Further, He went on to say to them, "You men keep on beautifully** (adroitly) **setting aside God's implanted goal** (impartation of the finished product within; inward directive and purposed destiny) **so that you can keep and maintain your tradition.**

10. **"For instance, Moses said, 'Be habitually honoring and constantly expressing value for your father and your mother,'** [Ex. 20:12] **and, 'Let the one habitually saying something worthless, of bad quality, corrupt, or evil to or about father or mother progressively come to an end by** (or: in) **death** (or: = be put to death).' [Ex. 21:17]

11. **"Yet you folks are yourselves constantly saying [that] a person** (a man) **can at any time say to father or mother, 'Whatever of mine by which you might have been helped or benefited [is] Corban** (or: a korban; = an oblation, offering or sacrifice)' **– which is an approach present** (a gift dedicated to God and usable for no other purpose).

12. **"You continue allowing him to no longer do a single thing** (or: And so you people still continue releasing him to do nothing) **for father or mother!**

13. **"This is habitually invalidating** (depriving of lordship; making void of authority) **the Word of God** (God's thought and idea; the message from God) **by** (or: in; with) **your tradition which you folks deliver and pass along** (or: handed down) **– and you are constantly doing many such things of this kind** (or: repeatedly performing many such similar [rituals] along this line)."

14. **So, calling the crowd to Himself again, He began saying to them, "Everyone listen to Me** (or: Hear Me – all of you folks –), **and understand** (or: let it flow together so as to get the meaning).

15. **"There is nothing** (not even one thing) **from outside a person** (a human) **which, progressively entering into him, continues having power** (is continuing able) **to make him ritually defiled or unclean** (or: can contaminate him or make him common). **But to the contrary, the things habitually issuing forth from out of the person** (human) **– these things are habitually ritually defiling** (contaminating; making common and unclean) **the person** (humanity). [comment: *cf* Hag. 2:4-19; here is a reverse-contagion: the Land is clean by the Spirit]

16. **"If anyone continues having ears to hear, let him continue hearing** (or: listening; or: = If someone can hear, let him pay attention to and obey what he is hearing)."

17. **Now when He entered into a** [other MSS: the] **house, away from the crowd, His disciples began asking** (or: inquiring of) **Him about** (concerning) **the parable** (the comparative illustration).

18. **So He is then saying to them, "Do you people also thus continue being without understanding** (a flowing together for perception and comprehension)? **Are you folks still continuing not to use your mind and intellect** (not to think or consider) **so as to perceive and comprehend that nothing proceeding to enter into the person** (human) **continues having power or ability to ritually defile him** (contaminate, pollute or make him common or unclean),

19. **because it is not passing on into his heart, but rather, into the stomach and intestines** (the cavity), **and then proceeds to pass out into the toilet** (evacuation seat; latrine)?" **Upon proceeding in cleansing** (making ritually clean) **all foods,**

20. now He continued saying, **"The thing normally issuing forth from out of midst of the person** (human)**: that thing habitually contaminates the person** (makes the person ritually polluted, unclean and common),

21. **"for you see, from inside of the person** (man; human) **– from out of the midst of the heart – the worthless reasonings** (base conversations; dialogues of poor quality; evil thoughts and schemes; bad ideas and designs) **constantly issue forth: [for example], prostitutions, acts of sexual immorality or involvements in fornication; thefts; murders;**

22. **"adulteries; situations of wanting more than one's share** (thoughts of greed; feelings of coveting), **bad conditions which bring pain, gushes of misery, anguish or hard labor** (or: acts of wickedness; malicious deeds; evil doings); **bait to catch someone with deceit,**

treachery, guile or fraud; loose conduct (indecency); **an evil eye** (= a focus toward malice or mischief); **villainous and light-hindering slander, harmful and abusive speech, or blasphemy** (a hindering of light); **pride, arrogance and haughtiness; acting without thinking** (or: imprudence; unreasonableness; inconsiderateness; lack of purpose; folly).

23. **"All these bad situations and misery-causing things are habitually issuing forth from within, and repeatedly contaminate the person** (continuously make the human common, polluted and ritually unclean)."

24. **Now from there** (or: from that place [= that house]), **after rising up, He went off** (or: away) **into the regions** (or: territories; districts) **of Tyre and Sidon. Then, upon entering into a house** (or: household), **He was intending that no one was to know it** (i.e., to learn that He was there). **Even so, He continued unable to escape notice or to elude [them].**

25. **On the contrary, at once upon hearing about Him, a woman set for goodness and well-being – whose little daughter continued having an unclean spirit** (or: was still holding in impure breath-effect; was yet having a vicious and unpruned attitude; was continuing to hold a disposition which reeked of dirt, refuse and the contents of a grave) – **upon entering, immediately prostrates** (falls forward) **toward His feet.**

26. **Now the woman was a Greek** (or: a Greek-speaking Gentile of the Hellenist culture; = a pagan) – **a Syrophoenician by birth** (= a native of Syro-Phoenicia) – **and she kept on begging Him that He would cast out** (expel) **the demon** [Hellenistic concept and term: = animistic influence/spirit/attitude; vss. 15 & 25 illustrate the term] **forth from the midst of her daughter.**

27. **Yet Jesus began saying to her, "First allow** (or: Let it flow off first for) **the Children to be fed until satisfied, for it is not appropriate** (good form; ideal; fine; beautiful) **to take the bread of** (or: which belongs to; from) **the Children and to throw [it] to the little house dogs** (or: pet dogs; puppies)."

28. **Now she considered a reply, and then says to Him, "Yes, Lord** (or: Sir; Master), **and yet** [with other MSS: O Lord, even] **the little house dogs underneath the table are normally eating from the crumbs** (morsels; scraps) **of the little children** (or: young servants)."

29. **At that He said to her, "Because of this idea** (thought; word; saying; = that remark), **go! The demon** (= spiritual influence) **has gone forth from out of the midst of your daughter."**

30. **So, after going away unto her house, she found the young girl** [with other MSS: her daughter] **prostrate, having been laid upon the bed** (couch; mat) – **the demon** (= inner malady) **having completely gone out.**

31. **Then, again, upon coming out from the boundaries** (territories) **of Tyre, He went through [those of] Sidon unto the sea of the Galilee [district], on up to the midst of the regions** (boundaries; territories) **of Decapolis**

> [or, with p45, A & other MSS: going out from the midst of the regions of Tyre and Sidon, He went into the sea of Galilee {district}, amidst the territories of {the} Decapolis {note: Greek cities}].

32. **Here folks proceeded bringing to Him a man with blunted hearing** (= deaf) **who also had some speech impediment, and they are continuing to call Him to their side, entreating Him so that He would place [His] hand upon him.**

33. **So, taking him away from the crowd, privately, He thrusts His fingers into his ears, and, upon spitting, He touched his tongue [with the spittle]** (or: took hold of his tongue; or: brought [it] in contact with his tongue), **so as to activate it.**

34. **Then, looking up into the sky and atmosphere** (or: the heaven), **He groaned** (or: sighs; or: took a deep breath) **and is then saying to him, "Ephphatha** [note: an Aramaic word]," **which is, "Be thoroughly opened up!"**

35. **And, set for well-being, his hearing abilities were at once opened up, and the bond** (fetter; thing of the binding) **of his tongue was loosed** (or: destroyed), **and he began speaking normally** (correctly; in a straight and upright way).

36. **And with that He Himself made full arrangements with them, cautioning them to the end that they could** (or: should) **be then telling no one; yet, as much as He kept on making**

these arrangements for them, cautioning them, they themselves much more kept on proclaiming it publicly to a greater degree.

37. **Indeed, they kept on being superexceedingly amazed and astonished beyond all bounds, repeatedly saying, "He has done all things beautifully** (has made everything ideally and finely)**: even the sensory blunted** (or: deaf) **ones He continues making to be habitually hearing, and speechless** (mute) **ones to be constantly speaking!"**

CHAPTER 8

1. **During those days – there again being a large crowd of folks [who] also [were] not at that time having anything they could be eating – upon calling His disciples to Himself, He continues in saying to them,**

2. **"I am again moved in my inner being** (inner organs) **with compassion on the crowd, because they continue remaining already three days with Me, focused toward Me, and they continue having nothing they can be eating.**

3. **"So if I should loose them away** (= send them off) **unto their homes, fasting** (= hungry, having no food)**, they will proceed falling apart in the road, being faint and exhausted – and some of them have arrived [here] from far away."**

4. **But then His disciples made a logical reply to Him, "From where will anybody here on [the] wilderness** (uninhabited, deserted, isolated or desert place) **be able to feed and satisfy these folks with loaves of bread?"**

5. **So He went on to ask them, "How many loaves of bread do you men presently have?" And they said, "Seven."**

6. **Then He proceeded in making an announcement to the crowd, instructing [them] to recline** (lean back) **upon the ground. Then taking the seven loaves of bread [while] expressing gratitude for the good gift** (or: the wellness from the ease of grace)**, He broke [them] in pieces and began giving [these] to His disciples so that they could proceed in placing [them] alongside [the crowd]. So they served the crowd, placing [the pieces of bread] beside [them].**

7. **They also were in possession of a few small fish. So, upon blessing them with good words, He told [them] to proceed in also placing these beside [the crowd], and to continue serving.**

8. **So they all ate, and fed until satisfied. Then they picked up the result of the surplus of the superabundance of broken pieces – seven hamper-size provision baskets [full]!**

9. **Now those eating were about four thousand men. After that He loosed them away** (dismissed them).

10. **Next, set for goodness, ease and well-being, upon stepping into the little boat with His disciples He immediately went into the parts** (= the vicinity or district) **of Dalmanutha.**

11. **Now at one point the Pharisees came out [to where He was] and began to be discussing and arguing with Him, repeatedly seeking to see a sign from the heaven** (or: from the sky) **at His side** (or: from beside Him)**, continuing in examining, trying and testing Him** (or: requiring proof [of His claim]).

12. **Then, sighing again in His spirit** (or: deeply groaning, inwardly by the effect of His breath and in His mood)**, He continues to say, "Why is this generation continually seeking** (constantly trying to find) **a sign? It is true!** (or: So be it; Amen; Verily; Count on it; Truly,) **I am now saying, As if a sign** (or: Make it so, I now lay it out, since a Sign) **will progressively be given to this generation–!"**

13. **And sending them away** (or: leaving them)**, upon again stepping into a little boat He went off into [the area of] the other side** (= the opposite shore).

14. **And it happened that they completely forgot, and thus neglected, to take** (or: get) **loaves of bread, and, except for one loaf, they continued having nothing with them within the boat.**

15. **Then He began instructing, and continued to be fully setting things in order for them, saying, "Be continuously looking and observing, so as to be seeing with perception! Be constantly taking note of and look out for so as to beware of the leavening agent** (or: the

yeast; = the pervading elements of fermentation and fomentation) **of the Pharisees as well as the leavening agent of Herod** [i.e., = the pervading doctrines and theology of the structured and organized religion, as well as current governmental politics]."

16. **So they began reasoning-through [this saying] and kept on presenting deliberations to one another, discussing [the situation] that they are repeatedly having no loaves of bread** [other MSS: ... that, "we constantly have no bread"].

17. **And becoming aware** (= noticing it), **He is then saying to them, "Why do you continue reasoning about and discussing [the fact] that you folks are repeatedly having no bread? Are you men not yet in the habit of directing your minds so as to perceive and understand? Are you neither making [sayings, thoughts or events] to continually flow together so that you can understand? Do you continue having your heart which has been turned to stone** (has been hardened or calloused so as to now be settled in a petrified state)**?**

18. **"Constantly having eyes, are you not continuing to observe so as to see? Constantly having ears, are you not continuing to listen so as to hear? And are you men not continuing to remember?**

19. **"When I broke the five loaves of bread into** (or: for the situation of) **the five thousand men, how many wicker hand-baskets full of fragments** (broken pieces) **did you men pick up?" They are then saying to Him, "Twelve."**

20. **"And when [I broke] the seven loaves into the four thousand men, how many provision-hampers filled with fragments did you men pick up?" And they are then saying to Him, "Seven."**

21. **So He continued in saying to them, "Are you not yet allowing [these things] to flow together so that you get the meaning?"**

22. **And so they proceed in coming into Bethsaida. Here people are now progressively bringing a blind man to Him, repeatedly calling Him to his side, continuing to urge and implore Him to function as a paraclete: that He would touch him.**

23. **So then, taking a hold upon the blind man's hand, He led him forth, outside of the village. Then, upon spitting into his eyes while placing [His] hands on him, He proceeded to ask him, "What, if anything** (or: Whatsoever), **are you now seeing?"**

24. **And looking up, he kept on saying, "I continue looking at the people** (humans); **I continue seeing [them] as trees continually walking around!"**

25. **Next, He again put [His] hands upon his eyes, and then he looked throughout and saw thoroughly** (= clearly), **and he was restored to his former state. He even kept on attentively looking at and seeing everything at a distance quite distinctly.**

26. **So He sent him away, unto his house, saying, "Neither should you enter into the village, nor yet may you speak to anyone centered in the village."**

27. **Next Jesus and His disciples went out into the villages of Caesarea Philippi. And on the way** (in the road) **He began questioning His disciples, saying to them, "Who are the people** (humans; men and women) **now normally saying** (speaking [of]) **Me to be?"**

28. **Now they said to Him, "[They] are repeatedly saying that [You are] John, the one who immerses. And others [are saying] Elijah, yet others that [You are] one of the prophets."**

29. **And then He continued inquiring of them, "But you yourselves, whom are you repeatedly saying Me to be?" So Peter, replying from discernment, is then decidedly saying to Him, "You Yourself are the Christ** (the Anointed One; = the Messiah) **– the Son of God!"** [other MSS omit: "the Son of God"; cf Jn. 6:69; 11:27]

30. **Then with complete graciousness, He respectfully gave admonition to them to the end that they should be telling no one about Him.**

31. **Next He began to progressively teach them that it is necessary** (it remains binding) **for the Son of the Man** (or: the son of man; = the Human Being) **to experience** (or: to be affected by; to suffer) **many things, and after being put to the test, to be disapproved and rejected under and by the elders** (older men, perhaps signifying members of the Sanhedrin), **the head** (or: chief; ranking) **priests, and the scribes** (Torah-teachers; experts in the Law; theologians), **then to be killed-off – and yet, after three days, to stand back up again** (or: to rise up, again).

32. **Now with boldness, in freedom of speaking as being a citizen, and by plainness of speech He was repeatedly speaking the message** (telling this word of patterned information). **Then Peter, drawing Him hospitably aside to himself, began to graciously and respectfully give corrective admonition to Him.**

33. **So Jesus, being turned about and seeing** (or: looking at; perceiving) **His disciples, graciously and respectfully gave instructive** (or: corrective) **admonition to Peter and says, "Be habitually bringing the things pertaining to the adversary under control behind Me**
     (or: Be continually leading under that which is adversarial [to a place] behind Me; or: Be gone, under [My] authority, and continue withdrawing behind Me [= Move out of My way],
     O [My] opponent {or: satan}), **because you continue not having a frame of mind which is disposed to the things of God, nor are you habitually directing your intellect to the issues which have their source in God, but to the contrary, [your frame of mind is disposed to and your intellect is applied to] the things pertaining to humanity** (or: which belong to and have their source in people)."

34. **Then, upon calling the crowd – together with His disciples – toward Himself, He said to them, "If anyone continues purposing** (intending; willing) **to come behind** (or: after) **Me, let him once for all completely renounce** (deny; disown; say "No!" to) **himself and pick up his cross** (or: torture and death stake; pole for suspending corpses), **and [thus] let him be continuously** (habitually; progressively) **following** (coming after and accompanying) **Me.**
35. **"For you see, whosoever may continue purposing** (intending; willing) **to save** (deliver; rescue) **his soul** (or: the soul-life pertaining to himself; or: the consciousness which is himself; his inner life) **will progressively destroy and lose it. Yet whoever destroys his soul** (or: soul-life; consciousness of the estranged self) **on account of Me and for the sake of the good news** (the message of ease, wellness and goodness) **will progressively deliver** (rescue; save) **it** (or: will continue restoring it to health, wholeness and its original state and condition).
36. **"For what continues benefiting a person** (or: progressively augments or repeatedly brings help or profit to humanity) **to gain** (acquire possession of) **the whole world** (ordered system of culture, religion, government or economy; universe) **and to undergo forfeiture of his soul** (or: to receive damage or detriment to its life, or to the consciousness which he/it is)**?** [Cf Lu. 9:25]
37. **"In fact, what can** (would; could; should; [other MSS: will]) **a person** (mankind) **give, as a result of a change-instead** (or: in exchange) **pertaining to his** (or: its) **soul** (or: as an effect corresponding to transformation of the consciousness of, and which is, himself/itself which makes him/it other than he/it is)**?"**

38. **"Furthermore, whosoever may be ashamed of, or embarrassed because of, Me and My messages** (Words; Thoughts; Ideas; Information) **within the midst of this adulterous and erring** (failing; mis-shooting; sinful; deviating) **generation, the Son of the Man** (or: the son of mankind; the Human Being; = the eschatological Presence, or, Son) **will also continue being ashamed of and embarrassed, because of him – whenever** (at the time that) **He may come within the midst of His Father's glory** (or: in a manifestation which calls forth praise for His Father) **along with the set-apart agents** (or: holy messengers; sacred folks with the message)."
1. **Then He continued saying to them, "Truly** (or: Assuredly; Amen; Verily), **I am now saying to you folks that there are certain ones** (or: some) **of those standing here who under no circumstances can taste** (may test by sipping; = experience; partake) **of death until they can** (should; may) **see God's kingdom** (God's reign and influence as King; the sovereign activity which is God) **being present, having already come within the midst of power and ability."**

CHAPTER 9

2. **Then, after six days, Jesus proceeds in taking along Peter, Jacob (James) and John, and continues leading** (or: bringing) **them up into a high mountain – privately [and] alone** (= by themselves). **And He was transformed** (or: transfigured; changed in form) **in front of them**
3. **– even his garments became continuously glistening** (radiantly shining as an effect of radiating very bright light), **exceedingly white as snow, such as no person on earth who cards, cleans and bleaches woolen clothes is able to thus whiten –**

4. **and next, Elijah was seen by them, together with Moses, and they continued being** (were existentially existing) **[there], continuing in conversation with Jesus.**

5. **Then, after considering, Peter proceeds in saying to Jesus, "Rabbi, it is a beautiful** (ideal; fine) **[situation for] us to continue being** (or: existing) **here! So we could** (or: should) **construct three tents** (tabernacles)**: one for** (or: to) **You, one for Moses, and one for Elijah."**
6. **You see, he had not perceived, so as to see, what considered judgment** (or: decided response) **he should make, for they became** [other MSS: were being] **so frightened** (or: became terrified; became ones responding out of reverential fear).
7. **And then a cloud formed, progressively overshadowing** (casting shade upon) **them. Next a Voice sounded** (came into existence; was birthed) **from out of the midst of the cloud, saying, "This One is** (ongoingly exists being) **My Son, the Beloved One. Be habitually hearing, listening to [and thus, obeying] Him!"**
8. **Then suddenly, upon looking around, no longer did they see anyone, except Jesus, alone with themselves** (or: they no longer saw even one person with themselves, except Jesus, only).

9. **And then during their progressively descending** (climbing down) **from out of the mountain, He expressly gave a distinct explanation to them to the end that they should be relating** (or: leading through the account of the incident) **to no one what they saw – except whenever the Son of the Man** (the Human Son; mankind's son; the eschatological Son [or: Presence]) **should arise** (would stand back up again) **from out of the midst of dead ones.**
10. **So they strongly held the word** (the information; or: = [Christ's] statement concerning not relating the matter) **to themselves, continuing in discussing and questioning** (speculating and debating) **together as to what is the [meaning or significance of the words], "to stand back up again** (or: arise again) **from out of the midst of dead ones."**
11. **And so they began to inquire of Him, saying, "[How is it] that the scribes** (= theologians of the Law; scholars) **are continually saying that it is necessary for Elijah to come first?"**
12. **Now He affirmed to them, "Elijah indeed, coming first, progressively moves and reintegrates all humanity away from where it has been placed** (or: put) **down, and from what has been firmly established. So how has it been written on** (or: concerning) **the Son of the Man** (mankind's son; the Human Being; = the son of Adam; = the eschatological Messianic figure) **that He should experience – and even suffer – many things and then be treated as nothing and with utter contempt and disregard?** [Mat. 17:11; Acts 3:21; Isa. 53:2ff; Phil. 2:7]
13. **"Nevertheless, I now say to you men that Elijah as well has come, so as to be here, and they do to Him** (or: did with him) **as many things as they were desiring and are still purposing – correspondingly as it has been written on Him** (or: concerning him)**."**

14. **Then, when coming toward the [other] disciples, they saw a large crowd around them – even scribes** (= theologians of the Law; scholars) **repeatedly making inquiries together, aimed toward them** (or: discussing with them; perhaps: arguing with them).
15. **And so, set for ease and well-being, upon seeing Him the entire crowd was astonished** (or: surprised [to see Him]; or: overawed; or: completely amazed), **and, progressively running toward [Him], they began to greet, salute and even embrace Him!**

16. **So He asked them** [Concordant Text: the scribes], **"Why do you continue making inquiries together, aimed toward them?** (or: What are you folks discussing with them?)**"**
17. **Then one out of the crowd decidedly answered Him, "Teacher, I brought my son to you. He continues having a speechless spirit** (or: a breath-effect which renders him incapable of speech; or: an attitude which results in his being mute),
18. **"so wheresoever it may seize him or get him down, it repeatedly dashes him [upon the ground]** (or: [inwardly] tears and rips him up), **and he continues frothing and foaming at the mouth, as well as grinding his teeth, and then he progressively withers** (either: becomes weak and limp; or: becomes rigid and stiff).
So I spoke to your disciples so that they would cast it out (or: throw if forth from out of the midst; eject it), **and yet they did not have the strength** (or: they are not strong [enough])**."**

19. **Now He, responding with a considered reply, is then saying to them, "O generation without faith and trust** (or: faithless, disloyal and unbelieving generation)! **Till when will I continue in being facing toward** (or: being with) **you folks? Till when am I continuing holding back with you** (or: = bearing or putting up with you people)? **Go ahead and bring him to Me."**

20. **So they brought him to Him, and at having seen Him, the spirit** (breath-effect; attitude; mood and internal disposition; result of a breath or of breathing), **at once set for well-being, violently convulses him and then, falling on the ground, he began rolling and wallowing** (or, as a passive: continued being rolled) **while continuously frothing at the mouth.**

21. **So He asked his father, "How much time** (or: How long) **is it that something like this has happened to him, and continued being thus for him?"**

22. **And [the father] said, "From childhood on. Further, many times it also throws him into fire or into places of water, so that it might destroy him** (or, possibly: that it can loose-away from him). **But now, if you continue having power and ability [to do] anything, in instant out-flowing of compassion upon us, come quickly to our aid, and help us!"**

23. **So Jesus said to him, "As to your 'if you continue having power and ability,' all things [are] possible to** (for; by; in; with) **the one habitually trusting** (or: progressively believing)."

    [or, reading with A & other MSS: "About the 'if': you continue being able (having power) to trust (or: to believe). Everything (or: All) {is} endued with power for the one continuously faithing and trusting (or: progressively believing; constantly having confidence)!"]

24. **The father of the young boy** (the lad), **set for ease and well-being, immediately is crying out, with tears was saying, "I continue trusting** (or: I habitually have faith; I am now believing)! **Be now helping me in the lack of faith** (or: Continue being my immediate aid in the unbelief, or for lack of trust and confidence; or: Help my unbelief; Give progressive aid [in the area of] the disbelief from me)!"

25. **Now Jesus, noticing** (or: seeing) **that the crowd is progressively running together upon [their position]** (or: rapidly converging on [them]), **at once spoke seriously but respectfully to the unclean spirit** (or: culturally-unpruned, and thus unproductive, attitude), **adding a charge**

    (or: Jesus respectfully penalized the unclean breath-effect; or: Jesus appraised the impure spirit and assessed an injunction upon it; [or, paraphrasing an interpretation: Jesus strongly speaks to the disabling mental, physical and psychological condition in reproof {censure, reprimand, or strict enjoining}]), **saying to it, "O speechless and dull spirit** (or: deaf-mute breath-effect), **I, Myself, am now making complete arrangements for you** (or: am presently setting an injunction upon you): **at once come forth from out of the midst of him, and no longer** (or: no more) **may you at any time enter into him."**

26. **Then, after crying out and throwing him into severe convulsions, it went out, and he became as if dead – so as for it to be said by the majority that he died.**

27. **Yet Jesus, taking a strong hold on his hand, awakens and raises him up, and he stood back up.**

28. **Then, upon His entering into the house, His disciples** (or: students; apprentices) **began asking Him privately, "Why were we, ourselves, unable** (or: having no power) **to throw** (or: cast) **it out?"**

29. **So He said to them, "This kind** (or: sort; species; race; progeny; offspring; family; lineage [note: does this indicate that it was perhaps an inherited condition?]) **is normally in no way able to come** (or: go) **out, except within the midst of speaking with a view toward having goodness, and thoughts that face well-being** (or: prayer; [other MSS add: and fasting])."

30. **And upon going out from there, they began traveling along through the Galilee [district], but He continued not intending that anyone should come to know [of it]** (or: but during this time He was wanting no one to come to know about it), **because He was continuing to teach His disciples.** [cf Isa. 53:6, 12, LXX, with 14:10-44 and 15:15, below]

31. **Then He began saying to them, "The Son of mankind** (The Son of the Man; humanity's son) **is in the process of being given over into the hands of people** (= control of humans),

and they will proceed in killing Him off. Then, having been put to death, after three days He will proceed to stand back up again (or: He will proceed in raising Himself up, again)."
32. However, they continued not understanding the effect of the saying, for they still had no insight or experiential knowledge of the result that flowed from the declaration and continued being afraid to question Him (or: and kept on fearing to ask Him [about it]).
33. So they came into Capernaum, and upon coming to be within the house, He began inquiring of them, "What had you men been reasoning-through and trying to settle (or: debating; arguing) among yourselves on the way (or: in the road)?"
34. Yet they continued silent, for on the way they had been discussing (or: debating) with one another [as to] who is being [the] greatest (= most important).
35. Then, upon being seated, He summoned (or: called loudly [to]) the twelve, and then continued, saying to them, "If anyone continues intending (purposing; willing; wanting) to be first, he will continue being last of all – even an attending servant of everyone (or: all)!"

36. Next, taking a little child, He placed (or: stands) it [Greek is neuter: = a boy or a girl] in their midst, and embracing it with His arms, He said to them,
37. "Whoever may (or: should; would) hospitably welcome and embracingly receive one of such little children upon [the basis or authority of] My Name, participates in welcoming Me with hospitality and continues receiving Me in his embrace. Further, whoever may (or: should; would) continue welcoming and receiving Me in this way is not [simply] giving Me a hospitable welcome and an embraced reception, but further, [he does this to] the One sending Me off with a commission (as a Representative and an Emissary)."

38. John began affirming to Him, "Teacher, we saw a certain man (or: someone) casting out (expelling) demons (Hellenistic concept and term: = animistic influences) in Your name, and we began trying to prevent him (or: kept on forbidding him) because he was not making it his habit to be following and accompanying us."
39. Yet Jesus said, "Stop forbidding him and trying to prevent him, for there is no one who will continue doing a powerful work (or: performing an act of ability) upon the [basis and authority of] My Name, and then will proceed in being able to quickly (or: soon afterward) speak badly or unworthily of Me.
40. "You see, the person who is not down on us or against us is for us (or: exists being [a shelter] over us).
41. "In fact, whoever may give you folks a cup of water to drink – within (or: in; centered in) [the] Name, because you are from, and belonging to, Christ
    (or: because you exist having Christ as your source; or: seeing that you folks are of [the]
    Anointing; or, as genitive of apposition {definition}: because you exist being that which is
    Christ), it is true (or: count on it; amen), I am now saying to you men that he can (or:
would) by no means lose (or: may in no way destroy) his wage (pay; compensation).
42. "And yet, whoever may be an entrapment for (or: give bait so as to entrap; = give cause for stumbling and becoming captured, trapped, held in bondage or enslaved) one of these little ones – those continuing with faith, who are habitually trusting, believing and being loyal – it is ideal rather (fine, instead) for him if a millstone, such as is turned by an ass, continues lying around his neck and throat, and he had been thrown into the sea!
43. "Further, if ever your hand should at some point be entrapping you (be giving cause for stumbling or becoming captured, trapped, held in bondage or enslaved), at once cut it off! It is ideal [for] you, yourself, to enter into the Life maimed, than, having the two hands, to go off into the Valley of Hinnom (or: Gehenna; [note: this is a ravine south of Jerusalem where fires were kept burning to consume the dead bodies of animals, criminals and refuse]) – into the fire which is not extinguished.
[note: Nestle-Aland, Westcott & Hort, Tasker, and Panin texts, following the oldest MSS, omit vss. 44 and 46, which are the same as vs. 48; MSS A D and others contain them:
    "'where their maggot (or: worm) continues not coming to the end [of its food], and the fire
    continues not being extinguished.']

45. "And if your foot should begin repeatedly entrapping you in some snare, at once cut it off! It is ideal [for] you, yourself, to enter into the Life lame and crippled, than, having the two feet, to be thrown into the Valley of Hinnom (Gehenna: the city dump).

47. "And if your eye should begin repeatedly entrapping you in some snare, throw (or: cast) it out! It is ideal [for] you, yourself, to enter into God's kingdom (the reign from God; the activities and influence which are God) one-eyed, than, having two eyes, to be thrown into Hinnom's ravine (Valley of Hinnom; Gehenna – the city dump outside of Jerusalem),

48.   "'where their maggot (or: worm) continues not coming to the end [of its food], and the fire continues not being extinguished.' [Isa. 66:24]

49. "Indeed, everyone (or: It follows that all humanity) will be salted (seasoned and preserved) in (with; by) fire! [some MSS add: – even every sacrifice is to be salted with salt]

50. "Salt [is] ideal (fine; beautiful), yet if the salt should ever become saltless (or: deprived of saltiness; savorless), in what way (or: with what) will you proceed fitting it for seasoning? Be constantly having and holding salt within and among yourselves, and habitually be at peace in the joining (or: keep or make joining-peace [= shalom]) in union with one another."

CHAPTER 10

1. Later, upon rising from that place, He proceeds in going into the border areas (regions, or, districts which were the boundaries) of Judea, and then [to the] other side of the Jordan [River]. And again crowds are progressively traveling together toward Him, so again, as He had been accustomed (had been in His usual habit), He went to constantly teaching them.

2. At one point, the Pharisees were coming toward [Him] and began questioning Him – being in the habit of repeatedly putting Him to the test, so as to examine Him, or even to tempt Him or to get Him off His guard – whether it is allowed, from [the time of Israel's] existence, for an adult male to loose-away (divorce; dismiss) a wife.

3. So He, giving a considered reply, asked them, "What did (or: does) Moses impart as a goal for you folks (or: give as the end in mind to you people)?"

4. And they said, "Moses turned it upon [us] (= gives it to our management, thus permitting [us]) to write a little scroll of divorce (of putting off and standing away in separation), and to loose [her] away (dismiss [her])." [Deut. 24:1, 3]

5. So now Jesus said to them, "He wrote this implanted goal (impartation of the finished product within; inward directive) for (or: to) you people with a view to (or: directed toward) the dryness and hardness of your hearts,

6. "however, from [the] beginning of creation
     'He made them (or: forms and constructs them) male, and female.' [Gen.1:27; 5:2]

7.   'On account of this, a person (a human; mankind; or: a man) will proceed completely leaving his/her father and mother,'

8.   'and the two people will proceed coming into an existence of being one flesh,' [Gen. 2:24]
     [note: Westcott & Hort and Panin follow the above reading of vs. 7, with Aleph, B & other MSS. The Concordant Text and Tasker include, while Nestle-Aland & Griesbach bracket the following addition to vs. 7:
     '... and will continue joined (glued; welded) together with and focused toward his wife,']
     [note: this latter reading suggests being matrilocal]

with the result that they no longer exist being two [people], but rather, one flesh.

9. "Therefore, what God yokes together, humanity (a person; mankind; a man) must not be continually separating (or: by customary action be putting apart)."

10. Then, [having entered] into the house again (= when indoors once more), the disciples kept on asking Him about this.

11. So He proceeds saying to them, "Whoever may loose-away (dismiss; divorce) his wife and should marry another woman proceeds to commit adultery on her.

12. **"Also, if she** [i.e., the wife], **upon loosing-away** (divorcing) **her adult male, should marry another man, she proceeds in committing adultery."**

> [comment: thus, it is the same for both husband and wife; in this verse, Jesus points out that the action could be initiated by the wife]

13. **Then people began repeatedly bringing little** (or: young) **children to Him, so that He would** (or: might; could) **touch them – yet the disciples respectfully chided and restricted them.** [comment: this was in emphasis of the value and importance of who He was]

14. **Now, seeing and perceiving [this], Jesus was physically and emotionally feeling pain, showing signs of much grief and displeasure** (or: irritation, indignation or resentment), **so He said to them, "Release and allow the little** (or: young) **children to proceed coming to Me. Stop hindering and preventing** (or: forbidding) **them, for you see, of such ones exists** (or: is) **the kingdom of God** (or: for it follows that God's reign as King, and the sovereign influence of God, continues being from, belongs to, and consists of, such as these).

15. **"Truly** (or: It is so; Count on it; Amen), **I am now saying to you folks, Whoever may** (or: would) **not welcome and receive as in one's arms the kingdom of God** (or: God's reign and actions) **as a little or young child, can under no circumstances** (or: may in no [other] way) **enter into it."**

16. **So, at once clasping them in turn, within the embrace of His arms, He continued in bring down words of blessing, ease and well-being while repeatedly placing [His] hands upon them.**

17. **Later, during His traveling out into [the] road** (or: a path; or: as He was setting out on His way), **a certain rich man, running toward [Him] and falling on his knees [before] Him, began asking Him, "Good Teacher! What should I do** (or: perform) **to the end that I can** (or, as a future: will) **inherit** (receive and enjoy an allotment of) **eonian life** (life pertaining to and having the qualities of the Age; life into the unseeable and indefinite future; life of and for the ages)**?"**

18. **Yet Jesus said to him, "Why, from reasoning, are you proceeding in terming Me 'good'? No one [is] good except One: God.**

19. **"You have perceived and are thus acquainted with the implanted goals** (impartations of the finished product within; inward directives),

> **'You should not murder; you should not commit adultery; you should not steal; you should not bear false witness** (give false testimony)**; you should not cheat or defraud. Be habitually honoring, valuing and respecting your father and mother.'"**
> [Ex. 20:12-13]

20. **So he affirmed to Him, "Teacher, I observed, guarded and maintained all these from out of my youth** (= since my boyhood)**."**

21. **Now Jesus, looking at him and seeing within him, loves** (accepts and urges toward reunion with) **him, and so said to him, "You yourself continue behind, and are thus lacking and coming short in, one thing. Withdraw** (or: Go off) **and progressively bring things under control. At once sell as many things as you continue holding** (possessing; having), **then at once give to the poor and destitute folks – and you will continue holding** (possessing; having) **stored up treasure within heaven** (or: in [your] atmosphere)**! After that, come here and be habitually following with Me** [other MSS add: picking up the cross (execution pole)]**."**

22. **Yet he, being somber and downcast with gloom upon [hearing] the word** (*logos*; message and information, with its thoughts and ideas), **went away being increasingly made sad with pain and distress, for he was being in the position of holding** (having) **many possessions** (the results of many acquisitions of goods and property).

23. **Then, after glancing around, Jesus proceeds speaking His thoughts to His disciples, "How difficultly and fretfully – as with those being peevishly hard to satisfy or please with regard to food – will those constantly holding** (possessing; having) **the effects of a wealth of money and useful things proceed entering into the kingdom of God** (or: the sphere and realm of God's reign as King; the sovereign influence and activity which is God)**!"**

24. **Now the disciples began being affected by an emotion of astonishment in which awe is mixed with fear, upon [hearing] His words which expressed His thoughts and reasoning. So Jesus, giving a considered response, continues again by saying to them, "Children,**

how difficult and fretful [a thing] it is (or: [the situation or process] continues to be [Texts omit, but other MSS add: {for} those having placed their confidence upon money or the effects of wealth]) **to enter into the kingdom of God** (the sovereign actions and influences from God).
25. **"It continues being easier for a camel to pass through the midst of a needle's perforation** (or: eye; hole bored or worn-through) **than for a rich person to enter into the kingdom of God** (God's sovereign reign and activities).
26. **"So they began being exceedingly struck out of their wits, being overwhelmed with bewilderment, saying to Him** [other MSS: to one another], **"So who is able** (or: So is any one [of them] with power) **to be saved** (rescued; delivered; made healthy and whole)**?!"**
27. **Upon looking at and within them, Jesus then is saying, "On the side of humans** (or: With people) **[it is] impossible, but on the other hand, not on the side of God** (or: not with God), **for all things [are] possible at God's side** (or: everything is able [to happen] with God)."

28. **Peter began to speak his thoughts to Him, "Look** (or: Take into consideration), **we ourselves at once abandoned everything and have followed You!"**
29. **Jesus affirmed, "It is so** (Amen). **I now say to you folks, there is not even one person who leaves** (or: releases; lets flow away) **a house, or brothers, or sisters, or mother, or father, or children, or fields** (or: farms; lands; estates) **on My account, and on account of the good news** (the message of goodness, ease and well-being),
30. **"who would** (or: may; should) **not get** (or: receive) **one hundred times as much now** (at the present time) **– within this appointed season** (or: fitting situation)**: houses and brothers and sisters and mothers and children and fields** (farms; lands; estates), **along with their pursuits** (or: with the effects and results of hurry, rapid motion and pressing after [things]; or: accompanied by persecutions), **then, within the progressively coming age, Life pertaining to that Age** (or: eonian life; life which has the qualities and character of the Age [of Messiah]; life whose source is the Age; life of and for the ages). [comment: = house, family & realm of God]
31. **"Yet many first ones will proceed being last ones, and the last ones first ones** (or: there are many [who are] first who will be existing last; and those last [who will be existing] first)."
> [comment: reversals seems to be a common ingredient to the kingdom; the Jews had been "in first place" and the good news came to them first; still, first and last describe a whole – all are included]

32. **Now they had been in the road, on the way progressively walking up into Jerusalem – and Jesus had been steadily leading the way ahead of them – and they began being filled with awe and continued being amazed, yet the folks who were still following along began fearing.**
Then, once again taking the twelve aside, He began to tell them the things [i.e., the events, the situations] **that were progressively being about to be suddenly in step together with Him, and to at once converge on Him,**
33. **"Look here** (or: See this), **and consider. We are progressively walking up into Jerusalem, and then the Son of the Man** (Mankind's Son; the son of humanity; or: = the Human Being) **will proceed in being given over and committed to the chief priests and to the scribes** (the theologians who are experts in the Law and the Scriptures). **Then they will proceed to condemn and sentence Him to death, and then will proceed giving Him over to the ethnic multitudes** (transmitting Him to the nations; commending Him among the Gentiles).
34. **"And those folks will repeatedly ridicule, mock, scoff at and make fun of Him, will repeatedly spit on Him and even repeatedly scourge** (severely whip and lash) **Him. Then they will proceed in killing [Him]. And yet, after three days He will progressively stand back up, again** (or: will proceed arising again)."

35. **Then at one point Jacob (= James) and John – the two sons of Zebedee – by habit continue to make their way toward Him [and] proceed to be laying out their thoughts to Him, saying, "Teacher, we continue wanting** (desiring; willing; intending) **that You would do for us whatever we should request of You."**
36. **So He said to them, "What are you now wanting** (wishing; or: repeatedly intending) **for Me to do for you?"**

37. **So they said to Him, "Grant at once to** (or: for) **us that we can** (or: may; should) **sit – one on Your right and one on Your left – within the midst of Your glory** (in union with Your manifestation which calls forth praise; centered in the assumed appearance from You)."
38. **Yet Jesus said to them, "You have not seen, so are not aware of what you [two] are now requesting. Do you now have power and do you continue able to drink the cup which I Myself am now progressively drinking, or to be immersed in** (or: baptized with) **the immersion** (baptism) **which I Myself am now progressively being immersed** (baptized)**?"**
39. **And they said to Him, "We now have power and continue able!"**
Yet Jesus replied to them, "You folks will progressively drink the cup which I, Myself, am now progressively drinking, and you will also be progressively immersed in (or: baptized with) **the immersion** (baptism) **which I, Myself, am now progressively being immersed, unto saturation** (baptized).
40. **"However, the [matter, situation or choice of] to sit down at My right or at My left is not Mine to give, but rather, [it is] for those for** (or: in; with; by) **whom it has been prepared and made ready."**

41. **Well then, hearing [of the incident], the [other] ten began to be indignant and resentful about Jacob** (James) **and John.**
42. **So Jesus, calling them to Himself, then proceeds laying out His thoughts, saying to them, "You men have seen and are thus aware that those of the ethnic multitudes** (or: of the nations, who are non-Jews, or "Gentiles") **[who] are habitually presuming** (or: are normally seeming, appearing or supposing) **to be constantly ruling, are habitually exercising full ownership of them while habitually bringing the effects of their lordship down on them, and their great ones are continually exercising complete authority for their positions, while putting them down under their dominion and coercion.**
43. **"Yet it does not exist** (or: it is not) **this way among you folks. To the contrary, whoever may continue intending** (wishing; desiring; wanting; purposing) **to become great** (or: a great or important person) **among you will continue existing being your attending servant.**
44. **"And whoever may continue intending** (desiring; purposing) **to be first among you folks will continue existing being a slave of everyone** (or: all).
45. **"You see, even the Son of the Man** (or: For it follows that the Human's son, as well,) **did not come** (or: does not go) **to be given attending service, but to the contrary, to give attending service, and further, to give His soul** (or: the consciousness from Him; the conscious life, that is him) **[as] a ransom payment – a loosener for liberation and release – for, as, in the place of, in exchange for, and which corresponds to, many people."**

46. **Next they proceed coming into Jericho. Then, during His continued journeying out away from Jericho [with] His disciples and a considerable crowd, Bar-Timaeus** (or: Bar-Timai) **– a blind beggar, the son of Timaeus** (Timai) **– was sitting, as was his habit, beside the road.**
47. **And upon hearing that it is Jesus the Nazarene** (i.e., the Jesus from Nazareth), **he started to repeatedly cry out, and to keep on saying, "O Son of David! Jesus! Mercy me** (or: Act in mercy to me)**!"** [comment: might this title indicate "Builder of the Temple"?; = Messiah]
48. **Then many began respectfully chiding and strongly admonishing him to the end that he would be silent. Yet he, to a much greater extent rather kept on crying out, "O Son of David! Mercy me** (or: Act in mercy to me)**!"**
49. **Then Jesus, standing [still], said, "You folks call him** (or: summon him)**!"**
So they proceeded to be calling (summoning) **the blind man, while saying to him, "Keep on taking courage and continue confident! Be rousing and proceed getting up! He is now calling** (summoning) **you."**
50. **Now at once throwing off his outer garment** (or: cloak), **he, leaping up, came toward Jesus.**
51. **Then, giving to him a discerning response, Jesus said, "What do you now want** (intend for) **Me to do for you?" So the blind man said to Him, "Rabboni** (= My Master), **[it is] that I can see again** (or: could recover my sight)**!"**

52. **So Jesus said to him, "Lead your way under [faith in this thought] and proceed going [home]. Your faith, confidence and trust have restored you to wholeness** (has rescued you [out of blindness]; has saved you)." **And so, set for well-being, he immediately sees again** (or: recovered his sight), **and he began following Him in the Way** (or: on the road).

CHAPTER 11

1. **Now when they are drawing near unto Jerusalem – [close] unto Bethphage and Bethany, facing toward the Mount of Olives – He is in process of dispatching two of His disciples**
2. **and says to them, "Be now going into the village down in the place opposite of you [two], and, set for goodness and success, upon immediately continuing on your way into it, you will proceed in finding a colt having been tied up** (or: bound; tethered) **upon which not even one human has yet sat** (= which has never been ridden). **Loose it at once and proceed in bringing it.**
3. **"And if anyone should say to you, 'What is this you are proceeding to do** (or: Why are you men in process of doing this)**?' say, 'The Lord** (The Master; perhaps = Yahweh; or: = the owner) **is presently having need of it, and He** (or: he), **set for goodness and success, is presently sending it off back here, right away.'"**

4. **So they went off and found a colt having been tied up** (tethered), **facing a door** (or: gate), **outside on the open street that goes both ways, and they engage in loosing it.**
5. **Then some of those standing there began saying to them, "What are you men doing in loosing the colt?"**
6. **Now they said to them accordingly as Jesus had told them, so they let them depart.**

7. **So they are progressively bringing the colt toward Jesus, then they, one after another, throw their cloaks or outer garments upon it, and He sat upon** (or: mounted) **it.**
8. **Next many folks at once spread their own cloaks and outer garment into the road** (path; way), **yet others began cutting or chopping soft foliage** (leafy twigs and boughs; reeds; field grasses) **from out of the trees, large bushes and fields, and continued spreading [them] into the road.**
9. **Then those progressively leading the way, as well as those continuing in following behind, began crying out and were repeatedly exclaiming,**
    "Hosanna [Aramaic word: Please save and deliver us now]**!" "Blessed and praised in having received the good word and message of ease and wellness [is] the One progressively coming in [the] Name of [the] Lord** (or: within [the] Owner's Name; = in union with Yahweh's Name [signifying His authority and character])**!"**
10.   **"Blessed and praised in having received the good word and message of ease and wellness [is] the progressively coming kingdom** (or: the continually advancing reign) **of our father David!" "Hosanna** (= O deliver us now) **within the midst of the highest [realms, or places]!"** (or: "O [You] within the heights above, please save us now!") [Ps. 118:25-26]

11. **So Jesus entered into Jerusalem, and then on, into the temple grounds** (or: courts). **And, upon glancing around upon everything** (or: after looking all about), **He went out into Bethany with the twelve, since the hour was already being late** (= evening had come).

12. **Then on the morrow** (or: the next day), **at their coming out, away from Bethany, He became hungry.**
13. **And from afar** (= in the distance) **having seen a fig tree having leaves, He went [to it], assuming He will be finding something in it** (or: on it). **But coming upon it, He found nothing except leaves, for it was not being the season of** (or: fitting situation for) **figs.**
    [note: on fig trees, a few first-fruit figs normally come before the tree fully leafs out, but the main harvest of figs comes later; *cf* Jer. 24:1-10; Hos. 9:10; Mic. 7:1]

14. Then, after considering, He said to it, "It is likely that no one may eat fruit out of (or: forth from) **you, on unto the Age." Now His disciples had been listening, and heard.**

15. So they proceeded on into Jerusalem, and upon entering into the temple courts and grounds, He started, one-by-one, to expel (drive out; cast forth) **those habitually selling, and those regularly buying or doing business as in a marketplace** (= the merchants and their customers) **within the midst of the temple courts and grounds. Then He overturned and upset the tables belonging to the money-changers as well as the seats** (chairs; benches) **of those constantly selling the doves** (or: pigeons). [cf Mt. 21:12; Zech. 14:21 in ESV or CVOT]
16. **Further, He was not allowing that anyone should carry merchandise, vessels, furniture or utensils through the midst of the temple courts or grounds** [e.g., to use that area as a short-cut between the shops and their houses; also: cf Targum Zech. 14:21]. Cf Jn. 2:15-16
17. **Next He began teaching, and kept on saying, "Has it not been written,**

>   'My house will continue being called a house of thoughts, and which are words,
>   toward having goodness, ease and well-being (or: of prayer) to, for and amidst all
>   the ethnic multitudes and nations (or: non-Jews; Gentiles; = pagans)'?** [Isa. 56.7]

"Yet you, yourselves, have made it 'a cave of robbers (or: a den of highwaymen, bandits, pirates and violent ones).'" [cf Jer. 7:11-15; a "prophecy of... destruction" – D. Chilton, p 231]

18. **Now the chief** (or: ranking) **priests and the scribes** (experts in the Law; theologians) **heard [about this] and began continuously trying to find how they could** (or: should) **destroy Him, for you see, they continued fearing Him, because all the crowd** (or: the entire throng) **was continually being struck from, and astounded** (astonished) **at, His teaching.**
19. **And then, when it became late [in the day]** (= evening), **they were proceeding out on their way, outside the city.**

20. **Then, while passing by early [in the morning], they noticed the fig tree being withered, having been dried out from [its] roots.**
21. **And so Peter, remembering** (it being called back up in his mind), **is then saying to Him, "Rabbi** (Teacher), **see the fig tree which You Yourself spoke a corresponding prayer to** (or: brought a vow down on; or: said a wish against; cursed) **has been dried out and is withered!"**
22. **Then from considering, Jesus proceeds saying to them, "Be constantly holding God's faith**

>   (or: Be habitually having trust which has its source in God; or, reading the genitive as in
>   apposition, with the verb as an indicative: You men continue possessing confidence
>   which is God)!   [*cf 1 Cor. 13:2]

23. **"Indeed, I am now saying** (or: I am truly saying now) **that whoever may say to, for or in this mountain*, 'Be picked up, and be cast** (thrown) **into the midst of the sea,' and may not be undecided or be divided in his discernment or judgment within his heart, but to the contrary, can** (or: may; would) **continuously trust and believe with confidence that what he is speaking is progressively occurring** (or: birthing itself; coming into existence), **it will proceed being [thus] for him** (or: by him; to him; in him; with him).
24. **"Because of this** (or: Through this) **I now say to you folks, All things** (Everything) **– as much or many as you are habitually thinking, speaking or acting toward having goodness, ease and well-being** (or: praying) **and repeatedly requesting – be constantly trusting and believing that you received or obtained [them], and it will continue existing for you folks** (proceed being in you people, with you folks as well as to or by you).
25. **"And whenever you are normally standing** (or: repeatedly take a stand), **being folks constantly thinking, speaking or acting with a view toward having goodness, ease and well-being** (or: being ones in the habit of praying), **continue habitually letting flow away whatever you folks are continuing to hold down on someone** (or: be repeatedly forgiving {abandoning [it]; sending [it] away} if you still have anything against anyone), **to the end that your Father, also – the One within the midst of the atmospheres** (or: in union with the heavens; centered in the skies) **– should let flow away** (would at once forgive and send away) **in you** (for you) **the effects of your falls to the side** (trespasses; offenses; transgressions)."

[note: vs. 26 omitted by Nestle-Aland, Westcott & Hort, Panin, Tasker – following Aleph, B, L, W, Δ & Ψ]:

[26.] [following A, (C, D), Θ & later MSS: **"So if you folks are not habitually forgiving and letting {things} flow away, neither will your Father – the One within the midst of the heavens – continue to forgive and send away the effects of your trespasses** (offenses).**"**]

27. **Later, they proceed coming again into Jerusalem. Then, during His progressively walking around within the midst of the temple grounds** (or: courts), **the chief** (or: ranking) **priests, the scribes** (theologians; experts in the Law; scholars) **and the elders** (or: older men) **proceed to be coming toward Him,**

28. **and they began saying to Him, "Within what authority** (right from being; privilege) **are you continuing to do** (or: perform) **these things and engage in these activities?"**

29. **So Jesus said to them, "I, Myself, will proceed also asking you men one word** (one question from reasoned thought; = one point). **You folks respond to me from your considered deliberation** (or: decided opinion), **and I will continue saying to you within what authority** (right from out of Being) **I continue doing these things and engaging in these activities:**

30. **"The immersion from John** (or: John's baptism)**: was it from out of heaven** (or: from [the] atmosphere), **or forth from humans, as a source? Give to me a decided reply** (or: a definite answer).**"**

31. **So they began reasoning with themselves in face-to-face dialogues, eventually saying, "If we should say, 'From out of heaven** (or: atmosphere),**' he will proceed in saying, 'Why** (Through what reasoning or situation), **then, did you men not trust him** (or: it) **or believe in him** (or: it)**?'**

32. **"But on the other hand, should we say, 'Forth from humans'?" They had been fearing the crowd, for everyone** (all [the] folks) **continued holding John as being real – that he had been a prophet** (or: progressively had it that John in reality was one having-light-ahead-of-time),

33. **and so, giving a considered response, they proceed saying to Jesus, "We have not seen** (have not perceived; have not been aware), **so we do not know."**

Then Jesus, with a decided reply, proceeds to say to them, "Neither am I, Myself, now laying out My thoughts in saying to you within what authority or right of Being I continue doing (performing; producing) **these things and engaging in these activities."**

CHAPTER 12

1. **And so He started** (or: begins) **to be speaking to them in parables** (illustrations from things cast or placed alongside for comparison)**:**

"A person (or: human) **planted a vineyard, then put** (or: places) **a fence around [it], dug a pit** (or: excavates a trough for a vat; [a place under the winepress where the extracted juice could be collected, or a hole to place a large press-vessel in, to steady it]) **and erected** (or: constructs; builds) **a tower. Next he leased it to tenant-farmers** (or: let it out to cultivators and vineyard keepers) **and traveled abroad.**

2. **"Now in the appropriate season he commissioned a slave and sent him off, as an emissary, to the tenant-farmers** (cultivators and vineyard keepers), **to the end that he could take** (or: receive) **some of the fruits of the vineyard from the tenant-cultivators.**

3. **"But taking hold of** (or: grabbing and seizing) **him, they scourged** (severely whipped and beat) **[him] and sent [him] off empty** (= empty-handed).

4. **"Now again he commissioned and sent off another slave to them, and they battered that one's head** [other MSS: they pelted with stones] **and they dishonored [him]** [other MSS: they sent {him} off in dishonor].

5. **"Then he commissioned and sent off another one, and that one they killed. And [there were] many other – some of whom [they] were, one after another, scourging** (whipping and beating), **on the one hand, yet others of whom, on the other hand, [they] kept on killing, one after another.**

6. **"He still had one person, and had kept on holding him: his beloved son. He then also commissioned and sent him off last, to them, collecting his thoughts and saying, 'They will proceed turning back on themselves to show deference to and be respecting my son.'**

7. **"Yet those tenant-farmers said to themselves and toward each other, 'This one is the heir** (the one receiving the allotment of the inheritance). **Come! Let us** (or: We should) **kill him, and the inheritance will proceed to be ours!'** [note: there was a law that the estate of a proselyte who dies and has no heir may be regarded as ownerless property which can be claimed by anyone, those presently occupying it having first choice – J. Jeremias]

8. **"So seizing [him], they at once killed him, then threw him out of [their] midst – outside the vineyard.** [comment: a prediction of His own treatment by the Judeans]

9. **"What will the owner of the vineyard proceed in doing? He will in succession be coming and then destroying the tenant-farmers! Next he will proceed to give the vineyard to other folks.** [comment: a prediction of A.D. 70]

10. **"Have you folks not yet read this Scripture? –**

> **'A Rock** (or: stone) **which the builders rejected and threw away after examining it, this one comes into being [the] Head of [the] corner** [note: could = the keystone, or, the cornerstone].

11. > **'This [head] came into existence from beside [the] Lord** [= Yahweh], **and He** (or: it) **is Wonderful** (or: marvelous; remarkable; or: Amazing) **in our eyes'?"** [Ps. 118:22-23]

12. **So they further continued seeking [a way] to take a strong grasp of Him** (= to arrest Him), **for in this experience they knew that He said the parable directing it toward them – and yet they were afraid of the crowd. Then, abandoning Him, they went off.**

13. **Next they commissioned some of the Pharisees and the Herodians** (members of Herod's political party) **and sent them off to Him so that they might catch** (or: trap, as in hunting or fishing) **Him by a word** (or: in a question; with an argument; by some verbal snare; in [His] message).

14. **On arrival, they proceeded to say to Him, "O teacher, we have seen and thus now know that you are constantly genuine** (habitually exist being real and true [perhaps here: = truthful]) **and [that] it is not a care or concern for you about anyone, for you are not continually looking into [the] face of humans**

> (here, may = not looking at men's outward appearance or being unduly influenced by man-made prestige; or: not showing consideration for people; or: not concerned for what response you get from mankind), **but to the contrary, [your eyes are] upon truth. You habitually teach God's way** (the path whose source is God [= the path of life which He directs]; the road of God [= the road He takes]). **[Tell us,] is it permitted, from [our current] existence, to give [the] poll tax to Caesar, or not?**

15. **"Should** (or: May) **we give** (= pay), **or should** (or: may) **we not give?"**

Now He, having seen and perceived, and thus now knowing their close inspection of the Scriptures and attention to details (or: their perverse scholarship and hyper-criticism; their discernment from a low position), **said to them, "Why do you men continue putting Me to the test** (or: continually trying to examine me)? **Bring Me a denarius** (a Roman silver coin) **so that I can see [it]." So they brought it.**

16. **He then says to them, "Whose [is] this image and inscription?" So they said to Him, "Caesar's."**

17. **So Jesus said, "Give back to Caesar what belongs to Caesar** (or: Pay off to Caesar the things that come from Caesar), **and to God what comes from and belongs to God." And they began marveling** (being amazed and astounded) **at Him** (or: upon who He is, and His ability in responding). [comment: "This story could have been important as a differentiator between the budding revolt and the Yeshua community" – Derek Leman]

18. **Now progressively approaching Him are [some] Sadducees – folks who normally say that there is to be no resurrection – and they began asking** (or: questioning) **Him, saying,**

19. **"O teacher, Moses wrote** (or: writes) **to us that,**

> **'If anyone's brother should die, and should leave-down-behind a widow** (or: wife) **and yet should not leave a child remaining, that his brother should receive the widow and take her as a wife and then should cause a seed** (= offspring; a posterity) **to rise up out [of their union] for** (or: to) **his brother.'** [Deut. 25:5-6]

20. **"There were seven brothers, and the first took a wife and, upon dying, leaves no seed** (offspring).
21. **"Next the second one took** (or: received) **her and then he died, leaving-down no seed, and the third similarly.**
22. **"So the seven also received** (took; got) **her and yet left behind no seed. Last of them all, the woman also died.**
23. **"In the resurrection, then, whenever they may be rising** (or: standing) **up, of which of them will she continue being a wife – you see, the seven had** (possessed) **her as a wife?"**

24. **Jesus affirmed to them, "Are you folks not, therefore** (for this reason), **constantly deceived and led astray, having not seen, perceived, and thus not knowing or being acquainted with the Scriptures – nor yet God's power** (or: the ability of God)**?**
25. **"For whenever they can be standing up again** (or: should be rising up) **from out of the midst of dead ones, men neither continue marrying** (taking wives), **nor [are women] continuing being given in marriage, but to the contrary, they continue being** (or: constantly exist being), **as it were, agents – within the atmospheres** (or: like messengers in the midst of the heavens; or: as folks with the message, centered in the skies)**!**
>   [comment: this may be foreshadowing the new arrangement where women are no longer "given" in marriage, but are equal, everyone being God's agents; cf Acts 23:8]
26. **"But concerning** (or: about) **the dead folks – that they are continually** (or: constantly; habitually; progressively; repeatedly) **being aroused and raised up – did** (or: do) **you folks not read within the scroll of Moses, at the thornbush, how God spoke to him, saying,**
>   **'I [am] the God of Abraham, as well as Isaac's God and Jacob's God'?** [Ex. 3:6]
27. **"He is not a God of dead folks, but to the contrary, of continuously living ones. You men are continuing much deceived, habitually wandering far astray** (= missing the point)**."**

28. **Now while approaching, one of the scribes** (experts in the Law; Torah interpreters; scholars; theologians), **hearing their discussing and questioning together [and] seeing** (perceiving) **that He beautifully gave a discerning answer to them, made inquiry upon Him, "Which and of what sort is [the] foremost** (= most important) **implanted goal** (impartation of the finished product within; inward directive) **of them all?"**
29. **So Jesus gave a decided reply to him, "Foremost** (= Most important) **is,**
>   **'Be habitually listening and hearing [and, thus, obeying], O Israel, [the] LORD [=** Yahweh] **[is] our God. [The] LORD** [Yahweh] **is** (continually exists being) **one**
>   (or: [The] LORD our God is one LORD). [note: the *Sh'ma*]
30.   **'And so, you folks will continue loving** (fully giving yourselves to; urging toward reunion with) **[the] LORD [=** Yahweh] **your God from out of the midst of your whole heart** (core feelings; seat of emotions), **and from out of the midst of your whole soul** (or: inner self-life; person; consciousness), **and from out of the midst of your whole intellect** (throughout the midst of your entire comprehension and full mental ability), **and from out of the midst of your whole strength.'** [Deut. 6:4-5]
31. **"[The] second one [is] the same** [or, with other MSS: And {the} second one [is] like this one],
>   **'You folks will continue loving** (participating in; unrestrictedly seeking union with) **your near-one** (or: neighbor; associate) **as he were** (or: like) **yourself.'** [Lev. 19:18]
There is no other investment with authorization (implanted goal; impartation of the finished product within; inward directive) **greater than these!"**

32. **The scribe** (scholar) **said to Him, "Teacher, in truth you spoke beautifully** (= you gave a fine answer)**, that He is one and there is no other more than** (or: besides) **Him.**
33. **"And this 'to be constantly loving Him' from a whole heart and from the whole understanding, even out of the whole strength, and then to be habitually loving** (seeing with unambiguous acceptance) **the near-one** (neighbor; associate) **as he were** (or: like) **oneself – it is excessively more than the effect of all of the whole burnt-offerings and sacrifices."**

34. **Then Jesus, seeing and perceiving him, that he responded intelligently from considered discernment, said to him, "You are** (exist being) **not far from God's reign** (the sovereign influence, activity and kingdom of and from God)**."
And so no one any longer continued daring to ask Him a question.**

35. **Then, in giving a considered response while continuing in teaching within the temple courts** (or: grounds), **Jesus began to say, "How are the scribes** (scholars; theologians) **normally saying that the Christ** (the Anointed One; = the Messiah) **is David's son** (or: a son of David; = a descendant of David)**?**
36. **"David, himself** (or: This same David), **within the midst of the Set-apart Breath-effect** (or: in union with the Holy Spirit; centered in the Sacred Attitude) **said,**
> **'The LORD** [= Yahweh] **said to my Lord** (Master), **"Continue sitting at My right, until when I should place** (or: put) **Your enemies down under Your feet** [other MSS: {as} a foot-stool for Your feet]**.'"** [Ps. 110:1]
37. **"David himself** (or: This very David) **keeps terming Him 'Lord'** ('Master')**; so from where** (from what source) **is He his son?"**
And the large crowd continued listening to Him with pleasure (or: delight).

38. **Then within His teaching He went on to say, "Be constantly noting** (looking out for; observing and considering; wary of) **the scribes** (scholars and theologians) **– those continually wanting to be walking around in robes and [desiring] greetings within the marketplaces,**
39. **"as well as front seats** (= places of honor) **in the synagogues, and prominent reclining places at dinners;**
40. **"those habitually eating-down** (devouring; consuming) **the houses of the widows and those constantly making long prayers** (words toward having ease and goodness) **as a 'front'** (for 'appearances;' as a pretense; for a pretext) **– these will continue taking to themselves and receiving a more excessive result of judgment** (effect from a decision)**!"**

41. **Later, sitting down opposite and across from but facing the [temple] treasury, He began watching how the crowd continued throwing** (casting; tossing) **copper coins into the treasury collection box, and [how] many rich folks, one after another, kept on throwing many [coins].**
42. **Now there is coming one woman – a destitute widow. She threw two small, thin copper coins** (leptons; mites) **– which is of very little value** (a quadrans; a farthing; = a value of a fraction of a Roman cent).
43. **So, calling His disciples to Himself, He said to them, "Truly** (Amen), **I now say to you men that this destitute widow threw more than all those continuously throwing [money] into the treasury collection box,**
44. **"for everyone threw from out of their exceeding excess** (or: surplus), **yet she, from out of her poverty** (need; want; deficiency; being behind) **threw [in] all, as much as she had – her entire livelihood** (the whole of what gives her a living)**."**

CHAPTER 13

1. **Later, while progressively making His way out of the temple grounds** (or: courts), **one of His disciples says to Him, "Teacher! See** (or: Look) **what kind of** (may = what magnificent) **stones and what sort of** (may = what wonderful or great) **buildings [these are]!"**
2. **However, upon considering, Jesus said to him, "You continue looking at these great buildings!** (or: Are you still observing these great buildings?) **Under no circumstances may be left here stone upon stone, which may not by all means be loosed down** (dislodged and torn down)**."**

3. **And then – [having come] into the Mount of Olives – during His continued sitting with the temple complex in view, Peter, Jacob** (James), **John and Andrew began inquiring of Him, privately,**

4. **"Tell us, when will these things proceed in being? And further, what [is/will be] the sign whenever all these things may be about to be progressively brought together and ended** (or: concluding; or: finished together and brought to their purposed goal – their intended end and destiny)**?"**

5. **So, giving a decided response, Jesus began progressively to lay it out for** (or: saying to) **them, "Be continuously observing, and see to it [that] no one can lead you folks astray** (or: should at some point deceive you people).

6. **"Many folks will continue coming [depending or basing their authority] upon My Name, repeatedly saying, 'I myself am'** (or: saying that, 'I, in contradistinction to others, am he [or: the one]') **– and they will successively be leading many folks astray** (or: deceiving many).

7. **"Yet, whenever you men may hear [the noise of] battles [nearby], as well as reports or rumors of wars [farther off], don't you folks be disturbed or alarmed, for it is necessary for it to happen, but nonetheless, [it is] not yet the end** (the goal; the consummation; the closing act; the finished product).

8. **"For ethnic group** (or: nation) **will proceed being raised** (or: roused) **up upon ethnic group** (or: nation), **and kingdom upon kingdom. There will successively be earthquakes** (or: shakings) **in one place after another. There will continue being famines and times of hunger. These things [are] a beginning of 'birth pains.'**

9. **"So as for YOU folks, continue looking to** (or: after) **yourselves, for people will repeatedly give you over unto sanhedrins** (the ruling councils, or courts, in the Jewish culture of that time), **as well as unto synagogues** (local religious and cultural centers). **[There] you folks will be repeatedly beaten and severely whipped** (or: lashed). **Also, you will continue being caused to make a stand upon [the demand] of governors** (rulers) **and kings – in consequence of involvement with Me – into the midst of a witness to, evidence for, and a testimony among, them.**

10. **"Further, it continues necessary for the good news** (the message of goodness, ease and well-being) **to be publicly proclaimed into the midst of all the ethnic multitudes** (unto all the Gentiles and the nations), **first.**

11. **"Then, whenever they may repeatedly bring or progressively lead you folks, while in process of giving you over, do not continue anxious or filled with worry beforehand as to what you folks should be speaking. On the contrary, whatever may be given to and in you within that hour, continue speaking this. You see, you folks are not the ones then speaking, but rather, [it is] the Set-apart Breath-effect** (or: Holy Spirit; Sacred Attitude).

12. **"And so, a brother will proceed giving over** (committing; delivering) **[his] brother into death, and a father [his] child. Also, children will progressively rise up upon** (or: repeatedly take a stand against) **parents and even will proceed putting them to death.**

13. **"Furthermore, you will continue being people constantly hated, repeatedly regarded with ill-will by everyone** (or: detached from all people) **– because of My Name. Yet, the one enduring and remaining under [these situations] on into the conclusion [of these things]** (or: unto the attainment of the goal; into the finished state of maturity; into the final act and end) **will continue being kept safe** (or: rescued; delivered; restored to health and wholeness; saved).

14. **"Now whenever you folks may see 'the abomination of the desolation'** (or: the detestable thing which results in a region becoming uninhabited, lonely and like a desert; or: the loathing and abhorrence which pertains to a wasted condition; [Dan. 9:27; 11:31; 12:11]) **standing where it is binding not [to stand]** (or: where it is not proper; where it must not) **– let the one reading continue directing his mind and using his intellect [here]** (= figure out what this means) **– then let those within the midst of Judea progressively take flight, and continue fleeing into the mountains** (or: hill country).

15. **"But now for the one upon the housetop: let him not descend** (step down), **neither let him enter to pick up anything from out of his house.**

16. **"And for the one [having gone] into the field, let him not return** (or: turn back) **unto the things [remaining] behind to pick up his cloak** (or: outer garment).

17. **"Yet woe to** (= it will be hard, perhaps even tragic, for) **the pregnant women, as well as for those still nursing [babies] in the midst of those days!**

18. **"So you folks be continuously thinking and praying toward having things go well, to the end that your flight** (escape) **may not occur** (happen) **in winter** (or: in the rainy season),
19. **"for it follows that those days will continue being pressure** (constricted squeezing; tribulation; affliction; oppression) **the sort of which, [even] such a kind as this, has not happened** (occurred), **and could in no way have come to be, from [the] beginning of [the] creation** (= the bringing of order from out of chaos; [comment: perhaps = the formation of Israel as a nation]) **which God framed and founded, until now!** [Joel 2:2; Dan. 12:1; Lu. 21:22]
20. **"And now – except [the] Lord** [= Christ or Yahweh] **cuts short** (maims; curtails; lops off; discounts) **the days – all flesh** (= people; [comment: likely a reference to Jerusalem and Judea in the 1st century AD]) **will not likely continue being kept safe or rescued. However, because of the chosen ones, whom He Himself picked out, He cuts short** (curtails) **the days.**

21. **"Then, at THAT time, if anyone among YOU folks should say** (or: if someone would say to You people), **'Look! Here [is] the Christ** (the Anointed One; or: the Anointing; or: = the Messiah)! **Or See, there [He is]!' – be neither trusting nor believing [him or her].**
22. **"You see, false 'Christs'*** (false anointed ones; counterfeit anointings) **and false prophets will continue being roused and raised up** (perhaps = come to prominence) **and they will be repeatedly providing signs and miracles** (wonders; portents) **[aiming] toward the accomplishment of leading-astray – if [they are] able – the chosen ones** (or: with a view to the situation for the selected and picked-out folks to wander off [the path] – since [it is] possible and [they are] having power). [*cf Josephus*: Menaham, the Zealot leader or John of Gischala]
23. **"So YOU people continue looking and keep on taking note** (= be on your guard). **I have foretold everything to you** (or: I have declared all things for you beforehand).

24. **"But further, after that pressure** (tribulation; stress; affliction) **within those days,**
    'The sun will be progressively darkened, and the moon will not continue giving her radiance, [comment: figure of the temple and the Jewish leadership; *cf* Gen. 37:9-10]
25. **'then the stars will proceed falling, one after another, from out of the heaven** (or: the sky), **and those powers within the heavens** (or: skies; atmospheres) **will be repeatedly shaken.'** [Isa. 13:10; 34:4; Ezk. 32:7; Joel 2:10; 3:4; 4:15; Hag. 2:6, 21]
26. **"Then, at that time, THEY will proceed seeing the Son of the Man** (son of the human; the Human Being) **progressively coming within the midst of clouds, with much power and a manifestation which incites praise** (glory; an assumed appearance). [Dan. 7:13-14]
27. **"Also, at that time, He will proceed to commission and send off** (cause to function as representatives) **His agents** (with other MSS: the messengers; **the folks with the message**) **and He will proceed completely gathering together** (convening; fully leading together; or: assembling-upon) **His chosen ones from out of the four winds – from the extremity of the Land** (= Judea, or Palestine; or: the territory; or: the earth) **to the extent of the extremity of [the] atmosphere** (or: the edge of [the] sky; or: the high point of heaven).

28. **"Now, learn the parable** (or: the illustration) **from the fig tree: whenever its young branch** (or: shoot) **should become tender** (soft and pliable) **and should progressively grow and sprout out the leaves, by experience you normally know that the summer is near at hand.**
29. **"Thus also, whenever YOU folks, yourselves, should see these things progressively occurring** (happening; coming into existence), **YOU will continue knowing from experience that it** (or: He) **progresses to be at hand – upon** (or: at) **the [city?] gates** (or: doors; entrances)!
30. **"Truly, I am now saying to you folks that THIS generation may under no circumstances pass on by until which [time; situation] ALL these things would come to be** (occur; happen; be birthed).
31. **"The heaven and the earth** (or: The sky and the land) **will progressively pass on by, yet My words** (or: thoughts and ideas; messages) **will under no circumstances pass on by.**
32. **"Now about** (concerning) **that day or the hour, no one has seen, nor knows – neither the agents in the midst of [the] atmosphere** (or: messengers within heaven; folks with the message, centered on the sky), **nor the Son – except the Father.**
33. **"Continue looking, observing, taking note – and be on your guard! Be constantly awake, watchful and alert! Be habitually thinking, speaking and acting with a view to**

having goodness, ease and well-being (or: Be continuously praying)! **You see, YOU folks have not seen and are thus unaware of when it is the appointed season** (or: the fitting situation; the *kairos*; the fertile moment).

34. **"[It is] like a person** (human), **a traveler** (one who journeys away from home and country), **leaving his home and giving the authority to his slaves – to each one his work – and imparts a directed goal in the gatekeeper** (or: to the doorkeeper; for the person in charge of the entry) **that HE should be constantly watchful and alert** (or: vigilant).

35. **"Therefore YOU people continue being watchful and alert, because you have not seen and thus you folks are unaware of when 'the Lord of the House'** (or: = the 'Owner/Master of the [Temple]') **is proceeding to come – whether [at] evening, or midnight, or [at] the crowing of the rooster, or early in the morning.** [comment: all describing times on a DAY of visitation]

36. **"Coming suddenly and unexpectedly, may He not find YOU folks continuing** (or: by habit) **fast asleep!**

37. **"Now what I am now saying to YOU PEOPLE, I continue saying for everyone** (to all), **'YOU folks continue being watchful and alert** (or: vigilant)**'!"**

CHAPTER 14

1. **Now the** [Feasts, or, festivals, of] **Passover and [of] the Unleavened Bread were two days off** (or: after two days), **and the chief** (or: ranking) **priests and scribes** (scholars and theologians of the Law) **were still seeking** (or: continuing in trying to find) **how they could kill Him off, [after] seizing [Him] in a trap using some kind of crafty device as bait.**

2. **You see, they kept on saying, "Not within the Feast** (or: festival; may = in the presence of the festival crowd), **lest at any time there will proceed being an uproar of the people** (or: a riot from the people)**."**

3. **And during His being in Bethany at the house of Simon the leper, while His lying down [at a meal] was continuing on, a woman came with** (having and continuing in holding) **an alabaster [case, or, vase] of perfumed ointment which was a pure and unadulterated extract from the roots of the spikenard plant** [note: native to India; may = lavender] **– very expensive. Upon crushing the alabaster [vase; case], she poured [its contents] down upon His head.**

4. **But there were some people being increasingly annoyed, to themselves** (or: Now certain folks continued expressing resentment and pained displeasure among themselves) **and kept on saying, "Why** (or: Into what [purpose]) **has this loss and destruction of the perfumed ointment taken place?**

5. **"Because it was being possible for this perfumed ointment to be sold for over three hundred denarii** (more than a year's wages)**... and to be given to the destitute** (poor folks)**!"** **And so they began, as it were, inwardly snorting** (perhaps: snarling) **and proceeded turning their fury and fretted agitation on her.**

6. **But Jesus said, "You men let her alone and let her flow [with this]** (or: Leave her)! **Why do you continue presenting her with [verbal] beatings? She performs a beautiful deed** (or: courtesy), **centered on Me** (or: She works a fine and ideal work within, and in union with, Me).

7. **"You see, you folks always continue having the destitute** (poor folks) **with yourselves, and whenever you may be in the habit of purposing** (wanting; intending) **[it], you continue able at all times** (or: always) **to do well for** (to; with) **them. Yet you folks do not continue always having Me.**

8. **"What she possesses, she performs** (or: What she had, she used). **She undertakes, beforehand** (in anticipation), **to anoint My body with aromatic ointment, with a view to the preparation of [My] corpse for burial.**

9. **"Now truly I am saying to you folks, Wherever the good news** (the message of ease and well-being) **may be publicly proclaimed – [even] into the whole ordered system** (world; realm of the secular and the religious) **– this also which this woman does** (or: performed) **will continue being spoken [leading] into a memorial of her** (or: a means of remembering her)**."**

10. **Later, Judah** (Judas) **Iscariot – one of the twelve – went off to the chief** (or: ranking) **priests, to the end that he should** (or: could) **transfer, commend and give Him over to them.**

11. **Now the men hearing [this] rejoiced** (were delighted) **and promised to give him silver** (= coins). **So he kept on seeking how he could conveniently transfer Him** (or: give Him over).

[* *cf* Lev. 23:5-6]

12. **Now on the first day of the Unleavened Bread*** (= in the first of the seven days for eating unfermented "matzah"), **when they were by custom sacrificing the Passover [animal], His disciples proceed asking Him, "Where are You now intending** (wanting; willing) **[that] we – upon going off – will make [things] ready and prepare so that You can eat the passover?"**

13. **So He gives two of His disciples a mission and sends them off, and proceeds saying to them, "Be progressively off under [these instructions] into the city, and a person** (a human) **progressively carrying a small earthenware vessel** (jar; pitcher) **of water will be encountering** (or: proceed meeting) **you. Follow after him,**

14. **"And wherever he might enter, say to the householder** (master or head of the house; or: = owner) **that the Teacher now says, 'Where is My guest-room where I can** (or: may; would) **eat the Passover with My disciples?'**

15. **"Then he, himself, will proceed pointing out and showing you [two] a large room upstairs** (or: an upper room) **ready with furnishings spread, and there you make the necessary preparations for us."**

16. **So the disciples went out and came into the city and found [everything] just as He said to them, and they prepared the Passover.** [comment: prepare for the new Exodus – D. Leman]

17. **Later, with the arriving of evening, He proceeds coming with the twelve.**

18. **Then, at their continued lying back** (reclining) **and while still eating, Jesus said, "Truly** (or: Count on it), **I am now saying to you men that one [person] from among you** (or: from your [group]) **– the person presently** (or: normally) **eating with Me – will proceed transferring, committing, and giving Me over** (or: delivering Me and handing Me along; turning Me in)."

19. **They at once began to be pained, grieved, made sad and distressed, then to be one after another saying to Him, "Surely not I!"** [other MSS: "It is not I, is it, Rabbi?"]

20. **Yet, giving a decided reply, He said to them, "[It is] one of the twelve – the person repeatedly** (or: normally) **dipping [a morsel] into the common bowl with Me**

   (or: presently dipping [the bitter herbs; Concordant Text: {his} hand] into the same [literally: the one] deep dish simultaneously with Me {or: after Mine}),

21. **"because, [you see], the Son of the Man** (the son of the human; the Human Being) **is indeed progressively leading the way under** (or: is now going away), **just as** (or: accordingly as) **it has been written about** (or: concerning) **Him, yet [there is] disaster** (woe; calamity; or: Alas!) **to** (for; in) **THAT person** (human; man) **through whom the Son of the Man is being progressively transferred** (committed; delivered up; given over)! **It was being beautiful in and ideal for Him – if THAT person** (human) **had not been given birth** (or: were not born)!"

22. **And during their continued eating, Jesus, taking a loaf of bread [and] saying a good word** (or: expressing the goodness, ease and well-being of the Word; or: speaking a blessing), **breaks [it] and gives [it] to them, then said, "You men take** (or: grasp) **this. It is My body."** (or: "Get hold of and receive [it]. This is My body.")

23. **Then, taking a cup – while speaking of the goodness and well-being of grace, and expressing gratitude [for it] – He gave [it] to them and ALL the men drank from out of it.**

24. **Then He said to them, "This is My blood pertaining to The Arrangement** (or: of the covenant; or: which is the will and testament; [with other MSS: This is My blood which is the source of the qualitatively New, Different and Innovative Covenant]) **– the [blood] being now progressively poured, scattered and diffused out over** [other MSS: around] **many people**

   (or: "This exists being My blood constantly being poured out over many folks – which is arrangement, and the covenant;

   or: This blood, in being presently poured out concerning [the situation and condition] of many people, continues being the arrangement from Me.")

25. **"Truly (Amen), I am now laying out my thoughts and saying to you that no longer, under any circumstances, can I** (may I; would I; should I) **drink from out of the product of** (birth-result, yield and offspring from) **the grapevine – until that day, whenever I can drink it**

(or: constantly drink it) **new in quality and kind, within God's reign as King** (or: in the midst of the kingdom of God; in union with God's sovereign activities, influence and way of doing things)."

26. **And after singing a hymn** (perhaps = singing the Hallel*; or: chanting a psalm), **they went out into the Mount of Olives.** [*perhaps: from Pss. 113-118 – Derek Leman]

27. **Then Jesus is laying out His thoughts and saying to them, "All you men will proceed being ensnared by the bait and caught in the trap, and thus stumble in your walk** [other MSS add: in union with Me, in the midst of this night], **because it has been written,**

> **'I will proceed to strike** (smite; hit) **the Shepherd, and the sheep will continue being thoroughly scattered and dispersed throughout.'** [Zech. 13:7; cf 50, below; Acts 8:1]

28. **"But nonetheless, after the [situation, or arrangement, or accomplishment for] Me to be aroused and raised up, I will proceed going ahead of you folks into Galilee."**

29. **Yet Peter affirms to Him, "Even if everyone [else] will proceed being ensnared and caught or made to stumble, still – nevertheless – I myself [will] not** (or: but, not I)!"

30. **So Jesus then says to him, "Truly (Amen), I am now saying to you that today – in this night, before a rooster** (cock) **crows twice – you, yourself, from a stance of contradiction and refusal will proceed utterly denying, disowning and renouncing Me, three times."**

31. **Yet Peter kept on speaking from excessive insistence, "More certainly, rather, if ever it may progress to where it is necessary to die for or with You, under no circumstances will I be utterly denying or renouncing You!" Now everyone began saying similarly, as well.**

32. **They later continued going into a small designated spot** (or: landed property; estate; freehold), **the name of which [is] Gethsemane*, and He is then saying to His disciples, "Sit down here while I may be praying** (or: until I can speak [to God] with a view toward having things be, or go, well)." [* Gethsemane means "oil press"]

33. **Then He proceeded in taking Peter, Jacob (James) and John aside** (or: along) **with Him and He began to be increasingly affected from out of a stunning sense of extreme awe and terrifying astonishment, and to be progressively depressed and sorely troubled with distress.** [cf Jn. 12:27; Pss. 42:11; 55:1-8]

34. **And so He then is saying to them, "My soul** (consciousness) **is encompassed with pain, grief and exceeding sorrow – to the point of death! Remain here and continue alert and watchful."**

35. **Then going forward a little distance, He was repeatedly falling upon the ground, and kept on praying with a view toward having things go well – to the end that, if it exists being possible, The Hour might pass by** (or: go to the side and divert) **from Him.**

36. **And He went on to say, "Abba** (= Dad; Papa) **– O Father – all things [are] possible for** (to; with; in; by) **You! Carry this Cup away from Me! But to the contrary** (or: Nevertheless) **not what I Myself am now wanting** (or: continue wishing; am repeatedly willing), **but rather and further, what You [are; want; will]!"**

37. **Later He proceeds coming and is then finding them down continuing fast asleep, so He then says to Peter, "Simon, are you continuing down fast asleep? Do you not have strength to continue staying alert and watchful [for] one hour?**

38. **"You men be constantly alert and watchful, and continue praying with a view toward having things go well – to the end that you folks will not continue coming** (or: going) **into a test** (or: a trial; an ordeal). **Indeed, the spirit** (the Breath-effect; or: the attitude) **[is] eager** (rushing ahead with passion), **yet the flesh** (= the estranged human nature; the alienated self; the person who has been molded and dominated by the System; [comment: = the old covenant, the Law that had formed them]) **[is] weak** (without strength and powerless; frail and infirm)."

39. **And then again, going off, He prayed, saying the very same word** (message, thought; idea; expression).

40. **Then, coming again, He found them down continuing fast asleep, for their eyes continued in being weighed down. And they did not know what reasoned response to give to Him.**

41. **And He repeats His coming, the third [time], and so is saying to them, "Are you men continuing in being down sleeping and resting up [for] the rest** (or: the remainder) **[of the**

night]? It [i.e., the hour] **continues holding off** (= it remains distant; perhaps: = the night is dragging on; from commercial usage of the phrase: He now has full payment from [them])... **The hour comes** (or: came). **Look, and consider** (See, and understand), **the Son of the Man** (the human son) **is being progressively given over into the hand of the sinners** (of the ones failing to hit the target; of the deviants missing the point; of those failing and making mistakes).

42. "**Now be wakened and aroused, and proceed to get up! We should lead the way, let us go! Look! The man handing** (or: transferring) **Me over has approached and is now at hand.**"

43. **Then set for goodness, all of a sudden while He was still speaking, Judah** (Judas) **Iscariot – one of the twelve – is presently coming to be at His side, and with him [there is] a crowd with swords and wooden weapons** [i.e., clubs or staffs], **[sent] from the chief priests, the scribes** (scholars; theologians; professional Torah teachers) **and the elders** [i.e., sent from a committee of the Sanhedrin].

44. **Now the man commending, transmitting, committing and handing Him over had given to them a prearranged** (or: agreed-upon) **signal, saying, "Whomever I should kiss** (show the outward expression of a greeting as a friend), **He it is. At once seize Him with a strong hold and proceed securely leading [Him] away.**"

45. **So upon coming set for goodness, after immediately approaching Him he is saying, "Rabbi!" Then he affectionately kissed** (or: = gave a prolonged kiss to) **Him.**

46. **Now those men thrust their hands upon Him and strongly seized Him.**

47. **However, a certain one of those that had been standing by** (i.e., beside [Him]), **upon drawing [his] sword, struck the slave of the chief priest and cuts away a little [portion of] his ear** [other MSS read: took off his ear].

48. **And yet Jesus, giving a decided response, said to them, "Do you men come out with swords and wooden weapons as upon a bandit** (highwayman; robber; or: a rebel; an insurrectionist; = a Zealot) **to arrest and apprehend Me?**

49. "**Day after day I was there facing you folks within the temple courts and grounds, repeatedly teaching – and you did not seize Me. Nevertheless, so that the Scriptures can** (or: may; would) **be fulfilled...**"

50. **And then, abandoning** (deserting) **Him, they** (= His disciples) **all fled.**

51. **Now a certain young man, having thrown** (or: loosely wrapped) **a fine linen sheet around [his] naked body, had been following-on together with Him and they kept on trying to grab a strong hold of him, so as to seize him.**

52. **But he, leaving the fine linen sheet behind to drop down** (or, perhaps: in their hands), **fled naked.**

53. **And they** [i.e., the armed crowd] **led Jesus off toward the chief priest. Then all the chief** (or: ranking) **priests – as well as the elders and the scribes** (scholars) **– one by one proceeded in assembling together.**

54. **Now Peter followed Him at a distance, until [having come] inside as far as [entering] into the uncovered courtyard of the chief priest, so he was continuing on there, sitting down together with the house attendants** (the [chief priest's] subordinates) **and continuing warming himself, facing toward the [fire; house] light.**

55. **Meanwhile the chief priests and the whole Sanhedrin** (the ruling council) **– looking for evidence against Jesus in order to issue a death sentence [on] Him – kept on trying to find a witness [to bring testimony or evidence] corresponding to and down on** (= against) **Jesus, but they were not finding [any].**

56. **You see, many kept on giving false testimonies** (or: evidence) **down on** (or: against) **Him, and yet the stories** (testimonies) **were not being consistent** (alike; equal; = in agreement).

57. **Further, certain folks standing up one after another were telling false stories in relation to, but down against, Him, in turn saying,**

58. "**We, ourselves, heard Him saying, 'I myself will proceed loosing-down and destroying this hand-made temple sanctuary** (the inner shrine), **and through the midst of** (or: during) **three days I will proceed building** (constructing) **another house not made with hands.'**"

59. **And yet neither, in this way, was their testimony** (or: story) **consistent** (= in agreement).

60. Then, rising up into the midst [of the group] and taking a stand, the chief priest questioned Jesus, going on to say, "Are you continuing to give a definite response to nothing (or: not to make a decided response to anything)? What (or: Why) are these folks repeatedly testifying down against you?"

61. Yet He continued silent and from considered decision did not respond anything. Again, the chief priest continued inquiring of Him and proceeds saying to Him, "Are you the Christ (the Anointed One; = the Messiah), the son of the Blessed One?"

62. Now Jesus said, "I am (or: I, Myself, am [He]); or: As for Me, am I?; or: Am I, indeed?; [some later MSS and quotes by Origen, read: You are saying that I am])! And furthermore, you men will (or: So will you folks) proceed seeing the Son of the Man (or: human's son; Human Being) by habit (or: continue) sitting at (or: forth from the midst of) [the] right [hand; section] of the Power, and progressively (or: repeatedly; as by habit) coming (or: coming and going) with the clouds of the atmosphere (or: the sky; the heaven)!" [Dan. 7:13; Ps. 110:1]

63. But at this the chief priest, ripping and tearing his inner garments (tunics; clothes), is then saying, "What need of witness or evidence do we still continue having?

64. "[other MSS add: Look!] You men hear (or: heard) the blasphemy (the abusive talk [before God]; this villainous speech; the harm-averring hindering of light; the injurious slander)! How is it now appearing to you folks (or: What continues evident to you; = What do you think of this)?" So they all made a decision down against Him (or: corresponding to pattern, evaluated and condemned Him) to be held fast within (under the control of; thus = liable to or deserving of) death.

65. Then some started to repeatedly spit on Him and then proceeded to put a covering around His face [so as to blindfold Him]. Next they continued to repeatedly beat Him with their fists all the while saying to Him, "Prophesy!" And [with] slaps (or: blows with a rod), the subordinates (deputies; court guards) took Him.

66. Now during Peter's being below within the courtyard, one of the servant girls (or: maids) of the chief priest is then coming,

67. and, seeing Peter continuing to warm himself, while looking straight at him is saying, "You, too, were with the Nazarene, Jesus!"

68. Yet he contradicts and denies (or: says, "No"; or: disowned; renounced) [it], by saying, "I have neither seen nor do I know [Him] – nor do I even understand now what you yourself are presently saying! (or: I neither know nor understand what you are saying {= meaning}; or: I neither know nor am acquainted with him. What do you mean?)" So he went forth outside into the forecourt (vestibule; entranceway). And then a rooster (cock) crows!

69. But then the servant girl (maid), seeing him [there], started to go on saying again to those that had been standing by, "This fellow is one from their group (or: one of them)!"

70. Yet he again began contradicting, denying and continued renouncing [it]. Then, after a little [while; time], those that had been standing by again began saying to Peter, "You really (certainly; truly) are one from their group, for you are a Galilean, also [other MSS add: and your speech is alike]!"

71. Now he started to be repeatedly speaking as though making an offering (or: cursing; or: anathematizing) and to continue swearing with an oath, "I have not seen nor do I know the person (the man; the human) of whom you folks continue speaking!"

72. And immediately a rooster (cock) crowed a second [time], and Peter recalled the effect which flowed from the saying (gush-effect in the declaration), just as Jesus said to him, "Before a rooster is to crow twice, you will utterly deny and disown Me three times." Then, casting [his thoughts and attention] upon [this], he began weeping
> (or: on setting [himself] on [the situation] he continued in lamenting, wailing and shedding tears; may = he broke down and cried; or: And then, throwing [himself] upon [the ground], he was crying; or: So, throwing [his mantle] upon [his head or himself], he was weeping).

CHAPTER 15

1. Then, set for a good position, as soon as it was dawn (or: early in the morning,) the chief (or: ranking) priests, upon forming (convening) a council (or: holding and conducting consultation; [other MSS: having prepared {= reached} a decision upon counsel]) with the

elders, the scribes (scholars; Torah specialists) and the whole Sanhedrin, [are] binding Jesus. They conducted [Him] away and turned (or: committed; transferred; delivered; gave) [Him] over to Pilate.

2. So Pilate asked Him, "You [spoken emphatically, perhaps with disbelief] are the king of the Judeans?" Now He, giving a considered and decided reply, is then saying to him, "You yourself are now saying [it] (or, may = If you say so; or: You [spoken emphatically] are presenting this thought and idea)." [cf Jn. 18:36]

3. Then the chief priests began bringing many charges and accusations against (or: down on) Him.

4. Yet Pilate continued with questioning Him again, saying, "Are you continuing giving no definite reply about anything? Consider how many charges and accusations they keep on bringing down on (or: against) you!"

5. But Jesus no longer made a response about anything – so that Pilate continued to be amazed (filled with wonder, astonishment and marvel).

6. Now corresponding to [the] festival (or: feast), he was customarily releasing to them one prisoner – whomever they had been requesting by petition.

7. And now there was the man being commonly called Bar-Abbas (the father's son) – being bound with the insurrectionists (insurgents; rebels; = a Zealot) who, themselves, had committed murder in the insurrection (or: the revolt; the rebellion).

8. So upon coming up, the crowd – shouting – started to be repeatedly requesting in accordance to what he was customarily always doing for them.

9. Yet Pilate put a discerning question to them, saying, "Are you folks presently intending (or: continuing in wanting) [that] I should release to you (or: set free for you people) 'the king of the Judeans'?"

10. You see, he had begun to be aware and continued recognizing from his personal experience that the chief (ranking) priests had turned (or: committed; transferred; delivered; gave) Him over because of envy and jealousy.

11. Now the chief priests stirred up and incited the crowd to the end that he would rather release to them (or: set free for them) Bar-Abbas (= "son of the father").

12. Yet Pilate again replied discerningly, continuing in speaking to them, "What, then, do you continue intending (or: are you presently wanting) [that] I should do [with; to] the fellow whom you folks continue calling 'the king of the Judeans'?"

13. Now those folks again made an outcry (or: shouted back), "Put him to death on a torture stake (or: Suspend him on a pole; Crucify him; Impale him) at once!"

14. But Pilate continued saying to them, "Why? What bad or worthless thing did he do?" Still they exceedingly made outcry, "Put him to death on a torture stake (or: Suspend him on a pole; Crucify him; Impale him)!"

15. So Pilate, wanting and intending to do that which was sufficient to satisfy the crowd, released to them (or: set free for them) Bar-Abbas, and – upon scourging (severely whipping) [Him] – turned (or: gave; transferred; committed; delivered) Jesus over so that He would be put to death on a torture stake (crucified).

16. Now the soldiers led Him away inside the courtyard – which is [part of the] Praetorium (i.e., the governor's headquarters, or palace) – and proceeded calling together the whole company of troops (squadron; battalion; detachment).

17. Then they proceed to clothe Him in a purple garment and, upon braiding (or: weaving) a thorny wreath, then proceed to put [it] on Him, around [His head – i.e., crowned Him].*

18. Next they started to repeatedly salute and greet Him, "Be constantly rejoicing (or: = Greetings and good day; or: Hail), O king of the Judeans!"*

19. They also began striking (hitting; beating) His head with a reed staff (or: cane rod) and kept on spitting on Him and, repeatedly kneeling, continued doing obeisance (bowing down; [pretending] worship)* to Him. [*Leman: Roman tradition in triumphal parades of prisoners]

20. And so, when they had ridiculed (made fun of; mocked) Him, they stripped the purple garment from Him and clothed Him with His own outer garments.

Then they are progressively leading Him out so that they could put Him on an execution stake (Hang Him on a pole; crucify Him). [*note: likely an eyewitness – R. Bauckham in Leman]

21. **A certain man – Simon* of Cyrene, the father of Alexander and Rufus – on his way coming from a field** (or: [the] countryside) **is continuing passing on by, and they proceed to compel his assistance** (to commandeer or conscript [him] into service) **to the end that he should pick up and carry His execution stake** (or: suspension-pole; cross).

22. **So they continue bringing Him [until they come] upon the place Golgotha, which is being normally translated and interpreted, "a place of a skull."**

23. **Then they began trying to give Him wine to drink which had been drugged with myrrh. But He did not take** (or: receive) **[it].** [Ps. 69:21]

24. **And so they continued in crucifying Him** (attaching Him to the execution stake; suspending Him from a pole). **Next they are proceeding to divide and distribute His outer garments, repeatedly casting a lot on them [to see] who would take what.** [Ps. 22:18]

25. **Now it was [the] third hour [of the day]** (= 9 A.M.) **when they crucified Him** (attached Him to the execution stake; suspended Him from a pole),

26. **and there was the inscription** (epigraph) **of the charge** (accusation) **brought against Him** (= identifying His crime), **having been written upon [the stake, or a placard]:**
    "THE KING of the JUDEANS."

27. **Furthermore, they continued the process of crucifixion** (hanging bodies) **by attaching two robbers [= Zealots] on stakes, together with Him – one on the right of Him and one on left.**

[vs. 28] [note: omitted by WH, Panin, Tasker, Nestle-Aland and Concordant, bracketed by Griesbach, but found in later MSS & included in the Received Text:
> And the Scripture is fulfilled, the one saying, "And He is being thought to be (considered or counted as) belonging with lawless men." *Cf* Lu. 22:37; Isa. 53:12b]

29. **Meanwhile people, as they continued passing by on their way, began repeatedly speaking abusively** (hurling insults; blaspheming; assessing villainy) **to and at Him, continuously shaking** (wagging; tossing) **their heads and repeatedly saying, "Ha** (or: Aha; Bah; Ooh)**! The one progressively loosing-down and destroying the inner sanctuary of the temple, and then progressively building [it] within three days!** [Ps. 22:7; Mk. 14:58; Jn. 2:19]

30. **"Immediately rescue** (save; deliver) **yourself by at once stepping down from the stake** (execution pole; cross)**!"**

31. **Likewise, the chief** (ranking) **priests with the scribes** (scholars; theologians), **also continuing in ridiculing** (making fun; mocking) **toward one another, kept on saying, "Other people he rescued** (saved, delivered and healed) **– himself he is not able** (has no power) **to rescue** (save; deliver)**!** [*cf Ps. 109:25; Heb. 12:3; 1 Pet. 2:23]

32. **"The 'Christ'! The 'King of Israel'! Let him step down now from the stake** (suspension/execution pole; cross) **so that we can see and may believe!"***
Even those having been attached to stakes (suspended on poles; crucified) **together with Him had been unjustifiably insulting and reproaching Him*** (or: charging Him with disgrace).

33. **Later, upon the coming of it being [the] sixth hour** (= noon), **darkness** (dimness and gloomy shadiness; obscurity) **came to be upon the whole land – until [the] ninth hour.**

34. **And at one point during the ninth hour, Jesus shouted in a loud voice,**
    > **"Eloi! Eloi! Lama [other MSS: Lema] sabachthani?"– which is normally being translated and interpreted, "My God! My God! Into what do You leave Me down within?"** (or: "Into what did You leave Me down to remain in union with?") [Ps. 22:1]

35. **Then, upon hearing, some of the folks that had been standing nearby began saying, "Look** (or: See; or: Consider)**! He is summoning Elijah!"**

36. **Now someone, running and soaking a sponge with wine vinegar** (or: sour wine that has a sharp taste) **[and] putting it around [the end] of a reed-staff, began trying to cause Him to drink** [Ps. 69:22], **while saying, "Let [him] be! We can see if Elijah is now coming to take him down."**

37. **But Jesus, letting flow a loud sound** (or: a great Voice), **breathes out** (or: expired; blows out [His] spirit; = died).

38. **And then the curtain** (or: veil) **of the inner sanctuary** ([divine] habitation) **of the temple was split** (torn; divided) **into two [pieces] – from above until below** (or: from top to bottom).

39. **Now the centurion** (Roman army officer in charge of 100 foot soldiers) **– who had been standing at the opposite side facing Him – upon seeing that He expired** (i.e., died; breathed

out His life breath) **this way, said, "Truly** (or: In reality; Certainly) **this man was God's Son** (or: a son of God!"

40. **But there were also women continuing in looking on from afar, among whom [were] also Miriam** (or: Mary), **the Magdalene** (or: from Magdala), **Mary the mother of Jacob** (or: James) **the younger** (or: the Little) **and of Yosi** (or: Joses), **as well as Salome**

41. **– those who had been following with** (accompanying) **Him and continued giving ministering service to Him when He was within the Galilee [district] – and many other women who had been walking up together with Him into Jerusalem.**

42. **Later, with it already coming to be late in the afternoon** (or: evening time), **since it was being a preparation [day] which is before a sabbath,**

43. **Joseph from Arimathea – a prominent and reputable counselor** (or: a member of the Council [the Sanhedrin]) **who showed good form, who himself also was habitually focusing and progressively moving toward receiving God's reign** (or: was constantly having a receptive, welcoming attitude toward the kingdom of God; was anticipating God's imperial rule) – **demonstrating courage, entered within, [going] to Pilate, and requested the body of Jesus.**

44. **Yet Pilate became amazed and wondered if He had already died. So, summoning the centurion to himself, he made inquiry upon him if He already died off.**

45. **So then, ascertaining [it] from the centurion, he granted** (freely gave) **the corpse to Joseph.**

46. **Then after buying some linen cloth from the marketplace, upon taking Him down he wrapped [Him] in the linen cloth and put Him within a memorial tomb which was one having been quarried from out of a rock-mass, then rolled a stone forward – upon the entrance** (opening; doorway) **of the memorial tomb.**

47. **Now Mary the Magdalene and Mary the [mother] of Yosi** (Joses) **continued watching and were noting where He had been put.**

CHAPTER 16

1. **So with the elapsing** (or: coming to be fully through) **of the sabbath, Mary the Magdalene, Mary the [mother] of Jacob** (James) **and Salome bought spices and oils which come from spices, to the end that upon coming, they could anoint** (or: besmear) **Him.**

2. **And very early, on one of the sabbaths** (or: in one of the sacred days of rest), **they continued approaching the memorial tomb with the rising of the sun.**

3. **And they began saying to each other, "Who will roll the stone away from out of the entrance of the memorial tomb for us?"**

4. **Then, upon looking up they continue gazing, noticing that the stone has been rolled back – for in fact it was tremendously large.**

5. **Next, upon entering into the memorial tomb, they saw a young man** (or: a fresh, new one [or: person?]) **continuing sitting down on [the places, or, furnishings] at the right, being a person having clothed himself with a bright, white, long flowing robe – and they were stunned from amazement.**

6. **Now he is then saying to them, "Stop being alarmed** (or: Don't continue being utterly amazed). **You are still looking for** (trying to find) **Jesus the Nazarene – the Man having been crucified** (attached to an execution stake; suspended from a pole). **He was aroused and raised up; He is not here. Look at** (or: See and consider) **the place where they put Him.**

7. **"But now, go and lead, under [this message]: say to the disciples – and** (or: even) **to Peter! – that He is progressively going ahead of you folks into the Galilee [area]. You will repeatedly see Him there, just as He told you people."**

8. **So coming out, they fled** (= ran away) **from the memorial tomb, for trembling and ecstasy** (a being put out of place and normal standing; a displacement of the mind) **continued holding them and [along the way] they said nothing to anyone, for they continued fearing** (being affected by reverential fear and respect).

    [Codices Aleph, B and other witnesses end Mark here; Codices A, C, D, L and W, along with later MSS and witnesses contain the following:]

9. **Now arising early in the morning, in the first [part] of [the] sabbath, He [later] appeared first to Mary the Magdalene, beside whom** (or: from the presence of whom) **He had thrown out seven demons** (Hellenistic concept and term: = animistic influences).

10. **That woman, upon going on her way, reported back to those being ones birthed to be** (or: having come to be; happening to have been) **with Him – folks continuously mourning** (expressing grief) **and repeatedly shedding tears.**

11. **At hearing that He continues living** (or: lives) **and was gazed upon** (observed) **by her, those folks were without faith** (distrusted; disbelieved).

12. **Yet after these things, He was displayed in clear light and manifested – in a different form – to two of their group, when they continued walking along, being on their way journeying into [the] country.**

13. **So those men, upon coming away, reported back to the rest, yet they were not trusting** (or: putting faith and belief) **in those men.**

14. **Now later on** (or: subsequently) **He was suddenly manifested in clear light to them – to the eleven, as they were continuing in reclining [at a meal]. Then He challenged their character in regard to their mistrust** (or: reproached their reputation of lacking faith) **and hardness** (or: roughness and dry condition) **of heart, because they did not put faith or trust in those attentively viewing Him as One having been aroused and now raised up from out of the midst of dead ones.**

15. **Then He said to them, "As you are journeying on your way** (or: As you are traveling) **into all the ordered system** (or: into the midst of all the aggregate of mankind: the world of religion, culture, government and secular society; the cosmos), **you men make a public proclamation of the good news** (or: herald the good message of ease and wellness) **to the entire creation** (or: in all the founded and civilized area that has been reclaimed from the wild).

16. **"The trusting and believing person – as well as one being immersed** (baptized) **– will continue being restored to health and wholeness** (be delivered, rescued, made safe, and returned to his original state and condition). **Yet the distrusting person** (the one being without faith; or: the faithless one) **will proceed being commensurately evaluated and correspondingly decided about** (or: be separated down according to the pattern; have a decision rendered against him; be condemned).

17. **"Now these signs will continue following along beside in** (or: by; with; for) **those trusting and believing: within and in union with My Name, they will be periodically casting out demons** (Hellenistic concept and term: = animistic influencess). **They will from time to time be speaking to new languages** (or: with, in and by strange, different, innovative tongues).

18. **"Further, they will progressively carry away and remove** (or: lift up) **serpents** [some MSS add: in or with {their} hands], **and if they should ever drink anything deadly it can** (or: may) **under no circumstances harm** (injure; hurt) **them. They will continue placing hands upon folks being without strength** (= sick people; disabled folks; infirm ones), **and they will progressively have [it] ideally** (or: will be possessing [themselves or situations] beautifully)."

19. **So then, after [times of] speaking with them, the Lord Jesus was taken back up again** (or: was received again) **into the midst of the atmosphere** (or: sky; heaven), **and sits** (or: sat down; = assumes the throne) **at God's right [side, or, hand].** [Ps. 110:1]

20. **Yet those men, in [their] going forth** (or: upon exiting [the area]), **made public proclamations of the Lord** (or: from the Lord; pertaining to the Lord) **everywhere – He continuously cooperating and working together, and repeatedly establishing** (setting on good footing) **the message** (the *Logos*; the Word; the thought; the idea; the conveyance of Meaning-bearing Information; the Flow of Information that is a Pattern-forming Influence) **through the consistently accompanying signs** (or: by means of the signs which continued attending as sequels).

[written circa A.D. 45-60 – Based on the critical analysis of John A.T. Robinson; Derek Leman notes from "Daily Portion," derek@TheHebrewNerd.com]

LUKE

CHAPTER 1

1. **Since it is admittedly true – and considering – that many people put their hand to and undertook to compile, collate and compose** (or: arrange back again and rehearse) **by** (or: for) **themselves a narrative that leads throughout the matters and facts** (the results and effects of events, practices, business, affairs and what has been done) **concerning the things having been brought to full measure** (or: having been fully accomplished) **among us,**
2. **just and correspondingly as the original** (the from [the] beginning) **eyewitnesses** (= personal examiners) **and assistants** (deputies and subordinates – "under-rowers," or, those under orders) **of the Word** (message; idea; Logos; Reason; thought; patterned flow, conveyance and transfer of Meaning-bearing Information) **gave, and transmit, [them] over to us** (or: pass along, commended and commit [them] among us),
3. **it seems [necessary; important; a good idea] also for** (or: to) **me – having followed alongside and accompanied closely from the earlier period – to write to** (or: for) **you, most excellent Theophilus** (or: most mighty friend and lover of God; or: O man most strongly loved of God), **all things consecutively** (or: point by point; systematically) **[and] accurately** (or: with details exact),
    > (or: – having from above {i.e., in descending order} intensively traced and investigated on all things – to write for you in logical order and with precise details {the course and movement}...),
4. **to the end that you can** (would; should; may) **fully know by experience and added insights about** (or: concerning) **the certainty** (the state of being secure from stumbling or falling; = reliability) **of the words** (ideas; informational messages; laid-out communications; = teachings) **which you were instructed** (orally resounded down into the ears so as to make the ears ring).

5. **Within the days of Herod, the king of Judea, there happened to be a certain priest, named Zechariah** (or: Zacharias) **– [a member] out of [the] daily [service division, or, routine section] of Abiah** (or: Abijah), **and his wife – her name [being] Elizabeth, a [descendent] from out of the daughters of Aaron.**
6. **Now both continued being** (or: were) **fair and equitable folks [who followed] the way pointed out in right and just relationships before** (in front of and in the sight of) **God, habitually going their way** (progressively journeying on) **within all the implanted goals** (impartations of the finished product within; inward directives) **and effects of equity** (or: results of just and rightwised dealings springing from right relationships) **whose source and origin is the Lord** [= Yahweh] (or: in union with all the Lord's [= Yahweh's] commandments as well as the results of being in the way pointed out) **[being] blameless** (or: un-blamable) **folks.**
7. **And yet, there was no child for them, corresponding to [the fact] that Elizabeth continued being infertile** (or: was sterile; barren) **and both were folks having walked forward, and were now being advanced, within their days** (= they were elderly).
8. **Now it occurred** (happened) **during the [situation for] him to be routinely performing the service** (acts; duties) **of a priest, in his arranged order and appointment of the daily [service division] within the presence of and facing before God,**
9. **[and] corresponding to and in accord with the custom of the priesthood** (or: the priestly functions, or office), **he obtained by lot the [duty] to burn incense, after entering into the [holy place] of the inner sanctuary of the Temple of the Lord** (= [Yahweh's] divine habitation).
10. **Also, during the hour of the incense offering** (the result of the burning of incense), **all the full capacity of the people normally praying was outside.**

11. **Now an agent of, and from, [the] Lord** (= Yahweh's messenger; [note: LXX uses *kurios* for Yahweh]), **standing to the right of the altar of incense, was seen by him,**
12. **and Zechariah** (or: Zacharias) **became troubled** (was made to shake and become unsettled) **– upon seeing – and fear fell upon him.**

13. **So the agent said to him, "Stop fearing** (or: Do not continue being afraid), **Zechariah** (or: Zacharias), **because your request in regard to your need was listened to – upon [its] entering into hearing – and so your wife, Elizabeth, will proceed in generating and giving birth to a son by and for you, and you will proceed calling his name 'John,'**

14. **"and he will continue being a joy and an extreme exultation to you** (or: and there will progressively be joy and exceeding elation for and with you), **and upon [the occasion of] his birth many people will progressively find joy and will continue rejoicing.**

15. **"You see, he will continue being great** (or: = important) **in the sight of** (or: before) **[the] Lord** [= Yahweh], **and he should under no circumstances drink wine or [other] strong drink** (= intoxicating beverage). **Also, he will be continuously filled with a set-apart breath-effect** (or: holy spirit; a separated and consecrated wind; a sacred Attitude) **still [not being] out from** (or: repeatedly filled, from [the] Holy Spirit, while yet from the midst of) **his mother's womb.**

16. **"Later, he will proceed turning many of the sons** (= people) **of Israel back upon [the] Lord** [= Yahweh] **their God.**

17. **"And so, he himself will continue advancing in His presence** (or: going forward in His sight) **– within and in union with a breath-effect** (or: wind) **and ability having the character and qualities of Elijah** (or: in association with Elijah's spirit and power; or: in an attitude and an ability which is Elijah [= God is Yah]) **– 'to turn back hearts of fathers upon children,'** [Mal. 3:23] **and stubborn folks** (or: incompliant ones; unpersuaded people) **in a thoughtful** (sensible; prudent) **frame of mind which has the characteristic qualities of fairness, equity, rightwised relationships, and justice which pertain to the Way pointed out: to prepare and make a people having been fully formed into vessels and utensils, as well as being completely furnished with, and supplied with equipment, by, for and in, [the] Lord** [= Yahweh]."

18. **And then Zechariah** (or: Zacharias) **said to the agent** (or: messenger), **"In association with** (or: According to; Down from) **what will I proceed in experientially knowing this for myself? You see, I myself am an old man** (aged; an elder) **and my wife [is] one having walked forward and [is] now being advanced within her days** (= she is elderly).

19. **And so, giving a decided response, the agent** (or: messenger) **says to him, "I, myself, am** (exist being) **Gabriel** [Hebrew = God is mighty; or: God's mighty One], **the one** (or: the person) **having been standing alongside in the sight and presence of God, and I was sent off as an emissary** (or: a representative; messenger; agent) **to speak to you and to declare these things to you as a message of good news and well-being.**

20. **"And now consider this! You will proceed being one continuing silent and unable to speak – until [the] day on which these things can be birthed** (or: should come to be) **– in an opposing response, concerning my words** (or: in return for the message from me) **which you do not trust or believe – [words] which will proceed being fulfilled** (progressively made full) **[as they are coming] into their fertile moment, appointed season and fitting situation."**

21. **Meanwhile, the people were continuing in keeping and eye open and directed forward, in watchful waiting and expectation for Zechariah. And so they began wondering in regard to the [situation] for him to be delayed** (caused to spend more time than usual) **within the midst of the inner sanctuary** (first chamber, or holy place, of the temple; or "divine habitation").

22. **Now upon coming out, he was unable to speak to them, and they fully realized** (or: recognized from this added experiential knowledge) **that he had seen a sight** (a vision; an appearance; = a theophany) **within the inner sanctuary. And through nods and gestures he, himself, was continuing in motioning, beckoning and making signs to them, and yet was remaining mute throughout [the episode].**

23. **Later, as the days of his public work and duties were fulfilled** (= completed), **it came to pass [that] he went off unto his house.**

24. **Now after these days** (= shortly afterwards; or: = following this) **Elizabeth, his wife, being together with [him] received so as to become pregnant** (or: conceived). **And so, she continued keeping herself secluded** (hidden and concealed on all sides) **[for] five months, repeatedly saying,**

25. **"[The] Lord** [= Yahweh] **has thus formed** (created; made; constructed; produced) **in me within [these] days** (or: This is the way [the] Lord has dealt with, and done for, me during [these] days) **in which He fixed His gaze and looked upon [me] to take away my humiliation and lack of public honor among people** (or: reproach in relation to humans)."

26. **Now during [her] sixth month, the agent Gabriel** [Hebrew = God's mighty One; or: God is mighty] **was sent off as an emissary** (sent away as an "apostle") **from God into a city, of the Galilee [district], which [is] named Nazareth,**
27. **to a virgin girl** (girl of marriageable age; unmarried woman) **having been engaged** (espoused; promised in marriage) **to an adult male named Joseph, from out of the house of David. And the name of the virgin girl [is] Mary** (or: Miriam).
28. **And so, after entering, he said to her** (or: upon coming in toward her, he says), **"Be constantly rejoicing** (note: also used as a greeting, can = Continuous joy to you; Shalom; Hi; Hello; Greetings), **O young lady having been favored and given grace** (acted upon to produce happiness and joy, which is granted as a favor)! **The Lord** [= Yahweh] **[is] with** (or: [continues being] in company with) **you** [other MSS add: you having been spoken well of and {are} blessed among women]."
29. **Yet she was thoroughly shaken** (deeply disturbed; completely agitated) **at the Word** (the Logos; the message and information; the thought and idea) **and began thoroughly reasoning and continued carefully considering what this sort of greeting might be** (= could mean).
30. **And so the agent** (messenger) **said to her, "Stop fearing** (or: Do not continue being afraid), **Mary** (Miriam), **for you see, you find** (or: found) **grace and joyful favor at God's side** (or: in the side of, and with, God).
31. **"And so, see and consider. You will proceed in yourself receiving together and conceiving within the midst of [your] womb, and then you will proceed giving birth to a Son, and you will continue calling His name, Jesus** [= Yahshua].
32. **"This One will proceed in being great** (or: a great One), **and He will continue being called 'Son of [the] Most High'** (or: a son of [the] Highest One), **and [the] Lord** [= Yahweh] **will proceed giving to Him the throne of David, His father** (= forefather; ancestor), [2 Sam. 7:13]
33. **"and He will continue reigning upon the house of Jacob – on into the ages. Furthermore, there will not proceed being an end of His reign** (or: a final act of His sovereign influence, or of the activity which is Him; or: a termination of the kingdom from Him)."
34. **But Mary** (or: Miriam) **said, to the agent** (messenger), **"How will this proceed in being, since I presently continue having no intimate, experiential knowledge with an adult male?"**
35. **Then, giving a decided response, the agent** (messenger) **says to her, "A set-apart** (or: holy) **breath-effect** (or: a consecrated wind; or: sacred spirit and attitude; [The] Holy Spirit) **will continue coming upon you, and a power** (ability; or: [the] Power) **from** (or: which pertains to; or: which has the qualities and characteristics of; or: which is) **[the] Most High will continue casting a shadow upon you. For that reason, also, the Set-apart One** (or: holy thing) **being progressively generated and born will continue being called God's Son** (or: a son of God; 'Son of God'; a son from God).
36. **"Now see, and consider. Elizabeth, your relative** (kinswoman), **has also herself received together and has conceived a son in her old age – and this is a sixth month for her: the woman being normally** (or: repeatedly) **called infertile** (barren)!
37. **"because at God's side** (or: from beside God) **every declaration** (gush-effect; result of the flow; saying) **will not proceed being impossible!"**
> (or: because in God's presence – *coram Deo* – nothing [of] every effect of *rhema* speaking will continue being void of power or ability!"
> or: for with God, no declaration [at] all will progress being a powerless impossibility!")
38. **So Mary** (or: Miriam) **said, "See and consider the slave girl that belongs to [the] Lord** [= Yahweh]. **May He birth Himself** (or: May it of itself come to be and happen) **down from** (or: in accord with; corresponding to; in the sphere of) **your declaration** (saying; or: the effect of your gushing flow)." **And then the agent** (messenger) **went away from her.**

39. **Now during these days, Mary** (Miriam), **after rising, went her way with haste and urgency** (or: eagerness) **into the hill country** (or: mountainous region) **– into a town of Judah,**

40. **and [there] she entered into the house of Zechariah** (or: Zacharias) **and then greeted and embraced Elizabeth.**

41. **And then it happened – as Elizabeth heard the greeting of Mary** (from Miriam) **– the baby** (fetus) **leaped, as for joy, within the midst of her womb, and Elizabeth was filled [with] a set-apart Breath-effect** (or: a holy spirit; or: [the] Holy Spirit; [the] sacred Attitude),

42. **and she exclaimed with a loud shout** (or: uttered up in a great voice), **and said, "You [are] a woman having been spoken well to and having been blessed among women! The fruit of your womb is also One having been spoken well to, having been blessed!**

43. **"And so from what place [comes] this [occasion] to** (for: with) **me, that the mother of my Lord** (or: from my Master) **should come to me** (or: would come face-to-face-with *me*)**?**

44. **"For look and consider! As the sound of your greeting was birthed into my ears, the child** (unborn infant; baby) **within my womb leaped in joy and extreme happiness!**

45. **"Also, happy – and blessed – [is] the woman trusting that there will proceed being a maturing to the intended goal** (or: believing, because there will come into existence an accomplishing of the finished work, a perfection of the complete performance and an actualization of destiny) **with regard to** (or: for; in; by) **the things having been spoken to** (or: for; into) **her from close beside [the] Lord** [= Yahweh]**."**

46. **Then Mary** (or: Miriam) **said, "'My soul** (The consciousness which is me) **is constantly magnifying** (or: is progressively making great and enlarging) **the Lord** [= Yahweh], [1 Sam. 2:1ff]

47. **"and the effect and result of my breath expresses extreme joy** (or: my spirit and attitude transports supreme happiness and exultation) **upon the God [who is] my Savior** (or: upon my God, the Rescuer; upon God, the One [being] my Deliverer; [based] on my Safe-keeping God),

48. **"because He looks upon the low status** (or: = had regard for the humiliation) **of His slave girl.'** [1 Sam. 1:11] **For take note! From now on every generation** (or: all the generations) **will continue blessing me and [making; considering; pronouncing] me happy,** [*cf* Mat. 5:3f]

49. **"because the Powerful and Able One – and set-apart** (or: holy; sacred) **[is] His Name – does great things to, for, with and by me** (or: formed, constructed and created great {= sublime; important; monumental} things **in me**)! [Deut. 10:21]

50. **"His mercy [is] also unto, and [extending] into, generations and generations on** (or: in; to; for; with; by) **the folks habitually being caused to fear, respect and reverence Him.**

51. **"He makes strength** (performs [with] might) **within His arm – He thoroughly scatters proud and haughty folks** (or: those arrogant people who hold themselves above [others]) **along with [the] intellectual insights of their hearts** (or: by [the] attitudes of their hearts; in the comprehension of their hearts). [Ps. 98:1; Ps. 107; Isa. 40:10]

52. **"He takes down folks of power and ability from thrones, and then lifts up high folks of low status** (or: He also exalts humble folks). [Ps. 113:7]

53. **"He in-fills with good things folks who are habitually hungry, and yet He sends out and away empty folks who are habitually rich.** [*cf* Mat. 5:6]

54. **"He, Himself, takes the place and position belonging to Israel, His boy** (or: He took for, and in, Himself the part of Israel, His servant boy; or: He supports and helps His servant Israel), **to have [them] reminded of mercy** (or: for mercy to be brought to mind and remembered),

55. **"just and correspondingly as He spoke [it] to our fathers – to Abraham and to his seed** (= descendants) **– on into the Age."** [Ps. 98; Isa. 41:8-9; Micah 7:20]

56. **So Mary** (Miriam) **remained together with her about three months, and then returned unto her home.**

57. **Now the time was fulfilled** (brought to full term) **for Elizabeth for her to bear and bring forth to birth, and she gave birth to a son.**

58. **And so the neighbors in the homes about her, as well as her relatives, heard that [the] Lord** [= Yahweh] **magnified and enlarged His mercy with her, and they began rejoicing with her.**

59. **Then it occurred on the eighth day [that] folks came to circumcise the little boy, and they began to call it Zechariah** (or: Zacharias), **[based] on the name of his father.**

60. **And yet his mother, making a decided response, said, "No! To the contrary, he will continue being called John."**

61. **Then they rejoined to her, "There is no one from your kinship group** (extended relatives) **who is normally being called by this name."**
62. **So they began nodding and motioning** (gesturing) **to his father, [to find out] what he would want him to be habitually called.**
63. **And so, asking for a writing tablet, he wrote, saying, "His name is John." And they were all amazed.**
64. **Now instantly his mouth was opened up and his tongue became useful, and he began speaking – continuing in saying good words about God.**
65. **Then fear** (reverent awe) **was birthed** (came to be) **upon all the folks dwelling in the neighborhood around them. Later, all these sayings** (= matters and rumors) **began being told within the whole mountain** (or: hill) **country of the Judean [district].**
66. **And all those hearing [this] placed** (= pondered) **[them] within their hearts, from time to time saying, "What will this little boy proceed really being?" You see** (For it follows that) **[the] Lord's** [= Yahweh's] **hand continued being also with** (or: in company with) **him.**

67. **And then Zechariah, his father, was filled with a set-apart Breath-effect** (or: a sacred spirit and attitude; or: a holy wind; or: [the] Holy Spirit), **and he prophesied, saying,**
68. **"'[The] Lord, the God of Israel** (= Yahweh, Israel's God), **is characterized by good words and blessings,'** [Ps. 41:13] **because He visits and closely looks upon with attentiveness, and also creates** (or: produced) **a loosing and liberation, for** (or: in; to; among) **His people.**
69. **"And He raises up a horn of deliverance** (rescue; safety; health and wholeness; salvation) **for us within the midst of the house** (or: household; = family) **of David, His servant boy,**
70. **"just and correspondingly as He spoke through [the] mouth of His set-apart prophets** (or: the holy folks having light ahead of time, from Him) **from [the previous] age,**
71. **"[about] a deliverance** (rescue; safety; health and wholeness; salvation) **from out of the midst our enemies, and from out of [the] hand of all those constantly hating us, radically detaching from us and repeatedly treating us with ill will,** [Ps. 106:10]
72. **"to do** (or: perform; form; construct; create; produce) **mercy with our fathers, and to have called to mind His set-apart** (or: holy) **arrangement** (thorough setting and placement; covenant; testament)**:**
73. **"an oath** (solemn promise) **which He swore to Abraham, our father,** [Gen. 12:2]
74. **"to give to us – upon being drug out of danger from [the] hand of enemies –**
75. **"to fearlessly render habitual sacred, public service to Him, in pious ways sanctioned by divine law and in accord to the way pointed out** (or: with [covenant] fairness, equity, justice and right relationships) **in His sight** (or: before Him and in His presence) **for all our days.**
76. **"Now you also, little boy, will proceed being called a prophet of [the] Most High, for you will continue to 'go your way before and in the sight and presence of [the] Lord** [= Yahweh], **to prepare and make ready His paths and roads** (or: ways, from Him)'**:** [Mal. 3:1; Isa. 40:3]
77. **"to give intimate, experiential knowledge and insight of deliverance** (pertaining to salvation, safety, rescue, and a return to the original state; or: from health and wholeness) **to and for His people, in conjunction with a sending away** (in union with a divorcing, an abandoning flowing away and forgiveness) **of their mistakes, failures, shortcomings, deviations and sins,**
78. **"through our God's inner organs which are composed of mercy** (or: because of His tender compassions which have the character and quality of mercy), **in union with and amidst which an upward performance and a rising** (or: a dawning and a daybreak) **from out of the midst of an exaltation** (or: from on high) **will progressively visit and caringly look upon us**
79. **"to at once 'shine upon the people continuously sitting within the midst of darkness** (the realm of the shadow and obscurity; dimness and gloom)' [Isa. 9:1] **– even within death's shadow; to cause our feet to be fully straight and to [walk] in correspondence to straightness, into the path** (way; road) **of peace** (or: from, and which is, a joining)."

80. **Now the little boy was continuing to progressively grow and increase, and was being progressively made stronger in Breath-effect** (or: by [the] Spirit; in spirit; with an attitude), **and later he continued existing within the midst of desolate places** (deserts; uninhabited areas; wildernesses) **until the day of his upward exhibit** (the raising aloft to show him) **to Israel.**

Luke

CHAPTER 2

1. **Now it occurred in those days, [that] a decree went out from beside** (= the court of)
**Caesar Augustus, [that] all the inhabited [domain of the Empire] is to proceed to register
themselves for public record** (enroll in a census).
2. **This first** (or: former; earlier) **registration occurred while Quirinius continued leading and
governing Syria.** [note: Quirinius governed twice; enrollment was every 14 years – A. Nyland]
3. **And so everyone began going their way to proceed to register themselves** (or: to be, in
turn, enrolled) **for the public record [of the census] – each one into his own city.**
4. **So Joseph also walked back up from the Galilee [district], from out of [the] town of
Nazareth, into the Judean [district], into a town of David which is normally being called
Bethlehem – because of the [fact of] his being from out of the house and lineage** (ancestry)
of David –
5. **to register himself** (or: be enrolled) **for the public record, together with Mary** (Miriam), **the
woman having been pledged in marriage for** (engaged to) **him – she being pregnant.**
6. **Now it happened, during their being there, [that] the days for her to give birth were
fulfilled** (brought to full term).
7. **And so she gave birth to her Son, the firstborn, and then she wrapped Him in long
strips of swathing cloth and made Him lie back in a manger** (feeding trough; [note: probably
in the house]), **because there was not a place for them in the guest room [of the house].**

8. **There were also in that same district** (or: region) **shepherds [that] were seasonally living
out of doors with temporary enclosures in the fields, and they were by turn guarding and
keeping watch upon their flock during [the] watches which divide the night.**
9. **And then – look and think of this! – all at once [the] Lord's** [= Yahweh's] **agent** (or: a
messenger from [Yahweh]) **took a stand upon [their encampment], in the midst of them** (or:
stood at their [side]), **and [the] Lord's** [= Yahweh's] **glory** (assumed appearance; Theophanous
manifestation; = manifest Presence) **shone** (gleamed and radiated) **around about them, and
they became afraid [with] a great fear** (= were struck with extreme reverence, or terror).
10. **And so the agent** (messenger) **says to them, "Stop being afraid** (or: Do not continue
fearing)! **Look, and consider this – for you see, I, myself, am now bringing and announcing
good news** (a message of ease and wellness) **to, for and among you folks: great joy which
will progressively be for all the people** (or: will continue existing in the entire general public),
11. **"because today, within the town of David, a Savior** (Deliverer; Rescuer; Restorer to
health, wholeness, and to your original state, condition and position) **was birthed and brought
forth to, for and among you folks Who is** (exists being) **Christ [the] Lord** (or: [the] Lord Christ;
or: an Anointed Lord, Master and Owner; an Anointed One, a Lord; = Messiah, [the] Lord)!
12. **"And now this [will be] a sign to and for you folks: you will proceed finding a Babe** (an
infant) **having been wrapped in long bands of swathing cloth, and continuing lying within a
manger** (feeding trough; [note: the average home kept domestic animals in the house at night])."
13. **Then unexpectedly and suddenly [the] fullness of a throng** (or: multitude) **of a heavenly
host** (or: a full number of an army which inhabits, and can be compared to, the atmosphere; [cf
Heb. 12:1a, 22-23]) **– of folks continuously praising God – came to be with the agent** (or:
came to exist and happened with the messenger), **and are repeatedly saying,** [cf 2 Ki. 6:16-17]
14. **"[This is] a reputation for God, in the highest places!**
> (or: Glory to God, in the midst of the highest [realms];
> or: [It is] a manifestation which call forth praise with God, among the highest [peoples];
> or: An assumed appearance and a manifestation by God, within the midst of a most
> elevated location;
> or: A notion and an imagination within [the] highest places in God);

and upon earth – among humanity (or: within mankind; in union with people) **– a peace and a
joining having the qualities and characteristics of well-thinking and goodwill**
> (or: harmony [= shalom] whose source is good opinions and imaginations of well-being;
> or: a peaceful joining which is a manifestation and a reputation of good and ease; or: a
> peace which belongs to good pleasure; joining from a disposition of goodness)!"

132

15. **And so it happened, as the agents** (messengers; folks with the message; [A, D, Ψ, TR & others add: – **even** (or: that is,) **the humans**]) **went away from them into the atmosphere** (or: the heaven), **[that] the shepherds began speaking to one another, saying, "We should by all means pass through now, clear to Bethlehem, and we can see this gush-effect** (the result of this flow; or: this 'rhema' declaration and saying) **that has happened** (been birthed; come to be), **which the Lord** [= Yahweh] **makes known to** (or: for; among; by) **us."**

16. **So they came hurrying and, after searching, finally found not only Mary** (or: Miriam) **and Joseph, but also the Baby** (or: new-born infant) **[which was] still lying within the manger** (feeding trough).

17. **Now after seeing [this], they made known about the declaration** (gush-effect; matter; result of the flow) **being spoken to them concerning this little boy.**

18. **And so all those hearing and listening marveled and wondered in astonishment concerning the things being spoken to them by the shepherds.**

19. **Yet Mary** (or: Miriam) **began keeping these gush-effects** (results of the flow; sayings; declarations) **together, watching and preserving [them], repeated tossing them together and pondering** (jointly comparing, conferring and reflecting [on them]) **within her heart.**

20. **Then the shepherds returned, glorifying** (building the reputation of) **and praising God on [the basis of] everything which they heard and saw – just as it was spoken to them.**

21. **And later, when eight days were fulfilled [bringing them to the ritual] to circumcise Him, His name was then called "Jesus," the name called by the agent** (messenger), **before the [situation and time for] Him to be conceived within the womb.**

22. **Further, when the days were fulfilled for their purification** [note: probably referring to Mary and Jesus] **– in accord with the Law** [= Torah] **of Moses – they led Him up into Jerusalem, to stand** (place) **Him beside** (or: = present Him to) **the Lord** [= Yahweh],

23. **just as it has been written with the Lord's** [= Yahweh's] **Law, that,**
> **"every male fully proceeding to open up the womb will be called 'set-apart to, for, in and by the Lord** [= Yahweh]',"** [Ex. 13: 2, 12, 15]

24. **and also to give** (= offer) **a sacrifice corresponding to that having been stated in the Lord's** [= Yahweh's] **Law,**
> **"a pair of** (or: a couple) **wild doves** (or: turtledoves; murmurers) **or two young pigeons."** [note: "the offering of the landless peasantry" – Richard Rohr]

25. **And now, look and consider this! There was a man within Jerusalem whose name [was] Simeon, and this man [was] just** (fair; equitable; in right relationships; in accord with the way pointed out) **as well as grasping things well** (or: well-received; taking it with ease and wellness), **habitually receptive to** (or: continuously welcoming and granting access to) **Israel's call to the side for relief, aid, comfort and encouragement** (or: the work and function of a Paraclete from Israel) **– and a set-apart spirit** (a holy wind; a separated Breath-effect; a sacred attitude) **was continuously being upon him.**

26. **Furthermore, it was for** (or: to; in; with) **him – having been transacted by dealings by** (or: under) **this set-apart Breath-effect** (or: the Holy Spirit; this Sacred Attitude) **– to not see or know death before he would see and know the Christ of, and from, [the] Lord** (= Yahweh's Anointed One, the Messiah).

27. **And so, within the midst of this Breath-effect and in union with the Spirit** (or: centered in this Attitude) **he came into the Temple courts** (or: grounds). **And within the [situation for] the parents to bring the little boy Jesus, for them to do and perform according to and in correspondence with the practice having been done by custom of the Law concerning Him,**

28. **he, himself, then received Him into [his] arms and spoke good words** (or: words of goodness, ease and well-being) **about God, and then said,**

29. **"At this time** (or: Right now) **You are in the process of loosing away, releasing and freeing Your slave, O Sovereign Owner, corresponding to Your gush-effect, in union with Peace** (or: the result of the declaration flowing from You within the midst of a Joining).

30. **"because my eyes see and perceive Your Deliverance** (Your Salvation; Your Safety; Your Health and Wholeness; Your Restoration to the original state and condition),

31. "which You prepared and made ready in correspondence with (or: true to and stepping with; following the pattern of; down in front of) [the] face of (or: face to face with; personally to; or: = openly before and in the presence of) all the peoples,
32. "a Light [leading] into an unveiling of (or: a revelation belonging to and pertaining to) ethnic multitudes (or: nations; non-Israelites), and [the] Glory (a manifestation calling forth praise; a reputation; an Appearance) of, from, and with a view to, Your people, Israel."

33. And so His father and mother were continuing in marveling, being amazed and wondering upon the things being one after another, and repeatedly, spoken about Him.
34. Then Simeon spoke good words to (or: laid out goodness for; blessed) them, and said to Mary (Miriam), His mother, "Look and consider! This One continues lying down into the midst of a fall, and then a standing back up again, of many people within Israel – and into a sign being constantly spoken in opposition to, and being repeatedly contradicted!
35. "Yet a long Thracian javelin (or: long sword) will be repeatedly coming and passing through your very soul (consciousness), so that thought processes, reasonings and dialogues from out of many hearts would be uncovered (unveiled; revealed; disclosed)."
36. And now there was Anna, a prophetess (a woman with light ahead of time), [the] daughter of Phanuel (or: Penuel), from out of [the] tribe of Asher – she having walked forward during many days (= was well advanced in years), living with a husband [for] seven years from her virginity (may = after her marriage, or, after her girlhood),
37. and then she [was] a widow until [now being] eighty-four years [old] (or: was a widow for eighty-four years) – who continued not withdrawing (or: departing; standing away; putting herself away) from the temple courts and grounds, repeatedly doing public sacred-service in fastings and by petitions (or: prayer requests) night and day.
38. And so, taking a stand on [the scene] in that same hour, she began – in [Simeon's] place – saying similar things to God (or: she began responding in like words while standing in the place for God; or: she continued in [His] presence making confessions in God) and kept on speaking about Him [either: God; or: the Child] to all the folks habitually having a view toward welcoming, granting access to, and receiving a liberation of Jerusalem (or: a release by payment of a ransom for Jerusalem; [with other MSS: a redemption in Jerusalem]).
39. And so, when they finished (ended) all the things corresponding to the Lord's [= Yahweh's] Law, they returned into the Galilee [district], unto their own town, Nazareth.
40. So the little Boy kept on growing, progressively increasing and steadily becoming strong by [the] Breath-effect (or: in spirit; with a [positive] attitude), being progressively filled with wisdom – and God's grace (or: favor, from God,) continued being upon Him.

41. Now as was [their] custom, His parents regularly went their way – year by year – into Jerusalem during the Feast (or: at the festival) of the Passover.
42. So when He came to be twelve years [old], after their finishing going up – according to the custom of the Feast (or: festival) –
43. and upon finishing the days, during their process of returning, the Boy Jesus continued to remain in Jerusalem.
44. Yet, inferring from custom for Him to be within the group journeying together (= in the caravan; company of fellow travelers), they went a day's way (path for a day; = a day's journey on the road) and then began seeking Him back among the relatives and acquaintances.
45. Then upon not finding Him, they returned into Jerusalem, continuing in searching again for Him.

46. Later, after three days, it happened [that] they found Him within the Temple courts (or: grounds), continuing in sitting within the midst of the teachers, constantly listening to them, as well as repeatedly making inquiries and putting questions to them.
47. Now all the folks continuing to listen to and hear Him began 'standing outside themselves' in amazement and were repeatedly astonished at His understanding (His ability to make things flow intelligently together) and discerning responses (or: decided answers).
48. And so, upon seeing Him, [His parents] were bewildered and overwhelmed (or: struck out [of their wits]), then His mother said to Him, "Child, why did you treat us in this manner?

Look, and consider, your father and I were caused constant pain and distress as we continued searching for you."
49. **So He said to them, "Why [is it] that you were trying to find Me? Had you not seen so as to now know that it continues binding and necessary for Me to be within the midst of the men belonging to My Father**
> (or: to constantly exist among the [realms] that pertain to, and are from, My Father; or: to continue being centered in, and in union with, those things which are My Father)**?"**
50. **And yet they, themselves, did not understand** (make flow together) **the result of the flow** (declaration; gush-effect) **which He spoke to them.**

51. **And so He walked back down with them and came into Nazareth, and continued being set in a supportive arrangement for them** (or: kept on being subject to and under them). **His mother also continued carefully watching, noting and keeping all these sayings** (gush-effects; results of the flows; declarations; matters) **within her heart.**
52. **And so Jesus kept on cutting a passage forward, making progress in** (or: by; with) **the Wisdom – as well as in maturity and physical stature – and in** (or: by; with) **grace and favor, beside God and mankind** (or: in the presence of God as well as people).

CHAPTER 3

1. **Now in the fifteenth year of the governmental leadership** (or: rule) **of Tiberius Caesar, while Pontius Pilate continued leading the government** (performed as governor) **of the Judean [district] and Herod [Antipas] filled the provincial office of 'tetrarch'** (= ruler of a fourth part of a kingdom) **of the Galilee [district] – yet Philip, his brother, continued ruling as 'tetrarch' of the province of Iturea and Trachonitis, as well as Lysanias continuing rule as 'tetrarch' of Abilene –**
2. **on the [occasion and term of the priesthood of] chief** (or: ranking) **priests, Annas and Caiaphas, a gush-effect which was God** (or: the result of a flow from God; God's spoken word; a declaration from God) **came into existence** (came to be; was birthed) **upon John, son of Zechariah, within the midst of the wilderness** (the uninhabited, desolate place).
3. **And so he came** (or: went) **into all [the] region around the Jordan [River], repeatedly making a public proclamation heralding an immersion** (or: baptism) **of a change of mind, way of thinking and state of consciousness [which also implied a return to God], into a flowing-away of failures**
> (a sending-away of mistakes; a letting-go and release of failed attempts to hit the target and attain the goal; abandonment of sins; a divorce from, and a forgiveness of, errors).
4. **As it has been and stands written within the scroll of [the] words of Isaiah the prophet, "A voice** (or: sound) **of someone repeatedly exclaiming and imploring loudly within the midst of the wilderness** (the desolate place):
   'You people at once make ready (or: 'Within the wilderness [now] prepare) **the Way (Road) of [the] Lord** [= Yahweh's Path]**! Be progressively making His worn thoroughfares and highways straight.**
5. **'Every ravine** (or: gully; place narrowly enclosed by cliffs) **will be progressively filled, and every mountain and hill** (or: all hill country and rising ground) **will continue being made low. Then the crooked things** (or: places) **will proceed in being [made] into straight ones, and rough and uneven places, into smooth roads!**
6. **'Then all flesh will proceed in seeing God's Deliverance** (Salvation; Rescue; health and wholeness; Returning [all; things] to the original state and condition)**!'"** [Isa. 40:3-5]
> [cf Rev. 1:7b]

7. **However, he** [i.e., John] **kept on saying to the crowds that were one after another going their way out to be immersed by him, "[You] offsprings** (or: Results of the births) **of poisonous snakes** (vipers), **who** (or: what) **privately suggested** (or: secretly showed; divulged; pointed out under [cover]) **to you folks to be at once taking flight** (fleeing) **away from the progressively impending inherent fervor** (internal swelling towards fruition, agitation of soul, or, anger and wrath [from God, or from humans] that is presently about to occur)**?**

8. **"Be at once, then, producing fruit of corresponding value to** (or: of equal worth of; worthy of) **the aforementioned change of mind and way of thinking! And so, you should not start** (or: begin) **to be repeatedly saying among yourselves, 'We continue having Abraham [as; for] a father,' for I am now saying to you folks that God continues able** (constantly has power) **to raise up children to** (or: for) **Abraham from out of the midst of these stones!**

9. **"Now the ax already continues lying [positioned with its aim] toward** (face to face with)) **the root of the trees. So then, every tree not seasonally producing beautiful** (fine; ideal; choice) **fruit is customarily cut out [of the orchard or garden] and is regularly being tossed into a fire [to heat or to cook]."**

10. **And so the crowds began putting questions to him, one after another saying, "What, then, should we be doing?"**

11. **So, giving a decided reply, he began saying to them, "The person habitually having two tunics** (undergarments), **let him at once share with the one not normally having [one]; and the person habitually having things to eat** (food), **let him regularly do likewise."**

12. **Now tax collectors** (or: government revenue contractors; customs agents) **also came to be immersed** (baptized), **and they said to him, "Teacher, what should we be doing?"**

13. **So he said to them, "Be habitually practicing** (thus: collecting, demanding or exacting) **nothing more besides the thing having been precisely arranged and prescribed for you** (= charge nothing beyond the standard rates)."

14. **And then soldiers** (men serving in the army) **also began putting questions to him, as a group saying, "What should we also be doing?"**
And he said to them, "You men should not at any time violently shake anyone (thus, also: intimidate, harass or extort from anyone), **nor should you at any time inform on, blackmail or falsely accuse [people]. Also, be habitually content and satisfied with your subsistence rations and pay."**

15. **Now during the people's continued anticipation – keeping an eye open and directed forward in watchful expectation – [and] while everyone kept on reasoning and debating in their hearts concerning John, whether perchance he might be the Christ** (the Anointed One; = the Messiah),

16. **John gave a decided response, repeatedly saying, "I, myself, on the one hand am in the process of immersing** (baptizing) **you folks in** (or: with) **water. Yet on the other hand, the Person stronger than I is now progressively coming – the lace** (or: strap; thong) **of Whose sandals I am not competent** (fit; sufficient) **to loosen or untie. He, Himself, will proceed immersing** (or: baptizing) **you folks within the midst of set-apart Spirit** (or: set-apart spirit; sacred attitude; Holy Breath-effect) **and** (or: even) **Fire –**

17. **"Whose winnowing shovel** (or: fork) **[is] in His hand to thoroughly clean** [other MSS: and He will thoroughly cleanse] **His threshing floor and to gather together** [with other MSS: He will collect] **the grain into His storehouse** (granary; barn) **– but then He will progressively burn down** (or: up) **the chaff** (husks and straw; = the useless remains of the dead plants) **with** (or: in) **an inextinguishable Fire."** [comment: the same fire as in vs. 16; *cf* 1 Cor. 3:7-17]

18. **Then, indeed, constantly calling the people alongside to give encouragement, exhortation and assistance** (or: repeatedly performing as a paraclete), **he kept on bringing and announcing many and different things as good news of ease and well-being.**

19. **Now Herod, the tetrarch** (district ruler) **– being repeatedly put to the proof** (or: being constantly questioned, as in a cross-examination, and refuted, exposed, convicted and treated with contempt) **by him concerning Herodias, the wife of his brother Philip, as well as about all [the] worthless, malicious and wicked things which Herod did and does –**

20. **added this also, upon everything [he had done]: he locked-down John within the midst of a prison** (or: jail).

21. **Now during the [period and situation for] all the people to be immersed** (baptized), **and with Jesus also having been immersed** (baptized) **and then continuing in prayer** (or: thinking with a view toward having goodness, ease and well-being), **[the time and situation] had come to be** (or: was birthed; occurred; happened) **[for] the heaven to be opened back up again,**

22. **and [for] the Set-apart Breath-effect** (or: the Holy Spirit; the Sacred Attitude) **to descend** (step down) – **in bodily perceptual appearance as a dove** (or: pigeon) – **upon Him, and [for] a Voice from out of the midst of heaven** (or: a Sound from [the] atmosphere, or sky,) **to birth Itself: "You, Yourself, are** (continuously exist being) **My Son – the Beloved One! I have good thoughts within the midst of You**

> (or: I take delight in You; I am disposed to good things and wellness in union with You; In You I think ease and imagine well-being; [instead of this last sentence, D reads, and this reading is found in various second and third century church fathers, over a wide geographic area from Spain to North Africa, to Palestine: Today I, Myself, have given birth to You])!"

23. **And so this same Jesus, Himself starting to rule** (or: progressively beginning), **was about thirty years [old], being a son – as it continued commonly supposed and established by Law, custom, and thus legally – of Joseph, [son] of** (or: from) **Eli,**
24. **[a son] of Matthat, [son] of Levi, [son] of Melchi, [son] of Jannai, [son] of Joseph.**
25. **[He was a son] of Mattathias, [son] of Amos, [son] of Nahum, [son] of Esli, [son] of Naggai,**
26. **[son] of Maath, [son] of Mattathias, [son] of Semein, [son] of Josech, [son] of Joda** (or: Yoda),
27. **[son] of Joanan, [son] of Rhesa, [son] of Zerubbabel, [son] of Shealthiel, [son] of Neri,**
28. **[son] of Melchi, [son] of Addi, [son] of Cosam, [son] of Elmadam, [son] of Er,**
29. **[son] of Jesus, [son] of Eliezer, [son] of Jorim, [son] of Matthat, [son] of Levi,**
30. **[son] of Simeon, [son] of Judah, [son] of Joseph, [son] of Jonam, [son] of Eliakim,**
31. **[son] of Melea, [son] of Menna, [son] of Mattathah, [son] of Nathan, [son] of David,**
32. **[son] of Jesse, [son] of Obed, [son] of Boaz, [son] of Salmon, [son] of Nahshon,**
33. **[son] of Amminadab, [son] of Arni, [son] of Hezron, [son] of Pherez, [son] of Judah,**
34. **[son] of Jacob, [son] of Isaac, [son] of Abraham, [son] of Terah, [son] of Nahor,**
35. **[son] of Serug, [son] of Reu, [son] of Peleg, [son] of Eber, [son] of Shelah,**
36. **[son] of Cainan, [son] of Arphaxad, [son] of Shem, [son] of Noah, [son] of Lamech,**
37. **[son] of Methuselah, [son] of Enoch, [son] of Jared, [son] of Mahalaleel, [son] of Cainan,**
38. **[son] of Enos** (or: Enosh), **[son] of Seth, [son] of Adam, [son] of God.**

> [note: Following Joseph, in vs. 23, each name of this genealogy is a genitive or ablative phrase. Thus, alternate renderings of the last part of vs. 38 are: ... belonging to, or from, Adam, belonging to, or from, God; or: ... whose source is Adam, whose source is God; or, as a genitive of apposition: ... who is Adam, who is God; comment: this last function of the genitive would indicate a continuity, from God, through Adam, and on through the rest of the genealogy]

CHAPTER 4

1. **So Jesus, full of a set-apart spirit and attitude** (or: a set-apart Breath-effect; [the] Holy Spirit; [the] sacred Breath), **turned back away from the Jordan [River] and began being led** (or: guided) **within the** (or: that) **Breath-effect** (or: in union with the Spirit; in that attitude) **within the midst of** [other MSS: into] **the wilderness** (desert; desolate and uninhabited place) –
2. **[for] forty days being constantly examined and tested** (or: tried and proved) **by, and under, the one who thrusts or hurls [things; thoughts] through [us]** (or: the adversary). **And He did not eat anything within those days, and so, at their being brought together to the purposed goal, and concluded, He became hungry.**

3. **So the one who thrusts through [folks]** (the adversary) **said to Him, "Since** (or: If) **you are** (exist being) **God's son** (or: a son from God; [the] 'Son who is God') **speak to this stone with the result that it can** (may; would) **come to be a loaf of bread."**
4. **And then Jesus gave a decided reply to him, "It has been written, 'Humanity** (or: The Man; or: The human being) **will not continue living upon bread alone, [but rather upon God's every gush-effect** (or: on every result of God's flow, spoken word or declaration).]'"** [Deut. 8:3]

5. **Then, upon leading Him up into a high mountain, the adversary** (thruster-through) **pointed out to Him all the kingdoms** (reigns; dominions; empires) **of the inhabited earth** (the civilized world; or: = the Roman Empire), **within a point of** (or: puncture or tattoo from) **time,**
6. **and then the adversary** (the thruster-through; or: that which was cast through the midst [of Him]) **said to Him, "I will proceed giving to you all this authority** (or: right and privilege from out of Being), **as well as their glory and reputation** (or: even that which is supposed to be from them; also that which appears and seems to be them; or: and also their imagination) – **because it has been given over and committed to me** (or: passed on by me; delivered in me), **and to whomsoever I may wish** (will; want; intend; purpose) **I am normally periodically giving it.**
7. **"Therefore, if you yourself would at some point bow down in homage or worship before me, it will all proceed being yours** (or: it will all continue existing being that which is you)**!"**
8. **And so, giving a decided answer, Jesus said to him, "Go submissively** (or: Sink down) **behind me, adversary! It has been written, 'You will continue being bowing down in homage and worship** (or: doing obeisance) **to [the] Lord** [= Yahweh], **your God, and to Him alone will you continue giving public sacred service.'"** [Deut. 6:13-14]

9. **So he** (or: it) **led Him into Jerusalem and stationed** (set; stood) **Him upon the little wing of the Temple complex, then said to Him, "Since you are** (or: If you exist being) **God's son** (or: a son from God; [the] 'Son who is God') **cast** (or: hurl) **yourself down** (= jump) **from this place,**
10. **"for it has been written that,**
> **'He will proceed imparting a goal in** (giving the end in view to) **His agents** (messengers) **about** (concerning) **you, [with the directive] to carefully protect, keep and guard you.'**
11. **"also, that,**
> **'Upon [their] hands they will continue lifting you, lest at some point you could** (or: might) **strike** (or: dash) **your foot toward a stone** (= stub your toe; or: =stumble).'"** [Ps. 91:11-12]
12. **So, giving a determined response, Jesus said to him, "It has been said,**
> **'You will not proceed in testing-out** (or: putting out on trial) **[the] Lord** [= Yahweh], **your God.'"** [Deut. 6:16]
13. **And then, upon concluding and bringing every test and all examination to its goal, the adversary** (the through-thruster) **withdrew and took a stand away** (defected) **from Him, until an appointed season** (or: a fertile moment; a fitting, convenient or opportune situation).
14. **Then Jesus returned – within the midst of and in union with the power of the Spirit** (or: the ability which is the Breath-effect; the power from the Attitude), **into the Galilee [district]. And so fame about** (or: news and rumor concerning) **Him went out down through the whole surrounding region.**
15. **And then He Himself began teaching within their synagogues, [He] being progressively held in honor, esteem and reputation, or imagination, by all people** (or: being constantly glorified with assumptions or opinions by everyone).

16. **Later He came** (or: went) **into Nazareth, where He had been brought up** (raised, supported, nourished, provided for, cared for, educated and prepared for adulthood), **and according to His custom on the day of the sabbaths, He entered into the synagogue. In time, He stood up to read.**
17. **So a scroll of the prophet Isaiah was handed to Him. Then, upon opening up the scroll, He found the place where it was written,**
18. **"[The] Lord's** [= Yahweh's] **Breath-effect** (or: [The] Spirit of [the] Lord; or: a spirit from [Yahweh]; or: a spirit and attitude which is [the] Lord) **[is] upon Me** [Old Syriac MS: you], **on account of which He anointed Me** [Syriac: you] **to bring and proclaim good news** (a message of ease and wellness) **to destitute folks – and so He has sent Me off as an emissary** (a missionary; one commissioned as His representative) **to cure and heal folks with [their] heart having been crushed, to publicly proclaim, as a herald, to** (for; among) **captives a release and liberation** (a letting go away) **and to** (for; among) **blind folks a seeing again** (a recovery of sight), **to send away with a mission those having been shattered by oppression, in a state of release and liberation,**

19.   "to publicly and loudly proclaim [the] Lord's [= Yahweh's] **year which is characterized by being welcomed, favorably received, approved and acceptable...!"** [Isa. 61:1-2a; 58:6; note: some see this as a reference to the 'year of Jubilee,' Lev. 25:10]

20.   **Then, upon rolling up the scroll [and] giving [it] back to the attendant, He sat down – and the eyes of everyone in the synagogue were staring intently at Him.**

21.   **So He started to be saying to them, "Today this scripture has been fulfilled in your ears** (= your hearing)." [cf 4Q278, 521 to compare with vss. 16-30, here]

22.   **And so everyone began giving evidence to Him, testifying against Him or giving witness about Him, and then continued stunned on these words just presently proceeding forth from His mouth concerning the grace** (or: astonished at these thoughts from, or ideas about, this favor), **so that one after another was saying, "Isn't this Joseph's son?!"**

23.   **Later, He said to them, "In all likelihood** (= Doubtless; By all means) **you folks will say** (or: quote; speak) **this illustration** (parable; = proverb) **for** (or: to; about) **Me, 'Healer** (or: Physician; Doctor), **cure** (or give attentive care to, or prescribe therapy for, or instigate ongoing treatment to) **yourself!' [and say,] 'Do now also here, within your home territory** (or: fatherland), **as many things as we heard birthed themselves into Capernaum** (= happened in Capernaum).'"

24.   **But then He said, "The truth is** (or: Amen; Truly), **I am now saying to, and laying it out for, you people, that not one prophet is welcome or acceptable** (or: a received one) **within His fatherland** (or: home territory; own country).

25.   **"Yet, [based] on truth** (or: = in reality) **I am now saying to you folks, there were many widows during the days of Elijah, in Israel, when the sky** (or: heaven) **was shut and locked for** (on [a period of]) **three years and six months, so thus a great famine occurred upon all the land –** [1 Ki. 17:1-18:1]

26.   **"and yet Elijah was sent to not one of them, except into Zarephath of the Sidon [territory], to a woman – a widow!** [comment: vss. 26 and 27 speak of grace to the Gentiles]

27.   **"and further, there were many lepers in Israel, on [the time of] Elisha the prophet, and yet not one of them was cleansed, except Naaman – the Syrian!"** [2 Ki. 5:1-19]

28.   **Then all the men in the synagogue, as they were hearing these things, were filled with a rush of emotion** (or: anger; fury; rage),

29.   **and after standing up** (arising) **they hustled Him out – outside of the town – then they led Him to a brow** (= an out-jutting cliff) **of the mountain** (or: hill) **upon which their town had been built, so as to shove Him down the precipice.**

30.   **But He Himself, after passing through their midst** (the middle of them), **continued on His way.**

31.   **So He went down into Capernaum, a city of the Galilee [district]. Then He was continuing in teaching them, during the sabbaths.**

32.   **And they kept on being struck out of themselves with astonishment at His teaching** (the skilled instruction from Him) **– that His word** (the *Logos* from Him) **was being in union with authority** (or: because His thought/idea was centered in right and privilege; that the meaningful message and the laid-out information from Him was existing in a sphere from out of [His] Being).

33.   **Further, in – and as a part of – the synagogue there was a man** (or: person) **contstantly having and holding a breath-effect** (spirit; attitude) **of an unclean demon** (Hellenistic concept and term: = a culturally unpruned animistic influence), **and he uttered up** (or: cried out) **with a loud voice,**

34.   **"Ah!** (or: Ha!) **What [is this] for us... and for You** (or: What [business is there] between us and You; What [is there in common] for us and for you; Why do you meddle with us), **Jesus, you Nazarene? You came to get rid of us!** (or: Do you come to destroy us?) **I have seen and know You... Who** (or: What) **you are! – God's set-apart One!** (or: the Holy man from, and whose source is, God; as a genitive of apposition: the Holy One {or: man} who is God!)"

     [comment: it has been assumed that when saying "us" this person was referring to the animistic influence; but was he perhaps referring to the Jewish culture, religion and political entity, of which he was a part? *Cf* Acts 16:16-18]

35.   **So Jesus gave a respectful directive** (or: spoke a value-based command) **to it, saying, "Be at once muzzled** (= Be quiet, or, silent) **and go** (or: come) **out – away from him." Then,**

after pitching (or: convulsing) **him into [their] midst, the demon** (= animistic influence) **went out – away from him – [in] nothing hurting or harming him.**

36. **And so there came to be amazement** (wonder, astonishment or bewilderment) **upon everyone, and they began conversing together, repeatedly saying to one another, "What word** (or: message; idea; information) **[is] this? – that in authority and power** (or: in union with privilege, or, prerogative, and ability) **He is now giving orders to the unclean breath-effects** (impure spirits or attitudes), **and they proceed coming** (or: going) **out!"**

> [comment: note that the people equate the concept of a "demon" with that of a spirit, or attitude]

37. **So a reverberating noise** (= an echoing report, or, rumor) **began proceeding forth concerning Him – into every place of the surrounding region.**

38. **Now upon rising up from the synagogue, He entered into Simon's house. But Simon's mother-in-law had been continuing gripped by and confined by a high fever, so they asked** (or: made request of) **Him about** (or: concerning) **her.**

39. **Then, upon taking a place over her, He spoke a respectful directive to the fever, and it released her and flowed away** (or: abandoned her). **Now without delay, after standing up, she began performing attending service to, for, and among them.**

> [comment: note that He responded to the illness in the same way that He did to the demon/spirit, in vs. 35, with a similar result]

40. **Now while the sun was setting, everybody – whoever were having folks being weak and infirm with various diseases – led them to Him. So He, placing [His] hands upon each one of them, was one, after, another treating, or curing, or giving attentive care to, or prescribing therapy to, or instigating ongoing treatment for, them.**

41. **And thus, demons** (= animistic influences) **also kept on going out from many folks, [as] one by one [of them] were uttering cries or exclamations, and then saying, "You, Yourself, are God's Son** (or: the Son from God)!" **And so, while speaking respectful directives, He was not permitting them to continue speaking, because** (or: to continue sounding forth that) **they had seen, and thus knew, Him to be the Christ** (the Anointed One; = the Messiah).

> [comment: note that Luke equates the terms "Christ" and "God's Son"]

42. **Now, when it came to be day, upon going out He went His way into a desolate** (desert; uninhabited) **place. And yet, the crowds kept on trying to find Him, and so they came to Him and they kept on detaining Him so that He would not be leaving them.**

43. **But He, Himself, said to them, "It is necessary and binding for Me to bring and declare the good news** (the message of Goodness, Ease and Well-being) **– God's reign**

> (or: the kingdom from God; the influence and activity of the sovereignty which is God;
> [note: reign/kingdom is in the accusative, and thus in apposition to the verb, so here
> "reign/kingdom of God" defines "the good news"]) **– in different towns and cities, as**

well, because I was sent off as an emissary (envoy; representative) **on this mission."**

44. **And so He was constantly making public proclamation [when entering] into the synagogues of the Judean [district].**

CHAPTER 5

1. **Now this happened** (it occurred; He came to be) **– during** (on) **the [situation, or time, that] the crowd continued pressing close and imposing** ([almost] lying) **upon Him in order to be listening to and hearing the Word of God** (or: God's thoughts and ideas; God's message; information from God) **– and He Himself was there, standing beside Lake Gennesaret.**

2. **Then He saw two sailing vessels moored beside the lakeside** (= at the shore), **but the fishermen, after disembarking from them, had started washing the nets.**

3. **So, stepping into one of the boats** (or: ships; sailing vessels) **– which was Simon's, He asked him to pull away** (or: lead back upon [the water]) **from the land a little. So, upon sitting down, He began teaching the crowds, from out of the sailing vessel.**

4. **Now as He ceases [the] session of speaking, He says to Simon, "Pull away again on [the lake], into the deep, and you men lower your nets into a catch."**

5. **And so Simon, in a considered reply, said, "Captain** (or: Commander; Chief; = Boss; or perhaps: Instructor), **after being wearied and spent with labor through the whole night, we took nothing. Yet, [based] upon Your spoken word** (on the result, and at the effect, of Your flow), **I will proceed lowering the nets."**

6. **Then, upon doing this, they shut up together and enclosed** (or: ensnared) **a huge multitude of fishes – and now their nets began tearing and ripping in two.**

7. **And so with hand gestures, they motioned to [their] business partners in the different boat to, upon coming, get together with them and help out** (assist). **So they came, and they filled both ships so that they began to progressively sink!**

8. **Now Simon Peter seeing [this], fell down at the knees of Jesus, while saying, "Go out, away from me, O Sir** (or: Lord), **because I am a man with the qualities of an outcast** (a man characterized by failure; a missing-the-target male; a sinful man; an adult male full of error, deviations and mistakes)!"

9. **You see, awe, fear and astonishment suddenly surrounded, engulfed and then overwhelmed him – as well as all those together with him – upon [the impact], at the catch of the fishes which they together took in hand.**

10. **Now [it was] likewise, also, [with] Jacob** (or: James) **and John – sons of Zebedee. They were partners and mates with Simon.**
Then Jesus says to Simon, "Stop fearing (or: Do not continue being afraid). **From now on you will be repeatedly catching humans** (or: [the] people) **alive!"**

11. **Then, after bringing the sailing vessels back down upon the land, abandoning all things, they followed Him.**

12. **Later, it happened for Him to be in one of the towns, and – look and think about this – an adult male full of leprosy [was there]. Now upon seeing Jesus, after falling upon [his] face, he begged** (or: from out of his need urgently asked) **Him, presently saying, "O Lord** (or: Sir; Master), **if you should continue willing [it]** (or: if you are now wanting to) **you continue able** (or: constantly have power) **to at once make me clean!"**

13. **And so, stretching out [His] hand He touched him, while saying, "I am now wanting [to], and continue willing and intending [it]. Be at once made clean!" Then immediately the leprosy went away from** (or: came off from; left) **him.**

14. **And then He gave to him a message at the side: to speak to no one [about this], but rather, "Upon going off** (or: away), **show yourself to the priest, and bear forward an offering concerning your cleansing – just as arranged and directed by Moses – with a view to evidence for** (or: unto a witness to and among [John D. Crossan suggests: against]) **them."**

15. **However, the account concerning Him began spreading throughout to an even greater extent and many crowds began gathering** (coming together) **to continue hearing, or to repeatedly listen, as well as to be cured by Him – or be given attentive care or be prescribed therapy or have instigated ongoing treatment – from their weaknesses, illnesses and diseases.**

16. **So He, Himself, was progressively withdrawing and repeatedly retiring into the desolate places** (deserts; uninhabited places) **and constantly praying** (thinking and speaking with a view to having {or: toward holding} goodness, ease and well-being).

17. **Then it occurred** (happened), **on** (or: during) **one of those days, that He Himself was progressing in teaching. Now there were Pharisees and teachers of the Law** [= Torah] **continuing in sitting [there] who had been coming out of every village of the Galilee [district] and Judea, and even Jerusalem. And [the] Lord's** [= Yahweh's] **power and ability continued being there for** (with a view to) **Him to be presently and continually healing.**

18. **And so, look and consider! Adult males carrying on a couch** (or: pallet; stretcher; bed) **a man who was one having been, and now remained, paralyzed and disabled, and they kept on seeking** (= attempting) **to bring him inside and to place him before Him** (or: in His sight).

19. **So, not finding some sort of way that they could bring him in through the crowd, upon climbing** (or: stepping) **up on the roof** (a flat house-top), **they lowered him down – together with the little couch** (cot; bed; pallet) **– through the midst of the clay tile roofing, [and] into the midst [of the gathering] right in front of Jesus.**

20. **And upon seeing and perceiving THEIR faith, trust and loyalty, he said, "Man** (or: O Human), **your failures** (mistakes; deviations; times of missing the target; errors; sins) **have been made to flow away for you** (or: have been divorced from you and sent away for you; have been made to abandon you and leave you forgiven and liberated)."

21. **At that, the scribes** (scholars; theologians; Law experts) **and the Pharisees began to be continuing in thorough consideration, reasoning and discussion, one after another saying, "Who** (or: What) **is this person who is now speaking blasphemies** (or: impious and irreligious statements; things abusive or irreverent to God)? **Who is now having power or ability to dismiss** (send away; forgive) **failures, mistakes or sins – except God alone?"**

22. **Now Jesus, with full intimate knowledge recognizing their reasonings and dialogues, in giving a discerning reply says to them, "What do you men continue reasoning and considering** (or: Why are you progressively debating) **in your hearts?**

23. **"Which is easier, to be saying, 'Your failures** (mistakes; times of missing the target; errors; sins) **have been sent away for you** (caused to flow off, be divorced, made to abandon and leave you liberated and forgiven),**' or to say, 'Proceed in getting up and continue walking about'?**

24. **"Yet, to the end that you men can have seen and so know that the Son of the Man** (or: Humanity's Son; = the eschatological Messianic figure; or: the human) **continues having [the] right and holding authority upon the earth** (or: constantly possesses privilege from out of Being, on the land,) **to at any point send away failures** (cause mistakes to flow off; divorce errors; cause missed shots to be abandoned, then leave [folks] pardoned and liberated; forgive sins) **..." He said to the paralyzed man, "I am now saying to you, Proceed in getting up, and then after lifting up your cot** (little pallet or bed), **continue going your way into your house."**

25. **And instantly rising up before them** (in their sight), **after picking up that upon which he had been lying, he went off into his house, while continuously giving glory to God** (or: verbally enhancing God's reputation with good opinions, while having imaginations from God).

26. **Then ecstasy seized them all, and they began expressing good opinions about God** (adding glory to God's reputation; having imaginations and impressions from God) **– and yet they were filled with awe and fear, repeatedly saying, "We saw things to the side of normal opinions** (incredible things; things that seem unusual; paradoxes) **today!"**

27. **Then, after these things, He went out and watched** (gazed at; observed) **a customs official** (or: tax collector; possibly: the tenant or lease-holder of the station; tax farmer) **named Levi** [also called Matthew, elsewhere] **sitting at the tax office** (or: toll and customs booth), **and then He said to him, "Be continuously following Me."**

28. **So, leaving everything down behind, after standing up he began following Him.**

29. **Later Levi prepared a great reception banquet for Him within his house. And there was a great crowd of many tax collectors, as well as others who were lying down while dining with them.**

30. **Then the Pharisees and the scribes** (scholars and theologians) **began grumbling with subdued talk and perplexed buzzing** (murmuring) **to His disciples about them, one after another saying, "Why** (Because of what [reason or situation]) **are you folks participating in eating and drinking with the tax collectors and outcasts**
> (folks who because of their lifestyle or means of making a living were considered as failures, or, 'sinners,' by the religious people; folks who did not by habit adhere to the religious customs of the Jewish culture)?"

31. **Then Jesus, giving a decided response, said to them, "The folks being normally healthy and sound are not normally having a need of a healer** (doctor; physician), **but rather those constantly having it badly** (= being constantly sick, or having a continuing illness).

32. **"I have not come to call 'righteous folks'** (= those who consider themselves rightwised in relation to God and mankind; = religious people), **but to the contrary, [to call] outcasts**
> (those considered 'sinners' by the religious community, and therefore rejected by them because of their lifestyles and practices; those who are failures and who continuously miss the goal [of life]; or: irreligious people) **into a change of thinking, a shift in consciousness with a new perspective, and a return to God."** [cf Rom. 12:2]

33. So they said to Him, "John's disciples are frequently fasting and constantly making petitions [to God]; likewise also those of the Pharisees; yet yours are continuously eating and drinking!"

34. Thus Jesus says to them, "You folks continue unable to make the sons of the wedding hall (= the bridegroom's friends and guests) to at any point fast while the bridegroom continues being with them.

35. "But days will continue coming when even (or: also) the bridegroom would (could; may) be lifted up away from them. They will then be habitually fasting during those days."

36. Now He also began telling an illustration to them (or: a parable directed at them), "No one is ripping (or: tearing) a patch from a new cloak (or: outer garment) [and] proceeding to sew [it] on an old cloak! Now if he does, he will proceed both tearing the new one, and the patch from the new one will not continue sounding together (agreeing, or being in symphony; voicing together; corresponding or matching) with the old one.

37. "Furthermore, no one normally puts just-made, new wine into old wineskins (skin bottles). Now if he does, the fresh, new wine will progressively burst and tear the wineskins, and it will proceed being spilled out, and also the wineskins will continue destroyed.

38. "To the contrary, freshly-made, new wine [is] drained into and stored in different, new, wineskins (used-for-the-first-time, or renovated, skin bottles), and then both are preserved.

39. "Also, no one continues wanting new (young, freshly-made [wine]) after immediately drinking [the] old (or: fully-aged), for he is then saying, "The old (or: fully-aged) continues being nicely useful and well adapted to it purpose, and is just fine (or: pleasant)!"

CHAPTER 6

1. Now on a sabbath He happened to be passing on His way through fields of sown grain, and His disciples began plucking (or: picking) the heads of grain, [then] proceeding to rub [them] in pieces between [their] hands, and then were eating [them].

2. So some of the Pharisees questioned, "Why are you people continuing in doing that which is not permitted, from [our] existing, to be done on (or: during) the sabbaths?"

3. Then, giving a decided response, Jesus said to them, "Did you men not even read this which David did when he, himself – as well as those with him – got hungry?

4. "How he entered into God's house, and upon taking the loaves of the Presentation (or: the Placing-before), he ate and gave [some] to those with him – which it is not permitted, forth from [Israel's] existence, to eat, except only [by] the priests?"

> [D adds: On the same day, upon noticing a certain person in the process of practicing his trade (working) on the sabbath, said to him, "Dear fellow (or: O man), if indeed you have seen, so as to now know, what you are continuing in doing (or: presently proceeding to do), you are presently happy (or: you exist being fortunate and blessed); yet if you have not seen, so that you do not know, [then] you are a person upon whom the curse has come, and are a transgressor (one who steps to the side, over the line) of the custom and the Law."]

5. And He went on to say to them (continued laying it out for them), "The Son of the Man (= Adam's offspring; = mankind; or: = the eschatological Messiah figure) is lord (Master; Lord) of the sabbath (or: = A human being is sovereign with respects to the sabbath)."

6. Now on a different sabbath, He happened to enter into the synagogue and [commences] to continue teaching (instructing). There was also a man there, and his right hand was dried up and withered.

7. So the theologians (scribes; scholars of the Law) and the Pharisees began attentively observing from the side, [to see] if He continues treating, caring for, curing or instigating therapy or ongoing treatment on the sabbath, to the end that they could find [something] to proceed to accuse and to bring a charge against Him.

8. **Yet He Himself had seen, and thus perceived, their reasonings and dialogues, so He said to the adult male – the one having the withered hand, "Proceed to get up, and put yourself into the midst [of us]." And so, upon standing up, he stood [thus].**
9. **Then Jesus said to them, "I now ask you men if on the sabbath it is allowed, from [Israel's] existence, to do good, perform virtue and produce excellence, or to do bad, perform worthlessness and produce ugliness; to heal** (deliver; restore to health and wholeness; save) **a person, or to destroy one** (or: to rescue someone, or to lose a soul)**?"**
10. **Then, after looking around at them all, He said to him, "Stretch out your hand."** **So he does – and his hand was moved from its fixed, static condition, and was returned to a normal condition** (or: restored) **as the other one.**
11. **But they, themselves, became filled with a lack of understanding** (an absence of mind, sound thinking, intelligence or good judgment; or: senselessness; madness; insanity), **and began thoroughly deliberating** (talking it over in detail) **to one another [about] what they could** (or: should; would) **do to, or with, Jesus.**

12. **Now it happened** (or: came to be) **during these days [for] Him to go out into the mountain** (or: hill country) **to have thoughts with a view towards having goodness, ease and well-being** (or: to pray), **and so He was continuing through the night within the midst of God's thoughts towards holding goodness**
> (or: in union with possession of the action of God which was directed toward ease; in the influence leading to having well-being, which was God; or: centered in the prayer from God).
13. **So when day was birthed** (or: when it came to be day) **He summoned His students, and was then selecting twelve from them whom He also named emissaries** (sent-forth ones; commissioned representatives)**:**
14. **Simon, whom He also named Peter** (Rock), **then Andrew, his brother, and Jacob** (James). **Also John, Philip and Bartholomew.**
15. **Then Matthew, as well as Thomas, Jacob** (James) **[the son of] Alphaeus, and Simon, the one being normally called Zealot** (or: a zealous person).
16. **Next Judah [the son of] Jacob** (James), **and then Judah** (or: Judas) **– who happened to be** (was birthed) **a person who pre-commits and gives in advance** (or: one who **gives-over** before, in front or **in preference**; or: one who abandoned in time of need; a pre-paid person).

17. **Then after walking down with them He stood upon a flat, level place, and a large crowd of His students** (learners; disciples) **[gathered around] – as well as a great multitude of people from all the Judean [district], Jerusalem, and the coastal regions of Tyre and Sidon, who came to hear Him and to be healed and cured from all of their sicknesses and diseases.**
18. **Even folks who were being continuously mobbed with trouble and annoyance from unclean breath-effects** (spirits; attitudes) **kept on, one after another, being treated or cured.**
19. **Then all the crowds kept on seeking** (= attempting) **to be one after another touching Him – because power and ability was continuously flowing** (or: issuing) **out from beside Him** (= from His presence; or: from at His side), **and it** (or: He) **continued healing everyone.**
20. **And then He, Himself, lifting up His eyes into the midst of** (or: = looking penetratingly and squarely at) **His disciples** (students), **began saying,**
"Happy and blessed [are you] poor and destitute folks! – because God's reign (or: sovereign influence and activity; kingdom) **is now yours** (or: belongs to you, as a group).
21. **"Happy and blessed folks [are] those at the present time being constantly hungry! – because you folks will be progressively fed until satisfied. Happy and blessed [are] the folks presently crying! – because you will proceed to be constantly laughing.**
22. **"You people continue existing being happy and blessed whenever the people** (the humans) **may hate you, detach from you or treat you with ill-will, and whenever they may mark you off by boundaries, so as to separate you, and may even insult or denounce [you], or defame [your] character and reputation, and then may even throw out your** (collective, or, individual) **name as worthless, harmful or wicked – on account of the Son of the Man** (= the eschatological Messianic figure; or: = Adam's son; the Son of mankind).

23. **"You folks be continuously rejoicing and then jump for joy** (or: frisk about) **within that day, for, look and consider! – the wage and reward** (or: the compensation) **belonging to you folks [is] much** (or: vast; great) **within the midst of and in union with the heaven** (or: in the atmosphere)! **You see, their fathers** (= ancestors) **kept on treating the prophets the very same way** (or: repeatedly did to the prophets in accord with the same things).

24. **"Nevertheless, tragic will be the fate for you rich** (wealthy) **folks, because your call to the side for help, supporting influence, encouragement and consolation continues being some distance away and is presently estranged** (or: = your times of prosperity are over), **and you currently have the fullness of what is due you.**

25. **"Tragic will be the fate for you folks who have been filled within and are at the present moment satisfied – because you folks will proceed being hungry** (or: continue going hungry)! **Tragic will be the fate of the people at this time being habitually merry and constantly laughing – because you folks will proceed mourning** (grieving; lamenting) **and you will continue weeping** (crying)!

26. **"Tragic will be the situation whenever all the people may speak well or nicely** (finely; beautifully; ideally) **[of; to; about] you folks, for you remember, their fathers** (= ancestors) **were habitually operating** (doing) **in accord with very same things to the false prophets** (= treating the lying prophets the same way).

27. **"But rather, I am now saying to you folks – the people continuing to listen, and constantly hearing – Be habitually loving your enemies** (accepting and giving yourselves to and for the folks that are hostile in regard to you); **be repeatedly doing ideally to** (constantly performing beautifully for; habitually making or creating finely among) **the folks habitually hating you, constantly radically detaching from you and repeatedly treating you with ill-will.**

28. **"Repeatedly speak words of goodness, ease, well-being and blessing to the people constantly cursing** (or: making negative prayers about) **you folks; be constantly thinking and speaking toward [their] having goodness and well-being: concerning** (or: habitually praying about) **the folks [that] repeatedly threaten, insult, mistreat or abuse you.**

29. **"To the person repeatedly striking and beating you upon the cheek or jaw, repeatedly offer** (or: present; hold to the side) **the other one, as well.**
"Also, from the one presently picking up and taking your cloak (outer garment) **you should not deny, refuse or withhold the tunic, as well** (or: even the undergarment; = shirt).

30. **"Be habitually giving to everyone constantly making requests from you** (or: begging from, or demanding [something] of, you), **and do not make it a habit** (or: cease your custom) **to demand it back** (or: repeatedly ask for it back) **from the person presently or repeatedly taking what is yours.**

31. **"And so, correspondingly and exactly as you folks are normally wanting and intending that these people** (or: folks in general) **should habitually do to and for you, you, yourselves also, be constantly doing likewise to and for them.**

32. **"Further, if you folks habitually love and unambiguously accept the people normally loving you, what sort of grace or favor is it by you** (or: for you; to you; among you)**? You see, the outcasts** (folks who by lifestyle or trade are habitually ceremonially unclean or repeatedly break the Law; people who constantly fail to hit the target, fall short of the goal, or make mistakes; sinners) **are also normally loving and accepting the folks who are habitually loving them.**

33. **"You see, if you folks should continue doing good [to; for; among] the people constantly doing good [to; for; among] you, what sort of grace or favor is it by you** (or: for you; to you; among you)**? The outcasts** (sinners; etc.) **are habitually doing the very same thing!**

34. **"And if you folks should lend [without interest] at the side, to people from which you normally expect to receive [back], what sort of grace or favor is it by you** (or: for you; to you; among you)**? For you see, outcasts** (sinners; etc.) **also are habitually lending to outcasts, with an expected result that they should** (or: can) **get back the equivalent.**

35. **"In any case, be continuously loving your enemies** (urging toward union with the ones hostile to you), **and be constantly doing good** (producing excellence; constructing beneficence;

performing virtue) **and also be habitually lending while expecting [to get] nothing back. Then your wage and reward will continue being much, and you folks will continue being sons** (= having the character and qualities) **of the Most High. You see, He Himself continues existing being benevolent, usefully kind and profitable upon the ungracious, unthankful and ungrateful, as well as [on] the useless, unprofitable, wicked or misery-gushed folks.**
36. **"Continue becoming compassionate people, just as your Father continuously exists being compassionate!**
37. **"And stop** (or: do not continue) **separating and judging, and then under no circumstances can you folks be separated and judged; and stop** (or: do not continue) **pointing down against right relationships and opposing fairness and equity and acting against the Way pointed out and condemning, and then under no circumstances can you be unjustly opposed, condemned or pointed down [at]. Be habitually unbinding and releasing, and you will proceed being loosed-away and repeatedly released.**
38. **"Be constantly giving, and it will continue being given to you – a beautiful, fine and ideal measure: one having been pressed and squeezed down, having been shaken back and forth, [and] continuing to be caused to gush out and spill over** (or: repeatedly made to overflow) **will they be progressively giving into your bosom** (= the pocket formed by tying the outer garment at the waist, then pulling the upper part out into a fold; or: pouring into your lap). **You see, the same measure with which you normally measure [out], will continue being [used to] measure in return** (or: in its place) **to, and for, you folks."**

39. **Now He also told an illustration** (parable) **for them: "A blind person is surely not able to continually lead or guide a blind person on the way. Will they not both proceed falling into a pit or be repeatedly dropping into a well?**
40. **"A disciple** (or: student; apprentice) **is not over the teacher, but yet upon having been thoroughly prepared and adjusted down** (fully instructed, trained and adapted), **he will continue being like** (or: as) **his teacher.**
41. **"So why are you constantly staring at and observing the small sliver of wood or straw that [is] in your brother's eye, yet the rafter** (beam; timber) **in your own eye you continuing not to notice or consider** (bring the mind down on)**?**
42. **"How do you continue able to repeatedly say to your brother, 'O brother, allow me to extract the sliver of wood** (or: straw) **which [is] in your eye,' while at the same [time] continuing not to see a rafter within your [own] eye? You overly-judging and critical person**

> (*hupokrites*; or: one who puts texts under close inspection to sift and separate and then give an answer, an interpretation, an opinion; or: one who lives by separating things yet who under-discerns; or: one who makes judgments from a low view; or: one who under-estimates reality; or: perverse scholar who focus on tiny distinctions)**! First at once extract the rafter from out of your [own] eye, and then you will proceed in seeing clearly to extract the sliver which [is] in the eye of your brother.**

43. **"You see, a fine, ideal** (choice) **tree is not normally producing rotten or diseased fruit, neither [is] a rotten or diseased tree normally producing fine, ideal** (choice) **fruit.**
44. **"Indeed, each tree is consistently being experientially known from its own fruit. For it follows that people are not normally gathering** (or: collecting) **figs from a thorn plant, nor are folks picking and harvesting a cluster of grapes from brambles.**
45. **"A good and virtuous person continually brings forth the good and virtuous thing from out of the midst of the good treasury of his heart, while the worthless** (wicked; spoiled; degenerate; unsound) **person normally brings forth the worthless and unsound** (wicked and degenerate) **thing from out of the midst of the treasury within his heart. You see from out of the midst of the effect from the surrounding abundance of [the] heart his mouth is continually speaking.**

46. **"So why are you folks constantly calling to** (or: summoning) **Me, 'Lord! O Master,' and yet you are not habitually doing what I continue saying** (laying out)**?** [Ezk. 33:29-33]

47. "Everyone who is continually coming to Me and repeatedly listening to and hearing My words (*logoi*, messages; thoughts; ideas; laid-out-patterns-of-information) and then proceeds in doing them – I will proceed in suggesting (or: intimating) to you folks to whom he is like:
48. "He or she is like a person proceeding in building a house, who dug [in the ground] and deepened [the trench], and then put [the] foundation upon the rock-mass. So with the occurring of a flood, the river burst on and dashed against that house – and it was not strong [enough] to shake it, because of the [foresight] for it to have been ideally and finely built.
49. "Yet the person, upon listening or hearing and then not doing, is like a person building a house upon the ground without a foundation, on which the river burst toward and dashed against [it], and it immediately collapsed (fell together) – and the result of the split, break-up and crash of that house became great!" [Isa. 28:14-18; Mat. 7:21-27]

CHAPTER 7

1. When He completed (made full) all His sayings (gush-effects and declarations) unto the hearing of the people (or: into the people's ability to hear), He entered into Capernaum.

2. Now a certain centurion (Roman officer, commander of one hundred soldiers) [owned] a slave who was valued, honored and respected by him, [but who was] continually having it badly (= having an illness; being sick): he continued being about to be progressively reaching his end (= living his last day).
3. So, upon hearing about Jesus, he sent off elders (or: older men) of the Jews with a mission to Him, making a request of Him so that, after coming, He would completely restore his slave to health and wholeness (or: bring his slave safely through [this illness]).
4. Now the men, coming along to Jesus, kept on entreating Him to speedily come to his aid, one after another saying, "He is worthy to (or: of corresponding value and deserving for) whom You should and will proceed in providing (or: holding to the side) this [favor],
5. "for You see, he continues loving (giving himself to) our ethnic group and nation, and he himself built (= authorized, supervised and paid for the building of) the synagogue for us."

6. So Jesus journeyed on with them. But at His already being then not far distant from the house, the centurion sent friends, [to be] presently saying to Him, "O sir (or: Lord; master), do not continue being bothered (or: having to take the trouble) [with this], for I am not fit (or: qualified [= ceremonially clean]; or: [important] enough; of sufficient [social standing]) that you should enter under my roof (or: covering).
7. "For this reason, neither do I consider myself worthy to come to you, but rather, speak by a message (or: in a communication; with a word), and let my servant be healed.
8. "You see I, myself, am a person continuing being set in order under authority – continuing in holding (or: having) soldiers under me. And so I normally am saying to this one, 'Be on your way,' and he proceeds on his way; and to another one, 'Be coming now,' and he proceeds coming; and to my slave, 'Do this at once,' and he proceeds to do [it]."
9. Now upon hearing these things, Jesus marveled and was amazed at him, and so, upon being turned to the crowd following Him, He says, "I am now saying to you folks, that not even in Israel do I find so much confident trust, faith and allegiance!"
10. Then, after returning unto the house, the men having been sent found the slave continuing healthy and being sound.

11. Later – it happened during the next [journey] (or: with other MSS: it occurred on the next [day]) – He traveled on into [the] town being normally called Nain, and a considerable number of His disciples, along with a large crowd, continued traveling together with Him.
12. Now as He neared (came close to) the town gate, – note, and consider this – a dead man, [being the] only-begotten son for his mother – and now she herself was a widow – was being progressively carried out [for burial], and a good-sized crowd from the town was continuing in being together with her.

13. **So, upon seeing her, the Lord** (Master; Owner) **was on the spot affected in His inner parts and felt tender compassion upon her, and so said to her, "Stop weeping** (or: Do not continue crying)**!"**

14. **Then, after approaching, He touched the bier** (an open frame funeral couch used to carry a dead person to burial), **so the folks proceeding in bearing [it] stood [still]. Next He said, "Young man, I am now saying for** (or: to) **you, Be at once aroused and raised up** (or, used intransitively: Rise; Get up)**!"**

15. **And then the dead man sat up and started to proceed speaking. So they gave him to his mother.**

16. **Now fear and respectful awe at once took them all in hand** (or: gripped them all), **and so they began adding to God's reputation, and continued giving God the glory** (credit; repute) **one after another saying, "A great prophet was aroused and raised up among us," and, "God visits and looks in on His people so as to closely observe and help them out!"**

17. **And so, this message** (*logos*; = story; report; communication; news) **went out within the whole of the Judean [district], as well as all the surrounding region, concerning Him.**

18. **Then John's disciples** (students) **reported back [to him] about all these things.**

19. **So, upon calling a certain two of his disciples** (learners) **to himself, John sent [them] to the Lord, saying [by them], "Are You, Yourself, the One who is now progressively coming, or should we continue anticipating and hoping for a different One?"**

20. **Now when coming to be alongside and facing Him, the adult men said, "John the immerser** (or: Baptist) **sent us off with a mission to You, saying [by us], 'Are You, Yourself, the One who is now progressively coming, or should we continue anticipating and hoping for a different One** [other MSS: another One of the same kind]**?'"**

21. **Within that hour He cured or gave attentive care to or prescribed therapy to or instigated ongoing treatment for many folks from sicknesses and diseases, as well as [from] scourges** (lacerating afflictions) **and worthless breath-effects** (miserable attitudes; bad spirits). **Also, He by grace granted favor for many blind people to be constantly seeing.**

22. **And so, with a discerning reply He said to them, "After journeying on your way, report back to John what things you men saw and heard: 'blind people continue seeing again; lame folks' continue walking around; lepers continue being cleansed. Also, 'deaf folks continue hearing;' dead people continue being raised up; 'destitute ones are constantly being brought the good announcement and told the message of goodness, ease and well-being!'** [Isa. 35:5-6; 26:14; 61:1; *cf. Messianic Apocalypse*, Dead Sea Scrolls *4Q521*]

23. **"Further, whoever should not be caused to trip the spring of a trap or to stumble into a snare of offense at** (or: in) **Me is** (continues being) **a happy and blessed person."**

24. **So, after the departing of John's agents** (messengers), **He began to continue saying to the crowds, concerning John, "What did you folks go out into the wilderness** (desert; desolate place) **to be watching? A reed being constantly shaken by a wind?**

25. **"But if not that, what did you go out to see? A person** (human) **having been clothed in soft** (= luxurious) **outer garments? Look around and notice, the folks in splendid** (magnificent; glorious; fashionable) **garments and constantly subsisting in luxury are in the royal environments** (or: palaces), **among the king's associates.**

26. **"But still, what did you go out to see? A prophet** (a person with light ahead of time)**? Yes, I am now saying to you people, even one exceedingly more than a prophet.**

27. **"This man is he concerning whom it has been written:**

> **'Look and consider! I am now sending off My agent** (messenger) **as an emissary** (representative) **before Your face** (= ahead of Your presence)**: he who will progressively construct, fully prepare, equip and put in useful order Your road** (path; way), **in front of You.'** [Mal. 3:1]

28. **"For truly, I now say to you folks, among the people born of women, no one exists being greater than John** [with other MSS: there is not even one prophet more important than John the immerser; or: no one continues being a greater prophet than John the Baptist]. **Yet the smaller** (= less significant) **person within the midst of God's reign** (or: centered in union with the sovereign kingdom and activities of God) **exists being greater** (= more important) **than he.**

148

29. **"And so all the people hearing [him] – as well as** (or: even) **the tax collectors** (or: customs and toll agents; tax farmers/contractors) **– by being immersed** (or: baptized) **showed** (or: declared) **that God is fair, equitable and just [through] John's immersion** (baptism).
30. **"Yet the Pharisees and the scholars of the Law, by not being immersed** (or: baptized) **under and by him, set aside** (displaced; invalidated; = disregarded or rejected), **unto** (into the midst of; to; for) **themselves, God's intent** (the design from God; the purpose of God).
31. **"So to whom, therefore, shall I compare the people** (or: these men) **of this generation, and what are they like?**
32. **"They are like little boys** (or: children; boys and girls) **who are habitually sitting in a marketplace and are constantly shouting to** (or: calling out to; accosting) **one another, who are repeatedly saying,**

'**We play the flute** (or: pipe a tune) **for you guys, and yet you are not dancing; we sing funeral songs** (or: wail), **and yet you do not cry** (= they would play neither games of festivals nor of funerals).'
33. **"You see, John the immerser** (or: Baptist) **has come neither habitually eating bread nor normally drinking wine** (= living the life of an ascetic), **and yet you men are constantly saying, 'He continues presently having** (or: constantly possesses) **a demon** (Hellenistic concept and term: = animistic influence).'
34. **"The Son of the Man** (Mankind's son; = Adam's son, or, the eschatological Messianic figure) **has come and is now here, constantly eating and habitually drinking** (= living the life of a normal person), **and you men are repeatedly saying, 'Look, and think of that! A person** (man) **[who is] a glutton** (or: = breaks diet codes) **and a drunkard** (person normally drinking too much wine); **a friend of** (one fond of, or, liking) **tax collectors and outcasts** (failures; sinners; irreligious folks who do not adhere to the conduct prescribed by custom and religious law)!'
35. **"And yet** (or: = For all that; or: All the same), **Wisdom is shown to be fair, equitable and just** (or: is vindicated and declared right) **from all Her children** (= offspring)!" [*cf* 1 Cor. 1:23-24]

36. **Now a certain man of the Pharisees had been making a request of** (or: kept asking) **Him, to the end that He would eat with him. So eventually, after entering into the Pharisee's house, He lay down on a couch [to eat].**
37. **Then – now look and consider this! – a woman who was certainly an outcast** (a sinner; not in compliance with the cultural and religious rules) **in the town, upon personally learning accurately that He is presently lying down [at a meal] within the Pharisee's house, is at once bringing an alabaster [container] of perfumed oil** (aromatic juices distilled from trees) **[which she had been] taking care of and attending to, so as to preserve [it], having acquired it as payment.** [note: final clause is a conflation from the semantic range of κομιζω]
38. **And so, taking a stand behind [Him] – beside the feet of Jesus – [and] continuously weeping, she started to be progressively making His feet wet with the tears! So then she began wiping [them] off with [the] hair of her head, and continued tenderly kissing His feet while continuing to anoint [them] with the perfumed oil.**

39. **Now the Pharisee – the one inviting Him – upon seeing [this], continued laying the matter out, saying within himself, "If this man were The Prophet, he would have been realizing** (or: recognizing) **and coming to a personal knowledge of who, and of what sort, [is] the woman who is certainly continuing to touch Him – that she is** (or: by habit continues being) **an outcast** (sinner; societal failure)!"
40. **And so Jesus, giving a discerning and decided reply, said to him, "Simon, I am progressively having** (or: I continue holding) **something to say to you."**
So the man is then affirming, "Teacher, say [it] (or: speak up; tell the rumor; utter an oracle)!"
41. **"Two men continued being debtors to a certain creditor** (moneylender). **The one continued indebted, still owing five hundred denarii** (silver coins; = 500 days' wages), **yet the one in the different situation [owed] fifty** [i.e., = one owed ten times the amount of the other].
42. **"At their continuing to not having [anything with which] to pay [him] back, he gave grace to both** (or: he deals graciously and favorably with both; or: = he freely cancelled the debts for both). **Therefore, which of them will proceed to be loving** (giving himself to) **him more?"**

43. **So giving a considered answer, Simon said, "As I take it under consideration, I am supposing that [it would be] the one to whom he gives the more grace** (or: = to whom he freely cancelled the greater debt)."
Now He says to him, "You decide and judge correctly (or: uprightly; in a straight manner)."
44. **With that, being turned toward the woman, He affirms to Simon, "Were you observing and are you now seeing this woman? I entered into your house – you did not give to Me water upon [My] feet! Yet this woman! She wets My feet with [her] tears, and then wipes [them] off with her hair!**
45. **"You do not give to Me a kiss of friendship. Yet this woman! From [the hour] in which I entered, she does not leave off** (cease; stop) **repeatedly kissing My feet tenderly!**
46. **"You did not anoint My head with olive oil** (= common oil). **Yet this woman! She anoints My feet with perfumed oil** (or: massages My *feet* with fragrant ointment)!
47. **"Pertaining to this gift, and from its grace, I am now saying to you, Her many failures** (mistakes; miss-shots; deviations; sins) **had been caused to flow away, and continue sent-off, divorced, forgiven – because she loved much** (or: so that she urges much for reunion)!
Now for whom little continues being caused to flow away (or: to whom little is habitually forgiven), **he continues habitually loving** (seeking reunion with acceptance) **little."**
48. **With this He says to her, "Your failures** (deviations; mistakes; times of missing the target; sins) **had been caused to flow away, and continue sent-off, divorced and forgiven."**

49. **At this, those folks reclining back together [at the meal] started to be saying among themselves, "Who is this man who also is now dismissing mistakes** (forgiving failures and deviations; sending away sins)?"
50. **So Jesus said to the woman, "Your trust and faith had restored you to health and now effect a condition of wholeness** (or: Your faithfulness had saved and rescued you, leaving you in a safe place). **Continue going on your journey into Peace of the Joining."**

CHAPTER 8

1. **Later it occurred that He Himself then began making His way through city by city and village by village, in consecutive order, repeatedly making public proclamation as a herald, and constantly bringing and declaring God's sovereign reign** (or: kingdom; the influence and activity of the ruling which is God) **as good news of ease and well-being – and together with Him, the twelve,**
2. **as well as certain women who were ones having been treated, cured or restored from bad attitudes** (worthless and misery-gushed breath-effects; malicious spirits) **and weaknesses** (or: illnesses)**: Mary, the one normally being called Magdalene – from whom seven demons** (Hellenistic worldview, concept and term: = animistic influences) **had gone out** (had departed),
3. **then Joanna, wife of Chuza, Herod's man-in-charge** (or: manager; steward; financial secretary), **and Susanna, as well as many different women, who continued giving attending and supportive service to them** [i.e., to Jesus and His comrades] **– from out of their personal possessions and resources.**

4. **Now with a large crowd being gathered together, and with the people keeping on making their way to Him from town after town, He spoke through an illustration** (a parable):
5. **"The sower** (= the farmer; the one normally scattering seed) **went out to sow his seed, and during the process of his sowing, one [handful] actually fell along the path** (or: beside the road), **and then the birds of the sky** (or: atmosphere; heaven) **ate it down** (or: devoured it).
6. **"Also, a different [handful] fell down upon the rock mass, and later, having been sprouted and caused to grow, it was dried out and caused to wither, because it was not having moisture.**
7. **"Then a different [handful] fell within the midst of the thorns, thistles and prickly weeds, then, after their being made to grow up together, the thorny plants choked it off.**
8. **"Still a different [handful] fell into the good soil, and later, having been sprouted and caused to grow, it produced a hundred times as much fruit as had been sown."** Upon **concluding in laying-out and saying these things, He then call out** (or: shouts), **"Let the**

person presently having ears to be now listening and hearing, continue to listen and hear!"

9. **Now His disciples began enquiring of Him what this illustration** (parable) **might be** (= might mean).

10. **So He said, "To** (or: For; With; In; Among) **you folks it has been given** (or: granted; gifted) **to intimately know from experience The Secrets** (or: mysteries) **of** (or: pertaining to; from and whose source is; or: which are) **God's reign** (or: kingdom; sovereign influence and activity). **Yet to** (for; in; among) **the rest** (the remaining folks) **[it is given] in illustrations** (parables; things cast alongside for comparison), **to the end that,**

> 'while constantly looking, they cannot (or: may not; would not) be presently seeing,
> and while repeatedly listening, they can (or: could; should; would) not make things
> flow together so as to understand (comprehend; = get the meaning).' [Isa. 6:9]

11. **"Now the illustration is this** (or: the parable means this)**:
The seed sown is God's Word** (the thought, idea, reason, laid-out communication of meaningful information and message, which is God; or: the *Logos* from God; the Blueprint-Pattern of God).

12. **"Yet those beside the path** (road; way) **are the folks [who] upon hearing [have] the adversary** (or: the person thrusting something through folks) **repeatedly coming, and it** (or: he; or: [that person]) **is constantly** (or: habitually) **picking up and removing the Word** (thought; message; information; *Logos*) **from their hearts so that they would not – upon** (or: in) **trusting and believing – be delivered** (rescued; made healthy and whole; saved; kept safe).

13. **"Now those upon the rock-mass [are] those who – whenever they should hear – continue welcoming and receiving the Word** (thought; message; information) **with joy. And yet, these do not continue having a root. They are folks who continue trusting and believing for a season, and then, during a season** (or: within a situation) **of testing and trial, they progressively stand off and position themselves away, continuing to be withdrawn.**

14. **"And now the [handful] falling into the midst of thorns: these are the folks [that] are at one point listening and hearing. And then, under anxieties** (cares; worries; concerns) **and by wealth and through pleasures** (enjoyments; gratifications) **of life** (= the daily functions of living and making a living, and the things that crowd our lives), **in continuing in going their way they are being progressively choked together and stifled – and then they are not continuing on to the goal of bearing mature fruit** (or: are not progressing to bear the finished product).

15. **"But the [handful] within the ideal soil – these are those folks who, at one point listening to and hearing the Word** (the thought; the idea; the message; the information; the *Logos*) **within an ideal** (beautiful) **and good** (virtuous) **heart, continue holding [it] down within and retaining [it] – and so they continue bearing fruit** (producing a harvest) **within the midst of a remaining-under, and in union with endurance** (or: centered in a persistent endurance which remains under [the task, burden or testing/trials] to give support).

16. **"Now no one, after lighting a lamp, is in the habit of covering it with a pot** (or: in a vessel; by an instrument or utensil), **or normally puts [it] down under a bed or underneath a couch; but to the contrary, he is normally putting [it] upon a lampstand, so that the folks progressively coming into the midst can continue seeing** (observing; casting a look at) **the light.**

17. **"For, you see, nothing continues being a hidden thing** (or: there is nothing hidden) **which will not proceed in coming to be visible and something seen in clear light. Neither [is there] something hidden away** (or: concealed) **which can** (or: should) **not at some point by all means be intimately and experientially known** (or: made known), **and can** (or: should) **come into a [situation that is] open, visible, apparent and seen in clear light.**

18. **"Therefore, keep on looking at and noticing how you folks continue hearing** (or: are habitually listening). **You see, whoever can continue possessing** (or: should habitually have and hold), **to him it** (or: He) **will continue being given; and whoever cannot continue possessing** (or: should or would not habitually have and hold), **even that which he constantly imagines** (thinks; supposes; presumes; or: seems; appears; or: is supposed) **to continue possessing will be progressively picked up and taken from him."**

19. **Now at one point His mother and brothers came along toward Him, and yet were unable to attain their aim to fall in with and meet with Him – because of the crowd.**
20. **So it was reported back to Him, "Your mother and brothers have been standing – and yet stand – outside, desiring** (wanting; intending) **to see You."**
21. **Yet, making a decided reply, He says to them, "My mother and brothers are now these folks – the people habitually listening to and hearing** [implying: obeying] **God's Word** (or: the *Logos* of and from God; etc.) **and then habitually doing** (performing; producing) **[it]."**

22. **Now it occurred on one of those days, [that] He, as well as His disciples, stepped into a sailing vessel** (ship; boat; bark) **and He said to them, "Let us pass through** (= cross) **unto the other side of the lake."**
23. **Then they were led up [upon the water]** (= they shoved off and set sail), **yet [after a time], during their sailing, He fell asleep. Later, a furious, violent windstorm** (squall; whirlwind; hurricane) **suddenly descended into the lake, and they began being completely filled** (swamped) **with [water] and continued to be in danger.**
24. **So then, after approaching, they got Him fully awake, repeatedly saying, "Captain** (or: Commander; Chief; = Boss; perhaps: Instructor), **O Captain, we are progressively losing ourselves** (or: we, ourselves, are presently perishing)!" **Now He, having been fully aroused, gave a respectful directive to the wind and to the violent surging of the water – and it came to be calm** (or: a stillness was birthed on the surface of the water).
25. **And so He said to them, "Where [is] your confidence, trust and faith?"**
Now, having been caused to fear (or: being afraid), **they marveled with amazement, in turn saying to one another, "Who really is this Man, that to even the winds and to the water He now applies directives** (or: gives orders and adds arrangements)? **– and in submissive hearing they continue giving obedience to Him!"**

26. **So then they sailed down into the region of the Gerasenes** [other MSS: Gergesenes] **which is across on the side opposite the Galilee [district].**
27. **But at His going out on the shore** (or: land), **a certain adult man from out of the town met up with Him – one continuously possessing** (having and holding) **demons** (Hellenistic concept and term: = animistic influences). **Now for a considerable period of time he did not clothe himself with a cloak** (outer garment; perhaps = clothing in general) **and by habit he was not staying** (remaining) **in a house, but rather, among the memorial tombs, instead.**
28. **Now, upon seeing Jesus and uttering up a cry** (or: crying aloud; screaming), **he fell toward Him. And then in a loud voice he said, "What [is there] for me and for You** (or: What [is the connection] to me, and in You; may = What do want with me), **Jesus, Son of the Most High God? I beg** (or: urgently request) **You... You should not test my qualities or cause me pain or distress!"**
29. **You see, He began passing on an announcement and continued giving instruction to the unclean breath-effect** (unpruned spirit, attitude or state of mind) **to at once come out of** (or: go forth from) **the man. For you see, many times it had seized and violently gripped him together** (= took control of him), **and he was from time to time being bound with and confined by chains and shackles** (ankle fetters), **being repeatedly guarded** (or: from time to time kept in protective custody). **And yet, repeatedly breaking the bonds in two, he kept on being driven** (or: urged forward; impelled) **off and away from** [other MSS: by; under] **the demon** (Hellenistic worldview, concept and term: = animistic influence; = an influence that was not part of him), **into the uninhabited places** (wilderness areas; desert regions; lonely places).
30. **So Jesus asked him, "What is [the] name for you?" Now the man said, "Legion** (or: An Army)," **because many demons** (= influences) **at some point entered into him.**
31. **Then THEY began calling Him alongside for aid and assistance, entreating Him to the end that He would** (might) **not add directives and apply arrangements for** (or: give orders to) **them to go off into the Deep** (the Abyss; [note: a term often used of the ocean]).
32. **Now there was a considerable herd of pigs** (hogs; swine) **being grazed** (pastured) **there, within the hill country** (or: on the mountain), **and so THEY entreated Him for assistance, to the end that He would proceed to allow** (or: progressively permit) **them to enter into those [pigs]. And so He gave permission to them.**

33. **So the demons** (= influences), **after going out from the man, entered into the pigs** (hogs; swine). **Next, the herd stampeded** (rushed headlong) **down the precipice** (cliff; steep bank) **into the lake – and it was choked, so as to drown.**

34. **Now the herdsmen, upon seeing what had happened, fled and reported back unto the town and into the fields** (= countryside).

35. **So people came out to see what had happened, and thus they came to Jesus and found the man, from whom the demons** (= influences) **went out, clothed with a cloak** (or: outer garments) **as well as sane and continuing in a sound and healthy frame of mind, remaining sitting beside the feet of Jesus – and they were made to fear** (or: were afraid).

36. **Then the folks having seen [it] explained to them the report of how the person being affected by demons** (= influences) **was made whole and restored to health** (rescued; delivered; saved).

37. **As a result, the whole fullness** (= the entire populace) **of the territory** (or: region) **surrounding Gerasenes** [other MSS: Gergesenes] **asked Him to go** (or: get) **away from them – because they began being constrained and hemmed in with a joint-possession, pressing them together by, with and in a great fear.**

38. **So He Himself, upon stepping into [the] sailing vessel, turned away. But the adult man – from whom the demons** (Hellenistic worldview, concept and term: = animistic influences) **had gone out – began begging and kept on asking to continue being together with Him. Yet He dismissed him** (loosed him away), **while saying,**

39. **"Proceed returning into your house** (or: unto your household), **and then make it a habit to fully relate and describe as many things as GOD did to, performed in and produced for you." And so he went off, down through the whole town, repeatedly making a public proclamation – as a herald – of as many things as JESUS did** (etc.) **to, in and for him.**

40. **Now it happened in the midst of the occurrence for Jesus to progress in returning, the crowd welcomed and favorably received Him – for you see, they were all progressively forming opinions about Him and continuing in anticipating Him.**

41. **Then – look, and consider! – an adult man whose name [was] Jairus – and this man existed being a leader** (or: ruler; presiding official) **of the synagogue – came, and upon falling at the feet of Jesus, began calling Him to his side for help, continuing to entreat Him to [come and] enter into his house,**

42. **because there was with and for him an only-daughter – about twelve years old – and she, herself, was progressively dying off. Now during the [situation for] Him to be progressively leading the way and bring things under control, the crowd continued crowding together around Him to the point of almost overwhelming and suffocating – as it were, [figuratively] strangling – Him.**

43. **At the same time** (or: In this situation), **[there was] a woman who – being continuously in a [condition of] a flowing issue of blood** (a discharge; a hemorrhage) **for twelve years [and] one who was spending [her] whole livelihood on physicians – had no strength, [and] from no one [was able] to be treated or cured.**

44. **Approaching from behind, she at one point touched the border** (or: edge; hem; fringe; tassel) **of His outer garment** (or: cloak) **– and the flowing issue of her blood** (her hemorrhage) **instantly stopped and stood firm, at the side of usefulness** (= stopped).

45. **Then Jesus said, "Who [was] the person touching Me?"**
Yet with the continued saying, "No," contradicting and denying from everyone, Peter and those together with him said, "Master (or: Commander; Chief; = Boss; perhaps: Instructor), **the crowds are continuously pressing together on You, hemming You in, and are constantly rubbing closely together, and You are saying, 'Who [was] the person touching Me?'"**

46. **But Jesus said, "Someone touched Me, for I Myself know by personal experience [that] power** (and/or: ability) **has gone** (proceeded) **out of the midst from Me."**

47. **Now the woman, upon seeing that she had not escaped notice, came trembling. And then, falling down toward Him** (or: prostrating to Him) **gave a report in the sight of all the people, explaining through what cause and reason she had touched Him, and so was instantly healed, to the side of usefulness** (or: for useful [service]).

48. So He said to her, "Daughter, your trust, faith and allegiance healed, delivered and restored you to health and wholeness (saved and rescued you). Continue traveling your journey into Peace of the Joining [or: = shalom]."

49. While He is still speaking, a certain associate of the synagogue leader is presently coming, then is saying, "Your daughter has died. Do not any longer continue bothering the teacher."
50. Yet Jesus, at hearing [this], gave a decided response to him, "Stop (or: Do not continue) fearing, only at once trust and be in faith (or: believe; be confident; be loyal), and she will proceed in being restored to health and wholeness (progress in being rescued and saved)."

51. Now upon coming unto the house, He allowed no one to enter with Him, except Peter, John and Jacob (James) – as well as the father and mother of the girl.
52. But all the people kept on weeping (crying and lamenting) and continued grieving, repeatedly beating their breasts, for her.
So [pausing], He said, "Stop crying (or: Do not continue weeping and lamenting), for you see, she did not die off, but to the contrary, she continues fast asleep."
53. And so they began ridiculing and laughing Him down with mocking – having seen, and thus knowing (perceiving), that she died off.
54. So He Himself, [after casting everyone outside and] then strongly taking hold of her hand, calls out loudly (shouts; voices in exclamation) by saying, "Young girl, be waking up and proceed arising [other MSS: rouse yourself and get up]!" [note: brackets not in oldest MSS]
55. And then her spirit (breath-effect; or: the result of her breathing) returns (turned around upon [her]) at once, and she instantly stood up for useful [service] (or: at the side of usefulness), so He gave directions and made thorough arrangements for her to at once be given [something] to eat.
56. And so her parents "stood out of themselves" in amazement and ecstasy.
But He gave instructions to them to tell to no one the [incident] having been birthed (or: [what] had been happening and was now occurring and existing).

CHAPTER 9

1. Now later, after calling the twelve together unto Himself, He gave to them power and ability, as well as authority (right and privilege from out of Being), upon all the demons (Hellenistic worldview, concept and term: = animistic influences) and thus (or: that is,) to be habitually giving care for, treating or curing sicknesses and diseases.
2. And then He sent them off with a mission (as emissaries) to be constantly making public proclamation, heralding God's reign (or: kingdom; dominion; sovereign influence and activity) and to be constantly (or: from time to time) healing the weak, feeble, ill and inadequate folks.
3. He also said, pertaining to (with a view to) them, "You men make it a habit to lift up and carry nothing into the path (road; way) – neither staff, nor food pouch (or: beggar's bag), nor loaf of bread, nor silver (= money), nor even to be having two tunics (undergarments) apiece.
4. "Then, into whatever house you folks may enter, you men continue staying (remaining; dwelling; abiding) there – and then periodically go out (or: venture forth) from that place.
5. "And yet, as many people as may perhaps not continue welcoming and receiving you folks, when going out away from that town, be continuously shaking off the dust from your feet – [pointing] unto evidence (into a testimony and a witness) upon (= against) them."
    [note: Hospitality in those times and countries involved having a servant wash the feet of their guests; further: Jews did this when they left a Gentile country, so this would indicate that this town was being regarded as polluted and unholy, and in the same category as the Gentiles]
6. So after going out (or: upon setting forth), they continued passing through – from village to village – constantly bringing and declaring the good news, as well as continuing to tend, give care to or cure [folks] everywhere.

7. Now Herod [Antipas], the tetrarch (= district governor), **heard of all the things continuing to be happening, and he continued being bewildered and thoroughly perplexed because of the [rumors] being repeatedly told by certain folks that John [the immerser] was raised up from out of the midst of dead folks,**
8. **yet by some, that Elijah had appeared, but then other folks [said] that some** (or: a certain) **prophet of the ancient ones had risen** (or: had stood back up again).
9. **So Herod said, "I, myself, beheaded John – but who is this man about whom I continue hearing such things?" And so he began trying** (or: seeking [a way]) **to see Him, and thus, to become acquainted with Him.**

10. **Later, upon returning, the men sent off on the mission** (or: the emissaries; the sent-ones; the representatives; the commissioned folks) **fully related and described to Him as many things as they had done, as well as whatever they had taught. So then, taking them along** (or: aside), **He privately withdrew into, and afforded an adequate place and room for, a town being normally called Bethsaida.**
11. **But the crowds, finding [this] out** (or: coming to know of [it]) **followed after Him. So, upon being favorably received and welcomed, He began speaking to them about God's reign** (or: sovereign kingdom and activities), **and continued healing or curing the folks having a need of a cure or treatment.**
12. **Now the day started to be progressively declining** (or: leaning and sloping down; = coming to a close), **so upon approaching, the twelve said to Him, "Loose-away** (Release; Dismiss) **the crowd so that they, after going on their way into the villages and fields round about, can** (or: may) **loosen-down** (= relax, camp or procure lodging) **and should find food and provisions, because we are in a desolate** (uninhabited; desert) **place here."**
13. **Yet He said to them, "You yourselves give them [something] to eat."**
But they said, **"There are not with** (or: for) **us more than five loaves of bread and two fishes – unless perhaps, upon going our way we could at a marketplace buy food [to dispense] into all these people." You see, there were about five thousand adult men.**
14. **So He says to His disciples, "Make them recline in groups of up to about fifty, in situations for a meal."**
15. **And then they did [it] in that way, and had them all recline for a meal.**
16. **Now after taking** (or: receiving) **the five loaves and the two fishes [and] looking up into the sky** (or: the atmosphere; the heaven), **He spoke words of blessing and well-being on them, then completely broke [them] down into pieces and began giving [them] to the disciples to set beside, for, and among, the crowd.**
17. **And so they all ate and were filled to being satisfied. Then the surplus was picked up by them: twelve hand-baskets of fragments** (results of the breaking into pieces).
18. **Later – it happened during the [situation for] Him to be continuing in communing toward having goodness** (or: praying), **in seclusion – the disciples came together to Him and Jesus inquired of them, saying, "Who are the crowds normally** (or: presently; continuing in) **saying [that] I am to be** (or: What do the crowds now make reference [of] Me being)?"**
19. **So they, giving considered responses, said, "John the immerser** (or: Baptist)." **Yet others [say] "Elijah." But still others [said] "that some prophet of the ancient ones has risen** (or: stood back up again)."**
20. **Then He said to them, "So you, yourselves – who are you folks normally saying [that] I am to be?"**
Now Peter, giving a considered response, said, **"God's Anointed One** (or: The Christ of, or who comes from, God; = God's Messiah)."
21. **Then He, after giving a respectful compliment** (or: assessing [the situation]; or: adding respectful admonition), **passed on the information [that] no one is to continue saying this** (or: made the announcement at their side: "No one is to presently tell this"),
22. **then saying that, "It continues being binding and necessary that the Son of the Man** (or: mankind's Son; = Adam's Son; = the expected eschatological Messiah; or: the Human Being) **is to experience many things** (= both good and neutral things, as well as suffering), **and then, from examination, scrutiny and testing, to be rejected by the elders, the chief** (or: ranking)

priests and scribes (scholars; theologians of the Law), **and finally to be killed off – and yet on** (or: in) **the third day to be aroused and raised up."**

23. **Now He went on to say toward all, "If anyone continues willing and intending to progressively come after Me, let him at once deny, disown and say, 'No,' to, himself** (or: in rejection, contradict her 'self'), **and then lift up and carry his execution stake** (or: pole from which to be publicly suspended; cross) **each day, and then be habitually following after Me.**
24. **"You see, whoever may** (or: would; can) **habitually will** (or: purpose; intend; want) **to keep his soul safe** (or: to rescue or save his self-life) **will be destroying it** (or: will progressively lose it). **Yet whoever can** (or: may) **at some point destroy his soul** (or: lose his self-life) **– on account of Me – this person will continue keeping it safe** (or: will progressively rescue, deliver and heal it, and thus return it to its original state and condition of health and wholeness).
25. **"For how or in what way is a person normally furthered or benefited by gaining, or making a profit of, the whole world** (organized system of economics, culture, religion or government; universe; adorned arrangement; aggregate of humanity) **while yet destroying** (or: losing) **himself or suffering detriment, loss, disadvantage, damage or forfeit?** [cf Mk. 8:36]
26. **"It follows that whoever may be ashamed of, or embarrassed by. Me and [of or by] My words** (messages; thoughts; ideas; conveyances of information), **the Son of the Man** (mankind's offspring; = Adam's son; or: the eschatological messianic figure) **will proceed in being ashamed of and embarrassed by this person – whenever He may come or go within His glory** (in union with His assumed appearance, which calls forth praise), **as well as the Father's**
     (or: can go in the reputation and opinion which belongs to Him and to the Father; or: should come in a glorifying thought from Him and from the Father; would come in the imagination which is Him and which is the Father), **and which belongs to the set-apart agents** (or: even from the sacred messengers; which pertains to the holy folks with a message).
27. **"Now I am presently saying to you folks truthfully** (or: I presently tell you folks, truly) **there are certain people of those now standing here in this place who can under no circumstances taste** (= partake of or experience) **death until they can** (or: would) **see and perceive God's reign** (or: the kingdom influence and activity from God; the realm of God)."

28. **So it came to be** (happened; was birthed) **– about eight days after these words – that, taking along Peter, John and Jacob (James), He walked up into the hill country** (or: climbed into the mountain) **to think and commune with a view toward having goodness, ease and well-being** (or: to pray).
29. **Then it happened! During that [occasion] for Him to continuing speaking toward having goodness** (or: praying), **the form** (external appearance) **of His face became different, and His clothing** (apparel) **continued flashing forth bright whiteness and brilliant luster.**
30. **Also – look, and consider this! – two adult men** (males), **who were and continued being Moses and Elijah, continued speaking with Him.**
31. **These men were being seen** (or: were being caused to be visible and were being observed) **in the midst of the manifestation which called forth praise and in union with [the] glory** (or: in an assumed appearance). **They kept on talking [about] His exodus** (His way out; His path from out of the midst; or: His departure) **which was progressively about to be filling up to completion within Jerusalem.**
32. **Now Peter and those with him had been men having been weighed down and burdened by sleep** (may = were half asleep; or: = were sound asleep), **yet, upon being fully awake and alert, they see His glory** (praise-inducing manifestation; assumed appearance) **and the two adult men standing together with Him.**
33. **And then – it happened during the [situation for] them** [= Moses and Elijah] **to progressively be thoroughly separated and detached from Him – Peter said to Jesus, "Master** (or: = Rabbi; Instructor; Chief; = Boss; [p45, X read: Teacher]), **it is a beautiful and fine [situation] for us to continue being here! So let us construct three tents** (or: Tabernacles): **one for** (or: to) **You, and one for** (or: to) **Moses, and one for** (or: to) **Elijah!" – [he was] not seeing, realizing or being aware of what he was then saying!**
34. **But at his being in the midst of saying these things, a cloud was birthed** (came to be; formed) **and began to cast a shadow upon, and then continued overshadowing, them. Now**

in the midst of the [situation for] them to enter into the cloud, they were made fearful (or: became wary and afraid; or: were filled with reverent awe).

35. And then a Voice was birthed (or: a Sound occurred) from out of the midst of the Cloud, progressively laying it out and saying, "This Man is (or: exists being) My Son, the Man having been selected, picked out and now being the Chosen One! From and of Him, you men continue hearing (or, as imperative: You folks be habitually listening to Him)."

36. And in the midst of the [situation for] the Voice to be birthed (or: the Sound to occur), Jesus was found alone. And so they, themselves, kept silent and within those days reported back to no one anything of what they had seen.

37. Now it happened on the next day, after their having come down from the hill country (or: mountain), [that] a large crowd met up with Him.

38. Then – look and consider [this]! – an adult man (male) shouted out from the crowd, by saying, "Teacher, I am now begging (urgently asking from my need) of You to look upon my son, because he is an only-begotten one for me,

39. and look, a breath-effect (or: spirit; attitude) is periodically (or: habitually) taking hold of him, and unexpectedly he suddenly cries out, and it repeatedly convulses and tears him, accompanied with foam – and it is normally withdrawing and departing away from him with hard labor, continuing to rub him [against things] and bruise him.

40. And so I begged of Your disciples so that they would throw it out – and yet they had no power and were unable."

41. So Jesus, giving a discerning and decided answer, said, "O undependable generation without trust, faith or belief and having been thoroughly twisted in two and fully turned (or: distorted into separate parts and perverted)! Until when shall I continue being facing toward, and focus upon, you people, and shall I Myself continue holding you up (or: holding up with you; or: = putting up with and tolerating you)? Bring your son over here to Me."

42. But while he is still approaching, the demon (Hellenistic concept and term: = animistic influence) burst forth [in] him (= tore and shattered his inner being) and then with [him] violently convulsed. So Jesus spoke a serious but respectful directive to the unclean breath-effect (or: unpruned attitude; or: = diseased spirit; = distorted life-force) and so healed the boy and gave him back to his father. [note: "demon" equates to "breath-effect/spirit"]

43. Now they all began being struck out of themselves with astonishment, continuing being amazed at and by God's greatness (on the magnificence from, and majesty of, God).

44. So at everyone's continued marveling in wonder and admiration upon all [the] things which He kept on doing (performing; making), He said to His disciples, "You, yourselves, put (or: lay [up]) these words (thoughts; ideas; messages) at once into your ears. You see, the Son of the Man (or: the Son of humanity; = Adam's offspring; or: = eschatological messianic figure; the Human Being) continues being about to be progressively given over (transferred; passed along; delivered) into [the] hands of mankind (or: = unto [the control] of humans)."

45. Yet they continued being ignorant (without personal, intimate knowledge and insight) [in regard to] this saying. In fact, it was continuing concealed, having been hidden at the side, away from them, so that they could not sense or notice it. And so they continued being afraid to ask Him about this saying (concerning the declaration in the gush-effect).

46. Now later, a reasoning and a discussion entered in among them – the [topic being] who might continue being [the] greatest of them (= most important among them).

47. So Jesus, seeing and thus knowing the reasoning and discussions of their hearts, after taking hold of a little child, stands it [note: Greek is neuter, = either a boy or a girl] beside Himself,

48. and then says to them, "Whoever may welcome and favorably receive this little child – upon the basis of (or: at) My Name – continues welcoming and favorably receiving Me. And whoever may welcome and favorably receive Me constantly welcomes and favorably receives the One sending Me off on a mission and as an emissary (a representative). You see, the one habitually subsisting inherently as one under the leader or subordinate to the chief, and thus the smaller and lesser person among you all, this person is a great one."

49. **So John, giving a considered response, says, "Master** (or: Captain; Instructor; Leader; = Boss), **we saw someone repeatedly casting out demons** (Hellenistic concept and term: = animistic influences) **in** (or: in union with; centered in) **Your Name, and so we were trying to forbid, hinder and prevent him, because he does not continue following with us."**
50. **But Jesus said to him, "Stop** (or: Do not continue) **forbidding, hindering or preventing. You see** (or: It follows that), **the person who is not down on or against you folks is [standing] over [and sheltering] you folks and is for you."**

51. **Now it came to pass – amidst the progression for the days to be filled together unto fulfillment pertaining to His being taken back up again – that He, Himself, firmly set [His] face** (= His decided focus and direction) **to proceed going His way** (journey) **into Jerusalem.**
52. **So He sent off agents** (messengers; Greek: *angelos*) **as representatives before His face** (= in advance of His presence). **And thus, after going their way, they entered into a village of Samaritans, so as to prepare and make ready for Him.**
53. **And yet they [i.e., the Samaritans] did not welcome or receive Him** (= offered Him no hospitality), **so that** (or: because) **His face** (= His decision or focus) **kept on being that of continuing in journeying on unto Jerusalem.**
54. **Now, upon seeing** (or: perceiving) **[this], the disciples** [with other MSS: His apprentices] **Jacob** (James) **and John said, "Lord, are You now desiring that we should tell 'fire to come down from the sky** (or: from the atmosphere, or heaven) **– and so to seize and take them up so as to overcome and ruin' them, even as Elijah did?"** [2 Kings 1:9-16]
55. **Yet, being turned, He respectfully spoke a stern admonition to them** [later MSS add: and said, "You do not see or know of what sort of breath-effect (spirit; attitude) you are. For the Son of the Man does not come to destroy {the} lives (or: souls) of humanity, but rather to rescue, heal, save and restore to health and wholeness"].
56. **And so they went their way** (journeyed on) **into a different village.**

57. **Later, upon their continuing in traveling** (journeying) **on their way on the road** (or: in the path or way), **a certain person said to Him, "I will continue following You wherever You may continue going off** [p45 and others read: may continue leading under control], **Lord!"**
58. **Then Jesus said to him, "The foxes are normally having burrows** (or: dens; holes), **and the birds of the sky** (or: atmosphere; heaven) **[have] nests** (or: roosts; places for 'tenting-down,' i.e., camping or lodging), **yet the Son of the Man is not normally or presently having [a place] where He may recline [His] head."**
[comment: here, He discourages the volunteer; next, He calls a different person]
59. **Now He said to a different person, "Be habitually following Me." Yet the person says, "Master** (or: Lord), **allow** (or: Permit) **me first, after going away, to bury my father."**
60. **But He said to him, "Leeave** (or: Abandon and allow) **the dead folks to bury their own dead people. Yet you, yourself, after going away, throughout [the land] and abroad be constantly announcing God's sovereign reign** (or: kingdom)." [note: stipulations are added]
61. **So a different person also said, "I will be following You, Lord, but first allow** (or: permit) **me to at once make arrangements** (or: set things off in order) **for myself, [going] unto my household so as to detach myself and say good-by to the people at home."**
62. **But Jesus said to him, "No one, after thrusting [his] hand upon a plow and then looking into the things behind, is well-fitted for** (or: well-placed in; thus: suitable or useful to) **God's reign** (or: kingdom; royal influences and activities)." [note: necessary "follower" qualities]

CHAPTER 10

1. **Now after these things, the Lord also indicated** (or: designates) **seventy** [other MSS: seventy-two] **different people by raising them up to be seen, and later sent them out as representatives on a mission, two by two, before His face** (= in advance of His presence) **into every town and place where He continued being about to be progressively coming.**
2. **So He began saying to them, "On the one hand, the harvest [is] much** (or: vast; = it is a very good crop); **on the other hand, the workers are few. Therefore, at once urgently ask**

(or: beg) **the Owner** (or: Lord; Master) **of the harvest so that He would** (or: should; could) **put out workers into His harvest.**

3. **"You people be off, and lead the way under [My word and direction] to progressively bring things under control. Look, and consider this: I am progressively sending you folks off as representatives** (emissaries; "*apostles*") – **as lambs among** (within the midst of) **wolves!**

4. **"Do not continue carrying a bag** (belt; purse) **for money, nor a food or beggar's pouch, neither sandals – and you should not embrace or greet anyone down along the path** (road; way). [comment: be barefoot priests: treat the Land as holy; villages as temples – Bruce Chilton]

5. **"Yet into whatever house you may enter, first always say, 'Peace of the Joining [=** Shalom] **to** (or: [We are] joined with; or: = The result of the joining [is] with and for) **this house.'**

6. **"And if a son of peace** [note: = a person having the character, qualities and spirit of peace and of being joined to Yahweh or the Messiah] **should be there, your peace** (the joining from you) **will rest and repose upon him – yet if not, it will bend back upon you people again.**

7. **"So you folks continue staying** (remaining; dwelling) **in this same house – repeatedly eating and drinking the things they provide, for the worker** (laborer) **is worthy** (of equal value; deserving) **of his wage** (pay). **[So] do not repeatedly change [locations] by stepping together and transferring from house to house.**

8. **"Also, into whatever town or city you may one after another be entering – and they may continue favorably welcoming and receiving you folks – habitually eat the things regularly placed beside you,**

9. **"and then continue treating, giving attentive care for or curing the sick and weak folks within it. Also, be constantly saying to them, 'God's reigning and activity of exercising sovereignty** (or: kingdom) **has drawn near and is at hand upon you people – close enough to touch** (= has arrived and is now accessible)!'

10. **"But into whatever town or city you may one after another be entering – and they may not continue favorably welcoming and receiving you folks – after going out into its broad, open streets** (plazas or squares), **be at once saying,**

11. **"'Even the dust being caused to cling unto our feet – from out of your town – we are now in the process of wiping off for you people** (= with regard to you folks; [*cf* note in 9:5, above])! **Furthermore, continue knowing this by intimate experience, that God's reigning** (or: the sovereignty from God; the kingdom activity, which is God) **had drawn near, is at hand, and is close enough to touch** (= has arrived; = is accessible)!'

12. **"I am now saying to you folks, that within** (or: on) **THAT day it will continue being more able to hold up in** (or: endurable and bearable for) **Sodom than in** (or: for) **THAT town or city.**

13. **"Tragic will be your fate, Chorazin! Tragic will be your fate, Bethsaida! If the expressions** (manifestations; works; deeds) **of power birthing themselves** (or: taking place) **within you had happened within Tyre and Sidon, they would have long ago changed their thinking with a change of their state of consciousness, and altered their lives by turning [to God] – while [dressed] in sackcloth and continuing to sit in** (or: on; among) **ashes.**

14. **"More than this, within the separating in evaluation and deciding** (or: centered on sifting and judging) **it will continue** (or proceed in) **being more able to hold up in** (or: more endurable for) **Tyre and Sidon than among** (or: for; with; within; united with) **YOU people.**

15. **"And you, Capernaum! You will not proceed in being 'lifted up** (or: exalted) **to heaven** (or: as far as [the] sky)!'... **'You will [instead] progressively climb down** (or: descend; subside; [other MSS: be mounted so as to be brought down]) **to the unseen** (or: as far as Hades [Heb. *sheol*, in the text of Isa.]; or to the state and condition of being unseen).' [Isa. 14:13, 15]

16. **"The person continuing to listen to and hear you folks is habitually listening to and hearing Me. And the person habitually setting you aside and disregarding you continues to set Me aside and disregard Me. Yet the person setting Me aside continues to set aside and disregard the One sending Me off with a mission and as a representative** (emissary)."

17. **Now the seventy** [other MSS: seventy-two] **returned with joy, one after another saying, "O Lord, even the demons** (Hellenistic concept and term: = animistic influences) **are continually being subjected to us** (or: set under and arranged below for us) **within and in union with Your Name!"** [comment: 70 in Judaism = "the non-Jewish nations" – Bruce Chilton]

18. So He said to them, "I began gazing and continued contemplating and repeatedly watching the adversary (opponent; or: *satan*) suddenly falling – as lightning from out of the sky (or: dropping down as lightning – from out of the atmosphere and heaven).

19. "So look, and realize – I have given to you folks the authority (privilege from Being) to habitually step up on and trample snakes (serpents) and scorpions – as well as upon all the power and ability of the enemy (or: from the hostile or adversarial person) – and nothing at all will proceed (or: in any circumstance will continue) causing you folks harm (or: wronging you or treating you unjustly).

20. "Nevertheless, do not continue rejoicing in this – that the breath-effects (spirits; attitudes; life-forces; winds) are being continually subjected to you people. Instead, be constantly rejoicing that your names have been written on and stand engraved (or: inscribed; [other MSS: were/are written]) within the heavens (or: in union with the atmospheres; centered among the skies)." [note: Jesus interprets "demons" of vs. 17 as "breath-effects," etc.]

21. Within the same hour, He expresses extreme joy (or: transports supreme happiness and exultation) to the Set-apart Spirit (or: in the set-apart Breath-effect; by the Holy Spirit; for the sacred spirit; with the Sacred Attitude), and says, "I am in Myself constantly speaking out the same thought, word and message by You (or: I am, Myself, habitually confessing out and acclaiming to You), O Father – Lord of the heaven (or: Owner of the atmosphere and sky) and the earth (or: Land) – because You carefully hid (or: conceal) these things from wise folks and intelligent people (clever and intellectual folks that can make things flow together to thoroughly comprehend), and then revealed (or: uncover; unveil) them to (or: in; by; for; among) babies (infants not yet able to speak). Yes, O Father, because thus well-thinking is birthed (or: it thus came to be an approved notion and an imagination of ease and well-being bringing good pleasure) in front of You (or: in Your presence)!"

22. Later, upon turning to face the disciples (apprentices), He said, "All mankind (humanity) and All things were given over, committed and transferred to (or: in) Me by, and under, My Father, and yet no one is in constant, intimate, experiential knowledge of Who the Son is (exists being), except the Father, nor Who is the Father, except the Son – and whomsoever the Son is now wanting and continuing intending to at some point unveil (uncover; reveal; disclose) [Him]."

23. And then, being turned toward the disciples (students; apprentices), He said privately, "Happy and blessed [are] the eyes [that] are constantly observing and seeing the things which you folks are now continually observing and seeing,

24. "for I am now saying to you that many prophets and kings wanted (or: felt an intense desire) to see (catch a glimpse of; or: see [the picture] of) the things that you folks are now looking at and presently seeing – and yet they did (or: do) not at any point see [them]; also to hear the things that you folks are now hearing – and yet they did (or: do) not at any point hear [them].

25. Later – look and consider! – a certain man versed in the Law (a lawyer and a legal theologian; a Torah expert) rose (or: stood) up, proceeding to put Him on trial and test [Him] out by saying, "Teacher, by doing what shall I proceed in inheriting eonian life (or: in what performing will I proceed to be enjoying an allotment of a life in, and which has the character and qualities of, the Age [of Messiah], even an age-enduring life)?"

26. So He said to him, "Within the Law, what has been written? How are you in the habit of reading [it] (or: How are you normally reading what stands written in the [Torah])?"

27. Now making a discerning reply, the man said, "'You will be constantly loving (fully giving yourself to; urging toward reunion with) [the] Lord [= Yahweh] your God from out of your whole (= entire) heart, and in union with your whole soul (or: consciousness, self and soul-life), and in union with and in the midst of your whole (= entire) strength, and in union with and within your whole (= entire) mind (intellect; comprehension; understanding)' – and 'your neighbor (the one close to you; your associate) as being yourself.'" [Deut. 6:4; Lev. 19:18]

28. So He said to him, "With discernment you answered correctly. Be habitually doing this and you will continue living."

29. **Yet he, still wanting to justify himself** (make himself 'right' [in the argument]; show himself to be righteous and on the right path; or: do himself justice), **said to Jesus, "And so, who** (or: Who, really,) **is my neighbor** (associate; the one close to me)**?"**

30. **So undertaking [a response], Jesus said, "A certain person** (human being) **was by habit** (or: progressively) **descending** (or: walking down) **from Jerusalem into Jericho and he fell encircled round about by bandits** (robbers; highwaymen), **who, after stripping him and putting blows upon** (= beating) **[him], went away, leaving [him] half dead.**

31. **"Now by coincidence, a certain priest was by habit** (or: progressively) **descending** (or: walking down) **on that road, and upon seeing him, passed by on the other side.**

32. **"And likewise also, a Levite, coming** [other MSS: happening] **down upon the place and seeing him, passed by on the other side.**

33. **"But a Samaritan – someone habitually traveling on the road – came down to him and at seeing [him and the situation] was moved in his inner organs with compassion.**

34. **"Then, after coming to [him], he bound down** (bandaged) **the results of his trauma and injuries** (wounds), **while pouring on olive oil and wine. Now after mounting him upon his own animal** (either: pack animal, or, mount) **he led him into a caravansary** (or: inn) **and took care of him** (or: had him cared for).

35. **"And then on the next day, thrusting out** (or: extracting and putting forth) **two denarii** (silver coins; [note: adequate for up to two weeks stay]), **he gave them to the caravansary host** (or: innkeeper – the one who welcomes everyone) **and said, 'Take care of him. And that which you may likely spend in addition, I myself will proceed in paying [it] back to you on the [occasion for] me to be normally coming back upon [this place]** (or: returning).'

36. **"Which one of these three now seems** (appears) **to you to have come to be a neighbor** (associate; close-one) **of the person falling into the midst of the bandits** (highwaymen)**?"**

37. **Now he said, "The person doing the mercy** (performing the [act of] compassion) **with him." So Jesus said to him, "Be now going** (journeying) **on your way, and you yourself be habitually doing** (performing) **likewise** (similarly; in the same way)**."**

38. **Now on the [occasion for] them to be progressively going** (journeying) **on their way, He entered into a certain village. And a certain woman, named Martha, welcomed Him under [her roof] and entertained Him as a guest, [after His entering] into the house.**

39. **Now for her there was also a sister being normally called Mariam** [other MSS: Mary] **who later, after sitting alongside near to and facing the Lord's** [other MSS: Jesus'] **feet, began listening and kept on hearing His word** (or: the thought, idea and message from Him).

40. **But Martha kept on being pulled from all around and was thus distracted concerning much serving** (or: = attending to many duties). **So, taking a stand upon [the situation], she said, "Lord** (or: Master), **does it not now matter to You that my sister is leaving me completely alone to be continuously giving attending service and dispensing? Speak to her, therefore, so that she would take hold together opposite me, and join in helping me."**

41. **But making a discerning response, the Lord** [other MSS: Jesus] **said to her, "Martha, O Martha, you continue being anxious** (overly concerned) **and constantly troubled** (upset) **about many things** [note: e.g., the courses of the dinner; Mary's inappropriate behavior],

42. **yet there is a need of [only] a few things [or: dishes; courses; situations], or of [just] one** (or: But few are necessary, indeed [only] one; [other MSS: Yet there is a need of {only} one]). **You see, Mariam** [other MSS: Mary] **selected** (or: picks and chooses out) **a good part** (virtuous portion; worthwhile share; [note: may = dish or course of the meal; may be a figure in reference to the anticipated Messianic banquet]) **which will not be chosen away or lifted from her.**

CHAPTER 11

1. **This happened later, on the [occasion] for Him to be within a certain place continuing in thinking, and/or speaking, with a view toward having goodness, ease and well-being** (or: prayer), **[that] as he ceased, a certain one of His disciples** (students; apprentices) **said to Him, "Lord** (Master), **teach us [how] to be normally thinking and speaking toward having goodness, ease and well-being** (or: praying) **– just as John also taught his disciples."**

2. **So He said to them, "Whenever you may be** [other MSS: are] **normally focused on having goodness, ease and well-being** (or: praying), **habitually say,**

    'Our Father [other MSS: O Father] **– [You] within the midst of the heavens** (or: centered in the atmospheres)! **Let your Name be separated, set-apart and kept holy** (or: regarded as sacred)! **Let Your reign, kingdom and sovereign influence come at once! Let the effect of Your will, purpose and intent be birthed** (come to exist) **at once – as in heaven** (or: within [the] atmosphere), **so also upon the earth** (or: Land)!

3.   **Repeatedly give** (or: Keep on giving) **to us our bread – the one that has been made upon being and has reference to existence** (or: the dole that is sufficient for today and the coming day), **the one that corresponds to and accords with [the] day.**

4.   **Also, at once send away** (divorce and cause to flow off; forgive) **for and in us our failures and mistakes** (sins; times and occasions of missing the target; deviations) **– for we, ourselves, are also habitually sending away** (causing to flow off and forgiving) **for everyone continually owing and being indebted to us. So would** (or: may) **You not at any point lead, bring or carry us into a [time or situation of] examination, testing or trial where we are put to the proof; but to the contrary, at once drag** (rescue) **us out of danger, away from the misery-gushed, worthless person, or the one of malicious intent or who has bad and unprofitable qualities** (or: the bad situation; the wicked person; the miserable condition; the painful labor; the unprofitable endeavor).'"

5. **Then He said to them, "Which person from among you folks will proceed in having a friend** (someone you are fond of and care about), **and you will from time-to-time go your way to him [at] midnight and then say, 'Friend, let me use** (= borrow) **three loaves of bread,**

6. **"'since, in fact, a friend** (or: loved one) **of mine happened along to me from out of the road** (path; way), **and I am not presently having something which I will proceed putting at the side for him** (= serving him to eat).'

7. **"And that person giving a decided reply from inside may be saying, 'Do not continue providing and holding out troubles and weariness for me** (= Stop bothering me)! **The door has already been shut and locked, and my young children are now [put] into bed with me – I am now unable** (have no power) **[to be; in] rising up to give [something] to** (or: for) **you.'**

8. **"I am now saying to you folks, [that] although he will not, after getting up, proceed in giving [them] to him because of the [situation of] him being his friend, [yet] because of the fact of his overly bold and shameless audacity** (or: *chutzpah*), **upon being aroused and raised up he will proceed giving to him as much as he is presently needing.** [*cf* Lu. 18:5]

9. **"And so I, Myself, continue saying to you folks, Be continuously asking – and it will continue being given to you. Be constantly seeking and trying to find – and you folks will be constantly finding. Repeatedly knock** (or: Keep on knocking) **and it will repeatedly be** (or: proceed in being) **opened up to** (or: for; in; among) **you people.**

10. **"You see, everyone continuously asking is continuously receiving; and the person constantly seeking is constantly finding; and to** (or: for; in; with) **the person repeatedly and continually knocking it will repeatedly be** (or: proceed in being) **opened up.**

11. **"Now [for] a certain [situation] from among you folks: the son will ask the father for bread – he will not give him a stone; or even a fish – will he instead proceed to be giving a snake** (serpent) **to him?**

12. **"Or further, he will** [other MSS add: if he should] **ask for an egg – will he proceed giving a scorpion to him?**

13. **"Since then, you folks, continuously subsisting being inherently misery-gushed, worthless, malicious or evil people, have seen and thus know to be habitually giving good** (virtuous) **gifts to your children, to how much greater an extent will the Father – the One from out of heaven** (or: from [the] atmosphere) **– be continuously giving a set-apart Breath-effect** (or: [the] Holy Spirit; or: a sacred attitude; a consecrated life-force) **to** (or: for; among) **the people habitually asking Him!"**

14. **Later, He was proceeding in expelling** (casting out) **a blunt, dull, mute demon** (Hellenistic concept and term: = animistic influence). **Now with the coming out of the demon, the [previously] mute and dull person spoke. And so the crowds marveled and wondered.**

15. **But certain ones of them said, "He continues casting out the demons in union with Beelzebul, the chief and ruler of the demons** (the *Archon* of the animistic influences)."
But He, giving a discerning reply, said, "How does the adversary (*satan*) **continue able and with power to continue casting out the adversary** (*satan*)?"
16. **Yet different folks** (= another group), **repeatedly testing and examining [Him], kept on seeking from His presence** (or: beside Him) **a sign out of [the] sky** (or: atmosphere; heaven).
17. **So He, seeing and knowing the results of their thoughts and imaginations** (what had gone through their minds), **said to them, "Every government** (reign; kingdom) **being divided in two, or into parts, upon itself is being progressively brought to desolation** (made to be an uninhabited wilderness or a desert), **and house is one after another falling upon house.**
18. **So if the adversary** (*satan*) **is** (or: were) **divided in two, into parts, upon itself** (or: himself), **how will its** (or: his) **reign** (government; kingdom) **continue standing** (or: keep on being firm and enduring) **– since you folks continue saying [that] I continue, in union with Beelzebul, to cast out the demons** (= animistic influences)?
19. **"Now if I, Myself – in union with Beelzebul – am constantly expelling the demons, in union with whom are your sons normally expelling [them]? Because of this, they will proceed, and continue, being your judges** (or: critics).
20. **"Yet if I, Myself – in union with 'God's finger'** (= minimal effort; [Ex. 31:18]) **– continue casting out the demons** (Hellenistic concept and term: = animistic influences), **consequently God's reign** (sovereign influence and activity; imperial rule; government; kingdom) **really makes progress and has advanced to be beforehand upon you folks** (or: has really made its way to and has overtaken you, so as to have arrived; or: outstrips [to be now] upon you people).

21. **"Whenever the strong person – being one that has fully armed and completely equipped himself – may habitually watch over, guard and protect his own courtyard, his possessions and the things that sustain him continue being in peace** (joined [to him]).
22. **"Yet as soon as** (or: if ever) **a person stronger than him, after coming upon [him], can conquer** (or: may overcome) **him, he progressively lifts up and carries off his full armament** (all the armor and weaponry) **upon which he had trusted and placed his confidence – and now progressively distributes his spoils** (booty).
23. **"The person not continuing in being with Me is down on Me** (or: The one not existing accompanied by Me exists being out of line and out of step with Me, and is thus against what is Mine) **– and the person not habitually gathering or presently leading [folks] together with Me is constantly scattering and dispersing.**

24. **"Whenever the unclean or culturally unpruned breath-effect** (spirit; attitude; life-force) **can** (or: should; may; would) **go out from the midst, away from the person** (human), **it is progressively** (or: constantly) **passing through waterless places, continuing to seek** (constantly trying to find) **a place or situation to rest** (cease-back; refresh; be still again) **– and yet habitually not finding [one] – it at that point is saying, 'I shall proceed returning into my house from where I came** (or: went) **out.'**
25. **"And then, upon coming, it is presently finding [it] continuing at leisure, in idleness, unemployed and not occupied – having been swept and cleaned with a broom, as well as having been put in order and adorned** (or: decorated).
26. **"At that point it continues going on its way and then proceeds taking along seven different breath-effects** (spirits; attitudes; life-forces) **more worthless, misery-gushed, bad and malicious than itself, and upon entering, it proceeds settling down in the house and continues dwelling there – and so the last [conditions and situations] of that person** (human) **progressively comes to be** (or: exist) **worse than the first ones."**

27. **Now it happened, during the [situation for] Him to be proceeding in saying these things, [that] a certain woman from the crowd, raising [her] voice, said to Him, "The womb [is] happy** (blessed; privileged) **that was carrying You, as well as the breasts which You sucked [when nursing]."**

28. Yet He said, "On the contrary, the people continually listening to and habitually hearing [so as to obey] – as well as watching over, guarding and keeping – God's Word (*Logos*; Thought; idea; message; information) [are the] happy, blessed and privileged folks."

29. Now with the progressive assembling (collecting; convening) of the crowds into a thick mass (or: a throng), He began to go on to say, "This generation is, and continues being, a worthless and misery-gushed (unsound; wicked; depraved; evil; malicious; disadvantaged; unprofitable; painfully bad; toil-bringing) generation. It is constantly seeking a sign (= insisting on a proof of My claims) – and yet no sign will proceed being given to it except Jonah's sign (or: the sign of Jonah; the sign which is Jonah; the sign from, or in relation to, Jonah).
30. "You see, just and correspondingly as Jonah came to be a sign to (for; among) the Ninevites, in the same way the Son of the Man (the Son of mankind; = Adam's son; = the Human Being; = the eschatological Messianic figure) will also proceed and continue being [a sign] to (for; among) this generation.
31. "A (or: [The]) 'Queen of (or: from) [the] South' will proceed being aroused and raised up in union with the decision (or: in this judging; in the midst of the sifting and separation for discerning) with (or: accompanying) the adult men of this generation, and she will continue making a corresponding decision about (condemning; bringing a down-judgment upon) them, because she came from out of the limits (or: boundaries) of the Land (or: earth; region) to listen to and to hear the wisdom of (or: from) Solomon, and – look and take note! – Something more than Solomon [is] here (or: in this place and situation)! [cf Mat. 27:52-53]
32. "The Ninevite adult men will proceed standing up (arising) in union with the sifting and separation for deciding (in the judging) with this generation and they will be proceed to commensurately decide about (condemn; bring a down-verdict upon) them, because they changed their thinking into [alignment with] the public proclamation (or: the result of the heralding) of Jonah, and – look and take note! – Something more than Jonah [is] here! [cf Heb. 12:1; Rom. 12:2]
33. "No one, upon lighting a lamp, normally puts [it] into hiding in a cellar or vault, nor under the measuring basket, but rather upon the lampstand, so that folks coming in on their way can see (or: may observe) the light and its radiance.
34. "The body's lamp is your eye. Whenever your eye may exist being (or: be) single (simple; = has focus that is not complex or compounded; not given to taking voyages), the whole body is also flooded with light (illuminated; shining and radiant). Yet, whenever it may be worthless and misery-gushed (unsound; miserable; wicked; depraved; evil; malicious; disadvantaged; unprofitable; painfully bad; toil-bringing; or: = stingy), your body also [is] dark (or: in the dark; full of darkness; shrouded with dimness from shadows).
35. "Continue alert and be habitually watchful, continually taking careful notice, therefore, [that] the light within you is not darkness (does not continue being dimness from shadows).
36. "If, therefore, your whole body [is] illuminated (flooded with light; or: luminous; composed of and full of light) – not having any part in the dark (or: full of darkness) – [the] whole will continue being illuminated (luminous; composed of light) just as whenever the lamp can (or: may) shine light on (enlighten; give light to) you by (or: in; with) [its] beam (ray; flashing)."

37. Now during this [situation for] Him to be speaking, a Pharisee kept on making a request that He would dine with him. So later, after entering, He fell back (or: reclines) [at the meal].
38. But seeing [this], the Pharisee was surprised and amazed (or: wondered) that He was not first ceremonially washed (or: baptized; dipped; [immersing of the hands up to the elbows for ceremonial purification]) before the dinner.
39. So the Lord said to him, "At this time you folks, the Pharisees, are normally (or: habitually) cleansing [by washing] the outside of the cup and the dish – yet the inside of you folks continues being brimming and crammed full (so as to be replete) of plundering (acquiring booty; seizing and carrying off; rapacity) and worthlessness and misery-gush
     (badness of conditions; unsoundness and miserableness; wickedness and depravity; evil and malice; disadvantageousness; unprofitableness; that which brings toilsome labor).

40. **"Thoughtless, unreasonable and senseless people! Did not the One making** (forming; constructing; producing) **the outside also make** (form; create; produce) **the inside?**

41. **"However** (or: Nonetheless; In any case), **give the things being within** (or: continuing being inside) **[as] a gift or expression of mercy** (= alms or charity), **then – look, and consider! – everything is** (or: all things are) **clean to** (or: for; among; with) **you folks.** [= a new purity code]

42. **"But in contrast, tragic will be the fate for you, the Pharisees** (or: among you, the Pharisees), **because you consistently give away one tenth** (or: habitually pay tithes) **from the mint and the rue, as well as every edible plant** (garden herb or vegetable), **and yet you folks are consistently** (or: continually) **bypassing the deciding which yields justice** (or: the process of evaluating and then judging) **and the love of God** (or: the acceptance from and the character pertaining to God; the whole being's drive and movement toward reunion, which is God). **Now it was continuing binding and necessary to do these things, and not to bypass** [other MSS: and yet not continue to {other MSS: not at any point} send away, or to the side,] **those things.**

43. **"Tragic will be the fate for you, the Pharisees** (or: among you, the Pharisees), **because you habitually love** (strive to unite with; give yourselves for) **the front place of sitting** (or: highly regard the prominent seat, i.e., the most important place in a meeting) **in the synagogues, as well as the greetings** (= deferential recognitions) **within the marketplaces.**

44. **"Tragic will be your fate, you scholars** (theologians; scribes) **and Pharisees – the overly judging and critical folks**

> (*hupokrites*; or: those who put texts under close inspection to sift and separate and then give an answer, an interpretation, an opinion; or: those who live by separating things yet who under-discern; or: those who make judgments from a low view; or: those who under-estimate reality; or: perverse scholars who focus on tiny distinctions), **because you exist being as the unseen** (or: = are unmarked) **memorial tombs** (= graves having the characteristics of Hades), **and so the people** (or: the humans) **habitually walking around on top [of them] have not seen and so do not know** (= without realizing) **[it]!"**

> [note: under the Law, contact with a grave rendered a person ceremonially unclean]

45. **Now a certain man of those versed in the Law** (a legal expert; a Torah lawyer and interpreter), **in giving a considered reply, is then saying to Him, "Teacher, in** (or: by) **constantly saying these things you continue invading our territory and outraging us by violating our rights – thus, insulting us, too!"**

46. **So He said, "Tragic will be the fate for you men versed in the Law** (Torah lawyers), **too, because you are constantly burdening people** (humans) **[with] cargos** (or: loads) **[that are] hard to bear** (= intolerable burdens), **and yet you folks are continuing not to even lightly touch the loads with one of your fingers!**

47. **"It will be so tragic for you, because** (or: It is so tragic among you, that) **you folks habitually build and erect the memorial tombs of the prophets, but your fathers** (or: forefathers; ancestors) **killed them off** (or: murdered them)!

48. **"Really** (or: Consequently; Accordingly, then), **you folks exist being witnesses** (or: continuously are folks who testify and give evidence) **and you are constantly approving, thinking well of and giving endorsement to the actions** (deeds; works) **of your fathers** (and: forefathers), **because they indeed killed them off, and now you yourselves continue building the [memorial] houses** [other MSS: their tombs]!

49. **"That is why** (or: On account of this) **the Wisdom of God also said, 'As emissaries I will proceed sending off prophets and representatives unto them** (or: into the midst of them) **– and they will proceed killing off [some] from out of their midst, and then they will proceed to pursue** (chase; press forward [on] and persecute; [other MSS: banish]) **[others].'** [Jer. 7:25ff]

50. **"So thus, the blood of all of the prophets – that having been** [other MSS: being constantly or repeatedly] **poured out from a casting down** (or: a founding; a foundation; or: may = a conceiving) **of an ordered system** (a world of culture, economy, religion and government; or: from an aggregate of humans; or: = a polity of Israel) **– can** (or: should; would) **at some point** (or: suddenly) **be searched out to be required and exacted from this generation:**

51. **"from Abel's blood until the blood of Zechariah – the man losing himself** (or: perishing; being destroyed) **between the altar and the House – yes, I continue saying** (or: am now saying) **to you folks, it will progressively be sought out and exacted from this generation.**
52. **"Tragic will be the fate for you experts in the Law** (Torah lawyers), **because you lifted up and carried away** (or: lift up and carry off; took and remove) **the Key of, and which is, the intimate, experiential, personal knowledge and insight** (or: the key from the *Gnosis*). **You, yourselves, do** (or: did) **not enter [so as to experience and gain insight] and you hinder, block, prevent and forbid the folks periodically entering** (or: going into its midst)."

53. **And from there** (or: Then from that time and place), **upon His going out, the scribes** (scholars and theologians) **and the Pharisees began to fiercely keep on holding** (or: hemming) **[Him] in** (or: started to progressively bring dreadful entanglement on [Him]) **and to repeatedly get Him to speak without [His first] thinking** (literally: speak from the mouth) **concerning more things,**
54. **repeatedly** (or: constantly) **lying in wait to ambush Him, constantly seeking to pounce on and catch** (or: trap) **something from out of His mouth** (= from His own words).

CHAPTER 12

1. **Under these circumstances, [with] a crowd of tens of thousands** (myriads) **being gathered together upon [the event] – so as to be time after time trampling** (or: stepping down on) **one another – He began a discourse TO, and facing, His DISCIPLES** (students) **first: "Be constantly holding your attention toward, and continuously guarding yourselves from, the yeast permeating the Pharisees, which is to put texts under close inspection, to sift and separate, and then give an answer, an interpretation, an opinion**
   > (or: to live by separating things yet, under-discern; or: being overly critical and making judgments from a low view; or: perverse scholarship which focuses on tiny distinctions).
   > [comment: their yeast would inflate them with pride]
2. **"Now there is nothing [which] continues having been completely concealed** (or: veiled and covered together) **which will not be progressively unveiled** (uncovered; revealed; disclosed), **and [nothing] hidden which will not continue being intimately and experientially made known.** [comment: the realm of God's reign does away with the mystery religions]
3. **"Instead, whatever** (or: as many things as) **YOU folks said** (or: say) **within the darkness** (or: in union with darkness) **will proceed being listened to and heard in the midst of and in union with the Light – and that which YOU speak** (or: spoke) **to the ear within the private rooms** (or: inner chambers) **will continue being heralded in public proclamation upon housetops** (or: roofs). [comment: Light brings an end to secret knowledge and hidden teachings]
4. **"So I am now saying to, and for, YOU, My friends, Do not** (or: You should not) **be afraid of** (or: caused to fear from) **the people presently** (or: in the process of) **killing off the body, and yet after these things are not having** (holding; possessing) **anything more excessive to do.**
5. **"Now I will continue expressly pointing out to** (indicating and even underlining for) **YOU people [him; the person] of whom YOU folks should be made fearful: Be made to fear** (be wary of; have respect for) **the person [who], after the killing off, continues possessing** (having and holding) **the right** (or: authority) **to throw YOU into the Valley of Hinnom** (Greek: Gehenna; = the City Dump, the garbage pit outside of Jerusalem; [= to dishonor you by giving no burial; to treat you as a criminal]). **Yes, I continue saying to YOU folks, Be afraid of this one** (or: Have serious respect for this person). [comment: this may have been a warning to Zealots]
6. **"Are not five sparrows normally being sold for two of the smallest copper coins** (an assarion; 1/16th of a denarius)? **And yet not one of them is forgotten in God's sight or presence.**
7. **"But in comparison, even the hairs of YOUR head have all been numbered** (or: given a number, and thus, counted)! **So then, stop fearing** (or: do not continue being caused to fear or be wary)! **YOU folks constantly carry through to be of [more] consequence and value [than] many sparrows.** [comment: thus, vs. 5 does not refer to God]
8. **"Now I am saying to YOU folks that everyone who will ever publicly confess** (avow; acknowledge; speak the same thing concerning) **union with Me – in front of the people** (or: the

humans), **the Son of the Man** (the Human Being; = the eschatological messianic figure) **will also continue publicly confessing** (acknowledging; avowing; speaking the same thing concerning) **union with him – in front of God's agents** (the messengers: folks with the message from God)!
9. **"But the person contradicting or declining Me** (or: denying, disowning or renouncing Me; or: saying, "No" to Me) **in the sight and presence of the people** (or: humans) **will continue being fully contradicted, or declined** (or: said, "No" to; disowned; written off; renounced), **in the sight and presence of God's agents and messengers** (the folks with the message from God).
10. **"And furthermore, everyone who utters a word** (declares a thought; speaks a message) **[aimed] into the midst of the Son of the Man** (the Human Being or: = a human), **it will be repeatedly forgiven and sent away for him** (or: made to flow off of him). **Yet for the one speaking abusively** (or: slandering; blaspheming; being a Light-hindrance) **unto the Set-apart Breath-effect** (the Holy Spirit; Sacred Breath or Attitude), **it will not be forgiven or sent away.**
11. **"Now whenever they may bring YOU folks into the midst, upon [some charge before] the synagogues** (or: public assemblies), **or [haul you up before] the government officials** (rulers) **and the authorities, YOU should not be anxious or overly concerned about how or what you should speak in YOUR defense, nor what you should say.**
12. **"You see, the Set-apart Breath-effect** (or: Holy Spirit; Sacred Breath and Attitude) **will continue teaching YOU within that very hour what things it is necessary to say."**

13. **Then someone out of the crowd said to Him, "Teacher, tell my brother to divide the inheritance** (or: the concerns and possessions acquired by lot) **into parts with me."**
14. **But He said to him, "Man** (perhaps: = Mister; Friend), **who appointed and set Me down [to be] a judge** (or: decider) **or a divider** (or: arbiter) **upon you folks?"**
15. **So He said toward them, "Be continuously seeing [the situation] and constantly watching over so as to guard yourselves from all greed and desire to have more, because for anyone, his life does not exist in the superabundance of the goods and possessions undergirding and being a subsistence for** (or: to) **him."**
16. **And so He told an illustrative story** (a parable) **to them, saying, "The farming space** (or: cultivated tracts of fields; the region) **belonging to a certain rich person produced well.**
17. **"Consequently he reasoned and debated** (dialogued) **within himself, presently saying, 'What should** (or: shall) **I do, [seeing] that I am not presently having [a place, or, room] where I will continue gathering** (or: collecting and storing) **my fruits (= crops)?'**
18. **"And so he said, 'I will proceed doing this: I will progressively pull** (or: tear) **down my barns** (storehouses; granaries) **and I will progressively build bigger ones. After that I will continue gathering and storing there all my grain and goods.**
19. **"'Then I will proceed saying to my soul** (interior self and life), **Soul** (Self), **you are now possessing** (having and holding) **many goods** (or: good things) **[that] continue lying [in storage] on unto** (or: into; = for) **many years. Continue resting and taking it easy: eat, drink, continue easy-minded and keep on being merry** (expanding the diaphragm with satisfaction).'
20. **"But God said to him, 'O senseless one** (foolish person [literally: one without a diaphragm {to expand}]), **on this night they are presently requesting** (or: demanding) **your soul** (interior self; person; or: consciousness and life) **from you. So whose** (or: for whom) **will the things continue being which you prepare and make ready?'**
21. **"This is how it is** (or: So it goes) **[with; for] the person constantly laying up treasure** (amassing and hording goods) **for** (or: to; in) **himself, while not becoming progressively rich with regard to God** (or: and yet not being habitually wealthy unto, and into the midst of, God)."
22. **Then He said to His disciples, "On account of this I am now saying to you folks, Quit** (or: Do not continue) **being anxious and overly concerned for the [other MSS: your] soul** (the consciousness, inner life and its concerns; or: your person) **– what you should eat! Nor for your body – what you should put on** (or: with what you can clothe yourselves)!
23. **"You see, the soul** (the consciousness, the inner being, the self and its life; [your] person) **is more than nourishment – and the body [more] than what is put on** (clothing).
24. **"Focus your mind down on and consider the ravens** (or: rooks; jackdaws) **– that they are not sowing seeds, nor are they reaping [the grain], [and for] which critters there is no storeroom nor yet a barn** (or: granary) **– and yet God constantly provides food to nourish them, and provision to maintain them. To what an extent and in how many ways are you**

folks rather constantly carrying through to be of [more] consequence and value [than] the birds (or: the flying creatures)?

25. "Now who of you, by being anxious and worrying, is able (or: has power) to add a cubit (about eighteen inches) upon the span of his life (or: to his size or stature)?

26. "Since (or: If), then, you folks continue being not even able (or: having power) [for the] least thing, why continue anxious and overly concerned about the rest (or: concerning the remaining things)?

27. "Focus your mind down on and consider the lilies. [Note] how it progressively (or: repeatedly) grows and increases. It is not constantly working hard (toiling; spent with labor), neither is it continuously spinning thread [for cloth]! Yet I am now saying to you folks, not even Solomon – in the midst of all his glory (splendor; manifestations which called forth praise; assumed appearance) – was arrayed (or: cast clothing around himself) as one of these!

28. "So if God continues thus clothing the vegetation – being in a field today, and proceeding in being cast into an oven (or: furnace) the next day (or: tomorrow) – how much rather [will He continue clothing and adorning, and thus, taking care of] you folks: people having little trust and with small faith and allegiance!

29. "And thus, as for you folks, stop constantly seeking what you can (or: should) eat, and what you can (or: should) drink – and stop being repeatedly unsettled and in suspense.

30. "You see, all the ethnic multitudes (the nations; the non-Jews; = the pagans) of the ordered system (world of governments, cultures, religions; and domination systems; secular society; aggregate of mankind) are habitually searching for and seeking out all these things – yet your Father has seen, and thus knows, that you folks constantly need these things.

31. "However, and more so, be continuously seeking out and progressively pursuing His [other MSS: God's] reign (sovereign influence and activities; rule; kingship; kingdom), and all these things will continue being set toward, and then added to, you people.

32. "Stop fearing (or: Do not continue being wary or afraid), Little Flock, because it delights the Father (or: because the Father thought it good, and thus, approved) to give the reign (rule; kingship; kingdom; sovereign influence and activities) to you folks.

33. "You folks at once sell your possessions (the things constantly providing subsistence for you), and then at once give a gift of mercy (or: a charitable donation; alms) – [and thus] at once make money pouches [that are] not progressively becoming old and worn out: an unfailing and inexhaustible treasury (or: storehouse for treasure or things of value) within the midst of the heavens (or: atmospheres), where a thief is not at hand and does not come near, nor is a moth constantly eating (consuming and thoroughly ruining).

34. "For you see, where your treasury is (exists), there also will continue being your heart.

35. "Let your loins (from the waist to the genitals) constantly exist being bound around and fastened (or: girded about; = be dressed and ready for work or prepared for battle) and your lamps continuously burning,

36. "and you, yourselves, [be] like people habitually focused toward anticipating, welcoming and receiving their own master (lord; owner) – whenever he can untie [himself], loosen up [his involvement] and break loose from the midst of the marriage banquet – so that, upon coming and knocking, they might immediately open up to (or: for) him.

37. "Those slaves [are] happy and fortunate whom the master (lord; owner) – upon coming – will proceed to find being continuously awake, alert and watchful. Truly (or: Amen; It is so; Count on it)! I say to you folks that he will proceed to gird himself about (as with an apron) and will continue in causing them to recline [at a meal]. Then, coming alongside, he will give attending service and dispense to them!

> (or, as a question: In truth, I am now asking you: Will he proceed to tie an apron around himself then have them lie back for dinner and then serve them?)

38. "And should he arrive in the second watch (= just before midnight) – or even during the third (= past midnight or in the early hours of the morning) – and might find [them, or, the situation] thus, happy and fortunate are those slaves! [note: this is all on the same Day]

39. **"Now you normally know this by personal experience** (or, as an imperative: But be coming to experientially know this), **that if the householder had seen, or by foresight had perceived so as to be aware, at what hour the thief is proceeding in coming, he would stay awake and be watchful – and thus not allow his house [wall] to be dug through** (= let his house be broken into). [note: also referring to one Day; also note the term "hour" in vs. 40]

40. **"And so you folks, yourselves, therefore progressively come to be ready and prepared – because in an hour in which you folks are not normally supposing** (or: in the habit of assuming or imagining), **the Son of Mankind** (or: the Son of the Human Being; = Adam's Son; = the anticipated eschatological messianic figure) **is habitually coming** (or: normally comes)."

41. **So Peter said, "Lord** (Master), **are you presently saying this illustration** (parable) **[aimed] toward us, or also, toward all people** (or: peoples; everyone)**?"**

42. **Then the Lord said, "Who, consequently** (or: really), **is the faithful** (trustworthy; reliable) **house manager** (steward; administrator who also enforces the laws of the house) **– the thoughtful** (sensible; considerate; prudent; discreet) **one – whom the lord** (master; owner) **will proceed to appoint and place down upon and over his household staff** (the group in charge of care, attending treatment and curing) **to keep on** (or: to repeatedly be) **giving [to them their] measure of grain** (= food allowance) **when it is due, and in the fitting, proper situation?**

43. **"That slave [is] happy and fortunate whom his lord** (master; owner), **upon coming, will continue to be finding [him; her] habitually operating in this way** (or: constantly doing thus).

44. **"I am now saying to you folks that truly** (or: certainly) **he will proceed in appointing and placing him down upon and over all his possessions and those things which sustain him.**

      [comment: all this comports a sense of immediacy]

45. **"Yet, if that slave should ever say within his heart, 'My lord** (master; owner) **continues taking a long time and delays [his] coming,' and then should begin both to habitually beat the boys and the maids** (= the male and female servants) **and to be constantly eating and drinking – even to be repeatedly getting drunk,** [note in vs. 46: day and hour, not year or age]

46. **"the owner** (lord; master) **of that slave will proceed in arriving on a day in which he continues not anticipating or suspecting [it], and in an hour in which he continues having no personal knowledge [of it]. Then he will proceed to cut him in two** (figurative: = severely punish him; perhaps: = sever him from his position after lashing him with a whip) **and next will proceed putting his part** (or: setting his position) **with the unfaithful and unreliable [slaves].**

47. **"Now that slave who by experience is knowing and personally understanding his owner's** (his lord's; his master's) **will and intent – and yet is not preparing** (or: making ready) **or performing with an aim toward his [owner's] will or intent – will proceed in being flayed** (severely whipped) **[with] many lashes.**

48. **"But the person not knowing or understanding – yet doing [things] deserving of blows** (or: a beating) **– will proceed in being flayed** (severely whipped) **[with] few lashes.**
So to everyone to whom much was given, much will continue being sought for from him (at his side or situation); **and to whom they set much alongside** (or: committed to and put in charge of much), **of him they will continue more excessively requesting and demanding.**

49. **"I came to throw Fire upon the earth** (or: I come to cast a fire upon the Land) **– and what am I now wishing, since it is already ignited** (or: and what do I intend, if it is already kindled)**?**

50. **"Now I continue having an immersion** (or: a baptism) **[in which] to be immersed and saturated** (plunged and baptized) **– and how am I continuing being held together, until it can be brought to its purposed goal and destiny?**
      (or: and how [greatly] I am being pressed together {or: constrained; sustained; held in custody; gripped} till it should be finished and accomplished!)

51. **"Do you folks continue supposing** (assuming; imagining) **that I came along** (or: was birthed to be present) **to give peace and joining [= shalom] within the Land** (or: on the earth)**? No, I am saying to you, to the contrary, complete division** (or: a thorough dividing).

52. **"You see, from now on, within one house there will proceed in being five people that are existing having been completely divided: three on** (= against, or, from) **two, and two on** (= against, or, from) **three.**

53. **"A father will continue being thoroughly divided on** (= from; or: about; against; or: on [decisions, issues or perspectives in regard to]) **a son, and 'a son on a father;' a mother on a daughter, and 'a daughter on a mother;' a mother-in-law on her daughter-in-law, and 'a daughter-in-law on the mother-in-law.'"** [Micah 4:6]
54. **And now He went on saying to the crowds, also, "Whenever you people may** (or: should) **see a cloud progressively arising upon** [other MSS: from] **the west** (or: on the western regions), **you are immediately saying that a rainstorm is progressively** (or: presently) **coming – and thus it comes to be** (or: it happens; it occurs).
55. **"And whenever a south [wind] continues blowing you are normally saying that there will proceed being heat** (or: a heat wave) **– and it comes to be** (or: happens; occurs).
56. **"O you the overly judging and critical folks**
> (*hupokrites*; or: those who put texts under close inspection to sift and separate and then give an answer, an interpretation, an opinion; or: those who live by separating things yet who under-discern; or: those who make judgments from a low view; or: those who under-estimate reality; or: perverse scholars who focus on tiny distinctions)**! You have seen and come to know [how] to constantly examine and discern, and then to assess and interpret the face** (or: outward appearance) **of the land and the sky** (or: the earth and the heaven), **yet you have not seen, and thus do not know, how to examine, discern and interpret this present situation and season** (or: fertile moment)**!**
57. **"So why are you people not also habitually discerning and deciding for yourselves [what is] right** (just; fair and equitable; what accords with the Way pointed out; neighborly)**?**
58. **"For example: as you proceed with your opponent in a suit at law** (perhaps: = a creditor) **to bring [a situation] under control before a magistrate** (or: civil ruler), **while on the way** (or: road), **make an effort** (take action; get to work; endeavor) **to have come to a settlement so as to have the situation or conditions completely changed and to be delivered from him** (or: be rid of him and the dispute for good), **otherwise he can continue to drag you down to the judge, and then the judge will proceed giving** (transferring) **you over to the court officer** (bailiff; constable), **and finally the court officer will proceed throwing you into jail** (or: prison)**!**
59. **"I tell you, you can** (or: may) **not come out from that place until you should pay back in full even the last fraction of a cent** (small brass coin; mite)**!"** [note context: this life; that society]

CHAPTER 13

1. **Now there were some present, on that same occasion and situation, [who were] reporting to Him about the Galileans whose blood Pilate had mixed with their sacrifices** (= whom Pilate slaughtered as they were offering sacrifices – perhaps as they were slaughtering the animals).
2. **And so, giving a considered reply, Jesus said to them, "Does it normally seem to you** (or: Do you continue to think, suppose, presume or imagine) **that these Galileans had come to be folks who missed the target** (sinners; failures) **more so than and beyond all the [other] Galileans, seeing that they have experienced and suffered such things as these?**
3. **"I am now saying to you, No. Nevertheless, if you folks should not progressively change your thinking and state of consciousness** [also = a return to Yahweh's heart] **you will all likewise proceed in destroying yourselves** [i.e., by coming into conflict with the Romans].
4. **"Or then, those eighteen people upon whom the tower in Siloam fell and killed them off – does it usually seem to you** (or: do you continue to imagine or suppose) **that they, themselves, had come to be debtors more so** (or: obligated from guilt of worse offenses) **than and beyond all the people permanently settling down in and inhabiting Jerusalem?**
5. **"I am now saying to you, No. Nevertheless, if you folks should not progressively change your thinking*** [implies consciousness of the Messianic Age with its new arrangement (in Christ); to be neighborly (Brueggemann)], **you will all similarly proceed in destroying yourselves** [i.e., by towers and walls falling; comment: = reference to Jerusalem, AD 70].
[* *cf* Rom. 12:2]
6. **So He went on to tell this illustration** (or: parable)**:**
"A certain man had a fig tree that was planted in his vineyard, and so he came seeking (or: searching all over) **within it for fruit – and he found none.**

7. **"Then he said to the person who took care of the vineyard, 'Look, for three years now I have been repeatedly coming, constantly searching for fruit within this fig tree, and I continue finding none. Therefore, cut it out [of the vineyard]. For what reason does it also continue making this spot of ground completely idle and unproductive?'**
8. **"But the [vineyard keeper], giving a considered response, then says to him, 'Master** (or: Sir; Lord), **leave it this year also, until which [time] I can dig and spread manure around it.**
9. **"'And then, if it should indeed produce fruit [as we progress] into the impending [season], [well and good] – yet if not, you will certainly proceed having it cut out.'"**

10. **Now He had been repeatedly teaching within one of the synagogues, on the sabbaths.**
11. **Then – look and consider this! – a woman continuously having a spirit of weakness** (or: constantly holding and possessing an aspect of sickness and impotence) **[for] eighteen years [came by], and she continued being constantly bent over** (or: bent double and together) **and completely unable** (or: having no power) **to bend back up** (or: to unbend).
12. **Now upon seeing her, Jesus called out loudly in summons, then said to her, "Woman** (Madam; Lady), **you have been loosed away and are now freed** (released) **from your weakness** (illness; infirmity; impotence)!"
13. **Next He placed** (or: put; laid) **[His] hands upon her – and instantly she was made straight and erect again** (or: was straightened back up) **and she began giving glory to God and enhancing God's reputation** (formed opinions and imaginations about God; credited God).

14. **Now making a critical remark, the presiding officer** (ruler; chief; ranking member; leader) **of the synagogue – growing indignant and displeased, resenting the fact that Jesus had given care and effected a cure on the sabbath – began saying to the crowd, "There are six days within which it continues necessary and binding to be habitually working** (performing acts)! **You folks continue the habit of receiving treatment and cures while normally coming on** (or: during) **them – and not on the sabbath day!"**
15. **So the Lord made a decisive reply to him, and said, "O you overly-judging and critical folks**

> (*hupokrites*; or: those who put texts under close inspection to sift and separate and then give an answer, an interpretation, an opinion; or: those who live by separating things yet who under-discern; or: those who make judgments from a low view; or: those who under-estimate reality; or: perverse scholars who focus on tiny distinctions)! **Does not each**

one of you folks normally loosen (or: untie) **his ox or ass from the stall** (or: stable; or: feeding trough) **on the sabbath – and then continuing in leading [it] off, he is habitually giving [it water] to drink?**
16. **"Now this woman – being a daughter of Abraham whom the adversary** (or: opponent) **binds, and consider it, eighteen years! – did it not continue binding and necessary for** (or: due) **[her] to be at once loosed from this bond on the sabbath day** (a day of rest and ceasing from labor)**?"**
17. **And with His continuing in saying these things, all those remaining in opposition to Him began being brought down in shame and complete disgrace – and yet all the crowd rejoiced at all the glorious** (splendid; remarkable) **things coming to be by, and taking place under, Him.**

18. **Therefore He went on to say, "To what is the reign of God like** (or: How and in what is God's kingdom activities similar), **and with what shall I liken it** (put it in resemblance)**?**
19. **"It is like a mustard seed which, upon taking, a person threw into his own garden** (or: [the] garden of himself), **and it grew and then became [like] unto a** [other MSS add: great] **tree, and then the birds of the sky** (or: atmosphere; heaven) **settled down** (took up lodging as in tents; = made temporary nests; pitched and set up a tabernacle) **within its branches."**
20. **Then, again, He said, "To what [else] shall I continue in likening God's reign** (rule, government and kingdom, or His kingship, sovereign influence and activity)**?**
21. **"It is like yeast** (or: leaven) **which, upon taking, a woman hid, [mixing it] into three seah-measures** (= about thirty-six quarts) **of ground wheat** (meal or flour) **– until where [the] whole [batch] was leavened** (then, fermented)."

22. **Later, He began journeying through, from city to city and from village to village, repeatedly teaching and then journeying on, progressively making His way on into Jerusalem.**

23. **Now at one point, someone said to Him, "Sir** (or: Master; Lord), **[I wonder] if [only] a few are proceeding in being saved**
> (or: if few are progressively being rescued; if the folks presently being healed and made whole are a small number)**?"**

So He said to them,

24. **"YOU folks be continually struggling and constantly exerting yourselves vigorously even to the point of agonizing, as contestants in the public games, to at once enter through the narrow gate, or door** (or: cramped entry), **because many people – I now tell you – will continue seeking to enter, and yet they will not continue having strength.**

25. **"From [the point or time] where the master of the house** (or: the owner and lord of the house; the householder) **may get up and lock off** (close and bar) **the door** (or: entry), **and then YOU folks should begin to stand outside and to repeatedly knock [at] the door** (or: entry), **repeatedly saying, 'Sir** (or: Master; Lord; [other MSS: Sir, sir! {or: Lord, Lord!}]), **open up to us** (or: for us)**!' And then, giving a decided reply, he will proceed in declaring to YOU folks, 'I have not seen, and thus do not know, YOU people. From what place are YOU?** (or: I am not acquainted with whence you are, what exists being your source, and why are you [here]!)**.'**

26. **"At that point YOU will begin to be saying, one after another, 'We ate and drank in front of you** (in your sight)**! Also, you taught in our town squares** (plazas; broad streets)**!'**

27. **"And yet, he will continue declaring, 'I am now saying to YOU, I have not seen, and thus do not know, from where you are, nor what exists being your source, nor why you are [here]. Stand off away from me, all workers of injustice and un-neighborliness**
> (laborers in that which is not right; unfair workmen; folks whose actions do not accord with the Way pointed out; un-neighborly workers void of rightwised relationships)**!'**

28. **"Whenever you folks may [other MSS: will] see Abraham, Isaac and Jacob – as well as all the prophets – within the midst of God's reign** (or: centered in sovereign activities and influence from God; in the kingdom of God; or: in union with the kingship which is God), **yet YOU yourselves are one after another being thrown outside, the weeping and the grinding** (or: gnashing) **of the teeth** (= the sorrow and regret) **will continue being [out] there, in that place.**

29. **"Not only that, people will continue arriving from eastern regions and western territories, as well as from [the] north and [the] south, and they will proceed in being made to recline back at a meal, within God's reign** (kingdom; sovereign projects and programs).

30. **"And so – now think about this – last folks are they who will continue being first ones, and yet first folks are they who will continue being last ones** (or: they continue being last ones who will proceed in being first ones; and they continue being first ones who will regress to being last ones)**."**

31. **In that very hour certain Pharisees approached, one after another saying to Him, "At once go out and continue on your way** (journey) **from here, because Herod is wanting and intending to kill you off!"**

32. **And yet He replied to them, "After going on YOUR way, say to this fox** (or: jackal), **'Look and take note! I continue throwing out demons** (Hellenistic concept and term: = animistic influences) **and finishing off** (or: completing) **healings today and tomorrow, and then on the third day I am proceeding in being brought to the purposed goal and destiny** (or: I am progressively being finished and made fully functional). [cf Jn. 19:28, 30]

33. **"Moreover, it continues being binding and necessary for Me to continue journeying today, tomorrow and on the following one [other MSS: in the one still coming], because it continues being inadmissible** (not acceptable or allowed; = unthinkable) **for a prophet to be destroyed** (or; be lost; or, middle: ruined himself) **outside of Jerusalem!**

34. **"Jerusalem, O Jerusalem! – the one constantly killing off the prophets, and repeatedly stoning the people having been sent off as emissaries** (missionaries; representatives) **to face**

her – how often (how many times) **I wanted and intended to at once completely gather together and assemble your children, in the manner in which a hen [gathers] her own brood** (or: chicks) **under [her] wings, and yet you people did not want or intend [it]!**

35. **"Look and consider this – your house** (or: House; = the Temple; or: household [a figure of the entire people]) **is being progressively left and abandoned** [other MSS add: {and} desolate – depopulated like a desert; *cf* Jer. 22:5] **to you people** (or: divorced, dismissed and sent away among you; or: is repeatedly forgiven for you folks)**! So I am now saying to you folks that under no circumstances can** (would; could; may) **you see or perceive Me, until you can** (or: should; would) **say,**

> **'The One progressively** (or: repeatedly) **coming in union with [the] Lord's Name** (centered in a Name from [YHVH; YHWH]; = in the authority of the Name of [Yahweh]) **is One having been blessed with good words of ease and well-being and now is continuing with goodness!'"** [Ps. 118:26]

CHAPTER 14

1. **Later, it occurred during the [situation for] Him to go** (or: come) **into the house of a certain one of the leaders** (or: rulers; officials; chief or prominent men) **of the Pharisees, on a sabbath, to eat bread** (= a meal) **– and they, themselves, were continuing in closely observing Him from the side, scrutinizing Him.**
2. **And then – look and take note! – there was [suddenly] a certain person** (human) **suffering from edema** (dropsy; excess swelling from fluid retention) **in front of Him.**
3. **And so, giving a discerning response, Jesus said to the men versed in the Law** (the Torah and legal experts) **and [to the] Pharisees, "Is it** [other MSS: Does it continue] **allowed, from [our] existence, to give care, attentively treat or cure on the sabbath, or not?"**
4. **But they were quiet** (or: kept silent). **And so, after taking a strong hold upon [him], He healed him and set [him] free** (or: loosed [the disease] off of [him]; or: released [him]; or: dismissed [him]).
5. **Then, making a discerning response, He said to them [either: to the men watching Him; or: to all present], "Which one of you folks, [if your] son** [other MSS: ass] **or ox will fall into a cistern** (sealed-in well; or: a pit) **on a sabbath day, will [you] not also proceed immediately pulling** (or: dragging) **him, or it, back up again [the same day]?"**
6. **And they did not have strength or ability** (were powerless) **to give a decided response in opposition to** (or: to direct back an answer in contradiction toward) **these [reasonings].**

7. **So He went on to tell an illustration** (a parable) **to the folks having been invited [to the meal] – as He was holding His attention on how, one after another, they continued choosing** (picking out) **for themselves the first reclining places** (= the most prominent seats that were considered places of honor and importance) **– saying to them,**
8. **"Whenever you may be invited** (or: called) **unto wedding festivities** (or: a marriage feast) **by someone, you should not recline** (= sit down) **into the first** (= most honorable or important) **place, lest at some point there may be a person having been invited by him [who is held] in more honor** ([who is] more distinguished) **than you,**
9. **"and then, upon coming [up], the person inviting both you and him will proceed saying to you, 'Give [the] place to this person.' And at that point you begin, with shame and disgrace, to continue holding down** (= occupying and retaining) **the last place** (= the place of least honor).
10. **"But instead, whenever you may be invited** (or: called), **after going on your way, fall back into** (= assume a position in) **the last** (= least distinguished) **place, so that, whenever the person having invited you may come, he will proceed saying to you, 'Friend, walk** (or: move) **on up to a higher** (more upward) **[position].' At that point there will continue being a manifestation of esteem for you** (or: there will proceed being glory on you; it will habitually be a good reputation to you) **in the sight and presence of all those reclining back [at the dinner] with you** (i.e., all your fellow guests),
11. **"because everyone habitually exalting himself** (lifting himself up; = promoting himself) **will be habitually brought** (or: made) **low** (be progressively humbled; be constantly demoted), **and**

yet the person habitually making and bringing himself low (humbling and demoting himself) **will be habitually exalted** (lifted up; promoted)." [Jas. 4:10; 1 Pet. 5:6]

12. **Now He also continued saying to the person having invited Him, "Whenever you should normally make** (or: provide; = give) **a luncheon or a dinner, do not be habitually** (or: stop) **summoning your friends, nor even your brothers, nor yet your relatives, and not rich neighbors – lest at some point** (or: lest perchance) **they themselves should be inviting you in return, and it could** (or: may; would) **become a repayment-effect to** (or: for) **you.**
13. **"But to the contrary, whenever you normally make a reception** (provide entertainment; = give a banquet; = throw a dinner party), **make it a practice to be inviting destitute folks, crippled, maimed or mutilated people, lame folks, [the] blind,**
14. **"and you will continually be a happy, blessed and fortunate person, because they continue having nothing [with which] to repay you, so you see, it will proceed being repaid to you within** (or: in union with) **the resurrection of the fair and equitable folks**
> (or: the standing, placing, putting or setting back up again of the just and rightwised people who are in right relationships and are in union with the Way pointed out)."
> [comment: this runs counter to *1 Enoch* 62:1-11; 1QSa 2:5-22; *The Isaiah Targum*]
15. **Now on hearing these things, someone of the fellow guests** (a certain one of those lying back together [at the meal]) **said to Him, "Whoever will continue eating bread** (= a meal) **within God's reign** (kingdom; royal rule and domain) **[will be] happy, blessed and fortunate."**
16. **But** (or: Yet) **He said to him, "A certain person** (human) **was in the process of preparing** (making) **a great dinner** (main meal of the day), **and he [had] invited many people.**
17. **"So he sent off his slave on an errand, at the hour of the dinner, to say to those having been invited, 'Be now progressively coming, because already the results of [our] preparation are ready.'** [comment: He is pointing to His present mission: the time had arrived]
18. **"And then one by one** (or: from one [mind or motive]) **they all began to proceed in making excuses and to beg off with declining requests. The first one said to him, 'I just bought a field and I continue having necessity of going out to see it. I am now asking you, Have me excused.'**
19. **"And a different person said, 'I just bought five yokes** (= pairs; teams) **of oxen** (or: cattle), **and I am presently on my way to prove them** (to examine and test them out), **I am now asking you, Have me excused.'**
20. **"Then still another person said, 'I just married a wife, and because of this, I am unable to come.'** [comment: these folks represent the Jewish leadership who refused Him as Messiah]
21. **"And so the slave, after coming to be alongside, reported back to his owner** (master; lord) **these [responses]. At that point the master of the house** (or: householder), **being indignant from the internal fervor of his natural disposition, said to his slave, 'At once go out quickly into the squares and streets of the city and at once lead and bring into the midst, here, the destitute folks as well as crippled, maimed and mutilated people, even blind folks and lame ones!'** [comment: such were the folks to whom Jesus gave the kingdom]
22. **"And so later, the slave said, 'Sir** (or: Master), **what you ordered and instructed has happened, and yet there is still a place** (= room).' [*cf* Isa. 49:5-12; 56:3-11]
23. **"So the owner** (lord; master) **said to the slave, 'At once go out into the roads and fenced areas** (or: hedgerows; boundary walls), **and at once COMPEL** (force; oblige) **[them] to come in, so that my house may be filled to capacity!'** [comment: a figure of Gentile inclusion]
24. **"You see, I am now saying to you folks that not even one of the adult men of those having been invited will proceed in having a taste of My dinner."** [*cf* Isa. 25:6-12 – messianic banquet; Mat. 21:43; Rom. 11:14-33]

25. **Now many** (or: large) **crowds** (= hordes of people) **continued traveling** (journeying on) **together with Him, and so, upon turning, He said to them,**
26. **"If anyone continues coming to** (or: toward) **Me, and does not habitually regard with a negative will** (or: radically detach from; or: = put lesser importance to; hate, in the sense of giving less preference to) **his father and mother and wife and children and brothers and sisters – and still [more], even his own soul-life** (the inner being, concerns and consciousness which is himself) **– he has no power and is unable to be My disciple** (student; apprentice)!

27. "Whoever is not habitually picking up and carrying his own execution stake (or: the cross of himself; the suspending-pole which pertains to, or is, himself) **and then continuing in coming behind Me – he or she has no power and is unable to be My disciple** (apprentice)!

28. "For example, who among you people – wanting and intending to build a tower – is not first sitting down [and] progressively calculating (reckoning by use of pebbles; estimating) the expense – [to see] if he continues having** (holding; possessing) **sufficient resources [to bring it] into completion?**

29. "– so that, after his laying a foundation and then not being [financially] strong enough to finish everything out, those folks continuing in watching might not at some point start to repeatedly ridicule, mock or make fun of him,**

30. "one after another saying, 'This person started to progressively build, and yet he was not [financially] strong [enough] to finish [it] out.'**

31. "Or, what king, continuing on his way** (journeying) **to progressively engage into the midst of a war with a different king, will not first – after sitting down – proceed taking counsel with himself** (consider, deliberate, ponder and plan) **[to see] if he is powerful and able to undertake a face to face meeting, [himself being] in the midst of ten thousand [troops], with the [king] constantly coming upon him with twenty thousand [troops]?**

32. "Now if in fact [he decides that he could] not, [at] his still being far away, through sending off a delegation of representatives he proceeds asking for the [terms that lead] toward peace** (a compact of union).

33. "Thus, then** (or: Therefore, in the same manner), **everyone from among you folks who is not in the habit of setting-off and arranging-away from himself all his own possessions which are continuing to be his subsistence, he continues with no power and is unable to be My disciple** (student; apprentice).

34. "To be sure, salt [is] excellent** (ideal; beautiful; fine). **Yet if the salt also should be made dull** (or: tasteless; insipid; flat), **in what [way or situation] will it proceed in being made fit for seasoning?**

35. "It is neither well placed** (thus: fit to be put) **into soil nor into manure. Folks normally throw it outside.**
Let the person presently having ears to now hear (or: to continue to listen and hear), **continue listening and habitually hearing."**

CHAPTER 15

1. **Now all the tax collection contractors** (or: governmental customs and tribute agents) **and outcasts** (cultural, religious and legal failures; those who by habit and lifestyle miss the mark; sinners) **were progressively drawing near to Him to continue listening and hearing Him,**

2. **Consequently both the Pharisees and the scribes** (scholars; theologians of the Law) **kept on privately grumbling, muttering complaint and discontent among themselves, one after another saying "This man is constantly receiving and giving welcoming-hospitality to outcasts** (sinners; etc.) **and is habitually eating with them."**

3. **So He spoke this illustration** (parable) **to them, progressively saying and laying it out:**

4. **"What person from among you folks, presently owning** (possessing) **one hundred sheep and then upon losing one of them, is not normally leaving the ninety-nine down within the wilderness** (open range; desolate and uninhabited place) **and then continuing on his way upon [the track of] the lost one – until he can** (or: may; would) **find it?**

5. **"Later, after finding [it], he proceeds to place** (or: lay) **it on his shoulders, amidst rejoicing!**

6. **"And so, upon coming into the house, he proceeds calling together [his] friends and neighbors, saying to them in turn, 'Celebrate** (or: Be glad and caused to rejoice) **together with me, because I have found my lost sheep** (or: the sheep having been destroyed from me)!'**

7. **"I am now saying to you folks that in this way there will continue being joy within the heaven** (or: the atmosphere) **upon** (or: on the occasion of) **a progressive changing of the mind** (or: a continued change in thinking, state of consciousness, and perspective, [accompanied by a return to the Lord])* **by one outcast** (habitual failure; person who constantly makes mistakes;

sinner) – **[more] than upon ninety-nine 'righteous and just folks'** (or: upright folks; people who are fair, equitable and in rightwised relationships in the Way pointed out) **who continue having no need** (or: necessity) **of a change of mind or state of consciousness [a return to Yahweh]!** [* cf Rom. 12:2]

8. **"Or then, what woman** (or: wife) **presently possessing** (having) **ten drachma coins, if she should lose one drachma, does not proceed to light a lamp and then continue sweeping the house and carefully looking and searching for [it] until she can** (or: may; would) **find it?**

9. **"And later, after finding [it], she proceeds calling together her women friends and neighbors, saying [to them] in turn, 'Celebrate** (or: Be glad and caused to rejoice) **together with me, because I have found the drachma which I lost!'**

10. **"In this way, I am now saying to you folks, joy is habitually birthed** (or: constantly happens) **in the sight and presence of God's agents** (or: the messengers from God; the folks with the message of God) **upon** (or: on the occasion of) **a progressive changing of the mind** (or: a continued change in thinking and state of consciousness, [accompanied by a return to the Lord]) **by one outcast** (habitual failure; person who constantly makes mistakes; sinner).**"**

11. **Now He said, "There was a certain man having two sons.**

12. **"And the younger of them said to [his] father, 'Father, give to me the part of the estate** (the existing substance; the property; the essence) **normally falling upon [me].' So he apportioned** (divided in two parts and distributed) **to** (or: for; between) **them the livelihood** (or: [the means of] living). [note: Jewish law allotted one-half as much to the younger as to the older]

13. **"Later, after not many days, upon gathering everything together the younger son traveled from his homeland into a far country – and there he squandered** (thoroughly scattered; dissipated) **his substance for existing** (or: essence; or: property; [portion of] the estate), **constantly living as one having no chance of safety or preservation** (one not being in a condition of health, wholeness or salvation; the disposition and life of one who is abandoned and reckless).

14. **"Now after his expending everything** (= using up all his money and possessions), **a severe famine was birthed down on that country** (or: occurred that extended throughout that region), **and he himself began to be caused to progressively fall behind so as to be in want and need** (= he became nearly destitute, facing starvation).

15. **"And so, after making his way [from place to place around the area], he was joined** (glued together) **to one** (= put in the service of a person) **of the citizens of that country, and [that person] sent him into his fields to continue tending and grazing young pigs** (hogs; swine).

16. **"As time went on, he kept on having a strong desire to be fed, until satisfied, from out of the little horn-shaped pods of the carob trees which the young pigs were habitually eating – and still, no one was giving [anything] to him.**

17. **"Now at some point, coming into** (or: to) **himself, he affirmed, 'How many of my father's hired workers are surrounded by an abundance of bread – yet I, myself, am progressively perishing** (loosing myself away) **in a famine** (or: by deprivation of food)!

18. **"'Upon rising, I will continue traveling** (journeying on) **to my father, and then I will proceed saying to him, "O father, I failed to hit the target [leading] into the heaven** (or: I missed my aim into the sky; or: I sinned in regard to the atmosphere), **as well as in your sight and before you.**

19. **"'"I am no longer worthy to be called your son. Make me as one of your hired workers."'**

20. **"And so, upon rising, he went toward his own father.**
Now while he continued being still a long way off (or: But during his progressive holding off yet far away), **his father saw him and was moved with compassion. Then, after running, [his father] fell upon his neck and tenderly kissed him** (or: expressed affection down on him).

21. **"So the son said to him, 'O father, I failed to hit the target [leading] into the heaven** (or: I missed my aim into the sky; or: I sinned in regard to heaven; or: I [sowed] failure into the atmosphere), **as well as in your sight and before you. I am no longer worthy to be called your son. Make me as one of your hired workers.'**

22. "But the father said to his slaves, 'Quickly! Bring out the first robe – the one that signifies the first arrangement with the first equipment and which places him in first place – and clothe him! Then give a ring into his hand, and sandals unto (= for) [his] feet.
23. "'Next, you folks proceed in bringing the grain-fed young animal (e.g.: fat and choice calf): at once slaughter (or: sacrifice) [it], and, after eating, we can be put in a good and easy frame of mind (or: we should be given thoughts of well-being, cheer and celebration),
24. "'because this one, my son, was existing being dead – and now he becomes back alive again (or: lives up, again); he was existing being one having been destroyed and lost – and now he is found!'
And so they began to be progressively put in a good and easy frame of mind and were continually given thoughts of well-being and cheer.

25. "Now his older son was continuing being in the midst of a field. Later, while progressively coming – as he drew near at hand to the house – he heard [the sound] of a symphony (a concert of musical instruments) and choruses (or: = music and choral dancing).
26. "And so, calling one of the servants to him, he began inquiring so as to ascertain what these things might be (or: mean).
27. "So the man told him, 'Your brother is now arriving, and your father slaughtered the grain-fed young animal (= the fat and choice calf), seeing that he got him back being still sound and healthy.'
28. "But now the [older brother] swelled with internal teeming, expressing his natural disposition with agitation and irritation (or: grew angry or enraged), and then was not willing (or: wanting; intending) to enter. So his father, upon coming out, began calling him to his side and continued entreating him.
29. "Yet the [older brother], making a judging reply, said to his father, 'Look, and think about it! For so many years I constantly slaved for (or: worked as a slave to) you, and not even once did I transgress (go to the side of) your implanted goal (impartation of the finished product within; inward directive) – and yet not even once did you give to (or: for) me a kid (a young goat), so that I could be put in a good and easy frame of mind (or: should be given thoughts of well-being, cheer and celebration) with my friends.
30. "'But when this son of yours came – the one eating down (or: devouring) your livelihood with prostitutes – you slaughtered (sacrificed) the grain-fed young animal (e.g.: fat and choice calf)!'

31. "So now the [father] said to him, 'O child, you yourself continue being with me always – and all my things continue being yours (or: everything [that is] mine is yours).
32. "'But it continued being binding and necessary to at once be in a good and easy frame of mind (or: be given thoughts of well-being, cheer and celebration) and to rejoice, because this one – your brother – was existing being dead, and now he comes to life; and was one having been lost and destroyed – and now he is found!'"

CHAPTER 16

1. So He went on saying to the disciples (students; learners; apprentices),
"A certain person was being rich who was having a house manager (administrator; steward), and this [manager] was at one point accused (thrust-through with charges brought by an adversary; [note: from this verb comes the noun "one who thrusts-through," commonly rendered "devil"]) to him [i.e., to the rich person] as habitually squandering his property, possessions and means of subsistence by thoroughly scattering and wasting [them].
2. "And so, upon summoning him, he said to him, 'What [is] this [that] I am continually hearing about you (or: Why am I now hearing this concerning you)? Turn in the account (= Hand over the books for an audit) of your management (administration; stewardship), for you are no longer able to be [the] manager of the household (or: the estate).'
3. "So the manager said within himself, 'What shall I do, because my master (lord; = employer) is in the process of taking the management (the administration) away from me? I

am not strong to be habitually digging; I am ashamed and feel disgrace to make a life of begging.

4. "'I know from experience what I will proceed in doing, so that, whenever I am actually transferred (or: may have my position changed) from out of the management (the position of administration), folks may welcome and receive me into their own houses (or: homes).'

5. "And then, after calling to himself each one of his own master's (lord's; = employer's) debtors, he was saying to the first one, 'How much do you continue owing to my master (lord; = employer)?'

6. "So he said, 'One hundred baths (Hebrew liquid measure: = about five to nine hundred gallons [estimates vary]) of olive oil.' So [the manager] said to him, 'Take in hand (= take back) your writings (the notes; the contracts; the invoices) and, after sitting down, quickly write [a new one for] fifty.'

7. "Next, he said to a different person, 'You there – how much are you continuing to owe?' So he said, 'One hundred cors (Hebrew dry measure: = about a thousand bushels) of grain.' He said to him, 'Take in hand (= take back) your writings (contracts; invoices), and write [a new one for] eighty.'

8. "And so the master (lord; = employer) commended (added praise and applause to) the estate-manager in regard to the disregard for what is right (the injustice; the actions which were not in accord with the way pointed out; the dishonesty), because he acted thoughtfully (or: performed intelligently in considering [the situation]), because, you see, the sons of this age (= the people who have the qualities and display the character of the current age and present period of time) exist being (or: are) more thoughtful, prudent and intelligent with common sense unto (or: in; respecting; with a view to) their own generation than are the sons of the Light (= people of the covenant with revealed knowledge of the Way of the Life).

9. "Now am I really now saying to you folks, At once make for yourselves friends from out of the midst of the Mammon (Aramaic: wealth and earthly goods; Syrian god of riches) that pertains to and has its source in the inequity (or: this aforementioned mammon of injustice and dishonesty) so that whenever it gives out (fails; falls short; is defaulting) folks can (or: they may, or would) welcome and receive you folks into the lifelong tents that have the qualities and characteristics of [this] age (or: the tabernacles that last for an undetermined duration)?

10. "The person [who is] faithful (reliable; trustworthy; loyal) in [the] least (or: smallest) also continues being (or: is) faithful (reliable; trustworthy; loyal) in much; and the person [who is] inequitable (unjust; dishonest) in [the] least (or: smallest) also continues being (or: is) inequitable (unjust; unfair; dishonest) in much!

11. "Therefore, if you folks do not come to be faithful and trustworthy in connection with the inequitable Mammon (the unjust wealth or unfair material possessions), who will proceed entrusting to you (or: in you) the Real and True?

12. "And if you folks do not come to be faithful and trustworthy in connection with the thing belonging to another, who will continue giving to you (or: for you; in you) the thing that is your own [other MSS: that is ours]? [cf Ps. 24:1]

13. "No domestic (household servant) continues able to habitually perform as a slave for (or: to; with) two owners (masters; lords); you see, he will either proceed treating the one with less preference and disfavor (with ill will; with disapproval and detachment; with hate) and will continue loving the other (urging union with the different one), or, he will continue holding himself instead to (= uphold; be attentive to; stay loyal to; support) [things] pertaining to one and then proceed despising (hold a down-oriented opinion and frame of mind toward) the other (the different one). You folks continue unable to keep on performing as a slave for (or: to) God and also to (or: for) Mammon (= wealth, money, or, the false god of riches).

14. Now the Pharisees, habitually being inherently fond of silver (= money-lovers), were listening to all these things, and so began turning out and up their noses while contemptuously sneering at Him.

15. Consequently He said to them, "You men are the ones constantly justifying yourselves in the sight of people (or: show yourselves as being fair and equitable to humans), but God continuously knows your hearts by intimate experience! The fact is, the thing

[which is] high and lofty among humans [is] a disgusting and nauseating thing (something which is the result of filth and nastiness) **in God's sight.**

16. **"The Law [= Torah] and the Prophets [continued in effect] until John [the baptist]. From that time on** (or: Since then), **the reign of God** (royal rule from God; kingdom which is God; God's kingship, sovereign influence and activity) **is being progressively brought and declared as the good news of well-being, ease and goodness – and everyone is one after another being pressed and forced into it** (or, as a middle voice: and so, without any recourse to law or customary right, everyone is progressively crowding himself into it)**!**

17. **"Still, it continues being easier** (or: Now it is less trouble and work) **for the sky or atmosphere and the land** (or: the heaven and the earth) **to pass on by or go to the side, than for one horn-like projection** (diacritical mark, such as an accent or breathing mark, or part of a Hebrew letter; a serif; = the smallest detail) **of the Law to fall.**

    [comment: this means that the Jewish leaders would receive the curses of the Law]

18. **"Every man repeatedly loosing-away** (dismissing; divorcing) **his [current] wife, and then proceeding in marrying a different woman is in the act of committing adultery. And also the man habitually** (or: one after another) **marrying a woman having been loosed-away** (divorced) **from a husband is in the act of committing adultery.**

    [comment: Jesus is here condemning the then current practices of the male-dominated marriage/divorce arrangements of those who followed the school of Hillel, which taught that a man could divorce his wife "for any reason"]

19. **"Now there was a certain rich man, and he was in the habit of dressing himself with purple fabric and fine linen** (a shiny white cloth made from bleached flax; used in Egypt for wrapping mummies; = costly garments) **while daily enjoying himself and being in a good frame of mind – [being simply] radiant** (or: [living] splendidly and magnificently).

20. **"Now in contrast, there was a certain destitute man named Lazarus, who, having been sorely wounded, had been flung [down] and cast [aside]** (or: having been afflicted with sores and being ulcerated, was normally placed) **in the proximity of and facing toward the large portico** (gateway and forecourt) **of his [house].**

21. **"And [this destitute man continued there] progressively experiencing strong desires to be fed and satisfied from the things [which were] from time to time falling from the rich man's table. Not only that, in contrast even the dogs – periodically coming – were licking his wounds** (or: sores and ulcers).

22. **"Now at one point it came to be [for] the destitute man to die off and for him to be carried away by the agents** (or: messengers) **into Abraham's place of safety and intimacy** (bosom; chest; garment folds; inlet or bay; valley [note: a figure of Paradise or the Messianic banquet]). **Now the rich man also died, and he was buried** (or: – he also was entombed).

23. **"Then, while undergoing the distress of being examined, tested and tried** (having the touchstone applied to check his composition) **within the midst of the unseen [realm]** (or: = the grave; the sphere or state of the dead; Greek: *hades*), **upon lifting up his eyes he continues seeing Abraham, from afar, as well as Lazarus within his places of intimacy, safety and acceptance** (or: bosoms; valleys; or: = within the *triclinium*; [cf Jn. 13:23, "bosom of Jesus"]).

24. **"And so he, shouting a call, said, 'Father Abraham, mercy me** (do at once that which will be merciful to me) **and at once send Lazarus** [means: God's helper; or: God is the Helper] **so that he can** (or: may) **immerse** (dip; baptize) **the tip of his finger [in] water, and then can cool down my tongue – because I continue being pained within the midst of this flame.'**

25. **"But Abraham said, 'O child** (or: My boy; Born one; or: Descendant), **be reminded that within your life** (or: lifetime) **you took away** (or: received from; or: got in full) **your good things** (or: the good things that pertain to you; the good things that had their source in you), **and Lazarus likewise the bad things** (the [experiences] of poor quality; the worthless things; the harmful and injurious [treatments]; the [conditions] as they ought not to be). **But at the present time, here he continues being called alongside and given relief, aid, comfort and consolation, yet you yourself continue being given pain.**

26. **"'Furthermore, in the midst of all these things [and conditions] a great, yawning chasm** (or: gaping opening) **has been set firmly in position and is now established between us and you people, so that folks presently wanting or intending to step through from here toward**

you people would continue being unable [to do so] – neither could folks pass over from there toward us.'

27. **"So he said, 'Then I am begging you, father** (or: O father, in that case I now ask you), **that you would send him into the house** (or: household) **of my father –**

28. **"'you see, I continue having five brothers – so that he can progressively bring a thorough witness** (give full testimony; or: show complete evidence) **to them, to the end that they would not also come into this place of painful examination and testing** (or: of the application of the touchstone, which tests our composition).'

> [Note: the touchstone (*lapis Lydius*) was applied to metals to determine the amount of alloy which was mixed in, and thus e.g. with a gold object, is a test to indicate the amount of pure gold in the piece. The process became a figure of the pain and discomfort of a person sick with palsy (Matt.8:60); of the difficulties and pressures in maneuvering against a strong wind and high waves (Matt. 14:24); of the hard work of rowing in a storm (Mark 6:48); of how Lot was distressed by lawless acts (2 Pet. 2:7-8); and of the pain of childbirth (Rev. 12:2) – all of which can be construed as "tests" given by God. The flame in the context of this parable calls to mind the fire of the "refiner and purifier of silver" and the purging of the gold by Yahweh (Mal. 3:3) in His dealing with the Levites. It is also interesting to note that "purple fabric and fine linen" were used as part of the vestments of the priests (Ex. 39), as well as by the rich.]

29. **"But Abraham proceeds to say, 'They continue having Moses and the Prophets – let them at once listen to, hear from, [and thus obey] them.'**

30. **"Yet he said, 'Oh, no** (or: = That's not enough; or: = They won't), **father Abraham. However, if someone from [the] dead people should go his way** (or: travel; journey) **to them, they will proceed to change their minds** (or: have a change in their way of thinking and state of consciousness) **[and be returning to Yahweh and covenant neighborliness]!'**

31. **"Still, he rejoined to him, 'Since** (or: If) **they are not in the habit of listening to or hearing [and thus obeying] Moses and the Prophets, neither will they proceed in being persuaded if someone should arise and stand up out from among [the] dead folks.'"**

CHAPTER 17

1. **So** (or: Now) **He said to His disciples, "It continues being inadmissible** (or: unallowable; or: unavoidable; or: = incredible) **that the entrapments and causes for stumbling are not to come. Nevertheless, tragic is the fate of the person through whom it continues coming**
> (or: It is inwardly unacceptable [that] snares [will] not be [set in place], but all the more, [it will be] a grievous experience for the person who keeps on [setting them])!

2. **"It continues being an advantage to, and a profit for, him** (or: It progressively looses him to the goal) **if a stone from a [hand] mill continues lying around** (= tied to and hanged from) **his neck and then he had been tossed** (or: pitched; hurled) **into the sea, than that he should cause one of these little ones to stumble, falter or be ensnared.**

3. **"Be habitually holding your attention and your selves toward each other, and thus be considerate of and devoted to one another. If your brother** (or: fellow believer; group or family member) **should make a mistake or fail** (may miss the goal or fall short; or: happens to sin or go into error), **respectfully give him honorable advice and let him know of his value. Then, if he should change his mind and his thinking [while turning to Yahweh and neighborliness], make the [issue] flow away from him** (or: forgive and release him).

4. **"Even if he should** (or: may) **be a failure unto you** (or: sin into you) **seven times a day, and then seven times should turn around to you, time after time saying, 'I continue in the process of changing my thinking [and am turning to neighborliness],' you will proceed making it flow away from him** (or: be repeatedly forgiving and habitually releasing him)."

5. **And later, the commissioned ones** (the emissaries; the sent-ones) **said to the Lord, "Apply faith for us**
> (= Be our faith; or: Apply trust in us; = Trust us; or: Put faith toward us; = Give us faith; or: Add faith to us; Increase trust in us; or: Deliver loyalty, allegiance and faithfulness to us; or: Attribute reliability to us; Set us toward confident faithfulness)."

6. **So the Lord said, "Since you folks continue having trust** (or: If you by habit hold faith and progressively possess confident faithfulness and loyalty) **as a grain of mustard, you could likely have been saying to this black mulberry tree, 'Be at once rooted out, and then be suddenly planted within the midst of the sea** (or: lake),' **and it would submissively listen to, and obey, you.**

7. **"Now which one [is there] from among you folks normally having a slave [who is] regularly plowing or tending [sheep, or, cattle], who – upon [his] entering from out of the field – will say to him, 'Upon coming by [the dining area], immediately recline back [for dinner]'?**

8. **"To the contrary, will he not rather proceed saying to him, 'At once prepare and make ready what I will eat for the evening meal, and, after girding yourself about** (e.g., putting on an apron; or: tightening your belt and tucking in your clothing), **continue giving me attending service until I can be eating and drinking. Then, after that, you yourself will proceed eating and drinking'?**

9. **"He does not continue having gratitude for** (or: holding favor to) **the slave because he did** (or: does) **the things being fully arranged** (specifically assigned and prescribed), **does he? I think** (assume; presume; imagine) **not!**

10. **"Thus also, whenever you yourselves may do all the things being fully arranged** (specifically assigned) **to you folks, be habitually saying, 'We are unnecessary, useless** (= good-for-nothing and unprofitable; or: = ordinary) **slaves. We have done that which we were constantly obliged and indebted to do.'"**

11. **Later – it happened during the [occasion for] Him to be proceeding on the journey into Jerusalem, and He had been passing through the midst of** (or: between) **Samaria and Galilee –**

12. **at His entering into a certain village, ten adult men – lepers – encountered Him. They stood up at a distance,**

13. **and they themselves raised a voice, together saying, "Jesus, Leader** (or: Sir; One-who-stands-upon/over-us; Boss), **mercy us** (do at once that which will be merciful to us)!"

14. **And so, upon seeing [them], He said to them, "After going your way** (journeying on), **at once fully exhibit** (show for examination) **yourselves to the priests!" And then it happened – during their proceeding to go under [His instructions] they were at once cleansed!**

15. **Now one from among their group, upon seeing that he was healed, turned around under [this awareness] with a loud voice constantly ascribing the glory to God, enhancing His reputation** (or: experiencing imagination and impressions – forming opinions about God),

16. **then fell upon [his] face at His feet, repeatedly giving thanks to Him – not only that, this same man was a Samaritan.** [cf 10:33, above; Luke emphasizes inclusion]

17. **Now giving a discerning response [to the crowd], Jesus said, "Were** (or: Are) **not the ten men cleansed? So where [are] the nine?**

18. **"Were none found returning to give glory to** (or: credit, opinion and repute for) **God, except this foreigner** (person of another birth, race or nation)**?"**

19. **And so He said to him, "After arising** (or: standing up), **continue going your way** (journeying on). **Your trust and faith has made you healthy and left you whole** (or: has healed, delivered and saved you so that you are now rescued from your prior condition)."

20. **Now later, upon being asked by the Pharisees [as to] when the reign and kingdom of God is proceeding to come, He gave a decided reply to them, and said, "The reign** (or: kingdom; royal rule; sovereign activities and influences) **of God is not proceeding in** (or: presently; progressively; in the habit of) **coming with a careful keeping watch from the side**
(or: by means of or accompanied by attentive or intensive observing; [note: this word was used of watching the symptoms of an illness, as well as about making observations of the sky]; = with visible signs).

21. **"Neither will folks continue saying, 'Look here!' or, 'There!' You see – now consider this, and understand – God's reign** (the kingdom and royal rule, which is God; the sovereign

influence and activity from God) **continually exists inside you folks** (or: is on the inside of you people; or: is within the midst of you folks, in your community; exists centered in you people)."
22. **Then He said to the disciples, "Days will proceed in coming when** (or: will continue going, in which) **you folks will continue strongly yearning and desiring to see one of the days of the Son of the Man** (the Son of Mankind; = Adam's Son; = the anticipated eschatological messianic figure) **– and yet you will continue** (or: proceed) **not seeing [it].**
23. **"And folks will continue saying to you, 'Look there!' or, 'See here!' You should not go off, neither should you follow after or pursue [it].**
24. **"You see, even as the brightness** (the brilliant beam; the bright shining; or: = lightning) **progressively lightening and with luster shining forth from under the sky** (or: atmosphere; heaven; = the clouds) **continues giving light unto the under-sky** (= the lower heaven and atmosphere which is under the clouds), **in this way** (or: thus; so) **will the Son of the Man continue being** (or: will the Son from Humanity keep on existing) **in the Day of, and from, Him.**
25. **"Yet first, however, it continues necessary and binding for Him to at some point experience, and suffer, many things – and even to be summarily thrown away as the result of testing, and be rejected away from this [present] generation.**
26. **"Also, correspondingly as** (just as; accordingly as) **it was birthed** (happened; occurred) **within the days of Noah, in this way** (thus) **it will also progress** (or: continue) **being – within** (in the midst of) **the days of** (from) **the Son of the Man** (= the eschatological messianic figure)**:**
27. **"they were eating, they continued drinking, they kept on marrying, they were habitually given** (or: taken out) **in marriage – until which day Noah at one point entered into the ark, and then the down-washing** (flood; cataclysm) **suddenly came and at once lost, ruined and destroyed them all.**
28. **"Likewise, just as it was birthed** (happened; occurred; came to be) **within the days of Lot: they were eating, they continued drinking, they kept on buying** (or: doing business) **at the marketplace, they were repeatedly selling, they were seasonally planting, they were periodically building...**
29. **"but on the day in which Lot came** (or: at once went) **out from Sodom, it suddenly rained fire and sulphur from [the] sky and atmosphere** (or: fire – even deity and the divine nature – from heaven), **and it at once lost, ruined and destroyed them all.**
30. **"Down from and in accord with the very same things will it proceed being – on the Day in which the Son of the Man** (= Adam's Son; = the eschatological messianic figure) **is being progressively unveiled** (or: continues being revealed and disclosed).

31. **"On** (or: Within; During) **that Day, whoever will continue being upon the housetop – even though his moveable belongings** (utensils, vessels, gear, possessions) **[are] within the house – let him not walk down** (or: descend) **to pick them up. Likewise also [for] the person in a field – let him or her not return unto the things [left] behind.**
32. **"Continue remembering Lot's wife!** [comment: a reference to God's judgment]
33. **"Whoever may endeavor to build an encompassing protection**
       (or: produce a perimeter of defense; or: make a form or a structure to encircle; or: set
          boundaries or lines of demarcation) **around his soul-life** (his inner being and
consciousness, with its will, desires, emotions, appetites, affections, passions; or: himself) **will be progressively loosing it away and destroying it. Yet whoever may be loosing it away** (or: destroying it) **will continue bringing it forth as a living creature** (will engender it to be a living being; will produce it alive as a child or offspring).
       (or: = "Folks who try to make their lives secure will lose them, but in contrast, a person
          who can free it will give it life.)
34. **"I am now saying to** (laying it out for) **you folks, in** (or: on; by) **this Night-Season** (or: this particular night; or: by figure: = this darkness), **there will continue being two people upon one bed** (or: couch)**: the one will proceed being taken in hand and seized at the side** (= caught and taken prisoner; or: will be taken along) **and yet the different** (or: other) **one will be let go**
       (pardoned and left behind; = allowed to flow away in peace; or: will proceed being
          abandoned, sent away, divorced or set aside).
35. **"There will continue being two women continuing in grinding grain into meal and flour, upon the same [mill]** (or: at the same [place])**: the one will proceed being taken in hand and**

seized at the side (= caught and taken prisoner; or: will be taken along) **but the different** (or: other) **one will proceed being let go** (pardoned and left behind; = allowed to flow away in peace; or: will proceed being abandoned, sent away, divorced or set aside)."
[36. note: this verse is missing in most texts and MSS]

37. **Then, making separated and uncertain responses, one after another kept on asking, "Where, Lord?"**
So He said to them, **"Where the body [is], there in that place the eagles will also proceed being gathered together on [it]** (or: there, too, the vultures will continue assembling)."
> [comment: a picture of judgment having come; possible reference to the Roman army]

CHAPTER 18

1. **Now He went on [and] told them a parable** (an illustration cast alongside) **with a view facing the [circumstances for] them, [that] it is of necessity at all times to be constantly thinking, speaking and active with an aim toward having goodness, ease and well-being** (or: keep praying), **and not to give in to the bad or worthless [situation or conditions]** (or: to dwell within an ugly mood or a disposition of poor quality; or: to respond badly in [something]),
2. **proceeding in saying, "A certain judge was living within a certain city [who was] not in the habit of fearing or reverencing God, and also was not normally respecting** (turning himself back upon so as to concern himself for; or: shamed by) **people.**
3. **"Now there was a widow in that city, and she kept on coming** (or: going) **to him, repeatedly saying, 'Decide the case from our custom and take up my cause by avenging and vindicating me from my adversary at law** (or: plaintiff)**!'**
4. **"And yet for some time he continued unwilling and would not. But after these [repeated pleas] he said within himself, 'Although** (or: Even if) **I am not normally fearing, being wary of or reverencing God nor respecting, concerned about, or shamed by, people,**
5. **'"yet in fact, because of the [situation with] this widow constantly holding wearisome labor at the side for me** (or: continually furnishing me with trouble and vexation while affording me personal cuts; or: = keeps pestering me), **I will proceed deciding the case for her and continue avenging her** (or: giving her justice, with a favorable ruling), **so that with [her] continual coming, unto [the] end [of the matter], she may not repeatedly hit me in the face [with it]** (or: = treat me severely and wear me out with pestering; or: = give me 'a black eye').'"

6. **So the Lord said, "Listen to, and hear, what the judge of the disregard for what is right** (the injustice; the actions which were not in accord with the way pointed out; = the dishonesty) **is here saying!**
7. **"Now [think about it]! Would** (or: Should) **not God by all means make the situation right** (or: do that which will bring the fairness; produce equity and justice) **for His picked out and chosen people – those constantly crying, or calling, out to Him day and night? And thus, does He continue pushing anger far away and is He repeatedly long before rushing with passion upon them?** (or: Also, is He now continuing to delay acting and keep them waiting?; or: And so, He continues with patient endurance on them).
8. **"I am now laying it out and telling you that He will proceed in quickly making the situation right concerning them** (or: doing that which will bring their justice; forming of and from them the fairness and equity that proceeds from the right and just Way).
But more than this, in coming and going (traversing), **will the Son of the Man** (= Adam's Son; = the anticipated messianic figure), **really** (or: consequently) **continue finding trust upon the Land** (or: faith and loyalty on the earth)**?"**
> (or: Moreover, when coming and going, the Human Being will in fact progressively find faithfulness on this country and region.")

9. **Now He also spoke this illustration** (parable) **to certain folks who had reached a settled, persuaded conclusion in which they continued confidently trusting upon themselves – that they are just, fair,** (decent; upright), **while continuing in right and legal relationships in**

the path pointed out by law and custom, and [they] continue considering and treating the rest (= other folks) as amounting to nothing, while despising and disregarding [them]:

10. "Two men walked up into the Temple courts to think or speak of having goodness, ease and well-being (or: to pray). The one [was] a Pharisee (a Separated One), and the different (or: other) one, a tax collector (or: a tribute or customs contractor; tax farmer).

11. "The Pharisee, standing [apart] by himself, began affirming to have these good things, referring to himself (or: praying these things to himself): 'O God, I continue giving thanks to You that I am not even as the rest of the people (humans) – extortioners, unjust folks, adulterers – or even as this tax collector!

12. "'I habitually fast twice a week; I continually tithe (give the tenth of) everything – as much as I continue acquiring.'

13. "But the tax collector (or: tribute contractor), standing far off (= remaining at a distance, in the background), continued unwilling even to lift up his eyes to heaven (or: unto the atmosphere or sky) – and in contrast kept on beating (striking) his chest, repeatedly saying, 'O God, at your mercy seat let me, the failure (the one who has deviated and missed the goal; the sinner), be sheltered and cleansed!' [Isa. 66:2]

14. "I am now saying to you folks, this man walked down into his home being one having been rightwised (delivered, turned in the right direction and placed in right relationship within the Way pointed out), rather than that one, because everyone [who is] constantly lifting himself up (exalting himself) will be brought low and humbled. Yet the person habitually humbling himself and placing himself in a low position will be lifted up and exalted." [Mt. 18:4; 23:12]

15. Now at one point, people began bringing (or: carrying) infants (or: new-born children) to Him, also, so that He would, one after another, touch them. Yet, upon seeing [this], the disciples began respectfully giving a stern and discouraging admonition to them.

16. So Jesus called them to Him by saying, "Allow the little children to continue coming to Me, and stop hindering and preventing them. You see, of such as these is God's reign (or: the kingdom and influence of God pertains to such as these; the royal rule and sovereign activity from God is belonging to such as these).

17. "Amen (or: It is true; or: Make it so; or: Count on it). I am now saying to you folks, Whoever may not welcome and receive God's reign and kingdom as (or: like; or: in the same way as does) a little child, can in no way (or: may under no circumstances) enter into it."

18. Then a certain ruler (or: chief; or: leading person of the ruling class) put a question to Him, saying, "Good teacher, by doing what can I be an heir of, and shall I proceed receiving an allotment in, eonian life (= life in the coming Age when the Messiah reigns; or: life which has the character and qualities of the Age; or: life in the ages and for an indefinite period of time)?"

19. So Jesus said to him, "Why do you now say [of] Me, 'good'? Not even one person [is] good, except One – God!

20. "You have seen and are thus acquainted with the implanted goal (impartation of the finished product within; inward directive; the *mitzvot*):

> 'You should not commit adultery. You should not commit murder. You should not steal. You should not give false evidence or bear false witness or testimony. Be habitually valuing and showing honor to your father and mother...'" [Ex. 20:12-13; Deut. 5:16-20]

21. So he said, "I observe and maintain all these – from out of my youth, on!"

22. Now upon hearing [this], Jesus said to him, "There continues remaining yet one thing left for (or: with; to; by) you (or: There is still one thing lacking in, and about, you). At once sell everything – as many things as you presently have – and distribute [the proceeds] to the destitute folks and you will continue possessing (having and holding) treasure within the heavens (or: among the atmospheres) and then finally, come back here; keep on following Me (or: continue being a follower to Me)."

23. The man, upon hearing these things came to be engulfed in pain, sorrow, grief, misery and despair – you see, he was extremely rich.

24. Now upon seeing and perceiving him, Jesus said, "How difficultly – as with disagreeable squeamishness concerning food – are the folks who are habitually having

money (or: the results of needs-based acquisitions) **progressively going their way into** (journeying on into the midst of) **God's reign** (kingdom; royal rule; sovereign activities).
25. **"It is, in fact, easier** (more comparable to easy labor) **for a camel to enter through a bored aperture** (an eye) **of a sewing or surgeon's needle** (or: projectile point) **than for a rich person to enter into God's reign** (kingdom; royal rule; sovereign influence and activities)."
26. **So the folks hearing [that] said, "And so who is now able** (or: Then does any such person continue with power) **to be saved or rescued** (kept safe; restored to health and wholeness; returned to their original state or condition)**?"**
27. **But He said, "The things [that are] impossible** (powerless; incapable) **from humanity's side [of the issue] continuously exist being** (or: are) **possible** (empowered; capable) **from God's side."**

28. **Now Peter said, "Look, and take us into mind – we, upon letting our own [plans; lives; possessions; desires] flow away** (or: after abandoning our own things) **– we follow with You!"**
29. **So He says to them, "It is true** (or: Amen; Count on it). **I am now saying to you folks that there is no one who abandoned** (or: lets flow away) **house, or wife, or brothers, or parents, or children on account of** (or: for the sake of) **God's reign** (kingdom; royal rule; sovereign influence and activities)
30. **"who would not by all means be getting back and receiving many times more, in this season** (or: fitting situation and opportunity; fertile moment), **and then within** (or: in union with) **the Age which is progressively coming, life pertaining to that Age** (or: eonian life; life with the qualities of the Age of the Messiah; life from and of that Age; or: life of and for the ages)."

31. **Now, taking aside the twelve, He said to them, "Look, and consider this. We are progressively walking up into Jerusalem, and all the things having been written through the prophets for** (or: pertaining to; concerning) **the Son of the Man** (= the eschatological messianic figure; = Adam's Son) **will progressively be brought to their purposed goal and destiny** (or: finished; completed; accomplished; perfected; made fully functional).
32. **"You see, He will proceed being passed along and transferred to the ethnic multitudes** (or: committed, **for** the nations; delivered over, among the Gentiles; given alongside and entrusted to the non-Jewish people groups), **and then He will continue being mocked, ridiculed and made fun of and He will progressively be insolently personally invaded with outrageous, violent and injurious treatment. He will even be repeatedly spit upon!**
33. **"Later, after severely lashing [Him] with a whip, they will proceed killing Him off. Then, on** (in; during) **the third day, He will proceed standing Himself back up again and arising."**
34. **However, not even one of these things did they make flow together so as to comprehend** (or: to understand the meaning of these [words]), **and so this gush-effect, and result of the flow** (spoken word; utterance; declaration; saying) **was continuing to be something having been hidden away from them, and they were not coming to personally know or have an intimate connection with the things being presently said and laid out.**

35. **Now later, during the [situation for] Him to draw near unto Jericho, it happened [that] a certain blind man was by habit sitting beside the road** (path; way), **periodically begging** (asking for something).
36. **So upon hearing [the noise] of a crowd progressively passing through, he began inquiring to find out what this might be** (= what was happening and what it might mean).
37. **Now they explained** (or: reported) **to him that Jesus, the Nazarene, is presently passing by.**
38. **Then he at once called out loudly** (or: cried out imploringly), **"Jesus! O Son of David, mercy me** (do that which will bring mercy to me)**!"**
39. **And then those in the lead, who continued preceding the group, began respectfully but sternly giving admonition to him so that he would be silent and keep still. However, he himself kept on shouting louder than ever, "Son of David, mercy me!"**
40. **So then, being brought to a standstill, Jesus set [them] in motion by urging him to be at once led** (or: brought) **toward Him. So, at his drawing near at hand, He asked him,**

41. **"What are you wanting or intending that I should do for you?" So he said, "O Lord** (or: Master), **that I could see again."**
42. **Then Jesus said to him, "At once see again! Your trust and faith has healed and made you whole** (saved and rescued you [from that condition]) **so that you are now restored to your original condition."**
43. **And at that very moment, and with usefulness, he saw again. And so he began to follow Him, repeatedly glorifying** (expressing a good opinion of) **God, and progressively enhancing God's reputation. Then all the people – at seeing [it] – gave praise to God.**

CHAPTER 19

1. **Later, after entering, he continued passing through the midst of Jericho.**
2. **And then – look, and consider this – an adult man normally being called by the name Zacchaeus [was present]. He was chief tax** (or: tribute; customs) **collector and contractor** (or: Superintendent of tax-farmers) **[for the district], and [was] a wealthy man.**
3. **Well, he kept on trying** (seeking) **to see who this Jesus is** (or: which one is Jesus), **and yet he was unable – because of the crowd – because he was short** (small in size, or, stature).
4. **And so, running forward into the [place] ahead [of the crowd], he climbed up on a fig-mulberry** (or: sycamore fig) **tree so that he could see Him – because He was about to continue passing through that [way].**

5. **Then as He came upon the place, upon looking up, Jesus said to him, "Zacchaeus, while hurrying, climb down at once, for it is necessary for Me to stay at your house today."**
6. **And so, making haste, he climbed down and received Him as a guest, under [his roof], while continuously rejoicing.**
7. **Then, upon seeing [this], all [the crowd] began buzzing throughout with muttered complaints, one to another saying, "He goes in** (enters) **to loose-down** (= relax and lodge for the night) **beside** (= in company with) **an adult man [who is] an outcast** (a sinner; one who by way of life fails to attain the goal of a culturally accepted life)**!"**
8. **Now being brought to a standstill [by this], Zacchaeus said to the Lord, "Look here, and consider! One half of my possessions** (the things normally giving me sustenance), **O Lord** (Master), **I am habitually** (or: now, from this moment) **giving to the destitute folks. And if I extorted anything from anyone through what appeared as threat of accusation, I am habitually giving back** (or: now, from this moment, repaying) **four times as much."**
>   [comment: an echo of the Law in Ex. 22:1. This would be an appeal to the Law, and
>   thus, an affirmation that he lived by the Torah, and was not really a "sinner"]
9. **So Jesus said to him, "Today salvation** (deliverance; health and wholeness; healing and restoration to an original state of being) **is birthed in this house** (or: happened to this house; came to be for this house), **in accord with the fact that he himself is also Abraham's son**
>   (= a son having the qualities and character of Abraham; or: = he is a true Israelite; or: =
>   **he is as much a son of Abraham as I am**).
10. **"You see, the Son of the Man** (= the eschatological messianic figure; = Adam's son) **came to seek after, and then to save, deliver and restore what is existing being lost, ruined, demolished and destroyed."**

11. **Now after their hearing** (or: with their listening to) **these things, He, placing more toward [them], spoke an illustration** (a parable) **because of the [situation for] Him to be near** (close to; at hand at) **Jerusalem, as well as [for] them to continue thinking and supposing that God's reign and kingdom proceeds about to, at that very moment and with usefulness, be progressively brought up to light and caused to fully appear.**
12. **Therefore He said, "A certain man of noble birth traveled** (journeyed) **into a far off country** (a distant land) **to take possession for himself** (or: to receive to himself) **a kingdom and its reign, and then to at once return.**
13. **"Now [before leaving], upon calling ten slaves to himself, he gave to them** (or: distributed among them) **ten minas** [a silver coin = about three months' wages; the sixtieth part of

a talent] **then said to them, 'Do business** (or: Engage in trade) **while** (in the midst of which) **I continue going and proceed coming [back].'**

14. **"Now** (or: However) **his fellow citizens began hating** (or: progressively detached from; or: continued with ill-will against) **him, and so they sent off a delegation** (a body of ambassadors) **after him** [note: presumably to the one who was to make him a king], **as a group [to be] saying, 'We continue not wanting or intending this one to reign as king upon** (or: over) **us.'**

15. **"Later, after receiving the kingdom and taking** (or: obtaining) **its reign, it occurred within the [situation for] him to come back that he spoke [a directive for] these slaves – to whom he had given the silver coins – to be summoned to him so that he might personally come to know what** (or: something about; what kind of) **business or trading they had fully arranged and conducted.**

16. **"So the first one happened along, saying, 'Master** (or: Sir), **your mina worked itself and earned ten more minas!'**

17. **"Then he said to him, 'Well done, [you are] an excellent slave! Because in a least thing** (within a small matter or situation) **you came to be loyal, faithful and trustworthy, be constantly holding** (or: having; possessing) **top authority over ten towns** (or: cities).'**

18. **"Next came the second one, saying, 'Your mina, sir** (master), **made five minas.'**

19. **"So he said to this one, also, 'And you, yourself, progressively come to be on top of five towns** (or: cities).'**

20. **"And then the different one came, saying, 'Sir** (or: Master), **look! [Here is] your mina which I continued having lying away reserved** (or: stored) **within a handkerchief** (or: piece of cloth; or: a rag).

21. **"'You see, I was constantly fearing and wary of you, because you are a harsh person** (or: an austere, severe, demanding man). **You habitually take or pick up what you did not deposit, and you are repeatedly reaping what you did not sow.'**

22. **"He is then saying to** (or: laying it out for) **him, 'From out of your own mouth I am now deciding about you, you worthless** (good-for-nothing, misery-gushed, malignant) **slave! You had seen so as to know, did you, that I, myself, am a harsh person – constantly withdrawing what I did not deposit and repeatedly reaping what I did not sow** (or: plant)**?**

23. **"'And so why** (through what reason or circumstance) **did you not give my silver coin upon a table** (= with the money changers, or, at a bank), **and I, upon coming, could make a transaction with it – together with what it produced** (offspring; = interest)**?'**

24. **"And so, he said to those standing by, 'Take the mina away from him and give [it] to the one now having the ten minas.'**

25. **"'But master,' they interposed to him, 'he [already] now has ten minas!'**

26. **"'I continue saying to you people, that to everyone presently and habitually possessing** (having and holding), **[more] will be given; yet from the one not presently or habitually possessing** (having or holding), **that which he continues holding [onto] will be lifted up and taken away.**

27. **"'What is more, You folks bring here these enemies of mine** (these folks [that are] hostile with regard to me) **– the ones not wanting me to reign as king over** (or: upon) **them – and at once slaughter them in front of me by slashing their throats!'..."**

28. **And then, after saying these things, He began to make His way** (journeying on), **ahead [of the crowd] and in front [of them], progressively walking up into Jerusalem.**

29. **Then it came to pass, as He neared Bethphage and Bethany – at** (or: facing toward) **the mountain being normally called Olivet** (or: the Mount of Olives) **– [that] He sent off two of the disciples on a mission, saying,**

30. **"Be now going, under [these directions], down into the village facing [us] within which, after entering, you will find a colt tied [there] – one upon which not even one person at any time sat down. And then, after loosing [it], lead it [here].**

31. **"And if anyone may be asking you, 'Why** (For what [purpose]) **are you now loosing [it]?' you will respond in this way, 'The Lord** (or: Master; = Yahweh?) **is now having need of it.'"**

32. **So, after leaving, those who were sent off found [it] just as He told them.**

33. **Now upon their having loosed the colt, its owners said to them, "Why are you now loosing the colt?"**
34. **So they said, "The Lord** (or: Master; = Yahweh?) **is now having need of it."**
35. **Then they led it to Jesus, and after throwing their cloaks** (or: outer garments) **upon the colt, they mounted Jesus on [it].** [cf Mat. 21:2-7]
36. **Now then, during His traveling** (journeying) **along, folks began strewing, scattering and spreading out their cloaks and outer garments on the path, under [Him].** [cf Mt. 21:7-9]

37. **But at His already progressively drawing near to the road descending the slope from the Mount of Olives, the entire multitude of the disciples started continuously rejoicing – to be repeatedly praising God, in a great** (or: loud) **voice, concerning all of the powers and abilities** (= works and deeds of power) **which they had seen and perceived,**
38. **repeatedly and one after another saying, "Having been spoken well of and blessed [is] the One presently and progressively coming** (or: going) **centered in, and in union with, the Name of [the] Lord** [= in Yahweh's authority]: **the King!** [Ps. 118:26] **Peace and shalom from the Joining within the midst of heaven** (or: A joining in [the] atmosphere), **and a manifestation which calls forth praise** (glory; a good reputation; an assumed appearance) **in union with the highest places, and in [the authority of the] highest Ones!"** [cf Ps. 118:19-28; Mk. 11:7-10]

39. **Then some of the Pharisees from the crowd said to Him, "Teacher, at once give [your] valued advice to your disciples [to restrain and silence them]!"**
40. **And yet, giving discerning and decided response, He said, "I am now saying to you folks, If these people will proceed to be silent and continue keeping quiet, the stones will proceed crying out, screaming and continue in exclaiming** (or: breaking into cheers)**!"**

41. **And then, as He came near at hand, upon seeing** (or: viewing and perceiving) **the City He wept** (or: wailed; or: lamented; or: cried, shedding tears as an expression of grief) **upon it** (= over its condition and situation),
42. **then saying, "If you, even you yourself, knew by intimate experience or had discerned in this day the things [leading, moving or tending] toward peace** (or: a joining; or: = shalom; [other MSS: your peace])**! – but at this time it is** (or: has been) **hidden from your eyes –**
43. **"that days will proceed arriving upon you, and your enemies will be progressively setting up an encampment beside you and will continue casting up a mound beside [you and] a staked fortification** (or: rampart) **on** (or: next to) **you, and next will proceed to encircle and surround you, then continue bringing and enclosing pressure on you from every side!**
44. **"Later, they will proceed in dashing you to the ground and razing you, as well as your children within the midst of you – then they will continue not leaving stone upon stone** (or: a stone on a stone) **within you – in return for what things? Because you do not know the season** (or: had no intimate or personal awareness so as to recognize the occasion; have no insights about the fertile moment) **of your visitation and inspection."**

45. **And next, after entering into the Temple courts and grounds, He started to progressively throw out** (or: chase and drive out; expel) **the folks engaged in selling in it – as well as those presently buying,**
    [comment: these actions were prophetic of the soon-coming overthrow by the Romans]
46. **while saying to them, "It has been written and presently stands on record, 'And My House will continue being a house of prayer,'** [Isa. 56:7] **yet you people make it a 'cave of robbers** (or: a den for highwaymen).**'"** [Jer. 7:11; comment: this is the reason for the prophecy of vss. 43-44]

47. **Later, He was repeatedly teaching, daily, within the midst of the Temple courts and grounds. But the chief** (or: ranking) **priests and the scribes** (scholars; Torah experts; theologians) **– along with the foremost folks** (or: leaders; ruling class) **of the people – kept on trying to find [a way] to destroy Him,**
48. **and yet they were not finding the [solution for] what they could do, for you see, all the people kept hanging on His [words]** (or: were suspended, from Him), **continuously listening.**

CHAPTER 20

1. **On one of the days during His continuing in teaching the people within the Temple courts** (or: grounds), **as well as declaring the good news of ease and well-being, it then happened [that] the chief** (or: leading; ranking) **priests and the theologians** (scribes; Torah-teachers; scholars) – **together with the elders – suddenly took a stand upon the scene.**
2. **Then they spoke up to Him, one after another saying, "Tell us at once in what sort of authority** (or: existing right) **you keep on doing these things,** (or: making these [statements]; producing these [actions?]), **or who is the person giving to you this right or privilege?"**
3. **So making a discerning reply, He said to them, "I, too, will myself proceed asking** (or: interrogating) **you men a** [other MSS: one] **question, and you tell Me** (and then you folks reply to Me):
4. **"The immersion conducted by John** (or: John's baptism) – **was it from heaven** (or: of [the] atmosphere), **or of human source?"**
5. **So then they reasoned together to each other, and drew conclusions, saying, "If we should say** (reply), **'From heaven,' he will continue saying, 'Why did you not trust and believe in him?'**
6. **"Yet if we should say** (or: reply), **'From humans,' all the people will proceed in hurling stones down on us, for they have been persuaded and remain confident that John is to be permanently [held as and reckoned] a prophet."**
7. **And so they gave the decided answer not to have seen and thus not to know from where** (= its source).
8. **Then Jesus replied to them, "As for me, neither am I laying it out and saying to you folks in what sort of authority** (in union with what privilege and right from out of Being) **I continue doing these things."**

9. **Now after that, He began to tell this illustration** (parable) **to the people:**
"A person planted a vineyard and then let it out to tenant-farmers (or: leased it to vine-dressers). **Next he left home on a journey** (or: travels abroad) **for an extended period** (a considerable time that is sufficient [for the vineyard to produce fruit]). [cf Isa. 5:1-6; Mk. 12:1-12]
10. **"And then, in the appropriate season, he sent off a slave to the tenant-farmers** (vine-dressers) **with the purpose that they will proceed giving to him [his portion] from the fruit** (or: crop) **of the vineyard. But the tenants** (vineyard workers; cultivators), **after whipping** (lashing) **and beating [him] to the point or removing skin, sent him forth** (or: out) **and away empty-handed.**
11. **"So next, he put forth a different slave to send. Yet that one also, after lashing and beating [him] – as well as dishonoring [him] – they sent forth and away empty-handed.**
12. **"Then he put forth a third one to send – but, after wounding, injuring and traumatizing this one, they threw [him] out.**
13. **"So the owner** (lord) **of the vineyard said, 'What shall I do?... I will proceed sending my son, the beloved one** (may signify: the only one). **All things being equal, chances are they will proceed being turned within so as to be showing respect to this one.'**

14. **"Now upon seeing him, the tenant-farmers** (vineyard cultivators) **began reasoning and deliberating with one another, one after another saying, 'This one is the heir! We should** (or: Let us) **at once kill him off, so that the inheritance can** (or: may) **come to be ours!'**
15. **"And so, after throwing him outside the vineyard, they killed [him]. What, therefore, will the owner** (lord) **of the vineyard proceed doing to them?...**
16. **"He will proceed in coming and will be progressively destroying these tenant-farmers, and then he will be progressively giving the vineyard to other folks."** [Isa. 5:5-6; Mat. 21:43] **Now upon hearing [this], they said, "May it not happen** (or: come to that)!"
17. **But He, looking intently at them** (or: staring in their [faces]), **said, "What, then, is the [meaning of] this having been written,**
     'A Stone which the builders rejected – after examining it – has come to be [placed] into [the] Head (= source) **of [the] corner** (or: ended up as the keystone)'?** [Ps. 118:22]

18. **"Every person at some point falling upon that Stone will continue jointly-bruised** (or: be progressively shattered-together, or dashed into pieces); **yet upon whom It may** (or: should) **fall, It will continue winnowing him [like grain]."** [Isa. 8:14-15: Mat. 21:42-44]

19. **At this, the scribes** (scholars and theologians) **and the chief priests sought** (tried to find [some way]) **to throw [their] hands on Him in that very hour, and yet they feared the people. You see, they realized that He spoke this illustration** (parable) **[with an aim] toward them.**

20. **Then, while watching [Him] closely from the side, they dispatched men [who were to be] let down within the midst [of His teaching] as spies and eavesdroppers, manifesting their own opinions and interpreting themselves to be in accord with the way pointed out** (or: critically judging themselves to be honest and upright), **with the purpose that could lay hold upon** (or: catch) **and seize His word** (or: message), **so as to hand Him over** (or: deliver and commit Him) **to the rule** (or: domain) **and authority** (or: privilege) **of the governor.**

21. **And so they questioned Him, saying, "Teacher, we have seen and so know that you habitually speak and are repeatedly teaching correctly** (or: straightly), **and you consistently do not receive folks or show partiality based on peoples' faces or appearances, but to the contrary you continuously teach the Way of God** (or: God's path) **based on truth and reality.**

22. **"[Therefore tell us:] is it allowed, from [our present] existence, for us to give** (= pay) **[the] annual land tax to Caesar** (i.e., the Roman Emperor), **or not?"**

23. **Now mentally pinning down their capabilities and contemplating what they were up to, He said to them,**

24. **"Why are you now testing Me? Show Me a denarius."**
So they showed [one] to Him, and He said, "Whose image and inscription does it have?"
So they replied, "Caesar's."

25. **And so He said to them, "Well then, give back Caesar's things** (or: the things from Caesar) **to and for Caesar – and God's things** (or: the things from God) **to and for God."**

26. **But they had no strength to get a grasp on [so as to comprehend] or to take a firm hold upon [so as to control or make use of] that which He spoke** (or: the effect of the flow of His spoken words) **in front of the people – and so they remained silent** (kept still), **while wondering in amazement, and marveling on His discerning response.**

27. **Now later, some of the Sadducees – folks normally saying there is to be no resurrection – upon approaching**   [cf Acts 23:8; 1 Cor. 15:40-54]

28. **posed a question to Him, presently saying, "Teacher, Moses wrote to** (or: for) **us, 'If anyone's brother should die off, and having a wife, this man may be childless, that his brother should take the wife** (i.e., the widow) **and should be raising up out of [her] a seed** (= offspring; progeny) **to and for his brother** (i.e., to preserve the man's family line).' [Deut. 25:5]

29. **"Now then, there were seven brothers; and the first, upon taking a wife, died childless.**

30. **"And so the second got the wife, and this one also died childless.**

31. **"Then the third took her. Now, similarly also, the seven men did not leave children behind, and also died off.**

32. **"Lastly, the woman also died off.**

33. **"Therefore, in the resurrection, of which of them does the woman become a wife – for you see, the seven men had her [as] a wife?"**

34. **So Jesus said to them, "The sons of this age** (= those now living and having the qualities and characteristics of this present time and arrangement) **are normally marrying and being given in marriage.**

35. **"Yet those folks being considered worthy** (of complete equal value) **of that Age – even to hit the target of the resurrection, the one out from among [the] dead folks – are neither normally marrying nor are being habitually given in marriage,**

36. **"for you see, neither are they any longer able to die off, for they exist being** (or: are) **the equivalence of agents** (or: identical to and the same thing as messengers) **and they are God's sons** (= the offsprings of God) **– being sons of the resurrection** (= the offsprings of, and from, the resurrection; or: = those having the qualities and characteristic of the resurrection).

37. **"Yet that the dead people are habitually** (or: repeatedly; or: continuously) **being raised up, even Moses divulged** (or: discloses) **at the thornbush, as he continues terming** (or: speaking of) **[the] Lord** [= Yahweh] **'the God of Abraham and the God of Isaac, and the God of Jacob.'** [Ex. 3:6]
38. **"Yet He is not a God of dead folks, but to the contrary, of continuously living ones – for you see** (or: for it follows that), **in Him** (and: with Him; and: by Him; and: to Him) **all people are continuously living."** [cf Jn. 11:25]

39. **Now, giving an approving response, some of the scribes** (scholars and theologians; Torah experts) **said, "Well said, Teacher** (or: [Rabbi], you answered beautifully and ideally)."
40. **You see, they were no longer daring, or having courage, to continue asking Him a single question** (or: anything).
41. **In turn, He said to** (or: laid it out, facing toward [and confronting]) **them, "How are they normally saying [that] the Christ** (the Anointed One; = the expected Messiah) **is to be David's son** (= a descendant of David)**?**
42. **"For David himself says in the scroll of Psalms,**
    '[The] Lord [= Yahweh] **said to my Lord, "Continue sitting, from My right** (= Be constantly ruling from out of My high positions of power and places of honor)
43.   **Until I should be placing** (setting) **those hostile to You [as] a footstool of Your feet.'** [Ps. 110:1; cf 1 Chron. 28:2; Ps. 132:7; Acts 7:49; Heb. 1:13; 10:13]
44. **"Therefore, David is habitually calling Him 'Lord** (Master; Owner),**' and so how is He his Son?"**
45. **Now, while all the people continued listening** (or: in the hearing of all the people), **He said to the disciples,**
46. **"Be habitually holding your focus and attention away from the scholars and theologians** (the scribes; the Torah, or, Bible experts) **– those continuously wanting to be habitually walking around in religious and stately robes and being fond of deferential greetings in the marketplaces** (i.e., in public, where folks often gather), **and [liking] prominent** (or: front) **seating in the synagogues** (places of corporate worship and study of the Scriptures), **as well as first places of reclining** (or: prominent or best couches; = the places of honor) **at banquets –**
47. **"folks who [in reality] are habitually devouring the houses** (or: eating down the households) **of the widows, and then in pretense** (or: for a front which is put to make a show or an appearance for pretext) **they are constantly making long prayers. These people will continue and progressively be receiving more excessive result of judgment** (or: will get a more abundant effect of the separating and the decision)."

CHAPTER 21

1. **Now later, upon looking up, He saw the rich people, one after another, tossing their gifts into the treasury** (a guarded collection box for offerings).
2. **But in contrast, He saw a certain needy** (impoverished), **working-class widow in the midst of dropping two mites** (small copper coins of very little value) **there,**
3. **and He said, "Really** (or: Truly), **I am saying to you folks that this destitute widow cast [in] more than all of them.**
4. **"For you see, all these folks tossed the gifts into [the treasury] from out of their surplus and the excess of wealth that continually surrounds [them], but this woman, from out of her [situation] of lack and want, dropped [in] all her livelihood** (= all she had to live on) **which she was normally** (or: presently) **having."**

5. **Later, while certain folks were in the midst of remarking about the Temple complex – how that it had been arranged and stands adorned with fine, beautiful stones and stonework, as well as the effects of things set up** (possibly: dedicated objects; votive offerings; memorial decorations) **–**

6. He said, "These things at which you folks continue gazing with attentive interest – days will progress in coming in which a stone will not continue being left here upon a stone, which will not be progressively loosed down in complete destruction."

7. So folks continued asking Him, "Teacher, when therefore will these things progress in being – and what [will be] the sign, whenever these things should progressively be about to continue happening?"

8. Now He replied, "Continue looking. You should not at any point be deceived or led astray. You see, many people will continue coming – on the [basis of] My name (i.e., claiming to be My representative and have My authority) – one after another saying, 'I am (or: I, myself, am [he; the one])!' and 'The appointed season (or: fitting situation) has drawn near and is now present!' You folks should not at any point go from place to place behind them.

9. "So when you happen to hear of wars and unsettled conditions (instability; unrest; turmoil; insurrections), you people should not be terrified or caused to panic with alarm. You see, it continues necessary, even binding, for these things to happen (occur; come to be) first, but still the end (or: the final act; the finished condition) [is] not immediately."

10. At that time He went on to say to them, "Nation (or: Ethnic group) will be progressively raised up upon nation (or: ethnic group), and kingdom (or: empire) upon kingdom (empire).
    (or: = A swarm will be progressively roused upon [the] nation [= the Jewish nation]; even [the] Empire upon [the Jews'] kingdom.)

11. "Also, there will continue being major earthquakes (or: great shakings), and in one place after another, there will proceed being pestilences (or: epidemics; plagues) and famines (= food shortages), besides fearful sights and dreadful events, as well as there being great signs from [the] sky (or: atmosphere; heaven). [cf Ex. 7-11; Rev. 15-16]

12. "Yet before all these things, people will continue laying their hands on YOU folks, and they will be repeatedly chasing and persecuting [you], handing over one after another unto the synagogues (places of worship and fellowship) and [into] jails and prisons, while you are repeatedly being led off, up before kings and governors – on account of My Name.

13. "Yet it will continue going away for (or: stepping off among) YOU folks, [leading] into a witness and a testimony (= an opportunity for giving your evidence).

14. "Therefore, YOU people put [it] in YOUR hearts not to be habitually premeditating or rehearsing beforehand to make [your] defenses.

15. "You see, I Myself will continue giving to YOU people a mouth (= ability and an opportunity to speak) as well as wisdom, to which all YOUR opponents, who are repeatedly lying in ambush against YOU, will not continue being able to at any point stand in opposition to or resist, nor to speak against or contradict.

16. "Now YOU people will even proceed in being turned in (or: handed over) by parents and brothers and relatives and friends – and folks will keep on putting some of YOU to death.

17. "Furthermore, YOU folks will continue being ones being constantly regarded and treated with ill will, radically detached and even hated, by all – because of My Name (= because of your association with Me, or, because you bear and proclaim My Name).

18. "And yet, not a hair from out of YOUR head can by any means be lost (or: should by no means be loosed-away or destroyed).

19. "Within the midst of your persistent, supportive remaining-under (or: In union with your patient endurance), be progressively gaining possession of YOUR souls (or: continue acquiring your inner life and consciousness; make it a habit to procure and possess yourself; [with other MSS: you folks will repeatedly gain and progressively acquire your conscious lives/selves]).

20. "Now later, when YOU folks see Jerusalem being continuously surrounded by encamped armies, at that time realize and know from that experience that her desolation has drawn near and is now present.

21. "At that point, let the people in Judea progressively flee into the hill country and mountains; then let the people within the midst of her [i.e., Jerusalem] proceed departing out of that place, and don't let (or: let not) the folks in the country or the district continue coming (or: going) into her,

22. **"because these are days of executing justice** (or: from deciding the case, with a view to the maintenance of right: whether vindication or retribution) **– of bringing about what is fair and right and of establishing what accords with the Way pointed out – with a view to have fulfilled ALL the things having been written** (or: for ALL that is written to be fulfilled)!

23. **"Tragic will be the situation for the women then being pregnant, and for the ones still nursing [babies] in those days. You see there will progressively be a great compressive force upon the Land, and inherent fervor bringing internal swelling emotion on THIS People.**

24. **"And so, THEY will keep on falling by [the] mouth of a sword, and [others] will proceed being led captive into all the nations** (or: into the midst to unite with every ethnic group) **– and Jerusalem will continue being progressively trampled by and under pagans** (non-Jews; those of the nations) **– until where they can be made full** (or: should be filled [up]; or: would be fulfilled). **And then there will progress being seasons of ethnic multitudes** (or: fitting situations pertaining to nations; or: occasions which have the qualities and characteristics of pagans; or: **fertile moments from**, and with regard to, **non-Jews**). [*cf* Rev. 11]

> [D omits: seasons of nations; with other MSS: … and then Jerusalem will continue existing being repeatedly trampled by nations up to the point where seasons of (or: appointed times from) nations can at some point be fulfilled or filled full]

25. **"Also, there will keep on being signs: in sun and moon and stars** [comment: a figure of a disruption of father, mother and brothers, i.e., social organization and leadership – Gen. 37:9-10], **and upon the Land** [comment: of Israel?] (or: earth; ground; soil): **a constraint from [the] non-Jews** (or: with a character of pagans; which is nations) **in the midst of a perplexity in which there seems no way out – [like being in the] roar and surging of a sea –**

26. **"pertaining to humans progressively breathing away and cooling off** (= fainting, or dying) **from fear and apprehension** (thoughts about what is going to happen) **pertaining to the things progressively coming upon the homeland** (the place being inhabited) **– for you see,**

> **'the abilities of the heavens** (or: the powers of the sky and atmosphere; [note: may = folks normally in charge of things]) **will be progressively shaken.'** [Hag. 2:6, 21]

27. **"And at that point** (or: time), **THEY will keep on seeing** (or: perceiving) **'the Son of the Man** (= Adam's son; the Human Being; = the eschatological messianic figure) **progressively coming within the midst of a cloud,'** [Dan. 7:13-14] **with power and much glory** (or: with ability and repute; or: along with power and a praise-inducing assumed-appearance).

28. **"Now as these things are beginning to be progressively happening, at once bend back up** (or: stand tall and erect), **and then lift up YOUR heads** (= hold YOUR heads high), **because YOUR setting-free** (the loosing-away and release of YOU folks from prison; YOUR redemption and liberation from slavery) **is presently at hand** (continues close enough to touch)!"

29. **And then** (or: Later; With that,) **He spoke an illustration to them** (or: told them a parable): **"Look at and perceive the fig tree – as well as all the trees.**

30. **"Whenever they may be already budding** (or: shooting forth sprouts), **in consistently seeing** (or: observing) **[this] for yourselves, you normally know from experience that the summer is already near** (at hand; close enough to touch).

31. **"In this same way, then** (or: also), **YOU yourselves: whenever YOU folks may see** (or: perceive) **these things progressively coming to be** (occurring; happening; being birthed), **be progressively knowing** (realizing) **from experience that God's reigning and activity of sovereignty** (or: the kingdom and royal rule of God) **is** (or: exist being) **close at hand – near enough to touch** (= has arrived and is accessible)! **It is true** (or: Amen; Count on it).

32. **"I now proceed telling YOU that THIS very generation can under no circumstances pass on by** (or: may by no means pass along) **until ALL these things can happen** (or: should occur).

33. **"The sky and the land** (or: This heaven and earth) **will be progressively passing on by, yet My words** (or: but the thoughts, ideas, messages and laid-out transfers of pattern-forming information from Me) **will under no circumstances proceed to be passing on by.**

34. **"So YOU people make it a habit to hold your attention to yourselves, and hold to each other, lest at some time YOUR hearts may be weighed down or burdened – in the midst of a hangover** (or: headache nausea or giddiness from an overindulgence in wine), **and in**

drunkenness (intoxication) – **as well as by anxiety** (or: care; concern; worry) **in the daily matters pertaining to living, and then THAT day take its stand upon YOU folks unforeseen** (with unexpected suddenness), **as a trap** (a snare; a net; something that will catch and hold).
35. **"You see, it will continue coming in upon** (or: enter on) **all the people normally sitting** (= presently dwelling) **upon [the] face** (= surface) **of the entire Land** (territory; or: all of the earth).
36. **"So YOU people be constantly staying awake, alert and watchful – in each season and every situation** (or: in union with every fertile moment and on every occasion) **– repeatedly asking with urgency, or begging, so that YOU can be fully strong to flee out and escape all these things being presently and progressively about to be happening, and then to be placed** (or: cause to stand) **in front of the Son of the Man** (the Human Being; = Adam's Son; = the eschatological messianic figure)."

37. **Now He was [during] the days repeatedly teaching within the Temple courts and grounds, yet [during] the nights, after going out into the mountain, He was making it a habit to spend the night** (camp out) **[in the midst of] the Mount of Olives.**
38. **And so, all the people kept on eagerly arising early in the morning, face-to-face with Him within the Temple courts** (or: grounds), **to continue listening to, and hearing, Him.**

CHAPTER 22

1. **Now the [seven-day] Feast of the Unleavened [Bread]** (or: festival of Matzahs) **– the one being normally termed Passover – had been progressively drawing near** (coming to be at hand). [note: commemoration of Israel's deliverance from slavery in Egypt; cf Ex. 12]
2. **And still, the chief** (head; ranking) **priests and the scribes** (scholars; theologians) **kept on trying to find how they could take Him up** (= assassinate Him) **– you see they were still fearing the people.**
3. **Now an adversary** (or: an opposing spirit, purpose or attitude; [cf Mat. 16:23]) **entered into Judah** (or: Judas) **– the man normally being called Iscariot, being [part] of the number of the twelve.** [Cf vs. 31, below]
4. **And so, after going off** (or: away), **he conferred** (or: confers) **with the chief** (or: head) **priest and military officers about how he could transfer and commit Him** (or: turn Him over) **to them.**
5. **Then they rejoiced and placed themselves together in agreement to give him silver coins.**
6. **And out of this same word** (or: discussion) **he consented, so then he began trying to find a good situation** (or: opportunity) **– without a crowd [around] – to transfer Him to them.**

7. **Now [during the period] of the Unleavened [loaves; cakes; matzahs], the Day came in which it was periodically necessary for the Passover to be slaughtered in sacrifice.**
8. **And so He sent off Peter and John on an errand, after saying, "After going your way, at once prepare and make ready the Passover for us, so that we can eat [it]."**
9. **So they asked Him, "Where are you presently intending [that] we should make [the] preparations?"**
10. **So then He replied to them, "Take note of this: after your entering into the city, a man carrying an earthenware container** (or: fired clay jar or ceramic pitcher) **of water will meet with you. At once follow him into the house into which he is proceeding to enter.**
11. **"Then you will proceed saying to the proprietor** (landlord; facility-master) **of the house, 'The Teacher** (= Rabbi) **is now saying to you, "Where is the guest room** (caravansary; dining room; khan-room) **where I can eat the Passover with My disciples?"'**
12. **"Then that man will show you a large upper room furnished with [couches] spread out** (= arranged). **Get things ready and make preparations there."**
13. **So after going away, they found [it] just as He had declared to them, and they prepared and made ready the Passover.**

14. **Later, when the hour occurred, He leaned back [at table, there] – as well as the twelve emissaries** (commissioned representatives), **together with Him.**

15. **Then He said to them, "With full passion and emotions I yearn and strongly desire** [note: the verb is repeated: a Hebrew idiom] **to eat this Passover with you folks – before the [occasion for] Me to experience suffering** (or: before My [time] to experience [what lies ahead]).

16. **"You see, I am now telling you folks that I can** (or: may; would) **under no circumstances be eating it** [other MSS: of or from it] **[again] until [the time] when it can** (or: until [the circumstances] in which it may or would) **be fulfilled in union with God's reign** (or: within the midst of the kingship from God; in the sovereign influence and activity which is God)."

17. **Then, after receiving and accepting a cup [and] speaking a word of the goodness of favor and grace** (or: upon taking in hand a cup [of wine], then giving thanks), **He said, "Take and receive this, and then distribute [it] into the midst of** (= among) **yourselves.**

18. **"You see, I am now saying to you [twelve] that, from now on, under no circumstances can I drink from the product** (the result of what is born; the offspring; the yield) **of and from the grapevine until which [time or occasion that] the kingdom of God would pass on [to others]** {Mat. 21:43} (or: God's reign comes [to you]; or: the sovereign influence from, and activity which is, God can set out and journey on)." [note: the verb ερχομαι has this semantic range]

19. **And then, taking in hand a loaf of bread – [and again] speaking a word of favor and grace** (or: giving thanks) **– He broke [it] in pieces and gave [it] to them, while saying, "This [bread] is** (or: = represents) **My body** (or: the body which is Me) **– the one presently and continuously being given over you folks** (or: that which is customarily given on your behalf and over your [situation]). **You folks are normally doing this unto My memorial** (or, reading as an imperative: Habitually do this with a view to My commemoration)."

20. **Also, the cup, as thusly with** (or: similarly after) **the [occasion] to eat the dinner, [He is] continuing in saying, "This, The Cup – [being; representing] the new arrangement** (or: the covenant which is new in character and quality) **in union with, centered in, and within the midst of, My blood** (or: the blood which is Me) **– [is] the one presently and continuously being poured out over you folks** (or: that which is customarily being poured out on your behalf).

21. **"Moreover, look and consider – the hand of the person in the process of transferring Me** (or: committing Me; giving Me over) **[is now] with Me upon the table** (= is present with us),

22. **"because indeed, the Son of the Man** (the Human Being; = Adam's Son) **is progressively going His way** (journeying) **– corresponding to and in accord with that which has been determined by marking off the boundaries. However, tragic will be the fate for that person through whom He is being passed along** (or: committed; transferred; given over)."

23. **And so they themselves began to seek, each one in face to face discussion among themselves, who really it could be from their [group] that is progressively about to be committing this thing.**

24. **Now this also birthed a readiness to quarrel resulting in a dispute** (or: a fondness for contention with a love for victory which spawned "mimetic rivalry" [– Walter Wink]) **among them about who of them is now seeming to be greater [than the rest]** (or: who is normally presuming to be the most important).

25. **So He said to them, "The kings of the nations and ethnic multitudes are habitually acting as their lords and owners, and those exercising authority** (rights, from out of being) **over** (or: among) **them are normally being called** (or: terming themselves) **'Benefactors.'**

26. **"Yet you men [are] not [to be] thus** (or: [are] not [to behave] in this way), **but to the contrary, let the greater among you come to be like** (or: as) **the younger; and the one normally leading like** (or: as) **the person normally giving attending service and dispensing.**

27. **"For who [is] greater? – the one normally reclining [at a meal], or the person that habitually serves [the meal]? [Is it] not the one normally reclining [at the meal]? Yet I Myself am in your midst as the person constantly giving attending service: dispensing.**

28. **"Now you yourselves are the men having remained throughout with Me, within and in union with My tests and trials,**

29. **"and so I, Myself, am now making an arrangement for you** (or: am progressively making a covenant with, to and in you folks), **just and correspondingly as My Father made the arrangement for a reign for Me** (or: made the covenant of a kingdom with, and in, Me) –

30. **to the end that you folks can continuously eat and drink at My table, in union with My reign and in the midst of My kingdom and sovereign activities, and now you can habitually sit** (or: be seated) **upon thrones** (or: chairs; seats), **repeatedly making separations in, evaluations of and decisions for the twelve tribes** (or: clans) **of Israel.**

[note: the twelve tribes had been scattered; the last clauses uses the present tenses]

31. **"Simon, O Simon! Look, and consider. The adversary** (or: opponent; *satan*; = Jewish leaders?) **makes** (or: made) **a request** [to God; *cf* Job 1:9-11; 2:4-5] **concerning you men: to winnow [you folks] as grain!**

32. **"But I Myself urgently asked [God] concerning you, [Simon], to the end that your trust, allegiance and faithfulness would not leave from out of [you]** (or: default; = give out). **And so at some point, you yourself, upon turning around, make your brothers immovable** (or: stabilize and establish your fellow members [of God's Family])."

33. **So then he said to Him, "Lord** (Master), **I am ready and prepared to proceed going** (journeying) **on with You, both into jail** (or: prison) **and even into death."**

34. **Yet He said, "I am now saying to you, Peter, a rooster** (cock) **will not proceed crowing today, until you will three times proceed in fully denying to have seen or known Me."**

35. **Next he said to them, "When I sent you men away on a mission – not having a purse or pack** (or: food pouch or beggar's sack) **or sandals – you did not lack anything, did you?" So they answered, "Nothing!"**

36. **So then He rejoined to them, "But in contrast now, the one normally having a purse – let him take [it] up; likewise also a food pouch** (or: pack; beggar's sack). **And the person not now having a sword – let him at once sell his cloak** (or: outer garment) **and buy [one].**

[comment: the situation has now changed and different conditions were imminent]

37. **"You see, I continue telling** (laying it out to) **you folks that it continues necessary and binding for the thing having been written to be brought to its goal and finished** (or: completed and accomplished) **in Me,**

> **'And He was logically counted** (or: classed; considered; reckoned) **with the lawless folks** (or: criminals),' [Isa. 53:12]

For also, that which concerns (or: = what [is written] about) **Me is presently having an end** (or: continues possessing a [or: the] final act; progressively holds a destiny)."

38. **So they said, "Look, Lord, here [are] two swords!" And so He replied to them, "It is enough** (or: That is sufficient)."

39. **Later, upon going out, corresponding to [His] custom** (or: as usual), **He went His way** (journeyed out) **into the Mount of Olives – now the disciples also followed with Him.**

40. **So, on coming to be at that place, He said to them, "Be habitually praying** (or: Be repeatedly expressing a wish with a view toward goodness and for having it well, so as) **not to enter into an attempt to bring you into a test which will put you to the proof or will try you."**

41. **Then He was dragged** (or: pulled) **away from them about [the distance] of a stone's throw, and kneeling, He began speaking toward having ease and well-being** (or: praying),

42. **saying, "O Father, if You continue purposing** (willing; intending) **[it], at once bear along** (or: carry aside) **this, the Cup, away from Me. However** (Yet more than that), **not My will or desire, but to the contrary, let Yours continue of itself progressing into being** (or: let Yours keep on happening to itself, and from itself come to be, then progressively take place for itself)!"

[note: vss. 43 & 44 are omitted in *p*75, Aleph1, A, B, N, T, W, 579, 1071*, and others, as well as writings by Marcion, Clement, Origen, Athanasius, Ambrose, Cyril John-Damascus, a Georgian MS, and others; Aleph*, D, L, later MSS, various church Fathers, and others include them; Griesbach and Nestle-Aland bracket them; UBS footnotes them in the apparatus]

43. **Now an agent from the atmosphere** (or: a messenger from heaven) **was seen by Him, continuously strengthening Him.**

44. **Then, coming to be within the midst of great inner tension and conflict** (or: agony and anxiety), **He continued praying more intensely and more stretched out, and so His sweat came to be as it were large drops and clots of blood, steadily dropping down upon the ground.**

45. **Later on, rising from the expression of having ease and goodness** (or: the prayer) **and going toward the disciples, He found them continuing outstretched in slumber, from the distress** (or: pain of sorrow).

46. **And so He said to them, "Why do you folks continue sleeping? Upon standing up** (or: rising), **carry on thinking of having ease and well-being** (or: praying), **so that YOU folks would not enter into a test or a trial."**

47. **Amidst His still speaking, look, a crowd! – and the man being normally called Judah** (or: Judas), **one of the twelve, was progressively coming before them. And then he drew near at hand to Jesus to kiss Him.**

48. **So Jesus said to him, "Judah** (or: Judas), **are you now in the process of committing** (or: transferring; giving over) **the Son of the Man** (= the expected Messiah) **with** (by; in) **a kiss?"**

49. **But upon seeing the [situation] that was going to exist** (or: perceiving what was going to happen), **the men around Him said, "Lord** (or: Master), **shall we strike with** (i.e., in [the use of]) **a sword?"**

50. **And then a certain one of them struck the slave of the chief priest, and took** (slashed) **off** (amputated) **his right ear.**

51. **Yet Jesus, making a decided response, said, "You folks continue allowing [them] – even as far as this** (or: Leave off from [doing] as much as this)!" **And then, handling the ear so as to modify and kindle [it], He healed him.**

52. **So then Jesus said to the folks arriving upon Him and at His side – chief** (or: ranking) **priests and officers of the Temple** [D reads: of the people], **as well as elders, "Do you come out with swords and clubs and staffs, as upon a robber** (bandit)**?**

53. **"During My being with you folks daily, within the Temple courts** (or: grounds), **you did not stretch out [your] hands upon Me. But now, this is your hour, and the privilege of** (from being) **the Darkness** (or: even the authority of the gloomy realm of shadow and obscurity)."

[comment: this second rendering equates the darkness to this adverse group]

54. **So, after taking Him into custody** (or: seizing, or apprehending, and arresting Him), **they led [Him off] and brought [Him] into the chief priest's house.**
Now Peter kept on following, at a distance.

55. **Now after their lighting a fire in [the] midst of the courtyard and sitting down together, Peter was sitting down in their midst.**

56. **So at seeing him sitting, facing toward the light** (= the glow of the fire), **and now staring intently at him, a certain serving girl** (maidservant) **says,**

57. **"This man was also together with him." Yet he denied** (or: contradicted, said, "No," and declined) **proceeding in saying, "I have neither seen nor do I know Him, woman!"**

58. **Later, after a short while, a different person, upon seeing him, affirmed, "You, yourself, are also [one] of them!" But Peter affirmed, "Man** (Buddy; Mister; My good fellow), **I am not!"**

59. **Then, after the intervening of about an hour, someone else began strongly insisting** (or: firmly maintaining), **then saying, "Of a truth** (or: Really; Quite certainly), **this man was with him, for he is a Galilean, too!"**

60. **So Peter says, "Man** (Sir; Mister), **I have not seen, so I don't know what you are now saying** (= what you mean)!"
Then, at the appropriate moment (or: immediately) **– while [he is] still speaking – a cock crows.**

61. **And then, after being turned, the Lord looked within** (or: on; at) **Peter, and Peter was reminded of the Lord's saying** (or: gush-effect; spoken word; declaration) **as He said to him, "Before a rooster** (or: cock) **is to crow today, with you will proceed fully denying and disowning Me** (or: adamantly saying, 'No,' concerning Me) **three times."**

62. **And so, after going outside, he wept bitterly.**

63. **Now the men – those continuing to hold Jesus in custody – began making fun of Him, treating Him like a child and jesting, while repeatedly lashing [Him].**

64. **Then, after putting a covering around** (perhaps: over) **Him, they continued asking, one after another saying, "Prophesy. Who is the person hitting you and treating you like a child?"**

65. **And so they went on saying many different things, while repeatedly blaspheming with vilifying, abusive, insulting and light-hindering speech to Him** (i.e., into His [face]).

66. **Eventually, as it became day, the body of the elders** (= the Sanhedrin) **of the people was led together** (was gathered and assembled) **– [including] both chief** (or: ranking) **priests and scribes** (scholars and theologians) **– and so they led Him away into their Sanhedrin** (the supreme Jewish council), **then saying,**

67. **"If you are the Christ** (the Anointed One; = the Messiah), **tell us!"**
So He said to them, "If I should tell you, you folks would by no means at this point believe or have allegiance (or: you certainly could not suddenly trust, have faith or be loyal).

68. **"Yet if I should be asking, there is no way you folks would make a decided or discerning reply, or release Me.**

69. **"However, from the present time** (from now on) **the Son of the Man** (the Human Being; = the expected Messiah) **will continue being continuously 'sitting out of the midst of God's right [hands; sides] of power** (or: permanently [positioned to rule] from the midst of the rights: from the power of, and which is, God).'"** [Ps. 110:1]

70. **So everyone [together] said, "Then you, yourself, are God's son!"** (or: Consequently all asked, "Are you, yourself, therefore the Son of God?")
Now He affirmed to them, "You, yourselves, are one-after-another saying that I am." (or: "Are you, yourselves, presently saying that I am?"; or: = a Greek idiom for, "Yes.")

71. **So they said, "Why do we still continue having a need for a witness?** (or: What further need do we now have of testimony?) **For we ourselves heard [it] from his own mouth!"**

CHAPTER 23

1. **And so, after standing up, the entire full count of them** (= the whole Sanhedrin and all assembled there) **led Him on to Pilate** [the Roman governor].

2. **Now [once there], they began to be progressively bringing charges and speaking down against Him, while accusing [Him], one after another saying, "We found this man time after time completely turning** (or: We find this person progressively subverting and inciting revolt for) **our nation and culture group – as well as habitually hindering and forbidding [folks] to continue paying taxes to Caesar – and repeatedly terming himself to now be Christ** ([the] Anointed One; = the Messiah), **a king!"**

3. **So Pilate questioned Him, saying, "Are you, yourself, the king of the Judeans?"**
Now making a decided response to him, He affirmed, "You, yourself, are now saying [it; so] (or: are proceeding in laying out [the issue])."

4. **Then** (or: Later,) **Pilate said to the chief** (or: ranking) **priests and the crowd, "I find not even one ground for a charge** (= no cause or reason for a case) **in this man."**

5. **But they began adding strength in their insistence, one after another saying, "He is constantly shaking, stirring up and agitating** (exciting) **the people! – continuously teaching down through the whole Judean [district], even starting from Galilee as far as here!"**

6. **On hearing [that], Pilate inquired if the man is a Galilean,**

7. **and so upon coming to know that He is from the jurisdiction of Herod, he sent Him back to Herod – he also being in Jerusalem during these days.**

8. **Now Herod, upon seeing Jesus, was exceedingly delighted** (overjoyed), **for he was for a considerable time constantly wanting to see Him because of hearing much about Him – and he was still hoping and expecting to see some sign presently happening by Him.**

9. **So he kept on questioning Him – in abundantly ample words – but He, Himself, gave not even one considered response to him.**

10. **But the chief** (ranking) **priests and the scribes** (Torah experts; scholars) **had taken a stand [and] kept on vehemently** (well-tuned at full stretch) **accusing Him and progressively bringing charges against Him.**

11. So Herod – together with his troops – while treating Him contemptuously as a nobody and then making fun of [Him], throwing a bright (or: brilliantly colored; shiny and resplendent; = magnificent) garment (or: robe) around [Him], [finally] sent Him back to Pilate.

12. Now both Herod and Pilate became friends with each other on that same day, for you see, before [this] they were being inherently at enmity toward each other.

13. Then Pilate, calling together to himself the leading priests and the rulers (ranking leaders; ruling class), as well as the (or: this) People, said to them (or: facing toward them),

14. "You People brought this man to me as one constantly turning the people away [from the right path] (perhaps: = inciting the people to revolt), and yet, look and consider: I, myself – re-examining and sifting [him] in front of you folks (or: in your presence) – found not one fault or ground in this man for the charges which you people keep bringing down on him!

15. "As further contradiction, neither [did] Herod, for he sent him back to us – and look! – there is nothing worthy (deserving) of death having been committed by him!

16. "Therefore, after disciplining and chastising (= flogging) him, I will release him (or: loose him away).

[17.] [this vs. omitted by most texts, but is in some MSS: Now he was normally having an obligation to release one {prisoner} to them, in accord with {the} festival.]

18. But they, as it were with one voice of an entire multitude, cried out – some screaming; some yelling; some shrieking – repeatedly saying, "Be lifting this one up (or: Proceed in taking this one away)!... yet at once release to (or: for) us Barabbas (meaning: the [or: a] father's son)!"

19. – which was a man having been thrown into the prison because of a certain rebellion (incident where folks took a stand and were posturing as for a riot or an uprising), occurring within the City, and [for] murder.

20. Now again, Pilate shouts to them – still wanting and intending to release Jesus –

21. but they kept on yelling and shouting [back], repeatedly saying, "Be crucifying!... proceed putting him to death on an execution stake (pole for hanging corpses)!"

22. Now [for the] third [time] he said to them, "Why? What evil (or: worthless thing) did this man do (or: = What has he done wrong; What crime has this man committed)? I find (or: found) nothing deserving of death in him. Therefore, after disciplining and chastising (= flogging) [him], I will proceed in releasing him."

23. But the men began and continued laying more on, pressing the issue in loud voices, repeatedly demanding Him to be crucified (put to death on an execution stake; to be hung and suspended from a pole). And their voices – along with [those of] the chief priests – continued increasingly strong, so as to prevail.

24. And so Pilate came upon a decision and gave sentence for their demand to come to be (to happen; to be birthed).

25. So he released the one whom they kept on demanding – the man having been thrown into prison because of insurrection and murder. But he turned over (transferred; committed; gave up) Jesus to their will and intent.

26. Later, as they led Him away, taking hold of (or: seizing) Simon – a certain Cyrenian [who was] presently coming from a field (or: [the] country; = [the] farming district) – they placed the execution stake (or: pole; cross) on him, to continue carrying [it] behind Jesus.

27. Now there continued following Him a huge multitude of the people – including women who, in their mourning, kept on striking their chests in lamentation, expressing grief, and were continuously wailing and singing funeral songs [for] Him.

28. Yet, being turned toward them, Jesus said, "Daughters of Jerusalem, do not continue crying for Me (or: stop weeping on and over My [account])! Much more be constantly weeping for yourselves and for your children (or: on your own [account] and over your children's [situation]),

29. "because – look and consider! – days are progressively coming in which they will proceed declaring, 'Happy [are] the sterile and barren women, and the wombs which do not give birth, and breasts which do not nourish!'

30. "At that time,

> 'They will begin saying to the mountains, "Fall at once upon us!" and to the mounds (or: hills), "At once veil (cover; = hide) us!"'" [note: quoting Hos. 10:8, referring to Israel's "high places" of idolatry]

31. "because if they continue doing these things in the wet wood (or: when the tree is green and moist – full of sap), what would happen (or: may occur; or: can be birthed) in the dried and withered one?"

32. Now two different men, criminals (evildoers; men whose works are ugly, of bad quality and worthless; or: may = social bandits or outlaws), were being progressively led together with Him to be lifted up (= executed by crucifixion, i.e., being hung on a pole). [cf Mat. 26:55; 27:38]

33. Then when they came upon the place being normally called "Skull (or: a Skull; [the] Skull)," they crucified Him (attached Him to the stake; suspended Him from a pole) there, along with the criminals – one on [His] right and one on [His] left.

34. Now Jesus kept on saying, "O Father, let it flow away in them (or: send it away for them; forgive them), for they have not seen, so they do not know or perceive, what they are now doing."

> "Now they cast a 'lot' (equivalent to: threw dice) in dividing and distributing His garments." [Ps. 22:18]

35. And so the people stood, continuing in watching and attentively observing, yet the rulers (leaders; chiefs; ruling class) 'began turning their noses up and out, sneering and mocking,' [Ps. 22:8] and one after another saying, "He rescued and healed other folks, let him rescue and restore himself – if (or: since) this man is God's Anointed One (or: the Christ of God; = the Messiah from God), the Chosen One!"

36. So the soldiers also, approaching, made fun of and ridiculed Him while repeatedly offering sour wine (or: vinegar) to Him, [Ps. 69:21]

37. and, one after another, saying, "If (or: Since) you, yourself, are the king of (or: the reigning one from among) the Judeans, rescue (restore; save) yourself!"

38. Now there was also an added inscription upon Him (or: = over Him):

> "THIS [is] THE KING of the JUDEANS (or: The king from among the Judeans [is] this one)."

39. And now one of the criminals being hung began speaking abuse and insults to Him, presently saying, "Are not you, yourself, the Christ? [Then] save yourself, as well as us!"

40. So the other [one], making a discerning reply proceeds adding a value judgment to him, affirming, "You yourself are not even now fearing God! For you are presently in the same result of judgment (effect of a decision)!

41. "... and we, indeed, rightly so (or: justly; fairly), for we are presently receiving back things that balance the scales corresponding to the things which we committed... yet this man committed nothing out of place (= improper)."

42. And then (D adds: turning to the Lord) he went on to say, "Jesus... remember me (other MSS add: O Lord,) whenever you may come into Your kingdom (other MSS: within Your reign; [D reads: in the day of Your coming and going])."

43. And so Jesus said to him, "Truly it is so (or: Count on it!)... I am now saying to you (or: laying it out for you; [D adds: Take courage])... Today (This very day) you will continue being (or: keep on existing) with Me... within the midst of (or: centered in; in the sphere of; in union with) Paradise (= in the Garden [note: used in the LXX for the Garden of Eden in Gen. 2:8])!"

44. And by now it was already about the sixth hour (= about noon) and darkness was birthed (or: a dim, gloomy shadowiness came to be) upon the whole Land – until [the] ninth hour (mid-afternoon),

45. with the leaving-out (or: excluding; failing; defaulting) of the sun [from the situation] (or: = at the ceasing [= departing] of the sunlight). Now the middle veil of the Temple (= the holy places; the inner sanctuary) was split and torn [apart] (or: So the curtain of the Divine dwelling place was torn [down the] middle).

46. **Then Jesus, shouting with a loud voice, said, "O Father... into Your hands I am now setting aside My spirit** (or: I proceed committing My Breath-effect and life-force)!" [Ps. 31:5] **Now upon saying this, He out-spirited** (or: breathed out; expired).

47. **Now the centurion** (Roman military officer), **upon seeing what was occurring, began** (or: kept on) **glorifying God** (continued giving a good opinion of God; began to enhance God's reputation; kept on experiencing impressions and observing imaginations about God) **in saying, "In reality and essential being, this man was innocent** (or: just; righteous; in right relationship; fair; exemplary of the way pointed out; practiced equitable dealings; = upright)!"

48. **And so, all the crowds [of] those presently come to be together at the side – upon the [occasion of] this spectacle** (or: sight) **– after attentively viewing** (or: watching) **the things that were happening, began returning [to the city, or, home], while repeatedly beating** (or: striking) **[their] chests [expressing sorrow and grief].**

49. **But all the folks acquainted with Him – those by intimate experience knowing Him as well as being known by Him – as well as the women normally** (or: habitually) **following Him, from the Galilee [district], had taken a stand and still stood, off at a distance, constantly looking and seeing** (or: perceiving) **these things** (or: events).

50. **And then, look and consider! An adult male named Joseph, a leader who was a member of the Council** (= the Sanhedrin); **a virtuous** (or: good) **and just** (fair; equitable; rightwised) **grown man –**

51. **this man was not one having put [a vote] down together** (= concurring; consenting) **with their wish** (will; intent; purpose) **nor [was endorsing their] performance** (= action; what they committed) **– from Arimathea, a town** (or: city) **of the Judeans, who was habitually receiving, constantly embracing, and kept on giving welcomed admittance to God's reign, kingship, dominion, and sovereign influence-and-activities** (or: the kingdom from God).

52. **This very man, upon coming to Pilate, made a request for the body of Jesus.**

53. **Later, after lowering [it]** (or: taking [it] down), **he wrapped** (or: rolled; folds) **it in** (or: with) **a linen sheet, then he put it** [other MSS: Him] **within a memorial tomb cut in stone** (or: a carved and polished stone sepulcher) **– where no one was lying as yet** (= which had never been used).

54. **Now it was a** (or: [the]) **Day of Preparation, and a sabbath was progressively approaching to shine upon [them].**

55. **So the women who were the ones who had come together with Him out of the Galilee [district], after following [them] down** (or: along the [path], and keeping step,) **viewed the memorial tomb and how His body was placed** (laid out).

56. **Now after returning, they prepared aromatic spices and perfumed oils. Then they indeed rested** (were calm and quiet) **[for; on] the sabbath – according to the implanted goal** (impartation of the finished product within; inward directive).

CHAPTER 24

1. **Now from deep, early pre-dawn, in** (or: on) **that ONE of the sabbaths, they came upon the memorial tomb, progressively carrying [the] spices which they had prepared,**
> [comment: the sabbath of 23:56, above, would have been the Day of Passover; the sabbath of this verse would then been the seventh day of that week, or, the weekly sabbath]

2. **and they found the stone having been rolled away from the tomb,**

3. **yet, upon entering, they did not find the body of the Lord Jesus.**

4. **And then – it happened in the midst of a perplexity for them to be without a way [to explain or understand] about this – look! two adult men** (human males), **in clothing that was constantly flashing and radiating beams of light, stepped up suddenly and stood by them.**

5. **Now in their immediately coming to be terrified and bowing [their] faces unto the ground** (or: So, at their suddenly becoming engulfed in fear and inclining prostrate – the faces [pressed] into the soil), **they** [i.e., the men] **said to them** [i.e., the women], **"Why are you women in the midst of looking for the Living One in the company of** (or: with; amidst) **the dead folks?**

6. **"He is not here. To the contrary, He was aroused and raised up! Be now reminded how He spoke to you folks, while yet being in the Galilee [district],**

7. **"repeatedly saying [of] the Son of the Man** (the Human Being; = Adam's Son; = the expected Messiah), **that it continued necessary for [Him] to be transferred** (or: delivered; committed; given over; commended) **into [the] hands of outcast humans** (people who fail to hit the target; men [that are] sinners), **and then to be crucified** (executed on a stake; hung to be a corpse on a pole) – **and yet on** (or: in) **the third day to rise and stand back up again!"**

8. **So thus were they reminded of His gush-effects** (the results of His flow in sayings and spoken words).

9. **Later, after returning from the memorial tomb, they reported all these things to the eleven, as well as to all the rest** (the remaining ones).

10. **Now they** [i.e., these women] **were the Magdalene Mary and Joanna and Mary, the one of** (or: belonging to or related to) **Jacob** (or: James), **as well as the rest of the women with them** (= their companions). **They, one after another, kept on telling these things to the folks that He had commissioned as emissaries** (sent-forth ones; representatives),

11. **and yet these gush-effects** (or: sayings; declarations) **seemed** (or: appeared) **in their sight to be as if nonsense** (or: wild talk; hysteria; or: a frivolous tale), **and they continued putting no trust in them** (i.e., the women; or: they were still not believing them; they were remaining without confidence in [the women]).

12. **So Peter, upon arising, ran [until he came] upon the memorial tomb, and then, bending forward beside [it], he continues looking** (observing) **only the linen wrappings** (swathings; = burial clothes). **And so he went off to himself, continuing in wondering [at] what had been happening** (or: he came away, still marveling to himself [about] that which had been coming to be).

13. **And now, look and consider! Two of them, on that same day, were progressively journeying into a village which is named Emmaus, being located at a distance of sixty stadia** (= seven miles) **from Jerusalem,**

14. **and they, themselves, kept on conversing with each other about all the things that had been coming about in step with one another** (= had happened in conjunction).

15. **And then it happened! In the midst of the [situation for] them to be in continued conversation and seeking together by progressive questioning and deliberation, Jesus Himself, upon drawing near at hand, also began journeying together with them,**

16. **but their eyes continued being held in a strong grip** (thus: restrained) **[so as] not to recognize or to fully experience knowledge of Him.**

17. **So then He said to them, "What [are] these words which you continue tossing back and forth to each other** (or: What [is] this you are saying as you exchange words and remarks with one another) **while walking along?"**
And so they paused and stood still, with stern and gloomy faces (looking depressed).

18. **So, giving a considered reply, the one named Cleopas said to Him, "Are you yourself temporarily lodging alone** (by yourself) **in Jerusalem and so you did not come to know about** (or: As for you, are you the only person presently visiting Jerusalem that does not know) **the things happening** (or: which have taken place) **in her in these days?"**

19. **And then He said to them, "Which** (or: What sort of) **things?"**
So they said to Him, "The things about (or: concerning) **Jesus – the one from Nazareth – a Man who came to be a prophet, powerful in deed as well as word** (or: able in work and expressed thought), **before** (in front of and in the sight and presence of) **God and all the people;**

20. **"and how our chief** (ranking) **priests and rulers** (or: leaders) **turned Him over** (committed and delivered Him; gave Him along; transferred Him) **unto a sentence** (or: judgment-effect) **of death, and then crucified Him** (executed Him on a stake; suspended Him from a pole).

21. **"Yet we, ourselves, had been expecting that He is the One being now about to be progressively loosing, redeeming and thus liberating Israel** (set Israel free, as in releasing

slaves by paying a ransom). **But surely, to the contrary and besides all these things, this makes the third day since these things occurred.**

22. **"Still, on the other hand, certain women from our group amazed us beyond comprehension, putting us out of place [in our thinking]! Coming to be at the memorial tomb early,**

23. **"and then not finding His body, they came, also repeatedly saying to have looked on and seen a sight: an appearance of agents** (or: messengers) **who kept on laying out and explaining [the situation for] Him to be or to continue living!**

24. **"And so, some of those with us set off [to come] upon the memorial tomb, and then found [it] thus, just as the women also said [it to be], but yet, they did not see Him."**

25. **Then He said to them, "O senseless** (or: unintelligent; mindless) **ones and folks slow at heart to be trusting and believing on all things which the prophets spoke!** [cf Gal. 3:1a]

26. **"Did it not continue necessary for the Christ** (the Anointed One) **to experience and suffer these things – and then to enter into His glory** (or: His assumed appearance)**?"**

27. **And so, beginning from Moses, and then from all the prophets, He continued to fully interpret and explain to** (or: for) **them the things pertaining to** (or: the references about) **Himself within all the Scriptures.**

28. **Later they came near at hand to the village where they were journeying, and He does as though** (or: acted as if) **to continue journeying farther,**

29. **and so with constraining force they pressured Him, the one after the other saying, "Stay** (Remain; Abide) **with us, because it is toward evening, and the day has already declined." With that, He went in to stay with them.**

30. **And then it happened – during the [situation for] Him to be reclining [at the meal] with them! After taking** (or: receiving) **the loaf of bread, He spoke words of goodness, ease, well-being and blessing. Then, after breaking [it], He began giving [it] to them.**

31. **At that their eyes were at once fully opened wide, and they experienced full recognition of Him. Then He, himself, at once became invisible** (or: vanished; disappeared), **away from them.**

32. **Later they said to each other, "Were not our hearts constantly burning as He continued speaking to us on the road** (or: in the path; with the way) **– as He continued fully opening up the Scriptures to** (and: for; with; or: in) **us?"**

33. **And rising up in that same hour, they returned into Jerusalem and found the eleven, as well as those having been collected together with them as a body,**

34. **[who were] then saying [to these two] that the Lord was existentially** (as a being; and: actually; in fact) **aroused and raised up, and then was seen by Simon."**

35. **So then they, themselves, began leading forth with a detailed explanation about the events on the road, and how He came to be known to them** (or: personally recognized by them) **in the breaking of the loaf of bread.**

> [comment: A.T. Robertson points out that the recognition did not come in His exegesis of Scripture, but at the meal and His serving them]

36. **Now upon their speaking these things, He** [other MSS: Jesus] **himself stood in their midst, and proceeds to say, "Peace** [A joining; = Shalom] **to** (or: [is] for; by; in; with) **you folks."**

37. **Yet as [some] were being startled, while [other] were being terrified – then [all] were becoming ones in the grips of fear – they kept on supposing** (imagining; assuming) **to be presently watching** (being a spectator of) **a spirit or life-force** (a breath-effect).

38. **Then He said to them, "Why are you folks shaken... troubled... disturbed? And because of what are reasonings and doubts repeatedly climbing up within the midst of your hearts?**

39. **"Look at My hands, and My feet... see and perceive that I, Myself, am He** (or: that I Myself continue existing; or: because, as for Me, I continue existing [as] Myself)**! Handle Me, and feel as you grope and touch, then perceive that spirit** (breath-effect; wind; life-force)

does not usually have flesh and bones – according as you folks continue viewing Me [as] continuously having."

40. **And while continuing in saying this, He showed** (displayed) **[His] hands and feet to them.**

41. **But at their still continuing in not trusting or believing** (or: disbelieving) **– from the joy and continued marveling, wondering and bewilderment – He says to them, "Do you presently have something edible** (or: = any food), **here in this place?"**

42. **So they handed a piece of broiled** (or: baked) **fish to Him.**

43. **Then, upon taking** (or: receiving) **[it], He ate [it] in front of them and in their sight.**

44. **Now He says to them, "These [were] My words** (thoughts; ideas; laid-out transmissions of information; or =: This [is] My message) **– which I spoke to you folks, while yet being together with you – That it continues binding and necessary for all the things having been written within the Law of Moses, and in the Prophets and Psalms, concerning Me, to be fulfilled."**

45. **At that time He fully opened back up again their minds to be habitually making the Scriptures flow together** (or: to continue putting the Scriptures together so as to comprehend [them]),

46. **And then He says to them, "Thus is has been written** [other MSS add: and thus it continued binding] **[about] the Christ** (the Anointed One): **He was to suffer, and then to rise** (or: stand back up again) **from out of the midst of dead folks – on the third day –**

47. **"and then, upon the [authority and basis of] His Name, a change of mind, thinking and state of consciousness –** [proceeding, or, leading] **into** [other MSS: and] **a flowing away of failures** (a sending away of mistakes; a forgiveness of sins; a divorcing of the situations of missing the target; an abandonment of guilt; a release from error) **– is to be proclaimed by heralds unto all the ethnic multitudes and nations** (or: the Gentiles; the non-Israelites), **beginning** (or: with folks starting) **from Jerusalem.** [cf Rom. 12:2]

48. **"You folks are witnesses of these things** (or: are people who can give evidence for these people).

49. **"And so, look and take note: I Myself am now progressively sending forth the Promise from out of the midst of, and from, My Father** (or: am out from within repeatedly sending forth My Father's promise, as an Emissary; [with other MSS: From where I now am, I now continuously send off the Promise, **which is My Father**]) **upon you people. So you, yourselves, sit down** (be seated) **within the City – until where** (or: which [situation] or: what [time]) **you can** (or: may) **clothe yourselves with** (or: enter within the midst of) **power and ability from out of the midst of exaltation** (or: height; elevation; perhaps: = on high)."

50. **Now He led them out [on the Mount of Olives] as far as facing toward Bethany** (or: to where [the road turns off] toward Bethany), **and then, after lifting up His hands on [them], He spoke words of goodness, ease and well-being, and blessed them.**

51. **Then – it happened during the [occasion for] Him to be blessing them – He stationed [Himself] at an interval from [His] former position, away from them, and then He was progressively carried back up into the atmosphere** (or: heaven; sky) **again.**

52. **And they themselves, after doing obeisance and paying homage to Him and bowing in worship, returned into Jerusalem, with great joy.**

53. **Later, they were through all [times and conditions] within the Temple grounds and courts, constantly praising God, and habitually speaking good words of ease and well-being. It is so** (Amen).

[written circa A.D. 57-62 – Based on the critical analysis of John A.T. Robinson]

JOHN

CHAPTER 1

1. **Within the midst of a beginning** (or: In [the] Origin, in union with Headship and centered in Sovereignty) **there was, and continued being, the Logos** (the Word; the Thought; the collection of thoughts; the Idea; the Reason; the discourse; the speech and communication; the verbal expression; the Message; the reasoned, laid-out and ordered arrangement).
And the Logos (the idea; the thought; the expression; the Word) **was, and continued being, facing, [directed, and moving] toward,** (or: continued being face to face with) **God.**
And the Logos (the Word; the thought; the idea; the reason; the expression) **continued being God.**

> (or: Originally, within the midst of the first principle, the Word, a Patterned Design, was existing and continued to be; and then the Word, or Patterned Design, was being [projected] toward God. And this Word, or Patterned Design… It continued existing actually and essentially being God;
> or: In command was Reason {the ontological "structure of the mind which enables the mind to grasp and transform reality" [Tillich]}, and Reason was staying with God, for Reason {this ontological mental structure} was just what God was;
> or: The Thought, or The Concept, was in the midst of [the] Source. The Thought, or The Concept, was oriented toward the Deity. And the Thought, or The Concept, was Deity;
> or: In beginning, the collected and put side by side Thoughts continued in progressive existence, and the collected and put side by side Thoughts continued being a progression to God, and God {"the Divine Mystery" – Paul Tillich's definition of *theos*} was in continued existence being those collected and put side by side Thoughts;
> or: In union with [the] beginning there was the continued existence of the laid-out Idea {the blueprint – Rohr}, and the laid-out Idea {blueprint} was continued existence face to face with God, and the laid-out Idea {blueprint} continued in existence being "the Divine Mystery;"
> or: At a starting point, the Word continued Being. Then the Word was Being [directed] toward God. And then {or: yet} the Word was Being God {essential Deity; Divine Essence};
> or: Within the power of beginning – which is the controlling principle and power of the entire process – there existed the Idea {the creative and unifying principle of the cosmos}, and the Idea was aimed at and moving toward God. Also, the Idea existed being God;
> or: The Logos continued being within Archē (Source; = The Son was in the midst of [the] Father; [note: I owe to Jean-Yves Leloup the connecting of Archē with the Father]), and the Logos continued being in a movement toward God (= The Son existed in a movement toward the Father), and the Logos continued being God (= The Son was [part of? Within?] the Father);
> or: = Centered in, and in union with, a starting of a Beginning, there was existing, and continued being, the transfer and input of Information that was conveying Meaning [= the Word and Will], and this transfer and input of Information that conveyed [purposed, causal] Meaning continued being projected with God as its Aim, and God continued in existence in this transfer and conveyance of Meaning-bearing Information {or: this "Flow of Information that is a Pattern-forming Influence;" = "God's self-expression in a creation"}). [note: I owe the concepts of these interpretive renderings in this final option to an essay, "The science of complexity: a new theological resource?," by Arthur Peacocke, citing John Macquarrie, in *Information and the Nature of Reality*, Paul Davies & Niels Henrik Gregersen, Editors, Cambridge Univ. Press 2010]

2. **This** (or: This One) **was continuing in existence, within a power of beginning and in union with Headship and Sovereign principle, facing [directed, and moving] toward** (or: staying with) **God.**

> (or: This [situation?] was existing {or: continued being} within the midst of Archē (Source; = Father), [aimed; progressing; being; moving] toward, and thus [to be] face-to-face with, God.)

3. **All things suddenly happened and came to be** (or: occur and come to be; were birthed) **by means of It, or Him** (or: He at some point gives birth to all humanity through It), **and apart from It** (or: Him) **not even one thing comes into being** (occurs; was birthed; came into being; happens) **which has come into being** (which has occurred; which has happened).

4. **Within It** (or: Him), **life was continuing and progressively existing**
> (or: In It was life [as a source]; [Aleph, D and other witnesses read present tense: In union with it there continues being life; Life progressively exists within the midst of It]). **And the life was continuing being, and began progressively existing as, the Light of the humans** (or: Furthermore, the Light progressively came to be the life known as {or: which was} the humans, and was for the human beings; or: Then later the life was existing being the light from the humans).

5. **And the Light is constantly shining in the dim and shadowed places, and keeps on progressively giving light within the gloomy darkness where there is no light** (or: within the midst of the obscurity of The Darkness where there is no light of The Day; or: = in the ignorant condition or system).

And yet the darkness does not grasp or receive it on the same level
> (or: Furthermore, the Darkness did not take it down, so as to overcome it or put it out; or: = the ignorant condition or system would have none of it, nor receive it down into itself [in order to perceive it]; But that darkness does not correspondingly accept It nor commensurately take It in hand so as to follow the pattern or be in line with Its bidding).

6. **A man came to be** (was birthed), **being one having been sent forth with a mission, as a representative, from God's side** (or: having been commissioned as an emissary and sent forth from beside God; having been sent forth to the side, as an envoy, whose source was God); **a name for him: John.**

7. **This one came into a testimony** (or: went unto evidence, a witness), **to the end that he may give testimony** (be a witness; show evidence) **about The Light, so that all humans** (or: everyone) **would at some point come to believe and trust through It** (or: by means of Him; or: through him).

8. **That person** (= He) **was not The Light, but rather [he came] so that he could give testimony** (would be a witness; should present evidence) **about The Light.**

9. **It was** (or: He was, and continued being) **the True and Genuine Light which** (or: Who) **is continuously** (repeatedly; progressively) **enlightening** (giving light to) **every person** (or: all humanity) **continuously** (repeatedly; progressively; constantly; one after another) **coming into the world** (or: the ordered system of culture, religion, economics and government; aggregate of humans; or: the universe)
> (or: It was the real Light, progressively coming into the world {organized system and aggregate of humanity}, which is progressively illuminating {or: shedding light on} every human).

10. **It was** (or: He was, and continued existing being) **within the world** (or: centered in the ordered system; in the midst of the aggregate of humanity), **and the world** (ordered system; etc.; or: cosmos) **came to be** (or: was birthed) **through It** (or: by means of Him), **and the world** (ordered system; etc.) **did not have intimate, experiential knowledge of It** (or: did not recognize Him; had no insight into It).

11. **It** (or: He) **came into Its** (or: His) **own things** (possessions, realms, or people), **and yet Its own** (or: His own) **people did not grasp, receive or accept It** (or: Him) **or take It** (or: Him) **to their side.**

12. **Yet, as many as grasp, receive or accept It** (or: took Him in hand; seized to possession Him) **– to, for and among the ones habitually trusting into Its** (or: believing and being faithful unto His) **Name – It gives** (or: He gave) **to them** (or: for them; in them; among them) **authority** ([the] right; or: privilege from out of the midst of Being) **to be birthed God's children** (or: to become born-ones from God),

13. **who are born** (or: were given birth) **not out of bloods** (or: [flows] of blood), **neither forth from the will of flesh** (or: from the intent of a flesh [ceremony]), **nor yet out of the will** (purpose; intent) **of an adult male, but to the contrary and in contrast, from out of the midst of God!**

14. **And so That Which had been Laid Out as a transfer of Information, i.e., The Word**
> (the Idea; the Thought; the Reason; the Discourse; the Message; The Collected Expression of Rational Logic; *The Logos*; = the meaning, plan and rational purpose of the ordered universe),
births Itself flesh
> (or: became flesh; came to be [in] flesh; came into existence being flesh; = God's thought, the ground of all real existence, became projected into creation as an immanent power within the world of mankind, inhabiting flesh), **and lives in a tent, within us** (or: set up a tent and tabernacled among us), **and we view** (attentively gaze at; looked at so as to contemplate) **Its** (or: His) **glory and assumed appearance**
> (Its manifestation which calls forth praise; Its appearance which creates and effects opinions in regard to the whole of human experience; His imagination; = His manifest presence): **a glory** (=

prestige and importance; reputation and opinion-forming appearance) **as of an only-begotten person** (or: like One that is an only kin, of a solitary race, in a by-itself-class) **at a father's side** (or: in the presence of, and next to, [the] Father), **full of grace and truth** (filled and replete with joy-producing favor, as well as reality and genuineness).

15. **John is continuing witnessing about It** (or: Him) **and has cried out, repeatedly saying, "This One was the One of Whom I said, 'The One progressively coming behind me has come to be in front of me** (or: has taken precedence of me),**' because He was existing first, before me** (or: 'that He was first [in place and station] in regard to me'),**"**

16. **because we all at some point receive** (take with our hands) **from out of the result of His filling** (or: the effect of Its full contents; that which fills Him up): **even grace in the place of grace** (or: favor corresponding to and facing favor; a [new fresh] gracious favor in the place of and replacing [the previous] gracious favor; [one] joyous favor after and exchanged for [another] joyous favor),

17. **because the Law was given through Moses, yet grace and truth are birthed** (or: joyous favor and reality came to be and exists) **through Jesus Christ** [= Messiah Yahshua].

18. **No one at any time has seen God. The only-begotten** (solitary-race, one of a kind) **God** [other MSS: Son] **– the One continuously Existing – THAT One ruled and led the Way forth into the Father's safe place of honored intimacy** (or: unto the midst of the breast and garment fold of the Father): **[He] interprets** (explains) **[Him] by unfolding and bringing Himself forth, out of the midst.**

19. **And this is** (or: continues being) **the testimony of John** (the witness from John), **when the [Sanhedrin, or religious authorities, of the] Judeans** (or: Jews) **sent forth the priests and the Levites** [note: thus, these may have included some Sadducees] **as emissaries out of Jerusalem toward** (or: to; to face) **him – to the end that they may ask him, "You, who are you?" –**

20. **and he confessed and did not contradict or deny, and even agreed that, "I am not the Christ** (the Anointed One; = the Messiah).**"**

21. **And so they asked him, "What, then? Are you Elijah?" And then he continues saying, "I am not." "Are you The Prophet?" Then he distinctly replied, "No!"**

22. **Therefore they said to him, "Who are you, so that we may give a decided reply to the ones sending us – what are you in the habit of saying about yourself?"**

23. **He affirmed, "I am a voice** (or: [the] sound) **of one repeatedly calling out loudly** (crying out; exclaiming; imploring) **within the desolate place** (the wilderness; the uninhabited region; the lonely place), **'Straighten the way of [the] Lord** (the Lord's road; the path pertaining to [the] Lord [= Yahweh or Christ, the Messiah])
> (or: habitually shouting, 'Make straight in the wilderness the way originating in [the] Owner [= Yahweh or Christ]')!' [Isa. 40:3]
just as Isaiah, the prophet, said."

24. **Now [some] folks having been sent as emissaries were from among the Pharisees.**

25. **And then they asked him, and said to him, "Why, then, are you continuously immersing** (or: baptizing), **since** (or: if) **you are not the Christ nor Elijah nor The Prophet?"**
> [note: by immersing folks, either John was treating the Jews as non-Jewish proselytes, or else it should be the Messiah, or His representative, initiating Israel into the new Age – if all the Jews were now supposed to be immersed]

26. **John replies distinctly to them, saying, "I am repeatedly immersing** (baptizing) **within water. He, Whom you men have not seen or perceived, and have no knowledge of or acquaintance with, has stood in your midst** [other MSS: continues presently standing in your midst].

27. **"He is the very One, Who, progressively coming behind me, has come to be in front of me, of Whom I am not worthy** (equal of value) **that I should loose the lace** (strap; thong) **of His sandal."**

28. **These things occurred** (or: came into being) **in Bethany, on the other side of the Jordan, where John was living his life** (or: was existing), **repeatedly immersing.**

29. **The next day** (or: On the morrow) **he is looking at and observing Jesus** [= Yahshua] **progressively coming toward him, and he begins saying, "Look!** (Pay attention, see and perceive)! **God's Lamb** (or: the Lamb from God; the Lamb having the character and qualities of God; or, in

apposition: the Lamb which is God), **the One continuously lifting up and progressively carrying away the Sin of the world, and removing the sin which belongs to and is a part of the System**

> (or: habitually picking up and taking away the failure and error brought on by the system and in the cosmos; progressively removing the falling short and the missing of the goal from the world of culture, religion, economy, government, society, and from the aggregate of humanity)!

30. **"This One is He over whose situation** [other MSS: concerning Whom] **I said, 'An adult male is progressively coming behind me Who has come to be in front of me,' because he was existing before me** (or: was continuously being first in rank and importance in regard to me).

31. **"And I myself had not seen Him to know, recognize or be aware of Him, but nevertheless, to the end that He may be brought to light in** (or: for; by) **Israel** (or: be manifested to Israel) **– because of this – I came continuously immersing** (or: baptizing) **in water."**

32. **John also testified** (gave witness), **repeatedly saying that, "I have viewed and continued gazing at, so that I can now visualize, the Spirit progressively stepping down** (or: the Breath-effect continuously descending), **as a dove, forth from out of [the] atmosphere** (or: as a pigeon out of the sky, or from heaven), **and It remains and dwells upon Him** (or: It abode [= nested] upon Him).

33. **"And yet, I had not seen Him to know or be aware of Him! But further, the One sending me to be habitually immersing** (baptizing) **in water, that One said to me, 'Upon whomever you may see the Spirit progressively stepping down** (or: the Breath-effect continuously descending) **and then continuously remaining** (dwelling; abiding) **upon Him, this One is** (continuously exists being) **the One progressively** (or: habitually) **immersing** (or: baptizing) **within a set-apart spirit** (or: in the midst of [the] Holy Spirit; in union with the Sacred Breath-effect and Attitude).'

34. **"And so I myself have seen and given witness, and thus now bear testimony, that this One is God's Son** (or: continuously exists being the Son which is God; or: the son having the character and qualities of God; or: the Son from God; The Son of The God)."

35. **The next day** (or: On the morrow) **John, and two from among his disciples, again had taken a stand and now stood [there].**

36. **Later, gazing upon Jesus** [= Yahshua] **progressively walking around, he is saying, "Look** (Pay attention and perceive; See and consider)! **God's Lamb** (or: The Lamb from, and whose origin is, God; or: the Lamb which is God)."

37. **And his two disciples hear** (or: heard; listen) **as he is speaking, and then they follow** (or: followed with) **Jesus.**

38. **Now Jesus, being suddenly turned and then viewing** (or: gazing at) **them following, is saying to them, "What are you seeking** (or: What do you habitually look for)?" **Yet they said to Him, "Rabbi," –** **which, being translated and explained, is normally being called** (or: termed) **"Teacher" – "where are you presently staying** (or: habitually remaining and dwelling)?"

39. **He replies to them, "Be coming, and you will proceed seeing for yourselves** [other MSS: Come and see (or: perceive)]." **They went** (or: came), **then, and saw** (or: perceived) **where He is presently staying** (habitually remaining and dwelling), **then stayed at His side** (or: remained with Him) **that day. It was about the tenth hour.**

40. **Now Andrew, the brother of Simon Peter, was one of the two hearing at John's side, and following Him.**

41. **This one** [i.e., Andrew] **is first finding his own brother, Simon, and is saying to him, "We have found the Messiah!" – which is presently being translated with explanation, 'Christ** ([the] Anointed One)' **– "so we now know Who and where He is!"**

42. **And so he led him toward Jesus. Looking within** (or: on) **him, Jesus said, "You are Simon, the son of John** [other MSS: Jonah]. **You will be called Cephas" – which is presently being translated and interpreted, "Peter (a stone)."**

43. **The next day** (or: On the morrow), **He decided** (or: He wants) **to go out into Galilee. And then Jesus is finding Philip and proceeds saying to him, "Be constantly following Me!"**

44. **Now Philip was from** (= had been living in) **Bethsaida, the city of Andrew and Peter.** [note: both Philip and Andrew are Greek names, a sign of Hellenization]

45. **Philip proceeds finding Nathaniel** [note: probably also called Bartholomew] **and says to him, "We have found the One of Whom Moses wrote within the Law and the Prophets: Jesus – Joseph's son** (or: a son of Joseph) **– the one from Nazareth!"**
46. **Then Nathaniel said to him, "Can anything good be** (or: Is anything virtuous normally able to exist) **from out of Nazareth?" Philip continues, saying to him, "Come and see."**
47. **Jesus saw Nathaniel progressively coming toward Him, and He begins saying about him, "Look, and pay attention: truly an Israelite, within whom exists** (or: there continues being) **no deceit** (bait or contrivance for entrapping; fraud; guile)**!"**
48. **Nathaniel says to Him, "From where** (or: what place) **are you having an intimate knowledge of me?** (or: Where do you know me from?)**" Jesus decidedly answers, and said to him, "Before Philip made a sound to call out to you, [you] being under** (beneath) **the fig tree, I saw you."**
49. **Nathaniel considered and replied to Him, "Rabbi, You – You are the Son of God! You – You are Israel's King!"** [note the equivalence of the appellations, in Nathaniel's view}
50. **Jesus decidedly answers, and said to him, "Because I said to you that I saw you down under the fig tree, you proceed believing** (or: are you now trusting with allegiance)**? You will continue seeing greater things than these."**
51. **And He is further saying to him, "It is certainly true** (or: Amen, amen; Most truly; Count on it). **I am presently laying it out, saying to you folks, you will proceed seeing the heaven** (or: sky; atmosphere) **being one that is opened back up again, and 'God's agents repeatedly** (progressively; continuously) **ascending** (stepping back up again) **and habitually** (progressively; continuously; repeatedly) **descending** (stepping down)**'** [Gen. 28:12] **upon the Son of the Man** (or: Mankind's Son; = the Son of Adam; the Human Son; = the Human Being; = the eschatological Messianic figure)**."**

CHAPTER 2

1. **And on the third day a wedding occurred** (or: a marriage and wedding feast took place) **within Cana of Galilee, and the mother of Jesus was there.**
2. **Now Jesus – along with His disciples – was also called into the wedding** (or: invited unto the marriage feast).
3. **Then later, there being a lack of** (a need of; a failing of sufficient) **wine, the mother of Jesus proceeds saying to Him, "They are not continuing to have** (= they're running out of) **wine."**
4. **So Jesus is replying to her, "What [is it] to Me and to you, madam** (or: What [is that] for Me and for you, O woman; or: = My lady, what has this got to do with us)**? My hour is not yet** (or: is still not) **arriving."**
5. **His mother proceeds speaking, saying to the attending servants, "Do at once whatever** (or: anything which) **He may be telling** (or: should be laying out for, or saying to) **you."**
6. **Now there were six stone water pots** (or: jars) **habitually lying there – corresponding to the cleansing** (or: purifying) **practice pertaining to the Jewish customs** (or: ritual and ceremony of washing, originating from the Judeans) **– having capacities for up to two or three liquid measures** (= 15 to 27 gallons).
7. **Jesus says to them, "Fill the water pots** (or: jars) **full, with water." And so they filled them up to the upper part** (back up to the top, or, brim).
8. **So then He continues speaking, saying to them, "Now bale out** (or: draw off) **[some] and proceed carrying** (bearing; bringing) **[it] to the head man** (or: chief) **of the dining room** (= the master or director of the festivities)**." And so then they brought [it].**
9. **Now as the head man** (chief) **of the dining room sipped and tastes the water existing having been made to be wine** (or: the water [which] had been birthed being [now] wine) **– now he had not seen to know from where it is, yet the attending servants, the ones having baled** (or: drawn) **out the water, had seen and thus knew – this director of the feast begins calling out** (continues shrieking; or: insistently summons) **the bridegroom**
10. **and proceeds, saying to him, "Every man habitually places the fine** (the beautiful; the ideal) **wine first, and whenever they may have been made drunk, then the inferior. You – you have guarded and kept the fine** (ideal) **wine until now** (the present moment)**!"**
11. **This beginning of the signs Jesus performed** (did; made; constructed; accomplished; produced) **within Cana, of the Galilee [district], and set His glory in clear light** (or: manifested His splendor so

as to create a reputation; gave light in a manifestation which calls forth praise and has its source in Him; manifested His assumed appearance), **and His disciples trusted, had faith and believed into Him.**
12. **After this, He and His mother – also His brothers and disciples – went down into Capernaum, but they did not remain** (stay; abide) **there many days.**

13. **Now the [annual observance of the] Passover [Feast; festival], which originated with and pertained to the Jews** (the Jewish people, religion and culture) **was near, so Jesus went up into Jerusalem.**
14. **Then within the Temple grounds** [probably the court of the Gentiles], **He found those habitually selling cattle, sheep and doves** (or: pigeons), **and those who [for a fee] exchanged foreign coins for acceptable Judean money** (money brokers) **continuously sitting [at their stations, or tables].**
15. **And so, after constructing a kind of whip out of small rush-fiber cords** (or: making like a lash of twisted rush-ropes), **He casts** (or: ejected) **them all out of the Temple grounds: both the sheep and the cattle** (or: He drove them all, both the sheep and the cattle, forth from the midst of the temple's outer courts). **And then He pours out the coins** (change; small pieces of money) **of the money changers** (= bankers for currency exchange), **and overturns the tables.**
16. **Next He said to the ones habitually selling doves** (or: pigeons), **"You folks at once take these things from this place! Stop making** (or: Do not habitually make) **My Father's House a house of merchandise** (a merchant's store; a market place; a house of business)**!"**

17. **Now His disciples are** (or: were) **reminded that it is standing written that**
    "the zeal (passion; the boiling jealousy) **of Your House** (or: from Your House; or: for Your House) **will 'completely consume Me'** (or: 'eat Me down and devour Me')**."** [Ps. 69:9]

18. **Then the [religious authorities of the] Judeans made a decision to respond to Him. And so they say, "What sign** (authenticating token or distinguishing signal) **are you presently showing** (pointing out; exhibiting) **to us, [seeing] that you are proceeding to do these things?"**
19. **Jesus considered then responds to them, and says, "Loosen** (or: Undo, and thus, destroy or demolish) **this Sanctuary** (Shrine; Divine Habitation; = the Temple consisting of the holy place and the holy of holies), **and within three days I will proceed to be raising it up."**
20. **Then the Judeans** (= Jewish religious authorities) **say, "This Sanctuary was built** (constructed to be the House) **and erected in** (or: over a period of) **forty-six years – and now you... you will proceed to be raising it up within three days?!"**
21. **Yet that One** (= He) **had been laying [things] out concerning, and speaking about, the Sanctuary which is His body** (or: the Divine habitation of the body belonging to, and which is, Him; the inner Temple pertaining to His whole corporeal and material substance).
22. **Then, when He was awakened, aroused and raised up forth from out of the midst of dead ones, His disciples were reminded that He had been repeatedly saying this, and they believed by the Scripture and put trust in the word** (message; idea) **which Jesus said** (proposed; had recited).

23. **Now as He was continuing being within Jerusalem during the Passover** [note: the feast of unleavened bread followed for seven days right after the Passover], **in the midst of the festival** (celebration; Feast) **many believed and put their trust into His Name, constantly gazing upon and critically contemplating His signs** (or: the authenticating tokens and distinguishing signals originating in Him), **which He was continuing to perform** (or: had been one-after-another progressively doing).
24. **Yet Jesus, Himself, was not habitually entrusting Himself to them** (or: had not been adhering Himself to them, or committing Himself for them; or: kept on refusing to trust Himself to them), **because of the [situation for] Him to be continuously** (habitually; progressively) **knowing all people by intimate experience and through insight,**
25. **and because He was not having** (had not been continually holding) **a need requiring that anyone should bear witness** (or: give testimony or evidence) **about mankind** (or: humanity; the [corporate] Man), **for He Himself was constantly** (had been habitually) **knowing by intimate experience what was continuing to be within mankind** (the human; the [corporate] Man).

CHAPTER 3

1. **Now there was a man from out of the Pharisees, Nicodemus by name, a ruler** (leader; chief; head man) **of the Judeans** (those of the Jewish culture, political organization and religion, in Judea).
2. **This one comes** (or: goes; came; went) **to Him by night, and says** (or: said) **to Him, "Rabbi, we have seen and thus know that You are a Teacher having come, and are here, from God, for no one is able** (or: continues having power) **to constantly be doing** (making; producing) **these signs** (or: habitually performing these authenticating tokens and attesting signals), **which You are constantly doing** (performing; producing), **unless God would continue being with him** (or: if God should not continue being existentially with him)."
3. **Jesus considered, and replies to him, saying, "Certainly it is so, I am saying** (= I now point out) **to you, unless anyone may** (or: someone would) **be born back up again to a higher place** (or: can be brought to birth again; or: would be given birth from above), **he continues having no power** (or: remains unable) **to see or perceive God's reign, sovereign influence, activity, or kingdom."**
4. **Nicodemus says to Him, "How does a man continue being able to be born, being an old man? He is not able** (or: remains powerless) **to enter into his mother's womb** (cavity; belly) **a second [time] and be born!"**
5. **Jesus decisively replies, "Certainly that is so. I am now saying** (laying it out; = pointing out) **to you, unless anyone may** (or: someone would) **be born forth from out of water and spirit** (or: – as well as Breath-effect and attitude –) **he continues being unable** (remains having no power) **to enter into God's realm** (or: reign; kingdom; sovereign activity and influence).
6. **"The thing being birthed, having been born forth from out of the flesh, is flesh** (or: from the estranged human nature, continues being the estranged human nature; or: = from out of a flesh system is a flesh system), **and the thing being birthed, having been born forth from out of the Spirit, is spirit** (or: what is birthed out of the Breath-effect continues being Breath-effect; or: what is born from the Attitude is an attitude).
7. **"You should not be amazed** (or: begin to marvel; at some point be filled with wonder; suddenly be astonished; or: Don't be surprised) **that I said to you, 'It is necessary and binding for you folks to be born back up again to a higher place** (or: for you people to be given birth from above).'
8. **"The Spirit** (or: Breath-effect, or, exhaled Breath; Attitude) **habitually breathes or blows where It** (or: He) **is presently intending** (willing; purposing), **and you continually hear Its** (or: His) **voice, but yet you have not seen, and thus do not know, from what source It continuously comes, and where It progressively goes and habitually brings [things and folks] under [Its] control.**

> (or: The wind constantly blows where it presently sets its will, and you constantly hear it's sound, but yet you have not seen and do not know from where it is coming, nor where it is going; or: = The wind continuously blows and the Spirit normally breathes {respires} – in the place that each has purpose. And so you are often hearing the sound that either makes, although you have not perceived from what place it is presently coming, as well as to what place it is presently leading, under [its influence or control].)

Thus is everyone (or: does everyone constantly exist being) – **the person** (or: the [corporate] Person [= the Second Humanity]) **being birthed, having been born forth from out of the midst of the Spirit**

> (or: In this manner exists all mankind, which is in the state of being born from the Breath-effect)."

9. **Nicodemus considered in reply, and says to Him, "How is it possible for these things to occur** (or: How can these things come to be; How is it repeatedly able [for] these to come to birth)**?"**
10. **Jesus decisively responded and says to him, "You yourself are the teacher of Israel, and yet you continue not knowing and being intimately familiar with these things!**
11. **"Certainly it is so, I am now saying to you, that which we have seen and thus know** (or: perceive), **we are constantly speaking** (or: telling; chattering [about]), **and what we have caught sight of and seen we repeatedly bear witness of** (constantly give testimony to), **and you folks continue not receiving** (or: none of you are laying hold of) **our witness** (or: testimony; evidence).
12. **"Since I tell** (or: If I told) **you folks the earthly things** (or: ones; situations), **and you folks are not continuing in belief** (do not presently believe; are not proceeding to trust), **how will you continue to believe or trust if I should speak to you the things** (or: situations; ones) **upon the heavens**

> (or: the super-heavenly occurrences; the fully-atmospheric things [taking place]; the things or folks being in a position of control upon the atmospheres)**?**

13. **"Furthermore, no one has ascended** (or: stepped up) **into the heaven** (or: atmosphere) **except the One descending** (or: stepping down) **from out of the midst of the atmosphere** (or: heaven)**: the Son of Mankind** (the Son of the human [= Adam]; Humanity's Son; the Son of man) **– Who is continuously being** (or: constantly existing) **within the midst of the heaven** (or: atmosphere).

> [with *p*66 & *p*75, Aleph, B and others: And yet not even one person climbed up into heaven (or: the sky), if not that person at one point descending from out of the midst of heaven (or: the sky) – the Human Being.]

14. **"And so, just as** (or: correspondingly as) **Moses lifted up** (elevated; raised up high) **the serpent, within the wilderness** (desert; desolate place) [Num. 21:7ff]**, thus it is necessary and binding for the Son of Mankind** (Humanity's Son; the Human Being) **to be lifted up** (elevated; raised up high; exalted),

15. **"with the result and end that all – this progressively believing and successively** (one-after-another) **trusting humanity – in union with Him** (or: in order that all humanity, who being constantly loyal, centered in and within the midst of Him), **would continuously have eonian Life** (life having the state of being, qualities and characteristics of the sphere pertaining to the Age [of the Messiah]; age-quality and eon-lasting life; Life in this lifetime and for a lifetime or an indefinite period of time)!

> [with other MSS: so that all, while continuously trusting into Him {others: on Him}, may not lose or destroy themselves, but rather may continuously hold age-abiding life (eonian life; life that continues on through the ages).]

16. **"For thus God loves** (or: You see God, in this manner, fully gives Himself to and urges toward reunion with) **the aggregate of humanity** (universe; ordered arrangement; organized System [of life and society]; the world), **so that He gives His** [other MSS: the] **only-born** (or: only-kin; unique-class) **Son,**

> (or, reading ωστε as an adverb: You see, in this manner God loves the sum total of created beings as being the Son: He gives the solitary-race One; or: reading ως τε: For you see, [it is] in this way [that] God loves the aggregate of humanity – even as it were His Son: He gives the by-itself-in-kind-One), **to the end that all humanity, which** (or: everyone, who) **– when progressively trusting and successively believing into Him and thus being constantly faithful to Him – would not lose or destroy itself, or cause itself to fall into ruin, but rather can continuously have** (or: would habitually possess and hold) **eonian life** (age-durative life with qualities derived from the Age [of the Messiah]; living existence of and for the ages).

> [note 1]: I have here given the "fact" sense of the *aorist* tense of the verbs "love" and "give" rather than the simple past tense. The statement by Jesus is a "timeless" fact of God; it signifies that the object of His love and His gift (that object being the cosmos, the universe, the world of men and created beings) is in view as a whole, and both the love and the gift are presented as fact, as one complete whole (punctiliar) which exists apart from any sense of time (i.e., coming from the realm or sphere of the "eternal," or, "the Being of God;"
> note 2): Paul Tillich defines "love" (*agapē*): the whole being's drive and movement toward reunion with another, to overcome existential separation; an ecstatic manifestation of the Spiritual Presence; acceptance of the object of love without restriction, in spite of the estranged, profanized and demonized state of the object; – *Systematic Theology III,* pp 134-138; Richard Rohr: Love; a drive to give yourself totally to something or someone] *Cf* Rom. 8:3

17. **"You see, God does not send forth His** [other MSS: the] **Son as a Representative or Emissary into the world** (or: System; aggregate of humanity) **to the end that He should continuously separate and make decisions about the world** (or: would at some point sift and judge the System, or the aggregate of humanity), **but to the contrary, to the end that the world would be delivered**

> (or: for the result that the System could be healed and made whole; so that the ordered arrangement should be restored to health; to the end that the aggregate of mankind may be saved – rescued and re-established in its original state): **through Him!**

18. **"The person habitually believing and progressively placing trust into Him is not being continuously sifted or evaluated** (is not habitually being separated for decisions or being judged), **yet the person not habitually trusting and believing has already been sifted and evaluated** (separated for a decision; judged) **and that decision yet exists, because he or she has not believed so that he trusts into** (or: had not been faithful and loyal unto) **the Name** [note: "name" is a Semitism for the person, or his authority, or his qualities] **of the only-born Son of God** (or: into the Name of God's Son – the only-kin and unique-class One, or the by-itself-in-kind One, or, the solitary-race One).

19. **"Now this continues being the** (or: So there continues being the same) **process of the sifting, the separating and the deciding** (the evaluating; the judging), **because the Light has come** (or: that the Light has gone) **into the world** (the aggregate of humanity; the ordered system and arrangement of religion, culture and government; or: the system of control and regulation; or: the cosmos), **and yet the humans love the darkness** (or: the men [= the leadership] love and fully give themselves to the dimness of obscurity and gloom; or: mankind loved and moved toward union with the shadow-realm) **rather than the Light, for their works** (deeds; actions) **were continuing to be bad ones** (unsound ones; wicked, wrongful ones; laborious ones; unprofitable and disadvantageous ones; malicious ones),

20. **"for it follows that everyone who is habitually practicing** (or: performing) **worthless things** (base, mean, common, careless, cheap, slight, paltry, sorry, vile things or refuse) **is continuously hating** (regarding with ill-will; radically detaching from) **the light, and is not coming** (or: going) **to the light** (or: the Light), **so that his or her works** (deeds; actions) **may not be tested and put to the proof** (and thus, exposed and perhaps reproved).

21. **"Yet the person habitually doing the truth** (constantly constructing the real; repeatedly making the genuine; progressively producing the non-concealed, actual state) **is constantly coming** (or: moving) **toward the light** (or: the Light), **so that his or her works** (deeds; actions) **may be set in clear light and manifested, because they exist being ones having been worked, accomplished or performed within God** (or: that it is in union with God [that they are] ones having been acted out)."

22. **After these things, Jesus and the disciples went** (or: came) **into the Judean territory** (land; country; region), **and He was wearing away the time there with them. He was also periodically immersing** (or: baptizing).

23. **Now John was continuing repeatedly immersing** (baptizing) **in Enon** (or: Ainon), **near Salim, because much water was** (or: many waters were) **there, and [folks] kept showing up alongside and were being immersed** (baptized),

24. **for not yet was John one having been cast into the guardhouse** (jail; prison).

25. **Then there arose** (came to be) **from out of John's disciples, thereupon, a discussion** (an inquiry; a seeking question) **with a Jew** (or: a Judean) **about cleansing** (ceremonial purification).

26. **So they went to** (or: come toward) **John, and said** (or: say) **to him, "Rabbi, he who was with you across** (on the other side of) **the Jordan [River], to whom you have borne witness** (or: for whom you have testified), **look** (see; consider), **this one is continually immersing** (baptizing), **and everyone is** (or: all are) **constantly coming toward** (or: going to) **him."**

27. **John deliberated in reply and says, "Man continues without ability** (or: Humanity remains unable) **to be receiving anything, unless it may have been existing being having been given to him** (or: it) **from out of the heaven**

> (or: A person is continually powerless to lay hold of and take anything, unless he was possibly being one having been given [ability] from out of the atmosphere and heaven in him).

28. **"You folks, yourselves, repeatedly bear me witness** (or: habitually testify for me) **that I myself said, 'I am not the Christ** (the Anointed One)**!' But rather that, 'I am one having been sent forth as an emissary** (one sent forth with a mission as a representative) **in front of That One.'**

29. **"The One continually holding** (or: constantly having) **the bride is** (exists being) **a Bridegroom** (or: [the] Bridegroom). **Yet the friend of the Bridegroom – the man having taken a stand, and continuing standing, and continuously listening and hearing from Him in joy – is constantly rejoicing because of the Bridegroom's voice! This joy – the one [that is] mine – has therefore been fulfilled** (or: This, then, my joy, has been made full).

30. **"It is necessary and binding for That One to be progressively growing and increasing, yet for me to be progressively less** (or: continually made inferior and decrease).

31. **"The One repeatedly coming back again from above** (or: habitually going again to a higher place) **is above upon all people** (or: constantly exists being up over upon all things). **The person continuously being forth from out of the earth [as a source] is** (or: constantly exists being) **from out of the earth, and is habitually speaking forth from out of the earth. The One continuously coming** (or: habitually going; repeatedly coming and progressively going) **forth from out of the midst of the heaven** (or: the atmosphere) **is, and constantly exists being, above upon** (= has authority and dominion over) **all people** (or: up over upon all things).

32. **"What He has seen and hears** (or: heard), **to this He continuously bears witness** (or: is repeatedly testifying, attesting and giving evidence), **and yet no one is presently grasping** (or: habitually takes in hand; continues receiving) **His witness** (or: testimony; evidence).

33. **"The one receiving** (grasping; taking in hand; accepting; getting hold of) **His witness** (testimony; evidence) **certifies – by setting a seal** (= giving attestation) – **that God is true** (real; genuine; truthful),

34. **"for He Whom God sends forth with a mission** (dispatches as an Emissary and Representative) **habitually is speaking the gush-effects from God** (the results of the flows of God; God's declarations or sayings), **for God is habitually** (or: continuously) **giving the Spirit** (Breath; or: Attitude) **[and] not from out of a measure** (= not by a measured portion or limit; = without measure and without limitation).

35. **"The Father continuously loves and fully gives Himself to the Son, and He has given all humanity** (or, as a neuter: all things) **[to Him] so that He has it** (or: them) **as a gift within His hand.**

36. **"The one habitually trusting into** (or: continuously going on confidently believing with loyalty unto) **the Son is now constantly holding and is presently, progressively possessing** (having) **eonian life**
> (life having the characteristics and qualities of the sphere of the Age; life of and for the ages; eon-lasting life; life whose source is the Age [of Messiah]). **Yet the person now continuing being unpersuaded by the Son** (or: presently being constantly incompliant, disobedient or disbelieving to the Son; being repeatedly stubborn toward the Son) **will not be catching sight of** (seeing; observing; perceiving) **[this] life. To the contrary** (or: Yet, nevertheless), **God's personal emotion and inherent fervor**
> (or: the teeming passion and **swelling desire, which is God**; the mental bent, natural impulse, propensity and disposition **from God**; or: the ire, anger, wrath or indignation **having the quality and character of God**)

presently continues remaining (keeps on resting, dwelling and abiding) **upon him."**
> [note: vss. 31-36 may be narrative by the author, John, and not continued sayings of the Baptist]

CHAPTER 4

1. **Then, as the Lord** (Master; [other MSS: Jesus]) **became personally aware** (or: came to know) **that the Pharisees heard that Jesus is progressively making and immersing** (baptizing) **more disciples than John –** [comment: "Jesus did not reject baptism, but neither did He require it" – Bruce Chilton]

2. **although, to be sure, Jesus Himself had not been immersing, but rather His disciples [were] –**

3. **He abruptly left** (or: abandoned) **Judea and went** (or: came) **away again into the Galilee [district]**.

4. **Now it was being necessary for Him to be progressively passing through Samaria.**

5. **He continues going, therefore, into a city of Samaria, called Sychar** (perhaps: Shechem), **near** (close to) **the small place** (or: the plot of ground [which could be bought, and then become an inheritance, or sold]; the freehold) **which Jacob gave to his son Joseph.**

6. **Now [the well of] Jacob's Spring** (or: a spring that had belonged to Jacob) **was located there. Jesus, therefore, being wearied from the journey, was sitting upon [the large capstone of]** (or: at) **the Spring. It was about the sixth hour** (= noon, mid-day).

7. **There presently is coming a woman of Samaria to draw** (or: dip up) **water. Jesus now says to her, "Would you give [some] to** (or: for) **me to drink?"**

8. **– you see, His disciples had gone away into the city so that they may buy food** (nourishing provisions) **in the market place –**

9. **The Samaritan woman is then saying to Him, "How is it that you, being a Jew, are requesting to drink from my side – me being a Samaritan woman? You know, Jews are not usually making common use [of vessels, or things] with Samaritans!"**

10. **Jesus considered and decidedly said to her, "If you had seen, so as to be aware of and now perceive God's gift, and Who is the One presently saying to you, '[Please] give [some] to me, to drink,' you would ask** (or: make request of) **Him, and He would give continuously living water to you."** [note: a figure for "flowing water"; metaphorically: water bringing life that continues to live within]

11. **She** [other MSS read: The woman] **says to Him, "Sir** (or: Master; = My lord), **you are not even holding** (or: having) **a bucket or any means of drawing, and the well is deep! From where** (or: From what source), **then, are you holding** (or: having; possessing) **the living water?**

12. **"You yourself are not greater than our father Jacob who gave the well to us, are you? Even he himself drank out of it, together with his sons and his nourished and reared ones** (i.e., his livestock)."

13. **Jesus considered and responds to her, and says, "Everyone repeatedly drinking from out of this water will repeatedly become thirsty again.**

14. **"Yet whoever may** (or: would) **drink from out of the water which I, Myself, will be continuously giving to him will not repeatedly become thirsty, on into the Age, but further, the water which I shall constantly give to** (or: in) **him will progressively come to be** (or: repeatedly become; continuously birth itself) **within him a spring** (or: fountain) **of water, constantly bubbling up** (continuously springing and leaping up) **into a life having the source, character and qualities of the Age** (life of and for the ages; eonian life; = the life of the Messianic age)."

15. **The woman is saying to Him, "Sir** (or: Master; = My lord), **give to me this water, so that I may not constantly become thirsty, nor yet be repeatedly coming over to this place to be constantly drawing** (or: dipping up)."

16. **He presently says to her, "Be going on your way. At once call out to** (or: summon) **your husband and then come to this place."**

17. **The woman thoughtfully replies, and says to Him, "I am not presently having a husband** (or: I do not continuously hold a man)." **Jesus then says to her, "Beautifully you say that, 'I am not presently having a husband** (or: I do not continuously hold a man),'

18. **"for you had five husbands** (or: at various points held five men), **and whom you now are presently holding** (or: having) **is not your husband. This you have said [is] true** (or: a reality; [other MSS: This you truly and truthfully say])."

19. **The woman now says to Him, "Sir** (perhaps, by now: Lord; Master), **in carefully observing, I am perceiving that you, yourself, are a prophet.**

20. **"Our fathers worshiped** (or: worship) **within this mountain** [i.e., Mt. Gerizim], **and you folks continually say that the place where it continues necessary** (or: is constantly binding) **to be habitually worshiping is within Jerusalem."**

21. **Jesus then says to her, "Be constantly trusting in Me** (or: by and with Me; or: Continue believing Me), **O woman** (madam; = dear lady), **because an hour is progressively coming when neither within this mountain nor within Jerusalem will you folks continue giving worship to the Father.**

22. **"You people are habitually worshiping what you have not seen and thus do not know. We [Jews] are presently worshiping what we have seen and thus know, because the deliverance** (the rescue and being restored; the health and wholeness; the salvation) **continues being** (habitually is; constantly exists being) **from out of the Judeans** (or: from among those of Judah {or: from the Jews}).

23. **"Nevertheless an hour is progressively coming – and now exists** (or: is; is being) **– when the true** (real; genuine) **worshipers will proceed to worship** (or: will habitually give worship to) **the Father within spirit and Truth** (or: in breath and reality; centered in the midst of [the] Spirit and a Fact; in union with and centered in Breath-effect, attitude and genuineness of non-concealed actuality), **for the Father is also constantly seeking after such folks** (habitually searching out such ones as this; continuously looking for and trying to find lost ones to be this kind) **– ones presently by habit worshiping Him!**

24. **"God [is] spirit** (or: [is the] Spirit; [gives] Breath; [becomes] Wind; [is] a Breath-effect and Attitude), **and it is binding** (or: necessary) **for the ones continuously worshiping Him to be constantly worshiping in union with spirit and Truth** (in Breath-effect and Reality; within the midst of [the] Spirit and [the] Fact; centered in [life]-attitude, as well as non-concealed genuineness and open actuality)."

25. **The woman then says to Him, "I [other MSS: we] have perceived** (or: seen) **and hence know that a Messiah repeatedly comes** (or: an anointed leader periodically comes; Messiah is presently coming) **– the One commonly called** (or: interpreted or translated) **'Christ'** (or: Anointed). **Whenever that one comes, he will bring back a report** (or: fully announce again a message; or: = explain) **to us about all humanity** (or: all things; or: [the] whole [matter])."

26. **Jesus then says to her, "I – the One presently speaking to you – I AM [the One; He]."**

27. **Now upon this [situation], His disciples came, and were** (or: had been and continued) **wondering** (or: amazed; astonished) **that** (or: because) **He had been and continued speaking with a woman. Of course** (or: Indeed, let me tell you), **no one said, "What are You presently seeking or looking for** (= What can we do for You)**?" or "Why are You speaking** (or: What are You now saying)

with her?"

28. **Then the woman left behind her water jar** (or: pot) **and went away into the city, and proceeds saying to the people,**

29. **"Come here! See a man who said to me** (or: told me) **everything which I did** (or: all [the] things which [other MSS: as much as] I do)! **Surely this one is not the Christ, is he?** (or: Is this one not the Christ?; Can this one be the Anointed?)"

30. **They came** (or: at once went) **forth out of the city, and were progressively coming toward Him.**

31. **Now in the meantime** (or: Meanwhile) **the disciples had kept on urging Him, repeatedly saying, "Rabbi, You must eat!"**

32. **Yet He says to them, "I, Myself, continually have** (or: hold) **food to eat which you men have not seen and hence do not know or perceive."**

33. **Thereupon, the disciples were saying to one another, "Did anyone bring Him something to eat?** (or: No one brought Him anything to eat!)"

34. **Jesus then says to them, "My food is** (or: exists being) **that I should do** (can perform; would produce; [other MSS: can continuously be doing; or: habitually do]) **the will, intent and purpose of the One sending Me, and that I should and would bring His work to its purposed goal and destiny** (or: can complete His act; may finish and perfect His deed).

35. **"Do you guys not commonly say that, 'It is still** (or: yet) **four months more, and then the process of harvesting progressively comes'? Consider** (or: Look and see)! **I am now saying to you men, 'Lift up your eyes and attentively view** (fix your eyes on, gaze at and consider) **the countryside and fields of cultivated tracts, that they are radiant** (brilliant; or: bleached light to white) **toward a harvest.'**

36. **"Already** (or: Even now) **the one habitually reaping** (normally or progressively harvesting) **is constantly receiving** (or: taking in his hand) **a compensation** (a wage; a reward; a payment), **and is constantly** (or: presently; progressively) **gathering** (collecting; bringing together) **fruit into a life having the source, character and qualities of the Age** (eonian life; life of, for and in the ages; eon-lasting life), **so that the one habitually** (or: progressively) **sowing and the one habitually reaping** (or: repeatedly harvesting) **may be continually rejoicing together [in the same place or at the same time],**

37. **"for within this [relation, respect, or, matter] the message** (or: Logos; saying; thought; verbal expression; word) **is genuinely true** (dependable; real; [other MSS: the truth]), **'The one is habitually sowing, and another is habitually reaping** (or: One is the sower, and another the harvester).'

38. **"I, Myself, sent you men off as commissioned agents** (or: representatives; emissaries) **to be constantly harvesting** (or: reaping) **[a crop] for which you folks have not labored, so as to be wearied from toil; others, of the same kind, have done the hard labor and are weary** (tired) **from the toil, and you men have entered into their labor** [i.e., into the results and fruit of their work and have thus benefited from it; = entered into the midst, joining with and fulfilling their labor]."

39. **Now many of the Samaritans from out of that city believed and put their trust into Him through the word** (the message; the communication) **of the woman constantly bearing witness that, "He said to me everything which** [others: as much as] **I did** (or: He tells me all things that I do)!"

40. **Therefore, as the Samaritans came toward** (or: to; face to face with) **Him, they began asking, and kept on begging, Him to continue remaining** (or: dwelling) **with them** (or: at their side). **So He stayed** (or: remained; dwells) **there two days.**

41. **And now many more folks believe through** (or: And so many people, in and by much [evidence], placed their trust, because of) **His word** (Logos; message; thought; communication; flow of information),

42. **and were saying to the woman, "We are no longer having faith, believing or trusting because of what you said** (your speaking; your speech), **for we ourselves have listened and heard from Him, and have seen to become aware and thus know that this One truly** (really; genuinely; actually) **is the Deliverer** (Rescuer; Savior; Healer and Restorer to health and wholeness) **of the world**
    (of the aggregate of humanity; of the ordered system of culture, religion, economy and
    government; or: of, or from, the dominating and controlling System; of the cosmos; or: = of all
    mankind), **the Christ** (the Anointed One; [= the Messiah])."

43. **Now, after the two days, He went out from there into the Galilee [area],**

44. **for you see, Jesus, Himself, bore witness** (or: testifies) **that a prophet** (one with light ahead of time) **continues to hold no honor** (or: is not in the habit of having value or worth; is not respected or rightly evaluated) **within his own country** (or: fatherland; native land).
45. **Now then, when He comes into the Galilee [district], the Galileans at once receive and welcome Him, being folks having seen everything: as many things as He did** (performed; produced) **at the Feast in Jerusalem – for they themselves, also, went into the festival** (Feast).
46. **So Jesus went back again into Cana, of the Galilee [area], where He made the water [to be] wine.**
Now there was a certain royal officer (king's courtier; or: relative of the king; royal one) **whose son was continuing sick** (infirm; without strength in a chronic ailment) **within Capernaum.**
47. **This man, upon hearing that Jesus is presently arriving from out of Judea into the Galilee [district], went off toward Him and began asking and kept on begging Him so that He would walk down** (or: descend) **at once and instantly heal** (or: cure) **his son, for he was progressing in being about to be dying** (or: was at the point of death).
48. **However, Jesus says to him, "Unless you folks see miraculous signs and unusual events** (wonders; portents; omens), **you people can in no way** (or: would under no circumstances) **trust, have confidence, believe or faith-it."**
49. **The royal officer** (courtier; king's attendant or relative) **continues, saying to Him, "Lord** (or: Sir; Master), **walk down** (or: descend) **at once, before my little boy dies!"**
50. **Jesus then says to him, "Be proceeding on your way** (or: Depart and continue traveling). **Your son continues living." The man trusts by, and believes in, the word** (Logos; message; statement; conveyed information) **which Jesus spoke to** (in; for) **him, and so he began proceeding on his way.**
51. **Now by** (or: during) **the time of his steadily descending, his slaves meet him, and so they report, saying that his boy continues living.**
52. **He then inquired from them the hour within which he began to better hold himself** (or: started to have better health; held a turn to a more trim and improved condition), **and they then said to him, "Yesterday [at the] seventh hour, the fever released from him** (or: let go away from him; divorced and abandoned him; emitted from him; flowed off him; [note: this verb is often translated "forgive"])**."**
53. **Then the father knew by this experience that [it was] in that hour within which Jesus said to him, "Your son continues living." And so, he himself believes** (or: experiences trust; or: held conviction; or: was loyal, with faith) **and, later, his whole household.**
54. **Now this, again, [is; was] a second sign [which] Jesus makes** (or: did; performed; produces), **upon coming from out of Judea into the Galilee [district].**

CHAPTER 5

1. **After these things there was a festival** (or: Feast) **pertaining to the religion and culture of the Jews, and Jesus went up into Jerusalem.**
2. **Now within Jerusalem, at the sheep gate [which is within the northern city wall], there is a constructed pool [for bathing or swimming] – the one being normally called** (or: named) **in Hebrew "Bethzatha"** (means: House of the Olive; [other MSS: Bethesda, which means: House of Mercy]) – **presently having five covered colonnades** (porticos; porches supported by columns).
   [note: that this structure existed when John wrote this (the verb is present tense) is evidence for this being written prior to A.D. 70 and the destruction of Jerusalem]
3. **Within these and filling them [was] a crowd of the sick** (weak; infirm) **folks, of blind people, of those being lame** (crippled; or: missing a foot), **[and] of withered** (dried up) **folks** [A & later MSS add: periodically receiving (reaching in and taking out) from the moving (or: agitation) of the water].
[4.] [this vs. omitted by WH, Nestle-Aland, Tasker, Panin, following p66 & 75, Aleph, B & other MSS (also absent in Old Syriac, Coptic versions & Latin Vulgate); it is present in A & others: for an agent of {the} Lord used to on occasion (or: corresponding to a season; in accord with a fitting situation) descend (or: step down) within the bathing (or: swimming) pool and it was periodically agitating the water. Then the first one stepping in, after the agitation of the water, became sound and healthy – who was at any time being held down by the effect of a disease (or: sickness).]
5. **Now there was yet a certain man there, having continuously [spent] thirty-eight years within his illness** (weakness; infirmity).

6. **Jesus, having seen this man presently** (or: habitually) **lying [there], and intimately knowing** (or: knowing from personal experience) **that he already continues having [spent] much time [thus], He says to him, "Do you continue purposing to become sound in health?"** (or: "Are you habitually intending or presently wanting to become restored to your original healthy condition?")

7. **The ill** (infirm; weak) **man considered and answers Him, "Sir** (or: Lord; Master), **I do not regularly have a man, to the end that he should cast me into the pool whenever the water may be disturbed** (or: stirred up; or, perhaps: = rippled by a wind). **But within which [time, or, situation] I [by] myself am in progress of coming** (or: going), **another one is always stepping down** (or: descending) **before me!"**

8. **Jesus then says to him, "Get on up** (or: Proceed to rise up), **pick up your pallet** (or: mat; cot) **and go to walking about!"**

9. **And immediately the man becomes sound and healthy, and he was raised up** (or: was aroused), **and at once takes up his pallet** (or: mat; cot) **and began walking about.**
    – now it was a sabbath on that day –

10. **The Judeans** (= religious authorities) **therefore, were saying to the man having been attended and cured** (having received the therapy and healing), **"It is sabbath** (or: It is a sabbath), **and it is not permitted, from [our] existence, for you to lift up or carry the pallet** (mat; cot)**."**

11. **Yet he considered and answers them, "The one making me sound and healthy: that one said to me, 'Pick up your pallet** (mat; cot) **and go to walking about.'"**

12. **They then asked him, "Who is the person** (or: fellow), **the one saying to you, 'Pick it up and go to walking about'?"**

13. **Now he, being the one being healed, had not perceived so as to know who He is, for Jesus, as a swimmer turning his head to the side, slipped out of the crowd being [there], within the place.**

14. **After these things, Jesus is presently finding him within the temple grounds** (or: courts), **and says to him, "Consider** (See; Take note), **you have come to be sound and healthy! No longer continue in error** (or: Do not further make it a habit to stray from the goal), **so that something worse may not happen to you** (or: to the end that something worse should not come to be in you)."

15. **The man then went away and told** [other MSS: informed] **the Judeans** (= religious authorities) **that Jesus is the one making him sound in health,**

16. **so on this account the Judeans** (= religious authorities) **kept in hostile pursuit and were persecuting Jesus** [other MSS add: and were seeking to kill Him], **because He kept on doing these things on a sabbath.**

17. **But Jesus decidedly answers them, "My Father is continuously working and keeps on being in action until the present moment** (or: up to right now); **I, Myself, also am continually working** (or: and so I, Myself, continue active, regularly performing in [His] trade)." [thus: it was not God's sabbath]

18. **On this account, therefore, the Jews** (= the religious authorities) **were all the more continuing in seeking to kill Him off, because not only was He habitually loosing and destroying** (or: breaking down; dismantling) **the sabbath, but further, He was also repeatedly saying that God [is] His own Father – making Himself equal to God** (or: casting Himself as the same thing as God; constructing Himself as even, on the same level, in God; formulating Himself as an equal with, or in, the Deity).

19. **Jesus therefore considered and replied, and began saying to them, "It is certainly so** (Amen, amen; It is so, it is so)! **I am now saying to you folks [that] the Son continues unable to do anything from Himself** (or: the Son, from Himself, habitually has no power to be doing anything [independently]) **except He can** (or: unless He should) **continue seeing something the Father is in process of doing** (or: if not something He may presently observe the Father making, producing, constructing, or creating), **for what things That One may likely be progressively doing** (making; constructing; creating; producing), **these things, also, the Son is likewise habitually doing** (or: is in like manner constantly making, producing, creating, constructing). [cf Heb. 4:3, 9; Isa. 11:10]

20. **"You see, the Father likes the Son** (or: continuously has affection for and expresses friendship to the Son) **and habitually points out** (constantly shows; progressively exhibits) **to Him** (or: in Him; or: by Him) **everything** (or: all things) **which He is constantly doing, and He will continue exhibiting in Him greater works than these** (or: He will point out to Him greater acts than these), **to the end that you folks may be constantly amazed** (filled with astonishment and wonder).

21. **"For, just as the Father is habitually** (repeatedly; constantly; presently) **raising up the dead folks, and is repeatedly** (continually; presently) **making [them] alive, thus also, the Son is habitually** (constantly; presently) **making alive which ones He is presently intending** (willing; purposing).
22. **"So it follows that, neither is the Father presently** (progressively; constantly) **separating and making a decision about** (evaluating; judging) **anyone, but rather, He has given all sifting and decision-making in the Son** (or: has granted all judging by the Son; has handed over all evaluating of issues to the Son),
23. **"to the end that everyone** (or: all humans) **may and can continuously be honoring the Son** (or: would habitually value, and constantly find worth in, the Son), **correspondingly as they are** (or: may be) **continually honoring the Father. The one not habitually honoring** (valuing; finding worth in) **the Son is not habitually honoring** (valuing; finding worth in) **the Father – the One sending Him.**
24. **"Most certainly** (Amen, amen), **I continue saying to you folks, that the person habitually listening to, repeatedly hearing and normally paying attention to My Word** (or: My message; the communication of the information, thought and idea from Me; the laid out concept {*Logos*}, which is Me), **and continuously trusting by** (or: progressively believing in; habitually being loyal to; faithing-it with) **the One sending Me, presently continues holding** (is progressively possessing; is continuously having) **eonian life** (life having the quality of the Age [of the Messiah]; age-lasting and eon-enduring life; life having its source in the Age; or perhaps: = life of the coming age), **and is not repeatedly coming into a separating or a deciding** (an evaluating; a judging), **but rather, he has proceeded** (has changed his place of residence; has changed his walk; has stepped over to another place) **forth from out of the midst of 'the Death,' into 'the Life,' and now exists in the midst of 'the Life.'**
25. **"Count on it** (Amen, amen), **I am presently continuing to say to you folks that an hour is progressively** (or: presently in process of) **coming, and even now exists** (or: = is now here), **when the dead folks WILL be repeatedly hearing the voice of God's Son** (or: the Voice from, and which is, the Son of God; or: the voice of the Son, Who is God), **and the ones hearing WILL proceed to be living!**
26. **"You see, just as the Father continuously holds** (or: constantly has) **Life within Himself, thus also, He gives in the Son** (or: to the Son) **to be continuously holding** (or: constantly having; progressively possessing) **Life within Himself,**
27. **"And He gives in Him** (or: to Him; for Him) **authority** (or: the right; the privilege; or: out of [His] essence and Being) **to be habitually separating and deciding** (to be constantly sifting and evaluating; to continuously be judging [issues]), **because He is a son humanity** (= because He is human – a member of the human race [= Adam's Son]; or: = because He exists being [the] eschatological Messiah).
28. **"Don't you folks be constantly amazed at this, because an hour is progressively** (or: presently; or: repeatedly) **coming within which all the people within the memorial tombs** (or: graves) **– will be continuously or repeatedly hearing His voice** (or: the Voice from, and the Sound which, is Him).
29. **"and they will proceed journeying out: the ones doing virtue** (producing, making or constructing good) **into a resurrection which is Life** (or: of, from, and with the quality of, Life); **the ones practicing careless** (base, worthless, cheap, slight, paltry, inefficient, thoughtless, common or mean) **things into a resurrection of separating and evaluation for a deciding** (or: a resurrection which is a judging).
30. **"I, Myself, am continually unable** (or: As for Me, I habitually have no power or ability) **to be doing anything from Myself: correspondingly as I am continuously hearing, I am habitually sifting, separating, evaluating and deciding** (or: judging), **and My deciding** (separating and evaluating; judging) **is right and just** (continues being in accord with the Way pointed out and is turned in the right direction of fairness, equity, justice and right relationship), **because I am not seeking My own will** (intent; purpose), **but rather the purpose** (intent; will) **of the One sending Me.**
31. **"If I, Myself, should be giving testimony** (can by habit witness or make claims) **about Myself, is My claim** (or: evidence and testimony) **not valid and true?** (or: My claim is not true or valid [by your standards]).
32. **"There is Another, of the same kind. He is presently** (or: constantly) **bearing witness** (testifying; giving evidence) **about Me, and I have seen, and thus know, that the claim which He is bearing witness about Me is valid and true** (or: credible).
33. **"You folks have dispatched [men] to John, and he has borne witness to the Truth** (or: testified by the Truth; made confirmation in the Truth; attested with reality),
34. **"yet, for Myself, I am not by habit taking the witness** (or: receiving testimony or claim) **from a person** (from [the] side of a human), **but rather, I presently say these things to the end that you folks**

yourselves may be delivered (or: could and would be rescued, saved, made healthy and whole, and restored to your original condition).

35. **"That person was continuing being the continuously burning** (ignited; lighted) **and constantly shining lamp, and you folks yourselves, for a short time** (for an hour), **want** (or: purposed) **to exult and rejoice in its light** (or: centered within his light).

36. **"Yet I, Myself, constantly hold** (or: am continuously having) **the Witness** (or: the evidence) **[that is] greater and more important than [that] from John** (or: the greater testimony compared to the one that John gives), **for the works** (or: actions; deeds) **which the Father has given in Me** (to Me; for Me; by Me) **– to the end that I may bring them to the goal** (finish, mature and perfect them to their destined purpose) **– the works themselves** (or: these same actions) **which I am continuously doing** (performing; producing) **continuously bear witness** (testify; make claim; give evidence) **about Me, that the Father has sent Me forth with a commission** (as a Representative, or Emissary).

37. **"Also, the One sending Me, that Father, has borne witness** (has testified) **about Me. You folks have neither heard His voice at any time, nor have you seen** (or: perceived) **His external appearance** (shape; figure of what is seen; = what He looks like),

38. **"and further, you people are not holding or possessing His** *Logos* **(His Message; His communication of His Thought and Idea; What has been Laid Out from Him; the Word which is Him) remaining** (or: dwelling) **continuously within you** (or: and you are not having His Word or Information abiding continually among you folks), **because Whom That One sent forth with a commission** (or: as a Representative) **in** (to) **This One you people are not presently trusting, believing** (showing loyalty).

39. **"You folks continuously search** (or, as an imperative: Be constantly searching) **the Scriptures, because within them you yourselves are habitually presuming to be presently and continuously holding eonian life**

> (or: because you folks are normally supposing for yourselves to be habitually having – in union with them – life pertaining to, and having the qualities and characteristics of, the Age [perhaps: = the life of the coming age]), **and those [Scriptures] are** (exist being) **the ones continuously testifying about Me** (constantly giving evidence concerning and bearing witness around Me).

40. **"And yet you people continue not willing** (or: presently refuse and habitually do not intend) **to come toward** (or: to; face to face with) **Me, so that you may presently be having Life** (or: would continuously take hold of and possess [this] life).

41. **"I have no habit of receiving glory from humans** (or: I am not continuing to take a reputation at the side of people, nor do I normally get opinions from [them]),

42. **"but rather, I have come to know you folks by personal experience, that you people do not continuously hold** (or: do not presently have) **God's love** (or: the urge toward reunion from, and which is, God; or: love and acceptance from, and pertaining to, God) **within yourselves.**

43. **"Now I, Myself, have come within my Father's Name, and you folks are not proceeding to receive Me; if another one may come within his own name, you will proceed to receive that one.**

44. **"How are you folks, yourselves, able to trust or believe, when habitually getting a reputation and receiving fame** (or: repeatedly taking opinions and glory) **from one another, and yet you folks are not constantly seeking the glory** (or: the reputation, opinion or manifestation which calls forth praise; or: the assumed appearance) **which comes from the only God** (or: from God alone)?

45. **"Stop thinking** (supposing; presuming; having opinions) **that I, Myself, will publicly speak down against** (or: accuse) **you folks to the Father; the one constantly accusing** (publicly speaking down against) **you people is** (or: exists being) **Moses, into whom you folks have put your expectation, and on whom you now rely.**

46. **"For if you folks had been trusting by, adhering to, having loyalty for and believing in Moses, you would have been trusting by, adhering to and believing in Me: for that one wrote about Me!**

47. **"Yet if you are not habitually trusting by, adhering to, having loyalty for and believing in that one's writings, how will [other MSS: do] you folks continue to trust by, have loyalty for, adhere to and believe in My sayings** (or: My declarations; My gush-effects; the results from flows in Me)?"

CHAPTER 6

1. **After these things** (= Sometime later), **Jesus went away to the other side of the Sea** (or: Lake) **of Galilee, the [area] pertaining to Tiberias.**

2. **Now a large crowd kept following Him, because they had been attentively viewing the signs which He had been doing** (making; constructing; creating; performing; producing) **upon those who were sick** (without strength; infirm; ill).

3. **So Jesus went back up into the mountain, and was continuing sitting there with His disciples.**

4. **– Now the Passover, the Feast** (or: festival) **of the Judeans** (from the Jewish culture and religion), **was drawing near –**

5. **Then, lifting up His eyes and observing that a large crowd was progressively coming toward Him, Jesus then says to Philip, "From what place may we purchase loaves of bread so that these folks may eat?"**

6. **– Now he was saying this in process of testing him**
(putting him to the proof; [note: the verb can also mean: to attempt; to try something. Was Jesus perhaps here "teasing" Philip?]), **for He had seen, and thus knew what He was being about to progressively do –**

7. **Philip considered and answered Him, "Two hundred denarii** [note: a denarius = a day's pay for a laborer, thus = about eight months' wages] **worth of loaves are not continuing adequate** (enough; sufficient) **so that each one might receive** (get; take) **a little** (a short piece).**"**

8. **One of His disciples, Andrew, the brother of Simon Peter, then says to Him,**

9. **"There is a young lad** (little boy; young fellow; or: servant; or: lass; young woman) **here who presently has five loaves of barley bread, and two small cooked** (or: dried) **fishes, but what are these unto** (or: for) **so many?"**

10. **Jesus says, "You guys make the people recline back, as at a meal." – Now there was a lot of grass and plants in the area** (or: the place) **– Therefore the adult men reclined back, about five thousand in number.**

11. **Then Jesus took the loaves and, expressing gratitude** (giving thanks; or: speaking well-being, favor and grace), **He distributes [it] to those presently lying back. Likewise, also from out of the small cooked fishes – as much as they wanted.**

12. **Now as they are being filled within and satisfied, He then says to His disciples, "Gather together** (or: Collect) **the excessive abundance of broken pieces** (fragments; or: crumbs), **to the end that nothing may be lost."**

13. **Therefore, they gathered** (or: collected) **[them] together and filled twelve wicker baskets of broken pieces** (fragments; or: crumbs) **from out of the five loaves of barley bread which were over-abounded to the folks having eaten.**

14. **Then the people, seeing the signs which Jesus did, began to say** (or: kept on saying), **"This One is truly** (or: really) **The Prophet – the One periodically** (or: presently) **coming into the organized system** (or: the world of culture, religion and government; or: the aggregate of humanity).**"**

15. **Jesus, therefore – experientially and intimately knowing** (or: coming to perceive) **that they are presently about to be coming and to proceed snatching Him away** (seizing and forcefully taking Him away) **to the end that they may make [Him] king – withdrew Himself, alone, back up** (or: retires; leaves the area and goes back up) **again into the mountain** (or: hill country).

16. **Now as it came to be evening, His disciples walked down** (or: descended) **upon the sea [shore],**

17. **and then, stepping within a boat** (or: boarding a small fishing craft), **they began going and continued coming to the other side of the sea** (or: lake), **unto Capernaum.**
Now it had come to be dim with darkness already (= it had grown dark) **– and Jesus had still not** (or: not yet) **gone toward them –**

18. **and now the sea** (or: lake) **was being progressively roused and stirred up from a great wind continuously** (or: progressively) **blowing.**

19. **Then, having been rowing forward about twenty-five or thirty stadia** (= three or four miles), **they noticed and kept on intently watching Jesus continuously walking around upon the sea** (or: lake; or, perhaps: = along the shore) **and progressively coming to be near the boat, and they became afraid** (or: were made to be terrified)!

20. **Yet He then says to them, "I am!** (or: It is I.) **Stop fearing!** (or: Don't continue being afraid.)**"**

21. **Then they began to be willing and proceeded purposing to receive** (or: take) **Him into the boat. And immediately** (or: instantly; all at once) **the boat came to be upon the land** (perhaps: = ran aground) **into which they had been proceeding under way.**

22. **The next day** (or: On the morrow) **the crowd – the one having stood, and still standing, on the other side of the sea** (or: lake) **– saw that there was no other little boat there, except one, and that Jesus did not enter in together with His disciples, but rather His disciples went** (or: came) **away alone.**
23. **And further, boats from out of Tiberias came near the place where they ate the bread, from the Lord giving thanks** (or: upon expressing gratitude, they ate the bread of the Master [or: = Yahweh]).
24. **Therefore, when the crowd saw that Jesus is not there, nor His disciples, they stepped within – into the little boats – and went into Capernaum, progressively seeking Jesus.**
25. **And later, upon finding Him – on the other side of the sea** (or: lake) **– they said to Him, "Rabbi, when** (or: at what time) **have you come to be here** (or: in this place)**?"**
26. **Jesus decidedly answered them, and says, "It is certainly true** (Amen, amen), **I am saying to you folks, you people continue seeking Me not because you saw signs, but rather because you ate from out of the loaves, and you were fed until satisfied.**
27. **"Stop continuously working or doing business for the food which is continuously disintegrating of itself** (loosing itself away; destroying itself), **but rather [for] the Food continuously remaining** (abiding; dwelling) **on into eonian Life**

> (or: unto life originating from, existing in, having the characteristics and qualities of, the Age [of Messiah]; age-enduring and eon-lasting life) **which the Son of the Man** (of Humanity; of the

human; of [Adam]; or: = the Human Being; or: = the eschatological messianic figure) **will continue giving to you** (or: in you; for you) **folks, for This One** (or: This Man) **Father God seals**

> (or: for God, the Father, put [His] seal [showing ownership and/or approval and/or authority] upon a person [doing] this; or: you see, this One the Father sealed: God)**."**

28. **Then they said to Him, "What should we be habitually doing, so that we would be habitually working God's works** (or: actions or labors having the character of, or pertaining to, God; or: the deeds from God; or: = the things God wants us to do)**?"**
29. **Jesus considered and answered, saying to them, "This is God's Work** (the Action which is God; the Deed from God), **so that you folks would continuously trust and progressively believe into** (or: the work of God: that you can remain faithful unto) **Him whom That One sends** (or: sent) **forth with a mission."**
30. **So then they say to Him, "Then what sign are you yourself doing** (making; performing; producing), **so that we can see and believe in** (or: trust and have faith by; be loyal to) **you? What are you, yourself, presently accomplishing** (or: actively working; habitually practicing)**?**
31. **"Our fathers ate manna within the wilderness** (in the desolate place of the desert), **according as it stands written, 'He gave to them bread from out of the atmosphere** (or: the sky; heaven) **to habitually eat.'"** [Ps. 78:24]
32. **Therefore Jesus says to them, "Count on this** (Amen, amen)**: I am now [emphatically] saying to you folks, Moses did NOT give the bread from out of the atmosphere** (or: the sky; heaven) **to YOU folks! But rather, My Father is presently** (or: continually; progressively) **giving the true, real, genuine Bread from out of the heaven** (or: the atmosphere) **to, for and among you people.**
33. **"For God's Bread is** (or: You see the bread which is God, and comes from God, exists being) **the One repeatedly descending** (continually or habitually stepping down) **from out of the midst of the atmosphere** (or: heaven) **and constantly** (or: habitually and progressively) **giving Life to the world** (or: in the organized system and secular society; or: for the aggregate of humanity and in the universe)**."**
34. **Therefore they exclaimed to Him, "O Master** (or: Sir; Lord), **always and ever give this bread to us!"**
35. **Jesus said to them, "I, Myself, am** (or: exist being) **the Bread of 'the Life'** (or: the bread which is the Life, and which imparts the Life). **The person progressively coming toward** (or: to; or: face to face with) **Me may by no means at any point hunger** (or: would under no circumstances be hungry), **and the one constantly trusting and believing into** (or being habitually allegiant and loyal unto) **Me will by no means continue thirsting** (under no circumstances be repeatedly thirsty) **at any time.**

36. **"But further, I say to you that you folks have also seen Me, and yet you continue not trusting or believing** [Concordant Greek Text adds: Me].

37. **"All, which** (may = whom [so, D.B. Hart]) **the Father is progressively giving to Me, will progressively move toward** (will one-after-another keep on coming face-to-face with) **Me to finally arrive here, and the person progressively coming toward Me I may under no circumstances** (or: would by no means) **throw forth from out of the midst** (eject; cast out) **[so that he will be] outside,**

38. **"because I have stepped down to this level, away from the atmosphere** (or: descended, separating off from the heaven), **not to the end that I should continue doing My will** (purpose; intent), **but to the contrary, the will** (intent; purpose) **of the One sending Me.**

39. **"Now this is the purpose** (intent; will) **of the One sending Me: that all that** (or: everything which) **He has given to Me, so that it is now Mine, I will proceed to** (or, as an aorist subjunctive: may; can; should; would) **lose nothing from out of it, but further, I will proceed to** (or: should; would) **raise it up to, in and with This Last Day** (or: by the Last Day; for the final Day).

40. **"You see, this is the purpose** (will; intent) **of My Father, to the end and intent that all mankind – which, in continuously watching** (or: the one repeatedly gazing at) **the Son, in contemplative discernment, and then progressively trusting** (believing) **into Him – would possess** (or: can have; may hold) **Life, Whose source is the Age** (or: eonian life; life having the qualities and characteristics of the Age [of Messiah]; an age-enduring and eon-lasting life), **and I will proceed to** (or: can; should; would) **be raising him up to and for this last Day** (or: in the Last Day; by and with the final day)." [note: on "watching/gazing at," cf Rev. 14:10, beholding the little Lamb, in His presence; Nu. 21:8-9]

41. **Therefore the Judeans** (= religious authorities of the Jews) **began a buzz of discontented complaining and critical comments, and were progressively murmuring like a swarm of bees concerning Him, because He said, "I, Myself, am** (or: exist being) **the Bread – the One stepping down** (or: descending) **from out of the midst of the heaven** (or: the atmosphere),"

42. **and they kept on saying, "Is this not Jesus, the son of Joseph, whose father and mother we have seen and know? How** [other MSS: How then] **is he now presently saying that 'I have stepped down** (or: descended) **from out of the midst of the heaven** (or: the sky)'?"**

43. **Jesus decidedly answered, and says to them, "Stop the grumbling buzz of murmuring** (undertoned mutterings of critical and discontented comments like a swarm of bees) **with one another!**

44. **"No one is able** (or: is presently having power) **to come toward Me unless the Father – the One sending Me – should drag him [as with a net]** (or: draw him [as drawing water in a bucket or a sword from its sheath]), **and I Myself will progressively raise him up** (proceed to resurrect him; continue standing him back up again) **within** (or: in union with) **this Last** (the eschatos) **Day.** [Cf vs. 65, below]

45. **"It exists having been written within the Prophets: 'And all humans** (all people) **will continue existing being God's taught-ones** (or: folks having had instruction from God).' [Isa. 54:13] **All humanity – which, in hearing from the Father** (or: the person listening at the Father's side), **and learning** [D and others read: progressively learning] **– is progressively coming toward Me!**

46. **"Not that anyone has seen the Father, except the person continuously being at God's side** (or: existing from God) **– this person** (or: One) **has seen the Father.**

47. **"It is certainly true** (or: Amen, amen), **I am saying to you folks, the person presently and continuously trusting** (or: constantly believing; progressively faithing-it; continuing loyal) **presently and continuously has and holds eonian Life** (life having its source, qualities and characteristics from the Age [of the Messiah]; age-enduring and eon-lasting life; or: = the life of the coming Age)!

48. **"I, Myself, am** (or: continuously exist being) **the 'Bread of the Life'** (or: the bread which is life and which gives and imparts life),

49. **"– your fathers ate the manna within the wilderness** (desert; desolate place), **and they died.**

50. **"This is** (or: continuously exists being) **the Bread which is repeatedly** (or: constantly) **stepping down from out of the atmosphere** (or: progressively descending from heaven) **to the end that ANYONE may eat from out of It and not die** (or: he can, or would, not die; [B reads: and he can continue not dying]).

51. **"I, Myself, am** (or: continuously exist being) **the continuously living Bread – the One stepping down** (or: descending) **from out of the midst of the atmosphere** (or: heaven). **If anyone should eat from out of this Bread, he will continue living on into the Age. Now also, the Bread which I, Myself, will continue giving, over** (or: for the sake of; on behalf of) **the life of the world** (the ordered

system; or: = 'the totality of human social existence' – Walter Wink; or: the aggregate of humanity), **is** (or: continuously exists being) **My flesh!"**

52. **Therefore, the Jews** (= religious authorities of Judea) **began violently arguing** (disputing; warring [with words]) **toward one another, constantly saying, "How is this one presently able to give us his flesh to eat?"**
53. **Then Jesus said to them, "Most truly** (Amen, amen) **I am now laying out the arrangement for** (or: saying to) **you people: unless you folks should at some point eat the flesh of the Son of the Human** (the Son of man; = the eschatological messianic figure), **and then would drink His blood** (or: since you would not eat the flesh which is the Human Being, and further, drink His blood), **you are continuing not holding** (or: habitually having or presently possessing) **Life within yourselves!**
54. **"The person habitually eating** (continuously chewing or masticating) **My flesh and drinking My blood is continuously possessing** (habitually holding; progressively having) **eonian Life** (life derived from and having the qualities of the Age; age-enduring and eon-lasting life), **and I Myself will proceed raising, resurrecting and standing him back up again in this Last Day** (or: for and by the last Day),
55. **"for My flesh is** (or: constantly exists being) **true** (real; genuine) **food, and My blood is** (or: continuously exists being) **true** (real; genuine) **drink.**
56. **"The person habitually eating** (constantly chewing [on]) **My flesh and repeatedly drinking My blood is continuously remaining** (abiding; dwelling) **within, and in union with, Me – and I Myself within, and in union with, him.** [*Cf* 15:1ff, below]
57. **"Just as** (or: In corresponding accordance as) **the continuously-living Father sent Me off** (or: forth) **as an Emissary** (or: commissions Me as a Representative and sends Me on a mission), **and I Myself am continuously living through** (or: because of) **the Father, likewise the person who is habitually eating** (repeatedly chewing and feeding [on]) **Me, that person will also continue living, through** (or: because of; by means of) **Me.**
58. **"This is** (or: continuously exists being) **the Bread: the One stepping down** (or: descending) **from out of the midst of heaven** (or: [the] sky and atmosphere) **– not according as the fathers ate and died. The person habitually eating** (continually chewing and feeding [on]) **this Bread will continue living** [*p*66 & others read middle: will in (or: of) himself continue living; D reads present: is continuously living] **on into the Age."**
59. **He said these things, while repeatedly teaching within a synagogue in Capernaum.**

60. **Therefore, many from out of His students** (the learners following His teachings), **upon hearing [this], said, "This word** (message; saying; thought; idea; communicated information) **is hard and rough – who is able to continue hearing from it** (or: listening to its [message])?"
61. **Now Jesus, knowing from having seen within Himself that His students** (disciples) **are continuing to buzz in discontented complaint** (murmur; grumble; hold puzzled conversations) **about this** (or: around this [subject]), **says to them, "Is this continuing to trip you folks up** (or: Is this now snaring or trapping you; or: = Is this a problem for you)?
62. **"Suppose, then, you could continuously watch** (contemplatively gaze at) **the Son of Mankind** (the Son of the Human; = the Human Being; messianic figure) **progressively stepping back up again** (or: presently ascending) **to where He was being before** (or: continued existing formerly)!
63. **"The Spirit** (or: Breath-effect; or: spirit; Breath; Attitude) **is** (or: continues being) **the One continuously creating Life** (or: repeatedly making alive; habitually forming life). **The flesh continues being of no help or benefit to anything** (furthers or augments not one thing). **The declarations** (gush-effects; spoken words; sayings; results of the Flow) **which I, Myself, have spoken to you folks are** (or: continue to be) **Spirit** (or: spirit; Breath-effect; attitude) **and they are** (or: continue being) **Life.**
64. **"But in contrast, there continue being some from among you folks who are not continuing faithful or habitually trusting** (or: not presently believing)." **For Jesus had seen, and thus knew from the beginning, which ones are those not habitually trusting or remaining faithful** (or: not presently believing), **and who is the one proceeding to transfer, commend and commit Him** (or: hand Him over).
65. **So he went on saying, "Because of this I have told you folks that no one is presently able** (or: continues having power) **to come toward** (or: face-to-face with) **Me, unless [the situation] may be**

existing of it having been granted or given to him from out of the Father (or: unless he or she should be a person having been given in Him, forth from the Father)."

66. **From out of this [saying, or, circumstance], therefore, many from out of His [group] of students went away into the things back behind** (or: went off to the rear) **and then were no longer continuing to walk about** (or: travel around; = make a way of life) **with Him.**

67. **Then Jesus says to the twelve, "You men also are not wanting** (or: intending) **to be going away** (or: to progressively withdraw), **are you?"**

(or: "Don't you men want to leave, too?")

68. **Then Simon Peter decidedly gave answer to Him, "O Lord** (Master; Owner), **toward whom shall we proceed to go away? You continue holding** (or: constantly have; habitually hold [out]) **gush-effects of eonian Life** (sayings and declarations of life whose source and origin are the Age [of Messiah]; results of the flows of things spoken pertaining to life of, in and for the ages)!

69. **– and we ourselves have trusted and are now convinced so as to now be believing, and we by personal, intimate experience have come to know that You, Yourself, ARE** (or: continuously exist being) **God's Holy One** (or: the Sacred One from God; the Set-apart One which is God)."

70. **Jesus considered and gave answer to them, "Do I Myself not select and pick you out – the twelve – for Myself** (or: Did I not choose you twelve Myself)? **And one from among you men is a person who thrusts things through [situations, or, people]** (or: is a devil)!"

71. **Now, He was speaking of Judah** (or: Judas), **[son] of Simon Iscariot, for you see, this person – one from among** [other MSS: being a part of] **the twelve – continued in being about to proceed in transferring, commending, and to keep on committing, Him** (or: to continue in handing Him over).

CHAPTER 7

1. **And after these things, Jesus continued walking about** (moved around) **within the Galilee [area], for He was not intending** (willing; purposing) **to be walking around within Judea, because the Jews** (or: the Judeans; or: = authorities of the second temple Jewish religion/culture of Judea, and its representatives) **had been trying to find Him** (seeking Him; searching for Him), **to kill Him off.**

2. **Now [the season for] the Jew's Feast of Tabernacles** (*Sukkoth*: the festival of Trumpets, the day of Atonement, and the erecting Booths, or pitching tents, which pertained to the culture and religion of the Jews) **was drawing near.**

3. **Therefore His brothers said to Him, "Change your steps from this place, and go away into Judea, so that your disciples will** [other MSS: can; might] **continue watching and thoughtfully observing your work** [= the miracles] **which you are habitually doing,**

4. **"for no one is in the habit of doing anything within a hidden place** (in hiding; under concealment) **and at the same time seeking for himself to be in public openness. If** (or: Since) **you continue doing these things, show yourself in clear light to the world** (cause yourself to be seen by the system [= the religious, cultural and political organizations of the area] and the aggregate of people)."

5. **– you see, not even were His brothers putting their trust into Him, and were still unbelieving –**

6. **Therefore, Jesus is presently saying to them, "My season** (My fitting situation; My *kairos*; My appointed occasion; My fertile moment) **is not yet existing at My side** (is not yet present or here), **yet your season** (the fitting situation belonging to you folks) **is always prepared and ready.**

7. **"The world** (The System; The organization; = the controlling religious, cultural and political society) **is not presently able to be habitually hating you** (to continue radically detaching from and regarding you with ill-will), **yet it is constantly hating and progressively detaching from Me, because I Myself am habitually giving testimony about it** (or: continuously bearing witness and showing evidence concerning it) **that its works are continuously unwholesome** (laborious and such that put others to trouble; apt to shrewd turns; mischievous; wicked; unsound; malignant; gushed with misery).

8. **"You men walk on up into the Feast** (or: festival). **I, Myself, am not yet walking up into the midst of** (= to be a focal point of) **this feast** (or: festival), **because My season** (or: fitting situation; fertile moment) **has not yet been fulfilled** (made full; filled up)."

9. **Now, after saying these things to them, He remained within the Galilee [area].**

10. **Yet, after** (seeing as) **His brothers walked up into the feast** (or: festival), **then later He Himself walked up, not as in clear light** (or: as clearly visible), **but rather, as within a hidden situation.**

11. **Then, the Judeans** (= religious authorities of the Jewish religion, and of Judea) **began persistently looking for Him within the festival, and they kept on saying, "Where is that man?!"**

12. **And there continued being a lot of subdued talk and perplexed buzzing** (murmuring) **about Him within the crowds. Some, on the one hand, kept on saying that "He is a good man** (a virtuous one)**." On the other hand, others were saying "No, to the contrary, he continues misleading** (deceiving; leading astray) **the crowd."**

13. **Of course no one was in public openness** (or: with the boldness of a citizen) **speaking about Him, because of the fear [which they had] of the Jews** [i.e., the religious/political Judean leaders].

14. **Now with it already being in the middle of the Festival** (or: = half way through the feast), **Jesus walked up into the Temple grounds** (or: courts; porches; sanctuary area) **and began teaching.**

15. **The Jews** (= religious professionals of the Judeans) **were therefore surprised and kept on being amazed** (or: astonished), **saying, "How has this one seen, and thus known [the] writings, not being one having learned** [i.e., having studied at the schools, to be educated and articulate]**?"**

16. **Jesus therefore replied distinctly to them, and says, "My teaching is not My own, but rather belongs to and comes from the One sending Me.**

17. **"Should anyone be habitually wanting or intending to continuously be doing His will** (intent; purpose), **he will progressively come to know by intimate experience concerning the teaching – whether it is and continues being from out of the midst of God** (or: from that which is God), **or whether I am continuously babbling on, just uttering sounds or randomly talking from Myself.**

18. **"The one continuously speaking or randomly talking from himself is normally seeking his own reputation** (or: appearance; glory); **yet the One constantly seeking the reputation** (or: glory; appearance) **of the One sending Him, this One is true** (continues being genuine and real), **and dishonesty** (injustice; that which is contrary to fairness, equity and rightwised relationships in the Way pointed out) **does not exist within Him.**

19. **"Did not Moses give the Law** [= Torah] **to you folks? And yet not one from among you folks is habitually doing** (or: performing) **the Law! Why are you constantly seeking to kill Me?"**

20. **The crowd considered and replied, "You're demon-possessed** (or: You possess a demon; You constantly hold a demon; You presently have a demon [note: a Hellenistic concept and term: = animistic influence]; = you are out of your mind)**! Who is constantly seeking to kill you?"**

21. **Jesus decidedly answered, and said to them, "I did one work** (or: I do one act [= miracle]) **and you all continue being amazed** (shocked and stunned with wonder) **because of this.**

22. **"Moses has given the circumcision to you – not that its source is from out of Moses, but rather from out of the fathers** (= ancestors) **– and yet, within** (or: on) **a sabbath you folks habitually circumcise a man.**

23. **"If a person** (a human; a man) **is normally receiving circumcision within** (or: on) **a sabbath so that the Law of Moses may not be loosened so as to fall apart** (be untied or undone; be destroyed; = be broken), **are you constantly bitterly angry and progressively enraged** (literally: filled with bile) **with Me because I make** (or: made) **a whole man sound in health within** (or: on) **a sabbath?**

24. **"Do not be constantly judging** (or: Stop making decisions or evaluations) **according to sight** (= external appearance), **but rather be habitually making just decisions** (or: be judging with fair evaluating which accord with the Way pointed out; form rightwised conclusions)**."**

25. **Then some of the inhabitants of Jerusalem said, "Is not this one he whom they** (= the group of leaders) **are presently seeking to kill?**

26. **"And look! He continues speaking in public openness** (boldly as though being a citizen) **– and they continue saying nothing to him. The chief rulers** (or: "the authorities"; the ruling class) **have not at some point come to really know personally that this one is the Christ** (the Anointed One; = the Messiah), **have they?**

27. **"On the contrary, we have seen, and thus, we know this one – what place and source he is from. Yet whenever the Christ** (the Anointed One; = the Messiah) **should proceed in coming, no one is getting to know what place or source he is from."**

28. **Therefore Jesus cries out** (or: spoke in a loud voice), **as He is proceeding with teaching within the Temple grounds** (court yards; porches), **and continuing, says, "You have both seen and know Me, and you have seen and know where I am from** (or: what is my source). **And yet, I have not come from Myself** (= on My own initiative or authority). **On the contrary, the One sending Me is Real** (True; Genuine), **Whom you folks have not seen, neither know.**

29. **"I, Myself, have seen and know Him, because I am from His side** (or: I continuously exist being at His side and in His presence) **– and that One sent** (or: that One also sends) **Me forth as an Emissary with a mission** (as a Representative)."

30. **Then they began seeking to catch hold of and arrest** (or: seize) **Him – but still no one laid a hand upon Him, because His hour had not yet come.**

31. **Now many, from out of the crowd, came to believe and so put [their] trust into Him, and so they began and continued saying, "Whenever the Christ may come, He will proceed doing** (performing; making) **no more signs than this Man does** (or: did)!"

32. **So the Pharisees heard the crowd buzzing with these low-toned conversations about Him, and the chief priests and the Pharisees commissioned and dispatched officers** (deputies; those who act under orders; = temple guards) **to the end that they might catch hold of and arrest** (or: seize) **Him.**

33. **Then Jesus says, "I am still with you folks for a little time, and then I am progressively withdrawing, bringing things, under control, toward** (or: face-to-face with) **the One sending Me.**

34. **"You people will continue seeking to find Me, but you will not be coming across, discovering or finding Me – and where I, Myself, am existing** (or: in what place I Myself continue being), **you folks presently have no power to come** (or: continue unable to go)."

35. **Therefore, the Jews** (= the authorities) **said to themselves** (= toward each other), **"Where is this fellow about to proceed journeying, that we will not be finding him? He is not about to be traveling into the Dispersion, among the Greeks** (= Greek-speaking Jews; or: = all those having been absorbed into the Greek culture and civilization), **and to continue teaching the Greeks, is he?**

36. **"What is this word** (discourse; saying; communication; expression) **which he said, 'You people will continue seeking to find me, but you will not proceed to come across, discover or find me – and where I, myself, am** (or: in what place I continue being), **you folks presently have no power to come** (or: continue unable to go)'?"

37. **Now within the last day – the great one – of the Feast** (or: festival), **Jesus, after having taken a stand, stood and then suddenly cries out, saying, "If ever anyone may continue being thirsty, let him be habitually coming toward** (or: face-to-face with) **Me, and then let the person continuously trusting and progressively believing into Me be constantly** (habitually; repeatedly) **drinking!** [cf Isa. 12:3; 55:1]

> (or: let him be progressively coming to Me and keep on drinking. The person habitually being faithful unto Me,)

38. **"Just as the Scripture says, 'Rivers** (or: Floods; Torrents) **of living water will continuously flow** (or: gush; flood) **from out of the midst of His cavity** (His innermost being or part; or: the hollow of his belly; [used of the womb]).'"** [cf Isa. 58:11; Ezk. 47:1; Joel 3:18; Zech. 13:1; 14:8]

39. **Now this He said about** (or: with regard to) **the Breath-effect** (or: Spirit; Attitude; [other MSS: Holy, or set-apart Spirit; Sacred Wind]) **of which** (or: of Whom as a source; [other MSS simple read: which]) **they – those trusting and believing into Him – were about to be continuously and progressively receiving. You see, the Holy Spirit** (set-apart Breath-effect; Sacred Wind and Attitude) **was not yet being One having been given** [note: reading with B; with p66c, p75, Aleph, and others: for you see, there was not yet Spirit in existence; D* and three others: for there was not yet a Holy Spirit upon them; *Textus Receptus*: You see, [the] Holy Spirit was not yet being or existing], **because Jesus was not yet glorified** (given repute and an assumed appearance; made into a manifestation which induces praise).

40. **Then from out of the midst of the crowd,** [p66 and others read: many] **after hearing these words, they began saying, "This one is certainly** (really; truly) **The Prophet!"**

41. **Others began saying, "This one is the Christ** [= Messiah]!" **Yet they** [other MSS: But others] **continued saying, "Surely the Christ** (the Anointed One) **does not normally come** (or: is not presently coming) **from out of the Galilee [area]!**

42. **"Does not the Scripture say that the Christ** (the Anointed One; = Messiah) **is proceeding in** (or: normally) **coming from out of the seed of David** [2 Sam. 7:12], **and from Bethlehem** [Micah 5:2], **the village where David was?"**

43. **Therefore a split-effect** (a tearing division) **occurred** (came into being; developed) **within the crowd, because of Him.**

44. **So some of them were wanting** (intending; willing) **to catch hold of and arrest Him, but yet no one laid hands on Him.**

45. **Therefore the subordinate officials** (officers; deputies; those who act under orders) **went to the chief** (or: ranking) **priests and Pharisees, and so those fellows said to them, "Why** (Through what [situation; reason]) **did you not bring him** (or: Wherefore do you not lead him [here])**?"**

46. **Then the subordinate officials** (= temple guards, or police), **after consideration, replied, "Never** (Not even once) **did a human** (a person; a man) **speak thus** (like this; in this way)**!"**

47. **The Pharisees then pointedly questioned them, "Have not you men also been led astray** (or: been deceived)**?**

48. **"Not anyone from out of the rulers** (chiefs; leaders) **or from out of the Pharisees put trust, confidence or belief into him, do they?**

49. **"But this crowd, which is having no habitual, experiential or intimate knowledge of the Law, continues being those under a curse** (are those upon whom a curse rests)**."**

[comment: they said this because they viewed the "crowd" as people who did not keep the Law]

50. **Nicodemus, the one previously going to Him – being one of them** (or: = a part of their group), **proceeds saying to them,**

51. **"Our Law** (or: custom) **is not in the habit of judging** (or: No law of ours is proceeding to decide about) **the person** (man; human) **unless it can** (or: except it should) **first hear from his side and can** (or: should; may; would) **know with intimate experiential knowledge what he is habitually doing** (repeatedly or presently practicing)**!"**

52. **They thoughtfully replied, and say to him, "You are not also from out of the Galilee [area], are you? Search** (or: Examine) **and see, that a prophet is not usually awakened** (not normally raised up) **from out of the midst of the Galilee [district]!"**

53. **And they went on their way, each one into his house** (= they all went home).

CHAPTER 8

1. **Now Jesus went on His way into the Mount of the Olives.**

2. **Yet at dawn** (at daybreak; early in the morning) **He came to be alongside, moving into the Temple courts** (porches; grounds; or: cloister), **and all the people began and kept on coming toward Him, and so, after sitting down** (taking a seat; [= teacher's posture]), **He began and continued teaching them.**

3. **Now the scribes** (specialists in the written Scriptures; theologians; scholars) **and the Pharisees are progressively bringing a woman** (or: a wife) **– a woman being one having been taken down** (grasped down with force; overpowered by hand, seized and forced) **upon in an act of adultery – and then, standing** (setting; placing) **her within the midst,**

4. **they proceeded in saying to Him, "Teacher, this woman** (or: this, the wife) **has been taken down, grasped, overpowered by hand and forced, upon the very act: being a woman having repeatedly been adulterated** (or: having the act of adultery habitually performed upon her; gang raped).

5. **"Now within the Law, Moses implanted a goal for** (imparted the end in view with; gave an inward directive to) **us to repeatedly stone this sort of woman. Therefore, what are you yourself now saying?"**

6. **– Now they were saying this, continuing in putting Him to the proof** (examining so as to test Him; = to trap Him) **to the end that they should continue holding** (or: having) **[something] to be constantly accusing** (or: progressively bringing charges) **pertaining to Him –**

So Jesus, stooping (or: bowing [His] head and bending) **down, began writing down into the dirt** (earth; soil; ground; = dust) **with the finger.**

7. **Now as they were persisting, remaining upon [the subject], continuing to question Him, He unbends back up** (or: straightens up) **and says to them, "Let the sinless one** (the one without failure or a miss of the target) **of** (or: among) **you folks [be] first [to] cast** (or: throw) **a stone upon her."**

8. **And again, bending** (or: stooping) **down, He was continuing to write into the dirt** (or: earth).

9. **So those hearing [Him] also being progressively convinced, then convicted by the conscience, began going out, one by one, beginning from the elders** (or: the older ones) **until the last ones. Then Jesus was left behind, alone, and also the woman** (or: the wife) **continuing being** [other MSS: standing] **in the midst [of the court, or cloister].**

10. **Now Jesus, unbending, straightening up and seeing no one but the woman, says to her, "O woman** (or: Madam; = Dear lady), **where are those, your accusers? Does no one condemn you?"**

11. **Then she says, "No one, sir** (or: O lord; or: Master)**." So Jesus says to her, "Neither am I, Myself, bringing a corresponding decision upon you** (or: proceeding to condemn you according to the pattern). **Be going on your way, and from this moment no longer make it a habit to miss the target** (or: from now on be failing no more; from the present moment no longer practice error or sin)**."**

12. **Jesus therefore again spoke to them** [i.e., to those whom He had just been teaching, in vs. 2, or at a later time], **saying, "I, Myself, am** (or: continuously exist being) **the Light of this ordered world**
> (or: of the aggregate of humanity; for the System of domination; of the cultural, political, and religious arrangements; from the cosmos; of 'the theater of history' – Walter Wink).

The one habitually and progressively following Me can by no means walk around (= under no circumstances live his or her life) **within, or in union with, the Darkness [of the old order]**
> (or: the dim and shaded areas; the gloom and obscurity due to the lack of the Light of the Day; the [realm] of the shadows; [note: = ignorance; = that situation which existed before the Light came; or, could also refer to the dim condition within the holy place of the Temple, or to the darkness of death, blindness or the womb]),

but, to the contrary, he will progressively possess (constantly have and hold) **the Light of 'the Life!'** (or: the light which is life; or: the Light from the Life.)**"**

13. **Therefore the Pharisees said to Him, "You yourself are continuing to bear witness** (or: are now giving testimony) **about yourself! Your witness** (testimony) **is not true** (real; valid)**!"**

14. **Jesus considers a reply, and then says to them, "Even if I, Myself, continue bearing witness** (or: am now giving testimony) **about Myself, My witness** (testimony) **is, and continues being, true** (valid; real; genuine) **because I have seen and thus know where** (or: what place) **I came from, as well as under where I progressively lead the way** (or: to where I am going). **Yet you folks, yourselves, have not seen and do not know from where** (or: what place) **I am progressively coming, nor under where I progressively lead the way** (or: to where I am departing and continuing to go).

15. **"You people, yourselves, continue making decisions based on the flesh** (or: constantly separate, evaluate and judge down from, on the level of, and in accord with [the realm and system of] the flesh). **I, Myself, am habitually judging** (sifting, separating, evaluating and deciding about) **no one.**

16. **"And yet, if I, Myself, ever proceed in judging** (or: if ever I, Myself, should evaluate or decide), **My deciding** (separating, evaluating and judging) **is, and continues being, true** (valid; real; genuine), **because I am not** (or: I do not exist being) **alone, but to the contrary, [it is] I, Myself, and the One sending Me: the Father.**

17. **"Yet even within your own Law it has been written that the witness** (testimony; evidence) **of two people** (humans; men) **is true** (or: exists being valid, genuine and real).

18. **"I, Myself, am the man now bearing witness** (or: habitually testifying; progressively giving evidence) **about Myself, and the Father – the One sending Me – is continuously bearing witness** (constantly testifying and giving evidence) **about Me."**

19. **Therefore they went on saying to Him, "[So] where is your father?" Jesus decidedly answered, "You folks have neither seen nor known Me, nor My Father. If you had seen and knew** (or: were acquainted with) **Me, you would also have seen and know** (or: be acquainted with) **My Father."**

20. **These declarations from the gush** (or: sayings which resulted from the flow) **He spoke within the treasury area, while teaching within the Temple courts** (or: grounds; porches), **and still no one caught hold of or apprehended Him, because His hour had not yet come, so as to be present.**

21. **Then He** [p66c & others: Jesus] **again said to them, "I Myself am progressively leading the way under** (or: I am Myself proceeding to withdraw and go away), **and so you folks will continue looking for Me** (or: seek to find Me) **and you yourselves will progressively** (or: one after another) **die and decay within your errors** (failures; misses of the target; deviations; sins). **Under where I, Myself,**

progressively lead the way (or: To where I am Myself proceeding to withdraw and go away) **you folks continue having no power to go** (or: are presently unable to come)."

22. **The Jews** (= religious authorities of Judea) **were therefore beginning to say, "Surely he will not proceed to be killing himself, will he, seeing that he is saying 'Under where I progressively lead the way** (or: To where I am proceeding to withdraw and go away) **you folks continue having no power to go** (are presently unable to come)'**?"**

23. **So He went on to say to them, "You folks, yourselves, continuously exist** (presently are) **from out of the things below** (or: You are yourselves presently forth from out of the downward places); **I, Myself, continuously exist** (have My being; am) **from out of the things above** (or: I am Myself forth from the midst of upward places). **You yourselves continuously exist from out of this System** (ordered arrangement; world of culture, economy, religion and politics; this System of control and domination); **I, Myself, do not exist** (do not have My being) **from out of this System** (world; etc.).

24. **"Therefore I said to you that you will progressively die and decay within your errors** (failures; sins; times of falling short or to the side of the target), **for, unless you come to trust and believe that I, Myself, am** (or: that, as for Me, I exist and continue being; or; that I am Myself Existence and Being; or, emphatically: that I AM), **you folks will progressively die and rot within your failures** (sins; etc.)!"

25. **They then began saying to Him, "YOU! – what** (or: who) **ARE you?" Jesus says to them, "That which I am even habitually telling you: the Beginning, the Origin, the Source and the Chief One** (or: The *Archē*; or, perhaps: Primarily that which I am also constantly telling you). [Cf 1:1, above]

26. **"I continuously hold and habitually have many things to be constantly speaking and deciding** (or: separating, evaluating and judging) **about you folks. However, the One sending Me is truthful** (exists being continuously real and true), **and I, what I hear from His side, these things I constantly speak and utter into the System** (into the world; unto the aggregate of humanity and the ordered arrangement of the culture, religion, economy and government; into the realm of the secular; or: unto the dominating systems of control; or: into the midst of the universe)."

27. **They did not know or understand that He had been speaking the Father to, and among, them.**

28. **Then Jesus says to them, "Whenever you folks may lift up high** (should raise aloft; would elevate; or: can exalt) **the Son of man** (Humanity's Son; = the Human Being; = the son of Adam; = the eschatological messianic figure), **then you will progressively come to know by personal experience that I, Myself, am** (or: I Myself continue existing; I Myself am Being and Existence; or, emphatically: I AM), **and I from Myself am habitually doing nothing** (not one thing), **but rather, according** (just; correspondingly) **as the Father teaches** (or: taught) **Me, I continue speaking** (uttering) **these things.**

29. **"And further, the One sending Me is constantly** (or: continuously exists being) **with Me. He does not leave Me alone** (or: He did not send Me off alone; He does not let Me go away alone; He does not divorce or abandon Me). **For this reason I, Myself, am always constantly doing the things pleasing to Him** (or: making pleasing things by Him; performing and producing the acceptable things in, and with, Him)."

30. **During His progressively speaking these things, many at some point believed, and came to put [their] trust and confidence into Him.**

31. **Therefore, Jesus began laying it out, saying to the Judeans who had trusted and were now believing by Him** (or: in Him), **"If you yourselves would remain** (can dwell; should abide) **within My word** (in union with My message and information; centered in the thought, idea: what is laid out by Me), **you folks are, and continue being, truly** (really; genuinely) **My disciples** (or: learners from Me),

32. **"and you will progressively come to know the Truth** (or: Reality; that which is unsealed, open and without concealment) **by intimate experience, and the Truth** (Reality) **will progressively liberate and make** (or: set) **you people free!"**

33. **The [Jewish leaders] considered and replied to Him, "We are Abraham's seed** (offspring; descendants), **and we have served as slaves to no one at any time. How are you now saying, 'You will progressively come to be free ones'?"**

34. **Jesus decidedly answers them, "It is certainly true** (Amen, amen). **I am now saying to you that everyone, who** (or: all humanity, which) **when, or by, habitually doing the failure** (constantly making the mis-shot; repeatedly performing the sin; progressively producing error), **is** (or: exists being) **a slave of the failure** (the error; the sin; the mis-shot; the mistake; the deviation).

35. **"Now the slave is not remaining** (dwelling; abiding) **within the House** (= having no perpetual place in the household) **on into the Age** (or: for life). **The son continuously remains** (dwells; abides) **on into the Age [of Messiah]** (or: for life).

36. **"Therefore, if the Son should** (or: would) **at some point liberate or begin to make** (or: set) **you free, you folks will progressively exist being actually, essentially and ontologically free people.**

37. **"I have seen and know that you people are Abraham's seed** (offspring; descendants), **but now you men continue seeking to kill Me, because My word** (message; thought; idea; discourse; laid-out information; *logos*) **is not continuing to have room and make progress within** (or: among) **you guys.**

38. **"I am habitually speaking things which I, Myself, have seen, [being] at the side of** (or: present with) **the** [other MSS: My] **Father, and you folks are yourselves therefore habitually doing** [*p75*: speaking] **things which you hear** (or: heard) **at the side of your father** [with other MSS: ... and so are you people then by practice doing what you have seen at the side of the Father?]."

39. **In calculated reply, they said to Him, "OUR father is Abraham!" Jesus then says to them, "If** (or: Since) **you folks are Abraham's children, be continually doing and performing Abraham's deeds** (actions; works).

> [other MSS: If you folks were Abrahams' children, were you ever doing Abraham's works (deeds; acts)?]

40. **"So now, proceed in seeking to kill Me!** (or: Yet now you are continually seeking to kill Me; [note: the verb "seeking" is either present imperative or present indicative]) **– a Man** (person; human) **Who has spoken to you the truth which I hear from** (or: heard at) **God's side** (or: in the presence of God). **Abraham does not do this** (or: did not do this).

41. **"You folks habitually do your father's works** (perform deeds and actions from your father)." **Therefore they said to Him, "We ourselves were not born out of prostitution** (or: fornication). **We have one Father: God!"**

42. **Jesus said to them, "If God were your Father, you folks would have been, and continued, loving and urging toward union with** (or: progressively giving yourselves fully to) **Me, for you see, I Myself came forth and am arrived here** (or: and here I am) **from out of the midst of God. For neither have I come or gone off from Myself** (= on My own initiative), **but rather that One sent Me away with a mission** (commissions and sends Me forth as an Emissary, [His] Representative).

43. **"How** (Through what [situation]) **is it that you folks consistently do not understand** (have personal, experiential knowledge of) **the matter of My discourse or the way I'm speaking** (= Why don't you understand what I'm saying)**? Because you presently have no power and continue unable to keep on hearing My word** (or: to progressively listen to My message, thought or information [*logos*]).

44. **"You folks, in particular, are** (continue existing, being) **from out of, and have your source in, the Ancestor who cast [something] through [someone]** (or: the adversary {devil} father; or: the father – the one thrusting [words or issues] through [folks/groups] and dividing them), **and you are habitually wanting** (willing; intending; purposing) **to be constantly doing your father's passionate cravings** (full-rushing over-desires). **That one was existing being a murderer** (a killer of humanity) **from [his; its; a] beginning** (or: from [the] start; from [its] origin; or: from headship, chieftainhood, government or rule), **and he/it has not stood and does not now stand within the Truth** (or: it had not made a stand in union with reality), **because truth is not** (openness and reality does not exist) **within him** (or: it). **Whenever he/it may be speaking the lie, he/it is continuing speaking from out of his own things – because he/it is** (or: continues existing being) **a liar, and its father** [note: either the father of the lie, or of the liar; Could this refer to what Paul called "the first man Adam" – 1 Cor. 15:45?].

45. **"On the other hand – because I, Myself, am continually saying the truth** (speaking reality)! **– you folks are not presently trusting Me or believing in Me, nor do you continue loyal to Me.**

46. **"Who of you is presently correcting Me about error**

> (or: demonstrating a proof about My being wrong; making a convincing argument which refutes
> Me and exposes Me about having missed the target; arraigning me concerning sin)**? Since** (or:

If) **I am habitually speaking truth** (reality), **how** (through what [situation]) **is it that you folks are not presently trusting Me, believing in Me or pledging allegiance to Me?**

47. **"The person continuing in being** (ontologically existing in essential being) **out of the midst of God is constantly hearing** (repeatedly and habitually listening and paying attention to [implies obeying]) **the effects of the things God says** (results of God's flow of declarations; spoken words from God).

Because of this, YOU folks are not presently in the habit of hearing (or: listening; paying attention [and obeying])**: because** (seeing that) **you are not presently existing from out of God."**

48. **The Jews** (= religious authorities of Judea) **calculated a reply and said to him, "Are WE not expressing it beautifully** (or: finely; ideally; precisely) **when we are saying that you yourself are a Samaritan** [note: a term of loathing and contempt – Barclay] **and constantly have** (or: continuously hold or possess) **a demon** (a Hellenistic concept and term: = an animistic influence)**?"**

49. **Jesus decidedly replies, "I, Myself, do not have** (or: habitually possess) **a demon, but to the contrary, I continuously honor** (bring value to) **My Father, and yet you yourselves are repeatedly dishonoring** (or: devaluing) **Me.**

50. **"Now by habit I am not seeking My glory or reputation. There is One constantly seeking [glory; repute] and continuously making decisions** (sifting, separating, evaluating and judging).

51. **"It is certainly so** (or: Amen, amen; Count on it)**! I am now progressively laying it out, and saying to you folks: If anyone should keep watch over, so as to hold in custody, protectively guard, observe and maintain My word** (message; thought; idea; information which is laid out; *logos*), **he or she can under no circumstances** (or: may, or would, by no means) **at any point gaze upon death, so as to contemplate it, be a spectator to it or look at it with interest and attention** [note: a Hebrew idiom for 'experiencing' death], **on into** (or: throughout) **the Age [of Messiah]."**

52. **The Jews** (= authorities of Judea) **said to Him, "Now we have come to personally know** (have intimate experiential knowledge) **that you presently have a demon** (= an animistic influence)**! Abraham died** (or: is dead), **also the prophets, and yet here you are now saying, 'If anyone should hold, protect, note and observe my word** (message; idea) **he by no means** (under no circumstances) **may taste of** (= partake of or participate in) **death, on into the Age.**

53. **"You are yourself not greater than our father Abraham – who died – are you? Even the prophets died! Who are you continually making yourself [to be]?"**

54. **Jesus decidedly replies, "If I should ever glorify Myself** (build a reputation for Myself), **My glory is** (or: My reputation exists being) **nothing. My Father – of Whom you keep saying, "He is our God"** [with other MSS: that He is your God] **– is actually the One continuously and progressively glorifying Me** (bringing a manifestation of Me which calls forth praise; building My reputation).

55. **"Now you have not intimately or experientially known Him, yet as for Myself, I have seen and thus know Him – and if ever** (or: even if) **I should say** (or: = Suppose I say) **that I have not seen nor know Him, I will be a liar, like you folks. But to the contrary, I have seen and know Him** (or: am acquainted with Him), **and I continuously hold in custody, protectively guard, observe and maintain His word** (*Logos*; message; laid-out thought; patterned idea; conveyed information).

56. **"Abraham, your father, was exceedingly glad** (or: exulted) **to the end that he could see My day, and he saw** (caught sight of; beheld; observed; perceived) **[it] and then was graced** (or: favored; or: rejoiced; was made glad)**."**

57. **Therefore the Jews** (= religious authorities of Judea) **said to Him, "You are not yet holding** (or: having) **fifty years – and you have seen Abraham** [p75, Aleph, Sin-syr & Coptic read: and Abraham has seen you]**?"**

58. **Jesus says to them, "It is certainly so** (Amen, amen; Count on it)**! I am telling you, before Abraham comes** (or: was to come) **into being, I, Myself, am** (or: I continuously exist; or: I repeatedly had being; or: I am Being; I am continuous Existence; I AM)**."**

59. **They therefore lifted up stones so that they could hurl** (throw; cast) **[them] upon Him. But Jesus had been suddenly concealed** (was at once hidden), **and then He went out from the Temple grounds** [Aleph, A & others add: even (or: and) passing through the midst of them as He was proceeding, and He thus was passing by].

CHAPTER 9

1. **Now continuing passing along, He saw a man [who had been] born blind** (blind from out of birth),
2. **and His disciples asked Him, saying, "Rabbi, who failed** (sinned; missed the mark; deviated), **this man or his parents, to the end that he should be born blind?"**
3. **Jesus judged the situation and replied, "Neither this man sinned** (missed the mark; failed) **nor his parents, but rather [it is] so that God's deeds** (the works of God; the acts from God) **could be set in clear light and manifested within him.**

4. **"It is constantly necessary** (or: binding) **for Me** [other MSS: us] **to be habitually performing the works** (accomplishing the deeds; active in the acts; doing the business) **of the One sending Me** [other MSS: us] **while it is day; night** (or: a night; = darkness; *cf* Gen. 1:5) **progressively** (repeatedly; habitually) **comes, when no one is able** (or: has power) **to continue performing work** (accomplishing deeds; doing business).

5. **"Whenever I may** (can) **continue being within the world** (aggregate of humanity and its ordered System; the religious and cultural arrangement), **I am the world's** (system's) **Light**

> (or: When I would progressively be within the System's ordered arrangement, I exist being the System's light)."

6. **After saying these things, He spits on the ground and makes clay mud from out of the spitted saliva, and then smears** (or: anoints; rubs on; [WH following B read: applies; puts... on]) **His clay mud upon the blind man's eyes,**

7. **then says to him, "Lead on under** (or: Go your way; Depart) **into the swimming-pool of Siloam"** [note: situated south of the Temple, fed by a subterranean tunnel] **– which is normally being translated and interpreted 'Being sent forth on a mission** (or: Commissioned; Being made representative)' – **"[and] wash yourself!" Therefore, he went off** (or: away) **and washed himself and came [back] seeing.**

8. **Then the neighbors, and those habitually observing** (being spectators of; carefully noticing) **him formerly – that he was existing being a beggar – began saying, "Is this one not the person normally sitting and constantly begging?"**

9. **Some were saying, "This is he." Others were saying, "No, but he is like him." Yet that man kept saying, "I, myself, am [he; the one]."**

10. **Then they began saying to him, "How, then, were your eyes opened up?"**

11. **That man decidedly replied, "The Man called 'Jesus' made clay mud and anointed** (smeared [it] on) **my eyes, and said to me, 'Lead on under into the Siloam, and wash yourself.' And then, upon washing myself, I looked up and saw again."**

12. **And so they said to him, "Where is that one?" He then says, "I have not seen so I don't know."**

13. **They are progressively leading him – the once-blind man – to the Pharisees.**

14. **Now it was on a sabbath day in which Jesus made the clay mud and opened up his eyes.**

15. **Again, then, the Pharisees also began asking him how he saw again** (= received his sight). **Now he said to them, "He applied clay mud upon my eyes, and I washed myself, and now** (or: the next thing), **I am seeing."**

16. **Some, from out of the Pharisees, therefore began saying, "This man is not on God's side** (or: from God; beside God; in God' presence), **because he is not keeping** (observing; guarding) **the sabbath." Yet others were saying, "How is a person who misses the mark** (a man, a sinner; an erring man; a man who is failing [in regard to the Law]) **able to be constantly doing such signs?" And there was a tearing split-effect** (= a division) **among them.**

17. **Therefore, they continued again saying to the once-blind man, "What are you yourself now saying about him, seeing that he opened up your eyes?" And the man exclaimed, "He is a prophet!"**

18. **The Judeans** (= religious authorities), **however, did not trust or believe concerning him, that he was blind and saw again** (or: received his sight), **until they summoned the parents of the man being made able to see again,**

19. **and they questioned them, saying, "Is this your son, who you say was born blind? How, then, is he presently seeing now?"**

20. **His parents considered, then replied, saying, "We have seen, and thus know, that this is our son, and that he was born blind.**

21. **"Yet how he now presently continues seeing, we have not seen and do not know, nor who opened his eyes we have not seen and do not know. You men ask him; he is of age** (has maturity; is an adult). **He will speak concerning himself."**

22. **His parents said these things because they had been fearing the Judeans** (= religious authorities; the ruling class), **for the Judeans** (= Jewish leadership) **had put it together and agreed, so**

that if anyone should ever confess (acknowledge; avow) **Him Christ** (or: express the same idea, that He is [the] Anointed), **he should come to be [put] away from the synagogue** (= be excommunicated; = be cut off from membership in the synagogue, and thus be considered an outcast).

23. **Because of this [situation], his parents said, "He's an adult** (He has maturity; He has come of age), **you men inquire upon him."**

24. **Then a second time they summoned the man who had been blind, and said to him, "Give glory** (the credit and reputation) **to God. We have seen and now know that this man is a sinner** (one who misses the goal; or: an outcast)**."**

25. **So then that man considered and replied, "I have not seen and do not know if he is a sinner** (one who does not comply with the religious rules, thus missing the goal; an outcast). **I have seen and know one thing: that I was existing being a blind man; at present** (or: just now) **I constantly see."**

26. **So then they said to him** [some MSS add: again], **"What did he do to you? How did he open up your eyes?"**

27. **He decidedly answered them, "I told you already, and you folks did not listen** (or: hear; = pay attention)! **Why are you now wanting to hear [it] again? You are not wanting to become his disciples, also, are you?"**

28. **So now they hurled abuse at him** (railed and reviled him) **and said, "You are now a disciple of that fellow, but we ourselves are disciples of Moses!**

29. **"We have seen, and know, that God has spoken to** (or: in) **Moses. But this fellow – we have not seen, nor do we know, where he is from."**

30. **The man insightfully replied, saying to them, "Accordingly indeed, in this [situation] is the marvelous thing** (the wonder; the astonishing state of affairs): **that you yourselves have not seen nor know where he is from, and yet he opened up my eyes** (= made me able to see)!

31. **"We have seen, and know, that God does not usually listen** (or: normally respond) **to sinners** (to those habitually missing the target; to those continuously being in error), **but rather if anyone may be one who reveres and stands in awe of God, and may be habitually doing His will** (intent; purpose), **He continuously listens to** (hears, or, responds to) **this one.**

32. **"From out of the age [past]** (= from of old; = in known history; = since our world began) **it is not heard that anyone opened up [the] eyes of one having been born blind.**

33. **"If this one was not being from God's side** (on God's side; at God's side), **he would not have been having power** (he would not have been able) **to be doing anything."**

34. **They decisively replied, and said to him, "You yourself were wholly born within sins** [idiom = You bastard!] **– and are YOU now teaching us?" And so they cast him out** (threw him outside).

35. **Jesus heard that they threw him outside, and so upon finding him, said to him, "Are you yourself now trusting or believing or putting faith into the Son of man**
(or: = the son of Adam; = the Human Being; or: = the eschatological messianic figure [A, L and others read: Son of God])**?"**

36. **And in considered response, that one says, "And who is he, sir** (or: my lord; master), **so that I can believe** (or, as a future: to the end that I will believe and progressively put trust) **into him?"**

37. **Jesus said to him, "You have both seen Him, and the One presently talking** (speaking) **with you, that One is He."**

38. **Then he began affirming, "I am now believing, Lord** (or: Master, I trust, and continue confident)!" **And he bowed down to the ground** (did obeisance), **kissing toward Him, and gave worship to Him.**

39. **Then Jesus says to him, "I came into this world** (or: ordered System of control and subjection) **into a result of sifting and deciding** (an effect of separation; a judgment): **to the end that the folks NOT habitually seeing and observing can** (or: may; would) **be constantly seeing and observing, and the ones habitually seeing and observing should** (or: would; may) **become blind ones."**

40. **And so those from out of the Pharisees – being with Him – heard these things, and said to Him, "We ourselves are not also blind ones, are we?"**

41. **Jesus says to them, "If you men had been and were continuing being blind ones, you were not holding and would not be having sin** (error; a miss of the goal; failure). **Yet now you continue saying that, 'We are continuously seeing and habitually observing.' Your error** (sin; failure; miss of the target; deviation) **continues remaining** (is habitually dwelling; constantly abides).

CHAPTER 10 [continuing the above discussion]

1. **"I tell you folks it is certainly true** (amen, amen; count on it)**: the person not habitually entering in through the door** (or: gate; opening for entrance/exit) **into the sheepfold** (the walled-in pen for the sheep), **but rather repeatedly climbing up elsewhere** (or: stepping back over [the wall] from another place), **that one exists being a thief and a plunderer** (one who seizes by violence; or: an insurrectionist; a brigand).

2. **"But the person habitually entering through the door is the sheep's own shepherd** [note: root meaning of 'shepherd' is 'to protect'].

3. **"The doorkeeper** (the one who takes care of the gate and has charge of the sheep in the fold at night) **is regularly opening up to** (or: for) **him, and the sheep are constantly hearing and listening to his voice, and he habitually summons** (or: calls out to) **his sheep, [each] by its own name, and is constantly leading them forth** (or: out).

4. **"And whenever he may drive out** (eject; herd forth) **all his own sheep, he is habitually passing on in front of them, and the sheep progressively follow him, because they have been acquainted with and recognize his voice.**

5. **"Yet to that [voice] belonging to another person they simply will not continue following; on the contrary, they will progressively take to flight** (flee) **from it** (or: him), **because they have not been acquainted with nor recognize the voice belonging to the other ones** (or: strangers)."

6. **Jesus told them this proverb** (common saying), **yet those did not intimately experience nor come to know or understand what things they were which He has been speaking to them.**

7. **Therefore, again, Jesus said to them, "I tell you, and it is certainly true** (amen, amen), **I Myself AM the Door for the sheep** (or: the sheep's Gate and Entrance).

8. **"All – as many as came – before Me are thieves and plunderers** (those who seize by violence; brigands; insurrectionists), **but yet the sheep did not listen to** (or: hear, pay attention or [obey]) **them.**

9. **"I Myself AM the Door** (or: Gate; Entrance); **if anyone should enter in through Me he will be constantly kept safe and protected** (made whole and returned to his original condition; rescued; delivered; saved), **and he will be habitually going in** (entering) **and going out** (exiting), **and he will continue finding pasture** (something to feed on).

10. **"The thief does not constantly come, except to the end that he may steal, slaughter** (slay for food – as for a feast – or, for a sacrifice) **and destroy** (utterly loose away). **I, Myself, come so that they can progressively possess** (would continuously have; could habitually hold) **Life, and may continue possessing [it] in superabundance** (or: and may have a surplus surrounding them in excessive amounts).

11. **"I, Myself, AM the Ideal Shepherd** (the Beautiful Protector of, and Provider for, the sheep). **The Ideal** (Fine; Beautiful) **Shepherd continually places His soul over the sheep** (or: habitually sets [p45 & others: gives] His inner life and consciousness for, and on behalf of the situation of, the sheep).

12. **"The hireling** (hired hand working for wages) **– not even being a shepherd [and] the sheep are not his own – continues attentively watching the wolf progressively coming, and proceeds to abandon the sheep and to take flight – and so the wolf continues ravenously snatching them away and progressively scattering and dispersing them –**

13. **"because he is a hireling and it is not a concern to him** (or: a care for him) **about the sheep.**

14. **"I, Myself, AM the Ideal** (the Beautiful; the Fine) **Shepherd, and I intimately know those [that are] Mine by experience, and those [that are] Mine are now intimately coming to know** (or: progressively are intimately knowing) **Me by experience –**

15. **"just as the Father has continuous, intimate knowledge of Me, and I Myself have continuous, intimate knowledge of the Father – and so I am constantly placing My soul-life over the sheep.**

16. **"And I constantly have** (hold; possess) **other sheep which do not exist** (or: are not) **from out of this fold** (or: sheep pen), **and it is binding** (or: necessary) **for Me to progressively lead those also, and they will continue listening to** (will habitually hear and pay attention to [implying: obey]) **My voice, and they** [other MSS: it; there] **will progressively become One Flock, One Shepherd.** [E 2:15]

17. **"On this account the Father continuously loves** (or: fully gives Himself to) **Me, because I Myself am constantly placing** (or: repeatedly setting) **My soul-life** (or: progressively laying My inner self, being and consciousness [over them]), **so that I may take it in My hand** (or: would receive it) **again.**

18. **"No one at any point lifts it** [with other MSS: Not one person is presently lifting it] **up and carries it away** (or: proceeds to remove it) **from Me; on the contrary, I Myself continue putting** (placing; setting; laying) **it away from** (or: off) **Myself. I constantly hold authority** (continuously have the right and hold the 'position'; or: continue possessing privilege from out of the midst of Being) **to place it** (put it; lay it), **and I constantly hold authority from out of being** (continuously possess the right, forth from [My] existence; = am in the authoritative position) **to take it** (or: receive it; resume it) **again. This implanted goal** (purposed impartation of the finished product within; inward directive and destiny) **I received from** (or: at) **My Father's side."**

19. **Then a tearing split-effect** (= a division) **occurred again among the Judeans** (= religious authorities; ruling class in Judea) **through these words** (or: on account of these ideas {*logoi*}).

20. **Now many of them began saying, "He continues having a demon** (a Hellenistic concept and term: = animistic influence) **and is insane** (mad; manic; crazy; deranged). **Why do you continue listening to** (or: hearing; = paying attention to) **him?"**

21. **Others were saying, "These are not the gush-effects of** (or: result of a flow from; spoken words of; declarations from) **a demoniac** (of one being constantly affected or afflicted by a demon). **A demon** (= an animistic influence) **is not able and has no power to open up blind people's eyes!"**

22. **At that time [the feast** (or: festival) **of] the Dedications** (or: celebration of renewals or rededication; Feast of Lights; Hanukkah) **occurred within Jerusalem – it was winter** (the rainy and stormy season).

23. **Jesus had been walking around in the Temple grounds, within Solomon's Colonnade** (Portico; covered porch attached to the Temple buildings).

24. **Then the Judeans** (= religious authorities) **surrounded** (or: encircled) **Him, and began to say to Him, "Until when are you continuing to lift up our soul** (= How long are you going to constantly keep us in suspense, or with high expectations)**? If YOU** (or: you yourself) **are the Christ** (the Anointed One; = the Messiah), **openly** (outspokenly; boldly and publicly, with freedom of speech, as a citizen) **tell us!"**

25. **Jesus directly answered them, "I did tell you folks, and you continue not trusting or believing with conviction. The works** (The deeds; The actions) **which I Myself am continually doing** (or: progressively performing; regularly producing) **within My Father's Name, these are continuously bearing witness** (giving testimony; showing evidence) **about Me.**

26. **"But you folks yourselves are not in the habit of trusting or believing, because you are not from among My sheep** (or: because you presently exist being no sheep of Mine), **just as I told you,**

27. **"because My sheep are constantly hearing and listening to** [implying: obeying] **My voice, and I Myself am progressively** (or: continuously) **knowing them by intimate experience, and they are progressively** (or: habitually) **following Me,**

28. **"and I Myself am continuously giving eonian life** (age-enduring life; life having the qualities and characteristics of the Age [of Messiah]; a life from, of and for the ages) **to and in them and so by no means** (or: under no circumstances) **can they at any point be lost or destroyed, or even cause themselves to perish; and further, no one will be snatching them** (or: taking them by force) **from out of My hand.**

29. **"My Father, Who has given [them] to Me, is greater than all** (or: everything; all things or people; [other MSS read: What My Father has given to Me is greater than all]), **and no one** (not even one person) **has power or is able to proceed to snatch from out of the Father's hand.**

30. **"I, Myself, and the Father are** (continuously exist being) **ONE** (or: I and Father: We are one thing [= essence, nature or being]; or: = unity; union).**"**

31. **Then the Judeans** (= leaders of the Jewish religion) **again picked up stones and brought them so that they could stone Him** (pelt Him with stones; or: kill Him with stones).

32. **Jesus discerningly replies to them, "I exhibited** (pointed out, showed, displayed) **to** (or: among; for) **you folks many beautiful works** (ideal acts; fine and noble deeds) **issuing from out of the midst of the** [other MSS: My] **Father. Because of what kind** (sort; character) **of work, of them, are you men proceeding to stone Me?"**

33. **The Judeans** (= religious authorities) **considered and answered Him, "We are not proceeding to stone you about beautiful works, but rather, about blasphemy** (villainous, impious slander; defaming communication and misrepresentation [of God]) **– even because YOU** (or: you yourself), **being a human** (a man), **continue making yourself God** (or: frame yourself [to be] a god).**"**

34. **Jesus judiciously replies to them, "Is it not standing written within your Law** [other MSS: the Law; = the Torah] **that 'I say, you people are** (or: exist being) **gods'?** [Ps. 82:6]

35. **"Since He said 'gods'** [= *elohim*] **to whom God's** *Logos* (the Word which was laid out from God) **came to be** (or: toward whom the Idea, whose source and origin is God, was birthed; toward whom God's message proceeded and was directed into existence) – **and it is not possible** (or: there is no power) **for the Scripture** [= the Tanakh] **to be loosened, to be undone so as to nullify, or to be destroyed** –

36. **"are you yourselves now saying to the One Whom the Father set apart** (consecrated as holy) **and sent forth as an Emissary** (on a mission; as a Representative) **into the organized domination-System** (into the world; into the cosmos; unto the religious, political and cultural complex; into the midst of the aggregate of humanity) – **that 'You are blaspheming** (speaking impious villainy and giving a false image [of God]),' **because I said, 'I am God's Son** (I exist being the Son of, and from, God)'**?**

37. **"If I am not habitually** (continually; progressively) **doing My Father's works** (deeds; actions), **do not make it a habit to put trust in Me** (or: Don't proceed to believe Me or give allegiance to Me).

38. **"Yet since I am constantly performing** (habitually doing; repeatedly making; progressively producing), **even if you folks cannot now be trusting and believing in Me or continue loyal to Me, continue to** [other MSS: at some point] **trust, believe and put faith in and by the results** (acts; works; deeds) **so that you may come to experientially know and habitually trust** (or: believe [other MSS: continue knowing]) **that** (or: because) **the Father [is] within Me, and I [am] within the Father!"**

39. **Therefore they kept on seeking [opportunity], again, to lay hold of and arrest** (or: seize; grasp) **Him at some point, but He went** (or: slipped) **forth out of their hands** (or: from their clutches).

40. **So He went off** (or: away), **again, to the other side of the Jordan [River], into the place where John had been habitually immersing [folks] the first time** (or: formerly), **and continued remaining** (abiding; dwelling) **there.**

41. **Then many came to Him, and they began saying, "John, indeed, did not perform a single** (or: one) **sign, yet all – whatever John said about this one – was true."**

42. **And so many believed and put convinced trust into Him** (or: were loyal unto Him) **there.**

CHAPTER 11

1. **Now there was a certain man being constantly ill** (habitually weak; progressively infirm; repeatedly sick) – **Lazarus, from Bethany, from out of the village of Mary and her sister Martha.**

2. **In fact, it was the Mary who at one time rubbed and anointed the Lord** (the Master) **with perfumed oil** (ointment) **and then wiped off His feet with her hair, whose brother, Lazarus, had been continuing ill** (weak; sick).

3. **So the sisters dispatched a message to Jesus, which was saying, "O Lord** (Master), **take note, he whom You habitually regard as a friend** (constantly treat with fondness and affection; continuously cherish and love as a congenial associate) **continues being weak and sick."**

4. **Now Jesus, hearing [this], said, "This weakness** (sickness; infirmity) **is not directed or leading toward death, but to the contrary [is] over [the issue of] God's glory** (or: reputation; appearance; manifestation; recognition), **to the end that through it God's** [other MSS: His; the] **Son would be glorified** (may receive recognition, a good reputation and a manifestation which calls forth praise)."

5. **Now Jesus was loving and continued in loyal appreciation of Martha, her sister, and Lazarus.**

6. **Even so, when He heard that he continues being sick and weak, He then, indeed, remained two days within [the] place in which He was [staying].**

7. **Thereupon – after this – He is saying to His disciples, "We should proceed going into Judea again."**

8. **The disciples are then saying to Him, "Rabbi, at the present time the Judeans** (= leaders of the Jewish religion) **have been seeking to stone You – and You are proceeding to go there again?"**

9. **Jesus decidedly replied, "Are there not twelve hours [in] the day** (= of daylight)? **If anyone may habitually walk around** (= live his life) **within the Day, he does not constantly stumble** (cut toward or strike against [something]), **because he continually sees** (looks at; observes) **the Light of this world, or from the aggregate of humanity**

(or: of this cosmos; this System's light; or: = because he progressively perceives the light and understanding that guides this System and secular society).

10. **"Yet, if anyone should habitually walk around within the Night, he constantly stumbles** (strikes against [things]), **because the Light is not** (does not exist) **within him."**

11. **He said these things, and after this He presently says to them, "Our friend Lazarus has been made to sleep** (or: has been lulled to sleep; has been caused to sleep; or, as a middle: has fallen asleep; has found repose), **but even so, I am setting out to proceed in journeying to the end that** (or: so that) **I can awaken him out of [his] sleep."**

12. **Therefore the disciples said to Him, "O Lord** (Master), **since** (or: if) **he has been caused to sleep** (or: fallen asleep) **he will be restored to health** (made to recover; saved; rescued; delivered)."

13. **Now Jesus had spoken** (made a declaration; = used the phrase) **about his death, yet they suppose** (imagine; think) **that He is saying [it] concerning** (or: is talking about) **the taking rest and repose of sleep** (slumber).

14. **Therefore, Jesus then plainly and openly said to them, "Lazarus died.**

15. **"And because of you folks I am progressively rejoicing that I was not there, so that you can trust** (or: would believe; could faith-it). **But now, we can** (or: should) **be going to him."**

16. **Then Thomas, the one being normally called "[the] Twin"** (or: Didymus), **said to [his] fellow disciples, "We should also be going, so that we can die with Him."**

17. **Consequently, upon coming into Bethany, Jesus found him having already been within the memorial tomb for four days.** [note: Jewish custom was to bury on the day of death]

18. **Now Bethany was near Jerusalem, about fifteen stadia** (= just under four miles) **away.**

19. **So many of the Jews** (or: Judeans) **had come to Martha and Mary in order that they could give a word of comfort, console and encourage them about their brother.**

20. **Then Martha, as she hears** (or: heard) **that Jesus is now coming, goes** (or: went) **to meet Him, but Mary continued sitting in the house.**

21. **So Martha said to Jesus, "O Lord** (Master), **if You had been here, my brother would not [have] died away.**

22. **"But even now, I have seen and recognize** (know; perceive) **that as many things as You may likely ask from God** (= whatsoever You could possibly request of God), **God will proceed giving to, or by, You!"**

23. **Jesus then says to her, "Your brother will proceed standing up** (arising back up again)."

24. **Martha now says to Him, "I have perceived and am aware that he will proceed standing up** (arising back up again) **within the standing back up again** (the resurrection; the arising) **within** (or: in union with) **the Last Day."**

25. **Jesus said to her, "I am the Resurrection** (or: the standing back up again; the Arising), **and** (or: that is to say,) **the Life. The one progressively believing and habitually putting trust into Me, even if he may die-off** (or: die-away), **will continue Living** (or: will proceed being alive)!

26. **"And further, everyone, who** (or: all mankind, which) **in presently living and progressively trusting-and-believing into** (or: regularly experiencing convinced faith into the midst of; being constantly faithful unto) **Me can by no means** (or: may under no circumstances) **die-off** (or: die-away), **on into the Age [of Messiah]. Are you presently believing this, trusting this and having convinced faith of, or in, this?"**

27. **She says to Him, "Yes, Lord** (Sure, Master). **I have trusted, and now believe, that You, Yourself, are the Christ** (Anointed One; = Messiah), **God's Son – the One habitually** (repeatedly; or: presently) **coming into the world** (into the ordered System; or: unto the aggregate of humanity)."

28. **And upon saying this she went off** (or: came away) **and summoned** (or: called) **Mary** (or: Miriam), **her sister, secretly** (covertly) **saying, "The Teacher is present** (= is now here), **and He is calling for** (or: summoning) **you."**

29. **So that one, as she heard, was quickly roused and was proceeding to go toward Him.**

30. **Now Jesus had not yet come into the village, but rather was yet** (still) **being within the place where Martha met Him.**

31. **Then the Judeans – those constantly being with her within the house, and repeatedly giving words of comfort, consolation and encouragement – seeing Mary, that she quickly stood up and**

went out, follow her, supposing [other MSS: one after another saying] **that she is on her way** (progressively going) **unto the memorial tomb so that she could cry** (or: weep; mourn) **there.**

32. **Then Mary – as she came where Jesus was – on seeing Him, falls at His feet, saying to Him, "O Lord** (Master), **if You had been here my brother would not [have] died away."**

33. **Jesus, therefore, as He saw her continuously weeping** (crying) **– and the Judeans coming with her [also] crying** (mourning; audibly weeping or wailing) **– inwardly snorted** (as with violent displeasure) **and groaned, being deeply moved in spirit** (or: by [the] Spirit; with Breath-effect; to an attitude and mood), **and then stirred Himself up** (shook Himself; or: disturbed and troubled Himself),

34. **and says, "Where have you folks laid** (put; placed) **him?" They proceed saying to Him, "Lord** (Master), **come and see."**

35. **Jesus sheds tears** (let tears flow; gave way to tears; or: bursts into tears).

36. **The Judeans therefore began saying, "Consider** (Look; See) **how he was feeling affection for** (how fond he was of; what affection he used to have for) **him."**

37. **Yet some of them said, "Was this one – the one opening up the eyes of the blind one – not able** (or: powerless) **to make also this one so that he would not die off?"**

38. **Jesus therefore, again continuing inwardly snorting, groaning and being deeply moved within Himself, is progressively going into the memorial tomb [area]. Now, it was a cave, and a stone was lying upon** (= against) **it.**

39. **Jesus is then saying, "Lift up** (Remove; Take away) **the stone."**
Martha, the sister of the one having come to his end (or: of the one having reached the goal; = of the deceased), **then says to Him, "O Lord** (Master), **he is already progressively giving off a smell** (or: there is already an offensive odor increasing), **for it is [the] fourth [day]."**

40. **Jesus proceeds saying to her, "Did I not say to you that if you would trust and believe** (faith-it) **you will be habitually seeing God's glory and appearance**
(God's manifestation which calls forth praise; or: a notion which is God; God's recognition and reputation; the vision and fancy of God; God's expectation; the imagination from God)**?"**

41. **Then they lifted up the stone and took it away. Yet Jesus lifted His eyes upward, and said, "O Father, I continually thank You that You hear and respond to Me,**

42. **"and I, Myself, have seen and thus know that You habitually listen and constantly hear Me at all times** (always), **but nevertheless, because of the crowd standing around, I spoke – to the end that they could trust, believe and have faith that You commissioned and sent Me forth as an Emissary** (Representative)."

43. **Upon saying these things, He suddenly shouted with a loud** (or: in a great) **voice, "Lazarus! Here! Outside!"**

44. **And out comes the man having been dead, still being bound, having been wrapped in grave-clothes** (with swaths, bands, or bandages of cloth, such as linen) **– even binding the feet and the hands – and his face having been wrapped around with a face-cloth** (or: sweat-cloth; handkerchief; napkin). **Jesus says to them, "You folks loose** (unwrap; unbind) **him and release him** (let him go off) **to proceed leading the way** (or: to be departing)."

45. **Therefore, many from out of the Judeans – those coming to Mary and being ones attentively watching what He did – put faith and trust into** (or: believed and were loyal unto) **Him.**

46. **Yet some of them went off to the Pharisees and told them what** [other MSS: how much; how many] **things Jesus did.**

47. **Consequently, the chief** (or: ranking) **priests and the Pharisees gathered [the] Sanhedrin** (= convoked a council of the leaders of the Jewish religious and political culture), **and they began to say, "What are we presently doing, seeing that this man is repeatedly doing many signs?**

48. **"If we let him go on in this way** (or: If we disregard him in this manner; or: Suppose we thus abandon, neglect or leave him alone), **all** (everyone) **will one-by-one put trust into him** (or: will continue believing, being allegiant unto him), **the Romans will proceed to come, and they will progressively take away both our place and our nation** (= political station, culture and corporate ethnic identity)."

49. **Yet one of them, Caiaphas, being chief priest of that year, said to them, "You people have not seen, nor perceived, nor know anything,**

50. **"neither are you logically reasoning or taking into account the fact that he is progressively bringing it together for you** (or: it is advantageously bringing things together for you), **so that one man**

can die over (or: to the end that one person should and would die away for the sake of [in the sense of "instead of"]) **the People, and not [that] the whole nation should destroy itself!"**

51. **Now, he did not say this from himself, but to the contrary, being chief priest of that year, he prophesied that Jesus was being about to be dying away over [the situation of]** (or: for the sake of) **the Nation** (or: ethnic group),

52. **and not over [the condition of] the Nation** (or: on behalf of the ethnic group) **only, but further, to the end that He could gather God's children together – those having been thoroughly scattered – into one** (or: so that He would lead together into unity God's divided, dissipated and disintegrated born-ones that have been dispersed throughout). [cf Gen. 11:8; Eph. 2:11-17]

53. **Therefore, from that day they deliberated and consulted together to the end that they should** (or: would) **kill Him.**

54. **Jesus, therefore, was no longer walking about publicly** (openly; with outspoken boldness as a citizen) **among the Judeans** (or: = religious authorities), **but rather, He went away from there into the country** (or: region; territory) **near the wilderness** (desert; desolate area), **into a city called Ephraim, and there He remained** (or: dwelled; [other MSS: was passing time]) **with His disciples.**

55. **Now the Passover of the Jews** (of the Jewish culture and religion) **was coming to be near, and many went up into Jerusalem from out of the region** (country; territory), **before the Passover, so that they could purify** (or: perform ritual cleansing for and of) **themselves.**

56. **Consequently, they began trying to find** (or: were looking out for or continued seeking) **Jesus and would periodically converse with one another, as they had been standing within the Temple courts, saying, "What do you think or suppose** (or: What is you opinion)?" **"Surely he is not likely to come into the festival** (or: Feast)!"

57. **As it was, the chief** (or: ranking) **priests and the Pharisees** (= the Sanhedrin) **had given goal-oriented directions, with imparted authority, so that if anyone may come to know where He is, he should disclose** (or: report) **it, so that they might lay hold of and seize Him.**

CHAPTER 12

1. **Accordingly then, six days before the Passover feast, Jesus came into Bethany where Lazarus – the one having died – was, whom Jesus raised up out from the midst of dead folks.**

2. **So they made dinner** (the evening meal) **for Him there, and Martha was serving [them]. Now Lazarus was one of those still reclining** (lying back) **[at the meal] with Him.**

3. **Then Mary, taking a pound** (Roman pound = about 12 oz.; about a pint) **of very costly** (of much value; precious) **genuine** (= pure) **perfumed ointment** (or: oil; aromatic juice distilled from plants) **extracted from the spike-nard plant, anoints and rubs** (as in preparing the body with oil for gymnastics) **the feet of Jesus, and then wipes His feet off with her hair, and so the house was filled full with** (or: from) **the fragrance** (aroma; odor) **of the perfumed ointment.**

4. **Now [other MSS: Then] Judah** (or: Judas) **of Simon Iscariot, one of His disciples – the one continuing about to proceed commending, and thus transferring and committing, Him** (or: giving Him over; turning Him in) **– proceeds in saying,**

5. **"Why** (Through what [reason; situation]) **was this perfumed ointment not sold for three hundred denarii** (= a year's wages) **and given to** (or: for) **destitute** (poor) **people?"**

6. **He said this, though, not because it was normally a care** (or: of interest) **to him about the destitute** (the poor people), **but rather, because he had been existing as a thief, and, normally holding** (or: having; [other MSS: used to be in possession of]) **the money box** (or: case; originally a receptacle for the "tongues" {i.e., mouth-pieces} of musical instruments), **had been regularly carrying** (or: bearing) **the things being repeatedly** (or: habitually) **deposited.**

> [note: the verb of being is the imperfect tense, and can refer to past practice; thus, John is not necessarily saying that Judas was currently a thief, but is pointing out his disposition toward money; the verb for carrying (bearing) can also be used in the sense of "bearing away," "removing," or "pilfering;" or, it can be used to signify "supporting; providing for" – this latter giving a different slant to John's words. Recall that Mark says that "some" had indignation, and Matt. says "the disciples" did, so Judas expressed a consensus. Also, in Matt. 26:6, they were in the same town, but at a different place – the house of Simon the leper – and an anonymous

woman enters while they are eating, and this time pours the costly ointment on His head. Jesus gives a response similar to below]

7. Then Jesus says, "Let her off (or: Forgive her; or: = Leave her alone) so that she can keep it in view (watch over, observe, take note of and guard it) on into the day of the preparation for My burial,

8. "for you see, the destitute ones (the poor people) you folks are always having with yourselves. Yet, you are not always holding (or: having) Me."

9. Then many of the common folks (or: the vast crowd) from out of the Jews (or Judeans) became aware (or: got to know) that He is there, and they come (or: came) – not only because of Jesus, but also so that they might see and become acquainted with Lazarus, whom He raised up from out of the midst of dead ones.

10. So the chief priests [note: representing the Sadducees] deliberated and resolved (or: purposed and made a plan) to the end that they should also kill off Lazarus,

11. because many of the Jews (or: Judeans) had been repeatedly going, on account of him, and then were progressively believing and continuing to put their trust and loyalty into Jesus (or: = believing what Jesus was saying; or: = being convinced that Jesus was the Messiah; = being followers).

12. The next day (or: On the morrow), the vast crowd going unto the Feast (or: i.e., the one coming into the festival) – upon hearing that Jesus is on His way into Jerusalem –

13. took the branches (or: fronds) of the palm trees (date palms) and went out into a meeting with Him, and they began and kept on shouting, "Ho-san'na [Heb. word meaning: Save now; Send your salvation]! O One having been blessed, now coming (or: repeatedly coming) in [the] Lord's Name (= in [the] Name which is Yahweh): even the King of Israel!" [Ps. 118:25, 26]

14. Now Jesus, finding a donkey colt (or: a small donkey, or, ass), sits down upon it – according as it stands, having been written,

15.   "Do not continue fearing (or: Stop fearing), O daughter of Zion! Look and consider, your King is progressively coming – presently sitting upon a donkey's colt." [Zech 9:9]

16. Now His disciples did not notice, become personally aware of, or understand these things, at the first, but when Jesus was glorified, recognized, made to appear, and became renowned (or: was given an assumed appearance) they were then reminded that these things were written upon Him (= had been written about Him), and that they did these things for Him (or: to Him; with Him).

17. Accordingly, the crowd of common folks – the one constantly being with Him when He summoned Lazarus forth from out of the memorial tomb and raised him out of the midst of dead ones – kept on bearing witness and giving testimony.

18. [It was] on account of this, [that] the [other] crowd also came to meet with Him, because they heard [that] He had performed (done; made; produced) this sign.

19. So the Pharisees said among themselves (to one another), "You are observing (noticing; or, as an imperative: Be watching and considering) that your efforts are futile (that you men are benefiting nothing; = that you are getting nowhere). Look and consider! The world (or: The mass of society; or: The system of our culture; or: The inhabitants of our organized society; or: This aggregate of humans) went off after (or: goes away behind) him!"

20. Now there were certain (or: some) Greeks (or: Hellenists; those of the Greek culture; or: Jews who had acculturated to Hellenistic philosophy or culture) out of (or: among) those progressively coming up so that they could worship in the Feast (or: pay homage at the festival).

21. These, then, approached Philip [note: this is a Greek name] – the one from Bethsaida of the Galilee [area] – and began inquiring with a request of him, saying, "Sir (or: My lord), we desire (or: wish) to see and become acquainted with (or: = have an interview with) Jesus."

22. Philip proceeds to go and he tells Andrew [note: also a Greek name]. Andrew and Philip then continue on to Jesus, and proceed telling Him.

23. Yet Jesus is deliberating a reply for them, [and] proceeds saying, "The hour has come and is here so that the Son of Mankind (Humanity's Son; = the Son of Adam; or: = the Human Being; or: = the eschatological Messianic figure) can be glorified (or: may be recognized with a reputation of renown; should be made a manifestation which incites praise; would be given an assumed appearance).

24. "Most assuredly (It is certainly true; Yes, indeed; Count on it; Amen, amen), I am saying to you folks [that] unless the grain of wheat (or: kernel of corn; = seed of an agricultural crop), upon falling

into the earth (the ground; the field), **should die, it by itself continues remaining alone. Yet if it should die, it proceeds to bear much fruit** (= it produces a harvest of many grains, or, seeds).
25. **"The person being constantly fond of** (maintaining an emotional attachment to; continuing in devoted affection for) **his soul** (or: soul-life; interior self; perceived image) **progressively destroys it, and yet in contrast, the one continuing to radically detach from and regard with less affection** (or: habitually hates with distaste) **his soul** (or: inner life; conscious self) **[that is] centered in this System** (world; ordered arrangement of cultural, political and religious society) **will safeguard** (keep in watchful custody and preserve) **it, into the midst of eonian life** (life of and for the ages; life having the qualities and characteristics of the Age; life for, pertaining to, and having its source in, the Age [of Messiah]).
26. **"If anyone would habitually give attending service** (raise dust throughout in hastening to provide for material needs) **to Me, let him habitually and progressively follow with Me, and then where I Myself AM, there My attending servant will also be** (exist; have his or her being). **If anyone would habitually give attending service to Me and provide for Me, the Father will value and honor him.**
27. **"At the present time, My soul** (the consciousness which is Me; My inner self, feelings, emotion and will; My inner being) **has been stirred up** (shaken; disturbed; troubled), **and what can** (or: should) **I say? O Father, deliver** (rescue; save) **Me from out of the midst of this hour!** (or: ?) **But to the contrary, on account of this I come into the midst of** (or: came unto) **this hour.**
28. **"O Father, glorify Your Name** (bring glory, recognition and a renowned reputation to Your Name in a manifestation which calls forth praise)**!" Then a Voice** (or: sound) **came from out of the midst of the heaven** (or: the sky; the atmosphere)**: "I both bring glory** (or: brought recognition and a reputation) **to [it], and I will continue glorifying** (bringing a manifestation that calls forth praise to) **[it] again!"**

29. **Hence the crowd of common folks, the [crowd] standing around and hearing [it], began to say that it had thundered. Others were saying, "A messenger** (or: An agent) **has spoken to him."**

30. **Jesus decidedly replied, and said, "This Voice** (or: sound) **has occurred** (happened; come to be) **not because of Me, but rather because of you folks** (= for your benefit).
31. **"At the present time** (or: Now) **is an evaluation OF and a decision PERTAINING TO** (or: a sifting of and separation for; or: a judging **FROM**) **this System** (or: this ordered arrangement; this world; this polity, culture and religion; or: this system of control and subjugation; or: this aggregate of humanity). **Now the Ruler** (the one invested with power; the **Leader**; the chief; the ruler; or: the Original One; **The Beginning One**; the **Prince**) **of this System** (or: cosmos) **will progressively be ejected outside**
> (or: At this time the Chief of this world of culture, religion and government, the Originator and Controlling Principle of this cosmos and ordered arrangement of the universe, will proceed in being thrown out, [to the] outside [of it]).
32. **"And thus I Myself: if** (when) **I should be lifted up from out of the earth** (or: can be exalted from the midst of this Land), **I will progressively** (or: one after another) **drag** [note: drag as with, or in, a net; or: draw, as drawing water with a bucket, or a sword its sheath] **all humans** (or: everyone) **to Myself."**
33. **Now He was saying this continuing to indicate, by a sign, by** (or: with; in) **what sort of death He was progressively being about to be proceeding to die.**

34. **Therefore the crowd considered and replied to Him, "We, ourselves, hear** (or: heard) **from out of the Law that the Christ continuously remains** (abides; dwells) **on into the Age; so how are you, yourself, now saying that it continues necessary and binding for the Son of Mankind** (= the Human Being; = the eschatological Messianic figure) **to be lifted up? Who is this Son of Mankind** (or: = son of Adam)**?"**
35. **Jesus then says to them, "The Light continues being** (or: is) **among you folks, yet a little time** (= for a little while). **Continue walking around** (= living your lives; = order your behavior) **while you folks continue having the Light, so that Darkness** (the dim shadow-land of obscurity; = the ignorance of the system of shadows) **can** (or: could; would) **not grasp you with force and take you folks down. And the one constantly walking around within the Darkness has not seen nor does he know under what place he progressively leads [his path]** (or: where he is humbly going; where he is constantly withdrawing).
36. **"While you continue having the Light, progressively trust and believe into the Light, to the end that you folks can yourselves come to be** (or: would yourselves be birthed) **sons of Light**

(= folks having the quality and characteristics of light; folks whose source is Light; [note: this could be considered a Hebrew idiom for 'enlightened people'])."

Jesus spoke these things, and then after going off, He was hidden (or, as a passive with a reflexive idea: kept Himself concealed) **from them.**

37. **Yet, [even with] His having performed** (done; made; produced) **so many signs in front of them, they were not proceeding to believe or place their trust into** (or: not continuing loyal unto) **Him,**

38. **to the end that the word of** (or: message laid out from) **Isaiah the prophet could** (may; should; would) **be made full** (or: fulfilled), **which he said:**

> **"O Lord [= Yahweh], who trusts or believes in our report** (tidings; the thing heard from us)**? And to whom was the Lord's [= Yahweh's] arm unveiled** (revealed; uncovered)**?"** [Isa. 53:1]

39. **On account of this they were unable** (or: they had no power) **to progress in trusting or believing** (or: to continue loyal), **because again** (= elsewhere) **Isaiah says,**

40. > **"He has blinded their eyes with the present result that they are still blind, and He hardened** (or: petrified) **their heart, to the end that they could** (or: should; would) **not see with [their] eyes nor could they direct [their] mind so as to perceive and get the thought in** (or: with) **the heart and be turned, so I, Myself, will proceed to heal** (or: will progressively cure) **them."** [Isa. 6:10]

41. **Isaiah said these things because he saw His glory** (or: appearance; splendor; manifestation) **and knew His recognized reputation, and so spoke about Him.**

42. **Just the same, however, many of the rulers also** (or: many, even from among the chiefs and ruling class) **believed and placed their trust into Him, but still, because of the Pharisees, they did not begin confessing** (= openly avowing their faith) **or keep on speaking in agreement – so that they would not become ones cut off from** (separated away from) **the synagogue,**

43. **for you see, they loved, held precious and accepted the opinion, esteem and reputation** (or: the recognition; the glory; the appearance; the manifestation which calls forth praise) **of the humans** (or: from the people) **rather than even the opinion, esteem and reputation** (or: the recognition; the glory; the appearance; the manifestation which calls forth the praise) **of, from, and which is, God.**

44. **Now later, Jesus suddenly gives out a loud exclamation** (or: cries out) **and says, "The person progressively believing and continuing to put trust into** (or: constantly being loyal unto) **Me is not continuously believing and placing loyal trust into Me, but rather, into the One sending Me;**

45. **"and further, the person continuing in attentively gazing at and contemplatively watching Me continues looking at** (contemplatively viewing; watching, discerning and seeing) **the One sending Me.**

46. **"I, Myself a Light, have come into, and am now within, the world** (the organized domination System of religion, culture and government; the ordered and adorned arrangement; or: secular society; or: the cosmos or universe; the aggregate of humanity), **to the end that everyone, who** (or: that all humanity, which) **in habitually trusting and progressively believing into Me, cannot** (should not; may not; would not) **remain** (abide; dwell) **within the midst of the Darkness, or in union with the dim shadiness, or centered in the obscurity.** [Cf 1:4-5, above]

> [note: darkness is perhaps a figure for their religious system, or for the world that does not know what God is really like, or for the Night, that period before the coming of the Day]

47. **"And yet, if anyone can listen to and would hear** [implying: obey] **results of the flow of My sayings and declarations** (the gush-effects said by Me) **and yet cannot** (may not; should not) **keep** (guard; maintain; watch-over and protect) **them, I Myself have no habit of separating him so as to make a distinction with him, or to evaluate, decide and then be judging him. For you see, I did not come to the end that I should** (could; would) **constantly separate, make distinctions, evaluate, then decide about and be judging the world** (the domination System; secular society; the arranged religious structure; aggregate of humans), **but to the contrary, to the end that I could, and will** [note: the verb form is both an aorist subjunctive and a future indicative], **progressively save the world**

> (restore the universe to its original state and condition; or: make the ordered System healthy and whole; rescue and deliver the ordered and adorned arrangement of religion, culture and secular society; or: heal the aggregate of mankind). [cf chapter 3:16]

48. **"The person habitually displacing, disregarding, rejecting or setting-aside Me, and not progressively taking in hand and receiving or getting the effects of what I have gushed in speech**

(the results of My sayings and declarations which flowed), **is constantly having that which is** (or: the One) **continuously evaluating, progressively deciding and repeatedly judging him: the Word** (the message, laid out *Logos*) **which I spoke** (or: speak)! **THAT will continue to sift, separate, evaluate and make a decision about** (or: be judging) **him – within** (or: in union with) **this** (or: the) **Last Day –**

49. **"because I Myself do not speak from out of the midst of Myself, but to the contrary, the One sending Me – [the] Father, Himself – has given an implanted goal** (an impartation of the finished, purposed product within; an inward directive of destiny) **to Me: what I could** (or: should; would; may) **say, and what I will proceed to** (or, as an aorist subjunctive: could, should, would or may) **speak.**

50. **"And I have seen and know that His implanted goal** (purposed impartation of the finished product within; inward directive of destiny) **is, and continuously exists being, eonian Life** (life of and for the ages; Life having the qualities and characteristics of the Messianic Age; an eon-lasting life which pertains to, and comes from, the Age). **Therefore, the things which I Myself am habitually** (or: continuously; periodically) **speaking, just and according as the Father has told Me** (or: declared to Me), **thus I am habitually and continually speaking** (= When I speak, I repeat what the Father has told Me)."

CHAPTER 13

1. **Now before the festival** (or: Feast) **of the Passover, Jesus, having seen and thus knowing that His hour comes** (or: came) **– to the end that He could** (or: should; may; would) **change His steps and move** (walk differently; transfer; pass over to another place) **from out of the midst of this world** (ordered System; secular society; human aggregate; cosmos) **toward the Father – in loving** (accepting and driving toward union with) **His own** [people? humans? friends? disciples? created ones?], **[i.e.,] those within the world** (the System; culture; ordered universe; aggregate of mankind), **He loves and fully gives Himself to them unto the end** (or: the goal and attained destiny; the finished, purposed product; the accomplished and completed work; the consummation; or: = to the uttermost extent).

2. **So, while the evening meal was progressively going on** [other MSS: with, or after, the occurring of the evening meal] **– the adversary** (the one who thrusts something through the midst of situations, or of people; traditionally: the devil) **having already thrust** (cast; hurled; thrown; = put) **[the idea or conviction] into the heart of Judah** (or: Judas), **[son] of Simon Iscariot, that he should transfer, commend and commit Him** (or: hand Him over; or: = turn Him in) –

3. **Jesus, having seen and now knowing** (or: being aware) **that the Father has given** [other MSS, aorist: gives/gave] **all humanity and all things to Him – into [His] hands – and that He came out from God – forth from the midst [of Him] – and now is continuously leading and bringing [all] under [His] control to God** (or: is progressively humbly withdrawing and continues underway, going back [to be] face to face with God), [Cf 1:1, above]

4. **He presently proceeds to get up** (or: arise) **from the meal** (dinner, or, supper), **continues to lay aside [His] outer garments, and then taking a linen cloth** (a servant's towel; [note: symbol of a priest's clothing?]) **He ties it around Himself** (around His waist; or: He girds Himself).

5. **Next, He proceeds to cast** (= pour) **water into the washbasin and was beginning to successively wash the feet of the disciples, and to continue to wipe [them] dry with the linen cloth** (or: towel) **with which He had girded Himself.**

6. **So then He continues coming toward Simon Peter, and that one then exclaims to Him, "O Lord, You, Yourself – are you preparing to wash my feet?!"**

7. **Jesus decidedly replies, and says to him, "What I Myself am presently doing, you yourself have not seen and do not understand at present** (or: just now), **yet after these things you will progressively gain insight and then intimately learn and realize through experience."**

8. **Peter then says to Him, "Under no circumstances can** (or: should) **You wash my feet ... unto the Age** (in this lifetime)!" **From discerning, Jesus replied and said to him, "Unless I can** (or: If I should not) **wash you, you do not continue to hold** (or: have) **a part** (portion) **with Me."**

9. **Simon Peter then says to Him, "O Lord ... not my feet only, but also [my] hands and [my] head."**

10. **Jesus in turn says to him, "The person being one having bathed himself or herself** (or, as a passive: being one having been washed and cleansed) **does not continue having a need to wash himself or herself – except the feet – but rather she or he continues to exist being wholly clean. And so you men continue being clean folks – however, not all [of you folks]."**

11. **For He had seen and knew about the person in process of transferring and committing Him** (or: handing Him over). **On account of this He said, "Not all you people exist being clean ones."**

12. **After He had washed their feet, He took His outer garments** (= He put them back on) **and reclined back again, [and] says to them, "Are you men coming to know and personally understand what I have done for you** (to you; in you; with and among you folks)**?**
13. **"You men are repeatedly addressing** (calling) **Me, 'Teacher** (= Rabbi)**' and 'Lord** (Master),**' and you keep on speaking** (or: saying [it]) **beautifully** (ideally; finely), **for I am.**
14. **"If I Myself, then, the Lord and the Teacher, wash your feet, you men also are constantly indebted** (obliged; continuously owe it) **to be habitually washing one another's feet,**
15. **"for I give** (or: gave) **an underlying example** (or: result of something pointed out as a specimen or illustration shown under your eyes) **to, and for, you folks, so that just** (accordingly; correspondingly) **as I, Myself, do** (or: did) **for** (to; in; among) **you, you men should also be repeatedly doing.**
16. **"Most assuredly** (It is certainly true; Amen, amen), **I am saying to you, a slave is not greater than** (superior to) **his lord** (owner; master), **nor [is] one sent with a mission** (an emissary; a representative) **greater than** (superior to) **the one sending him.**
17. **"Since** (or: If) **you have seen and know these things, you are happy** (continue being blessed and fortunate) **ones – if you can** (or: would; should) **be habitually doing** (performing; producing) **them.**
18. **"I am not now speaking about all of you men. I Myself have seen and thus know which ones** (or: whom) **I select and pick out for Myself, but to the end that the Scripture may be fulfilled** (made full; filled up): **'The one habitually eating** (crunching; chewing) **My bread** [other MSS: the bread with Me] **lifts** (or: lifted) **up his heel on** (= walked away from; or, = turned against) **Me.'** [Ps. 41:9]
19. **"From now** (or: this moment) **on, I am saying [it] to** (or: telling) **you folks before the [situation for it] is to come to be** (is to be birthed; is to occur; = before it happens), **so that when it may come to be** (happen; occur) **you can** (or: would) **continue trusting and believing that I am** [what I say I am; He] (or: I AM; because I Myself am Being; for I am continuous Existence; or: that I continue existing).
20. **"Most assuredly** (It is certainly true; Amen, amen), **I am saying to you, the person habitually receiving** (taking with the hand, embracing and accepting) **whomever I will send** (or: may send) **is continually receiving Me** (welcoming, embracing and accepting Me). **Now the one habitually receiving Me is continually receiving** (welcoming, embracing and accepting) **the One sending Me."**

21. **[On] saying these things, Jesus was shaken by the Spirit** (or: troubled in mood or disturbed in the spirit; or: **stirred with** the Breath-effect and Attitude), **then gave witness** (testified) **and said, "Most assuredly** (It is certainly true; Amen, amen), **I tell you** (I am saying to you) **that one from among you men will proceed in transferring, commending and committing Me** (or: handing Me over)."
22. **Therefore the disciples began to glance and continued looking into one another, being perplexed** (at a loss; confused) **about whom He is speaking.**
23. **Now one from among His disciples, whom Jesus had been loving** (progressively urging for accepting union, as being on common ground; giving Himself to), **was by habit lying back** (reclining at the table) **at the chest** (or: on garment fold; = close at the right, the place of honor/intimacy) **of Jesus.**
24. **Therefore Simon Peter repeatedly nodded to this one, and then says to him, "Tell who it is** [other MSS: Ask which one it might be], **about whom He is now saying [this]."**
25. **Therefore that one, thus leaning back upon the chest of Jesus, says to Him, "Lord** (Master), **who is it?"**
26. **Jesus considers and then replies, "It is that one for whom I, Myself, will dip the morsel** (bit of bread) **and will give [it] to him." Then, after dipping the morsel in, He continues taking it in His hand and proceeds to give [it] to Judah** (Judas), **[son] of Simon Iscariot**
27. **– and with** (accompanying) **the morsel, at that time, the adversary** (opponent; "*satan*") **enters into that one. Therefore Jesus proceeds to say to him, "What you are in process of doing** (or: proceeding to do), **do more quickly** (or: promptly)."
28. **Now none of those presently reclining knew** (at any point had personal knowledge) **toward what end He said this to him.**
29. **Some in fact thought** (supposed; imagined), **since Judah** (Judas) **had been holding** (in possession of) **the money box, that Jesus is saying to him, "Buy at the marketplace things of which**

we presently have need, with a view to the feast [days]," or, "for the destitute folks," so that He could give something.

30. **Then, upon accepting** (or: receiving) **the morsel, that one went out set for goodness, ease and well-being** (or: a straight, direct, upright and true one; or, as adverb: immediately). **Now – it was night.**

31. **Then, when he went out, Jesus proceeds to say, "Now is** (or: At this moment was) **the Son of Mankind glorified** (or: given an appearance, a recognized reputation and caused to receive opinions), **and God is** (or: was) **glorified** (or: made to appear; recognized; receives opinions and a reputation; given a manifestation which will call forth praise) **within Him** (or: centered in union with Him),

32. **"and God will progressively glorify Him within** (in union with) **Himself, that is, He will continue giving Him an assumed appearance set for goodness, ease and well-being** (or: and He will keep on manifesting Him as a straight, direct, upright and true One which calls forth praise).

33. **"Little children, I am with you yet a little while** (or: longer). **You folks continue seeking, and trying to find Me, and just as I said to the Jews** (= Judean leaders), **'To the place that I Myself progressively lead under** (or: am going away), **you yourselves are continuing unable** (still have no power) **to go** (or: come),' **I am also now saying to and for you right now** (at present).

34. **"I am giving to you men a new implanted goal** (an inward purposed directive different from that which had been formerly; an impartation of a finished product and destiny that is new in kind and character)**: that you folks are to be continuously and progressively loving** (or: should constantly accept, and give yourselves to,) **one another, just as** (correspondingly as; to the same level as; in the sphere as) **I love, accept, and fully give Myself to, you folks so that you also may constantly** (or: would habitually) **love, accept, fully give yourselves to, and drive toward union with, one another.**

35. **"Within this, all people will come to know by personal experience and insight that you are** (or: continue being) **My disciples** (students; learners; apprentices) **– if you should constantly hold love centered in, and in union with, one another** (or: have acceptance which overcomes separation and drives toward union among yourselves)."

36. **Simon Peter then says to Him, "Lord** (Master), **to what place are you proceeding to lead under** (or: where are you going)**?" Jesus decidedly answered, "To what place I proceed leading under** (or; departing) **you continue unable** (still have no power) **to follow Me now, but you will keep on following afterwards** (will subsequently proceed following).

37. **Peter now says to Him, "Lord** (Master), **why** (through what situation or circumstance) **am I not presently able to keep on following you right now? I will continue placing my soul over You** (or: I will proceed to be laying [down] my soul-life, inner being, and conscious self for Your sake)."

38. **Jesus continues in discerning reply, "You will continue to place your soul over Me** (or: lay you soul-life and self [down] for My sake)**? Most assuredly** (It is certainly true; Amen, amen; Count on it), **I now say to you, a cock** (or: rooster) **will** [other MSS: can] **under no circumstances crow until you will proceed to disown** (renounce; deny) **Me three times. Don't let the heart of the group be continually shaken or concerned** (unsettled; agitated; troubled; disturbed; distressed)."

CHAPTER 14

1. **"You folks are constantly trusting, believing and continue faithful unto God; you are also progressively trusting and believing on into Me**

> (or, as an imperative: Keep on believing and putting faith into the midst of God, and also keep on putting your trust, confidence and loyalty into Me). [cf 2 Cor. 5:1-2, 4, 6, 8]

2. **"Within My Father's house** (or: household) **are many abodes** (staying places; dwelling places; homes; rooms). **Now if not, I would at once tell you folks, because I am progressively passing** (or: traveling) **along to prepare and make ready a place in you** (or: for you; with and among you folks).

3. **"Even if I should journey on and prepare** (make suitable, fit and appropriate) **a place** (or: a spot; a position; a role) **in you folks** (or: with, among and for you), **I am now presently** (or: progressively; repeatedly; habitually) **coming again, and then, I will progressively take you folks in My arms and receive you to Myself, directing you toward Myself so as to be face to face with Me, to the end that where I, Myself, am** (or: exist) **you folks also can continue being** (or: would ongoingly exist).

4. **"And to the place under, where I Myself am progressively leading the way** (or: where I am submissively going), **you have seen and know the Way** (or: path; road)."

5. Thomas then says to Him, "O Lord (Master), **we have not seen nor do we know under what place You are leading the way** (or: where You are humbly going), **so how are we able to have seen and** [other MSS: how do we] **know the way?"**

6. Jesus then says to him, "I, Myself, AM (exist being) **the Way** (or: Path), **the Truth** (the Reality) **and the Life** (or: = I am the way to really live). **No one is presently going to, or progressively coming toward, the Father, except through Me** (through means of Me, or, through the midst of Me).

7. **"Since you men have personally and experientially known Me** (or: If you folks had insight of Me or were acquainted with Me), **you also will continue personally and experientially knowing and perceiving My Father** [other MSS: you would likely have seen and now know (or: perceive) My Father, as well]. **And so from right now** (this moment) **you are intimately, experientially and progressively knowing and recognizing Him** (or: you folks continue gaining insight of Him), **and have seen Him."**

8. Philip then says to Him, "O Lord (Master), **show us the Father** (point the Father out to us), **and it is continuing to be sufficient** (adequate; enough) **for us."**

9. Jesus is then saying to him, "I continue being (I am) **with you folks so much time, and you have not come to intimately and experientially be aware of, know and recognize Me, Philip? The person having discerned and seen Me has seen, and now perceives, the Father! How are you now saying, 'Show us the Father'?**

10. **"Are you not continuing to trust and presently believe that it is continuously** (it constantly exists being) **I, Myself, within the midst of the Father, and the Father within the midst of Me** (or: I Myself centered in union with the Father, and the Father centered in union with Me)? **The gush-effects** (results of the flow; or: utterances, declarations, words spoken) **which I, Myself, am constantly saying to you men, I am not constantly saying from Myself. But the Father, continuously dwelling and remaining** (abiding; staying) **within the midst of Me, is habitually** (constantly) **doing** (making; constructing; creating; forming; performing; producing) **His works** (actions; deeds).

11. **"Keep on trusting and progressively believe Me** (or: by Me and in Me,) **that [it is] I within the midst of the Father, and the Father within the midst of Me** (or: that I [am] in union with the Father, and the Father [is] in union with Me). **Otherwise** (or: But if not), **keep trusting and constantly believe Me** (or: in Me) **because of the works** (actions; deeds) **themselves.**

12. **"It is certainly true** (Most assuredly; Amen, amen), **I am saying to you folks, the person habitually trusting and progressively believing into Me, the works** (actions; deeds) **which I Myself am constantly doing** (habitually performing; progressively making, constructing, creating, forming) **that person also will proceed doing** (performing; making; creating; producing), **and he will progressively be doing and producing greater than these, because I Myself am progressively journeying** (constantly going from one place to another) **toward** (or: facing; face-to-face with) **the Father.** [Cf 1:1]

13. **"And because** [reading 'οτι αν] **you would have sought in petition within My Name** (or [reading 'o τι αν]: Also whatever you could seek in petition in union with My Name), **I will proceed doing it: to the end that the Father can** (could; would) **be glorified** (recognized; be given a good reputation, a good opinion and a manifestation which incites praise; have an assumed appearance) **within the Son.**

14. **"If you folks should petition Me for something** (or: anything) **within, in union with, and centered in, My Name, I Myself will proceed performing** (doing; making; creating; forming) **this.**

15. **"If you folks are habitually loving and accepting Me** (or, as a subjunctive: would continue seeking union with, and fully giving yourselves to, Me), **you folks WILL continue observing** [other MSS, subjunctive: you folks can or should observe (or: note and keep watch over; guard and preserve; keep in view; hold in custody); other MSS, the imperative: Keep in view and take note of] **My implanted goals** (impartations of the finished product within; inward directives; interior purposes and destiny),

16. **"and I Myself will continue asking** (making a request of) **the Father, and He will proceed to be giving another Helper** (One called alongside to give assistance, relief, comfort and encouragement; Paraclete), **of like kind, to you folks – to the end that He** (or: It) **can continue being** [other MSS: would be constantly remaining and dwelling] **with you folks on into the midst of the Age –**

17. **"the Spirit of the Truth** (or: the spirit and breath of reality; the Breath-effect and Attitude which is this Reality), **whom** (or: which) **the System** (world; ordered arrangement of religion, politics and culture; the system of domination) **has no power** (is not able) **to receive, because it is not habitually gazing upon It** (or: Him) **with contemplation** (continually viewing and watching it with attentive interest), **nor is it coming to intimately and experientially know It** (or: Him). **Yet YOU folks are progressively knowing It** (or: Him) **by intimate experience, because It** (or: He) **is continuously dwelling** (remaining;

abiding) **alongside you folks – in your presence – and It** (or: He) **continuously exists** (or: is; [other MSS: will continue being]) **within, in union with, and among you people.** [*Cf* 2 Cor. 5:5]

18. **"I will not be leaving you abandoned or be sending you off as orphaned ones** (or: folks without family). **I am repeatedly** (or: habitually) **and now progressively coming to** (or: face to face with; toward) **you people.**

19. **"Yet a little [while; longer] and the domination System** (world; ordered arrangement of religion and culture) **no longer continues viewing** (attentively watching) **Me, but YOU people are constantly watching** (attentively and contemplatively viewing) **Me. Because I, Myself, am continuously living, you folks will also continue living** [other MSS: will also from, or in, yourselves keep on living].

20. **"Within That Day you yourselves will personally be coming to progressively realize and then be knowing that I Myself [am; exist] within the midst of My Father, and you folks within the midst of and in union with Me, and I Myself within the midst of and in union with you people.**

21. **"The person continuously holding** (or: constantly possessing and having) **My implanted goals** (impartations of the finished product within; inward directives; interior purposes and destiny) **and habitually observing** (watching over to keep, protect and maintain) **them – that one is** (exists being) **the person continuously loving, and fully giving himself to, Me. Now the one continuously loving and accepting Me will continue being loved, accepted and urged toward union** [*p*75 reads: watched over and cared for] **by** (or: under) **the Father, and I Myself will continue loving that person and I will progressively** (or: habitually) **cause Myself to be seen in clear light in him or her**

> (or: will continue inwardly manifesting Myself by her/him; will continuously inwardly make Myself visible to her/him; will progressively show Myself within for him/her; or: = will continue showing to, in, or by him/her what I am really like)."

22. **Judah** (Judas) **– not Iscariot – is then saying to Him, "Lord** (Master), **what has come to be** (or: has happened) **that you are now about to progressively and continually show Yourself plainly** (make Yourself to be inwardly seen in clear light) **to us** (or: in us) **and not to** (or: in) **the world** (or: domination System; ordered arrangement of the religious and political culture; aggregate of humanity)?"

23. **Jesus conclusively replies, and says to him, "If anyone continues** (or: may be habitually) **loving, accepting, fully giving himself to, and urging toward union with, Me, he WILL continue constantly watching over so as to observe, guard, preserve keep and maintain My word** (*logos*: thought, idea and message; laid-out, patterned information), **and My Father will continue loving, fully giving Himself to, and urging toward union with, him, AND, facing toward him, We will continue coming to him and will be progressively making** (constructing; forming; creating; producing) **a home** (an abode; a dwelling place; a place to stay) **with him** (or: at his side and in his presence).

24. **"The one not habitually loving or fully giving himself to Me is not habitually observing, watching over or keeping My words** (laid-out thoughts, ideas and messages), **and the word** (that which has been laid out; *Logos*; thought; idea; message) **which you folks are continually hearing is not Mine, but rather belongs to, is from and pertains to the Father [Who is] sending Me.**

25. **"I have spoken these things to you folks while constantly remaining** (dwelling; abiding) **with you** (in your presence; at your side or at your house).

26. **"Now the Helper** (the One called alongside to aid, comfort, encourage and bring relief; the Paraclete), **the set-apart Spirit** (or: the Sacred Breath; the holy Breath-effect; the holy attitude), **which the Father will proceed sending within, and in union with, My Name, that One will be progressively teaching you all things** (everything) **and will continue reminding you of** (calling to your mind and causing you to think about) **everything** (all things) **which I, Myself, said to you.**

27. **"I am continuously sending off** (releasing away; hurling off) **peace** (joining) **to** (or: for; by; in; with) **you people. My peace I am constantly giving to you** (or: in, by, for you folks). **I, Myself, am not giving [it] to you the way** (or: according as) **the System** (the world of religion, politics and culture) **continually gives [it]. Do not let the heart of the group be constantly shaken, disturbed or agitated, neither let it be habitually timid** (shrinking; responding cowardly). [Deut. 31:8; Josh. 1:9]

28. **"You heard that I, Myself, said to you, 'I am progressively leading away under** (or: humbly departing, but bringing things under control), **and yet I am presently progressively** (or: repeatedly; habitually) **coming toward** (face-to-face-with) **you folks.' If you had been loving and giving yourself to Me, you should have at some point been caused to rejoice, because I am progressively journeying toward the Father, because the Father is greater** (or: = more important) **than I.**

29. **"And now** (at the present time) **I have told you** (declared [it] to you) **before it comes to be** (is birthed; occurs), **so that whenever it would come to be** (or: should occur) **you people would trust, can believe, should be loyal and may faith-it.**
30. **"I will no longer converse** (be speaking) **with you folks [about] many things, for the ruler** (the one in first place; the chief) **of the System** (or: of this ordered arrangement of the political, economic, religious and cultural world) **is progressively coming, and yet he is holding nothing within Me**
   (or: it [i.e., the domination system] continues to have and possess nothing in Me and has no hold on Me; or: = he [note: this could refer either to the chief priest, or to Pilate] has nothing to do with Me, and there is nothing in Me that is to his advantage),
31. **"but rather, even correspondingly as the Father gave an implanted goal and destiny in Me** (imparted the finished purpose within and gave an inward directive to Me), **thus and in this manner I continue habitually performing** (constantly doing and producing), **to the end that the System** (the ordered arrangement of the world; the system of control; religious and secular society) **can come to know by experience that I am continuously loving, and fully giving Myself to, the Father.**
Be progressively caused to rise up, and be habitually awake and excited (or, as a middle: Now rise up). **We can** (or: should) **now progressively lead the way from this place** (or: = Let's get out of here)."

CHAPTER 15

1. **"I, Myself, AM** (or: exist being) **the true** (genuine; real) **Grapevine, and My Father is** (continues being) **the One who tends the soil** (the Farmer; the One who tills and works the Land; the Cultivator, Gardener, Husbandman).
2. **"Every tender branch** (shoot or twig which can easily be broken) **within Me not habitually bearing** (bringing forth; = producing) **fruit He regularly lifts up and takes it away. And every one consistently bearing the fruit He periodically clears and cleans** (or: seasonally cleanses) **by pruning, to the end that it can continue bearing more** (a greater amount of) **fruit.** [cf Mat. 25:46]
3. **"You folks, yourselves, are already clean** (cleansed), **cleared and pruned ones through and because of the word** (*Logos*; laid-out message; thought; idea; pattern-conveying information) **which I have spoken to you** (in you; for you; among you) **folks.**
4. **"You folks remain** (dwell; abide; stay) **within and in union with Me – and I, Myself, [will remain] within and in union with you. Correspondingly as the tender branch is not being consistently able** (having continuing power) **to repeatedly bear fruit from itself unless it should continually remain** (stay; dwell) **within** (in union with; on) **the grapevine, in the same way, neither [can] you folks, unless you may constantly remain** (stay; dwell) **within** (in union with; centered in) **Me.**
5. **"I, Myself, AM the Grapevine; you folks [are] the tender branches** (shoots or twigs that can be easily broken). **The person continuously remaining** (dwelling; abiding) **within the midst of Me – and I within the midst of and in union with him – this one is repeatedly bearing** (bringing forth; = producing) **much fruit. [It is the case] that apart from** (or: Because separated from) **Me you folks continue having ability and power to do** (make; construct; create; form; perform; produce) **nothing!**
6. **"If anyone would** (or: may; should) **not continuously remain** (dwell; abide; stay) **within the midst of and in union with Me, he or she is cast** (or: thrown) **outside, in the same way as the tender branch** (or: like that twig or shoot). **And thus, it** (or: he/she) **is caused to dry up and wither, and then they are constantly gathering** (or: leading) **them** [other MSS: it] **together ["synagogue-ing" them, or it, as in a bundle]. Later, they are normally throwing** (or: casting) [p66 adds: **them**] **into the fire – and it** (or: he) **is progressively kindled** (repeatedly ignited; or: habitually lit and progressively burned).
7. **"If you people can** (or: would; should) **remain** (abide; dwell; stay) **within the midst of and in union with Me – and My gush-effects** (results of spoken words) **can** (should; would) **remain** [with p66 and others: and the flow of My declarations continues abiding] **within the midst of and in union with you – seek in petition** [other MSS: you will continue asking) **whatever you folks may habitually purpose** (constantly intend; repeatedly will; continuously want or desire), **and it will proceed coming to be in and among you folks** (or: will progressively occur for you people; will continue being birthed by you folks; will habitually happen to you folks).
8. **"In this is** (or: was) **My Father glorified** (caused to appear and be recognized; given a good reputation and a manifestation which calls forth praise)**: that you men can continuously bear** (or: would keep on bringing forth) **much fruit, and thus can** (or: would) **come to be** [with other MSS: will continue

becoming] **disciples** (learners; students; apprentices) **by Me** (or: in Me; to Me; for Me; with Me; [other MSS: My disciples]).

9. **"Correspondingly as** (or: In the same sphere as; To the same degree as) **the Father loves and accepts Me – and I, Myself, also love and accept you folks – at once begin to remain** (abide; dwell; stay) **within the midst of** (and: in union with; centered in) **My own Love** (acceptance; drive toward reunion)! [comment: His Love is the Vine – vss. 4-5, above – and He is the Love – vs. 10, below]

10. **"Whenever** (or: If) **you would** (can) **observe, watch over, guard, keep in view and maintain My implanted goals** (impartations of the finished product within; inward directives; interior purposes and destinies), **[by this] you will continue remaining** (abiding; dwelling) **within the midst of, in union with, and centered in the Love which is Me** (My love; the acceptance and urge toward union, from Me), **correspondingly as** (or: to the same level as) **I, Myself, have watched over, observed, guarded, keep and now maintain My Father's implanted goals** (impartations of the finished product within; inward directives; interior purposes and destinies) **and continuously remain** (or: dwell) **within the midst of the Love, acceptance, Self-giving and urge toward union, from, and which is, Him.**

11. **"I have spoken these things to you to the end that My joy would** (or: can; should) **remain and continuously exist within the midst of you people, and that your joy may be filled full** (or: fulfilled).

12. **"This is My implanted goal** (impartation of the finished product within; inward directive; interior purpose and destiny)**: that you keep on loving, urging toward union, and accepting one another – correspondingly as** (to the same degree as; in the same sphere as) **I love and accept you folks.**

13. **"No one continues holding** (or: having) **greater Love** (full self-giving; urge toward reunion) **than this: that someone should place** (set; lay; put) **his soul** (or: inner being; self; person; consciousness which is him) **over [the situation or circumstances of; = cover]** (or: on behalf of) **his friends.**

14. **"You folks are** (exist continuously being) **My friends! So if you can – or would – [simply] keep on doing** (or: be habitually producing) **whatever I, Myself, am constantly imparting as the goal in you** (or: repeatedly giving as inner direction to you; progressively implanting as the goal and end for you; now implanting as the interior aim, purpose and destiny by you)! ...

15. **"I am no longer calling** (or: terming) **you people slaves, because the slave has not seen and does not know** (or: is not aware of) **what his owner** (lord; master) **is habitually doing. Yet now I have declared you folks friends, because I make intimately and experientially known to you everything** (or: all things) **which I heard and hear at My Father's side and in His presence.**

16. **"You yourselves did not choose Me, but to the contrary I, Myself, selected and picked out** (or: chose) **you folks and placed** (or: set) **you, to the end that you would** (or: can; may) **progressively lead and bring [situations] under control** (or: humbly go your way) **and would** (or: can; should) **be constantly bearing** (bringing forth) **fruit, and your fruit may continuously remain** (stay; abide), **so that whatever you people may seek in petition from the Father – in** (or: centered in) **My Name – He at a certain point would** (or: may suddenly; [other MSS: will proceed to]) **give [it] to you folks.**

17. **"I repeatedly give you these goal-oriented, inner directions** (or: I am progressively imparting these purposed aims leading to the union-centered end-and-destiny, by, for and among you folks) **so that you can and would habitually be Loving** (accepting; seeking union) **with one another.**

18. **"Since** (or: If) **the System** (world; controlling ordered arrangement of the political and religious culture) **is constantly regarding you folks with ill-will** (or: hating or radically detaching you), **you continue knowing by experience** (or, as an imperative: be now knowing) **that it has socially detached Me, hated Me and still regards Me with ill-will first – before you people.**

19. **"If you had been and yet had your being from out of the domination System** (or: world of culture, religion and government) **as a source, the System** (world of control by religion and economy) **would have been being friendly toward and fond of its own production and possession. Yet now, because you do not exist from out of the System** (cosmos) **as a source – but to the contrary I have selected** (or: chosen) **and picked you out from the midst of the System** (world's organization: culture, religion and politics) **– on account of this, the System** (world; institutional religion; society; government) **continues treating you with ill-will** (or: habitually hates you and socially detaches you).

20. **"Continually bear in mind** (or: Keep on remembering) **the *Logos*** (Word; thought; message and information that was laid out) **which I, Myself, said to you. A slave is not greater than** (does not exist being superior to) **his owner** (lord; master). **Since they pursue and persecute Me, they will also continue pursuing and persecuting you folks. If they keep** (or: observed and cared for) **My *Logos*** (Word; laid-out message), **they will also proceed to be keeping** (observing and caring for) **yours.**

21. "But to the contrary, they will proceed doing (accomplishing; making; performing; producing) **all these things unto you and bringing them forth into the midst of you folks, on account of My Name, because they have not seen nor do they know the One sending Me.**
22. "If I did not come and speak to (or: among) **them, they had not been holding failure** (or: were having no sin or error; continued possessing no deviation). **But now** (at this time) **they continue holding nothing which like a specious and deceptive cloak appears in front around their sin**
>   (or: they are not continuing to hold that which is put forward to hide the situation concerning their failure; they are not habitually having an excuse or pretense about their deviation, error and miss of the target).
23. "The one who by habit hates Me, detaches from Me or treats Me with ill-will also continues hating My Father, habitually treats Him with ill-will and keeps on radically detaching from Him.
24. "If I did not do (perform; produce; create) **the works** (actions; deeds) **among them or within them – which no one else** (or: no other one) **did** (performed; produced) – **they were having no sin or error** (they had not been holding a failure or a miss of the target). **But now** (at this time) **they have both seen and hated with radical detachment from both Me and My Father.**
25. "But then, [this is] so that the *Logos* (Word; message; pronouncement; blueprint) **having been written in their Law would** (could; should; may) **be fulfilled: 'They hated, treated badly and radically detached from Me for no cause** (for no reason at all; gratuitously).' [Ps. 35:19; 69:4]
26. "Whenever the One called alongside to aid, comfort, encourage and bring relief (the Helper; the Paraclete) **can** (or: may; should would) **come – the Spirit of the Truth** (or: the Breath-effect of, and which is, Reality; the attitude which is genuineness) **Which** (or: Who) **is constantly** (habitually; progressively) **proceeding and traveling out from beside the Father** (= emanating from the Father's presence; or: from a presence which is the Father), **[and] Which** (or: Whom) **I, Myself, will continue sending to you from the Father's side** (or: from the presence which is the Father) – **that One will continue bearing witness** (giving testimony; showing evidence) **about Me.**
27. "Now you folks, also, continue giving witness (are habitually testifying; are progressively being evidence), **because – from [the] beginning** (= the start or the outset) – **you are with Me** (or: because you constantly exist, being with Me from [the] origin)."

CHAPTER 16

1. "I have spoken these things to, for and among you folks so that you would (could; may; should) **not at any point be caught in a snare** (or: trap) **by surprise, or be made to stumble or falter.**
2. "They will continue making you gathering-outcasts (synagogue-exiles) – **ones turned away from the synagogues** (= they will continue cutting you off from the rights and privileges of the Jewish society). **But further, an hour is progressively coming with the result that everyone in the process of killing you folks off may imagine** (suppose; hold the opinion of; think) **[himself] to be proceeding in presenting** (bearing forward) **an offering of sacred service to, and for, God,**
3. "and they will continue doing (or: performing) **these things because they neither personally know** (or: intimately or experientially recognize; have insight into) **the Father, nor Me.**
4. "Nevertheless, I have spoken these things to you so that whenever their hour may (or: should; would) **come, you folks can call them to mind** (or: would remember them), **that I, Myself, told you. Now I did not tell you these things originally** (from out of [the] beginning; from [the] start; = at first), **because I was being with you.**
5. "Yet now (at this time) **I am progressively leading [the way] under** (or: humbly going away) **toward the One sending Me, and no one from among you folks is presently asking** (or, as a subjunctive: should keep on inquiring of) **Me, 'To what place are you progressively leading [the way] under** (or: submissively departing)?'
6. "But now because I have spoken these things to you people, grief, sorrow and sadness has **filled the heart of you folks** (or: = the core emotion of the group; or: = your hearts).
7. "Nevertheless, I, Myself, am telling you folks the Truth (or: speaking reality to, for and among you folks). **It progressively bears together for you people** (It continues being advantageous and expedient in you; It is now for your benefit) **that I should go away. For if I should not go away, the One called alongside to aid, comfort, encourage and bring relief** (Helper; Paraclete) **will not come** [other MSS:

may by no means come] **to you and be face to face with you folks. Yet if I should journey on** (or: would travel on to another place) **I will be repeatedly sending Him to you folks.**

8. **"And upon coming, that One will be progressively testing and putting the domination System** (or: the aggregate of humanity; or: the world of culture, society, religion, economy and politics) **to the proof** (or: exposing and presenting convincing arguments about the aggregate of humanity) **concerning error** (failure; deviation; missing the target; sin) **and about fairness and equity in rightwised relationships which comprise the Way pointed out** (or: concerning eschatological deliverance that produces covenant inclusion) **– and about dividing and separating** (sifting) **for evaluating and deciding** (or: concerning judging). [comment: thus, the Paraclete replaces the Law]

9. **"About error** (failure; missing the mark; sin; deviation), **on the one hand, because they are not constantly trusting, continuing faithful, or progressively believing into Me.**

[comment: this now defines sin and failure to hit the Target (Christ)]

10. **"About justice, fairness and equity in rightwised relationships of the Way pointed out** (or: concerning eschatological deliverance that produces covenant participation), **on the other hand, because I am progressively leading [everything] under control by withdrawing toward** (or: to; [to be] face-to-face with) **the Father, and so you folks are no longer continually gazing upon and contemplatively watching Me.**

11. **"And about dividing and separating** (sifting) **for evaluation and decision, because the ruler** (one in first place; chief) **of this System** (world of culture, economics, religion or politics; domination system) **has been sifted, separated, evaluated and decided about, and now stands judged**

(or: Yet concerning judging, because the Prince and Leader of this universe and the aggregate of humanity has had a decision made about Him, and He now stands judged [by the System]).

12. **"I still have** (or: hold) **many things to be progressively telling** (laying out for; informing) **you folks, but yet, you continue not yet being able** (or: having no power) **to habitually or progressively pick it up and carry** (or: bear) **it right now** (at present).

13. **"Yet, whenever that One – the Spirit of the Truth** (or: the Breath-effect from Reality; the attitude which is genuineness) **– would come** (or: Nonetheless, at the time when that spirit which is truth and reality should come), **It** (or: He) **will constantly be a Guide and will progressively lead you on the Path** (or: it will continue leading the way for you) **directed toward and proceeding on into all Truth and Reality** (or: into the midst of every truth and genuine reality) **– for It** (He; it) **will not habitually speak from Itself** (or: Himself), **but rather, as many things as It** (He; it) **continuously hears, It** (He; it) **will proceed speaking, and will continue reporting back to you the things presently and progressively coming, as well as those that are habitually coming and going.**

14. **"That One will progressively glorify Me** (will keep on giving Me an assumed appearance, recognition, and a good reputation, with a manifestation of Me which calls forth praise), **because It** (He; it) **will constantly take from out of what is Mine** (or: receive from the one from, and which is, Me) **and will repeatedly report back to you folks** (or: will continue announcing to and informing you).

15. **"All things – as many and as much as the Father continuously possesses** (or: whatever the Father has and constantly holds) **– progressively, then continuously, exists being Mine. On this account I said that from out of what is Mine It** (or: from the one from, and which is, Me, He) **is continuously receiving** (habitually taking) **and will continue reporting back** (announcing) **to, for, and among, you folks.**

16. **"A little [while; time], and then no longer do you folks continue attentively watching** (gazing at) **Me, and yet then again a little [while; space of time], and you will continue seeing Me."**

17. **Therefore some of His disciples said to one another, "What is this which He is presently saying to us, 'A little [while], and then you do not continue attentively watching Me, and yet then again a little [while] and you will continue seeing Me'? And, 'Because I am progressively bringing [everything] under control and departing toward the Father'?"**

18. **Hence, they went on saying, "What is this** (= What does this mean) **which He is saying, 'In a little [while]'? We have not seen nor do we know what He is speaking** (= what He is talking about)."

19. **Jesus knew** [with other MSS: then came to know] **that they were wanting and intending to be questioning** (or: asking) **Him, so He said to them, "Are you folks continuing to seek with one**

another (among yourselves) **about this, because I said, 'A little [while] and you do not continue attentively watching Me, and yet then again a little [while], and you will continue seeing Me'?**
20. **"Most assuredly** (It is certainly true; Amen, amen), **I now say to you folks that you yourselves will continue to weep** (shed tears and lament) **and will be from time to time shrieking out** (wailing in mournful funeral songs), **yet the world** (controlling System of culture, religion and politics; or: religious and secular society) **will continue rejoicing. You yourselves will periodically be made sad and distressed with grief, but yet your sadness, grief and distress will repeatedly birth itself into joy.**
21. **"The woman, whenever she may be progressing in giving birth, is progressively having pain and distress** (sorrow and grief), **because her hour comes** (or: came). **Yet, whenever she may give birth to the little child** (infant), **she continues no longer calling to mind** (remembering; bearing in mind) **the pressure** (the squeezing, anguish and tribulation) **because of the joy that a human being** (a person) **is born** (or: was given birth) **into the world** (the system of culture; or: the universe).
22. **"And you yourselves, therefore, are now progressively having** [other MSS: will continue having] **sadness, distress and grief. Yet I will repeatedly see you folks again, and your heart will repeatedly rejoice, and no one will continue lifting up and carrying** [other MSS: now takes] **your joy away from you folks.**
23. **"And within that Day you will continue asking Me nothing** (or: will not repeatedly request even one thing [from] Me). **Most assuredly** (It is certainly true; Amen, amen), **I am now saying to you, if you folks should petition the Father for anything** (or: whatever you people may corporately request of the Father), **He will proceed giving [it] to you corporately, within** (or: in union with) **My Name.**
24. **"Until the present time** (right now) **you folks petitioned nothing within** (or: in union with) **My Name. Be habitually making petitions, and you folks will habitually receive, to the end that your joy may constantly exist being having been filled full and continuing filled up** (or: complete).
25. **"I have spoken these things to you within comparative illustrations** (in figures of speech, proverbial sayings, similes, and veiled language placed alongside the course of the way). **An hour is progressively coming when I will no longer continue speaking to you in comparative illustrations, but rather, I will proceed in outspoken freedom of speech, as a citizen, reporting back to you folks about** (or: concerning) **the Father.**
26. **"Within that Day you will continue making petition within My Name – and I am not saying to you that I, Myself, will continue asking** (or: requesting of) **the Father about you folks,**
27. **"for the Father, Himself, continuously likes, has fond affection for, and is constantly friendly to you people, because you have liked and been friendly to, and even have shown fond affection for Me, and further, you folks have trusted and still believe that I came out from God's side** (or: came forth from beside God; [other MSS: the Father]).
28. **"I came from out of the midst of** [other MSS: I went forth from beside] **the Father and I have come back** (or: again [*palin*]) **into the ordered arrangement** (the world; the System of culture, religion, economics and politics; or: the aggregate of humanity).
    (or: reading *palin* modifying *aphiēmi*: **Furthermore** {or: Again}) **I am continuing in forgiving the world and aggregate of humanity** (or: releasing [*aphiēmi*] the system of culture and religion; or: leaving this ordered arrangement), **and then I am progressively journeying on** (traveling to another place), **directed to and facing toward the Father."** [note: *palin* can modify either "come" or "forgive"]
29. **His disciples are then saying to Him, "Look!** (See!) **You are now speaking in [the] outspoken boldness of speech of a citizen, and are saying not even one comparative illustration.**
30. **"Now we have seen and continue to know that You have seen and know all things** (or: everything) **and have no need that anyone should questioning You. Within this we constantly trust and progressively believe that You came forth from out of God."**
31. **Jesus discerningly replied to them, "At present** (or: Right now) **you continue trusting and believing with loyal allegiance** (or: Just now you are believing!?).
32. **"Look and consider. An hour is progressively coming – and it has come and is here – to the end that you folks should be scattered and dispersed [as sown seed], each one into his own [places; life; home; paths; destiny; things], and Me you folks can let go off alone** (or: should leave and send off alone). **And yet I am not alone, because the Father is constantly being with Me.**
33. **"I have spoken these things to you so that you may continuously have** (hold; possess) **peace and a joining centered in, within the midst of, and in union with, Me. Within the System** (dominating and controlling world of culture, religion, economy and government; or: among and in union

with the aggregate of humanity) **you normally have pressure and stress** (or: continually have squeezing; repeatedly have tribulation and oppression), **but nonetheless, be confident and take courage! I, Myself, have overcome and conquered the System** (dominating world; organized arrangement of religion and society; aggregate of humanity) **so that it stands a completed victory!"**

CHAPTER 17

1. **Jesus speaks** (or: spoke) **these things and then, lifting up His eyes into the sky** (or: the atmosphere; the heaven), **says, "O Father, the hour has come and is now here: bring glory** (give a good reputation; bring an assumed appearance and a manifestation which calls forth praise) **to Your Son, to the end that the Son can bring glory** (or: may give a recognized appearance and a good reputation; would bring a manifestation which calls forth praise) **to and for You.**

2. **"Correspondingly as You give** (or: gave) **to Him right, privilege and authority from out of Being concerning ALL flesh** (= people) **to the end that ALL, which You have given to Him and that He now possesses, to THEM He will continue** (or: one-after-another be) **giving** [other MSS: would at some point give] **eonian Life** (life having its origin in, and the characteristics and qualities of, the Age [of Messiah]; or: age-enduring life; life of, for and in the ages).

3. **"Now THIS is** (or: exists being) **eonian Life** (living existence of and for the ages; life pertaining to the Age [of Messiah]): **namely, that they may progressively come to intimately and experientially know You, the only** (or: sole) **true and real** (genuine) **God – and Jesus Christ, Whom You send forth as an Emissary** (or: as well as Jesus [as the] Anointed One, whom You sent off as a Representative).

4. **"I Myself glorify You** (or: brought a recognized appearance for You; present a good reputation with a manifestation which called forth praise to You) **upon the earth** (or: the Land), **finishing and perfecting** (bringing to its goal, purpose, destiny and fruition) **the Work** (the Deed; the Act) **which You have given to** (or: in; for) **Me, to the end that I could do** (or: would perform; may produce) **[it].**

5. **"So now You Yourself, O Father, glorify** (bring a good reputation and a manifestation which calls forth praise to) **Me alongside Yourself** (or: with the presence of Yourself) **in, by and with the glory** (recognition; good reputation; manifestation which calls forth praise) **which I was having** (or: used to hold) **and continued holding at Your side and in Your presence, before the universe** (or: system; world of culture, religion and government) **is continuing to have being** (or: which I was constantly possessing, alongside Yourself, before the aggregate of humanity continued to exist with You).

6. **"I brought Your Name to clear light and manifest it to the humans** (people) **whom You gave to, and for, Me from out of the midst of the System** (or: aggregate of humanity; organized culture and religion; world of a dominated society). **They were existing in You** (or: with You; by You; for You; [given] to You) **and to Me** (for Me; in Me) **you give** (or: gave) **them, and they have kept, observed, taken care of and watched over Your** *Logos* (Word; thought; laid-out idea; message; blueprint).

7. **"Now** (or: At this moment) **they have intimately and experientially known that all things – as many** (or: much) **as You have given to Me, so that I now possess – continuously exist from You and are at Your side, in Your presence,**

8. **"because I have given to them the gush-effects** (results of the flow; spoken words; sayings; declarations) **which You gave to Me, and give in and by Me, and they themselves took and received** (accepted) **[them], and they intimately and experientially know truly** (or: with reality) **that I came out from beside You** (or: went forth from Your presence), **and they trust and believe that** (or: they are faithful because) **You, Yourself, sent Me forth as an Emissary** (a Representative).

9. **"I, Myself, am now requesting about** (or: concerning) **them. I am not presently requesting about the System** (religious, political and cultural world; or: society; the aggregate of humanity; system of domination), **but rather, about** (or: concerning) **those whom You have given to Me, and I possess,**

10. **"because they continuously exist** (or: are) **in You** (or: by You; for You; with You). **Thus, all My possessions are Yours, and Your possessions are Mine, and I have been – and remain – glorified** (made to be a recognized appearance and a manifestation which calls forth praise) **in and among them.**

11. **"Also, I am no longer within the System** (or: And yet I no longer exist being in union with, or centered in, the world of culture and religion, or the domination arrangement), **and yet they themselves are continuing to be within the System** (world; ordered arrangement of the current society) **– and I, Myself, am progressively going toward You** (or: constantly coming face to face with You). **O Father, O Set-apart and Holy One, watch over and care for them** (observe, keep and guard them) **within, and**

in union with, Your Name – which You have given to Me, and I now have – to the end that they can (or: would) **continuously exist being one, correspondingly as** (just as; in the same sphere as; to the same degree as; on the same level as) **We Ourselves [are].** [Cf vs. 22, below]

12. **"When I was being with them** [other MSS add: within the System], **I Myself was continually watching over, caring for, observing, keeping, guarding and maintaining them in union with** (or: centered in) **Your Name – which You have given to Me, and I now have – and I protected [them], and NOT ONE from among them lost himself** (or: destroyed himself), **except** (or: since not) **the son of "the loss"** (the son of the dissolution, or, from the destruction; the person having the characteristics of loss, dissolution or destruction), **so that the Scripture could and would be fulfilled.**

13. **"Yet now** (at this moment) **I am progressively coming toward You, and I am repeatedly speaking these things aloud, within the System** (world of culture, politics and religion; aggregate of humanity), **so that they can continuously hold** (or: would habitually have) **My own joy** (the joy that is Mine) **existing having been filled full** (made full and continuing full) **within the midst of themselves.**

14. **"I, Myself, have given Your *Logos*** (Your Word; the thought and idea from You; the laid-out message and blueprint, which is You) **to them, and the domination System** (world of government and religion) **hates them** (treats and regards them with ill will; detaches from them), **because they do not exist from out of the dominating System as their source** (= are not being a product of that world), **correspondingly as I, Myself, am not from out of the dominating System, as My origin** (or: just as, in Myself, I do not exist [springing up] from the midst of the world of religious or governmental dominance).

15. **"I am not now making a request to the end that You should pick them up and carry** (or: remove; take) **them out of the System** (world; ordered arrangement of culture, religion, economy and government; human aggregate), **but rather that You should observe, guard, protect, maintain, care for and keep them out of the worthless or bad situation, the sorry plight, the effect of the knavish and good-for-nothing person, the oppressive toil and the base or evil influence.**

16. **"They do not exist** (are not being) **from out of the System** (world of society, religion or politics) **as a source or origin, just as I, Myself, am not from the System** (world) **as a source or origin.**

17. **"Set them apart** (or: Make them different from the norm) **within the midst of the Truth** (or: in union with, and centered in, reality). **Your *Logos*** (Word; blueprint; patterned idea) **exists being Truth**
> (or: Your thought, patterned information and expressed message of divine rational meaning and purpose is Reality; Your laid-out, communicated reason continues with Being [as] Reality).

18. **"Correspondingly** (or: Just; In the sphere; On the level) **as You sent Me into the System** (world of religious and political dominance; human aggregate) **as an Emissary, I Myself also send them forth as emissaries** (representatives) **into the prevailing, organized system of the human aggregate,**

19. **"and I, Myself, am continuously setting Myself apart over them** (progressively making Myself different from the norm, in their behalf) **to the end that they themselves, also, can** (may; would) **continuously exist being ones having been set-apart within the midst of reality** (centered in Truth).

20. **"I am not now making a request about these only, but further about those habitually trusting and progressively believing into Me through their word** (or: *logos*; message; what they lay out),

21. **"to the end that all humans would** (or: all people can and should) **continuously exist being one, correspondingly as You, O Father** [other MSS: Father], **[are] within the midst of Me, and I [am] within the midst of You – so that they, themselves, may and would also continuously exist being within the midst of Us, to the end that the aggregate of humanity** (the System: world of culture, religion and government; or: secular society) **can** (may; could) **continuously trust and progressively believe that** (would continue faithful because) **YOU sent Me forth as an Emissary with a mission.**

22. **"And I, Myself, have given to them** (or: in them), **and they now possess, the glory** (the notion; the opinion; the imagination; the reputation; the manifestation which calls forth praise) **which You have given to Me, and which I now possess, to the end that they can continuously exist being one correspondingly as** (just as; according as; to the same level as; in the same sphere as) **We are one:**

23. **"I within the midst of and in union with them and You within the midst of and in union with Me, to the end that they would** (or: could; should; may; can) **continuously exist being folks having been perfected** (brought to the destined goal; finished; completed; matured and purposed) **into one – so that the human aggregate** (or: the domination System) **can** (or: could; would) **progressively come to experientially know that** (or: experience insight [*gnosis*], because) **YOU commissioned and sent Me forth, and You love, accept, and urge toward reunion with, them correspondingly as** (or: just as; in the same sphere and to the same level as) **You love, accept, and give Yourself fully to, Me.**

24. **"Father, I continue purposing and intending** (or: willing; wanting) **that those also, whom You have given to Me and that I now possess, would continuously exist being with Me where I, Myself, AM** (or: where I AM, and continuously exist Being), **so that they can** (or: may; could; would) **constantly look upon and keep on contemplatively watching My own glory** (assumed appearance; manifested Presence which incites praise), **which You have given to Me as a possession because You loved** (accepted; fully gave Yourself to) **Me before [the; a] casting-down of [the; a] universe** (or: tossing down of a world; or: [the] founding of an organized system; a sowing [as seed] or [impregnating] of [the] aggregate of humanity; founding of [the] system of culture and society; or: a casting corresponding to and in agreement with an ordered disposition of [the] Dominating System).

25. **"O fair and equitable Father** (O Father, who are the paradigm of justice, uprightness, honesty and rightwised relationship – the source of what is right; O deliverance-bringing Father who puts things right), **though the aggregate of humanity** (System; world of culture, religion, economy and government) **does not have intimate, experiential knowledge of You, yet I Myself experientially and intimately know You** (or: the world, also, did not know you by experience, yet I personally knew You), **and these people personally know that** (recognize because) **YOU sent Me forth as a commissioned Emissary,**

26. **"and I made Your Name intimately known to, for, in and among them – and I will continue making It experientially known, to the end that the Love** (acceptance; urge toward union with, and Self-giving to, [all]) **[in; with] which You love** (accept; give Yourself to) **Me can** (would; may; could) **continuously be** (or: progressively exist) **within the midst of and among them – and I Myself within the midst of, among, in union with, and centered in them."**

CHAPTER 18

1. **[After] saying these things, Jesus, together with His disciples, went out to the other side across the winter flow of the Kedron** (the "brook, torrent or wadi of the Cedars"; or: the Kidron Valley) **to where there was a garden** (a place planted with trees and herbs), **into which He Himself – and His disciples – entered.**

2. **Now Judah** (or: Judas) **– the one presently transferring, commending and progressively committing Him** (or: handing Him over) **– also had seen and knew the place, because Jesus had many times** (or: frequently; often) **been gathered there with His disciples.**

3. **Therefore Judah** (Judas), **getting and taking the detachment** (or: squad [of Roman soldiers]) **and subordinates** (those who act under orders; deputies; Temple guards or Sanhedrin officers) **from the chief** (ranking) **priests and from the Pharisees, is proceeding to come there with lanterns, torches and weapons** (or: arms).

4. **Then Jesus, having seen and being aware of** (or: knowing) **all the things progressively coming upon Him, went out and proceeds saying to them, "Whom are you folks presently seeking** (looking for; or: What things are you men now trying to find)**?"**

5. **They decidedly replied, "Jesus, the Nazarene." He then says to them, "I AM** (or: I, Myself, am; or: I am Being)**"** [B reads: "I am Jesus."]. **Now Judah** (Judas) **– the one transferring, commending, committing and handing Him over – had also been standing with them,**

6. **then, as He said to them, "I, Myself, am** (or: I AM; I am continuous Existence),**"** he [other MSS: they] **went off into the rear** (into the [area] back behind) **and they suddenly fell to the ground.**

7. **Then He again inquired of them, "Whom are you presently seeking** (looking for; or: What things are you men now trying to find)**?" Now those men say, "Jesus, the Nazarene."**

8. **Jesus decidedly replies, "I told you that I, Myself, am** (or: I AM). **Since** (or: If), **then, you men are presently seeking Me, allow these men to proceed departing,"**

9. **so that the word** (or: saying; that which was laid out) **may be fulfilled which He said: "I lose** (or: destroyed) **not one from out of them whom You have given to Me as a possession."**

10. **Then Simon Peter, holding** (or: having) **a small sword, suddenly draws** (or: unsheathed) **it and hits** (struck) **the chief priest's slave, and cuts off his right ear. Now the name of the slave was Malchus.**

11. **Therefore Jesus says to Peter, "Thrust the small sword into the sheath** (scabbard). **The cup which the Father has given to Me and which I now have – should I not by all means drink it?"**

12. **Then the detachment** (or: squad [of Roman soldiers]) **and the military commander** (tribune; commander of a thousand soldiers) **and the subordinates** (deputies) **of the Judeans** (= religious authorities) **together seized** (apprehended; arrested) **Jesus and bound Him** (tied Him up),

13. **and then they led Him first to Annas** (or: Hannas), **for he was father-in-law of Caiaphas, who was [the] chief priest of that year.**

14. **Now Caiaphas was the one joining in counsel with and advising the Judeans** (= religious authorities) **that it is progressively bearing together as an expedient advantage for one man to be dying over [the situation of]** (or: on behalf of) **the People.**

15. **So Simon Peter and another disciple kept on following Jesus. Now that [other] disciple was personally known by** (or: intimate with; or: = a close friend of) **the chief priest, and he went in together with Jesus into the courtyard of the chief priest's house.**

16. **Yet Peter had been, and remained, standing outside, facing toward the gate** (or: door). **Therefore the other disciple – the one well-known to the chief priest – went out and spoke to the girl who kept** (or: guarded) **the gate** (portress; doorkeeper) **and then leads Peter into the midst.**

17. **Then the young woman** (or: young female servant) **– the gate keeper** (portress) **– says to Peter,** "Are you not also one of this man's disciples?" **That one then says, "I am not!** (or: No, I'm not.)"

18. **Now the slaves and the subordinates** (deputies; those under orders), **having made a charcoal fire and keeping the embers going because it was cold, had been standing and kept on warming themselves, and so Peter, also, was standing with them and continued warming himself.**

19. **Then the chief priest questioned Jesus about His disciples and about His teaching.**

20. **Jesus considered and replied to him, "I, Myself, have publicly** (outspokenly with boldness and freedom of speech which is the right of a citizen) **spoken in the System** (or: to the world of religion, culture, economics and government; for the cosmos). **I at all times taught in a synagogue, and within the Temple courts, where all the Jews are habitually coming together, and I have spoken nothing within a hidden place.**

21. **"Why are you men now proceeding in questioning Me? Question those being ones having heard what I spoke to them. See and consider** (or: Look [to them]), **these people have seen and know** (are aware of) **what things I, Myself, said."**

22. **Now [upon] His saying these things, one of the subordinates** (deputies, or Temple guards) **[who] had been standing at the side gave a striking blow to Jesus, with some instrument [such as a rod or a whip], saying, "Are you answering thus** (or: in this way) **to the chief priest?"**

23. **Jesus considered and replied to him, "If I spoke inappropriately** (in an ugly way; badly; meanly; basely; worthlessly; abusively), **testify** (give evidence) **concerning the inappropriateness** (bear witness about the abuse, the base words, the mean and ugly attitude, the bad thing). **Yet if ideally** (beautifully; appropriately; excellently), **why are you now lashing Me** (flaying Me so as to remove My skin; beating Me)?"

24. **At that, Annas** (or: Hannas) **sent Him off** (or: away) **– having been bound** (tied up) **– on their mission to Caiaphas, the chief priest.**

25. **Now Simon Peter was yet standing and warming himself. Then they said to him, "Are not you yourself, also, from out of His disciples?" That one says, "No," contradicts and denies** (or: disowns), **and says, "I am not."**

26. **One from out of the slaves of the chief priest – being a relative of the one whose ear Peter cut off – is then saying, "Did I not see you within the garden with him?"**

27. **Then again, Peter contradicted** (denied; disowned) **– and immediately a cock** (rooster) **crowed.**

28. **They then are progressively leading Jesus from Caiaphas into the Roman governor's headquarters** (the Praetorium). **Now it was early in the morning** (between 3 and 6 A.M.), **and they did not enter into the governor's headquarters so that they would not be polluted** (defiled; made ceremonially impure), **but rather could still eat the Passover meal.**

29. **Therefore, Pilate went forth outside to them and began his interrogation: "What accusation** (formal charge) **are you presently bringing with regard to** (or: which pertains to; [other MSS add: against]) **this man?"**

30. **So they decided a reply and said to him, "If this one were not continually doing an inappropriate thing** (habitually doing bad or wrong), **we would not commit or give him over to you."**

31. **Then Pilate said to them, "You men, yourselves, take him and decide about** (or: judge) **him corresponding to** (or: in accord with) **your Law." The Jews** (= religious Judean authorities) **said to him, "It is not allowed, or permitted from [our] existing, for us to kill anyone,"**

32. **so that the word of** (laid-out message and information from) **Jesus could be fulfilled which He said, repeatedly indicating by signs** (showing by symbols, omens, signals and tokens) **by what kind of death He was being about to be progressively dying away** (or: off).

33. **So Pilate entered again into the governor's headquarters** (the Praetorium) **and summoned Jesus and then said to Him, "You are yourself the king of the Judeans?** (or: So YOU are the king of the Judeans.)"

34. **Jesus considered and replied, "Are you yourself now saying this from yourself, or did others tell you about Me?"**

35. **Pilate considered and replied, "Surely I myself am not a Jew** (or: Judean)! **Your nation** (ethnic group) **and the chief priests committed and gave you over to me. What did you do?"**

36. **Jesus decidedly replied, "My kingdom** (My sovereignty; the realm and activity of My reign and influence; My kingship) **is not** (does not exist being) **from out of this System** (world of organized government, culture, economics or religion; or: universe) **as its source or origin. If My kingdom** (or: reign, realm and sovereign influence) **were from out of this System** (or: world of government, culture, religion and economy; secular society), **as a source or origin, My subordinates** (deputies; officers; those under My orders) **would have been progressively contending, struggling and fighting, to the end that I could** (or: would) **not be commended, committed or given over to the Jews** (= religious Judean authorities). **But now** (= As a matter of fact, and as it is) **My kingdom and reign is not** (sovereign influence does not exist being) **from that source** (from within this place; thence or hence)."

37. **Therefore Pilate said to Him, "Are you yourself not, then, a king?** (or: So then... you are yourself a king!)" **Jesus discerningly replied, "You yourself continue saying that I am a king. Into this [position, or purpose] I, Myself, have been born, and I have come into this System** (world and culture; social arrangement; cosmos) **and continue being present: to the end that I could and would bear witness to Reality** (or: give testimony to and evidence of the Truth). **Everyone being** (or: who is existing) **from out of Reality** (or: the Truth) **is habitually hearing, progressively listening [and thus: continually obeys] My voice."**

38. **Pilate then says to Him, "What is Reality** (or: Truth)?"
And upon saying this, he again goes out to the Jews (= religious Judean authorities), **and then says to them, "I, myself, continue finding not one cause for accusation** (or: fault, responsibility, or reason for a case) **within him.**

39. **"Now for you people there is a joint custom of intimate friendship and intercourse, for our mutual use, to the end that I should release one man to you within** (at; during) **the Passover. Are you men therefore continuing deliberately intended and purposed to the end that I should release to you the king of the Judeans?"**

40. **Then they all yelled again, saying, "Not this fellow, but rather, Bar-Abba** [meaning: a father's son, or: the son of the father]!" **Now Bar-Abba had been a robber** (one who appropriates what is not his by violence, and openly; = a Zealot; = an insurrectionist; cf Mk. 15:7).

CHAPTER 19

1. **Thereupon** (or: At that time), **therefore, Pilate took Jesus and scourged** (with a whip [having pieces of metal embedded, so as to rip off flesh] severely flogged) **[Him].**

2. **And then the soldiers, upon weaving** (intertwining; braiding) **a victor's wreath from [branches] out of a thorn-bush** (or: prickly weeds; thistles), **placed [it] upon His head, and threw a purple cloak** (outer garment; robe; [note: Matt. 27:28 reads: scarlet robe – the color robe worn by Roman officers of rank]) **around Him,**

3. **and they kept coming toward Him and were repeatedly saying, "Be rejoicing** (= Hail; Greetings), **O King of the Judeans** (or: Jews)!" **And they kept on giving Him slaps in the face with the open hand** (or: strikes with a whip, rod or club).

4. **So Pilate goes outside again and says to them, "Look and consider! I am leading him outside to you, so that you folks can come to know by experience that I am still finding no cause for accusation** (no fault, responsibility or reason for a case) **within him."**

5. **Then Jesus came forth, outside, still wearing the thorny victor's wreath and the purple garment** (cloak; robe). **And he** [i.e., Pilate] **says to them, "Look at the man!"** (or: "See and consider this person.")

6. **When, then, the chief priests and the subordinates** (deputies; Temple guards) **saw Him, they yelled and shouted, repeatedly saying, "Crucify [him]** (or: Suspend [him] from a pole; Impale [him] at once; affix [him] to the stake)**!" "Crucify** (Suspend; Hang) **[him] on a pole!"**

Pilate then says to them, "You, yourselves, take him and you crucify (hang) **[him] on a pole, for I, myself, am still finding no cause for accusation** (no fault, responsibility or reason for a case) **in him."**

7. **The Jews** (= religious Judean authorities) **decidedly replied to him, "We, ourselves, are continuously holding** (or: having) **a Law, and corresponding** (or: according) **to the Law, he continues bound** (indebted; obliged) **to be dying away, because he makes** (constructed; creates) **himself God's son** (or: [the] Son of God)**!"**

8. **Then, when Pilate heard this statement** (word; what was laid out), **he was made more afraid,**

9. **so he enters again into the headquarters** (the Praetorium), **and asks Jesus, "As for you, from what place are you?** (or: From whom were you, yourself, born and what is your origin?)**" Yet Jesus gives him no reply.**

10. **Hence Pilate continues saying to Him, "You are not speaking to me? Have you not seen to know that I continually hold authority** (the right) **to release you? I also constantly have authority** (the right) **to crucify you** (impale you; attach you to, or suspend you from, a stake)**!"**

11. **Jesus decidedly replied to him, "You were** [other MSS: continue] **holding no authority at all** (or: in even one thing) **down on** (or: against; with regard to; in the sphere of) **Me, except that it is existing having been given to you from above** (or: from [One; someone] above [you]). **Because of this, the person commending, committing and giving** (transferring) **Me over to you continues holding a greater mistake** (or: having a greater failure, error, sin or miss of the target).**"**

12. **From out of this, Pilate was continuing to seek to release Him, but the Jews** (= religious Judean authorities) **yelled and shouted, repeatedly saying, "If you should release this fellow, you are not Caesar's friend! Every man progressively making himself the king is progressively speaking in opposition to** (or: continues to declare himself against and in the place of) **the Caesar!"**

13. **Pilate, therefore, hearing of these words, led Jesus outside and sat down upon [the] elevated place – a platform, or stage, which is ascended by steps and from which men spoke to public assemblies, or judges and public officials performed their duties – into a place normally being called "The Stone Pavement," yet in Hebrew, "Gabbatha."**

14. **Now it was [the] preparation** (= the Preparation Day) **of the Passover** [Feast; Festival], **being about the sixth hour** (= noon time), **and he proceeds saying to the Jews** (or: Judeans), **"Look at and consider your king!"**

15. **Therefore those men yelled and shouted, "Lift [him] up at once and carry [him] away!" "Lift [him] up and carry [him] away!" "Crucify** (Suspend; Hang) **him** (Put him to death on the stake)**!"**

Pilate says, "Shall I proceed to crucify (suspend and put to death on the stake) **your king?"**

The chief (ranking) **priests decidedly answered, "We are not having a king** (or: we continue holding no king) **except Caesar!"**

16. **At that time, therefore, he** [Pilate] **committed Him, and gave Him over to them, to the end that He would be crucified** (hung on a pole; suspended and put to death on a stake).

They then took (or: received) **Jesus alongside and led Him away.**

17. **So, carrying, supporting and progressively bearing away the cross** (torture pole; execution stake) **by Himself, He went out into the commonly-called "Skull's Place"** (or: the place of a skull), **which is normally called "Golgotha," in Hebrew,**

18. **where they crucified Him** (hung or suspended Him; attached Him to a pole; impaled Him), **and with Him two others – [one] on each side** (or: hence and hence) **– yet Jesus in the middle.**

19. **Now Pilate also wrote a notice** (or: title) **and posted it upon the cross** (stake; execution pole). **And that which stood written was:**

"Jesus the Nazarene, the King of the Judeans."

20. **Therefore many of the Jews** (or: Judeans) **read this notice** (title), **because the place where Jesus was crucified** (hung on or suspended from a pole) **was near the city, and that which stood written was in Hebrew, Latin** (the Roman language) **[and] in Greek** (or: the Hellenist language).

21. **Then the chief priests of the Jews** (Judeans) **began and persisted in saying to Pilate, "Do not be writing 'The King of the Judeans,' but rather, 'That one says, "I am King of the Judeans."'"**

22. **Pilate considered and replied, "What I have written, I have written!"**

23. **Then the soldiers, while they crucified Jesus** (during the time Jesus was affixed to the stake, or was hung from a pole), **took His outer garments and made four shares** (or: parts) **– for** (or: to) **each soldier a share** (part) **– also the tunic** (inner garment). **Now the tunic was seamless, out of those [kinds] woven from above** (= the top) **on throughout the whole.**

24. **Therefore they said to one another, "We should not tear** (split; rend) **it, but rather let us cast** (or: draw) **lots concerning it, to decide whose it will be," so that the Scripture could** (or: would) **be fulfilled – the one saying,**

> **"They divide** (or: divided) **up My garments among themselves, and on My vesture** (apparel with beauty, being more or less stately and costly) **they cast [the] lot."** [Ps. 22:18]

Indeed, the soldiers then did these things.

25. **Now His mother, the sister of His mother** (= His aunt), **Mary the [wife] of Clopas, and Mary the Magdalene had been and remained standing beside the cross** (torture stake/pole) **of Jesus.**

26. **Jesus, therefore, seeing and perceiving [His] mother – and the disciple whom He was habitually loving and accepting, standing by** (or: in their presence) **– He says to His mother, "Woman** (or: Dear lady; Madam), **look at and consider your son."**

27. **Next, He says to the disciple, "Look at and consider your mother." So from that hour the disciple took her into** (or: unto) **his own home** (or: place; things). [*cf* Lu. 13:32b]

28. **After this, Jesus, having seen and knowing** (being aware) **that already He has been brought to the purposed goal, His destiny – and now remains completed, finished and perfected [for; as] all humanity** (or: [in] all things) **– in order that the Scripture could be finished** (would be at once ended; should be brought to its purposed and destined goal and perfected), **He now says, "I am thirsty."**

29. **Now a vessel** (container) **full of cheap sour wine** (a common, inexpensive vinegary wine, with a sharp flavor, that was a popular thirst-quenching drink) **was lying [close by]. Therefore, putting a sponge, full of the vinegary wine, around a hyssop stalk** [one MS reads: javelin], **they brought it to His mouth.** [*cf* Ps. 22:15; 69:21]

30. **Then, when Jesus received the cheap sour wine, He said, "It has been finished** (or: It has been brought to its goal and end), **and now stands complete** (having been accomplished, perfected, ended and now is at its destiny)!" **– and so, bowing [His] head, He transferred the Spirit** (or: committed [His] spirit and life-force; or: gave over and surrendered to the side the Breath-effect). [*cf* Lu. 13:32]

31. **Then the Judeans** (= Judean leaders) **– since it was [the] Preparation – made petition of Pilate to the end that their** [i.e., of those crucified] **legs could at once be broken and they could soon be lifted off and carried away, so that the bodies would not remain upon the cross** (torture stake; upright suspension pole) **on** (or: within) **the sabbath, for the day of THAT sabbath was a great one.**

32. **The soldiers therefore came** (or: went) **and indeed broke the legs of the first one, and of the other one who was crucified with Him.**

33. **Yet coming upon Jesus, as they saw and perceived Him being already having died, they did not break His legs,**

34. **but rather, one of the soldiers pierced** (jabbed; punctured) **His side through the rib cage with the head of a javelin** (or: spear), **and at once** (straightway; immediately) **blood and water came out** (or: went straight out).

35. **Now the man having seen [this] has borne witness** (given testimony), **and his witness is true, and that one has seen and knows that he is normally speaking true, so that you folks, also, can yourselves keep on loyally trusting and believing** [other MSS: can come to trust and believe],

36. **for these things came to be** (occurred; happened) **so that the Scripture could be fulfilled,**

> **"A bone belonging to Him will not proceed in being worn down, crushed or broken,"**
> [Ps. 34:20; Ex. 12:46; Nu. 9:12]

37. **and again, a different Scripture says,**

"They will proceed seeing, catching sight, and perceiving into Whom they deeply pierce forth (or: lance from out of a stabbing)." [Zech. 12:10]

38. Now after these things, Joseph from Arimathea – being a disciple of Jesus, yet being one having been hidden because of the fear of the Judeans (= religious Judean authorities) – made petition of Pilate, to the end that he could lift up and carry away the body of Jesus. And so Pilate gave permission. Therefore they [other MSS: he] came (or: went) and carried away His body.

39. Moreover, Nicodemus also came – the one coming to Him by night, at the first – bringing a mixture [other MSS: roll, or, package] of myrrh and aloes, roughly 75 to 100 pounds [of it].

40. They then took the body of Jesus and bound (or: tied) it in (or: with) swaths of linen bandages, along with spices and aromatic oils – according as is the custom for (or: with; among) the Jews (or: Judeans) to normally prepare [one] for burial.

41. Now within the area where He was crucified (suspended from a pole/stake) there was a garden, and within the garden an unused memorial tomb within which, as yet, no one had been placed.

42. Therefore, on account of the Preparation pertaining to the Jews' [Feast; festival; high sabbath], they placed Jesus there, because the memorial tomb was nearby.

CHAPTER 20

1. Now on one of the sabbaths [note: Passover was one sabbath, and the seventh day of the week was another sabbath], Mary the Magdalene is progressively coming early into the memorial tomb [area] – there yet being darkness (or: dimness) – and begins seeing and observing the stone, [already] having been lifted off and moved from the [opening of the] memorial tomb.

2. She therefore begins running (or: racing) and progressively going toward Simon Peter – and toward the (or: that) other disciple for whom Jesus was continuing feeling friendly affection and showing devotion – and [upon arriving] she is then saying to them, "They lifted up and carried the Lord (or: the Master) out of the memorial tomb, and we have not seen nor do we know where they put Him!" [note: she says "we;" cf "the other Mary" in Matt. 28:1; also Mark 16:1 and Lu. 24:10]

3. Peter and the (or: that) other disciple then went out, and were progressively coming into the memorial tomb [area].

4. Now the two had been running (or: racing) alike (the same; thus: together), and yet the other disciple raced more quickly before Peter, and he came first into the memorial tomb [area],

5. and then, upon stooping down alongside, is seeing and continuing observing the swathing strips of linen bandages (or: winding sheets) still lying [there], though he did not enter.

6. Then Simon Peter, progressively following him, is now coming and he enters into the memorial tomb and continues intently gazing at the bandages (strips of linen) still lying [there],

7. also the handkerchief (face-cloth; napkin) – which had been upon His head – not lying with the linen bandages, but rather having been separately rolled (or: folded) in one place apart.

8. Then, therefore, the other disciple – the one coming first into the memorial tomb [area] – also entered, and saw with perception, and believed (faithed-it; trusted; experienced faith).

9. You see, they had not seen and did not as yet discern (perceive; know) the Scripture that it is necessary for (binding upon) Him to rise up (to stand up; to arise) forth from out of the midst of dead ones.

10. Therefore the disciples went off (or: came away) again, toward themselves (face-to-face with themselves; or: = to their own places and things; or: = met together, privately).

11. Now Mary had taken a stand outside, facing the memorial tomb, and still stood there, continuously weeping and expressing strong inner emotions. As, then, she was continuing to weep, she stooped alongside [it] to peer into the tomb,

12. and continues intently gazing at and carefully observing (watching) two agents (or: messengers) in brilliant, shining white (as being in a bright light), remaining sitting down – one toward the head, and one toward the feet – where the body of Jesus had been lying.

[note the picture of this setting: within this set-apart chamber, the place where He had been lying corresponds to the ark of the covenant, with His blood on the mercy seat; the two agents are at the positions of the cherubim, at each end, sitting on the top of the ark]

13. **And they are now saying to her, "Woman** (or: Dear lady; or: O married one), **why do you continue weeping?** [A*, D & others add: Whom are you presently seeking?]" **She says to them, "They took away my Lord** (or: Master; or: owner; the one having authority over me; or: my legal guardian and master of my house), **and I have not seen nor know where they put Him."**

14. **Upon saying these things, she was suddenly turned around** (or: felt impelled to turn [and look]) **into the midst of** (or: unto) **the things behind [her] and continues intently gazing then carefully observing** (watching) **Jesus standing [there] – and she has not perceived, to be aware that it is Jesus.**

15. **Jesus now says to her, "Woman** (or: Dear lady; or: O wife), **why do you continue weeping? Whom are you continuing to look for** (or: presently seeking)**?" That one, supposing** (or: imagining; thinking) **that He is the gardener, then says to Him, "Sir, if you yourself removed and carried Him away, tell me where you put Him, and I myself shall lift Him up and bear Him away."**

16. **Jesus then says to her, "Miriam** [other MSS: Mary]**!" Now, at once twisting herself about, spinning and springing to [Him]** (or: being [inwardly] turned), **that one** (= she) **is exclaiming to Him, in Hebrew, "Rabboni!" – which is normally translated and interpreted, "O Teacher** [D reads: My lord (or master), my teacher]**!"'**

17. **Jesus then says to her, "Stop holding** (or: Do not continue hanging on and clinging to) **Me, for I have not yet stepped back up again so as to be ascended toward** (or: to; face to face with) **the** [other MSS: My] **Father. Now be going on your way toward** (or: to) **My brothers** (family, from the same womb; or: = fellow members), **and say to them [that I said], 'I am progressively stepping back up again** (or: now ascending) **toward My Father – even the Father of you folks – and My God: even** [the] **God of you people** [note: this would be Yahweh]**!'"**

18. **Miriam** [other MSS: Mary] **the Magdalene is progressively coming, repeatedly announcing** (reporting; giving the news; spreading the message) **to the disciples, "I have seen the Lord** (Master)**!" – and [that] He said these things to her.**

19. **Then, it being late in that day** (or: evening on that day) **– on one of the sabbaths – and the doors having been shut and locked** (or: barred) **where the disciples were gathered together, because of the fear of the Judeans** (= the Judean religious authorities), **Jesus came and suddenly stepped into the midst** (or: came into the midst and stood {or: took a stand}) **and is then saying to them, "Peace, from the Joining,** [or: = Shalom] **to you folks** (or, in our idiom: Hi)**!"**

20. **And upon saying this, He also pointed out** (or: shows) **His hands and side to them. Therefore, upon seeing** (or: at perceiving) **the Lord, the disciples rejoiced.**

21. **Then Jesus again said to them, "Peace** (or: Harmony and prosperity [= Shalom], from the Joining,) **to and for you folks! Correspondingly** (or: Accordingly; On the same level; In the same sphere; In line with) **as the Father has sent Me forth with a mission and as an Emissary** (Representative), **I Myself also am progressively** (or: repeatedly; or: one after another) **sending** (dispatching) **you folks."**

22. **And after saying this, He suddenly blows on, and says to, them** (or: He breathes within [them], so as to inflate them [note: same verb as used in Gen. 2:7, LXX], and is saying to them), **"Receive a set-apart spirit!** (or: Get [the] Holy Spirit!; take the Sacred Breath-effect!; or: Receive a sacred attitude).

23. **"If you folks should send away** (dismiss; allow to depart; forgive; pardon; divorce; let go) **the mistakes** (sins; errors; failures; deviations) **of certain ones, they have been sent away for them** (or: have been and remain pardoned in them; let go for them; have been dismissed or divorced by them). **If you would continue holding fast and controlling** (or: should keep on grasping and exercising strength; or: can restrain, hinder, hold back) **those of certain ones, they have been and continue being held fast and controlled** (seized; grasped; restrained)."

24. **Now Thomas – one from among the twelve, the one normally called, "Twin** (Didymus)**" – was not with them when Jesus came.**

25. **Consequently the other disciples kept telling him, "We have seen the Lord** (Master)**!" Yet he said to them, "Unless I can see and perceive the mark** (impression; print; exact replica) **of the blow of the nails** (spikes) **within His hands, and can thrust my finger into the impression** (or: mark) **of the nails and thrust my hand into His side, I can in no way** (or: I will by no means) **trust or believe."**

26. **And then, after eight days, His disciples** (students; apprentices) **were again indoors** (or: inside), **Thomas also with them. The door having been shut and locked** (bolted), **and being yet that way, Jesus is progressively coming, and then suddenly steps into the midst, and says, "Peace** [or: = Shalom] **of a Joining to, for and among you folks!"**

27. **Next, He is saying to Thomas, "Bring your finger here** (to this place) **and see** (or: perceive) **My hands; and bring your hand and thrust [it] into My side, and do not continue becoming unbelieving** (or: stop becoming without trust), **but to the contrary, believing** (trusting and faithful)**!"**

28. **Thomas decidedly replies, and said to Him, "O my Lord** (or: Owner) **and my God!"** (or: "O my Master!," and, "O my God!"; or: = "My [Yahweh]!... even, my God!")

29. **Jesus then says to him, "Because you have seen Me, you have trusted and believed!** (or: ?) **Happy and blessed [are] those trusting and believing, although not also seeing or perceiving."**

30. **To be sure** (Indeed), **then, Jesus also performed** (made; did) **many other signs in the sight and presence of the disciples – which things are not written within this scroll.**

31. **Yet these things have been written to the end that you folks can** (or: may; would) **continue trusting and keep on believing** [other MSS: should come to trust and believe] **that** (or: should progressively be faithful, because) **Jesus is the Christ** (Anointed One), **God's Son** (or: the Son of The God and from God), **and so that in continually trusting, believing and being loyal, you can continuously hold** (would progressively have) **Life** [other MSS: eonian life (or: life from, and in the realm of, the Age; age-lasting life)] **within, in the midst of, in union with, and centered in, His Name.**

CHAPTER 21

1. **After these things, Jesus at one point manifested Himself** (or: displays and discloses Himself; causes Himself to be seen in clear light) **again to the disciples, upon [the shore] of Lake** (or: the Sea of) **Tiberias. Now He manifested** (or: manifests) **in this way:**

2. **Simon Peter, Thomas – the one normally being called "the Twin"** (Didymus), **Nathaniel – the one from Cana of the Galilee [area], the [sons] of Zebedee and two others of His disciples, had been continuing being together, in the same place.**

3. **Simon Peter is then saying to them, "I am under way** (departing; going off) **to continue my habit of fishing!" They are then saying to him, "As for us, we are also coming together with you!" So out they went and stepped straight into the boat** (or: and immediately boarded the ship). **But during** (or: within) **that night, they caught nothing.**

4. **Now already, with [the] progressive birthing of morning coming to be, Jesus [comes] into the seashore** (or: unto the beach) **[and] stands [there]. The disciples, however** (or: of course), **had not clearly seen or perceived, so as to know that it is Jesus.**

5. **Jesus then says to them, "Lads** (or: Fellows), **are you not holding anything eatable** (or: Boys, do you have nothing, such as fish, to add to your bread)**?" They considered, and replied to Him, "No."**

6. **So He said to them, "You men cast the net into the areas at the right of the boat... and you will be finding [some]." Therefore, they cast [it], and were no longer having the strength to draw** (or: drag; tug) **it away from the great number of fish** (or: because of the multitude of the fishes).

7. **Then, that disciple whom Jesus was loving says to Peter, "It is the Lord** (or: He is the Master)**!" On hearing that it is the Lord, Simon Peter at once put on his fisherman's shirt** (an outer garment), **tucking it under his girdle – for he was stripped for work** (partially clad; naked, i.e., not having the "outer garment" on) **– and threw himself** (plunged) **into the lake** (or: sea).

8. **Yet the other disciples came in the** [Concordant text adds: other] **little boat – for they were not far from land, in fact, about three hundred feet** (two hundred cubits) **away – progressively dragging in the net of fish** (or: which had the fishes).

9. **Then, as they stepped off** (disembarked) **onto land, they continued staring** (looking) **at a charcoal fire lying there with cooked fish** (food fish) **still lying upon [it], and bread.**

10. **Jesus is then saying to them, "Bring away some of the fish** (food fish) **which you just now caught."**

11. **Simon Peter therefore went back** (or: stepped up) **and dragged ashore** (onto land) **the net, filled and distended with one hundred fifty-three large** (or: big) **fish. And yet, [with there] being so many of them, the net was not split** (torn; rent).

12. **Jesus says to them, "Come folks! Have breakfast!" Now not one of the disciples was daring to inquire of Him, "You... who are You?"** – **having seen to perceive and so being aware and knowing that it is the Lord** (or: He is the Master).

13. **Jesus is then coming and proceeds taking the bread, and likewise the fish, and continues presently giving [it] to them.**

14. **Now this [is] already [the] third [time** (situation) **in which] Jesus was manifested** (was displayed in clear light) **to** (or: for; among) **the disciples [after; since] being raised up from out of the midst of dead folks.**

15. **Then, when they had finished breakfast, Jesus says to Simon Peter, "Simon of John** [other MSS: Jonah], **are you continuously loving Me** (accepting Me without restriction; fully giving Yourself to Me) **more than these things** (or: = more than you love these folks; or: more than these folks love Me)**?"**
He [Peter] says to Him, "Yes, Lord (Master), **You, Yourself, have seen and know that I am fond of** (or: like) **You and am Your friend."**
He [Jesus] says to him, "As a herdsman, be habitually feeding (or: grazing) **and tending My young lambs!"**

16. **Again, a second [time], He continues, saying to him, "Simon of John** [or: Jonah], **are you continuously loving Me** (is your whole being progressively driving toward accepting union with Me)**?"**
He [Peter] says to Him, "Yes, Lord (Master), **You, Yourself, have seen and know that I am fond of** (or: like) **You and am Your friend."**
He [Jesus] says to him, "Constantly shepherd (herd for grazing; = lead, protect, care for, nourish) **My sheep** [other MSS: small sheep]**!"**

17. **"Simon of John** [or: Jonah]**," He continues, a third [time] saying to him, "Do you like Me and are you habitually My friend, having fondness and affection for Me?"**
Peter was made to grieve and be sad and sorry, because He said to him, the third [time], "Are you habitually My friend, liking and having fondness and affection for Me?" So he said to Him, "O Lord, You, Yourself, have seen and know all things and all humans. YOU continue knowing by progressive intimate experience and insight that I like You and continue as a friend with affection and fondness for You."
Jesus says to him, "As a herdsman, be habitually feeding (or: grazing) **and tending My sheep** [other MSS: small sheep]!

18. **"Most assuredly** (Amen, amen) **I say to you** [note: singular; = Peter], **when you were younger, you used to clothe and gird yourself, and you habitually walked around where you were consecutively setting your will** (intending; purposing). **Yet whenever you may grow old and decrepit, you will proceed stretching out your hands, and another will continue clothing and girding you, and will proceed carrying you where you are not intending** (willing).**"**

19. **Now He said this showing by a sign** (or: signifying) **by what sort of death he [Peter] will continue bringing glory** (a manifestation which calls forth praise, recognition, and a good reputation) **to God. And after saying this, He continues in saying to him, "Continue following Me!"**

20. **But Peter, being turned around, continues looking at the disciple progressively following along behind** – **[the one] whom Jesus was loving and accepting, who also leaned back upon His chest during supper and said to Him, "O Lord, who is the one transferring, committing and giving You over?"**

21. **Peter, therefore, seeing and perceiving this one, says to Jesus, "Lord** (Master), **now** (or: but) **what [of] this man?"**

22. **Jesus then says to him, "If I am intending** (willing; purposing) **him to continue remaining until I am progressively coming, what [is it] to you** (or: what [effect comes] toward you)**? As for you, you be habitually following Me!"**

23. **Then this word** (saying; message; idea) **went forth unto** (or: into the midst of) **the brothers** (= fellow believers; members of the group) – **that that disciple continues not dying off. Yet Jesus did**

not say to him that he continues not dying off, but rather, "If I am intending (willing; purposing) him to continue remaining until I am progressively coming, what [is it; effect comes] to you?"

24.   **This is the disciple: even the one constantly witnessing and testifying about these things, even the one writing these things – and we have seen and know that his witness** (testimony) **is true** (genuine; real).

25.   **Now there are also many other things which Jesus did** (performed; made; created; produced), **which things – if ever it could be progressively written, one by one** (= in full detail) **– I am imagining** (or: continue evaluating and supposing) **that not even the organized System** (world; society at large; arranged order; cosmos) **itself will [be able] to contain the scrolls being constantly written.**

[written circa 40-65 – Based on the critical analysis of John A.T. Robinson]

ACTS
[OF THE SENT-OFF FOLKS]

CHAPTER 1

1. **Indeed, I made** (did; produced composed) **the first** (or: former; previous) **account** (word; narrative; message; laid out and arranged collection of thoughts, information, ideas, expressions and statements; logos), **O Theophilus** (or: O friend and lover of God; or: O man loved of God), **concerning everything** (or: about all [the] things) **which Jesus both began to continuously do** (or: started to progressively make, construct and produce) **and to habitually and progressively teach,**

2. **until a** (or: [the]) **day in which He was taken** (or: received) **back up again, after – through a set-apart Breath-effect** (or: [the] Holy Spirit) **– imparting the goal and destiny within the folks sent off with a mission** (giving the purposed end in view to the emissaries; implanting union-centered, inner directives for the representatives), **whom He selected** (picked out and chose) **for Himself,**

3. **to whom also – within many fixed marks of substantial, irrefutable and certain proof – He presented Himself** (or: among whom He placed Himself alongside) **still living** (or: continuing alive) **after the [situation causing] Him to suffer, from time to time repeatedly appearing to, and being seen by, them at intervals throughout [a period of] forty days, and continuously saying the things concerning God's reign and sovereign activities** (or: and progressively laying out the patterned thoughts about the kingdom from, and realm of, God, as well as the ruling influence, which is God).

4. **And so, being repeatedly collected together to the assembled crowd, and periodically eating with them, He at one point passed along the message to them not to be presently separated** (or: caused to depart) **from Jerusalem, but rather, to continue remaining with regard to, and waiting around for, the Father's promise** (or: the promise pertaining to, and from, the Father; or, as a genitive of apposition: the promise which is the Father), **"Which you people heard Him repeatedly saying through My mouth** [reading with D*; other MSS: "Which you folks heard from Me],

5. **"because John, indeed, immersed in** (or: baptized with and by) **water, but you yourselves will proceed being immersed within the midst of [the] Holy Spirit**

    (or: dipped into the midst of to the point of being saturated in a set-apart Breath-effect; baptized in a holy attitude; immersed in a union with a sacred wind; [D* adds: which, also, you are presently about to continuously receive]), **after not many [of] these days** [D* adds: – until Pentecost]."

6. **So then these folks, having come together, indeed kept on asking Him, one after another saying, "Lord** (or: Master), **are You in this time progressively moving the kingdom away from where it has been put down** (or: off its established position and away from the current situation and condition) **and now restoring the sovereignty in** (or: the reign to and for) **Israel?"**

7. **So He said to them, "At this point it is not yours** (or: it does not pertain to you) **to personally know times or seasons** (or: periods or situations) **which the Father put within His own authority** (or: places in His own jurisdiction and privilege; set within the midst of His personal right from out of Being).

8. **"Nevertheless, you folks will progressively receive power and will continue taking to yourselves ability: a sudden** (point of time) **added, full coming [= Parousia] of the Set-apart Breath-effect** (the Holy Spirit and Sacred Attitude) **upon you folks – and you will keep on being My witnesses** (those who testify and give evidence of what they have seen and experienced; = you will continue telling about Me), **both within Jerusalem and within all Judea and Samaria... even as far as [the] end of the Land** (or: an extremity of the region, or a farthest point of the earth)." [cf Rom. 8:11b]

9. **Then, after saying these things – during their continued looking and uninterrupted seeing – He was suddenly exalted** (or: raised upon [them]; lifted up to a higher status), **and then a cloud from underneath [Him] took and received Him** (or: He was at once hoisted on and fully lifted up, and even a cloud took Him in hand, from below)**... away from their eyes.**

10. **Next, as they were continuing in staring intently, straining and stretching with a fixed gaze into the sky** (or: the atmosphere; heaven) **during His progressively going on His way – and now look and consider! – two adult men** (males of the human race; or: husbands) **had taken a position and now stand beside them in bright white garments,**

266

11. **who also said, "Men! Galileans! Why do you stand continuously looking into the sky** (or: the atmosphere; heaven)**? This Jesus – the One being taken** (or: received; taken in hand) **back up away from you folks into the atmosphere** (or: the sky; heaven) **– will thus be periodically coming and going, [in the] manner [in] which you gaze at Him progressively going His way into the atmosphere** (or: will in this way be continuing to go, [by] which [in] turning, you watched Him continue journeying into the heaven)**."**

12. **At that time they returned into Jerusalem from [the] mountain being normally called The Olive Grove** (or: Olivet; or: = the Mount of Olives) **– which is near Jerusalem – having a way to go** (or: path [to travel]) **which corresponded to a sabbath's [allowable distance** (= 2000 yards, just over a mile)**].**
13. **And so when they entered [the city], they went up into the upstairs room where they were residing** (or: continuing to stay) **– both Peter and John, as well as Jacob** (James) **and Andrew, Philip and Thomas, Bartholomew and Matthew, Jacob** (James) **Ben-Alphaeus and Simon the Zealot, also Judah** (Judas) **Ben-Jacob** (or: [son] of James).
14. **All these men were continuing to be carrying on forward with strength and with the same passion and temperament constantly persisting in the prayer with a view to goodness – together with [the] women, as well as Mary** [other MSS: Mariam], **the mother of Jesus, and with His brothers.**

15. **Later during these days, after rising** (or: standing) **up within the midst of the brothers** (= the assembled brotherhood) **– now there was a group at the same [place] of about one hundred and twenty names** (= people; [note: these were probably outside; further: in Jewish local government, at least 120 persons were needed to constitute a council]) **– Peter said,**
16. **"Men! Brothers** (= Fellow believers)**! It was continuing necessary and binding for the Scripture to be fulfilled in which the Holy Spirit** (or: the Set-apart Breath-effect and Sacred Attitude) **foretold** (or: spoke in advance) **through the mouth of David, concerning** (or: about) **Judah** (or: Judas) **– the one coming to be a guide for** (or: to) **the folks seizing and arresting Jesus –**
17. **"because he was one having been actually numbered** (or: counted down; = enrolled and assigned) **among us** (or: within our [group]) **and thus he obtained by lot the allotted portion** (or: share) **of this attending service."**
18. **– This man, indeed therefore, acquired a small parcel of ground** (a farm; an estate; a freehold: a place not subject to allotment which could be bought or sold) **from out of wages of injustice** (that which is contrary to solidarity and the Way pointed out; inequity; unfairness), **and so, having come to be flat on his face** (prostrate), **[his] heart** (the core of his being in the midst of him) **broke and his deep feeling and affections were poured forth** (or, literally: mid-section ruptured and all his intestines were poured out).
19. **And it came to be known to** (or: by; among) **all those normally inhabiting Jerusalem, so that small parcel of ground** (freehold) **came to be called "Akeldama." In their language** (or: dialect [of Aramaic]) **this is "a bloody piece of ground** (or: Field or Freehold of Blood)**" –**
20. **"You see," [continued Peter], "it has been** (or: it stands) **written within [the] Book** (or: scroll) **of Psalms,**

> **'Let his encampment** (unroofed place where he spends the night; or: sheepfold; unwalled village; homestead) **at once come to be desolate** (abandoned and lonely; a desert), **and let there not continue being the permanent resident with it,'** [Ps. 69:25]

also,

> **'Let a different person take** (or: receive) **his function of visitation and supervision** (or: of keeping an eye fixed on a distant object or goal; of a watcher who takes note of a situation and provides care).'** [Ps. 109:8]

21. **"Therefore, it continues binding and necessary that of those adult men coming together to us and assembling with us during all the time in which the Lord** (or: Master) **Jesus entered upon our [situation], and then exited** (or: came in and went out [among] us) **–**
22. **"beginning from the immersion originated by John** (or: John's baptism) **until the day in which He was taken back up** (or: received again), **away from us – one of these is to become a witness** (one who gives testimony and presents evidence) **together with us, in regard to His resurrection."**

23. **And so they set** (or: placed; = nominated) **two men: Joseph, the one normally being called Bar-Sabba – who was surnamed Justus, and Matthias.**

24. **Then, in praying, they said, "You, O Lord** (Master; or: = [Yahweh]) **– Knower and One experiencing the hearts of all people, raise up to point out** (or: exhibit and indicate) **one from these two men, whom You picked out and chose for Yourself**

25. **"to receive** (or: take in hand) **the place** [other MSS: lot] **pertaining to** (or: of) **this attending service of dispensing and sending-forth** (or: releasing on expedition) **– from which Judah** (or: Judas) **stepped aside, to journey into his own place."**

26. **So then they gave lots for** (or: on; to; among) **them** [D* and other MSS: they gave their lots], **and the lot fell upon Matthias. Then** (or: And so) **he was voted on by placing pebbles down together, and thus was jointly numbered and reckoned with** (= being a part of) **the eleven sent-forth folks.**

CHAPTER 2

1. **Later, during the progression for the day of Pentecost** (= Feast of the harvest; = the Festival of Weeks) **to be filled together unto its full measure, they were all alike together, in the same place, at the same time, [and focused] on the same thing.**

2. **Then suddenly and unexpectedly there came to be** (or: was birthed) **from out of the midst of the atmosphere** (or: sky; heaven) **a roaring noise** (or: sound) **as of a continued rushing and driving of a violent wind** (or: exactly like a continual carrying of a forcible breath), **and it filled** (pervaded; permeated; saturated) **the whole house where they were sitting.**

3. **Then progressively dividing and self-distributing tongues – as if of fire – were seen by them, and He** (or: it) **sat down** (or: and then one is seated) **upon each one of them.**

4. **And so they all were filled with a Consecrated Breath-effect** (or: [the] Holy Spirit; or: a set-apart attitude), **and they started** (or: began) **to continuously** (or: repeatedly) **speak in, by and with different tongues** (= languages) **– accordingly and correspondingly as the Breath-effect** (or: the Spirit) **kept on giving** (or: granting) **to, in and for them to keep on** (or: be intermittently) **uttering out loudly and clearly** (or: chanting, croaking, screeching or ringing-out [as in response]; or: progressively declaiming).

5. **Now there were Jews permanently residing** (continuously housed-down; or, perhaps: staying) **in Jerusalem – well-received adult men who take hold well [on things]** (or: pious, reverent, devout and circumspect adult husbands [thus: wives or women implied]; plural: = people) **from every nation and ethnic group under the sky** (or: heaven). [note: these were patrilineal, male-dominated cultures]

6. **But upon the occurring of this sound, the multitude came together and were mingled with perplexity, bewilderment and confusion – because each one of them kept on listening and heard [the disciples] continually** (or: repeatedly) **speaking in his own language and dialect.**

7. **So they all began being put out of place** (or: set out of themselves) **with amazement, and continued being caused to wonder with admiration and astonishment – one after another saying, "Look, and think about it** (or: See here)! **All these folks who are presently speaking are Galileans, are they not?**

8. **"And so how are we ourselves now hearing – each one of us – in his own language and dialect, [the one] in which we were born** (= native vernacular)?

9. **"[There are] Parthians, Medes and Elamites** [= portions of the Persian empire]; **even folks presently dwelling in Mesopotamia... both Judea, as well as Cappadocia... Pontus, as well as Asia** [= principally the kingdom of Pergamus, including Lydia, Mysia, Caria and Phrygia],

10. **"both Phrygia and Pamphylia; Egypt and the parts of Libya which is down toward Cyrene, as well as the temporary residents from Rome** (or: the repatriated Romans); **both Jews and proselytes** (converts to Judaism), **Cretans and Arabians** (or: Arabs) –

11. **"we continue hearing their speaking the magnificent things of God** (or: God's great deeds; the mighty [discourses; messages; announcements] from God) **in our own tongues** (= languages)!"

12. **So they all continued being put out of place** (or: set out of themselves) **with amazement and were fully bewildered** (or: thoroughly at a loss and perplexed; divided, without means for a solution), **[some] saying one to another, "What is this now purposing** (or: intending; resolving) **to be?"**

13. **Yet folks of a different class, while thoroughly joking, jesting and taunting, began to say, "They are folks having been filled full** (glutted; tanked; are brimful) **of sweet wine** (or: musk)."

14. **So Peter, having stood together with the eleven, raised his voice** [D* adds: first] **and [from inspiration – vs.4] uttered loudly and clearly** (or: declaims) **to them, "Men! Jews!** (or: Gentlemen! Judeans!) **– and all those presently residing in Jerusalem! Let this be known to you folks, and let the effects of my flow** (or: the result of my declarations) **at once sink in your ears** (= listen carefully)!
15. **"For these folks are not being drunk, as you folks are presently undertaking to suppose, for you see it is the third hour of the day.** [note: Jews did not breakfast until after morning prayer, at nine]
16. **"On the contrary, this is the thing** [= oracle; prophecy] **having been spoken through the prophet** (one who had light ahead of time and spoke before folks) **Joel,**
17.   **'And so it will proceed being** (or: existing) **within** (or: during) **the last days,' – God is now saying – 'I will progressively pour** (or: diffuse; shed) **from out of the midst of My Breath-effect** (Spirit; attitude) **upon all flesh** (= humans, people) **and then your sons and your daughters will proceed prophesying, and your youths** (older girls and boys; young people) **will continue seeing sights** (or: visions), **and your old folks** (or: elder ones) **will be repeatedly dreaming** (or: interpreting – Nyland) **dreams** (or: communications received while sleeping).
18.   **'In fact, I will continue pouring from out of the midst of My Breath-effect** (or: diffusing from My Spirit and Attitude) **even upon My slaves – both men and women – and they, too, will continue prophesying** (speaking light ahead of time and before people).
19.   **'Later I will keep on giving miracles** (wonders; omens; portents) **within the sky** (or: atmosphere; heaven) **above, and signs upon the Land** (or: territory; earth; ground) **below – blood and fire and vapor [pillars] of smoke** (or: a mist composed of smoke; [note: these three are a figure to illustrate bloodshed and destruction on earth, specifically referring to their Land]);
20.   **'the sun will proceed being converted into darkness** (or: twisted with [itself, and move] into gloomy dimness and obscure shadowiness) **and the moon into blood – before the great and fully-apparent day of [the] Lord** [= Yahweh] **is to come in full and clear light.**
21.   **'Then it will continue being** (or: existing) **[that] everyone – whoever can** (or: may in any single situation) **call upon the Name of [the] Lord** [= Yahweh's name]! **– will proceed being rescued and progressively restored to wholeness** (or: kept safe; healed; delivered; saved).'
       [Joel 2:28-32; comment: they were now in vss. 17-18; vss. 19-21 would come in AD 66-70]

22. **"Men! Israelites!** (or: Men of Israel!) **Continue listening and hear these words** (expressions of information; [plural of *logos*])! **Jesus the Nazarene, a mature Man having been fully pointed out unto you and continuing publicly exhibited and demonstrated [to be] from God** [D* reads: proved unto us, after testing and examination, and thus approved, from God] **– in powers and by abilities, together with miracles** (wonders; omens; portents) **and signs which God did and performs through Him within your midst – just as you yourselves have seen, and thus are aware and know.**
23. **"This Man, given forth** (or: lent out; provided out of the Midst [of God]; given out [in marriage]; given from the midst [of one's house]; issued forth [in birth]; or: surrendered; or: **This Fully-given, Emerged and Emptied One**) **in and by the specific, determined, bounded** (limited) **plan** (intended purpose, design and counsel) **and foreknowledge** (intimate knowledge which was experienced beforehand) **of God** (or: whose source and character was God; or: which pertained to and was God), **you folks – through the hand** (= agency) **of people not bound by the Law** (= folks without knowledge of and not living in accordance to the Torah) **– took up and assassinated by fastening [Him] to [an execution stake** (or: a cross)],
24. **"Whom God resurrected** (raised up; caused to stand back up again), **after loosing** (untying; = releasing and freeing from) **the birth-pangs** (or: birth-throes) **of the death** (or: the Death; [or, with D and other witnesses: after destroying the cords of the Unseen {Hades}]) **– corresponding to the fact that it was not possible for Him to be held fast by it** (or: it was not continuing to be powerful or capable for Him to be possessed under its strength).
       [comment: death gives birth to life]
25. **"You see David is constantly laying out words [that lead] into Him:**
       'I was continuously foreseeing the Lord in my sight, through everything (or: I habitually held [Yahweh] in sight, before my eyes, in the course of all things and through all people; or: I was previously seeing the Lord, before me and in my presence continually), **because He is** (or: continuously exists) **at my right hand – to the end that I can** (or: may; should; would) **not be shaken** (or: caused to waver or totter; agitated).

26.   'Through (or: Because of) **this, my heart was made cheerful, glad and in a healthy frame of mind, and then my tongue was constantly expressing extreme joy! Now still, even my flesh** (= natural existence) **will continue pitching its tent and residing upon expectation** (or: = But yet, also my body will live its life with expectant hope),

27.   'because (or: that) **You will not continue leaving my soul** (my interior self; my existential life) **down in** (or: abandon me into) **[the] Unseen** (or: Hades, the unseen abode of the dead), **neither will You proceed giving Your loyal one** (a person sanctioned by God's law, and by nature; a pious and devout person) **to see** (= experience) **corruption** (thorough ruin, rot and decay).

28.   'By intimate experience You make paths of life known to me (or: You personally made known to me [the] Life's ways; You give insights for me of roads which are life); **with Your face** (= Your presence and attention) **You will continue filling me with gladness, cheer, euphoria and a healthy frame of mind – a disposition of well-being.'** [Ps. 16:8-11]

29.   "Men! Brothers (= Fellow Believers; or: = Fellow Israelites)! **It continuing permitted, from [our] being and existence, to speak to you folks, with freeness of speech and with outspoken frankness and boldness, concerning the patriarch David: he both came to [his] end and was buried, and his memorial tomb is among us until this day.**

30.   "Being inherently a prophet (one who had light ahead of time), **however, and thus seeing and knowing with perception that God swore and affirms to him with an oath to at some point seat [One] upon his throne [that is] from out of [the] fruit of his loins** (reproductive organs),

31.   "seeing and perceiving beforehand, he spoke concerning the resurrection of the Christ, that **He was neither left down within the midst, in** (or: [sinking] into) **the Unseen** (or: Hades; = Hebrew: sheol; the realm or abode of the dead; often used for "the grave"), **nor did His flesh** (= body) **see** (= experience) **corruption or decay.**

32.   "God resurrected (raised; made to stand back up again) **this Jesus – of which and of Whom we are all witnesses** (folks who saw what happened and who now give evidence and testimony)!

33.   "Being, then, lifted up high by the right hand of God, and exalted to, and thus being at, God's right hand – as well as receiving the Promise of the Set-apart Breath-effect** (or: from the Holy Spirit; or: which is the Sacred Spirit and Attitude) **at the side of, and from, the Father – He poured out this** (or: THIS He pours out,) **which you folks are now both continuously seeing** (or: observing) **and keep on hearing.**

34.   "For you see, David did not climb up** (or: it [was not] David [who] ascended) **into the heavens** (or: skies; atmospheres), **yet he himself continues laying it out and saying,**

       'The Lord [= Yahweh] **said** (or: says) **to my Lord** (or: my Master),
       "Continue seating Yourself at My right [hand; plural: = positions of power, honor and authority],

35.   "until I may place (put; set) **Your enemies** (folks hostile to You) **[as] a footstool for Your feet."'** [Ps. 110:1]

36.   "Therefore, let all [the] house of Israel, for a certainty and without slipping or tripping, come to progressively know by intimate experience that God made and constitutes Him [to be] both* Lord** (Master; Owner) **and Christ** ([the] Anointed One; [= Messiah]) **– this Jesus, whom you folks put to death on a stake** (publicly suspended from a pole; crucified)!"

       [*note: "both" omitted by p91]

37.   **Now, upon hearing [this], they were pierced down to the heart** (the core of their being), **and so said to Peter and the rest of the commissioned and sent-forth folks** (or: emissaries), **"Men... brothers** (folks from the same womb), **what can or should we do?"**

38.   **So Peter at once affirms to them, "At once change your way of thinking** (your frame of mind and point of view; change to a new state of consciousness* [by customary use this implies: and turn to Yahweh]). **Then at once let each one of you folks be immersed** (baptized) **within the Name** (= in union with the identity, the character, the authority, the essence) **of Jesus Christ** (or: of [the] Anointed Jesus; which is Jesus [the Messiah]) **– into the midst of a release and sending away, a divorce and an abandonment, a cancellation and a forgiveness: of your failures, your mistakes, your times of missing the target, your errors, your deviations and your sins – and then you will proceed receiving and continue taking in hand the free gift** (the gratuity) **of the Set-apart Breath-effect** (or: which is the Holy Spirit; or: which is from, and has the character of, the Sacred Attitude). [* cf Rom. 12:2]

39. "For you see, the Promise is (continuously exists being) to, for, with and in you folks, as well as to, for, with and in your children – even to, for and in all people: to, for and in the folks [being] a long way off – in such an amount as [the] Lord [= Yahweh] our God would call toward [Himself]!"
40. Besides [this], he gave full testimony, completely laying out the facts of the case, with different thoughts and ideas, and by many more words. Then he kept on calling one after another to his side, repeatedly urging, encouraging and admonishing them, while saying, "You folks can be rescued and kept safe, away from this generation which has become warped and crooked from drying out ([cf Jn. 15:6]; or, and as an imperative: Be restored to health and wholeness – be at once saved – as you are separated from this perverse generation)!" [cf Mat. 16:4; Mk.8:38]
41. Therefore the people who indeed, as it were with their hands, took away and fully received, welcomed and embraced his word (his account; his message; the information from him) were at some point immersed (baptized). And so on (or: during) that day about three thousand souls (= people) were added [to the group and community] (or: were placed and set toward [the goal]).
42. So they were continuing strongly focused toward and persevering in and by, while devoting themselves to, the teaching of the sent-forth folks (the emissaries; the representatives) and to the common existence and in the common being, to sharing, partnering, contributing and in the participation in the breaking of the loaves of bread (= eating meals), as well as to, in, with and by the thoughts, words and deeds that were focused and aimed toward having goodness, ease and well-being (or: the prayers).

43. Now reverence, awe, respect and fear began to be birthed in every soul (or: continued coming to be on every person), and many miracles (or: portents; omens) and signs began occurring through the sent-forth folks (the emissaries; the representatives).
44. So all the folks continuing in trusting, believing and being faithful were alike together, in the same place, at the same time, [and focused] on the same thing, and they continued having and holding all things in common and with joint-participation (in a fellowship of partnership).
45. Furthermore, they began, and from time to time continued, selling (disposing of) the possessions and acquisitions, as well as the properties and things that support their existence, and then were thoroughly dividing and distributing them to everyone – in correspondence to, and to the degree of, anyone who would continue having a need.
46. Not only daily continuing strongly focused and persevering while devoting themselves in like passion and with one accord – in union, centered in the Temple courts and grounds – but also regularly breaking bread (= having meals) from house to house (or: home by home; or: in accord with [their] homes), they were sharing and partaking together of food (nourishment) in the midst of great rejoicing and with the evenness and smoothness of a heart without a stone,
47. constantly praising God and habitually having grace with and facing – also holding favor for, with reference to and toward – the whole People. Now the Lord [= Christ or Yahweh] kept on adding and placing toward [the goal] the folks being from day to day rescued (saved; delivered; made whole; restored), at the same [place and time] [other MSS add: within the called-out community].

CHAPTER 3

1. Now during those days Peter and John – as was their habit – were progressively walking up [i.e., ascending the terraces] unto the Temple courts and grounds in the afternoon, as it was coming upon the hour of the prayer, the ninth (three o'clock) [note: the time of the evening sacrifice and the prayer which accompanied the offering of incense; there were three hours of prayer: the third, the sixth, the ninth].
2. And now a certain adult man, being inherently lame (or: crippled) from out of his mother's womb (= since birth), was in the process of being carried, whom they were in the habit of daily placing near and facing toward the gate (entrance) of the Temple courts – the one normally being called "Beautiful"
     (or: Timely [from the noun: hour]; Seasonable; Lovely [note: the term is used figuratively of a
     virgin ready for marriage; the entrance is elsewhere called the Gate of Nicanor; an external
     gate leading into the court of the Gentiles]) – in order to continue asking for an act of mercy
(= to beg for alms, i.e., a charitable gift of money) at the side of the folks normally going their way into the Temple grounds and courts,

3. **who, upon catching sight of Peter and John being about to be entering into the Temple complex, began requesting to receive a gift of mercy** (alms; = money) **[from them].**

4. **So Peter, together with John, staring intently into him, said, "Look unto** (or: into) **us!"**

5. **Now the man began holding [his] attention on them, progressively anticipating to at once receiving** (or: take) **something from them.**

6. **However, Peter said, "Silver and gold [coin] is not normally a subsistence for me** (or: is not a possession with me), **yet what I do continuously have, this I am presently giving to you: Within, and in union with, the Name of Jesus Christ the Nazarene, start walking, and then keep on walking about** (around)!"

7. **And so, taking a firm grasp on him by [his] right hand, he raised him up. Now instantly and with usefulness the bases of his feet** (the part directly under his legs) **and the ankle bones were made firm with strength, and were given stability.**

8. **Then, after repeatedly leaping forth, he stood a moment, then began walking around. Next, together with them, he entered into the Temple courts – constantly walking around and leaping and praising God!**

9. **And so all the people saw him continuously walking around and praising God.**

10. **Now they began to recognize him, and were fully perceiving that this man was the one customarily sitting for gifts of mercy** (alms; = money) **at the Beautiful Gate of the Temple complex – and they were filled with wondered astonishment and ecstasy, being internally put out of their normal position of understanding things – upon the thing having stepped together with him** (= at what had happened to him).

11. [conflated with D:] **So as Peter and John proceeded going out, and with his continued going out with them, clinging** (firmly holding fast) **to Peter and John, the entire [crowd of] people – overawed and out of their wits – ran together to them at the portico** (or: porch) **normally called Solomon's Colonnade** [note: built on a remnant of the ancient Temple].

12. **Now Peter, upon seeing [this], gave a decided reply to the people: "Men! Israelites!** (or: Men of Israel!) **Why do you folks continue amazed with wonder upon this [occurrence; or: man]? Or, why do you continue staring and gazing intently at us – as if by our own power and ability or godliness** (religiousness; devout conduct; piety) **[we] had been making him to be walking around?**

13. **"The God of Abraham, of Isaac and of Jacob – the God of our fathers – brought glory** (a manifestation which calls forth praise) **and a good reputation to His Servant** (or: Boy) **Jesus, Whom indeed you folks turned over** (passed along and committed; delivered; [D adds: unto judgment]) **and renounced** (or: disown; denied) **before Pilate's face – [he] having decided to be releasing that One!**

14. **"But then you yourselves renounced** (disowned; denied; or: contradicted; said, "No" to) **the set-apart and fair Person** (the holy and just One Who personified the Way pointed out; this consecrated and rightwised One), **and instead you demanded for yourselves an adult man [who is] a murderer – to be at once graciously surrendered to you, as a favor.**

15. **"So you folks killed-off the Inaugurator of the Life** (or: Life's Originator; this Author, Founder, Leader, Prince and Initiator of the Life) **– Whom God raised up out from among the midst of dead folks, of which and of Whom we ourselves are witnesses, and continue being both evidence and testimony.**

16. **"Consequently, by the faith from** (or: in the trust which has its source in; with the loyalty and reliability of) **His Name, His Name at once made this person firm, solid and stable – whom you now continue watching and gazing at, and have seen so thus know** (or: recognize) **– and the faith, trust, loyalty and faithfulness that [is] through and by means of Him both gave and gives to him the entire allotment of whole and complete soundness... in front of you all!**

17. **"And so now, brothers, I have seen and so know that you acted and committed [it] in accord with and down from ignorance** (lack of knowledge) **– even as also your rulers** (chiefs; leaders) **[did].**

18. **"But what God fully announced-down in advance** (or: before) **through the mouth of the prophets** (those who have light ahead of time and speak before people) **– [the situations which] His Anointed One** (or: Christ) **was to experience and suffer – He thus, and in this way, fulfilled.**

19. **"Therefore, at once change your way of thinking** (change frame of mind and point of view; pass beyond the known to a new state of consciousness; have after-thought and after-perception; [by custom: and turn back to Yahweh]), **and then turn around toward [the situation for] your failures** (errors; times of missing the target; sins; deviations) **to be anointed out and wiped forth from your midst, so that**

seasons of cooling again, as well as fitting situations and fertile moments of refreshing could, should and would come from [the] face (= personal presence) of the Lord [= Yahweh or Christ],
20. "and that He would send forth in (or: to; for; with; by; among) you folks the One having been handpicked beforehand to be ready and at hand, Christ (= Messiah) Jesus,
21. "Whom indeed it continues necessary and binding for heaven to welcome, accept and embrace (or: for [the] atmosphere to grant access, admit, receive and take to itself) until times of a movement away from all things that have been firmly put down, set and established and until the periods of successive events which occur in passing moments, moving all mankind away from having been placed and positioned down as well as from the state or condition of all things that had been determined from an indefinite period of time (or: from a [particular] age) – of which things God spoke (or: speaks) through [the] mouth of His set-apart prophets (those sacred folks who spoke light ahead of time). [cf Mat. 17:11; Mk. 9:12; 2 Cor. 5:18-20; Eph. 2:16; Col. 1:20, 22;]
22. "Indeed, Moses said,

> '[The] Lord [= Yahweh] God will proceed raising up for (or: to; among) you folks a Prophet from out of the midst of your brothers, as (or: like) me. You people will continue listening to His [words] and hearing (= obeying) Him in regard to (or: in accordance with) all things – as much (or: as many) as He may be speaking to you folks!

23. > 'So it will continue being [that] every soul (= person) which may (or: should; or: will) not listen to or hear (= obey) that Prophet will progress being completely brought to destruction (or: ruin and loss) from out of the midst of the People.' [Deut. 18:15-16]

24. "Now all the prophets also fully announced these days, from Samuel on, and as many as consecutively (in order according to succession) spoke.
25. "You yourselves are the sons of (= descendants from) the prophets and of the thorough arrangement (or: from the covenant), which God fully arranged (or: covenanted) to, and with a view toward, your [other MSS: our] fathers (= ancestors), progressively saying to Abraham,

> 'And so, within and in union with your Seed, all the families (or: kinship groups; clans; tribes) of the earth (or: land) shall proceed being blessed and will continue having words of goodness, ease and well-being spoken to and about them.' [Gen. 22:18; 26:4]

26. "To you folks first, God, in raising up His Servant (or: Boy), sent Him forth continually blessing you people and repeatedly speaking words of goodness, ease and well-being within the [situation for] constantly and progressively turning each one away from your misery-gushed situation of worthless conditions, laborious works, painful relationships, malicious deeds (or: from these wicked ways, as well as from the evil thoughts, plans and dispositions of you people)."

CHAPTER 4

1. Now during their continued speaking to the people, the chief (or: ranking) priests, the officer of the Temple guard (= the Controller/Commander of the Temple), and the Sadducees stood near them, in opposition, and at last took a stand upon [the scene],
2. being progressively annoyed, exasperated, vexed through and through, and in a thoroughly worthless and knavish attitude because of their continuing to teach the people, and to be bringing down the announcement and be fully proclaiming in [the case of] Jesus (or: in union with Jesus; in the sphere [or: authority] of Jesus) the resurrection from out of the midst of dead folks.
3. And so they thrust [their] hands on them and they were placed into custody (in ward) overnight, since it was already evening.
4. However, many of the folks presently hearing the word (message; information; the Logos) trusted and believed, and so the number of the men (or: adults) came to be about five thousand.

5. Now it happened on the next day [that] their rulers and the elders, along with the Torah scholars (scribes; theologians; doctors of the Law) were to be gathered together in Jerusalem.
6. And Annas, the chief (or: ranking) priest, as well as Caiaphas, John, Alexander and as many folks who were of the chief priest's family (kinsfolk) [were also present].
7. So then, standing [Peter and John] in their midst [note: the Sanhedrin sat in a semicircle], they began by inquiry to investigate and ascertain: "Within, or in union with, what sort of power or ability – or in what kind of name (= in whose authority or invoking whose power) – did you people do this?"

8. **At that point Peter – being filled full of [the] Set-apart Breath-effect** (or: a holy spirit and a separated attitude; [the] Holy Spirit) – **said toward them, "Rulers** (or: Chiefs; Leaders) **of the People, and elders!**

9. **"Since** (or: If) **we ourselves are in the process of being investigated and thoroughly examined on [the matter of] a good deed** (a beneficial act of well-being) **pertaining to a weak and disabled person – within Whom and in union with what this man has been healed, and now stands made whole** (or: saved; rescued) –

10. **"let it be now progressively known to all you men and to all the people of Israel, that in** (within and in union with) **the Name of Jesus Christ** (or: of [the] anointed Jesus), **the Nazarene, Whom you yourselves executed on a stake** (publicly suspended from a pole; crucified), **Whom God raised up from out of the midst of dead folks – within and in union with this Man** (or: [Name]), **this man has stood near, and is standing restored, sound and healthy at the side, in your sight and presence!**

11. **"This One is the Stone – the One being treated as nothing** (or: with scorn and contempt) **and being disregarded by and under you folks, the builders** (or: the 'architects'); **the One coming into [the position of] being 'Head of [the] corner** (or: Source of [the] angle; = the Corner Foundation Stone from which the walls are built; or: = Headstone, or, Keystone; = the Summit of the building)!' [Ps. 118:22]

12. **"And thus, the rescue and deliverance – the restoration to health and wholeness, the safety and salvation, and the return to our original state and condition – is in absolutely no other person! And it follows that neither is there a different name under the [dome of the] sky** (or: heaven) **that has been given, and now exists as a gift, among mankind** (or: in the midst of humans; centered in people), **within which, it continues binding and necessary for us to be saved** (healed and restored to health and wholeness; delivered and kept safe; rescued and returned to our original state and condition)!"

13. **Now as they continued watching and observing the bold confidence and outspoken freedom of speech of Peter and John – and grasping that they were uneducated** (= without the effects of technical training in the professional rabbinical schools of Hillel or Shammai) **and untrained people** (= laymen; common laborers or folks of some trade, or, of the peasant class) **– they began marveling and continued filled with wonder, and they began to fully realize** (or: recognize) **[about] them, that they had been** (or: used to be) **with Jesus.**

14. **Besides, while continuing to observe the man who had been cured standing with them, they were having nothing to say in rebuttal or in contradiction.**

15. **So after ordering them to go forth outside of the Sanhedrin [hall], they began tossing [their thoughts and ideas] together** (= conferring and consulting) **with one another,**

16. **one to another saying, "What can or should we do to or with these men? Because, for a fact, a known and noteworthy sign has occurred through them – one that [is] apparent** (obvious and manifest) **to all the folks presently inhabiting Jerusalem – so we are unable to keep on denying** (or: contradicting) **[it].**

17. **"Nevertheless, so that it may not all the more be disseminated and spread abroad, on into the People [at large], let us make threats to them [that they] no longer are to continue speaking on** (= about, or, on the authority and basis of) **this Name to even one individual of humanity!"**

18. **And so, after calling them, they ordered [them] to cease making any utterance at all, as well as to terminate teaching anywhere, on [the authority or basis of] the Name of Jesus.**

19. **But Peter and John, giving a decided reply, said to them, "You men judge and decide whether it is right** (in accord with the Way pointed out) **in God's sight to continue listening to** (and thus: obeying) **you rather than God.**

20. **"For you see, we ourselves are unable not to be constantly speaking [about] the things which we saw and heard** (or: perceive as well as hear)."

21. **So, after projecting menace and adding threats, they released them – continuing to find nothing [to solve] "the how"** (= the means) **[so that] they could prune or curb them** (= cut back their activities) **– on account of the people, because they were all continuing in glorifying God** (enhancing God's reputation) **[based] on the thing** (= the healing) **having occurred** (having come to be).

22. **You see, the man upon whom this sign had occurred was more than forty years [old].**

23. **Now being released** (loosed away), **they went to their own [group; company; association; family and friends; home] and reported back as many things as** (or: whatever) **the chief priests and the elders said to them.**

24. **So upon hearing [it], the [group] unanimously with the same mind and like-passion lifted up a voice** (or: sound) **to God and said, "O Sovereign Owner – absolute in power – You, 'the One making** (or: constructing; producing) **the heaven** (or: the atmosphere and sky) **and the earth** (or: the land; soil) **and the sea as well as all the things within them,'** [Ps. 146:6]

25. **"the One saying – through means of [the] Holy Spirit** (or: a set-apart breath-effect and a sacred attitude) **– from [the] mouth of our father** (= ancestor) **David, Your servant** (or: Boy),

'**To what end or purpose did** (or: do) **the ethnic multitudes** (or: nations) **snort, neigh and stomp around [as a high-spirited horse]** (or: behave arrogantly or with insolent and haughty airs) **and peoples show care for and take interest in empty things** (or: concern themselves over meaningless [activities]; or: mumble empty [phrases]; or: practice useless [rituals]; or: meditate on, give careful thought and attention to and then devise futile [schemes] or hollow [projects])**?**

26. '**The kings of the land** (or: earth; territory) **took a stand** (or: stood by; i.e.: placed themselves alongside to be at folks' disposal), **and the rulers** (or: the leaders; the officials) **were gathered together at the same [time and place]** (or: = joined forces upon the same [purpose and intent]; or, perhaps: = as one) **– down against the Lord** [= Yahweh] **and down against His Anointed One** (or: the Christ which was Him; the [Messiah] from Him).**'** [Ps. 2:1-2]

27. **"For in truth** (actuality; reality) **both Herod and Pontius Pilate, together with ethnic multitudes and [the] People of Israel – [coming] upon** (= against) **Your set-apart Servant** (or: holy Boy) **Jesus, Whom You anointed – were gathered together** (thus: were made to join forces) **in this city**

28. **"to do whatever** (or: as many things as) **Your hand and Your counsel** (purpose; plan; intent; design) **previously marked out the bounds for and limited beforehand to be happening** (to come to be; to occur).

29. **"And so at this time, O Lord** [= Yahweh], **gaze upon** (= take note of and attend to) **their threats, and then give** (or: at once grant) **to Your slaves to continue speaking Your *Logos*** (or: message; idea; thought; Word; pattern-forming Information) **with the right of complete freedom from constraint, and with all boldness to be publicly open and frank, as citizens,**

30. **"during** (in; in union with) **the [situation and circumstance for] You to continue stretching out** (or: forth) **Your hand unto** (or: into the midst of a) **healing, and while signs and miracles** (or: portents; wonders; marvels) **continue to be birthed** (come to be; happen; occur) **through means of the Name of Your set-apart Servant** (or: holy/sacred Boy) **Jesus."** [cf 5:12, below]

31. **Then, after their urgently making their needs known in [this] prayer** (or: while they are still presenting their earnest requests in prayer), **the place – within which they were continuing assembled, having been gathered together – was suddenly shaken** (moved to and fro, vibrated and then put into a state of moving in a wave), **and then they were all filled full of the Set-apart Breath-effect** (or: the Holy Spirit; or: with the consecrated attitude). **Later they kept on speaking God's *Logos*** (the message and information from God; the Word of, and which is, God) **with a citizen's right of complete freedom from constraint, and thus with all boldness being publicly open and frank.**

32. **Now pertaining to the fullness of the trusting, faithing, loyal and believing multitude of folks, there was one heart and soul** (= they were united at their core and in their will, feelings and beings) **and not even one person was saying [that] anything of the things belonging to, or sustaining for, him continued to be his own – but to the contrary, all things were common to and for them** (or: things held in partnership and shared by them).

33. **And thus, with great power and ability, the sent-forth folks** (the representatives; the emissaries) **continued giving away** (rendering; handing over in answer to an expectation) **the evidence of** (or: witness about; testimony from) **the resurrection of the Lord Jesus. Furthermore, great favor and enormous grace continued being upon them all.**

34. **In fact, "there was not even anyone** [p8 D E and others: Your see, not even any was continuing to subsist inherently] **in persistent need** (poverty-stricken; destitute; indigent) **among them"** [cf Deut. 15:4], **for whoever** (or: as many as) **had been owners** (possessors) **of pieces of land or houses, upon from**

time to time selling [them], were periodically bringing the proceeds (= the money paid for the value and price) **of the things being occasionally sold,**

35. **and they habitually placed** (deposited) **[them] beside the feet** (= at the disposal) **of the sent-forth folks. So then it was from time to time being distributed** (or: given throughout)**: to each person in proportion to any need he or she would occasionally** (or: routinely) **have** (or: for as much as someone would from time to time, or customarily, have a need).

36. **Now Joseph, the one from among the sent-forth folks being surnamed "Barnabas** (or: bar-Nabas)**" – which is normally being translated and interpreted "A son of comfort, consolation and encouragement** (or: One who has the character and qualities of being an aid-giver and a helpful assistant; a son of a paraclete {or: the Paraclete})**" – a Levite, a Cyprian by country of origin,**

37. **upon selling a field belonging to him, brought the money and placed** (deposited) **[it] beside the feet of the sent-forth folks** (= set it to be at the disposal of the representatives).

CHAPTER 5

1. **However, a certain adult man – Ananias by name – together with Sapphira, his wife, sold a possession**

2. **and he secretly put aside** (kept back funds; embezzled) **for himself from the proceeds** (the price received for its value) **– [his] wife having seen [it] with [him] and thus also knowing [about it] – and then bringing a certain part [of it], he placed [it] beside the feet** (= deposited it for the disposal) **of the sent-forth folks.**

3. **So Peter said, "Ananias, why** (or: through what [situation or circumstance]) **did the adversary** (or: *satan*; = a spirit of greed; = an attitude of selfishness) **fill your heart** (= the core of yourself) **to lie to the Set-apart Breath-effect** (or: play false to the Holy Spirit; speak that which is not true, with the Sacred Attitude), **and thus to secretly put aside** (keep back funds; embezzle) **for yourself from the proceeds of the piece of ground** (the field; the property; the homestead; the freehold)**?**

4. **"Was it not by all means continuously abiding** (remaining; dwelling) **with you while it continued remaining [yours]? And then, upon being sold, it continued in your authority and control. Why [is it] that YOU put** (or: fix) **this worthless matter** (this affair of poor quality; this bad performance-effect) **within your heart** (= the place where anti-communal and adversarial thoughts arise)**? You did not play false and lie to humans** (people), **but rather** (or: but on the contrary) **to God!"** [= to Christ in them all]

5. **Now after progressively hearing these words, Ananias, immediately falling [down], at once breathed out [his] soul-life. Then great fear and reverence came to be upon all the people presently** (or: one after another) **hearing [about it].** [comment: perhaps a heart attack, from shame]

6. **So after standing up, the younger men enwrapped him for burial, then, after carrying [him] out, they buried [him].**

7. **Now it occurred [after] about an interval of three hours that his wife entered – not having seen or known of the thing having occurred** (or: not being aware of what had happened).

8. **So Peter made a decisive response to her, "Tell me if you folks sold** (or: gave from yourself [as a price]) **the property for such-and-such."**
So she said, "Yes, for so much."

9. **Then Peter [said] to her, "Why [is it] that it came in symphony to you folks** (or: was voiced together by [both] of you) **to make [this] attempt [with] the Spirit of [the] Lord** (or: to test [Yahweh's, or, Christ's] Breath-effect)**? Look and see! The feet of the folks just now burying your husband [are] at the door** (or: gate), **and they will proceed in carrying you out!"**

10. **Now she instantly fell to** (or: toward) **his feet and she breathed out [her] soul-life. So upon entering, the youths found her dead. And then, after carrying [her] out, they buried [her] face-to-face with her husband.** [comment: perhaps a heart attack, from the shame of exposure]

11. **Consequently great fear and awe was birthed** (or: came to be) **upon the whole called-out community – as well as upon all the people hearing these things.**

[comment: due to the grace-effect of a word of knowledge or of discernment; 1 Cor. 12:4-11]

12. **Now through** (or: by means of) **the hands of the sent-forth folks** [*cf* 4:30, above] **many signs and miracles** (or: portents; wonders) **kept on happening** (or: were being birthed from time to time) **among the people. And so they all continued being with one accord and with similar emotions** (like-minded and with the same passions) **within Solomon's colonnade** (a roofed portico).

13. **But concerning the rest of the folks [in the city], no one was daring or brave enough to be permanently united with** (or: closely joined [as with furniture] or glued [as in sexual union] to) **them. Nevertheless, the people [of the city] continued speaking highly of them – as well as great things about them.**

14. **Yet, more than that, multitudes** (= large numbers) **of both men and women** (or: husbands and wives) **– folks continuing to trust, to believe, to faith-it, and to be loyal – kept on being added by the Lord** [= Christ or Yahweh] (or: to the Lord; or: for the Lord; or: in the Lord).

15. **Therefore** (or: So then) **[folks] continued to be carrying out the sick and weak** (infirm) **folks even into the plazas and city squares or broad streets, then to be putting them on little beds and cots** (small couches used by the poor), **so that at Peter's repeated** (or: usual; habitual) **coming and going, at the very least [his] shadow** (or: even if the shadow) **will overshadow** [other MSS: might cast a shadow on] **some one of them** [D adds: **for you see, they were one after another changed or transformed to be other than they were away** (or: = set free and healed) **from all sicknesses and infirmities according as each one of them had been having**].

16. **So the multitude – from towns and cities roundabout – also continued coming together, constantly bringing sick people and folks being constantly disturbed by unclean spirits or breath-effects** (or: repeatedly affected under the [influence of] crowds and culturally impure mob spirits and attitudes) **– all of whom, one after another, were being tended, given treatment or cured.**

17. **Now having arisen, the chief** (ranking) **priest and all those together with him – the existing sect of the Sadducees – were filled with jealousy** (or: with boiling zeal),

18. **and they thrust [their] hand upon** (= arrested) **the sent-forth folks** (the emissaries) **and put them in [the] public [place] of custody and observation.**

19. **But during [the] night, an agent of [the] Lord** (= Christ's messenger, or an agent from Yahweh; perhaps: = a person doing the Lord's bidding and then delivering His message) **opened the gates** (or: doors) **of the prison** (or: jail; place of being under guard). **Then, after leading them out, he said,**

20. **"You folks be going your way, then later, upon taking a stand within the Temple courts** (or: grounds), **continue speaking to the people all the gush-effects of and results of the flow from** (or: sayings and declarations about) **this Life."**

21. **So after hearing [this], they entered into the Temple complex under the [light of] daybreak** (or: the early dawn) **and began** (or: continued) **teaching.**
Now later, after arriving (or: coming along), **the chief** (ranking) **priest and those with him called together the Sanhedrin** (the Jewish High Council; the governing body) **and all the assembly of the older men** (persons of age and influence invited to sit with the Sanhedrin; = the senate) **of the sons of Israel** (= Israel as a tribe, nation or ethnic group), **and they sent forth [men] unto the prison** (jail; place for bound folks) **to have them brought.**

22. **But upon arriving** [D adds: **and opening up the prison**], **the subordinate officers did not find them in the jail** (or: prison). **So after returning, they gave a report, saying,**

23. **"We found the prison** (or: jail) **shut in all security, having been firmly barred and locked, and the guards standing at the doors – yet upon opening [them] up, we found no one inside."**

24. **Now as they heard these words, both the captain of the Temple complex and the head** (chief; ranking) **priests became utterly perplexed** (divided and without a solution) **about them and continued bewildered as to whatever this might come to be** (or: what would come of this).

25. **But then someone just arriving reported to them, "Look, and consider** (or: Hey)! **The men whom you folks put in the prison are presently within the Temple courts** (or: grounds), **standing and continuing in teaching the people!"**

26. **At that point the captain, after going off with the subordinate officers, proceeded in leading them, [bringing them] without force or violence – for they were fearing the people, lest they could** (or: should; would) **be stoned.**

27. **So after leading them, they had [them] stand in the Sanhedrin [hall], and then the chief** (head; ranking) **priests questioned them, saying,**

28. **"We commanded to you men, with a direct order, not to keep on teaching upon the [authority and basis of] this Name – and look! – you folks have filled Jerusalem with your teaching, and now you continue purposed and determined to bring upon us** (= hold us responsible for) **the blood of this man!"**

29. **So Peter, along with the sent-forth folks, in giving a decisive reply, said, "It continues binding and necessary to with persuaded faithfulness habitually obey and yield to God as the Ruler and Origin, rather than to humans** (people)!

30. **"The God of our fathers** (= ancestors) **raised up Jesus – Whom you men yourselves intensely manhandled with intent to kill, hanging [Him] on a wooden pole** (or: suspending [Him] upon a tree).

31. **"God exalted and lifted up high this Originator** (or: Beginning Leader; Inaugurator; Founder; Chief Agent; Prince) **and Deliverer** (Savior; Rescuer; Restorer of health and wholeness; Returner to the original sphere and state of being) **to** (or: by; with) **His right hand** (= power and authority; [D reads: glory]) **– to give** (or: grant) **a change of mind and way of thinking [which results in a return to Yahweh] to** (or: for; in) **Israel, and a sending away of mistakes and deviations** (a divorcing of failures; an abandoning of sinning; a flowing away of the results from times of missing the target; a forgiveness of errors; [D adds: within {or: among} them])**!**

32. **"And we ourselves are evidences and witnesses of these gush-effects and results of the flow** (or: saying and declarations; spoken words) **– as well as the Set-apart Breath-effect** (or: Holy Spirit; consecrated attitude) **which** (or: Whom) **God gave** (or: gives) **to** (or: in; for; among) **the folks who in persuaded loyalty are continually obeying and yielding to Him as the Ruler and Origin."**

33. **Now the people hearing [this] began being divided in two by a saw** (sawn through; = cut and torn apart emotionally so as to be enraged) **and began intending** (wanting and purposing) **to "lift them up"** (= haul them off and kill them).

34. **But, after standing up, a certain man in** [other MSS: belonging to] **the Sanhedrin – a Pharisee named Gamaliel, a Law professor** (a respected teacher of the Torah; [note: the grandson of Hillel]), **one esteemed and honored by all the People – gave an order to put the men outside for a little while** (or: briefly).

35. **And then he said to them** [D reads: to the leaders (rulers) of the Sanhedrin], **"Men! Israelites!** (or: Men of Israel!) **Hold [this matter] to yourselves [in your mind] and put your attention upon these men, being careful as to what you are presently about to be committing or performing** (= doing to them).

36. **"You see, before these days Theudas** (or: Todah) **arose, repeatedly saying of himself to be somebody** [D adds: great (= important; significant)] **– to whom men numbering about four hundred were inclined** (= rallied in support) **– who was "taken up"** (= hauled off to be killed – [perhaps by hanging or crucifixion]) **and everyone, whoever was loyally submitting to him and obeyed him, were at once disbanded and dispersed, and so it came to be nothing** (or: unto nothing did it occur).

37. **"After this, Judah** (or: Judas) **the Galilean, in the days of the registration** (or: census; the enrollment for the Roman tax), **also established a people off behind him** (= got some people to defect to him). **That one also destroyed himself – then all** [p45 & D omit: all], **whoever was loyally submitted to him and obeyed him, were fully dispersed and are scattered abroad.**

38. **"And so, [with] the present [circumstances and events]** (or: = in this instance), **I am now telling you men, Stand away from these men and leave them alone** (or: let them go off; divorce [yourselves] from them; allow them; [D adds: {do} not {be} staining {your} hands]), **because if this counsel or this work should be from humans** (or: have people as its source or origin) **it will be utterly undone and demolished.**

39. **"Yet if it is from out of God, you folks will not be able or have power to dismantle or demolish them** [D adds: neither we nor kings nor tyrants. Therefore, hold yourselves away from these men] **– and** [D* omits: and] **may you not at some point be found [to be] fighters [against] God!"**
And so they were persuaded by him.

40. **Next, upon calling the sent-forth folks to their presence, after severely lashing** (flogging; whipping) **[them], they gave orders not to continue speaking upon the [authority and basis of the] Name of Jesus. Then they released them.**

41. **Therefore the sent-forth folks indeed went their way, away from the face** (= presence) **of the Sanhedrin** (the High Council), **repeatedly rejoicing because they were counted** (deemed; regarded; put down and recorded as being) **worthy** (of corresponding value) **to be dishonored and treated as being without value and despised – over** (for the sake of) **the Name.**

42. **And so every day – within the Temple complex, as well as from house to house – they were not ceasing** (they continued without letup) **in repeatedly and progressively teaching and announcing**

the good news of the ease and well-being: the message about Christ Jesus (or: the news which came by, and is, Jesus, the Anointed One [= the Messiah]).

CHAPTER 6

1. **Now in these days, during a progressive multiplying** (= increasing the number) **of the disciples** (students; learners; apprentices), **a discontented muttering of grumbling and complaints occurred** (was birthed) **from the Hellenists** (Greek-speaking Jews, and/or, folks of the Hellenistic culture) **aimed toward the Hebrews** (the Hebrew/Aramaic-speaking folks, and/or folks living in accord with the Jewish culture) **because their widows kept on being overlooked** (= neglected and disregarded) **in the daily attending service of dispensing hospitality and serving meals.**

2. **So the twelve, after summoning the full multitude of the disciples** (students; apprentices) **to themselves, said to them, "It is not acceptable** (satisfactory; approvable) **[for] us to be constantly serving [food] at tables** (also: = supervising the distribution of supplies), **thus neglecting** (or: leaving down; completely abandoning) **the Word of God** (or: the *Logos* which is God; the message from God)!

3. **"Thus, brothers** (= fellow believers and members of the community), **look about carefully upon and inspect so as to select from your [ranks] seven adult men [who are] constantly being attested and certified by witnesses [to be] full of Breath-effect** (or: [the] Spirit; Attitude) **and of wisdom, whom we will proceed situating** (setting or placing down) **upon this need.**

4. **"Yet we ourselves will continue enduring strongly focused on and loyally persist in the thought, speaking and action aimed at having goodness, ease and well-being** (or: with prayer) **and the attending service of the Word** (and: the dispensing pertaining to the Idea and from the Message which originates in the *Logos*)."

5. **And the idea** (word; thought; *logos*) **brought satisfaction in the eyes** (in the sight; = in the judgment and view) **of all the full multitude, and so they selected** (picked out; chose) **Stephen, an adult man full of trust** (and: faith; or: trustworthiness) **and set-apart Breath-effect** (or: Holy Spirit; or: a consecrated attitude), **as well as Philip, Prochorus, Nikanor, Timon, Parmenas, and Nicolas, a proselyte of Antioch,** [cf 21:8, below]

6. **whom they made stand before the sent-forth folks. Then, while envisioning having goodness and speaking of ease with well-being** (or: praying), **they placed [their] hands on them.**

7. **And so the *Logos* of God** (or: God's idea, message; the Word from God, which was God) **kept on progressively growing and increasing** (also: = God's Reason was spreading out like a growing Vine), **and thus the number of disciples** (students; apprentices) **continued tremendously multiplying** (= increasing in number) **within Jerusalem. Furthermore, a vast throng of the priests** [note: these would have been Sadducees] **kept on submissively listening to and hearing** (thus: paying attention to and obeying) **the Faith** (or: heeding the Faithfulness; [note: noun with the article, thus this would signify trust and belief in the resurrected Jesus as the Messiah and His act of faithfulness which brought liberation]).

8. **Now Stephen, full of grace and power** (and: favor and ability), **repeatedly performed great miracles and signs among the people.**

9. **Yet certain men rose up – from the [members] of the synagogue being normally termed "Freedmen"** (or: Libertines; Jews who had been enslaved in the Syrian wars but were later freed), **also [composed] of Cyrenians, Alexandrians and people from Cilicia, as well as [the province] of Asia – repeatedly arguing and debating** (or: inquiring and discussing together) **with Stephen,**

10. **and yet they were not continuing strong [enough] to withstand** (= hold their own position against) **the wisdom and the spirit in which** (or: with which; or: the Breath-effect or Spirit by which) **he continued speaking.**

11. **At that point they underhandedly and secretly induced men to be saying, one after another, "We have heard him repeatedly speaking blasphemous** (or: slanderous; defaming; harmful; abusive; light-hindering; villainous) **gush-effects** (or: declarations) **unto Moses and God** (or: directed into [the Law with its religion and culture, which is represented by] Moses, and [into] God)."

12. **And so they stirred up** (agitated; moved and shook together like an earthquake) **the people – as well as the elders and the scholars** (scribes; theologians of the Law) **– and so, having been standing**

near upon [him], they, as a group, suddenly took him by force (gripped, seized and snatched him) then led [him] unto the Sanhedrin (High Council).

13. Here they set up (or: put on the stand) false witnesses, one after another saying, "This man is not ceasing from continually speaking gush-effects (or: declarations) down against this set-apart (or: holy; sacred) place and the Law.

14. "For instance, we have heard him repeatedly saying that Jesus the Nazarene will destroy (demolish; dismantle) this place and he will change the customs which Moses handed down to (and: for) us." [comment: Stephen is here pictured as a "proto-Paul" – cf C.H. Rieu, The Acts, 1957 p 128]

15. Then, staring intently at him (or: into [Stephen]), all the men presently sitting in the Sanhedrin (High Council) saw his face (and: countenance) as if [it were the] face of an "agent" (or: countenance and presence of [God's] messenger).

CHAPTER 7

1. Yet the head (chief; ranking) priest said [D adds: to Stephen], "Do these matters continue holding thus (or: Are these things so; = Is this the case)?"

2. So he affirmed, "Men... brothers and fathers, listen, and now hear!
[note: what follows is "the Jewish idea of proving something in the present from a similar occurrence in the past" – C.H. Rieu, ibid]
The God of the glory (or: The God of the manifestation which called forth praise; or: The God which pertains to, and is, the glory [of Israel]; The God from the assumed Appearance) was perceived (or: seen) by our father (or: forefather; patriarchal ancestor) Abraham – [he] being in Mesopotamia, before the [situation for] him to settle down (= take up residence) within Haran –

3.   'and He said to him, "At once go forth from out of the midst of your land and your relationships with family (or: your relatives and the fellowship of kinfolks; your common origin), and then come on into the Land which I would then be pointing out and showing to you."'
[Gen. 12:1]

4. "At that point, after going forth out of the land of [the] Chaldeans, he settled down and took up residence in Haran. Then from there – after the [occurrence for] his father to die off – He caused him to change residence into this Land in which you yourselves are at this time presently residing (continuing settled down).

5. "And yet He did not give to him an allotted permanent inheritance [for him] to possess and enjoy – 'not even a raised public platform or step for a foot (or: = a space, or a chance, for a foot to step)!' [Deut. 2:5] And yet He promised to 'give it to him – [leading] into a holding it down for a possession – and also to his seed (= offspring; descendants), after him,' [Gen. 12:7; etc.] while there was not presently being a child by and for him.

6. "But God also spoke thus [other MSS: to him]: that his 'seed (descendants) would be alien residents (sojourners) in a foreign land – and [the foreign people] will proceed to be enslaving them and will continue treating [them] badly [for] four hundred years.

7. "'And yet I Myself will proceed to be judging the nation to (or: for) which they will continue performing as slaves,' said God, 'and after these things they will proceed coming out (or: going forth from the midst), and then they will continue rendering sacred service to (or: hired service for) Me – in this place.' [Gen. 15:13-14, 16]

8. "He also gave to him a full arrangement of circumcision (a covenant which is circumcision; or: a settlement that pertains to, has the characteristics of, is marked with, and is disposed by circumcision). And thus, he generated (effected the birth of) Isaac, and then circumcised him on the eighth day – and [likewise] Isaac [generated; sired] Jacob, and then Jacob the twelve patriarchs.

9. "Then the patriarchs, becoming jealous of Joseph, gave [him] away by selling [him] into Egypt – and yet God continued being (or: was existing) with him. [comment: Jesus was sold to the priests]

10. "And so He took him up out (extricated him) from the midst of all his pressures (or: squeezing compressions; tribulations; afflictions), and then 'gave to him grace and favor, as well as wisdom, before (in front of; in the sight of) Pharaoh, king of Egypt, who established him (appointed and placed him down) [as the] one to continue exercising leadership upon and being governor over Egypt, as well as his whole house (or: household and palace affairs).' [Gen. 41:37-44; comment: Jesus was raised to the highest position in God's household – cf Rieu, ibid p 129]

11. "'Now a famine came upon the whole of Egypt and Canaan,' [Gen. 41:54] **and [there was] great pressure** (stress and affliction), **and so our fathers** (forefathers; ancestors) **kept on not finding provisions** (foodstuffs and sustenance-effects for people or provender and pasture for cattle).

12. **"So upon hearing of there being [stores of] grain in Egypt, Jacob sent out our fathers on a first mission** (or, with other MSS: Thus, at hearing of there being grain, Jacob sent forth our ancestors into Egypt a first [time]).

13. **"Then during the second [mission] 'Joseph was made known to his brothers,'** [Gen. 45:1] **and so Joseph's race** (family stock; kindred group) **came to be apparent and manifest to Pharaoh.**

14. **"So now Joseph, dispatching [them], called** (or: summoned) **Jacob, his father, and all [his] relatives** (the group of common birth) **from that place – consisting of seventy-five souls** (= people) [note: Stephen follows the LXX here].

15. **"Thus Jacob walked down into Egypt. Later he came to his end – he and our fathers –**

16. **"and they were transferred into Shechem, then they were placed within the memorial tomb which Abraham [in the person of Jacob] purchased for a price** (or: a certain sum) **– in silver – from the sons of Hamor, in Shechem.**

17. **"Now just as the time of the Promise** (the succession of time pertaining to the Promise) **– that which God covenanted in speaking the same Word, consenting agreement** [*p*45, D & others: promised], **to** (for; in) **Abraham – drew near at hand, the People 'grew** (increased in number) **and was multiplied,' within Egypt,**

18. **"until which [time] 'a different king stood up upon Egypt – one who had not seen or known Joseph.'** [Ex. 1:7-8]

19. **"This one, devising shrewdly** (cleverly plotting to outwit and deal insidiously) **against our race** (family stock; kindred group), **treated the fathers** (the ancestors) **badly – to be habitually making their infants** (or: newborn babies) **[to be] placed outside and exposed, unto the [result for them] to not continue to be kept alive as a living being** (= to be abandoning their babies in the open so they would die) –

20. **"in the midst of which opportune situation and appointed season, Moses was born, and he was well-bred and refined** (with the qualities of an urban person [as opposed to an ill-bred country urchin]) **by God** (or: handsome to God; attractive for God), **and who was nursed and nurtured** (reared up) **for three months in his father's house.**

21. **"So, at his being exposed by being placed outside** [D adds: beside (E reads: into) the river], **the daughter of Pharaoh took him up for herself, and then she nourished him and reared him into [being] her own son.**

22. **"Then Moses was child-trained, disciplined and educated in and by all the wisdom of and from [the] Egyptians. Now thus he was being powerful and able in his words, thoughts, ideas, patterns of information, and verbal expressions – as well as in his acts, works and deeds.**

23. **"Now as forty years' time was progressively being fulfilled to** (or: for; in; by; with) **him, it walked up upon his heart** (= it occurred in the core of his being) **to visit and look upon** (or: see for himself and inspect) **his brothers** (= his fellows; his countrymen) **– the sons** (= the people) **of Israel.**

24. **"Then, upon seeing someone** [D, E add: of his kinsmen (or: fellow tribesmen)] **being repeatedly injured and treated wrongly** (unjustly; unfairly), **he at once defended [him] and took revenge for the person being abused** (worn down by exhaustive labor and knavish treatment), **striking a fatal blow on the Egyptian** [D* adds: and hid him in the sand].

25. **"Now he had been assuming from what was customary [that] the brothers** (= his people) **would then be grasping that God was presently giving deliverance to them through his hand** [note: e.g., in his striking the Egyptian] **– but they did not put that together so as to comprehend [this].**

26. **"And so, on the following day, he was seen by them as [some] men continued fighting** [D* adds: and he saw them behaving unfairly and bringing injury], **and thus he began attempting to negotiate with them a change into peace, saying, 'Men! You are brothers** (= fellow countrymen)! **Why [is it] that you continue injuring one another and behaving unfairly** (or: unjustly)**?'**

27. **"But the one presently hurting** (and: treating unfairly) **the associate** (or: neighbor) **pushed him away, saying,**

'Who established you (set you down) **[as the] ruler and judge** (or: arbitrator) **upon us?**

28. "'You... you are not presently desiring or intending to lift me up (= kill me) **in the same manner as you lifted up** (= killed) **the Egyptian, yesterday – are you?'** [Ex. 2:14]
29. "Now in [view and consideration of] this expressed thought (word; verbal expression; information), Moses fled and came to be an alien resident (a sojourner) within [the] land of Midian, where he generated (effected the birth of; sired) two sons.

30. "And then – with forty years having been filled full (or: fulfilled) – within the midst of the desolate place (the wilderness; the desert) of Mount Sinai, an agent (or: messenger; [D & others add: of the Lord]) – in union with [the] flame of a fire in a bramble (or: thornbush) – was seen by him.
31. "So Moses, upon seeing [it], was shocked and filled with wonder, marveling at the sight (or: vision; or: the result and effect of what was seen). **Now during his progressive approaching to take note and focus his mind down [on it], a Voice of [the] Lord was birthed** (or: a sound of [Yahweh] occurred, or, came to be; [D reads: the Lord {= Yahweh} spoke to him, saying]),
32. "'I Myself [am] the God of your fathers (= ancestors): the God of Abraham and of Isaac and of Jacob.' So Moses, coming to be in a tremble was not continuing to have courage to be focusing [his] mind or taking notice, or considering [what was happening]!
33. "And the Lord [= Yahweh] further said to him,
    'At once loosen (or: untie) the sandals from your feet, for you see, the place upon which you stand is set-apart ground (sacred soil; consecrated earth; a holy land). [note: the priests were barefooted while serving in the Temple]
34. "'In seeing, I saw the bad treatment of (worthless conduct to; evil handling of) My People who are in Egypt. I also heard their groaning, and so at this time I stepped down to at once by Myself take them up from out of the midst (or: extricate them). Thus come here now; I can send you off with a mission (or: as an emissary) into Egypt.' [Ex. 3: 6-10]

35. "This Moses – whom they contradicted, refused and disowned, saying,
    'Who established you (set you down) [as the] ruler and judge (or: arbitrator) [some MSS add: upon us]?' [Ex. 2:14] –
This one God has sent off on a mission (or: as an emissary) [as] both a ruler (or: chief) and a redeemer (ransomer) – together with (= in association and co-operation with) [the] hand (= agency; help) of [the] agent (or: a messenger) – the one being seen by him within the midst of the bramble (thornbush).
36. "This one led them forth from out of the midst after doing (or: performing) miracles (portents; wonders) and signs within the land of Egypt, and in the midst of [the] Red Sea, as well as in the wilderness (desolate place; desert) [for] forty years. [cf the miracles performed by Jesus – Rieu, ibid]

37. "This one is the Moses saying to the sons of Israel,
    'God will proceed to be raising up for (or: to) you people a Prophet from out of the midst of your brothers – like me! (or: will proceed appointing and setting up a prophet {one who has light ahead of time and speaks it before the people} like me from your people; [D, C & others add: You will continue hearing and listening to Him!])' [Deut. 18:15]
38. "This one is the man coming to be in the midst of the called-out community which was our fathers within the desert (which consisted of our ancestors in the desolate places of the wilderness) – along with the agent (or: messenger), the one continuing in speaking to him in Mount Sinai – he who received continuously living little Words (or: thoughts; ideas; verbal expressions; oracles) to give to you folks [other MSS: to us] (or: to grant for you people; to deliver among you; to bestow in you) –
39. "to whom our fathers were not willing to become obedient with submissive hearing, but to the contrary, they pushed [him] away and within their hearts they were turned around, into Egypt
    (or: to which [words] our ancestors were not wanting or intending to be birthed submissively obedient in hearing [them], but rather, they thrust [them] away – and thus they were turned back to Egypt, in the midst of their hearts),
40. "saying to Aaron,
    'Make (Construct; Create; Produce; Form) at once for (or: to) us gods who will continue going their way before us, since this Moses who led us forth from out of the midst of Egypt – we have not seen, so we don't know, what has happened to him.' [Ex. 32:1, 23]

41. **"And so they made** (constructed; formed; created; produced) **a calf in those days, and then they brought** (or: led) **up a sacrifice to the idol. Thus they were in a good frame of mind and began to enjoy themselves and celebrate, being made glad in the works of their hands.**

42. **"So God turned and handed them over** (committed them) **to be habitually rendering sacred service, as hirelings, to the host of the sky** (= by the sun, moon and stars; or: for the military company of that atmosphere; with heaven's army), **just as it has been written in the scroll of the prophets,**

> **'O house** (= people) **of Israel, it was not to or for Me [that] you people offered slaughtered victims and sacrifices [for] forty years, within the midst of the wilderness** (desolate place; desert)!

43. **'"Later you took up the tent** (or: tabernacle; or: covering shadow) **of Moloch and the star** (or: constellation) **of your god** [B, D and other witnesses read: the god] **Raiphan** (or: Rompha; Remphan; Reifan) **– the models and beaten replicas which you made** (formed; fabricated)' **to repeatedly** (or: habitually) **be worshiping and doing obeisance to them. 'Consequently I will proceed causing you to change houses** (change your abode; = deport and exile you people) **beyond'** [D*: upon the district of] **Babylon.** [Amos 5:25-27, LXX]

44. **"The Tent** (tabernacle; covering shadow) **of the Witness** (evidence; testimony) **was with** (or: for; in the midst of) **our fathers within the wilderness** (desert) **– just as the One then periodically speaking to Moses personally prescribed** (thoroughly arranged and set in order) **[for him] to make** (or: construct) **it: according** (and: corresponding) **to the model** (replica; pattern; type) **which he had seen,**

45. **"which, later on, our forefathers** (or: ancestors), **receiving [it] in succession with Joshua, led** (or: brought) **in within the possession of the ethnic multitudes** (or: nations; = the peoples of Canaan) **whom God drove out** (expelled; thrust forth) **from the face** (= presence) **of our fathers, until the days of David**

46. **"– who found grace and favor in the sight of** (or: before) **God, and so he asked to find a camping site** (a tenting place; the results and effects of pitching a tabernacle; = a place for a habitation with covering shade) **for the God** [p74, B, D and other MSS read: in the house] **of Jacob.**

47. **"However, Solomon built** (constructed) **a house for Him.**

48. **"Nevertheless, the Most High is not continuously settling down to perpetually dwell in houses made by hands – just as the prophet continues saying,**

49. **'The heaven** (or: sky; atmosphere) **[is] a throne for** (or: to) **Me, and the earth** (or: land) **[is] a footstool for My feet. What kind** (or: sort) **of house will you folks proceed constructing for Me,' [the] Lord** [= Yahweh] **continues saying, 'or what is [the] place of My stopping down to rest?** [cf 1 Chron. 28:2; Ps. 132:7; Heb. 1:13; 10:13]

50. **'"Did not My hand make all these things?** (or: My hand forms and constructs all these, does it not?)' [Isa. 66:1-2]

51. **'"Stiff-necked** (= Obstinate and proud) **men' and 'people uncircumcised in hearts and ears!'** [Ex. 32:9; Lev. 26:41] **You yourselves are ever repeatedly falling in opposition against** (or: are always by habit resisting and clashing with) **the Set-apart Breath-effect** (or: the Holy Spirit; Sacred Attitude)! **– as your fathers** (or: ancestors), **so also you folks!**

52. **"Which one of the prophets** (those who had light ahead of time and spoke before the people) **did your fathers** [D* reads: those men] **not persecute and pursue? And they killed off those predicting concerning** (or: bringing down the announcement in advance about) **the coming of the Just One** (the Fair, Equitable, Right One that is in rightwised relationships that accord with the Way pointed out) **– of Whom you yourselves now became people who pre-commit and give in advance** (or: folks who **give-over** before, in front or **in preference**; or: ones who **abandoned** in time of need; people who [were] pre-paid), **even murderers:**

53. **"the very ones who received and took in hand the Law – [leading] into [situations] thoroughly arranged and fully set in order by [His] agents and messengers – and yet you people did not observe it, maintain it, keep it or guard it!"**

54. **Well now, while progressively hearing these things, they were being progressively sawn in two in their hearts** (= emotionally ripped and cut to the core so as to be filled with rage), **and so they**

began and continued to grind and gnash [their] teeth on him (= at his words) **with noises as of a wild animal eating greedily.**

55. **Yet he, continuing in being inherently full of set-apart Breath-effect** (or: of [the] Holy Spirit; or: filled with a consecrated attitude), **gazing intently into the atmosphere and sky** (or: heaven) **saw God's glory, and Jesus** [D adds: the Master (or: Lord)], **standing at God's right [hand, or, side]**
(or: fixing his eyes into the heaven, sees a manifestation of God which calls forth praise – even Jesus, having taken a stand from out of the midst of God's place of honor and power),
56. **And so he said, "Look! I am presently watching the atmosphere and skies** (or: the heavens) **having been fully opened up... and the Son of the Man** (the Human Being; = Adam's Son; [p74 reads: God's Son]) **standing at God's right [hand, or, side]** (or: having taken a stand from out of the midst of the right [parts] of God)!" [Ps. 110:1]

57. **So now, screeching and crying out in a great voice** (with a loud sound; = at the top of their lungs), **they pressed [their hands on] their ears and uncontrollably rushed upon him with one accord** (in like passions).
58. **Then after casting [him] forth, outside of the city, they began stoning [him]** (throwing stones at him to kill him).
And the witnesses put off their outer garments, [depositing them] beside the feet of a certain young man being normally called Saul.
59. **Then as they continued stoning Stephen, [he] continued making an appeal and repeatedly saying, "O Lord Jesus, at once welcome and receive my breath-effect** (or: spirit)!"
60. **Now kneeling, he cried out with a great** (or: loud) **voice, "O Lord** [= Christ or Yahweh], **You should not place** (or: set; cause to stand) **this mistake** (failure; error; sin) **to** (or: on) **them** (= do not charge this sin against them)!"
Then, after saying this, he fell asleep (euphemism: he died).
Now Saul was endorsing (approving in; thinking well together [with them] about) **his assassination** (at his lifting up; in his murder).

CHAPTER 8

1. **Now on that day great persecution, pursuit and** [D adds: pressure] **was birthed** (occurred) **upon the called-out community [that was] within Jerusalem, so they were all – except for the sent-forth emissaries** (representatives) [D* & 1175 add: who alone remained in Jerusalem] **– dispersed and scattered as seeds down among the regions** (or: territories) **of Judea and Samaria.**
2. **– Yet cautious but respected men joined together and collected Stephen and carried [him] in to be prepared for burial, and then they made a great lamentation** (grieving and beating the chest) **upon him** (= at his situation and the loss of him) –
3. **But Saul had been devastating, then continued laying waste and bringing havoc to the called-out community, repeatedly making his way into and invading one house after another. Constantly dragging away and pulling along both men and women by force, he routinely handed [them] over into prison** (or: transferred and committed [them] to a jail).
4. **Nonetheless, those being scattered and dispersed went throughout, from place to place, progressively bringing the Word as good news, and announcing the message of goodness: the** *Logos* (the patterned information; the Idea with the Reason).

5. **Now Philip, upon going down into the** [or: a] **city of Samaria, continued publicly proclaiming to them the Christ** (the Anointed One; = the Messiah). [note: this would apparently include non-Jews]
6. **And the crowds, with one accord and like-passion, continued attentively holding to [themselves and their minds] the things being progressively spoken by Philip, at hearing them, and then [with] repeatedly seeing** (looking at; observing) **the signs which he kept on doing** (or: performing; producing).
7. **You see, many of the folks habitually having unclean breath-effects** (unsifted spirits; unpruned attitudes) **kept on crying out, then shouting for joy, with a loud voice, [as] they** [i.e., the spirits], **one after another, were coming** (or: going) **out.**
Now many folks – being people having been paralyzed, as well as lame ones – were cured and healed.

8. **So, much joy was birthed** (or: a great deal of happiness came to be) **within that city.**

9. **Now a certain man named Simon had been previously subsisting in the city [by] habitually practicing magic** (or: using sorcery) **and repeatedly amazing the nation** (or: ethnic group) **of Samaria, constantly saying [of] and presenting himself to be someone great** (= important) [note: such folks were often considered spiritual advisors, and may have had an official position],

10. **to whom everyone, from small to great** (= from the unimportant to the very important), **kept on attentively holding [themselves] and giving heed, one after another saying, "This man is normally being called God's Great Power** (or: This one continuously exists being God's Power – that usually termed Great One)**!"**

11. **So they kept on heeding and holding themselves focused to him due to the considerable time [he had] to have been displacing [things] and amazing them by the magical acts** (or: with [his] magic).

12. **But when they came to trust and then believed – by Philip progressively bringing and declaring the good news of ease and well-being pertaining to the reign and kingdom of God, and [about] the name of Jesus Christ** (or: Jesus [the] Anointed One) **– they were being from time to time, and one after another, immersed** (or: baptized)**: both men and women.**

13. **So Simon himself also trusted and came to believe, and then, after being immersed** (or: baptized)**, he was constantly attached to Philip** (or: habitually persistent at standing by waiting and ready to assist Philip) **and continued amazed and moved out of his position** (beside himself) **while continually watching and observing both signs and great powers** (or: abilities; or: may = works and deeds of power) **continually happening** (or: one after another being birthed into existence).

14. **Now upon hearing that [the regions of] Samaria had welcomely received, accepted and taken to themselves the Word** (*Logos*; Idea; message and information) **of, and from, God, the sent-forth folks** (emissaries and representatives) **in Jerusalem sent off Peter and John on a mission to them,**

15. **who, after walking down, thought and spoke concerning, and with a view toward, their having goodness** (or: prayed about them)**, so that they would receive a set-apart Breath-effect** (or: in what manner and by what means they could accept or should take hold of [the] Holy Spirit and a sacred attitude),

16. **for you see, it** (or: It; He) **had not yet fallen upon even one of them, yet, only being folks having been immersed, they were continually subsisting and were progressing from under that beginning into the Name of the Lord Jesus**

> (or: they continued being a possession, progressing into the Name, which is the Owner, Jesus; or: Now only having been baptized, in making a beginning they continued belonging unto the Name which pertains to the Master: Jesus).

17. **At that time they began placing** (kept laying) **hands upon them, and so, one after another, they began** (or: kept) **receiving a set-apart Breath-effect** (or: [the] Holy Spirit; a sacred attitude).

18. **Now Simon, upon seeing that the [p45, A & other MSS add: set-apart (or: Holy)] Breath-effect** (or: Spirit; Attitude; Breath) **is repeatedly being given through the placing or laying on** (or: the imposition) **of the hands of the sent-forth folks** (the emissaries or representatives)**, he brought** (or: offered) **useful things** (or: money; properties) **to them,**

19. **repeatedly saying, "Give at once also to me this authority and right, so that on whomever I also should place [my] hands he may receive a set-apart breath-effect** (or: [the] Holy Spirit)**!"**

20. **But Peter said to him, "Your silver might** (or: could) **continue being with [you, as you yourself progress on the path] into loss or destruction, seeing that you suppose and presume from custom to proceed to obtain and acquire God's free gift** (or: gratuity) **through useful things** (or: money; properties; = by buying it).

21. **"There is neither a part nor a lot for you within this Word** (or: this *Logos*; this Idea and Reason; this expressed verbal communication; or: this message; or: this matter). **You see, your heart is not straight and level with a position answering to God** (or: in front of God, in His presence).

22. **"So change your mind** (way of thinking; state of consciousness) **– away from this worthlessness** (or: ugliness; baseness; badness of quality; malice) **of yours – and then at once urgently ask of the Lord** [= Christ or Yahweh] **if consequently** (or: since in that case) **the thought and purpose of your heart will be caused to flow away** (or: will be divorced from [you]; will be forgiven and sent away),

23. **"For you see, I am presently seeing you existing** (continuously being) **[drawn] into [the] bile** (or: gall) **of bitterness as well as a close joint-bond of injustice** (inequity and unfairness; that which is not in right relationship and contrary to the Way pointed out)."

24. **So, making a decided response, Simon said to them, "I am now asking for help: would you men at once urgently make a request over me** (or: on my behalf; for my situation; [D: concerning me]) **to the Lord** [= Christ or Yahweh; D reads: God] **so that not even one of the things which you have said can** (or: would) **come upon me?"** [D adds: – {He} could not cease shedding many tears.]

25. **Therefore, after indeed fully giving evidence** (thoroughly witnessing and certifying) **and speaking the Word of the Lord** (or: = Yahweh's thoughts and ideas; = the message about Christ [p74, A & others read: God]; the *Logos* from The LORD), **these men began returning unto Jerusalem, also repeatedly bringing the good news and announcing the message of goodness, ease and well-being [to] many villages of the Samaritans.**

26. **However, an agent of, and from, [the] Lord** [= Yahweh's or Christ's messenger] **spoke to Philip, presently saying, "At once arise** (or: stand up) **and continue traveling down south** (or: at noon) **on the road descending from Jerusalem unto Gaza." This is a desert** (or: desolate, uninhabited) **[road].**

27. **And so, upon arising, he went his way and – look, consider this – an adult man – an Ethiopian eunuch who had power** (= a high court official) **of [the] Kandake, [or] Queen, of [the] Ethiopians, who was upon** (= had control of) **all of her treasury – who had come unto Jerusalem in order to be worshiping.**

28. **Now he was in the midst of returning and was presently sitting on his chariot** (or: carriage) **while continuing in reading aloud the prophet Isaiah.**

29. **Now the Breath-effect** (or: Spirit) **said to Philip, "Approach and be joined** (glued) **to this chariot."** [comment: was this Breath-effect the same "agent/messenger" of vs. 26, above?]

30. **So upon running up to [it], Philip heard his reading aloud [of] Isaiah the prophet, and then he said, "Are you presently personally-recognizing and progressively understanding [the] things which you are now progressively reading** (experientially knowing-again)?"

31. **But he replied, "Actually, how would I likely be presently able [to], unless someone will progressively lead and guide me on the path?" And so he asked Philip to assist [him], after climbing up to sit with him.**

32. **Now the passage** (context) **of the Scripture which he was reading was this:**
   "As (or: Like) **a sheep, He was led onto [the] slaughter, and as** (or: like) **a lamb [that is] set in position against the person shearing it [is] without a voice** (or: mute; voiceless; = silent), **in like manner He continues not to open up His mouth.**

33. **"Within the midst of the low status and the experience of being abased and humiliated, His justice** (either: the opportunity for a fair trial; or: the chance or ability to divide, separate and make decisions; or: the judging) **was lifted up and taken away. So who will continue fully taking over the lead of His generation** (or: will proceed conducting a thorough narration to recount His generation), **because His life is now being taken up, away from the earth** (or: taken away from the Land)?" [note: a paraphrase of Isa. 53:7b-8, LXX; *cf* Lu. 22:37]

34. **So the eunuch, making a discerning response, said to Philip, "Now my question to you is, About whom is the prophet now saying this – about himself, or about someone else?"**

35. **Well Philip, opening his mouth and beginning from this Scripture, presents to him Jesus, as the news of goodness, ease and well-being** (or: declared to him the good news about Jesus).

36. **So as they continued going their way down the road, they came upon some water, and the eunuch affirms, "Look! Water! What continues preventing** (hindering) **me to be at once immersed** (or: baptized)?"
   [note 1: vs. 37 is missing in texts of Nestle-Aland, WH, Concordant, Panin, Griesbach, Tasker, and is not in the ancient Syriac; note 2: apparently Philip was not adhering to Judaism, for the Law did not allow a eunuch to be a member of the congregation – Deut. 23:1; Isa. 56:1-5 prophesied of the change that would come with the new covenant (Isa. 55:3b-5)]

38. **And thus, he ordered the chariot to halt** (or: stand still), **and they both walked down into the water – both Philip and the eunuch – and [Philip] immersed** (or: baptized) **him.**

39. **Now when they walked up out of the water, [the] Lord's** [or: = Yahweh's] **wind** (or: a Breath-effect or Spirit [of Christ]; or: a spirit from [Yahweh]) **suddenly snatched Philip away** (i.e.: carried him off), **and the eunuch did not see him any longer for he kept on going on his road, continuously rejoicing.**
40. **But Philip was found** (or: discovered) **[entering] into Ashdod** (or: Azotus), **and then continuing in going throughout [the territory], he was repeatedly bringing and announcing the good news to all the towns and cities – till the [occasion for] him to come into Caesarea** [the Roman capital of Judea].

CHAPTER 9

1. **Now Saul, still continuously inhaling and breathing** (or: in-spiriting and blowing [out]; animated with the spirit of) **threatening and murder** (or: slaughter) **into the midst of the Lord's** [= Yahweh's or Christ's] **disciples** (or: students; learners), **after going to the head** (chief; ranking) **priest,**
2. **requested from him letters [to take] into Damascus – to the synagogues – so that if he should be finding anyone being [a part] of** (or: belonging to) **the Way** (or: the Path; the Road), **he could lead [them] – both men and women – bound** (= as prisoners) **into Jerusalem.**

3. **Now it happened, during [the occasion for] him to be progressively traveling [and] to be nearing Damascus, that with unexpected suddenness a light from out of the midst of the atmosphere** (or: sky; heaven) **flashed around him as lightning,**
4. **and having fallen upon the ground, he heard a Voice** (or: sound) **repeatedly saying to him, "Saul... Saul... Why do you continue pursuing and persecuting Me?"**
5. **So he said, "Who are You, Lord** (or: Sir; Master)**?"**
Now He replied, **"I, Myself, am Jesus... Whom you continue pursuing and persecuting!**
6. **"Nevertheless, at once stand up and then enter into the city. Then it will proceed being spoken to you that which it continues binding and necessary for you to continue doing."**

7. **Now the adult men who were presently accompanying him on the journey had stood speechless and continued standing dumbfounded – while hearing the voice** (or: sound; = Paul speaking?), **and yet still, as spectators, gazing at not even one person** (or: yet not viewing anyone)**!**
8. **But then Saul got up from the ground, and yet with his eyes having been opened up, and continuing open, he was seeing nothing! So, in progressively leading him by the hand, they conducted him on into Damascus,**
9. **and he was three days still not seeing. He also neither ate nor drank.**
[comment: "the three days of darkness are like three days in the tomb"—Rackham, in Rieu, ibid p 134]

10. **Now there was a certain disciple** (student; apprentice) **in Damascus named Ananias, and within a vision the Lord** [= Christ] **said to him, "Ananias!" So he said, "Look, I [am here], O Lord!"**
11. **So then the Lord [said] to him, "At once get up and go on your way upon the alley** (or: narrow street) **being normally called 'Straight,' and look for** (seek; try to find) **within [the] house of Judah** (or: Judas) **a person from Tarsus named Saul, for you see, look and consider! – he is presently thinking with a view toward having goodness, ease and well-being** (or: continuously praying),
12. **"and within a vision** (the effect of something seen) **he saw an adult man named Ananias coming in and putting [his] hands upon him so that he can look up, and see again!"**

13. **But Ananias discerningly answered, "O Lord! I hear** (or: heard) **from many people about this adult man... how many vile and bad** (worthless and evil; ugly and malicious) **things he did to Your set-apart folks** (Your saints) **in Jerusalem!**
14. **"And here in this place he is presently having** (or: holding) **authority from the chief** (head; ranking) **priests to bind all those habitually calling upon Your Name!"**

15. **Yet the Lord** [= Christ] **said to him, "Be presently going** (or: Go, and continue on your way), **because this one is** (exists being) **a vessel of choice to Me** (or: a picked-out and chosen instrument by and for Me) **to lift up and carry My Name before** (in the sight and presence of) **the ethnic multitudes** (or: nations; Gentiles; non-Israelites) **– as well as [before] kings and [the] sons** (= people) **of Israel.**

16. **"For you see, I Myself will proceed underlining and pointing out** (or: plainly showing) **to him how many things it continues being binding and necessary for him to experience and be suffering – over [the situation of]** (or: for; on behalf of) **My Name."**

17. **So Ananias went off and entered into the house, and after placing [his] hands upon him, he said, "O Brother Saul! The Lord – Jesus, the One being seen by you on the road in which you were coming – has sent me with a mission so that you can look up and see again, and then you can be filled with [the] set-apart Breath-effect** (or: [the] Holy Spirit; a consecrated attitude)!"
18. **And immediately there fell off from his eyes [something] like scales** (or: hulls; shells; rinds; incrustations; [Greek *lepris*; note: *lepra* is the word 'leprosy'; *lepros* is a leper]). **And so he looked up and could see again** (or: recovered his sight). **Next, after standing up, he was immersed** (or: baptized). **Later on, upon receiving food** (or: nourishment), **he was inwardly strengthened and invigorated.**

19. **Now he came to be** (was birthed into an existence; = spent some time) **with the disciples in Damascus [for] some** (or: certain; [*p45* reads: enough]) **days,**
20. **then straightway** (at once) **began publicly proclaiming Jesus within the synagogues – continuously heralding that this Man is** (exists being) **God's Son** (or: the Son which has the character and qualities of, and whose origin is, God)! [*cf* vs. 22b, below]
21. **Yet all the folks presently listening and hearing [him] continued amazed and astonished** (literally: standing out of themselves), **and were one after another saying, "Is not this man the person [who] in Jerusalem was laying waste** (devastating; ravaging; trying to kill) **the people habitually calling upon this Name? And now he has come here, into this place** (or: unto this purpose), **so that after [their] having been bound, he could lead them on to the head** (chief; ranking) **priests!"**

22. **But Saul kept on being more exceedingly empowered and was progressively given inner abilities, and so he kept on pouring and diffusing [thoughts; ideas; Scriptures] together – [to the point that] he was creating an uproar among, and was confounding** (or: throwing into confusion and perplexity) **the Jews presently living and permanently dwelling in Damascus – progressively causing [his arguments] to stand together, thus proving conclusively that this Man is** (exists being) **the Christ** (the Anointed One; = the Messiah; [note: = "God's Son," of vs. 20, above]).

23. **Now as a considerable number of days were, one after another, being fulfilled** (or: = coming to a close; thus: = quite some time later), **the Jews consulted together to assassinate him** (to "take him up"). **However, their plot became known to Saul.**
24. **Now they also kept on closely watching and covertly guarding the gates both day and night so that they could capture and assassinate him.** [*cf* 2 Cor. 11:32-33]
25. **So his students** (disciples), **by night taking [him] through [an opening or window in] the wall, let him down by gradually lowering [him] in a hamper** (possibly: a basket made of braided ropes).

26. **Now later, coming to be present [after entering] into Jerusalem, he kept on trying to be closely joined to the disciples** (students; apprentices), **and yet everyone continued fearing him, still not trusting or believing that he is now a disciple.** [note: i.e., that he is now one of them, a follower]
27. **So Barnabas, taking on [the problem]** (or: taking him on [as a friend]; or: taking him by the hand), **led him to the sent-forth folks** (the emissaries) **and then he [i.e., Saul] fully related to them how he saw the Lord on the road, and that He spoke to him** (or: he spoke to Him) **and how in Damascus he spoke in the Name of Jesus with the right of complete freedom from constraint, and with all boldness being publicly open and frank.**
28. **And so he continued being with them, going his way into Jerusalem, as well as traveling out.**
29. **Repeatedly speaking in the Name of the Lord with the right of complete freedom from constraint, and with all boldness being publicly open and frank, he continued both speaking and making joint-deliberations to the Hellenists** (the Jews who spoke Greek or had adopted the Greek culture, or both). **Yet these folks began taking in hand to assassinate him.**
30. **So, upon coming to be personally aware and to accurately know [of this], the brothers led him down into Caesarea, and then sent him forth with a mission into Tarsus** [note: capital of Cilicia].

31. **So then the called-out community down through [the] whole of Judea, Galilee and Samaria continued having peace from the joining** (or: began possessing tranquility), **progressively being built as a house and continuously edified, as well as habitually going their way, in and by the fear of the Lord** [= Christ or Yahweh]. **And so, in and by the comforting and encouraging relief and assistance of the set-apart Breath-effect** (or: the Holy Spirit and Sacred Attitude), **it continued being multiplied** (or: was progressively increased and made full). [note the trans-regional single community]

32. **Now while Peter continued going through all [the territories]** (or: fully traversing through the midst of all people groups [or: towns]), **he happened to go down also to the set-apart folks** ([to be] face-to-face with the saints) **presently inhabiting** (or: permanently settled in) **Lydda** (or: Lud).

33. **Now there he found a certain man named Aeneas, who was one having been paralyzed, continuously lying down upon a cot** (or: pallet; = bed-ridden) **for eight years.**

34. **So then Peter said to him, "Aeneas, Jesus Christ** (the Anointed One) **is presently healing** (or: has healed) **you. At once stand up** (or: arise; get up) **and spread** (= make up) **[your bed] by yourself** (or: prepare the couch [for a meal] for yourself)**!" And so he immediately got up** (arose; stood up).

35. **Later all the folks presently inhabiting** (residing in) **Lydda and the [plain of] Sharon saw him, which folks [also] turned back upon** (= returned their lives to having a focus on) **the Lord** [Christ or Yahweh].

36. **Now in Joppa there was a certain female disciple named Tabitha – which, being translated, is normally called Dorcas** (= Gazelle). **She was full of good works and noble, virtuous acts – as well as deeds of mercy and gifts of compassion – which she was habitually doing** (regularly performing).

37. **But in those days, after becoming weak and ill, she happened to die. So, upon washing** (bathing) **[her], they placed her in the upper room** (or: story; chamber).

38. **Now with Lydda being near to Joppa, the disciples – upon hearing that Peter was in [Lydda] – sent off two adult men to him, calling [him] to their side for help, urging, "You should not delay or be slow to pass through to us** (or: hesitate to come through as far as us; = include us in your travels, and don't delay)**!"**

39. **So after arising, Peter went with them, whom – upon [his] arriving – they led up into the upper room** (or: the upstairs chamber). **Then all the widows presented [themselves] to him and stood by, weeping and exhibiting tunics and outer garments** (= dresses and coats) **[and] whatever Dorcas used to make [while] still being with them.**

40. **But after causing everyone to be put forth outside and then kneeling down, Peter prayed** (focused toward [her] having well-being). **Next, turning around and facing toward the body, he said, "Tabitha! Get up** (or: Stand up; Arise)**!" So she opened up her eyes, and, seeing Peter, she sat up.**

41. **And so, giving her a hand, he raised her up** (or: helped her stand up). **And now, after summoning the set-apart folks** (the saints; the holy people) **and the widows, he stood her alongside** (or: presented her), **now living.**

42. **So it came to be known down through [the] whole of Joppa, and many folks placed trust upon** (or: believed and had faith on) **the Lord** [= Christ or Yahweh].

43. **Now it turned out [for] him to remain and dwell in Joppa – alongside of a certain Simon, a tanner – for a considerable number of days.**

CHAPTER 10

1. **Now in Caesarea there was a certain adult man named Cornelius, a centurion** (a Roman officer in charge of 100 men, i.e., one sixth of a cohort) **that was a part of the band** (or: cohort; squadron; – an army division of 600 men) **which is normally being called "Italian,"**

2. **a person of well-directed reverence** (or: devout and virtuous conduct; observation of Jewish religious customs) **and by habit fearing God, along with all his household, constantly performing many acts of mercy and making lots of gifts that express [his] compassion to the people, as well as repeatedly making requests of God** (or: from God) **throughout all times and situations.**

3. **In the midst of a vision** (a result of something seen) **– just about the ninth hour of the day** (three o'clock in the afternoon) **– he clearly saw an agent of** (or: messenger from) **God entering toward** (or: coming in, face to face with) **him, and then saying to him, "Cornelius!"**

4. **So he, gazing intently at him and then coming to be in reverent fear, said, "What is it, sir** (or: [my] lord)**?"**
Now [the agent] replied, "Your thoughts, words and actions toward having goodness (or: prayers) **along with your gifts and acts of mercy ascended into a situation that has caused you not to be forgotten** (or: unto a remembrance) **in front of and facing** (or: before) **God's presence.**

5. **"And so, at this time send adult men into Joppa, and then send after** (or: change the sending to summon) **Simon, a certain man who is now surnamed Peter.**

6. **"This man is currently being entertained as a guest at the side of Simon, a tanner, for whom there is a house beside [the] sea** (or: ocean)**."** [note: a tanner's trade kept him ceremonially unclean]

7. **So as soon as the agent** (messenger) **that had been speaking to him went away, upon summoning two of the household servants and a devout soldier** (a warrior with well-directed reverence) **of those being constantly in loyal attendance to him** (or: regularly attached to his service),
8. **and then leading them through a detailed narrative of all the things [that occurred], he sent them off on the mission, into Joppa.** [note: Gentiles coming to a perpetually unclean house, for Christ]

9. **Now the next day, while those [three] were in progress of traveling on the road and were presently drawing near to the city, Peter went up onto the housetop to pray** (think and speak towards having things go well and be at ease) **– [it was] about [the] sixth hour** (about noon).
10. **But he became very hungry – almost ravenous – and began desiring to at once taste** (= eat) **[something]. Now during their being in the midst of preparing [a meal], an ecstasy happened** (an out-of-place state of being was birthed [*p*45 reads: came]) **upon him,**
11. **and he is now – as a spectator – watching the sky** (or: heaven; the atmosphere) **– having been opened up – and in the process of descending [is] some container, like a large, fine linen sheet** (or: sail-cloth; bandage), **being gradually but progressively lowered down onto the ground** (or: Land; earth) **by [its] four corners** (extremities; origins; beginnings),
12. **within the midst of which were continuing under [the directive, or, power] of [their] origin all the four-footed animals, as well as creeping things** (perhaps: insects; reptiles) **of the ground** (or: land; earth) **and flying creatures of the sky** (or: atmosphere; heaven).
13. **Then a voice was birthed to him** (or: occurred, [directed] toward him), **"After getting up** (or: Upon arising), **Peter, slaughter** (or: sacrifice) **and then at once eat [it]!"** [*cf* Lev. 11:1-47; Deut. 14:3-21]
14. **But Peter said, "Not even one [of those], Sir** (or: Lord; Master; or: = Yahweh?), **because I never eat** (or: ate) **all [that is] common** (= what is not set-apart as food for Israelites and is forbidden by the dietary rules of the Law; profane) **and unclean** (meaning: ceremonially unclean)**!"**
15. **Then again, a voice, forth from a second [one, saying] to him: "You are not to continue making, deeming or considering common** (or: profane) **[the] things which God cleansed** (or: cleanses) **and made** (or: makes) **clean!"** [*cf* Mk. 7:18-19]
16. **Now this happened on a third [time]** (or: So this occurred three times), **and immediately the container was taken back up again, into the sky** (or: the atmosphere; heaven).

17. **Now as Peter was continuing thoroughly perplexed** (bewildered and at a loss, as when not knowing what road to take) **within himself [as to] what the vision** (or: sight) **which he saw would likely be** (= mean) **– now look and consider this! – the men who had been sent off on the mission by Cornelius, after sorting out by making inquiry throughout [the town] and ascertaining [the location of] Simon's house, approached and stood by at the portal** (or: vestibule; gateway).
18. **Then calling out loudly, they kept inquiring if Simon – the one surnamed Peter – is still being entertained as a guest** (or: continues lodging) **in this place.**
19. **Now during Peter's repeatedly going through various feelings about the vision** (what he saw), **continuing engrossed in pondering the effects of that which was seen, the Breath-effect** (or: Spirit) **said to him, "Look, and take note! Three [B reads: Two] men are presently seeking you!**
20. **"But now, after getting up, you at once go downstairs** (descend; climb down) **then continue going your way together with them – doubting nothing and continuing in making no diverse**

judging, nor discriminating, nor divided evaluating, nor separating yourself in even one thing – because I Myself have commissioned them and sent them off on this mission."

21. So after walking downstairs to the men, Peter said, "Look, I myself am [the person] whom you are presently looking for. What [is] the cause for which you men are now present?"
22. So they said, "Cornelius – a centurion (army officer), a just, fair and equitable man who lives in accord with the way pointed out, as well as being habitually God-fearing (= an "observer of Jewish religious customs" – C.H. Rieu) besides being a person constantly attested (reported by witnesses; = highly regarded) by the whole nation of the Judeans (or: ethnic group of the Jews) – was given useful and practical instructions on this matter, by a set-apart agent (or: sacred messenger): to send you over unto his house, and then to listen face-to-face to gush-effects of your spoken words and declarations (or: to [the] effects of the flow, at your side; or: = to hear in person what you have to say)."
23. Therefore, upon inviting them in, he entertained and lodged [them] as guests.
So on the next day, after getting up, he went with them – and some of the brothers (= fellow believers) from Joppa accompanied him.
24. The following day (or: On the day after that) he entered into Caesarea. Cornelius, of course, was looking forward in anticipation for them, calling together to himself his relatives and the indispensable intimate friends.
25. So it happened as Peter was [about] to enter, Cornelius, upon meeting with (or: encountering; intercepting) him, in falling prostrate at [his] feet did obeisance (showed respect and offered homage) [to him].
26. Yet Peter raised him up, while saying, "Get up (or: Stand up; Rise)! I myself also am the same as you – a human!"

27. And so, while continuing to converse with him, he entered and is then finding many people having come together and now assembled.
28. Thus he affirmed to them, "You folks continue well versed [in the fact] and are well aware of how illicit and inappropriate (impermissible and forbidden by [our] Law and contrary to [our] established order) it is for an adult man [who is] a Jew (or: is of the Jewish culture) to be intimately joined to, or to regularly come to (or: visit and associate with), a person from another race or tribe. And yet God pointed out and demonstrated to me not to continue saying [that] even one human [is] common (or: profane; = socially or ceremonially unhallowed or defiled) or unclean (or: impure).
29. "Wherefore – and without speaking against it or debating the matter – I come (or: came), being sent over. I am now, therefore, inquiring to ascertain for what reason (or: to what matter or issue; by what word; with what *Logos*) you folks sent over for me."

30. Then Cornelius brought the matter to light: "Four days ago, exactly to this very hour, I was in the midst of thinking and speaking with a view toward having goodness and well-being (or: praying) within my house, at the ninth [hour] (three in the afternoon), and – now consider this! – an adult man (male human being) in bright, shining clothing stood before me
31. "and proceeds to utter, 'Cornelius, your thoughts, speech and deeds toward having goodness and well-being (or: prayer) came into hearing (or: [entering] into the midst were heard; or: were listened into), and your gifts, as well as acts, of mercy were remembered in God's sight and presence.
32. "'Therefore, send into Joppa and call over Simon, who is normally being surnamed Peter. This man is currently being lodged and entertained as a guest in the house of Simon, a tanner, by [the] sea.'
33. "Thereupon I immediately sent to you [D adds: urging you to come to us and help us], and you did beautifully (or: ideally) in [D adds: quickly] coming to be at [our] side. At this time, then, we ourselves are all present – in the sight and presence of God – to at once hear all the things having been commanded to you from, and now arranged for you by, the Lord [= Yahweh; p74, D & others read: God]."

34. At this Peter, opening his mouth said, "[Based] upon truth and reality, I continue grasping with force and fully receiving [understanding] that God is neither partial nor takes folks at face value (does not receive faces or appearances or show favoritism), [cf Deut. 10:17b]

35. **"but to the contrary, within every nation and ethnic group the person habitually reverencing and fearing Him, as well as repeatedly doing works and performing acts of fairness, equity, justice, deliverance, or rightwised relationships which accord with the way pointed out** (= covenant principles) **is and continues being welcome and acceptable to Him.** [*cf* Eph. 2:11-17]

36. **"He sent forth the *Logos*** (the Word; the laid-out Idea; the Thought; the Reason; the Message; the patterned Information) **to, and then in, with, among and by the sons of Israel – repeatedly announcing the good news of ease and well-being: peace and harmony from the joining, through Jesus Christ** ([the] Anointed One). **This One is Lord** (Master) **of all humans, and Owner of all things!**

37. **"You yourselves have seen and thus know the thing happening** (coming to be) **– [the] result of the flow** (or: spoken word; or: = the subject talked about) **[going] down through the whole of the Judean [district], beginning from Galilee, after the immersion** (or: baptism) **which John, as a herald, publicly proclaimed –**

38. **"Jesus, the One from Nazareth – even as how God anointed Him with [a/the] set-apart Breath-effect** (or: Holy Spirit; Sacred Attitude) **even for** (or: and with) **power and ability – Who went throughout repeatedly doing works bringing goodness, ease and well-being, as well as constantly healing all the folks being continuously held down under power** (tyrannized and oppressed) **by the one that casts things through folks** (the accuser, slanderer, adversary)**... because God was with Him.**

39. **"And we ourselves [are] witnesses** (or: folks who give evidence) **of all [the] things which He did** (and: performed; produced), **both within the country of the Judeans, and in Jerusalem – Whom also they lifted up and assassinated, hanging [Him] upon a wooden pole** (or: stake; tree).

40. **"This Man** (or: Person) **God raised up on** (or: in; [D reads: after]) **[the] third day, and He gave** (or: gives) **Him to become** (or: be birthed) **visible within the midst** (or: inwardly apparent) **–**

41. **"not among** (or: in; by) **all the people, but rather among** (or: in; by) **witnesses** (or: disclosed – not to all the people, but rather to, in and by folks giving evidence) **having been previously hand-picked and elected by God – in us** (or: to and by us) **who ate and drank together with Him, after the [occasion for] Him to stand back up** (rise again) **out from the midst of dead folks.**

42. **"And He passed along the directive** (the announced instructions) **for us to publicly proclaim, as heralds – to, and among, the people – and to solemnly certify and vehemently argue, by personal evidence in thorough testimony and with witnessing throughout, that this Man is and continues being the very One having been definitely marked out and specified by God [as] He who decides** ([the] Evaluator; a Sifter; Judge) **concerning presently living folks, and currently dead people.**

43. **"To this Man** (or: Person) **all the prophets** (those who had light ahead of time) **continue bearing witness, giving testimony and presenting evidence: through** (or: by way or means of) **His Name, everyone** (or: all humanity) **– keeping on placing trust and faith into Him, progressively believing into the midst of Him, or remaining faithful unto Him – [comes] to receive** (obtain) **a divorce from failures** (a sending-away of mistakes; a cancellation of errors; a forgiveness of sins; a flowing-off of deviations)**."**

44. **During the middle of Peter's still speaking these gush-effects and results of the flow** (or: declarations), **the set-apart Breath-effect** (or: the Holy Spirit; the Sacred Wind) **fell upon all the folks presently listening to and hearing the *Logos*** (the message; the Word). [note: = a Gentile Pentecost]

45. **Then the trusting** (full of faith and loyal) **folks from among [the] Circumcision** (= those of the Jewish culture and religion) **who came with Peter "stood out of themselves" in shocked amazement, that the free gift** (the gratuity) **of** (or: which is) **the set-apart Breath-effect** (the Holy Spirit) **had been poured out upon the nations** (the ethnic multitudes; the non-Jews) **as well,**

46. **for you see, they kept on hearing them continuously and repeatedly speaking with tongues** (in languages; by ecstatic glottal utterances) **and repeatedly magnifying** (speaking great things about) **God.**

47. **At that point Peter gave a decisive and insightful response: "Surely not anyone continues able to cut off the water [that] any of the [group] is not to be immersed – these who received the set-apart Breath-effect, even as we ourselves [have]** (or: Perhaps a certain One has Power to withhold the water with a view to these – who receive the Holy Spirit, just as also we – not to be immersed)**!"**

48. **So he gave instruction toward arranging them to be immersed: centered within the Name of Jesus Christ** (or: be dipped unto envelopment and saturation in union with the Name, Anointed Jesus). **At that point they requested him to stay on and remain some** (or: certain; = a few more) **days.**

CHAPTER 11

1. **Now the sent-forth folks and the brothers** (= fellow believers or members of the brotherhood) **who were down throughout Judea heard that the ethnic groups of the nations** (the non-Jews; Gentiles) **also welcomingly received and embraced the *Logos* of God** (or: the Word which is God; the message and information from God; God's thought, idea and reason).

2. **So when Peter went up into Jerusalem, the men from among [the] Circumcision** [note: i.e., the Jews adhering to the Jewish culture and religion: these may or may not have been a part of the called-out community] **continued their evaluation [of propriety] for a complete distinction and separation [between Jews and non-Jews], and so began taking sides against him to make a cleavage, contending and debating the issue with him,**

3. **[and, speaking about Peter,] were saying that he had gone into [a house] to men still having foreskins and he had eaten with them.** [other MSS have this as a direct address: "You entered to men that are uncircumcised, and you ate with them!"]

4. **At this Peter, in making a beginning, began setting [the matter] out for them consecutively** (or: expounding a deliberate and detailed narrative to them, point by point), **saying,**

5. **"I myself was in the city of Joppa, continuing in prayer** (thinking and speaking towards having things be well), **and I saw – within an ecstasy** (a displaced state of being) **– a vision** (a sight)**: some container in the process of descending, like a large, fine linen sheet, being gradually but progressively lowered down from out of the sky** (or: atmosphere; heaven) **by [its] four corners** (extremities; origins; beginnings), **and it came right down to me,**

6. **"after gazing intently, stretching [my eyes] into which, I began considering and fixing my mind down [on it], and then saw** (or: perceived) **the four-footed animals of the land** (or: earth), **and the little wild animals that are trapped and hunted, also creeping things** (insects and reptiles), **as well as the flying creatures of the sky** (or: heaven; atmosphere).

7. **"Now I also heard a voice, saying to me, 'Get up** (Stand up; Arise), **Peter! Slaughter** (or: Sacrifice) **and eat [something] at once!'**

8. **"But I said, 'Not even one [of those], Sir** (or: Lord; Master; or: = Christ or Yahweh?), **because common** (= what is not set-apart as food for Israelites and is forbidden by the dietary rules of the Law; profane) **and unclean** (meaning: ceremonially unclean) **never entered into my mouth!'**

9. **"Yet a voice forth from a second one** (or: = a second time; out of a second [directive]) **responded decidedly from out of the heaven** (or: atmosphere; sky), **'You are not to continue considering common** (making profane) **things which God cleansed** (or: cleanses) **and made** (or: makes) **clean!'**

10. **"Now this occurred three times, and then everything was pulled** (or: drawn) **back up again into the sky** (or: atmosphere; heaven).

11. **"Furthermore – now consider this! – out of that very [moment], three men, being the ones sent off on the mission from Caesarea to me, stood at the house in which we presently were** [other MSS: I presently was].

12. **"So the Breath-effect** (or: Spirit) **told me to at once go with them – doubting nothing and making no diverse judging, nor discriminating nor separating myself in even one thing. Now these six brothers also went together with me, and then we entered into the house of the man.**

13. **"Now he at once reported back to us how he saw the agent** (messenger) **standing within his house, and then saying, 'Send off into Joppa, then send after Simon, the one now surnamed Peter,**

14. **"'who will be speaking to you gush-effects and results of the flow** (or: declarations; spoken words) **within the midst of which you yourself will be made whole** (saved; rescued; healed and returned to your pristine state of being) **– as well as all your household!'**

15. **"However, within the midst of my starting to continue speaking, the set-apart Breath-effect** (or: Holy Spirit) **fell upon them – even as also upon us, in the beginning.**

16. **"At this I was reminded of the results of the flow and the gush-effects** (or: words spoken) **by the Lord, as He was repeatedly saying, 'John, indeed** (or: for his part), **immersed in water, yet you yourselves will be immersed** (baptized) **within the midst of set-apart Breath-effect** (or: in [the] Holy Spirit; in union with a sacred attitude).' [note: a contrast between immersion in water and in Spirit]

17. **"Since** (or: If), **therefore, God gave to** (or: gives in; grants for) **them, as also to** (or: in; for) **us, the equal free-gift** (the gratuity that is equal in quality, measure and rank)**: faithing, believing and putting**

their trust upon the Lord, Jesus Christ (or: [the] Anointed Jesus) – who or what [am] I? Was I able to cut off or hinder God?!"

18. Now upon hearing these, they were quiet (silent; still), and then they gave glory to, and enhanced the reputation of, God, as a group saying, "Consequently, God also gave (or: gives; grants) to the non-Jews (the ethnic multitudes of the nations; the Gentiles) the change of mind (or: change in thinking, attitude and state of consciousness) into Life!"

19. So then, as to the folks being scattered and dispersed from the pressure, affliction and tribulation being birthed on [the situation regarding] Stephen, they went throughout [the country, or, area] as far as Phoenicia, Cyprus and Antioch [capital of the Roman Province of Syria], by custom speaking the *Logos* (the Word; the message; the idea and information) to no one except to Jews only.

20. Yet there were certain folks from among them – adult men from Cyprus and Cyrene – who, upon coming into Antioch, began also speaking to the Greeks [reading with p74, Aleph2, A and D*: = Gentiles, non-Jews, people of the nations; but B, D2, and other MSS read: Hellenists (= Greek-speaking Jews, as well as others of the Greek culture)], continuously bringing and announcing [to them] the Lord Jesus as the news of goodness, ease and well-being.

   [note: it is not clear from the text whether this happened before, simultaneously with, or after
   Peter visited Cornelius; further: these folks seemed to be operating on their own, with no
   "official" sending or commissioning]

21. Furthermore, the hand (= the power and activity) of [the] Lord [= Yahweh, or Christ] was with them, and a great number -- the faithing, trusting and believing – turned [themselves and their lives] back around (or: returned), upon the Lord.

22. Now the account concerning them was heard in the ears of the called-out community then being in Jerusalem, and those folks sent forth Barnabas out on an errand, all the way to Antioch,

23. who, upon coming to be at [their] side and seeing the joyous grace and favor – that which has its source in God, and which has the qualities and characteristics of God, and which in fact is God – at once rejoiced and began calling everyone to his side so that he could assist and encourage them to habitually remain oriented to and focused in the Lord [= Christ and Yahweh] – with (or: by) the plan and purpose of the heart!

24. Because you see, he was a man [that was] good (virtuous; having quality) and [was] full of set-apart Breath-effect (or: [the] Holy Spirit; a sacred attitude), and faith (trust; conviction; loyalty). And thus, a considerable crowd was set toward (or: added to) the Lord.

25. So he went forth into Tarsus to hunt up (to seek up and down as well as back and forth for; = to make a thorough search for) Saul,

26. then, upon finding [him], he brought (or: led) [him] into Antioch.
Now it also came to be (or: happened) for them to be gathered together among (or: within the midst of) the called-out community [there for] a whole year, and to teach a considerable crowd [of people]. Furthermore, [it happened] in Antioch for the first time to employ the useful appellation "Christians (little anointed ones; = Messianics; = associates or followers of the Christ)" [to; for] the disciples (or: students; apprentices).

27. Now during these days, prophets (folks having light ahead of time who spoke this light before folks) came (or: went) down from Jerusalem unto Antioch.

28. And now one from among them, named Agabus, upon rising and taking a stand, through means of the Breath-effect (or: Spirit) began indicating by signs and symbols [that] a great famine is to be progressively impending, [which] is going to birth itself into existence upon the whole inhabited land (= the whole Roman empire) – something which occurred upon [the reign] of Claudius.

29. So they determined a plan (marked off the horizon) [that] each of them, according as any of the disciples prospered and thrived (= could afford), is to send [something] unto a relief service (or: to a dispensing of aid) for the brothers (= fellow members of the called-out community) presently settled permanently (or: dwelling) in Judea,

30. which also they did, sending [it] off to the older men (or: elders) through [the] hand (= by the means or personal agency) of Barnabas and Saul.

Acts

CHAPTER 12

1. **Now down through that season and during that particular situation, Herod** [Agrippa I] **the king [had his subordinates] thrust [their] hands on** (= arrest) **certain of the folks from the called-out community** (or: the [local Messianic] communit[ies]; [D adds: in Judea]) **to mistreat [them].**
2. **And so he took up Jacob** (or: James), **the brother of John, and assassinated [him] with a** (or: by [the]) **sword.**
3. **Now upon seeing that [this] was pleasing to the Judeans** (= the Jewish leadership and their sympathizers), **he set himself with a focus to seize** (take together with the hands) **Peter, also – now [these] were the days of Unleavened Bread** [= during the Feast following Passover],
4. **whom, after taking a firm hold on [him], he put into prison** (or: jail), **turning [him] over** (committing [him]) **to four [shifts] of four soldiers [each] to continue guarding him, presently intending to lead him back up** (= present him) **to the people, after the Passover.**

5. **Therefore Peter, consequently, continued being kept in custody** (remained under guard and was being watched) **within the prison** (or: jail), **yet thoughts and speech toward having things be well [for him]** (or: prayer) **continued being repeatedly birthed** (or: was continuously coming to be) **extendedly** (i.e., in a way or manner that stretched forth from out of [their] midst; or: intensely) **focused on God around him** (or: toward God concerning him), **by the called-out community.**
6. **So when Herod was being about to bring him forth** (or: produce him [to them]), **during that night Peter – being bound with two chains – continued sleeping between two soldiers, besides [the] guards before the door [who] continued watching over and guarding the prison** (or: jail).
7. **And yet, look, and consider this! An agent of and from [the] Lord** (or: [Christ's or Yahweh's] messenger) **made a stand upon [the scene;** D reads: stood by Peter], **and light shown** (or: a light shines) **within the midst of the room** (= prison cell). **Now tapping Peter's side, he** (she; it) **raised him up, while saying, "Get up quickly!" Then his chains at once fell off from [his] hands.**
8. **Now the agent** (messenger) **said to him, "Gird yourself** (= Fasten your garments with your belt, so as to be ready to walk) **and bind on your sandals." So he did so. Then he** (she; it) **says to him, "Throw your outer garment** (robe; cloak) **around [you] and keep following me."**
9. **And thus, after going out, he continued following, and yet he had not seen or perceived so as to know that the [incident] presently happening by means of the agent** (messenger) **is real, so he continued thinking** (imagining; supposing) **[himself] to be seeing a vision** (effect of something seen).
10. **Now, after passing through [the] first guard station, and then a second one, they came upon the iron gate, [which] now is leading into the city – which automatically** (spontaneously; by self-acting) **was opened up to** (or: for) **them. And so, having gone out, [D adds: they descended seven steps and then] they proceeded [along] one narrow street** (lane; alley) **– then suddenly the agent** (messenger) **stood away** (or: withdrew; departed) **from him.**
11. **Next, Peter, suddenly coming to be within** (= coming to) **himself, said, "Now I have truly seen, and thus am really aware, that the Lord** [= Yahweh or Christ] **sent forth His agent** (messenger) **out on a mission, and he extricated me** (plucked me out) **from the midst of Herod's hand** (= power and authority), **and from the entire anticipation of the Judean people** (or: from everything the people of Judea were focusing their thinking to and looking toward)."

12. **And then, after perceiving [the various aspects of his situation] and consciously considering [it], he came upon the house of Mary, the mother of John – the one surnamed Mark, where quite a few people** (or: those having attained competence) **had been gathered and were crowded together continuing in thinking or speaking toward having things be well and go with ease** (i.e., praying).
13. **So after his knocking [at; on] the door or the portal** (or: gateway; entrance), **a servant girl named Rhoda came to [the entry] to answer** (to obediently hear [the reason for the knock] and to respond; [p74: to go to meet {him}]).
14. **Then, upon recognizing** (accurately knowing) **Peter's voice, from the joy [of the realization] she did not open up the gateway, but instead, immediately running into [their] midst, reported [that] Peter is standing before the gateway** (or: entrance).
15. **Yet they themselves said to her, "You are either manic, or you are out of your mind!" But she continued strongly asserting and thoroughly insisting [that] thus [they] are to continue having [it]** (= that it was so). **So those folks kept on saying, one after another, [D adds: to her], "[D adds:**

Perhaps] **it is his agent** (or: The messenger is from him; or: It is the agent that pertains to him; It is the messenger that has his characteristics)!" [*cf* Mat. 18:10]

16. **Now Peter continued remaining at [the door], repeatedly knocking. So when they opened [it] up, they saw him and were standing outside of themselves in astonishment** (or: beside themselves in amazement).

17. **But, after gesturing** (motioning downward) **with [his] hand for them to hush and keep silent, he thoroughly related to them how the Lord** [= Christ or Yahweh] **led him forth out of the prison. Then he said, "Report these things back to Jacob** (James) **and the brothers** (or: brotherhood)." **And then, after going out, he went his way into a different place.**

18. **Now with the birthing of** (or: at its coming to be) **day, there was no little** (small; slight) **commotion** (stir; agitation; disturbance) **among the soldiers – about what had really become [of]** (or: had in fact happened [to]) **Peter.**

19. **So Herod – after making a thorough search for him and not finding [him] – [and] upon examining and interrogating the guards, ordered [them] to be led away [and punished, or, executed]. Later, after going down from the Judean [district] into Caesarea, he continued wearing through [the fabric of the days]** (= he idled away, or spent, some time [there]).

20. **But he was continuing in a rushing passion for battle** (or: progressing to a furious fighting mood) **in regard to the people of Tyre and of Sidon. So with like mind and purpose, they kept on being present with [their faces] toward him. Then upon persuading** (convincing; coaxing; conciliating; winning over) **Blastus – the king's personal attendant who is in charge of his sleeping quarters – they kept on asking for peace, because their country [had the situation] to be normally receiving [their] food supplies from the territory and authorization of the king** (or: via royal discretion).

21. **Now on an arranged** (set; appointed) **day, Herod – having dressed** (or: clothed) **himself [in] royal attire** (garments; apparel; [note: A.T. Robertson comments that Josephus says it was a robe of silver tissue]) **– being seated upon the dais** (an elevated platform, ascended by steps, for public address; here: = a throne or a judgment seat), **was in the midst of giving a speech to them.**

22. **In response** [D adds: his being changed from enmity to friendship by the people of Tyre], **the populace gathered [there] began shouting, "[This is] a voice of a god, and not of a human!"**

23. **So without delay an agent of [the] Lord** [= Yahweh or Christ] **from necessity struck him, in return for that [situation] – [since] he did not give the credit** (or: glory) **to God. Later, having come to be consumed** (or: eaten) **by worms, he expired** (breathed out).

24. **But the** *Logos* **of God**
>   (God's Word, thought and idea; or: the message pertaining to and the source of which is God;
>   the verbal expression which is God [B reads: the Lord {= Christ or Yahweh}]) **kept on growing** (increasing) **and continued being multiplied.**

25. **Yet Barnabas and Saul, after returning out of** [D reads: from; other MSS: into] **Jerusalem** [E and other witnesses add: into Antioch], **[are] fulfilling the dispensing and attending service – having taken along with [them] John, the one surnamed Mark.**

CHAPTER 13

1. **Now there were prophets** (folks who had light ahead of time and spoke it before folks) **and teachers within the midst of Antioch, down in** (or: corresponding to; or: to accord with) **the called-out community currently being [there]: both Barnabas and Simeon – the one normally being called "[the] Black"** (or: Niger) **– as well as Lucius, the man from Cyrene** (a Greek colony in north Africa; or: Cyrenian, being the name of another man there), **and Manaen** (or: Manahen) **– a person who was brought up with** (or: a foster brother of; a childhood companion of; one educated and nurtured with) **Herod, the tetrarch** (provincial or district ruler) **– and Saul.**

2. **So, in the midst of their continually doing public work** (service for the people) **for** (or: in; to; by; with) **the Lord** [= Christ or Yahweh], **as well as periodically fasting, the set-apart Breath-effect** (or: the Holy Spirit) **said** (spoke; told [them]), **"Now therefore, you folks section off** (mark off boundaries so as to define; same verb used in Nu. 8:11, LXX, for sectioning-off the Levites) **Barnabas and Saul – to** (or: for; by; in; with) **Me – into the work toward which I Myself have called** (or: summoned) **them."**

3. **At that time then, after fasting and praying** (speaking and thinking toward things going well), **and then placing their hands on** (or: to) **them, they loosed** [them] **away** (disbanded and released [them]).

4. **They themselves indeed therefore – being sent out from the midst by the set-apart Breath-effect** (or: under the Holy Spirit) **– went down into Seleucia. Then from there, they sailed away unto Cyprus.**

5. **And so, upon coming to be in Salamis, they began bringing God's *Logos* down**
> (or: thoroughly announcing the message and proclaiming God's Word, Idea and thought; [note: the prophets brought the Word of God down from heaven, and to the people]) **within the**
synagogues of the Jews. Now they also continued having John [as] an attendant ("under-rower;" = an aid, for support and assistance).

6. **Now after going through the whole island up to Paphos, they found a certain man – a magus** [note: originally of the Persians, Medes and Babylonians as priests and wise men, magi specialized in the study of astrology and enchantment and were often employed as official spiritual advisers; some were sorcerers] **[and] a false prophet – a Jew named Bar-Jesus** (son of Jesus),

7. **who was in association with the proconsul** (= regional governor under the control of the Roman senate) **Sergius Paulus – an intellectual and intelligent man. This man, having called to himself Barnabas and Saul, earnestly sought to hear God's *Logos*** (the Word of God; the thought, idea, reason and verbal expression which came from, had the characteristic of, and was God; the message from God; the pattern-forming information about God). [*cf* Jn. 1:1ff]

8. **But Elymas** (Arabic meaning: the wise one), **the magus – for in this way is his name being normally translated and interpreted – kept on standing in face-to-face opposition to them, repeatedly seeking to twist in two and thoroughly turn the proconsul away from the faith.**

9. **Yet Saul – the [same] man also [being] Paul – being filled full of set-apart Breath-effect** (or: being filled with [the] Holy Spirit and a sacred attitude), **after staring intently into him, said,**

10. **"O you son of an adversary** (of one who throws something through another person; = one who has the character and qualities of a devil), **all full of fish-bait** (or: filled with every fraud and deceit) **and every thing that is done adroitly and with ease** (knavish schemes and roguish tricks) **– enemy of all fairness, equity, rightwised behavior and just relationships which constitute the Way pointed out** (= covenant principles)! **You will not of yourself cease thoroughly perverting and twisting in two** (or: distorting) **the straight ways and paths of [the] Lord** [= Yahweh, or, Christ],

11. **"and so at this moment, look and consider: [the] hand of [the] Lord [is] upon you, and you will proceed being a blind man, not seeing the sun – until an appointed season, and a fitting situation!"** So instantly, and from the necessary [situation], a thick mist (also: a medical term for a failure of sight) **and darkness** (obscure dimness and shadowed gloom) **fell upon him, and then, continuously going around, he kept seeking people to lead him by the hand.** [~ Paul in 9:9, above]

12. **At that point the proconsul, having seen what had happened, at once was convinced, believed and is trusting – being progressively struck out the midst of himself** (or: = struck out of his [wits]), **and astounded, upon** (or: at) **the Lord's** [= Christ's or Yahweh's] **teaching** (or: teaching about the Lord, and from the Lord).

13. **Now having been led back up [upon the sea] away from Paphos, they – around Paul – came into Perga of Pamphylia. Yet John, withdrawing from them and departing, returned unto Jerusalem.**

14. **They themselves, however, after passing on through from Perga came along unto the Pisidian Antioch. Then having gone into the synagogue on the day of the sabbaths, they sat down.**

15. **Now after the public reading of the Law and the Prophets, the synagogue leaders** (rulers; chiefs) **sent a message over to them, saying, "Men** (= Gentlemen), **brothers, if within or among you folks there is any word** (or: *logos*; message; idea; information) **of relief, comfort, encouragement or exhortation to the people, be now speaking [it]** (= you are invited to be speaking at this time)."

16. **So, arising** (or: after standing up) **and gesturing – making a downward motion – with [his] hand, Paul said, "Men** (= Gentlemen), **Israelites – as well as the folks fearing God** (i.e., the God-fearers: Gentile proselytes) **– listen, and hear.**

17. "The God of this people Israel picked out and chose our fathers (= ancestors), then exalted (put up high) the people during [their] period of living as alien residents (as foreigners) within the land of Egypt. Next He led them out of it with an uplifted (high) arm,

18. "and then for about forty years' time He carried them in His arms as a nurse [reading with p74, A, C and others; Aleph, B, C2, D and others read: put up (or: was tolerant) with their behavior, disposition, moods and manners] within the midst of the wilderness (desert; lonely and desolate place).

19. "Later, after pulling down seven nations (or: demolishing seven ethnic groups) within the land of Canaan, He distributed (or: ceded) [A, C, D2 and others add: to them] their land [D* reads: the land of the foreign tribes], by lot, as an inheritance

20. "– for about four hundred and fifty years.
Then after these things, he gave [them] judges – until Samuel, the prophet (the one who had light ahead of time, and spoke it before folks).

21. "And from there they asked for a king, and so He gave them Saul, son of Kish, a man out of the tribe of Benjamin – [for] forty years.

22. "Then, upon changing the standing of (or: deposing; dismissing) him, He raised up David to (or: for) them, unto [the position of] king – about whom He also said, showing evidence and giving testimony,

> 'I found David, the [son] of Jesse, a man corresponding to and in accord with My heart, who will continue doing all the effects of My will (or: who will progressively produce and habitually perform all the results of My intent, purpose and desire).' [Ps. 89:20]

23. "From the seed of this one (or: From this person's descendant) – corresponding to and in accord with [the] promise – He brought to (or: for; in; by) Israel a Deliverer (Savior; Rescuer; Restorer to health and wholeness), Jesus.

24. "John's previous heralding – before His personal entrance – was publicly proclaiming an immersion (a dipping; a baptism) which pertained to a change of mind (a change in thinking, attitude and state of consciousness, with a return of their focus to Yahweh) to and for all the people [of] Israel.

25. "Yet as John continued fulfilling [his own] race course (= completed [his] career), he kept on repeatedly saying, 'What or who are you people continuing to secretly think (or: repeatedly conjecturing; presently supposing) me to be? I myself am not [what you think] (or: not [the One])! To the contrary, look and consider! One is progressively coming – after me – the sandals of Whose feet, I am not worthy to loosen or untie.'

26. "Men! Brothers! Sons of the race (or: family) of Abraham as well as those among you continuously revering and respecting God (or: [who] are God-fearers; proselytes)! The Logos (Word; message; idea; matter laid out; pattern-forming information) of this deliverance (salvation; rescue; return to health, wholeness and our original state of being) was sent forth out to us [other MSS: you]!

27. "You see, those presently residing (dwelling; having a permanent home) in Jerusalem, along with their rulers, not knowing this or even the voices of the prophets – those being regularly and repeatedly read in accord with every sabbath – they fulfilled [them] in judging [Him]

> (or: not recognizing or knowing, and being ignorant about, this One, by judging [Him] they fulfilled the voices of the prophets which are continuously being read, down on every sabbath).

28. "And even though not finding in Him even one cause for (or: grounds deserving) death [D* adds: after judging Him they turned {Him} over to Pilate {and}], they asked Pilate to take Him up to be executed.

29. "So as they ended (brought to fruition; brought to its goal and destiny; finished; completed the final act and purpose of) all the things having been written concerning Him, after taking [Him] down from the wooden pole (stake; cross), they put [Him] into a memorial tomb.

30. "Yet God aroused and raised Him up from out of the midst of dead folks,

31. "Who was from time to time seen on many days by those walking back up together from Galilee into Jerusalem – who at this time continue being witnesses of Him (or: evidence for Him; His folks who give testimony) to the people.

32. "And thus we ourselves continue bringing and declaring [to] you folks the good news [about] the Promise that was being birthed to (or: was coming into existence, or occurring, toward) our fathers (= ancestors),

33. **"that God has filled this out of [our] midst** (or: has fully fulfilled this) **for** (or: to; in) **our children** [other MSS: us, their children,] **in raising** (resurrecting; standing back up again) **Jesus – even as it has been written in the second Psalm,**

'**You are My Son; I Myself have given birth to You today** (or: today I Myself have become Your Father).' [D adds: You see then, request of Me and I will proceed giving to You the ethnic multitudes (nations and people groups) {for} Your allotted inheritance, and the limits and uttermost parts of the earth {as} Your firmly held possession.] [Ps. 2:7]

34. **"Now, seeing that He raised Him up** (resurrected Him; stood Him back up again) **from out of the midst of dead folks – no longer being about to be progressively returning** (or: not anymore continuing about to be constantly or repeatedly turning below, or under) **into corruption and decay. Thus He has declared,**

'**I will proceed giving to and among you people the faithful and trustworthy qualities and aspects of pious and benign loyalty which belonged to David.**' [Isa. 55:3]

35. **"Wherefore also, in a different [Psalm], it continues saying,**

'**I will not proceed in giving Your Pious and Benignly Loyal Person to see** (= experience) **decay or corruption.**' [Ps. 16:10]

36. **"You see David, on the one hand – in his own generation – after rendering subordinate service to** (or: in; by; for; with) **the counsel, purpose and express will of, and from, God, fell asleep** (= died) **and was placed facing toward** (or: was added to) **his fathers – and then saw** (= experienced) **decay and corruption.**

37. **"On the other hand, He whom God aroused and raised up did not see** (= experience) **decay or corruption.**

38. **"Therefore be it now known to you and progressively experienced by you folks – men... brothers – that through This One is being continuously and progressively announced, as a message come down to** (or: for; among) **you people, a flowing-away of mistakes**

(a sending away of failures; a divorce from sins; an abandoning of errors; a forgiveness from situations of missing the target; a release from deviations),

39. **"even** (or: also) **from all things of which** (or: from which) **you folks, in union with** (or: within; centered in) **[the] Law of Moses, had no power or ability to at any point be rightwised** (eschatologically delivered or turned in the right direction; made right, fair, equitable and in right relationships within the Way pointed out). **In union with, centered in, and within This One, everyone – the habitually trusting, the repeatedly faithing, the normally believing, or the continuing faithful**

(or: all humanity – which when habitually trusting, repeatedly faithing, progressively believing or continuing faithful) –

is being progressively rightwised (eschatologically delivered, turned in the right direction, and habitually placed in covenant relationships which accord with the Way pointed out; or: continuously made right, fair, just and equitable).

40. **"Therefore see to it [that] the thing having been declared within the Prophets** (= the writings of those who had light ahead of time) **may not be coming upon you folks,**

41. '**Continue looking and keep on directing your eyes, you scorners and despisers who maintain a down frame of mind, and be at once wondering and marveling in amazement – and then be caused to disappear** (be made invisible), **because I Myself am progressively accomplishing a work in your days – a work which you folks cannot trust or put your faith in** (or: would not believe) **even if someone would relate [it] in detail to you.**'" [Hab. 1:5]

[D adds: And they {i.e., those hearing him} were silent.]

42. **Now at their being out from the midst of the synagogue, folks began asking them to come to their sides for assistance [and for] these gush-effects** (or: sayings and declarations resulting from the flow) **to be spoken to them [during the days] between, [leading] unto the next sabbath.**

43. **So with the breaking up of the gathering** (the dissolving of the synagogue assembly), **many of the Jews and the reverent proselytes** (Gentiles who wished to embrace the Jewish faith) **followed Paul and Barnabas who, in continuing to speak to them, began persuading and convincing them to be habitually remaining focused toward God's grace and favor.** [D adds: Now accordingly it happened {for} God's *Logos* (Word; message; idea; reason) to go throughout the whole of the city].

44. **So on the coming sabbath almost all the city was led together to listen to and hear the *Logos*** (Word; message; information) **of the Lord** [= Yahweh or Christ; other MSS: God; D reads: to hear Paul delivering a long message concerning the Lord].

45. **Yet upon seeing the crowds, the Jews were filled with jealousy and began contradicting the things being spoken by Paul, while repeatedly speaking abusively** (or: arguing with slander and invectives; speaking light-hindering misrepresentations; defaming with accusations of villainy).

46. **Continuing bold, expressing the inherent right to speak the whole truth publicly with freedom from reprisal, both Paul and Barnabas said, "It was a matter of constraint, compulsion, and pressed indispensability [for] God's *Logos*** (Word; message; idea) **to be spoken to you folks first! Yet since you folks continue to push it away from yourselves, and are repeatedly judging** (or: deciding) **yourselves [to be] not worthy of the eonian life** (the life pertaining to the Age [of Messiah]; the life whose source and character is from the Age), **look! We are now being turned** (or, as a middle: progressively turning ourselves) **unto the nations** (the ethnic multitudes; the Gentiles; the non-Jews).

47. **"You see, thus has the Lord [= Christ or Yahweh] inwardly directed to** (set a goal for) **us:**
     'I have placed (or: set) **you unto [being] a light of nations** (ethnic multitudes; non-Jews), **[in order for] you to be [placed] into the midst of a deliverance** (a rescue and a return to health and wholeness; a restoring to the original state of being and condition) **as far as [the] last [point] of the earth!'"** [Isa. 49:6]

48. **Now upon hearing [this], the non-Jews** (the [folks of the] nations and ethnic groups) **began rejoicing and continued glorifying** (enhancing the reputation of) **the message from God** (God's *Logos*: God's Word and idea). **And so they trusted and believed – whoever were folks having been set and arranged into an eonian life** (or: into life which has its source and quality from the Age [of Messiah]).

49. **So the message of, from, and about, the Lord** [= Christ or Yahweh] (or: the Lord's Word and idea; the *Logos*, which is the Lord) **began being carried through the midst in all directions – and continued thus throughout the whole country** (or: region).

50. **But the Jews incited and spurred on the reverent, respectable** (or: reputable; influential; of good form and decorum) **women, as well as the leading** (principal; foremost) **men of the city, and they aroused** (raised up; mounted) **a pursuit and persecution upon Paul and Barnabas, and then threw them out of their midst – away from their boundaries** (= city limits; or: territory; district).

51. **So, after shaking out** (or: off) **the dust from their feet on them** (= as a repudiation, signifying that their city was like the unclean heathen), **they went into Iconium.**

52. **Furthermore, the disciples** (the students) **continued being repeatedly, or progressively, filled with joy and a consecrated attitude** (a holy spirit; a set-apart Breath-effect; or: [the] Holy Spirit).

CHAPTER 14

1. **Now in Iconium, the same thing happened [for] them: to enter into the synagogue of the Jews, and then to speak to them in such a way so that a great multitude of both Jews and Greeks** [thus: non-Jews] **at once came to trust and to believe!**

2. **Yet the Jews [who] were at that point being unconvinced** (or: stubborn) **rose up on [the situation**; D reads: But the synagogue leaders of the Jews, and synagogue rulers brought persecution upon them – against those of the rightwised Way –] **and acted in a worthless manner so as to badly effect the souls** (inner lives) **of the non-Jews** (folks of the nations; = the Greeks that were involved) **in a negative manner in regard to the brothers** [= either those with Paul and Barnabas, or, those of the synagogue who had become brothers; D adds: but the Lord soon granted peace {to the situation}].

3. **Therefore, as a result, they spent adequate time constantly and repeatedly speaking out freely, boldly and openly in public – as is the right of respected citizens – upon** (or: on [the authority and basis of]; or: [with trust and reliance] on; or: = about) **the Lord** [= Christ or Yahweh], **[Who] was continuously giving evidence for, testifying by, and bearing witness to, the *Logos*** (Word; message; idea; pattern-forming Information) **of, and which is, His grace and from His favor, by repeatedly giving signs and granting miracles** (or: portents; wonders) **to be happening through their hands.**

4. **However, the multitude** (= population) **of the city was split** (rent [in two]), **and so, on the one hand, folks were with the Jews** (= on their side), **yet on the other hand, [there were] folks [who sided] with**

the sent-forth folks [D reads: folks continuing closely joined with the sent-forth folks by the *Logos* (Word; message) of God].

5. **So as a rushing onset occurred of both the non-Jews** (ethnic folks; = Greeks) **and Jews – together with their leaders** (or: authorities; rulers) **– to outrage** (to violate, manhandle, or treat insolently) **and to pelt them with stones,**

6. **they, becoming aware [of it], fled down for refuge into the cities of Lycaonia, Lystra and Derbe – as well as the surrounding country,**

7. **and there** (= in those places) **they were continuously bringing and declaring the good news** (the message of goodness, ease and well-being) [D adds: And the whole multitude was moved over the teaching. So Paul and Barnabas continued spending time in Lystra].

8. **Then, in Lystra, a certain adult man was sitting, impotent** (without power; = disabled) **in [his] feet – lame from out of his mother's womb** (= from birth), **who had never walked around.**

9. **This man kept on listening to the continued** (or: repeated) **speaking of Paul – who, looking intently at him and then seeing that he is progressively having faith pertaining to being healed** (made whole; restored to health; rescued; saved),

10. **said in a loud voice** [C & D add: I say to you in the name of the Lord Jesus Christ], **"Stand up erect upon** (or: upright on) **your feet!" And so he immediately leaped** (sprang up) **with a single bound, and continued walking around.**

11. **Besides this, upon seeing that which Paul did, the crowds lifted up** (elevated) **their voice in [the] Lycaonian language, repeatedly** (or: one after another) **saying, "The gods, being made to resemble humans, stepped down** (or: descended) **to us!"**

12. **Furthermore, they began calling Barnabas, "Zeus," yet Paul, "Hermes," since he himself continued being the one constantly taking the lead with reference to the Logos** (or: was the leader of the message; or: continued taking the lead from the Word; or: was repeatedly guiding the discourse).

13. **More than this, the priest of Zeus – the [idol and temple] being in front of [their] city – upon bringing bulls, as well as wreaths and garlands, proceeded in intending to be progressively slaughtering and then offering sacrifices, together with the crowds.**

14. **Now upon hearing [of this], the sent-forth men, Barnabas and Paul, leaped forth into the midst of the crowd while at the same time ripping** (or: tearing) **their outer garments** (or: cloaks) **in two, crying out loudly,**

15. **and [both] saying, "Men** (= Gentlemen)! **Why are you now doing these things? We ourselves are also humans: men with similar experiences and like emotions as you folks! Men presently bringing and progressively declaring the good news to you people:** [D adds: the God by what means] [with p45: you are to at once stand away and separate] **– to then progressively turn away from these fruitless** (vain; groundless; purposeless; useless) **things** (or: practices) **and to continue turning [your focus and attention] on a** [other MSS: the] **living God, Who makes** (or: formed; constructs; produced) **the heaven and the earth** (or: the sky and the land) **– as well as all the things within them,**

16. **"Who, within the generations having gone by, permitted** (let; allowed; let be; committed) **all the ethnic groups** (nations; non-Jewish multitudes; i.e.: left [the non-Israelites] alone) **to continue going in their ways** (or: to progressively travel on their paths),

17. **"although He did not leave** (or: abandon; neglect; let go from His care and attendance of) **Himself without evidence** (= proof; or: testimony; or: a witness) **by repeatedly doing good works** (or: producing benevolent deeds): **regularly giving to** (or: for) **you people rains from heaven** (or: [the] sky), **and thus fruit-bearing seasons, constantly filling the core of your beings full of food** (or: nourishment) **and your hearts with gladness and a frame of mind** (or: disposition) **characterized by ease and well-being in the midst of togetherness."**

18. **And so, by saying these things, they with difficulty caused the crowds to bring [the proceedings] down to an end and fully stop – [so as] not to continue in sacrificing to them** [C adds: but rather [for] each one to proceed on their way unto their own homes].

19. **So** [C, D & E add: during their continuing to spend time {there} and repeatedly teaching, certain] **Jews from Antioch and Iconium came upon [the scene], and** [with other MSS: from their repeated arguments, publicly] **persuaded the crowds** [other MSS add: to separate from them, saying that they

were not even speaking truth, but rather were all constantly lying]. **And so, after stoning Paul, they proceeded to be violently dragging [him] outside of the city, continuing in presuming him to have died.**

20. **However, with the disciples' forming a circle, surrounding him, upon arising** (or: after standing back up again; or: upon resurrecting) **he entered into the city. Then on the next day he went out, together with Barnabas, into Derbe.**

21. **Continuing in bringing and declaring the good news to that city as well, and making a considerable [number of] disciples** (or: students; apprentices), **they returned into Lystra, then into Iconium, and finally into Antioch,**

22. **progressively establishing** (fixing and making to stand) **the souls** (inner lives) **of the disciples** (or: students), **repeatedly calling [them] alongside to give relief, aid and comfort while encouraging [them] to continue abiding and remaining in place by The Faithfulness** (or: in this trust, reliance, confidence and assurance; with the loyalty of conviction), **and [saying] that, "It continues binding and necessary for us to enter into the reign of God** (or: God's kingdom; the sovereign activities which are God) **through the midst of many pressures, squeezings, tribulations, afflictions and oppressions."**

23. **So while extending** (or: stretching out) **their hands to** (or: on; or: with) **them, in accord with the older men in each called-out community, while speaking toward having things be well** (or: praying) **– along with** (or: accompanying) **fastings – they committed them to the Lord** (or: put them at [their] side, in the Lord [= Christ or Yahweh]; or: deposited them for the Lord; or: set them along [the path] by the Lord) **into Whom they had faithed, believed then placed their confident trust, and were now loyal.**

24. **Later, passing through the Pisidian [district], they came into Pamphylia.**

25. **Next, after speaking the** *Logos* (Word; message) **in Perga, they walked down into Attalia.**

26. **From there they sailed off into Antioch – the place from where they had been, and continued, given over to** (or: commended by; committed for; passed along in; transferred with) **the grace of, and favor from, God, into the work which they fulfilled** (made full; = fully performed).

27. **Now upon coming to be alongside** (= present) **and after gathering the called-out community together, they began recounting [to them] whatever God did** (performed; produced) **with them** [D reads: with their souls], **and that He opened up a** (or: [the]) **door of trust with the ethnic multitudes** (or: from faith among the nations; of confidence for the non-Jews; from Faithfulness to the Gentiles).

28. **So they continued spending not a little time** (= stayed a long time) **together with the disciples** (students; apprentices).

CHAPTER 15

1. **Later, certain men, having come down from Judea, began teaching the brothers that, "Unless you folks should** (or: would) **get circumcised within** (or: by) **the custom of Moses** [D reads: and should habitually walk (= order your lives) in (by) the custom of Moses], **you continue without power to be saved** (or: you continue unable to be healed, made whole or returned to the original state and condition, or delivered)."

2. **But** [p74, A & others: Therefore] **with there coming to be no little occurrence of taking positions** (making stands in the dissension) **as well as of debating, disputing and seeking a resolution [to the question] by** (or: with; or: to) **Paul and Barnabas, face to face with them, they made arrangements for Paul and Barnabas – and certain others from among them – to now go up unto Jerusalem, to the sent-forth folks and older men concerning the effect of this seeking** (or: about this question)

> [D reads: ... face to face with them, for Paul, insisting firmly, continued telling {them} to remain thus, according as they had believed. Yet the men who had come from Jerusalem passed on instruction to them for Paul and Barnabas – and some other folks – to now go up to face the sent-forth ones, even {the} elders, in Jerusalem so that they could have a decision made upon them about this matter in question].

3. **Accordingly** (or: Indeed, therefore), **after being sent forward** (or: = being helped forward [on their journey]; or: being escorted [part way]) **by the called-out community, they themselves continued passing through both Phoenicia and Samaria, repeatedly relating in detail the turning about** (= the conversion) **of the ethnic multitudes** (the non-Jews; the [people] of the nations). **And thus they**

continued producing (making; causing; creating) **great joy for** (in; to) **all the brothers** (= fellow believers).

4. **Now on having come to be alongside** (= upon arriving) **into the midst of Jerusalem, they were welcomely received as part of the group by the called-out community – even the sent-forth folks, including the older men** (or: the elders) **– and so they recounted** (or: reported) **whatever** (or: as many things as) **God had done** (or: produced; accomplished) **in accompaniment with them.**

5. **Yet certain men from the sect of the Pharisees – being ones who had believed and were now trusting – stood up out of the midst, [as a group] saying that it continues binding and necessary for them** [i.e., the non-Jews] **to continue with circumcision, besides to continue to be observing the Law of Moses.**

6. **So the sent-forth folks and older men** (or: elders) **were gathered together to see about this idea** (expressed thought; Word; laid-out communication; *Logos*; or: = matter).

7. **Now after there coming to be much seeking [of a solution], questioning and disputing, Peter – after standing up – said to them, "Men! Brothers! You yourselves continue well versed** (standing upon so as to comprehend) **that from the days of the beginning God chose among you folks [for] the ethnic multitudes** (or: nations; non-Jews) **to hear the *Logos*** (Word; idea; message) **of the good news** (the message of goodness, ease and well-being) **through my mouth – and then, to at once trust and believe!**

8. **"And God, One who knows** (or: has insights into) **the heart by intimate experience, has given evidence for** (or: bore witness to; gave testimony in) **them in** (or: when) **giving the set-apart Breath-effect** (or: the Holy Spirit) **to [D reads: upon] them, just as [He did] to us, also!**

9. **"Furthermore, He made not even one separation of any kind** (or: He made a distinction in nothing; or: He makes no dividing decision in even one thing) **between both us and them, at once cleansing** (or: purifying) **their hearts by faith** (with trust; in The Faithfulness [of Christ]; to and for convinced reliance)!

10. **"Therefore, why are you folks at this time** (or: now) **continuing to test** (or: constantly trying; repeatedly examining and attempting to prove) **God [by attempting] to put** (place; set) **upon the neck of the students** (disciples; apprentices) **a yoke which neither our fathers** (= ancestors) **were, nor we ourselves are, strong enough [even] to pick up, [much less] to carry?**

11. **"But to the contrary, through the grace and gratuitous favor of the Lord** (or: Owner) **Jesus** [C, D & others add: Christ] (or: which has its source and character in [Yahweh] – Jesus; or: which is the Lord Jesus) **we continue trusting and believing to at once be delivered or rescued or saved or made whole, in accordance with which manner those people also [are]**
    (or: But rather, we ourselves habitually trust to be wholly restored to health and returned to our original state and condition, through the joyous grace which has the character and qualities of Jesus, the Lord – in the same way as those folks [were], also).**"**

12. **So** [D adds: with the older men (or: elders) now accepting and consenting to the things having been spoken by Peter,] **the entire multitude became silent, and they began listening to Barnabas and Paul progressively unfolding and leading [the folks] out, [through] a description of whatever** (or: however many) **signs and miracles** (wonders; portents) **[which] God did** (produced) **among the ethnic multitudes** (or: nations; non-Jews) **through them.**

13. **Now after the [time for] them to become silent, Jacob** (or: James) [D adds: upon arising] **discerningly responded, presently saying, "Men! Brothers! Hear** (or: Listen to) **me!**

14. **"Simeon led [us] out and unfolded, relating in detail, how God first** (or: first of all; in the first [place]) **made a visit** (and: took an attentive look characterized by complete care) **to at one point take from out of the midst of the ethnic multitudes** (or: nations; folks who were non-Jews) **a people for His Name** (= as His representatives and for His glory; or: by His Name [= power and authority]; in His Name [= possession and realm of being]; with His Name [= character and reputation]; to His Name).

15. **"And with this** [D reads: thus] **the words** (or: messages; *Logoi*) **of, or from, the Prophets** (= the writings of those who had light ahead of time) **continue sounding together in agreement and symphony, just as it has been – and stands – written,**

16.   **'After these things I will proceed turning back again** (or: return), **and I will progressively build back up again** (rebuild as a house) **the tent** (or: tabernacle) **of David – the one having fallen down. Then I will continue building back up again** (rebuild as a house) **its things having been turned upside down – also I will keep on making it straight and erect again**

17.   'so that the rest of humanity would seek out and earnestly try to find the Lord [= Yahweh] – even all the ethnic multitudes (nations; non-Jews), upon whom My Name has been called upon and remains surnamed and attached: upon them, continues saying [the] Lord [= Yahweh] – the One constantly doing these things.' [Amos 9:11-12; Rev. 21:3]

18.   "[These have been] known from an indefinite period of time (from [the; this] age) by insight and personal experience.

>   [or: with other MSS: "Known in (or: with; or: to; by) the Lord {= Yahweh or Christ}, by intimate experience and insight from the indefinite past, are His deeds and works.]

19.   "Hence (or: Because of which), I myself am now judging and deciding not to continue making it more difficult for, or to be troubling or harassing, the folks from the ethnic multitudes (the nations; the non-Jews) [who] are progressively turning upon (= turning around to) God,

20.   "however (or: but yet), to send word by a letter for them to be habitually holding themselves away from (constantly abstaining from) the effects of ceremonial pollution from (or: belonging and pertaining to) the idols – as well as from the prostitution (or: whoring; [note: may also have reference to temple idol worship]; or: sexual immorality; [p45 omits this phrase]) – and from [something that was] strangled [i.e., where the blood was not drained out], also from blood

>   [comment: these were prohibitions from the Law, in Lev. 17 & 18; D adds: Also, whatever you would not normally want to be happening to yourselves, do not do to others].

21.   "For you see, Moses – from out of [the] original (beginning; = ancient) generations – continually has folks repeatedly making public proclamation of him [= of his laws], in city after city within the synagogues, being habitually read aloud in correspondence with every sabbath."

22.   At that point it seemed [good; favorable] to the sent-forth folks and the older men (or: elders), together with the whole called-out community, to send adult men – folks picked out (or: chosen; selected; spoken-forth) from among their midst – into Antioch along with Paul and Barnabas, [namely], Judah – the one normally being called Barsabbas – and Silas (probably = Silvanus), men normally taking the lead among the brothers (= fellow believers),

23.   after writing [D adds: a letter] by their hand [D adds: presently containing this]:
"[From:] The emissaries (sent-forth folks) and the older men (or: the elders) – brothers (or: the older brothers; [other MSS: as well as the brothers {= fellow believers; = your brothers}]),
To: The brothers down in Antioch, Syria and Cilicia – to those from out of the ethnic multitudes (nations; non-Jews) – to continue to be rejoicing! (= Greetings!)

24.   "Since we hear (or: heard) that certain folks going out from among us disturbed (agitated; troubled; perplexed) you folks with words (or: by messages; in thoughts) progressively dismantling (breaking up the camp of; bankrupting by removing the furniture of; remodeling) your inner lives (souls) [CEΨ and others add: repeatedly saying to be circumcised and keep the Law] – to whom we of ourselves gave no distinctive decision, thorough arrangement, determined instruction or assignment –

25.   "in coming to be like-minded (of one accord; unanimous), it seemed [good; productive] to us, by choosing men out from ourselves, to send [them] to you, together with our beloved Barnabas and Paul:

26.   "men having given over (= dedicated) their souls (inner lives: will, desire, intellect – and very breath) over (= for the sake of) the Name of our Lord, Jesus Christ ([the] Anointed One).

27.   "Therefore we have sent off (dispatched with a mission) Judah and Silas, and so they themselves are now reporting the same things verbally (by word; through Logos) [to you].

28.   "You see, it seemed [good; productive] to the set-apart Breath-effect (or: in the Holy Spirit) and to (or: among) us to have not even one more burden to be placed upon you folks – besides these necessary and essential things:

29.   "to habitually abstain and hold yourselves away from idol sacrifices (or: things [i.e., foods] sacrificed to idols) and from blood, and from things that were strangled, and from sexual immorality (whoring; fornication; prostitution; = infidelity) – out from which things, by practice carefully keeping and habitually thoroughly guarding yourselves, you folks will perform well (be well-engaged; prosper)

>   [D reads: and whatever you do not normally wish or purpose for yourselves to progressively become or to have happen, do not keep on doing to other folks, {and} from which things in continuously keeping yourselves thoroughly {away}, commit acts of ease and well-being, being

folks constantly carried along within the set-apart Breath-effect (or: the holy wind; the Holy Spirit)]. **Be ones having been strengthened and made firm** (or: = Good health to you)**!"**

30. **Therefore accordingly upon being released away** (= dismissed), [D adds: in a few days] **these men went down into Antioch and – after gathering the multitude together – they handed the letter [to them].**
31. **So, upon reading [it], they burst into rejoicing at the helpful and encouraging [message] of comfort and relief.**
32. **Both Judah and Silas – they also being prophets – assisted, gave relief to, comforted and encouraged the brothers** (= fellow believers; members) **through much discourse** (*Logos*)**, and they established [them]** (or: they helped and made the brothers to settle and rest upon [the *Logos*; the Word] through many a word, thought and idea).
33. **Now after performing** (accomplishing; = laboring) **a period of time, they were released away – with peace of a joining, from the brothers – to the folks having sent them off on the mission.** [34. missing in most MSS, but C D and others add, by parts, this conflation: Yet Silas decided to remain on with them, and Judah continued on his way alone unto Jerusalem.]
35. **However Paul and Barnabas continued spending time in Antioch, constantly teaching and repeatedly bringing the good news – declaring the *Logos*** (Word) **of, and from, the Lord** [= Christ or Yahweh]**: the message of ease and well-being – along with many different folks, also.**

36. **Now after some days, Paul said to Barnabas, "In returning** (= retracing our journey), **doubtless we can and should visit and look in on the brothers, city by city, in every one in which we brought the message down, and announced the *Logos* of the Lord** (or: the Word from [Yahweh]; the idea of which is the [Christ]; the message about the Lord), **[to see] how they continue holding [it]** (or: how they progressively have [it]; or: = how they are now getting on)**."**
37. **However, Barnabas kept on wanting – and stuck with intending – to take along together with [them] also John, the one normally being called Mark.**
38. **Yet Paul kept on thinking it not fitting** (of appropriate worth) **to continue taking along with them this one – the person having withdrawn from them, away from Pamphylia, and not going together with them into the work** [D adds: into which they were sent].
39. **So there occurred a sharp dispute, with the result for them to at once be pulled apart and disunited from one another. And thus at that point Barnabas, taking along Mark, set sail unto Cyprus.**
40. **But Paul, choosing for himself Silas, went forth from [their] midst, being given over to** (or: committed by; commended with; passed along for; transmitted in) **the grace and favor of [the] Lord** [= Christ or Yahweh; p45 C E and others read: God] **by the brothers.**
41. **And so he continued passing on through Syria and Cilicia, progressively establishing the called-out communities** [D adds: while one by one passing on the goals/directives from the older folks].

CHAPTER 16

1. **So** [with D: after going through these ethnic (= non-Jewish) countries,] **he came down into, and arrived at, Derbe, and then at Lystra – and now consider this! – a certain disciple** (student; apprentice) **was there, named Timothy – [the] son of a faithful** (loyal; trusting; believing) **Jewish woman, yet of a Greek father –**
2. **who was constantly being attested** (or: repeatedly witnessed of, well reported on and recommended) **by the brothers** (= fellow believers) **in Lystra and Iconium.**
3. **[It was] this man [that] Paul had wanted and now intended to go out with him, and so after taking [him], he circumcised him because of the Jews – the ones presently being in those places – since they had all seen, and were thus aware, that his father was** (or: had been) **a Greek.**

4. **Now as they continued traveling through the villages and cities,** [D adds: they continued heralding and repeatedly dispensing the Lord Jesus Christ to them publicly, with all the boldness and freedom of a citizen, while at the same time] **they kept on delivering to** (or: handing over for; transmitting among; passing along to) **them the effects of the opinions and the decision, [regarding]**

what seemed appropriate [for them] to be observing and maintaining – which had been decided upon by the sent-forth folks and elders (or: older men) who were in Jerusalem.

5. The called-out communities were indeed, therefore, being progressively made strong, firm, solid and stable by The Faithfulness (or: in union with the trusting conviction; with loyalty), and they kept on increasing and superabounding in number daily.

6. So they went through Phrygia and [the] Galatian province [note: possibly the ethnographic area of the Gauls or Celts who dwelt in North Galatia], having been restrained (or: prevented) by the set-apart Breath-effect (or: the Holy Spirit) from speaking the message (the *Logos*; the Word; [D reads: not even one word of God]) within the [province of] Asia.

7. Now upon coming down [to] Mysia, they made efforts [D reads: they continued wanting and intending] to travel on into Bithynia, and then the Breath-effect (or: Spirit) of Jesus did not let (permit; allow) them.

8. So, skirting alongside (or: bypassing) Mysia, they went down into Troas.

9. Then, during one night, a vision (or: sight; effect and result of something seen) was seen by (or: in) Paul: [D adds: as it were] a certain Macedonian man was standing [D adds: before him] and calling him to his side for assistance, and repeatedly saying, "After crossing over into Macedonia, run to us with aid, in response to our cry for help!" [note: this was a call to come to Europe]

10. Now as [soon as] he saw the vision [D reads: Then, being aroused he related the vision in detail to us and we understood.] we immediately endeavored to go forth into Macedonia, progressively putting [aspects of the vision] together and mutually concluding that God [D and others read: {the} Lord] had called to us, to bring them [D reads: those in Macedonia] the good news – the message of goodness, ease and well-being.

11. Therefore, setting sail and putting out to sea, from Troas we followed a straight course (i.e., were sailing before the wind) unto Samothrace, but on the following [day we went] to Neapolis,

12. and from there unto Philippi, a colony [of Rome] which is a foremost (principle) city of [that] part of Macedonia. Now we were within this city, continuing to spend time, for some days.

13. And then, on one of the sabbath days, we went forth outside the [city] gate beside [the] river [Gangites (or: Gargites); about one mile west of town] where we had been supposing (or: inferring from custom) there to be a place of prayer (may = a synagogue; a place devoted to imparting goodness and to speaking toward things being well). And so, after sitting down, we [note: implies each of the four men] began speaking to the women being come together [there].

14. Then a certain woman named Lydia – a seller (or: dealer) of purple fabrics, from the city of Thyatira, [and she was] a woman who stood in awe of God

> [D* reads: the Lord {= Yahweh, or, Christ}; note: = a convert to Judaism, or, a "God-fearer;" the
> word was also used to designate a group (including males and females) separate from
> proselytes and native Jews, yet considered as members of a synagogue] – began hearing

and continued listening, whose heart (core of her being) the Lord [= Yahweh, or, Christ] at once completely opened up (or: opened back wide) to continue holding to, attentively accepting and being devoted to the things being presently and progressively spoken by (or: under) Paul.

15. Now as soon as she had been immersed (or: baptized) – along with [D adds: all] her household – she at once called [them] to her side, saying with entreaty, "Since (or: If) you men have sifted and separated me, then decided (judged) me to be trusting in the Lord (or: faithful to the Lord; full of faith by the Lord [= Christ or Yahweh; D reads: God]), upon entering into my house, continue remaining (abiding; dwelling)." And thus she strongly urged us [to accept her hospitality].

16. Once it happened, during our going our way unto the place of prayer (= synagogue; or: the place devoted to imparting well-being and to speaking toward having things be well), [that] a certain servant-girl (or: maid) – continuously holding a python spirit

> (or: repeatedly having a python breath-effect; = a serpent attitude and orientation; = an
> animistic practitioner; [note: in Greek mythology, Python was a giant snake guarding the
> oracular sanctuary at Delphi until slain by the god Apollo; later, the term came to refer to
> divination, ventriloquism and oracular spirits]) suddenly comes to meet with us (or: comes

from under to confront us face to face), who, by habitually performing many acts of the craft of divining, fortune-telling and casting spells, had been consistently providing a steady source of income for her owners (or: masters; lords).

17. **This girl, repeatedly following Paul and [the rest of] us down [to the river], kept on crying out and shrieking, constantly saying, "These people** (or: humans) **are slaves of the Most High God** [= El Ha Elyon], **who are constantly and progressively bringing the news down and are announcing to you folks** [other MSS: to us] **a way** (or: path) **of safety and deliverance** (or: health, wholeness and salvation)."

18. **Now she kept on doing this for many days. So, being thoroughly wearied and exasperated [from this], and finally turning around [toward her], Paul says to the breath-effect** (or: spirit; or: said in and by the Breath-effect and Spirit), **"I am now giving a directive to you** (or: passing on an announcement for you) **– within and in union with [the] Name of Jesus Christ** (or: the Anointed Jesus) **– to go out and away from her at once!" And thus, it went out that very** (or: same) **hour** [D reads: it went out at once].

19. **Well, her** [D reads: the servant-girl's] **owners** (masters), **upon seeing** (or: perceiving) **that the expectation of their business** (= the source of their income) **went out from the midst** [D reads: had been deprived from them which they had been having through her], **after seizing Paul and Silas, they forcibly dragged [them] into the marketplace [and] before [the station of] the authorities** ([city] rulers).

20. **And so, after leading them forward to the civil magistrates, they said, "These men, being** (or: belonging to; making a beginning as) **Jews, continue completely stirring up** (or: are repeatedly bringing forth a disturbance [in]) **our city!**

21. **"Furthermore, they are habitually bringing down an announcement of customs which are not permitted, from [the time of our] existence, for us to habitually accept and embrace at our sides, nor to continue doing or practicing, [we] being Romans."**

22. **Then the crowd rose up together,** [with D: taking a stand in attack] **against them** [with D: repeatedly crying out against them], **and the civil magistrates, after stripping** (or: ripping) **off the cloaks and outer garments from them, began giving orders to proceed beating [them] with rods.**

23. **Besides imposing** (inflicting) **on them many blows** (or: stripes), **they threw them into jail** (or: prison), **passing along instructions to the jailer** (or: prison guard) **to continue keeping them guarded securely,**

24. **who, upon receiving such an order, cast them into the more interior prison** (or: jail), **and then fastened their feet into the wooden stocks.**

25. **Now at about midnight, Paul and Silas, continuing in thinking toward having the situation go well** (or: praying; imparting words with a focus on ease and well-being), **began singing hymns** (or: praise and festive songs) **[to] God** (or: were continuing on by creating odes [about] God). **So then, the prisoners kept on attentively listening [to what came] from them.**

26. **Now suddenly and unexpectedly, a great** (or: violent) **shaking** (= an earthquake) **occurred so that foundations of the prison** (the place of the bound ones) **were caused to move to and fro** (made to totter and be rendered unstable). **So now, instantly for use, all the doors were at once opened and the bonds of everyone were loosened** (allowed to go up or back so as to relax and be slack; [D reads: unfastened]).

27. **So the guard of the bound ones** (the jailer; the warden), **coming to be awakened** (aroused out of sleep) **and having seen the doors of the prison being opened up** (= standing open), **on drawing [his] sword was about to proceed in killing himself, continuing in assuming – from what normally happens – the prisoners to have fled out** (escaped).

28. **But Paul shouted in a loud voice, saying, "You should perform nothing bad to** (or: on) **yourself** (or: May you execute nothing worthless for yourself; = Don't harm yourself) **– we are all in here!"**

29. **So, after asking for lights, with a leap he rushed into [their] midst, and then coming to be in the midst of a tremble** (or: inwardly trembling), **he fell down toward** (or: prostrated to; [D adds: the feet {of}]) **Paul and Silas.**

30. **Next, after leading them outside** [D adds: and upon securing the rest {of the prisoners}], **he said to them, "Sirs** (or: [My] lords; Masters) **what is it now necessary for me to continue doing or keep on performing so that I can be kept safe** (or: rescued)**?"**
31. **So these men said, "At once place your trust and confidence upon the Lord Jesus** (or: the Master, Jesus), **and then you as well as your household will be kept safe** (or: rescued and kept from trouble or danger [from the consequences of these events])**."**

32. **Later, they spoke God's** [other MSS: the Lord's {= Christ's or Yahweh's}] **Word** (or: God's idea and thoughts; God's *Logos*; the message and information from God) **to him [and] to all the folks within his house** (or: household), **together.**
33. **Then, taking them along in that very hour of the night, he washed [the bruises from] the blows, and bathed [their] stripes. Next he himself was immersed** (baptized), **along with all his folks** (= family, or, those belonging to him; [p45 reads: his whole house]), **instantly and effectively.**
34. **Besides this, leading** (or: bringing) **them up into the house, he placed beside [them] a table** (= fed them a meal). **Then, after having put faith on God, and now being in a state of confident trust in and loyalty to [Him], he expressed extreme gladness, leaping and skipping in ecstatic delight, along with all the household.**

35. **Now, with it becoming day, the civil magistrates dispatched the constables** (those who had the rods: both an emblem of the office, as well as a means for executing the judgments of the magistrates), **saying [to them], "Release those men."**
> [D reads: At daybreak, the civil magistrates came together at that time into the market place, and recalling the earthquake which had happened, they became afraid and so dispatched the court-officers, who said, "Release those men."]

36. **So the guard of the bound ones** (the jailer; the warden) **reported back these words to Paul: "The city magistrates have sent off [a message] to the end that you men should be released. At this time, therefore, upon going out, be going your way in peace."**
37. **Yet Paul affirmed to them, "After lashing** (or: beating) **us in public, uncondemned** (or: not having gone through a legal trial) **– men who are Romans – they threw** (cast) **[us] into prison** (or: jail)**! And now they are proceeding in throwing us out secretly and unnoticed? No indeed! To the contrary, upon coming [here], let they themselves lead us out!"**

38. **So the constables reported these results of the flow** (or: sayings) **back to the city magistrates. Now they grew fearful upon hearing that they were Romans,**
39. **and then, after coming, they entreated them, calling them to their sides. Next, having led them out [of the prison], they kept on asking [them] to go off** [other MSS: out], **away from the city.**
> [D reads: and so, upon arriving unto the prison – accompanied by many friends – they entreated them to go forth, saying, "We were not aware (had no personal knowledge) of the situation regarding you folks, that you are just men (men of blameless character)." And so, having escorted them out, they entreated them, saying, "Go forth out of this city, otherwise folks may gather together again and turn on you, repeatedly shouting threats against you."]

40. **So then, after coming out of the prison** (or: jail), **they went unto [the home], to face and be with Lydia. Then, upon seeing the brothers** (= fellow believers; folks from the same Womb), [D adds: they fully related everything that {the} Lord did for them {and}] **they called [them] to their sides, encouraging them. Later they departed** (went out [of the city]).

CHAPTER 17

1. **So after making their way through Amphipolis and then Ampollonia, they came into Thessalonica – where there was a synagogue of the Jews.**
2. **Now corresponding to the custom having been normally practiced by Paul, he went into [their] midst to face them** (= to join their meeting), **and thus, upon three [consecutive] sabbaths he laid out thoughts and ideas to them through reasoning from the Scriptures** (or: he held thorough discussion with them from out of the writings; he led a dialogue through [a path] from the midst of the Scriptures for them),

3. **thoroughly and progressively opening [them] up and repeatedly placing [them] side-by-side** (= explaining and setting forth proofs) **that it had continued binding and necessary for the Anointed One** (the Christ) **to experience, and at some point to suffer, but then to rise** (stand back up again) **from out of the midst of dead folks – and [saying] that "This Jesus, Whom I myself am now fully announcing to** (or: progressively publishing down among) **you folks, is the Anointed One** (the Christ; = the Messiah)."

4. **And so certain folks from among them were persuaded and became convinced – including a great multitude of reverent** (or: "God-fearing") **Greeks** [i.e., those who, without becoming "Jews," attended the synagogue to worship the true God], **as well as not a few of the leading** (most prominent) **women [of the city]** (or: first-[ranking] women; = women of the upper class or aristocracy) **– and thus had their lot cast with Paul and Silas.**

5. **Now the** [D adds: unpersuaded; unconvinced] **Jews, becoming jealous and taking to themselves certain worthless men** (= degenerates) **from the market-place loafers** (ones who are idle and hung out on the streets) **as associates and forming a mob, began starting a riot in the city. Then, after assaulting the house of Jason** [note: probably Paul and Silas' host], **they continued in seeking to lead them before the populace** (or: into the midst of the mob).

6. **Yet upon not finding them, they began violently dragging** (or: forcefully trailing) **Jason and certain brothers before the city rulers** (or: politarchs; magistrates; officials), **repeatedly yelling, "The people that are causing the inhabited areas of the Empire to be roused up out of its situation** (or: are inciting tumults and insurrections in the State; or: = are upsetting the inhabited land, causing folks to get up and take a stand) **– these folks are now present in this place also;**

7. **"men whom Jason has received under [his roof] and has shown hospitality! And yet all these people are constantly practicing and committing [acts; things] contrary and in opposition to the decrees of Caesar, repeatedly saying there is now to be a different king: Jesus!"**

8. **So they stirred up** (unsettled; agitated and provoked; shook together and threw into confusion) **the crowd and the city officials** (rulers) **[that were] presently listening and hearing these things.**

9. **And so, after receiving sufficient security** (or: obtaining enough bail; taking considerable bond) **from Jason and the rest, they released them.**

10. **So then the brothers** (= fellow believers) **immediately sent both Paul and Silas out by** (or: through [the]) **night into Berea** (or: Beroia), **who, upon arriving unto the synagogue of the Jews, continued being away [there].**

11. **Now these folks were** (or: existed being) **more noble** (well-born; = noble-minded and having the character that comes from being raised in a good family) **than those in Thessalonica. [They were] folks who received and welcomed the** *Logos* (the Word; the message; the idea) **with all eagerness** (rushing forward), **repeatedly examining again, separating back and sifting up and down the Scriptures – day by day – to determine if these continue having it thus** (or: holding it in this way).

12. **Indeed, therefore, many from out of their midst trusted and believed – and from the respectable** (those who had good form, decorum, manners and propriety; reputable; may = prominent and influential) **Greek women and men, not a few** [D reads: a considerable number became loyal].

13. **Now as soon as the Jews from Thessalonica came to know** (or: learned) **that the** *Logos* **of, and from, God** (or: God's Word and message; information about God) **was proclaimed by** (or: brought down as a public announcement under) **Paul in Berea also, they came there as well, repeatedly shaking** (agitating) **and stirring up** (disturbing) **the crowds** [D adds: not ceasing].

14. **So at that point, the brothers immediately sent Paul out from [their] midst, to continue traveling away – as far as the sea. Other than this, both Silas and Timothy remained there, under cover yet persevering and supporting [the situation].**

15. **Now the folks progressively conducting Paul brought [him] as far as Athens. Then, after receiving** [D adds: from Paul] **a directive to Silas and Timothy that they should come to him as quickly as possible, they departed** (they were progressively forth from the midst [of that place]).

16. **Yet during Paul's waiting for them and progressively taking in [the scene] from the midst of the people and the situation within Athens, his breath-effect** (spirit; attitude) **began being**

progressively on edge (sharpened; stimulated; or: spurred on and encouraged; or: irritated or incited) **within the midst of him, while being a spectator and steadily observing the city being full of idols**
(or: as he was progressively beholding the city continuously existing in a correspondence to idols; or: repeatedly noticing the city as existing in the sphere of concepts and mental images of forms, fancies and appearances, as well as being followers along the line of perceptions).
17. **Consequently, he began to reason and dialogue** (hold discussions) **with the Jews and with the reverent, religious folks within the synagogue, and then, day by day in the marketplace, to those happening along** (or: toward people whom he is happening to meet, at the side).

18. **Now certain folks – both of the Epicurean and of the Stoic philosophers – began throwing [comments; thoughts; ideas] together to** (or: took to conversing with; were intermittently tossing remarks at) **him, and some had been saying, "What could this seed-collector** (or: seed-layer; or: = a bird or a gleaner that picks up scraps in the market place or fallen seeds in the field; or: = a chatterer who gathers scraps of knowledge and repeats trifling thoughts and ideas) **now possibly intend** (or: want) **to continue saying?" While others [said], "He seems to be an announcer of** (publisher for; one putting forth a case about) **foreign** (or: alien; strange) **demons** (a Hellenistic concept and term: = animistic influences; here may refer to foreign divinities)," **because he had been announcing the message of goodness, ease and well-being: Jesus and the resurrection!**
19. **So** [other MSS: Along with this; D adds: after a few days,] **after taking a hold on him, they brought [him] up on the Areopagus** (or: a meeting of the council of the Areopagos [a body similar to a municipal or colonial senate]), **various ones saying, "Are we able** (or: Can we) **get to know what this strange, innovative, new teaching [is] which is being repeatedly spoken by you?**
20. **"For you see, you continue importing into our hearing some things being presently strange and foreign. Therefore we are now wishing and intending** (we are resolved) **to personally know and experience** (or: gain insight about) **[what] these certain things are progressively intending** (purposing; resolving) **to be."**
21. **In fact, all Athenians and the foreigners repeatedly being temporary residents** (or: sojourners; folks continuing as resident aliens) **were habitually spending leisure time** (or: good opportunities; seasons of ease) **[invested] into nothing different than to be saying** (or: telling) **something or to be hearing** (or: listening to) **something stranger and innovatively newer** (= the latest novelty).
22. **So Paul, being made to stand in the middle of the Areopagus, affirmed [to them],**
"Men (some scholars suggest that this term = Ladies and Gentlemen), **Athenians! I continue watching and observing you people as [being] most reverencing of the animistic powers** (or: more religious than usual in regard to the fear of demons [a Hellenistic concept and term: = an animistic influence] and unseen forces),
23. **"for while passing through, and then continuing in contemplation during carefully observing one after another of your religious objects** (items of reverence; effects of veneration, devotion and worship), **I also found an elevated spot within which it had been inscribed, 'To** (or: For) **an Unknown** (or: Unknowable) **God.' To Whom then, while continuing ignorant, you make it a habit to give reverent worship and dutiful support, this One am I myself presently announcing** (bringing down a clear proclamation of) **to you folks** (or: Therefore, to what you people continue unknowingly giving godly devotion, this same One do I myself continue publishing among you).
24. **"The God making** (forming and constructing; producing) **the ordered system and arrangement of the universe, and all the things within it – this One continuously being from the start: Lord of heaven and of earth** (or: this Owner and Master, repeatedly and progressively being the subsisting and originating source, the under-beginning, of sky and land) **– is not now** (or: habitually) **taking up residence within handmade shrines, sanctuaries or temples!**
25. **"Neither is He continuously provided for, attended or habitually served by human hands – as constantly being in want, or having a need of something – He Himself being the One constantly giving to all people, and things, life and breath and all things** (or: everything; the whole [universe])!
26. **"Besides this, He made** (formed; or: constructs; or: produced) **from out of one [man, or, source**; D and other MSS add: blood] **every ethnic group of mankind, to continue dwelling** (or: to be repeatedly residing) **upon all [the] face of the earth** (or: land) **– while setting a boundary for** (or: defining; determining; specifying) **[the] seasons and fitting situations** (or: fertile moments and opportunities) **which have been set and arranged with [predetermined] aspects** (or: facing toward [specific purposes]), **as well as [the] limits and bounds of their dwelling place** (residence; habitat) **–**

27. "[D adds: most of all] **to be continuously seeking God** [D reads: the Deity], **since really, in fact, they could feel about and grope, and then at some point might** (or: possibly) **find Him! And, to be sure, [He] is continuously being an Originator** (or: He is constantly subsisting, being inherently [the] Under-Beginner; = [the ground of Being]) **not far away** (or: a long distance) **from each one of us!**
28. **"For you see, within the midst of and in union with Him we continuously live** (or, as a subjunctive: could be constantly living), **and are constantly moved about and put into motion, and continue existing** (experiencing Being). **Even as certain of the poets down among you people have said,**

> **'You see, we are also a family of the One** (or: we even continuously exist being a race whose source is the One; or: we also are His species and offspring; we are even a family which is composed of the One and which is the One).' [a quote of Aratos, and of Keleanthes]

29. **"Therefore, continuously and inherently subsisting from under a beginning, being God's family** (a species of God; a race whose source is God; [the] kind of being having the qualities and characteristics of God; [the] offspring birthed from God), **we continue indebted** (or: we ought) **not from custom to be habitually presuming or inferring the Deity** (or: the Divine Nature) **to be like gold or silver or stone – a result of engraved or sculpted work of art or craftsmanship, or even of human inner rush of emotion, feeling, passion, sentiment, reflection or concept.**

30. **"Indeed then, upon looking over, seeing above and perceiving on behalf of** [D reads: taking no notice of] **the times of this ignorance, in regard to the present conditions and situations, God is presently and progressively passing along** [other MSS: bringing back] **this announcement to, for and among, the humans: all people** (or: humans), **everywhere, are to be progressively changing [their] thinking, mindset, attitude and state of consciousness!** [*cf* Rom. 12:2]
31. **"In accord with that, He set** (or: established) **a Day within which He continues about to proceed evaluating and deciding about** (or: judging) **the inhabited area [of the Empire], in fairness and equity of an eschatological deliverance and liberation** (or: in union with rightwised relationships for making things right and in accord with the Way pointed out; or: centered in covenant inclusion; or: within establishment of covenant participation) **– within a Man,** [D adds: Jesus,] **Whom He definitely marked out, furnishing faith to all people** (providing trust and confident assurance among, and for, all humans; tendering fidelity, loyalty and faithfulness in all) **by raising Him back up again from the midst of dead ones** (or: causing Him to stand up: out of, or forth from among, dead folks)."

32. **Now upon hearing [of] a resurrection** (or: standing back up again) **of dead people** (or: a standing up from out of, or forth from among, dead folks), **indeed, some folks began sneering and mocking, yet others said, "We will listen and hear from you about this again, also."**
33. **Thus** (or: Under these circumstances), **Paul went out from the midst of them, yet certain men** (= adults, or, ladies and gentlemen) **trusted and believed – being glued** (joined; attached; welded) **to him,**
34. **Among whom [were] also Dionysius, the Areopagite** (a member of the court of Areopagus), **and a woman named Damaris, as well as different folks together with them.**

CHAPTER 18

1. **After these events [and] having been separated from out of Athens, Paul came into Corinth.**
2. **Then, upon finding a certain Jew named Aquila – a native of Pontus recently having come from Italy along with Priscilla, his wife, because of the order that Claudius [Caesar] had carefully arranged to be prescribed for all the Jews to progressively be separated from Rome – he** [D reads: Paul] **came to them,**
3. **and, because of [his happening] to be by occupation practicing a like craft – you see, they were tentmakers by trade – he continued staying** (remaining; dwelling) **at their side** (or: with them) **[and] they continued working [together]** [*p*74, Aleph2, A, D and others read: he began working {there}].

4. **Now he continued dialoguing and reasoning in the synagogue on every sabbath, [and] was repeatedly persuading and convincing both Jews and Greeks.**
> [D reads: Now repeatedly going his way into the synagogue on every sabbath, he continued holding discussions and habitually implanting the Name of the Lord Jesus and repeatedly persuading and convincing not only Jews but also Greeks.]

5. **So, as both Silas and Timothy came down** [D reads: arrived] **from Macedonia, Paul continued being held together by the** *Logos* (or: was constantly being compressed, so as to be confined, in the Word; or, as a middle: held himself focused on Information and attuned to the message), **repeatedly witnessing and progressively giving evidence to the Jews [for] Jesus to be the Christ** (= certifying that Jesus is the Anointed One [= the Messiah]).

6. **But with their constantly setting themselves in face-to-face battle array for opposition against [him] and then repeatedly speaking abusively [to him], while suddenly shaking out [his] garments** [note: a symbolic act denoting disassociation], **he said to them, "Your blood [is] upon your head! I myself [am] clean** (= I have no blame in this situation, and am not responsible for your lives). **From now on I will be going unto** (or: into the midst of) **the ethnic multitudes** (the nations which are non-Jews)."

7. **And so, walking over from that place** [D reads: from {the residence of} Aquila], **he came unto [the] house of** (= [the] home belonging to) **a certain man named Titus Justus, who by way of life reverenced God** (= a convert to Judaism; a "God-fearer," i.e., one in awe of the [true] God), **whose house had a common wall, or boundary, with** (or: was adjoined or adjacent to) **the synagogue.**

8. **Now Crispus, the presiding member** (or: leader; ruler) **of the synagogue, believed by the Lord [= Christ], then put trust into the Lord, and became loyal to the Lord – along with his whole household. Furthermore, many of the Corinthians, continuing in hearing [the message] and listening to [the** *Logos*] **began trusting and believing, and, one after another, were being immersed** (baptized).

9. **Now at one point, through a vision** (the result of something seen), **during [one] night, the Lord [= Christ or Yahweh] said to Paul, "Stop being caused to fear. To the contrary, keep on speaking; and you should not at any point become silent,**

10. **"because I, Myself, am with you, and not even one person will set himself upon** (= assault; attack) **you with the intent to treat you badly** (harm you; behave in a worthless manner to you; injure or ill-treat you), **because within this city there are many people in Me** (or: for Me; with Me)." [Gen. 15:1]

11. **So he took a seat** (as a teacher) **and was seated** (= installed) [D adds: in Corinth] **one year and six months, habitually teaching the** *Logos* **of** (Word which is; message from) **God among them.**

12. **Now while Gallio** [brother of Seneca, Nero's tutor] **was being [the] proconsul** (regional governor) **of Achaia, the Jews,** [D adds: after talking together,] **with one accord and like rushing-passion, took a stand down upon** (or: made a concerted assault on) **Paul and,** [D adds: laying hands on {him},] **led him up on the raised public platform where legal cases were tried** (the dais), **[before Gallio],**

13. **one after another** [D adds: repeatedly shouting in complaint and] **saying, "By persuading folks back** (or: again) **[to a different belief], this person continues inducing** (inciting; urging) **the people to habitually worship and show reverence to God [in a manner that is] to the side of the Law** (or: = outside the law; = in illegal ways; or: = against the Torah)."

14. **But then, at Paul's being about to be opening up [his] mouth, Gallio says to the Jews, "O Jews! If this were actually the result of something unfair** (inequitable; injurious; contrary to what is right; or: = a violent crime), **or the effect of a worthless act of villainy** (e.g.: fraud; unscrupulousness; reckless action), **in accord with reason** (or: corresponding to [such] account) **I would hold myself back and tolerate you people** (or: your [issue and behavior]).

15. **"Yet since it is the results of questions and controversies concerning a word** (or: a message; a thought; an idea; information) **and names, or even a law or custom of that which relates to you people, you yourselves will proceed seeing [to it]! I myself am neither wishing nor intending to be a judge of these matters!"**

16. **Then** (or: And so) **he drove them away from the court** (the elevated public platform; the dais).

17. **So** (or: Then) **they all, after suddenly grabbing Sosthenes, the [current] presiding leader** (or: chief ruler) **of the synagogue, began beating [him] in front of the court area** (the dais). **And yet no one of these things came to be a concern or was of interest to** (or: for) **Gallio.**

18. **Now Paul, after remaining** (or: staying on) **yet a considerable number of days face-to-face with the brothers** (= fellow believers), **upon separating himself and saying good-bye proceeded to sail forth unto Syria – Priscilla and Aquila also with him – shearing [his] head** (cutting his hair in the manner of shearing a sheep) **in Cenchrea, for you see, he continued holding** (or: having) **a good thought for well-being** (or: a wish for/prayer of goodness which he claimed and professed; or: a vow).

312

19. **So they came down opposite unto** (or: arrived into the midst of) **Ephesus and** [D adds: on the next sabbath] **he left those folks there, yet he himself, upon entering into the synagogue, had dialogues and reasoned with the Jews.**
20. **Yet at their repeated asking [him] to stay on more time** [D and others add: with them], **he did not nod in consent,**
21. **but rather, upon arranging for himself to be off** (or: away) **while saying good-bye and saying,** "[D and others add: Now it continues binding for me to by all means do (or: perform) the feast – the one periodically coming into Jerusalem, but] **I will proceed coming back again to you folks, God's continuing in willing and intending [it],"** he set sail from Ephesus.
22. **Then, after coming down into Caesarea and walking up [to be] one-after-another greeting and embracing [the folks of] the called-out community, he walked down into Antioch.**
23. **And then, after creating** (or: doing; = spending) **some time [with the folks there], he went forth, passing consecutively through the Galatian province and the Phrygia, progressively setting and establishing** [D and others read: further establishing] **all the disciples** (students; apprentices).

24. **Now a certain Jew named Apollos came down unto** (or: arrived into the midst of) **Ephesus, a native of Alexandria – an adult man of reason, thought, and a gifted speaker** (or: a learned and eloquent man; a man well-trained in rhetoric) **being able and powerful in the Scriptures.**
25. **This man was one having been orally instructed in the way** (or: path) **of the Lord** [= Yahweh], **and continuing boiling hot** (= fervent) **in** (or: by; for; with) **the Breath-effect** (the Spirit), **he kept on speaking and teaching accurately the things concerning** (or: about) **Jesus – continuing being versed in and acquainted with only the immersion** (or: baptism) **carried out by John.**
26. **More than this, this person started to be consistently speaking boldly, as with the right of a citizen, within the synagogue. So after hearing him, Priscilla and Aquila took him to themselves and more accurately exposed** (or: expounded; set out from the midst) **God's Way** (or: path).

27. **Now at his continuing in desiring and intending to pass through into Achaia, the brothers** (= fellow believers), **themselves promoting and encouraging [him; or: it], wrote to the disciples to, from acceptance, welcome and receive him – who, upon coming to be at [their] side, in giving much help threw himself [into the work] with the folks having trusted, faithed-it, believed now continue loyal through the grace and on account of joyous favor,**
28. **for you see he, at full stretch and with intense vigor, began thoroughly reasoning the case down to a conclusive proof to, and continued completely refuting, the Jews publicly, by** [p38 and D add: continuously reasoning and] **progressively giving a complete demonstration** (or: a full exhibition) **through the Scriptures [for] Jesus to be the Christ** (the Anointed One; = the Messiah).

CHAPTER 19

1. [D and p38 read: Now upon Paul's desiring – according to {his} personal wish and intent – to continue traveling into Jerusalem, the Breath-effect (or: Spirit) told him to be progressively turned back into Asia]. **So it happened during the [occasion] for Apollos to be within Corinth, [that] Paul, passing through the upper parts** (= mountainous or highland regions; or: = by an inland route), **came down into Ephesus. Then, upon finding certain disciples, he said to them,**
2. **"Since** (or: If) **in or upon** (or: when) **at some point trusting, believing or being loyal, did you folks accept or receive a Set-apart Breath-effect** (or: take in hand and possess [the] Holy Spirit; or: take possession of a holy spirit or grasp a sacred attitude)**?" Yet these [said] to him, "To the contrary, we have not even heard if there is** (or: exists) **a Set-apart Breath-effect** (or: Holy Spirit; or: sacred spirit and attitude; [D* and p38 read: we have not so much as heard of any one's receiving a holy spirit])**."**
3. **So he said, "Into what, therefore** (or: then), **were you folks immersed** (or: baptized)**?" And they said, "Into the immersion that originated with** (or: which had the character of and pertained to; which was carried out by) **John."**
4. **Yet Paul said, "John immersed** (or: baptized) **[into] an immersion** (a baptism) **of a change of thinking for the people, repeatedly saying that they could and should at once put their trust in, believe and place loyalty into the One progressively coming after him – that is, into Jesus."**
5. **Now, upon hearing [this], they were at once immersed** (or: baptized) **into the Name of the Lord Jesus.**

6. **Then, after** (or: during) **Paul's placing [his] hands upon them, the Set-apart Breath-effect** (or: the Holy Spirit) **came** [*p*38 and D read: immediately fell] **upon them and they began speaking in languages** (or: with tongues), **and then began** (or: and continued) **prophesying** (speaking light ahead of time and in front of people).

7. **There were about twelve adult men, [in] all.**

8. **Now upon entering into the synagogue,** [D adds: in union with great power and ability] **he began speaking publicly with the boldness and freedom which comes from citizenship – making this a habit for about three months – repeatedly holding discussions while thoroughly laying thoughts out with reasonings, as well as habitually seeking to persuade and endeavoring to convince** [folks; other MSS read: {about} things], **concerning the reign of God** (or: about God's kingdom; sovereign influences and activities which are God).

9. **Yet, as certain folks were being progressively dried up and began to be made hard and stiff, they continued unconvinced** (unpersuaded) **and began being uncompliant and obstinate, repeatedly speaking bad, worthless and malicious things about the Way before the crowd** (or: multitude) [D adds: of the ethnic groups (or: nations). At that point,] **immediately withdrawing from them, he set boundaries to separate the disciples** (the folks who were learning) **away from [them], continuing in daily holding discussions while thoroughly laying thoughts out with reasonings** [D adds: from eleven o'clock in the morning until four in the afternoon] **in the school** (or: lecture hall or auditorium; or: place for leisure) **of** (or: belonging to) **Tyrannus.**

10. **Now this took place for two years, so that all the folks permanently living in** (or: normally inhabiting) **[the province of] Asia [had the chance] to at some point listen to and hear the** *Logos* **of the Lord** (or: = Christ's Word; or: [Yahweh]'s thought and idea; or: the message and information about, and which is, the Lord) **– both Jews and Greeks.**

11. **More than this, God kept on performing** (or: continued making and constructing) **uncommon** (or: extraordinary; what one doesn't experience every day) **abilities and expressions of power through the hands of Paul,**

12. **so that even sweat cloths** (or: face cloths; handkerchiefs) **or workman's** (or: servant's; artisan's) **aprons from the surface or proximity of him** (= from his skin or having grazed his body) **came to be periodically carried away [and placed] upon the folks being habitually without strength** (= weak; infirm; ill; sick; incapable), **even thus to cause the sicknesses and diseases to be transferred away from them** (or: to be changed and transformed so as to be other than they were, and be away from them), **and furthermore to cause the miserable spirits** (or: the breath-effects and attitudes which cause pain, bad conditions, unsoundness, wickedness and evil) **to journey out of the midst** (or: to progressively travel out and depart), **one after another.**

13. **So certain folks who were a part of the constantly wandering** (or: periodically roving; habitually vagabond) **Jews – being practicing exorcists** (folks who exacted or administered oaths; people who pronounced incantations) **– also took in hand** (= ventured; undertook) **to be repeatedly naming the Name of the Lord Jesus upon folks continuing in having miserable spirits** (breath-effects or attitudes which bring pain, bad conditions, unsoundness, wickedness and evil), **habitually saying, "I am now administering as an oath upon you folks** (or: adjuring and solemnly charging you people by) **the Jesus whom Paul is now repeatedly proclaiming** (publicly heralding)**!"**

14. **Now there were seven sons of a certain Sceva** (or: Sceuas), **a Jewish chief priest, repeatedly performing this** [D and *p*38 read: desired to do this].

15. [D and *p*38 add: They continued having a habit (or: custom) such as these things, to proceed in performing an exorcism. And so, upon entering to face the person affected by a demon (a Hellenistic religious word and concept), they began to repeatedly have the Name called upon, repeated saying, "In union with {the} Jesus, whom Paul continues preaching, we are now commanding and passing along this announcement to you, to come (or: go) out at once!"] **But making a discerning reply, the miserable spirit** (or: the malicious and mischievous breath-effect) **said to them, "Indeed, from experience I recognize and have insight about Jesus, and I am learning of, and becoming increasingly acquainted with, Paul, but now who** (or: what [sort of] men) **are you folks?"**

16. **And then suddenly leaping** (springing like a panther) **upon them, the man within whom was the miserable breath-effect** (the bad spirit or attitude) **– in coming down as master and owner of both of**

them (= two at a time; or, thus: = all of them, one after another) – **exerted [his] strength down on and against them** (= prevailed over them), **with the result that, naked and having been wounded and traumatized, [they managed] to make an escape** (to flee out) **from that house.**

17. **Now this [incident] came to be known to** (or: by) **everyone – both Jews and Greeks – normally residing in Ephesus. And so fear fell upon them all, and then the Name of the Lord Jesus began becoming great and continued enlarging.**
18. **More than that, many of the folks having believed, trusted and come to be full of faith and loyalty, continued coming, one after another, constantly making open confession** (speaking out agreement) **and continuing in reporting again their practices in public announcements.**
19. **So a considerable number of the folks practicing the meddling arts** (acts or works concerning [other folks]; things that work around [nature or people]; or: = sorcery or magic arts), **after bringing together the scrolls, began burning [them] down** (= up) **in the sight of all** (or: before everybody). **Then folks calculated the prices** (or: values) **of them and they found [them worth] fifty thousand [pieces] of silver** (= a day's wage per piece of silver).
20. **Thus, down with force and in accord with [the] might of the Lord** [= Yahweh, or, Christ], **the** *Logos* (Word; idea and message; pattern-forming, laid-out Information) **continued growing and increasing – and It increasingly exerted strength so as to prevail.**

21. **Now as these things were being fulfilled** (or: made full), **Paul put himself in the attitude** (or: set himself in union with the Breath-effect; or; placed within the spirit for himself [the intent]) **to continue journeying into Jerusalem – after passing through Macedonia and Achaia – saying, "After the [situation] occurs [for] me to come to be in that place** [i.e., Jerusalem], **it continues binding and necessary for me to see Rome at some point, also."**
22. **So after sending off Timothy and Erastus – two of the folks normally giving him attending service** (= two of his assistants) **– on a mission into Macedonia, he himself held on [for] a period of time** (= stayed longer), **[eventually passing deeper] into the [province of] Asia.**

23. **Now corresponding to that particular situation [in Ephesus]** (or: Now during that season) **there occurred no slight disturbance** (agitation; trouble) **about** (or: concerning) **the Way.**
24. **You see, a certain silversmith named Demetrius was habitually furnishing a continual supply of no small working profit** (or; trade; business for gain; income) **to** (or: for) **the craftsmen** (or: artisans) **– by constantly making silver temples** (or: shrines) **of Artemis –**
25. **whom convening into a crowded body** (or: assembly) **– as well as the workers and laborers involved with such things** (= workers in similar trades) **– then says, "Gentlemen! You men continue well knowing and habitually stand upon [the fact] that from out of this trade** (vocation; business) **is prosperity** (a good means of passing through life; = wealth and a high standard of living) **for us.**
26. **"And yet, you folks continue as spectators gazing with contemplation, and you are constantly hearing that not only in regard to Ephesus, but as it pertains to nearly all of the [province] of Asia, this Paul, by persuading, caused a considerable crowd to change positions and stand with a changed opinion, now continually saying that they are not gods which are periodically coming into being** (or: existence) **by means of [people's] hands.**
27. **"Now not only this, but the part for us** (= the trade done by us) **is now progressing in danger** (or: peril) **to come into discredit** (refutation and disrepute), **but further, even** (or: also) **the temple of the great goddess Artemis will come into being logically considered nothing, and reckoned of no account. Besides this, her magnificence – which the whole [district or province of] Asia and the inhabited area [of the empire] continues adoring with godly fear and worship – also proceeds in being about to be progressively pulled** (or: brought) **down and demolished."**

28. **Now at hearing these things and coming to be full of rushing and violent emotions** (or: impetuous passion leading to indignation and fury) [D adds: then (or: while) running (or: dashing; rushing out forward) into the street], **they began crying out, one after another repeatedly saying, "Great [is] Artemis of [the] Ephesians!"** (or: they continued making exclamations of entreaty, constantly saying, "O Great Artemis of Ephesus!")
29. **So the city came to be filled with the confusion that comes with the actions of a disorderly mob** [D reads: And thus the whole city was being poured together with the sense of shame and disgrace].

What is more, with similar emotions and passion they rushed headlong (or: stampeded) **into the theater, having suddenly and violently seized and drug away Gaius and Aristarchus – the Macedonian traveling companions of Paul** (or: folks traveling abroad with Paul).

30. **Now at Paul's persistent desiring and intending to go inside unto the people of the local society, the disciples** [D: began preventing (hindering)] **[and] continued not letting him [do so].**
31. **Moreover, even some of the annually elected officials who presided over and funded the public games and religious festivals in the province of Asia** [note: called Asiarchs, they acted as high priests of the cult of the goddess Roma, and of the Emperor cult], **being friendly to him and having affection for him, were sending [word] to him, continuing in offering assistance, as well as entreating him** (= kept on insisting for him) **not to give himself unto the theater** (or: not to venture into the theater).
32. **Indeed, other folks then kept on crying out some other thing – for you see, that called-out group was one having been commingled into a state of confusion, and the majority had not seen, and were thus unaware of, what reason or account they had come together.**
33. **So folks of the Jews, thrusting him forward, together made Alexander stand out of the crowd. Thus now Alexander, gesturing** (or: motioning) **downward with [his] hand, was wanting and intending to be defending himself to the people** (or: populace).
34. **Yet upon recognizing** (or: coming to clearly know) **that he is a Jew, one voice was birthed** (= arose) **forth from the midst of all of them,** [like a flock of gulls] **continuously crying out for about two hours, "Great [is] Artemis of [the] Ephesians** (or: O Great Artemis of Ephesus)**!"**

35. **Finally, upon quelling and composing the crowd** (or: throng), **the city recorder** (or: town clerk; [note: this was the chief elected magistrate of the city]) **continued saying, "Gentlemen! Ephesians! Now really, who is there of mankind who does not continue with personal, experiential knowledge and insight [that] the city of [the] Ephesians continues being the temple keeper** (warden; custodian; sexton; official in charge of keeping the temple clean, decorated and in repair) **of the great Artemis, and of the [stone; statue] fallen from Zeus?**
36. **"Therefore, with these things being undeniable** (indisputable; beyond question of being spoken against), **it continues being binding for you folks to be from the source submitted** (or: to be submitted from the beginning; = be calm), **being ones having been quelled and composed, and to continue practicing** (committing; performing) **nothing rash or reckless** (as though from falling headlong toward something).
37. **"For you see, you folks led these men [here], [who are] neither robbers of temples nor folks blaspheming** (slandering; speaking abusively or contemptuously of) **our goddess.**
38. **"Indeed, therefore, if Demetrius and those artisans** (craftsmen) **with him continue having** (or: holding) **a matter aimed toward someone** (= a case or a charge against anybody), **court sessions are regularly being convened, and there are proconsuls** (= governors of the Roman provinces); **let them continue to call in the cases** (= bring the charges) **to** (or: for; = against) **one another.**
39. **"If, however, you folks continue seeking** (or: searching for) **anything beyond that** [other MSS: concerning different things], **it will be released** (= resolved and settled) **in the lawful assembly,**
40. **"for we also continue being in danger** (or: peril; at risk) **to be now arraigned and indicted** (or: accused and charged) **for a rebellious posture** (a stance which signifies civil insurrection) **concerning today's [affair; commotion; events], possessing** (or: there inhering [D reads: there being]) **not one cause concerning which we will be able to render a reason** (an account; a word; a thought; = an explanation) **about this turning-together** (= a conspiracy, a riot, or a disorderly mob)**."**
41. **And so, upon saying these things, he dismissed** (loosed-away) **the assembly.**

CHAPTER 20

1. **Now with** (or: after) **this [intervention] to cause the uproar, milling and disorderly tumult to cease, Paul – after summoning the disciples to himself, then comforting and encouraging [them], and finally giving a farewell embrace – went out to continue [his] journey into Macedonia.**
2. **So, after passing through** [D adds: all] **those parts and [at the same time] comforting, assisting and encouraging them with many a word and message** (or: with much *Logos*, thought and patterning Information), **he came into Greece.**

3. **Along with this, after doing** (= spending) **three months [in that area, and] there coming to be a plot against him by the Jews** (or: under [the direction of the leaders of] the Jewish [religious leaders]), **being progressively about to set sail unto Syria, he suddenly came to be of the informed opinion and of the experienced decision** [D reads: he intended to go back again into Syria, but the Breath-effect (Spirit) told him] **to be now returning through Macedonia.**

4. **Now** [D: therefore with his being progressively about to depart], **it continued being arranged for him to be met, as far as [the province of] Asia, [by] Sopater, [the son] of Pyrrhus, a Berean. Now [there was] also Aristarchus and Secundus, from Thessalonica, and Gaius from Derbe, as well as Timothy. Then, from [the province] of Asia, [there were] Tychicus and Trophimus.**

5. **So these, having come before us** [other MSS: after going on], **continued waiting** (or: were for a while remaining) **in Troas,**

6. **yet we** [= Paul and Luke?] **put out to sea** (or: set sail) **from Philippi after the days** [= the Feast] **of Unleavened [Bread] and then within five days came to them, [upon entering] into Troas, where we spent seven days.**

7. **Now on that one particular sabbath** (literally: in the one of the sabbaths), **at our having been gathered together to break bread** (= share a meal), **Paul began dialoging with** (or: discussing and reasoning through a discourse to) **them. [He was] being about to depart on the next day, so he continued prolonging the message** (stretching out beside [them] the thoughts and reasons of, and from, the *Logos*) **until midnight.**

8. **So in the upper room** (or: chamber; = upstairs or in the upper story) **where we were gathered together, there were quite a few lamps.**

9. **Now a certain young man named Eutychus, remaining seated upon the window [sill]** (or: little door [opening]; [note: likely opened due to the crowd as well as from the heat and smoke from all the lamps]) **[and] being made to increasingly sink down in a deep sleep during Paul's discoursing still more** (= for a long time), **upon being caused to collapse from the sleep, he fell down from the third story – and was lifted up dead!**

10. **So Paul, descending the steps, fell on him and, after taking [him] in his arms and embracing [him], said, "Stop wailing and do not continue causing a tumult, for his soul** (the inner life of his being) **continues existing** (or: being) **within the midst of him!"**

11. **Now after walking back up and breaking bread, then tasting** (= sipping and eating) **for a considerable time, besides conversing until daybreak, without further ado, he went out.**

12. **So** [D adds: after their embracing and saying good-bye], **they took the young man [home] alive** (or: living), **and thus were relieved and comforted beyond measure.**

13. **Now we ourselves** (= the rest of us), **going ahead by boat, sailed on to Assos, being about** (= planning; intending) **to take up Paul – for thus [he] had arranged, [as] he himself was being about to continue going on, [taking a shortcut], by foot.**

>   [note: this was a journey of about twenty miles over a paved Roman road, and was less than half the distance of the sea voyage around Cape Lectum]

14. **So as [soon as] he was joining us in Assos, after taking him up** (= on board), **we went into Mitylene.**

15. **Then from there, sailing away on the succeeding [day], we arrived down in front of and face to face with Chios. Yet on a different day, we threw alongside and touched into Samos, but then on the following [day], we came into Miletus.**

16. **You see, Paul had decided to sail on, passing beside Ephesus, so that it would not happen for him to linger or run out of time in the [province of] Asia, for he was continuing to hurry on [so as] to come to be [entered] into Jerusalem [for] the Day of Pentecost – if it would be possible for him.**

17. **Now by sending from Miletus unto Ephesus, he summoned the older men of the called-out community [there] to journey over to him.**

18. **So when they arrived and came to his side** [D & *p*74 add: at their being in the same place], **he said to them, "**[D adds: Brothers,] **you yourselves continue being fully acquainted with and are well versed about how I came to be** (= lived and acted [during]) **the whole time with you folks, from the first day on which I stepped into the [province of] Asia –**

19. "constantly performing as a slave for the Lord (or: continually serving as a slave-servant to [Christ, or, Yahweh]), with all submissive humility (the frame of mind as of being in a low position) and [with] tears and [with] harassing ordeals (or: tests and trials) which from time to time walked along with me (= happened to me) during, and in the midst of, plots originating from the [religious leaders of the] Jews –

20. "how [in] nothing (or: under no circumstances) did I arrange myself under (= out of public view) and hold myself away [from the issue] (or: shrink or draw back) from repeatedly bringing [thoughts and information] together to recount to (or: for) you and to teach you folks in public, as well as from house to house,

21. "to both Jews and Greeks constantly certifying with thorough testimony about, and full witness of, the change in thinking, mindset, attitude and state of consciousness, with a turning into God, as well as faith, trust and loyalty unto our Lord, Jesus [p74, Aleph, A, C & D add: Christ].

22. "And so now, look and consider this! I myself, having been bound by the Breath-effect (or: in the Spirit; to [my] spirit and attitude; with the [realm of] spirit; for the breath-effect) – and still being thus – I continue proceeding on my journey into Jerusalem, not seeing or knowing [p41 & D read: having insight about] the things that will progressively be meeting together with me (or: that will proceed falling together in opposition to me) within the midst of her (or: it),

23. "except that down through each city (or: from city to city) the Set-apart Breath-effect (or: Holy Spirit) keeps repeatedly giving full witness and evidence to me, continually saying that bonds (= imprisonments) and pressures (oppressions; afflictions; tribulations) continue remaining and are still awaiting me.

24. "Nevertheless, from not even one thought do I habitually make my soul of value to myself (or, with other MSS: neither do I now hold a word or idea for me, nor do I continuously make my inner life or self valuable or precious to me), until I can finish my course (complete my trek and perfect my career; bring my run to its purposed destiny; or: [with other MSS: so] I would bring my race-course to its goal), as well as the attending service, which I received from beside the Lord Jesus: to (or: for) myself make full witness of and give thorough evidence for the good news (the message of ease, goodness and well-being) which is God's grace (or: which has a source in, and the character of, the undeserved joyous favor of God).

25. "And thus now, consider this. I have seen and am thus aware that all you folks, among whom I passed through constantly and progressively making public proclamation heralding the reign and kingdom [D adds: of Jesus; E and others read: of God], will no longer see my face.

26. "Hence (or: Because of this) I am now testifying to you men – in this very day – that I continue being clean from the blood of all people,

27. "for you see, I did not draw back from recounting to, for, and among you folks all the purpose, will and counsel of God (or: from the [situation] to at some point announce again all God's design and determination for you people).

28. "Continue holding focused toward and taking attentive care – to and for yourselves, as well as for all the little flock among whom the Set-apart Breath-effect Itself (or: the Holy Spirit Himself) set you folks [as] ones who look around over people for their welfare and oversee situations – to be continuously (or: habitually) acting as shepherds of God's [other MSS: {the} Lord's {= Christ's or Yahweh's}] called-out community which He built and produced as a surrounding for Himself (or: made to encompass Himself), through (or: by means of) His own blood.

29. "Now I myself have seen and am aware that, after (or: with) my spreading forth as dust and ashes (= going away, so as to be out of reach), heavy (burdensome and oppressive; fierce; vicious) wolves will enter into the midst of you folks – folks by habit not sparing (or: treating with tenderness or forbearance) the little flock,

30. "and men from among you yourselves (= from your own community) will of themselves proceed standing up, repeatedly speaking things having been thoroughly turned and twisted (things that are distorted and not straight), to progressively drag (or: draw; [D & p41 read: turn]) away the disciples behind (thus: after) themselves.

31. "Therefore, constantly keep your wits about you (be continuously awake, alert and watchful) while continuously bearing in mind through remembrance that three-year period [when] night and

day I did not cease – with tears – repeatedly and progressively placing [thoughts; ideas; information; admonition] in the minds of each one [D & E add: of you folks].

32. "And these present things I am presently placing beside you folks, by (or: in; with) the Lord [= Christ or Yahweh; other MSS: God], even by (or: in; with) the *Logos* (Word; thought; idea; message) of His grace and from His undeserved, joyous favor which is continuously having power and ability to at any point edify and build the house, and then to at once give the enjoyment of the allotted inheritance within the midst of (or: in union with; or: among) all the folks having been set-apart (or: consecrated, made holy and dedicated to sacred service).

33. "I did not covet, have an over-desire for, or set my heart upon silver or gold or clothing which belongs to even one person.

34. "You yourselves continue knowing by personal experience that these very hands subserved to my needs, as well as [giving service] to those being with me.

35. "I demonstrated under your observation, giving you an object lesson for all situations and for all people, that by thus laboring it continues binding and necessary to habitually take things in hand so as to assist in the stead of the weak and infirm folks, besides to be constantly bearing in mind through remembrance the words (thoughts; ideas; messages; patterns of information; *logoi*) of, and from, the Lord Jesus, that He said, 'It is a happy and blessed [state and situation] to be habitually giving, rather than to be continually receiving!'"

36. Then, after saying these things, upon bending his knees together with all of them, he spoke toward having things being well, with ease and goodness (or: he prayed).

37. So there came to be considerable weeping and lamentation from all of them, and one after another, after falling upon Paul's neck, were successively giving down expressions of affection and fondly kissing him,

38. being presently pained by mental and emotional distress – especially upon the word (or: at the *Logos*; on the information) which he had declared, that they were about to no longer be periodically gazing upon his face. Thus they began escorting him, sending [him] forward unto the boat.

CHAPTER 21

1. Now as it happened [for] us finally to be put out to sea – after having been torn away from them – in running a straight course we came into Cos, but then on the succeeding [day] into Rhodes, and from there into Patara [p41 & D add: and Myra].

2. Later, upon finding a boat in the process of passing through, ferrying into Phoenicia, after climbing on board we were sailed away.

3. So then, with Cyprus coming up into view, then later leaving it behind on the port side (the left), we continued sailing on into Syria and came down into (= put into port at) Tyre – for it was there [that] the boat was unloading the cargo.

4. Now after searching and having found the disciples – who through means of the Breath-effect (or: on the basis of the Spirit) repeatedly told Paul not to continue stepping on [board] (or: embarking) unto Jerusalem – we prolonged our stay there seven days.

5. So when there came to be the days to furnish us (fit us out [with provisions] and put us in appropriate condition), after going out, we continued on our journey – all of them, together with women and children, progressively sending us forward and accompanying us till outside of the city. Then, kneeling upon the beach (or: seashore), after speaking toward having things go well for us (or: praying)

6. we at once pulled away from one another in saying goodbye (exchanging farewells) and then we stepped into (or: boarded) the boat – yet those folks returned into their own [homes and affairs].

7. Now we ourselves, finishing the voyage, descended to arrive from Tyre into Ptolemais and, after greeting the brothers, we remained one day with them.

8. So after setting out on the next day, we came into Caesarea. Then, upon entering into the house of Philip, the one who brings wellness and announces goodness and ease (or: good news) – being [a part] of the seven – we remained (or: stayed) with him. [cf 6:3-6, above]

9. **Now by this man there were being four daughters – virgins** (unmarried girls, of marriageable age) **– [who] were from time to time prophesying** (speaking light ahead of time and in front of people).

10. **Yet during the prolonging of our stay [several] more days, a certain prophet** (one who speaks light ahead of time) **from Judea, named Agabus, came down,**
11. **and then, after coming to us and picking up Paul's girding attire** (sash or leather belt; girdle with which he wraps himself) **[and] upon binding his own feet and hands, he said, "Thus is the Set-apart Breath-effect now saying** (or: Now the Holy Spirit is progressively laying out these things), **'In this way will the Jews in Jerusalem proceed binding the man who owns this girding attire – and they will continue in turning [him] over** (transferring and committing [him]) **into [the] hands of [the] ethnic multitudes** (or: nations; people groups that are non-Jewish)!'"
12. **So as we heard these things, both we ourselves and the folks in the place began entreating him not to continue walking up into Jerusalem.**
13. **At that point Paul made a discerning and decisive reply: "What are you folks proceeding in doing by continuing to weep and to progressively crush my heart to pieces? You see, I myself readily make it a habit to be holding [myself] prepared not only to be bound** (or: = imprisoned), **but more than that, at once also to die [upon entering] into the midst of Jerusalem for the sake of** (or: over [circumstances concerning]) **the Name of the Lord Jesus!"**
14. **So at his not being convinced or persuaded, we grew calm and became silent, [all; or: various ones] saying, "Let the will** (or: desire, intent, resolve, design) **of the Lord** [= Yahweh or Christ] **come to be** (be birthed; = be [done])."

15. **Later, after these days, upon furnishing, preparing and packing on our baggage, we began walking up into Jerusalem.**
16. **Now some of the disciples from Caesarea also came with us, proceeding in leading [us]** [D adds: later coming into a certain village] **to a certain Mnason** [Aleph reads: Jason] **of Cyprus, a disciple [from the] beginning with whom we would lodge and be received as guests.**
17. [D reads: Then departing from there], **with our coming to be [arrived] into the midst of Jerusalem, the brothers** (= community of believers) **favorably and gladly welcomed and received us.**
18. **So on the following [day], Paul was proceeding to be entering in with us to [meet with] Jacob** (or: James). **All the older men** (or: elders) **came to be present, as well.**
19. **Then, after greeting and embracing them, he began leading out with a detailed account, unfolding one by one each of the things which God had done among the ethnic multitudes** (= the non-Jews of the nations) **through his attending service.**

20. **Now after hearing [these things] they began giving the glory and ascribing the reputation to God** [D and other MSS: the Lord (= Yahweh, or, Christ)]. **Besides this, they said to him, "Brother, you are now observing and noticing how many tens of thousands there are among the Jews of those having trusted and are continuing in believing – and they all continue humbly from their beginning being zealots of the Law** (or: zealous about the Law).
21. **"Yet they have been orally instructed concerning you, that you are repeatedly** (or: habitually) **teaching all the Jews down through the ethnic multitudes** (or: nations; non-Jews) **an apostasy away** (a revolt; a standing away) **from Moses, constantly telling them not to be circumcising [their] children, nor even to be living their lives** (continually walking about) **in** (by; with) **the customs.**
22. **"What therefore is it** (= What is to be done; What is the solution)**? At any rate** (or: By all means) **it is now compelling for a multitude to come together, for they are going to hear that you have come.**
23. **"Therefore, at once do this which we are now saying to you. With us are four men presently having a vow** (or: holding a religious commitment on behalf of well-being) **[placed] upon them** [or, with other MSS: from themselves (= voluntarily taken)].
24. **"Taking these men along, be ritually purified together with them and pay the expenses for them to the end that they will proceed shaving [their] heads – and everyone will proceed in coming to know that what they have been orally instructed concerning you** (= that the rumor about you) **is nothing, but to the contrary you yourself are also habitually observing the elements and keeping in line, constantly watching, guarding and maintaining the Law!** [cf Heb. 5:12; 2 Pet. 3:10]
25. **"Now concerning those of [the] ethnic multitudes** (or: nations; non-Jews) **[who] have believed and now trust,** [D adds: they presently having nothing to say to you, for you see,] **we ourselves sent**

forth a letter which we wrote, deciding and giving our judgment for them to be constantly **guarding themselves against** (= habitually avoid and abstain from) **both idol sacrifices** (or: meat sacrificed to idols) **and blood, as well as something that was strangled** [i.e., so the blood was not drained out], **and also sexual impurity** (or: fornication; prostitution; infidelity; [cf Lev. 18:3, 6-23])."

26. **Thereupon on the next day, after taking the men along then being ceremonially purified together with them, Paul entered into the Temple complex and continued being there while giving thorough notice [to the priests or Levites] of the date when the period of purification would be completed** (or: the [number] of days [remaining] for the fulfillment of the cleansing period), **at which time an offering would be presented** (or: a sacrifice would be offered) **over** (= on behalf of) **each one of them.**

27. **So as the seven days were being about to be concluding, the [fanatical and extremist religious] Jews from the Asian [district], upon catching a view and gazing upon him** [i.e., Paul] **in the midst of the Temple complex, began pouring [themselves into the midst], together with [the] whole crowd, to mix and stir up confusion – then they laid [their] hands on him,**

28. **repeatedly crying out, "Men! Israelites! Come help [us]... now** (Run immediately to our cry)**! This man is the person who is constantly teaching all people everywhere against the People** [= Jews or Israelites] **and the Law and this** [Concordant text adds: holy] **Place! Still more than this, he also brought Greeks into the Temple complex and has thus made this set-apart and sacred Place common** (= profane, contaminated and defiled)**!"**

29. **You see, they were folks who had been previously seeing Trophimus the Ephesian together with him** [i.e., Paul] **in the city, whom they had been presuming – from what is customary – that Paul had brought into the Temple complex.**

30. **And so with this, the whole city was set in violent motion** (or: disturbed and stirred up) **and there came to be a running together of the people. Then, with getting a hold on** (or: grabbing) **Paul, they began dragging him outside of the Temple complex – and at once the doors were closed and bolted** (or: locked) **[by the Levites].**

31. **And then, while [they were] seeking to kill him, a report that [the] whole of Jerusalem was being progressively poured together in turmoil reached the commander** (or: tribune) **of the battalion** (or: squadron – normally 600 Roman soldiers),

32. **who from that same moment ran** (or: rushed) **down upon them, taking along soldiers and centurions** (officers in charge of 100 men)**. Now upon seeing the commander and the soldiers, they at once stopped beating Paul.**

33. **At that point the commander** (or: tribune), **drawing near at hand, took hold of him** (= arrested him)**. Then he gave orders [for him] to be bound with two chains, and began inquiring who he might be and what it is he had done.**

34. **Now some within the mob began shouting out one thing, other folks something else. So with his not being able to know the certainty [of the matter] because of the uproar and tumult, he gave orders for him to be led into the barracks** (or: fortress).

35. **But when he came to be upon the stairs, the situation presented the need for him to proceed by being picked up and carried by the soldiers – because of the violence of the crowd,**

36. **for you see, the great mass of the people kept following, repeatedly crying out, "Take him up and be doing away with** (= killing) **him!"**

37. **But just as he is about to be led into the barracks, Paul proceeds in saying to the commander, "Is it permitted, from [my] existing [situation], for me to say something to you?" So he affirmed, "You know Greek!**

38. **"Consequently, you are certainly not the Egyptian – the one who was stirring up a revolt and then leading the four thousand 'men of the dagger'** (= assassins or terrorists) **into the desert some time ago** (or: before these days)."

39. **So Paul said, "I myself am in fact a Jew, a man from** (= a native of; [D adds: having been born in]) **Tarsus in Cilicia, a citizen of a distinguished and illustrious** (or: no insignificant) **city. So please, will you permit me to speak to the people?"**

40. **Now after his giving permission, Paul, standing on the stairs, gestures – motioning down with [his] hand – to the people. Then, with it becoming perfectly quiet, he shouted to [them] in the Hebrew** [*p*74 & A read: in his own] **language** (or: dialect), **saying:**

CHAPTER 22

1. **"Men! Brothers** (= Fellow Jews) **and fathers! Listen, and hear my defense to you now!"**

2. **Well, upon hearing that he was now loudly addressing them in the Hebrew language** (or: dialect), **they provided even more quietness of behavior** [D reads: became more calm and tranquil]. **And so he continued affirming,**
3. **"I myself am a man [who is] a Jew having been born in Tarsus of Cilicia, but having been nourished, trained and educated in this city at the feet of Gamaliel – disciplined and instructed corresponding to and in accord with the strictness, accuracy and precision of the ancestral Law** (or: the Law received from the fathers); **continuing under a beginning of being God's zealot** (or: progressing from a humble beginning, being zealous concerning God), **just as all of you yourselves are today!**
4. **"I – who quickly gave pursuit and persecuted this Way, to the extent of death, repeatedly binding and handing over** (committing; transferring) **into prison both men and women,**
5. **"as both the chief priest and the entire body of elders continue bearing witness** (or: giving testimony) **to** (or: for; with) **me, from whom also receiving letters to** [D adds: all] **the brothers** (= fellow Jews) **– I was continuing my journey into Damascus, intending to be bringing also those [of this Way] being there, bound** (= as prisoners), **into Jerusalem, so that they could** (or: would) **be punished.**

6. **"Now it happened to me, during going my way and when drawing near to Damascus, at about midday, suddenly and unexpectedly from out of the sky** (or: forth from the midst of heaven; out of the atmosphere) **a bright and intense Light flashed all around me like lightning!**
7. **"At this, I fell onto the road** (literally: the bottom), **and I heard a Voice repeatedly saying to me, 'Saul... Saul! Why do you continue pursuing and persecuting Me?'**
8. **"So I myself gave a considered reply, 'Who are You, Lord** (or: Master; Sir)**?' Then He said to me, 'I am** (or: I Myself Am) **Jesus, the Nazarene, Whom you yourself continue pursuing and persecuting!'**

9. **"Now the men being with me indeed had a view of and gazed at the Light** [D and others add: and came to be afraid], **yet they did not hear the One presently speaking to me.**
10. **"At that I said, 'What should or can I do, or shall I proceed doing, Lord** (Master)**?' So the Lord said to me, 'After standing up** (or: Upon rising), **continue on your way into Damascus, and there it will be spoken to you about all things which it has been arranged and aligned for you to do.'**
11. **"So, since I continued being in a condition of not seeing – from the glory** (= dazzling brightness) **of that Light – I came into Damascus, being progressively led by the hand under [the directing and assistance] of the folks being with me.**

12. **"Now Ananias, a certain well-received adult man who took a good hold on things that corresponded to the Law, [which fact] was being constantly attested by all the Jews normally dwelling** [*p*41 and others add: in Damascus] **so that he was held in high regard.**
13. **"Upon coming to me and standing near, he said to me, 'Brother Saul** (or: Saul, my brother)**! Look up and see again!' And I myself at once looked up into him and saw again** (or: recovered my sight) **– in that very hour** (= right then)**!**
14. **"So he said to me, 'The God of our fathers** (or: ancestors) **took you in hand beforehand** (or: handled you in advance; or: hand-picked you ahead of time) **to know His will and to gain insight about the effect of His intent, and the result of His design and purpose, by intimate experience, and then to see the Fair and Equitable One** (the One who is Rightwised, Just, in right relationships, and who embodies the Way pointed out), **and to hear [the] voice forth from His mouth,**

15. "'because (or: that) **you will be a witness for** (or: to; with; by) **Him to all mankind** (or: you will be evidence about Him with a view toward all humanity) **of what** (or: concerning which things) **you have seen and heard** (or: and now hear).

16. "'**And so now, what are you presently waiting for** (or: why do you continue delaying)**? Upon rising, at once wash yourself – and thus wash off your mistakes** (your failures to hit the target; your sins) **– in and by calling upon His Name!**

> (or: While standing up, through calling upon His Name immerse yourself [in this Name; in this knowledge and purpose; in Him], and so wash away your errors).'

17. "**Now it happened to me, after returning into Jerusalem and then during my continuing in projecting thoughts and words toward having events and situations being well** (or: praying), **within the midst of the Temple complex, I came to be** (or: was birthed) **within an ecstasy**

18. "**and then to see Him presently saying to me, 'Hurry up and get out of Jerusalem quickly, because they will not accept your testimony** (or: witness; evidence) **concerning Me.'**

19. "**And so I myself said, 'Lord, they themselves continue being well-versed and understand that in one synagogue after another I myself was repeatedly imprisoning and flaying** (flogging) **the folks trusting and believing upon You.**

20. "'**Then when the blood of Stephen, Your witness, was being progressively poured out, I myself was also standing by and continuing in consenting** (approving; endorsing) **as well as guarding the outer garments of those in the process of assassinating** (murdering) **him.'**

21. "**Then He said to me, 'Get on your way, because I Myself will be sending you off with a mission, out into the ethnic multitudes** (or: nations; non-Jews; Gentiles) **afar off.'"**

22. **Now they kept on listening to his [speech; presentation] – down to this word! Then they suddenly raised their voice, [together and one after another] repeatedly saying, "Be lifting the likes of him away from the earth** (or: Be taking such a person off the Land), **for he has not continued fit or suitable** (it has not reached the level) **for him to keep on living!"**

23. **More than this** [p74, Aleph, D and others read: Now], **with their continued crying out and one after another throwing, tossing and flinging off [their] robes and outer garments, then continuing in casting dust into the air,**

24. **the commander** (tribune) **gave orders to proceed in taking him inside, into the barracks, saying [for] him to be progressively interrogated and thoroughly examined with whips** (= to undergo scourging) **so that he can personally come to fully know through what cause** (or: for what reason) **the people were continuing to shout against him in this way.**

25. **Yet as they extend and stretch him forward with the thongs** (or: straps), **Paul says to the centurion, "If a person [be]** (or: Since a man [is]) **a Roman and [is] uncondemned, is it permissible, from out of [his] being [so], for you to be scourging [him]** (= Is it legal for you to flog a Roman who has not been condemned)?"

26. **Well, upon hearing this the centurion, after approaching, reported to the commander, saying,** "[D adds: Consider] **what you are about to be doing, for this man is a Roman [citizen]!"**

27. **So after approaching [Paul], the commander said to him, "Tell me, are you a Roman [citizen]?" So [Paul] affirms, "Yes."** [D reads: So he said, "I am."]

28. **Now the commander, after considering, responds, "I myself, with much capital** (= a large sum of money), **procured for myself this citizenship!" But Paul affirmed, "Yet I myself have even been born [one]** (or: But I by heredity)."

29. **Immediately, therefore, the men being about to be interrogating him at once withdrew** (stood away) **from him. Then the commander** (tribune) **became afraid after becoming fully aware that he is a Roman [citizen], and that** (or: because) **he was the person having bound** (or: imprisoned) **him.**

30. **So on the next day, continuing being determined to know** (or: = find out) **the certainty of the [matter] – just why he continues being accused by the Jews, he loosed him** (unshackled him and released him from prison) **and then commanded the chief priests and all the Sanhedrin** (High Council) **to come together** (to assemble). **Next, bringing Paul down, he had inserted [him] into the midst, making [him] stand among them.**

CHAPTER 23

1. **So Paul, looking intently** (riveting his gaze) **at the Sanhedrin** (Jewish High Council) **said, "Men! Brothers** (= Fellow Jews)! **I myself have lived and behaved as a citizen in all good conscience to and for God** (or: with a completely clear joint-knowledge and with virtuous shared-sight, I have conducted my citizenship in God and managed the affairs of [His] city for God), **up to this day!"**

2. **But Ananias** [note: son of Nebedaeus], **the chief priest** [note: nominated as high priest by Herod, King of Chalcis in A.D. 48], **placed a directive upon those standing beside him to proceed in striking his mouth.**
3. **At that point Paul said to him, "God is now about to be striking you, you whitewashed wall! And so you yourself are now sitting, continuing in judging me according to the Law, and at the same time [you are] transgressing the Law** (acting illegally) **[by] proceeding in ordering me to be repeatedly struck** (or: beaten)!"

4. **So those standing by say, "Are you now reproaching and reviling God's chief priest?"**
5. **At this Paul affirmed, "Brothers, I had not seen so I was not aware that he is a chief priest, for it has been written,**
        'You will not continue speaking badly [of] a ruler of your people.'" [Ex. 22:28]

6. **Now Paul, knowing from personal experience that in the Sanhedrin** (High Council) **the one part** (or: party) **is of [the] Sadducees, yet the different part [is] of [the] Pharisees, suddenly cries out, "Men! Brothers** (= Fellow Jews)! **I myself am a Pharisee, a son of Pharisees! I myself am presently being judged** (or: am now standing on trial) **concerning [the] expectation – even [the] resurrection of dead people!"**
7. **Well, during his saying this, there came to be a taking of a stand creating a dispute between Pharisees and Sadducees, and so the whole group was split** (torn apart).
8. **You see, Sadducees are indeed normally saying there is not to be a resurrection: not even agent nor spirit** (or, similar to D.B. Hart: neither [as] a messenger nor [as] a breath-effect). **Yet Pharisees normally concede both** (or: consent and agree to both those things). [cf Mk. 12:18, 25]
9. **So a great outcry broke out with shouts and screaming, and then standing up, some of the scribes** (theologians; Torah experts) **of the party of the Pharisees began fighting through the midst, contending vehemently, as a group saying, "We continue finding nothing wrong** (bad; worthless) **in this person! Now since** (or: if) **a spirit** (or: breath-effect) **or an agent** (or: messenger) **spoke** (or: speaks) **to him..."**
10. **Yet, with so much commotion and dispute occurring and becoming so violent, the commander – fearing [that] Paul would at some point be torn in two** (or: pulled apart) **by them – commanded the troop** (band of soldiers) **to bring [him] into the barracks after descending to snatch him out of the midst of them.**

11. **Now in the following night, the Lord** [= Christ or Yahweh], **while standing by him, said, "Be increasingly receiving courage and confidence, for as you delivered a thorough witness of the things concerning Me into Jerusalem, in this way it continues binding and necessary for you yourself to deliver a witness** (a testimony; evidence) **into Rome also."**

12. **But with it becoming day, those** [other MSS: certain ones of the] **Jews, constructing a plot, placed themselves under an oath, all swearing neither to eat nor to drink until which [time, or, occasion] they would kill off Paul.**
13. **Now there were more than forty men forming this oath-bound conspiracy,**
14. **who, upon coming to the chief priests and the older men** (or: elders), **said, "We placed ourselves under an oath in a gift devoted [to God] to taste nothing until which [time, or, occasion] we can kill off Paul.**
15. **"Now therefore, you men make it appear** (show it in such a light so as to convey the idea) **to the commander along with the Sanhedrin** (High Council) **as though [you are] intending to continue**

investigating, being now about to thoroughly examine and more accurately know the things concerning him – so that he would bring him down to you folks. Yet before the [situation for] him to draw near to be at hand [*p*48 adds: to you] (= before he gets here), **we ourselves are ready and prepared to assassinate him.**

16. **However, the son of Paul's sister, upon hearing about the ambush – while happening to be present at the side – then, after entering into the barracks, reported [it] to Paul.**
17. **So Paul, calling one of the centurions to him, said, "Take this young man to the commander** (tribune), **for he is having something to report to him."**
18. **Therefore he indeed, taking him along, led [him] to the commander and proceeded affirming, "The prisoner Paul, upon calling [me] to himself, requested me to lead this young man to you. [He] has something to speak to you."**
19. **So the commander, upon taking a hold on his hand and withdrawing apart, back to his own quarters, began inquiring privately, "What is it which you now have to report to me?"**
20. **So he said, "The Jews have set themselves together joining in agreement to ask you, so that tomorrow you would lead Paul down unto the Sanhedrin as though you [were] being about to ascertain something more accurately about him.**
21. **"As for you, therefore, you should not be persuaded by them, for you see more than forty men from their midst continue lying in wait to ambush him – folks who placed themselves under an oath neither to eat nor to drink until which [time, or, occasion] they can assassinate him. And at this time they are ready and prepared, continuing in waiting to receive the promise from you."**

22. **The commander indeed, therefore, released the young man, having charged [him] "to speak out to no one that you have made these things clear to me."**
23. **Then upon calling to himself two specific centurions, he said, "Get two hundred heavy-armed infantry soldiers prepared and ready so that from the third hour of the night** (= at nine o'clock tonight) **they can march clear to Caesarea – also seventy mounted cavalry and two hundred spearmen.**
24. **"Besides this, provide riding mounts so that being mounted, they can bring Paul safely through to Felix the governor."**
25. **[Then] writing a letter having this form** (or: model), **[he said]:**
26. **"Claudius Lysias to the strongest and most mighty governor Felix: Greetings** (Be rejoicing)!
27. **This man, being taken in hand together by the Jews, was also being about to be murdered by them. Standing by with the troop of soldiers, I myself extricated** [*p*48 reads: rescued] **[him], having learned that he is a Roman [citizen].**
28. **Besides this, wishing to fully know the cause for which they had been accusing him, I led him down into their High Council** (Sanhedrin).
29. **I found him being presently accused** (or: indicted) **concerning questions of their Law, but having not even one charge worthy of death or of bonds** (or: imprisonment).
30. **Now with it having been divulged to me [that] there will be a plot against the man, I at that very hour sent [him] to you, also commanding the accusers to be speaking those things against him in your presence. Be strong and in good health** (= Farewell)."

31. **Therefore indeed, having taken things up according to that which had been fully arranged for and ordered to them, these soldiers brought Paul by night into Antipatris.**
32. **But on the next day they returned unto the barracks, allowing the mounted cavalry to continue going off with him,**
33. **who, upon entering into Caesarea and after handing over the letter to the governor – and then, Paul to him – stood at the side.**

34. **Now upon reading [it] and inquiring from what province he is, then ascertaining that [he is] from Cilicia,**
35. **he affirmed, "I will be fully hearing from you whenever your accusers should come to be present also," [then was] commanding him to be guarded within the praetorium of Herod** (Herod's headquarters and official residence).

CHAPTER 24

1. **Now after five days, Ananias the chief** (or: ruling) **priest came down** (or: descended; or: walked down) **with a group of older men** (or: elders) **and Tertullus, a certain forensic orator** (or: lawyer; barrister; advocate), **who as a group brought things to light** (or: gave information; = gave evidence and presented their case) **against Paul to the governor.**

2. **So, at his** [i.e., Paul's] **being called, Tertullus began to proceed in making accusation, by saying, "Happening upon and continuing to experience** (or: enjoy) **much peace and tranquility through you, as well as [the] effects of reforms** (the results of the setting-right of situations and conditions) **continually taking place in and for this nation through your forethought – both in every [way]** (or: at all [times]) **and in all places –**

3. **"we continue receiving from [this] and welcomingly accept [it] with all thankfulness and the goodness of favor, O most strong and mighty Felix!**

4. **"Now, so that I should not cut-in on or interrupt you any further** (or: detain you any longer), **I am now entreating you, in your abundant, lenient reasonableness and fairness, to listen to us briefly.**

5. **"You see, [we have been] finding this man [to be] a plague and a pest – also repeatedly putting insurrections in motion among the Jews down through the inhabited land** (= the Empire), **besides [being] a spearhead** (or: ringleader; one standing in the first rank) **of the sect** (or: party; or: heresy) **of the Nazarenes,**

6. **"who also tried to profane** (ritually defile; desecrate) **the Temple, whom also we seized.**

    [note: 6b through 8a not found in early MSS and omitted by most texts; found in TR; bracketed by Griesbach; represented only by E and later MSS which add: "and intended to judge according to our Law. But Lysias, the commander, upon arriving with a great force, led {him} away out of our hands, commanding his accusers to come and appear before you]

8. **"from whose** [i.e., Paul's] **presence at your side, you yourself, by examining and again judging, will be able to fully come to know in person about all of these things of which we ourselves continue accusing him."**

9. **With that, the Jews also joined together in the attack** (or: the charge; the indictment), **continuing in alleging these things to continue holding thus** (= to be true).

10. **Following this, with the governor nodding to him to be now speaking, Paul gave a discerning response:**
    "Being fully versed in the knowledge of you being a judge of this nation for many years, in a good spirit and with passion I readily proceed making a defense about the things concerning myself.

11. **"With your being able to fully recognize and verify for yourself that for me there have not been more than twelve days since I walked up into Jerusalem, intending to be worshiping,**

12. **"and that they found me – neither within the Temple complex, nor within the synagogues, nor down through the city – neither dialoging or arguing with anyone, nor in the act of creating a tumult by collecting folks to be taking a stand on some issue, and thus making a mob of the crowd.**

13. **"Nor even are they now able to substantiate to you** (or: set beside you [evidence]) **concerning that for which at this time they continue accusing me.**

14. **"Yet this I now speak in agreement** (or: confess) **to you, that according to the Way** (or: corresponding to the Path) **– which they are normally calling a sect** (or: maintaining [to be] a party; or: terming heresy) **– in this way am I habitually performing sacred service to the God of** (or: pertaining to) **the fathers** (or: the ancestral God), **constantly trusting, believing and being loyal to all the things corresponding to the Law** (= the Torah) **and having been written within the Prophets –**

15. **"habitually holding** (or: constantly having) **an expectation [directed] into** [other MSS: with a view toward] **God, which also these men themselves continue anticipating and entertaining: a resurrection presently continues to be impending [which] will continue to be of both fair and equitable people as well as of unfair and inequitable folks**

(or: there now is about to be a resurrection. [This] will continue to be {or: [It] will progress to exist being} both of rightwised folks who are in right relationship in the Way pointed out, and of unrightwised folks who are not in right relationship nor in union with the Way pointed out).

16. **"Within this I myself also habitually exercise, exert myself, train and make endeavors: to be constantly having** (or: habitually holding) **a conscience free from striking toward [others], being inoffensive to God as well as [to] humanity – through all [situations] and at all [times].**

17. **"So intending, through the midst of more years, to make gifts of mercy and offerings unto my nation** (or: ethnic group), **I finally arrived and was present,**

18. **"within which [activities] they found me, having been ceremonially purified, within the Temple complex – not with a crowd, nor with a tumult or uproar!**

19. **"But [there were] certain Jews from the [province of] Asia for whom it continued binding to be present before you, and to be making accusations – if they might continue having anything against me.**

20. **"Or else let these men themselves say what result of wrong-doing, injustice, injury or unfairness they found at my standing before the Sanhedrin** (Jewish High Council),

21. **"other than about this one voice with which I cried out, standing in the midst of them: 'Concerning a resurrection of dead people I myself am presently being judged** (or: separated for a decision) **today, before you people!'"**

22. **However, Felix, perceiving more exactly and being acquainted more accurately with the matters concerning the Way** (or: the Path), **thrust them back from himself** (= postponed and adjourned the proceedings, putting them off), **saying, "Whenever Lysias the commander can come down I will continue more thoroughly coming to know the matters involving you folks."**

23. **Making precise arrangements with the centurion, [he] was giving orders for him to be kept in custody and maintained, besides to continue having a relaxation [in regard to confinement] with both ease for refreshing and privileges, as well as to continue preventing** (or: hindering) **no one of his friends to regularly attend to him and give him assistance.**

24. **So after some days, Felix, happening by with Drusilla his wife – [she] being a Jewess** (or: a Judean woman) **sent for Paul and then heard from him about the faith, trust and confident reliance [being placed] into Christ Jesus** (or: the loyalty unto [the] Anointed Jesus [= Jesus the Messiah]).

25. **Yet during his dialoging and discoursing about eschatological deliverance and justice** (or: being rightwised with righted relationships from covenant inclusion and participation within the Way pointed out), **inner strength and self-control, and then the impending effect of judgment** (separation and evaluation which is about to result in a decision), **Felix – coming to be alarmed with inner fear – gave a decided response: "For the present, be now going your way while continuing to hold this [subject]. Now then, upon getting a fitting opportunity with [you], I will keep on calling for you,"**

26. **– at the same time continuing in expecting that money** (or: the effect of something useful; = a bribe) **will be given to him by Paul, on account of which, repeatedly sending for him even more frequently, he kept on conversing with him.**

27. **Now with two years being fulfilled** (= at the end of two years), **Felix received a successor, Porcius Festus. Yet continuing in desiring to lay up favor for himself with the Jews, Felix left Paul behind imprisoned** (or: bound).

CHAPTER 25

1. **Then Festus, having stepped up to assume the governorship of the province, after three days went up from Caesarea into Jerusalem.**

2. **Along with this, the chief** (ruling; ranking) **priests and the leading** (or: foremost) **men of the Jews brought things to light** (or: gave information; = gave evidence and presented their case) **against Paul and began entreating him,**

3. **repeatedly asking for themselves a favor in regard to him, so that he would himself send after [Paul], [to bring] him into Jerusalem – all the while [themselves] laying an ambush to assassinate him along the road.**

4. Nonetheless, Festus gave a discerning reply, [that] Paul is to continue being kept and observed in Caesarea and that he himself is now soon about to be departing on his way quickly (in haste; = without delay).

5. "Therefore, let those in power among you," he affirmed, "after coming down together, continue making accusations of him – if there is anything out of place in the man."

6. Now after spending no more than eight or ten days among them, then descending into Caesarea, on the next day, when sitting upon the elevated platform in the public court area, he gave orders for Paul to be brought [to him].

7. So at his coming to be present, the Jews who had come down from Jerusalem stood round about him progressively bringing down many and weighty reasons for accusations and results of charges against [him] – which they were having no strength of argument to demonstrate or prove,

8. with Paul's presently refuting in defense, that "Neither unto the Law (= Torah) of the Jews (or: Judeans) nor unto the Temple, nor unto Caesar did I commit any sin or do anything in error or failure, nor commit any wrong to offend!"

9. Now Festus, presently desiring and intending to lay up favor with the Jews (or: Judeans), in making a calculated response to Paul, said, "Are you now willing to be going up into Jerusalem, to be judged there before me concerning these matters?"

10. But Paul said, "I am taking a stand (or: I am presently standing) before the court of Caesar, in which place it is binding for me to be judged (or: where I must stand trial)! I have done not even one thing wrong [to the] Jews (or: pertaining to Judeans) as you yourself are now fully coming to find out in finer fashion (or: are presently more ideally recognizing).

11. "If, then on the one hand, I am habitually doing wrong (committing injury, injustice or unfairness) and have practiced anything worthy of death, I am not now seeking to be excused from dying (or: presently refusing to die). But since (or: Yet if), on the other hand, there exists not even one thing of which these men continue accusing me, no one has power (or: is able) to hand me over (or: surrender me) to them as a favor. I am now calling upon (or: appealing to) Caesar!"

12. At that point Festus, after conferring with the gathered council, answered decidedly, "You yourself have called upon (or: appealed to) Caesar; before Caesar you will proceed in going!"

13. Now with the elapsing of some days, Agrippa the king and Bernice arrived in Caesarea, paying their respects to Festus.

14. So, as they were spending more days there, Festus submitted the matters regarding Paul to the king, saying, "There is a certain man left a prisoner by Felix

15. "concerning whom, at my coming to be in Jerusalem, the chief (or: ranking) priests and the older men of the Jews (or: elders from the Judeans) brought to light information, while repeatedly asking a decision (or: judgment) of condemnation against him.

16. "– to which men I made the decided reply that it is not [the] custom for Romans to hand over any person as a favor before the one being accused might have the accusers face to face, as well as receive a place for (= have opportunity to make) a defense concerning the indictment (or: charge).

17. "Therefore, with their coming together in this place, on the following [day] – making not one postponement or delay – while sitting on the dais (raised platform in the public hearing area) to convene court, I gave command for the man to be brought [in],

18. "concerning whom, at their being made to take the stand, the accusers were not bringing even one cause for accusation (or: ground for a charge) of [the] bad things (= serious crimes) of which I myself had been supposing (or: suspecting; surmising),

19. "but instead they continued holding (or: having) certain questions aimed at him concerning [their] own reverencing of the animistic powers (or: fear of demons [Hellenistic concept and term: = animistic influence] and superstition of unseen powers) and about a certain Jesus – a person having died – whom Paul keeps on alleging to be alive (or: was continuing in claiming to be living now).

20. "So, I myself, continuing in being perplexed (without means or a way) concerning these questions and disputes, proceeded to ask if he might be willing to be journeying into Jerusalem and there to be judged (= stand trial) concerning these [matters].

21. "But at Paul's personally calling upon (or: making an appeal) to be kept and reserved unto the investigation and determination (= judicial hearing) by the August One (or: Venerable One; Revered;

= Augustus; = the Emperor), **I gave orders for him to be kept and observed until which [time, or, situation] I can** (or: would) **send him up to Caesar."**

22. **And so Agrippa said to Festus, "I myself was also wanting and intending to listen to** (or: hear) **this person." "Tomorrow," [Festus] affirms, "you will** (or, as an aorist subjunctive: may; can; should) **proceed to be hearing him."**

23. **Therefore, on the next day, at [the] coming of Agrippa, as well as Bernice – with much pageantry for making an "appearance" – and their entering into the audience hall, together with both military commanders** (tribunes) **and the prominent men of the city, and then with Festus giving the command, Paul was led [in].**

24. **Then Festus affirms, "King Agrippa, and all you men being present with us, you are now looking at this person about whom the entire multitude of the Jews interceded** (or: petitioned) **to me, both in Jerusalem and in this place, repeatedly shouting [that] by all means it continues necessary and binding for him to continue living no longer.**

25. **"Now as for myself, I grasped** (caught; = found out about) **him to have committed nothing worthy** (or: deserving) **of death, yet when this man himself was calling upon** (= making an appeal to) **the August One** (= the Emperor), **I decided to proceed in sending [him] –**

26. **"concerning whom I continue having nothing certain to write to [my] Lord** (= the Sovereign; or: [our] Owner). **On this account I bring him forth before you people – and most of all, before you, King Agrippa – so that with the examination having taken place, I would have something to write.**

27. **"For it now seems illogical and unreasonable for me** (or: absurd to me), **while proceeding in sending a prisoner, not also to give a sign of** (or: to give some sign indicating) **the charges against him."**

CHAPTER 26

1. **So Agrippa affirms to Paul, "It is now permitted for you to proceed in speaking concerning** [other MSS: over; on behalf of; = for] **yourself." At that point Paul, while stretching out [his] hand, began to make a defense:**

2. **"King Agrippa, I have considered myself fortunate, happy and blessed at now being about to proceed in making a defense before you, today, concerning all [the] things of which I am being repeatedly charged by [these] Jews** (or: indicted under Judeans),

3. **"especially with you being an expert with personal experience and knowledge, being versed both [in] all the customs and also [the] questions** (results of seeking [understanding], and, controversial issues) **which relate to Jews** (= Jewish culture and religion). **For this reason, in my need I now beg you to listen and hear me with indulgence** (or: being long before rushing into strong emotions; patiently).

4. **"So then: all the Judeans** (or: all these Jews) **have seen and are thus acquainted with my kind of life, and its course, springing into being out of my youth with a beginning from within the midst of my nation** (or: ethnic group), **and more so within Jerusalem,**

5. **"previously having a personal acquaintance and intimate knowledge about me from that earlier period [so as] to continue testifying, giving witness one after another – if they would continue being willing – that in accord with the strictest sect** (or: party) **of this ritual and form of worship** (or: religious discipline; system of external observances) **of ours, I lived** (or: I live) **a Pharisee.**

6. **"And yet now I stand being repeatedly** (or: constantly) **judged** (or: put on trial) **based upon [the] expectation** (or: hope) **of the promise having been birthed into our fathers** (= ancestors) **by God –**

7. **"unto which [promise] our twelve-tribed [people], constantly rendering sacred service in earnest perseverance night and day, is continuously hoping and expecting to attain. Concerning this expectation I am now being indicted** (or: charged) **by the Jews, O king.**

8. **"Why does it continue being judged unbelievable** (or: decided [as] incredible) **by** (or: among) **you folks – since** (or: that) **God periodically** (or: habitually; constantly) **raises dead people?**

9. **"Therefore within myself I, for one, used to think it to continue binding** (or: had the opinion [that] it was then necessary) **to commit** (or: perform) **many acts in opposition against the Name of Jesus, the Nazarene,**

10. **"which I did, even in Jerusalem. Furthermore, I myself also locked up many of the set-apart folks** (holy ones; saints) **in prisons, receiving the authority from the chief** (or: ranking) **priests, and more than this, I brought down a pebble** (= cast my vote) **against them – when one after another they were being taken back to be killed.**

11. **"Then, while continuing in punishing them in vengeance – down through the [various] synagogues – I kept on trying to force** (or: compel) **[them] to blaspheme** (speak abusively about [God]), **besides keeping them in the midst of insane rage which completely surrounded them, and continued pressing forward to persecute [them] even into the cities outside [Palestine].**

12. **"Within the midst of which [activities], while traveling on my journey unto Damascus with [the] authority, as well as a commission which gave permission, from the chief** (or: ranking) **priests,**

13. **"[being] down on the road at midday, I saw, O king, a light from [the] sky** (or: from heaven) – **more intense than** (or: above) **the brightness and brilliance of the sun – shining and flashing around me and the folks then traveling with me.**

14. **"Next, at all of us falling down to the ground, I heard a Voice proceeding in saying to me in the Hebrew language** (or: dialect) **'Saul, O Saul! Why do you continue pressing forward to persecute Me? To keep on kicking [your heel] toward [the] goads** (sharp points; e.g., as with an ox-goad; = futilely resisting or 'flogging a dead horse') **[makes it] hard for you** (or: = can hurt you)!'

15. **"So I myself said, 'Who are you, Sir** (or: Master; Lord)**?' But the Lord** (or: The Owner; [= Christ]) **said, 'I Myself am Jesus** (or: I exist in Myself being Jesus) – **Whom you continue pressing forward to persecute!**

16. **"'But now, get up and stand upon your feet! You see, into this [situation; commission] and unto this [purpose] I became seen by you** (or: was made to appear to you)**: to take you in hand beforehand** (or: to handle you in advance; or: to hand-pick you ahead of time) **[to be] a subordinate** (one who is a rower of a ship's crew) **and a witness** (one who testifies and gives evidence) – **both of things in which you saw Me, and of things in which I will continue being seen by** (or: in; with) **you –**

17. **"'now Myself choosing you from out of the midst of the People** (or: repeatedly taking you from out of the midst of, i.e., rescuing you from, the People), **as well as from out of the midst of the ethnic multitudes** (or: nations; non-Jews) **unto whom I Myself am progressively sending you off with a mission:**

18. **"'to open back up their eyes again; to turn [their eyes; or: them] back: away from darkness** (a realm of the shadow; dimness and obscurity) **into Light, even from the authority and privilege of the adversary** (or: that is, from the right which comes from out of being the opponent), **and upon God; to receive a flowing away of deviations and a release from failures, mistakes and occasions of missing the goal** (or: a forgiveness of sins) **and an allotted inheritance among and in union with the folks having been – and now remaining – set apart in the trust into Me and for the loyalty unto Me**
    (or: centered within the people made holy by The Faithfulness – [received] into the midst of Me; or: within those having been consecrated for fidelity, sanctified with faith and now set apart to trusting conviction – unto Me).'

19. **"Wherefore, O King Agrippa, I did not come to be unpersuaded in** (or: become disobedient to) **the heavenly sight** (or: the vision from the atmosphere,) **which was seen,**

20. **"but to the contrary, both to the folks in Damascus, first, and then in Jerusalem – besides all the country of Judea – and later to the ethnic multitudes** (the nations; the non-Jews) **I kept on reporting the message to be progressively changing one's way of thinking, mindset, perspective and state of consciousness, as well as to be turning back upon** (= oriented to) **God, while habitually performing works** (or: constantly committing deeds and practicing acts) **worthy of that change of mind and state of consciousness, that embody the value equal to [a turn to God].**

21. **"On account of these things, a group of Jews – upon seizing me within the Temple complex – on their own began attempting at once to thoroughly manhandle [me], and probably kill [me].**

330

22. "But then, all of a sudden obtaining the help and assistance from God which was right on target, I have taken a stand – and still stand until this day – repeatedly testifying (attesting and giving evidence) to both small and great, continuously saying nothing outside of those things which both the Prophets and Moses spoke (or: speak) concerning people being presently about to be birthed, and with regard to progressively impending [events] to be one-after-another occurring:

23. "that the Christ [would be] a suffering [Messiah, and] (or: that the Anointed, [is] One subject to experience and suffering, [and]) that He, [as] first forth from out of a resurrection of dead people, [would] continue about to be repeatedly and progressively announcing Light* to the public, as a herald – both to and for the People [= the Jews and Israel] as well as to, for and among the ethnic multitudes (the nations; the non-Jews; the Goyim; the Gentiles)." [*2 Tim. 4:1b]

24. Now with his progressively making [his] defense [in] these [statements], Festus then affirms with the voice elevated (= shouts loudly), "You are progressively going insane (stark raving mad), Paul! The many writings (or: = the effects of much learning) progressively spin you around into madness (mania and insanity)!"

25. But Paul is then affirming, "I am not going insane (proceeding into mania or madness), O most mighty Festus, but to the contrary I have been presently uttering an elevated and weighty discourse of declarations and gush-effects about reality (or: truth) and a sound, healthy frame of mind which has been restored to its original perspectives with saved and healed thought patterns (= true sanity)!

26. "You see, the king – to whom I am now speaking, continuing in the outspoken freedom with the rights of a bold citizen who has no fear of retribution – continues being adept and well versed concerning these [matters], for I continue persuaded and convinced that not one of these things continues to elude him or escape [his] notice. You see, this is not a thing having been committed in a corner (= obscurely, as in some back alley).

27. "Do you continue faithful and loyal to the Prophets (or: Are you presently trusting and believing in the Prophets), King Agrippa? I have seen and so know that you continue faithful and loyal [to] (or: presently trust and believe) [the Prophets]."

28. Yet Agrippa [said] to Paul, "In a little [time] and within a few [words] are you now proceeding in persuading me – to make [me] a Christian? (or: You continue convincing, in a small [way], to make me a Christian!)"

29. So Paul [responds], "I would ever claim it for the goodness in God (or: speak in boast to the well-being [that is] by God) [for] both in a little [time] as well as even in a great (= long) [space of time] not only you, but further also all those presently hearing me today, to at some point come to be folks of such a sort as I myself presently am – with the exception (or: yet at the outside) of these bonds!"

30. [As a group] both the king and the governor, along with Bernice and the folks that had continued sitting together with them, arose,

31. and as they were withdrawing they kept on speaking to one another, [each one] in turn saying that this person continues committing (or: practicing; performing) nothing warranting (or: deserving; worthy of) death or even bonds (= imprisonment).

32. So Agrippa affirmed to Festus, "This man was able to have been released, if he had not called upon (or: appealed to) Caesar."

CHAPTER 27

1. Now as it was decided for us to be presently sailing off into Italy, they handed over (transferred; committed) Paul, besides also some different prisoners (= folks who were prisoners for reasons different than for Paul), to a centurion (Roman officer normally in charge of 100 soldiers) named Julius, who was a part of an Augustan military cohort (or: [the] Imperial regiment or squadron).

2. So after stepping on [board] the boat (or: ship) [on its way from the seaport] in Adramyttium [which was] presently about to continuing sailing into the places down along the [province of] Asia, we were put out [to sea] – there being with us Aristarchus, a Macedonian man from Thessalonica.

3. **After this, on a different [day], we were put in at** (or: led down [from the high sea] into) **Sidon. With this, Julius, dealing kindly and being helpful and humane to Paul, permitted [him] to obtain and enjoy casual care and attention which hit the spot – after [his] going on his way [to visit] the friends** (= either personal acquaintances who had affection for him, or, fellow believers who were referred to in this way).

4. **Later, from there, upon putting out [to sea] we sailed under the [lee, or, shelter] of Cyprus, because of the winds being contrary.**
5. **After this, sailing through** (= across) **the open sea – down along Cilicia and Pamphylia – we put in at** (or: made our way down into) **Myra in Lycia.**
6. **And there, with the centurion finding an Alexandrian ship in route sailing unto Italy, he had us board it** (or: step on into the midst of it).
7. **Then, after continuously sailing slowly and with difficulty during a considerable number of days, after coming to be down by Cnidus** [note: on a peninsula of the southwest part of Asia Minor] **with the wind continuing in not allowing us to approach, we sailed under the** [lee, or, shelter, of] **Crete, down by** (= off the coast of) **Salome** (or: Salmone),
8. **and then, with difficulty, progressively skirting** (or: coasting along) **it, we came into a place [that was] by some folks being normally called Ideal Harbors** (or: Fine and Beautiful Seaports; Fair Havens), **near which was [the] city [of] Lasea.**

9. **Now with a considerable amount of time having elapsed** (i.e., having passed by, and so was now lost), **and sailing being already hazardous – because even the Fast** [i.e., part of the Day of Atonement feast] **had already passed by** [note: thus, around early or mid October, the season of perilous navigation in that area] **– Paul began strongly advising and making recommendation, saying to them again and again,**
10. **"Gentlemen, I continue watching and am noticing that the voyage is soon about to be with damage and much loss** (or: detriment) **– not only of the cargo and of ship, but also of our souls** (= ourselves; or: persons among us)."
11. **Yet the centurion continued being persuaded by the helmsman** (or: pilot; navigator) **and the ship owner** (or: the man chartering the ship; or: shipmaster) **rather than by the things being repeatedly said by Paul.**
12. **Now with the harbor possessing no good placement and being unsuitable with a view toward wintering through the stormy season, the majority gave counsel to at once set sail from there, since somehow they might be able to reach Phoenix** [note: about 40 nautical miles away; approximately 12 hours of sailing with a good wind; this town could also be Phineka or Phenice] **– a harbor of Crete looking down [the] northeast and [the] southeast** [note: depending on whether reading looking into the wind, or looking down the line of the direction the wind is blowing, some interpret this as meaning northwest and southwest] **– to spend the winter.**
13. **So at the south wind blowing gently, folks supposing to have gotten into [their] power the intended purpose, upon weighing** (or: hoisting) **[anchor] they began skirting** (or: coasting along) **very close to Crete.**

14. **However, after not much [time or distance] a hurricane** (or: typhoon) **wind, called a "northeaster"** (or: Euroaquilo), **thrust down against it** [i.e., the ship] **[from mountainous Crete].**
15. **So with the ship being violently gripped and snatched together [amidst the waves], and then not being able to continue keeping the eye face to face to the wind** (or: look the wind in the eye; = keep the boat's head facing into the wind), **after yielding, we began being borne** (or: carried) **along.**
16. **Now upon running under [the lee, or, shelter, of] a small island called Cauda** [other MSS: Clauda], **we had strength – with difficulty – to come to be in control of the dinghy** (or: skiff) **[at the stern],**
17. **after hoisting which, they began using emergency devices** [e.g., ropes; tackle] **for support, continuing in undergirding the ship with braces. All the more continuing in fearing lest they should fall out [of line]** (= stray off course and run aground) **into the shoals** (or: Syrtis, a gulf full of shifting sandbanks and quicksand), **upon lowering the gear** (or: container; perhaps: anchor), **they in this way continued being borne** (or: carried) **along.**

18. **Yet with our continuing in being violently tossed and battered by the storm, on the following [day] they began throwing [things] overboard** (jettisoned [first nonessentials, later, the cargo, to lighten the ship]),
19. **then on the third [day] they hurled out the ship's equipment** (gear; furnishings; tackle) **overboard, with their own hands.**

20. **Now with neither sun nor stars** (or: constellations) **making their normal appearance to shine upon [us, or, the sea] for many days – besides no small winter's storm and rain continuing in lying upon [us] – all hope and expectation of the [situation or chance for] us to continue being kept safe and sound** (or: to proceed to be saved or rescued) **began being taken away from around [us]** (or: being removed as a surrounding environment).
21. **Added to this, with [their] continuing under the rule [of this situation] from its beginning with much lack of appetite, and thus a long period of abstinence from food, Paul, at that point taking a stand within their midst, said, "O gentlemen! It was continuing being a necessity, by being yielding to me as to one in authority and in being persuaded, not to have been put out to sea from Crete – to acquire, besides this damage, also the loss** (detriment and forfeit).
22. **"And yet, in the present circumstances, I am now strongly advising and urging you to be constantly in good spirits with your emotions at ease, for you see, there will be not even one casting away of a soul** (or: throwing off of a person; = loss of life) **from out of your midst, more than** (= except) **the ship,**
23. **"because there stood by me, in this night, an agent of** (or: a messenger from) **the God from Whom as a source I continue existing** (or: of Whom I am and to Whom I belong) **and to Whom, for Whom, in Whom and by Whom I perform as a servant,**
24. **"presently saying, 'Do not be fearing now, Paul. It continues necessary and binding for you to stand beside Caesar – and now, consider this! God has in grace favored, along with you** (or: to you; for you), **all the folks presently sailing with you.'**
25. **"On this account, men, continue being in good spirits and with emotions at ease! You see, by God I continue trusting** (or: I keep on believing in God; I habitually rely on God) **that thus it will continue being – corresponding to the turn of events of what has been spoken to me.**
26. **"So it continues now necessary and binding for us to at some point fall out** (= be cast ashore from running aground) **into some island."**

27. **Now as the fourteenth night fell, during our being continuously carried throughout while tossed first this way then that in the midst of the [Sea of] Adria, down on through to the middle of the night the sailors began suspecting and continued sensing for them to be now leading toward some region or strip of land.**
28. **And so, upon taking soundings** (dropping weighted lines), **they found [the depth of water to be] twenty fathoms** (about 120 feet), **yet after proceeding through a short interval and again taking soundings, they found [it to be] fifteen fathoms.**
29. **With this, progressively fearing lest we should** (or: would) **fall out somewhere down on rough or uneven places** (or: = crash upon some rocks), **having hurled four anchors out of the stern, they continued thinking of having well-being and claiming day to be birthed** (or: to have come to be; [i.e., that it was daytime even though dark]).
30. **So when the sailors continued seeking** (= attempting) **to escape out of the boat and were lowering the dinghy** (or: skiff) **into the sea under pretense** (or: putting forth words as truth) **as though being about to be stretching out anchors from the bow** (or: prow),
31. **Paul said to the centurion and the soldiers, "Unless these men should remain in the ship, you men yourselves are not able to be kept safe** (rescued; delivered; saved)**!"**
32. **At that point the soldiers cut off the ropes of the dinghy** (or: skiff), **and they allowed it to fall off.**

33. **Now until day was progressing in being about to be birthed, Paul kept on encouraging everyone to take their share of food** (nourishment) **at some point, repeatedly saying, "Today [is the] fourteenth day [that] you folks are continuing through to completion without food, constantly focusing [your] imagination toward apprehension and suspenseful anticipation – taking nothing to yourselves at any point.**

34. "Because of this, I continue encouraging you folks to take a share of food (nourishment) at some point, for this is now leading as a support (or: originating as an undergirding), with a view to your personal safety and preservation. You see, not a hair from the head of one of you folks will proceed in being lost!"

35. So upon saying these things and then taking a loaf of bread, he spoke of the good favor in God and gave thanks to God, in the sight of them all, and after breaking it he then started to eat.
36. Then, with everyone coming to be in good spirits and with emotions at ease, they themselves took food (or: nourishment), too.
37. Now we were, all [together], two hundred seventy-six souls (= people) in the ship,
38. and upon being satisfied with food (or: nourishment; = having eating their fill), they began lightening the ship by progressively throwing the grain (= the cargo) out into the sea.

39. So when it came to be day, they continued still unable to recognize (or: accurately know) the land, yet some began to notice and consider a bay having a beach into which they continued deliberating whether they might continue able (or: they were planning, if they now could,) to drive out (= to run aground and beach) the ship.
40. And so, upon removing the anchors from around [the ship] (= casting off), they allowed [them to fall] into the sea while at the same time giving slack to the lashings of the rudders (or: steering paddles). Then, after hoisting the foresail to the wind, they began holding [the ship] on course, steadily heading down into the beach.
41. Now upon falling about into a place (a reef, shoal or sandbank) formed where two opposing currents of the sea flow together, they ran the sailing vessel (or: craft) ashore and the prow (or: bow) – indeed becoming immovable and firmly fixed – remained unshakable, yet the stern began being loosened and destroyed by the violence of the surging waves and continued being smashed up under the pounding of the surf.
42. So [the] counsel (intended plan) of the soldiers came to be that they should kill off the prisoners, lest anyone by swimming out to land could escape through the midst.
43. But the centurion, wanting and intending to bring Paul safely through (or: to fully rescue Paul and keep him safe and sound throughout [the ordeal]), prevented them from [their] intention. Besides that, he gave orders for those being able, after diving off, to proceed to be swimming [and thus] to be out upon the land first,
44. and then [for] the rest [to follow] – some in fact upon planks, yet others upon various pieces from the ship. And in this way it happened for everyone to be brought safely through and be preserved on the land.

CHAPTER 28

1. And so, after having been preserved through the midst [of the sea], we at that point recognized (or: learned; or: came to accurately know by experience) that the island is normally being called Melita.
2. More than this, the foreign-speaking people (or: barbarians; non-Greek-speaking natives or local inhabitants) happening to meet [us] continued to extend to us extraordinary human kindness and affection, for after kindling a fire, they took us all [in] (= extended hospitality to all of us) because of the imminent rain, and because of the cold.

3. Now at Paul's gathering together a large bundle of some dry sticks and then placing it upon the fire, a viper (poisonous snake), coming out [of the bundle] away from the heat, fastened [itself] down on his hand.
4. So as the native people (barbarians; non-Greek speakers) saw the little beast hanging and continuing suspended from his hand, they began saying to one another, "Undoubtedly (or: By all means) this person is a murderer whom – though having been brought safely through from out of the sea – Justice does not allow to continue living."
5. But then, after shaking the little beast off into the fire, he experienced nothing bad,
6. yet they continued apprehensively anticipating (or: expecting) him to be about to be caused to swell and burn with a fever and inflammation, or else to suddenly fall down (or: drop) dead. So

with their continuing in anticipation for a long time and yet observing nothing out of place (= unusual) **being birthed into** (or: happening to) **him, then progressively casting themselves into a change [of perspective and opinion], one after another they went to laying out [the conclusions for] him to be a god** (or: they went to speaking [of] him being a deity, or, a divine person).

7. **Now in the [areas; regions; (= neighborhoods)] around that place were estates** (or: properties) **belonging to the first man** (= foremost resident; or: = governor [as a title]) **of the island, named Publius, who – after taking [us] up and welcomingly receiving [us] with embraces – lodged us as guests [for] three days, in a loving and friendly manner.**
8. **But it had happened** (or: occurred) **[for] the father of Publius to be constantly bed-ridden** (continuously lying down) **while being continuously gripped by intermittent fevers and dysentery** (an intestinal infection), **to whom Paul was entering and then speaking toward having goodness and well-being** (or: praying). **After placing [his] hands on him, he healed him.**
9. **So in relation to this happening, the rest of the folks in the island also, [who were] presently having weaknesses and illnesses, began approaching in a steady procession, and then were being treated or cured, one after another –**
10. **who also honored us with many things of value** (gifts), **and later, while proceeding in being put to sea, they loaded on [board] the things with a view towards [our] needs.**

11. **So now, after three months, we were put to sea in an Alexandrian ship – with the ensign** (figures painted on each side of the prow) **"Sons of Zeus** (or: Castor and Pollux; Dioscuri)**" – which had wintered in the island.**
12. **Later, putting into port at Syracuse, we remained [there]** (or: stayed) **three days.**
13. **From there, tacking about, we arrived at Rhegium. Then with a south wind coming on [us] after one day, we came into Puteoli on the second day,**
14. **where, upon finding brothers** (= fellow believers), **we were called to [their] side and encouraged to stay on [for] seven days. And so in this way we came into Rome.**
15. **And now from there, the brothers** (= fellow believers there) **– after hearing the things about us – came unto a meeting with us** (or: = came to meet us), **as far as the Market Place of Appius** (or: Appii Forum) **and Three Taverns** (or: Inns; Shops), **upon seeing whom, Paul, while speaking of the good favor in God** (or: in giving thanks to God), **received courage and confidence.**
16. **Now when we entered into Rome, it was permitted for Paul to continue dwelling** (or: to proceed staying; to be remaining) **by himself, along with the soldier presently guarding him.**

17. **Then, after three days, he happened to call to himself the folks being the foremost** (those in the leading circle in the community) **of the Jews. So upon their coming together, he proceeded to say to them, "Men... Brothers! I myself, having done nothing contrary** (or: not one thing in opposition) **to the People nor to the customs of the fathers** (or: the paternal and hereditary traditions), **was from the midst of Jerusalem handed over** (transferred) **[as] a prisoner into the hands of the Romans,**
18. **"which folks, after fully examining me and coming up with a decision, were wanting and intending to release [me], because not even one cause for death is to proceed in making a foundational beginning or to continue being an undergirding possession within me.**
19. **"Yet with the Jews incessantly speaking against [this], I was compelled to call upon** (or: appeal to) **Caesar – yet not as though having anything [of which] to be now accusing or bringing charges against my own ethnic and cultural group** (or: nation).
20. **"Therefore, because of this accusation** (or: this reason), **I called you folks to my side: [for you] to see [the situation] and to address [it]** (or: to see [you folks] and to speak to [you]), **for you see, I continue with this chain lying around me** (or: continue lying encompassed by this chain) **on account of the hope and expectation of Israel."**

21. **So they said to him, "We ourselves neither received letters concerning you from Judea, nor has anyone of the brothers** (= fellow Jews) **coming along reported back or spoken anything harmful** (disadvantageous; malicious; bad) **about you.**
22. **"But we continue considering it valuable** (worthwhile; deserving) **to hear from you, at your side** (or: personally), **what things you are normally thinking and what things compose your disposition and frame of mind. Indeed, you see, concerning this sect** (= denomination; chosen opinion; heresy),

it is personally known to us that it is continuously being spoken against and contradicted everywhere."

23. Then, having themselves arranged a day with him, more folks came to him, into [his] place of lodging, to whom he continued setting forth, explaining from out of [his] midst, while progressively giving thorough evidence and double witness of God's reign (or: the sovereign influence, actions and kingdom of God), besides constantly using persuading and convincing [reasoning with] them concerning Jesus – both from the Law (= Torah) of Moses and from the Prophets – from early morning until evening.

24. And so [some] folks, on the one hand, began being progressively persuaded and convinced by (or: in) the things being continuously spoken and laid out, yet on the other hand, [other] folks continued without faith and trust (or: persisted in unbelief).

25. So, continuing in being out of harmony (dissonant; discordant; without symphony; = at odds and in disagreement) toward one another, they began loosing themselves away (continued dismissing themselves, one after another) with Paul's speaking one gush-effect (or: comment; declaration): "The set-apart Breath-effect (or: Holy Spirit) beautifully (finely; ideally; aptly; fittingly) speaks (or: spoke) through Isaiah the prophet – to your fathers – saying,

26. "'Go your way at once to this People and say, "By listening (or: In hearing), you people will continue hearing (or: listening) and yet by no means would you understand (or: could you make things flow together). And then, while constantly looking and observing, you folks will continue looking and observing, and yet by no means would you see (or: could you perceive).

27. "You see, the heart of this People was made fat and thick (fleshy and stout; clotted and coarse; massive and gross; = thick-witted and stupid) and with [their] ears they hear heavily (= with difficulty and without response), and they squint or close their eyes – lest at some point they would (or: could) see with [their] eyes and should hear with [their] ears, and would understand (make things fit together) with the heart, and then could turn about and return – and so, I will proceed progressively (or: one-after-another) healing them!'" [Isa. 6:9-10]

28. "Therefore, continue letting it be known by you folks that this restoration to health and wholeness – this rescue, deliverance and salvation – was (or: has been) sent off to, for, and among the ethnic people groups (the multitudes of the nations)! And they themselves will keep on listening, then in and for themselves will continue (or: be progressively) hearing!"
[vs. 29 not in any early MSS]

30. Now he remained in his own hired house two whole years, and continued welcomingly receiving all the folks periodically or regularly coming their way in to him,

31. continuously and progressively making public proclamation and heralding the reign of God (or: God's kingdom and sovereign influence), as well as habitually teaching the things concerning the Lord [p74 reads, instead of "Lord": the salvation and deliverance which comes from] Jesus Christ (or: the Lord, Jesus [the] Anointed One [= the Messiah]) – unforbidden and without hindrance, with all the bold outspoken freedom of speech which is the right of a citizen!

[Written circa A.D. 57-63 – Based on the critical analysis of John A.T. Robinson]

ROMANS

CHAPTER 1

1. **Paul, Jesus Christ's slave** (or: a slave servant of and from [the] Anointed One, Jesus; a slave belonging to Jesus [the] Anointed [= Messiah]), **a called person, one sent forth with a mission** (or: an ambassador or emissary by invitation), **being one having been marked off by boundaries** (fully parted and determined by bounds; separated away and limited off; delineated; defined) **unto God's good news** (or: into a message of goodness and well-being which is God),

2. **which He Himself previously promised through His prophets, within [the] set-apart writings** (or: holy and sacred Scriptures),

3. **about** (concerning; with reference to) **His Son – the One coming into existence** (or: birthing Himself) **from out of David's sperm** (or: Davidic seed; = David's descendant), **down from and in the line of succession of flesh** (or: = in the sphere of the natural realm);

4. **the One being bounded** (marked off, thus defined; separated, and so designated; divided away, and so determined; or: appointed) **God's Son** (or: a Son Who is God; or: a Son from, or having the character and qualities of, God; = God's Regent, cf Ps. 2; 2 Sam. 7:14) **immersed within the midst of power and in union with ability, down from** (or: corresponding to and on a level with; in the sphere of) **a Breath-effect of set-apartness** (or: an attitude of holiness and sacredness; a spirit pertaining to being set apart) **forth from out of a resurrection** (a standing back up again) **of** (or: from among) **dead folks – Jesus Christ, our Lord** (Master and Owner),

5. **through Whom we receive grace, as well as a sending off with a mission [leading] unto faith's obedience** (or: obedience that springs from trust and loyalty; [the] paying attention associated with loyal allegiance; or, as apposition: "obedience which faith is" – Rudolf Bultmann) **among all the ethnic multitudes, over [the essence, reality and power of] His Name**

> (or: through means of Whom we at one point received a joy-producing act of favor, and then suddenly took in hand a commission as emissaries with a view to a humble and submissive hearkening – along with an appropriate response, which is faithfulness – and a giving-of-the-ear from beneath [Him], with compliant listening and paying attention that has its source in trust and involved commitment, within all the non-Jewish nations for the sake of and in behalf of His Name [and reputation]),

6. **within the midst of which peoples** (or: among whom) **you yourselves are continuously existing, being also called folks of Jesus Christ** (or: Jesus Christ's invited ones) –

7. **to** (or: for) **all those being in Rome: God's loved ones** (folks accepted of God), **set-apart** (holy) **called one. Joyous grace and peace to you** (or: favor and harmony from the joining [are] in and with you) **from God, our Father and Lord, Jesus Christ** (or: from our Father God, and [the] Master, Jesus Christ; or: from God our Father, even [the] Owner – [the] Anointed Jesus).

8. **First, indeed, I am constantly giving thanks to my God** (or: expressing the well-being and goodness in the grace and favor by my God) **– through Jesus Christ – about** (with reference to; concerning) **all of you folks, because** (or: that) **your faith, trust and loyalty are being repeatedly proclaimed** (or: announced) **down within** (= throughout the midst of) **the whole ordered System** (world of culture, economy, government and religion; or: = the Roman Empire).

9. **For you see, God is my Witness** (or: continuously exists being my Evidence) **– to, in and with Whom I continuously render service** (or: for Whom I am hired to constantly work), **within my spirit** (or: in union with my Breath-effect; in my attitude), **within His Son's good news** (or: in

union with the message of goodness, ease and well-being pertaining to, coming from, having the character of, and which is, His Son) – **how unintermittingly** (without intervals in between; unceasingly) **I am habitually constructing a memory** (or: producing a recollection) **pertaining to you** (or: making mention of you folks),

10.   **always upon my thoughts and expressions toward having things go well** (or: my prayers), **continuously requesting** (or: asking) **if by any means** (or: somehow), **at length, I shall sometime be prospered along the path within God's will and purpose to come to you folks and be face to face with you,**

11.   **for I constantly long** (or: am increasingly yearning) **to see you, to the end that I may share and exchange some spiritual effect of favor with you folks** (or: mutually partner in the impartation to you people, and among you, of some gift that is a result of grace and which has its source in the Breath-effect) **[leading] into the [situation for] you to be established** (firmly settled and made steadfast; stabilized).

12.   **Now this means to be called together to be side-by-side for an interchange of aid, encouragement or consolation among you folks, through the faith and trust within each other – both yours and mine.**

13.   **Yet I do not want you to continue to fail to know** (or: be unaware or remain ignorant), **brothers** (= fellow believers and members of the Family), **that I often set before myself** (purposed and proposed) **to come** (or: go) **to you – and I was prevented until now** (up to this point) **– to the end that I may have** (or: could hold and enjoy) **some fruit within you folks** (or: among you), **correspondingly as also [I do] within** (or: among) **the remaining ethnic multitudes** (or: the rest of the nations – the non-Israelites; the Gentiles).

14.   **I am** (or: I continue being) **a debtor to** (or: for; or: with) **both Greeks** (Hellenists) **and to** (for; with) **barbarians** (non-Hellenists: those who do not possess Greek culture); **to** (or: for; with) **both wise ones and to** (for; with) **those without understanding** (unintelligent ones; foolish ones; folks who lack sense).

15.   **In this condition** (or: Thus so) **– commensurate with me, the ready** (willing; eager) **one – [I] myself [desire and intend] to also bring and proclaim** (or: announce) **the message of goodness, ease and well-being** (or: Good News) **to and among you folks** (or: for you folks) **in Rome, for you see, I am not in the habit of being ashamed of** (= I am proud of and thrilled about) **the Good News** (message of goodness, ease and well-being; [other MSS add: of, from and which is Christ]).

16.   **You see, God's power** (or: [the] ability of God; capacity from God; or: **a power which is God) is unto deliverance** (or: exists [leading] into rescue, salvation, health, wholeness and restoration to the original state and condition) **for everyone** (or: in all; to everyone) **– to, for, in and with the person continuously having faith and trusting** (or: believing and relying upon [it]; being faithful)**: both for** (to; in) **[the] Jew first, also for** (to; in) **[the] Greek** (or: = non-Jew)
      (or: – to not only the believing/trusting Jew, but also, firstly {or: primarily}, to the Hellenist as well) –

17.   **for by Him** (or: in it) **God's justice** (solidarity in fair conduct; equity; righteousness; [covenantal] qualities of the Way pointed out; way of righting what is wrong; right relationship [with us]; or: a means of turning us in the right direction by an eschatological deliverance, which is God,) **is continuously and progressively being unveiled** (revealed; disclosed), **from out of faithfulness** (or: forth from the midst of faith, trust, conviction and loyalty), **[reciprocally proceeding] into faith, trust, conviction and loyalty, according as it has been written,**

"But the one righteous (or: just) **out-of-faith/faithfulness will himself continue living** (or: Yet the Just One will experience life in himself from faith/faithfulness; or: Now the one in accord with the Way pointed out from trust, will in himself be living; or: And the person rightwised from out of faith will continuously live; or: So the One being fair and equitable from trust will progressively receive life into Himself from that trust).**" [Hab. 2:4]

18. **But you see, God's personal emotion** (or: mental bent; natural impulse; teeming desire and swelling passion; temperament; disposition; or: anger; wrath; or: an inherent fervor, which is God,) **is continuously and progressively being unveiled** (revealed; disclosed) **from heaven upon every irreverence** (lack of awe or absence of pious fear; disrespect) **and injustice** (wrongdoing; unrighteousness; situation or behaving that is contrary to the Way pointed out) **of people** (or: that arises from humans) **– the folks continuously holding down** (restraining; stopping while possessing) **the Truth** (or: reality) **in the sphere of** (or: within the midst of) **injustice** (unrighteousness; that which is not right; unfairness and inequality) **–**

19. **simply because the thing experientially known** (or: personally knowable; able to be gained by insight) **pertaining to God** (or: from, and which has its origin in, God; which is God) **is continuously made visible** (made apparent; manifested by light) **within** (or: among) **them, for God at one point made** (or: makes) **it visible** (manifests it) **to them** (or: for them; in them; by them; among them).

20. **For you see, from [the] creation** (framing; founding of order out of chaos; settling) **of [the] ordered System** (cosmos; universe; or: world of culture, religion and government) **His invisible things** (unseen [qualities and attributes]) **– both His imperceptible** (unobservable, but effecting-all) **power, ability and capacity, as well as divinity** (Godship; God-state) **– are habitually seen down the line** (or: are normally correspondingly perceived), **being continually apprehended** (grasped by the mind; mentally conceived) **in the results and by the effects of things which are made or done, in order for them to be continuously defenseless** (without an excuse),

21. **simply because, although at one point experientially knowing God with insight, they did** (or: do) **not glorify** (imagine; esteem; suppose; fancy; conjecture about; hold an opinion of; repute) **[Him] as God, or even thank [Him]** (or: give thanks in joyously expressing the goodness and well-being inherent in [His] grace and favor). **And so in contrast, they were made futile** (vain; fruitless; without profit; empty; useless; worthless; subject to a process of meaningless frustration; subject to exercises in futility) **in their reasonings** (or: thought processes; dialogues; ideas that went throughout in every direction), **and their [collective] unintelligent** (stupid; unable-to-put-things-together) **heart was darkened** (= the core of their being was made to experience an absence of light in a dim, shadowy gloom of obscurity [= ignorance]).

22. **[So] continuously claiming** (asserting; alleging with pretense) **to be wise ones, they were made to be dull** (sluggish; moronic; stupid; foolish)   [*vs. 23, below: cf Ps. 106:19-20; Ex. 32:4]

23. **and they at once changed** (or: exchange in barter; make other than it is) **the glory** (or: splendor and praise-inducing manifestation; or: esteem; opinion; imagination; supposition; thought; appearance; honorable consideration) **of the imperishable** (un-ruinable; unspoilable and incorruptible; non-decayable) **God within the result of a likeness** (resemblance; conformed similarity; copy-effect) **of an image** (form; appearance) **of a perishable** (corruptible; spoilable) **human, as well as of flying things and of four-footed [animals]* and of creeping things.**

24. **Wherefore** (or: On which account) **God gave** (or: hands) **them over** (or: delivered or transfers them into another's power), **within the full passions** (or: rushing passionate cravings; added earnest desires, wants and wishes; or: compiled angers and complete wrath) **of their**

hearts, into uncleanness (or: ritual impurity), **to be continuously dishonored and shamed –
with respect to** (or: pertaining to) **their bodies – among** (or: within) **themselves,**
25. **whichever folks altered or exchange God's truth** (or: the reality from and which is God,
and which pertains to God) **to and for something else, within** (or: in union with) **The Lie, then
they were adored and venerated with dread, and next rendered religious service to and for
the creation** (or: creature; or: forming, framing, founding and settling which brought order from
chaos) **alongside** (or: to the side of; parallel to; or: = rather than) **the Creator** (The One framing
and founding) **Who is** (continuously exists being) **well spoken of** (praised; blessed; eulogized;
or: is One filled with thoughts of goodness and well-being) **on into the ages. It is so** (Amen)!

26. **Because of this** (or: Wherefore) **God gave, or hands, them over** (delivered, or transfers,
them into the power of someone else) **into experiences of dishonor** (or: ignoble sufferings;
situations of being unvalued; unworthy passions), **for even their females at one point altered**
(or: alter; change or exchange) **the natural use into the [use which is] off to the side of** (or:
beside; = other than) **nature** (or: a natural condition; natural production; a generated situation).
27. **And likewise** (or: So in like manner) **also the males, sending away** (or: abandoning;
leaving) **the natural use of the female, were set aflame within their cravings unto** (or: into)
one another; males in males continuously producing (accomplishing; effecting; working
down) **shameless indecency, and constantly taking away** (or: receiving back) **the necessary
retribution** (return compensation; the opposite of a reward; the anti-payment) **of their
wandering** (or: the corresponding wage which is binding, pertaining to their straying and
deception) **within the midst of, or among, themselves.**
28. **And then, correspondingly as they did not** (or: to the same degree as they do not) **put
God to the proof and so approve [Him] as fit and suitable, to be continuously holding
[Him] within full experiential knowledge** (or: having [Him] in union with added intimate insight;
or: possessing [Him] in recognition and acknowledgment), **God gave them over** (or: transfers or
delivers them) **into a mind which fails to meet the test** (a disqualified mind) **to continuously
do** (practice; make) **things that consistently are not fitting** (not reaching the proper level),
29. **being people having been filled with all injustice – so that they are now full of every
inequity and unfairness which lacks rightwised relationships and right actions – [as well
as] worthlessness** (or: criminality; unprofitableness; badness of condition; misery-gushed
existence), **inordinate, anti-social desire for more** (or: ruthless, aggressive and self-assertive
greed for advantage), **ugliness** (poorness of quality; malice); **folks very full of** (or: replete with)
jealousy and envy, murder, strife (or: contentiousness), **bait for entrapment, [and] with a
settled habit of evil and a disposition of depravity.**
30. **[They are] whisperers** (or: gossipers, i.e., folks who disseminate detrimental information
about other people), **slanderers, haters** (detesters) **of God, overbearing and outrageous
folks, haughty and arrogant people, ostentatious and vainglorious ones, inventors of ugly,
worthless and bad things, [being] incompliant** (stubborn; disobedient) **to parents,**
31. **unintelligent** (stupid; unable to cause things to flow together), **covenant-breakers** (or: folks
bound by no arrangement or who are false to agreements; not put-together), **folks without
natural affection, people unwilling to make a treaty** (or: implacable), **unmerciful folks,**
32. **those who, fully knowing by experience** (being fully aware of) **the effect of God's justice**
(or: the result of God's fairness and equity; or: the result of what is right, from the way pointed out,
which is God; or: God's decree of the Way pointed out) **– that those continually performing**

(committing; executing) **such things are folks deserving** (worthy; of equivalent value) **of death – not only keep on doing the same things, but also are constantly mutually approving, taking pleasure in and consenting with those habitually performing** (or: committing; practicing) **them.**

CHAPTER 2

1. **Wherefore** (or: Because of which) **you continue to be without a defense or an excuse, O human – everyone continually judging** (pronouncing a judgment; separating, evaluating and making decisions; determining) **– for within that which you continue judging the other person** (or: the different one), **you are correspondingly evaluating** (or: commensurately deciding about; condemning) **yourself, since you who are continually judging are constantly performing** (committing; practicing) **the very same things!**

2. **Now we have seen and thus know** (or: are aware) **that result of God's judgment** (decision rendered; separation; determination) **is down from, in line with and accords to Truth and reality, [coming] upon those habitually performing or committing such things.**
3. **Yet you continue logically thinking** (reckoning; counting on) **this, O human – the one continuously judging those who are normally performing or committing such things, and yet are also a person habitually doing the same things – that you will proceed in making an escape out of the result of God's judgment** (the effect of a decision from God)**?**
4. **Or, are you continually having a "down-oriented" frame of mind** (or: despising; thinking with disrespect or a negative disposition) **concerning the riches** (or: wealth) **of His kind and gentle usefulness** (sweetly-disposed benevolence; kindness), **of the tolerant delay in holding back with forbearance, and of the pushing far away of anger in patient longsuffering? [Are you] continuing ignorant that God's kind and gentle usefulness** (sweetly-disposed benevolence) **is continuously leading you into a change of mind and purpose** (a shift to a new state of consciousness; or: a change of thinking, with a turn toward God and His reign)**?**
5. **Yet down from your hardness** (or: in line with and in accord to your obstinacy) **and an unrepentant heart** (= unchanged thinking and affection in the center of your being) **you habitually collect and lay up stores of personal emotion in yourself** (or: progressively treasure up to yourself inherent fervor, passionate impulse and a mental bent or a disposition; or: periodically bank for yourself anger, indignation or wrath) **within a day of personal emotion** (fervor; passion; anger; etc.) **and of an unveiling of a decision of rightwising from God**
    (or: of a revealing of God's verdict regarding fair and equitable dealing; of an uncovering of a just judgment which is God; of a disclosure of a separation for a decision having the character of the Way pointed out from God; of a disclosure from God's right evaluation),
6. **Who will progressively award in each person** (or: habitually give back to or pay for each one) **down from** (in line with; in accord to; to the level of) **his works** (actions; deeds)**:**
7. **in those** (to those; for those), **on the one hand, in accord with [the] patient endurance** (humbly remaining under for persistent support) **of a good work** (or: virtuous action) **[who] are constantly seeking glory** (a good reputation; a manifestation of that which calls forth praise) **and honor** (value; worth) **and incorruptibility** (or: incorruption) **– life which belongs to, is connected with, and is proper to the Age** (or: eonian life; the life of and for the ages).
8. **Yet, on the other hand, in those** (to those; for those) **out of a work for ambitious, factious**

or contentious purposes, and in (or: by) **being continuously incompliant** (disobedient; unwilling to be persuaded) **to** (or: by) **the Truth** (reality; veritable essence), **but constantly compliant** (obedient; persuaded) **in, to, by and for the injustice** (inequity; that which is not in accord with the Way pointed out), **[there will be] personal emotion** (or: inherent fervor; passionate impulse; anger; indignation; wrath; a habit of mind; a mental bent or disposition) **and rushing of feelings** (or: intense passion of the mind; violent breathing; glowing animation; turbulent commotion of the mind; or: rage; fury),

9. **pressure** (affliction; trouble; tribulation; ordeal) **and squeezed narrowness** (tight restriction; distress; anguish) – **upon every soul of mankind which is persistently in himself working down and effecting the bad** (the ugly; the worthless; the evil; the injurious; the bad situation; the worthless quality; the malicious intent) – **both of a Jew, first, and also of a Greek** (or: one of the Hellenist culture);

10. **but yet glory** (a manifestation of that which calls forth praise; a creditable reputation) **and honor** (value; worth) **and peace** (or: harmony; [=Shalom]) **in, to, for and with everyone habitually working and accomplishing in or for himself the Good** (or: the virtuous and excellent) **both in, to, and for a Jew, first, and then also in, to and for a Greek** (or: to not only the Jew, but also, firstly {or: primarily}, to the Hellenist);

11. **for partiality** (favoritism; receiving on the basis of faces, countenances or personalities) **does not exist alongside of God** (or: by God's side; = with God or in His presence and dealings). [*cf* 8:1-4, below]

12. **For you see, as many as** (or: however many) **miss the goal** (or: sin; fail; or: erred; missed the target due to lack of ability or through distraction) **without (a) law [= Torah?], without (a) law will progressively lose and continue destroying themselves; and as many as** (or: however many) **within law** (or: within [the] Law [= Torah]) **miss the goal** (sin; sinned; fail; deviated), **through law** (or: [the] Law) **will be judged** (separated, evaluated and decided upon),

13. **for [it is] not the hearers of [the] Law** (= the ones instructed in the Law, or who listen to the Torah) **[that are] just ones** (rightwised folks who are in right relationships in accord with the Way pointed out; fair and equitable ones) **by God's side** (= with God and in His sight and presence), **but rather the doers of [the] Law** (= the folks performing deeds of the Torah, and producing the character and qualities of the Law) **[who] will continue being made right and just** (constituted in the Way pointed out; or: pronounced as being fair, equitable and in right relationship).

14. **You see, whenever ethnic multitudes** (or: [certain] Gentiles; or: [some] non-Israelite nations; = pagans) – **those not having a law** (or: [the] Law) **by nature – may normally do the things of the Law** (= Torah), **these, [although] not having a law** (or: [the] Law), **are in and among themselves a law** (or: continuously exist being a principle, or custom, for or to themselves),

15. **which very ones continuously display** (exhibit; show outward proof by demonstration) **the work of the Law** (or: action and conduct of that law and principle) **written within their hearts, their conscience** (the knowing with themselves; awareness; integrated recognition from what has been seen) **continually bearing joint-testimony** (giving confirming witness and evidence, together), **and, in between each other's calculations** (or: logical thoughts), **also constantly accusing** (speaking down [against] in the assembly) **or defending themselves** (or: and in the mean time one another's reasonings and reckonings constantly accusing, or even repeatedly

excusing themselves).

16. **God is presently judging** (or: continues deciding and is progressively separating off and evaluating) **the hidden things of humanity** (or: the things concealed from humans, [but which] belong to people) **within, and in union with, the Day – commensurate with my good news** (or: according to and following the pattern of my message of goodness, ease and well-being) – **through Jesus Christ** [with other MSS: by means of Jesus [the] Anointed [= Messiah]).

[with other MSS: In a day when God will continue judging people's hidden {agendas}...]

17. **So since** (or: But if; [other MSS: Consider this,]) **you yourself are habitually calling** (naming; classifying) **yourself a Jew and are continuing to rest** (lean back) **upon [the] Law** (= Torah), **and are even from time to time boasting** (expressing pride) **in God,**

18. **and you are progressively knowing the Will by personal experience and insight, and are constantly testing in order to prove** (or: approve) **the things that carry through, by habit** (i.e., the essential things which matter and are different in that they are of greater value), **while being a person regularly undergoing oral instruction from out of the Law** (= Torah),

19. **[and] likewise** (or: besides) **you have confidence in yourself** (or: you have persuaded yourself) **to be a guide or an escort of blind folks on the way or in the path; a light within [the] darkness** (obscurity of the shadow areas; dimness of the gloom),

20. **a trainer** (instructor; corrector; discipliner; educator) **of senseless ones** (folks without will, heart or guts; imprudent ones; foolish ones); **a teacher of infants** (ones not yet able to speak), **while habitually having** (or: holding) **the outward form** (outline; framework; semblance) **of the experiential knowledge and of the truth** (or: possessing the rough sketch of personal insight, from unconcealed reality) **within, or in union with, the Law** (= Torah)**...**

21. **You then, the one habitually teaching another** (a different one), **are not habitually teaching yourself! You, the one constantly preaching** (proclaiming; heralding), **"Do not steal," are habitually stealing!**

22. **The person continually saying not to be committing adultery, you are habitually committing adultery! You, the one repeatedly detesting idols** (responding to forms, shapes or concepts as an abomination, as something that is foul and stinks), **are in the habit of robbing temples** (despoiling or profaning the sanctuary)**!**

[note: vss. 21-22 can also be rendered as questions]

23. **You who are boasting in law** (or: [the] Law [= Torah]; or: a law), **through the transgression of** (stepping across the line of; stepping to the side of; deviating from) **the Law, you are constantly dishonoring** (devaluing) **God,**

24. **for according as it has been, and stands, written [in the Tanakh** (Hebrew Scriptures)**],**
> **"Because of you, God's NAME** [Yahweh?] **is continuously being blasphemed** (vilified; misrepresented; slandered; given a false image which hinders the Light) **among the ethnic multitudes** (nations; non-Jews; Gentiles)**."** [Isa. 52:5; Ezk. 36:20]

25. **Now you see, circumcision, indeed, continues being beneficial** (continues to profit, to help), **if you should continue practicing** (or: observing) **[the] Law** (= Torah). **But if you should be a transgressor** (side-stepper; violator) **of [the] Law, your circumcision** (cutting around) **has become uncircumcision** (literally: the foreskin).

26. **Therefore, if the Uncircumcision** (= non-Jews) **should be habitually on watch to guard** (have in keeping and maintain) **the effects of justice and equity** (the results of being pointed in the right direction; the fair and equitable dealings; the acts which result from what is right) **of or from the Law** (= customs from neighbor-based equity), **will not his uncircumcision continue**

to be logically considered and accounted (reckoned; calculated) **into circumcision** (or: credited to his account for circumcision)**?**

27. **And so the Uncircumcision, out of natural instinct** (out of nature or native conditions; = naturally) **habitually bringing the law to its goal** (or: completing or fulfilling the Law), **will continue judging** (or: making a decision and a separation regarding) **you – the one [who] through Letter and Circumcision [is] a side-stepper** (a transgressor; a violator) **of [the] Law,**

28. **for you see, the Jew is not the one in the visibly apparent or outwardly manifest** (or: For not he in the outward appearance is a Jew), **neither [is] circumcision that [which is] visibly apparent** (outwardly manifest) **in flesh** (= in body),

29. **but rather, a Jew [is] the one within the hidden [place]** (or: [that which is] in the concealed [realm]) **and circumcision [is] of [the] heart** (= core of our being) **– in union with Breath-effect** (or: within [the] spirit; in attitude), **not in letter – whose praise** (applause; full recommendation; [note play on words: Jew is a derivative of "Judah," which means "praise"]) **[is] not from out of mankind** (humanity), **but rather from out of God.**

CHAPTER 3

1. **What then [is] the advantage** (the thing given by the surplus of abundance which results in pre-eminence, prerogative and superiority) **of the Jew, or what [is] the furthering benefit of the circumcision?**

2. **Much, in accord with every turn** (i.e., from every angle, or, in every way), **for first [of all]** (or: in the first place; foremost; mainly), **indeed, that they were** (or: are) **entrusted with God's brief utterances** (little words; [note: the diminutive of Logos; often translated: "oracles"]).

3. **So, what if certain ones refuse** (or: if some at one point refused) **to believe** (or: disbelieved; are unfaithful or disloyal; were without faith; are faithless)**? Will not their unbelief** (faithlessness; lack of trust; disloyalty) **proceed in causing God's faithfulness** (or: trustworthiness; loyalty; trust; faith) **to be idled-down** (rendered useless and unproductive)**?**

4. **Certainly not!** (May it not come to be!; "Heaven" forbid!) **Now God must repeatedly come to be true** (or: let God continually be birthed genuine and real), **though every human [be] a liar – even as it has been written:**

> **"So that You should be justified** (seen as fair and equitable – in accord with the way pointed out) **within Your words** (or: sayings), **and You will repeatedly overcome** (conquer) **within the [situation or time for] You to be periodically judged and decided about** (or: You will be winning the case when You are tried)." [Ps. 51:4 & 6]

5. **However** (or: But; Now) **if our injustice** (disregard for what is right; behavior contrary to the Way pointed out) **continues to stand together with** (is jointly establishing; habitually commends) **God's solidarity in fair and equitable dealings** ([covenantal] justice; Way pointed out; rightwised direction), **what shall we continue saying** (or: declaring)**?**

God, the One continuously bringing the personal emotion (inherent fervor; impulse; or: wrath; anger; indignation), **[is] not unjust! – after the manner of a man** (down from [my] humanity) **I am now laying this out**

> (or: [Is] not God, the One repeatedly bringing on the personal emotion against mankind or anger in correspondence to humanity, unjust? I proceed saying this from a human perspective;
>
> or: God [is] not unfair by being the one constantly bringing this inherent fervor and impulse against a person, is He? I am presently speaking on the level of humanity)!

6. **Certainly not** (May it not come to be)! **Else** (or: Otherwise), **how is God constantly making decisions about and repeatedly judging** (or, as a future: how will God continue separating, evaluating and judging) **the ordered System** (controlling world of society, economy, government and religion; human aggregate)**?**

7. **But** [other MSS: For] **if in the result of my lie** (or: falsehood-effect) **God's truth and reality encircles** (or: surrounds) **for superabundance into His glory** (or: [leading] unto His enhanced reputation and a manifestation which calls forth praise), **why am I also still being continually separated** (judged; evaluated) **as one failing to hit the target** (as a sinner or an outcast)**?**

8. **Now [it is] not according as we are constantly being slandered** (abusively spoken of so as to hinder the Light) **and according as certain folks habitually affirm us to be continually saying, "We should constantly be doing** (or: producing) **the bad things** (the ugly, worthless and evil things) **so that the good things may come [of it]!"**
Concerning whom the result of the judgment (or: Whose evaluation-effect, separation [of the issue] and decision) **is fair** (equitable; in accord with justice and deserved)**!**

9. **What, then** (or: therefore)**? Do we continue holding an advantage** (habitually have something ahead; or, as a passive: are we continually surpassed)**?**
Not entirely (or: Not in every respect; or: Not at all), **for we already charged** (previously accused) **all mankind, both Jews and Greeks** (or: Hellenists), **to be** (to continuously exist) **under [the direction, power and control, or result, of] failure** (the missing of the target by falling short or shooting astray through lack of skill and ability or by distraction; or: error; a mistake; sin),

10. **according as it has been, and stands, written,**
    "There is not a just man (There is none fair or in right relationship; or: No one exists being in accord with the Way pointed out), **not even one!**

11.   **"The one understanding does not exist** (or: There is no man bringing it together to understand)**!**
    The one habitually seeking God does not exist (or: There is none continually looking for or repeatedly searching-out God).

12.   **"All bend out of the regular line** (turn aside; or: avoid [God]), **[and] at the same time they are made useless;**
    there is no one habitually doing useful kindness (or: kind usefulness);
    there is not as much as one. [Ps. 14:1-3; 53:1-3]

13.   **"Their throat [is] an opened grave; by their tongues they were consistently baiting for entrapment** (or: to deceive); [Ps. 5:9]
    venom of asps (vipers) **[is] under their lips,** [Ps. 140:3]

14.   **"whose mouth constantly is crammed full of a wishful curse and of bitterness.** [Ps. 10:7]

15.   **"Their feet [are] swift** (or: sharp) **to pour out blood.**

16.   **"The results of crushing** (bruising; shattering) **and misery** (wretchedness) **[are] in their paths** (or: ways),

17.   **"and the road of peace** (path or way of shalom) **they do not experience** (intimately know). [Isa. 59:7-8; Prov. 1:16]

18.   **"There is no fear of or respect for God before** (in front of) **their eyes."** [Ps. 36:1]

19. **But we know from having seen, that whatever the Law** ([Torah]; or: custom) **continues**

saying, it continues speaking to and for those within the Law and [its] custom,
(or: Now we are aware that as much as the Law repeatedly lays out to those centered in the Law, it keeps on speaking) **to the end that every mouth may be shut** (fenced in; hedged around; stopped; barred; silenced)! **And then all the world** (ordered System of religion, culture, economy, and government; or: secular society; or: = all humanity) **can come to be "under fair and equitable dealings," in God**
(or: would become subject to a just decision and a pointing out of the Way, by God; or: should come to be liable to God, "under what is right"; or: may be brought to a just trial with God).

20. **On account of that** (or: Wherefore), **no flesh** (= person) **[at] all will proceed to be rescued or put right** (be rightwised or turned in the right direction; or: be considered justified; be freed from guilt and placed in the covenantal Way pointed out by being eschatologically liberated) **before Him** (in His sight; face to face with Him in His presence; *corem Deo*) **from out of works of Law** (or: deeds or accomplishments springing from Law; performance of Laws' cultus; or: observance of custom or Torah), **for you see, through Law [comes] a full, clear, exact, added and experience-gained knowledge of sin** (or: from failure; having the character of a missing of the target; which is deviation and error).

21. **Yet now, apart from Law** (or: custom; habitual practice; ordinance made by authority; or: = Torah), **a righteousness of God** (God's just action of eschatological deliverance; God's solidarity, with moral integrity in fair and equitable dealings; a turning in the right direction that comes from God; God's covenantal faithfulness, justice and pointing out of the Way; a rightwisedness and right relationship, which is God) **has been manifested and remains displayed in clear light – being continuously attested in witness by means of** (or: under) **the Law** (= Torah) **and the Prophets –**
22. **yet a righteousness of God** (or: a right relationship and solidarity with, and which is, God; justice from God; God's fair and equitable dealings in accord with the Way pointed out; a rightwised condition effected by God; God's eschatological deliverance which brings covenant justice, inclusion and participation) **through Jesus Christ's faithfulness** (or: trust-faith; convinced, faithing loyalty and allegiance) **unto all humanity – as well as upon and unto all those presently believing** (or: habitually trusting [in God]), **for you see, there exists no distinction** (no difference; no divided arrangement)!
23. **You see, all people at one point veered off the mark** (or: all folks deviated; or: everyone fails; all humanity sins), **and so** (or: that is,) **they are continually posterior to, falling short of, inferior to and wanting of, God's glory** (of the manifestation of God which calls forth praise; of a reputation which comes from, and has the character of, God; of God's opinion and imagination; of [having] the appearance of God; of the glory from God; of the assumed appearance of God),
24. **while being folks presently and progressively being made right, freed from guilt, placed in solidarity within the Way pointed out, and continuously set in right relationship** (or: being [all] one-after-another delivered and rightwised; being ones habitually turned in the right direction; being [all] presently justified [by covenant inclusion]) **freely** (as a gift; gratuitously) **by His grace** (or: in His favor; with His grace; by His gratuitous act which brought joy) **through means of the process of a release-from-an-enslaved-condition and a liberating-away-from-imprisonment, which is resident within Christ Jesus** (or: by the setting-free which is centered in [the] Anointed Jesus; or: through the redemption that is union with Jesus [the] Messiah),

25. **Whom God publicly set and places before [us]** (or: before put-forth; purposed) **[as] a sheltering, cleansing covering** (lit.: the lid of the ark, place of mercy; = act of atonement) **through the faithfulness** (or: the trust, the faith; or: that loyalty and allegiance) **resident within His blood** (or: centered in the blood which is Him) **– into a demonstration which points out the proof of His solidarity by the rightwising deliverance** (or: His fairness in covenantal justice and rightness, and His just act which accords with the Way pointed out), **through** (or: on account of and because of) **the letting flow-aside, and the releasing-to-the-side, of the effects of errors** (or: the deliverance from the results of sinful acts or offenses against the Law, and the divorcing from the effects of mistakes) **having previously occurred** (being ones having been before brought into being) **during the midst of the holding-back and support from God –**
26. **toward the demonstration which points out the proof of His eschatological, rightwising deliverance, in solidarity and with fair and equitable dealing** (His justice; His rightwising righteousness; His compliance with the Way pointed out) **within the present season** (in the current fitting situation; in union with the current fertile moment), **for Him to be just** (or: One in covenantal solidarity that accords with fair and equitable dealings which comprise the Way pointed out) **and the One liberating, progressively turning in the right direction, making just and freeing from guilt while constantly placing in the Way pointed out which is righted, covenantal relationship and justice** (or: The Right-wiser and Justifier of) **the person [issuing; being born] forth from out of the midst of Jesus' faithfulness** (or: from [the] trust, faith, loyalty, and trustworthiness [emanating] from, and [the] allegiance which is, Jesus)!
27. **So then where [is] the loud-spoken boasting? It is shut out** (or: was excluded). **Through what kind of law, custom or teaching? Of works** (or: The one concerned with, composed of and pertaining to acts; The one whose source and involvement is deeds and actions)**? No!** (or: By no means!) **But rather through Faith's law and principle**
>   (or: To the contrary, by means of a principle of trust and loyalty, manifested in
>   faithfulness and coming from confident reliance; = a law and custom which was
>   displayed in the confident loyalty of Christ in His act of solidarity with the human
>   condition)**!**
28. **For you see,** [some MSS: Now] **we continue logically concluding** (reckoning and reasonably accounting) **a person** (or: mankind; humanity) **to be continually made right and freed from guilt, placed in solidarity in the Way pointed out, and kept in a right social bond of relationship** (or: rightwised; justified; eschatologically delivered and included in covenant) **by faith and in trust** (or: with [the] faithfulness and allegiance [of Jesus]), **apart from works of law** (or: [the] Law's deeds; or: actions which are a law; or: = observance of Torah, or acts associated with custom and habitual practice, or pertaining to ordinances made by authority).
29. **Or, [is He] the God of [the] Jews only? [Is He] not also of the ethnic multitudes** (nations; Gentiles; non-Jews)**? Yes, of the ethnic multitudes** (nations) **also,**
>   (or: Or to the contrary, [is He not] the God of only Jews? [He is] not also [the God] of
>   non-Jews, is He?
>   Yes! [He is the God] of non-Jews, as well,)
30. **since indeed** (or: if after all; [other MSS: seeing that] **God [is] One** (or: [there is] one God; [it is the] one God; = God [is; tends toward] Union; [Deut. 6:4, *Shema*]) **Who from out of faithfulness** (or: forth from [His] faith, trust and loyalty) **will, by rightwising [them], progressively make Circumcision right, just and free from guilt, placing them in the Way pointed out and setting them in solidarity within right relationships – and** (or: as well as)

Uncircumcision through means of the [same] faithfulness (by means of this trust, faith and loyalty).

31. **Then are we habitually rendering inactive and useless** (idling-down and rendering unemployed) **law or custom** (or: [the] Law) **through the faith and trust** (or: by means of [God's] faithfulness)? **Certainly not** (May that not come to be)! **But rather, we are constantly establishing law** (or: a law; setting a custom in its fixed place and making a principle stand).

CHAPTER 4

1. **What then shall we declare Abraham – our forefather according to the flesh** (or: the first founder of our family, in line with natural descent) **– to have found?**

> (or: That being so, what will we be saying is to be discovered [concerning] Abraham, "our founding father," in accord to flesh?
>
> or: What, consequently, will we say? Is Abraham found [as] our preferred father on the level or sphere of *flesh*?)

2. **You see, if Abraham was rightwised, placed in right relationship, and declared just and in accord with the Way, from out of [his] works** (or: made right, turned in the right direction and justified by actions; = included in covenant from [his] deeds), **he yet holds something to boast about** (a ground or right for boasting), **but not toward** (or: face to face with) **God.**

3. **For what is the Scripture saying?**

> **"Now Abraham believed and was faithful by God, trusted in and was loyal to God and from logical consideration it was and is entered into the leger of his story, in him, into participation in a generous act of right relationship within the path that [God] was indicating**
>
> > (or: it was considered, concluded and reasonably viewed for him and an account was credited to him [to have entered] into a right relationship with behavior in accord with the Way pointed out, which was comprised of fairness and equity from being turned in the right direction [progressing] into properly-ordered living of rightwised covenant-participation)" [Gen. 15:6]

4. **Now to** (or: for; with) **the person habitually working** (practicing a trade; accomplishing a work), **the wage** (or: pay) **is not being credited** (reckoned; put on an account; considered) **as corresponding to** (or: in accord with) **an undeserved, gratuitous gift** (or: grace; a favor), **but on the contrary, as commensurate with and coming down from a debt** (something owed; an obligation).

5. **But to** (or: for; with) **the person not habitually working, yet constantly believing** (actively placing [his] trust and reliance) **upon the One [Who is] habitually delivering and making right the irreverent** (or: the One habitually rightwising, pointing in the right direction, putting in right relationship, justifying, and placing the profane person in the midst of the [covenantal] Way pointed out), **his faith** (trust; convinced, confidence and loyal allegiance) **is logically being considered and viewed** (or: constantly reckoned and credited on account) **into** (unto; for) **right behavior in accord with the Way pointed out** (justice; fairness; right, equitable and well-ordered living).

6. **Exactly as David also is telling of the happiness and blessedness of the person in whom** (to whom; for whom) **God is constantly counting** (reasonably concluding; logically considering) **rightwised existence in accord with the Way pointed out** (justice; righteousness; solidarity; fair and equitable dealing), **apart from works** (or: independent of [Law] activities):

7.   **"Happy and blessed [are] the people whose lawlessnesses** (transgressions; violations of the Law; lawless deeds) **were and are sent away** (dismissed; discharged; divorced; pardoned) **and whose failures** (errors; situations of missing of the target; sins) **were and are covered over** (concealed with a veil or lid)**!**

8.   **"Happy and blessed [are the] adult males of whom** [other MSS: to whom; for whom] **the Lord** (= Yahweh) **may by no means logically consider a failure** (take into account or conclude a missed target; reasonably calculate or reckon a sin).**"** [Ps. 32:1-2]

9.   **So then, [is] this happiness** (or: blessedness) **upon the Circumcision, or upon the Uncircumcision as well** (or: also)**? Emphatically we are habitually reiterating,**

> **"The faithfulness and trust in and by Abraham were from logical consideration entered into the leger of his story: into a participation in a generous act of right relationship within the path that [God] was indicating**
>
>> (or: was considered, concluded and reasonably viewed for him and an account was credited to him [to have entered] into a right relationship with behavior in accord with the Way pointed out, which was comprised of fairness and equity from being turned in the right direction [progressing] into properly-ordered living of rightwised covenant-participation).**"** [Gen. 15:6]

10. **How then is it or was it logically considered or calculated** (or: How then was it put to the account, credited and reckoned) **– with [his] being** (= when he was) **in circumcision, or in uncircumcision? Not in circumcision, but on the contrary, in uncircumcision!**

11. **Then later he received** (or: took hold of; obtained) **circumcision as a mark and a sign** (or: circumcision's sign) **– a seal** (or: a stamped impression of a seal or signet ring which shows ownership, possession, identification or authority) **of and from the accordance with the Way pointed out, which is faithfulness** (or: of a rightwised relationship with fair and equitable dealings from trust and which has the character and qualities of convinced fidelity; or: from faith's own righteousness), **pertaining to the [situation of being] within the uncircumcision** (or: = the right covenantal relationship corresponding to the faith he had while in his uncircumcised state), **in order for him to be a father of all the people habitually believing and trusting by way of uncircumcision [and moving them] into [the place for] the accordance with the Way pointed out** (or: the rightwised relationships characterized by fair and equitable dealings; the well-ordered life that is pointed in the right direction; = covenantal inclusion) **to be logically considered in them** (or: reckoned and reasonably concluded to them; calculated, accounted and credited for them) **also –**

12. **and as well, a father of [the] Circumcision, [yet] not to** (or: for) **those out of circumcision only, but rather also to** (for; in; by; with) **those continuously advancing in line with the elements of the faithfulness** (or: walking orderly by the first principles which are faith, trust and reliant allegiance) **– in the footprints of our father Abraham – within uncircumcision** (or: in uncircumcision, in union with the footprints of the faith of our father Abraham).

13. **For not through** (a; or: [the]) **law [is/was] the Promise to** (for; in) **Abraham, or to** (for; in) **his seed** (offspring; posterity), **[for] him to be an heir of [the] aggregate of humanity** (or: the one receiving and enjoying an allotted System of culture: the world of society), **but on the contrary, through a [covenantal]-rightwisedness by a generous act of [God's] eschatological intervention, which is faith and which creates faithfulness**

> (or: faith's righteousness and justice; a placing in right relationship and a keeping in the Way pointed out which belongs to and comes from faith, reliance and trust; trust's way of

life which results in just and equitable dealings; fairness and equity from conviction).

14. **You see, if the ones out of law** (or: = those who have [the] Law as their origin) **[are] heirs** (inheritors and enjoyers of the allotment), **[then] the faith has been made empty** (void; vain) **and is now without content, and the Promise has been rendered useless** (has been permanently unemployed and idle; has been annulled and is inoperative).

15. **For you see, the Law is by labor constantly effecting personal emotion from intrinsic fervor or natural propensity** (or: is progressively working-down anger and wrath, repeatedly producing indignation and by habit fully accomplishing a teeming, passionate impulse or a disposition of desire). **Yet** (or: Now) **where no law is existing** (or: where there is no custom), **neither [is there] a stepping to the side** (a transgression; a violation; a breach).

16. **Because of this [i.e., there being no law, the Promise comes] out of [Christ's] faithfulness,** (or: from faith/trust/fidelity), **to the end that [it is] down from, in line with and according to grace: a joy-producing act of favor [leading] into the [situation for] the Promise to be continuously firm** (steadily walked; secured, confirmed and established; guaranteed as valid and made sure) **in all** (or: to all; for all) **the seed** (or: = realized by all the offspring), **not in the person** (or: to or for the [group]) **[coming] out of the Law only** (or: by that only from out of custom), **but rather also in the [seed]** (or: to the [group]; for the person; or: by that) **from out of [the] faithfulness and trust of Abraham – who is a father of all of us,**

17. **according as it has been and stands written,**

> **"A father of many multitudes** (nations; ethnic groups) **I have placed** (put; set; deposited) **you"** [Gen. 17:5]

[Now while he was being] down in the midst of and facing [the One] Whom he believed, which was God

> (or: down in a place that was in opposition, from which he trusted in [the message] which was God, and he relied upon [the idea] which [came] from God; or: in line with and in union with, yet being on the opposite side of the matter, he gained confidence from God)

– the One continuously (habitually; or: repeatedly; periodically) making the dead ones alive, and (or: even) continuously calling (or: repeatedly and habitually summoning) the things not existing as existing (or: = not being into continuously being) –

18. **who, to the side of expectation** (or: more than or beyond expectation; beside hope; near the side of expectation), **trusted** (believed; relied; was faithful; put faith) **upon expectation** (or: expectant hope) **into the [situation for] him to become** (to bring himself into being) **a father of many multitudes** (nations; ethnic groups), **in accord with** (down from and in line with) **that having been and still being spoken** (or: declared), **"Thus shall progressively be your seed** (or: offspring; descendants)." [Gen. 15:5]

19. **And so, not being weak** (without strength; infirm) **in this faith, trust and loyalty, he attentively considered** (studied, thought and perceived down upon) **his own body by this time** (or: already) **having been made dead** (or: deadened), **subsisting in the circumstances of** (or: beginning to be under the possession of) **about one hundred years, as well as** (or: also; and; even) **the state of deadness** (or: deadening) **of Sarah's womb.**

20. **Yet he was not divided in his judgment by unbelief with a view to God's Promise** (or: But by and in lack of trust he was not separated or undecided in view of, and with regard to, God's Promise; or: Yet unto God's Promise he did not waiver or doubt in disloyalty), **but on the contrary, he was empowered and enabled by faith** (or: in trust; for conviction; with loyalty), **giving glory** (or: an opinion; an estimation; credit) **to God and a reputation for God,**

21. **and being carried to full-convicted assurance** (completely convinced) **that what He had promised He continuously exists being capable and powerful to do, create and perform.**
22. **Wherefore** (or: Through which; For this reason), **also, from logical consideration it was and is entered into the leger of his story, in him, into participation in a generous act of right relationship within the path that [God] was indicating**

> (or: was viewed in him as having been brought into an eschatological deliverance; is reasonably credited into righteous existence; or: was accounted to him [to have entered] into right thinking and conduct; or: is concluded for him as being turned in the right direction; or: = was reckoned into rightwised covenant-participation).

23. **Now it was not written because of him only, that, "it was and is logically considered for him** (reckoned, concluded and accounted to him; it was put to his account)," [Gen. 15:6]
24. **but rather** (or: on the contrary) **because of us also, for whom, in whom, with whom and to whom it is constantly about to be logically considered** (or: it continues being about to be put on account) **for, in and to the folks continually believing, constantly trusting, habitually expressing covenant allegiance and progressively relying upon the One rousing and raising Jesus, our Lord, forth from out of the midst of dead folks –**
25. **[He] who was handed over** (or: transmitted; delivered; passed along; or: given to [our] side) **through and because of the effects of our falls to the side** (or: with a view to and for the sake of the results of our stumblings aside, transgressions and offenses), **and yet was roused and raised up through and because of our eschatological deliverance, being placed in the Way pointed out and turned in the right direction**   [cf 5:9, below; Gal. 2:17; Phil. 3:9]

> (or: for the benefit of our being made to be just; or: on behalf of our justifying, leading to freedom from guilt; or: for the purpose of our being brought into equity and right relationship: a rightwising of solidarity in covenant inclusion and participation).

CHAPTER 5

1. **Being, then, folks that were eschatologically delivered and rightwised** (placed in the right relationship of covenantal solidarity in the Way pointed out and made fair, equitable, just, free from guilt and turned in the right direction) **from the midst of [His] faithfulness, out of trust and from conviction, we continuously hold and progressively have** [other MSS: let us (or: we can and should) habitually retain and enjoy] **peace and a joining, face to face with God** (or: a harmonious joining [directing and conducting us] toward God), **through our Owner and Lord, Jesus Christ** (or: Master, [the] Anointed Jesus),
2. **through Whom, also, we have had and now hold the conducted approach and access** (or: the act of bringing toward to gain entrée), **by [His] faithfulness** (or: in this trust; with that confidence; for loyalty), **into this grace and joyous favor within which we have stood and in union with which we now stand, and so we keep on celebrating, speaking loudly and boasting upon the expectation** (or: expectant hope) **of God's glory** (the manifestation from God which calls forth praise; from the splendor, which is God [filling His Temple]; and: from God's good reputation; of the opinion from God; from the imagination which has the quality of God).
3. **So not only this, but further, we also keep on celebrating, speaking loudly and boasting within the pressures, while exulting in ordeals, afflictions and tribulations, having seen and thus knowing that the pressure** (or: the ordeal, affliction or tribulation) **is habitually producing** (working down; accomplishing) **a relentless remaining** (or: abiding and dwelling) **under [situations and circumstances]** (or: humble and persistent endurance and fortitude as

we get through it, as well as the patient ability to give support).

4. **Yet the remaining and abiding under [produces] a quality of being approved by testing** (= maturity of character); **in turn, the quality of being approved by testing [produces] expectation and hope.**

5. **Now the expectation** (or: expectant hope) **does not habitually bring down shame** (disgrace; dishonor; thus: disappointment), **because God's love** (the urge toward reunion and the unambiguous, uniting acceptance from God; God's giving of Himself to [us]) **has been poured out in a gush and shed forth so that it now floods within our hearts, permeating the core of our being, through the Set-apart Breath-effect** (or: Holy Spirit; Sacred Attitude) **being given to us** (in us; for us).

6. **For during our yet existing [as] weak folks and continuing in being without strength** (or: [B reads: Since in fact] when we were infirm, and thus helpless), **Christ, still corresponding to and in accord with [the] appointed season** (or: down from a *kairos*; in the sphere of and down into the level of a fitting situation; in line with a fertile moment), **died for the sake of the ungodly and irreverent** (or: died over [the situation of] and on behalf of those without awe of God).

7. **Now you see, with difficult toil and pain** (or: For hardly, scarcely or rarely) **for the sake of** (over [the situation of]; on behalf of) **a just person** (a righteous one; one in accord with the Way pointed out; someone in right relationship; a rightwised one) **will someone** (anyone; a certain one) **proceed to be dying. For over** (for the sake of) **the good** (noble; virtuous) **person or cause, perhaps** (or: possibly) **someone** (or: a certain one) **may continue being brave enough** (daring; courageous) **to die.** [*cf 8:31-39, below]

8. **Yet God constantly stands together with His own love* [flowing] into us** (or: But God continuously puts the urge for accepting-reunion, from, and which is, Himself, together into the midst of us), **because during our still continuing to exist being** (= while we were yet) **failures** (folks deviating from the goal; ones missing the target and making mistakes; sinners; outcasts), **Christ died over our [condition and predicament]** (or: on our behalf; for the sake of us).

9. **Much more, then – being NOW** (at the present time) **eschatologically delivered and rightwised** (turned in the right direction; placed in right relationships of solidarity; righted and made fair within the Way pointed out; or: justified and made free from guilt; or: = placed in covenant) **within His blood** (or: in union with the blood from, and which is, Him) **– through Him we will continue being rescued** (saved; delivered; made healthy and whole; returned to our original state and condition; kept safe), **away from the [conditions or situations of] personal emotion** (inherent fervor; natural mental bent or disposition; teeming passion and swelling desire; or: [our] anger and [human] wrath). [cf 4:25b, above; Gal. 2:17; Phil. 3:9]

10. **For you see, since** (or: if) **while continuously existing being actively hostile ones** (or: enemies [of people, or of God]) **we were suddenly changed from enmity to friendship by God** (or: conciliated to God; or: changed to be wholly other and to be in line, consistent and compatible IN God) **through His Son's death, much more** (or: all the more, then) **we will continue being kept safe and will be progressively delivered** (rescued; saved; cured and restored to the health and wholeness of our original state and condition) **– being folks that were conciliated** (fully changed from enmity to friendship and made totally other than we were) **within His Life** (or: in union with the life which is Him).

11. **And not only that, but further, we also are now folks constantly celebrating, speaking loudly and boasting within, and in union with, God, through our Owner** (or: Lord; Master), **Jesus Christ – through Whom we NOW receive** (or: actively seize; grasp; take-down and hold by hand) **the [aforementioned] act of being changed from enmity to friendship**

(or: the full exchange of being changed to be in line, consistent and compatible, where we are totally other than we were; the reconciliation; the commensurate exchange; the change, [induced by the action of God,] which came down [upon us]).

12. **Because of and through this** (or: Therefore; That is why), **just as through one man** (or: So it is that, even as through the act or agency of one person,) **The Sin** (or: the failure, miss of the target and deviation from the goal) **entered into the aggregate of humanity** (ordered system of religion, culture, society and government; or: world; cosmos), **and through The Sin** (failure; the mistake; the miss of the target; the deviation) **The Death [also], in this way The Death thus also passed through in all directions** (or: came through the midst causing division and duality; went throughout) **into all mankind** (or: into the midst of humanity; or: to all people), **upon which [situation, condition, and with the result that] all people sin** (or: whereupon, everyone failed, missed the target and fell short of the goal, and thus all make mistakes and deviate from the path)
13. **– for you see, until** (or: you see, up to the point of; for prior to) **Law** (or: custom), **sin** (failure; missing of the target; deviation from the goal) **continued existing within the ordered System** (world of religion, government, economy and culture; or: organized societies; or: cosmos), **yet sin** (failure; missing; deviating) **is not continuing to be logically considered** (is not being taken into account; is not habitually being put on one's account or ledger; is not continually counted), **there being** (or: existing) **no law** (or: custom).
14. **But nonetheless The Death reigned** (or: holds royal and kingly rule) **from Adam as far as and as long as Moses** [= Law], **even upon those not sinning** (failing to hit the target; deviating from the goal) **upon** [B and other MSS: within] **the result of that which is conformed to** (upon the occasion of the effect of the similarity of, or in the likeness of) **the stepping aside** (or: the transgression) **of Adam – who is, and continues being, a replication** (an impress; a pattern; a type; a prefigure) **of and from the One being repeatedly** (or: always; or: progressively) **about to ... [be (?) come (?) do something (?)]** (or: the One habitually impending)

> (or: which exists being an impression made by a blow from the [situation; Person; creation; realm; arrangement] progressively being about to [exist]).

15. **Yet to the contrary, [it is] not in the same way [with] the effect of grace** (result of favor; the thing graciously given) **as [it was with] the effect of the fall to the side** (or: = the result of the stumbling aside and the offence is not simply balanced out by the result of the joyful gift of grace – the gratuitous favor). **For you see, since** (or: if) **by** (or: in) **the effect of the fall to the side** (the result of the stumbling aside and the offense) **of the one THE MANY** (= the mass of humanity) **died, MUCH MORE** (= infinitely greater) **[is] the Grace of God** (God's Grace; favor which is God), **and the gift** (or: gratuitous benefit) **within Grace – a joy-producing act of Favor – by that of the One Man, Jesus Christ, surrounded** (or: encircles) **into encompassing superabundance** (extraordinary surplus and excess) **into THE MANY** (= the mass of humanity).
16. **And further, [it is] NOT [with] the effect of the gush and flow of the gratuitous gift as [it was] through one missing of the target** (failing; deviating; sinning). **For you see, on the one hand, the effect of the decision and judgment** (result of the separating, evaluation and verdict) **[was] from out of one [failure and deviation, which led] into a commensurate effect of a decision** (a corresponding result of a negative evaluation which fell in line with the decision and followed the pattern which divided [us] down). **But on the other hand, the effect of the grace** (the product of the gratuitous favor and the resulting joyous benefit) **[is] from out of the effect of many falls to the side** (result of many stumblings-aside and offenses) **into the effect of a rightwising deliverance into covenant inclusion in the Way and making things right**

(the result of a liberating placing into right relationships within the Way pointed out; or: the effect of an act of justice; an effect of equity; a just award; or: a result of fairness, removal of guilt, and justification, while being turned in the right direction; an amendment of what was wrong; a just-effect; = the effect of covenant inclusion and participation).

17. **For since** (or: if) **by the effect of the fall to the side** (or: in the result of the stumbling aside; with the effect of the offense) **of the one The Death reigned** (or: reigns; rules as king) **through that one, much more, rather, will the peoples** (= the masses of humanity) – **in continuously receiving and seizing upon** (taking in hand) **the surrounding superabundance** (encircling, extraordinary surplus and excess) **of the Grace and of, from and which is the gratuitous gift of the liberated Rightwisedness** (of the solidarity in fair and equitable treatment; from the placement in right [covenant]-relationship in the Way; of the justification and freedom from guilt while being turned in the right direction and made right) – **continue reigning** (or: ruling as kings) **within and in union with Life through the One, Jesus Christ.**

18. **Consequently, then, as [it was] through the effect of one fall to the side** (or: the result of one offense) **[coming] into all mankind** ([permeating] into all humanity; = [extending] into the whole race) **[bringing them] into a commensurate effect of a decision** (a corresponding result of a negative evaluation which fell in line with the decision and followed the pattern which divided [us] down), **THUS ALSO and in the same way, through one just-effect and the result of one right act which set [all humanity] right and in accord with the Way pointed out** (through the result of one act of justice, equity and solidarity; through a single decree creating rightwised relationships; through one effect of rightwising which turns [people] in the right direction) **[it comes] into ALL MANKIND** (all humanity; all people; = the whole race) **[bringing them] into a setting right of Life and a liberating rightwising from Life [including them in covenant community]**

> (or: Life's turning [folks] in the right direction resulting in right relating, equity and justice which is in accord with the Way pointed out; a making of situations and conditions to be right, which pertain to Life; an expressing of fairness and equity, which is LIFE; a rightly directed solidarity coming from Life; a just-acting deliverance having the qualities of life).

19. **For you see, JUST AS through the unwillingness to listen, or to pay attention, resulting in disobedience** (or: the erroneous hearing leading to disobedience) **of the one person THE MANY** (= the mass of humanity; note: cf Weymouth NT in Modern Speech, 1909 Edition) **were rendered** (established; constituted; placed down and made to be) **sinners** (failures; ones who diverge and miss the target), **THUS – in the same way – ALSO through the submissive listening and paying attention resulting in obedience of the One, THE MANY** (= the mass of humanity) **will continue being rendered "set-right folks"**

> (placed down and established [to be] just ones; constituted folks who have been rightwised to be people in the Way pointed out; made righteous ones who are guilt-free, fair, equitable, and rightly-turned in the solidarity of covenant relationships).

20. **Now Law and custom at one point entered in alongside** (or: intruded into the situation by the side) **to the end that the effect of the fall to the side** (or: so that the result of the offense and the stumbling aside) **would increase to be more than enough** (should greatly abound and become more intense). **But where the Sin** (the failure; the divergence and missing of the target) **increases** (or: abounded to be more than enough; becomes more intense) **THE GRACE** ("the act producing happiness, which is granted as a favor" – Jim Coram) **at once super-exceeds** (or:

hyper-exceeded) **over and above, surrounding to excessive abundance and overflow,**
21. **to the end that JUST AS the Sin** (the failure; the erroneous act; the deviation and digression which issued in missing the goal) **at one point reigned** (or: ruled as king; exercised sovereign sway) **within, and in union with, the Death, THUS SO** (or: in THIS way) **also the Grace and joyous favor would reign** (should rule as king; can exercise sovereign sway) **through an eschatological deliverance that created rightwisedness** (or: by means of being rightly-turned into an existence with equity in [covenantal] solidarity of right relationships which accord to the Way; through a liberating Justice-[expression]) **[which leads] into Life which belongs to, pertains to and has the characteristics of the Age** (or: eonian life; Life of the Age [of Messiah]; a life for the ages) **– through Jesus Christ, our Owner** (Lord; Master).

CHAPTER 6

1. **What, then** (or: consequently), **shall we continue saying** (or: declaring)**? Should we continue prolonging our remaining** (or: May we stay longer, remain on, habitually abide or persist) **in the Sin** (with the failure; by the missing of the target; centered in the error; in relation to the deviation from the goal), **to the end that the Grace and Favor may increase to be more than enough?**
2. **Certainly not** (May it not come to be; May it not happen)**! We, the very ones who once died by the Sin** (or: died with the Sin; die in deviation; died with reference to missing the target; died to failure; die in error), **how shall we** [other MSS: could we] **still** (or: yet) **continue living within it, centered in it, or in union with it?**

3. **Or are you continuing to be ignorant** (are you remaining without experiential knowledge; do you continue not knowing) **that as many as are immersed** (or: were at one point soaked or baptized) **into Christ Jesus are immersed** (or: were then baptized) **into His death?**
4. **We, then** (or: consequently), **were buried together** (entombed together with funeral rites) **in Him** (or: by Him; with Him), **through the immersion** (baptism) **into the death, to the end that just as** (or: in the same manner as) **Christ was roused and raised forth from out of the midst of dead folks THROUGH** (through means of) **THE GLORY** (the glorious manifestation of splendor which calls forth praise; the imagination; the assumed appearance) **of, from, and which is, The Father, thus also we can walk around** (or: we also should likewise conduct ourselves and order our behavior) **within newness of life** (in union with life characterized by being essentially new in kind and quality, and different from that which was former).

5. **For since** (or: You see, if) **we have been birthed** (have become; have come to be) **folks engrafted and produced together** (or: planted and made to grow together; brought forth together; congenital) **in, by, to and with the result of the likeness of** (or: the effect of the similar manner from) **His death, then certainly we will also continue existing [in and with the effects of the likeness] of The Resurrection**
      (or: which is the resurrection; or: from, and with qualities of, the resurrection),
6. **while constantly knowing this by intimate experience, that our old, former humanity is crucified together** (or: was simultaneously and jointly impaled and put to death on an execution stake) **with [Him], to the end that the body of the Sin** (the body belonging to the failure; the corporal manifestation that pertains to the deviation; the group of people [Adam] who missed the target) **could and would be rendered useless and inoperative** (idled-down to be unproductive;

made null, inactive and unemployed), **for us to no longer continually be a slave to the Sin** (or: perform as a slave in the failure, for the Sin, or by deviating and thus missing the goal),

7. **for you see, the One at one point dying** (or: the person at some point experiencing death) **has been eschatologically released and rightwised away from the Sin**

> (or: set in the Way pointed out, away from the Failure; turned in the right direction, away from the deviation and missing of the target; placed into equity and right relationships, away from error; = has been delivered and moved away from The Sin, and has been brought into participation in covenant relationship). [*cf* vs. 18, below]

8. **Now since we died** (or: if we die) **together with Christ, we are continuously believing** (relying; trusting) **that we will also continue living together in Him** (by Him; for Him; to Him; with Him),

9. **having seen and thus knowing and perceiving that Christ, being aroused and raised forth from out of the midst of dead folks, is no longer dying. His death is no longer exercising ownership** (or: Death is no longer being lord or exerting mastery pertaining to Him; or: From Him, death is no longer functioning as a lord, owner or master),

10. **for it follows that what He died** (or: You see, [the death] which He died) **He died for the Sin** (or: by the Failure; in the deviation; to the Sin; with the Error) **at once and for all [time, and people]** (or: once and only once); **yet what He lives** (or: Yet [the life] which He continues to live), **He continues living in God** (for God; to God; by God; with God).

11. **Thus you folks, also, be logically considering** (reckoning, accounting and concluding) **yourselves to exist being dead ones, indeed, by the failure to hit the target** (or: in the Sin; or: to the deviation), **yet ones continuously living by God** (in God; for God; to God; with God), **within Christ Jesus, our Owner** (or: in union with [the] Anointed Jesus, our Lord and Master).

12. **Do not, then, let the Sin to continue reigning** (or: Therefore, stop allowing the failure, the mistake, or the deviation from the goal to continue on the throne ruling as king) **within your mortal body, [leading] into the continual listening in submissive obedience to its earnest desires** (or: its full rushing of emotions, passions and lusts).

13. **Also stop constantly placing your members** (or: body parts) **alongside** (providing and presenting them) **[as] tools** (or: instruments) **of injustice** (disregard for what is right; activities discordant to the Way pointed out); **but rather, you folks at once place yourselves alongside for disposal to God** (or: stand yourselves with God, at [His] side; by and in God, present yourselves; set yourselves alongside [each other], for God) **as it were being folks continually alive forth from out of the midst of dead ones, and your members [as] tools** (instruments) **of fair and equitable dealing in the Way pointed out in and by God** (of justice and solidarity, for God; of being turned in the right direction, to God; of rightwised covenant relationships with God),

14. **for your sin** (your failure; your missing of the target) **will not continue exercising mastery** (or: You see, deviation from the goal shall not exert ownership and rule as your lord), **for you folks are not under Law** (or: do not exist being subject to [Torah] or custom), **but rather under Grace** (or: the Act which produced happiness, which was granted as a favor).

15. **What, then? Should we** (May we; Can we) **occasionally sin** (miss the target; fail), **because we are not under law** (subject to [Torah] or custom), **but rather under grace** (the act yielding happiness, granting joyous favor)? **Certainly not** (May it not come to be or happen)!

16. **Have you not seen and thus know** (Are you not aware) **that to whom** (for whom; or: in what) **you habitually place yourselves alongside, presenting and providing yourselves as**

slaves into submissive, obedient hearing, you folks are, and continue being, [his or its] slaves – to whom (in what; for which) you habitually submit in obedient hearing – whether of failure (of sin; of missing the target) into death, or of submissive, hearing obedience into fair and equitable dealings of rightwised relationship in the Way pointed out ([covenant] justice).
17. But Grace by God (or: Now [this is] happiness granted as favor in God): that you folks were existing, continuing to be slaves of the Sin (slaves of failure; slaves belonging to the missing the target), yet now you submissively hear and pay attention, so as to obey – from out of heart! – [the] type of instruction (or: chiseled and imprinted pattern of teaching) into which you are (or: at one point were) given over (transferred; delivered; committed).
18. Now, being set free (or: liberated) from the Sin (failure; error), you folks are (or: were suddenly) enslaved (made slaves) to justice (= to covenant participation in solidarity)
(or: in the Way pointed out; for fair and equitable dealings; by the Well-ordered, Righteous Existence [in Christ]; to rightwised relationship and [covenantal] behavior).

19. I am speaking humanly because of the weakness or sickness of your flesh (or: = your human condition; or: = the self that had been distorted by the System): for even as you folks presented (placed and provided alongside) your members [as; being] slaves by (for; in; to) the Uncleanness and by (for) the Lawlessness, [leading] into that Lawlessness (or: in one illegal act to [another] illegal act), in this manner (thus) now you folks must place (provide; present) your members alongside [as] slaves of the Way pointed out (slaves of rightwised relationship in fair and equitable dealings; slaves of justice and righteousness) [leading] into the quality and sphere of being set-apart (or: into a holy consecration and a state of being sacredly different).
20. For when you folks were existing being slaves of the Sin (slaves from failure; slaves of deviation from the goal), you were existing [as it were] being free [as; with regard] to the Way pointed out (= being not owned by rightwised relationships, fairness, equity and justice).
21. What fruit, then, were you having (did you used to hold or possess) at that time, upon which [situation or condition] you folks now continue to be ashamed and embarrassed? For, indeed, the outcome (the end; the goal; the fruition; the consummation; the destiny) of those things [is] death.

22. But now being folks set free from the Sin (from failure; from error; from missing the target; from deviation) yet being enslaved by (to; in; for) God, you folks continue having (habitually hold and possess) your fruit unto the quality and sphere of being set-apart (into a sacred difference). Now the outcome (goal, end and destiny) [of this is] life which belongs to, is proper to, pertains to and is connected to the Age (eonian life; Life of and for the ages).
23. For you see, the subsistence pay (the ration money; the allowance) of the Sin (failure; the missing of the target; the deviation) [is] death, but God's grace-effect (or: the result of the joyous and gracious gift of and from God; the effect of the favor, which is God,) [is] life which belongs to, is proper to, pertains to and is connected to the Age (eonian life; Life of and for the ages) within Christ Jesus, our Owner (or: in union with [the] Anointed Jesus, our Lord).

CHAPTER 7

1. Or are you continuing to be ignorant (are you remaining without experiential knowledge and insight), brothers (= fellow covenant members) – for I am speaking to those having intimate experiential knowledge of Law (= those who understand Torah) – that the Law (or: culture;

Torah) **continuously performs as lord** (owner; master) **of the man for as long as he is living?**
2. **For instance, the married woman** (the woman under subjection to a husband or to an adult male) **has been bound and remains tied up by Law and custom to the living husband** (or: has been wrapped up and stands tied to law [= Torah; or: custom] by the living man). **Yet if the husband may die, she has been released from employment and stands idle** (or: has been brought down to living without labor and rendered inactive; she is discharged and brought down to unproductivity, being idled down) **away from the husband's law** (or: from pertaining to the Law [= Torah] and custom of the adult man).
3. **Consequently** (or: Accordingly), **then, [with the] continued living of the husband, she will be dealing as an adulteress** (or: bear the title "adulteress") **if she should become [attached] to, or [a lover] for, or [involved] with a different man** (or: husband); **but if the husband may die, she is free** (she exists in a state of freedom) **from the Law** [= Torah], **not to be an adulteress, pertaining to her becoming [a wife]** for (or: to) **a different man** (or: husband).
4. **So that, my brothers** (folks from the same womb), **you folks also were made dead to the Law** (or: were put to death by the Law [=Torah] and with the Law), **through the body of the Christ, [proceeding] into the situation to become [the wife] for** (or: to; in; with) **a different One – in** (to; for) **the One being roused and raised forth from out of the midst of dead folks – to the end that we may bear fruit by God** (or: produce a harvest in, for, to and with God).

5. **You see, when we** [= Adam/Israel] **were existing within the flesh** (or: = in the old alienated Adamic existence, with the flesh sacrifices and markers of the Law), **the effects, impressions, emotions and impulses from the experiences, passions and suffering of the failures** (from the sins and deviations which caused misses of the target) **– the things through means of the Law** [the Torah] **– were continually operating** (working within; energizing and effecting) **within our members into the condition to produce fruit by Death** (in death; to death; for Death).
6. **But now** (at the present time), **we** [= Israel] **are** (or: were instantly) **rendered inactive** (brought down to living without labor, released from employment, made unproductive; discharged) **away from the Law** (= the Torah; [some MSS add: of Death]), **dying within that in which we were constantly being held down** (held in possession and detained), **so that it is [for] us to be habitually performing as slaves within newness of spirit** (a newness pertaining to spirit and has its source in the Breath-effect; freshness and new quality of attitude) **and not in oldness** (obsoleteness; outdatedness) **of Letter** (or: not in outwornness of written Scripture).
7. **What, then, shall we say** (or: declare)**? [Is] the Law** (or: custom) **sin** (error; failure to hit the target; deviation from the goal)**? Certainly not** (May it not come to be)**! Instead** (or: But rather) **I did not** (or: do not) **at any point experientially and intimately know the Sin, if not through Law** ([= Torah]; or: custom). **For besides, I had not seen and thus had not known** (become conscious of) **the full passion** (earnest desire; lust; coveting; emotion upon something) **if the Law and the custom were not continuously saying** (or: except the [Torah] kept on saying),

> **"You will continue not putting strong emotions upon something** (or: You shall not repeatedly have a strong impulse or desire; You will not constantly crave or covet [other folks' possessions or their gods])**."** [Ex. 20:17; Deut. 5:21; comment: the "I" of this passage = Adam (Gen. 3)/Israel (Ex. 32)/Paul (in his pre-Christian experience)]

8. **Yet the Sin** (or: the failure; the error; the mistake; the missing of the target; the deviation from the goal), **taking** (receiving in the hand and thus, getting) **a starting point** (a base of operation; an occasion; a means of beginning) **through the implanted goal** (impartation of the finished product within; inward directive; commandment [to Adam, then to Israel]), **works** (or: worked)

down to effect and produce within me every full passion, strong impulse, over-desire and craving emotion upon things – for apart from Law (or: a custom; or: [Torah]) **sin** (error; failure; missing the target; deviation) **[is] dead** (or: [was] lifeless).

9. **Now I was at one time** (or: formerly) **habitually living apart from Law** (or: I was once alive, independent from custom and [Torah]); **yet, in connection with the coming of the implanted goal** (of the impartation of the finished product within; of the inward commandment and directive), **the Sin becomes alive again** (or: deviation, failure, error and the missing of the target revived and comes back to life), **but I die** (or: and I died; yet I die).

10. **Also, the implanted goal** (impartation of the finished product within; inward directive; commandment) **– the one [meant to lead] into Life – this was found by me** (for me; in me; to me) **[to be leading] into death.**

11. **For the Sin** (failure; error; the miss when shooting at a target; the deviation from the goal), **taking a starting point** (receiving an occasion and base of operation) **through the implanted goal** (impartation of the finished product within; inward directive; commandment [to Adam, then to Israel]), **completely makes me unable to walk the Path** (made me incapable to walk out [customs of the Law]; thoroughly cheats and deludes me, making me lose my Way; deceives me; [comment: reference to Eve in Gen. 3:13]) **and through it kills me off** (or: slaughtered me).

12. **And thus** (or: Consequently) **the Law** [= the Torah], **indeed, [is] set-apart** (holy; sacred; consecrated) **and the implanted goal** (impartation of the finished product within; inward directive; commandment) **[is] set-apart** (holy; sacred) **and in accord with the Way pointed out** (fair; equitable; just; = related to covenant) **and good** (virtuous).

13. **Then did the good come to be death for me** (in me; to me)**? Certainly not** (May it not come to be)**! But rather, the Sin** (failure; error; the miss; the mistake; the deviation) **– to the end that sin** (failure; error; deviation) **may be brought to light and made visible** (or: in order that it may be made to appear and be shown as being sin) **– is constantly producing** (or: working down) **death through the good** [i.e., the commandment], **to the end that the Sin** (failure; the miss; error; the deviation), **through the implanted goal** (impartation of the finished product within; inward directive; commandment), **could come to be in accord with a throwing-beyond that is missing the target** [cf 5:20; above]

> (or: should happen according to excess which is failing; may become extremely erroneous; should come to be in line with a deviating shooting over the goal; or, substantively: would become an exceeding failure, an excessive sinner or a total outcast). [cf Gal. 2:19-20]

14. **For you see, we have seen and are aware** (or: on the one hand I recognize and know) **that the Law** (= Torah; or: law; custom; principle) **constantly exists being spiritual** (is pertaining to spirit; is having the qualities of a Breath-effect; is relating to attitude), **yet** (or: on the other hand) **I** [= Israel? or, Adam] **myself am** (or: exist being) **fleshly** (composed of flesh; carnal; flesh-oriented; or: = affected by the alienated self), **being one having been and now remaining sold under [the power and control of] the Sin** (under failure and the miss of the Target [of Torah?]).

15. **For what I am constantly producing** (habitually working down to accomplish; [= keeping customs of the Torah]) **I do not intimately know** (experience in my understanding). **You see, that which I continually will** (habitually intend and purpose), **this I do not habitually practice. But rather, that which I constantly hate, this I continue to do or repeatedly perform!**

16. **Now if what I am not continually willing** (not habitually intending), **this I am habitually doing or producing, I am constantly concurring with** (conceding; agreeing with; a prophetic voice with) **the Law** [= the Torah], **that [it is] ideal** (fine; excellent; beautiful).

17. **Yet now** (= as the case really stands) **I myself am no longer habitually producing** (continuously working down and effecting) **this, but rather the Sin** (the failure; the personified error of missing the Target; the deviation [from Torah and its boundary markers]) **[which is] continuously housing herself** (or: making its home; inhabiting; dwelling; = living) **within me.**

18. **For I have seen and thus know that good** (or: virtue) **is not habitually making its home** (housing itself; dwelling; = living) **within me – that is, within my flesh** (= alienated self; or: = life under Torah) **– for the [ability or condition] to will** (or: intend; purpose) **is continually lying near beside me, but the [ability, condition or circumstance] to constantly produce** (work down, effect and accomplish) **the ideal** (the fine; the excellent; the beautiful) **[is] not.**

19. **For that which I constantly intend** (will; purpose) **– a good thing** (a noble deed; a virtuous act) **– I do not normally do** (or: I am not consistently doing what I continually will, intend and purpose: [something] good), **but rather, that which I continuously do not intend** (or: will) **– a worthless** (ugly; ignoble; base; bad; evil) **thing – this I habitually put into practice!**

20. **Yet if that which I am not willing** (intending), **this I am constantly doing, I, myself, am no longer producing** (working down and effecting) **it, but rather, [it is] the Sin** (the failure; the error; the missing of the Goal; the deviation [from Torah-keeping]) **continuously housing herself** (making its home; dwelling) **within me** [= Adam, or an Israelite, personified].

21. **Consequently I keep on finding the principle** (or: this law) **in me – in the person normally willing** (purposing; intending) **to habitually do** (perform; produce) **the ideal** (the beautiful; the fine) **– that in me** (or: with me; for me) **the worthless** (the ugly; the ignoble; the base; the evil) **is constantly lying close by.** [cf 8:3b, below, re: the Sin in the flesh]

22. **For habitually I am pleased with** (take enjoyment and delight with) **the principle and law which is God** (or: the principle of God; or: the Law from God), **down in** (or: in correspondence with; on the level of) **the inner human** (or: the interior person within; the inside humanity),

23. **yet I constantly see** (or: observe) **a different principle** (or: law), **within my members, [which is] by the Law** (or: custom; or: [= Torah]) **repeatedly taking the field to wage war against my mind** (or: warring in opposition to, and in the place of, the law of, and which is, my mind), **and repeatedly taking me prisoner and leading me into captivity within the principle** (or: in union with the Law) **of the Sin** (the failure; the error; the miss of the Target; the deviation from [Torah-keeping]) **– the one continuously existing** (or: now being) **within my members.**

24. **I [am] a wretched** (callous-weighted [from hard work], miserable, distressed, enduring-severe-effort-and-hardship) **man** (or: human)**! What will be progressively rescuing me from out of the body of this death** (or: from out of this body of the death; out of this body which pertains to death and which has its origin, character and qualities in death)**?** [comment: Paul continues his rhetoric of impersonating Adam's and Israel's predicament; cf 2 Cor. 5: 1-8]

25. **Grace! The Grace of, and the joyous favor from, God! – through Jesus Christ our Owner** (or: by means of [Messiah] Jesus, our Lord; through Anointed Jesus, our Master)**!**
> [other MSS: The grace of {the} Lord; other MSS: Yet {there is} grace and favor in God (or: by God; with God), through Jesus Christ our Lord (or: Master); other MSS: I habitually give thanks to, and speak of the goodness of grace in, God!] **Consequently then, I myself in** (or: by; with) **the mind, indeed** (or: on the one hand), **continuously perform as a slave to and for the principle and law which is God** (or: in God's Law; by and with God's principle), **yet in** (or: on the other hand by and to) **the flesh** (= with the self which is oriented to society and the System; or: = customs and cultus of the Torah), **to, for and in a principle of failure** (with a law of sin or error; or: for a law from missing the Target; or: by Sin's law).

CHAPTER 8

1. **Nothing, consequently, [is] now a result of condemnation in** (or: a commensurate effect of a decision for; a corresponding result of a negative evaluation which falls in line with a decision or follows the pattern which divides [folks] down, with) **those within Christ Jesus**

(or: In that case, therefore, [there is] now not one thing [that is] really an effect of a downward-judging to, in or with the folks in union with or centered in [the] Anointing of Jesus)! [A, D & later MSS here add: {They} are not habitually walking around (= living their lives) in accord with (or: corresponding to) flesh] [Aleph2, D2 & later MSS here add: but to the contrary, in the sphere of spirit and attitude (or: Breath-effect; or: {the} Spirit).]

2. **For the principle and law of, from and which is the spirit and attitude of 'The Life within Christ Jesus'**

(or: For you see, the Law of Life's spirit, joined with [the] Anointing of Jesus; or: For the Spirit's law of life within Christ Jesus; or: the Law [= Torah] from the Breath-effect, which is Life in union with [the] Anointed Jesus)

frees you away from the Law of the Sin and of the Death (or: immediately set you [other MSS: me] at liberty from the principle of the failure, or of the missing of the target, and from the death; exempts you from this code involved with error and deviation from the goal, as well as from the death; emancipated you from this law from the mistake, and which is the Death). [comment: This law from sin and from death refers both to the principle of the old Adamic life and to Israel's Torah; *cf* 1 Cor. 15:53-54; 2 Cor. 3:6; 5:4]

3. **You see, [because of] the powerlessness and inability of the Law** (from the written code; = associated with Torah) – **within which it kept on making [folks] weak and feeble** ([note: the active voice]; but as an intransitive: in which [incapability] it was constantly falling sick and continued being without strength) **through the flesh** (= the alienated self oriented toward the System; or: = Torah culture and cultus, with boundary-marker observances) – **in sending His own Son** (or: by sending the Son, Who is Himself) **within a result of a likeness of flesh that is connected with sin** (or: in an effect of being made similar to sin's flesh; = in union with a result from being made like the alienated existence that came from failure), **and concerning sin**

(or: **encircling** failure and error; to address a missed target; **surrounding** deviation; [note: or, as a technical term for the sin offering: = to be the sin-offering; see: Lev. 4:32; 5:6-9; 2 Chr. 29:24; Ps. 40:6; Ez. 42:13, LXX]; *cf* 7:11ff, above; Jn. 3:16), **God gives a commensurate decision from a corresponding negative evaluation which falls in line with and follows the pattern which divides down** (or: condemned; gives a down-oriented verdict; passed down a sentence on and gave judgment against) **the Sin within the flesh [system]**

(or: the failure, the error, the miss of the target and the deviation [which is] in union with the human condition; or: = the mistake of the estranged, System-dominated self),

4. **to the end that the effect of the just Deed of deliverance in which wrong was set right, resulting from being liberated and turned in the right direction within the Way pointed out, which is the principle,** (or: so that the effect of the fair relationships which come from [His] law and custom; or: in order that the result of the equity and rightness of the Law) **can** (would; could; may) **be fulfilled and become full within us – in those habitually walking about** (or: = for the folks ordering their behavior/living their lives) **not in accord with flesh** (or: = not corresponding to the human condition; or: = on the level of Torah-keeping boundary-markers), **but rather in accord with spirit** (or: down from [the] Spirit; corresponding to [His] Attitude; on the level of and in the sphere of Breath-effect). [*cf* 2:1-11, above; 2 Cor. 3:3; 5:16; Gal. 4:4-5]

5. **You see, those continuously existing in accord with flesh** (or: = in correspondence to Torah-keeping and cultural boundaries; or: = the human condition) **habitually think about, have an understanding and outlook based upon, are inclined to, set their mind on and are disposed to the things of the flesh** (= the human condition with its cultural traditions, religious cultus and national boundary markers), **yet those in accord with spirit** (or: down from [the] Spirit; on the level of Breath-effect; in line with [His] Attitude) **[think about; have an outlook from] the things and matters of the spirit** (or: the Spirit; Breath-effect; the Attitude).

6. **For the result of the thinking** (mind-set; effect of the way of thinking; disposition; result of understanding and inclination; the minding; the opinion; the thought; the outlook) **of the flesh** (= from the human condition or the System of culture and cultus; or: = Torah keeping) **[is; brings] death, yet the result of the thinking** (mind-set; disposition; thought and way of thinking; outlook) **of the spirit** (or: from the Spirit; which is the Breath-effect) **[is; brings] Life and Peace** (joining).

7. **Because of that, the result of the thinking** (disposition; thought processes; mind-set, outlook) **of the flesh** (= attention to Torah boundary-markers, custom and cultus; or: = from the human condition) **[is; brings] enmity, alienation and discord [streaming] into God** (or: hostility unto, or active hatred with a view to, God), **for it continues not being humbly aligned and supportive** (habitually placed under and submitted; or, as a middle: subjecting, humbly arranging or marshaling itself) **to the principle and law which is God** (or: in God's principle; by the Law from God), **for neither is it able nor does it have power.**

8. **Now the folks continuously existing in the midst of** (or: So people being in union with, or centered in,) **flesh** (= the alienated human condition; or: = the religious system involving flesh sacrifices, Torah boundary-markers/customs) **have no power and are not able at any point to please God** (or: to fit or adapt to God; or: to be content with God; or: to be acceptable in God).

9. **Yet you folks are not constantly existing within the midst of flesh** (or: you are not in union with nor centered on [the alienated human condition, or Torah-keeping with flesh sacrifices]), **but rather within spirit, in union with Breath-effect and centered on [His] attitude, since indeed God's Spirit** (or: if so be that [the] Breath-effect which is God; or: if as is the fact that an attitude which corresponds to God) **is continuously housing Itself** (making His abode; residing; dwelling; by idiom: cohabiting; living together as husband and wife) **within and among you folks. Yet if anyone is not continuously having, or not habitually and progressively holding, Christ's Spirit and [the Messiah's] Attitude** (or: So if a certain person is not regularly possessing a Breath-effect which is Anointed), **this one is not habitually existing from Him as his Source** (or: is not now having His character or qualities; or: presently is not His).

10. **But since Christ** (or: Yet if [the] Anointing) **[is] within you folks, on the one hand the body is dead** (lifeless) **BECAUSE OF sin** (through failure, deviation and missing the target), **yet on the other hand, the Spirit, Attitude and Breath-effect [is] Life BECAUSE OF an eschatological act of justice that brought a rightwising deliverance into equitable, covenantal relationships within the Way pointed-out** (or: on account of the covenantal Faithfulness of a liberating Turn into the Right Direction of the Living Way/Path).

11. **Now since the Breath-effect** (or: Spirit; Attitude) **of the One arousing and raising Jesus forth from out of the midst of dead folks is continuously housing Itself** (making His abode; residing; making His home; by idiom: living together as husband and wife) **within, and in union with, you folks, the One raising Christ Jesus forth from out of dead ones will also continue progressively giving Life to** (or: will even habitually make alive) **the mortal bodies of you**

folks (or: your mortal bodies) **through the constant indwelling of His Spirit** (or: the continual in-housing of His Breath-effect; the continuous internal residing of the Attitude, which is Him,) [other MSS: because of His habitually-indwelling Spirit] **within and among you folks.**
[*cf* 2 Cor. 4:14; 5:4-5; Acts 1:8]

12. **So then brothers** (or: Consequently then, fellow believers), **we do not continue being debtors to the flesh** (or: we are not folks under obligation in the [alienated human condition, or by the system of flesh sacrifices and Torah observance]), **[i.e.,] of the [situation] to be continually living down on the level of and in accord with flesh,** [*cf* 2 Cor. 3:3; 5:16]

13. **for you see, if you folks are continuously living down on the level of, and in accord with, flesh** (= the alienated self, or, the system of flesh sacrifices and Torah observance), **you are progressively about to be dying away. Yet since** (or: if) **in spirit** (or: by [the] Breath-effect; with [His] Spirit; for [the] Attitude), **you folks constantly put to death** (or: deprive of life; extirpate) **the practices and activities of the body** (= works of flesh traditions; Torah cultus) **you will continue living** (or: will be continuously living and progressively possessed of vitality).

14. **For it follows that as many as are being continuously led by God's Spirit** (or: habitually brought or conducted in [the] Breath-effect which is God; progressively driven along with an attitude from God), **these folks are God's sons** (these continuously exist being sons of God; or: = these are folks who have the character and qualities of God). [comment: echo of the Exodus]

15. **For you folks did** (or: do) **not receive again a spirit of slavery to fear** (or: get slavery's spirit or breath-effect again, unto fear; or: take an attitude which personifies being a slave [as in Egypt or under the Law, leading] into fear again), **but rather you received a spirit of being placed as a son** (or: a Breath-effect which set you in the position of a son; or: you receive an attitude of one having been adopted [in accord with Greek or Roman law]), **within which** (or: in union with Whom) **we are habitually crying out, "Abba (Dad), O Father!"**

16. **The same Spirit** (or: spirit; or: The Breath-effect Himself; or: This very attitude) **is constantly witnessing together with our spirit** (is continuously bearing joint-testimony to our spirit; is habitually co-witnessing for our spirit; is progressively adding confirming testimony and evidence in our attitude) **that we are, and continuously exist being, God's children** (ones born of God; children from God [not of the child-escort {Gal. 3:24}], by natural descent).

17. **Now since children** (or: Yet if ones born by natural descent), **also heirs** (possessors and enjoyers of an allotted inheritance; those who hold sway over the allotted portion): **on the one hand, God's heirs, on the other, Christ's joint-heirs**
> (or: indeed possessors and enjoyers of an allotment pertaining to God and from God, yet possessors and enjoyers together in an allotment pertaining to Christ and belonging to Christ) **if so be** (or: provided) **that we are continually affected by sensible experiences together – feeling together; receiving impressions, undergoing passion or suffering together – to the end that we may also be glorified together**
> (or: can be given a shared appearance; would together receive a manifestation of that which calls forth praise; should be given a joint-approval and a joint-reputation; may be thought of and imagined together [in covenant relationship]).
[*cf* 2 Cor. 4:8-9; Col. 3:4; 1 Jn. 3:2]

18. **You see, I have come to a reasoned conclusion** (or: I am reckoning and logically considering) **that the effects of the sensible experiences – sufferings, impressions, passions or feelings – of the current season** (or: of the situation fitted to the present time) **[are] not equivalent** (do not balance the scales; are not of equal value or worth), **[being] face to**

face with the glory (or: [are] of insufficient weight when put in balance to the manifestation which calls forth praise as well as the reputation and good opinion) **which is progressively about to be disclosed unto us, and for us** (or: unveiled into our midst; revealed to and [enter] into us).

19. **For the departure of, and liberation from, head-thinking – which is the cessation and a moving-away from [human] imagination, opinions and assumptions – in the head of the creation is constantly receiving and taking away from out of the unveiling of God's sons**

> (or: = the uncovering and revealing of folks who have the character and qualities of God; or: the disclosure pertaining to the sons of God; or: the unveiling and revelation which belongs to God's sons; or, as an ablative: **the disclosure from God's sons**).

20. **For you see, the creation** (or: that which was formed, framed and founded; [note: can be a figure for Israel under the Law]) **was placed, arranged and aligned under subjection in the empty purposelessness** (or: subordinated to vanity and by futility; made supportive to fruitless nonsense: in worthlessness, for nothingness), **not voluntarily or willingly** (from out of [its] being), **but rather because of** (through; on account of; for the sake of) **the one** (or: the One) **placing [it] under and arranging [it] in subjection** (or: in supportive alignment) **– based upon an expectation** (or: expectant hope) **–**

21. **because** (or: that) **even the creation** [note: can = Israel and the Law] **itself will continue being progressively set free** (will be habitually liberated and constantly made free) **from the slavery of, and from, decay – even the bondage of deterioration which leads to fraying and ruin – [and released] into the freedom of the glory and splendor of God's children**

> (or: into the liberty of the manifestation of that which calls forth praise from, and a good opinion which pertains to, God's born-ones; or: unto the freedom coming from God's imagination pertaining to God's children; or: into the midst of the freedom of the glory from the children [who] belong to God; or: toward centering in the liberty from the glory, which is God, [and] belongs to the children). [*cf* Jn. 1:12, 13; 3:3, 7, 10; 2 Cor. 5:16-17]

22. **You see, we have seen, and thus know and are aware, that all the creation** [note: = Old Covenant Israel] **keeps on sighing, groaning or querulously moaning together, and yet progressively travailing together as in childbirth** (continues suffering common birthing pains) **until now** (to the point of the present moment). [*cf* 2 Cor. 5:2, 4]

23. **Yet not only [this], but further, even we ourselves – constantly holding** (or: having; possessing) **the firstfruit of, and which is, the Spirit** (or: the Firstfruit from the Breath-effect; or: the first offering, or first portion, which is spirit and breath, and is from the Attitude) **– we ourselves also continually sigh and groan within** (in the center of) **ourselves, continuously accepting and with our hands taking away from out of** (or: fully receiving) **a placing in the condition of a son** (or: [the] deposit of the Son; a setting in place which is the Son; a constituting as a son; a placing in the Son)**: the process of the release of our body from slavery**

> (or: [and] the loosing from destruction pertaining to the [corporate, old covenant] body, which is us; or: = the unbinding and release of the body [of Adam; of humanity], which belongs to us). [*cf* 2 Cor. 5:4]

24. **For in the expectation and with hope we are suddenly made whole and healthy**

> (or: You see, by the expectation we are delivered and saved; or: For we were at one point rescued to expectation; or: To be sure, we were kept safe for this expectation)!

Now expectation (or: expectant hope) **being continuously seen or observed is not expectation or hope, for who continues hoping in expectation for what he also constantly sees or observes?**

25. **Yet since** (or: even if) **we continue expecting what we are not seeing** (or: observing), **we**

continue taking away and accepting from out of (or: fully receiving from) **it through remaining under [our present situation and circumstances]** (or: through patient, humble, persistent, supportive endurance).

26. **Now similarly** (or: likewise; in like manner), **the Spirit also** (or: even the Breath-effect; the Attitude) **habitually takes hold together on the opposite side of a situation so as to assist in our weakness** (or: joins with a helping hand in our lack of strength and infirmity; [note: = old covenant weakness of the Law, or of Adam; *cf* 1 Cor. 8:7, 10-12; 9:20-22; 15:43; 2 Cor. 12:9; 13:4; Gal. 4:9; Heb. 7:18]), **for we have not seen, and thus do not know nor are aware of, the thing which we should think, speak or do toward having things go well unto goodness – to accord with what must be** (or: can pray commensurately to what is necessary and down from what is binding), **but rather the Spirit Himself** (the Breath-effect Itself; this Attitude itself) **from above constantly and repeatedly hits the target within us** (or: falls in on our behalf; instead of us hits within; falls in for and over us; or: makes hyper-intercession) **with unexpressed, unutterable or inexpressible groanings**

> (or: in sighs too deep for words; with wordless and inarticulate battle cries of deep emotion; in shouts of victory from the core of His Being).

27. **But the One continuously searching** (tracing; exploring; trying to find out [concerning]) **the hearts has seen, and thus knows and is aware of, what [is] the effect of the mind-set and way of thinking of the Breath-effect** (or: This Spirit's opinion and thinking; or: the frame of mind and thought of the [person's] spirit and attitude), **because** (or: that) **down from God** (or: in accord with God; on the level of and commensurate with God) **He** (or: It; it) **continually hits on target within** (encounters and falls in union; obtains within while interceding), **over [the situation of] and for the sake of [the] set-apart folks** (saints; holy ones; sacredly different people).

28. **Now [look], we have seen, and thus know and are aware, that to those habitually or progressively loving and giving themselves to God – to the folks being called and invited according to [the] purpose**

> (or: for, in and with the people progressively experiencing participating acceptance in, unambiguous love for, and the urge toward union with, God – in, with, by and for the people being invited down from an advanced placing, congruent with a design and corresponding to a before-placing and a prior setting forth)

– He is constantly working all things together into good and is progressively working all humanity together into that which is advantageous, worthy of admiration, noble and of excellent qualities,

> [with other MSS: Yet we know that God is continuously joining everything together (or: working together with everything) into goodness by those continuously loving God...]

29. **because those whom He foreknew** (whom He knows from previous intimate experience), **He also marked out beforehand** (determined, defined and designed in advance) **[as] copies** (joint-forms) **of the image** (material likeness; portrait; form) **of His Son** (or: He previously divided, separated and bounded conformed patterns from the image/form of His Son) **into the [situation for] Him to be** (or: to continually exist being) **the Firstborn among, within the center of, and in union with many brothers** (= a vast family from the same womb; Gal. 4:26)!

30. **Now [in fact, consider this]: those whom He at one point before-marked-out** (or: designates beforehand; [A reads: knew from prior intimate experience; note: may refer to Israel]), **these He also at once called** (or: calls; invited), **and whom He called** (or: calls; invites), **these He also in one stroke rightwised by an eschatological deliverance** (or: makes and sets right, frees from guilt and liberates from bondage, while making them fair and placing them in

[covenant] relationships in the Way pointed out). **Now further, those whom He rightwised** (or: liberates and turns in the right direction; or: = included in covenant), **these He also instantly glorified**

> (or: makes of reputation which calls forth praise; gives a splendid appearance; gives honorable thoughts and imaginations; clothes with splendor).

31. **What, then, shall we say to** (or: declare in the face of) **these things? Since** (or: If) **God [is] over, and above, us** (or: on our behalf; for us), **who or what [is; will be; can be; will appear]** (or: [is] anyone) **down against us?** [Nobody! Nothing!]
32. **Surely** (or: Actually; In fact; Certainly), **He Who at one point did not spare** (or: is not using thrift concerning) **His own Son, but further, over [the situation] of us all** (or: on behalf of all of us), **He at one point transmitted Him** (or: commends and commits Him; hands Him along; delivers Him), **how will He not also, in grace and joyous favor, freely be constantly and progressively giving all things** (or: The Whole) **to us, together with Him?**
33. **Who will bring charges down on** (institute proceedings against) **God's selected and chosen ones** (the folks picked out by God; the ones gathered out and laid in order, who belong to God)**?** [note: the charges would proceed from the Law; *cf* Jn. 5:45]
God [is] the One continually and progressively rightwising [them] (or: constantly liberating and turning [humanity] in the right direction, repeatedly placing [folks] in the Way pointed out and keeping them in righted relationships, or: = now freeing [them] and including [them] in covenant).
34. **Who [is] the one habitually bringing commensurate evaluations or corresponding decisions** (or: constantly condemning and giving a verdict down against; or, as a future: will be separating by following the patterns so as to be indicting or passing sentence)**?**
Now Christ Jesus [is] at the same time the One dying, yet very much more being aroused and raised [some MSS add: forth from out of dead ones], **Who also exists** (or: is) **within God's right side** (at God's right hand or position; [note: the place of honor, power and offensive weapons, yet also the place of acceptance and receiving]), **Who also continuously hits on-target within** (or: falls in with the situation and addresses the concerns) **over our [situation and predicament] and on our behalf!** [or as a question, and with other MSS: {Will; Would} Christ, the One dying... for us {do this}?]
35. **Who or what will be separating, dividing or parting us away from the Love of and from Christ** (or: the separation-overcoming acceptance which is Christ; [other MSS: the God's fully giving of Himself, within Christ Jesus])**? Pressure** (squeezing; affliction; tribulation; oppression), **or confinement in a narrow, tight place** (distress; difficulty; trouble), **or pursuit** (the chase of persecution), **or famine** (or: hunger; deprivation of food), **or nakedness** (lack of sufficient clothing; deprivation of necessities), **or danger** (peril; risk), **or sword** (or: large butcher knife; or: curved weapon for close combat)**?**
36. **Accordingly as it has been written,**

> **"On Your account** (For Your sake; By reason of You) **we are progressively being put to death the whole day! We are logically considered** (accounted) **as sheep which belong to slaughter** (are associated with slaughter)**."** [Ps. 44:22]

37. **But rather** (or: On the contrary), **within all these things we are habitually over-conquering** (we are remaining completely victorious; we continue more than overcoming) **through the One loving, urging toward reunion with, and giving Himself to, us.**
38. **For you see, I have been persuaded and now stand convinced that neither death, nor life** (or: living existence), **nor agents** (or: messengers), **nor sovereignties** (rulers; those in prime

position; or: beginnings), **nor things being now here** (being placed within, at present), **nor things about to be** (impending, or about to consecutively come), **nor powers** (or: capabilities), 39. **nor height** (effect of being high), **nor depth** (or: deep places), **nor any other or different created thing** (or: founded thing; institution; = the Law; = old covenant; = adversaries) **will be having power or be able to separate, divide or part us from God's Love** (or: from the acceptance from God; from the urge toward reunion, which is God; God's full giving of Himself to us) **which is within Christ Jesus, our Owner** (Lord; Master; Possessor). [*cf* 5:8, above]

CHAPTER 9

1. **Truth I presently speak within Christ** (or: I am constantly speaking reality in union with [the] Anointed One; centered in [the] Anointing), **I am not now lying** (or: I do not habitually lie), **my conscience** (my joint-knowing from having seen together) **habitually giving joint-witness** (testifying together; giving corroborating evidence) **to me** (in me; for me; with me) **within [the] Holy Spirit** (or: in a set-apart spirit and attitude; in union with a Sacred Breath),

2. **that to me** (or: for me; in me) **a great distressing sorrow** (or: an annoying grief), **as well as unintermittent** (unceasing) **consuming pain, continues being in my heart.**

3. **For you see, I kept on claiming, while having goodness, holding well-being and possessing ease, that I myself am to be** (or: to continuously exist [as]) **a result or an effect of something set up as an offering devoted to God** (= a sacrifice; [comment: this would correspond to Jesus telling His disciples to follow Him, bearing their crosses]), **forth from the Anointing** (or: = [thus being separated] from [the body] of Christ; or: arising from the Christ) **over [the situation of]** (or: for the sake of) **my brothers, my relatives** (kinsmen; joint or commonly born ones; fellow countrymen) **according to flesh** (= in the sphere of natural human birth),

4. **the very ones who are Israelites, whose [is/was] the placing in the condition of a son** (or: the deposit of the Son; the setting in place which is the Son; the constituting as a son) **and the glory** (the things which call forth praise and bring a splendid reputation) **and the arrangements** (or: covenants; [other MSS: the Covenant) **and the placing of the Law** (or: even the setting of custom and legislation by/as [Torah]) **and the sacred service and the promises,**

5. **whose [are] the fathers** (= ancestors) **and forth from out of the midst of whom [is] the Christ** (= the Messiah), **the [descendant] down the line of flesh** (or: on the level of the human realm) **– the One continuously being upon all mankind: God, worthy of praise and blessing on into the ages! It is so** (or: – corresponding to natural descent – [is] the Anointed One [= the Messiah] who exists being God: One with a message of goodness, ease and well-being – superimposed on all things – on into the indefinite time periods! Amen – count on it)**!

6. **Yet [it is] not such as that God's Word has fallen out** (fallen from the midst, or: fallen out [of line]; or: drifted off course; or: = failed in its purpose), **for in consideration of all the folks [springing] forth from out of Israel – not [all] these folks [are] Israel!**

7. **Neither because they exist being seed of Abraham [are] all children! But rather** (or: To the contrary),

> "**In Isaac shall a seed** (= a descendant) **continue being called in you** (or: For you, a seed will continue being named in Isaac; To you, offspring will continue being invited in union with Isaac).**" [Gen. 21:12]

8. **That is,** [some MSS: That is because] **the children of the flesh** (= those born physically by humans; or: = the self that is produced by influence from the alienated System) **– these [are] not the children of God! But rather, He is continually considering "the children of The**

Promise" into [being] seed (or: He is constantly counting into [the] Seed; [that] is habitually reckoned and reasonably concluded for a seed).

9. **For the Word** (or: message) **of Promise [is] this:**

> **"Corresponding to** (or: At; In line with) **this season** (or: In accord with this fitting situation and fertile moment) **I will be coming, and then a son will be existing for Sarah** (or: shall progressively be by Sarah and will be existing in Sarah)." [Gen. 18:14]

10. **Yet not only so, but further, Rebecca, also, continued having a marriage-bed** (= was habitually having sexual intercourse and conceiving children) **from the midst of one man, Isaac, our father** (= ancestor).

11. **For you see, not as yet being born ones, nor ones practicing** (performing; accomplishing) **anything good or vile** (mean; sorry; careless; bad [*p*46 reads: worthless; of bad quality; corrupt; evil]) **– to the end that God's purpose and aim, which He designed and set beforehand, may continually remain** (abide; dwell) **down from** (corresponding to and in accord with) **election** (a selection; a choosing-out; a choice), **not forth from out of works** (or: actions), **but instead from out of the One repeatedly calling** (or: from the continual summoning) **–**

12. **It was said** (or: declared) **to her that,**

> **"The greater** (by implication: the older) **will continue performing as and be a slave to and for the smaller** (by implication: the younger; the inferior)." [Gen. 25:23]

13. **Just as it has been written,**

> **"Jacob I love** (participate in and accept as on the same ground), **yet Esau I regard with ill-will** (detach from; hate; am unfriendly to; esteem with little affection)." [Mal. 1:2-3]

14. **What, then, shall we continue saying? Not [that there is] injustice** (behavior contrary to the Way pointed out) **with God? Of course not** (May it not come to be)!

15. **For He is saying to Moses,**

> **"I will continue being merciful to** (will progressively relieve the distress and misery of) **whomever I should presently be merciful** (or: I may continuously relieve of distress and misery), **and I will continue being compassionate to whomever I should** (or: may; would) **be continuously compassionate."** [Ex. 33:19]

16. **Consequently, then, [it is] not of or from the one constantly exercising [his] will** (or: [it does] not pertain or belong to habitually intending or designing), **nor of the one constantly rushing forward** (or: nor does it pertain or belong to the one continuously running or habitually racing), **but rather of, from, pertaining to and belonging to God, the One constantly being merciful** (or: but from God's habitually and continuously relieving from distress and misery; or: but to the contrary, [it is] from the One repeatedly dispensing mercy, which is God).

17. **For the Scripture is saying to Pharaoh that,**

> **"Into this itself** (or: For this very thing) **I roused you forth** (I awakened and stirred you to come out), **so that I may** (or: would) **display and demonstrate in you My power and ability, so that My Name would be thoroughly proclaimed** (preached and published far and wide) **within all the land** (or: in the entire earth)." [Ex. 9:16]

18. **Consequently, then, on whom He from time to time wills** (or: to whom His will is presently directing) **He is continuously merciful** (He constantly relieves from distress and misery). **Yet whom He from time to time wills** (intends; designs), **He continues progressively hardening.**

19. **You will ask me** (or: protest to me), **then, "Why, then, is He still blaming and continuing to find fault? For who** (which one; what) **has resisted** (stood against or in place of) **His intention** (the effect of His deliberated purpose and resolve) **and is yet still so standing?"**

20. **O man** (or: human)! **On the contrary, even more, what** (or: who) **are you – the one habitually answering back to God** (or: replying against God; from a position of standing instead and in opposition, judging for God; disputing with God)**?**

> **"The thing molded and formed will not proceed to be saying to the One molding and forming, 'Why do you make me thus** (or: did you create and construct me this way)**?'"** [*cf* Isa. 29:16; 45:9; 64:8]

21. **Or does not the Potter hold authority or have a right pertaining to clay, forth from out of the same kneaded mixture** (effect of uniform mixture) **to make the one a container** (a vessel; an instrument; a utensil) **into honor and value, yet the other into an unhonored one** (a worthless one; one without value; one deprived of privileges; or: = one for common use)**?**

22. **Now since** (or: So what if) **God – habitually willing** (or: repeatedly intending) **to display and demonstrate inherent fervor, natural impulse, propensity and disposition** (or: teeming passion; swelling desire; or: anger, wrath and indignation), **and also to make known by personal experience His power and ability – in much long-suffering** (long-breathing state of inner quietness; forbearance; pushing anger far away) **bears and carries** (or: brought forth and produced; or: enduringly supports while moving) **containers** (vessels; instruments; utensils) **of natural impulse** (belonging to a passionate disposition; displaying inherent fervor; from teeming passion and swelling desire; or: of anger; having the character of wrath; owned by indignation), **being folks having been fully outfitted, thoroughly prepared and made correspondingly adequate for loss** (or: having equipped, adapted and adjusted themselves down into ruin, waste and destruction [of their well-being]), **and now continuing in this condition,**

23. **[it is] to the end that He could and would** (or: may) **also at some point make known by intimate experience the wealth of His glory** (or: of His manifestation of that which calls forth praise; of the glory which is Him; which pertains to His reputation; from His imagination and opinion) **upon containers of mercy** (instruments of mercy), **which He beforehand prepares into [being]** (or: made ready and provides into the midst of) **a manifestation of [that] glory**

24. **– even us, whom He calls** (or: at one point summoned; invites), **not only from out of the Jews, but further, even from out of the nations** (or: out of the ethnic multitudes, also; forth from the Gentiles, too).

25. **And so, as He is saying in Hosea,**

> **"The one [that is] not My people, I will be continually** (or: one-after-another) **calling, 'My people,' and her being one that had not been loved** (accepted), **'Beloved one;'**

26. > **"and it will proceed being in the place where it was declared to them, 'You folks [are] not My people,' there they will continue being called 'sons of [the] Living God.'"** [Hos. 2:23; 1:10]

27. **Now Isaiah is repeatedly crying out over Israel,**

> **"If ever** (or: Even if) **the number of the sons of Israel may** (or: should; would) **be as the sand of the sea, [even] the destitute remainder** (or: the fully forsaken; [even] the minority under the effect of lack; the subjected, left-behind surviving group; the failing part left below) **will continue being delivered** (saved, healed and made whole; rescued);

28. > **"for the Lord [= Yahweh] will progressively produce a Word of bringing ends together** (or: will repeatedly construct a thought of completing combinations; will continue doing an accounting of combining goals together; will continue creating [the] message of finishing things together; will habitually perform [the] Logos of combined maturities and joined destinies) **and of cutting things together** (of combined or summary cuttings) **upon the land** (or: earth).**"** [Isa. 10:22-23]

29. **And further, just as Isaiah before declared,**

"**Except the Lord** [= Yahweh] **of Hosts left a seed down within for us** (or: conserved a seed in or by us), **we would become as Sodom, and we would be made like as** (or: likened to) **Gomorrah."** [Isa. 1:9]

30. **What, then, shall we continue declaring? That [the] nations** (ethnic multitudes; Gentiles; non-Israelites) – **the ones** *not* **constantly pursuing** (pressing forward rapidly after) **rightwisedness** (eschatological liberation and covenant inclusion which is right and fair relationship with equitable dealings in accord to the Way pointed out; a turning in the right direction on the Path) – **overtook, seized and took-down this rightwisedness as a possession: yet [it is] a rightwising, eschatological act of deliverance** (a "being turned" to equity and justice in the Way; = liberation with covenant membership and participation) **that [is] forth from out of the midst of faithfulness** (or: having its source in [God's] faithfulness/[Christ's] faithful act; or: from loyal trust and confident faith; from having been centered in fidelity)**!**

31. **However Israel, habitually pursuing a Law which was a rightwisedness from right activities** (or: pertaining to fair relationships with equitable dealings in accord to the way [which the Law] pointed out [to them]; or: of a the path to eschatological deliverance) **did not precede [the others] into [that] principle or custom** (or: did not outstrip or sooner arrive unto [such] a law or custom) **of rightwised, eschatological deliverance** (or: which is comprised of being turned in the right direction)

(or: = did not reach, ahead of other folks, the righted results of what the Torah had promised).

32. **Through what cause** (or: Why)**? Because [the pursuit was] not forth from out of a source of faithfulness** (or: fidelity, trust, conviction or faith), **but rather as from out of a source of works** (actions). **They dash against, trip and stumble on** (or: by) **"the Stone that caused the Stumbling-effect,"** [Isa. 8:14; Lu. 2:34; Hos. 14:9; 1 Pet. 2:7-8]

33. **Just as it has been written,**

"**Look and consider! I am repeatedly placing in Zion a 'Stone of Stumbling,' and a 'Rock of a trap-snare.' And the one habitually believing upon Him** (or: It) **will not continue being brought to shame, disgrace, or disappointment."** [Isa. 28:16]

CHAPTER 10

1. **Indeed, brothers** (= family, or, fellow believers)**, the good thinking** (pleasure; consuming desire; good will; delightful imagination) **of my heart, and the request** (plea; petition) **[directed] toward** (or: face to face with) **God over them** (or: for their sake) **[is; leads] unto deliverance** (salvation; health and wholeness; restoration to their original state and condition) **[for them].**

2. **For I am habitually testifying and giving evidence among them, because they continue possessing a zeal from God** (or: For you see, I can repeatedly bear witness to and for them that they constantly hold God's zeal and they continuously have a boiling jealously and hot aspiration concerning God), **but however, not down from** (or: on the level of and in accordance with) **full and accurate experiential knowledge, recognition or insight** (*epi-gnosis*).

3. **For they, being continuously ignorant of God's rightwising act of deliverance** (or: habitually failing to recognize the rightwisedness and fairness of the Way pointed out, which is God, and the right relationships from God in His covenant justice of eschatological liberation) **and constantly seeking to establish** (to set and make to stand) **their own way pointed out with a view to eschatological deliverance** (or: plan of right cultic activity and relational dealings [that

are informed by the Law]), **were not placed under to be humbly and supportively aligned to God's eschatological act of deliverance in the eschatological liberation that came from God** (or: subjected to God's just path and Way of fairness, or arranged under the rightwisedness from God [= brought into God's covenant participation in resurrection life]),

4. **for you see, Christ [is] an end of Law** (or: for Christ [is] Law's goal and destiny; for [the] Anointing [is] termination from [the] Law; for Christ [was the] final act of [the] Law) **[leading] into the Way pointed out in fair and equitable dealings, and rightwised [covenant] relationships of justice in eschatological liberation, to, for and in everyone habitually trusting and believing**

> (or: because Christ [entering] into the pointed-out Way – in everyone normally exercising faith with conviction, and with each person remaining loyal – [is; brings] Law's climax).

5. **For Moses is writing [about] the way pointed out** (the equitable dealings, right relationship and cultic observance) **[which is] out of the Law** [= Torah; some MSS read: from the midst of law], **that,**

> **"The person** (human) **doing** (performing) **the same things** (or: these very things) **will be constantly living** (passing his existence; exercising functions of life) **within them** (or: in union with them [other MSS: it] he shall continue living and will be possessed of vitality)." [Lev. 18:5]

6. **Yet the rightwised act of eschatological deliverance** (the condition of being liberated and turned in the right direction in the Way pointed out; the fairness and equity of [God's] justice and right relationship; or: = covenant inclusion/participation) **[coming] from out of the midst of faithfulness** (or: trusting fidelity; [Christ's] confident loyalty) **is constantly saying thus** (is habitually speaking in this manner)**:**

> **"You should not say in your heart, 'Who will ascend** (climb back up) **into the Heaven** (or: the sky; or: the atmosphere)**?'"**

– **that is, to lead, convey, carry or bring Christ** [= the Messiah] **down;**

7. **Or,**

> **"'Who will descend** (climb down) **into the Deep** (the Abyss)**?'"**

– **that is, to lead, convey, carry or bring Christ back up again from out of the midst of dead ones.**

8. **But rather, what is He** (or: it) **saying?**

> **"The result of the flow** (the gush-effect; or: the saying; the declaration; that which is spoken; the speech) **is** (or: exists) **near you – within your mouth and within your heart!"** [Deut. 30:11-14]

– **that is, the effect of the gush from The Faithfulness** (or: the result of the Flow which is the saying that pertains to the conviction of trust; the effect of the flux and movement of that Faith; or: that which is spoken which is trust; or: the speech and declaration which comes from [Christ's] Fidelity) **which we are habitually announcing publicly** (proclaiming extensively),

9. **namely that whenever you can speak the same gush-effect** (or: because if you would agree with the result of the Flow) **within your mouth, that "Jesus Christ [is] Lord,"**

> (or: because if at any time you should confess in your mouth the declaration that Jesus [is] Lord; [with other MSS: because if ever you should suddenly avow in your own mouth, "Lord Jesus!"]) **and then can trust, in union with your heart,** (or: could believe and have confidence within the core of your being) **that God raised** (or: because God aroused and awakened) **Him forth from out of the midst of dead folks, you will proceed being healed and made whole** (or: will keep on being delivered, kept safe, rescued, saved, and will progressively

be restored to your original state and condition).

10. **You see, in** (or: by; with) **[the] heart** (= core of your being) **it is progressively believed and trusted** (or: a person is repeatedly made loyal and given confidence) **[leading] into a rightwised, eschatological deliverance** (or: unto being turned in the right direction – with equitable dealings and right relationships – from having been placed within the Way pointed out, which includes covenant inclusion and participation), **yet by** (or: in; with) **[the] mouth the same thing is being repeatedly said** (or: it is agreed and habitually confessed and professed) **[leading] into the midst of health and wholeness** (a rescue; salvation; deliverance into safety).

11. **For the Scripture is saying,**

> **"Everyone habitually believing** (putting trust) **upon Him will not continue being disgraced, put to shame, humiliated or be disappointed."** [Isa. 28:16]

12. **You see, there is no distinction or separation made by putting asunder in order to define or distinguish between Jew and Greek, for the same Lord** (Owner; Master) **of everyone** (or: for the same One [being] Lord of all) **is continuously being enriching unto**

> (or: is constantly abundantly furnishing [Himself] into; or, reading πλουτων as a gen. pl. noun: You see this very Owner of all treasures [is proceeding] into the midst of) **all the**

folks habitually, in and for themselves, calling upon (or: summoning) **Him for help and assistance.**

13. **For thus it follows,**

> **"Everyone – whoever may at some point call upon the Name of the Lord** [= Yahweh] **– will proceed being delivered** (kept safe; rescued; saved, healed and made whole)**!"** [Joel 2:32]

14. **How, then, can** (may; should; would) **they at some point call unto** (= invoke) **One Whom** (or: that which) **they do not trust or believe** (or: did not have faith in)**? And how can** (may; should; would) **they believe where they do not hear** (or: trust in Whom they did not hear)**? And how can they at any point hear apart from a person continually making public proclamation** (habitually publishing and extensively heralding)**?**

15. **Yet how can they publicly proclaim unless they may be sent forth as representatives with a mission** (or: as emissaries)**? Just as it has been and stands written,**

> **"How timely and seasonable [are] the feet of the folks continually bringing and announcing goodness** (or: the good news of ease and well-being)**: the good and excellent things!"** [Isa. 52:7]

16. **But, to the contrary, everyone did not put the ear under hearing obedience** (or: However, not all listen in obedience) **to the good news** (or: message of goodness, ease and well-being). **For Isaiah is saying,**

> **"O Lord** [= O Yahweh], **who believes** (which one adhered and trusted) **in our hearing** (or: by our hearing; in the thing heard from us)**?"** [Isa. 53:1]

17. **Consequently, the faithfulness** (or: the trust and faith; confidence; loyalty) **[comes or arises] from out of the midst of, or from within, hearing, yet the hearing [comes] through a gush-effect of Christ, even through the result of a flow which is Christ** (or: through Christ's utterance; through something spoken concerning Christ; or: by means of a declaration which is anointed, or from Christ; through a word uttered which is Christ; [other MSS: God's speech]).

18. **But, I ask, isn't it rather that they didn't pay attention or hear? On the contrary!** (or: However, I am saying, do they fail to hear? Most certainly!)**:**

> **"Their clear, distinct sound** (as vibrations of a musical string; = their voice; = their utterance) **comes out into all the earth** (or: went out into the entire land), **and their**

gush-effects (results of the flow; or: sayings; the things spoken by them; their declarations) **into the boundaries** (limits; extremities) **of the inhabited area."** [Ps. 19:4]

19. **But further, I am asking, isn't it rather that Israel did not recognize, come to know or gain insight** (or: However, I say, did not Israel fail to experientially and intimately know)**? First Moses is saying,**

"**I will progressively bring rivalry, envy and jealously alongside you folks** (or: I will provoke you to jealousy) **upon [the situation of] a non-nation** (a no-nation; upon one not a multitude)**; upon [the situation of] an unintelligent** (stupid; unable-to-put-things-together) **ethnic multitude I will proceed bringing an impulsive mental attitude, anger, a vexing indignation and inherent fervor alongside you folks."** [Deut. 32:21]

20. **Yet Isaiah is daring and risking without restraint, and is saying,**

"**I am** (or: was) **found by, among and within those not seeking or trying to find Me; I become** (or: became; was birthed) **apparent** (visible; obvious to sight; manifest) **in** (or: by; to; with; among) **the ones not inquiring about Me."** [Isa. 65:1a]

21. **Now toward Israel He is saying,**

"**The whole day I stretch and spread out my hands toward a consistently disobeying** (noncomplying; refusing to believe) **and habitually contradicting** (refuting; speaking instead-of; speaking back against) **people."** [Isa. 65:2]

CHAPTER 11

1. **I am asking** (or: saying), **then, God does not** (or: did not) **thrust away His people, does He** (or: did He)**?** [cf Ps. 94:14] **Certainly not** (May it not happen)**! For I myself am also** (or: also exist being) **an Israelite, forth from out of the seed of Abraham, of the tribe Benjamin.**

2. **God does not** (or: did not) **thrust away His people – whom He by experience intimately foreknew! Or have you not seen, and thus perceive, in [the passage of] Elijah, what the Scripture is saying as he is repeatedly encountering in God** (or: hitting on target when conversing with God), **concerning the sphere and condition of** (or: down against) **Israel?**

3. "**O Lord** [= O Yahweh], **they kill Your prophets! They dig down under** (thus: undermine to demolish) **Your altars! And as for me, I was left under, alone** (or: I'm the only one left below), **and they continually seek** (are continuously trying to find) **my soul** (my breath; = they want to kill me)**."** [1 King 19:10, 14]

4. **To the contrary, what does the useful transaction** (the deliberative instruction; the oracle) **say to him?**

"**I leave down** (or: reserve) **to Myself** (for Myself; in Myself) **[other MSS: They have been leaving for Myself] seven thousand adult males, those men who do not bend a knee to Baal."** [1 Kings 19:18]

5. **Thus then, also, within the present season** (or: In this way, therefore, even in the current appropriate situation and in union with the present fertile moment) **a destitute remainder** (or: a forsaken minority under the effect of lack; a left-behind surviving group; a worn-smooth, plain, inferior, unsculptured, unembossed part; a remnant) **has been birthed** (has come to be and exists) **down from a selection of grace** (in accord with an election which is grace and a choosing-out for favor).

6. **Now since** (or: if) **[it is] by grace** (in a gift of favor), **[it is] no longer from out of works** (deeds; actions)**! Otherwise grace** (the joyous gift of favor) **comes to be no longer grace** (or: Else grace is no longer birthed, or comes to be, grace; [some MSS add: but if from out of works, it

is no longer grace, otherwise the work is no longer work]).

7. **What, then? That which Israel is constantly searching for** (or: seeking out), **this it did not encounter** (or: did not hit upon the mark, and thus, obtain), **yet The Selected One** (the Picked-out and Chosen One; or: the choice collection; the elect – that which is chosen out) **hit upon the mark, encountered and obtained it. But the rest** (the folks remaining) **were petrified** (were turned into stone; were made calloused and were hardened),

8. **just as it has been and now stands written,**

    "**God gives** (or: at one point gave) **to them a spirit** (breath-effect and attitude) **of stupor, from receiving a piercing blow** (or: deep sleep; a senseless mental condition), **eyes of the [condition] not to see, ears of the [condition] not to hear, until this very day** (or: until today's day)." [Deut. 29:4; Isa. 29:10]

9. **And David is saying,**

    "**Let their table be birthed into a snare** (a trap) **and into a wild beast trap-net and into a trap-stick, even into an effect of repayment to them** (for them; in them).

10.   "**Let their eyes be darkened, not to see, and let them bend** (or: bow) **their back together [in bondage] through all** (or: every [situation])." [Ps. 69:22-23]

11. **I am asking, then, they do not stumble [on the racetrack] so that they should fall, do they? Certainly not! On the contrary, by** (or: in) **the result of their fall to the side the Deliverance** (the Rescue, Salvation, health and wholeness; the restoration to the original state and condition) **[is] in, for, to and among the nations** (the ethnic multitudes; the non-Jews; the Gentiles; the pagans) **unto "the [situation] to bring jealousy alongside them** (or: in order to provoke them to jealousy)." [Deut. 32:21]

12. **Now since** (or: if) **the effect of their fall to the side [brings, or, is] enrichment of the world** (universe; = all humanity; or: the realm of the secular; or: the ordered System [outside of Israel]) **and the effect of their discomfiture [in the games] and the resultant lessened position** (the result of their defeat and loss from being overthrown) **[brings, or, is] enrichment of the nations** (ethnic multitudes; non-Jews; Gentiles), **how much exceedingly more the effects of their filled-full condition** (the result of their full measure with the entire contents)!

13. **So I am presently speaking for and to you, the nations** (the ethnic multitudes; the non-Jews; the Gentiles). **In as much as** (or: For as long as), **indeed then, I myself am an emissary** (envoy; missionary; one sent on a mission with a commission) **pertaining to and belonging to [the] ethnic multitudes** (nations; non-Jewish groups; Gentiles; pagans), **I am continually building the reputation, appearance and notions of my service and dispensing** (or: I am glorifying the function and execution of my attending in waiting upon [you folks]),

14. **if somehow, possibly, I may arouse my own flesh** (= my own people) **to jealousy and can deliver** (or: should save; as a future: I will proceed in rescuing and making whole) **certain folks** (or: some) **from among them.**

15. **You see, since** (or: if) **their casting away** (or: their rejection [of the good news]) **[is, means or brings the] conciliation of the aggregate of humanity** (the changing of the universal system to another level of existence; the complete change for the arranged order to be other than it was; the world's change from enmity to friendship), **what [will be] the receiving** (the acceptance; the taking or drawing toward one's self as a companion or associate) **[of them, (or: the receiving of it)] if not life forth from out of the midst of dead folks?!**

16. **Now since** (or: But if) **the Firstfruit [is] holy** (set-apart and consecrated; sacred), **the kneaded mixture** (the result of the lump which is mingled and reduced to a uniform consistency by treading, kneading or beating) **also [is]; and since** (or: if) **the Root [is] holy** (set-apart, sacred, different from the norm), **so also [are] the branches** (the shoots; the boughs).

17. **Now since some** (or: if certain ones) **of the branches are broken off** (or: were at one point broken out of [the tree]), **yet you yourself, being a wild olive tree of the field or forest, you are** (or: were) **grafted in within** (or: among) **them, you also came to be** (are birthed; are become) **a joint-participant** (a partner taking in common together with; a co-partaker) **of the Root and of the Fatness** (= sap) **of The Olive Tree** (or: of the oil of the olive).

18. **Stop boasting against** (or: Do not be constantly vaunting or exulting over) **the branches! Now since you are habitually boasting and exulting** (priding yourself), **you yourself are not bearing** (supporting; sustaining; carrying) **The Root, but rather, The Root you!**

19. **You will say** (or: declare), **then, "Branches are broken off** (or: were broken out of [the tree]) **to the end that I may be grafted in."**

20. **Beautifully [put]!** (Ideally [said]!; Well [conceived]!) **In lack of faith or trust** (or: By unbelief; Because of lack of allegiance) **they are broken off** (or: were broken out of the midst), **yet you yourself stand in faith** (or: by trust; with confidence). **Stop being haughty** (Don't constantly have high opinions; Do not continually think lofty things), **but to the contrary, [be constantly having] an attitude and mindset of respectful awe** (or: [Godly] fear; healthy respect)!

21. **For you see, since** (or: if) **God spares not** (or: was not thrifty with) **the natural branches** (the branches down from, or, in accord with, nature), **neither will He continue sparing you!**

22. **Observe, perceive and consider, then, God's useful kindness** (benevolent utility) **and abruptness** (sheer cutting-off; rigorous severity) **– on the one hand upon those falling: abruptness** (sheer cutting-off); **on the other hand** (or: yet) **upon you: God's useful kindness** (benign, profitable utility), **provided** (or: if) **you should persistently remain in** (or: with; by) **the useful kindness** (or: = continue to be kind and useful). **Otherwise you, also, will proceed in being cut out!**

23. **Now they also, if they should not persistently remain in the lack of faith and trust** (or: unbelief), **they will proceed in being grafted in, for God is able** (capable; is constantly powerful) **to graft them back in again!**

24. **For since** (or: if) **you yourself were cut out of the olive tree [which is] wild** (of the field or forest) **by nature, and then to the side of nature** (perhaps: = outside of, or contrary to, nature) **you are** (or: were at one point) **grafted in – into a fine** (beautiful; cultivated; garden) **olive tree – to how much greater an extent** (or: for how much rather) **will these, the ones in accord with nature, proceed in being engrafted into their own olive tree!**

25. **You see, I am not willing for you folks to continue being ignorant of this secret** (or: mystery), **brothers** (= fellow believers; family) **– in order that you folks may not continue being prudent, thoughtful or discreet by** [other MSS: among or within; other MSS: beside] **yourselves** (or: = be conceited) **– that a petrifying, from a part** (a stone-like hardening in some measure; a callousness [extending over] a part), **has been birthed and come into existence in Israel** (or: has happened to Israel) **until which [time]** (or: to the point of which [situation]) **the effect of the full measure** (or: the result of the entire contents; or: = the full impact and full compliment of forces) **from the nations** (or: of the ethnic multitudes; or: – which are the Gentiles –) **may enter in.**

[comment: Does the last clause refer to the entrance of the Roman legions into Jerusalem? Or, is this referring to the fullness of all ethnic multitudes, which now includes Israel, entering into the kingdom, since vs. 32, below, says that God has locked up all mankind in disobedience, etc., so as to have mercy upon all?]

26. **So then, thus, in this manner and with this result: all Israel will progressively be delivered** (rescued, saved, made whole and restored to their original position [in the olive tree]), **according as it has been written,**

> **"The One continuously dragging out of danger and drawing to Himself** (The Rescuer; The Deliverer) **will repeatedly arrive and be present from out of Zion; He will continue turning irreverence away from Jacob.**

27. **"And this [is] the arrangement for them from beside Me** (or: And this [will be] My covenant in, to and for them) **when I take away their failures** (deviations; sins; mistakes; misses of the target; shooting amiss of the goal)." [Isa. 59:20-21; 27:9]

28. **Corresponding to** (With respect to; In accord with; Down from) **the Good News** (the message of goodness and well-being), **on the one hand, [they were] enemies** (hostile ones; ones regarded as enemies) **because of** (or: through; with a view to) **you folks; on the other hand, according to** (in accord with; down from; corresponding to) **the selection** (the choosing out; the election) **[they are] loved ones, because of** (with a view to) **the fathers** (= ancestors),

29. **for you see, the grace-effects and the calling of God** (or: because the results of God's joyous favor and invitation) **[are] void of regret and without change in purpose** (or: unregretted; not to be regretted afterward; are not subject to recall; = are never taken back).

30. **For just as you folks were once** (or: at one time) **incompliant to God** (or: unconvinced, disobedient, unwilling to be persuaded and stubborn by God), **yet now** (at the present time) **you folks are** (or: were) **mercied** (made the recipients of mercy) **by** (or: in; with) **the incompliance** (disobedience; stubbornness; lack of being convinced) **of these folks.**

31. **Thus, also, these now** (at the present time) **are incompliant** (stubborn; disobedient; unconvinced) **by** (or: for; to) **your mercy, to the end that they also may now be mercied** (would be the recipients of mercy).

32. **For you see, God encloses, shuts up and locks all mankind** (everyone; the entire lot of folks) **into incompliance** (disobedience; stubbornness; lack of being convinced), **to the end that He could** (or: would; should) **mercy all mankind** (may make everyone, the all, recipients of mercy)!

33. **O, the depth of [the] riches** (wealth; resources) **and wisdom and intimate, experiential knowledge and insight of God** (or: from God; which are God)! **How unsearchable** (inscrutable) **the effects of His decisions** (results of the distinctive separations, judicial awards, judgments and evaluations from Him), **and untrackable** (untraceable) **His ways** (paths; roads).

34. **For,**

> **"Who knows** (knew by intimate experience) **the Lord's** [= Yahweh's] **mind?**
> **Or, who becomes** (or: came to be) **His planning adviser** (His design counselor; the one who makes determinations with Him)?" [Isa. 40:13]

35. **Or,**

> **"Who gives to Him first, and it will continue being repaid to him?"** [Job. 41:3]

36. **Because, forth from out of the midst of Him, then through the midst of Him** (or: through means of Him), **and [finally] into the midst of Him, [is; will be] the whole** (everything; [are] all things; or: = Because He is the source, means and goal/destiny of all things – everything leads

into Him)!

By Him (In Him; To Him; For Him; With Him) **[is] the glory** (the manifestation of that which calls forth praise; the reputation; the notion; the opinion; the imagination; the credit; the splendor) **on into the ages. It is so** (Amen; So be it; Count on it)!

CHAPTER 12

1. **Consequently, brothers, I am repeatedly calling you folks alongside to advise, exhort, implore and encourage you, through God's compassions to stand your bodies alongside** (or: to set or place your bodies beside) **[the] Well-pleasing, Set-apart** (Holy; Different-from-the-usual), **Living Sacrifice by God** (or: in God; for God; to God; with God), **[this being]** your **sacred service which pertains to thought, reason and communication** (or: your reasoned and rational service; the logical and Word-based service from you folks; or: = temple service).
2. **And stop constantly conforming yourselves in fashion** (or: external show or appearance; guise; scheme) **to** (or, as passive: So then, quit being repeatedly molded by, fashioned for or patterned together with) **this age** [with other MSS: and not to be continuously configured to this age, or not to constantly remodel yourself for this time-period], **but on the contrary, be progressively transformed** (transfigured; changed in form and semblance) **by the renewing** (or: in the renewal; for the making-back-up-new again) **of your mind** [with other MSS: from The Mind; of the intellect; pertaining to the faculties of perceiving and understanding; of the mindset, disposition, inner orientation and world view] **into the [situation and condition for] you folks to be habitually examining in order to be testing and, after scrutiny, distinguishing and approving what [is] God's will** (design; purpose; resolve; intent): **the good and well-pleasing, even perfect** (finished, complete and destined)!
   (or: = the thing [that is] virtuous, satisfying and able to succeed in its purpose.)

3. **For, through the grace and favor being suddenly given to me, I am saying to** (or: for) **everyone being among you folks not to be continually over-opinionated or elated** (to be constantly hyper-thinking to the point of being haughty, arrogant or having a sense of superiority; to be habitually over-thinking issues; to constantly mind things above; to be overweening) **beyond what is necessary** (binding; proper), **but rather to think** (mind; be disposed) **into the disposition to be sane and of a sound mind, as God divides, apportions and distributes** (or: parted) **to, in and for each one a measure of faith** (a meted amount of firm persuasion; a measured portion of trust; a [specific or allotted] ration of confidence and loyalty).
4. **For you see, just as** (or: according to what is encompassed) **in one body we continuously have** (constantly hold and possess) **many members, yet all the members do not have the same mode of acting** (do not constantly hold the same function),
5. **thus we, the many, are and continue to exist being one body within Christ** (in union with [the] Anointed), **yet individually** (or: the situation being in accord with one), **members of one another** (or: but still, [being] on one level, [are] members whose source is, and who belong to, each other).

6. **Now constantly holding** (having; possessing) **excelling grace-effects** (or: gracious results of favor that carry-through), **down from, in accord with and to the level of the grace and joyous favor being given to us, in us and for us, whether prophecy – [let it be] down from**

and in line with the above-word of the faith
> (or: in accord with the analogy of the loyalty; according to the proportion of trust; following the pattern of the corresponding relationship that pertains to the Faith; down along the upward-thought of faith or the up-message of the belief; in accordance with conformability from the faithfulness; on the level of the correspondence and ratio of confidence);

7. **or whether serving** (thoroughly dispensing in attendance on a duty) – **[let us be, or live] in the service** (the attendance to the duty; the arrangement for provision; the aid through dispensing); **or whether the one constantly teaching – [let the person continue] in the teaching** (the instructing or training);

8. **or whether the person normally performing as a paraclete** (one habitually calling alongside to aid, admonish, encourage, exhort and give relief) – **[let the person flourish] in the calling alongside to give relief and aid, as well as for admonition, encouragement and exhortation;**
the one habitually sharing (imparting; giving together) – **in simplicity** (singleness; or: = with generosity);
the one constantly setting himself before [a situation] or being a caregiver (or: standing in front and presiding; or: being in charge of giving care or aid) – **in diligent haste** (= eagerly);
the one continuously mercying (applying mercy) – **in cheerfulness** (pleasantness; gleeful abandon).

9. **Love** (or: The inner movement toward overcoming existential separation) **[is] not overly critical and [does] not [make] hyper-distinctions or excessive divisions or separations** (or: [is] unfeigned, unhypocritical and [does] not play a role as an actor).

With abhorrence (or: strong detesting) **[be] constantly shrinking away from the worthless thing** (the bad situation; the painfully toilsome endeavor; the base, cowardly or evil thing) **[and be] habitually gluing or welding yourself** (attaching yourself and adhering) **to The Good One** (or: the profitable situation; the virtuous endeavor).

10. **In sisterly love** (or: By fond affection, as for members of a family,) **unto one another, [be] tenderly affectionate folks who express warm regard, being people constantly taking the lead in the honor** (by and with the estimation of value or worth) **of one another**
> (or: habitually esteeming one another first in value; constantly giving preference to one another in respect).

11. **[Be] eager and in diligent haste – not slothful, lazy or hesitating folks. In the Breath-effect** (or: By the Spirit; With this attitude), **[be] people constantly boiling hot! For the Lord** (or: In the Owner; By the Lord; To the Lord [= Yahweh or Christ]; [D* F G & others: For the situation; In the season]), **[be] folks constantly slaving** (repeatedly performing as slaves)!

12. **In and with expectation** (or: By expectant hope) **[be] people continuously rejoicing; in pressure** (squeezing; tribulation; compression) **[be] folks constantly remaining under to give support** (or: humbly enduring); **in thinking or by acting, and with speaking, toward having goodness, ease and well-being** (or: by and with prayer) **[be] people habitually persevering** (persisting in adherence and engagement).

13. **To the** (or: For the; In the) **needs of the set-apart folks** (the holy ones; the saints) **[be] people continuously sharing** (contributing/participating in partnership from common existence). **[Be] folks habitually pursuing** (rapidly following; eagerly pressing toward) **the love of and for**

foreigners (or: Follow the course of hospitality by fondness expressed in kindness to strangers).
14. **You folks keep on speaking well of** (or: repeatedly think goodness for; continue blessing)
the people consistently pursuing and persecuting you: be continuously blessing (speaking
well of [them] or thinking goodness for [them]) **and stop cursing** (or: you must not continue
praying down on, or wishing anything against, [things, situations or people])!
15. **Practice** (or: Be constantly) **rejoicing with those who are presently or habitually**
rejoicing, and constantly weep (or: cry; lament) **with those presently** (or: habitually) **weeping;**
16. **in this very same vein, continue being folks who are focusing your thinking into one**
another: not being those constantly setting their minds on the high positions or elite
social statuses (or: don't be corporately arrogant), **but rather, being folks consistently led**
away together to the low, humble ones (or: by the humble people; in the low things; =
associate with folks of low social standing).

You folks must not habitually become people of a particular mind-set (or: Stop engendering
corporate arrogance or producing opinionated folks) **side-by-side with, and among, yourselves**
(or: = Stop being those who are wise or conceited in their own opinions and in their own eyes)!

17. **To no person practice giving away** (returning or repaying) **evil in exchange for evil** (ugly
in the place of ugly; worthless, bad, ill, unsound, poor quality over against the same)!
Habitually being folks taking thought in advance for fine things (or: constantly providing
ideal things; continuously giving attention ahead of time with regard to things of good form and
quality; repeatedly having forethought for beautiful [situations]) **in the sight of all humanity,**
18. **since [you are] full of power** (or: if capable; if or since able) **regarding that which has its**
source in you folks (or: as to that which proceeds from yourselves corporately), **[live] being**
folks continuously at peace with all mankind (or: in joined harmony in the midst of all people),
19. **not being folks habitually getting justice for yourselves** (not maintaining what is right
concerning yourselves; not avenging yourselves), **beloved ones, but on the contrary, you folks**
must yield the position held in anger (or: give a place for [His] natural impulse, propensity,
passion and personal emotion; give place to [His] intrinsic fervor; relinquish [your] right to anger
or wrath), **for it has been written,**

> **"'In Me** (or: For and By Me; With Me) **[is] maintenance of justice** (execution of the Way
> pointed out; working out of the right; awarding just decisions [to all parties]; effecting
> rightwised fairness of the Path); **I Myself will continue giving away, instead** (or: I will
> progressively be making a recompense [to you]; or: I will continue taking the opposing
> position of giving [it] away; or: in its place, I Myself will repeatedly repay [you]),**' the Lord**
> [= Yahweh] **is habitually saying."** [Deut. 32:25]
> [comment: if we are not to practice giving away evil in exchange for evil (vs. 17, above),
> then we should not expect the Lord to do this]

20. **But further,**

> **"If your enemy** (the one hostile to you) **should perhaps be hungering** (or: continues
> hungry), **continue feeding him morsels** (supplying him with food); **if he may continue**
> **thirsting** (be constantly thirsty), **continue giving drink to him** (causing him to drink), **for**
> **while constantly practicing** (performing; doing) **this you will progressively pile on**
> **and heap up burning coals** (embers) **of fire upon his head."** [Prov. 25:21-22]
> [comment: the directives of feeding and giving drink correspond to what was to be done
> for brothers in Matt. 25:35, 40; the metaphor of heaping coals may correspond to Isa. 6:6

where a coal from the incense altar purged sin, so being put on his head may be a picture of purging his thinking; Wuest suggests this as supplying a needed source of fire for someone's home, meeting a desperate need – *Word Studies*, vol. 1, p. 220; as the first two are blessings, I suggest that this latter also is]

21. **Do not be habitually conquered under** (or: Stop being overcome by) **the worthless** (the bad of quality; the ugly and unsound; the evil), **but to the contrary, be constantly conquering** (overcoming; victorious over) **the worthless** (the unsound, the bad and the ugly; the evil) **[by being] in union with The Good One** (or: [a participant] within what is profitable; or: in the midst of virtue).

[comment: this verse points to a positive interpretation of the burning coals in vs. 20]

CHAPTER 13

1. **Every soul** (or: = Everyone) **is to be continuously placed and arranged, or aligned, in a supportive position by superior** (or: excelling) **authorities** (or: must be subjected to rulers holding dominion and jurisdiction above [him]; [*p*46, D*, F, G, it, & Ire. read: To every superior authority you folks must subject yourselves]). **For an authority does not exist except under God** (or: For there is no authority, except by God), **and the existing ones are those which have been arranged and set in order, under God** (placed in their relative positions by God).

2. **As a result, the one constantly placing himself in opposition to the authority** (or: the man resisting and posting an array as to battle against or to stand instead of the authority) **has taken a stand against God's precise and complete arrangement** (or: institution), **and the ones having taken an opposing stand, and remaining in determined resistance, will progressively take to themselves** (or: will continue receiving in themselves) **a result of a decision** (the effect of that which [God] decides to do or to bring to pass; a judgment-effect; a result of separating for evaluation).
3. **For the chief ones** (those in first position or headships; the princes or rulers; the magistrates) **are not a fear to the good work** (or: for virtuous and profitable action; [F*, Ethiopic: worker of excellence]), **but rather, for the worthless** (the ugly; the base; the evil; the one of poor quality).

Now are you not wanting to constantly fear and be wary of (or: So are you normally desiring to be unafraid of) **the authority? Keep doing the good** (the virtuous; the profitable), **and you will continue having praise** (applause; commendation) **forth from it** [i.e., the authority],
4. **for it is God's servant** (attendant who renders service or does a duty; an aid in dispensing; one who arranges for provision) **for you** (or: to you), **[directing you] into the good** (the profitable; the virtuous). **Yet if you should be constantly doing the worthless** (the evil; the base; the thing of poor quality; the ugly), **be fearing with a healthy respect, for it is not purposelessly** (aimlessly; vainly) **continuing to bear the sword! For it is God's servant, a maintainer of what is right** (an obtainer and executor of justice) **into a fruitful fervor** (to a strong personal emotion; unto an angry result; unto [its] personal bent) **for** (or: in; to) **the person constantly practicing or performing the worthless** (the ugly; the poor of quality; the evil).
5. **On which account** (or: Wherefore) **[there is] compelling necessity** (or: compression) **to constantly be subjected and humbly aligned in support** (or, as a middle: to be subjecting and aligning oneself; to place oneself under; to humbly subordinate oneself), **not only** (or: solely)

because of (or: through) **strong personal emotion** (intrinsic fervor; natural disposition; swelling desire and teeming passion; or: indignation, anger or wrath), **but further, also, because of** (or: through) **the conscience** (the mutual knowing from the together-seeing).

6. **For you see, because of this you folks continually fulfill the obligation by paying tribute-taxes brought on by a foreign ruler – for they are God's public servants** (officials; officers), **men constantly attending to** (staying by and persisting at) **this very thing** [i.e., duties].

7. **Render** (give away in answer to a claim; pay) **the debts** (the duties; what is owed) **to everyone: to the tax [collector], the tax; to the [one collecting] civil support tax, the civil government tax; to [whom] fear** (or: reverence) **[is due], fear** (or: reverence)**; to the one [due] honor and value, honor and value.**

8. **You folks are not to be continual debtors** (or: do not be in the habit of owing even one thing) **to anyone, except to be constantly loving and accepting one another, for the person continually loving the different one** (or: urging toward reunion with, and fully giving himself to, the other person) **has made full the Law** (has fulfilled law [or: = Torah] and custom)

   (or: You see, the one constantly loving has fulfilled the other, different law).

9. **You see, the [Law, or Torah, says or prophesies],**
   > **"You will not continue committing adultery,"**
   > **"You will not continue committing murder,"**
   > **"You will not continue stealing,"**
   > **"You will not continue to over-desire** (crave; covet; lust),**"** [Ex. 20:13-14; Deut. 5:17-18]

and if any different implanted goal (impartation of the finished product within; inward directive), **it continues being brought to a head, summed up and united again in this word, namely,**
   > **"You will continue loving your near one** (participate with uniting and unambiguous acceptance with your close one, associate, or neighbor) **as yourself."** [Lev. 19:18]

10. **Love** (or: Giving oneself to another in an unambiguous drive toward reunion) **is not habitually working [the] worthless** (poor quality; base; bad; evil; harm) **for** (or: to; with) **the near one** (the associate; the neighbor). **Love** (or: Acceptance, etc.) **[is], then, that which fills up Law's full measure** (the entire contents of law and custom; [the] Law's [= Torah's] fulfillment).

11. **This also – being folks having seen and thus knowing the season** (the fit of the situation; the appointed fertile moment) **– that [it is] by this time** (or: already) **an hour to be aroused** (or: awakened) **out of sleep, for now our rescue** (our deliverance; our wholeness, health and salvation) **[is] closer than when we came to trust** (or: we believed with faith and conviction).

12. **The night advances, and the day has approached and is presently at hand** (close enough to touch; accessible). **We should therefore put the acts of the Darkness** (works from the realm of the shadows; actions that belong to dimness and obscurity) **away from ourselves** (or: take off and put away the deeds pertaining to darkness; = ignorance; that which was before the light arrived), **and clothe ourselves with the instruments** (tools; weapons; implements; [some MSS: works; deeds]) **of Light** (or: The Light).

13. **As within [the] Day, we should** (may; can) **walk about** (= live our lives) **respectably** (reputably; decently; with good form; mannerly; pleasing to look upon; presentably) **– not in festive processions** (or: orgies; revelries; excessive feastings; carousing) **and collective drunkenness** (intoxications)**; nor in beds** (i.e., sexual interludes) **and outrageous behaviors** (shamelessness; vice; loose conduct; indecencies)**; not in strife** (or: contentious disposition) **and**

in jealousy (or: envy) –

14. **but rather, you folks must clothe yourselves with** (or: enter within and put on) **the Lord, Jesus Christ, and stop** (or: do not continue) **making forethought** (constructing provision; planning ahead; performing provident care) **into excessive desires of the flesh** (= into rushing upon emotions which pertain to the inner self or the estranged humanity; = into the setting of feelings and longings upon something of the human nature that is oriented to the System).

CHAPTER 14

1. **So constantly reach toward and receive in your arms** (take as a companion, admit to your home, society and friendship, and then partner with) **the one continuing without strength in the faith or by the Faithfulness** (or: the person weak in trust, confidence and loyalty) – **not [putting him] into separated distinctions** (or: not [pushing the issue] into disputed discriminations for a decision) **based upon or pertaining to opinions** (or: reasoned considerations; thought processes; dialogues or disputes; things being thought through; thoroughly considered and settled accounts).

2. **One person, indeed, is habitually trusting** (is continually believing; continues to have faith) **to eat everything, yet the person being constantly weak** (without strength) **continues** (or: is normally) **eating vegetables.**

3. **The person habitually eating the one thing must not constantly make nothing out of** (= look down on) **the person not eating. And the person not normally eating the one thing must not constantly make a decision about** (separate away from; make a distinction between; pass judgment on) **the one habitually eating, for God reaches toward him and takes him in His arms** (receives him as a companion and a friend, and has taken him as a partner).

4. **You, who are the person constantly judging** (separating away; making a distinction or a decision about) **another man's house-servant** (domestic)! **By** (In; To; For; With) **his own Lord** (Master; Owner) **he continues standing, or, he is falling. Yet he will repeatedly be made to stand, for you see, the Lord** [= Yahweh or Christ] **is constantly able** (perpetually powerful) **to make him stand.**

5. **One person, on the one hand, is habitually discriminating** (deciding; separating; passing judgment; making a distinction)**: a day from** (or: beside) **a day** (or: = [one] day more than, or compared with, [another] day). **Yet, on the other hand, another is habitually deciding for every day** (or: is constantly separating each day [as alike, or, as set-apart]). **Let each one habitually be fully led within his own mind** (or: Each person must constantly be carried to full measure in union with his own mind [on this matter]).

6. **He who is habitually minding** (being disposed to; being opinionated about) **the day, in the Lord** [= Yahweh] **is continuously opinionated** (or: for the Lord [= Christ] is he [thus] minding or being disposed; [some MSS add: and yet the person not minding the day, to, for or in the Lord he is not minding it]). **And the one habitually eating, in the Lord** [= Yahweh or Christ] **is he eating, for he habitually gives thanks to God** (constantly expresses gratitude by God, for God and in God). **And the one not eating is not eating in God** (to God; for God), **and habitually expresses gratitude for God** (in God; gives thanks to God).

7. **You see, not one of us is living to himself** (for himself; by himself; in himself), **and not one is dying away by himself** (in himself; for himself; to himself).

8. **For it follows, both if we are** (or: should be) **living, in the Lord** (or: for, to and by the Lord [=

Yahweh or Christ]) **we are** (or: could and should be) **living, and then, if we may** (or: would) **be dying, in, for, to and by the Lord we would be dying. Then, both if we are living, and if we may be dying, we are the Lord's** (we constantly exist being of [Yahweh]; we continuously belong to the Lord; we are from the Owner).

9. **For into this [situation] Christ not only died away, but also now lives** (= came back to life again), **to the end that He would** (or: should) **be Lord** (Owner; Master; Possessor) **both of dead folks as well as of living people.**

10. **But you! Why are you constantly judging** (discriminating against; separating away; making a decision about) **your brother** (= fellow believer; or: = fellowman)**? Or why are you also habitually making light of** (making nothing out of; setting at naught; treating with scorn or contempt) **your brother?**

For you see, we will all continue standing in attendance alongside on God's elevated place (platform or stage which is ascended by steps, from which one speaks in a public assembly; or: we will all repeatedly present ourselves at the seat, dais or throne which is God [some MSS: Christ]),

11. **for it has been written,**

> **"I, Myself, am continuously living. The Lord** [= Yahweh] **is saying that in Me** (by Me; to Me; for Me) **every knee will repeatedly bend in worship, or, to sit down** (or: I live, says the Lord, because every knee will repeatedly bend to sit down in Me), **and every tongue will continue to agree, bind itself and promise to God** (speak out of the same word in God; publicly acclaim/acknowledge God; openly profess by God)." [Isa. 45:23]

12. **Consequently, then, each one of us will continue giving a word** (presenting a message; rendering an account) **about himself to God** (or: for God; by God; in God).

13. **No longer, then, should we continue judging** (making decisions about; discriminating against; separating away) **one another, but rather, to a greater extent you folks must decide this: not to continue placing** (or: setting) **the stumbling-block** (that which results in tripping) **for or in the brother; neither a snare** (a trap-spring; a cause for tripping or becoming trapped).

14. **I have seen to know** (or: have perceived), **and I have been persuaded and now stand convinced in union with [the] Lord Jesus, that nothing** (not one thing) **[is] common** (profane; ceremonially defiled; unclean; contaminating; = the opposite of set-apart or holy) **through itself, except to** (in; by; for) **the person considering** (or: logically accounting and reckoning) **anything to be common** (profane; etc.); **to** (for; in; by) **that one [it is] common and unclean.**

15. **For instance, if because of solid food** (or: the effect of something eaten) **your brother is continually made sad** (made sorry, distressed or grieved), **you are no longer continuing to walk about** (= living your life) **in accord with** (or: down from and on the level of) **Love** (or: you are not yet habitually walking [your path] in participation with transcendent unity of unambiguous, uniting acceptance toward others). **Do not, by your food** (or: for your solid food), **progressively destroy away** (lose by ruining; bring to loss) **that person over whom Christ died.**

16. **Do not cause your good thing** (or: the excellence and virtue which pertain to you) **to be slandered** (defamed; insulted; blasphemed; vilified; have its light hindered),

17. **for you see, God's kingdom** (or: the reign-and-dominion which is God; the expression, influence and activity of God's sovereignty) **is not** (or: does not exist being) **solid food and drink, but rather, eschatological deliverance into fair and equitable dealing which brings justice and right relationship in the Way pointed out** (being turned in the right direction;

rightwisedness; also = covenant inclusion and participation), **peace and harmony from the joining** (= shalom) **and joy** (or: happiness; rejoicing) **within set-apart Breath-effect** (or: in union with and amidst a dedicated spirit and a sacred attitude; or: in [the] Holy Spirit).

18. **You see the one continuously slaving for and in the Christ in this [realm, sphere or regard] [is; continues being] well-pleasing** (well-satisfying; fully acceptable) **to** (or: in; by; with) **God, and approved** (after examination and testing) **by people** (or: among mankind).

19. **Consequently, then, we are continuously pressing forward and pursuing the things pertaining to, belonging to and which are the peace and harmony from the joining, and the things pertaining to, belonging to and which are the act of building a house, pertaining to [input] into one another** (or: which [effect] edification [infusing] into each other).

20. **Stop tearing down** (dissolving; loosing down; demolishing) **God's work for the sake of solid food** (or: on account of the effect of what is eaten). **Indeed, all things [are] clean** (= ceremonially pure; [Aleph2 adds: to the clean ones]), **but on the other hand, [it is] bad** (harmful; unsound; base; wicked; evil; not as ought to be) **for** (or: to; in; with) **the person who by habitually eating [experiences] an effect of [or causes] stumbling through it.**

21. **[It is] beautiful** (fine; as it ought to be; profitable; ideal) **not to eat meat** (animal flesh), **neither to drink wine, nor even that in which your brother habitually stumbles** (strikes himself against [it]), **or is being constantly snared, or is continually weak.**

22. **The faith, trust, confidence and fidelity which you yourself continue to have, hold it in accord with** (in line with, on the level of, and corresponding to) **yourself in God's sight and presence** (or: = Keep your personal faith between you and God). **Blessed and happy [is] the one not constantly judging himself** (evaluating himself; separating and dividing things within himself; criticizing himself; making decisions or determinations about himself) **within that which he is habitually examining to test and to prove** (or: in what she normally approves).

23. **Now the person continually wavering with diverse evaluations, being undecided, has been and remains correspondingly evaluated** (or: commensurately decided about; separated by following the pattern and judged accordingly; condemned), **if he should eat, because [it is] not forth from out of faith** (or: it does not have trust as its source). **And everything which [is] not forth from out of faith** (or: [does] not arise from trust and conviction) **is a failure to hit the target** (exists being an error; is a deviation from the goal; continues being sin and a mistake).

CHAPTER 15

1. **Now we ourselves, the able ones** (the powerful people), **owe and thus are constantly obliged** (or: are continually indebted) **to pick up and habitually carry** (or: embrace) **the weaknesses** (the results of being without strength) **of the unable ones** (the powerless or disabled people; the incapable), **and not to constantly be pleasing ourselves.**

2. **Let each one of us be habitually pleasing to the near one** (or: be continuously accommodating for [his] neighbor or associate), **[leading] into The Good, toward building the House** (or: unto [his] good, virtue and excellence: toward edification).

3. **For Christ also did not please Himself** (or: For even the Anointed One does not make accommodations for Himself), **but rather, just as it has been written,**

> **"The insults** (unjustifiable verbal abuses; reproaches) **of those habitually insulting You fell** (or: fall) **upon Me."** [Ps. 69:10]

4. **You see, as much as was written before was written [leading] into the teaching** (the

instruction and training) **[which is] ours** (or: was written unto and for our instruction), **to the end that through the persistent remaining-under to give support** (the humble yet relentless endurance in handling the blows), **and through the calling-alongside of the Scriptures** (or: through the Scriptures' comfort, consolation, relief, aid, support and performance as a Paraclete) **we may constantly hold expectation** (or: can continue having the expectant hope).

5. **Now may the God of the persistent remaining-under to give support** (or: Who has the qualities of this humble, patient and relentless endurance of the blows) **and of the calling-alongside for comfort, relief, consolation, aid and support** (or: the God Who is humble, persevering endurance and is the essence of the encouraging performance of a Paraclete) **give to** (or: grant for) **you folks to be constantly mutually disposed** (to be minding the same thing; to be of this very opinion) **within and among one another, down from** (or: in accord with and in the sphere of) **Jesus Christ** [other MSS: [the] Anointed Jesus; = Jesus the Messiah],

6. **to the end that at the same time, with a unanimous rush of passion, you folks may** (or: would) **in one mouth continuously glorify** (or: progressively enhance the reputation of and the opinion about) **the God and Father of our Lord, Jesus Christ.**

7. **Wherefore, be constantly reaching out with your hands and taking one another in your arms** (welcoming and receiving one another as partners), **just as the Christ** (or: the Anointed) **also in this way receives you as partners** (takes you [B, D* & P read: us] in His arms; took you to Himself), **into God's glory** (or: the glory from, and which is, God)!

8. **For I am saying and laying out the idea [that] Christ has been birthed to become, and remain, a Servant and Dispenser from circumcision** (or: an Attendant, Helper and Minister of and pertaining to [the] Circumcision [i.e., God's covenant people]), **over [the situation of] God's reality** (or: Circumcision's Dispenser of provisions for the sake of a truth from and about God, and a reality which is God), **into the standing to confirm** (stabilize; make good; cause to stand by stepping in place on a good footing; or: to guarantee the validity of) **the promises from, which pertain to, and which belong to, the fathers** (or: the patriarchal promises),

9. **and on the other hand [to place on good footing and confirm the standing of] the ethnic multitudes** (the nations; the non-Israelites; the pagans), **[for them] to glorify God** (to enhance the reputation of and the opinion about God) **over [the situation of] mercy** (for the sake of [His] mercy), **just as it has been written,**

> **"Because of this I will continue openly professing and acclaiming You** (speaking out of the same word for and to You; agreeing and promising) **within ethnic multitudes** (among nations that are pagans and Gentiles), **and I will continue playing music** (striking the string; making melody; singing with musical accompaniment) **to, for and in Your Name."** [2 Sam. 22:50; Ps. 18:50]

10. **And again he is saying,**

> **"Be of a good frame of mind** (Be merry and glad; Have thoughts of wellness), **you ethnic multitudes** (non-Jews), **together with His people."** [Deut. 32:43]

11. **And again,**

> **"You folks – all the multitudes** (all nations; all of the Gentiles) **– be continually praising the Lord** [= Yahweh]." [Ps. 117:1]

12. **And again, Isaiah is saying,**

> **"There** (or: He) **will continue being The Root** (or: the Sprout from the root) **of Jesse, even the One habitually standing up** (placing Himself back; raising Himself up) **to**

continue being Ruler (being The Chief; to repeatedly be the Beginner) **of multitudes** (ethnic groups; of nations; of Gentiles). **Upon Him ethnic multitudes** (non-Jews; nations) **will continue placing their expectation** (will rely; will hope)." [Isa. 11:10]

13. **Now may the God of Expectation** (or: the God Who is the Expectant Hope) **make you full of all joy and peace of the joining, within the midst of constant trust and in union with continual operation of faith and believing, [leading] into the midst of continually surrounding you with abundance within The Expectation** (or: in union with expectant hope) – **within [the] power of a set-apart spirit** (or: within [the] Holy Spirit's ability; or: in union with a power which is, and whose source is, set-apart Breath-effect and sacred attitude).

14. **Now, my brothers** (Family members; fellow believers), **I myself also have been persuaded and remain convinced about you that you yourselves are** (or: exist being) **folks stuffed full of goodness** (bulging with excellence and quality), **being those having been filled and remaining full of all The Knowledge** (intimate, experiential knowledge and insight; [with other MSS: all gnosis]), **being folks continuously able and empowered, also, to habitually put one another in mind** (or: to place [thoughts] in each other's mind; to advise or admonish).

15. **Yet I more daringly write to you** (or: Yet with assumed resolution I outspokenly write to you; [other MSS add: brothers; = fellow believers]) **partly as habitually calling you back to full recollection** (causing you to be completely remembering) **because of the grace and favor being given to me from** [other MSS: by; under] **God,**

16. **into the [arranged ability for] me to be Christ Jesus' public servant into the nations** (a public worker of Jesus Christ unto the ethnic multitudes and pagans), **constantly doing the work of a priest for God's good news** (or: habitually functioning as the Temple for the message of the goodness, which is God), **to the end that the offering composed of the ethnic multitudes** (or: the act of bearing forward gifts from the pagans; the approaching of the nations as an offering) **can become well-received and pleasingly acceptable, it being [an offering; a carrying toward] having been set-apart and remaining sacred within the midst of holy spirit and a sacred attitude** (or: in union with a set-apart Breath-effect; within [the] Holy Spirit).

17. **I have and continuously hold, then, the boast** (the glorying; the exulting) **within Christ Jesus** (or: in union with Anointed Jesus) **about the things facing toward** (or: with a view to; face-to-face with) **God.**

18. **You see, I will not venture to speak** (or: tell) **anything of which** (or: what) **Christ does not** (or: did not) **work down, produce and bring into effect through me [leading] into a submissive giving of the ear** (or: humble, obedient hearing and paying attention) **from [the] ethnic multitudes** (or: of non-Jews, nations and pagans) **by an arranged speech and message as well as by a work** (or: in word and in action or deed) – **in a power of signs and of miracles, [that is], in [the] power of God's Spirit** (or: in union with an ability from God's Breath; in an ability from an Attitude which is God [other MSS: in the midst of set-apart Breath-effect]) –

19. **with a view for** (in the purpose for) **me to have filled [the region] from Jerusalem even, around in a circuit, as far as Illyricum [with] the good news of, from, and concerning the Anointed One** (or: the message of goodness, ease and well-being – which is Christ).

20. **Now thus** (or: in this manner) **am I constantly loving the honor, which is my driving ambition, to habitually be proclaiming the message of goodness and well-being where Christ is** (or: was) **not named, to the end that I should not be building upon another person's foundation.**

21. **But just as it has been written,**
>   **"They, to whom it was not reported concerning Him, will progressively see!**
>   **And they who have not heard will progressively understand from things flowing**
>   **together."** [Isa. 52:15]

22. **For this reason** (Wherefore), **also, I was repeatedly being cut-in on** (interrupted; hindered) – **many times and by many things – in regard to coming to you folks.**

23. **Yet now I am no longer holding a place** (or: having a territory; or: = having an opportunity) **within these regions, but am holding** (or: having) **a great longing to come to you – for many years –**

24. **as whenever I may be traveling** (journeying; proceeding) **into Spain. For I continue expecting to gaze on you** (or: hoping to get a look at and view you), **while passing through, and to be escorted** (or: sent forward with funds and supplies) **there by you, if first I can be filled within, in part, from you** (or: could be in some measure satisfied by your company).

25. **But now I am progressively traveling into Jerusalem, continually performing as a servant in dispensing** (or: functioning as an attendant; or: supporting and supplying necessities) **to the set-apart folks** (the holy ones; the saints; sacred people).

26. **You see, Macedonia and Achaia take delight and were well-pleased to make some common sharing** (a certain participating contribution from partnership in common existence) **into the poor** (unto the destitute) **of the set-apart folks** (holy ones; saints) **in Jerusalem.**

27. **For they take delight and were well-pleased, and are their debtors, for since the ethnic multitudes** (the nations; the Gentiles; the non-Jews) **have common participation and shared existence in their spiritual things, they also continue indebted to perform communal service to and for them in things pertaining to the material life** (or: fleshly things).

28. **Bringing this, then, to fruition** (or: Attaining this goal; Coming upon completion, then, of this) **and myself sealing** (or: stamping an identifying mark) **to them** (or: on or for them; [omitted by p46 B]) **this fruit, I will proceed going away, through the midst of you folks, into Spain.**

29. **Now I have seen and thus know** (or: am aware) **that when coming** (or: going) **to you I will continue coming** (or: going) **in an effect of the fullness of Christ's message of Goodness**
>   (or: within that which fills up pertaining to [the] good word {*Logos*} about Christ; in a result
>   of the entire contents of well-speech from [the] Anointing; in union with an effect of the
>   filling of [the] Blessing, which is [the] Anointed One).

30. **So I am calling you alongside** (entreating and encouraging you), **brothers, to struggle together with me** (or: to contend and fight by my side, as in the public games), **through our Lord** (Master; Owner), **Jesus Christ, even through the Spirit's love** (or: and by means of the uniting and accepting love which is the Breath-effect; or: as well as through the full, unrestricted giving of yourselves in an urge toward reunion from this Attitude), **within the thoughts and words toward having goodness and well-being [directed] toward God over me** (or: in union with prayers, face to face with God, for my behalf),

31. **to the end that I may be dragged out of danger from the habitually incompliant** (disobedient; stubborn; unconvinced) **folks within Judea, and that my attending service of dispensing which is directed into Jerusalem may come to be well-received by, and acceptable to, the set-apart people** (holy ones; saints; sacred folks)

32. **in order that, in coming to you in joy through God's will and purpose, I myself will proceed to be taking rest, repose and refreshing in company with you folks.**

33. **Now the God Who is The Peace** (the God Who has the characteristics of Peace; the God of and from harmony [= Shalom]) **[is] together with all of you folks. Count on it** (It is so; Amen)!

CHAPTER 16

1. **Now for** (or: with) **you folks I continue standing together with Phoebe, our sister** (or: Now I am placing Phoebe, our sister, with you people; Now I am recommending Phoebe, our sister, to you [community members]), **she being also an attending servant of the called-out community** (or: a dispenser to the assembled congregation) **[which is] in Cenchrea,**
2. **to the end that you folks would welcome, provide hospitality, and may reach out with your hands and take her in your arms, within [the] Lord** [= Yahweh or Christ], **worthily** (in a manner of equal value) **of the set-apart folks** (of the saints; of the holy ones), **and may stand beside her within whatever matter** (practice-effect; event; affair; result of a transaction) **she may continue having need of [from] you folks, for she also became one who stands before many** (or: a leader or presiding officer over many; = a champion, protector or patron of many) – **even of me, myself!**

3. **Greet Prisca and Aquila, my fellow workers within Christ Jesus,**
4. **who, over my soul** (= person, or, life), **placed their own necks under the axe, to whom not I alone am constantly giving thanks, but further, also all the called-out communities** (summoned-forth congregations) **of the nations** (belonging to the ethnic multitudes of the Gentiles), **as well as the called-out community down at their house** (or: which also follow the pattern of their house-assembly).
5. **Greet Epanetus, my beloved one, who is a firstfruit of the [province of] Asia [entering] into Christ.**
6. **Greet Mary** (or: Mariam), **who wearily labored many things unto and into you folks.**
7. **Greet Andronicus and Junia** (p46 and others read: Julia), **my relatives** (or: fellow-countrymen) **and fellow-captives, who are ones bearing a distinctive mark** (a sign) **upon them** (or: = that are well-known or famous) **among those sent out with a mission** (the representatives; the emissaries), **ones that were birthed within Christ before me.**
8. **Greet Ampliatos, my beloved within [the] Lord.**
9. **Greet Urbanus, our fellow-worker within Christ, and Stachus, my beloved one.**
10. **Greet Apelles, the tried and approved one in Christ. Greet the people from out of those belonging to Aristobulus' [household]** (or: from Aristobulus' folks).
11. **Greet Herodion, my relative** (or: fellow-countryman). **Greet those from out of the people of Narcissus – those being within [the] Lord.**
12. **Greet Tryphena and Tryphosa, the women habitually wearied and spent with labor within [the] Lord. Greet Persida, the beloved woman who is weary from much labor within [the] Lord.**
13. **Greet Rufus, the chosen one in the Lord, and his mother, and mine.**
14. **Greet Asyncritus, Phlegon, Hermes, Patrobas, Hermas and the brothers** (= fellow believers) **with them.**
15. **Greet Philogos and Julia, Nereus and his sister, and Olympas and all the set-apart** (holy; sacred; different-from-what-is-common-and-usual) **folks with them.**
16. **Greet one another in a set-apart expression of affection** (or: a holy kiss which is different from the common one). **All the called-out communities of Christ are greeting you folks.**
17. **So I am calling you folks alongside to encourage and exhort [you], brothers** (= fellow believers), **to constantly view attentively and mark** (or: watch out for) **those continually**

causing the divisions, dissensions or standings-apart, and the snares (those occasions for stumbling and becoming entrapped; or: = obstacles and difficulties) **to the side of** (= which are a counterfeit of and a distraction to) **the teaching which you yourselves learned by instruction, and thus you folks must slope forth** (or: incline out; deflect; hold aloof) **away from them** (or: = shun or avoid them),

18. **for such folks are not habitually performing as slaves for our Lord Christ, but rather for their own belly** (cavity; bowels or stomach; = appetite), **and through the useful smooth talk** (profitable words) **and complimentary speech** (blessings!) **they continuously deceive** (mislead; seduce) **the hearts of the folks without malice** (those with no bad qualities; blameless and innocent ones).

19. **You see, [the report of] your obedient hearing and compliance has reached** (or: arrived) **unto all people. Therefore I constantly rejoice upon you** (or: = over [this news of] you), **yet I am wanting you folks, on the one hand, to be wise [leading] into the midst of The Good, yet, on the other hand, unmixed into the bad** (mixtureless as to the worthless, evil and ugly).

20. **And now the God Who is The Peace** (the God of harmony Who is the source of shalom; the God whose character and quality is this peace) **will progressively rub together, trample and crush the adversary** (beat the opponent to jelly; shatter satan) **under your feet swiftly! The grace and joyous favor of our Lord Jesus [is, and continues] with you folks.**

21. **Timothy, my fellow-worker, is greeting you. Also Lucius, Jason and Sosipater, my relatives** (fellow-countrymen).

22. **– I, Tertius, the one [being the amanuensis** (or: scribe; secretary) **and] writing down the letter, am greeting you in [the] Lord –**

23. **Gaisu, my host, and the whole of the called-out assembly, greets you. Erastus, the city manager** (administrator; steward) **greets you. Also Quartus, the brother.**
[vs. 24 – omitted by the oldest MSS – repeats vs. 20b]

25. **Now by the One** (in the One; to the One) **being continuously able and powerful to set you steadfast** (to make you stand firm and settled) **in accord with** (or: corresponding to; in the sphere of; in line with) **my message of goodness and well-being – even the preaching and public heralding of the message of and from Jesus Christ – down from** (in accord with; in line with) **an unveiling of a secret** (or: a revelation and a disclosure of a mystery) **that had been being kept silent** (or: quiet) **in eonian times** (or: for time periods of the [preceding] ages; to [the] times [that would] pertain to the Age [of Messiah]),

26. **but now is being brought to light and manifested, and through prophetic Scriptures, down from** (in accord with, on the level of and in line with) **a command of the eonian God**
        (from the God Who exists through and comprises the ages; of God in relation to the ages;
        or: = from the God who created, inhabits, owns and rules the ages), **[which leads] into hearing obedience from faith as well as a humble listening and paying attention belonging to trust, pertaining to confidence and which comprises loyalty – suddenly being made known unto all the ethnic multitudes** (nations; Gentiles; pagans; non-Israelites),

27. **by God** (or: with God; in God), **alone wise, through Jesus Christ, in Whom [is] the glory** (by Whom [is] the reputation) **on into the ages of the ages. It is so** (Count on it; Amen)!

[Written circa A.D. 57 – Based on the critical analysis of John A.T. Robinson]

FIRST CORINTHIANS

1. **Paul, a called** (or: summoned) **one – one sent forth with a mission** (a representative; an emissary) **of, and from, Jesus Christ** [other MSS: Christ Jesus' ambassador] **through God's will** (purpose; intent) **– and** (or: with) **Sosthenes, the brother** (one from out of the same womb),
2. **to God's called-out community** (or: summoned-forth, covenant group that has God as its source, and which belongs to God), **the one being within Corinth;**
> **to those having been set-apart within Christ Jesus** (or: made holy, sacred, different from the normal and sanctified, in union with an Anointing of, and from, Jesus)**;**
> **to called** (or: summoned) **folks [and] to set-apart people** (holy ones; saints; sanctified folks; sacred ones) **– together with all those in every place constantly calling upon the Name of our Lord** [note: the phrase applied to Yahweh in Gen. 12:8; Zech. 13:9]**,**
> **Jesus Christ** ([the] Anointed One) **– their [Lord and Messiah], as well as ours:**
3. **With, among, for and to you folks [are] grace** (the influence of favor, kindness, goodwill in the joy-producing gratuitous act) **and peace-of-the-joining from God, our Father and Lord, Jesus Christ** (or: from our Father, God, and [the] Owner, [Messiah] Jesus).

4. **I always and progressively give thanks to** (or: for) **my God**
> (or: experience gratitude in my God; express the ease of grace by my God; experience the happy fortune of abundant favor with my God; = observe my God's competent and prosperous grace) **concerning you folks, upon the basis of God's grace** (favorable influence) **[which is] being given to you folks within and in union with Christ** (or:
[the] Anointed One,) **Jesus,**   [*, vs. 5, *cf* 2 Cor. 9:11; Rom. 2:4; 11:33; Phil. 4:19]
5. **because in** (or: that within the midst of) **everything, and in union with all humanity, you folks are** (or: were) **made rich* within, and in union with, Him* – within every thought** (in the midst of all [the] *Logos*; centered in all reason and information; in every word, idea, expression, eloquence and message) **and in all intimate, experiential knowledge and insight** (*gnosis*) **–**
6. **correspondingly, and in proportion, as Christ's witness** (or: the testimony pertaining to and from the Anointed One; or: the evidence which is the Anointing) **was made certain, stable and established on good footing** (or: validated and confirmed) **within, and among, you folks,**
7. **and as you people are not continuing trailing behind or constantly late, so as to be deficient or fall short – not even in one effect of grace** (or: result of favor) **– being ones habitually receiving and taking away into your hands from out of our Lord's** [= Yahweh's, or Christ's] **unveiling: Jesus Christ**
> (or: from the midst of the uncovering and revelation of our Lord, Jesus [the] Anointed; or: forth from the disclosure from our Lord, which is Jesus Anointed),
8. **Who will continue making you folks stable, certain and established on good footing until maturity** (attainment of the purposed goal; accomplishment of the intended and destined results; finished)**: people not [being] open to accusation** (or: those not in the midst of a [legal] charge, not being called into account, or considered in some category; unimpeachable ones), **within the midst of and in union with this Day of our Lord – Jesus Christ!**
> (or: in the, or this, Day which is our Lord, Jesus Christ; or: in the day of [Yahweh], which is our Master, Jesus [the] Anointed.) [comment: the phrase "the day of the LORD" was used by the prophets to signify God's influence and activity upon people]
9. **God [is] full of faith, trustworthy, loyal and faithful – through Whom you folks were called** (summoned) **into a common being of and existence from** (or: partnership, participation, fellowship, sharing and communion with) **His Son, Jesus Christ, our Lord** (Owner; Master).

10. **Now I am constantly performing as a paraclete, calling you alongside to aid, comfort and encourage you, brothers** (= fellow members), **through the Name of our Lord – Jesus Christ – to the end that you can** (should; may; would) **all keep on speaking the very same thing, and there may not continue being tearing splits-effects** (divisions; schisms; rifts)

among you folks, but you should (or: would) **progressively be folks having been mended, knit together and restored so as to be adjusted down, attuned on the same level, fitly and completely united within the very same mind and in union with the very same result of knowing** (consensus of intent; opinion of purpose; effect of personal insightful-knowing [*gnōmē*]).
11. **For it was made evident and is clear** (or: was declared by intelligible communication) **to me about** (or: concerning) **you folks, my brothers** (= family of believers), **by those of Chloe's [people; group; household], that there continue being quarrels** (situations of strife; discordant debates) **among you people** (or: contentious dispositions within you folks).
12. **Now I am saying this because each of you is in the habit of saying, "I, myself, am indeed [a follower] of Paul," yet [another], "I myself belong to Apollos," and [another], "As for me, I [am] of Cephas' [group]," but [another], "I, myself, [am] of** (or: from) **Christ."**
13. **Christ has been parted and remains divided into fragments!** (or, as a question: Has Christ been fragmented and portioned out into divided parts?)
Paul was not crucified (suspended from a pole; executed on a stake) **over** (on behalf of; [other MSS: concerning]) **you folks! Or were you baptized** (immersed) **into the name of Paul?**
14. **I continue with goodness of grace** (or: thankful; [other MSS: I constantly thank {others add: my} God] **that I baptized** (immersed) **NOT ONE of you folks – if not even Crispus and Gaius!**
15. **– so that NO ONE could say that you folks were immersed** (other MSS: that I baptized) **into MY OWN name!**
16. **Now, did I even baptize** (immerse) **the household of Stephanas? Furthermore, I have not seen or know whether** (or: if) **I immersed some other person!**
17. **For you see, Christ did not send me off with a commission to be constantly baptizing** (immersing), **but rather to habitually announce the message of goodness** (to repeatedly bring the message of abundant well-being; to progressively declare the news of fortunate and ideal ease), **[though] not in cleverness of word** (within [wisdom] of a message or an idea; not in skillfulness of rhetoric) **– in order that the cross of the Christ** (the Anointed One's execution-stake) **cannot** (or: would not) **be made empty or void of content and purpose [by rhetoric].**
18. **You see, the message** (the word; the *Logos*) **of the cross** (or: the idea from, and the concept pertaining to, the execution-stake/suspension-pole) **is and continues being, on the one hand, stupidity** (nonsense; foolishness) **to** (or: for; in; with) **those folks constantly, progressively destroying themselves** (or, as a passive: being habitually lost or progressively undone); **yet, on the other hand, it is and continues being God's power** (or: the ability of and from God; the power which is God) **in us, to us and for us: in the folks being presently delivered**
> (or: for those being continually rescued, repeatedly saved and progressively restored to health and wholeness; or: with the ones being now salvaged and progressively restored).
19. **For it has been written, and thus stands,**
> **"I will undo** (untie and loose away; destroy) **the wisdom and cleverness of the wise ones, and I will set aside** (or: displace; invalidate) **the intelligence** (comprehension; understanding) **of the intellectual** (intelligent; comprehending) **people."** [Isa. 29:14]
20. **Where [is] a wise one? Where [is] a scribe** (one learned in the Scriptures; [the] scholar or theologian; Isa. 19:11f)**? Where [is] a collaborating seeker** (a co-investigator; a learned sophist; a reasoner; a dialectician) **of, or from, this age? Does not God prove** (or: make) **stupid** (foolish; nonsensical) **the wisdom** (attitude; cleverness; learned skill) **of this ordered arrangement** (aggregate of humanity; domination System; world of culture, society, religion)**?**
21. **For since, in view of the fact that – within the Wisdom of God** (or: centered in the wisdom from God; in the midst of the Wisdom which is God) **– the ordered arrangement and System of secular and religious culture** (or: the aggregate of humanity) **did not come to have an intimate, experiential knowledge of God through means of this Wisdom**
> (or: You see, in as much as – in union with God's wisdom – the world of mankind did not recognize, or have insight into, God through means of [human] wisdom), **God delights and considers it profitable** (thinks it thoroughly competent and easy; imagines it well-done) **to deliver** (or: save; rescue; salvage and restore to health, wholeness and their original state and condition) **the folks habitually trusting, repeatedly faithing, progressively believing and constantly being loyal, through the stupidity of the proclamation**

(or: the aforementioned foolishness of that which is proclaimed; or: the dullness of the effect of heralding; or: the "nonsense" of the result of the message preached),

22. **in as much as, in fact, Jews constantly request** (habitually demand) **signs, while and Greeks** (those of the Hellenistic culture) **constantly seek** (habitually try to find) **wisdom!**
23. **Yet as for us, we are constantly proclaiming** (habitually heralding) **Christ: One having been terminally crucified** (or: an executed, hung from a pole Anointed One) **– indeed, a trap-spring** (or: a snare; thus: an obstacle or cause for stumbling or being ensnared) **to** (or: with; for; among) **Jews** (those of the Jewish culture and religion); **yet stupidity** (foolishness; nonsense) **to and for [the] multitudes** (among [other] ethnic groups; in [the] nations; with the non-Jews),
24. **and yet [it is] Christ: God's power and ability, as well as God's wisdom**

(or: and so [we see the] Anointed One – a power from, and which is, God, as well as understanding insight and skillful cleverness from, and which is, God), **to, for, in, with and among those [who are] the called** (or: these summoned) **ones, both Jews and Greeks!**
25. **Because God's stupid thing [or: plan; idea]** (or: the foolish act of God; nonsense from God) **continues being wiser than the humans** (or: [than] from people), **and God's weak act** (or: the weak [thing; plan; idea] from God) **[is] stronger than the humans** ([than] from people).
26. **For, take a comprehensive look at** (or: as an indicative: To be sure, you folks are progressively seeing and observing) **your calling** (or: summoning; vocation; social role) **brothers, that [there are] not many wise folks – according to flesh [= the world's wisdom]**

(or: corresponding to a flesh [system of philosophy or religion]; on the level of [the estranged human situation]; with a consciousness oriented toward a domination System), **not many powerful ones** (those with [political or financial] ability), **not many well-born ones** (ones born to social ease and profit; those of noble birth; folks with distinguished genealogy),
27. **but to the contrary, God collects His thoughts and speaks forth** (or: selects and picks out; chose) **the stupid things** (or: the foolish ones) **of the organized System** (the world of religion, culture and its secular society; or: the cosmos; the universe), **to the end that He could** (or: would; may) **habitually disgrace and bring shame down on the wise ones; and God collects His thoughts and speaks forth** (or: selects, picks out and chooses) **the weak things** (or: the powerless or sickly ones) **of the System** (world; arranged order), **so that He would bring disgrace and shame down on the strong things** (or: the robust and mighty ones),
28. **and God collects His thoughts and speaks forth** (or: selects, picks out and chooses) **ignoble things**

(or: those of no family; those without known ancestry; the base ones; or: the things that are unborn or have not happened; the occurrences that have not come to be) **pertaining to the controlling System** (or: from the world or government, politics, religion or culture; of the realm of the non-religious; which are the social and religious outcasts), **and those that are looked down on, despised and regarded as having come from out of nothing – even those being nothing** (nonentities; or: the things not existing; or: the things that are "nothing") **– in order that He could make ineffective** (bring to "nothing"; bring down to idle uselessness) **the existing things** (or: the things that are "something"; or: = [domination systems] presently having being),
29. **so that no flesh [nature, government or religious system] – [including, or at] all – could boast in God's sight or presence** (or: before God).

30. **Now you folks are, and continuously exist being, forth from out of the midst of Him – within and in union with Christ Jesus, Who came to be** (or: is birthed) **wisdom in and among us** (or: to us; for us), **from God: both a rightwising, eschatological deliverance into righted, covenantal existence in fair relationships of equity in the Way pointed out** (or: likewise a just covenantal Act from God) **and a being set-apart to be different** (a being made sacred), **even a redemptive liberation** (an emancipation; a loosing-away from [a condition of bondage]) **–**
31. **to the end that, correspondingly as it has been and stands written,**

"The one constantly boasting: let him habitually boast and constantly take pride in [the] Lord [= Yahweh]." [Jer. 9:23]

CHAPTER 2

1. **And I myself, in coming toward you, brothers** (= fellow members), **did not come repeatedly announcing the message of God's secret** (or: constantly proclaiming the news of the mystery [other MSS: witness; testimony] from God) **down to you as down from an elevation of thought** (or: according to superiority of word [*logos*]), **or of wisdom and cleverness** (= with a message of transcendent rhetoric or philosophical subtlety and brilliance),

2. **for I decided not to see, perceive or know anything within or among you folks, except Jesus Christ – and this One being one having been crucified** (suspended from a pole)!

3. **So I, myself, came to be with and toward you, and faced you folks, in lack of strength** (or: in union with weakness), **and in fear – even in much trembling and agitation of mind** (or: very nervous; shaking with reverence and respect; or: = with earnestness and much concern),

4. **so my message** (the *Logos*, or word, thought and Information, from me) **and my public proclamation [were; consisted] not in persuasive words of wisdom** (or: ideas from cleverness [MSS add: of, or from, a human]), **but to the contrary [were; consisted] in demonstration of spirit and attitude, as well as of power and from ability**
    > (or: in the midst of a display of clear and logical proof from [the] Spirit, consisting of power and ability; in union with a documented manifestation which was Breath-effect and which was a means of influence and capability),

5. **to the end that your trust would not be in human wisdom** (your faith and reliance would not exist in cleverness of people), **but rather in God's power, means, influence and ability.**

6. **Now we habitually speak wisdom among the mature folks** (or: in the midst of the finished, completed people; or: in union with perfected ones who have arrived at the goal and destiny), **yet not a wisdom of, from or belonging to, this age, neither of the rulers** (chief people; leaders) **of this age – of or from those progressively and successively being brought down to idleness and ineffective uselessness** (or: gradually nullified and rendered inoperative; = brought to nothing; = being ones fired from their jobs).

7. **To the contrary, we habitually speak God's wisdom within the midst of a secret** (or: we normally speak – in [the form or realm of] a mystery which only the initiated understand – the wisdom which is God): **the [wisdom] having been hidden away and remaining concealed, which God marked out in advance and set its boundaries** (or: previously designed) **– before the ages – [leading] into our glory and assumed appearance** (praise-inducing manifestation),

8. **which [wisdom] not one of the rulers** (leaders; chief people) **of this age know** (or: came to know) **by intimate experience or insight. For if they knew, THEY would not likely have crucified** (hung or suspended on a pole) **the Owner of, and Who is, the glory** [*cf* Col. 2:15]
    > (or: For if they know, they would not stake-execute the Lord of the Manifestation which calls forth praise, and Who is the Appearance with a good reputation).

9. **But to the contrary, according as it has been and stands written,**
    > **"Things which an eye has not seen and an ear does not hear, neither does it ascend** (climb up) **upon [the] heart of a human, so as to conceive – so many things God prepares and makes ready in, for and by the folks habitually loving** (accepting and urging toward reunion with; fully giving themselves to) **Him."** [Isa. 64:3; 52:15]

10. **Yet** [other MSS: For you see] **God unveils [them] in us** (reveals [them] to us; uncovers [them] for us; discloses [these] among us) **through the spirit** (or: the Spirit; the Breath-effect), **for you see, the spirit** (or: the Spirit; the Breath-effect; the Attitude) **constantly and progressively searches, examines and investigates all humanity, and everything – even the depths of, from, which pertain to, and which are, God!**

11. **For who, of humans** (from people), **has seen so as to know the things of the human** (or: the [matters] pertaining to the person), **except the spirit of the human** (or: the person's spirit) **– the one within the midst of him? So, too, no one** (or: not one) **experientially or intimately knows** (or: came to know or have insight and exercise "*gnosis*" regarding) **the things of God** (God's matters), **except the Spirit of God** (or: God's spirit; the Breath-effect which is God).

12. **Now we did not receive** (or: do not accept or take to ourselves; do not take control of or grasp hold of) **the spirit of the System** (the world's spirit and atmosphere; the attitude of or from the domination system of government, economy or religion), **but to the contrary, that spirit** (or: the Spirit, Breath-effect or Attitude) **[which is] from out of the midst of God – to the end that**

we can see and know the things being freely and joyously given to and for us in grace (or: being graciously bestowed, and favorably given in us) **by God,**

13. **which things we are also habitually speaking – not in words** (*logoi*) **taught from human wisdom** (or: not centered in learned thoughts, ideas or messages instructed which pertain to human wisdom; or: not among those taught in, by or with words, patterns of information, or reasons which are human wisdom), **but rather in those [words] taught from spirit** (or: in union with and among those folks taught of [the] Spirit – from the effect of a Breath and an Attitude), **habitually evaluating, combining, contrasting and comparing, and then deciding spiritual [matters] together by spiritual [means] and with qualities inherent in the Breath-effect**

> (or: constantly matching or comparing/contrasting things pertaining to attitude with things in spirit, or by [the] Spirit; or: progressively making collective assessments of pneumatic [concepts] to and for pneumatic people; interpreting spiritual things in spiritual [terms]).

14. **But a soulish person** (one dominated by, or living focused on, his breath [= the transient life], or by those things which characterize the soul [emotions; will; intellect; physical life; internal welfare; the self; the ego] or psyche; = a nonpneumatic one) **does not normally accept** (or: habitually get or welcomingly receive the offer of) **the things of God's Breath-effect** (or: which have the character and quality of the Spirit of God; pertaining to God's spirit and attitude), **for they are stupidity to him** (foolishness for him; nonsense in him), **and he continues unable and habitually has no power to intimately and experientially know [them] or get insight, because they continue being sifted and held up for close spiritual examination**

> (are normally evaluated spiritually above; are constantly brought back for spiritual separation and attitudinal discernment; are progressively re-evaluated through means of the Breath-effect and comparison to the Attitude; or: are pneumatically interpreted).

15. **Yet the spiritual person** (one dominated by and focused on spirit or the realm of the Spirit, and characterized by the qualities of spirit: the Wind which continuously moves across the land; or: the pneumatic person) **is, on the one hand, continuously sifting and re-evaluating** (habitually separating and deciding from above on; progressively holding things up for close examination of) **everything and all humanity, yet, on the other hand, he is being sifted and held up for close examination or decision by no one.**

16. **For,**

> **"Who intimately knows** (or: experientially knew) **[the] Lord's** [= Yahweh's] **mind? Who will proceed to co-habit with** (or: so that he will mount or come together so as to unite and be knit with) **Him?"** [Isa. 40:13, LXX; note: for **mind** the Heb. text has Spirit]

Yet we, ourselves, are continuously holding (or: progressively having) **Christ's mind** (a mind which is Anointed, and which is Christ [other MSS: {the} Lord])**!**

CHAPTER 3

1. **And yet I myself, brothers, was not able to speak to you folks as to spiritual people** (= having the effect of the Breath; led by the Spirit/Attitude), **but to the contrary as to fleshly folks** (= people of flesh, being focused thereon; = as "natural" people, unaffected by the Breath/Spirit) – **as to infants in Christ** (or: babies/adolescents in Anointing).

2. **I gave you folks milk to drink, not solid food, for you were continuing not as yet being able or having power. But then, neither are you yet now** (at present) **able** (or: having power), **for you are still fleshly ones** (= people of flesh, focused on ordinary life, with natural thinking).

3. **For you see, in which place** (or: insofar as) **[there is] jealousy and strife and folks standing apart** (divisions and disunities) **among you folks – are you not existing being fleshly folks** (people adapted to flesh and self), **even constantly walking around** (= living your life) **according to, on the level of, in the sphere of, and corresponding to, humanity?**

4. **For whenever anyone repeatedly says, "I myself am indeed of Paul** (belong to Paul; have my association with Paul)**," yet a different one [says], "I, myself, of Apollos" – are you not continuing being fleshly humans** (= people acting like the estranged flesh; = non-spiritual)**?**

5. **What, then** [other MSS: So then, what], **is Apollos? And what is Paul? [They are] attending servants and dispensers of [spiritual] provisions, through whom you folks came to believe and trust – even as the Lord** [Christ; Yahweh] **gave** (or: gives) **to and in each one.**

6. **I myself plant** (or: planted), **Apollos irrigated** (or: waters; caused [you] to drink), **but then God was causing [it/you] to progressively grow up and increase** (be augmented).

7. **So that neither is the one habitually planting anything [special]** (anyone [of importance]), **nor the one habitually irrigating** (watering; giving drink), **but rather God: the One habitually and progressively causing growth and increase.**

8. **Now the one continually planting and the one continually irrigating are one** (exist being a unit), **yet each one will receive his own wage** (pay; compensation) **corresponding to his own labor** (toil).

9. **For we are God's fellow-workers** (or: we are co-workers of, and from, God, and are people who work together with God; we exist being workings-together who belong to God, synergies of God; attending deeds which are God). **You folks are God's farm** (or: field under cultivation), **God's building** (or: construction project from God; structure which is God; or: act of building pertaining to God).

10. **Corresponding to, in accord with and to the level of, God's grace and favor [which are] being given to** (or: by) **me, as [being] a skillful master-carpenter** (wise chief-builder; clever head-artisan; learned, competent leading-stonemason; like a wise architect, engineer, foreman or director of works) **I lay** [other MSS: have laid] **a foundation** (or: laid a foundation [Stone]), **yet another is progressively building a house upon [it]. Now let each one continue watching to observe** (= take care) **how he keeps on building the house upon [it]** (or: upon the house),

11. **for you see, no one can** (or: continues able to; is having power to) **lay another foundation** (or: to place or set another foundation [Stone] of the same kind) **beside** (or: in addition to and distinct from) **the One lying** (or: continuing being laid): **which is** (continues being) **Jesus Christ** (Jesus [the] Anointed One; = Jesus, [the] Messiah).

12. **Now if anyone proceeds building a house** (a superstructure) **upon the** [other MSS: this] **Foundation – gold and silver [with] precious** (valuable) **stones; wood [and] thatching: herbage** (or: grass; hay) **[or] stalk** (or: straw; stubble) –

13. **each one's work will make itself to be visible in clear light** (or: will become apparent), **for the Day will continue making [it] evident** (showing [it] plainly). **Because it is being progressively unveiled** (continually revealed) **within the midst of Fire, and the Fire, Itself, will progressively test, examine and put to the proof what sort of work each one's exists being.**

14. **If anyone's work which he or she built upon [it] will remain, he or she will proceed in receiving wages** (pay; compensation).

15. **If anyone's work will be burned down, he or she will proceed in incurring a loss** (sustaining the damage; forfeiting), **yet he himself or she herself will be saved** (rescued and delivered; healed; restored; made whole; kept safe), **and as in this way – through Fire!** [cf 5:5, below; Job 2:6, LXX]

16. **Have you folks not seen, to now know, that you people continuously exist being God's Temple** (Divine habitation; holy place and holy of holies; inner sanctuary), **and God's Spirit is constantly dwelling** (God's Breath is making Its home; the Wind which is God is housing Himself; the Attitude from God is progressively co-habiting) **within the midst of you folks?**

17. **If anyone habitually spoils, ruins, wrecks or corrupts God's Temple, God will spoil, ruin, wreck and corrupt this person; for you see, God's Temple – which you folks, yourselves, are** (exist being) **– is set-apart** (holy; sacred; different from the common).

18. **Let no one continue to be completely cheating, tricking, deceiving or deluding himself:** **if anyone among you folks habitually imagines** (thinks; supposes; presumes) **[himself] to be wise** (to exist being a clever one) **within this age** (this era; this period of time), **let him come to be** (or: birth himself) **stupid** (dull; foolish; a fool) **– to the end that he can come to be** (or: may birth himself) **wise.**

19. **For you see, the wisdom** (cleverness; skill) **of this world System** (or: pertaining to this ordered and controlling arrangement of cultures, religions and politics; or: from this society of domination; of the aggregate of humanity) **is stupidity** (exists as nonsense and foolishness) **[when put] beside or next to God** (or: in God's presence). **For it has been written,**

"He is the One habitually laying hold of and catching in His fist the wise (clever) ones, within the midst of their every act (or: capability and readiness to do or work; cunning; craftiness)." [Job. 5:13]

20. **And again,**

"**[The] Lord** [= Yahweh] **continues, by intimate experience, knowing the reasonings** (thought processes; designs) **of the wise ones, that they are and continue being fruitless, useless and to no purpose.**" [Ps. 94:11]

21. **Hence** (or: And so), **let no one continue boasting in people** (among, or in union with, humans)**. You see, here it is: all things [are] yours** (or: all things pertain to you),

22. **whether Paul, or Apollos, or Cephas; whether [the] world** (System of culture, religion, economy or government; human aggregate), **or life, or death; whether things standing or having been placed within [your situation], or things being about to be** (impending things), **all things [are] yours** (or: everything pertains to you, belongs to you, and [is] from you folks),

23. **yet you folks [are] Christ's – yet Christ [is] God's!**

(or: Now you have your source and origin in [the] Anointed, and [the] Anointed has His source and origin in God; or: But you belong to [Messiah]; [Messiah] belongs to God.)

CHAPTER 4

1. **Thus, let a person** (a human) **continue logically considering** (or: measuring and classifying) **us as God's subordinates** (God's deputies; those under God's orders; God's under-rowers) **and house-managers** (or: administrators) **of God's secrets** (or: mysteries from God which require initiation for receiving; secrets which are God).

2. **In this situation, furthermore, it is constantly being looked for and sought after, in house-managers** (administrators), **that this person may be found [to be] full of faith** (loyal; reliable; trustworthy; faithful).

3. **Now to** (or: for) **me, it is of little importance** (a very trivial matter) **that I am being constantly critiqued** (sifted, critically reviewed and evaluated; put up for judgment) **by you folks, or by a human day** (= day of reckoning; man's tribunal or day in court). **In contrast, by habit, neither do I set myself up for critique** (or: review, evaluate or judge myself).

4. **For, in and regarding** (or: [as] to; for) **myself, I have been conscious of nothing; but yet [it is] not in this [that] I have been set forth as** (or: made to be) **fair and equitable** (just and rightwised with right relationship in the Way pointed out). **Now the One continually setting me up for evaluation** (sifting, reviewing and deciding about me) **is [the] Lord** [= Christ or Yahweh].

5. **Hence** (or: And so), **do not be constantly evaluating** (or: stop judging, making decisions about or critiquing) **anything before [its] season** (before a fitting, due or appointed situation; prior to a fertile moment)**: until the Lord** [= Yahweh or Christ] **would come – Who will continue giving light to** (or: shine upon and illuminate) **the hidden things of the Darkness** (or: the hiding things which are things in the shadows and dimness of obscurity), **and will progressively set in clear light** (or: keep on manifesting) **the intentions and purposes** (designs, dispositions, motives and counsels) **of the hearts – and then the praise and applause from God will repeatedly be birthed** (happen; come into being) **in each human** (or: for every person)**!**

6. **Now I refashioned these things** (or: transposed and transfer these things into a figure; change the distinctive form to apply and exemplify; or: = changed the form of the metaphor), **brothers – with a view to Apollos and myself – because of you folks, to the end that in us you could learn not to set your thoughts** (be disposed; put your intellect and opinion; entertain sentiments) **on things over and above things which have been written, so that you do not continue being puffed up – one over and above another, [and] down on the different one.**

7. **For who continues making you to discriminate** (or: who is now thoroughly separating or dividing you through the midst, for evaluation; or: who is repeatedly discerning or distinguishing you; or: what makes you completely different, separated or exceptional)**? And what are you habitually holding** (constantly having) **which you did not receive? Now since** (or: if) **also you received [it], why do you continue boasting, as though not receiving [it]?**

8. **You folks already continuously exist being ones having become completely satiated, with the result that you are now fully satisfied. You are already suddenly rich. You people suddenly reign as kings** (or: attained sovereignty) – **apart from us!** [note: these three statements could also be questions: Are you... Are you... Do you...?] **And would that you surely did reign** (function as kings) **so that we could also reign as kings together with you!**

9. **Indeed, it continues seeming to me that** (or: I regularly suppose that; I am presently thinking that) **God shows us off** (exhibits us) – **the last ones sent off with a mission** (or: displayed the emissaries and representatives last) – **as men condemned to die in the public arena** [e.g., as gladiators, or as thrown to the lions], **because we were made to be a theater** (= an observed public spectacle) **for the world** (or: to the organized, domination System of culture, religion, economy and politics; or: in the cosmos!), **even to messengers** (or: for [government] agents; among folks with the Message), **and for humans** (or: to and among peoples [in general]).

10. **We [are] stupid folks** (fools; ones led by nonsense) **because of Christ, yet you folks [are] sensible and intelligent ones** (ones with understanding) **within, and in union with, Christ; we [are] weak ones, yet you people [are] strong ones; you [are] folks in glory and illustrious reputation, yet we [are] dishonored and unvalued ones.**

11. **Until the present hour** (or: Up to now – this very minute), **we also continue being hungry, constantly thirsty, habitually naked** (= scantily clothed), **repeatedly being struck on the ear with a fist** (= treated roughly) **and are continuously unsettled** (= homeless and wanderers).

12. **Further, we continue toiling** (laboring) **to weariness – habitually active in work with our own hands** [note: the Greek culture despised manual labor]. **Being constantly insulted** (reviled; cursed; verbally abused), **we are repeatedly speaking words of goodness** (or: blessing); **being habitually pursued and persecuted, we are continuously holding up and bearing [it]** (or: holding back [i.e., from retaliation]);

13. **being incessantly defamed** (slandered; plied with ill-rumors; [other MSS: blasphemed]), **we regularly called them to our sides** (normally entreated and offered assistance). **We were made to be as that which comes from cleaning all around** (as the off-scouring results; as the filthy refuses) **of the world** (from the organized System of culture, religion, economy and government) – **wiped-off filth and scum of all things and all people – until right now!**

14. **I am not continuing to write these things [to be] constantly shaming you folks** (or: turning you back within yourselves), **but to the contrary, as my beloved children** (accepted born-ones to whom I urge for reunion), **I am progressively placing things in your minds.**

15. **For should you folks proceed to have a vast multitude** (a myriad; ten thousand) **of child-escorts and guardians within Christ** (or: tutors or educators in an Anointing), **in contrast [you do] not [have] many fathers** (or: parents), **because in one moment I myself fathered** (gave birth to; generated) **you people within and in union with Christ Jesus – through means of the message of abundant wellness** (the news of fortunate, ideal ease and goodness).

16. **Therefore, I am repeatedly performing as a paraclete for you** (calling you to my side to aid, comfort, encourage and advise you). **Progressively come to be** (or: Keep on becoming) **my imitators** (ones who copy or mimic me).

17. **Because of this, I sent Timothy to you folks – he who is my beloved child** (accepted born-one) **and one full of faith** (or: a loyal, reliable, faithful and trustworthy person) **within and in union with [the] Lord** [= Christ or Yahweh], **who will continue calling you back to remembrance** (will be repeatedly reminding you) **of my ways** (roads; paths) – **the ones in union with an Anointing** [other MSS: in the midst of Christ Jesus (or: in {the} Anointing of Jesus); others: within {the} Lord Jesus; others: in Jesus] – **correspondingly as** (according as; along the lines as and to the level as) **I am habitually teaching everywhere, within the midst of every called-out community** (ecclesia; summoned forth covenant assembly).

18. **Now certain ones were puffed up** (= became arrogant; were bloated [from pride or self-esteem]), **as though I [were] not proceeding to be coming to you.**

19. **Yet I will proceed quickly** (speedily) **coming to you folks, if the Lord** [= Christ or Yahweh] **should intend** (purpose; will) **[it], and I will progress in knowing by intimate experience not the word** (thought; idea; message; verbal expression; information) **of, or from, those having been puffed up, but to the contrary, [their] ability and power.**

20. For God's reign (or: the kingdom which is God; the sovereign influence or activity from God) **[is; lies] not within an idea** (a *logos*; information; a thought; a word; a message; a verbal expression), **but rather within ability, in union with capability, or in the midst of power.**
21. What do you folks want (presently desire; normally intend; by habit purpose)**? Should I come to you people within [the realm of] a rod** (staff; = with corrective measures)**, or within love** (solidarity)**, and in a spirit of gentle friendliness and tender kindness** (or: meekness)**?**

CHAPTER 5

1. It is actually (or: generally; everywhere) **being repeatedly heard [that there is] prostitution among you folks – and such a sort of prostitution which is not even being mentioned** (or: named) **among the ethnic multitudes** (nations; non-Jewish groups)**: so as someone continues to hold** (or: a certain person is repeatedly having) **[his] father's woman** (or: wife; or, thus: [his] stepmother)**!** [*cf* Lev. 18:8]
2. And now you folks, yourselves, have been puffed up and remain inflated with pride! And still you do not rather mourn and grieve (or: lament and express sorrow)**, so that the man performing this act would** (or: that the man practicing this deed should) **at once be caused to depart** (or: be picked up, removed or taken away) **from out of your midst.**
3. For I myself, indeed, continuing being absent – in the body – yet continuously being present alongside – in (or: by; with) **the spirit** (or: Breath-effect; or: attitude) **– have, as being present, already sifted, evaluated and decided about the man thus working down to this effect:**
4. [Upon] your being gathered together within the Name of our Lord, Jesus Christ, then together with my spirit – in, by and with the power and ability of our Lord Jesus –
5. [you are] to commit (surrender; hand-over) **such a man, with the adversarial [spirit]** (or: in the adversary; by the opponent; or: to *satan*)**, into a loss of the flesh** (or: an undoing and destruction of this [distorted human nature]; a loss of [his "dominated existence" – Walter Wink]) **– to the end that the spirit may be saved** (rescued; delivered; restored to health, wholeness)**: within the midst of and in union with the Day of** (or: in this day from, or, which is) **the Lord** [= Christ or Yahweh; other MSS add: Jesus; others read: our Lord, Jesus Christ]. [*cf* 3:15, above; 1 Tim. 1:20; Job 2:6]
6. The effect of your boast is not beautiful, fine, ideal or good form. Have you not seen so as to know that a little leaven (or: yeast) **progressively leavens** (permeates) **[the] whole lump of dough** (the result of that which has been uniformly mixed and kneaded together)**?**
7. At once completely clean out the old leaven, so that you folks would progressively be a fresh, new lump of dough with uniform mix-effect, just as you are free from ferment
(or: in that you have continued being an aggregation which has been freshly mixed and kneaded together – correspondingly as you are continuing being unleavened ones). **For also Christ, our Passover** [= Passover lamb]**, was slaughtered** (or: sacrificed; slain for food).
8. Consequently, we can (or: should) **be continuously keeping and celebrating the Feast** (7-day Festival of Unleavened Bread) **– not in union with old leaven** (or: yeast in old dough from the previous batch)**, neither in union with or in the midst of a leaven of bad quality** (worthlessness; ugliness; what ought not to be; malice) **and painful misery** (hard labor; evil disposition; mischief; wickedness) **– but in contrast, in union with and in the midst of unleavened cakes** (matzah) **of genuineness** (or: which are integrity and sincerity; from that which has been tested by sunlight and found to be pure and unadulterated) **as well as truth and unhidden reality.** [*cf* Deut. 16:3; Lu. 12:1; Rev. 5]
9. I wrote to you folks, in the letter: not to keep on mixing yourselves together again with men who make a practice of whoring, or who are male prostitutes (or: not to be repeatedly intermingled again with male paramours or boys who sell themselves) **–**
10. and [I am] not wholly or altogether [referring] to this world's (or: secular society's) **prostitutes**
(or: the male prostitutes of this cultural, religious and political system [note: the concept of sexual misconduct also has a figurative aspect in Scripture, denoting unfaithfulness to God])**; or to those who are greedy and want to have more than, and to take advantage of, others and/or [are] folks who snatch things away, as extortionists; or [who**

are] idolaters (or: hirelings of the idols). **Otherwise, in that case, you folks continue under obligation to consequently exit the System** (go forth from out of the midst of the world of religion, culture and society) –

11. **yet at this time** (or: so now) **I write for you folks not to continue mixing yourselves back together with anyone being regularly recognized as** (usually designated; habitually named or called) **a "brother," if he should continue being a prostitute, or a covetous and greedy person, or an idolater, or a verbally abusive one, or a drunkard, or a snatching one** (or: an extortioner) – **not even to be habitually eating with such a person.**

12. **For what [right is it] for me to be making decisions about or judging those [who are] "outside"? Are you yourselves not repeatedly sifting and critiquing** (or: separating and judging) **those "inside"? Now those "outside" God habitually sifts and makes decisions about** (is constantly judging).

13.   **"Lift up out and carry forth** (Expel; Remove) **the degenerate person** (the misery-gushed, worthless, base or evil one who brings pain) **out of the midst of yourselves."** [Deut. 13:5; 17:7; etc.]

CHAPTER 6

1. **Does anyone of you folks [who] are continuing holding a result of some deed done** (or: the effect of a practice; or: = a court case) **toward someone else**
    (or: are now having a business transaction focused toward another; continue in having a dispute or law-suit proceeding toward the different person) **now dare or boldly presume to continue to be judged upon the basis** (or: = in the place or court) **of unjust folks** (people who are unfair and are not in the way pointed out; = those outside the called-out community), **and not upon the [basis; place; court] of the set-apart folks** (the saints; the holy ones)**?**

2. **Or have you not seen so as to know that the set-apart folks** (the saints; the holy, sacred people; the different-from-the-profane folks) **will habitually sift, separate, evaluate and decide about the organized System** (the world of culture, religion and government; or: secular society; or: = the Empire)**? So since** (or: if) **centered in, among and in relation to, you folks the domination System is being habitually** (progressively; repeatedly) **evaluated or judged, are you people unworthy or unfit in regard to deciding about very trivial controversies**
    (or: not of equal value to the smallest standards by which to sift and evaluate; or: of [holding the] least tribunals or places for court)**?**

3. **Have you not seen so as to know that we shall continue sifting, separating, evaluating and making decisions about agents** (or: will continue judging messengers, i.e., folks with the message) – **why not, indeed, the affairs and business matters of everyday life?**

4. **Indeed, therefore, if you may continue having tribunals** (places or situations for trying things; or: standards for evaluating controversies) **pertaining to life's affairs and business matters, make it a practice to seat [as judges] those in the local called-out community [who] have been regarded as amounting to nothing and are treated with contempt and scorn** (those least esteemed and of humble station in life).
    (or, as a question: are you making it a practice to seat [as judges] those looked down upon, disregarded or without repute and "standing" within the congregation?)

5. **I am saying [this] to direct you folks toward turning back within [your community or yourself, and so, to reconsider]. Is there thus not one wise person** (one skilled with insight) **among you folks who will continue able to thoroughly sift and hold up [things] for evaluation and decision** (to adjudicate back) **in his brother's midst?**

6. **But to the contrary, a brother is constantly being brought to court** (sued; judged; evaluated and decided about) **with a brother** (= by a fellow believer; or: member of the same family) – **and this upon [the basis and situation] of unbelievers!**

7. **Indeed, it is already** (or: to begin with [= even before going to court]) **therefore wholly an effect of a lessened condition in** (or: a defeat: a result of a diminishing from an overthrow for) **you folks – that you continue having lawsuits with one another. Why not rather continue suffering wrong** (or: be repeatedly treated unfairly and unjustly)**? Why not rather continue being defrauded** (or: being deprived from; or, as a middle: allowing yourselves to be cheated)**?**

8. **Yet instead, you yourselves are constantly committing wrong** (being unfair and unjust; living contrary to the Way pointed out) **and are repeatedly defrauding** (cheating; depriving from [someone]) **– and this [to] brothers** (folks from the same womb; = believers, in the Family)!

9. **Or have you not seen so as to know that unfair** (unjust; inequitable; wrongly-turned) **folks will not proceed to inherit a kingdom from God** (or: receive an allotment in God's sovereign reign or activities)**? Do not be repeatedly misled or constantly caused to wander** (or: be deceived). **Neither sexually licentious folks** (paramours; fornicators; [note: may also refer to men associating at idol temple-feasts]), **nor idolaters, nor adulterers** [may = participation in pagan religions; cf Isa. 1:21; Ezk. 16:15], **nor unmanly** (men who wear soft clothes [Mat. 11:8]; soft, delicate, weak folks; = untrained and undeveloped, so unable to bear a load?), **nor men who lie in beds** (= lazy folks? or: sex-traffickers? [note: meaning uncertain; cf LXX: Lev. 18:22; 20:13 have been associated with these passages; = those following an off-target direction?]),
10. **nor thieves, nor greedy** (covetous) **ones; not drunkards, not verbal abusers, not people who ravenously snatch, swindle or extort, will proceed to inherit a kingdom from God** (or: will continue in receiving an allotment in God's sovereign reign and activities).
11. **And some of you were these things. But now you folks bathed yourselves off** (took a bath to cleanse things away). **Even more than that, you were set apart** (made holy; sanctified). **But yet more, you were eschatologically delivered, rightwised and placed in the Way pointed out** (turned in the right direction, made just, and then joined in right, covenantal relationship with God and mankind) **in union with and within the midst of the Name of our Lord, Jesus Christ – even in union with and within the midst of the Spirit of our God** (or: that is, centered in the Breath-effect from our God and the Attitude which is our God)!

12. **To me, all things are presently out-of-Being** (or: All things continue from existence for me; or: All is authorized, right and permitted by and in me). **But yet not everything proceeds to bear together for advantage, profit, help, or are for the best. To me, all things are authorized, permitted and out of [His] Being, but still I myself will not proceed in being brought under authority by anyone.**
> (or: With, to and for me, all is from the source of Being, and continues with right and privilege. However, all is not habitually carrying together. With, to and for me, all is from the source of Being, and continues with right and privilege; nonetheless, I will not continue being put in subjection to rights and privileges under any person or under any certain thing, pertaining to me.
> or: All have rights with me, but on the other hand, not all things are advantageous. All, from [his, her or its] existence, has privilege with me, although, as for me, I will not proceed in being subdued under anyone's privilege.)

13. **The foods** (The things eaten) **[are meant] for the stomach, and the stomach [is meant] for the things eaten, yet God will make both it and them useless and unprofitable** (or: will also bring this and these down to being idle).
Now the body [is] not for prostitution (or: sexual immorality; or: = idolatry), **but rather for the Lord – and further, the Lord [is] in** (or: for; with) **the body.**
14. **Yet God both aroused** (awakened) **and raised up the Lord, and He is presently and progressively** (or: one-after-another repeatedly; or: keeps on) **arousing and raising us up out of the midst** [reading with p11.46*, A, D*, P and others; or: p46c2, B and others read: He fully aroused and raised us up (or: at one point arouses and raises us up out); or: p46c1, Aleph, C, D2 and others read: He will continue raising us up out] **through His power and ability.** [cf 15:29]

15. **Have you folks not seen so as to know that your** [other MSS: our] **bodies are** (exist being) **members** (body parts) **of Christ? Upon lifting up and carrying off** (or: bearing away) **the members** (body parts) **of the Christ, will I proceed then in making** (or: could or should I at any point yield) **[them] members** (body parts) **of a prostitute? May it not come to be or happen** (= Heaven forbid; = No way)!
16. **Or, have you folks not seen so as to know that the man continually joining himself** (or: being habitually glued in intimate union) **to** (or: in) **a prostitute exists being one body [with her]? For, He says,**

"The two will continue existing, being [joined] into one flesh." [Gen. 2:24]
17. **Now the person continually joining himself** (or: being habitually glued in intimate union; in himself being continuously welded) **to** (or: in; with) **the Lord exists being one spirit** (or: one Breath-effect; one Attitude; one Spirit).
18. **Constantly flee** (Repeatedly take flight [from]) **the prostitution.** [note: this would also apply to idolatry in pagan temples which used prostitutes as part of the idol worship] **The effect** (or: result) **of every sin** (failure to hit the target; error; mistake; deviation) – **whatsoever a person may do – exists being outside of the body. Yet the one habitually committing prostitution** (practicing sexual immorality) **is habitually sinning** (sowing errors and mistakes) **into his own body.** [note: both his physical body, and the body of the called-out community]
19. **Or, have you folks not seen so as to know that your body** (or: the body of you folks) **is a temple of the set-apart spirit** (or: a sanctuary belonging to the Holy Spirit; a holy place and a holy of holies which pertains to the Sacred Breath; or: that the body, which is you folks, exists being a divine habitation which has the qualities and characteristics of the Holy Attitude) – **within the midst of you** (or: in union with you folks; or: among you people) – **which you people constantly hold and progressively possess from God? And further, you are not folks belonging to yourselves** (or: Also then, you people do not exist from yourselves),
20. **for you people were bought, as at a marketplace: [there was] value and honor involved in the price** (or: [you are] of value)
    (or: = you see, you folks were bought and paid for; or: it follows that from a valuable price you folks were bought at market).
By all means then, glorify God (bring a good reputation to God; manifest that which calls forth praise to God) **within your body** (or: within the midst of the body which you folks are)!

CHAPTER 7

1. **Yet concerning the things which you folks wrote: "Is it fine for a man to by habit not touch a woman so as to hold or kindle her as a wife?"**
    (or: = Now about what you wrote: "Is it ideal for a man to live in celibacy as a way of life?")
2. **Well, because of prostitutions** (= the dangers of sexual immorality, or the lure of pagan temple prostitutes), **let each man continually hold and be permanently having a wife** (or: woman) **for himself, and each woman be constantly holding and permanently having her own husband.**
3. **Let the husband habitually render** (give away in answer to claim and expectation) **to the wife [her] due** (what is owed to her; the obligation; the debt), **yet likewise the wife, also, to the husband.**
4. **The wife continues having no right or authority pertaining to her own body, but to the contrary, the husband [does]. Now likewise the husband, also, continues having no right or authority pertaining to his own body, but to the contrary, the wife [does].**
5. **Do not habitually deprive** (defraud; rob) **one another, except anytime** (or: unless perhaps) **it should [be] from out of mutual consent** (spoken agreement) **with a view toward a specific period** (or: appointed season; fertile situation or condition) **so that you [both] may be at leisure in activities that lead toward having goodness and well-being** (or: could be otherwise unoccupied for prayer; can give each other time for thoughts of ease or to be unemployed with a view to wellness), **and then you [both] may proceed being** [other MSS: should come together] **again [putting your attention] upon this very thing [i.e., resume your physical relationship], so that the adversary** (the opponent; the adversarial [situation or attitude]) **may not keep on testing you** (endeavoring to put you to the proof; trying you; tempting you) **because of your lack of strength** (through your lack of control; because of your incontinence).
    [note: continued sexual relations in marriage was a duty, under Jewish law and custom; failure to do so was grounds for divorce – Ex. 21:10-11; vs. 4 is a step toward equality]
6. **Now I am saying this in accord with the common knowledge of experience, not down from an arrangement put upon [you]** (or: not in response to an imposed disposition or injunction).

7. **You see** [other MSS: Now], **I normally want** (keep on wishing; repeatedly set my will for) **all people** (all mankind; all humans) **to habitually exist being even as myself! But of course each one continues having and holding his own effect and result of grace and favor** (or: gracious gift) **from out of God: on the one hand, one person in this way, and on the other hand, another in that way.**

8. **Now I am saying to the unmarried** (= single; without a spouse, i.e., not married; can refer to: widowed, or, separated – Alain Decaux) **people, and to the widows, that [it is] fine for them** (or: beautiful in them; ideal to them) **if they can** (may; should; would) **remain even as I [am].**

> [note: from Acts 26:10, where Paul says "I cast my vote," being a member of the Sanhedrin, he would have been a married man at that time]

9. **Yet if they are not habitually having inner strength and control, [then] they must at once marry, for it is better to proceed to marry** (or: to continue married) **than to be repeatedly set on fire** (or, as a middle: to progressively burn oneself [= with passion and desire]).

10. **Now beside this, I – not I myself, but rather, the Lord** (or: Master) **– am giving an added message to those being married: a wife is not at any point to be separated** (disunited so as to be apart from) **[her] husband**

11. **– yet, even if she should get separated or be caused to depart, let her remain unmarried or else she must at once be reconciled to [her] husband – and a husband is not to proceed in divorcing** (or: leaving, or sending away) **[his] wife!**

12. **Now to the rest, I, myself – not the Lord** (or: Master) **– am speaking: if any brother is having an unbelieving wife** (or: a woman not full of faith; or: unfaithful?), **and she continues mutually content** (habitually thinks it jointly profitable and easy; with [him] is agreeable and approving) **to continue dwelling and making a home with him, let him not proceed to divorce her** (or: leave her, or send her away). [note: observe the equality in vss. 12-16]

13. **And a wife who is having an unbelieving husband** (or: a man not full of faith; or: unfaithful?), **and this man continues mutually content to continue dwelling and making a home with her, let her not divorce** (or: leave or send away) **[her] husband.**

14. **You see, the unbelieving husband** (man void of faith) **has been made set-apart and remains holy and sacred within** (or: in union with) **the wife, and the unbelieving wife** (woman void of faith) **has been made set-apart and remains holy and sacred within** (or: in union with) **the brother** (= the believing husband) **– otherwise, the consequence is your children being unclean. Yet now they are set-apart** (holy and sacred ones; folks different from the common).

15. **So if the unbelieving** (or: faith-lacking; trust-void) **one proceeds to be separating** (disuniting so as to be apart), **let this one continue separating and departing: the brother or the sister has not been nor is now enslaved** (has not been bound in servitude nor is under compulsion) **within such situations – for God has given you** [other MSS: us] **a permanent call within the midst of, and in union with, peace that is centered in harmony of the joining.**

16. **For what have you seen or how do you know, O wife** (or: dear lady; O woman) **– whether you will bring health and wholeness to** (or: will rescue, save and deliver) **[your] husband** (or: man)? **Or what have you seen and how do you know, O husband** (or: dear sir; O man) **– whether you will bring health and wholeness to** (or: will rescue, save and deliver) **[your] wife** (or: woman), **except as the Lord** [= Christ or Yahweh] **has divided, apportioned and distributed** [other MSS: parts and distributes] **a part to** (or: in; for) **each one?**

Let each one thus be habitually walking about (= continue living your life in this way), **as God has permanently called** (summoned) **[him].**

17. **And thus am I habitually arranging throughout** (or: thoroughly setting in order; fully prescribing or distributing; or: arranging the troops) **– within the midst of** (or: in union with) **all the called-out communities** (or: among all the summoned-forth folks).

18. **Was anyone called** (invited; summoned) **being a person having been circumcised? Let him not be de-circumcised** (have the marks of circumcision covered over)! **Has anyone been called [being] in [the condition of, or, among the group termed] uncircumcision? He is not to proceed in being circumcised!**

19. **The circumcision is nothing, and the uncircumcision is nothing – but to the contrary [what matters is the] observing and keeping of the goals implanted from God** (or: the impartations of the finished product within, which is God; or: God's inward directives to [His] end).
20. **Let each person – within the midst of the calling** (vocation; = station, position, situation or circumstances) **in which** (or: to which) **he was** (or: is) **called** (summoned) **– keep on remaining** (dwelling; abiding) **within this.**
21. **Were you called** (summoned) **[while being] a slave? Quit letting it be a concern or worry for you** (Do not continue to let it be a care to you). **But nonetheless, if you also continue to have the power and ability to become free** (or: a freeman), **make very much use of** (or: all the more employ) **[it]!**
> (or: Instead, even if you presently have means to come to be at liberty, [choose] rather to use [your present situation].)

22. **In fact, the person within the Lord** [= Christ or Yahweh] **– being one that was called** (summoned) **[when being] a slave – is [the] Lord's freed-person** (or: exists being [Christ's or Yahweh's] emancipated slave). **Likewise, the person being one that was called** (summoned) **[when being] free, or a freedman, is Christ's slave.**
23. **You folks were bought, as at a marketplace: [you are] of value** (or: [there was] value, worth and honor involved in the price). **Do not continue becoming slaves of humanity** (or: Do not repeatedly come to be slaves of people).
24. **Let each person, brothers** (folks from the same womb; = fellow believers; family members) **– within that in which he was** (or: she is) **called** (summoned) **– keep on remaining** (dwelling; abiding) **at God's side and presence within the midst of this.**

25. **Now about the virgins** (or: unmarried girls of marriageable age) **and celibate women, I do not hold** (or: have) **an arrangement put upon [you]** (or: an imposed disposition or injunction) **which originates from [the] Lord** [= Yahweh, or Christ], **but I continue giving [you] the result of experience-gained knowledge, as being one having been mercied** (shown mercy) **by** (or: under) **[the] Lord, to exist being one full of faith** (or: to be trustworthy, loyal and faithful).
26. **I therefore reason from custom [that] this continues to be inherently beautiful** (fine; ideal; good form) **– because of the present necessity which has been placed within through compulsion** (= a time or circumstance of stress) **– that it is ideal** (fine; beautiful) **for a person to continue being thus** (= as he is; or: for humanity to continue existing in this way)**:**
27. **Have you been bound together so that you are now tied to a wife? Stop** (or: Do not continue) **seeking loosing or release. Have you been released so that you are now loosed from a wife? Stop** (or: Do not continue) **seeking a wife.**
28. **Yet even if you should marry, you are not making a mistake** (or: missing the goal). **And if the virgin or celibate woman should marry, she does not fail** (is not making a mistake or missing the goal). **Still, such folks** (= those who do) **will continue or proceed having pressure and constricting stress, in the flesh** (= their natural lives) **– and as for myself, I [would] spare you folks [that]** (or: I advise thrift and restraint [in this] for you people).

29. **Now I forcefully declare this, brothers** (folks from the same womb; = family)**, the season** (fitting and appointed situation; fertile moment) **now exists being one that has been contracted** (drawn together so as to be shortened, curtailed and limited)**! So that for the remaining [time]** (for the rest of [the season]; henceforth), **those presently having wives** (or: the men now holding a woman) **should proceed in being as not presently having [them],**
> [note: in the culture and time which Paul is here addressing, the term "married," or, "having a woman" referred to both formal marriage, and to a man and a woman living together]

30. **and those presently weeping** (lamenting; shedding tears), **[should be] as [if] not weeping, and those presently rejoicing, [should be] as [if] not rejoicing, and those habitually buying at the market place, [should be] as [if] not constantly holding on to it** (owning it; keeping it held down; retaining it; = not being possessive),
31. **and those habitually employing** (making use of) **the System** (the ordered arrangement and world of culture, economy, religion and government; or: secular society) **as not folks who are constantly using it down** (exploiting it; making excessive employment or over-use of it), **for**

the outward fashion, mode of circumstance, condition, form-appearance (or: character, role, phase, configuration, manner) **of this System** (ordered world of culture, religion and society) **is progressively passing by** (= the present scheme of things is changing and passing away).
32. **Now I intend** (purpose and want) **you folks to constantly exist being free from anxiety** (care; concern; worry). **The unmarried one** (= the person who is not co-habiting; the single person) **is habitually concerned about and caring for the Lord's things** (= the issues pertaining to Yahweh; the matters that come from and belong to Christ): **how he or she can please** (be accommodating to) **the Lord.**
33. **Yet the one being married is constantly concerned about and repeatedly caring for the involvements of the System** (the issues pertaining to his world of culture, religion, economy and government): **how he can please and be accommodating to the woman** ([his] wife), **and thus, he has been divided so as to be distributed in parts!**
34. **Further, the unmarried** (or: = single) **woman – as well as the virgin** (or: unmarried mature young woman of marriageable age) **– is habitually concerned about and caring for the Lord's things** (= issues; matters): **[i.e.,] that she may continually exist being set-apart** (holy; sacred; different from the profane) **– both in [her] body and in [her] spirit** (or, with other MSS: so that she would be sacred with the body as well as with the spirit; that she should be holy both for the Body, and for the Spirit). **However, the woman being married is constantly concerned about and repeatedly caring for the involvements of the System** ([her] world): **how she can please and be accommodating to the man** ([her] husband).
35. **Now I am saying this with a view toward your personal advantage** (that which brings benefits together to your very selves) **– not so that I can throw a noose** (a lasso; or: a halter; = a leash) **upon you folks! To the contrary, [it is] with a view toward good form** (the well-fashioned [life]; the scene of ease and competent-appearing action) **and a good seating, [being] undistracted beside the Lord** (or: a close seat of ease, undistractedly sitting in the Lord).
36. **Now if anyone continues reasoning about custom [so as] to go on bringing the appearance of bad form** (or: is behaving dishonorably or indecently – that which is contrary to the accepted fashion) **upon [the situation of] his virgin [daughter; or: fiancée] – if she may be over her prime** (= beyond marriageable age; past the bloom of youth) **– and thus** (or: in this way) **he has obligation [for it] to proceed in occurring, let him continue to do what he is wanting and intending – he is not making a mistake or missing the goal: let them be marrying.**
37. **Now [he] who has been standing firm and is now settled in the seat of his heart – presently having no necessity** (continuing to hold no compulsion) **but holds authority concerning** (or: has a right pertaining to) **his own will and has decided this in his own heart – to continue keeping watch over and guarding his virgin** [daughter; fiancée; or, perhaps: his own virginity], **will be doing beautifully** (finely; ideally).
38. **Consequently, also, the one giving his virgin [daughter] in marriage** (or: the one marrying his virgin [fiancée]; or: the one giving the virginity of himself in marriage) **is doing** [other MSS: will be doing] **beautifully, and yet the one not giving in marriage or getting married will be doing better.**
39. **A wife, by law and custom, has been bound upon and remains tied to her husband for as much time as he continues living. Yet if the husband may fall asleep in death, she exists being free to be married to whom she continues intending** (willing; purposing) **– only within** (or: centered in; in union with) **[the] Lord.**
40. **Yet, she continues** (or: exists) **being happier** (more blessed) **if she remains as she is, according to the knowledge gained from my experience. Now I also continue seeming to hold** (or: have; possess) **God's spirit** (or: a Breath-effect from God [on this matter])
> (or: For I, myself, am also continuing to presume to constantly possess God's Spirit and Attitude).

CHAPTER 8

1. **Now concerning [foods] that were offered in sacrifice to idols, we** (or: I, indeed,) **have seen and know that we all continue having insight and knowledge** (*gnosis*) **gained by personal experience.** [note: this may have been a quotation from their letter to Paul]

The (or: This) **knowledge** (*gnosis*) **keeps on puffing [you; us] up** (progressively inflates), **but** (or: yet) **The Love** (*agape*: urge toward unambiguous, participating, accepting reunion; fully giving of oneself to others in solidarity) **progressively edifies and builds up the house!**
2. **If anyone continues imagining** (supposing; presuming) **to have come to know anything through his experience, he not as yet knows according as it continues binding and necessary [for him] to personally know** (or: he does not yet have insight in the sphere as, or correspondingly as, he ought to have insight).
3. **Yet if anyone is continuously or habitually loving** (urging toward union with; fully giving oneself to) **God, this person has been personally and intimately known by God and continues under the experience of His knowledge** (or: this One has been intimately known by him [i.e., by the one progressively loving God]).
4. **Therefore, concerning the eating of the [foods] that were offered in sacrifice to idols, we have seen and know that an idol [is] nothing** (or: = meaningless) **within [the] System** (or: not even one idol [exists] in the world of [our] culture or religion, or within the midst of the created universe, or among the aggregate of humanity), **and that [there is] no other God, except One.**
5. **For even though certainly there are ones being habitually termed, called or laid down in ideas as "gods" – whether within heaven or upon earth** (or: in sky and atmosphere, or on land) **– just as there are many "gods" and many "lords"** (or: masters; owners),
6. **to the contrary, to us** (or: for us; with us) **[there is] one God, the Father, from out of the midst of Whom [is] the whole** (the All; or: [are] all things) **– and we [proceeding] into Him – even one Lord** (or: as well as one Owner and Master), **Jesus Christ: through Whom [is] the whole** (or: [are; exist] all things) **and we through means of and through the midst of Him!**

7. **Nevertheless, this intimate, experiential knowledge, insight and awareness** (*gnosis*) **[of this is presently] not within** (or: centered in; resident in) **everyone** (or: all folks). **Now some – by joint custom and mutual habit pertaining to the idol, until right now – are continually eating [food] as something sacrificed to an idol, and their conscience** (integrated inner knowing; perceptive awareness) **being weak is repeatedly being stained** (polluted; defiled).
8. **Yet food** (something eaten) **will not proceed placing us beside, nor continue causing us to stand in the presence of, God. Neither if we should not eat are we continually behind time or being in the rear** (also = falling short or failing to attain, thus being inferior), **nor if we should eat are we constantly attaining superabundance** (surrounding ourselves with more than enough; exceeding; = spiritually or morally advancing ourselves).
9. **So continue to be on watch and take notice lest somehow this "right"** (privilege and authority from out of existence; license; = liberty) **of yours should come to be a tripping-effect to, or an obstacle that results in, stumbling for, or in, the weak folks.**
10. **For if anyone should see you – the one presently having** (continuing in holding and in possession of) **experiential, intimate knowledge or insight** (*gnosis*) **– repeatedly lying down** (habitually reclining at a meal during a sacrificial banquet) **within an idol's temple dining room, will not his conscience** (or: integrated inner knowing; perceptive awareness) **– he being a weak person – be progressively "built up" unto the [rationalizations for him] to be habitually eating [foods] having been offered in sacrifice to idols?**
11. **You see, [thus] the one being habitually weak is being progressively lost-away, brought to loss and ruined** (or: is destroying himself) **by** (with; in; for) **your "knowledge"** (*gnosis*) **– the brother** (Family member from the same womb) **because of whom Christ died!**
12. **Now by continually doing error** (repeatedly failing and missing the goal; habitually sinning or acting amiss; proceeding in deviation) **unto the brothers** (or: So while from time to time [casting this] mistake into the [hearts] of [your] fellow believers from the same womb and Family) **in this way, and repeatedly beating or striking and thus wounding their weak conscience** (awareness), **you folks are constantly doing error** (failing; sinning; acting amiss) **unto Christ!**
13. **Because of this very reason, if food is habitually being a snare-stick to entrap my brother** (= fellow believer; Family member) **or cause him to stumble, I should under no circumstances eat meat** (flesh [i.e., referring to what was offered to idols]) **– on into the midst of the Age! – so that I should not be a snare-stick to entrap my brother** (or: group member) **or cause him to stumble.**

CHAPTER 9

1. **Am I not free** (Do I not exist being a free man)**? Am I not one sent forth with a mission** (a representative; an emissary; a commissioned agent)**? Have I not seen Jesus, our Lord** (Owner; Master)**? Are you folks not my work within the Lord** (or: = in union with Christ or centered in Yahweh)**?**
2. **If I am not one sent off with a mission to or for other folks, nevertheless I surely am to and for you people – for you, yourselves, are my seal of the expedition** (or: = the validated document of my sent-off mission), **within, and in union with, the Lord** (or: centered in the Master).
3. **– this is my defense** (my verbal reply) **to or for those continuously examining me and sifting the evidence about me –**
4. **Are we not in any way continuing to have [the] right** (privilege from out of being; authority) **to eat and to drink?**
5. **Are we not in any way continuing to have [the] right** (authority; privilege from existence) **to be habitually leading around a sister [as] a wife – as also the rest of those sent out on a mission and the Lord's brothers, and Cephas?**
6. **Or, are only Barnabas and I continuing to have no right** (privilege; authority; license) **not to be habitually active in a trade** (not to be constantly working)**?**
7. **Who is at any time habitually performing military service** (serving as a soldier) **at his own expense** (by his private rations)**? Who makes a habit of planting a vineyard and then is not eating its fruit? Or who habitually tends** (or: shepherds) **a flock and then is not eating** (nourishing himself) **from out of the flock's milk?** [cf 2 Tim. 2:6]

8. **Am I not speaking these things to accord with [what is] human** (or: in line with and in the sphere of humanity)**? Or is not the Law also saying these things?**
9. **For you see, within the Law of Moses it has been written:**
    > **"You will not continue muzzling an ox** (bull; cow) **[that] is progressively treading in threshing."** [Deut. 25:4]
    Is the attention and concern to (or: by; for) **God [here perhaps] not about the oxen?** (or: It is not a care with God that has reference to bulls!)
10. **Or, is He** (or: it) **undoubtedly saying [this] entirely** (everywhere and in all circumstances) **because of us? Because of us! For it was written that the one progressively plowing ought normally** (or: is constantly obliged) **to be habitually plowing upon [the basis of] an expectation** (or: expectant hope), **and the person habitually threshing [to do so] on an expectation of the [result]: to continue participating in his share [of the produce].**
11. **Since, upon [the ground of] an expectation, we ourselves sowed the spiritual things in** (to; for; with; among) **you folks, [is it] a great thing if we ourselves shall reap a harvest of your fleshly things** (= natural or material goods pertaining to the material life)**?**
12. **Since (If) others are continually sharing and participating in your right from existing** (privilege), **[why] not rather** (or: all the more) **we? But to the contrary, we do not** (or: did not) **make use of this right** (privilege from being; authority), **but rather we are habitually putting a roof over, and thus covering** (perhaps: = putting up with) **all people, and all things [or: situations], so that we should not give any hindrance to the progress of Christ's good news**
    > (or: would not offer any incision which blocks the way for the message of abundant goodness, wellness and fortunate ease which pertains to and has its origin in the Anointing, and which is the Anointed One).

13. **Have you folks not seen so as to know that those habitually working at** (performing the duties of; engaged in the business pertaining to) **the sacred things of the temple are habitually eating from out of the things of the temple** (the holy place of the sanctuary)**? Those constantly sitting beside and attending to the altar are habitually sharing jointly in a portion of the altar** (= the offerings sacrificed there).
14. **Thus also, the Lord** [= Yahweh or Christ] **thoroughly arranged for those habitually bringing down the announcement of the message of goodness** (of the abundant wellness,

good fortune and ease) **to be continuously living from out of the message of goodness** (= the announcement of ease, well-being and goodness is to be the source of their living).

15. **Yet I myself have not made use of nor do I now employ even one of these things – and I do not write these things so that it should come to be thus in me** (or: = in my case)**: for to me [it would be] fine** (beautiful; ideal; good form), **rather, to die than that anyone should** [other MSS: shall proceed to] **make the result of my boast empty and void,**

16. **for it is not the result of a boast for** [other MSS: for is it not grace to...?] **me if I should habitually announce good news, for you see, a compressed necessity** (a compulsion) **is continues laid upon me. For it is a woe** (a condition or situation at which I would say, "Alas!") **to and for me, if ever I should not constantly bring/announce the message of Goodness.**

17. **For if I willingly continue performing this** (voluntarily from my being keep on executing this action), **I continue having compensation** (pay; a wage; a reward). **However, since** (or: if) **unwillingly, involuntarily, and not from my being I have been persuaded, caused to believe [in] and given faith [for] the management of a Household** (or: entrusted [with] a stewardship),

18. **what then is my compensation** (pay; wage; reward)? **That while repeatedly bringing and announcing the message of Goodness, I will continually** (or: can) **deposit** (put; set; place) **the good news** (the message of abundant wellness and fortunate ease) **without cost** (or: expense; or: = free of charge), **[leading] into the [situation so as] not to make downright use of my right or privilege within the good news** (or: not to fully employ or abuse my authority from being in union with the message of Goodness).

19. **You see, continually being free from out of the midst of all things and from all people** (or: independent of everyone and from everything), **I enslave myself to all people** (or: to everything and for everyone), **to the end that I can** (may; would) **gain [all] the more folks.**

20. **So I come to be** (or: became) **as a Jew for** (or: to; with; among) **the Jews, to the end that I can** (would; may) **gain Jews; as under Law for** (or: to; with; among) **those under Law, to the end that I can** (or: would; should; may) **gain those under Law;**

21. **as without law** (or: as lawless) **– [though] not continually being without a law pertaining to God, but to the contrary, within a principle which is Christ** (or: Christ's law; the custom which has the character and quality of Christ; or: [the] law which is [the] Anointing) **– to those without law** (for and with the lawless ones), **to the end that I will progressively** [other MSS: can; may; would] **gain the folks without law** (the lawless ones).

22. **To** (For; Among; With) **those without strength** (the weak ones), **I become** (or: came to be) **as without strength** (weak), **to the end that I would** (can; may) **gain those without strength** (the weak ones). **I have become and continue to be all things for** (to; among; with) **all folks** (or: peoples), **to the end that I can** (would; may) **by every means** (in every way; under all circumstances; entirely; everywhere) **save** (rescue; deliver; restore to health, wholeness and their original condition) **anybody!**

23. **Now I habitually do all things** (or: everything) **because of the message of abundant wellness** (the good news; the message of prosperous and ideal ease, and goodness), **to the end that I would** (could; can) **for myself come to be its** (or: His) **joint participant** (co-partner; sharer-in-common, along with others; equal fellow in communion and common Being).

24. **Have you folks not seen, so as to know, that those progressively running, on the race-course within a stadium, are indeed all progressively running** (or: constantly and repeatedly racing), **yet one normally** (= each time) **grasps** (takes; receives) **the contest prize** (victor's award)? **Be habitually running** (progressively racing) **so that you folks can** (may; would) **seize and take [it] down in your hands!**

25. **Now every person habitually engaging in a contest** (participating in the violent struggle of the public athletic games) **constantly exercises inner strength and self-control in all things, and among all folks: those, of course, therefore [do it] so that they may** (can; would) **grasp** (take; receive) **a corruptible wreath that will soon wither, yet we an incorruptible** (un-withering) **one.**

26. **So now, I myself am constantly running** (racing) **in this manner – not as without clear visibility of the goal** (not in an uncertain or aimless manner which lacks clear purpose); **thus I am habitually boxing – not as repeatedly flaying** (thrashing; = punching) **air.**

27. **To the contrary, I am repeatedly "striking my face below my eyes and beating my body black and blue"** (= treating my body severely by discipline and hardship) **and continually leading [it] as a slave** (or: causing it to lead the life of a slave), **lest somehow, while proclaiming** (heralding; preaching; [note: at the games it means to announce the rules of the game and call out the competitors]) **to** (or: for; among) **others, I myself should** (can; may; would) **come to be one that does not stand the test** (or: unproved; or: without the approval which comes from testing; or: disapproved and disqualified).

CHAPTER 10

1. **So I am not intending** (or: willing; wanting) **you folks to continue being ignorant, brothers, that our fathers** (= ancestors) **were all continually existing under the cloud, and everyone passed completely through the midst of the sea,**
2. **and so they all immersed themselves into Moses** (or: got themselves baptized [other MSS: were baptized] unto Moses), **within the cloud and within the sea,**
3. **and they all ate the same spiritual food,**
4. **and they all drank the same spiritual drink, for they kept on drinking from out of a spiritual bedrock** (or: cliff rock; rock mass) **– one continually following along behind** (or: progressively accompanying [them]). **Now the bedrock** (or: cliff rock) **was the Christ** (or: the rock mass was existing being the Anointing).
5. **But still, God did not take delight** (was not well-pleased; did not approve) **in the majority of them, for it followed that, they were strewn down flat on the ground** (scattered and laid low) **within the midst of the wilderness** (desolate place; desert; uninhabited place).
6. **Now these things were made to be types of us** (or: were birthed to be examples for, and typological figures pertaining to, us), **[directed] into this [goal]: [for] us not to habitually be those who set their strong passions** (rushing emotions; ardor; cravings) **upon worthless things** (ugly things of bad quality), **just** (correspondingly; along the same lines) **as those also set their passionate emotions and cravings on [such things].**
7. **Neither continue on to become** (or: Stop becoming) **idolaters, just** (or: correspondingly; along the same lines) **as some of them, even as it has been written,**
    > **"The people sit down to continually eat and drink, and they stand up** (arise again) **to repeatedly engage in childish play** (sport; amusement)**."** [i.e., play around the idol – the golden calf; Ex. 32:6]
8. **Neither may we continue practicing prostitution just** (correspondingly; in the same sphere) **as some of them practiced prostitution – and twenty-three thousand fell in** (or: on) **one day.**
    > [note: this prostitution involved the idolatry of Baal worship – Num. 25:1-9]
9. **Neither should** (or: may) **we keep on putting the Anointed One** (or: Christ) **to outrageous tests** [with other MSS: put the LORD [= Yahweh] to the proof, out of {personal motives}; with others: try-out God] **just as some of them tested and tried [Him] – and they kept on being destroyed** (lost and ruined-away) **by the serpents, day by day.** [Num. 21:5-9]
10. **Neither continue habitually murmuring** (grumbling with a buzz of under-toned mutterings of critical and discontented comments; [Num. 16:41]) **exactly as some of them murmured – and lost and ruined themselves away** (or: affected their own destruction) **by the Destroyer** [note: same word used in Ex. 12:23, LXX].

11. **Now all these things went on progressively** (or: from time to time) **stepping together among** (or: to; with) **those folks by way of types** (as examples; figuratively), **and it was written with a view toward a placing [of them] into the minds of us: ones unto whom** (directed into the midst of whom) **the ends** (= conjunctions; or: consummations; goals) **of the** (or: these) **ages have come down to** (or: arrived at and meet) **and are now face to face [with us].**
    > [note: "the ends," plural, may describe a picture of a succession, where "one end" meets "another end," this latter being really the beginning of another indefinite time-period, stretched out like a rope; each rope in the time-line having "two ends."]
12. **Consequently, let the person habitually supposing** (thinking; imagining) **to have taken a stand – and presuming to still be standing – be continually taking notice and observing so as to heed [that] he should** (or: [and] he would) **not fall.**

13. **No trial** (or: ordeal; temptation; putting to the proof; effect of probing and testing) **has laid hold of or seized you folks except a human one** (something pertaining to the human nature and situation).
Now God [is] faithful, loyal, trustworthy, and full of faith and trust – One who will not permit (let, allow; or: let go; leave alone) **you folks to be tested, tried, tempted or made to undergo an ordeal above** (or: over; = beyond) **that which you people continue having ability and power [to handle or endure], but to the contrary, together with the trial** (or: ordeal), **He will also continually make the way out** (the egress; or: He also will habitually do the stepping forth from out of the midst; or: He will even progressively construct the out-come) **to continually enable and repeatedly empower you folks to undergo [it]** (to bear up under [it]; to carry on under [it], sustain [it], and lead on).
14. **Wherefore by all means, my beloved ones, be habitually fleeing away from the idolatry** (the religious service of form, figures or image, and of what is seen; phantoms of the mind; impressions or fancies; ideas and concepts).
15. **I am now saying [this] as to and for sensible and thoughtful people** (ones with a prudent and intelligent frame of mind; discreet and discerning folks)**: you, yourselves, sift and decide about** (or: separate and judge) **what I continually affirm and mean.**
16. **The cup of The Blessing** (or: The cup which is the Word of Goodness, ease and well-being; the cup of the Idea from Goodness) **which we are habitually blessing** (speaking well of; speaking of with reference to goodness, ease and wellness), **is it not** (does it not exist being) **the common existing and sharing with, participation in, fellowship of, communion of being with and partnership of, and from, Christ's blood** (or: the blood which is the Anointing)**?**
The bread (or: loaf of bread) **which we are habitually breaking, is it not** (does it not exist being) **the common existing and sharing with, participation in, fellowship of, communion of being with, and partnership of, and from, Christ's body** (or: the body which is anointed)**?**
17. **Because we, The Many, are** (exist being) **One Bread** (one loaf of bread), **One Body, it follows that we, The All** (the all of humanity), **are continuously holding a share with others and are co-partaking from out of the One Bread** (or: this one loaf of bread).

18. **Take an extended look at Israel, according to [the] flesh, and be observing [their cultural situation]: are not those habitually eating the things sacrificed common-beings of the altar** (partners, partakers and ones who share common participation pertaining to the altar)**?**
19. **What, then, am I now meaning and affirming? That what is sacrificed to an idol is anything? Or, that an idol is anything** (= something more than just an idol)**?**
20. **To the contrary** (or: Not at all!)**: that which the multitudes of ethnic groups** (the nations; the pagans; the Gentiles) **habitually sacrifice, they continue sacrificing to, for or by demons** (Hellenistic concept and term: = animistic influences; personified concepts), **and not to, for or by God** (or: even to or by a non-god, or a no-god), **and I am not intending for** (willing; wanting) **you folks to proceed to becoming partakers of and thus common-beings with the demons**
    (= partners and ones who share common participation pertaining to the animistic
    influences [possibly: = evil or deranged spirits, mental conditions or attitudes]).
21. **You folks are unable to continue to drink** (or: You cannot habitually drink) **[the] cup of the Lord** (or: the Owner's cup; or: = the cup pertaining to Christ; or: [Yahweh's] cup; cf John 18:11) **and a cup of demons** (or: a cup pertaining to animistic influences [possibly: = evil attitudes; deranged mental conditions; evil spirits]); **you are unable to continue to** (or: to habitually) **hold a share with and co-partake of [the] Lord's** [= Christ's or Yahweh's] **table and also a table of demons** (pertaining to or having its source in animistic influences [possibly: = evil attitudes or qualities]).
    [note: Mal. 1:7 refers to the altar of burnt-offering as "the table of the Lord;" Isa. 65:11,
    Jer. 7:18 and Ezk. 16:18; 23:41 use the term "table" with reference to pagan idol-feasts;
    Paul may be using the terms "cup" and "table" figuratively, and not referring to specific
    ceremonies]
22. **Or are we proceeding to cause the Lord's emotions to boil over the side** (constantly inciting the Lord [= Christ, or Yahweh; cf Deut. 32:21, LXX] to jealous indignation)**? We are not stronger than He!**

23. **All things are presently out-of-Being** (or: All things continue from existence; or: All is authorized, right and permitted), **but yet not all things proceed to bear together for advantage, profit or expedience. All things are authorized, permitted and out of [His] Being, but yet not all things progressively edify or build up the house**
>   (or: All exists from out of [His] Being, but not all keeps on bringing [things] together; all is from Existence, but not all continues to edify).

24. **Let no one be habitually seeking the [interest, advantage, profit, welfare or edification] of, or pertaining to, himself, but to the contrary, the [interest, advantage, profit, welfare and edification] of the other** (or: pertaining to the different) **person.**

25. **Go on habitually eating everything that is normally being sold in** (or: at) **a meat market, while examining nothing because of** (or: sifting not one thing back through) **the conscience,**

26. **for it follows from,**
>   **"the earth** (or: land; soil) **and the results of its filling** (entire contents; that which fills it up) **belong to and have their origin in the Lord** [= Yahweh]." [Ps: 24:1; etc.]

27. **If anyone of the unbelievers** (or: of those not full of faith and void of trust) **is periodically inviting you folks [to be his guest], and you are wanting** (or: intending) **to go, keep on habitually eating everything that is normally being placed beside** (or: = set before) **you, while examining nothing because of** (or: sifting not one thing back through) **the conscience.**

28. **Yet if anyone should say to you folks, "This is [meat; something] offered in a temple or a sacred sacrifice to an idol," do not proceed to eat [it], because of that person pointing it out** (disclosing it) **and [on account of] the conscience** (integrated inner knowing; awareness).

29. **Now I am not speaking [about] your own conscience, but rather the other person's. For to what purpose is my freedom now being decided by another person's conscience?**

30. **If I myself am continuously participating** (holding a share with [others] and co-partaking) **in grace and favor** (or: with gratitude), **why am I being repeatedly blasphemed** (spoken abusively about; vilified; injuriously misrepresented; or: hindered in regard to the Light) **over what I myself am habitually receiving in good grace and for which I am expressing gratitude?**

31. **Therefore whether you folks are habitually eating or continually drinking, or anything you are constantly doing, be continuously doing all things unto God's glory**
>   (or: performing everything [directed toward and leading] into a good reputation pertaining to God; making all things into a manifestation which calls forth praise to God; forming all people into an assumed appearance from God).

32. **Progressively come to be people who are not obstacles or causes for stumbling** (= become inoffensive) **– both to, or among, Jews and to Greeks** (or: among those of the Hellenistic culture), **as well as to God's called-out community** (or: God's called-out person),

33. **correspondingly as I myself am also habitually accommodating and pleasing all folks in all things, not continually seeking the thing that bears together for advantage, profit, welfare and expedience of myself, but to the contrary, that which pertains to The Many – to the end that they can and would be saved** (rescued, delivered, healed, kept safe, made whole and restored to their original state and condition)!

1. **Progressively come to be imitators of me, correspondingly as I, myself, also [am] of Christ and from [the/an] Anointing.**

CHAPTER 11

2. **Now I am continually commending and appreciating** (or: applauding; adding praise upon) **you folks because you have called to mind and still remember everything that originated with me** (or: that came from and had its source with me; that is mine and of me), **and habitually keep possession of** (or: hold down and retain) **the traditions** (things handed on; cf vs. 23, below) **just as I handed [them] on** (or: transmitted [them]) **to** (or: for; among) **you people.**

3. **Now I continue intending** (willing; wanting; purposing) **you folks to be aware, from having seen and thus knowing, that the Christ is** (or: exists being) **the Source** (or: Head) **of every adult male** (or: the Anointing is the head of every husband); **in turn the adult Male [was] a source of Woman** (or: the husband [is] a head of a wife); **and yet God [is the] Source of the Christ, and the Anointing** (or: [is] Head of the Anointed One)!

4. **Every adult male** (or: husband) **habitually speaking to having well-being** (or: praying) **or prophesying while holding down [the; his] Source** (or: having [a head-covering] on, down from [his] head), **is continually bringing shame** (disgrace; dishonor) **to his Source** (or: Head).

> [note: according to A.T. Robertson (*Word Pictures in the NT*, vol. 4, p.159) there is no certainty that the *tallith* was used at this time]

5. **Now every woman** (or: wife) **normally speaking to having well-being** (or: praying) **or prophesying [publicly] with the head uncovered** (or: [her] source not veiled down) **is continually bringing shame** (disgrace; dishonor) **to her head** (or: source), **for it is one and the very same thing with the woman having been shaved.**

> [note on shaved: a dishonor as punishment for adultery; a custom for women slaves]

6. **You see, if a wife** (or: woman) **is not habitually covering herself down with a veil, let her also shear herself. Now since** (or: if) **[it is] ugliness** (deformity [of custom]; thus: a social disgrace, shame, dishonor and bad form) **for** (or: to) **a wife or a woman at any point to shear or shave herself, let her habitually veil herself down** (or: completely cover herself).

7. **So a husband** (or: a mature Male), **on the one hand, is continually obligated not to be covering [his] Source** (or: veiling down the head) **– [he] being inherently** (or: constantly being under the rule and headship of) **God's image** (resemblance; likeness; portrait) **and glory** (reflection; reputation; manifestation which calls forth praise; assumed appearance). **On the other hand, the wife** (or: Woman) **is, and continuously exists being, a husband's** (or: a mature Male's) **glory** (reflection; reputation; praise-inducing manifestation; mirrored appearance).

> [note: a reference to Gen. 1:28; 2:26; *cf* 2 Cor. 3:18]

8. **You see, [the] mature Male is not** (or: a husband does not exist being) **forth from out of the midst of Woman** (or: a wife), **for to the contrary, [the] Woman** ([the] Wife) **[is] forth from out of the midst of [the] mature Male** ([the] Husband)! [Gen. 2:21, 22]

> (or: It follows that one is not a husband from a wife, but [one is] a wife from a husband.)

9. **For also, [the] mature Male** (or: Husband) **was not created through** (or: because of) **the Woman** (or: Wife), **but to the contrary, [the] Woman** (or: Wife) **through** (or: because of) **the mature Male** (or: the Husband).

10. **Because of this, the woman** (or: wife) **is continually obligated to be habitually having privilege and right from being** (or: permission) **upon [her] head – because of the agents**

> (or: normally ought to constantly hold authority from out of being herself, [based] upon the Source, [as shown] through the messengers [= ancestors and prophets]). [comment: she ought to veil her glory, just as Moses veiled the glory that was on him – 2 Cor. 3:13]

11. **Nevertheless** (Of course), **in union with – and in the midst of – the Lord** [= Christ or Yahweh] **neither [is] Woman severed, separate or apart from mature Male** (or: a wife disunited from a husband), **nor [is] mature Male severed, separate or apart from Woman** (or: a husband disunited from a wife).

12. **For you see, just as the Woman [was] forth from out of the midst of the mature Male, in the same manner, the mature Male [is] through the Woman – yet all things [are]** (or: the whole [comes]) **forth from out of the midst of God.** [*cf* Rom. 11:36]

13. **Sift, sort-out and decide among yourselves: is it appropriate** (fitting and proper) **[for; in] a woman** (or: wife) **to [in public] be habitually praying uncovered** (not veiled down) **to God?**

14. **Does not even the essence and nature of what our culture has produced, itself, consistently teach you folks that if an adult male should ever plume himself or give himself airs with long hair** (tresses or long ringlets; = hair ornamentally arranged like a woman's style) **it is a dishonor to him** (is degrading for him)**?**

15. **Yet if a woman should have plumes or long, luxuriant hair** (tresses and long ringlets that are ornamentally arranged) **it is a glory to her** (is a good appearance, reflection and reputation for her; is splendor and a manifestation which calls forth praise for her), **because the long, ornamentally arranged hair has been given to her as a permanent endowment, instead of an article of clothing or mantle cast around [her head, or as a coat or cloak].**

16. **Still, if anyone continues presuming to be habitually fond of quarreling** (likes to argue, dispute or be contentious and cause strife), **we ourselves do not habitually hold to** (or: have) **such a custom or mutual habit – neither [do] God's called-out folks** (or: communities).

17. **Now while bringing along this announcement** (giving this notification to [your] side), **I do not now bring praise, or offer applause and commendation upon [you], because you folks are not continually coming together into more strength and for the better, but to the contrary, into the inferior: a diminished situation** (= the less profitable; = your gatherings do more harm than good).

18. **You see, in the first place, in your repeated coming together within an assembly of the called-out, I am constantly hearing there to be the results of tearing, and split-effects** (= separations into cliques; divisions), **continually inherent among you folks – and a certain part of it I am now believing!**

19. **Then you see, it also continues to be necessary and binding for there constantly to be choices and options among you folks** (or: For there must even be sects, factions, a mixture of doctrinal stances, or even heresies in your midst), **to the end that those who have been examined, tested and approved among you may also come to be** (or: be birthed) **manifested ones** (folks shown in clear light).

20. **So then, on the [occasion] of your periodically coming together at the same [time and place], it is not to be eating an evening meal having the character or qualities of the Lord** (or: a supper for, or pertaining to, the Owner; or: a Lord's [= Yahweh's or Christ's] dinner; a supper belonging to the Master; an evening meal validating, and directed by, the Master).

21. **for each person, in the midst of the progressive eating, is habitually taking his own meal before [another person], who, in this second case, is also constantly hungry, [or] who, in another situation, is repeatedly drunk** (or: constantly intoxicated).

22. **So do you folks by no means continue having houses for the habitual eating and drinking? Or are you constantly despising** (holding a negative attitude toward) **God's called-out community, and are you repeatedly pouring shame and disgrace down on those presently having nothing? What should I say to you? Am I supposed to now praise and commend you folks? In this I am not now sending praise, applause or commendation upon [you]!**

23. **For you see, I myself received to myself and accepted from the Lord** [= Christ or Yahweh] **that which I also passed along** (or: transmitted; commended; committed; hand on as a tradition; *cf* vs. 2, above) **to you folks, that the Lord Jesus, within the night in which He was in process of being handed over** (or: transferred), **received and took a loaf of bread,**

24. **and then, with gratitude and expressing the ease of grace, broke it in pieces and said,** "[some MSS add: You folks take {it}; eat {it}.] **This is My body, being now broken over [the situation and condition of] you folks** (or: for you people; on your behalf). **Keep doing this, into the calling up of the memory pertaining to Me** (or: with a view to remembering Me; or: unto a remembering of what is Mine)." [cf 12:13b, below]

25. **Similarly, [He took] the cup also, after the eating of the supper, saying, "This cup is the new arrangement within My blood** (or: exists being the thorough placing and setting – which is new in kind and character – in the sphere of My blood; or: is the different covenant [being made] in union with My blood). **Keep on doing this, whenever you may be normally drinking, into the calling up of the memory pertaining to Me** (or: with a view to remembering Me)."

26. **For whenever** (or: as often as) **you folks may be repeatedly eating this loaf of bread and may be habitually drinking the [other MSS: this] cup, you are continuing to proclaim and bring down the announcement of the death of the Lord – until which point He may come** (or: up to the point at which He should come; or: until the time where He would suddenly come).

27. **So that whoever may habitually eat the loaf of bread, or should be drinking the cup, pertaining to** (or: with reference to) **the Lord in a manner or situation without equal value** (or: unworthily; unsuitably), **he or she will proceed in coming to be one held within** (or: embraced by and possessed within the sphere of; or: will continue being a possession that is engulfed within) **the body and the blood of the Lord.**

28. **So let a person habitually examine, test and evaluate himself** (or: regularly approve and accept himself [i.e., his attitude and behavior in the occasion]), **and in this manner let him be habitually eating from out of the loaf of bread and drinking from out of the cup,**

29. **for the one continually eating and drinking in a manner or situation without equal value** (or: in an unworthy or unsuitable way) **is repeatedly eating and drinking the effect of an**

evaluation and the result of a decision (or: a sifting and a judgment) **in** (or: to; for) **himself –
by not habitually discerning the body**

> (or: in not continuing to separate throughout the body; not completely evaluating the
> body; not discriminating for, discerning about, or making a distinction of, the body [of
> believers]; not now passing judging throughout the body; [other MSS add: of the Lord]).

30. **Because of this, many among you folks [are] without strength** (or: weak and infirm) **and
without health** (ailing; chronically ill), **and a considerable number** (or: quite a few) **are
habitually asleep** (or: continuously sleeping; or: = dead).

31. **But if we were** (or: had been) **in the habit of thoroughly evaluating, sifting throughout
and passing discerning judgment on ourselves, we would not have been being sifted,
separated, evaluated and judged.**

32. **Yet, being folks habitually being sifted, separated, evaluated and judged by, and
under, the Lord** [= Christ or Yahweh], **we are being continuously child-trained, educated,
disciplined or corrected [by the Lord or His agent], to the end that we should not at any
point be correspondingly evaluated or commensurately decided about** (separated-down or
condemned; or: = have sentence passed on us) **together, and in company with, the organized
and controlling System** (the world of culture, religion, economy, government and mankind).

33.   **So that, my brothers** (= fellow believers; folks from the same womb), **while repeatedly
coming together into the [situation or occasion] to be normally eating, be constantly
receiving from out of one another, taking them in your arms and welcoming them from out
of the midst [of the group].**

34. **Now if anyone is habitually hungry, let him be regularly eating at home, so that you
may not be constantly coming together** (gathering) **into a result of judgment** (the effect of a
separation, an evaluation and then a decision).

**But I will myself thoroughly set the remaining matters [which you asked about] in order
whenever I can come.**

CHAPTER 12

1. **Yet once again** (or: Now then), **brothers** (= fellow believers, or, members of the Family), **I do
not intend** (purpose; want; desire) **you folks to continue being ignorant concerning the
things** (or: matters) **of the spirit and attitude**

> (or: the [qualities; characteristics] which are the Spirit; the [aspects] of, or [workings] from,
> the Breath-effect; or: spiritual folks).

2. **You have seen, and know, that when you were being** (or: continued existing being) **ethnic
multitudes** ([the] nations; Gentiles; non-Jews) **how you were folks being constantly led astray**
(or: led off [the path] and away) **toward the voiceless idols** (silent images; mute forms; silent
rituals) **– as often as you were being periodically and progressively led** (or: conducted up).

3. **Wherefore, I am now proceeding to make known to you folks that no one – speaking
within God's Spirit** (or: speaking in union with the Breath-effect of God; speaking in the sphere
of a Breath which is God) **– is in the habit of saying, "Jesus [is] a result of something set up
as an offering to a deity** (or: Jesus [was] devoted as a sacrifice to God; or: accursed)!" **And no
one is able** (normally has power) **to say, "Jesus [is] Lord** (or: O Lord Jesus; or: O [Yahweh]…
Yahshua [= Yah is Savior])!" **except within and in union with [the] Holy Spirit** (or: in the midst
of a set-apart Breathe-effect; in consecrated spirit and attitude; centered in [the] Sacred Breath).

4. **Now there continue being different distributions** (divided-out, assigned apportionments) **of
the effects of favor and the results of grace, yet the same Spirit** (Breath-effect; Attitude),

5. **and there are different distributions of attending services** (divided-out apportionments and
assignments of dispensings), **and yet the same Lord** (or: Owner; Master; [= Christ or Yahweh]);

6. **also there continue being different assigned distributions of the results of inner
workings** (effects of inward operations), **and still, the same God – the One continuously
working inwardly** (progressively activating) **all things within and in union with all humans** (or:
constantly energizing, activating and operating the whole, centered within the midst of all things).

7. **Yet in** (to; for; with) **each person the manifestation** (clear display in light) **of the Breath-
effect** (from, and which is, the Spirit) **is continuously being given with a view to and [leading]**

toward progressively bringing [folks; things] together, face-to-face with the constant mutual bearing-together for benefit, advantage, expedience and the common good.

8. **For you see, on the one hand, in** (or: to; for; with; by) **one person a word** (a thought, message or expression; *logos*) **of wisdom** (or: patterned information from Wisdom; reason which is wisdom; a wise idea) **is repeatedly or from time-to-time or progressively being given. In** (To; For; With; By) **another person, on the other hand, [is given] a word** (thought; expression; reason) **of, and from, intimate, experiential knowledge, insight or realization** (*gnosis*) – **in accord with** (or: down from; in the sphere of; in line with) **the same Breath-effect** (or: Spirit).

9. **In** (To; For; With; By) **a different person [is given] faithfulness** (trust; loyalty; belief; faith; conviction; trustworthiness), **within and in union with the same effect of the Breath** (or: Spirit; Attitude); **yet in** (to; for; by; with) **another the effects of grace, and the results of joyous favor, which result in healings** – **within and in union with the one Breath-effect** (or: Spirit; Attitude).

10. **Yet in** (to; for) **another person [is given] the effects and results of inner workings and operations of abilities, powers and influences; still in** (to; for; by) **another [is given] a prophecy** (or: light ahead of time), **and in** (to; for; by) **another [is given] thorough discernings, distinguishings, discriminations or evaluations pertaining to spirits**

> (or: separations from spirits throughout [oneself]; [the] siftings and complete separations which lead to a thorough decision or judgment of spirits or attitudes). **Yet, in** (to; for; by) **a different person [are given] races and species** (families; classes; kinds) **of languages** (or: tongues), **then in** (to; for; by) **another one [are given] translations and interpretations of languages** (tongues).

11. **Now the One and the same Spirit** (or: Breath-effect; Attitude) **is habitually working within** (energizing, activating and operating) **all these things, constantly dividing, apportioning and distributing in** (to; for) **each person his own [effect of grace], correspondingly as He** (She; It) **progressively intends** (is habitually willing; continuously purposes; keeps on pleasing [to do]).

12. **You see, correspondingly as the [human] body is one [body] and continuously has** (possesses; holds) **many members** (body parts), **and all the members of the one body** – **being many** – **are one body, in this way, also, [is] the Christ** (or: even thus [is] the Anointed One and the Anointing).

13. **For indeed** (or: also) **we, ourselves** – **within the midst of one Spirit** (or: in union with one Breath-effect and Attitude) – **are all submerged into one Body** (or: were all immersed into, so as to be enveloped by, one body) – **whether Jews or Greeks** (or: Hellenists), **whether slaves or free folks** – **and we all are** (or: were) **made** (or: caused) **to drink one Spirit** (or: spirit; Breath-effect; Attitude). [*cf* 11:25-26, above]

14. **It follows then, the Body is not one member** (or: part), **but to the contrary, [it is] many.**

15. **In case the foot should ever say, "Because I am not a hand, I am not from out of the midst of** (= a part of) **the Body," not for this reason is it not from out of the midst of the Body** (or: = it is not from this statement that it does not exist with the body being its source and that it is not a part of the body)!

16. **And if the ear should ever say, "Because I am not an eye, I am not forth from** (= a part of) **the Body," not alongside of this** (= not for this reason) **is it not forth from** (= a part of) **the body!**

17. **If the whole Body [were] an eye, where [would be] the hearing** (or: ear; ability to hear)? **If [the] whole [were] hearing** (the ability to hear), **where [would be] the sense of smell?**

18. **Yet, at this present time** (or: = But as things are), **God, for Himself, places** (or: at once set in Himself) **the members** (or: parts) – **each one of them** – **within the midst of and in union with the Body, just as He intends** (purposed; wills).

19. **Now if the whole** (or: all) **were one member, where [would be] the Body?**

20. **But, at this present time** (now) **[there are], indeed, many members** (or: parts), **yet one Body.**

21. **Now the eye continues unable** (habitually has no power) **to say to the hand, "I continue having no need of you," or, again, the head [cannot say] to the feet, "I continue having no need of you [two]."**

22. **On the contrary, much rather, the members of the body habitually seeming or appearing to be inherently weaker are** (or: exist being) **pressingly necessary and indispensable,**

23. **and ones which we habitually presume** (or: suppose; deem; think) **to be less valuable and less honorable [parts] of the body, we are constantly surrounding these with more abundant honor** (or: habitually place [things] of exceeding value around these), **and so our unattractive** (deformed; indecent; unfashionable) **[members] are constantly having** (habitually holding) **more exceeding and abundant good form** (or: presentability; respectability; modesty; good appearance).

24. **Now our well-formed** (or: respectable; presentable; profitably fashioned) **[members] continue having no need, but God mixed and blended the Body together, giving more abundant value and honor to those habitually or repeatedly being left behind in the rear** (or: being made defective, deficient, or below standard),

25. **to the end that there should be no tearing split-effect, causing division, within the body, but rather that the members should constantly show the same care over, and have the same concern about, the welfare of one another.**

26. **And further, whether one member is continuing to experience the effect of something, or constantly undergoes suffering, all the members continually experience the effect or the suffering together with [it; her; him]; or if a member is being constantly glorified, normally given an assumed appearance, or is progressively receiving a good reputation, all the members are continuously rejoicing together with [him; her; it].**

27. **Now you folks yourselves are, and continuously exist being, Christ's Body** (or: a body which is Anointed; or: a body whose source and character is Christ, and which is Christ) **– and [you folks are] members of** (or: from out of) **a part [of it] –**

28. **whom also God Himself, indeed, placed in union with the covenant community** (or: set, centered within the called-out). **[Now] first [it was] those sent off on a mission** (emissaries; representatives); **second [it was] folks who have light ahead of time and speak it before others publicly [on behalf of God]** (spokesmen [for God]; prophets); **third [it was] people who teach. Then after that [He gave] abilities and powers, adding then effects of grace which result in cures and healings. [He also gave] folks who take [things] in hand, in place of another, and grasp with their mind and apprehend the replaced [situation] and exchange**
  (or: those who lay hold of the other side of something in order to aid and assist; or: occasions of receiving in turn or in exchange; or: = helpful services; supports given in turn) **[and provided] situations and skills for steering the course** (or: abilities to guide and direct action; acts of pilotage; helmsman abilities and services; wise counsel and guidance; = administrative and managerial skills). **[He then gave] species** (or: families; races; kinds) **of languages** (or: tongues).

29. **[So you see that] not all [are] folks sent off on a mission** (representatives; envoys; emissaries). **Not all [are] those who have light ahead of time and speak it before others in public** (prophets). **Not all [are] people who teach** (teachers; instructors). **Not all [have] abilities or powers**.

30. **Not all constantly hold** (habitually have or possess) **effects of grace which result in cures and healings. Not all habitually speak in multiple languages** (or: are constantly speaking by tongues; or: normally talk to tongues [figure of people groups of other cultures]). **Not all are continually interpreting** (or: habitually translating).

31. **Yet, you folks be constantly boiling with fervor** (or: are habitually fervent in zeal) **[for; seeking; supporting; in devotion to] the greater effects of grace and favor! And still, I am now progressively pointing out and showing you folks a path** ([the] Way) **corresponding to transcendence**
  (or: a road which accords with a casting-something-over [someone] on their behalf; a pathway in the sphere of excess and extravagance; = an incomparable way)**:**

CHAPTER 13

1. **If ever I could habitually speak** (or as an indicative: If I continuously speak) **in or with the languages of the human groups** (or: by the tongues of mankind) **– or even of the agents** (or: messengers) **– yet am not constantly having and continuously holding Love** (a drive toward reunion with, unrestricted acceptance of, and full giving of myself to, others) **I have come to be a**

continuously sounding (or: blaring; booming out; resounding) **[piece of] brass** (or: copper; bronze) **or a repeatedly clashing basin or a continuously clanging cymbal!**

2. **Even if I am continuously holding light ahead of time** (or: repeatedly have prophecy), **and I may have seen, and thus know, all the secrets** (or: every mystery) **and all the intimate knowledge** (or: insight; *gnosis*), **and if I now continuously possess all the faith and trust – so as to repeatedly transport mountains** (or: to change the place and position of mountain after mountain) **– yet do not habitually possess** (or: progressively have) **Love and unambiguous, unrestricted acceptance, I am** (I exist being) **nothing!** [*cf* Mk. 11:23]

3. **If further I should dole out all my habitual subsistences in morsels of food – even if I should hand over** (commit) **my body! – so that I could boast** [C, D and other, later MSS read: so that I will be burned], **and yet do not habitually possess and progressively have Love, I continue being benefited** (furthered; augmented; helped; profited) **in not even one thing.**

> [note: love (*agapē*) – "unambiguous love;" "an ecstatic manifestation of the Spiritual Presence;" "the drive toward reunion;" "participation in the other one;" "the acceptance of the other one as a person... the power of reunion with the other person as one standing on the same ultimate ground..." – Paul Tillich, *Systematic Theology III*, pp 134-137; *Perspectives on 19th and 20th Century Protestant Theology*, p 200]

4. **The Love** (or: This unrestricted acceptance, etc.) **is habitually even-tempered, taking a long time to be in a heat of passion** (is constantly long-enduring/suffering and patient; keeps on putting anger far away; continues slow to progress toward rushing emotions which cause violent breathing; continues passionately persevering unto the goal) **– it continues being usefully kind. The Love** (or: This urge toward unambiguous, accepting reunion and giving of oneself) **is not constantly boiling with jealousy and envy. The Love is not continuously bragging or "showing off" – it is not habitually being puffed up; it is not conceited or arrogant.**

5. **It is not repeatedly indecent in manner or behavior** (it does not continually display lack of [good] form, rudeness or improper demeanor); **it is not habitually self-seeking** (or: not constantly pursuing its own interests or rights); **it is not continually caused to be sharp [in response] nor aroused to irritation or upset emotions; it is not habitually keeping account of the worthless thing, nor logically considering something of bad quality, nor counting the injury.**

6. **It does not continue to rejoice upon [seeing or hearing of] the injustice, nor is it happy about dishonesty, inequity, or lack of the qualities of the Way pointed out, yet it repeatedly rejoices with the Truth** (or: takes delight together in Reality).

7. **[Love] continuously covers all mankind; it is habitually loyal to all humanity; it constantly has an expectation for all mankind; it is continuously remaining under and giving support to all people.**

> (or, since "all" can also be neuter: It [i.e., unambiguous acceptance] progressively puts a protecting roof over all things; it is habitually trusting in, and believing for, all things; it is continually hoping in or for all things; it keeps on patiently enduring all things.)

8. **The Love** (or: This unrestricted, self-giving drive toward reunion) **never – not even once – fails** (collapses or falls into decay; = becomes ineffectual; [other MSS: falls out or lapses]). **Now, whether prophecies** (or: situations of light ahead of time) **will be rendered useless and unproductive** (or: idled-down to be inactive and unemployed, discarded or, nullified) **or languages will stop themselves** (or: tongues will restrain themselves so as to cease [speaking]; "utterances of ecstasy" will cease of themselves), **or whether intimate or experiential knowledge** (or: insight; *gnosis*) **will be rendered useless and unproductive** (be idled-down to be inactive and unemployed, discarded or, nullified)

9. **– for we are progressively gaining intimate and experiential knowledge from out of a part** (insight from a piece or a fragment; *gnosis* from the midst of a portion of the whole), **and we are habitually prophesying** (speaking publicly before others and sharing light ahead of time) **from out of a part** (a portion; a fragment; a piece of the whole) **–**

10. **still, whenever the destined goal** (the mature person; the finished product; maturity; the complete attainment of the purpose; perfection) **comes** (arrives) **that which is out of a part** (a piece; a portion; a fragment; partial) **will progressively be rendered useless and unproductive** (idled-down to be inactive, unemployed or discarded). [*cf* Eph. 4:13-14]

11. **When I was an infant** (a baby; a non-speaking one), **I used to babble and make vocal utterances as a non-speaking infant. I used to habitually be in the frame of mind, take thought with the intellect and understand as a non-speaking infant** (baby). **I continued taking account, reasoning and logically considering things as a non-speaking infant. Yet when I had come to be an adult male, I had permanently made inactive** (idled-down so as to be no longer used and discarded) **the things which pertain to a non-speaking infant** (infantile things).

12. **For you see, at the present moment we continue seeing and observing through means of a metal mirror, within the midst of an enigma** (the result of something obscurely expressed, hinted or intimated, giving an indistinct image), **but at that point, face to face. Right now I am progressively coming to intimately and experientially know from out of a part** (gain insight from a piece; be acquainted with a portion of the whole), **but thereupon I shall continue accurately knowing and recognizing, from full intimate experience and added insight, correspondingly as I am also fully and accurately known, by intimate experience.**

13. **So at the present time trust** (or: faith; loyalty; trustworthiness), **expectation** (or: expectant hope) **[and] love** (unrestricted acceptance which overcomes existential separation – Tillich) – **these three – continue remaining and habitually dwell [with us], yet the greatest of these [is] the Love** ([God's] urge toward unambiguous, accepting reunion – Tillich; self-giving – Rohr). **You folks make haste to progressively run after and continuously pursue this Love!**

CHAPTER 14

1. **Now with boiling fervor and affection, be habitually welling-up and zealous in regard to the things of the spirit**
    (or, as an indicative: So, you folks are constantly with your hearts set on the matters pertaining to the Spirit; or, as a subjunctive: Now you should keep on being ardently devoted in aspects having the character of Breath-effect), [cf 12:1, above]
and especially (or: yet even more) **that you folks would be habitually prophesying**
    (or: would keep on speaking publicly before others, speaking Light ahead of time; or: = should on behalf of God, be repeatedly proclaiming His message),

2. **for the person habitually speaking in a language is not speaking to or for humans, but rather, to, by and with God – for you see, no one continues listening so as to pay attention or obey. Yet for [the] Spirit** (or: by Breath-effect; with attitude) **he goes on speaking secrets.**
    (or: for he or she that repeatedly speaks in a tongue is not speaking to people or for mankind, but to the contrary, in, to, for or with, God – for your see, no one continues listening [to him or her] – and yet in spirit he or she continues speaking mysteries!)

3. **Now the one habitually prophesying** (or: normally publicly speaking [God's message] and sharing Light ahead of time) **is constantly speaking an act of building** (a construction; an edification) **– even a calling to the side to give relief, aid and comfort and encouragement** (or: a speaking as, and doing the work of, a paraclete), **as well as a speech of stimulation, soothing and gentle influence or incentive – to people** (or: among humans; for mankind).

4. **The person habitually speaking in a tongue** (or: language) **constantly upbuilds and edifies himself, yet the person constantly prophesying** (publicly speaking [God's message] before others) **continuously upbuilds, edifies and constructs the called-out community.**

5. **Now I continue intending** (purposing; willing; wanting) **all you folks to be habitually speaking in tongues** (or: with languages), **yet preferably that you would be constantly prophesying** (or: should keep on speaking publicly before others [as God's spokesmen, proclaiming God's message]), **for the one repeatedly prophesying [is] of greater [importance; influence] than the one habitually speaking in tongues** (or: with languages) **– outside of this exception: [that] he should continue on to interpret** (or: translate), **so that the called-out assembly can receive an upbuilding** (or: may take hold of, and get, edification; would grasp [the] construction).

6. **So now, brothers** (= fellow believers), **if I should come to you repeatedly speaking in language after language** (or: continuously speaking in tongues), **what will I be benefiting, augmenting or furthering you folks – unless instead I speak either on an unveiling** (a

revelation; a disclosure), **or in intimate knowledge based upon my experience and insight, or with a prophecy** (a proclamation of Light [from God]), **or by a teaching?**

7. **Likewise, [with] the inanimate** (soulless; = lifeless) **things [which] are normally giving a sound – whether a flute or lyre** (or: a wind instrument or a stringed instrument)**: how will it proceed being known [what] is being played on the flute or on the lyre unless it should give a distinction in the tones**

> (a set order throughout with a difference made through divisions in the arrangement or the sending of the sounds apart)**?**

8. **For also, if a military trumpet should give an indistinct** (uncertain; dubious) **sound, who will proceed to prepare and make himself ready for battle or war?**

9. **In the same way also, unless you, yourselves, should give an easily understood word** (intelligible expression of patterned information; a *Logos* that gives clear meaning) **through the language, or by means of the tongue, how will the thing** (or: matter) **that proceeds in being spoken be personally understood and experientially known, with insight? So you will [just] proceed being a person continuing to speak or babble into [the] air.**

10. **Since, as it happens to be, there are so many kinds of voices in [the] world** (or: sounds centered in the system of cultures, religions and societies, or in the midst of the aggregate of humanity) **– and not one of them voiceless** (= silent or without a language or meaning) **–**

11. **if then, I may not have seen so as to know the ability of the voice** (or: power of the sound; = force and meaning), **to the one presently speaking** (or: for the speaker [i.e., in his perception]) **I shall continue being a barbarian** (one who utters confused or unintelligible sounds; = a foreigner), **and in me** (or: in my case or view) **the one speaking [will be] a barbarian** (gibberish talker; = a foreigner).

12. **In the same way also, since you, yourselves, are folks boiling with fervor and affection in regard to spirit things** (or: from attitudes; pertaining to spirits; [in matters] which are Breath-effects), **be constantly and progressively seeking, [focused] toward the upbuilding, edification and construction of the called-out community – to the end that you folks can progressively surround yourselves with abundance** (or: be constantly superabounding).

13. **Therefore, let the one constantly speaking in a language, or a tongue, habitually pray that** (or: focus his thoughts on having goodness and well-being [of the group] so) **he can presently continue on, to translate** (or: may proceed to interpret) **[it].**

14. **So if I am habitually praying in a language** (or: speaking or thinking toward having goodness, with a tongue), **my spirit** (or: attitude; Breath-effect) **is continually praying, yet my mind continues being unfruitful** (or: my intellect is without fruit; = useless).

15. **Which** (or: What) **is it, then? I will constantly pray** (or: focus my thoughts on having goodness and speak toward things going well; [other MSS: I should pray]) **in and by the spirit** (or: with the Spirit; to the Breath-effect; for the Attitude), **yet I will [other MSS: should] also repeatedly think and speak toward having good results in** (or: pray by and with) **the mind. I will continue striking the strings and sing** (or: making melody) **in and by the** (or: = my) **spirit** (or: attitude; or: the Breath-effect), **yet I will also habitually strike the strings and sing** (make melody) **in and by the** (or: = my) **mind.**

16. **Else, if you may continue to speak a good word in spirit** (or: to utter eulogies within [the] Spirit; to be blessing in union with Breath-effect), **how will the one normally filling up the place of the private life of a non-specialist**

> [note: = one who occupies the ordinary position of the "average person," being unskilled, uneducated, uninitiated into the secrets of life in the kingdom or the mysteries of Christ]

normally say, "It is so! (or: Amen; Make it so!)" at your speaking of the ease and wholesomeness of grace, and your expression of gratitude – since he has not perceived and does not know what you are presently saying?

17. **For you yourself are indeed constantly expressing the ease and wholesomeness of grace and showing gratitude in a beautiful, fine and ideal way – but still the different person is not being progressively built up** (edified)!

18. **I am habitually speaking of the ease and wholesomeness of grace in** (or: by; with) **God, and giving thanks to God – I am habitually speaking in languages** (or: constantly babbling in tongues) **more than all of you folks!**

19. **Nevertheless, within the called-out assembly I constantly intend to speak five words by my mind** (with my intellect and understanding) **– to the end that I may also sound-down instruction on others – rather than an innumerable number** (myriads) **of words** (the plural of "*logos*"; ideas; thoughts; patterned information) **within a language** (or: [ecstatic] tongue).

20. **Brothers** (= Fellow members of the community)! **Stop becoming little boys and girls in or by [your] way of thinking and use of intellect, but still be infants – non-speaking babies! – in the worthless, the ugly and the poor of quality or the evil. Yet progressively come to be mature as folks which manifest the purpose** (full-grown; perfect; ones having reached the goal and express the destiny; or: = adults) **in [your] way of thinking and use of intellect.**

21. **It has been written within the Law that,**
> **"In different** (= foreign) **languages** (tongues) **and with different** (= foreign) **lips shall I proceed in speaking to** (with; in) **this people – and not even in this manner will they proceed in paying attention to Me, or listen into and obey Me," [the] LORD** [i.e., = Yahweh] **is saying.** [Isa. 28:11]

22. **Consequently the languages** (tongues) **are [pointing] unto and [leading] into a sign – not for believers** (or: to those constantly trusting), **but rather for unbelievers** (or: to those without trust or faith) **– yet the prophecy** (the publicly spoken message [from God]; the speaking of light ahead of time) **[is] not for** (or: to) **unbelievers, but rather for believers** (or: to those habitually trusting, progressively believing with conviction, and continuing loyal).

23. **Therefore, if the whole called-out community** (the entire local assembly) **should come together at the same [place], and everyone** (or: all) **should be speaking in languages** (or: with [ecstatic] tongues), **but then ordinary folks** (= unlearned people of the private sector) **or unbelievers should at some point enter, will they not proceed in saying that you folks are presently being crazy** (continuing to behave as insane people; now acting raving mad)?

24. **Now if everyone may be prophesying, one after another, and some unbeliever** (person without faith) **or an ordinary uninstructed person may at some point enter, he is progressively being given the proof [of the situation], being exposed to convincing arguments, by everyone – [and] by everyone continues being sifted, sorted and held up so that a decision [regarding the situation] can come to him!**

25. **The hidden things of his heart are now progressively coming to be set in clear light, and thus – falling upon [his] face – he will proceed to be doing obeisance to** (or: paying respect tot; worshiping) **God, progressively proclaiming back [to you] that God is existentially within, essentially in union with, and is presently being among you folks!**

26. **What, then, is [the conclusion], brothers** (= fellow members)? **Whenever you folks may at some point come together: each one of you habitually has a psalm** (song; tune played on a stringed instrument, with a poem); **has a teaching; has an unveiling** (revelation; a disclosure); **has a language** (or: a tongue); **has a translation** (or: interpretation) **– all things** (everything!) **and every person [directed] toward edification, upbuilding and construction – let it habitually happen** (normally come to be; constantly occur)!

27. **So if anyone is habitually speaking in a language** (or: with a tongue) **– let it be** (or: to the extent of) **two, or three, at the most – and then** (or: also) **let one be normally translating** (or: interpreting). [comment: 2 or 3 – the number of true witness]

28. **Now if there may be no translator within [this] assembly of the called-out, let him or her continue in silence,** (or: Yet if he should not be an interpreter he must keep still in an assembly), **yet let him or her continue to speak to** (or: in) **himself, and to** (or: in; with) **God.**

29. **Now let two or three prophets be speaking, one after another, and let the other folks continue thoroughly sifting and sorting so as to fully evaluate and reach a decision.**

30. **Yet if it may** (or: should) **be unveiled** (revealed; disclosed) **to another being seated, let the first hush, and keep silent,**

31. **for you all continue able** (constantly have power) **to be repeatedly prophesying, one by one, to the end that everyone** (all) **can be learning, and everyone** (all) **can be called alongside to receive relief, aid, comfort and encouragement** (may receive the benefits of the Paraclete).

32. **Also – [the] spirits and attitudes of the prophets are normally humbly aligned with [other] prophets, or, to [the] Prophets**

(or: breath-effects of those having fore-light are constantly subjected and subjoined to the arrangements [made] by [the] folks having fore-light),

33. **for God is not the source of instability, but to the contrary, of peace** (or: for God does not exist being unrest, disorder or turbulence, but rather, [is] harmony and joining [= shalom]) – **as [He is] within all the called-out communities of the set-apart ones** (or: as [it is] among all the called-out folks who are the sacred people that are different from what is common)....

[note: some scholars have suggested that the following is a quote from the letter sent from Corinth to Paul, not the position of Paul, himself; or, reading the last phrase of vs. 33 as an introduction to vs. 34-35: As {is the custom} among all the called-forth groups of the holy people {= Israel},]

34. **"Let the wives** (or: women) **habitually hush and continue silent [when] within the midst of the local assemblies of the called-out, for it continues not being allowed or permitted for them to be constantly babbling or habitually holding conversations, but rather, let them be habitually humbly aligned** (or: be supportively attached and subordinate themselves) – **correspondingly as also the Law** (or: the custom; or: = [the Torah]) **continues saying.**

35. **"Now if they are still desiring and intending to continue learning something, let them be habitually asking** (inquiring of) **their own husbands** (or: adult males) **at home** (within [the] house), **for it is, and continues being, bad form and shamefully offensive for a wife** (or: woman) **to be constantly babbling or habitually holding conversations within the midst of the local assembly of the called-out."**

[note: D, F, G and other MSS place vss. 34-35 after vs. 40. Some scholars consider this as evidence of an early introduction into the text. If the author is referencing the Torah, in vs. 34, then this would have been a Jewish custom; if merely citing custom, he could have referred to the local custom in Corinth, or to the *Talmud*; cf 11:5, above]

36. **What? Or, really, did this "thought or message from God" come forth from you folks?** (or: Was it from YOU [that] this "word of God" came forth?) **Or into only you people did this reach down and attain?**

37. **If anyone habitually presumes** (continues in assuming; normally imagines [himself]) **to be a prophet or a 'spiritual one,' let him continue to fully know and acknowledge the things which I am now writing to you folks, because they are [the] Lord's implanted goals** (impartations of the finished product from [the] Master; inward, directives which are [the] Lord)!

38. **Yet if anyone continues being ignorant or mistaken [of this], let him or her continue without knowledge** [other MSS: he or she continues being left ignorant and mistaken].

(or: Now if anyone is habitually without experiential understanding or insight, [this] continues being not known [by him], or he/she remains unknown.)

39. **Consequently, my brothers** (= fellow members and family), **with boiling fervor and affection, be habitually zealous for the prophesying** (the proclaiming [of God's message] before others; or: the having and/or speaking light ahead of time), **and do not be in the habit of cutting off, forbidding or hindering the habitual babbling in languages** (or: speaking or conversing in tongues).

40. **Yet let all things be progressively occurring** (or: coming to be) **with good form** (respectably; with good appearance and propriety) **and corresponding to an arranged order** (or: in the sphere of an aligned arrangement).

CHAPTER 15

1. **Now I am progressively making known to you, brothers** (= fellow called-out folks; = Family, from the same Womb), **the good news** (the message of goodness, ease and well-being) **– which I myself announced as glad tidings for you** (or: the message of goodness to you; the directive of ease and well-being among you) **– which you also accepted and embraced, as well as within which you have taken a stand, and in union with which you now stand,**

2. **[and] through means of which you folks are also progressively, and one after another, being rescued, delivered, and made whole** (saved, preserved and restored to your original state and condition) **– since you people are continuously keeping [it] in possession and retaining [it] – [even] by which, and in which, Word** (or: *Logos*; expressed message; laid-out idea) **I, myself, announced these glad tidings to you people: the message of goodness for**

you! [Now this is] outside of this exception: [that] you placed your trust randomly (or: Unless, in fact, you folks did believe to no purpose and express conviction feignedly)!

3. **For I handed on** (or: give over as tradition; transmit and commit) **to** (or: among) **you folks, among [the] first** (or: primary) **things** (or: = above all things), **that which I also accepted and embraced: that Christ died over [the situation and circumstances of] our failures** (on behalf of our mistakes, deviations and sins) – **corresponding to the Scriptures** –

4. **and that He was buried, and that He has been awakened and raised in** (or: on) **the third day, and He remains thus – corresponding to the Scriptures** –

5. **and that He was seen by** (or: was caused to appear and made visible to) **Cephas – next** (or: later) **by** (or: to; among; within) **the Twelve.**

6. **After that He was seen by** (or: was caused to appear and made visible to, among or within) **over five hundred brothers** (= fellow believers) **at one time – of whom the majority continue remaining until right now** (the present), **yet some fell asleep** (= died; passed away).

7. **After that He was seen by** (or: was caused to appear and made visible to) **Jacob** (= James), **next by all the sent-forth folks** (or: the representatives; the emissaries sent off with a mission).

8. **Yet last of all [these] folks, He was seen by** (or: was caused to appear and made visible to) **me, also – as if it were** (or: just as if) **by one born prematurely**
    (or: as though in a miscarriage; = born too soon, and thus weak and not fully developed, or, born dead, or, aborted; or: with that from out of a festering wound).

9. **So it follows that I myself am the smallest** (thus: the least one) **of the sent-forth people** (envoys; representatives), **who am not adequate to reach [the stature] to be normally called a sent-off representative or emissary, because I pursued and persecuted God's called-out** (or: the community of the summoned-forth God, which has the character of God).

10. **Yet in** (or: by; for; with) **God's grace, and joyous favor which is God, I am what I am, and His [placed]-into-me grace** (or: [birthed]-into-me joyous favor) **was not birthed to be empty, but on the contrary, I toiled to exhaustion by hard labor in excess of them all – yet not I, but rather God's grace and favor** (or: the grace from God; the joyous favor, which is God) **together with me** [other MSS read: which {is} with me].

11. **Whether therefore I or those, in this way we are constantly proclaiming the message, and in this way you folks trusted, believed, experience loyalty and are faithful.**

12. **Now since** (or: if) **Christ is habitually being publicly proclaimed** (heralded as a message) **that He has been, and remains, awakened and raised up from out of the midst of dead folks, how are some among you folks repeatedly saying that there is** (or: there presently exists and continues being) **no resurrection of dead people?**

13. **Yet now if there is presently no resurrection of dead people** (or: if there continues being no resurrection of dead ones; if a resurrection of dead ones does not constantly exist), **neither has Christ been awakened and raised up.**

14. **So if Christ has not been awakened and raised up, our message which we proclaim [is] consequently empty and without content – and your** [other MSS: our] **faith and trust [is] empty and vacuous,**

15. **and further, we [thus] continue to be found being false witnesses, from and concerning God, because we bring testimony and evidence down from God that He awakened and raised up the Christ – Whom, consequently, He did not raise up, if indeed** (= as they say) **dead ones are not really being habitually** (or: periodically; one after another) **awakened and raised up!**

16. **For you see, if dead ones are not habitually** (or: presently, one after another; periodically) **being awakened and raised up, neither has Christ been awakened and raised up.**

17. **And if Christ has not been awakened and raised up, your faith, trust and loyalty exists being devoid of success and results – you are still within the midst of and in union with your mistakes, failures, deviations, failures to hit the target, and sins!**

18. **Consequently, also, those falling asleep within the midst of and in union with Christ lose themselves** (or: loose-away and destroy themselves). [cf 2 Cor. 5:14b]

19. **If we are folks having placed an expectation in Christ within this life only** (or: If in this life only we are placing expectant hope centered in Christ), **we are, of all humanity** (or: mankind; people), **the ones most to be pitied and in need of mercy and compassion.**

20. **Yet now – at this present time! – Christ is roused and awake from having been raised up from out of the midst of dead people: a Firstfruit** (= the first of the harvest; the Sheaf Offering, signally the beginning of the harvest [Lev. 23:10]) **of those having fallen asleep, and are yet sleeping** (reposing).

21. **For since through a person** (or: a human; or: humanity) **[came] death, through a Person** (or: a Human), **also, [comes] resurrection** (a standing back up again) **of dead people.**

22. **For just as within Adam all humans keep on** (or: everyone continues) **dying, in the same way, also, within the Christ, all humans will keep on being made alive** (or: in union with the Anointed One, everyone will one-after-another be created and produced with Life) [*cf* Rom. 5:18]

23. **– yet each person within the result of his or her own set position [in line]** (or: effect of ordered placement; appointed class; arranged time and turn, or order of succession; = place in a harvest calendar, thus, due season of maturity)**: Christ a Firstfruit** (a First of the harvest), **next after that, those belonging to the Christ** (or: the ones who have their source and origin in the Anointing; those who are [a part] of the Christ) **within the midst of, and in union with, His presence,** [Phil. 3:16]

24. **thereafter** (next, in order of sequence,) **the purposed goal and destiny**
     (the finished work; the embodiment of maturity and perfection; the fulfillment; the result; the outcome; the end and purpose attained; the realization of the perfect discharge; or: the end; the closing act; the consummation), **when He would continue passing on the sovereign influence and activities by God** (or: can progressively restore and continue transferring or returning the reign to God; may, with and in God, repeatedly transmit the kingdom; should keep on committing, handing over and relating the dominion, for God) **even [the] Father** (or: in [His] God and Father), **at the time that He would suddenly bring down to idleness** (make unemployed and ineffective; nullify; abolish; render useless and unproductive) **every rulership of government** (all headship and sovereignty), **even all authority and power** (or: every existing right, privilege and what comes out of being – as well as, able-ness and capability)!

25. **For it is binding and necessary for Him to be continuously reigning** (ruling as King; exercising sovereignty) **until which [time or situation]** (or: until where) **He would put** (or: may place; could set) **all the humans that have or hold ruin** (or: the enemies) **under His feet.**

26. **[The] last holder of ruin** (or: A final enemy or quality having ill-will) **being progressively brought down to idleness** (made unemployed and ineffective; rendered useless and unproductive) **[is] the Death** (or: Death, a last enemy, is being presently nullified and abolished).

27. **For you see,**
     "He completely arranges, humbly aligns and then appends and puts under shelter all humanity (or: subjoins, supportively arranges in subordination, and brings under full control, all things) **under His feet** (= as supporting forces in His kingdom)." [Ps. 8:6]
Now when He would say, "All humanity (or: everything) **has been completely aligned and arranged under full, subjected and sheltered control," [it is] evident** (clearly visible) **that [it is] with the exception of, and outside of, the One subjecting the whole** (or: arranging all things and situations in humble, subordinate, attached alignment) **in, by and for** (or: to) **Him.**

28. **Now when the whole** (or: all things) **would be completely supportively-aligned in Him** (or: attached and appended to Him; subordinately sheltered and arranged by and for Him), **then the Son Himself will also continue being supportively aligned to, fully subjoined for and humbly attached under as an arranged shelter in, the One subjecting, appending and sheltering the whole in Him** (or: attaching all things to Him), **to the end that God can be all things within the midst of and in union with all humans** (or: may be everything in all things; or: should exist being All in all; or: would exist being everything, within the midst of everyone).

29. **Otherwise, what will the folks now being baptized** (immersed) **continue doing – or what will they continue producing – concerning** (over [the situation] of; for the sake of) **the dead people? If dead folks are not altogether** (actually; absolutely; generally speaking) **being habitually awakened and presently raised up, then why are these folks even being repeatedly baptized** (or: presently immersed, as a normal practice) **concerning them** (over their [situation]; for their sake; in connection with them)**?** [*Cf* 6:14, above]
     [comment: this vs. has been a quandary for most scholars, but I suggest that it presents the perspective held by first century believers, and was a common practice, regarding

422

their perceived relationship with those who died before coming to hear of the Christ, and thus be baptized – and it appears that their view was one of solidarity with them]

30. **And why are we constantly taking risks and being in danger all through every hour?**
31. **Daily I am repeatedly facing death** (or: progressively dying)! **Brothers, I swear** (strongly affirm) **by my reason for boasting!** [other MSS: On the basis of your own reason for boasting] – **which I continually possess** (hold), **centered in Christ Jesus, our Lord** (Owner; Master) –
32. **if I fight** (or: fought) **in accord with human [means, methods or purposes] with wild beasts in Ephesus, what [is] the benefit for or to me** (or: how am I furthered by it)**? If dead people are not habitually** (or: continuously; periodically) **being awakened and raised up,**
    "we should eat and drink, for tomorrow we continue dying away!" [Isa. 22:13]
33. **Stop being led astray** (or: Do not continue being deceived and caused to wander)! **"Worthless associations, conversations or interminglings in a crowd** (or: Companionships of corrupt quality [note: this can refer to sexual encounters]; Bad company or communication) **habitually and progressively corrupt, decay, spoil and ruin useful habits, kind customs and profitable characters."** [note: a quote from a play by the poet Menander]
34. **Sober up by returning your senses into the Way pointed out, with fairness, equity and rightwised relationships, and stop sinning** (do not continue in error or failure), **for some** (or: certain folks) **continue holding an absence of an intimate knowledge of God** (or: habitually possess an ignorance pertaining to God). **I am now saying this with a view toward a turning back within [the situation] by you people** (or: facing shame and humiliation for you folks).
35. **But still someone will say, "How are the dead ones being habitually** (or: presently; periodically; continuously) **awakened and raised up? And in what sort of body** (or: with what kind of material organism) **are they continuing to come** (or: one-after-another going)**?"**
36. **You idiot!** (or: You senseless and stupid fellow!) **What you are habitually sowing is not being progressively brought to life unless it should die off.**
    [comment: thus death is the path toward resurrection]
37. **And further, that which you continue sowing: you folks are not progressively sowing the body** [= the organism] **which shall be coming into being** (or: that will be developing), **but rather, a naked seed** (a bare kernel, or grain without clothing), **whether it may hit the target of wheat** (= perchance of wheat), **or any one of the rest [of the grains].**
38. **Yet God habitually gives a body to** (or: for) **it, according as He wills** (intends; purposed), **and to** (or: for; with) **each of the seeds its own body.** [comment: each kind of seed yields its own kind of plant; Paul is speaking here of classes of seeds/plants]
39. **Not all flesh [is] the same flesh, but to the contrary, [there is] indeed one [flesh] of humans** (of people; of mankind), **yet another flesh of tamed animals** (or: of livestock), **still another flesh of birds** (or: flyers), **and another of fishes.**
40. **And then [there are] imposed, heavenly bodies** (bodies having the characteristics of that upon the dome of the sky, or the upper heavens, the celestial), **and earthly bodies** (bodies which exist upon the land; terrestrial bodies), **but [they are] indeed different: the glory of, and from, the imposed, heavenly [is] one thing, while the glory** (assumed appearance) **of, and from, the earthly [is] different.**
41. **[There is] one glory** (or: splendor; assumed appearance) **of [the] sun, and another glory of [the] moon, and another glory of [the] stars, in fact star continues differing from star, in glory and splendor** (or: for you see, [one] star is progressively carrying through and bearing apart in excellence and assumed appearance from [another] star).
42. **Thus also** (or: In this way too) **[is] the resurrection of the dead people. It is habitually** (repeatedly; presently; one after another) **being sown [as a seed] within corruption** (or: in union with decay and ruin; in perishability); **it is being habitually** (or: presently; repeatedly; one after another) **awakened and raised up within incorruption** (non-decayability; imperishableness).
43. **It is constantly being sown within dishonor** (in union with lack of value; in the midst of worthlessness), **it is being habitually** (or: repeatedly; constantly; progressively; one after another) **awakened and raised up within, and in union with, glory** (a manifestation which calls forth praise; an assumed appearance of good repute). **It is constantly being sown within weakness** (in union with lack of strength), **it is being habitually** (or: repeatedly; constantly; one after another; progressively) **awakened and raised up within, and in union with, power and ability.**

44. **It is habitually** (continually; repeatedly; presently) **being sown a body having the qualities and characteristics of a soul** (a body with the life of a soul and a consciousness of self; or: = a body animated by soul; or: = a natural, psychical entity); **it is habitually** (repeatedly; constantly; presently; one after another) **being awakened and raised up a spiritual body** (a body determined by the characteristics of the Breath-effect, or spirit; = a spiritual entity). **Since there is a soulish** (soul-animated) **body, there also is** (or: exists) **a spiritual** (spirit-animated) **one.**
      [comment: note the germinal connection between the two – they are a progression of the same body, from seed to plant; the Seed is Resurrection Life – vs. 42a, above]

45. **Thus also** (or: In this way also), **it has been written, "The first human** (or: man), **Adam, came for existence** (or: was birthed) **into [being] a living soul"** [Gen. 2:7]; **the Last Adam into [being] a continuously life-making** (life-producing; life-creating; life-forming) **Spirit** (or: Breath-effect; Attitude). [comment: the first Adam is the "sowing;" the "Last Adam" is the Resurrection]

46. **Nevertheless, the spiritual [is] not first, but rather the one having the qualities and characteristics of a soul** (the soulish; psychical), **then afterwards, the spiritual** (that pertaining to and having the qualities of Breath-effect and Attitude).

47. **The first human** (person; humanity) **[was/is] forth from out of the earth** (Land; ground; soil), **made of moist soil and dust** (or: having the quality and character of moist dirt that can be poured or mounded; soilish); **the Second Human** (Person; Humanity; [other MSS add: {is} the Lord]) **[is made] out of heaven** (or: [is] from atmosphere and sky; [p46 reads: {is} spiritual]).
      [note: the phrases describing the materials, or the origins, of the two humans are parallel constructions in the Greek MSS from which I have given the bold rendering]

48. **As [is] the person made of and having the character and quality of moist soil or dust** (mounded or poured dirt), **of such sort also [are] the people [who are] made of and have the character and quality of moist soil or dust** (soil-ish folks); **and likewise, as [is] the Added, Imposed, Heavenly Person** (or: the one made of and having the quality and character of the added-heaven), **of such sort also [are] the added, imposed, heavenly people – those made of and having the quality and character of the added, imposed, heaven** (or: the finished and perfected atmosphere, or the added sky).

49. **And correspondingly as we bear and wear the image** (likeness; form) **of the mounded, dusty person,** [p46 adds: doubtless] **we can and should** [B reads: will continue to] **also bear and wear the image** (likeness; form) **of the Added, Imposed, Heavenly One** (or: belonging to the One having the quality and character of the finished, perfected atmosphere; or: from the fully-heaven [sphere]; of the added-sky person).

50. **Now I am saying this, brothers** (= fellow members and believers), **that flesh and blood** (= humans in their estranged condition; = people of dust who have not been resurrected) **have no power and continue unable to inherit or receive and participate in an allotted portion of God's reign** (kingdom or sovereign action) **– neither is corruption and decay** (the perishable) **continuing on to inherit** (participate in the allotment of) **the Incorruption** (Imperishability).

51. **See** (Look and consider)! **I am progressively telling you a secret** ([the] mystery)! **We, indeed, shall not all continue falling asleep, yet we all will continue being changed**
      (or: On the one hand, not all of us will continue [dying], but on the other hand, we all will be progressively altered; or: We all shall not continue being put to repose, and so we all shall keep on being transformed; or: All of us shall not continue sleeping, but we all will continue being rearranged to be another or made to be otherwise),

52. **within the midst of an instant** (or: in union with what is uncut and indivisible), **in a rapid sweep, blink or glance of an eye, within, or in union with, the midst of the last or final trumpet. You see, the trumpet will continue sounding** (or: For He will proceed to be trumpeting; Indeed, it will keep on trumpeting), **and the dead people will one-after-another be awakened and raised up** [A, D and others: will keep on standing back up again; will continue being resurrected] **incorruptible** (imperishable). **And so we ourselves will keep on, one-after-another being changed** (or: progressively be made otherwise, altered and transformed).

53. **For it continues being necessary** (it is habitually binding) **for this perishable and corruptible to at some point plunge** (or: sink) **in and clothe itself with** (or: slip on; put on) **incorruption and imperishability, and for this mortal** (one that is subject to death) **to at some point plunge and sink in and clothe itself with** (or: put on; slip on as a garment) **immortality** (or: the absence of death; deathlessness; undyingness).

54. **Now whenever** [other MSS add: this corruptible would (or: may) put on incorruption and] **this mortal would** (or: may) **plunge, sink in and clothe itself with** (or: slip on; put on) **the Immortality, then will continue taking place** (or: proceed being birthed; successively come into existence) **the word** (the thought; the message; the saying) **which has been written,**

"**The Death was drunk down and swallowed into Victory** (or: overcoming)!" [Isa. 25:8]

55. "**Where, O Death, [is] your victory** (or: overcoming)**?**

Where, O Death, [is] your stinger (sharp point; sting; drover's goad; spur)**?**" [Hos. 13:14; TR reads "O Unseen (Hades)" in the second line, following the LXX and Heb.]

56. **Now the sharp point and stinger of** (or: the sting, thus, the injection from) **the Death [is] the Sin** (the mistake; the error; the failure), **and the power and ability of the Sin [is] the Law.**

57. **But grace and joyous favor [is] in God** (or: by and with God) **– the One presently and progressively** (or: in the process of) **giving the Victory** (or: continuously bestowing the overcoming) **to us, in us and for us through our Lord** (Owner; Master), **Jesus, [the] Christ!**

58. **Consequently, my beloved brothers, progressively come to be seated and settled folks – immovable and unswerving people – continuing to always be surrounded by more than enough** (or: superabounding) **within the midst of the Lord's work** (= [Yahweh's or Christ's] deed or act), **having seen and now knowing that your fatiguing labor** (or: toil) **does not exist without contents** (is not empty) **within and in union with [the] Lord** [= Christ or Yahweh].

CHAPTER 16

1. **Now concerning the collection [being gathered] into the midst of the set-apart folks** (or: for the holy ones; unto the saints), **just as I thoroughly arranged in** (or: for) **the communities of the called-out of [the province of] Galatia, you yourselves do** (perform; make) **the same:**

2. **on one day of the week** (or: on one of the sabbaths) **let each one of you have the habit of putting [something] beside himself** (= at home), **continually storing up that in which he may be repeatedly prospered** (or: has been led, along a good path; other MSS: can be well-guided along the way) **so that whenever I may come, no collections may continue to happen at that time.**

3. **So whenever I should come to be at your side, whomsoever you folks may approve – after having examined and tested them – through letters [of introduction and recommendation] I will send these folks to bear** (carry) **off your grace into** (the favor from you folks [in the form of a gift] unto) **Jerusalem.**

4. **And if it should be appropriate** (or: worthwhile) **for me also to be traveling on [there], they will continue journeying [there] together with me.**

5. **Now I shall come to you folks whenever I can** (or: may; = should happen to) **pass through Macedonia, for you see, I am repeatedly passing through Macedonia.**

6. **So perhaps I shall aim toward you folks to temporarily lodge, or even spend the winter, so that you folks can yourselves send me forward** (= give me funds and supplies for my journey), **wherever I may continue traveling.**

7. **For I am not presently intending** (purposing; willing) **to see you right now, while passing by, for I continue expecting to stay on with you folks some time, if the Lord** [= Yahweh or Christ] **should turn [circumstances] upon [this plan]** (or: may turn [the outcome] upon [us to decide]; or: should instruct, or permit).

8. **Yet I am now continuing to remain on within Ephesus, until the [feast; festival] of Pentecost,**

9. **for a door, great and energetic** (working within; activated and operative), **has been opened for me, and stands wide open to me: even many men constantly lying in opposition**

(or: for you see, a great and inwardly effectual entrance has been opened back up in me, and remains open again in me, and yet many folks [are] ones habitually lying in the opposite position).

10. **Now if Timothy can** (or: may; should) **come, be constantly seeing [to it] that he should come to be fearless toward you folks, for he continues actively working** (or: performing as a worker on/in) **the Lord's** [= Christ's or Yahweh's] **work** (deed; action), **as I also [do].**

11. **No one, then, should make nothing of him** (scorn, despise or treat him with contempt; slight him), **but should send him forward in peace from the joining** (= with shalom) **with**

funds and supplies, so that he can (may; should) **come toward me, for I continue receiving [benefit] from out of him, together with the brothers** (folks of the same womb; = believers).
12. **Now concerning Apollos, the brother, I called him to my side many [times] to give aid, comfort and encouragement** (or: = I strongly urged him), **to the end that he should go to you folks with the brothers, and yet there was not altogether a purpose so that he should go now** (or: but it was not wholly [his] will {or: it was undoubtedly not [His] intent} that he should go at the present time), **yet he will proceed in going** (or: coming) **whenever there may be a good situation** (or: he may have an opportunity).

13. **You folks be habitually awake and constantly watching** (= be alert and with your wits about you)! **Continue standing fast in union with the Trust, and within the midst of The Faithfulness** (or: Constantly stand firm, centered in loyal confidence)! **Progressively come to Manhood** [= Adulthood] (or: = Be constantly courageous)! **Continue being strengthened.**
14. **Let this continuously occur: all of you folks [be] in union with Love** (Let it be repeatedly birthed: all centered in your unrestricted, self-giving urge toward reunion, with accepting solidarity; or: Let all from you folks happen, and come to be, in Love that participates in the other person as standing on the same ultimate ground, in spite of the distorted state of the other – Tillich)!
       [*cf* chapter 13, above]
15. **Now I continue calling you to my side to help and encourage you** (or: So I am now performing as a paraclete), **brothers** (= my fellow believers; folks from the same Womb) – **you have seen and known the household of Stephanas and Fortunatus, that it is [the] firstfruit of Achaia, and they orderly arranged themselves into attending service for and among the set-apart folks** (holy ones; saints; sacred people) –
16. **so that you folks can also be progressively aligned with humility to** (or: habitually arranged under to give support for and among, and to be attached to) **such folks** (persons of that kind), **and for everyone habitually working together** (or: with all those constantly co-operating) **and exhaustively laboring** (toiling).
17. **Now I continue rejoicing at the presence of Stephanas and Fortunatus and Achaicus, because these men fill up the deficiency belonging to you** (the result of your shortcoming; the effect of your being behind and in the rear; [other MSS: our deficiency]),
18. **for they rest, refresh and soothe my spirit – as well as yours. Therefore, come to progressively know and recognize such folks completely, by personal intimacy and continued experience with them.**
19. **The called-out folks** (or: called-out communities) **of the [province of] Asia habitually greet and embrace you folks. Aquila and Prisca** [other MSS: Priscilla] **continue giving you many embraces and much greeting, within [the] Lord** [= Yahweh or Christ], **together with the called-out assembly down in their house.**
20. **All the brothers** (folks of the same Womb) **constantly greet and embrace you folks! Continue to greet and embrace one another with a set-apart** (holy; saintly; sacred) **expression of affection** (or: kiss).
21. **This greeting to embrace you [is] in** (or: by; with) **my own hand – Paul's.**
22. **If anyone continues having no fondness or affection for the Lord, let him constantly be a person placed up [in prayer to be consecrated before the Lord] – [you see,] our Lord is present** (has come).
23. **The joyous favor and grace of the Lord Jesus, [the] Christ** (or: from [the] Anointed Master, Jesus,) **[continues] with you folks!**
24. **My love** (unambiguous acceptance and drive toward union) **[is] with all of you folks, centered in, and in union with, Christ Jesus. It is so** (Amen; Count on it)!

    [written circa A.D. 55 – Based on the critical analysis of John A.T. Robinson]

SECOND CORINTHIANS

1. **Paul, one sent off as a representative from Jesus Christ** (or: an emissary of Jesus [the Messiah]; an envoy belonging to [the] Anointed Jesus) **through the effect of God's will and purpose, and Timothy, the brother** (Womb-mate). **To God's called-out, covenant community** (or: the congregation of God) **– the one being** (existing) **within the midst of Corinth – together with all those set apart** (the holy ones; the saints or sacred people) **being** (existing) **within [the] whole [region of] Achaia:**
2. **Grace** (The act producing happiness, which is granted as a favor) **and peace from the Joining** (or: harmony; [= shalom]) [are] **with, in, and for you folks, from God, our Father and Lord, Jesus Christ** (or: from our Father, God, and Owner, Jesus, [the] Anointed [= Messiah]).

3. **The God and Father of our Master, Jesus Christ** (or: which is our Lord and Owner, Jesus [the] Anointed One [= Messiah]) **[is] One full of words of ease and thoughts of wellness** (or: [is] well-spoken of and blessed)**: the Father of the compassions and sympathetic acts of pity, and God of every entreaty and of every calling to one's [or: His] side for aid, relief, comfort, consolation and encouragement** (or: a God who is all the functioning of a Paraclete),
4. **the One continuously calling us to receive aid, relief, comfort, consolation and encouragement at [His] side** (or: the One habitually functioning as our Paraclete) **upon [the occurrence of] all our squeezing pressure** (or: our every affliction, tribulation and oppression), **[then] to progressively enable** (to constantly give power to) **us into the [sphere or situation] to keep on performing as paracletes in repeatedly giving aid, relief, comfort, consolation and encouragement for those within the midst of every** (or: all) **pressure** (oppression; squeezing, affliction and tribulation) **– [and this] through means of the [same] assistance with which we, ourselves, are being constantly called alongside by God to receive as aid, relief, comfort, consolation and encouragement [from Him]** (or: from which we, ourselves, are habitually being given the services of the Paraclete by God) **–**
5. **because correspondingly as the effects and results of** (or: from) **the Christ's experiences and sufferings are progressively superabounding into** (or: encompassing in full measure unto) **us, in the same way, through the Christ** (or: the Anointed One; [= the Messiah]; or: the Anointing), **our calling [folks] to our side to give [them] help, relief, comfort and encouragement is also progressively superabounding so as to surround us in full quantity** (or: the work of the Paraclete constantly environs in abundance from us, by the Anointing)**!**

6. **Now whether we are being continually squeezed and compressed, or oppressed in tribulation, over and on behalf of your assistance** (or: a calling to [His] side for relief, aid and comfort) **and deliverance** (salvation, rescue, health, wholeness and restoration), **or whether we are repeatedly being given relief, intimate assistance, comfort and encouragement over and because of your assistance and comfort – referring to [that aid and encouragement] which is continuously performing inward work and operation within the midst of [that] persistent remaining under in endurance of the very effects of experiences and results of sufferings which we, ourselves, also are habitually experiencing, or suffering –**
7. **either way, our expectation** (or: expectant hope) **[stands] on good footing** (or: [is] stable, unwavering, with feet firmly planted; or: [stands] guaranteed as valid; [remains] a confirmation of a certification of the purchase) **over and with regard to you folks, having seen and continuing to know that just as you are – and continue to be – people of common existence** (partners, participants and sharers of Being) **from the effects of experiences and the results of sufferings, in the same way [are you] of the relief, aid and encouraging comfort, as well.**

8. **For we do not continue intending** (or: wanting; purposing) **for you folks to continue being ignorant** (unaware or without intimate knowledge), **brothers** (folks from the same Womb), **over** [other MSS: concerning] **our squeezing pressure** (tribulation; affliction; oppression) **– referring**

to [that] which happened [other MSS add: to us] in [the province of] Asia – that corresponding to an act of overshooting or throwing beyond the target (= something extreme and excessive) over and above [our] power and ability, we were weighted down (burdened [with difficulty]) so as to be without an exit (with no way out) for us, even to continue living!

9. Further yet, we ourselves had held and continued having, within ourselves, the result and effect from a decision of the Death (or: from a judgment which meant death; or: the considered decision and insightful response in regard to death) – to the end that we may not exist being ones having put trust and confidence upon ourselves, but to the contrary, upon the God Who is continually (habitually; periodically; repeatedly; or: presently) awakening and raising up the dead people!

10. He Who snatched (dragged so as to rescue) us from out of the midst of the very prime (or: peak) of Death (or: out of a death of such proportions) will also repeatedly rescue and drag us to Himself – into Whom we have placed our hope and expectation so as to yet rely that He also will Himself continue still dragging us further toward Himself.

11. Your habitually cooperating and working together in undergirding support over us (= on behalf of us, or, concerning our situation), even in the need (or: and by the [or: your] petition regarding [our] need), [gives the result] that forth from out of [other MSS: in] many faces (= people; or: = outward appearances) [and] through (or: by means of) many folks, the effect and result of grace and favor can (or: may; would) be sent (or: given) unto us in the goodness, ease and well-being of grace (or: from favor) over our [situation] (or: may be given in gratitude on our [other MSS: your] behalf).

12. For you see, our boasting (or: expression of a reason for being proud) is this – [and it is] the witness and testimony of our conscience (integrated inner knowing): that within the midst of the System (dominating world of religion, culture, economy, and government; or: the aggregate of humanity), and especially (or: more exceedingly) in our relationship with you folks, we were turned back and caused to live our lives and conduct ourselves centered within, and in union with, God's singleness (single, uncompounded quality having no folds; [other MSS: quality of being set apart]) and clearness from being judged (discerned and evaluated) in sunlight (or: in a sincere and clear integrity from, and which, is God) – and this not within fleshly wisdom or cleverness, but to the contrary, centered within the midst of and in union with God's grace (or: the favor from, and which is, God).

13. So then, we are not now writing other things to you, but rather either (or: other than) what you continue reading and recognizing, or even what you folks continue progressing to full, intimate knowledge and insight about (or: what you presently recognize and acknowledge as added knowledge and complete *gnosis*). Yet I continue expecting and hoping that unto the purposed and destined goal (until maturity and the finished product) you will continue to additionally, accurately and intimately realize and know by experience,

14. just as you recognized with added personal knowledge about us, partly, that we have as much cause to be proud of you, exactly as you also [have] of us – resident within and in union with this Day which pertains to, is from, and is, our Lord (Master; Owner), Jesus.

15. So, with (or: in; by) this persuaded confidence, I had previously continued intending (planning and purposing) to come to you folks, so that you folks could have (or: may hold) a second grace (influence and boon of joyous favor, kindness and goodwill; [other MSS: {occasion for} joy]),

16. and then to pass on through you [i.e., through your city] into Macedonia, and to come back again to you from Macedonia, and [then] to be sent forward with funds and supplies (perhaps: to be accompanied or escorted on part of the journey) by you folks into [other MSS: from you unto] the Judean [area].

17. Therefore, continuing in determining, planning and intending this, surely I do not consequently engage in joking (employ lightness; or: = resort to fickleness or irresponsibility), do I? Or the things which I habitually plan and purpose, am I normally planning down from [the] flesh (or: = in accord with estranged human nature; or: = on the level oriented to the System or the old covenant), so that it may be with me, "Yes, yes," and "No, no!"?

18. **Now God [is] full of faith and reliable** (loyal; faithful; trustworthy)! **[With] that, our message** (or: Because the *Logos*, or Word, from us) **toward you folks is not** [other MSS: did not come to be] **"Yes," and then** [or, at the same time] **"No,"** [*cf* 1 Cor. 1:9; 10:13b]
19. **for the Son of God, Jesus Christ** [= Jesus the Messiah] **– the One within the midst of, among, and in union with you folks – being heralded and publicly proclaimed through us, [i.e.,] through Silvanus** [this may = Silas], **Timothy and me, did not come to be** (or: was not birthed) **"Yes," and yet, "No," but to the contrary, [the divine] "Yes" has been birthed and remains in existence within Him** (or: in union with Him, "Yes" has happened and continues being; or: within the midst of Him, [the] "Yes" has come into being and remains)!
20. **So you see, as many as [be] God's promises, [they are] the "Yes," within and in union with Him. Wherefore also, through Him [is] The Amen** (or: the affirmation; the "Count on it!"; the "It is so") **in** (or: by; with; or: to) **God, with a view to** (or: face to face with) **glory** (an assumed appearance; a good opinion or reputation, and a manifestation inciting praise) **– through us.**
21. **Now God [is] the One repeatedly placing us on good, firm footing** (constantly stabilizing and establishing us; or: confirming, guaranteeing and validating us as possessed by a purchase) **and completely** (or: instantly, in one point in time) **anointing us, together with you folks, into Christ.** [*cf* 5:5, below]   [*cf* Rev. 7:3ff; 13:16]
22. **He [is] also the One completely** (or: instantly, in one point in time) **sealing us** (stamping us with an identity-mark; imprinting us for ownership; or: validating/guaranteeing our genuineness;*), **even** (or: and; or: and then) **completely** (instantly, in one point in time) **giving the advance transaction of the agreement** (or: the pledge and down payment guaranteeing full payment for purchase; or: a dowry) **of the Spirit** (or: which is the Spirit; or: from the Breath-effect; or: which belongs and pertains to the spirit; which pertains to the Attitude) **within the midst of our hearts.**

CHAPTER 2

23. **Now I, myself, continue to call upon God [to be] a witness** (or: [as] evidence) **upon my own soul** (mind, will, emotions; inner life; self; or: = I stake my life on it!), **that in my continuing in holding back and sparing you folks, I no longer came** (or: I did not yet go) **into Corinth.**
24. **Not that we are constantly acting like your owners or and exercising lordship with regard to the Faithfulness** (or: performing like masters over your loyalty, faith and trust), **but to the contrary, we exist being** (or: we are) **fellow workers regarding and pertaining to your joy, for you folks have taken a stand and now stand firm by the Faithfulness** (or: in and for the Trust; or: with this faith and confident loyalty)!

1. **So I decided this in** (or: for; by) **myself: not to come** (or: go) **to you folks again in anxiety** (or: grief; sorrow; sadness; = to make another painful visit).
2. **For since** (or: if) **I, myself, continually cause you anxiety** (sadness; sorrow; grief; pain), **who** (or: which one) **[is] the person constantly putting me in a good frame of mind** (habitually cheering me and putting my mind at ease), **if not** (or: except) **the one being constantly made sorrowful, sad, upset, anxious and caused painful grief by me?**
3. **And so I write** (or: wrote) **this very thing, so that in coming I may** (or: should; would) **not have anxiety, sadness or grief from those concerning whom it was being necessary and binding for me to unceasingly rejoice, having been persuaded and now placing trust and confidence upon you all, because my joy has its source in all of you folks** (or: my joy exists being what pertains to all of your [situations]).
4. **You see, I write** (or: wrote) **to you from out of the midst of much pressure** (squeezing; affliction; tribulation; oppression) **and compression** (or: confinement) **of heart – through many tears – not so that you may be made anxious or sad, but rather to the end that you can** (or: may; should; would) **experience intimate knowledge and personal insight of the love** (the participating, self-giving, unrestricted, accepting drive toward reunion) **which I progressively possess and superabundantly hold [being directed] into the midst of you folks.**

5. **Now if anyone has been the cause of anxiety, pain, grief, distress, sorrow or sadness, he has not upset, caused grief or distressed me, but rather, to an extent, all of you – so**

then, I should not continue to be adding weight upon [you folks] (or: but to the contrary, in part – not that I would now belabor [the point] – [it has been done to] you all).

6. **This assessment** (or: added evaluation) – **the one [held; given] by the majority – [should be] sufficient** (or: enough) **for** (or: with; to) **such a person,**

7. **so that in its place – and to a greater degree – you folks are to extend favor and grace, and then to perform as paracletes** (call him alongside giving aid, relief, encouragement, and comfort/consolation), **lest somehow such a person may be swallowed up by more excessive anxiety** (or: drunk down in, and to, more abundant sorrow, grief, pain, distress and sadness).

8. **Therefore, I continue to call you folks alongside** (or: I am habitually being a paraclete, encouraging and entreating you) **to affirm** (make valid; ratify; authoritatively confirm) **love unto him** (unrestricted acceptance and urges toward reunion, into the midst of him),

9. **for I write, also, into this [purpose], to the end that I can personally** (intimately and experientially) **come to know the proof** (evidence) **from your testing – whether you folks continue being those who submissively listen and pay attention unto all people** (or: hear and obey as you proceed into all situations; or: humbly pay attention, with a view to all [that has been said]).

10. **Now to whom you repeatedly extend grace or deal favorably [concerning] anything** (or: Now for whom you constantly deal graciously or give forgiveness [in] anything), **I also [do], for you see, in whatever I myself have also been extended grace, treated graciously or forgiven – since I have been extended grace, favor or forgiveness for something** (or, as a middle: for what I myself have extended grace – if I have extended grace for anything) – **[it is] on account of and for the sake of you folks, within the presence of Christ** (or: in union with the face of the Anointing; = in sync with what the anointing looks like),

11. **to the end that we may** (or: can; would) **not at some point be held or possessed in more things or situations by the adversary** (or: be made, under "*satan*," to claim to have more than other folks; or: be overreached by [our] opponent, so as to desire personal advantage), **for we do not continue being without intimate and experiential knowledge of the effects from its directing peoples' perceptions, concepts and understanding** (or: we are not still ignorant, unaware or without *gnosis* about the results from directing one's mind from it).

12. **Now on coming** (or: going) **into Troas – [continuing] on into the midst of Christ's good news** (the message of goodness, ease and well-being, which is the Anointing), **there also having been opened up, and still standing open, a door to and for me, within [the] Lord** [= Christ or Yahweh] (or: by and with me, in union with [the] Master, centered in [our] Owner) –

13. **I had not had a release** (or: a relaxing; a letting flow; a relief) **in** (or: by; to; for; with) **my spirit** (or: inner breath-effect; attitude) **regarding my continuing not to find Titus, my brother, but instead, on sending off arrangements for myself among them and bidding them farewell, I went off into Macedonia.**

14. **Now grace and favor [are] in, with and by God – in, by and with the One constantly celebrating us with a victory procession** (or: progressively exhibiting us in a triumphal procession) **at all times, within and in union with the Christ, and progressively** (or: habitually) **setting in clear light** (manifesting) **the fragrance** (aroma; odor; perfume) **of His intimate knowledge** (or: of the experience of intimacy and insight which has its source in knowing Him; or: the knowledge and *gnosis* from, and which, is Him) **through us in every place,**

15. **because within** (or: by) **God, we continuously exist being Christ's sweet fragrance** (or: because, with God, we are an aroma of well-being from an Anointing; or: because for God we continue being an odor of ease, and a smell of goodness, which is Christ) **within and among those being progressively delivered** (habitually rescued; continuously made whole and restored; repeatedly saved; constantly kept safe) **– yet also within and among those being progressively loosed-away** (or: habitually destroying themselves; or: repeatedly being lost):

16. **to** (in; for; with) **these [latter ones], a stench from out of Death, [leading] into death** (or: from the midst of [one] death on into [another, or, more] death); **yet to** (in; for; with) **those [former ones] a fragrance from out of Life, [leading] into life** (or: from out of the midst of [one] Life] on into [another, or, more] life). **So who [is] adequate, sufficient or qualified [in facing or approaching] toward these matters?**

17. **You see, we are not – as the majority [are] – ones performing as hucksters in shameful traffic for unworthy gain, constantly peddling and marketing God's message** (God's thought and idea; the Word of God; the *Logos* from God), **but to the contrary, we are constantly and habitually speaking as from out of the midst of that which is decided about when viewing in clear sunlight – and further, as from out of the midst of God; down within, in union with, and in the place of, God – within Christ!** (or: but in contrast, as out of clear integrity, we are progressively speaking in an Anointing – as [being] forth from God [and] in God's presence!)

CHAPTER 3

1. **Are we beginning again to continue commending ourselves** (giving ourselves a standing together with [you folks]) **as if we, like some, now need letters of recommendation to you, or from you?**
2. **You yourselves are and continue being our letter – being one having been written** (inscribed; imprinted; engraved) **within your hearts** [other MSS: our hearts]; **one progressively being experientially known and continuously read** (or: periodically recognized and experienced again) **by all people** (human beings) –
3. **because you are and continue being those continuously set in clear light and progressively manifested: Christ's letter** (a letter whose source is Christ, and which is Christ), **being one dispensed in attending service by us, being one having been written** (inscribed; imprinted; engraved), **not in black** (= not with ink), **but rather, by** (or: in; with) **God's Spirit: One continuously living** (or: in a Breath-effect which has its origin in God, Who is constantly living); **not in stone tablets** (or: on tablets composed of stone), **but rather within tablets which are hearts made of flesh** (or: on tablets in hearts composed of flesh). [*cf* Rom. 8:26-27]

4. **Now through the Christ we continuously possess** (or: So, by means of the Anointing we progressively have and hold) **this sort of persuaded trust and faith-based confidence [directed and leading] toward God** (or: face to face with God)
5. **– not that we are competent** (adequately enough; sufficiently qualified) **from ourselves to logically evaluate or count anything as it were forth from out of ourselves – but to the contrary, our competency** (adequacy; sufficiency; qualification) **[is] forth from out of the midst of** (having its source in) **God,**
6. **Who also adequately qualifies us** (or: made us fit, competent and sufficient) **[to be] attending servants and dispensers of an arrangement that is new in quality** (or: pertaining to a new kind of covenant that has a different, innovative character and is fresh and effective) **– not of [the] letter** (or: not from Scripture, or pertaining to the result of that which is written down; not having its source in Scripture or the effect of a written text), **but in contrast, of a Breath-effect** (or: pertaining to the result of [the] Spirit; having its source in and being the effect of spirit and attitude), **for the effect of letter habitually kills** (or: Scripture, the result of writing something into a text, repeatedly puts away in death), **yet the Spirit** (or: the spirit; the Breath-effect; the Attitude) **continuously produces Life** (or: repeatedly makes alive; progressively forms life; habitually creates Life)! [*cf* Rom. 8:2, 6]

7. **Now since** (or: if) **the attending service of the Death** (or: the dispensing of provision from death; the serving of provisions and support, which is the Death) **– being one that has been formed by a beaten impression of types and the outlines of patterns that exists as engravings within letters and the effects of written texts** (Scriptures) **chiseled on stones – was birthed and came into existence within glory** (a manifestation eliciting praise; reputation; in an assumed appearance), **so that the sons of Israel came to be continuously unable** (or: habitually having no power) **to intently gaze into the face of Moses, because of the glory and manifestation which came from his face – which [glory] was being progressively unemployed so as to be brought down to having no work, to be ineffective and nullified –**
8. **how shall not rather the attending service and dispensing of the provision of the Spirit** (or: which has its source in the Breath-effect; marked by, pertaining to and being the effect of the spirit and attitude) **continue being within glory** (existing in the midst of a manifestation eliciting praise; centered on and in union with a good reputation and with an assumed appearance)**?**

9. **For since** (or: if) **the attending service and dispensing of the corresponding evaluations and commensurate decisions which follow the pattern** (or: separations for condemnation; judgments which are down-decisions against folks) **[had] glory, to a much greater degree does the attending service and the dispensing of the eschatological deliverance into fairness and equity in rightwised relationships** (or: righteousness from covenantal inclusion: that which corresponds to the Way pointed out, and which turns us in the right direction) **progressively surround and continuously exceed in glory** (or: habitually overflow with a manifestation which calls forth praise and brings a good reputation for and by its assumed appearance)!

> [comment: it would seem that Paul is casting the Law as a dispenser of condemnation, and is contrasting that to the Good News – casting this latter as a dispenser of "righteousness" and a servant for folks being turned in the right direction]

10. **In fact, even that which had been made glorious, [by comparison] has not been glorified so as to now be glorious – in this respect: on account of the transcending glory which is constantly surpassing [that one], and is progressively over-casting [us].**

11. **You see, since that which was being progressively unemployed and brought down to doing no work – even being made ineffective and nullified – [came] through glory, to a much greater extent is the continuously remaining one** (the dwelling, abiding and enduring one) **[existing] within the midst of glory, and in union with [greater] imagination** (repute).

12. **Therefore, in progressively possessing** (while continuously having and holding) **an expectation** (or: expectant hope) **such as this, we habitually use much freedom of speech and bold lack of reserve** (or: are constantly telling it all with absolute unreservedness, based upon our citizenship), **unlike Moses.**

13. **He kept on putting a head-covering (veil) upon his face so that the sons of Israel were not to gaze intently into the purposed and destined goal** (the end; the result; the termination; the fruition) **of that which was being progressively unemployed and brought down to doing no work and being made ineffective, nullified and abolished.** [Ex. 34:29; 33-35]

14. **But further, the results of their perceptions, concepts and understanding** (effects of directing the mind and thought processes) **were petrified** (were hardened into a stony concretion and made callous [note: a medical term for being covered with thick skin]), **for until this very day the same head-covering (veil) continues remaining** (dwelling; abiding) **upon the reading of the old covenant** (arrangement; thorough placement) **– it** [i.e., the reading of the old, or the old covenant itself] **continues not being uncovered or unveiled – because it** [i.e., the old covenant and arrangement] **continues being progressively and fully unemployed and brought down to doing no work and being made useless, ineffective and nullified within Christ** (or: [the old arrangement and covenant] is abolished in union with an Anointing, and in the midst of Christ).

15. **Still furthermore, until today, whenever Moses should be habitually read** [e.g., in the synagogue], **a head-covering (veil) continues lying upon their heart** (= the innermost being of the group).

16. **Yet whenever the time should be reached when it** [= the heart] **can** (or: would; may; should; or: shall at some point) **twist and turn upon, so as to face toward, [the] Lord** [= Christ], **"the head-covering (veil) is progressively taken from around [it]."**

> [note: an allusion to Ex. 34:34, LXX, where Moses would enter in to speak with Yahweh; the same act was performed by the husband, on the bride, after the wedding ceremony]

17. **Now the Lord** [= Christ or Yahweh] **continuously exists being the Spirit** (or: Yet the Breath-effect is the LORD), **so where [the] Lord's Breath-effect** (Spirit; Attitude) **[blows, there is] freedom** (or: and so in the place in which the Breath-effect – the Spirit – which is [the] Lord [= Christ or Yahweh] [blows; exists], liberty [comes; arises]).

18. **But we all, ourselves – having a face that has been uncovered and remains unveiled** [note: as with Moses, before the Lord, Ex. 34:34] **– being folks who by a mirror are continuously observing, as ourselves, the Lord's glory** (or: being those who progressively reflect – from ourselves as by a mirror – the assumed appearance and repute of, and from, [our] Owner), **are presently being continuously and progressively transformed into the very same image and form, from glory unto glory – in accord with and exactly as – from [the]**

Lord's Breath-effect (or: from [the] Spirit and Attitude of, and which is, [the] Lord).
>[comment: considering the context of this chapter, this may refer to the transformation from glory of Moses, into the glory of Christ; or, it may be speaking of a from-time-to-time transfiguration from the glory of humanity into the "**glory, imagination and assumed appearance**" of the Anointing, on an individual and/or corporate basis; *cf* Mat. 17:1-8]

CHAPTER 4

1. **Because of this – while continuously possessing** (having and holding) **this attending service and dispensing of provision – correspondingly as we were mercied** (shown mercy), **we do not habitually behave with a bad attitude, or perform in a worthless manner, or act from out of a mood or motive that is poor in quality, or, become discouraged.**
2. **To the contrary, we speak-away from ourselves** (or: spurn; renounced; disowned) **the hidden things pertaining to the shame** (or: whose source is [our] shame; that result in dishonorable conduct or bring disgrace), **not habitually walking around** (= living our lives) **in craftiness or guile** (or: in union with a capability for every work; within readiness to do anything), **neither constantly distorting, diluting or adulterating God's message** (the thought from God; Word of, *Logos* which is, God), **but rather, in a manifestation of the Truth and by a setting of the Reality in clear Light, we are progressively placing ourselves together in addressing every conscience of mankind** (or: commending ourselves toward every human awareness), **in God's sight and presence** (or: before, or, in front of, God; in the midst of a viewing from God).

3. **Now if the good news coming from us** (or: our message of goodness, ease and well-being) **continues being covered from having been veiled with a head-covering, it continues being thus covered in union with, within the midst of and centered in those on their way to ruin** (being progressively lost; repeatedly loosing-away, undoing and thus, destroying themselves),
4. **within and among which folks the God of this age** (or: the God [ruling] this indefinite time-period; the God Who is in relationship with this eon) **blinds** (or: deprived of the ability to see) **the effects of the perceptions, concepts and understanding** (or: the results of directing the mind to something) **of those without faith** (of the un-trusting ones; of the unbelieving and disloyal), **[leading them] into the [situation that] the shining forth of light and the illumination of** (or: the beaming forth of enlightenment from) **the good news of the glory of the Christ** (or: of the message of goodness, ease and well-being from the assumed appearance which is the Anointed One; from the glad tidings pertaining to the manifestation which calls forth praise of the [Messiah]) **– Who continuously exists being God's image** (a resemblance and likeness of [Concordant Text adds: the unseen; the invisible] God) **– would not shine forth as the dawn to irradiate them.** [*cf* Mat. 13:11-15; Jn. 12:40; Rom. 11:7-12, 25]
5. **For you see, we are not constantly preaching** (proclaiming; heralding) **ourselves, but rather, Christ Jesus [as] Lord** (or: [the] Anointed Jesus, [the] Lord, Master and Owner; or: = [the] Lord Jesus [as the] Messiah), **yet ourselves [as] your slaves, because of Jesus,**
6. **because the God suddenly saying** (or: the God Who once was saying), **"Light will shine forth** (give light as from a torch; gleam) **from out of the midst of darkness** (dimness and shadiness; gloom and the absence of daylight)," **[is] the One who shines forth within the midst of our hearts, with a view to illumination of the intimate and experiential knowledge of God's glory – in a face of Christ**
>(or: [is] He Who gives light in union with our hearts, [while] facing toward an effulgence and a shining forth which is an intimate knowing of the praise-inducing manifestation and assumed appearance whose source and origin is God, and which is God, [while] in union with face to face presence of Christ [other MSS: Jesus Christ]).
7. **Now we presently and continuously hold** (have and possess) **this treasure within containers** (jars; pots; vessels; equipment) **made of baked clay** [e.g., pottery; bone ware] **so that the transcendence of the power may habitually originate its existence in God – and not from out of us** (or: the over-cast of ability can be that which is God – and not of us; or: the overwhelming which comes from the Power would exist with the character and quality of God – and not from what characterizes us)**!**

8. **We are people being constantly pressed [as grapes] on every [side]** (or: squeezed and constricted within the midst of everything; given affliction, oppression and tribulation by everyone), **but yet not constantly confined by a narrow space or a tight place so as to be restricted or hemmed in** (or: = not cramped beyond movement); **we are those being repeatedly made to be without resources, a place to walk or a means for conveyance** (or, as a middle: we are habitually at a loss about things, in doubt and perplexed), **but yet not continuously caused to be living utterly without resources or absolutely with no way out or place to walk or means for conveyance** (or, middle voice: but still, we are not continually living at a total loss, being in complete doubt, being greatly perplexed or in utmost despair);

9. **we are folks being constantly pursued and persecuted, but yet not habitually left in the lurch, being forsaken down within some situation; we are those being repeatedly thrown down** (or: rejected) **but yet not continuously caused to fall apart** (be loosed-away into ruin; be undone so as to be destroyed) – [*cf* Rom. 8:18]   [*cf* Gen. 50:25; Ex. 13:19]

10. **at all times continuously carrying around** (or: bearing about) **among** (or: centered in) **the [corporate] body* Jesus' being put to death** (or: within [our] body the deadening, deadness and state of death, which comes from Jesus; or: within the midst of the body the dying associated with Jesus; or: the dying which is Jesus, in union with the body), **to the end that the Life, also, of Jesus** (or: so that also the life which comes from and is Jesus; or: so that Jesus' Life) **can** (or: could; may; would) **be set in clear light and manifested, within our body** (or: in the midst of the body, which is us)!

11. **For we, ourselves – the continuously living ones – are ever being repeatedly handed over and committed into death** (or: = continuously delivered into life-threatening experiences) – **because of Jesus – to the end that the Life, also, of Jesus** (or: so that also the life which comes from and is Jesus; or: so that Jesus' life) **can** (may; could; would) **be set in clear light and manifested – within our mortal flesh!**   [*cf* Phil. 2:17]

12. **So then** (or: Consequently), **the Death is repeatedly and progressively operating and inwardly working within us*, yet that Life [is constantly operative] within you folks.**

13. **Now continuously possessing** (having and holding) **that faith's very Breath-effect and the same Spirit of fidelity** (or: the Spirit which itself is the Trust; or: the spirit and attitude which itself comes from the Faithfulness [of Christ]), **corresponding to that which has been written,**

> **"I trust and am faithful, therefore I speak** (or: I believed and was loyal, [and] for this reason I spoke)," [Ps. 116:10]

we ourselves, also, are constantly faithful and loyal, habitually trusting and progressively believing; therefore we also keep on speaking,   [*cf* Rom. 8:11; Phi. 3:10-11]

14. **having seen, and now knowing, that the One at one point arousing and raising Jesus** [other MSS: the Lord Jesus] **will also continue arousing and raising us up together with** [other MSS: through] **Jesus and will continue making us stand alongside** (placing us beside; positioning us parallel, [for disposal]; setting us by, [for support]), **together with you folks,**

15. **for you see, all things [are]** (the whole – everything – [is]) **because of you folks, to the end that the grace and favor – increasing and becoming more than enough through the greater part** (the majority) **of the people – can** (should; would) **cause the benefits of grace** (or: the goodness, ease and wellbeing from grace; or: this attitude of gratitude; or: the expression of thanksgiving) **to be surrounding in superabundance, unto God's glory** (or: [proceeding] into the praise-inducing manifestation of, and assumed appearance from, God)!

16. **For this reason we do not habitually behave with a bad attitude, or perform in a worthless manner, or act from out of a mood that is poor in quality, or become discouraged. But to the contrary, even if** (or: since also) **our outside person** (or: outer humanity; = body of flesh) **is being progressively wasted away** (is constantly being decayed and brought to ruin and corruption), **certainly our inside [person]** (= inner humanity; Eph. 2:15) **is day by day** (or: from day to day; on a daily basis) **being progressively made new again** (or: renewed) **in kind and quality so as to have a different character that is fresh and effective.**

17. **So you see, the momentary light [aspect or character]** (or: lightness) **of the pressure and squeezing** (the affliction, oppression and tribulation) **is progressively working down in us a corresponding** (commensurate) **and consecutively transcending eonian weight of glory**

> (or: is repeatedly producing for us a heavy burden of glory, down from one over-casting

on into another over-cast, each of which pertains to the Age; or: is now accomplishing with us an according, age-lasting weight of a good reputation – [each] a transcending one [leading] into [another] transcending one; or: is continuously effecting in us – on the level of "surpassing leading into surpassing" – a weight which has the quality of the realm of [Messiah's] Age, and which belongs to a praise-inducing, assumed manifestation),

18. **while we are not constantly fixing our gaze on or carefully noting the things that are being constantly seen or repeatedly observed, but rather, [we are continuously looking at] those things not being constantly seen or repeatedly observed, because the things being constantly seen and observed [are] for a season** (temporary; set toward a certain situation; transient), **but those things not being habitually seen or observed pertain to and have their source in the Age** ([are] eonian; [continue] age-lasting). [cf 5:7, below; Eph. 2:7; 3:9-11, 21]

CHAPTER 5

1. **You see, we have seen, perceived and know that if our House – from the Tabernacle which was pitched on the Land – would at some point be dismantled** (or: that whenever our house, which is this tent upon the earth, should be loosed down), **we constantly have** (continuously hold; presently possess) **a dwelling structure or place** (a building for an abode; or: **a household**; = a family or a possession) **forth from out of the midst of God: an eonian act of building a roofed house** (or: a covered building for dwelling having qualities and character which pertain to the Age [of the Messiah]; a structure of edification for, and pertaining to, the ages) – **not made by hands** [cf Heb. 9:1-8, 11; Dan. 2:34, 45; Eph. 2:11; Col. 2:11] – **resident within the atmospheres** (or: in union with the heavens). [cf 6:16, below; 1 Tim. 3:15; Heb. 9:24]

2. **It follows that also, in union with** (or: centered in) **this, we are continuously groaning, utterly longing and constantly yearning to fully enter within and to completely clothe upon ourselves our dwelling-house** (habitation) – **the one [made] out of heaven** (or: the one from, or of, atmosphere; the [inhabited or settled place] from the midst of [the] sky)

3. **since, in fact, also being folks at some point entering within and clothing ourselves** (or: being dressed, also), **we shall not continue** (or: proceed) **being found naked.** [cf Ps. 84:1-4]

4. **For we also, being** (continually existing) **within the tent, are continuously groaning, being the ones constantly weighed down** (burdened). **Upon which [situation] we are not wanting to go out from** (to unclothe, strip or undress ourselves) **but rather to fully enter within and to add clothing upon ourselves, to the end that the mortal** (or: this mortal thing) **may be drunk down and swallowed under** (or: by) **The Life.** [cf Isa. 25:6-9; 1 Cor. 15:53-54; Rom. 13:14]

5. **Now the One working this down, commensurately producing and correspondingly fashioning US into this very thing** (situation and condition) **[is] God, the One giving to us the pledge and guarantee** (earnest deposit; security; first installment) **which is the Breath-effect** (or: of the Spirit; from the Attitude). [cf 1:22; 4:10ff, above; Eph. 1:13-14; Isa. 28:14-29; Ex. 15:16]

6. **Being, then, at all times and always courageous and of cheerful confidence, and having seen, perceived, and thus knowing, that continuously staying at home** (dwelling within the district of our own people), **in union with and centered in that body we are continually exiles, away from the Lord's home** (we are out of the Lord's district) [Heb. 11:14; 12:22; 1 Thes. 4:17]

7. **– for we are habitually walking about** (= living our lives) **through faithfulness and trust** (or: faith; [His] loyalty) **not through perception of the appearance of external form –** [4:18]

8. **yet we are constantly courageous and of cheerful confidence, even continuously delighting and thinking it good to a greater extent** (with exceeding preference) **to be away from home** (to be out of the district of our normal home and people), **forth from out of that body, and to be staying at home** (to be dwelling in the district of our new home and people) **[with orientation] toward, and face to face with, the Lord** [= Christ or Yahweh; cf Rev. 22:4].

9. **Therefore we are constantly loving the value** (or: ambitious for the honor), **also – whether staying at home** (dwelling within our district) **or being away from home and people** (out of our district) **– to constantly be folks [who are] well-pleasing to Him** (who give satisfaction for Him),

10. **for it continues** (or: is repeatedly) **necessary for us – the all-people** (the whole of humanity) **– to be manifested in front of Christ's elevated place** (a step, platform, stage, or place ascended by steps to speak in public assembly in the center of a city; or: = an official bench

of a judge or public official), **to the end that each one may himself take into kindly keeping, for care and provision** (= be responsible for), **the things [done] through** (or: by means of; or: [during our passing] through the midst of) **the Body – [oriented] toward, and facing, what things he practices** (or: she accomplishes), **whether good or bad, whether serviceable or inefficient, whether fair or foul, whether capable or careless.**

> (or: for you see that it continues binding for us all to be set in light so as to be clearly seen in the presence of the judgment seat which is Christ, so that each should keep and provide for the things performed throughout [His] body, with a view to, and face to face with, what things [were practiced], whether virtuous or vile). [*cf* 1 Cor. 3:9-17]
>
> [* *cf* Deut. 6:5, 13; Heb. 10:31; 12:28; 1 Jn. 4:18]

11. **Being, then, folks having seen, perceived, and thus knowing, the Lord's respect** (or: the reverence from, and which is, the Owner and Master [= Christ]; the reverential fear*, regard and recognition pertaining to or coming from [Yahweh]), **we are constantly persuading people** (habitually convincing people; one after another making humans confident). **So we have been, and thus remain, manifested** (set in the light so as to be clearly seen) **in God** (by God; for God; to God; with God), **yet I am also continually expecting** (or: hoping expectantly) **to have been manifested** (set in clear light) **within** (centered in; in union with) **your consciences.**

12. **We are not again recommending ourselves to you** (or: making ourselves stand together for you), **but rather, continue giving you a starting point and an occasion** (a base of operations and an incentive) **from the effect of boasting over and being proud of us** [other MSS: you] **– to the end that you folks may constantly possess** (have and hold) **[a position; a response; a defense] toward those continuously boasting in a face** (in presentation; in personal appearance; in a surface facade) **and not in [the] heart.**

13. **For whether we are beside ourselves** (standing without; = out of our minds), **[it is] for God** (in God; to God; by God; with God); **or whether we remain sane** (of sound mind; reasonable), **[it is] for you** (to you; with you) **folks,**

14. **for you see, Christ's love** (urge toward accepting reunion; full giving of Himself to [us]) **continuously holds us together.**
[We are] deciding (discerning and concluding; judging) **this: that** [some MSS add: since] **One Person** (or: Man) **died over [the situation of] all people** (or: for the sake of all humans); **consequently all people died** (or: accordingly, then, all humans died). [*cf* Rom. 5:12, reversed]

15. **And further, He died over all people** (over [the situation] of, and for the sake of all humans) **to the end that those living can** (or: may; could; would) **no longer live for themselves** (to themselves; in themselves; by themselves), **but rather for** (or: in; by; to; with) **the One dying and then being awakened and raised up over them** (over their [situation]; for their sakes),

16. **so that we, from the present moment** (or: from now) **[on], have seen and thus know** (or: perceive; or: are acquainted [with]) **no one on the level of flesh** (= in the sphere of the estranged human nature; = in correspondence to the self that is enslaved to the System; = according to the old covenant), **if even we have intimately, by experience, known Christ** ([the] Anointed One) **on the level of flesh** (or: = in the sphere of estranged humanity; or: = in correspondence to a self oriented to the System; = according to the old covenant), **nevertheless we now** (in the present moment) **no longer continue [thus] knowing [Him or anyone].** *[12:2]

17. **Consequently, since someone [is]*** **within Christ** (or: So that if anyone [is] in union with [the] Anointed One; or: And as since a Certain One [was] in Christ), **[there is] a new creation** (or: [it is] a framing and founding of an essentially different kind; [he or she is] an act of creation having a fresh character, a new quality)**: the original things** (the beginning [situations]; the archaic and primitive [arrangements]) **passed by** (or: went to the side). **Consider! New, essentially different things have come into existence** (have occurred and been birthed; or: It has become new things that are essentially different from what was habitual, before; or: He has been birthed and now exists being ones of a different kind, character and quality). [Rev. 21:5]

18. **Yet further, all things [are]** (or: the Whole [is]; = all the things that exist [are]) **forth from out of the midst of God – the One transforming us to be completely other [than we were]**

> (or: bringing us into another place or state of being; changing us to correspond with other [perceptions and conceptions]; altering us to be conformed to another [person]; changing us from enmity to friendship; reconciling us) **in Himself** (or: with Himself; by Himself; to

Himself; for Himself), **through Christ, and giving to us the attending service of, and the dispensing from, the complete transformation [for folks] to be other [than before]**
> (or: the change into another [position]; the changing to correspond with other [situations; perceptions]; the alteration to be another [person]; the change from enmity to friendship; the reconciliation), [*cf* Rom. 8:19-21]

19. **as that God was existing within Christ** (God was and continued being centered in, and in union with [the] Anointed One) **progressively and completely transforming [the] aggregate of humanity** (or: world) **to be other [than it is]**
> (or: progressively bringing [the] ordered System into another level or state; repeatedly changing [the] universe to correspond with other [conditions; perceptions]; progressively altering [the] ordered arrangement of culture, religions, economy and government to be in line with another one; habitually and progressively changing [the] secular realm [of humanity] from enmity to friendship; reconciling [the] world [of mankind]) **in Himself, to Himself, for Himself, by Himself and with Himself, not accounting to them** (not putting to their account; not logically considering for them; not reasoning in them) **the results and effects of their falls to the side** (their trespasses and offenses), **even placing within us the Word** (the *Logos;* the Idea; the Reason; the message; the pattern-forming information) **of the corresponding transformation to otherness** (or: the full alteration; the change from enmity to friendship; the conciliation).

20. **Over [the situation] in regard to Christ, then** (or: Therefore, on behalf of Christ), **we are elders of God, performing as ambassadors from God, as [Him] continually calling alongside to give comfort and relief** (performing as a Paraclete) **through us. We are constantly begging and urgently asking, on behalf of Christ** (or: for Christ's sake)**: "Be fully transformed in, be correspondingly altered by, be changed from an enemy to be a friend with, be reconciled to, and be altered to be another [person] in, by, and with, God!"** [6:1]
> (or: "You folks be completely exchanged with God; or: Be conciliated to, and for, God!"),

21. **for you see, He made** (or: formed) **the One not at any point knowing failure** (sin; error; mistake) **by intimate experience [to take the place of; to be] failure over us and our [situation]** (or: He constructed and produced a sin [offering], for our sake, the Person who was not having an experiential knowledge of missing the target or making a mistake), **to the end that we may be birthed God's just and rightwising act of eschatological deliverance** (or: would come to exist in righted, liberated relationships of equitable fairness; would become God's justice, the Way pointed out; could become participants in the new covenant from God: expressions of well-ordered living of the way it should be, which is God), **within Him and in union with Him.***

CHAPTER 6

1. **Now we, habitually** (or: continuously) **working together [with Him], are constantly calling you folks alongside to aid, comfort, direct, and urge/encourage you not to accept/receive God's grace into a void** (or: an empty or vain [situation; way of life]), [note: this continues 5:21*]

2. **for He continues saying,**
> **"At an acceptable season** (or: In an appropriate situation; For an agreeable *kairos*) **I fully hear and respond in regard to you, and within a day of deliverance** (on a day of health, restoration and salvation), **at your cry for help, I run to give aid to you** (I run with help for you)**."** [Isa. 49:8]

Consider (Look)**! [It is] now** (at this moment) **an especially acceptable season** (a fitting situation well-directed toward acceptance; a fertile moment of ease and face-to-face reception)! **Consider** (Look)**! [It is] now** (at this moment) **a day of deliverance** (of health, rescue, safety, salvation and restoration to the wholeness of the original state and condition)!

3. **[We are] normally giving no one a cause for striking [a foot] against something so as to stumble** (or: a reason or occasion for making a cutting attack toward someone) **– not in even one thing – so that the attending service and dispensing of provision would not at any point be found flawed so as to be discredited or censured,**

4. **but to the contrary, in the midst of every [situation] and in every [way], [we are] continuously placing and standing ourselves together, and recommending ourselves, as God's attending servants who dispense provisions: within the midst of much patient**

endurance and steadfast remaining under [the situation] for support; in compressed squeezings, pressures, afflictions and tribulations; within the midst of constraining necessities and compulsions; within tight spots that cramp, restrict and hem us in;

5. in [the receiving of] blows or beatings [as with a rod] or lashings; within prisons (or: times of being in custody); in the midst of unsettled situations (conditions of disorder; turbulences; political instabilities; riots); within toilsome, vexing and exhausting labors; in sleepless nights (or: vigils); within times without food (or: fasts; times of hunger).

6. [We have served and dispensed] with pureness (or: centered in [a life of] purity); in personally experienced knowledge; with forbearing patience (in taking a long time before becoming emotional or rushing with passion); with useful kindness; in a set-apart (holy) spirit (or: within the midst of [the] Holy Spirit; within a hallowed breath-effect; in a set-apart attitude); centered in, and with, uncritical love (or: acceptance that is free from prejudice and from a separating for evaluation; love that is not based on making distinctions, fault-finding or judging)

7. with a *Logos* and in a message of Truth (or: centered in a thought, idea and Word of Reality; in union with pattern-forming information from Reality); within God's power and ability; through means of the tools and instruments (or: weapons; utensils; implements) of and from the liberating deliverance, rightwised relationships and with the justice and equity of the Way pointed out in new covenant participation – on the right hand and on the left;

8. through a good reputation, and [by means of] dishonor (or: through means of glory and a praise-inducing manifestation, as well as [by] absence of value or respect); through words of ill omen and [by] words of good omen (or: through bad reports and defamation, and [through] good reports and praise); as wanderers and yet real (or: as [considered being] men who deceive and lead astray, and yet [being] true);

9. as continuing being unknown (nonentities) and yet constantly being ones fully known, recognized; as being those continually or progressively withering and dying, and yet look and consider: we continue living; as being those progressively being disciplined, trained and educated as young boys, and yet not being ones regularly delivered (put) to death;

10. as those being repeatedly made anxious, sad, vexed, distressed or in pain, but yet ever rejoicing; as constantly being people that are poor, destitute and living as beggars, but yet repeatedly making many rich (or: enriching many folks); as those possessing (having or holding) nothing, and yet continuously possessing all things to the full (or: habitually having and retaining everything in a firm grasp; or: repeatedly holding fast to all folks)!

11. Our mouth has been opened up and continues open toward you, O Corinthians: our heart has been broadened and is now enlarged.

12. You folks are not being constantly restricted into some limited place within us (= in our hearts), but you are being repeatedly squeezed into restrictions in your own inner sensitivities and deep feelings (within your interior organs).

13. Now I am speaking as to children: [let's have] the same fair exchange of recompense. You folks also be broadened and enlarged!

14. Do not of yourself continue (or: Stop) becoming yoked differently (or: unevenly yoked; yoked with ones of a different sort) with folks without faith (or: by those without trust; to unbelievers; with disloyal people), for, what mutual holding (having-with: sharing; partnership; communion; membership) [have] rightwised living and lawlessness (or: fairness/equity, and a lack of following rules; deliverance to right relationship which accords with the Way pointed out, and [the] inequity or wrong which come from violation of law), or what common existing (participation; partnership; sharing of Being) [is] in Light [directed] toward, or face to face with, darkness (or: [is there] for light with dimness from murky obscurity in the realm of shadows)?

15. And what joining of voice (concord, agreement and harmony of sound) has Christ [when faced] toward *belial* [Hebrew word for "worthlessness;" not a proper name]? Or what part for one full of faith and trust (or: portion in a loyal believer) [corresponds] with one who lacks faith (an unbeliever; one who is not trustworthy or loyal)?

16. Now what mutual deposit (or: concurrence or agreement arrived by group decision) [does] God's Temple [have] with idols (or: external forms or appearances; or: phantoms of the mind;

unsubstantial images or forms)**? For you see, we ourselves** [other MSS: you folks]
continuously exist being (indeed we/you are) **a temple of [the] living God, just as God said,**
"I will proceed to make My home and will continue walking about within and among
them (or: I will habitually reside {dwell}, as in a house, and live My life within and among
them), **and I will continue existing being their God, and they will continue existing**
being My people." [Lev. 26:12; Rev. 21:3]

17. **On which account [the] Lord** [= Yahweh] **says,**
"Instantly go forth from out of their midst and be instantly marked off by
boundaries so as to be defined and restricted – and do not continue (or: stop)
touching what is unclean (= ceremonially defiled), [Isa. 52:11] **and then I, Myself, will**
constantly admit you folks and receive you into [Myself; My family], [Ezk. 20:41]

18. **"and so I will proceed into being a Father for you, and you will proceed in being** (or:
will continue being) **sons and daughters in Me** (by Me; to Me; for Me), **says [the] Lord**
[= Yahweh] **the All-strong** (Almighty)**."** [2 Sam. 7:14; Isa. 43:6]

1. **Therefore, beloved ones, continuing in possessing** (having and holding) **these – the**
[aforementioned] promises – we can and should cleanse ourselves off from every stain,
pollution or ceremonial defilement of flesh (= the estranged human nature; = a self oriented to
the System) **and of spirit** (or: from flesh as well as from a spirit or attitude; or: pertaining to an
alienated persona or an attitude bound to a domination System), **while progressively bringing**
the state and condition of being set-apart (sacredness) **to a successful completion** (or: in
continuing to perform dedicated consecration amidst its destined goal), **centered in a reverence**
from God (or: in union with respect, with regard to God; in God's fear; [p46 reads: in God's love]).

CHAPTER 7

2. **You folks make room** (create space; set up an environment) **for us! We wrong no one** (We
at no point related to anyone unfairly or contrary to the Way pointed out; We act unjustly to no
one). **We spoil no one** (We caused no one to decay or be corrupted). **We have more than no**
one (or: We overreached no one so as to have an advantage over him or her; We exploit none).

3. **I am not now speaking with a view toward condemnation** (a decision to bring [you] down),
for I have said before that you folks continuously exist (or: are) **within our hearts – into the**
[situations of both] to die together and to be continuously living together!

4. **[There is] much freedom of speech, frankness, outspokenness and boldness in me,**
toward you folks. [There is] much boasting in me, over (in regard to) **you! I have been**
filled full so that I am stuffed with relief, encouragement and comfort – I continue
overflowing from the progressive flood of superabundance which encircles me in joy –
which tops all our pressure and tribulation (or: by the joy upon every squeezing, ordeal,
affliction and oppression).

5. **For even upon our coming into Macedonia, our flesh** (= physical selves, or inner natural
beings) **had not had a let-up or slackening** (a release so as to be at ease; relief), **but to the**
contrary, among all people and in every situation and manner [we were] ones being
continuously pressed, rubbed together, afflicted and oppressed: outside, fights and
battles; inside, fears!

6. **Nevertheless God, the One continuously performing as a Paraclete for the low ones**
(i.e., repeatedly calling the humbled and downhearted to [His] side to give them aid, relief, ease,
comfort and encouragement), **paracleted** (comforted, assisted and encouraged) **us in the arrival**
and presence of Titus,

7. **yet, not only in his presence, but further, also within the relief, comfort and**
encouragement (the influence of a paraclete) **in which he was paracleted** (comforted and
encouraged) **upon you folks [i.e., over your situation], repeatedly reporting back to us your**
longing (strong and anxious love with fond regret), **your grievous expression of anguish and**
remorse, your fiery zeal (ardor) **over me – with result that it caused me rather to rejoice –**

8. **because even if I made you sad and anxious** (or: cause you grief, pain and sorrow) **in the**
letter, I am now not regretting or changing my purpose of conduct – even if I had been
regretting and altering my purpose of conduct – for I see (observe) **that that letter made**
you sad and anxious (grieved, pained and sorrowful), **even if for an hour.**

9. **Now I continue rejoicing – not just that you folks were at one point made sad or anxious** (pained or sorrowful) **– but rather, that you were made sad and anxious [leading you] into a change in thinking and frame of mind, for you were saddened and made anxious down from, in the sphere of, in line with, and in correspondence to, God, to the end that you could in nothing be disadvantaged through loss, injury or damage due to** (or: from) **us.**

10. **For you see, the anxiety, sadness and pain down from** (or: in the sphere of; in line with; in correspondence to) **God continuously works, habitually effects and progressively produces a change in thinking and state of consciousness: [in turn, leading] into a deliverance and wholeness of health** (a rescue and restoration to the original state and realm; salvation) **void of regret and without change in purpose. Yet the anxiety, sadness, pain and sorrow which belongs to the world** (or: from the dominating, organized System of religion, culture, or government; which pertains to the aggregate of humanity) **is continuously working down the production of death** (or: is in line with repeatedly and progressively bringing about death).

11. **For consider** (or: look)! **This very thing – the [experience for] you to be made sad and anxious down from and in accord with God – to what extent it accomplished** (produces; worked down and effects) **[qualities] of haste to earnest diligence in you folks; but further, verbal defense** (apologetics); **but still further, indignant displeasure [with the whole situation]; yet further, fear and respect!; but then, longing** (strong and anxious love with fond regret); **on the other hand, fiery zeal and enthusiasm; yes, in fact, righting of what is wrong** (maintaining equity out of rightwised relationships from the fairness of the Way pointed out; awarding of justice [to all parties]) **– within the midst of everything, in every respect, in union with every situation, as well as among all people, while placing yourselves, and standing, together to continuously exist being pure in this practice-effect** (or: results of the matter).

12. **Consequently, even if I write** (or: although I wrote) **to you, [it is] not on account of the one doing wrong** (or: the person behaving contrary to the Way pointed out, acting unjustly or being injurious; the offender), **nor either on account of the one being wronged** (the person being treated unfairly or unjustly; the one being injured; the victim), **but rather on account of the [opportunity] to set in clear light and manifest to you folks your haste to earnest and diligent care – that which [was] over us and on our behalf – in God's sight and presence. Because of this we have been, and remain, encouraged and comforted** (we have received the influence of a paraclete).

13. **Yet, in addition to our encouragement and comfort, we rejoice still more abundantly due to the joy of Titus, because his spirit has been rested up and continues refreshed by all of you folks** (or: from you all),

14. **because if I have made any boast to him, over you folks, I have not been brought down in shame or disgrace, but to the contrary, as we speak all things to you folks in truth and reality, thus also our boasting on Titus came to be truth** (produced reality)

15. **and so his innermost feelings and compassions** (literally: internal organs; intestines) **are progressing more abundantly unto you folks, while progressively calling back to mind the submissive hearing and humble obedience of you all – as with fear and trembling** (or: respect and attentive concern) **you received him.**

16. **I continue rejoicing, that in everything I am constantly with good courage and confidence in you – that I can keep on depending and relying on you folks.**

CHAPTER 8

1. **Now, brothers** (folks from the same Womb; = family), **we are progressively making known to you God's grace** (the joyous favor from, and which has the character and quality of, God; the GRACE which is God), **which has been given and now continues as a gift among the called-out folks** (or: in union with the called-out communities) **of Macedonia,**

2. **how that within the midst of much testing and proving which came through pressure** (or: tribulation, oppression and affliction), **the superabundance of their joy – also contrasted with the depth of their destitution** (poverty, and/or life as beggars) **– superabounds into the wealth** (or: riches) **of their singleness [of heart and purpose] and the simplicity** (un-complexity; integrity; or: openness and sincerity in generous sharing with others) **from them,**

3. **because – I continue bearing witness and testifying that – corresponding to [their] power and in accord with [their] ability, and even beyond [their] actual power and ability, [they are] those who act spontaneously and voluntarily from their own initiative,**
4. **with much appeal and calling of us to their side to give us relief, assistance and encouragement** (the performance of a paraclete), **repeatedly and constantly begging of us, and from us, the grace** (or: the favor) **and the common participation** (partnership and sharing from common existence) **of the attending service which pertains to the dispensing into the set-apart folks** (the holy ones; the saints; the sacred people).
5. **And not according as we expected, but rather they gave themselves first to the Lord** [= Christ or Yahweh; p46 & others read: God], **and next even** (or: also) **to and for us, through the effect of God's will and a result of purpose, which is God,**
6. **[leading] us to assist and encourage** (to paraclete) **Titus, so that, just as he did before in the beginning, thus, as well, he should fully finish and complete also this favor unto you folks** (or: he should bring this GRACE to its goal, even into the midst of you people).
7. **But further, even as you folks continuously superabound within everything and among everyone – in faith** (or: with trust; by loyalty) **and in word** (or: by thought, idea, reason, and message; with information) **and in experiential knowledge and by insight, as well as with all haste to earnest diligence, and in the Love** (with unrestricted acceptance; by self-giving) **from out of the midst of us in union with you** [other MSS: the love from you [that is] within us] **– that you may be progressively superabounding, centered in this grace** (amidst this favor), **also.**

8. **I am not now saying [this] down from some arrangement added or put upon [you], but still [I am] also continuing in testing and proving the legitimacy of the birth** (or: the genuineness) **of the Love** (self-giving urge toward unrestricted acceptance and union), **which belongs to, and pertains to, you folks, through means of the haste to earnest and diligent care about** (or: pertaining to; or: from; of) **different folks.**
9. **For in fact, you people continue knowing by experience and insight the grace of Jesus Christ** (or: the favor from, and which is, Jesus [the] Anointed), **our Lord** (Master; Owner), **that although continuously existing being rich** (wealthy), **because of, and for the sake of, you folks He became destitute and led the life of a beggar, to the end that by, in and with the destitution and poverty of That One, you yourselves could** (or: should; may; would) **come to be rich** (wealthy).
10. **And so, in this [testing and proving], I am now offering an effect of knowledge and insight gained from my experience** (conclusion from *gnosis*), **for this [effect] is progressing to bring things together for you, to your benefit and expedience – you who from a year ago were first in making a beginning not only to do, but even to desire and purpose [it],**
11. **even so now – bring the doing to its goal** (fully accomplish the performing and the producing), **so that, even as the eagerness to will** (or: the propensity to rush ahead from the purposing), **thus also [may be] the accomplishing of the goal** ([situation] to fully complete), **from out of [your] possessions and holdings** (or: from the [situations] to normally have).
12. **You see it follows that, since** (or: if) **the eagerness continues lying before [a person], [it is] well-embraced and very acceptable – in proportion to whatever one may normally possess** (have and hold), **not corresponding to what he does not normally have.**
13. **For, you see, [the situation is] not that to** (or: for; in; with) **other folks [there is] a letting up with relief and ease, yet to** (or: for; in; with) **you folks [there is] pressure with tribulation, oppression and affliction** (or: = hardship),
14. **but to the contrary, out of the fairness and equity of equality within the present season** (or: from an equalization in the current occasion and situation), **your superabundance** (or: your encompassing surplus-result) **[can flow] into the lack resulting from the shortcoming of those folks** (= offset their deficiency), **keeping in mind that the superabundance** (or: surplus-effect) **of those folks could also at some point birth itself into the lack resulting from your shortcoming** (= offset your deficiency), **so that an equalizing can occur** (or: by that means there would come to be equality).
15. **[This is] just as it has been written,**
    "the person [who gathered] the great quantity did not have too much, and the person [who gathered] the small amount did not have too little." [Ex. 16:18]

16. **Now grace [is] in and with God** (or: Yet favor [is] by God; or, perhaps: But thanks [be] to God) – **in** (or: by; with) **the One constantly imparting within the heart of Titus this very same haste and earnest, diligent care over you folks,**

17. **because [Titus] indeed embraced and responded to the comfort, relief, assistance and encouragement** (the influence of the Paraclete), **and being inherently quicker to earnest diligence, spontaneously and of his own accord went forth to you folks.**

18. **So we sent together with him the** (or: his) **brother whose full approval** (praise and added applause) **in connection with the good news** (the message of goodness, ease and well-being) **[has spread] in every direction through all the called-out folks** (or: called-out communities)

19. **– yet not only [this], but further, [he is] also one having had hands extended, spread wide and pulled tight** [note: either, in love, or in "selecting" him] **by the called-out folks, [being] our traveling companion within this grace and favor** [other MSS: together with this grace] **which is being progressively dispensed and constantly given in attending service by us [moving with a view] toward the Lord's glory** (to the good reputation and manifestation which calls forth praise of Christ and Yahweh; or: face-to-face with the Master's assumed appearance), **and [to] a rushing forward with strong emotion and eagerness which pertains to us** (or: toward our Owner's glory and propensity to eagerly rushing with strong feelings) –

20. **[we] being those progressively ordering and arranging this for ourselves: [that] no one can find fault with us** (or: may find flaws or defects in us) **in connection with this ripe maturity which is being progressively dispensed in attending service by us.**

21. **For you see, we**
> **"habitually give forethought for providing beautiful things, ideal [situations] and fine [insights] – not only in [the] Lord's** [= Yahweh's] **sight and presence, but also in the sight and presence of people** (humans)." [Prov. 3:4 LXX]

22. **Now we send** (or: sent) **our brother** (person from the same Womb), **together with them, whom we often tested and proved as continually being quick to be earnest and diligent in many things, yet now much more quickly and with more earnest diligence, but with great confidence, which [he imparts] into** (or: that [he brings] unto) **you folks.**

23. **So whether concerning Titus – my partner** (person of common being and existence) **and co-worker [dispensing] into you people – or whether our brothers** (= fellow believers), **[they are] those sent forth pertaining to the called-out folks: Christ's glory** (or: [are] delegates and representatives who belong to, and are from, the called-out communities – a good reputation and assumed appearance of the Anointed One, and a manifestation which brings Him praise).

24. **Therefore, show within** [other MSS: be continuously being ones showing within] **the display and demonstration of your love** (selfless solidarity) **– and of our boasting over you – into the face** (= presence, or persons) **of those called-out folks** (or: called-out communities).

CHAPTER 9

1. **So indeed it follows that it is superfluous for me to be writing to you folks concerning this attending service and dispensing of this into the set-apart folks** (unto the sacred folks).

2. **For I have seen, and thus know, your eagerness** (fore-spiritedness; forward bent in passions and emotions) **– concerning which I am constantly boasting over you folks to [the] Macedonians – that "Achaia has prepared itself and stands ready since last year** (from a year ago)," **and your zeal stimulates the majority [of them].**

3. **Yet I send the brothers** (= fellow members of the Family), **so that the effect of our boasting over you may not be made void** (empty; to no purpose) **in this respect** (or: on this part), **so that you may be folks who have prepared yourselves – just as I have been saying –**

4. **lest by any means, if Macedonians should come with me and they should find you folks unprepared, we ourselves – not that we should proceed to mention you folks! – should be completely brought down in disgrace and be embarrassed in this underlying assumption** (or: substructure) **of boasting.**

5. **Therefore I considered it compelling to call the brothers alongside and to urge them so that they would come** (or: go) **unto you folks in advance and then that they could thoroughly adjust, prepare and arrange in advance "the blessing"** (or: idea and word of goodness, ease and well-being; reasonable goodness; plausible act of giving) **from you folks**

(or: your bountiful yield), **which had been previously promised and was being fore-announced, [and for] this to continually be ready, thus: as a blessing** (or: bountiful gift; or: word of goodness/act of generosity) **and not as one who has advantage in having more** (or: not grudgingly, from greed; possibly: not as the result of a scheme of extortion).

6. **Now this [is the reality]: the person who is habitually sowing sparingly** (thriftily; in a limited way) **will also continue reaping** (or: harvesting) **sparingly; and the person who is habitually sowing on [the basis of] good thoughts and words** (or: with or for added blessings; or: bountifully; with things well and fully laid out and arranged for ease and a reasonable yield) **will also continue reaping upon [those] good thoughts and words** (or: with added blessings; or: bountifully; with things well laid out and arranged for added ease and a reasonable yield) –

7. **each one [doing; giving] correspondingly** (or: accordingly) **as he has before chosen in** (or: by) **the heart, not from out of anxiety** (sorrow; pain; distress) **nor compulsion, for**

"**God habitually loves** (seeks reunion with) **a cheerful** (merry) **giver.**" [Prov. 22:8 LXX]

8. **Moreover, God is constantly able with continuous power to furnish all grace to surround and to make every favor superabound unto** (or: into the midst of) **you folks, to the end that, continuously having every ability in yourselves to ward things off and constantly holding all self-sufficiency and complete contentment at all times [and] within every [situation] and in union with every person, you can** (or: may; should; would) **continuously superabound into every good action, excellent deed and noble work,**

9. **just as it stands written,**

"**He scattered abroad and widely disperses; He gives to the ones who work hard for their bread, and yet are poor; His eschatological deliverance** (rightwised dealings and relationship which correspond to the Way pointed out, in covenantal faithfulness) **continuously remains and constantly dwells, on into the Age.**" [Ps. 112:9]

10. **Now the One habitually adding further supply and fully furnishing "seed to** (or: for) **the one habitually sowing** (the constant sower) **and bread unto eating** (= for food)," **will continue supplying and furnishing – He will even continue to multiply and give increase to fullness – your seed, and He will continue causing the offspring and produce** (or: product; yield) **of, and from, your eschatological deliverance** (justice in rightwised relationships of the Way pointed out: covenant participation) **to grow and increase** (be enlarged and amplified),

11. **being progressively enriched unto abundance within every person*** (or: in union with everything) **[leading] into complete singleness [of purpose] and simplicity [of being] for all generosity** (liberality), **which constantly produces** (works down; accomplishes) **thanksgiving to and for God through us, and through our midst** [or, with B: which repeatedly works in accord with God's ease of grace, instilling gratitude through the midst of us], [* cf 1 Cor. 1:5]

12. **because the attentive serving and dispensing of this public duty and service is not only repeatedly replenishing** (aiming toward filling back up again) **the needs** (results of defaults; the effects of shortcomings, lacks or deficiencies) **pertaining to the set-apart folks** (the holy ones; the saints; or: the sacred [communities]), **but further is also progressively superabounding** (bringing excessive amounts that overflow) **through many expressions of gratitude to God** (or: by means of many examples of the goodness of grace in God)

13. **through the evidence which is shown by this attending service and dispensing: [they are] folks constantly glorifying God and praising His reputation because of** (or: based upon) **the subjoined, humble alignment, supportive arrangement and subjection in appended shelter – which is your accordance to the message and agreement in thought** (and thus: your profession of saying the same thing), **[showing] assent unto Christ's message of goodness, ease and well-being, as well as by [the] simplicity and generosity from this partnership of common-existence sharing unto them, and into the midst of all people,**

14. **even by their request over [the situation of]** (or: on behalf of) **you folks – from people constantly longing and yearning for you. [It is] because of God's transcendent favor and surpassing grace [resting] upon you people –**

15. **grace and joyous favor, in and by God, [resting; based] upon His free gift** (the gift which is Him) **– a wonder beyond description** (or: added to His indescribable gratuity)!

CHAPTER 10

1. **Now I myself, Paul, am making a personal appeal in continuing to call you to my side to encourage and entreat you folks through Christ's gentle friendliness** (mild kindness; tender meekness) **and abundant, lenient reasonableness and fairness** (or: considerate suitableness) **– I, who indeed [am] humble and lowly when face to face** (= in person) **among you, yet, being absent, am constantly showing bold, cheerful courage and confidence unto you –**
2. **and am normally requesting, [that] when being present, not to have a situation where I need to be bold or courageous with** (or: in; by) **the assured confidence in** (by; with) **which I am reasonably considering** (or: counting on) **to be with resolved daring upon certain folks: those constantly counting or considering us as folks [who] are habitually walking around** (= living and behaving) **in the sphere of, or corresponding to, flesh** (= governed by human principles or conditions; or: = on the level of old covenant existence [T. Denton]; or: = in line with a self in bondage to the System).
3. **For though habitually walking about** (ordering our behavior) **within flesh** (= in the physical, human condition), **we are not now serving as a soldier** (or: continuing in military service) **in correspondence and accord to flesh** (= on the level of estranged/enslaved humanity, or in line with the human condition; or: = in the sphere/mode of old covenant Jewish reasonings),
4. **for you see, the tools and weapons of our military service** (campaign) **[are] not fleshly** (= do not pertain to our human condition; ["are not the weapons of the Domination System" – Walter Wink]), **but rather, [are] powerful and capable ones in God** (or: by and with God), **[focused] toward [the] pulling down** (demolition) **of effects of fortifications** (or: strongholds; strongly entrenched positions [of the "Domination System" – W. Wink, *Engaging the Powers*]),
5. **progressively tearing down and demolishing conceptions** (concepts; the effects of thoughts, calculations, imaginations, reasonings and reflections) **and every height** (or: high position; high-effect) **and lofty [attitude, purpose or obstacle] that is habitually lifting itself up against** (or: elevating itself up on so as to put down) **the intimate and experiential knowledge of God, and then taking captive every effect of perception, concept and understanding** (result from directing one's mind) **– one after another – and leading them prisoner into the hearing obedience of the Christ** (or: the humble attentive listening, which comes from the Anointed One; or: the submissive paying attention, which is the Anointing),
6. **even continuously holding [them] in a ready state and prepared condition to support justice and equity, while maintaining rightwised relationships from out of the Way pointed out, for every mishearing** (or: hearing-aside; setting of our attention to the side; or: disobedience) **– whenever your hearing obedience may be made full** (or: as soon as the humble attentive listening and submissive paying attention can be brought to full measure, would be completed and thus fulfilled, from, and with regard to, you folks)!

7. **You folks constantly look at things according to external appearances!** (or: Are you now regarding things in the sphere of surface meanings?; or: Keep on seeing the things that face [you]!) **If anyone has trusted and now continues persuaded for himself to exist belonging to Christ** (or: with himself to be from Christ; or: in himself to be with the qualities of the Anointing), **let him continue considering and reckoning this again upon himself: that just as he belongs to Christ, with the qualities of the Anointing, in this same way [do] we, also.**
8. **For besides, if I should boast somewhat more excessively concerning our privilege from out of Being** (or: right and authority) **– which the Lord** [= Christ or Yahweh] **gives us with a view unto edification and up-building** (construction into being a house), **and not unto your tearing down or demolition – I shall not be put to shame or be disgraced,**
9. **in that I would not seem, as it were, constantly to be completely intimidating you folks** (or: as if to be repeatedly making you really alarmed or afraid) **through the** (or: [my]) **letters.**
10. **"Because," one person is** [other MSS: they are] **constantly saying, "the letters [are] indeed weighty and strong** (or: = severe and violent), **but the presence of the body [is] weak, and the *Logos*** (Word; idea; information; message) **has been collected from out of nothing** (or: and [his] expression continues being scorned, despised and disregarded)!"
11. **Let such a person take this into account, that the kind of person we are in *Logos*** (word, etc.) **through letters, being absent, such also [are we], being present, in action.**

12. **Of course we are not daring to classify ourselves among, nor compare or explain ourselves with, some of those setting themselves together for commendation. But in fact they, themselves, are constantly measuring themselves among** (or: within) **themselves, and are repeatedly comparing themselves with themselves – they continue not comprehending or understanding!**

13. **Now we ourselves will not boast into what is not measured** (or: about the things that cannot be measured), **but rather, corresponding to the measure of the measuring rod** (rule; standard; canon; = sphere of allocated influence) **which God divided and gives as a part to** (in; for) **us – of a measure** (or: = sphere of influence) **to reach even as far as upon you folks.**

14. **Certainly we are not progressively overspreading** (or: overstretching) **ourselves – as if not being repeatedly reaching-on into you folks – for we advanced beforehand as far as even you people in the declaring of Christ's good news** (or: the message of goodness, ease and well-being pertaining to and having its source in the Anointed One).

15. **No, we are not men habitually boasting into what is not measured [off for us] – in labors** (toils) **belonging to other folks – but are continuously holding an expectation and having expectant hope of a progressively growing increase of your faith, trust and loyalty to be made great and enlarged within you** (or: among and in union with you folks) **– in line with and corresponding to our measured-out range and area** (= sphere of allocated influence) **– [leading] into abundance** (being surrounded with overflowing excess),

16. **[increasing] into the [regions] beyond those of your area, to yourselves** (or: to ourselves) **cause the good news to be proclaimed – not in the midst of a measured-out range and area** (= sphere of allocated influence) **belonging to another – [and] to boast into things [that have been] prepared and made ready,**

17. **so, "the one [among you] that is habitually boasting is to be habitually boasting in the Lord** [= Christ or Yahweh]." [Jer. 9:24]

18. **Now it follows that, the person constantly placing himself with others – so as to be commended – is not that one who is qualified or approved, but rather, he whom the Lord** [= Christ or Yahweh] **consistently includes and commends.**

CHAPTER 11

1. **I wish that you folks were continuing to put up with a little something of my thoughtlessness** (or: unreasonableness; lack of common sense; foolishness; imprudence). **But in fact, you are also always patiently tolerant of me** (or, as an imperative: Still further, be also patiently tolerant of me),

2. **for I continue with hot zeal** (ardor; eager vehement passion) **concerning you in, with and by God's fervent zeal** (ardent, passionate affection which is God), **because I myself joined you folks in marriage to one Husband** (or: Man), **to make** (place) **a pure virgin** (= unmarried girl) **to stand alongside in and with the Christ** (or: by the Anointed One; as the Anointed [body]).

3. **Yet I continue fearing lest somehow, as the serpent thoroughly deceived** (or: seduces; fully deludes; cheats) **Eve within its capability for every work** (its cunning ability in all crafts and actions; its readiness to do anything), **the results of directing your minds** (or: effects of your perceptions, concepts and understanding) **should be decayed** (could be ruined; would be spoiled or corrupted) **away from the singleness [of commitment] and simplicity [of being] – even the purity – which [focuses us] into the Christ** (or: with a view to the Anointing).

4. **For if, indeed, the person periodically** (or: presently) **coming is habitually preaching** (normally heralding or proclaiming) **another Jesus – whom we do not preach** (or: did not herald and proclaim) **– or, [if] you folks are continuously receiving a different breath-effect** (or: are repeatedly laying hold of a spirit or attitude that is different in kind and nature) **which you did not receive, or a different "good-news"** (a message of ease and well-being which is different in kind and character) **which you did not welcome and accept, are you repeatedly holding back from [him] in an ideal way?** (or: you folks are beautifully putting up with and tolerant of [it]! [other MSS: were you finely holding back from {him; it}?]).

5. **Now you see, I am habitually considering and counting myself to have been in nothing inferior to or deficient from those "very-overly [pretentious and condescending] emissaries** (or: super-folks sent forth with a mission)."

[note: Paul is probably referring to the Judaizers – those sent out from the Jews]

6. **Yet even if [I am] non-professional** (ordinary and unskilled) **in word and expression – though certainly not in the intimate and experiential knowledge and insight** (*gnosis*) **– still, we are men manifesting Light into you folks: in every situation [and] in all things** (or: in every person – in union with and in the midst of all people; in every respect, among all folks).

7. **Or, do I make a mistake** (or: did I commit a sin) **[by] repeatedly humbling** (or: lowering; abasing) **myself so that you folks can** (or: would) **be lifted up** (exalted) **because I announce as good news a free gift – God's good news – to you folks** (or: because without cost I declare the message of ease and well-being in and among you: a message of Goodness, which is God)**?**

8. **I encroached upon and took the goods of** (or: rob; despoil) **other called-out folks** (or: groups), **taking** (or: receiving; getting) **rations** (provisions; subsistence pay) **with a view toward the attending service and dispensing pertaining to you people.**

9. **Further, being present and facing you, and being put in need** (being made to lack and fall short of means), **I was not a "dead weight" on** (= an idle encumbrance, hence, a financial burden to) **even one person, for the brothers** (= fellow believers) **coming from Macedonia replenished the lacks resulting from my being in need, and in everything I kept and shall continue keeping myself "weight-free" to** (= free from being a burden for) **you folks.**

10. **Christ's reality** (or: Truth pertaining to, originating in, and which is [the] Anointed One) **continuously exists within me, so that this boast** (or: boasting) **will not be constantly fenced in or hedged about** (thus: stopped or blocked) **unto** (or: for) **me within the slopes** (= regions) **of Achaia!**

11. **Why** (Through what reason or situation)**? Because I am not continuously loving** (giving myself to; urging toward union with) **you folks? God has seen and thus knows!**

12. **So what I am habitually doing I will still continue doing, to the end that I can cut out the starting point, base of operations, and occasion of those repeatedly wanting and intending a starting point** (base of operations, or, an occasion), **so that they can be found also just as we** (= equal to us), **within that which they are constantly boasting** (= proud)**!**

13. **For such folks [are] false emissaries** (pseudo-representatives) **– fraudulent and deceitful workers – constantly changing their outward fashion and transforming themselves into emissaries of Christ** (representatives of [the] Anointed One).

14. **And no wonder** ([it is] no marvel or cause for astonishment), **for the adversary** (opponent; *satan*) **itself is repeatedly changing its form and outward fashion** (transforming itself) **into a messenger** (person with a message) **of light** (or, as a passive: is from time to time being transformed and changed in its outward expression into an agent from, or that is, [the] Light).

15. **Therefore, [it is] no great thing if its attending servants and dispensers also repeatedly change their form and outward fashion, as though [being]** (or: are habitually transforming or transfiguring themselves [to be] like) **attending servants of eschatological deliverance, justice and equity** (dispensers of the rightwised way pointed out; = ministers of the new covenant) **– whose finish** (or: end in view; finished product; attained goal; consummation; accomplished end) **will proceed in being in accord with, along the line of, to the level of and corresponding to their works and actions** (or: = their outcome will constantly be what they reap from their deeds).

16. **I say again** (or: I repeat), **no one should presume to imagine or suppose me to be a senseless fellow** (a fool; one devoid of intellect; an imprudent man). **Still – if not in fact – even if as senseless** (foolish; idiotic; imprudent), **accept and receive me, so that I myself also can boast of something!**

17. **What I am presently speaking I am speaking not down from or in accord with [the] Lord** (Master; Owner; [= Christ or Yahweh]), **but to the contrary, as within senselessness** (foolishness; imprudence) **– within this assumed position as a basis for boasting:**

18. **since many folks are habitually boasting – according to the flesh** (or: = on the level of the natural being; or: = in the sphere of estranged humanity) **– I myself should also boast,**

19. **for with pleasure you folks – continuously being intelligent, sensible and prudent folks! – habitually put up with the senseless** (foolish; idiotic; imprudent) **people!**

20. **In fact, you constantly put up with anyone if he is progressively bringing you down to slavery** (or: is completely enslaving you as his habit) **– if someone is repeatedly devouring; if**

someone is constantly taking [you] in hand; if someone is progressively elevating himself or lifting himself up upon [you]; if someone is continuously bringing the lash into your face (flaying you with a whip so as to remove the skin and eat into the face)!

> (= you folks constantly tolerate tyranny, abusive insults, pride and arrogance, as well as being drained of resources, being manipulated and being restrained.)

21. **I am saying [this] down from dishonor** (or: in accord with being devalued), **seeing** that (or: as though) **we, ourselves, had been weak [among you]! Yet in whatever anyone is habitually daring – I say this in senselessness** (I'm talking foolishly and unreasonably) – **I, too, am habitually daring!**

22. **Are they Hebrews? So [am] I! Are they Israelites? So [am] I! Are they a seed of Abraham? So [am] I!** [comment: this is the "boasting on the level of flesh" in vs. 18, above]

23. **Are they Christ's attending servants** (dispensers of Christ)**? – I am speaking as one being beside himself** (or: insane) **– I over and above [them]** (or: I more so; = I surpass [them])**! In toilsome labors and weariness more exceedingly; in prisons** (jails) **more often; in blows** (stripes; beatings) **surpassingly; in deaths** (or: near-death situations) **many times** (or: often).

24. **Five times by Jews** (or: under Judeans) **I received forty [stripes; lashes], less one.**

25. **Three times I was beaten with rods; once I was stoned; three times I was shipwrecked – I have done night and day within the midst of the depth [of the sea], even hitting bottom;**

26. **on journeys often** (many times)**; in dangers** (perils) **of rivers** (or: floods)**; in dangers of robbers** (perils of plunderers or insurrectionists; = Zealots)**; in dangers from out of [my] race** (kindred)**; in dangers from out of the multitudes of ethnic groups** ([the] nations)**; in dangers within city; in dangers within a desolate place** (wilderness)**; in dangers at sea; in dangers among false-brothers** (= pseudo-believers; or: = Family members who lie and deal falsely);

27. **in exhaustive labor and wearisome toil; in lack of sleep** (or: sleeplessness; or: vigils) **often; in hunger** (or: scarcity of food; or: famine) **and in thirst – in situations of deprivation or need of food** (or: in fastings), **many times; in cold and in lack of sufficient clothing** (or: nakedness);

28. **apart from these external matters** (or: apart from those things [just mentioned] – besides the outside –) **[there is] the thing rushing in on me and giving cares** (the pressure) **from day to day: the anxiety, concern and divided distraction pertaining to all the called-out folks** (or: summoned-forth communities):

29. **Who is continuing weak and I am not proceeding to be weak** (= sharing their weakness)**? Who is habitually snared and caused to stumble or be entrapped, and I, myself, am not being repeatedly made fiery hot** (or: caused to be incensed)**?**

30. **If** (or: Since) **it is necessary to boast, I will boast concerning the things pertaining to, from, and which are, my weakness.**

31. **The God and Father of the Lord Jesus** (or, in apposition: which is the Master, Jesus) **– the One continuously being a blessed One** (or: the One constantly existing [as] a Word of ease, a Message of well-being and [the] *Logos* of goodness) **on into the ages – has seen and thus knows that I am not lying.**

32. **In Damascus the ethnarch** (tribal governor; ruler of that culture) **under Aretas, the king, had been watching with guards to garrison the city of Damascus, intending to seize and arrest me,**

33. **and through a window** (or: small opening) **I was lowered through the wall in a braided hamper** (like a fish-basket [of ropes or wicker]), **and escaped** (fled out of) **his hands.**

CHAPTER 12

1. **It is necessary** (or: binding) **for one to boast from time to time – though indeed not beneficial or expedient – so I will proceed in coming unto [the subject of] visions and unveilings of [the] Lord** (or: disclosures from, pertaining to, or given by, [Christ or Yahweh]).

> (or: [other MSS: If (or: Since) it is necessary to continue boasting, {it}; still other MSS: Now to repeatedly boast] indeed does not normally bring [people] together, so I will continue moving on to sights, apparitions and appearances, as well as revelations and disclosures, whose source and origin are [the] Lord, or, which are [the] Lord).

2. **I have known, and am acquainted with, a person** (or: a man; a human being) **in Christ** (or: within the midst of Christ; in union with [the] Anointed) **more than fourteen years ago – whether in body** (or: in a body), **I am not aware; whether outside of the body, I am not aware; God has seen and knows** (is aware) **– being snatched away** (dragged off; seized and taken) **as such, as far as [the; or: a] third heaven** (or: atmosphere). [*cf* 5:17, above; 1 Thes. 4:17]

3. **Further, I have seen and know such a person** (man; human) **– whether in body or apart from the body, I know not; God knows –**

4. **that was snatched away** (seized and taken) **into the Paradise and heard inexpressible gush-effects and utterances** (unutterable sayings and results of a flow; unspeakable results of movement and flux; inexpressible matters and declarations) **which are not being from out of existence** (or: which are not continuing from within the midst of being; or: which it continues being not right; or: for which there is no privilege or authority; which are not being possible; which are not being allowed) **in a person** (to mankind; for a human) **to at any point speak.**

5. **I will boast over such a person, yet over myself I will not continue boasting – except in my weaknesses,**

6. **for if I should ever want or intend to boast, I shall not be senseless** (unintelligent; unreasonable; imprudent), **for I will continue declaring reality** (truth). **Yet I continue being reticent** (continue refraining, with thrift,) **and so no one should account** (overestimate) **into me above** (or: over) **what he continues seeing [in] and observing [of] me, or hearing from me.**

7. **And now, in the excess of the unveilings** (or: with the transcendence of the revelations; by the extraordinary amount and surpassing nature of the disclosures), **through this [situation] and for this reason – so that I could not be progressively exalted** (or: would not continue being overly lifted up [in myself or by others]) **– something with [its] point in [my] flesh is given in me** (or: an impaling-stake for the human nature was given for me; or: a thorn to the natural realm, and a splinter by alienated humanity, was assigned to me)**: an agent of, and from, the adversary** (or: an adversarial person with a message), **to the end that he could** (or: should; would) **repeatedly beat me in the face** (or: slap me on the ear) **with his** (or: its) **fist.**

> [comment: this personification of the irritation may well be metaphorical and may refer to his social or cultural-religious situation]

8. **I called the Lord** [Christ or Yahweh] **alongside for relief, ease and comfort, and entreated [Him] three times over** (or: about) **this, so that he would** (or: should) **at once stand away and withdraw from me,**

9. **and yet He has said to me – and His declaration stands, "My grace is continuously sufficient in you** (or: My joyous favor is constantly adequate to ward [it] off for you), **for you see, the ability** (or: the [other MSS read: My] power) **is habitually brought to its goal** (or: finished; perfected; matured) **within the midst of weakness** (or: in union with lack of strength and infirmity)**." Most gladly, therefore, I will rather continue boasting in** (or: centered within the midst of; and in union with) **the** [other MSS: my] **weaknesses, to the end that the ability of, and from, the Christ** (or: the Anointed One's power; the ability which is the Anointing) **can pitch its tent** (or: would tabernacle) **upon me** (or: = set up residence upon me; = fulfill the Feast of Tabernacles with me; or: = be my house from heaven; [*cf* 5:1, above; Rev. 21:3])**!**

10. **Wherefore I habitually delight and take pleasure in weaknesses** (or: in union with lacks of strength and infirmities); **in the midst of outrageous insults and ignominious situations of mistreatment; in union with pressured necessities; in the midst of pursuits for persecution and cramped situations over and on behalf of Christ, for whenever I continue being** (or: may periodically be) **weak, then I am powerful** (or: I then exist being capable)**!**

11. **I have become unreasonable** (senseless; imprudent; foolish) **– you, yourselves, compel me** (press and force me; = drive me to it!) **– for I myself ought to have been being constantly recommended** (placed together with and commended) **by you folks, because not even in one thing did I come behind** (or: am I deficient from or inferior to) **the "very-overly" [pretentious and condescending] emissaries** (or: representatives), **even though I am nothing** (or: since I also exist being nothing!).

12. **Indeed, the signs of the emissary** (the sent-forth representative) **were produced and accomplished among you folks in every [situation] of humbly remaining under to give**

support (or: in all patient endurance) – **as well as by signs and wonders** (portents; marvels) **and powers** (or: in abilities and capabilities).

13. **So what is there in which you folks were treated as inferior, or made worse off, above** (= more than) **the rest of the called-out folks** (or: communities), **except that for myself, I myself was not a "dead weight" for** (= and idle encumbrance, hence, a financial burden to) **you folks? Give grace to me for this unfairness** (wrong; injustice)!

14. **Look** (or: Consider)! **This third time I continue holding [myself] ready and prepared to come to** (or: go toward) **you folks – and I will not proceed in being "dead weight"** (an encumbrance or burden), **for I am not habitually seeking your "things"** (your possessions), **but to the contrary, you. For the children ought not to be habitually storing up and accumulating [material resources] for the parents, but rather, the parents [should do this] for the children.**

15. **So I myself most gladly shall spend** (pay the expenses) – **even be completely spent** (exhausted; bankrupted) – **over** (on behalf of) **your souls. Even if I am constantly loving you excessively, I am habitually being loved or accepted less.** (or: And since I am continuously loving you and seeking union with you more abundantly {or: too much}, am I being loved less?)

16. **Yet, let it continue to be** (or: so be it; be that as it may). **I myself do not** (or: did not) **overburden or weigh you down. Nonetheless, being inherently ready to do anything and capable for every work, [you say that] I caught you, taking you by bait** (as used for fish)!

17. **Not anyone whom I have sent off to you folks [did this]! Did I take advantage of you through him?**

18. **I called Titus alongside, urged [him] and sent [him] off, together with the** (or: [his]) **brother** (or: = fellow believer and member of the Family), **as an emissary** (sent-off representative). **Surely Titus did not take advantage of you! Do we not walk about in the same Spirit** (or: = Do we not live and order our lives with the same attitude)? **Not in the same footprints?**

19. **All this time** [other MSS: Again] **do you folks continue thinking** (supposing; presuming) **that we are repeatedly making a verbal defense to YOU? Down [here] in God's stead and place, we are constantly speaking within Christ and in union with [the] Anointing! And the whole** (all [these] things), **beloved ones, [is** (are)**] over** (on behalf of) **your edification** (your upbuilding; the construction of your house).

20. **So you see, I continue being afraid, lest somehow – on coming – I may not find you folks such as I habitually intend** (purpose; desire) **– and I myself may be found by you [to be one] such as you folks continue not desiring – lest somehow [I may find] strife** (contention; quarreling), **jealousy, outbursts of emotions or swellings of anger, selfish ambition and factious rivalry, backbitings** (down-babblings; slanderous conversations), **whisperings** (occasions of malicious gossiping), **situations of puffing up** (inflations of pride), **disorders** (situations of unrest; turbulences; losses of tranquility; instabilities).

21. **My God will** [other MSS: may] **not again be repeatedly humbling me toward you folks, at my coming, and yet I may mourn and grieve over many of those having previously been failing** (missing the goal; sinning), **continuing thus and not at any point changing thinking* to a new state of consciousness and attitude regarding the uncleanness and fornication** (sexual immorality; prostitution) **and loose conduct** (licentiousness) **which they practice.**

[* *cf* Rom. 12:2]

CHAPTER 13

1. **I am habitually coming to you folks – this third time, now!**
   "Upon [the] mouth of two witnesses – and of three – every effect of a flow (gush-effect; matter; declaration; saying) **will continue being made to stand."** [Deut. 19:15]

2. **I have said before, and I continue foretelling** (laying it out beforehand) **– as if continuing present, the second time, and yet now continuing absent – to those having before failed** (deviated; sinned), **and still continuing thus – and to all the rest – that if I should ever come again into the [area], I will not continue to being thrifty, so as to spare or refrain,**

3. **since you continue seeking a proof of the Christ continuously speaking within and in union with me – Who [having come] into you folks is not being weak, but rather continues powerful** (or: capable) **within and in union with you folks.**

4. **For even though He was crucified** (or: hung and put to death on a torture stake) **from out of the midst of weakness, yet in contrast, He is continuously living from out of the midst of God's power and ability. For you see, we ourselves also continue being weak, within** (or: in union with) **Him, but still we will continue on living together with** [other MSS: within] **Him, unto** (or: with a view to) **you folks, from out of the midst of God's power and ability.**

5. **Keep on examining and making trial of yourselves, since you exist being in union with the Faithfulness** (or: whether you continue being centered within the midst of this Trust); **repeatedly test and assay yourselves so as to approve of yourselves and come to meet the desired specifications. Or are you not now fully aware nor presently recognizing yourselves, with accurate insight: that Jesus Christ constantly exists being within the midst of, and in union with, you people? – since you are surely not unable to stand the test, nor are you unproven or disapproved!** (or: – except you are somewhat disqualified.)
6. **Yet I continue expecting that you folks will progressively come to know by intimate experience that we ourselves are not unable to stand the test, nor are we unproven, disapproved or disqualified!**
7. **Now we habitually hold good thoughts, having wishes of ease and well-being face-to-face with** (or: toward) **God, asking [that] you folks do nothing worthless or of bad quality – not so that we, ourselves, can appear** (or: should be made to be seen) **as proven, approved or qualified, but rather so that you yourselves can** (or: should; would) **be habitually doing** (performing; creating) **that which is beautiful** (or: constantly constructing the ideal; repeatedly making what is fine), **even though we ourselves may be as ones unproven, disapproved and disqualified** (= should look as if we had failed the test and are discredited),
8. **for it follows that we continue with no power** (are unable and incapable) **[to do] anything against** (or: [to be] putting down) **this Reality or the Truth, but to the contrary, [we have power and ability] for the sake of the Truth, and over [the situation] of this Reality.**
9. **So we are constantly rejoicing whenever we ourselves may continue being weak, yet you, yourselves, may continue being able and powerful. We are also constantly holding this good thought, asking with wishes of ease and well-being: your complete adjustment** (your thoroughly being knitted together, made completely equipped in full readiness, and adapted in perfect unity).
10. **Therefore, being absent, I am now writing these things, to the end that [when] being present I may not severely employ the rights that accord with the authority** (or: harshly behave in the sphere from out of [my] existence; act in a cutting-off way along the line of what is out of Being) **which the Lord** [= Christ or Yahweh] **gave, and gives, to and in me, with a view into building the house up** (construction of a household), **and not into tearing [it] down.**

11. **As to the rest, brothers** (= fellow believers and members – Family), **be habitually rejoicing** (or: be progressively happy); **be continuously adjusted so as to be completely equipped and fully made ready while being thoroughly knitted together into perfect unity; be repeatedly called alongside to give, or be given, aid, relief, comfort and encouragement; constantly mind the same thing and agree, being of the same opinion** (have the same frame of mind and be mutually disposed); **continuously dwell in and with peace** (habitually maintain the joining; be and live in joined-harmony) **– and the God of the Love and Peace** (or: the God Who is the Self-giving urge toward reunion and joining-harmony) **will continue being with you folks.**
12. **Greet and embrace one another within a set-apart expression of affection** (or: centered in or in union with a holy and sacred kiss; in the sphere of [the] Sacred Kiss).
13. **All the set-apart folks** (holy ones; sacred people) **constantly embrace you folks and send you their best.**
14. **The grace and joyous favor of, from and which is the Lord, Jesus Christ – even the Love which is God** (or: and the unambiguous, uniting acceptance and participation of, from and which characterizes God), **and the common-existence, partnership, sharing, communion and participation which is the set-apart Breath-effect** (or: of and from the Holy Spirit and that sacred spirit-attitude) **– [continue being; are] with all of you folks. It is so** (Count on it; Amen)!

[written circa A.D. 56 – Based on the critical analysis of John A.T. Robinson]

GALATIANS

1. **Paul, one sent as a representative** (emissary; envoy) – **not with a commission from people, nor through a human being, but rather through Jesus Christ, as well as Father God** (or: through Jesus, [the] Anointed One, and God [the] Father), **the One arousing and raising Him forth from out of the midst of dead folks –**
2. **and all the brothers** (= fellow believers; folks from the same Womb; [cf 4:26, below]) **together with me, to the called-out folks** (or: to the called-out communities and gatherings; for the summoned-forth congregations of people) **of [the province of] Galatia:**

3. **In, for and with you folks [are]** (or: To you people [be]) **grace and joyous favor, as well as peace** (a joining) **from God, our Father and Owner, Jesus Christ** (or: from our Father God, even [the] Lord, Jesus Christ; or: from God our Father, and [the] Master, Jesus [the] Anointed)
4. **– the One at one point giving Himself, over [the situation of]** (or: on behalf of; for the sake of; [p46, Aleph*, A, D & other MSS read: concerning]) **our failures** (situations and occasions of falling short or to the side of the target; deviations; mistakes; errors; sins) **so that He could carry us out from the midst of the present misery-gushing and worthless age**
> (or: bear us forth from the indefinite period of time – characterized by toil, grievous plights and bad situations – having taken a stand in [our] midst; or: extricate us from the space of time having been inserted and now standing in union with base qualities),

corresponding to (or: down from; in accord with; in line with; in the sphere and to the level of) **the effect of the will** (or: intent; purpose; design) **of our God and Father,**
5. **in Whom [is] the glory** (or: by Whom [is] the manifestation which calls forth praise; for Whom [is] the reputation; with Whom [comes] an appearance which creates and effects opinions in regard to the whole of human experience) **on into the indefinite times of the ages** (or: into the [crowning and most significant] eons of the eons). **It is so!** (Count on it; Amen!)

6. **I am constantly amazed** (or: I continue astounded, with wonder) **that you folks are so quickly being progressively transplanted** (or, as a middle voice: are thus now quickly transferring yourselves or changing your stand) **from the One** (or: that [message]) **calling** (summoning) **you people, within Christ's grace** (or: in [the] favor of the Anointed One), **on into a different sort of "message of goodness"** (unto a different evangel; into an alternative "good news," or gospel; = into an imitation and fake message of goodness, ease or well-being) **– which is NOT "another" one of the same kind** (= not just another version) –
7. **except that, there are certain folks – the ones constantly agitating** (stirring up; disturbing) **you folks – even repeatedly wanting** (or: intending) **to alter and distort** (turn so as to change; pervert; reverse) **Christ's message of goodness, ease and well-being** (or: the good news which is the Anointed One; or: the evangel about and from the [Messiah]).

8. **However, even if we – or an agent from the atmosphere or sky** (or: a messenger from out of the midst of heaven)! **– should ever bring or announce something as "good news"** (as the message of goodness; as being the evangel or gospel) **to you folks which is to the side of that which we bring and announce** (or: is parallel to what we proclaimed) **to, for and among you folks in the message of goodness, ease and well-being, let it be placed on the altar before the Lord** (set up as a result of a divine offering [i.e., to see if it is "accepted" by God, or "rejected," as Cain's was]; or, possibly: cursed).
9. **So as we have said before** (or: = above [in vs. 8]), **and I am right now presently saying again, if anyone is habitually announcing** (proclaiming) **as "good news" that which is to the side of that which you receive** (or: took to your side), **let it be placed on the altar before God** (set up as a result of a divine offering [to see if it's acceptable]; or, possibly: cursed).

10. **Come now, am I at the present moment habitually appealing to human beings, or God?** (or: am I right now constantly trying to convince and persuade people, or God ?) **Or, am I repeatedly seeking to keep on pleasing and accommodating people** (human beings)**? If I had been still continuing to please, appease or accommodate people** (human beings), **I would not have been being Christ's slave.**

11. **You see,** [other MSS: Now] **I am habitually making it intimately known to you folks by experience, brothers: that the message of goodness, ease and well-being – the one being brought, announced and proclaimed as "good" news by** (or: under) **me – is not down from or according to a person** (or: is not corresponding to something human; is not on the level of or in the sphere of a human being),

12. **for I myself neither received it to my side from a human being** (or: from beside a person), **nor was I taught [it], but to the contrary, [it came] through an unveiling of Jesus Christ** (or: through an uncovering pertaining to Jesus [the Messiah]; through a revelation from Jesus Christ; by means of a disclosure which is [the] Anointed Jesus).

13. **For you hear** (or: heard) **about my former way of life** (one-time conduct and behavior) **within the traditional Jewish culture and religion** ([Second Temple] Judaism), **that corresponding to excessive action** (a throwing over and casting beyond) **I was hastening in hostile pursuit, continuing to persecute God's called-out group of people** (the community whose source is God; the ecclesia pertaining to God), **and I kept on trying to lay it waste** (or: continued sacking and devastating it).

14. **And so I was progressively cutting forward and kept on advancing within Judaism** (the culture and religion of the Jews) **over and above many contemporaries** (folks of the same age) **within my race, being inherently more exceedingly zealous pertaining to the traditions of my fathers** (or: for the things handed over, given alongside or delivered which originated with my ancestors).

15. **Yet when God – the One marking off boundaries to separate and sever me from out of my mother's womb** (or: cavity; [comment: a figure of the religion of the Jews]), **and calling [me] through His grace and favor – thought well** (or: delights and takes pleasure)

16. **to unveil** (reveal; uncover; disclose) **His Son within the midst of me** (or: in union with me), **to the end that I in myself** (or: for myself; by myself) **would bring, announce and proclaim the message of goodness, [which is] Him, within the ethnic multitudes** (or: may bring and tell the message of ease and well-being: Him [now] among the nations), **I did not immediately place myself back toward flesh and blood** (= present my cause up for the approval of other people; consult anyone; seek communication or advice from my race, kin or religion),

17. **neither did I go up into Jerusalem, toward those [who were] people sent off** (= to face and be with the commissioned representatives) **previous to me, but rather, I went off into Arabia, then later I again returned into Damascus.**

18. **Later on, after three years, I went up into Jerusalem to become acquainted with** (or: to inquire of, examine and get information from) **Cephas** [some MSS: Peter] **while visiting him and relating my story to him, and then stayed on with him for fifteen days.**

19. **Yet a different one of** (or: another one from) **those sent with commissions** (the envoys; the representatives) **I did not see, except Jacob** (= James), **the Lord's brother.**

20. **Now what I am presently writing to you folks** (or: for you folks), **consider! In God's sight, I am not lying!**

21. **After that, I came into the slopes of the regions of Syria and Cilicia,**

22. **yet I was continuing being personally** (or: experientially) **unknown, by face, to the called-out groups** (the summoned-forth communities) **of the Judean area: folks within Christ.**

23. **Indeed, they were only hearing from time to time that, "The one once habitually pursuing and persecuting us is now habitually bringing and announcing as good news the Faithful One** (or: the fidelity and allegiance; or: the faith, trust and belief) **which once he kept on besieging, laying waste and devastating."**

24. **And in me [i.e., in my case or situation] they kept on glorifying God** (or: began giving credit to God and expanding His reputation; or: So they began presuming, imagining and then continued regarding God [as being] within the midst of, and in union with, me).

CHAPTER 2

1. **Later, after a period of fourteen years, I again walked up into Jerusalem with Barnabas** (bar-Nabas), **taking Titus, also, along with [us].**
2. **Now I walked up** (or: made the ascent) **[there] corresponding to and as directed by** (or: in accord with and in the sphere of; down from and in response to), **an unveiling** (or: a disclosure; a revelation), **and I put up to them** (set back again for them; submitted among them) **the message of goodness, ease and well-being, which I am habitually bringing and proclaiming as a public message within the multitudes** (or: among the nations and ethnic groups – non-Jews; Gentiles) – **yet [I did so] privately, to those continuing to be disposed to thinking and imagination** (or: for those being supposed to continue with a reputation; or: to ones yet forming opinions), **lest somehow I am progressively rushing forward and running, or had run, into emptiness** (or: for an empty thing; into something without content; = to no purpose; or: = in vain).
3. **However, not even Titus – the one with me – was compelled or even strongly urged to be circumcised, although being a Greek!**
4. **Yet, through the led-in-at-the-side** (or: smuggled-in) **false brothers** (or: = deceitful or lying fellow believers; or: = imitation members) – **folks who entered alongside to spy out** (to attentively look down and around, observe and take note of) **our freedom which we continuously possess** (constantly have and hold) **within Christ Jesus, to the end that they will utterly enslave us** (or: with a purpose that they will proceed to bring us down into slavery) –
5. **to whom** (or: for whom), **now, we did** (or: do) **not for even an hour give place to, make a way for, or simulate by humble alignment, subordination, submission or subjection, so that the reality** (the Truth) **of the message of goodness may abide throughout** (or: thoroughly remain; fully dwell; be permanent in continuing) **focused toward, and be face to face with, you folks!**

6. **Now from those continuing to be disposed to thinking and imagination** (or: from those being supposed to continue with a reputation; or: from the folks yet forming opinions) – **whatever sort of men they formerly** (or: once) **were being matters nothing** (makes no difference; carries nothing through) **to me** (or: for me) **[because] God is not in the habit of receiving a person's face** (= taking people at face value; or: responding to man's outward appearance or presentation). **So you see, those continuing to be disposed to thinking and imagination** (or: those being supposed to continue with a reputation; those yet forming opinions) **of themselves put nothing new forward for me** (or: from themselves placed forward [as a suggestion] nothing back in me; = contributed or added nothing to me).
7. **But rather, on the contrary, seeing that I had been persuaded by and convinced of** (or: perceiving that I had been entrusted with) **the message of goodness, ease and well-being concerning** (or: with reference to; in consideration of; pertaining to; separated for; belonging to; having characteristics and qualities suited to; for the context of; relative to; as it relates to) **the Uncircumcision** (literally: [cultures] of the foreskin; = those not of the Jewish religion, being from pagan religions or Hellenistic culture), **correspondingly as Peter, concerning** (or: with reference to; in consideration of; pertaining to; separated for; belonging to; having characteristics and qualities suited to; for the context of; relative to; as it relates to) **the Circumcision** (= the Jews, or those of the Jewish religion and culture [who cut off the foreskin]) –
8. **for it follows that, the One working within** (being active in; operating within; energizing) **Peter unto a sending for a mission concerning** (in reference to; which is) **the Circumcision, also by and in me inwardly works** (energizes; is inwardly active and operative) **unto the ethnic multitudes** (into the midst of the nations – the non-Jewish groups; the Gentiles) –
9. **then Jacob** (or: James), **Cephas and John – those continuing to be disposed to thinking and imagination** (or: those yet forming opinions) **and seeming, by reputation, to be pillars** (or: supportive columns [note: a figure of a living temple]) – **recognizing** (or: coming to know) **by intimate experience the grace and favor being given by me** (or: to me; in me; for me), **gave to**

me and to Barnabas [the] right [hands] of common partnership, from common participation, in regard to common existence/situation and which signified equal belonging in fellowship, community and sharing, to the end that we [would continue] into the nations (multitudes; ethnic groups; Gentiles; non-Jews) – yet they, into the Circumcision – 10. [the] only [concern being] that we would habitually be mindful of the poor ones (or: should keep on remembering the destitute folks), which very thing, also, I was eager and made every effort to do.

11. Now when Cephas came into Antioch, I took a stand opposite to him in relation to the appearance of the external situation (or: I resisted him face to face; or: I stood face to face with him, on his behalf), because he was continuing in a state of having been discovered to be down [over an issue] (or: he continued being one having been observed and known to be in a negative experience; or: was being found at fault; or: was being recognized as being prejudiced), 12. for you see, prior to the coming of some from Jacob (or: James), he had been habitually eating together with those of the multitudes (the nations; the non-Jewish ethnic groups; the Gentiles). Yet when they came, he began steadily withdrawing, and continued separating by marking off boundaries for himself, constantly fearing those from among [the] Circumcision (or: reverencing folks from the Jewish culture and religion). 13. And so the rest of the Jews (and/or Judeans) also, as a group, came under the decision to separate with (or: to) him, so that even Barnabas was jointly brought along (or: led away together) by their [Law]-based separation (or: in their perverse judgment which ended in a base decision; with their hyper-critical, under-discerning discrimination; or: = hair-splitting, legalistic behavior). 14. But then, when I saw that they did not continue walking straight (having a straight foot[print]; walking an upright course) toward the Truth (or: face to face with the reality) of the message of goodness and ease, I said to Cephas, in front of everyone (or: all), "If you, being inherently a Jew are now habitually living as the ethnic multitudes (like the nations; as a Gentile), and not like a Jew, how is it [that] you are continuing to compel (to strongly urge) the multitudes (the nations; the non-Jewish ethnic groups; the Gentiles) to be now Judaizing (progressively living according to Jewish custom and religion)?

15. We – Jews by (or: in) nature, and not outcasts (ones who miss the target or deviate from the goal; failures; sinners) from out of the multitudes (herds; nations; ethnic groups; Gentiles) – 16. having seen and thus knowing that humanity (or: mankind; or: a person) is not normally being eschatologically liberated, put in right relationship or turned in the right direction
> (made fair and equitable; made free from guilt and set into the Way pointed out; rectified; rightwised and made to be a just one; = being presently brought into covenant) from out of works of Law (or: forth from a law's observances or customs), except rather, through Jesus Christ's faithfulness (or: a faith and trust that belongs to, is from, and which is Christ Jesus), even we ourselves believe and place trust – into Christ Jesus – that we should and would be delivered and can be put in right relationships of the Way pointed out
> (or: and so we suddenly trusted and were at once loyal unto Jesus [the] Anointed One, to the end that we would be liberated and made just-fair-equitable, be released from feelings of guilt, be rightwised and placed into new covenant membership) from out of the midst of Christ's faithfulness, as a source and sphere (or: forth from trust and conviction, which are Christ), – NOT from out of the midst of works of Law, as a source and sphere, because from out of the midst of works of Law (or: so that, forth from a law's observances corresponding to custom, or from out of actions which comprise [the] Law) "no flesh (= person or human) at all will proceed being delivered or continue being put in right relationship
> (liberated and made to be just, fair and equitable; freed from guilt; rightwised or turned in the right direction from being placed into the Way pointed out; = put in covenant)." [Ps. 143:2]

17. Now since (or: if) we, in habitually seeking to be delivered and put in right relationship (placed into the Way pointed out; made to be just, fair and turned aright; also = made to be participants in the covenant; or: seeking to be freed from guilt) within Christ (or: in union with

[the] Anointed One [= the Messiah]), **were ourselves also found to be failures** (ones who miss the target; those who deviate; sinners; outcasts), **[is] Christ, consequently, an attending servant of failure** (sin's servant; a dispenser of error; a minister to the missing of the target)**? May it not happen** (or: It cannot come to be; Certainly not)**!** [*cf* Rom. 4:25b; 5:9; Phil. 3:9]

18. **For if I should continue building up again** (or: would repeatedly reconstruct) **these things which I loosed down and demolished, I myself continue standing together with a transgressor** (or: I proceed to exhibit myself as one who steps out of the Way and to the side).

19. **You see** (or: For it follows that) **I, myself, through [the]** (or: through means of by) **Law died by [the] Law** (or: to Law; in [the] Law; with [the] Law), **to the end that I could and would live by God, in God, for God, to God and with God!** [*cf* Rom. 7:13-23]

20. **I was crucified together with Christ** [= the Messiah], **and thus it remains** (or: I have been jointly put on the execution stake in [the] Anointed One, and continue in this state)**... yet I continue living! [It is] no longer I, but it is Christ continuously living and alive within me!** (or: No longer an "I," and ego – now Christ constantly lives in the midst of, and in union with, me). **Now that which I, at the present moment, continue living within flesh** (= a physical body), **I am constantly living within [His] faithfulness – in and by that [faithfulness] which is the Son of God** (or: in union with the trust and confidence that is from God's Son; [with other MSS: in the faith and fidelity belonging to God and Christ]), **the One loving me and giving Himself over to another for the sake of me** (or: even transmitting Himself, over my [situation and condition]; or: also passing Himself along for me; committing and transferring Himself over me).

21. **I make it no habit to displace** (shove aside; upset; thus: reject; thwart; repudiate; nullify) **God's grace and favor! For if rightwising deliverance into justice, equity and freedom from guilt with right relationships within the Way pointed out** (= transforming-inclusion into the new covenant) **[is] through Law** (= by legalistic behavior or religious works), **then as a consequence Christ died as a mere gratuity** (= for nothing; to no purpose).

CHAPTER 3

1. **O senseless, unreflecting and foolish Galatians! Who suddenly harmed you with malicious words, or bewitched you folks with the evil eye – before whose eyes Jesus Christ was graphically placarded** (= as though portrayed in writing before your own eyes) **one having been crucified on a stake** (suspended on an execution pole)**?** [*cf* Lu. 24:25]

2. **This only am I intending** (wanting; purposing; willing) **to learn from you people: Did you receive the Spirit** (or: get the Breath-effect; take in hand the Attitude) **from out of works of Law, or from out of a hearing of a report about faithfulness** (= [the] faithful One)

   (or: from the midst of faith's hearing; or: from a hearing of a proclamation that was characterized by [Christ's] fidelity; or: out of a listening from trust or loyalty)**?**

3. **Are you so senseless, unreflecting and foolish? Being folks making a beginning inwardly by spirit** (or: in breath-effect; by [the] Spirit; with [the] result of [the] Breath) **are you folks now being progressively brought fully to the goal** (being totally finished, perfected and brought to your destiny) **by flesh** (or, as a middle: are you now continuing to accomplish completeness in yourselves in, or with, flesh)**?**

   [note: Paul is using the word "flesh" here as a figure for "works of Law" (vs.2, above), with its circumcision, animal sacrifices, etc.; for other religions it would refer to "religious works" of those particular systems (including Christianity, in the following centuries)]

4. **Did you folks experience or suffer so many things randomly, for no cause or purpose – if in reality [there] even [is] "for no cause," or "by random happenings"?**

5. **The One, therefore, continuously furnishing and supplying to** (or: for; in) **you folks the Spirit** (or: the spirit; the breath; or: = attitude and vitality), **and constantly and effectively energizing, being active, working and producing abilities and powers within you people – [is its source] from out of works of Law, or out of a hearing of a report of faithfulness,**

   (or: The one, then, constantly supplying the Breath-effect for you folks, and repeatedly working powers among you – [does he do it] from out of deeds based on [the] Law and of observances of [Torah], or from out of faith's attentive listening or a hearing from trust,)

6. **just as Abraham, "was faithful to God** (or: believed by God; trusts in, and with, God), **and he is/was at once logically considered and viewed by Him [that he had come] into a right relationship** (or: and it was counted for him into a rightwised, equitable and covenantal relationship with [God] which aligned with the Way [that God had] pointed out)"**? [Gen. 15:6; *cf* Rom. 4:3ff]

7. **Be assured consequently, by your experiential knowledge and insight,** (or, as an indicative: Surely you are coming to know) **that the folks [springing] forth from out of the midst of Faithfulness** (or: whose source is [His; his] faith, trust and confident loyalty), **these are Abraham's sons!**

8. **Now the Scripture – seeing before [as a picture] that God is now progressively liberating the nations into rightwised relationship** (delivering the ethnic groups of non-Jews into the Way pointed out and freeing them from guilt) **from out of Faithfulness – announced to** (or: for) **Abraham beforehand the message of goodness, ease and well-being**

> (or: And further – the Scripture perceiving in advance and making provision that He is presently making the multitudes fair and equitable {or: = including the Gentiles in the covenant} from faith, trust, conviction and loyalty – God brought-before in Abraham the glad tidings of goodness {a gospel; an evangel}), **namely that,**
> **"All the nations, ethnic groups and multitudes will continuously and progressively be inwardly blessed** (receive the inner Word of wellness; participate within the Good Word) **in a union with you** (or: within you; in you; or: = in relation to you; or: = as in your case)." [Gen. 12:3; 22:18]

9. **So then, those from out of Faithfulness** (or: = folks who are derived from [Christ's] faith, trust and confidence and who come from the place of [His] loyal allegiance) **are being constantly blessed** (repeatedly given the Word of wellness; continuously made to participate in the Good Word) **together with the full-of-faith and faithful Abraham** (or: the trusting, believing, convinced and loyal Abraham).

10. **You see, however many people continue their existence from the midst of observances and works of Law** (= Everyone who lives by deeds and actions based upon the Torah) **are continuously under a curse** (a negative, down-focused or adversarial prayer; an imprecation), **for it has been and now stands written, namely that,**

> **"A curse** (or: an adversarial prayer; imprecation) **[is settled] upon all** (or: [is] added to everyone) **not constantly remaining within all the things having been and standing written within the scroll of the Law** [= Torah], **in order to do them."** [Deut. 27:26]

11. **Now [the fact] that within [the] Law no one is in process of** (or: in union with [the] Law or or custom is no one presently) **being eschatologically delivered and rightwised** (put in right relationship; made just, freed from guilt, or, placed within the Way pointed out which is covenant membership and life) **at God's side** (or: with God) **[is] clearly visible and evident, because,**

> **"the fair and equitable man** (the One in right relationship within the Way pointed out; the Just One) **will continue to live from out of faithfulness** (or: the one [who is] just from out of trusting fidelity, and loyal conviction, will progressively live)," [Hab. 2:4]

12. **yet the Law is not** (or: [Torah] does not have its existence) **[springing] forth from out of faith and trust, but to the contrary,**

> **"the one 'doing and performing' them shall be constantly living [his life] within them** (or: will continue living, in union with these things)." [Lev. 18:5]

13. **Christ bought us [back] out** (or: redeems and reclaims us out [of slavery] and liberates us) **from the midst of the curse** (or: adversarial prayer; imprecation) **of and from the Law, while becoming** (or: birthing Himself to be) **a curse** (or: an accursed One; an [embodied] adversarial prayer) **for our sakes** (or: over our [situation]) – **for it has been and now stands written:**

> **"A curse** (an adversarial prayer) **[is settled] upon all** (or: [is] added to everyone) **continuing hanging upon a tree** (or: wood; a stake or pole)" [Deut. 21:23, omitting the phrase "by God," after the word "curse"] –

14. **to the end that the Good Word** (the Blessing; Good *Logos*, Word of goodness, ease and well-being) **pertaining to Abraham** (belonging to and possessed by Abraham; from, and whose intermediary source is, Abraham) **could within Jesus Christ suddenly birth Itself** (or: may from Itself, within Anointed Jesus, at once come into being [and be dispersed]) **into the multitudes**

(the nations; the ethnic groups; the Gentiles), **so that we** [note: "we" = the new "one" mankind; *cf* Eph. 2:11-16] **could receive the Spirit's promise through the Faithfulness [of Christ]**
(or: to the end that we [all] may take in hand the Promise from the Breath-effect, through faith and trust; or: in order that we [Jew and Gentile] can lay hold of and receive the Promise – which is the Spirit – through that loyalty; [*cf* Isa. 44:3]).

15. **Brothers** (= fellow believers; family), **I am now speaking humanly** (in accordance with and on the level of mankind; = with an illustration of common human practice). **Like with the situation of a human settled arrangement** (or: will; contract; covenant; or: will and testament deed of gift)**: [when] existing as having been validated** (authoritatively confirmed; legally ratified; publicly affirmed), **no one is proceeding to displace it** (to annul it; to set it aside) **or modify it or add stipulations** (super-add an injunction; add a codicil; introduce additions, amendments or arrangements throughout it).
16. **Now the promises were declared** (said; spoken) **to** (or: for; in) **Abraham, and to** (or: for; in) **his Seed** (Descendant). **It** (or: He) **is not saying, "And to the seeds** (descendants),**" as upon many, but rather, as upon One, "And to, for and in your Seed,"** [Gen. 12:7; 13:15; etc.] **Who exists being Christ** (or: which is [the] Anointed One [= the Messiah], and an Anointing).

17. **Further, I am now saying and meaning this: the Law** [= Torah], **being that having come into existence after four hundred and thirty years, is not invalidating** (depriving of authority; annulling; abolishing) **into the situation to idle-down** (render ineffective, useless, unproductive or inoperative) **the Promise – a settled arrangement** (contract; covenant; will and testament deed of gift) **existing as having been previously validated** (confirmed; legally ratified) **by, and under [the authority of], God!**
18. **For if the inheritance** (the possession and enjoyment of the distributed allotment) **[is] from out of Law** [= Torah], **[it is] no longer from out of Promise. Yet God has Himself graced [it]** (has for Himself, in favor, freely granted [it]), **so that it now stands as a favor of grace, to** (or: for; in) **Abraham through a Promise** (or: by a promise).

19. **Why, then, the Law** [= Torah] **of The Transgressions? It was at one point set aiming at, and thus provided a view to, grace and favor**
(or: Why, then, the Law? It was placed close and applied {imposed; added}: grace on behalf of the walks to the side of [the path];
or: What, therefore [is] the Law [= Torah]? Something set, as a favor, face-to-face with the over-steppings and transgressions to the side of and beyond [the Way])
– being precisely arranged and thoroughly prescribed and mandated by injunction through means of agents (or: messengers; folks with the message) **within the midst of [the] hand of a mediator** (or: in an umpire's hand; within [the] hand of an arbitrator or an intermediary in a middle position) **– as far as to where** (or: until which place or time) **the Seed would** (or: should) **come, to Whom, for Whom, with respect to Whom and by Whom the promise had been made** (or: in Whom He had been promised).
20. **Now there is no mediator of one** (= when only one person is concerned or is acting alone). **Yet** (or: Now) **God is One.**
[note: to make a promise, one is sufficient – there is no need for a middleman]
21. **Is the Law, then, following the pattern of** (or: down from; or: down against; or: on a par with; commensurate with; corresponding to) **God's promises? May it not happen** (It could not come to be; = Of course not)**! For if a law** (or: [the] Law) **were given which continued having power or being able at any point to make alive** (to construct or create living folks; to engender living ones; to impart life), **really, the eschatological deliverance of fairness and equity resulting in righted relationships** (the liberating and rightwising qualities of justice, freedom from guilt, and life as it ought to be within the Way pointed out; or: = new covenant inclusion) **was likely being from out of the midst of [the] Law** [= Torah; other MSS: residing within law].
22. **But to the contrary, the Scripture encircles and encloses [as fish in a net] all things, shuts them up together and locks the whole** (the totality of everything) **under** (or: by) **failure** (error; deviation; the missing of the target; sin), **to the end that, from out of Jesus Christ's faithfulness**

(or: forth from the midst of the faith from Jesus Christ; from the midst of the trust and conviction which is Jesus, [the] Anointed One),
the Promise would suddenly (or: could at some point) **be given to** (or: in; for; by) **the folks habitually experiencing trust** (or: progressively believing with faith's conviction). [*cf* Rom. 11:32]

23. **So before the [time, or, event for] the Faithful One to come** (or: prior to the coming of this faith, trust, assurance, conviction and loyalty), **we were being continuously restrained, confined and held in custody under the watch of a guard, being folks constantly encircled, enclosed, shut up and locked together by and under Law, with a view to, aimed at, and moving into the midst of, the Faithfulness** (or: the Act of Trust) **being about to be unveiled** (or: revealed; disclosed),

    [*cf* Ex. 19:17 (LXX): "under the mountain (i.e., Sinai)"]

24. **so that, consequently, the Law** (= Torah) **had come to be** (had been birthed into existence) **and continued being our supervising guardian and attending, custodial escort unto, with a view to, and [pointing] into Christ, to the end that we could** (or: would) **be delivered by the Just Act and then rightwised to be in the new covenant of right relationships with justice and fairness that characterize the liberty in the Way pointed out, from out of Faithfulness** (or: an act of loyalty, trust and faith).

25. **So now with the coming of the Faithful One, we no longer continuously exist** (or: are) **under [the] supervising guardian or an attending escort** [comment: = the Law; Torah]!

26. **For you folks are all** [i.e., Jew and non-Jew; male and female; slave and freeman] **God's sons, through the faithfulness located and resident within Christ Jesus** (or: by means of the trust in union with an Anointing from Jesus; [*p46*: through Jesus Christ's faithfulness])**!**

    (or: You see, all you folks [who are] located and centered in Christ Jesus exist being sons of God, by means of that Faithful One!)

27. **For you see** (or: It follows that) **as many of you folks as were immersed into Christ, at once clothed yourselves with Christ** (or: were plunged into so as to be enveloped by, then saturated and permeated with, Anointing – or, the Anointed One – instantly entered within and put on [the/an] Anointing)**!**

28. **Within** [Him; us], **there is not** (there does not exist) **Jew nor Greek** (or: Hellenist); **within, there is not** (does not exist) **slave nor freeman; within, there is not** (does not exist) **'male and female'; for it follows that, you folks all exist being one within Christ Jesus** (or: for you see, all you people are one person, centered in, and in union with, an Anointing from Jesus).

29. **Now since you folks belong to Christ** (or: have [the] Anointing as your source and origin; or: So since you people have the qualities and character of Christ, and [are] that which is Christ), **you are straightway and consequently Abraham's Seed: heirs** (possessors and enjoyers of the distributed allotment), **down from, corresponding to and in the sphere of Promise!**

CHAPTER 4

1. **Now I continue saying, for** (or: upon [the length of]) **as much time as the heir** (the apparent possessor of the distributed allotment) **is progressing from being an infant to a minor** (one having either no ability, or no right, to speak; = continues being under legal age) **he continues essentially differing nothing from a slave, [though] continuously being owner** (lord and master) **of everything** (of all),

2. **but further, he exists being under those to whom the trust is committed** (guardians; ones entrusted with control and right to turn upon their charges) **and house managers** (estate stewards; administrators) **until the father's previously set** [time or situation].

3. **Thus also we ourselves, when we were progressing from infants to minors, we continued being folks having been enslaved under** (or: by) **the System's elementary principles** (the rows, ranks and series of the organized system and world of culture, economy, government in secular society and religion; or: the rudimentary things pertaining to the cosmos; [note: a probable reference to the Law, 3:24, above; vss. 4-5, 9-10, below]).

4. **Yet when the effect of the filling of the time came** (or: that which was filled up by time reached full term), **forth from out of a mission** (or: from out of the midst of [Himself]), **God sent-**

off His Son, being Himself come to be born from out of a woman, being Himself come to be born under [the rules, authority and influence of] Law, [*cf* Ex. 19:17, LXX: "under {Sinai}"]
5. **to the end that He could** (or: would) **buy out** (release by purchase; redeem; reclaim [from slavery]) **those under [the] Law – so that WE could and would receive and take away into possession the placing in the condition of a son** (or: the deposit of the Son; the setting in place which is the Son; the constituting as a son; the placing in the Son). [*cf* Rom. 8:3-4; Jn. 3:16]
6. **Now, because we exist being** (are presently and continuously) **sons, God at once sends forth** (or: at one point sent off from out of [His] midst) **His Son's Spirit** (or: the Breath-effect, which is His Son) **as an emissary into the midst of our hearts, repeatedly crying out** (habitually calling out or exclaiming in an inarticulate cry; even: screaming, shrieking [verb also means: croak, as a bird]), **"Abba** (Aramaic: = Dad, or, Daddy!), **O Father!"**
7. **So that, you are** (you exist being) **no longer a slave, but rather, a son, and since a son, also an heir** (a possessor and an enjoyer of the distributed allotment) **through** (or: through means of) **God** [other MSS: God's heir through Christ].

8. **But on the other hand, at that time, in fact, having not perceived and thus not knowing God, you folks were, and performed as, slaves to** (or: for) **those [who], by nature, are not gods.**
9. **Yet now, coming to know God by intimate experience and personal insight – or, rather, being known intimately by God – how are you folks progressively turning around again, upon the weak** (feeble; infirm; diseased; impotent) **and poor** (beggarly) **elementary and rudimentary principles to which** (for which; in which) **you people are presently wanting** (and progressively intending) **to again become, and perform as, slaves anew** (or: back again)?
10. **You are for yourselves and in yourselves continuously watching closely and observing days** [e.g., sabbaths; days for fasting] **and months** (or: new moons) **and seasons** (or: appointed situations [e.g., feasts]) **and [sacred] years!** [*cf* vs. 21a, below]
11. **I continue fearing for you, lest somehow I have, to the point of exhaustion, labored in vain** (for no purpose) **into you folks.**

12. **Brothers** (= Fellow believers; = O family), **I beg of you, progressively become as I, for I also [was; am] as you folks. You did me no wrong** (or: You folks treat me unfairly in nothing).
13. **Now you have seen and known that through weakness** (impotence; sickness; infirmity; feebleness) **of the flesh** (or: = pertaining to [my] imperfect human nature; = whose source is the self which was affected by the System; = which is the deficient inner person) **I formerly brought and announced the message of goodness, ease and well-being to you folks,**
14. **and yet you folks did not despise or treat as nothing your** [other MSS: my] **ordeal** (or: trial; testing) **– located within my flesh** (= in my human weaknesses) **– nor did you spit it out** (= reject it as loathing; [note: perhaps referring to the practice of spitting to break the spell of "an evil eye" – a common pagan belief]), **but to the contrary, you took me in your arms and welcomed me as God's agent** (or: messenger; Greek: *angelos*) **– as Jesus Christ!**
15. **Where, then, [is] your happiness** (or: the blessedness, which is you folks)? **For, I continually bear witness to you folks** (or: give testimony for you) **that, if possible** (if [you were] able), **upon gouging** (digging) **out your eyes you would give [them] to me!**
16. **So then, by habitually being real and speaking Truth to you** (constantly telling you the truth; progressively speaking reality to you), **have I come to be your enemy?**

17. **They are constantly zealous over you folks** (= These folks are constantly showing you great attention in order to win you over) **– [though] not beautifully** (or: ideally; in a fine or seemly way; = not with good form). **But on the other hand they are constantly willing** (intending; wanting) **to shut you out** (to exclude or alienate you), **so that you folks might be habitually zealous over them** (= trying to win their favor).
18. **Now [it is] always ideal** (fine; beautiful) **to be normally made zealous** (or: to continue having a ferment of spirit) **within a beautiful** (fine; ideal) **thing or situation, and not only within the situation for me to be present** (or: at your side) **and focused toward you folks.**

19. **O my little children** (born ones), **with whom I am progressing, again, in childbirth labor** (travail; labor pains) **until Christ may be suddenly formed within you folks** (or: = until the Anointing would at some point come full term and be birthed, centered and in union with you)!
20. **Yet I was wanting** (or: intending) **to be present** (at your side) **and focused toward you right now!... and then to alter** (change; make otherwise) **my voice** (or: tone; sound)... **because I continue without a way or path to bring myself in union with you folks** (or: = I am now perplexed, uncertain, disturbed and at an impasse in your case).

21. **Go on telling me, those of you constantly wanting or intending to be under Law** (or: exist [controlled] by a legalistic custom or system, or [Torah]), **do you not continue listening to and hearing the Law** (or: paying attention to the [Torah])**?**
22. **For it has been, and stands, written that, Abraham had two sons: one forth from out of the servant girl** (the maid; the female slave), **and one from out of the freewoman.**
23. **But, on the one hand, the one from out of the servant girl** (the maid) **had been born** (generated and birthed) **down from** (in accord with; on the level of; in the sphere of) **flesh** (= by human means); **on the other hand, the one from out of the freewoman [was] through Promise** (or: a promise)
24. **– which things are habitually being allegorized** (or: are normally being expressed in an allegory; are commonly spoken of as something other [than what the language means]) **– for these women are** (= represent) **two settled arrangements** (covenants; contracts; wills)**: one, on the one hand, from Mount Sinai, habitually** (repeatedly; continuously) **giving birth into slavery** (or: bondage) **– which is Hagar.** [cf Ex. 19:17 (LXX)]
25. **Now this Hagar is** (= represents) **Mount Sinai, within Arabia, and she continuously stands in the same line** (or: keeps step in the same rank; marches in a column; walks or stands in a parallel row; or: is habitually rudimentary together; or: = corresponds to) **with the present Jerusalem, for she continues in slavery** (or: functioning in bondage) **with her children.**
26. **Yet, on the other hand, the Jerusalem above is** (continues being) **free, who is** (or: which particular one continues being) **our mother.**
27. **For it has been and stands written,**
> **"Be made well-minded** (Be given a competent way of thinking; Be made glad; Be turned to a good attitude), **barren** (or: sterile) **woman, O woman consistently not bringing forth** (not bearing; not giving birth; not producing)**! Break forth** (or: Shatter) **in pieces and shout for joy** (or: implore aloud), **O woman consistently not having labor pains** (birth pangs), **because many [are] the children** (the born-ones) **of the desolate woman** (of the abandoned woman of the desert), **rather than of the woman continuously having** (holding; possessing) **the husband."** [Isa. 54:1, LXX]
28. **Now we [other MSS: you folks], brothers** (= fellow believers; = my family), **down from** (or: corresponding to; in the sphere and manner of) **Isaac, are** (continuously exist being) **children of Promise** (or: ones-born from [the] Promise).
29. **But nevertheless, just as then, the one being born down from** (in accordance with; corresponding to; on the level of; in the sphere of) **flesh** (= human efforts) **was constantly pursuing and persecuting the one down from** (in accordance with; corresponding to; in the sphere of) **spirit** (or: Breath-effect), **so also now.**
30. **Still, what does the Scripture yet say?**
> **"Cast out** (or: At once expel) **the servant girl** (the slave-girl; the maid) **and her son, for by no means will the son of the servant girl** (the slave-girl; the maid) **be an heir** (take possession of and enjoy the distributed allotment) **with the son of the freewoman."** [Gen. 21:10]
31. **Wherefore, brothers** (= fellow believers; family), **we are not** (we do not exist being) **children of a slave-girl** (a servant girl; a maid), **but, to the contrary, of the freewoman.**

CHAPTER 5

1. **For the [aforementioned] freedom, Christ immediately set us free** (or: [The] Anointed One at once frees us in, to, for and with freedom)**! Keep on standing firm, therefore, and do not**

again be habitually held within a yoke of slavery (or: a cross-lever [of a pair of scales] whose sphere is bondage)

> (or: Continuously stand firm, then, in the freedom [to which the] Anointing sets us free, and let not yourselves be progressively confined again by a yoke pertaining to servitude)!

2. **See and individually consider! I, Paul, continue saying to you folks, that if you should proceed to being circumcised, Christ will continue benefiting you nothing** (or: an Anointing will continue of use to you [for] not one thing)!

3. **Now I continue solemnly asserting** (attesting; affirming; witnessing), **again, to every person** (or: human) **proceeding to be circumcised, that he is, and continues being, a debtor** (one under obligation) **to do** (to perform; to produce) **the whole Law** [= the entire Torah]!

4. **You people who in union with** (or: centered in; [remaining] within) **Law continue being "liberated, rightwised and placed in covenant," were at once discharged** (made inactive, idle, useless, unproductive and without effect; or: voided, nullified, exempted) **away from Christ** (or: [the] Anointing) – **you folks fell out from the grace** (or: fall from the midst of the favor)!

5. **For you see, in union with [the] Spirit** (or: by [the] Breath-effect; with [the] Spirit; or: in spirit) **– forth from out of faithfulness** (or: [the] trust-faith-loyalty) **– we, ourselves, continuously** (or: progressively) **receive by taking away, as with our hands, from out of [the] expectation which belongs to, comes from and which is [the] rightwising, eschatological deliverance within the Way pointed out** (or: forth from the midst of [the] expected hope, which is the state of being liberated, pointed in the right direction, and included as a participant in the new covenant),

6. **for within Christ Jesus** (or: for you see, in union with [the] Anointed Jesus) **neither circumcision continues having strength, for competence or effectiveness, to be availing** (or: be of service for) **anything, nor [does] uncircumcision, but rather, [it is the] faithfulness** (or: trust; faith; loyalty): **of itself continuously working effectively** (operating; being inwardly active and productive) **through Love** ("[God's] acceptance of the object of love without restriction, in spite of the estranged, profanized and demonized state of the object; the whole being's drive and movement toward reunion with another, to overcome existential separation; an ecstatic manifestation of the Spiritual Presence" – Paul Tillich, ibid., on *agapē*; or: [God's] fully giving of Himself to [us] – Richard Rohr; brackets added; *cf* John 3:16; 1 Cor. 13:4-8).

7. **You folks have been running beautifully** (finely; ideally; with good form)! **Who** (or: What) **cut in on you folks, to hinder or thwart you, [for you] not to continue to be persuaded** (convinced) **by** (or: in; with) **the Truth and this reality?**

8. **This "art of persuasion"** (or: The enticement; or: The yielding to [their] persuasion) **[comes] not from out of the One continuously calling, and summoning, you folks.**

9. **A little yeast** (or: leaven) **is progressively permeating so as to ferment** (to be leavening) **the whole batch of kneaded dough.**

10. **I myself have been convinced so as to be confident** (have come to a settled persuasion), **with a view into you folks – within [the] Lord** (Owner; [= Yahweh, or Christ]; or: I am confident in [the] Lord, [directing my thoughts] into you) – **that you will [in] nothing continue being disposed otherwise** (or: that you will have not [even] one other opinion or frame of mind). **Now the person constantly agitating and disturbing you people will lift up and progressively carry** (or: bear) **the effect of the decision** (or: result of [his] sifting and judgment), **whoever he or she may be.**

11. **Now as for me, brothers** (= fellow believers; = my family), **if I am still habitually preaching circumcision as the message, why am I still being constantly pursued and persecuted? If that has been the case, then the snare** (trap-spring; bait-stick; = offense; = a stumbling-block) **of the cross** (the execution-stake/suspension-pole) **has been, and remains, discharged** (made inactive, down-idled, useless, unproductive and without effect; or: = removed or abolished).

12. **Would that** (or: I wish that) **those continually unsettling you** (causing you to rise up as in an insurrection; thus: disturbing or exciting you folks) **will also, one after another, cut themselves away** (i.e., amputate themselves from your body [of believers]; or: cut themselves off [note: some read this to mean to mutilate themselves or castrate themselves])!

13. **For it follows that you folks were called** (summoned) **upon the foundation of** (on the basis of; for the purpose of) **freedom, [my] brothers. Only not** (or: Just not) **the freedom [which is leading] into a starting point** (or: unto an opportunity, occasion or incentive; to a base

of operation) **for** (to; in; by; with) **the flesh** [comment: = circumcision with the flesh ordinances and ceremonial laws of Judaism; or: = personal license for the estranged human nature], **but to the contrary, through** (or: by means of) **the Love** [agapē: cf vs. 6b, above] **be continuously slaving for one another** (serving and performing the duties of a slave to each other),
14. **for you see, the entire Law has been fulfilled and stands filled up within one word** (or: centered in one thought or idea; in union with one Logos and blueprint-message) – **within this:**

> "**You will continue loving** [agapaō; cf vs. 6b, above] **your near-one** (your associate; your neighbor; the one close by your position), **as** (in the same way as; or: as he/she were) **yourself."** [Lev. 19:18; comment: this one "expressed thought" is the idea and purpose of the Word]

15. **Now since, or if, you folks are habitually biting and repeatedly eating one another down, watch out, lest you may be used up and consumed by** (or: under) **one another.**
16. **So I continue saying, be habitually walking about** (= living your life) **in spirit** (or: by [the] Spirit; with a Breath-effect), **and you should under no circumstance** (or: would by no means) **bring to fruition** (carry to its goal; end up with; bring to maturity) **the full rushing passion** (the over-desire; craving) **originating in flesh**

> (= pertaining to the estranged human nature, or the self which has been dominated by a system of culture or religion; or: corresponding to flesh-[righteousness]; belonging to [a religious system] of flesh-works).

17. **For the flesh [system or nature] is constantly rushing passionately down upon** (or: against) **the spirit** (or: Breath-effect), **and the spirit** (or: Breath-effect) **down on** (or: against) **the flesh [nature, or, system of religion], for these things are constantly lying in opposition to each other** (lying set to displace each other), **so that – whatever you may habitually be intending** (wanting; willing; purposing) **– these things you repeatedly cannot be doing.**

> [comment: either because of the estranged flesh nature, or, because of the rules and/or teachings of the system]

18. **Yet since** (or: if) **you folks are continuously being led in spirit** (by [the] Spirit; to [the] Spirit; with a Breath-effect), **you do not exist** (you are not) **under Law** (or: custom; = Torah; = the flesh system of works; = the Mosaic covenant). [cf Rom. 8:14]

19. **Now the works** (actions; deeds) **of the flesh [religion]** (or: = whose source and origin are the estranged human nature; or: pertaining to the flesh [system, or, nature]; or: = whose results and realm are the self in slavery to a system) **[are] seen and made apparent in clear light, which are, and continue being, the works of a prostitute** (or: actions by the Prostitute [cf Rev. 17]): **uncleanness** (or: waste or worthless material, as of decayed flesh; a never-pruned tree; material that has not been sifted), **excess** (immoderation; outrageous behavior),
20. **idolatry** (being a servant to or worshiping external forms or appearances, phantoms of the mind, unsubstantial or reflected images, or conveyed impressions) **sorcery** (employment of drugs and enchantments; magic rites; witchcraft), **hostilities** (enmities; alienations), **strife** (contentious disposition), **jealousies** (or: zealous emotions), **stirring emotions** (rushing passions; furies), **factions, standings-apart** (divisions), **sects** (religious denominations; parties with a particular opinion; the making of choices from preferences),
21. **envies, murders, intoxications** (times of being drunk), **festal processions** (or: excessive feastings), **and things like to these [whether religious, or personal], which things I continue predicting** (saying beforehand; or: = giving warning) **to you folks, just as I said before, that those habitually practicing** (or: performing) **such [religious, or personal,] things will not be inheriting** (receiving and enjoying a distributed allotment of) **God's reign** (kingdom; sovereign influence and activities).

22. **Now the Spirit's fruit** (or: So the fruit from the Spirit; But the fruit which is Breath-effect; Yet the fruit of the Attitude) **is: love** (unrestricted, self-giving acceptance; the drive to overcome existential separation; etc.), **joy, peace** (or: harmonious joining), **length before a stirring of emotion** (slowness of rushing toward something; long-enduring; longsuffering; patience; putting anger far away), **useful kindness, goodness** (virtuousness), **faith** (or: faithfulness; trust; trustworthiness; loyalty; reliance; reliability; allegiance; fidelity),

23. **gentle friendliness** (absence of ego; mildness), **inner strength** (self-control). **[The] Law is not down from such things** (or: In the sphere of such things [the] Law does not exists; There is no law against such things; Law does not correspond to and is not on the level of such things).
24. **Now those whose source and origin is Christ Jesus** (or: those who belong to the Anointed Jesus) **crucified the flesh** (or: put the flesh [system] on an execution stake; or: = associate their old estranged human nature as being put to death along with Christ Jesus), **together with the results and effects of the experiences** (emotions; feelings; sufferings; passions) **and the over-desires** (those rushing passionately upon things in full-rushing emotion).
25. **Since** (or: If) **we continue living in and by spirit** (or: for [the] Spirit; to Breath-effect; or: with Attitude), **we also can habitually advance orderly in line in regard to, or amidst, elementary principles** (or: [observing] rudimentary elements), **in and by spirit** (or: for [the] Spirit; by Breath-effect; with Attitude; or: = walk in rank following [the footsteps] behind the Spirit). [cf Rom. 4:12]
26. **We can** (or: should) **not repeatedly** (or: habitually) **come to be** (or: Let us stop becoming) **folks with empty glory** (or: a vacuous reputation; = to be egotistical or conceited), **continually being those challenging one another [as to combat], constantly envying one another.**

CHAPTER 6

1. **O brothers** (= Fellow believers; = My family)! **Even if a person may be at some point overtaken** (caught; laid hold of before; be surprised) **within the effect of some slip or falling to the side** (or: the result of some offense, lapse or mistake), **you folks – the spiritual ones** (people influenced by the Breath-effect and Attitude; pneumatics) **– repeatedly** (or: continuously) **thoroughly restore, reconcile, adjust, align, mend or repair such a one so as to thoroughly prepare and equip him** (or: her) **within a spirit of gentle friendliness** (an attitude void of ego; breath of mild kindness), **as you each are constantly keeping a watchful eye on yourself** (carefully noting yourself with regard to the goal), **and thus you folks may not at some point be put to the proof** (or: and you, yourself, would not be tried, tested or harassed by some ordeal).
2. **You folks be habitually lifting up and carrying one another's heavy burdens and oppressive matters** (grievous weights of and from one another), **and thus, you will continuously fulfill** [or, with other MSS: In this way, at once fill up and fulfill] **Christ's Law**
     (or: the law which is Christ; the law of the Anointing; [other MSS: and in this manner, at
     once fill up the law from the Anointed {or: pertaining to, and with character of, Christ}]).
3. **For you see, if anyone, being presently nothing, continues imagining** (supposing; presuming) **himself to be something, he continues leading his own mind astray** (he keeps on deceiving himself; he misleads and cheats his intellect and way of thinking).
4. **So let each one habitually put his own work to the test for approval** (examine and prove the deeds and actions which he does), **and then he will continue having a cause for exultation-effects** (or: hold a sense of achievement) **in regard to himself alone, and not in comparison with the other person,**
5. **for you see, each one will lift up and progressively carry** (or: shoulder) **his own specific little load** (or: pack; small thing to be borne).

6. **Now let the person being habitually orally-instructed** (being sounded down [from above] into the ears so that they ring) **in the Word** (the message) **constantly express common being to** (or: hold common partnership in and fellowship for; share equally with) **the one regularly giving the oral instruction** (sounding down and making the ears ring), **in all good things.**
7. **Do not be continually led astray** (or: Stop being caused to wander and being deceived); **God is not one to be sneered at** (to have a nose turned up at; to be scorned, mocked or treated like a fool), **for "whatever a person is in the habit of sowing, this also he will reap,"**
8. **because the person continually sowing into the flesh of himself** (= his estranged inner being), **will progressively reap corruption** (spoil; ruin; decay) **forth from out of the flesh** (= the estranged inner being);
     (or: the one habitually sowing into the flesh [system], of himself will continue to reap
     decay from out of the flesh [system];)

yet the one constantly sowing into the spirit (or: the Breath) **will be progressively reaping eonian life** (life having the characteristics of the Age [of Messiah]; or: life from the Age that lasts on through the ages) **forth from out of the spirit** (or: the Spirit; the Breath-effect; that attitude).
9. **So – not being people [who are] let loose out from** (or: set free from out of) **[the laboring]** (or: not being made unstrung or exhausted so as to be relaxing [from laboring]) **– we should not in worthlessness be remiss** (or: act badly by failing; be despondent; in bad quality, give up) **in habitually doing** (making; constructing; producing) **the beautiful** (the fine; the ideal; the noble), **for in our own appropriate situation** (or: in our own appointed season; or: to or by our own fitness and proportion) **we will progressively gather in a harvest** (or: will continue reaping).
10. **Consequently, then, as we are continuing to hold a fitting situation** [or, with other MSS: while we may continue having occasion or a fertile moment], **we can keep on actively working the good** [other MSS: we should habitually be performing the excellent; we can continue in the business of the virtuous] **toward all people – and especially toward the families and the households of the Faithful One** (or: characterized by the faith-trust [arising] from [His] loyal act)!
11. **Consider** (or: See) **how large [are the] letters** [i.e., of the alphabet] **[which] I write to you, in** (or: by; with) **my [own] hand!**

> [comment: Paul is doing this to make his point, i.e., he is "shouting" at them via the script, so that they will take note of the point he is making]

12. **As many as continually want** (intend; will; purpose) **to make a good impression** (a pleasing appearance; a fair face, front or facade) **within flesh** [i.e., in a flesh system or religion], **these are habitually urging, or trying to compel or force, you folks** (or: making you feel obliged) **to proceed to be circumcised – only so that they may not be continually pursued and persecuted for** (or: in; with) **the cross of Christ Jesus** (or: by the execution stake that pertains to the Anointed Jesus).
13. **For not even the folks being presently** (or: currently getting) **circumcised** (or, as a middle: habitually circumcising [people]; requiring [the practice of] circumcision; [other MSS: having been circumcised]) **are themselves habitually keeping** (guarding; protecting; observing; maintaining) **[the] Law, but even so, they constantly want and intend you folks to proceed to be circumcised, so that they may have cause for boasting in your flesh [ritual or religion].**

14. **Now may it not happen to me** (or: in me) **to take up the practice of boasting, except within the cross of our Lord, Jesus Christ, through Whom** (or: through which [i.e., the cross]) **the organized System** (or: the world of culture, economy, government and religion) **has been, and continues being, crucified in me** (or: to me; for me; by me; or: through Whom the aggregate of humanity has been, and is now, crucified with me), **and I by** (to; in; with; for) **the domination System** (the world; = their culture, secular society, religion, and government).
15. **For you see** [some MSS add: within Christ Jesus], **neither circumcision nor uncircumcision** (literally: having a foreskin) **continues being anything, but rather: a new and different creation** (a founding and settling [as a village] with a new character and quality, in a place that was wild and without order; an innovative, new act of framing and building).
16. **So as many as are habitually** (or: are one-after-another) **advancing** [other MSS: will advance; can advance] **in line by ranks, corresponding to this measuring rod**

> (or: continue belonging to the rank living in conformity to this rule; or: shall in this standard progressively observe the rudimentary elements or elementary principles and walk in line with them), **Peace** (Harmony of the Joining) **and Mercy [are continually]**

upon them – even (or: that is) **upon the Israel of, and from, God** (or: God's Israel).
17. **Pertaining to the rest** (or: In regard to what is left over), **let no one continue offering hard labor to me** (or: let no one be making trouble for me or be holding me to his side for a beating), **for I myself continuously carry the brand marks [of a slave or a soldier, showing ownership] of Jesus, within** (or: the effects of being stuck by a point from Jesus, on) **my body!**
18. **The grace and favor of, and whose origin and source are, our Lord, Jesus Christ [are continually] with your spirit** (or: the Breath-effect belonging to you folks), **brothers** (= fellow believers; = [my] family)! **It is so!** (Amen; So let it be; Count on it!)

[written circa A.D. late 56 – Based on the critical analysis of John A.T. Robinson]

EPHESIANS

1. **Paul, a sent-forth person belonging to Jesus Christ** (or: an emissary from, and a representative pertaining to, Jesus, [the] Anointed One [= Messiah]) **through and by means of God's will** (resolve; determined purpose; resultant choice), **to and for all** [other MSS: omit "all"] **those who continue being set-apart folks** (or: holy ones; saints) [other MSS add: within Ephesus], **as well as to** (or: who are also) **believing folks** (or: even for and among trusting, loyal people) **within, in union with, and centered in Christ Jesus** (Anointed Jesus)**:**
2. **Grace and peace of the joining to you** (or: Favor and harmony [are] with, among, for, and in you folks) **from God, our Father and Lord, Jesus Christ** (or: from our Father-God, even the Owner, Jesus [the Messiah]; or: from God, our Father, and [the] Lord Jesus Christ).
3. **Characterized by and full of thoughts of well-being, good words and messages of ease** (or: Worthy of being spoken well of) **[is] the God and Father of our Lord, Jesus Christ – the One speaking Good to** (or: blessing; expressing thoughts of well-being to) **us within every spiritual good word** (or: thought of well-being and blessing having the qualities of the Breath-effect) **within the things and among the people situated upon the heavens** (or: in the midst of the phenomena upon the atmospheres; in the full, perfected heaven-people; in union with the celestial people; among the folks [residing] in the imposed atmospheres) **centered in, resident within, and in union with, Christ** ([the] Anointed One),

> (or, taking *eulogētos* in apposition with a predicative force: The God and Father of our Owner, Jesus [the] Anointed One, [has] the qualities of a Word of goodness. He [is] the One speaking goodness, ease and well-being [to] us in every thought, word and expression of goodness which embodies the qualities of [the] Breath-effect resident within the superimposed atmospheres [that are] centered within the midst of Christ, and [are] in union with [His, or the] anointing,)

4. **even as He chose us out** (or: selects and picks us out) **within Him, and in union with Him** [F, G: for or in Himself] **before [the]** (or: prior to a) **casting down** (or: a laying of the foundation; a conception) **of [the] ordered system** (world; universe; cosmic order; or: human aggregate), **[for] us to continuously be set-apart ones** (or: to progressively exist being sacred and dedicated people) **and flawless folks** (people without blemish or stain; blameless ones) **in His sight and presence** (or: in the midst of the sphere of His gaze) **in union with, and centered in, Love** (unrestricted acceptance with participation) [or, putting this last phrase at the beginning of vs. 5:]
5. **In love** (an unambiguous urge toward reunion) **[He was] marking us out beforehand** (or: definitively appointing us in advance; before-setting our boundaries and defining us, with a designation) **[and directing us] into a placing in the condition of a son** (or: a deposit of the Son; a setting in place which is the Son; the constituting as a son; a placing in the Son) – **through and by means of Jesus Christ – [moving us] into the midst of Himself, according to** (or: down from; in correspondence with; following the pattern of) **the good thought, the intention of well-being, and the well-imagined delight of His will** (determined purpose).

6. **[This was] with a view unto praise of His grace's glory** (or: This [led] into [the] praise of [the] reputation and honorable consideration of His favor; or: [leading] into the midst of glory which is, and is from, His joy-producing act of favor) **in and with which He graced us** (or: favors and gifts us with joyous grace) **within the One having been, and continuing being, loved**

> (or: in the midst of the Beloved One; or: in union with the One having been given and now expressing the essence and qualities of love; [some MSS: within His beloved Son]),

7. **within and in union with Whom we continuously have** (constantly hold; progressively possess) **the release into freedom from slavery or imprisonment** (the liberation from our predicament) **through His blood – the sending away** (causing to flow off; forgiveness; dismissal) **of the effects and results of the fallings-aside** (the stumblings by the side; wrong steps; offences; transgressions), **in accordance with** (or: down from; corresponding to; in

keeping with; to the level of; commensurate with) **the wealth of, and which is, His grace and the riches of the joy-producing act of His favor** (or: of the favor/grace which is Him),

8. **which He caused to superabound around [and] unto us** (or: which He makes to be more than enough unto us; which He excessively supplied and then lavishes into the midst of us) **within the midst of, in union with and centered in all wisdom** (or: in every wise thing) **and thoughtful prudence** (gut-intelligence; mindful purpose; considered understanding).

9. **[This occurred] while making known to us** (acquainting us by intimate, experiential knowledge; suddenly making us to realize) **the secret** (mystery; hidden knowledge) **of His will** (determined purpose; resolve) – **in accord with** (or: down from and following the pattern of; corresponding to; in line with) **His good thought which He before placed within Himself**

> (or: – corresponding to the measure of His pleasing imagination and intent of well-being which He designed beforehand and determined by setting it forth in union with Himself),

10. **[leading] into an administration, implementation and realization from a detailed plan of the effects of that which fills up the appointed seasons and fertile moments**

> (or: unto a dispensing of the entire contents of the opportune situations; [leading] into a house-law of the result from the full measure of the fitting situations and a management of the household of the complement of the seasons; into an administration of the full effect from the eras), **[designed] to itself bring back again all things up under one**

Head (or: to gather everything around the main point and sum it all up in unity; to unite and return all things to the Source) **within and in union with the Christ: those things upon** [other MSS: within] **the heavens** (or: the atmospheres) **and the things upon the land** (earth) – **centered in, within the midst of, and in union with, Him!**

11. **Within and in union with Whom we were** (or: are) **also chosen** (or: randomly assigned or appointed) **by casting a lot** (or: were made an allotted portion; or: received an inheritance; or: had our lot cast), **being previously marked out** (or: being before designated) **in keeping with** (or: down from; corresponding to; in accord with) **a before-placed** (or: predetermined-by-setting-forth; destined) **aim, design and purpose of the One continuously operating** (effecting; energizing) **all things** (or: the whole) **in accord with** (or: down from; in line with; in correspondence to; following the pattern of) **the deliberated purpose** (intent; design; plan; determined counsel) **of His will** (or: resultant decision of His resolve; effect of His desire),

12. **[leading] into the [situation for] us to continuously be** (or: exist) **[immersed] into the midst of praise and approval from His glory** (or: from His manifestation which calls forth admiration and which yields a good opinion; which pertains to His imagination; of a reputation which is Him) – **[we] being the folks having before** (or: fully) **placed expectation within the Christ and who have left our expectation there** (or: who have continued expectantly hoping in advance [of others]).

13. **Within and in union with Whom you folks also, upon hearing the Word of the Truth** (or: the thought and idea of Reality; the message from the Truth; the Logos which is Reality) – **the good news** (the message of goodness, ease and well-being) **of your** [other MSS: of our] **deliverance** (rescue; return to health and wholeness; salvation) – **within and in union with Whom also, upon trusting and believing, you people are stamped** (or: were sealed; marked for acceptance, or with a signet ring; = personally authorized) **by the set-apart Breath-effect of The Promise** (or: with the holy attitude of assurance; in the sacred essence from the promise; or: for the Holy Spirit which is the Promise) [cf 2 Cor. 5:5]

14. **– Which is continuously a pledge and guarantee of our inheritance** (or: Who remains being an earnest deposit, a security and the first installment of our portion which was acquired by lot) **– [leading] unto a release into freedom** (liberation from slavery or imprisonment) **from that which was made to surround [us/you]** (or: of the encircling acquisition; or: which is that which has been constructed as a perimeter around [us]), **[being immersed] into the praise and approval from** (or: which is) **His glory** (or: from His manifestation which calls forth admiration and which yields a good opinion; which pertains to His imagination; of a reputation which is Him)!

15. **On account of this, I also, on listening to** (or: after hearing) **– along with and in accord with you folks** (or: in the same sphere as you; down from you; on the same level with you people) **– the faith resident within the midst of the Lord Jesus** (or: the trust centered in the

Owner, Jesus; the loyalty based on union with the Master, Jesus), **as well as the love and unrestricted acceptance [being dispersed] unto all the folks set apart** (holy ones; saints),
16. **[I] do not pause** (or: cease; stop myself) **in continuously giving thanks over you folks** (or: speaking good favor on your behalf; or: expressing the well-being of grace because of your [situation or condition]), **constantly making mention** (constructing a recollection; producing for myself a mental image) **upon the [occasions] of my speaking and thinking toward having wellness and goodness** (or: imparted desires; prayers),
17. **to the end that the God of** (or: pertaining to; or, reading the genitive as in apposition: Who is) **our Lord Jesus Christ, the Father of the Glory** (or: the founder and archetype of, and which is, this manifestation which calls forth praise), **would give** (may suddenly impart; should at some point grant) **to you folks a spirit** (or: breath-effect; attitude) **of wisdom and revelation** (unveiling; uncovering; disclosure) **within the midst of a full and accurate experiential and intimate knowledge of Himself**
> (or: in a full realization of Him; or: within and in union with His full, personal knowledge; or: centered and resident within an added insight from Him, and which is Him),
18. **the eyes of the heart of you folks** (= the insights and perceptions of the core of your [corporate] being) **having been and continuing enlightened** (or: now being illuminated into a state of enlightenment) **into the [situation for] you folks to have seen and thus perceive and know what is the expectation** (or: expectant hope) **of His calling** (or: from HIS calling; belonging to His summons; from the invitation which is Him) **and what [is] the wealth and riches from the glory** (or: of the imagination and opinion; pertaining to the reputation) **of and from the enjoyment of His lot-acquired inheritance within, in union with, and among the set-apart, sacred people** (the holy ones).

19. **And further, [I pray that you may know] what [is] the continually surpassing greatness** (or: the constantly transcendent, repeatedly overshooting and thrown-beyond huge extent) **of His ability and power [being given] unto, and into, us – the people continuously believing, progressively trusting and constantly loyal – in accord with** (or: down from; corresponding to) **the operation** (or: energizing; internal working) **of force** (or: might) **of His strength,**
20. **which is operative** (or: which He exerted and inwardly worked) **within the Christ** (the Anointed One; = the Messiah), **awakening and raising Him forth from out of the midst of dead folks and then seating Him within** (or: = at) **His right [hand]** (or: in union with the place of honor, strength and receiving – which is Him), **within the things** (or: places or realms) **situated upon the heavens and in union with the imposed atmospheres**
> (or: in the added heavens; within the full, perfected heavenlies; in union with the celestial people; among the folks [residing] in the imposed atmospheres),
21. **up over** (or: back above) **every primacy** (or: ruler; principality; government; controlling effect; or: beginning; origin) **and authority** (or: right and privilege from out of being) **and power** (or: ability) **and lordship** (or: ownership), **as well as every name being continually named – not only within this age, but also within the impending one** (the one being presently about to come) –
22. **and then placed and aligned all people in humbleness under His feet** [Ps. 8:6b; LXX]
> (or: and arranges everyone in a supportive position by His feet; or: then by the feet –
> which are Him – He subjects all things), **and yet gives** (or: gave) **Him, [as] a Head** (or: Source; origin and beginning of a series; or: extreme and top part) **over all humanity and all things, for the called-out community** (or: and as a Head over all humanity, gave Him to the summoned and gathered assembly; or: and then by the called-forth congregation He gives Him [to be the] Source over [the situation] of, and for, all humanity),
23. **which [community] is His body, the result of the filling from, and which is, the One Who is constantly filling all things within all humanity** (or: humans)
> (or: which continues existing being His body: the resultant fullness, entire content and full measure of Him [Who is] progressively making full and completing all things in union with all things, as well as constantly filling the whole, in – and in union with – all people).

CHAPTER 2

1. And you folks [who were] continuously existing being dead ones in (or: to; with; or: by) **the results and effects of your stumblings aside** (offenses; wrong steps) **and failures to hit the mark** (or: mistakes; errors; times of falling short; sins; deviations)

2. – within the midst of and in union with which things you once walked about (= lived your lives) **in accord** (or: in keeping; corresponding) **with** (or: as directed by) **the age of this ordered System** (or: down through this time period of the world of secular culture, religion, economy and government; or: in the sphere and to the level of this age of the aggregate of humanity), **in line with the primary directive of the right and privilege of the air** (or: corresponding to the Ruler out of Being with regard to air) **from the Breath-effect of the One at the present time continuously operating within the sons of The Disobedience**

> (or: down under the controlling aspect of the authority of "the blowing" of the Spirit of the One now progressively working internally in union with people having the character and qualities of noncompliance;
>
> or: in correlation to the chief and leader from the privilege which comes from the Blowing, which is the attitude which expresses a lack of persuasion, or of not being convinced, which repeatedly energizes at this present time;
>
> or: in keeping with the original one with regard to the right concerning the atmosphere – the attitude now habitually effecting inward action within the midst of people displaying non-conviction or a non-compliant disposition),

3. immersed among which folks we all also were once twisted up (or: entangled; overturned; upset) **within the cravings** (full longings; over-desires) **of our flesh** (= the estranged human nature, or the alienated self; or: = system of our works and sacrificial religion), **continually doing the will** (or: producing the intentions) **of the flesh** (= our existence while in bondage, or the duties of religion), **and of the divided thoughts and things passing through the mind. Furthermore, we were continuously existing in essence** (in natural condition; by instinct) **being children of natural impulse** (natural disposition; inherent fervor and swelling passion; teeming desire; or: anger; wrath) **even as** (or: as also) **the rest** (the remaining ones) **[were].**

4. But God, continuously being wealthy and rich in mercy, because of His vast (much; great in magnitude and quantity; outstretched; long-lasting; repeated) **Love**

> (*agapē*: the unrestricted and unambiguous drive and movement toward reunion and acceptance which overcomes existential separation; participation in the other one; the acceptance of the other one as a person; the power of reunion with the other person as one standing on the same ultimate ground; the urge toward unambiguous, accepting
>
> reunion, in spite of the estranged, profanized and demonized state of the object – Paul Tillich, *Systematic Theology III,* pp 134-138; full giving of Himself) **in** (or: with) **which He**

focused love on (or: loves, accepts and gives Himself to) **us** [*p*46 reads: had mercy on us],

5. even us, being continuously dead ones by (or: in; to; with) **the results and effects of stumblings aside** (wrong steps; offences)

> [*p*46 reads: ... in (to; by) the bodies; other MSS: by the failure(s) to hit the mark (sin/sins);
>
> B reads: within the stumblings aside and the cravings (lusts)], **He made alive together by** (or: joins us in common life **with,** for and in; [*p*46, B: within; in union with]) **the Christ – by** (with; in) **the Grace and joyous favor you continually exist, being folks having been delivered** (rescued and saved, so that you are now safe; made whole)! –

6. and He jointly roused and raised (or: suddenly awakens and raises) **[us] up, and caused [us] to sit** (or: seats [us]; = enthroned [us]) **together in union with, and among, the heavenly people, and within the things situated upon** [thus, above] **the heavens**

> (or: centered in the full, perfected heavenlies; or: among those comprising the complete and perfected heavenlies; in union with the celestial people; among the folks [residing] upon the atmospheres) **within and in union with Christ Jesus,**

7. to the end that within the continuously oncoming ages (the indefinite time periods continually and progressively coming upon and overtaking [us]) **He may exhibit** (display; point out; give proof of) **the continuously transcending** (being cast beyond; overshooting) **riches**

and wealth of His grace and favor, in useful goodness (beneficial kindness) **[flooding] upon us, within Christ Jesus** (or: in union with [the] Anointed Jesus).

8. **For you see, by** (or: to; in; for; with) **the grace and joyous favor you are** (you continuously exist being) **folks having been delivered** (rescued; kept safe; saved; made whole; restored to your original state and condition) **so as to now be enjoying salvation through** [some MSS add: the] **faithfulness** (or: loyalty; trust; faith; confidence), **and even this not forth from out of you folks, [it is] the gift of and from God** (or: the gift which is God; or: the gift pertains to God),

9. **not out of works** (or: not forth from the midst of actions or deeds done; = not self-produced; = not from the Law or the old covenant), **to the end that no one could boast,**

10. **for the fact is, we are** (continually exist being) **the effect of what He did** (or: His creation; the thing He has constructed; the result of His work; His achievement; His opus; the effect of His Deed)**: people being founded from a state of disorder and wildness** (being framed, built, settled and created; being changed from chaos to order), **within and in union with Christ Jesus; [founded and built] upon good works** (virtuous actions; excellent deeds) **which God made ready** (prepared; or: prepares) **beforehand, to the end that we may, could, should and would walk about** (= live our lives) **centered within and in union with them.**

11. **On which account** (or: Wherefore; So then), **you folks must continuously call to mind** (or: keep in mind; remember) **that once you, the nations** (multitudes; ethnic groups; Gentiles; non-Israelites) **in flesh** (= in your physical beings and cultural heritages) **– the ones habitually termed** (spoken of as; called; said to be) **"uncircumcision" by the one** (or: that) **habitually being termed "circumcision," in flesh** (= body, culture and religion), **[i.e.], made by hand –**

12. **that** (or: because) **you were, and continued on being for that season** (or: in that appointed situation), **apart from Christ** ([the] Anointed One; = [the] Messiah)**: people having been alienated from the state of being a citizen** (or: estranged from citizenship in the commonwealth and society) **of, and which is, Israel and [being] strangers pertaining to the arrangements of** (or: foreigners from covenants and testamentary dispositions whose origin is) **The Promise and the assurance, continually having no expectation** (or: hope), **and [were] folks without God** (or: godless; atheists) **within the ordered System** (centered in the world of culture, religion and governments; or: in union with the aggregate of humanity).

13. **But now, within, in union with and centered in Christ Jesus, you – the folks once being** (continuously existing) **far off** (or: at a distance) **– came to be** (were birthed; are generated; are suddenly become) **near, immersed within and in union with the blood of the Christ** (the Anointed One; = the Messiah).

14. **You see, He Himself is our Peace** (or: continuously exists being our joining and harmony [= Shalom]) **– the One making** (forming; constructing; creating; producing) **The Both [to be] one, and within His flesh** (= physical being; or: = system-caused crucifixion) **is instantly destroying** (unbinding; unfastening; loosing; causing to collapse) **the middle wall of the fenced enclosure** (or: the partition or barrier wall)**: the enmity** (cause of hate, alienation, discord and hostility; characteristics of an enemy),

15. **rendering useless** (nullifying; rendering down in accord with inactivity and unemployment) **the Law** (or: the custom; = the Torah) **of the implanted goals** (or: concerning impartations of the finished product within; from commandments; which was inward directives) **consisting in decrees** (or: prescribed ordinances), **to the end that He may frame** (create; found and settle from a state of wildness and disorder) **The Two into One qualitatively New and Different** [*p*46 & others: common] **Humanity centered within the midst of, and in union with, Himself, continuously making** (progressively creating) **Peace and Harmony** (a joining; = shalom);

16. **and then should fully transfer, from a certain state to another which is quite different, The Both – centered in, and within the midst of, One Body in God** (or: make completely other, while moving away from what had existed, and fully reconcile The Both, in one Body, **by, to**, with and for **God), through the cross** (execution stake) **– while in the midst of Himself killing the enmity and discordant hatred** (or: killing-off the characteristics of enemies within it).

17. **And so upon coming, He brings goodness and proclaims as good news** (or: as a message of ease and well-being), **Peace** (harmony from the joining; lack of discord; [= shalom]) **to you, the folks far off, and Peace** (a joining; harmony; = [shalom]) **to the people nearby,**

18. **that** (or: because) **through Him we, The Both, continuously have** (hold and possess) **the procurement of access** (conduct toward the presence; admission, being led), **within one Spirit** (or: in union with one Breath-effect and Attitude), **to** (or: toward; face to face with) **the Father.**

19. **Consequently then** (or: Thereupon), **you folks no longer continuously exist being strangers** (foreigners) **and sojourners** (folks being or living beside a house; temporary residents in a foreign land), **but in contrast, you continually exist being fellow-citizens of those set apart to be sacred people** (or: folks residing together in a City belonging to, and composed of, the holy ones)**: even God's family** (members of God's household),

20. **being fully built as a house upon the foundation from the sent-forth representatives** (or: emissaries) **and prophets** (folks who had light ahead of time), **Jesus Christ continuously being a corner-foundation [stone] of it** (or: there being an extreme point and head of the corner, or, capstone/keystone: Jesus Christ Himself),

21. **within, and in union with, Whom all the home-building** (all the construction of the house; or: = every house that is constructed, or, the entire building), **being continuously fitted [and] progressively framed together** (closely and harmoniously joined together; made a common joint by a word), **is continuously and progressively growing into a set-apart temple** (or: separate, different and holy inner sanctuary) **within [the] Lord** [= Christ, or, Yahweh]**:**

22. **within the midst of** (or: in union with) **Whom you folks, also, are continuously and progressively being formed a constituent part of the structure** (or: being built together into a house) **– into God's down-home place** (place of settling down to dwell; abode; permanent dwelling) **within [the] Spirit** (or: in spirit; or: in the midst of a Breath-effect and an attitude).

CHAPTER 3

1. **For this gracious cause** (or: In favor of this; For this pleasure) **I, Paul, [am] the bound one** (or: prisoner; captive) **of, from and belonging to Christ Jesus in behalf of** (or: over [the situation of]) **you folks, the nations** (non-Jewish ethnic multitudes; the Gentiles).

2. **Since indeed** (or: If at least; or: Certainly) **you folks heard** (or: hear; listened to) **[and thus, obey] the house-law** (or: detailed plan; the dispensing within the household; the administration; management of the household; or: the distribution) **of the grace of God** (or: from the grace which is God; which is God's grace; or: which is favor from God) **– which is being given by me unto and into you folks** (or: given to me with a view to you folks) **–**

3. **that, in accord with an unveiling** (or: down from and in line with a revelation; in keeping with a disclosure), **the secret** (or: mystery) **was made known to me – even as I before wrote** (or: wrote aforetime), **in brief –**

4. **toward which [end] you, the folks continually reading** (or: habitually reviewing and recognizing; progressively gathering up knowledge), **are constantly able and continue with power to comprehend** (conceive; understand; apprehend) **my understanding** (insight; confluence; my sending insights together) **in the secret** (or: mystery) **of the Christ** (or: which is the Anointed One [= the Messiah]; from the Christ; with the character of the [Messiah]),

5. **which to other generations** (or: for births of a different kind; in and during generations of another nature) **was not made known to the sons of mankind** (humanity; the humans) **as it is now** (at the present time) **uncovered** (unveiled; revealed) **in spirit** (or: within a Breath-effect; or: in union with [the] Spirit) **by** (or: to; in; among) **His set-apart emissaries** (or: consecrated representatives that were sent forth from Him) **and prophets** (folks having light ahead of time),

6. (or, reading the phrase "in spirit" with the next phrase rather than the previous one:) **In spirit the nations** (the Gentiles; the ethnic multitudes; non-Jews) **are to continuously be joint-heirs** (fellow-participants by allotment) **and a Joint Body** (sharing together the same body) **and joint sharers** (partakers; participants) **of The Promise – [along with the rest], resident within** (or: of the assurance in union with) **Christ Jesus through the good news** (or: [spreading or coming to be] throughout the midst by means of the message of goodness, ease and well-being)

7. **of which I came to be** (was birthed; became) **an attendant** (a server; one who renders service and dispenses) **in accord with, down from, in the sphere of and commensurate with the gift of God's grace and the joy-producing act of favor – that being given to me** (or: by me) **in accord with** (or: down from; corresponding to; to the level of; in line with; in the sphere of) **the operative, effective, internal working energy of His power and ability!**

8. **To me, the one far inferior to** (or: less than the least among) **all of those set apart** (or: the saints; the holy people), **was given this grace and joyous favor: to myself address the nations** (non-Jews; Gentiles; ethnic multitudes) **with the good news of** (or: whose source is) **the untrackable** (untraceable; or: not-searched-out and unexplored) **riches of the Christ**

> (or: to for myself declare and bring to the ethnic groups the message of goodness, ease and well-being of the unexploreable wealth which is the Anointed One),

9. **and to illuminate all people** (give light to everyone) **[as to] what [is] the execution of the detailed plan and household administration of the secret** (or: mystery) **pertaining to that having been hidden** (concealed) **away, apart from the ages** (or: disassociated from the [past] periods of time), **within the midst of God – in the One forming and founding** (framing, building and settling from a state of disorder and wildness; creating) **all things** (the Whole; everything) –

10. **to the end that now** (at this present time), **in union with the heavenly people, God's greatly diversified wisdom** (the exceedingly varied in colors [as in a tapestry or the Veil] wisdom which is God; or: the many-phased wisdom from God) **could be made known – through the called-out community – to the governments** (or: rulers; sovereignties; chief ones) **as well as to the authorities and folks with privilege among those situated upon elevated positions**

> (or: made known by the agency of the summoned and gathered congregation: by the original members and the folks who have the right, that is, among the imposed-heaven folks; or: made known by means of the ecclesia with the founders and people having the privilege – in union with these celestial people, within the midst of the things situated upon the atmospheres and among the folks [residing] in the added atmospheres),

11. **in accord with** (or: down from; corresponding to) **a purpose of the ages** (a fore-designed aim, plan and object [which He is bent on achieving] of the unspecified time-periods) **which He formed** (forms; made; constructs; creates; produced) **within the Christ by our Lord and Owner, Jesus** (or: in union with Jesus the Anointed One [= Messiah], within the midst of and for our Lord and Master),

12. **within, and in union with, Whom we continuously have** (progressively possess and hold) **the freedom of speech** (or: boldness, which comes with citizenship, to publicly speak the truth of a matter – without fear of reprisal) **and conducted access** (escorted admission), **in the midst of trust** (confident reliance and loyalty), **through His faithfulness, trust, confidence and loyalty!**

13. **Wherefore I myself continually ask** (or: request) **not to be constantly despondent** (or: repeatedly fainthearted) **within my pressures and squeezings on behalf of you folks** (or: over your [situation]). **Whatever, it is [for] your glory and reputation** (or: – something which is a manifestation which calls forth praise with regard to you).

14. **On account of this I continually bend my knees** (= in loyalty, respect and reverence) **to** (toward; or: face-to-face with) **the Father** [other MSS add: of (or: Who is) our Lord Jesus Christ],

15. **forth from Where** (or: out of the midst of Whom) **every family** (lineage; kindred; descent; paternal group) **within heaven and upon earth** (or: in [the] sky or atmosphere, and on [the] land) **is one after another being named** (or: spoken of, or to, by name; or: designated),

16. **to the end that He would give to you folks, in accord with** (or: down from; in correspondence to and on the scale of) **the riches of His glory** (or: the wealth of the glory which is Him), **to be strengthened** (rendered strong; reinforced; made to grow strong and acquire strength) **in power and with ability – through His Breath-effect – for the interior person** (or: by means of the Spirit, which is Him, [proceeding] into the midst of the humanity within,)

17. **to inhabit** (dwell down in; take up permanent abode in) **the Christ** (or: to house the Anointed One; or: to make a house in the sphere of the Anointing), **through the faith and by means of the trust within your hearts, being folks having been rooted** (or: having taken root) **and now established and placed on a foundation within the midst of and in union with Love** (or: having been grounded and rendered firm, centered in love and unambiguous acceptance).

18. **To this end, may you folks be fully powerful and thus act out of strength to grasp** (receive down for yourselves; take possession of so as to comprehend), **together with all the set-apart folks** (saints; holy ones), **what [is] the width and length and height and depth,**

19. **and thus to know – and gain insight by intimate experience – the love of, from, and which is, the Christ [that is] continuously transcending** (overshooting; being thrown over and beyond; surpassing) **personal experiential knowledge and insight, so that you folks would be filled unto all the effect of the fullness of God and the result of the filling from God**
> (or: could be filled up, unto the saturation point, with the result from the entire contents of
> God; or: into all God's full extent; or: unto all the effects pertaining to God's filling [you])
[or, with *p*46, B, 0278, 33: to the end that all the fullness of, or from, God could and would be filled up {33 adds: into the midst of you folks}].

20. **But by** (or: Now in) **the One being continuously able and powerful to do** (make; form; create; produce) **above and beyond all things – surpassingly above, over and beyond things which we are repeatedly asking for ourselves or are normally grasping with the mind** (apprehending; imagining; considering; conceiving) **– in accord with** (or: down from; corresponding to; in the sphere of and along the line of) **the power and ability [which is] continuously operating** (making itself effective; energizing itself; working and developing) **within us, and in union with us,**

21. **by Him** (to Him; for Him; in Him; with Him) **[is] the glory** (the manifestation which calls forth praise; the assumed appearance; the reputation) **within the called-out community** (the summoned-forth congregation) **as well as within Christ Jesus: unto** (or: [proceeding] into) **all the generations** (births; progenies) **of the Age of the ages** (= the most significant, or crowning, Age of all the ages)! **Make it so** (or: Amen)!

CHAPTER 4

1. **I myself – the prisoner** (or: bound one; captive) **within, in union with, and centered in [the] Lord** [= Christ or Yahweh] **– am therefore repeatedly calling you folks, as it were, alongside: exhorting, admonishing, imploring and entreating you to walk [your path]** (= behave; = live your life) **worthily pertaining to** (or: in a manner suitable to the value of) **the calling and invitation in regard to which you folks are called** (or: from which you were summoned),

2. **with all lowliness of attitude** (or: humility in frame of mind) **and gentle kindness and friendliness, with longsuffering** (even-tempered, forbearing patience; a long wait before rushing in passion; putting anger far away; passionate perseverance unto the goal), **continuously holding one another up** (or: bearing with each other with tolerance) **within the sphere of, and in union with, love** (unqualified acceptance and the urge toward union),

3. **repeatedly hurrying to make every effort to constantly keep** (watch over to guard and protect; maintain) **the Spirit's oneness** (or: the unity from the Breath-effect, and of spirit; the oneness which is the Spirit; = agreement of [your] attitude) **within the Bond** (the link, tie and connection that joins two things; the binding conjunction which results in union) **of the Peace** (or: which is from THE JOINING),

4. **[making] ONE BODY and ONE SPIRIT** (attitude and effect of the Breath), **according as you folks were** (or: are) **also called** (summoned) **within the midst of ONE expectation** (or: in union with one expectant hope) **of your calling** (or: from your summons; which is your invitation),

5. **[with] ONE LORD** (or: Master; Owner), **ONE FAITH** (or: faithfulness, fidelity, loyalty, reliability, confidence, conviction, assurance, and trust), **ONE effect of SUBMERSION and envelopment which brings absorption and permeation to the point of saturation,**

6. **ONE God and Father of all humans – the One upon all people and [moving] through all people, and within the midst of all humanity and in union with all people and all things.**

7. **But to and for each one of us was given** (or: Now in each one of us is imparted and supplied) **the grace and the joy-producing act of favor down from, in accord with and to the level of** (or: commensurate to) **the measure of the undeserved gift of the Christ** (or: the gratuity from the Anointed One; or: the free benefit, which is the Anointing; or: the present from the [Messiah]).

8. **For this reason He** (or: it) **is constantly saying,**
> **"Going up** (or: Stepping up; Ascending) **into a height** (unto [the] summit) **He led** (or: leads) **captive a captive multitude** (or: He led 'captivity' captive). **He gave** (or: gives) **gifts to mankind** (or: for, in and among the humans; to humanity)." [Ps. 68:18]

9. **Now** (or: Yet) **this "He went up (ascended)," what is it if not** (or: except) **that He also** [other MSS add: first] **descended** (stepped down) **into the lower parts** (or: the under regions) **of the earth** (or: which is the land; or: from the Land; or: of the ground)**?**

10. **The One stepping down** (descending) **is Himself also the One stepping up** (ascending) **far above** (back up over) **all of the heavens** (or: atmospheres; skies), **to the end that He would at once fill the Whole** (permeate and saturate everything; or: make all things full; bring all things to full measure and completion).

11. **And He Himself at one point gave** (or: gives; [p46: has given and it now exists as a gift]), **on the one hand** (or: indeed), **the folks sent off with a commission** (the emissaries; the representatives), **yet also those who have light ahead of time and speak it before others** (the prophets), **and on the other hand those who announce goodness and well-being and bring good news, and then the shepherds, and finally teachers** (or: the shepherds-and-instructors),

12. **facing and with a view toward the bringing down of the fresh and timely, for the preparation** (mending; knitting together; adjusting; fitting; repairing; perfectly adjusting adaptation; equipping; completely furnishing) **of the set-apart folks** (the saints; the holy ones) **unto a work** (or: into an action; into the midst of a deed or task) **of attending service and dispensing, [leading] unto** (or: into) **construction** (house-building) **of the body which is the Christ** (or: whose source, character and quality is from the Anointed One; or: the body formed by the Anointing),

13. **[to go on] until we – the whole of mankind** (all people) **– can** (or: would) **come down to the goal** (or: attain; arrive at; meet accordingly; meet down face-to-face)**: into the state of oneness from, and which is, The Faithfulness** (or: the unity of, that belongs to and which characterizes that which is faith; or: the lack of division which has its source in trust, confidence and reliability, has the character of and is in reference to the loyalty and fidelity), **even which is the full, experiential and intimate knowledge** (or: and from recognition; and of discovery; as well as pertaining to insight) **which is** (or: of; from; in reference to) **the Son of God, [growing] into [the] purposed and destined adult man** (complete, finished, full-grown, perfect, goal-attained, mature manhood) **– into** (or: unto) **[the] measure of [the] stature** (full age; prime of life) **of the entire content which comprises the Anointed One**

(or: which is the result of the full number which is the Christ; of the effect of the fullness from the [Messiah]; from the effect of that which fills and completes that which refers to the Christ; of the result of the filling from, and which is, the Christ) – [cf 1 Cor. 13:10-11]

14. **to the end that no longer** (or: no more) **would or should we exist being infants** (immature folks; not-yet-speaking ones), **continuously being tossed by** (= being caused to fluctuate from) **[successive] waves and repeatedly being carried hither and thither** (or: around in circles) **by every wind of the teaching** (or: from what is taught) **within the caprice** (the throw of the dice; versatile artifice; games of chance; the trickery) **of mankind, in readiness to do anything** (amoral craftiness; working everything; or: = while stopping at nothing) **with a view toward and leading to the methodical treatment** (or: the systematizing or technical procedure) **of The Wandering** (the straying; the deception; [A adds: of the thrusting-through; or: from the person who casts {divisiveness or harm} through the midst of folks]).

15. **But continuously being real and true** (living in accord with reality and the facts; holding to, speaking, pursuing and walking in Truth; truthing it) **within, and in union with, Love** (or: centered in unambiguous acceptance; a full giving of ourselves with an urge toward union), **we can grow up** (enlarge; increase) **into Him – the ALL which is the Head: Christ** (or: [and] we would in love make all things grow up into Him Who is the head and source: [the] Anointed One)**!**

16. **– from out of Whom** (or: out from the midst of Which) **all the Body** (or: the entire body) **being continuously fitted and framed together** (made a common joint by a word; laid out and closely joined together) **and constantly being knit together and caused to mount up united through every fastening** (or: joint) **of the supply of rich furnishings** (or: through every assimilation of the full supply of funds; through every touch {kindling; setting on fire} of the completely supplied requirements) **in accord with** (or: down from; commensurate to; in the sphere and to the degree of) **the operation** (operative, effectual energy) **within [the] measure of each one part** [other MSS: member], **is itself continually making** (or: is for itself progressively producing and forming) **the growth and increase of the Body, [focused on and leading] into**

house-construction (or: unto building [up] and edification) **of itself within the midst of, and in union with, love** (full self-giving in an unambiguous urge toward union or reunion; acceptance)

17. **This, then** (or: therefore), **I am continually saying** (laying it out) **and giving evidence of** (or: attesting to) **within the Lord: no longer are you folks to be continuously walking [your path]** (i.e., conducting yourselves; adjusting your behavior) **according to the way that the nations** (the multitudes; the non-Israelites; the Gentiles; the ethnic or special or pagan groups) **are continuously walking around** (behaving; living) – **within the empty purposelessness** (vanity; futility; nonsense; idle nothingness; fruitless worthlessness) **of their mind** (or: intellect),
18. **being folks having been, and still yet being, darkened in** (or: by) **the divided thought and the thing passing through the mind, having been and continuing being alienated** (estranged) **away from the Life of God** (or: God's life; or the life which is God) – **through the ignorance continuously existing** (or: being) **within them [and] through the petrifying** (becoming stone; callousness; = insensitivity from dulled perception) **of their heart,**
19. **which certain people, being folks having ceased to feel pain** (being insensible, dulled or callous), **gave themselves over** (transferred, committed and abandoned themselves) **to outrageous behavior** (excessive indulgence; wantonness; licentiousness), **into every unclean performance** (work, trade, business or labor of impurity) **in greed** (always wanting more; covetousness; schemes of extortion; = wanting more than one's due, in disregard for others).

20. **But you folks did not learn the Christ in this way,**
21. **since, in fact, at one point you heard and so listen to Him, and within Him as well as in union with Him and centered in Him you were and are taught – just as Truth and Reality continuously exist within Jesus** (or: in union with the One, Jesus) –
22. **to put off from yourselves** [as clothing or habits] **what accords to the former entangled manner of living** (or: twisted up behavior): **the old humanity** (or: the past, worn-out person) – **the one continuously in process of being corrupted** (spoiled; ruined) **down from and in accord with the passionate desires** (the full-covering, swelling emotions) **of the deceptions** (or: seductive desires) –
23. **and then to be continuously renewed** (or: from time to time, or, progressively made young again) **by** (or: in; with) **the spirit** (or: attitude; breath-effect) **of your mind** (or: from the mind which is you folks; or: by the Spirit which is your [collective] mind),
24. **and to enter within** (or: clothe yourselves with) **the new humanity** (or: the Person that is different and innovative in kind and quality) – **the one in accord with and corresponding to God** (or: the person at the Divine level) – **being formed** (framed, built, founded and settled from a state of disorder and wildness; created) **within the Way pointed out** (or: in union with fair and equitable dealings with rightwised relationships, justice, righteousness and covenant participation; centered in [His] eschatological deliverance) **and reverent dedication** (or: benign relationship with nature) **pertaining to the Truth** (or: in intrinsic alignment with reality, which is the Truth).

25. **Wherefore, upon at once putting the false away** (or: being folks having at one point set the Lie off) **from yourselves** [as clothing or habits], **you folks be continuously speaking Truth and Reality, each one with his associate** (the one near him; his neighbor), **because we are** (we continually exist being) **members [as of a body] of one another** (or: limbs or body parts belonging to one another and having our source in each other).
26. **You folks be habitually aroused by the internal pulse of life** (or: be constantly impulsive in reaction to your natural disposition and character; or: Continue corporately being made indignant or even angry), **yet be not folks continuously missing the target** (making mistakes; sinning; failing; erring; deviating). **Do not let sun be repeatedly setting upon your angry mood** (or: on the provoking exasperation, irritation or embittered anger at the side of you folks),
27. **neither be folks constantly supplying nor repeatedly giving a place or position** (or: so don't go on allowing opportunity, a chance, or a room in which to expand) **for** (or: to; in) **the person who thrusts things through [folks or situations]** (or: the slanderer; the adversary; the accuser; the devil; or: that which casts [harm or division] through the midst of folks).
28. **Let the person habitually stealing no longer continue stealing, but rather let him or her be normally spent with labor, constantly working** (performing; doing the business of) **the**

good (the profitable; the virtuous; quality) **by his or her own hands, to the end that he or she can continuously have** (or: possess) **[something] – [in order] to repeatedly share with the one constantly having a need.**

29. **Do not continue allowing every rotten word** (or: putrefied idea; bad quality message; unprofitable communication; unfit thought) **to be proceeding** (or: issuing) **out of the mouth of you folks, but rather if anything [is] good** (profitable; virtuous; [having] quality), **[speak it] toward house-construction** (building [up]; edification) **which pertains to the need, to the end that it may impart** (or: can give) **favor to and grace among those listening and hearing.**

30. **Also, don't you folks have the habit of grieving** (distressing; giving sorrow or pain to; or: = troubling) **God's set-apart Spirit** (or: the Holy Breath-effect which is God), **within Whom** (or: in union with Which) **you folks were** (or: are) **sealed** (at one point stamped with a seal; suddenly marked; imprinted; = personally authorized) **into the midst of a Day associated with and arising from the liberation of a releasing-away from slavery or imprisonment** (or: a Day which is emancipation pertaining to a dismissal and a loosing-away into a freeing from bondage).

31. **So let every bitterness, swelling negative emotion** (inherent fervor; or: natural propensity, disposition and impulse; or: wrath), **enraged impulse, clamorous outcry, and blasphemy** (slanderous, abusive or light-hindering speech; malignment, vilifying defamation; harm-averment) **be at once lifted up and removed from you folks, together with all worthlessness** (that which ought not to be; that which is of bad quality; malice; ugliness; badness; depravity)

32. **and keep on becoming kind folks** (or: So progressively come to be {or: be birthed to be} useful and obliging ones) **unto one another – people [who are] tenderly compassionate – folks constantly dealing graciously, extending favor among yourselves** (or: forgiving yourselves), **according as God also, within and in union with the Christ, was and is gracious** (or: deals favorably) **to and with** (or: freely forgives) **you folks** [other MSS: us].

CHAPTER 5

1. **Keep on becoming** (or: Progressively come to be), **then, imitators** (those made exactly alike so as to portray, express and represent by means of imitation) **of God, as beloved** (or: like loveable) **children,**

2. **and so, keep on walking** (walking around; = progressively living and maintaining your life) **within, and in union with, Love** (self-giving acceptance and the urge for union), **according as the Christ also loves** (or: to the same level and commensurately as the Anointed One loved, accepted and achieved reunion with) **you folks, and also gives** (or: gave) **Himself over in our behalf** (or: then commits and transfers Himself over us and our [situation]; [other MSS: you])**: a bearing toward and a bringing to be face to face, even an offering by** (or: in; with; or: to; for) **God [turning] into a fragrant odor** (or: and unto a sweet-smelling incense-sacrifice amid God).

3. **But all sexual vice** (cultic prostitution, which involved idolatry; fornication; sexual acts contrary to custom, e.g., Mosaic Law) **and uncleanness** (impurity), **or greed** (desiring or having more than one's due; gaining and having advantage over others; an insatiable drive to acquire), **let it continuously not even be named among** (or: within) **you folks – according as it is constantly appropriate** (proper; conspicuously suitable and befitting) **for set-apart people** (or: holy and sacred folks) --

4. **as well as obscenity** (ugliness; indecency; indecorum; shamefulness; baseness), **or even stupid** (moronic; foolish) **speaking** (talking) **or coarse joking** (vulgar talking; insinuation; wittiness; quickness in making repartee; making a good turn), **which things it has not been proper or fitting to have come up – but rather** (in preference), **giving of thanks** (or: conversation marked by grace, gratitude and favor in well-being).

5. **For this you people constantly know** (or: perceive), **habitually recognizing by experience, that every prostitute** (or: male prostitute; paramour), **or unclean** (impure [in character]; morally indecent) **person, or greedy one** (person who is covetous: insatiably desiring advantage or more than one's due), **[i.e.,] the person who exists as** (or: that is; or: = which means) **an idolater, is not now holding enjoyment of an inheritance** (does not currently continue having use of an allotment) **within the Christ's and God's reign or sphere of sovereign activity** (or: in union with the kingdom of the Anointed One [= the Messiah], as well as

of God; or: centered in the royal influence from the Christ, and from God; [*p46*: within the reign of God]).

6. **Let no one keep on deceiving** (or: seducing) **you folks by empty words** (or: messages; reasons; thoughts; ideas), **for because of these things, God's inherent fervor** (natural impulse and disposition; intrinsic teeming desire and swelling passion; or: anger; indignation) **is continuously coming upon** [note: *cf* John 3:36] **the sons of The Disobedience** (the incompliance; or: = folks having the quality of not being convinced or being disobedient and stubborn).

7. **Stop, therefore, becoming** (or: Therefore you folks are not to continuously come to be) **their joint partakers** (their joint members or partners; ones sharing together with them),

8. **for you folks were once existing being darkness** (dimness; obscurity; gloom; shadiness), **yet** (or: but) **now [you are] Light, within and in union with [the] Lord** [= Christ or Yahweh].

9. **Be constantly walking about** (= Habitually conduct yourselves) **as children of Light** (born ones from light) – **for the fruit of the Light** [other MSS: **Spirit**] **[is] in union with** (or: [exists] within the midst of and is centered in) **all Goodness** (virtue; beneficence; kindness), **Justice** (fair and equitable dealing in rightwised relationships which accord with the Way pointed out; eschatological deliverance in covenant participation) **and Truth** (or: Reality) –

10. **repeatedly testing so as to prove and approve** (or: continuously showing proof of) **what is** (or: continually exists being) **fully pleasing and compatible** (happily acceptable; well pleasing; good pleasure) **to** (or: for; in; with) **the Lord** [= Christ or Yahweh].

11. **And do not continually participate together** (involve yourselves in joint communion or community; or: Stop having fellowship together) **in unfruitful acts** (works; deeds; performances) **of the Darkness** (dimness in the shadows; gloom and obscurity; [comment: = the ignorance; = the lack of light; may refer to past religious acts]), **but rather even be continually questioning and cross-examining to expose** (unmasking and making facts known), **refute and reprove to bring conviction** (= bring light to them),

12. **for you see, it is obscene** (base; ugly; indecent; shameful) **to habitually even be speaking of the things [which] secretly** (or: in a hidden manner) **may be coming into existence** (be occurring; be being birthed) **by them.**

13. **Now everything** (or: the whole), **while being continuously exposed to show fact, being refuted and/or reproved unto conviction, is by the Light** (or: the light) **being continuously manifested** (clearly displayed, made apparent and shown for what it is),

14. **for you see, all that is continuously being manifested** (clearly displayed, made apparent and is progressively shown for what it is) **is, and continually exists being, Light. Wherefore He is now** (or: it keeps on) **saying,**

> **"Let the sleeper** (the person continuously down and being fast asleep) **be waking up,
> continue rousing, and then stand up** (arise) **from out of the midst of the dead ones,
> and the Christ will continue shining upon you** (progressively enlightening you)!"

15. **Therefore** (or: So then,) **be continuously observing exactly** (or: accurately), **brothers** (= fellow believers; members of the Family), **how you habitually walk about** [or, with other MSS: Be continually observing, then, how accurately you are conducting yourselves]: **not as unwise folks, but rather as wise ones,**

16. **making it a habit [to be] intensively buying-out for yourselves** (as at a market, exhausting the supply; redeeming; reclaiming) **the season** (fitting situation; opportunity; fertile moment), **because the days** (= present times) **are of a bad quality** (or: a gush of misery; unsound; harmful; or: in a sorry plight; or: toilsome).

17. **On account of this, stop becoming** (or: Do not continually come to be) **foolish ones** (folks not having common sense; people without reflection or intelligence; imprudent ones; thoughtless and inattentive folks), **but rather, be constantly understanding** (sending your perceptions together to comprehend) **what [is] the will** (result of the resolve; determination of what shall be done; design; effect of the purpose) **of the Lord** (= Christ or Yahweh; [other MSS: God; Christ]).

18. **And stop being made drunk** (or: Do not be continuously made intoxicated) **by wine, within which exists the disposition of one having no hope of safety** (unsavingness; dissipation and

ill health; desperation), **but rather be continuously or repeatedly filled full in spirit** (within [the] Spirit; within the midst of [the] Breath-effect; in the sphere of attitude; in union with [the] Breath),
19. **continuously speaking** (making vocal utterances) **among** (or: = to each other; or: to; within) **yourselves in, with or by psalms and hymns** (or: songs of praise; festive songs) **and spiritual odes** (songs; chants), **continually singing and playing stringed instruments** (making music; psalming; sharply touching or plucking [the strings or chords]) **in** (or: by; with; or: for) **your hearts to** (or: for; by; with: in) **the Lord** [= Christ, or, Yahweh],
20. **constantly giving thanks** (expressing gratitude; or: speaking of the well-being that is in grace and favor) **to God, even [the] Father** [p46 & others: to the Father, even God] **at all times** (or: always; = on all occasions) **concerning all things** (or: for everything; or: over all mankind), **within the midst of and in union with the Name of our Lord, Jesus Christ** [= the Messiah],
21. **while continually setting and arranging yourselves under** (placing yourselves in humble alignment; subordinating yourselves; being submissive) **so as to support one another, in respect for Christ**
> (or: in union with the reverence which is an Anointing; within Christ's fear; in reverence pertaining to, and the source of which is [the] Anointed One [other MSS: God]).

22. **Wives** (or: Women) **[are] to** (or: with; for) **their own husbands** (or: adult males), **as to** (or: with; for; in; by) **the Lord** (or: the Owner; or: = Christ, or, Yahweh)
> [note: this reading follows p46, B, Clement, Origen, other church fathers & other MSS, and is the reading in Westcott and Hort, Panin, Nestle-Aland, Tasker, and is bracketed by Griesbach; however, the following reading is also in Clement, Origen, other church fathers and MSS, as well as in Aleph and A: Let the wives be by habit humbly aligned and placed subordinate so as to be supportive to their own husbands, in the same way as to (or: in; by; for; with) the Lord],
23. **because a husband exists being a head of** (or: is a source with reference to) **the wife as also** (or: even as) **the Christ [is] Head** (or: Source) **of the called-out community** (the ecclesia; the summoned-out assembly); **He Himself is** (continually exists being) **[the] Savior** (Deliverer; Rescuer; Restorer to health and wholeness) **of the Body.**
24. **But, just as the called-out covenant community** (summoned-forth assembly) **continuously humbly aligns and places itself under for** (or, as a passive: is normally subjected in support to) **the Christ, thus also the wives to** (or: for; with) **the husbands, in everything** (or: within all; among all mankind).
25. **O husbands, be constantly loving, and urging to unity with, [your] wives** (or: Men, continue giving yourselves for and accepting the women), **accordingly and correspondingly as the Christ also loved** (or: to the degree that, and commensurately as, the Anointed One loves and unambiguously accepts) **the called-out community, and gave Himself up** (or: commits and transfers Himself over) **in behalf of** (for the sake of; over [the situation of]) **her,**
26. **to the end that He may set her apart** (separate her; consecrate and make her holy), **cleansing** (purging) **[her] by the bath of the Water [that is] within a result of a flow** (or: in union with a gush-effect; or: in the midst of a spoken word, a declaration, or an utterance),
27. **so that He Himself could place beside Himself** (or: should present to and make to stand alongside in and with Himself) **an inwardly-glorious and honorable** (or: held in honor and high esteem; in-glorious-array; or: inwardly-reputable; centered-in-glory) **called-out community – [which] is continuously having neither spot** (or: stain), **nor wrinkle, nor any of such things, but to the contrary – to the end that she would continuously exist being set-apart** (holy; different from the 'ordinary and profane') **and flawless** (unblemished; or: unblamable).
28. **Thus** (or: In like manner; In this way) **the husbands also are continuously indebted** (thus: obligated) **to constantly love** (give themselves to) **their wives as their own bodies** (= persons). **The one constantly loving** (accepting) **his own wife continues loving and accepting himself,**
29. **for you see, no one ever yet** (at any time) **hated** (or: hates; radically detaches from) **his own flesh** (= his body and interior self) **but rather continually intensively nourishes** (feeds and supports) **and warms** (cherishes; comforts) **it, according as also the Christ [does] the called-out community,**
30. **because we are** (we exist continuously being) **members of His Body** [other MSS add: from out of His flesh and from out of His bones; cf Gen.2:23].

31. **Answering this** (or: In the place facing this [situation or reality]),

> **"a man will continue leaving behind his father and mother, and he will be progressively glued** (welded) **to his wife, and the two will continue being [made] into one flesh** (= one physical unit as though being one body)." [Gen. 2:4]

32. **This secret** (or: mystery) **is great** (= important), **but I am speaking unto** (or: into; with a view to) **Christ, even** (or: and; as well as) **unto** (or: into; with a view to) **the called-out community** (or: the called-out person; or: the summoned-forth covenant assembly).

33. **Moreover, you men also, individually, each one thus** (in this way) **be continually loving** (or: accepting) **his own wife** (or: woman) **as** (or: as she were) **himself, and so the result will be that the wife would continually have deep respect for** (or: may habitually stand in reverential awe of; can normally be fearing with a healthy respect for) **the husband** (or: adult man).

CHAPTER 6

1. **You children make it a habit to humbly listen and pay attention to, and thus submissively obey, your parents** (begetters; those who birthed you into existence) **in union with the Lord** [= Christ or Yahweh], **for this is the Way pointed out** (is fair, right and just).

2. > **"Be continuously honoring** (holding in respect; valuing; reverencing; treating as precious and with dignity) **your father and mother,"**

which very one is a foremost implanted goal (impartation of the finished product within; inward directive) **within an act of promising** (or: in [the] promise; or: = that embodies assurance),

3. > **"to the end that it may come to be well and easy for** (or: to; in; with) **you and you will continue existing a long time upon the land** (or: earth)." [Ex. 20:12; Deut. 5:16]

4. **And so you fathers** (= parents): **do not continually bring along inherent fervor to** (or: irritate; exasperate to anger; bring impulse alongside) **your children, but rather be continually nourishing them within child-training discipline and education, and then the placing** (or: setting) **of the Lord** [= Christ or Yahweh] **in the mind** (or: as well as the Master's mind-set; or: and the Owner's admonition; or: and instruction about the Lord).

5. **Slaves: you folks be continually paying attention, listening humbly to and obeying [your] owners** (masters) – **those [being such] in respect to the flesh** (= this human condition and natural realm) – **with fear** (or: respect, reverence, = earnestness) **and trembling** (= concerned focus), **joined with singleness** (simplicity; uncompoundedness; = pureness of substance) **of your heart** (= with the core of your being willing one thing [comment: which is Kierkegaard's "the Good"]), **as though to** (or: as if for; as being in, and with) **the Christ,**

6. **not in accord with eye-service** (or: in line with slavery to the eyes [of folks watching]; or: = doing it only when being watched) **as folks desiring to please men, but rather as slaves of Christ, constantly doing** (performing; producing) **the will and intent of God – from out of [the] soul** (= with the whole inner being: mind, will, emotion, life-force; or: = spontaneously) –

7. **with a good disposition and intention** (well-mindedness; a good will and attitude; or: enthusiasm), **habitually serving** (or: being; working) **as a slave, as for** (or: to; in; with) **the Lord** [= Yahweh or Christ], **and not for** (or: to) **people** (humans; mankind),

8. **having seen and thus knowing** (perceiving; being aware; recognizing) **that each person, if she or he may do some good thing** (produce some excellence and quality; [other MSS: that whatsoever virtuous act each one would perform]), **this [good thing]** (or [for] this) **she, or he, will continue fetching and conveying to, for and in herself or himself – as a recompense: a kindly keeping, provisioning, attending and preserving of herself or himself – from beside the Lord** [= from Christ's or Yahweh's presence]: **whether [this person be] slave or free.**

9. **And now for the owners** (lords; masters): **be practicing** (continually doing) **the same toward them, constantly being lax** (loosening up) **in the threatening, knowing** (having seen; being aware) **also that their Owner** (Lord; Master) – **as well as yours – is continuously existing within [the] atmospheres** (or: heavens), **and partiality through respect or acceptance of faces** (= persons) **does not exist alongside of Him.**

10. **Of the remainder** (or: Concerning the rest; Finally), **be constantly empowering yourselves within** (or: finding or engendering ability within yourselves), **centered in and in union with [the] Lord** [= Christ or Yahweh] – **even within, and in union with, the force** (or: strength) **of His might** (or: the mightiness of His strength and forcefulness)**:**

11. **you folks must at some point, for yourselves, enter within** (or: clothe yourselves with) **the full suit of armor and implements of war** (panoply; the complete equipment for men-at-arms) **which is God** (or: which comes from and belongs to God), **in order for you to be continuously able and powerful to stand** (or: to make a stand) **facing toward the crafty methods** (stratagems; schemes; intrigues) **of the adversary**

> (or: = which throw folks into dualism with divided thinking and perceptions; or: from the person that throws something through the midst and casts division; or: which is the person who thrusts things through folks; or: from the slanderer who accuses and deceives; or: that have the quality of [what is commonly called] the "devil"),

12. **because for us** [other MSS: for you] **the wrestling is not against** (toward; with a view to) **blood and flesh** (= physical bodies), **but rather against** (toward; i.e., "face to face" with) **the beginning controls and rules**

> (or: original rulings; or: rulers and controllers; governments; those things or people in first position; the beginning things or people; the original ones; the princes) **and face to face with the rights and privileges** (or: liberties to do as one pleases; or: authorities; or: aspects from out of existence), **with a view to the strengths of the System** (or: strengths of the ordered arrangement; or: universal powers of domination; the world's strong-ones; or: the strengths from the aggregate of humanity) **of this darkness** (realm of shadows, gloom and dimness; [comment: = ignorance]), **facing** (toward; or: with a view to) **the spiritual aspects** (or: breath-effected attitudes; or: conditions and qualities of a spirit) **of the worthlessness**

> (the badness of conditions; the unsoundness and miserableness; the wickedness and depravity; the evil and malice; the disadvantageousness; the unprofitableness; the thing that brings toilsome labor and a gush of misery) **among those situated upon imposed,**
elevated positions and centered among the imposed "heavenly people"

> (or: situated within the heavenly positions or places; among the imposed "heavenly" realms; positioned in union with the "celestials and heavenly ones"; resident within the midst of added atmospheres; among the folks [residing] in the imposed atmospheres).
>> [note: this verse could be speaking about the ruling authorities of the religious world of ignorance, with its now worthless sacrifices, or, about the political system of darkened strength which was currently in power, bringing bad situations; Walter Wink, in *Engaging the Powers*, uses the phrase "against suprahuman systems and forces" for part of this verse]

13. **On account of this, you folks are to again take in hand and receive back** (or: at once take up) **the full suit of armor** (panoply; implements of war) **which is God** (or: which belongs to and has its source in God), **to the end that you would have power and be able to withstand and resist** (to stand opposite, over against as facing an opponent; or: stand in [other folks'] place, instead of [them]) **within the harmful and misery-gushed day** (or: this day of bad conditions), **and then accomplishing all** (achieving and effecting everything [the whole]), **to stand firm.**

14. **You folks must** (or, as a subjunctive: can; should) **stand** (or: at once take your stand), **then, after girding yourselves around your waist** (or: loins) **in union with Truth and within the midst of Reality, and then, entering within** (putting on; clothing yourself with) **the breastplate armor** (cuirass; corslet) **of fair and equitable dealing of the eschatological deliverance**

> (or: which is the rightwised relationships of the Way pointed out; the Righteousness; the Justice; also = covenant inclusion and participation),

15. **and next, sandaling** (or: binding under) **the feet in readiness and in union with preparedness which comes from, has the character of and which belongs to the good news** (or: message of goodness, ease and well-being) **of the Peace** (or: which are peace and harmony [= shalom]; from the joining) –

16. **within all things and situations** (or: in union with **all people**) – **[be] at once receiving again** (or: taking back up) **the large oblong shield which is the Faithfulness** (or: of Trust; which has the quality of Faith; that belongs to Confidence and Assurance; from the Loyalty),

within which you will continue having power and be progressively able to extinguish all the fiery arrows of and from the worthless person
> (or: evil one; unsound and miserable situation; disadvantageous and unprofitable condition; malicious and depraved attitude; toilsome labor that is gushed with misery).

17. **And at once accept** (or: receive and retain) **for yourselves the helmet of the Deliverance** (or: which comes from the Salvation; that belongs to health and wholeness; which is the restoration to the original realm and condition) **and the Spirit's sword** (the short sword from the Attitude; or: the dagger which is spirit; the dirk which is the Breath-effect) – **the one being God's gush-effect**
> (or: which is the result of the flow from God; the one existing [as] a result of a flux or an effect of a continuous movement, the source of which is God; or: which is a spoken Word of God; or: that being an utterance or declaration which is God).

18. **By means of all thought, desire, imparted message or action toward having things be well** (or: Through every prayer) **and request** (or: declaration) **regarding need, [be] folks continuously thinking, speaking and acting toward goodness and well-being** (or: praying) **within every season** (in union with every fitting situation; on every occasion; in the midst of every fertile moment) **within and in union with [the] Spirit** (Breath-effect; Attitude), **while maintaining a constant alertness** (or: in spirit being constantly vigilant and abstaining from sleep), **also, to that end, in all focus to unremitting and stout continuance** (or: in union with every view to resolute, potent perseverance which brings control) **and request regarding need concerning** (or: surrounding) **all of the set-apart folks** (holy ones; saints; sacredly different people),

19. **and further, in behalf of me, so that to me a word** (or: message; thought; idea; logos) **would be given, in the midst of opening my mouth in freedom of speaking openly in public and with the boldness and rights of a citizen, to make known the secret** (or: mystery) **of the good news** (or: which is the message of goodness, ease and well-being),

20. **over which I am an old man in a manacle** (or: on behalf of which I continue performing the duties of an elder and an ambassador – in a chain!) – **to the end that within Him** (or: it) **I may speak freely** (or: openly in public, boldly as a citizen), **as it is necessary for me to speak.**

21. **Yet so that you also may know** (can have seen, so as to perceive) **the things that [come] down to** (or: on) **me** (= my circumstances and affairs), **what I am continually involved in** (what matters or business I am transacting; what I'm doing), **everything** (or: all) **will proceed being made known to you [by] Tychicus, the beloved brother and faithful attending servant within the Lord,**

22. **whom I send** (or: sent) **to you for this very purpose, to the end that you may come to know our concerns** (or: our circumstances; = how we are doing) **and [that] he may call your hearts alongside** (assist, admonish, encourage, comfort and give relief to your hearts; = do the work of a paraclete for the cores of your beings).

23. **Peace and harmony** [= shalom] **to** (or: Peace from the joining [is] with, among and by) **the brothers** (= family or fellow believers; [p46 reads: the set-apart folks]), **and love** (unrestricted acceptance; [A reads: mercy]) **along with faith, trust and loyalty from God, [the] Father and Lord, Jesus Christ** (or: from Father God, and {or: even} [the] Lord Jesus Christ; or: [are] proceeding from God – from a Father and an Owner/Master, Jesus [the Messiah]).

24. **Grace and favor, in union with incorruption** (or: within a state or condition of being unspoiled, and being incorruptible [note: see 1 Cor. 15:42]), **[are] with all the people continuously, unrestrictedly loving, fully giving themselves to, and experiencing the urge toward reunion with, our Lord** (or: Owner; Master), **Jesus Christ** ([the] Anointed Jesus). **Amen** (It is so; Count on it)!

[written circa A.D. 58 – Based on the critical analysis of John A.T. Robinson]
Subscription [some MSS]: To Ephesians. [others add]: Written from Rome, through Tychicus.
Possibly a circular letter to the assemblies in first century Asia Minor

PHILIPPIANS

1. **Paul and Timothy, slaves of Christ Jesus for** (or: to) **all the set-apart folks** (the holy ones; the saints; sacred peoples) **within and in union with** (incorporate in) **Christ Jesus, to and for those being in Philippi, together with care-givers** (folks keeping a watchful eye upon [people and situations]; those noting and being concerned for others; overseers) **and attending servants:**

2. **Grace and peace** (or: Favor and harmony from the joining) **to you folks from God, our Father and Lord, Jesus Christ** (or: from God, our Father, and [the] Lord, Jesus [the] Anointed).

3. **I constantly give thanks to** (or: habitually speak of the goodness of grace in and by) **my God upon every memory** (or: recollection; or: mention) **of you folks,**

4. **at all times** (or: always) **in my every request** (or: petition) **over [the situation of] you all** (or: on behalf of all of you folks), **habitually making the request** (or: petition) **with joy**

5. **upon [the basis of] your common being and existence, as well as the partnership, participation, communion, sharing, fellowship and contribution [from you] into the message of goodness, ease and well-being** (or: good news), **from the first day on until the present moment** (now),

6. **being persuaded and convinced of this very thing: that the One inwardly beginning** (making an inward start; inciting; inwardly originating [note: in the context of sacrifices, this word meant "to begin the offering"]) **a good work, a virtuous action or an excellent deed within you people** (or: among you folks; or: in union with you [all]), **will progressively bring it to the completed goal** (will keep on bringing perfection upon it; shall continue upon it to the final act and finished product: its completion; will continue bring upon its destiny; [note: this was a technical term for the ending of the sacrifice]) **– on until** (or: right up to) **[the; a] Day of or from Christ Jesus** [with other MSS: as far as {the} Day which is Jesus Christ]! – [cf 3:12, 15, below]

7. **just as** (or: correspondingly as) **it is fair for me** (or: it is right in me; it accords with the Way pointed out to me) **to habitually think this regarding all of you folks** (or: to continuously have this opinion and disposition over you all), **because of the [situation for] me to constantly hold** (or: have) **you folks within my heart, both within my bonds** (fetters; chains) **and within the verbal defense** (a word spoken from and on behalf of) **and legally valid confirmation** (the placement on a good footing to establish and make firm and steadfast) **of the message of goodness, ease and well-being – you all being my co-participants** (common partners; fellow-sharers together) **of the grace and joyous favor!**

> (or: ... to continuously possess you people in the midst of the core of my being – you all being my joint-partners of this grace, both in union with my imprisonments and in verification of the good news!)

8. **You see, God [is] my witness** (or: evidence), **how I continually long** (or: yearn) **for all you folks within the inner seat of Jesus Christ's tender emotions** (upper internal organs – heart, liver, lungs; = compassions).

9. **And this I habitually think and speak toward having things be well** (or: pray)**: that your love may continually grow with excess and would progressively encompass [you and your world] with surpassing abundance still more and more, within full and accurate experiential and intimate knowledge and all insight and sensible perception,**

10. **into the [situation for] you folks to habitually test, examine, distinguish and determine** (or: make sure by proving) **the things that carry through and are thus of consequence or make a difference, so that you may constantly be** (continually exist being) **folks judged by the light of the sun** (thus: clearly sincere and with integrity) **and ones [that are] not stumbling or jarring against [anything] nor striking toward [someone] and causing trouble, on into the midst of a Day of, and which is, Christ** [p46: the Day from Christ (or: an anointing)],

11. **being people having been filled full with [the] Fruit of fair and equitable dealings which bring right relationship within the Way pointed out** (or: = from covenant inclusion)**: the one [that is] through Jesus Christ [that is] leading into God's glory** (good reputation and manifestation of that which calls forth admiration) **and praise** (approval and commendation)
> (or: being those filled full of fruit of the eschatological deliverance of a rightwised nature through Jesus Christ, which proceeds into glory and praise that belongs to and pertains to God; or: ... through Jesus Christ, with a view to inhabiting the qualities and characteristics of God's reputation and praise).

12. **Now I am constantly intending** (purposing and deciding for) **you folks to habitually know through intimate experience, brothers, that the affairs pertaining to me have rather come, and yet remain, into an advancement** (a progression; a striking ahead) **of God's message of goodness and well-being,**

13. **so that my bonds** (prison fetters) **[are] clearly seen** (visible; apparent; illuminated so as to be widely known) **to be within Christ, within the whole of the praetorium** (the living quarters of the emperor's guards), **and among all those left over** (the rest; the remaining ones),

14. **and by my bonds most of the brothers** (= the majority of the fellow believers), **having become persuaded and now being confident in the Lord, [are] to a greater degree** (or: more exceedingly) **courageously daring to be fearlessly continuing to speak the Word of God** (or: God's thoughts and message; the Reason from God; the Idea which is God)**!**

15. **Certain folks** (or: Some), **indeed, are also habitually proclaiming** (or: are even heralding publishing and preaching) **the Christ through** (or: because of) **envy, jealousy and rivalry, as well as strife** (discord; debate)**; yet also, certain ones** (or: some) **through delight** (or: because of a good disposition and a good opinion [about it]; or: through thinking well [of it and/or people]; because of approval [of the message]; or: = because they are pleased to do it).

16. **These, on the one hand, forth from out of love – having seen and thus knowing that I am constantly lying into** (or: repeatedly located with a view to; habitually being laid down, and thus set into the midst of) **a defense of the news of well-being and message of goodness.**

17. **Yet those, on the other hand, from out of faction** (partisan purposes; contentiousness; or: from self-interest, or from a motive of financial gain, or to enhance their careers) **are habitually announcing in accord with the message of the Christ, not purely** (= with pure motives) **– being ones habitually presuming** (or: supposing) **to be repeatedly arousing and raising up squeezing** (pressure; affliction; tribulation; oppression) **to** (or: for) **my bonds** (or: in my imprisonment).

18. **For what?** (or: So what?; = What difference does it make?) **That moreover, in every direction** (or: by every turn; by every method), **whether in pretense** (as a cloak for other purposes) **or in truth** (reality; essential essence), **Christ is continually being correspondingly announced, and in this I constantly rejoice.**

19. **For I am aware** (have seen and thus know) **that this will continue stepping away into deliverance** (rescue; health and wholeness; salvation) **for me** (and: in me) **through your request and the supply** (support; provision) **of the Spirit of Jesus Christ** (or: from the attitude pertaining to and having the characteristics of Jesus Christ; of the Breath-effect which is Jesus, [the] Anointed),

20. **in accordance with my premonition – in liberation from intuitive opinion – and an expectation, that within nothing will I proceed being put to shame** (embarrassment; disgrace). **To the contrary, within all freedom of speech** (boldness and public openness which comes from being a citizen) **– as always, even now** (at the present moment) **– Christ will progressively be unloosed and made great** (be greatened and magnified; be enlarged and set free to be huge) **within my body, whether through life, or through death!**

21. **For you see, to me, to be living [is] Christ** (or: For the [situation] in me and for me, life [is the] Anointed One), **and to be dying [is] gain** (advantage; profit).

22. **Yet since** (or: Now if) [*p46*, D: Whether] **the [situation] is to continue living within flesh** (= in a physical body in the natural realm), **this for me** (or: in me) **[will be] a fruit from work** (produce relating to [my] action) **– and so what** (or: which) **I will proceed choosing** (taking to myself in preference; [*p46*, B: I should and could choose]) **I am not presently making known.**

23. **So I am being continuously held together** (or: caught; squeezed) **from out of the two: constantly having the craving** (holding the strong desire and impulse) **into the [situation] to untie and loose back up again** [as in loosing tent pins and ropes when striking camp, or loosing moorings to set sail], **and to be** (to exist being) **together with Christ – for [that is] rather to a much higher rank** (a more advantageous situation; a more profitable thing; [it is] much better)!
24. **Yet the [situation] to be staying** (remaining-on) **in the flesh [is] more necessary** (indispensable; a more forced constraint) **because of you folks.**
25. **So, having been persuaded and still being convinced of this, I have seen and thus know that I will continue remaining on, and shall continue abiding** (dwelling so as to be ready to give aid) **together alongside with** (or: among) **all you folks – on into your progress** (or: cutting or striking a passage forward; advancement) **and joy that comes from, belongs to and has the characteristics of the Faith** (or: which is the trust, conviction and loyalty),
26. **to the end that, in me – [that is], through my presence again face to face with you – your loud-tongued exultation-results** (or: your justification for boasting) **in Christ Jesus** (or: in union with [the] Anointed Jesus) **may surround [you] in excessive abundance.**

27. **Only, by habit live** (or: continue living) **worthily, as citizens with behavior corresponding in value to Christ's good news** (message of goodness), **so that whether coming and seeing so as to become acquainted with you folks, or continuing absent, I may go on hearing about you folks** (the things concerning you)**: that you are constantly and progressively standing firm within the midst of and in union with one Breath-effect** (or: = steadfastly united in spirit and attitude), **continuing to be corporately striving in one soul** (by one inner life competing side-by-side as in the public games) **by the faith that comes from the good news**
     (or: in the conviction that belongs to and pertains to the message of goodness and well-being; or: by the trust which is the message of wellness and ease),
28. **even constantly being folks [that are] in nothing startled, intimidated or frightened by** (or: under) **the opponents** (the ones continuously lying in the opposing position) **– which is a public indication** (a pointing-out as of display; or: a showing within) **of loss** (ruin; destruction) **for** (or: to; among) **them, yet of deliverance** (wholeness, health, rescue and salvation) **to, for and among you folks** [other MSS: in and among us; other MSS: of your deliverance], **and this [is] from God,**
29. **because to you folks it is given by grace** (or: He graciously was given in you people, as a favor for you people), **over the [issue] of, and on behalf of, Christ, not only to be progressively believing and habitually trusting into Him** (or: continuing faithful unto Him), **but further, also, to be repeatedly having sensible experiences over Him**
     (or: to constantly experience feelings and impressions on behalf of Him; to habitually suffer and be ill used for His sake; to be continuously affected on account of the things pertaining to Him) –
30. **constantly having the very** (or: continuously holding the same) **contest [as] in the public games** (or: race in the stadium; agonizing struggle in the gathered assembly) **such as you saw** (or: perceive) **within me and now are presently hearing in me** (or: and at this moment are repeatedly hearing [to be] in me).

CHAPTER 2

1. **If, then, [there exists] any calling-alongside to receive relief, aid, encouragement, consolation, comfort or supporting influence** (or: any receiving of the work of a paraclete) **within Christ or in union with [the] Anointing, if [there is] any spoken comfort and consolation of love** (belonging to love; from a drive toward accepting-reunion with another; or: which is love), **if any common being and existence** (common participation; fellowship; partnership; communion; sharing) **of Breath-effect** (or: belonging to spirit; from the result of [the] Breath), **if any tender emotions** (literally: upper internal organs) **and compassions** (or: pities),
2. **fill my joy full, so that you folks may be continually having the same frame of mind** (may be mutually disposed; may have the same opinion; may mind the same thing), **habitually holding** (or: having) **the same Love: folks joined together in soul** (inner life of feelings, will,

heart and mind), **continuously minding The One** (or: habitually holding one opinion; constantly thinking one thing; regularly disposed to one [purpose]; [other MSS: the same]) –

3. **nothing down from** (or: along the line of; corresponding to; or: descending to) **party interests** (hireling-like contention; faction; self-serving; or: from a motive of financial gain, or to enhance one's career) **nor down from** (or: along the line of; corresponding to; or: descending to) **empty reputation** (futile opinion; vainglory; fruitless appearance; vacuous conceit) – **but rather, in humility** (or: by an attitude of being in a low station; in humbleness of disposition and way of thinking) **constantly considering one another** (or: each other) **[as] those habitually holding [a position] above yourselves** (or: [as] being superior in regard to yourselves),

4. **not each one continuing to attentively view** (keep an eye on and look out for) **the things or interests pertaining to themselves, but to the contrary, each one also [looking out for] the things and interests pertaining to others** (or: of different folks; of people that are different).

5. **You see, this way of thinking** (this attitude and disposition) **is continuously within and among you folks** (or, as an imperative: So let this minding be habitually within you folks) – **which [is] also within Christ Jesus,**

6. **Who, starting and continuing as inherently existing** (or: beginning under; subsisting) **within God's form** (or: in an outward mold which is God), **He does not consider the [situation] to be equals in and by God a plunder** (or: a pillaging; a robbery; a snatching; or: a thing or situation seized and held),

> (or: Who, [although] constantly humbly and supportively ruling in union with an external shape and an outward appearance from God, did not give consideration to a seizure: the [situation] to continuously exist being the same things with God, even on the same levels in God, or equal [things; aspects] to God,)

7. **but to the contrary, He empties Himself** (or: removed the contents of Himself; made Himself empty), **receiving** (or: taking; accepting) **a slave's form** (external shape; outward mold), **coming to be** (or: birthing Himself) **within an effect of humanity's** (mankind's; people's) **likeness.**

8. **And so, being found in an outward fashion, mode of circumstance, condition, form-appearance** (or: character, role, phase, configuration, manner) **as a human** (a person; a man), **He lowers Himself** (or: humbled Himself; made Himself low; degrades Himself; levels Himself off), **coming to be** (or: birthing Himself) **a submissive, obedient One** (one who gives the ear and listens) **as far as** (or: to the point of; until) **death – but death of a cross** (torture stake)!

9. **For this reason, God also lifts Him up above** (or: highly exalted Him; elevates Him over) **and by grace gives to Him** (or: joyously favors on Him) **the Name – the one over and above every name! –**

10. **to the end that within The Name: Jesus!** (or: in union with the name of Jesus; in the midst of the Name belonging to [Yahweh-the-Savior]), **every knee** (= person) **– of the folks upon the heaven** (of those belonging to an imposed heaven, or [situated] upon the atmosphere) **and of the people existing upon the earth and of the folks dwelling down under the ground** (or: on the level of or pertaining to subterranean ones; [comment: note the ancient science of the day – a three-tiered universe]) **– may bend** (or: would bow) **in prayer, submission and allegiance,**

11. **and then every tongue** (= person) **may speak out the same thing** (or: would openly, and joyfully agree; can confess, avow and with praise acclaim) **that Jesus Christ [is] Lord** (Master; Owner) **– [leading] into [the] glory of Father God** (or: unto Father God's good reputation; into the midst of a praise-inducing manifestation and assumed appearance which is God: a Father)!

12. **Consequently, my loved ones, according as at all times** (or: as always) **you folks submissively listened, paid attention and humbly obeyed, not as only in my presence, but further, now** (at this moment) **much more in my absence – in company with reverent fear and trembling** (or: = earnestness and concern) **– be habitually working commensurately with the deliverance** (or: be constantly producing on the level and sphere of the wholeness and well-being which are the outcome of the rescue and salvation) **of, or pertaining to, yourselves,**

13. **for you see, God is the One habitually operating with inward activity, repeatedly working within, constantly causing function and progressively producing effects within, among and in union with you folks – both the [condition] to be habitually willing** (intending;

purposing; resolving) **and the [situation] to be continuously effecting the action, repeatedly operating to cause function and habitually setting at work so as to produce – for the sake of and over the pleasing good form and the thinking of goodness in delightful imagination.**
14. **Be habitually doing** (accomplishing; constructing; producing) **all things apart from grumbling complaints** (or: murmurings) **and reasoned considerations**
      (or: designing thoughts; divided reckonings unto the settlements of accounts; arguments
      which permeate the environment or go in every direction),
15. **so that you folks may come to be blameless ones** (those without defect), **even unmixed** (unblended; artless and sincere) **children of God – unblemished** (flawless) **people in the midst of a crooked and distorted** (as having been misshaped on the potter's wheel) **generation** (or: a twisted family which has been altered and turned in different ways so as to be dislocated), **within which** (or: among whom) **you folks are continuously shining** (giving light; or: appearing; made visible by light) **as illuminators** (sources of light; or: luminaries) **within [the] dominating, ordered System** (or: centered in a world of secular culture, religion, economics and government; or: **in union with the aggregate of mankind**), [cf Dan. 12:3]
16. **constantly holding upon** (or: having added; keeping a good grip on and fully possessing) **Life's Word** (or: a *Logos* of Life; a message which is life; Reason and Patterned Information from Life; an idea with reference to Life; a laid-out thought that has the character of Life), **[leading you] into loud-tongued exulting-effects** (boasting; vaunting) **for me** (or: in me), **on into Christ's Day** (a day of [the] Anointed; or: a day which is anointed), **because I do not** (or: did not) **run into emptiness** (that which is without content; a void), **nor do I** (or: did I) **become weary or struggle in labor into emptiness** (unto that which is without content; into the midst of a void).

17. **But even more, since** (or: if) **I am also repeatedly poured out as a drink offering upon the sacrificial offering and public service pertaining to your faith** (or: which comes from your trust; in regard to the faithful loyalty which comprises you people), **I am constantly rejoicing** (or: glad) **– even continually rejoicing** (glad) **together with all of you!** [cf 2 Cor. 4:12]
18. **Now in the same way, you yourselves also be constantly rejoicing – even continually rejoicing together with me.**

19. **Now I continue expecting – in the Lord Jesus – to quickly send Timothy to you folks, so that I also may continue well in soul** (in good cheer; in good spirits), **knowing the [situations and circumstances] concerning** (or: the things about) **you folks.**
20. **You see, I presently have no one equal-souled** (of the same soul; = equally sensitive) **who will proceed to legitimately** (or: genuinely) **divide his mind so as to continue having his thoughts anxious about your interests and to keep on caring for the [circumstances] concerning** (or: the things about) **you folks.**
21. **For all those [others] are constantly concerned with** (looking out for; are seeking) **their own interests** (or: things), **not with the interests and things pertaining to and belonging to, or having the qualities and characteristics of, Jesus Christ.**

22. **Yet you folks continue knowing by experience his proof by scrutinized examination and testing, that as a child for a father, he slaves** (performs as a slave) **together with me, into the message of goodness, ease and well-being.**
23. **I continue expecting, indeed then, to send this one immediately** (out of the very time or situation) **– as soon as I can look away from the things around me** (or: see-off the [situations and] things concerning me).
24. **So I have been persuaded and am confident within [the] Lord** [= Christ or Yahweh] **that I myself, also, shall quickly proceed in coming to you folks.**

25. **Now I consider it necessary and pressing to send to you Epaphroditus, my brother and co-worker** (joint-operative) **and fellow soldier, yet your envoy** (representative; emissary; sent-forth agent), **and a public servant of my need,**
26. **since he had been continuously having great affection and longing to see all of you folks, even being repeatedly dejected and deeply troubled because you heard** (or: hear) **that he fell sick** (or: is ill).

27. **For he even fell sick** (or: also is ill) **as being a consort near alongside of death. But contrariwise, God had mercy on** (or: mercies) **him – yet not only him, but further, me also – to the end that I should not have pain and sadness upon pain and sadness** (or: = major and added sorrow).

28. **More diligently** (earnestly; eagerly), **then, I send** (or: sent) **him, so that in seeing him again, you may be glad and rejoice – and I may be more relieved of pain and sadness.**

29. **Be focusing on him, then, to welcome and continue receiving him within the Lord with all joy, and be constantly holding such people in honor and value,**

30. **because through Christ's work** (with other MSS: on account of [the] Lord's Act) **he drew** (or: draws) **near, as far as death, with [his] soul casting himself to the side** (or: in [his] inner being handing himself over and risking [his] life; = throwing self aside, he gambled [his] life), **so that he might fill back up your deficiency** (your lack; your coming too late; = what you were unable to do) **in the area of public service toward me** (= civic sponsorship and funding me).

CHAPTER 3

1. **As for the rest** (or: For what remains), **my brothers** (= family; = fellow believers), **continue rejoicing** (be habitually glad and delighted) **within [the] Lord** (centered in union with [Christ or Yahweh]). **To be repeatedly writing the same things to you** (or: To continue writing these very things for you) **[is] surely not troublesome for me** (or: delaying me or causing me to hesitate), **and for you [it is] something to secure you from stumbling.**

2. **Constantly keep your eyes on and be aware of the dogs** (= impudent, shameless or audacious folks; = people whose uncleaned natures are like little wild animals/beasts; [cf vss. 17-19, below; Ps. 22:16, 20; Isa. 56:10b; Rev. 22:15]); **habitually be observing so as to take heed of worthless workers** (craftsmen of bad quality; laborers who are not as they ought to be); **keep on seeing so as to continually observe and be aware of [the party of] the down-cision** (the mutilation; the cutting-into; the sacrificial meat-hacking; the wounding or maiming; or: = folks who cut things down or off; [comment: a sardonic slur = the circumcision]). [1Cor. 3:9-17; Rev. 2:9]

3. **For you see, we ourselves are** (exist being) **The Circumcision: the people** (or: those) **continuously rendering sacred service in a spirit of God** (or: by God's Breath-effect; to God's Spirit; with God's breath; [some MSS: service to God in spirit; p46 omits "God," so simply: serving in spirit]) **and constantly making our boast** (being loud-tongued, vaunting and exulting) **within, and in union with, Christ Jesus; even folks** (or: those) **being people having been persuaded and thus continuing to put no confidence within flesh**

> (= no reliance on the physical: e.g., religious works or natural heritage; or: the estranged human nature; [comment: may = animal sacrifices or old covenant cultus/purity codes]).

4. **Even though I myself continue holding** (or: having) **[grounds for] trust and confidence also within flesh, if any other man is in the habit of thinking** (or: is constantly seeming) **or presuming to have come to a settled persuasion, thus having confidence within [his] flesh, I to a greater degree** (more so; for a better reason; rather more):

5. **in circumcision, on [the] eighth day;**
> **out of race** (from posterity; by birth; as to class or species), **of Israel;**
> **of Benjamin's tribe; a Hebrew out of the midst of [the] Hebrews**
> (or: = a supreme Hebrew);
> **in accordance to Law, a Pharisee** (or: down from custom, a Pharisee);

6. **in accordance to zeal, one constantly pressing, pursuing and persecuting the called-out community;**
> **in accordance to fairness and equity in the way pointed out in the Law, one coming to be, of myself, without defect** (one becoming blameless).

7. **But to the contrary, whatever things** (or: things which) **were being gains** (advantages; assets) **to, for or in me, these things I have esteemed and now consider** (or: regard) **as a loss** (a penalty; a forfeit; disadvantage; a bad bargain; a detriment) **because of the Christ** (or: on account of the Anointed One [= the Messiah] and the Anointing).

8. **But further – indeed, then, as a matter of fact – I even am habitually considering** (or: regarding) **all things** (all; everything) **to be a loss** (a disadvantage; a bad bargain; damage; a

forfeit; a penalty) **because of** (on account of; for the sake of) **the thing that is constantly holding things above and thus having all-surpassing value and superiority: that which pertains to and comes from the experience of the intimate knowledge of my Lord, Jesus Christ** (or: of, from and which is Christ Jesus, my Owner) – **because of, on account of and for the sake of Whom I undergo loss of** (experience the forfeit of; receive as a disadvantage) **all things** (everything; the whole life-experience, environment and possessions) **and I continue considering** (or: regarding) **them to be [either] a lot of refuse and filth** (pieces of dung; a pile of manure) **[or] things that are cast away from the table to the dogs** (garbage), **to the end that I may have the advantage of Christ** (or: could maintain the gain of [the] Anointing; enjoy the assets of and profit from [the Messiah]), [cf vs. 2, above; 2 Cor. 5:2, 4; cf Rom. 5:9]

9. **and may be found within Him** (or: in union with Him; centered in Him) – **not continuing having** (or: holding) **my [previous] pointed-out way** (my fairness and equity; my relationships; my basis for what is right; my own righteousness) **from out of the Law or custom, but to the contrary, the [Way pointed-out which was a rightwising deliverance] through means of Christ's faithfulness** (or: the trust-conviction which is Christ; the faith of and from [the Messiah]): **the rightwising, eschatological deliverance into the new covenant fairness and equity of righted relationships within the Way pointed out [which is] forth from out of the midst of God as a source** (or: the just Act from the midst of God) **[and based] upon that Faithfulness** (or: [Christ's/God's] loyal allegiance; or: the Trust and confident faith) – [cf 2 Cor. 5:3, 8]

10. **to intimately and with insight experientially know Him, and the ability – even the power – of His resurrection and also the** [other MSS: a] **common existence** (participation; partnership, sharing and fellowship) **of the results and from the effects of His experiences** [note: these include good times/feelings and passions, as well as sufferings] – **being a person that is being continuously conformed by** (being progressively brought together with the form of; being habitually configured to) **His death,** [cf Col. 1:24]

11. **since this is how I can fully meet face-to-face, participate and reach into the midst of** (or: since in some way I would attain the level [to be] into the midst of; or: if by any means I may arrive and meet with the corresponding sphere [leading] into) **the full resurrection** (or: the arising and standing back up again from out of the midst; or: the out-resurrection) – **the one [arising] forth from out of the midst of dead folks.** [cf 2 Cor. 4:14; 5:4]

12. **[Now this is] not because I already take it by the hand** (grasp, lay hold of it; or: obtained; [p46 & D add: or [because] I have already been rightwised and made to be one in accord with the Way pointed out with justice and equity]) **or even have been already brought to the purposed goal and destiny** (matured unto perfection and finished). **But yet, I am consistently pursuing** (running swiftly in order to catch), **since I can** (or: if I would) **take down by the hand** (fully seize; forcefully grasp and gain possession of) **even [that] upon which I also was** (or: am) **taken down by hand** (fully seized; forcefully grasped and taken possession of) **by, and under [the control of], Christ Jesus.** [cf 1:6, above]

13. **Brothers** (Womb-mates; = Fellow believers)**! I am not** [other MSS: not yet] **calculating** (logically considering; reckoning; viewing) **myself to have taken it down by hand** (seized, fully grasped or gotten hold of it in order to have it), **yet [there is] one thing: habitually forgetting, on the one hand, the things behind** (or: in the back; vss. 4-8, above; = the old covenant), **and on the other hand constantly reaching and stretching myself out upon the things in front** (or: ahead),

14. **I am continuously pressing forward, pursuing down toward** [the; or: an] **object in view** (a mark on which the eye is fixed): **into the awarded contest prize of God's** (or: the award which is God's) **invitation to an above place** (or: the prize from, and which is, the upward calling from, and which is, the God) **within the midst of and in union with Christ Jesus.** [cf 2 Cor. 5:1]

15. **Therefore – AS MANY AS [are] people who ARE mature** (ones who HAVE reached the goal, being finished and complete) – **WE should constantly be of this frame of mind** (have this attitude and opinion; think this way; be minding and paying attention to this). **And if you folks are habitually thinking differently** (are continuing differently minded; are continually having a different attitude or opinion), **God will also proceed in progressively unveiling this to you** (or: uncovering and revealing, or disclosing, this for and among you folks). [cf 1 Cor. 13:10-11]

16. **Moreover, into that which we precede [others]** (or: into what we went before in; into what we come ahead so as to arrive at; = unto whatever stage we have reached) **in the very same thing [our goal is] to be habitually drawn into a straight line and consistently advance within our ranks**

> [Aleph2 and other MSS add phrases to read as follows: Besides, into what we outstrip {others}, by the same standard (measuring rod; rule) {it is for us} to habitually advance in line (i.e., frame our conduct in an orderly routine; or: consider the elements and observe the rudimentary principles by the same standard) – to constantly be intent on and keep thinking of the same thing (or: be of the same frame of mind and attitude)]. [1 Cor. 15:23]

17. **Brothers** (Folks from the same womb; Family; Fellows), **be progressively birthed to be joint-imitators of me** (or: unite in becoming my imitators), **and continually keep a watchful eye on and take note of those habitually walking about thus** (i.e., those who thus live their lives), **according as you folks continue having us as a pattern** (model; example; type).
18. **For you see – I was often telling you about them, yet now I am also presently weeping** (lamenting) **in saying it – many continue walking about** (i.e., are living their lives) **as enemies of the cross of the Christ** (the Anointed One's execution-stake and suspension-pole), [Rev. 3:9]
19. **whose goal** (eventual end; closing act; final stage; result; finished discharge) **[is] ruin and loss** (or: waste and destruction), **whose god [is their] cavity** (or: belly) **and [whose] reputation** (or: glory; opinion) **resides within their shame** (disgrace; embarrassment) – **people continually thinking about** (habitually being intent on; constantly minding) **the things existing upon the earth** (or: upon the Land; or: = folks whose minds are earthbound). [Rom. 8:6-8; Hos. 4:7; 7:13]

20. **You see, our citizenship** (result of living in a free city; or: commonwealth-effects; political realm) **continues inherently existing** (or: continues humbly ruling; continuously subsists; repeatedly has its under-beginning) **resident within the midst of [the] atmospheres** (or: heavens), **from out of where** (or: which place) **we also continuously receive and take away in our hands from out of a Deliverer** (a Savior; One restoring us to the health and wholeness of our original state and condition)**: [the] Lord** (or: a Master), **Jesus Christ,** [cf 2 Cor. 5:1, 4, 6, 8]
21. **Who will continue transfiguring** (progressively refashioning and remodeling; continuously changing the form of) **our body from the low condition and status** (or: the body of, and from, our humiliation; or: **the body which is us**, pertaining to this lowliness) **[to be] joint-formed in, and conformed by, to and with, the body of His glory** (or: from, and which is, His assumed appearance; [other MSS: into the {situation} for it to be brought into existence conformed to, and having the same form together with, His body, from that which calls forth praise and imagination for His character and good repute]; cf 2 Cor. 3:18), **down from** (or: in accord with; in the sphere of; to the level of; following the pattern of; in stepping with; commensurate with; as directed by) **the inwardly-centered operation** (functioning energy; inner-working) **of the [conditions, situation or sphere for] Him to be continuously able** (or: to progress with power) **also to humbly align The Whole to and in Himself** (or: to subject and subordinate all things for Himself; to arrange everything under so as to have full control and to support [it] by and with Himself).
1. **Consequently, my brothers** (= fellow believers; Family) **– loved ones and longed-for folks** (people missed with a craving), **my joy and winner's** (or: festal) **wreath – thus** (in this way) **you constantly stand within [the] Lord** [= Christ or Yahweh]**: [as or being] loved ones!** (or, as an imperative: be habitually standing firm in this manner: in [the] Lord, [B adds: my] beloved!)

CHAPTER 4

2. **I am calling Euodia alongside, and I am calling Syntyche alongside, admonishing** (entreating; begging; assisting) **[you two] to be habitually thinking about the same thing** (minding and being intent on the same thing; disposed in the same way; or: = agreeing and maintaining a common mind), **within, and in union with, the Lord.**
3. **Yes, I am asking you, too, O genuine and legitimate yokefellow** (or: O loyal Synzugus; O Suzugos, one born in wedlock; O paired star who rises as I set; O joined and united one belonging to [my] birth group), **be consistently taking these women together to yourself to aid and assist them – which women toil together with me** (or: compete [as] in the public

games along with me, and contend on my side) **within the message of goodness and well-being** (good news), **with Clement and the rest of my fellow workers, whose names [are] within Life's Book** (or: in a book of life; a book which is Life; [comment: = participation in life]).

4. **Be constantly rejoicing within, and in union with, [the] Lord** [= in Yahweh or in Christ], **at all times** (or: always)! **Again, I will repeat declaring it, Rejoice** (or: You folks be habitually rejoicing)!
5. **Let your gentle fairness, lenience, considerateness and suitable reasonableness be intimately and experientially known to all mankind** (or: by and for all humans). **The Lord** [= Christ or Yahweh] **is near** (close by – at hand, close enough to touch, and available)!
6. **Do not be habitually worried, anxious or overly concerned about anything! On the contrary, in everything** (and: within every situation), **by thinking and speaking toward having goodness and having things go well and with ease** (or: in prayer) **and in expression of need – together with thanksgiving – repeatedly let your requests be made known to** (toward; face to face with) **God,**
7. **and God's peace** ([shalom] from God; or: the harmonious joining, which is God), **which is continuously having a hold over** (habitually having sway over; or: constantly being superior and excelling over) **all mind and inner sense** (or: every intellect; all power of comprehension; or: all process of thinking), **will continue garrisoning** (guarding; keeping watch over; protecting) **your hearts and the results from directing your minds** (or: effects of your perceptions, concepts, thoughts, reasonings and understandings; or: dispositions; designs; purposes; [p16 adds: and bodies]), **centered within, and in union with, Christ Jesus** [p46: {the} Lord Jesus].

8. **In conclusion** (or: Finally; or: What [is] left), **brothers** (= fellow believers; [my] family), **as much as is true** (or: as many things as are genuine and real), **as many as [are] awe-inspiring** (serious; respectable; noble; dignified by holiness), **as much as [is] rightwised** (put right; fair, equitable; just; in right relationship within the Way pointed out), **as many as [are] pure and innocent, as much as [is] affection-inducing** (friendly; directed toward what is liked; lovable or lovely; agreeable; well-regarded; winsome; engendering fondness; attractive; kindly disposed; loveable), **as many as [are] well-spoken-of** (commendable; reputable; of good report; the effect of fair speaking; renowned), **if [there is] any excellence and nobleness** (virtues of braveness, courage, good character, quality, self-restraint, magnificence, benevolence, reliability) **[in them] and if [there is] any praise applied** (expression of high evaluation; honor paid; approval or applause) **[to them], be habitually thinking about these things in a logical way** (repeatedly make these things the focus of careful consideration and analysis; continuously take these things into account)!
9. **Keep on practicing and accomplishing these things which you folks both learn and accept** (or: learned and received alongside) **– even [what] you heard and saw within me. And, the God of the Peace** (or: And God, the source and quality of peace [= shalom]; Then the God which is joined-harmony) **will continue existing in company with you folks** (or: will constantly be with you folks).

10. **Now I greatly rejoice** (or: rejoiced) **within the Lord** [= in union with Christ or Yahweh] **that now, at last, you folks shoot up to flourish to the extent to be constantly focusing your thinking over me** (to continuously have my concerns intently in mind; to repeatedly take thought on my behalf) **– upon which, also, you folks were progressively thinking, yet you continued without a fitting situation** (you were being out of season; you kept on lacking the opportunity).
11. **Not that I am suggesting a need, for I learned and so know to be self-sufficient** (to be contented by warding-off my own [needs]; or: to have independent provisions) **within whatever circumstances or situations [that] I am.**
12. **I am aware of [what it is like] to be repeatedly made low [on provisions], as well as aware of [what it is like] to be continuously surrounded by more than enough**
    (or: I have seen, and thus know, both to be humbled, and I have seen, and thus know, to
    be constantly and excessively abounding). **I have been instructed to shut the mouth, and I am initiated into the secret** (or: mystery): **within everything and within the midst of all things** (or: among all people), **both to be** (or: [how] to be) **habitually feeding until satisfied,**

and to be (or: as well as [how] to be) **habitually hungry; both to be** (or: [how] to be) **constantly and excessively abounding** (continuously surrounded by more than enough), **and to be** (or: as well as [how] to be) **repeatedly in need** (or: lacking).

13. **I constantly have strength for all things among all people, [from being] in union with and within the midst of the One continuously enabling me** (empowering me; infusing me with power and ability)**: Christ!**

14. **Moreover you folks performed beautifully** (acted ideally; did virtuously; produced finely), **sharing** (partnering; participating; having common association) **together with me in my pressure** (squeezing; tribulation; trouble; oppression).

15. **Now you Philippians have seen, and thus are aware** (or: know), **that within the original period** (or: the beginning) **of the message of goodness, ease and well-being** (good news), **when I went** (or: came) **out from Macedonia, not one called-out community expressed common being** (or: communicated; participated; partnered; held common association; shared) **with me** (or: for me), **[leading] into a discourse** (or: with regard to an account or a matter of discussion; = injecting a thought) **of giving and of receiving** (or: of getting; of taking), **except you folks, alone** (or: only),

16. **because even in Thessalonica both once, and even twice!, you folks sent [provision] into my need.**

17. **Not that I am in the habit of really seeking the gift! But rather, I am in the habit of really seeking the constantly abounding fruit which is overflowing into your discourse** (or: your account; your word; your matter of discussion; your message; your thought).

18. **But now I am continually holding possessions from** (collecting; or: = receiving payment for what is due me from) **all things and from all folks; I am even constantly superabounding** (being surrounded by more than enough). **I have been filled full, receiving from beside Epaphroditus the things from your side: an odor of a sweet fragrance** (a fragrant aroma), **an acceptable sacrifice, well-pleasing to God** (or: with God; for God; in God).

19. **So my God will continue and progressively be filling to the full your every need** (or: will keep on making full all lack which pertains to you folks) **down from His wealth [being] within [the] glory [that resides] within Christ Jesus**

> (or: that accords to His wealth that resides within the opinion or imagination [which is] within Christ Jesus; to the level of His riches, within a manifestation of splendor which calls forth praise, within Christ Jesus; down through His abundance, within the reputation [arising from] within the midst of Christ Jesus; in the sphere of and in line with His riches [which are] in union with a glory centered in an anointing from Jesus).

20. **Now in our God and Father [is] the glory**

> (or: Now for our God and Father [is] the reputation; Yet by our God and Father [is] the manifestation which calls forth praise; So to our God and Father [is] the good opinion; But with our God and Father [is] the imagination and the assumed Appearance) **on into the indefinite and unseen time periods of the ages! Count on it, for it is so!**

21. **You folks gladly greet and embrace as a dear one every set-apart person** (every holy one; every saint) **within Christ Jesus. The brothers** (= fellow believers; = the family) **with me are habitually greeting and warmly embracing you folks.**

22. **All those set-apart are habitually greeting and warmly embracing you folks – yet especially those of Caesar's house** (= household).

23. **The grace of** (or: The joy-bringing favor belonging to and having its source in; The grace which is) **our Lord** [with other MSS: the Owner and Master], **Jesus Christ, [is] with the spirit of you folks** (or: [is] with your corporate breath-effect; or: [is] with the character and attitude manifested through you folks; [other MSS: {is} with all of you]). **It is so!**

[written circa A.D. 58 – Based on the critical analysis of John A.T. Robinson]

COLOSSIANS

1. **Paul, one sent with a mission pertaining to Christ Jesus** (or: an envoy of [the] Anointed Jesus; an emissary and a representative from Christ [= Messiah] Jesus) **through God's will, and Timothy, the brother** (or: = fellow believer; or: Timothy, the one from out of the same womb),
2. **To the set-apart folks** (the holy ones; the sacredly different people) **within Colossae – even to ones full of faith** (or: to faithful and trusting people) **– to [the] brothers within Christ** (or: and to loyal womb-mates [who are] in union with [the] Anointed [other MSS add: Jesus])**:**
With, among, to and for you folks [are] grace and joyous favor (or: The act that produces happiness, which was granted [to all] as a favor), **as well as peace and the harmony from the joining, from God our Father** [other MSS read: from God, our Father and Lord, Jesus Christ].

3. **We habitually express gratitude for the goodness in grace, and give thanks to God, the Father** [other MSS: to the God and Father] **of our Lord, Jesus Christ, at all times continually thinking and speaking goodness and well-being concerning** (or: praying about) **you folks,**
4. **upon hearing of your faithfulness, loyalty, trust and faith [being, resident, or having its source] within Christ Jesus** (or: centered in, and in union with, [the] Anointed Jesus) **and the love** (acceptance; urge toward union) **which you folks habitually have and hold [extended] unto and into the midst of all the set-apart folks** (or: holy ones; saints; sacred people)
5. **because of the expectation** (or: expectant hope) **– the one continuously lying stored away as a reserve – resident within the atmospheres** (or: heavens), **which you folks already heard** (or: heard before) **within the word** (message; discourse; or: Logos) **concerning the Truth** (or: the word of truth; the idea belonging to and having its source in Reality; the collected and laid-out thoughts which are truth and reality) **which originates in and pertains to the message of ease, goodness and well-being** (or: which belongs to the good news).
6. **This [Word; message] is being continuously present alongside [and proceeding] into you folks, just as it is also continuously existing within all the ordered System** (within the every world of culture, society, religion, economics and government; centered in the entire aggregate of humanity, the whole universe and all the Roman Empire), **repeatedly bearing fruit of itself and constantly being grown and caused to be increasing, just as also within you folks, from [the] day in which you heard and at once fully experienced – in intimate knowing and accurate realization – the grace of God, within Truth** (or: God's favor resident within [the] truth; God's grace in the midst of reality; or: the favor which, in reality, is God).

7. **Just in this way, you folks [were taught and] learned from Epaphras, our beloved fellow-slave, who is full of faith and loyal, an attending servant of the Christ on our** [other MSS: your] **behalf** (or: who is a faithful dispenser of the Christ [who is] over us [or: you folks]),
8. **the person also clearly showing and making evident to us your love in spirit and attitude** (or: your love, centered in a Breath-effect; your acceptance in union with [the] Spirit).

9. **And because of this** (or: So that is why) **we, from the day on which we heard, are not ceasing constant praying** (thinking and speaking toward having things being well) **over your [situation] and asking** (or: making a request) **on behalf of you folks, to the end that you may** (or: would) **be filled full with the entire contents of the accurate, full, experiential, intimate knowledge and insight of His will** (His design, purpose, plan and intention; or: so that you may know and experience all that He wants you to know and experience) **within the sphere of all wisdom and spiritual understanding** (comprehension; a junction of that which is sent together; discernment; being able to make the pieces fit together).
10. **[Thus we pray for you] to walk about worthily** (i.e., to live your life with corresponding value) **with regard to the Lord** (the Owner; [= Yahweh or Christ]) **[progressing] into all pleasing** (or: into every desire to please; into the midst of entire pleasure) **within every good work or virtuous action, while habitually bearing fruit and constantly being folks [that] are**

being progressively caused to grow and increase in the full, accurate, experiential and intimate knowledge of, and from, God (or: with God's full experience of intimate knowledge and insight; or: by the added insight and experiential knowledge **which is God**),

11. **being continuously empowered in every ability** (being ones progressively enabled within all power) **corresponding to the strength of His glory**

> (or: down from and in the sphere of the might pertaining to and having its source in His reputation or His manifestation of that which calls forth praise; or: = the strength coming from His manifested presence [= His Sh'khinah]) **[leading] into every [situation of]**

persistent remaining under [difficulties] to humbly give patient support (or: unto all relentless endurance) **and long-waiting before rushing into emotions** (or: long endurance in putting anger far away; a long time before breathing violently with passion; or: perseverance; tolerance towards others), **accompanied by** (or: together with) **joy.**

12. **[We are folks who are] constantly giving thanks to the Father: the One calling you** [other MSS: us] – **as well as making [you; us] competent** (sufficient; qualified; fit; suitable) – **into the divided share of the lot of the inheritance** (or: into the part and portion of the allotted possession) **of the set-apart folks** (or: pertaining to the holy ones; belonging to the saints; from the sacred people; which is the different-from-the-ordinary folks) **within the Light;**

13. **He who drags us out of danger** (or: rescued us) **forth from out of the midst of the authority of the Darkness** (from Darkness's jurisdiction and right; from existing out of gloomy shadows and obscure dimness; = the privilege of ignorance), **and changes [our] position** (or: transported [us], thus, giving [us] a change of standing, and transferred [us]) **into the midst of the kingdom and reign of the Son of His love**

> (or: into the midst of the sovereign influence of the Son Who has the characteristics and qualities of His accepting love; into union with the sovereign activities of the Son Whose origin is His love; or: into the sphere of the reign of the Son of the Love which is Him; into the center of **the kingdom** of the Son, **which is His love and drive toward union**),

14. **in Whom** (or: in union with [which Son]) **we continuously have and hold the release into freedom from slavery or imprisonment** (the liberation from our predicament) **[which results in] the sending away of the failures** (or: the dismissal of the errors pertaining to falling short and straying to the side of the target; the flowing away of the sins; the divorce from mistakes).

15. **It is [this Son] Who is the Image** (portrait; the Exact Formed Likeness; the Figure and Representation; visible likeness and manifestation) **of the not-seen God** (or: the unable to be seen God; the invisible God), **the Firstborn of all creation**

> (or: of every creature; or: of every framing and founding; of every act of settling from a state of disorder and wildness; or: pertaining to the whole creation; or: = the Inheritor of all creation Who will also assume authority over and responsibility for every creature [note: this is the duty of the firstborn]),

16. **because within Him was created the whole** (or: in union with Him everything is founded and settled, is built and planted, is brought into being, is produced and established; or: within the midst of Him all things were brought from chaos into order) – **the things within the skies and atmospheres, and the things upon the earth** (or: those [situations, conditions and/or people] in the heavens and on the land); **the visible things, and the unseen** (or: unable to be seen; invisible) **things: whether thrones** (seats of power) **or lordships** (ownership systems) **or governments** (rulers; leadership systems; sovereignties) **or authorities** – **the whole has been created and all things continue founded, put in order and stand framed through means of Him, and [proceeds, or were placed] into Him** (or: = He is the agent and goal of all creation).

17. **And He is before** (prior to; or: maintains precedence of) **all things and all people, and the whole has** (or: all things have) **been placed together and now continues to jointly-stand** (stands cohesively; is made to have a co-standing) **within the midst of and in union with Him,**

18. **and so He is the Head** (or: Source) **of the body – which is the called-out community** (the ecclesia; the summoned congregation) – **Who is the Beginning** (or: the Source, Origin and Ruling Principle; the Beginning Power and Ability of the process), **a Firstborn forth from out of the midst of dead folks, to the end that He would be birthed** (may come into existence; or: could come to be) **within all things and in all people: He continuously holding first place**

(or: constantly being preeminent; or: habitually being the First One; or: continuing being the First Man [note: this phrase has in Greek literature been used as a title for a person]),

19. **because WITHIN Him all – the entire contents** (the result of that which fills everything; all the effect of the full measure [of things]) **– delights to settle down and dwell as in a house** (or: because He approved all the fullness [of all existence] to permanently reside within Him) [cf 2:9]

20. **and THROUGH Him at once to transfer the all** (the whole; = all of existential creation), **away from a certain state to the level of another which is quite different**

(or: to change all things, bringing movement away from being down; to reconcile all things; to change everything from estrangement and alienation to friendship and harmony and move all), **INTO Him – making** (constructing; forming; creating) **peace** (harmonious joining) **through the blood of His cross** (execution stake/pole): **through Him, whether the things upon the earth** (or: land) **or the things within the atmospheres and heavens!**

21. **And so you folks, being at one time people having been alienated away** (being estranged; being rendered as belonging to another; = having been put out of the family) **and enemies** (or: hated ones) **by the divided thoughts** (in the dualistic perceptions and things going through the mind in every direction) **within** (or: in the midst of; in union with; or: = in the performance of) **the miserable deeds** (gushes of wicked actions; laborious and painful works) –

22. **yet now He at once reconciled** (or: changed and transferred to a different state; [p46 & B read: you folks were reconciled]) **within the body of His flesh** (= His physical being), **through His death, to place you folks alongside, down before Him and in His sight: set-apart** (holy) **folks and flawless** (unblemished; blameless) **ones, even people not accused, with nothing laid to your charge** (or: unaccusable ones; unimpeachable ones; folks without reproach),

23. **since in fact** (or: inasmuch as) **you folks are continually remaining on** (or: are constantly persisting) **by this trust, with this confidence, in that faith and for the loyalty, being ones having been provided with a foundation so as to continue grounded, even seated so as to be settled ones, and not people being repeatedly moved elsewhere** (shifted; removed; or, as a middle voice: shifting yourselves) **away from the expectation** (or: expectant hope) **pertaining to, belonging to and having its source in the message of ease, goodness and well-being of which you hear** (or: heard): **the [message] being heralded** (announced; publicly proclaimed and preached) **within all creation which is under the sky** (or: heaven) **– of which I, Paul, am myself come to be a herald, an emissary, and an attending servant** (or: a dispenser).

24. **I am at this moment continuing to rejoice within the effects of experiences and the results of my sufferings over your [situation] and on your behalf, and I am progressively filling back up in turn – so as in [His] stead to replace, supply and balance out, within my flesh** (or: = with the means of my natural situation) **– the deficiencies** (or: results from what is lacking; effects from need) **with regard to the pressures** (or: from the squeezings, tribulations and tight spots) **that pertain to the Anointed One** (or: that belong to and affect Christ; or: from the [Messiah]) **over [the situation of] His body, which is the called-out, covenant community** (which exists being the summoned-forth congregation – the ecclesia)

(or: Now I am progressively filled with joy – in union with the feelings coming from passion over you folks – and am habitually filling up again, to bring balance, the effects of what is lacking, resulting from the distresses of Christ – resident within my flesh – concerning His body, which is the invited-out assembly),

25. **of which I am come to be an attending servant** (or: a dispenser), **corresponding to** (or: down from; in the sphere of) **God's household administration** (or: God's directives for the tasks of a household manager; the stewardship whose source is God and pertains to His house; God's economy; God's scheme and arrangement which He planned for His household) **– the [detailed plan] being given by me unto you** (or: to me [and infused] into you) **– to fulfill God's Word** (or: to make full the message pertaining to God; to make a full presentation of God's message; to deliver God's laid-out thought and idea in full; or: with a view to you fulfilling God's idea):

26. **the Secret** (or: sacred mystery) **having been hidden away and remaining concealed away from the ages** (or: from [past] eons), **as well as away from the [past] generations, yet now** (at the present time) **is set in clear light in His set-apart folks** (or: was manifested to His holy ones; is caused to be seen by His saints; is shown for what it is, for His sacred people),

27. **to whom God wills** (or: at one point purposed; or: intends) **to make known by intimate experience, what [are] the riches of the glory of this Secret** (or: the wealth which has its source in this sacred mystery's manifestation which calls forth praise) **within the multitudes** (among the nations; in the Gentiles; IN UNION WITH the swarms of ethnic groups), **which is** (or: exists being) **Christ within you folks, the expectation of and from the glory**

> (or: which is [the] Anointed in union with you people: the [realized] hope of the manifestation which called forth praise; or: which is [the] Anointing [and the Messiah] within the midst of you folks – the expectation which is the glory),

28. **Whom** [other MSS: Which] **we ourselves habitually proclaim down the line** (or: announce in accord with the pattern), **constantly putting [Him] into the minds of every person** (or: human) **and repeatedly teaching every person** (or: human), **within the sphere of all wisdom, to the intent that we may place every person** (or: human) **finished** (mature; perfect with respect to purpose; complete; as having reached the goal of destiny) **by [our] side, within the midst of, centered in, and in union with, Christ** [other MSS add: Jesus],

29. **unto which [goal] I habitually work hard** (or: progressively toil on) **and become weary, constantly struggling as in a contest, corresponding to** (or: down from, yet on the level of) **His inward working** (or: energy and operation)**: the One continuously operating** (energizing and inwardly working) **within me – within power and in union with ability.**

CHAPTER 2

1. **You see, I continue wanting you folks to have seen and thus perceive** (realize; know) **[the] size of and how extensive a contest I am having and how intense a struggle I constantly hold** (or: continue to have) **over [the situation of] you and the folks in Laodicea, and as many as have not seen my face in [the] flesh,**

2. **to the end that their hearts may be called near, alongside, for comfort, relief, aid and encouragement – being joined cohesively** (jointly knitted; welded together; literally: mounted together in copulation) **and united in love and an acceptance with the urge toward union – even into all the riches** (or: wealth) **pertaining to the state of having been brought to fullness** (or: of the full assurance and conviction) **from the comprehension** (or: which is the joint-flow of discernment; of the junction of that which is sent together for a person to be able to catch on and understand) **[leading] into full, accurate, intimate and experiential knowledge and added insight of God's Secret: Christ**

> (or: of the secret of the God, who is Christ; or: of the secret from God, which is [the] Anointing; [with other MSS: of the sacred mystery of the God and Father, in relation to the Christ {or: having its source in [the] Anointing; or: belonging to Christ}]),

3. **within Whom** (or: in which) **are** (continually exist) **all the hidden-away** (or: concealed) **treasures** (or: treasure chests or vaults; storehouses) **of the wisdom and experiential, intimate knowledge and insight.**

4. **Now I am presently saying this so that no one may be derailing you in a persuasive discourse or reasoning, by logic and reasoning that are off to the side and thus cheats by false reckoning,**

5. **for though** (or: even if) **I am presently absent** (or: being away) **in the flesh, nevertheless I continue being together with you folks in the spirit** (or: by the Spirit; in union with the Breath-effect), **constantly rejoicing and seeing** (or: observing) **your arranged succession** (or: drawing up of rank and file for an ordered disposition in battle array; or: post and place in line; also: = a body of soldiers or militia) **– as well as the solid body having a backbone which is the result of strengthening unto firmness – of your trust and faith** (or: pertaining to your faithfulness and loyalty; which have the qualities of confidence and conviction of you folks) **[which is being placed] into Christ** (or: [which flows] into [the] Anointing).

6. **Therefore, as you folks take along and receive** (or: took to your side and accepted) **the Christ – Jesus, the Lord** (the Owner; the Master) **– continue walking about** (i.e., ordering your life) **within Him** (and: in union with Him; centered in Him),

7. **being people having been rooted** (or: having been caused to take root) – **even ones being constantly and progressively built upon The House** (i.e., added to the structure) – **within Him; also being folks repeatedly made steadfast and progressively stabilized with good footing within the faith** (or: confirmed by the conviction; made secure for trust and loyalty), **just as you are taught** (or: were instructed), **continuously superabounding** (being surrounded by more than enough) **within it – within gratitude and thanksgiving** (or: in an expression of the ease and goodness of grace, as well as the well-being of favor).

8. **Keep watching out for and beware that someone will not be the one progressively** (or: repeatedly) **carrying you off captive** (after stripping you of arms and seizing your goods, proceed in kidnapping you as booty or a prey) **through the philosophy and empty seduction** (or: a deceitful trick having no content) **being handed down from and being in line with the tradition of the people** (or: corresponding to the thing handed along from humans), **down from** (or: in line with and corresponding to) **the elementary principles** (or: rudimentary teachings and fundamental assumptions) **of the organized System** (the world of culture, religion, government, secular society or economy), **and not down from Christ** (or: in accord with the sphere of, and in line with, Christ; corresponding to an Anointing),

9. **because within Him all the effect of the fullness of the Deity** (the result of the filling from the Godship and feminine aspect of the Divine Nature) **is repeatedly corporeally** (or: bodily, as a whole; embodied; as a body) **settling down and progressively taking up permanent residence** (or: is continuously dwelling in person), [*cf* 1:19a, above]

10. **and you folks, being ones having been filled up** (or: made full), **are** (or: exist) **continuously within, and in union with, Him, Who is** (or: exists being) [other MSS: the One being] **the Head of** (or: the Source of) **all government and authority** (or: of every beginning and right; of all rule and privilege which comes from being; all Origin, as well as what is from Being),

11. **within Whom you folks were also circumcised** (or: in union with Whom you are cut around and off) **by** (or: in; to; with) **a circumcision not done by hands** (not handmade): **in the sinking out and away from** (or: the stripping off and undressing of; the going out and away from) **the body of the flesh**

> (= the corporate body of the Jewish religion and national heritage; or: = the natural body, or, the body pertaining to the natural realm; or: = the estranged human nature and alienated self) **– in the circumcision of the Christ** (in Christ's circumcision; in the

circumcision which was done to Christ; or: in the circumcision which is the Anointing),

12. **being buried together in Him** (jointly entombed with Him) **– within the placing into** (in the immersion and saturation, and its result; in the plunging for permeation; within the overwhelming; in the dipping into; within the baptism) **– within the midst of Whom you folks were awakened and caused to rise up together through the faithfulness which is** (or: belonging to; coming from) **the inward operation of God** (or: the trust belonging to the effectual energizing from and which is God): **the One awakening and raising Him up, from out of the midst of dead folks.**

13. **And you folks – continuously being dead ones within** [other MSS: by] **the results and effects of falls to the side, and in** (or: by) **the uncircumcision of your flesh** (= physical bodies or national heritage; or: = estranged human nature and alienated self) **– He makes** (or: made) **alive together: you** [other MSS: us] **jointly together with Him, gracing us, granting joyous favor to us [for; in] all the effects of the falls and stumbling to the side** (= false steps),

14. **anointing and wiping out the handwriting in the decrees** (bonds; bills of debt; ordinances; statutes) **put down against** (or: with regard to the effects of the thoughts or suppositions, and the results of the appearances of what seemed [to be], corresponding to) **us, which was continuing to be under, within and set in active opposition to us, and He has picked it up and lifted it from out of the midst, nailing it to the cross** (or: on the execution stake; with the corpse-pole),

15. **after Himself causing the sinking out and away of** (or: stripping off and away [of power and abilities]; undressing [them of arms and glory]; putting off and laying away [of categories and classifications]; or: divesting Himself of) **the governments and the authorities** (or: the ruling folks or people of primacy, and the privileged folks). **And then He made a public exhibit, in a citizen's bold freedom of speaking the truth, leading them in a triumphal procession within it [i.e., the cross/suspension-pole].**

(or: Undressing Himself {or: Stripping [them] off from Himself}, He also made a public display of the rulers and the authorities, with boldness leading them as captives in His victory procession in it {or: in union with Him}.) [*cf* 1 Cor. 2:8]

16. **Therefore, do not let anyone habitually pass judgment on you** (or: make decisions for you) **in [matters of] eating and drinking, nor in a part of a festival, or of a new moon, or of sabbaths** (= concerning [identity markers] or things that are of a religious nature or cultus),

17. **which things** (= cultic markers) **are** (exist being) **a shadow of the things being about to be** (or: in regard to [what had been] the impending existence), **[which is] now, the body of the Christ**

> (or: and now the physical form is from, and belongs to, the [Messiah]; or: Yet the corporeal reality has the qualities of the Anointing; or: Whereas the corresponding embodiment of the idea, its mass and its substance [is] Christ; or: So then the body pertains to the [Messiah]; [note: A.T. Robertson views this construction, "the body," as the object which is casting the shadow; Vincent is similar; *cf TDNT*, VII, p 1039-40]).

18. **[so] let no one be acting as an umpire, or an arbiter in the public games, so as to decide down against you, or to disqualify you, in regard to the prize** (or: to award the prize [to you] unjustly – Eduard Lohse) **– in lowness of understanding, intellect, frame of mind and deportment, continuously wanting [you] also [to be] in ritual-relating to the agents**

> (or: constantly delighting in religious activity originating from the messengers [note: e.g., old covenant rituals]; or: repeatedly taking pleasure by cultic religious service about, or external worship of or through the "angels"), **while continuously stepping randomly and rashly into** (or: entering purposelessly, thoughtlessly or feignedly into; or: = being initiated into) **things which he has** [other MSS: he has not] **seen** [note: this may refer to being initiated into cultic secrets or mysteries], **progressively being made natural and instinctual by the inner senses and perceptions of his flesh**

> (or: habitually being puffed up under [the influence of] the mind of his flesh [= his natural abilities and conditions, or by his alienated self, or by the human nature that has been conformed to the System]),

19. **and thus not continuously** (or: terminating the continuum of) **getting strength from** (or: apprehending and becoming strong by) **the Head** (or: the Source), **from out of Whom all the body** (or: the entire body) **– being constantly fully furnished and supplied to excess with funds and nourishment, and progressively joined cohesively** (welded together; knitted and compacted together; united and made to go together as in mounting for copulation) **through the instrumentality of the joints** (connections; junctures; fastenings) **and links** (things bound together, as by ligaments) **– goes on growing and increasing God's growth**

> (or: the growth of God; the growth having its source in God; the growth pertaining to God; the growth and increase which is God; or: the growth from God).

20. **Since** (or: If) **you folks died together with Christ, away from the world's system of elementary principles** (or: the rudimentary teachings and fundamental assumptions of the organized System [e.g., world of religion, secular society, education or culture]), **why, as living in a world** (in an organized, controlling system), **are you constantly being subjected to** (or, as a middle: submitting to; binding yourself to) **rules** (decrees; commands; or: effects of thoughts or results of imaginations; "dogmas" [of the system])**:**

21. **"You should not** (or: may not) **touch** (handle; light or kindle), **nor yet should you** (or: may you) **taste by sipping** (= partake of or enjoy), **nor yet should you** (or: may you) **come into contact!"**

22. **– which are all things [that are proceeding] into decay and ruin** (thus: corruption) **by consuming and being used up or misused – down from and corresponding to the effects of commands** (or: on the level of the results of purposed directives and imparted instructions), **as well as teachings and trainings, of humans** (whose source is mankind; from people)**?**

23. **– which things, indeed, having a message** (a word; an expression; may = a promise or reputation) **of wisdom in self-imposed observance of ritual or self-willed form of worship, and in humility** (= self-abasement), **even in asceticism** (unsparing) **of [the] body, [yet are] not of any value or worth [and lead] toward a filling up of the flesh to the point of satiation**

(= a gratification of the alienated self; = a satisfying of the estranged human nature; or: = a bringing of religious works to the full; or: [and have] no honor, facing a fullness and plenty which are flesh; or: = are worthless, with a view to having enough in the natural realm)!

CHAPTER 3

1. **Since, therefore, you folks were awakened and are raised up together in the Christ** (or: If, then, you are aroused and raised with the Anointed One), **be constantly seeking and trying to find the upward things** (or: the things being above), **where the Christ is** (exists being), **continuously sitting within the right [side]** (or: at the right [hand]; = at the place of receiving, and in the place of honor and the power) **of God.**
2. **Be constantly minding** (thinking about; setting your disposition and sentiments toward; paying regard to) **the upward things** (or: the things above), **not the things upon the earth,**
3. **for you folks died, and your life has been hidden so that it is now concealed together with the Christ, within the midst of God** (or: in union with God).
4. **Whenever the Christ, our life** [other MSS: your life], **can be brought to light** (or: may or should be manifested), **you folks also will proceed being brought to light** (or: will keep on being manifested), **together with Him, within the midst of glory** (or: in union with a manifestation which calls forth praise; or: in a good reputation; or: = in His manifest presence).

> (or: When Christ, the Anointing, can be manifested, then your life – even you yourself, together with Him – will continue being manifested in His assumed appearance). [1 Jn. 3:2]

5. **Make dead** (Put into a state of deadness; Deaden; = Kill), **therefore, these** [other MSS: your] **members** (body parts; = aspects of your life) **upon the earth** (= that pertain to this earthly existence)**: prostitution** (fornication; sexual immorality), **uncleanness, [unbridled] passion** ([uncontrolled] feeling or [excessive] emotion), **worthless over-desire** (rushing upon bad things; obsessive, evil cravings), **and the desire to have more and gain advantage over another** (or: selfish, greedy, grasping thoughts and behavior) **– which is idolatry** (the worship of forms, shapes, images or figures; or: service to pagan concepts)
6. **– because of which things God's inherent fervor** (natural impulse and propensity; internal swelling and teeming passion of desire; or: anger; wrath) **is repeatedly** (or: continuously; progressively) **coming** [other MSS add: upon the sons of The Disobedience (or: those having the condition of being unpersuaded; or: the stubbornness); note: "the disobedience" could refer to Adam and Eve eating from the tree, and thus, the "sons of the disobedience" could refer to all of mankind] **–**
7. **within** (or: in union with) **which things you folks also at one time** (once; formerly) **walked about** (= lived your lives), **when you were living within these things.**
8. **But now, you folks as well, at once put all these things away from [you, as of clothes put off and laid away]** (or: set off; = renounce or get rid of)**: inherent fervor**

> (or: So at this time you yourselves in one stroke set away and get rid of all the [following]: even natural impulse, propensity, internal swelling and teeming desire; or: Yet now, you
>
> people at once lay aside all intense anger, rage and wrath), **strong passion** (rushing of emotions; outbursts of rage), **worthlessness** (poorness of quality; influence of the bad; hateful intentions), **[and] from out of your mouth: blasphemy** (abusive and injurious talk; slander) **[and] foul-mouthed abuse** (obscenity; ugly words; deformed and shameful language).

9. **Do not keep on** (or: Stop) **lying unto one another! [Be] folks at once stripping off from yourselves** (undressing yourselves from; or: go out and away from) **the old humanity** (the old human; = the old Adam), **together with its practices,**
10. **and then [be] suddenly clothing yourselves with** (or: entering within) **the new one** (the fresh one which existed only recently), **the one being continuously** (or: repeatedly; habitually; progressively) **renewed** (made back up essentially new again -- different in kind and character) **into full, accurate, added, intimate and experiential knowledge and insight which is down from and corresponds to the image** (an exactly formed visible likeness) **of its Creator** (of the One framing and founding it from a state of wildness and disorder),

11. **wherein** (or: in which place) **there is no Greek** [figure of the multitudes who are non-Jews, and of those who are cultured and civilized] **and Jew** [figure of a covenant people of God], **circumcision and uncircumcision** [figure for religious in-groups and out-groups; there is no longer a covenant people versus non-covenant people], **barbarian** [foreigner who speaks a different language], **Scythian** [figure or example of wild, uncivilized groups], **slave, freeman, but to the contrary, Christ [is] all, and within all**
> (or: Christ [is] all humanity, and within all mankind; or: Christ [is] everything or all things, and within everything and all things; [note: the Greek is plural, and is either masculine, signifying "mankind," or neuter, signifying all creation, in these phrases]).

12. **Therefore, as God's chosen, set-apart and beloved ones** (or: God's sacred, loved and chosen people; or: as elect... ones from God), **clothe yourselves with** (or: enter within) **bowels** (internal organs; = the tender parts; seat of deep feelings) **of compassion, kindness** (adaptable usefulness), **humility** (the minding and disposition of things of lowness or of low station), **gentleness** (meekness; mildness), **waiting long before rushing with emotions** (even-temperedness; long-suffering; putting up with people/situations; pushing anger far away),
13. **being folks continuously holding up [things or situations] pertaining to one another** (or: habitually holding yourselves up, belonging to one another; constantly putting up with one another) **and incessantly giving grace to or doing a favor for** (dealing graciously with and among) **yourselves, if ever anyone may continue having** (or: holding) **a complaint toward someone. Just as the Lord** [= Christ or Yahweh; some MSS: Christ; Aleph* & some Vulgate MSS read: God] **also gave** (or: gives) **grace to and favor for you** (deals graciously in, with and among you folks), **thus also you folks [do the same].**
14. **Now upon** (= on top of) **all these things [put on; superimpose] the Love, which continues being** (or: is) **a joining link and uniting band of perfection**
> (a tie which binds together and pertains to the goal of maturity, being the result of fruitfulness; [the] fastening connection of the finished product; [the] bond producing perfection and destiny; a binding conjunction which brings union, which is the goal).

15. **Furthermore, let the peace** (or: joining; [= *shalom*]) **of the Christ** (belonging to and originating in the [Messiah]; the harmony which is the Anointing [other MSS: God]) **continuously umpire** (act as a judge in the games) **within your hearts** (= in union with the core of your being) **– into which [peace] you folks are called** (were called; were invited), **within one body. And progressively come to be thankful people** (or: continue becoming folks expressing gratitude for the goodness, ease and well-being that comes in grace; be habitually graceful folks).
16. **Let Christ's Word** (or: the *Logos*, which is the Christ; the Idea which is the Anointing; or: the message of and from the Christ [other MSS: of God; of {the} Lord]) **be continuously making its home within you folks** (or: progressively indwelling and residing – centered in and in union with you) **richly, within the midst of and in union with all wisdom, habitually teaching [it] and placing [it] in the minds of yourselves by psalms, in hymns, by spiritual songs and odes, within grace and amidst favor constantly singing within your hearts to, for and with God**
> (or: habitually singing in, by and to God [other MSS: to {the} Lord], in union with the grace resident within your hearts {= the core of your being}).

17. **And everything – whatsoever you may be habitually doing, in word or in action** (within a thought or message, or within a work or deed) **– [do] everything** (all; all things) **within and in union with [the] Name of [the] Lord, Jesus** [other MSS: of Jesus Christ; others: of {the} Lord, Jesus Christ], **constantly giving thanks** (expressing gratitude) **to Father God** (or: in union with God, [the] Father) **through Him.**

18. **Wives, be habitually aligned to humbly support** (or, as a middle: place and arrange yourselves in order, under) **[your] husbands** (or: Women, continue subjecting yourselves to the adult males [note: this was culturally appropriate at that time]), **in the same way as there has progressively come again to be a connection in [the] Lord** (or: since there has been an arrival back in union with [our] Master and Owner).

19. **Husbands, habitually love [your] wives** (or: Adult males, be constantly showing loving acceptance to the women), **and do not become repeatedly sharp toward them** (or: stop being rough, bitter or insensitive to them).

20. **Children, continue submissively hearing** (or: paying attention), **being constantly obedient to the parents in regard to all things** (corresponding to every situation), **for this continues being well-pleasing, within the Lord.**

21. **Fathers, do not constantly excite** (or: continuously incite or stimulate; repeatedly irritate, vex or provoke) **your children, so that they would not become habitually without strong passion** (discouraged and timid; without motivation; dispirited, listless, moody or sullen).

22. **Slaves, in regard to all things continue submissively hearing, paying attention and being constantly obedient to those [being] owners** (masters; lords) **on the level and the sphere of flesh** (= human, or "earthly," masters) **– not within eye-slavery** (bondage to eyes; = slavery to doing in order to be seen, or working only when someone is watching), **as desiring to please people** (or: wanting to be pleasing to people so as to win their favor; human-pleasers), **but rather within simplicity** (or: singleness) **of heart** (or: single-hearted sincerity), **constantly being folks reverenced by the fear of** (or, as a middle: being ones habitually engendering reverence because of respectful fear toward) **the Lord** [= Yahweh or Christ; p46 & other MSS: God].

23. **Everything – whatever you folks may be habitually doing – be constantly working** (doing business; practicing a trade; earning a living) **from out of soul** (from the whole being: intellect, emotions, will), **as to** (for; in; with) **the Lord** [= Yahweh or Christ] **and not for people** (to mankind),

24. **having seen, and thus, knowing that you folks will continue receiving back** (regaining what is due) **from the Lord** [Yahweh or Christ] **and taking away the corresponding and specifically matching compensation of, from and which consists in the enjoyment of the allotted inheritance. Be constantly slaving in, for and with Christ, the Owner** (Lord; Master) [or, with other MSS, and as an indicative: For you are constantly performing as a slave in (or: by; with) the Lord, in {the} Anointed One].

25. **Certainly, the person habitually doing wrong** (constantly acting unjustly or inequitably; repeatedly being unfair and walking contrary to the Way pointed out) **will continue receiving in himself what he wrongly does** (or: will progressively take for his own dealing what inequity and unfairness he did) **– and there is no partiality** (favoritism; consideration because of personal appearance or of the face presented; receiving of a facade; taking of personage into account).

CHAPTER 4

1. **Owners** (Masters; Lords), **continuously hold at your side and present the right** (the just; the fair; the equitable) **and the equal** (what is the same as something else) **to and for [your] slaves – [from] having seen, and thus knowing, that you folks also continuously have an Owner** (Master; Lord) **within heaven** (or: [the] atmosphere; [other MSS: {the} heavens {or: atmospheres}]).

2. **Be habitually occupied diligently in prayer** (or: Be constantly stout toward thinking with a view to having well-being; Be continuing persistent and persevering by speaking toward having goodness [in situations]) **within an expression of gratitude** (or: thanksgiving), **continuously watching and remaining awake and alert in it,**

3. **at the same time also progressively praying** (speaking to having ease and goodness) **about us, to the end that God may open a door of the Word for us to speak the secret of the Christ** (or: may open a door pertaining to the message, for us to speak the mystery which has its origin in the Christ – the secret which is the Christ), **because of which** [B G F read: Whom], **also, I have been bound** (or: tied; = imprisoned),

4. **so that I may set it [i.e., the secret] in clear light** (can bring it to light; would manifest it), **as it is continuously binding me** (making it necessary for me) **to speak.**

5. **Be habitually walking about within wisdom** (= living your lives in union with Wisdom): **toward those outside** (or: to outsiders; = those not a part of the called-out community), **being ones constantly buying for yourselves – as from out of the market place – the fitting**

situation (or: redeeming the season within yourselves; purchasing the fertile moment for yourselves; or: = making the best use of the opportunity in the public concourse),
6. **[with] your word** (your conversation; your message) – **at all times within grace** (or: = always favorable) – **being one having been prepared and fitted by salt** (or: seasoned in salt; or: = one being interesting and not insipid), **[and for you] to have seen, and thus be aware, how it continues binding for you folks to be habitually answering each person with discernment** (or: making a decided reply to or separating [issues] away in order to respond with a decision for each individual).

7. **Tychicus, the beloved brother and faithful** (or: loyal; trustworthy) **attending servant – even fellow slave – within [the] Lord** [= Christ or Yahweh], **will proceed personally making known all the things with reference to me,**
8. **whom I send toward you folks unto this very thing, so that you might intimately become acquainted with the things about** (or: concerning) **us** [with other MSS: so that he may come to intimately experience and know the things about and concerning you], **and that he may call your hearts to his side for comfort, relief, aid and encouragement** (or: so he can be a paraclete for you folks).
9. **Together with Onesimus, the faithful and beloved brother – who is from among you folks – they will personally and intimately continue acquainting you with** (making known to you) **all the things here.**
10. **Aristarchus, my fellow captive** (the one taken at spear-point, together with me), **continues embracing and greeting you folks, as does Mark, cousin of Barnabas, concerning whom you received goal-oriented directions [that] if he should ever come to you, receive** (accept and hospitably welcome) **him,**
11. **and Jesus, the one habitually being designated** (or: termed) **Justus – these being the only folks from among** (or: out forth from) **the Circumcision** (= Jews of the Jewish religion) **[who are] fellow workers [laboring] into God's reign and kingdom – which folks came to be a soothing emollient** (a consoling exhortation; a solace) **to me** (for me; in me).
12. **Epaphras – the one from among you folks; a slave of Christ Jesus – continues embracing and greeting you folks, at all times** (or: always) **in constant struggle as in a contest over [the circumstances of] you folks, within prayers** (speaking to having goodness and well-being), **to the end that you can stand** [other MSS: would at once be set and placed] **[as] mature folks** (or: complete people; finished ones; those having reached the purposed goal and destiny; perfect ones) **and people having been brought to fullness** (or: carried to the full measure) **within, and in union with, all God's will, intent, design and purpose.**
13. **You see, I am presently bearing witness for him that he constantly has** (or: continuously holds) **toil-caused pain** (misery; travail; anguish) **over you folks and those within Laodicea, and the people within Hierapolis.**
14. **Luke, the beloved healer** (or: physician) **continues embracing and greeting you folks – also Demas.**
15. **Embrace and greet the brothers within Laodicea, also Nympha and the called-out gathering** (or: community) **that corresponds to her** [other MSS: from their] **house.**
16. **And whenever the letter** (or: epistle) **may be read** (caused to be known again) **beside you** (= in your presence and to you), **you folks make an arrangement to the end that it may also be read within the set-apart community of the Laodiceans; and so that you folks may also read the one from out of Laodicea.**
17. **And say to Archippus,**

> **"Be constantly observing and seeing to the attending service which you received and took to your side, within [the] Lord** [= Christ or Yahweh], **to the end that you may make it full** (or: fulfill it)."

18. **The embrace and greeting [is] by my hand – Paul's. Call to mind** (Remember; Be mindful of) **my bonds** (= chains; = imprisonment).

Grace and favor [are] (or: [The] act producing happiness, which is granted as a favor [is]; – Jim Coram) **with you folks! It is so** (Count on it; Amen).

[written circa A.D. 58 – Based on the critical analysis of John A.T. Robinson]

FIRST THESSALONIANS

1. **Paul, Silvanus** (or: = Silas; D reads: Silbanos), **and Timothy, to the called-out community of the Thessalonians within, and in union with, God our Father, even** (or: and) **[the] Lord Jesus Christ: grace, and peace of the joining** (or: joyous favor and harmony with the absence of conflict; = shalom [peace and prosperity]) **to you** [other MSS add: from God, our Father and Lord, Jesus Christ (or: God our Father, and {the} Owner, Jesus {the} Anointed)].

2. **We are continuously experiencing the well-being of grace in God, and are mindful of the favor of goodness and ease with God, always, which encircles and surrounds all of you** (or: We are constantly always expressing gratitude and feeling thankful to and for God concerning you all), **continuously making mention of you folks upon our thinking and speaking towards having things be well** (or: remembering and being mindful of you people at [times of] our prayers) **in regard to**
3. **your incessantly remembering** (or: being mindful, without leaving-off throughout,) **of our Lord Jesus Christ's act of faithfulness** (the process of the trust; the work from the loyalty), **the wearisome toil of the Love** (the beating and cutting off involved with the acceptance, and with the urge toward union; the burdensome labor from the total giving of the self to [others]) **and persistent patient endurance from expectation, in front of our God and Father**
>   (or: ...upon our prayers, unceasingly mentioning, in the presence of our God and Father, the process of your faith {or: the work which is conviction and trust} and of the love's exhausting toil {or: the hard labor that is love which has unambiguous acceptance}, as well as of steadfast remaining under for support of {or: pertaining to} our Lord Jesus Christ's expectation {or: the expectant hope which is our Lord Jesus, [the] Anointed}).

4. **O Brothers** (= ones sharing members of the community – J.D. Crossan; or: = family), **folks having been loved and still being accepted by God, knowing and perceiving your election** (the choosing or selection and picking-out of you people; or: the speaking-out pertaining to you),
5. **how that the message of the goodness of, and from, our God** (or: our God's good news; the message of ease and well-being, which is God; [other MSS: the good news from us]) **was not birthed into you within word or thought only, but rather also within power and ability, even within a set-apart Breath-effect** (or: in union with [the] Holy Spirit; in the midst of [the] Sacred Breath), **as well as in much assurance having been brought to full measure, according as you have seen and perceived** (or: by extensive absolute-certainty and with much bearing and wearing to the full, just as you know and are aware). **Of such sort we were birthed** (produced; brought to be) **to, for and among you for your sakes** (because of you folks),
6. **and within much pressure** (or: squeezing; oppression) **you yourselves were birthed** (produced, made to be) **imitators of us and of the Lord, receiving** (taking in hand) **the Word** (or: idea; thought; message;) **with [the] joy of [the] set-apart Breath-effect** (or: from [the] Holy Spirit; or: the Sacred Breath's joy; or: accompanied by gracious joy which is a sacred attitude),
7. **so that you folks became a pattern for** (model [other MSS: models] to) **all those constantly trusting, being loyal and progressively believing, within Macedonia and in Achaia.**
8. **You see, from you the Word of the Lord** (or: [Yahweh's or Christ's] message) **has been loudly sounded forth not only in Macedonia and Achaia, but even within every place your faith, faithfulness and trust toward God** (or: the faith and loyalty from you which is face-to-face with God) **has gone forth** (or: out), **so that we have no need to be speaking anything!**
9. **For you see, they themselves are continuously reporting concerning us of what sort an entrance** (or: introduction) **we had toward you, and how you turned about toward God from the idols** (forms; images seen; external appearances; pagan concepts and world views) **to continuously be a slave to, for and with, a living and true** (or: real) **God,**
10. **even to constantly dwell and remain again** (or: abide back; fully lodge; or: stay up) **[with] His Son – [living] from out of the heavens** (or: His Son, whose origin is from the midst of the

atmospheres) – **Whom He raised from out of the midst of dead folks, Jesus, the One constantly rescuing** (or: repeatedly and progressively dragging) **us to Himself from out of the midst of** (other MSS: away from) **the repeatedly** (or: periodically; continuously; progressively) **coming and going inherent fervor** (or: violent emotion; mental disposition of teeming desire; passionate impulse; or: anger; natural bent or agitation; outburst of rage; wrath).

CHAPTER 2

1. **For you yourselves have seen and perceived** (thus: know; are aware), **brothers** (= fellow members of the Body), **that our entrance** (or: way into; introduction) **toward you has not been produced, birthed or come to be empty** (without contents; void; = useless or without results),
2. **but rather, after previously experiencing ill treatment and being outraged** (subjected to insolent, riotous, or insulting behavior) **in Philippi, according as you are aware, we spoke freely and boldly – publicly, as is the right of citizens – within, and in union with, our God, [proceeding at once] to utter God's message of goodness** (or: the good news from God; the message of ease and well-being, which is God) **toward you in the midst of much striving** (conflict; arguing; or: [as] within a large stadium or racecourse, in much agony of struggle).
3. **You see, our calling alongside to assist** (our appeal, admonition and encouragement; our work as paracletes) **[is] not out of wandering** (from being led astray; from deception), **neither out of uncleanness, nor yet within a bait for entrapping or with guile or craftiness,**
4. **but rather, to the degree that, and according as, we have been approved by testing under God to be entrusted [with] the message of goodness, ease and well-being, thus we are continuously speaking: not as constantly pleasing to people, but rather [as] to the God [Who is] repeatedly testing** (or: giving proof of) **our hearts!**
5. **For neither did we at any time become centered in a message** (word) **of flattery, according as you saw and are aware, neither within pretense** (by a false front; with a held-forward specious cloak) **from greed: God [is] a witness!**
6. **Neither [are we] continuously seeking glory** (or: a reputation) **from among people** (human beings) **– neither from you, nor from others – all the while being able [to be] burdensome** (or: as constantly having power in weighty [matters]), **as representatives of Christ** (or: emissaries of [the] Anointed One; sent-off folks from [the Messiah]).
7. **But rather, we were birthed babes** (or: became infants; [other MSS: we were made to become gentle and kind ones]) **within the midst of you folks, as whenever a nursing mother would constantly or repeatedly cuddle to impart warmth to her own children.**

8. **Thus, continuously being your affectionately "attached-ones"** (ones having a like-flow [of nourishment from our Nursing Mother]), **we were habitually delighted** (thinking it good; well-pleased) **to share or impart to you not only God's message of goodness and well-being** [other MSS: the good news which is Christ], **but rather even our own souls** (= inner beings and lives; or: = selves), **because you have been birthed** (or: come to be) **beloved ones to us** (or: folks urged to union by us; or: = very dear to us, accepted by us and appreciated by us).
9. **For you are remembering, brothers** (= fellow believers), **our exhausting labor** (or: = the trouble to which we went; toil; hardship; or: beating) **and hard work, continuously working night and day towards not being burdensome** (or: a weight) **upon any of you, [and] after the manner of a herald we proclaimed God's message of goodness** (the good news from God; or: the message of ease and well-being which is God) **into the midst of** (or: unto) **you folks.**
10. **You and God [are] witnesses of how appropriately and loyally** (or: benignly; in accord with universal law), **justly** (or: fairly; rightwisedly), **and blamelessly we were caused to be to you** (or: for you folks), **the ones continuously trusting and believing with loyal conviction.**
11. **With reference to which you have seen and are aware of how [we treated] each one of you folks, continually calling you alongside to give assistance or relief and to exhort or encourage** (perform as a paraclete), **as well as speaking gentle influence and comfort at your side, as** (just like) **a father [to] his own children,**
12. **even continuously giving evidence** (witnessing; confirming by testimony) **unto you folks to be continuously walking about worthily of the God** (= living your lives in a manner equal in value with regard to the God) **[Who is] continuously calling** (or: repeatedly inviting) **you people**

into His own royal activity (or: reign; sovereign influence; kingdom) **and glory** (or: reputation; manifestation which calls forth praise; or: opinion and imagination; or: = manifest presence).
13. **And so, on account of this, we ourselves also continuously give thanks to God** (or: affirm the goodness of the grace and favor in God) **by an unvarying practice** (or: incessantly; unintermittingly), **because in receiving** (or: taking to [your] side; accepting) **God's Word and message, from a hearing from us at our side, you welcomingly accepted not a word of or from people** (or: a human message), **but rather, according as it really and truly is, a *Logos* of God** (God's Message; an idea from God; patterned information which is God), **Which** (or: Who) **also** (or: even) **is continuously in-working** (being active; operating; energizing) **within and among you folks – in those continuously faithing, trusting and progressively believing with loyalty** (or: with the people continuing faithful).
14. **For you, brothers** (= fellow community members), **were birthed** (or: were made to be) **imitators of God's called-out folks** (or: summoned-forth communities) **– the ones within Christ being** (or: existing) **in Judea – because you also at one point experienced** (or: suffered) **the very same things by** (or: under) **your own fellow-tribesmen, just as they also [did] by** (or: under) **the Judeans** (= the religious leaders of Second Temple Judaism),
15. **even from those killing-off the Lord Jesus, as well as the prophets; even from those driving us out and continuously displeasing God, and from folks contrary to** (or: in opposition against) **all human beings** (or: peoples),
16. **while continuously cutting us off and forbidding us to speak to** (or: preventing us from speaking among) **the nations** (ethnic multitudes; Gentiles) **– to the end that they may, and would, be delivered** (saved; rescued; healed and made whole) **– always [advancing] unto that which fills up their own failures** (errors; deviations; sins)! **But inherent fervor precedes upon them unto a purpose** (or: swelling passion with teeming desire has arrived upon them into a final act and end; or: ire, agitation, anger and wrath overtook them into the midst of a destined goal).

17. **Now we, brothers** (sharers in community), **being deprived** (or: orphaned; bereaved; torn-away) **from you for a fitting situation of an hour** (or: for an hour's season; = for a short spell, during a specific situation) **– by face** (= in presence), **not by or in heart – we more exceedingly made diligent haste to see your face, in much full-desire** (or: added passion)!
18. **On that account we intended** (purposed, willed) **to come toward you – indeed I, Paul, once, even twice – and the adversary** (or: "the accuser;" = the enemy or opposer; *satan*; [note: perhaps a code name for the hostile Jews, as in Rev. 2:9 and 3:9]) **struck within us** (cut in on us; cut obstructions across our path; or: brought hindrance among us).
19. **For who** (or: what) **is our expectation** (or: expectant hope) **or joy, or shall continue being a crown** (victor's wreath; encirclement) **of boasting and glorying in front of our Lord Jesus, in His presence** (or: in the place facing toward our Master, Jesus, within the midst of His being present alongside [us]), **if not even you folks?**
20. **For you see** (or: For it follows that), **you yourselves are our glory** (or: reputation; assumed appearance; manifestation which calls forth praise) **and joy!**

CHAPTER 3

1. **Wherefore** (or: For this reason), **no longer keeping a lid on [our desires]** (or: bearing it no longer), **we thought it a good idea to be left down alone in Athens,**
2. **and then sent Timothy, our brother and God's fellow-worker in Christ's message of ease and goodness, to perhaps set you firmly** (make you stable) **and possibly call you alongside** (to aid, encourage, exhort, console and give relief; to perform as paracletes) **over the [situation] of your trust and faith** (or: conviction; loyalty; faithfulness),
3. **that no one be continuously wagged as a tail** (= shaken or agitated) **within these pressures** (contractions, constrictions; oppressions), **for you yourselves have seen and are aware that we are continually laid into** (or: repeatedly situated and set for) **this!**
4. **You see, even when we were with you we were predicting** (laying it out and telling beforehand) **to you that, "we are about to be continuously pressed** (or: squeezed; afflicted; oppressed)," **just as it also happened** (or: came to be), **and you have seen and know.**

5. **On account of this I also, no longer keeping a lid on [my desires]** (or: when I could bear it no longer), **sent to find out about your faith, trust and loyalty, lest** (or: in case) **somehow the One continuously putting [folks] to the proof** (or: the trier; [note: this could refer to God, or to one of His instruments, as with Job]) **put you to the proof** (tried or tested you), **and our exhausting labor** (or: = the trouble to which we went; toil; hardship; or: beating) **may be birthed into a void** (or: come to be [entered] into an empty place; or: exist in vain; = be to no purpose).
6. **Yet at the present moment, Timothy, upon coming to us from you and announcing the good news** (message of ease and well-being) **to us of your faith and love** (the urge toward reunion; acceptance; self-giving) **[said] that you always continuously hold** (or: have) **a good remembrance of us, continuously having strong desire to see us – even as we also you!**
7. **On account of this, brothers** (= folks who share, as family), **on [the occasions of] all our choking necessity and pressure, by means of the ministry of a paraclete** (or: the Paraclete) **we were comforted and encouraged through your faithfulness, trust and loyalty,**
8. **so that now we can be** (or: are) **living, since** (or: if, as is expected,) **you folks continue standing firm, within the midst of, centered in, and in union with, [the] Lord.**
9. **For now, what gratitude** (or: expression of the goodness of grace and favor) **we continue able to give back to God in return – concerning you folks, upon [the occasion of] all the joy for which** (or: in which) **we are continually rejoicing because of you – before** (or: in front of; in the place facing toward and in the presence of) **our God,**
10. **while night and day, over-excessively repeatedly begging regarding our need to see your face** (= to see you face to face), **and then to freshly adjust to correspondence** (or: thoroughly equip, fit, knit together, mend and bring into agreement) **the things lacking** (the deficiencies) **from your faith, or the shortcomings concerning the faithfulness of your trust!**
11. **But our God and Father Himself, even** (or: that is,; or: as well as; and) **our Lord Jesus, might suddenly, or at some point, make** [note: verb is 3rd person singular; = He might guide] **our road** (path; way) **straight toward** (or: to) **you folks.**
12. **Now the Lord** [= Yahweh or Christ] **might at some point make you increase** (or: be more than enough; be augmented; [note: in quality and/or quantity]), **even to abundantly surround and furnish** (or: and cause super-abundance) **with Love** (or: to self-giving; in love; by love; for acceptance) **unto each other and unto everyone** (or: all humans), **even as we also unto you,**
13. **unto this [end]** (the [goal])**: to establish** (or: to the firmly fixing immovable and setting fast [of]) **your hearts blameless and without defect** (or: to make stable your unblamable hearts) **in set-apartness** (or: holiness; sacredness) **in front of our God and Father, within, and in union with, the presence of our Lord Jesus with all His set-apart folks** (holy peoples). **Count on it!**

CHAPTER 4

1. **The remainder** (What is left; or: Finally), **then, brothers** (people from the same womb), **we are continuously asking and paracleting** (calling you alongside to aid, encourage, exhort and comfort) **you folks in the Lord Jesus, according as you took to your side** (or: received and accepted) **from us how** (or: in what manner) **it is binding [for; upon] you to normally walk about** (= live your lives) **and to be continuously pleasing to God – just as you are even now continuously walking about – to the end that you would progressively superabound to a greater extent** (or: can rather habitually excel and surround [yourselves] by more than enough).
2. **For you have seen and are aware what passed-on announcements** (or: instructions) **we gave to you through** (or: by means of) **the Lord Jesus.**
3. **You see, this is the will** (intent, purpose) **of, and from, God: your state of being set apart from the common use or condition** (or: sacred difference; = covenant living); **you are to continuously hold yourself from** (be distant from; abstain from) **all of the prostitution** [note: figuratively, the worship of idols or false religions, and a break from covenant].
4. **Each one of you [is] to have seen and thus learned how, know and be aware of his own equipment** (gear; utensils; instruments; vessel; = means of making a living), **to progressively acquire** (procure for one's self) **in set-apartness** (or: holiness) **and honor** (value, worth),
5. **not in a feeling of excessive desire** (or: in union with an experience of full-rushing passion), **just as also the nations** (ethnic multitudes; non-Israelites) **[do] who, having not perceived, do not know** (aren't aware of; aren't acquainted with) **God.**

6. **Thus, no one is to be continuously overstepping and have more** (hold advantage) **in his brother's affair** (result of doing; transaction-effect; development from a matter; = cheat his fellow believers in business dealings), **because [the] Lord** [= Yahweh or Christ] **[is] a maintainer of right** (an executor of justice and equity from the Way pointed out) **concerning all these people and things, just as we also told you before and certified with solemn witness throughout.**
7. **For God did not call us on the basis of uncleanness** (or: does not invite us [to be] on [a path lived in] a soiled condition or a dirty environment), **but rather within the sphere of set-apartness** (or: sacred difference; = in a manner commensurate to covenant living).
8. **Consequently, then, the person continuously setting aside** (or: displacing) **is not setting aside** (or: displacing; or: = disregarding) **a human** (or: person), **but God, even the One continuously giving His Sacred Breath into us** (or: repeatedly imparting His Spirit, the Holy One, unto us; constantly gifting the set-apart Breath-effect from, and which is, Him, into us).

9. **But now concerning loving one like a brother** (or: brotherly love; = fondness for fellow sharers of the community), **we have no need to continually write to you, for you yourselves are folks continuously taught by God** (God-taught ones) **to continuously love** (accept; urge toward reunion with; totally give yourselves to) **each other,**
10. **for you are even continuously doing this unto all of those brothers within the whole of Macedonia. But we are constantly paracleting** (calling you alongside to encourage, urge, exhort and comfort) **you, brothers, to progressively superabound to a greater extent** (or: rather to habitually excel and surround [yourselves] by more than enough [brotherly affection]).
11. **and then to habitually be fond of honor and value [and] to be repeatedly quiet** (or: to be progressively ambitious to live in settled peace), **and by habit to be engaged** (or: involved) **in your own affairs** (or: matters), **and then to constantly work with your own hands** (idiom: = work at it actively), **according as we passed on announcements and instructions to you,**
12. **to the intent that you may continuously walk about in good form** (= live your life respectably) **toward those without** (with a view to outsiders; = face to face with those that are not a part of your community), **and then you would continually have need of nothing.**

13. **Now then, we are not wanting** (or: willing, intending) **you to continue ignorant, brothers, concerning the folks who are from time to time falling asleep** [other MSS: those having been put to sleep (= passed away; died), and continuing made to be sleeping], **to the intent that you would not continue being pained, grieved or sad according as even** (or: just like also) **the rest** (those remaining), **the folks normally holding no expectation** (or: not possessing a hope).
14. **For you see, since** (or: if) **we habitually believe that Jesus died and then arose** (or: stood up again), **thus** (in this manner) **also, through Jesus, God will continue** (or: keep on progressively) **leading** (guiding; conducting), **with Him, those being ones caused to sleep.**
15. **For this we continue saying to** (laying out for) **you in a word of the Lord** (or: centered in the Lord's Word; in the midst of a *Logos*-message which is [the] Lord; or: in union with a blueprint from [our] Owner), **that we, the presently living** (or: the ones continuing alive) **– the folks presently continuing left around** (or: behind) **into the midst of the Presence of the Lord** (or: unto the Lord's presence; into the Presence, which is the Lord) **– can by no means advance before** (precede; have advantage over; outstrip) **the folks being ones caused to sleep,**
16. **because the Lord** [= Yahweh or Christ] **Himself will continue habitually descending** (or: repeatedly descend) **from [the] atmosphere** (or: heaven) **within the midst of** (or: in union with) **a shout of command, within the midst of [the] Chief Agent's** (or: in union with an original messenger's or a chief and ruling agent's) **voice, and within the midst of** (or: in union with) **God's trumpet** [note: figure of a message or a directive for action], **and the dead people within Christ** (or: in union with an Anointing) **will continue raising themselves up first** (or: will one-after-another be standing up again in [the or their] first place).   [*cf 2 Cor. 12:2; ** Heb. 12:1]
17. **Thereupon** (or: After that; As a next step) **we, the presently living folks, the ones continuing left around** (or: behind), **will – at the same time, together with them – continue being seized and snatched away* within clouds**** (or: carried off by force, in union with, and among, clouds,) **into the midst of [the] air** (air that we breathe in; mist; haze; [the] atmosphere around us; [note: located in the earth's lower atmosphere, the place where there is air]) **– into the Lord's away-meeting** (an escorting-off, from the Lord; a face-to-face encountering which is the

Lord). **And thus** (in this way and such a manner) **shall we always continue being** (or: continue existing at all times) **together with [the] Lord.** [*cf* 2 Cor. 5:6]
18. **So that** (or: Consequently) **you must constantly call each other alongside to give relief, encouragement and comfort, as a paraclete, within these words** (or: thoughts; reasons).

CHAPTER 5

1. **But concerning these** (or: the) **times and these** (or: the) **fitting situations** (or: specific seasons or occasions; fertile periods; mature moments), **brothers** (folks from the same womb; = sharers in community), **you have no need [for it] to be continually written to, or for, you,**
2. **for you yourselves are accurately aware** (know exactly from having seen) **that a day of, from, and which is, the Lord** [= Yahweh] **thus continually comes** (is habitually and repeatedly coming and going; is presently, progressively coming) **as a thief in a night** (or: within [the] night).
   [comment: the day of Yahweh was a term that figured a time of judging and hard times, in the Old Testament; e.g., *cf* Joel 1:15 and 2:1-2; Jer. 30:7; Amos 5:18; Zeph. 1:14-18]
3. **So whenever they may be repeatedly saying, "Peace** (A Joining) **and security** (or: safety; stability)**," then** (at that time) **sudden and unexpected ruin** (or: a surprise of destruction) **is presently standing upon them, just as the birth-pang for the pregnant woman** (or: to the one having [a child] in the womb), **and they may by no means flee out or make an escape.**
4. **Yet you yourselves, brothers** (= believers), **are not continuously in darkness** (dimness from being in a shadow; obscurity of gloom; absence of daylight) **to the end that the Day may** (or: would) **suddenly take you down** (grasp or seize you in a corresponding manner) **as a thief,**
5. **for you see, you all are** (or: exist being) **sons of** (from; associated with and having the qualities of; or: which are) **Light and sons of** (from; associated with and having qualities of; or: which are [the; this; a]) **Day! We are** (exist) **not of night, nor of darkness** (or: we do not belong to or have the characteristics of night, nor to or of dim obscurity from shadows and gloom).
6. **Consequently, then, we may not continuously fall asleep [into death? in awareness?] even as the rest** (= as other folks), **but rather, we can and should continuously be aroused and stirred up from sleep** [comment: thus, awake to be alertly watchful and vigilant; also a figure for being alive] **and sober** (or: clear-headed).
7. **For it follows that the folks continuously falling asleep** (or: drowsing) **are sleeping at** (or: from [the]) **night, and the ones continuously being made drunk are becoming drunk at** (or: from [the]) **night.**

8. **We, on the other hand, being of Day** (belonging to, having characteristics of, and existing from [the] Day), **can and should continuously be sober** (clear-headed), **putting on** (or: clothing ourselves with; enveloping ourselves in; entering within) **a breastplate of faithfulness and love** (or: a thorax which is faith and trust, along with acceptance urging toward union; from fidelity and a giving of self) **and, as a helmet, an expectation** (or: expectant hope) **from deliverance** (which is health and wholeness; of rescue and being kept safe; pertaining to salvation),
9. **because God did not** (or: does not) **place or set us into anger** (inherent fervor; violent emotion; wrath; or: teeming, passionate desire), **but rather, into an encompassing of deliverance** (or: unto establishing a perimeter of safety; into making health and wholeness encircle [us]; into the forming of an encompassing salvation around [us]) **through our Lord, Jesus Christ –**
10. **the One dying concerning and on behalf of us** (or: = while encompassing our [situation]; [other MSS: over our {condition}]), **to the end that whether we can or would exist being continuously awake** (attentively watching) **or continuously falling asleep** [note: a metaphor for "being alive or being dead"], **we can at the same time be alive** (or: live) **together with Him** (= share His life).
11. **Wherefore, keep on performing as a paraclete by calling each other to [your] side** (to encourage, aid, urge, comfort or exhort), **and by habit let one person build up** (or: edify) **the [other] person** [comment: a one-on-one endeavor], **just as you are even continuously doing.**
12. **Now we are continuously asking you, brothers** (folks of the same womb; = fellow-believers), **to have seen** (or: observed) **and thus to know and perceive those normally toiling wearily among you folks and continuously standing or setting themselves publicly in front**

of you to guard, support, defend, care for or direct you (or: presiding over you) **in [the] Lord, and then keeps on putting the Mind in you** (or: putting you in mind; or: admonishing you),
13. **and thus, to continuously lead them above, from out of an abundance in love** (or: lead the mind through a reasoning process to the conclusion to consider them exceedingly distinguished, centered in an urge toward acceptance and union) **because of their work. Keep on being at peace** (or: Continue joining, to cultivate harmony [= shalom]) **among yourselves.**
14. **But we are continually calling you to [our] side** (to encourage, entreat and admonish), **brothers: continually admonish and warn** (put a mind into; or: put in mind) **the disorderly ones** (the unarranged; those out of line; those not in battle position or deserters); **continually address** (speak alongside persuasively to and cheer up) **the little-souled folks** (those of small consciousness; = faint-hearted); **continually hold yourselves directly opposite** (or: hold against one's self; or: = stand your ground as a shield in front of) **the folks without strength** (the weak ones); **continually be even-tempered and tolerant** (patient; long-passioned unto the goal while keeping anger far away; long before breathing violently) **toward everyone** (or: all people).
15. **Make it a habit to see** (or: observe) **[that] no one may** (or: would) **give back** (render, discharge, repay) **evil in place of evil** (or: something ugly as opposition to something ugly; worthlessness in exchange for worthlessness; what not ought to be in return for what ought not to be; poor quality for poor quality; wrongdoing with wrongdoing; injury in the face of injury) **to anyone, but to the contrary, continue to always pursue** (follow rapidly; run swiftly to acquire; chase after) **the good** (the excellent; the virtuous) **unto [the benefit of] each other as well as unto all people.**
16. **Be continuously rejoicing – always** (or: = Find joy in every [situation]; Always express constant joy)!
17. **Continuously think, speak and act with a view toward having ease, well-being and goodness – unceasingly** (or: By habit be praying unintermittingly).
18. **Within the midst of everything, be continuously giving thanks** (or: In union with all people, be habitually expressing the goodness of grace and the well-being from favor), **for this is God's intent** (will, purpose) **unto you in Christ Jesus** (or: [proceeding] into the midst of you folks, in union with [the] Anointed Jesus).
19. **Do not continually extinguish** (put out; quench) **the Breath-effect** (or: Spirit; spirit).
20. **Do not continually make nothing out of** (set at naught, despise, disdain or scorn) **prophecies** (expressions of light ahead of time),
21. **but be continuously examining and putting all things to the proof** (or: yet habitually test every person) **– [then] constantly hold tightly to the beautiful, the ideal, the fine!**
22. **Habitually hold yourself away** (or: abstain) **from every form** (external appearance; shape; figure) **of what is misery-gushed, useless and unprofitable, or brings wearisome labor, or is mischievous, malicious, harmful or disadvantageous** (or: from evil's every form).

23. **Now may the God of the Peace** (the Joining) **Himself** (or: Yet the very God who is peace and joined-harmony can) **set you folks apart [being] completely whole** (or: wholly perfect; entirely mature; wholly finished and at the goal), **and may your whole allotment** (= every part) **– the spirit, the soul and the body – be blamelessly kept** (unexceptionally guarded and maintained) **within, and in union with, the Presence of our Lord** (Master), **Jesus Christ.**
24. **The One continuously calling you is faithful** (trustworthy; loyal; full of faith and trust), **Who will also perform** (do, make, form, construct, create, produce) **[it; this]!**
25. **Brothers** (= Fellow believers; = Family), **you must also continuously pray concerning us** (think and speak with a view to having goodness, ease and well-being around us).
26. **Draw to yourselves and enfold in your arms all the brothers** (those from the same womb; = fellow believers) **in a set-apart expression of affection** (or: a holy kiss).
27. **I adjure** (lay the duty on) **you folks [in; by] the Lord [that] this letter** (or: epistle) **be read to** (be made known again for; be recognized by) **all the set-apart brothers** (the sanctified [fellow believers]; sacred folks from the same womb; [Gal. 4:26]).
28. **The grace of and from our Lord** (or: the favor which is our Lord), **Jesus Christ, [is] with you folks. Amen** (Count on it; It is so)!

[written circa A.D. 50 – Based on the critical analysis of John A.T. Robinson]

SECOND THESSALONIANS

CHAPTER 1

1. **Paul, Silvanus** (or: Silas), **and Timothy, to the called-out, covenant community of [the] Thessalonians within God our Father, even** (or: and) **[the] Lord** (or: in union with God, our Father and Lord), **Jesus Christ:**

2. **Grace and peace** (or: Favor and harmony from the Joining) **to you from God, our Father and Lord** (or: our Father, and [the] Lord), **Jesus Christ** ([the] Anointed One [= Messiah])!

3. **We continue being indebted to be constantly expressing gratitude to God** (or: We are continually owing [it] to be habitually acknowledging the goodness of grace and the well-being from the favor in and by God) **– always – concerning you, brothers** (= fellow believers; = Family members), **according as** (or: to the same degree as) **it is continually valuable** (pushes the scales down; is worthy), **because your trust** (or: faith, conviction and loyalty) **is constantly flourishing** (growing above; over-growing; exceedingly increasing) **and the love of each one of you all continuously abounds** (exists in abundance) **unto and into the midst of each other,**

4. **so that we ourselves boast in you folks among God's summoned-forth ones** (among those called-out from God; or: in union with the called-out, covenant communities of God) **over your steadfast remaining under to give support** (or: persistent, patient endurance), **as well as faithfulness** (or: loyalty; or: trust and faith), **within all your pursuits** (or: chasings, persecutions and harassments) **and the pressures** (squeezings; constrictions; contractions; tribulations; oppressions; ordeals) **which you habitually have again** (or: sustain; hold up [in]; bear).

5. **[This is] a display-effect** (result of pointing-out; demonstration) **of God's fair and equitable** (just; in accord with the Way pointed out) **deciding** (separating for an evaluation or a judging), **[leading] unto your being deemed fully worthy of God's kingdom** (or: of commensurate value, from God's reign and from the influence which is God), **over** (or: on behalf of) **which you also continue having sensible experiences** (or: normally feel emotions; or: repeatedly suffer),

6. **since in regard to a person who observes the Way pointed out – a rightwised person – [it is right] in the presence of God** (or: if [it is], after all, the right thing with and beside God [= on God's part]), **to repay pressure** (or: squeezing and oppression; ordeal; trouble) **to those continuously pressuring** (squeezing; oppressing; troubling) **you folks,**

7. **and to** (or: for; in) **you – the folks being continuously pressed – relaxation** (ease; a relaxing of a state of constriction; relief), **together with us, within the midst of the uncovering of** (unveiling, laying bare and revelation from; disclosure which is) **the Lord Jesus from [the] atmosphere** (or: sky; heaven), **along with agents of His power** (or: with His agents of ability) **–**

8. **within Fire, of a flame** [with other MSS: in union with a blaze from fire] **continuously giving justice** (or: repeatedly imparting the effects of fair and equitable dealings from out of the Way pointed out, while maintaining equity from what is right) **among** (or: for; in; with; to) **those not knowing** (or: perceiving) **God, even among** (or: for; in; with; to) **those not continuously listening to or paying attention and obeying the message of goodness and well-being, which is our Lord, Jesus** (or: which comes from and pertains to our Master and Owner: Jesus).

9. **These certain folks who will proceed paying the thing that is right** (incur justice, fairness and equity)**: ruin in, and pertaining to, the Age [of Messiah]** (or: an unspecified period of ruin or destruction; or: ruin for an age; eonian destruction having the character of the Age; or: life-long ruin) **[coming] from the Lord's face** [= the Christ's or Yahweh's presence], **even from the glory and assumed appearance of His strength** (or: spreading from the manifestation which calls forth praise regarding, and having the character of, His strength) **–**   [*cf* Rev. 14:10-12]

10. **whenever He may come and go, to be made glorious within** (to be glorified in union with; to have repute centered in) **His set-apart folks** (holy and sacred people) **and to be wondered at** (marveled at; admired) **within all the folks believing, in that day, seeing that our testimony** (or: evidence), **[being placed] on you, was believed** (received with faith) **and is trusted.**

11. **Unto which end we always continuously pray** (think or speak toward having goodness, ease and well-being), **also, concerning you in order that our God would account you worthy of The Calling** (or: of equal value to this invitation) **and would fulfill every delight** (intent from

508

good thought; imagined well-being) **of virtue** (from goodness) **and work of faith in power** (or: may make full every good disposition of excellence and action from trust, in union with ability),
12. **so that the Name of our Lord, Jesus** [other MSS add: Christ], **may be invested with glory** (glorified; made to be a manifestation and a reputation which calls forth praise) **within you folks, and you within Him, according to** (down from; in line with; on the level of) **the grace and favor of our God and Lord, Jesus Christ** (or: from our God, and [the] Owner/Master, Anointed Jesus).

CHAPTER 2

1. **Now we are asking** (or: requesting) **you, brothers, over [the topic of] the** (this) **Presence of our Lord, Jesus Christ** (or: concerning our Master, Jesus Christ, [being] present), **and our being gathered together** (or: being fully led together and assembling) **upon Him:** [Heb. 10:25]
2. **in regard to this, you are not at any point to be quickly shaken** (tossed, as by the sea, or caused to totter, like a reed) **away from The Mind** (or: mental senses of perception; the ability to be aware and reason; wits; intelligence), **nor to be continuously disturbed** (alarmed; startled), **neither through a spirit** (or: a breath-effect; an attitude), **nor through a word** (or: a thought; a patterned message; an idea; a blueprint), **nor through a letter – as [if] by** (through) **us – as though the Day of the LORD** [= Yahweh] **has been set in place** (placed in; made to stand in; has stood within so as to be here). [comment 1: this may have come in AD 70]
   [comment 2: the Day of Yahweh was a term that figured a time of judging and hard times, in the Old Testament; e.g., *cf* Joel 1:15 and 2:1-2; Jer. 30:7; Amos 5:18; Zeph. 1:14-18]
3. **May no one at any point beguile or seduce you folks from a deception – not even down from one turn** (or: not according to one method; not in the sphere of a manner or disposition) – **because should not the standing-away-from** (the departure; the setting away; or: the rebellion; the Revolt) **come first, and thus the human from the lawlessness – the person of the failure**
   [some MSS: the Man who missed the mark – sinned; the human being with the qualities and character of error and mistake; other MSS: the person owned by lawlessness or associated with illegal acts] – **be uncovered** (unveiled; revealed; disclosed): **the son of the loss** (= the person having the qualities of, or the character pertaining to, The Destruction),
4. **the one continuously occupying an opposite position** (or: constantly lying as the opposing counterpart) **and repeatedly lifting** (or: raising) **himself up over all** (or: upon everything) **being normally called God or an effect of worship** (or: reverent awe), **so as to cause him to be seated – down into the midst of the temple of God** (or: God's dwelling place) – **continuously displaying himself, that this/it is God** (or: continuously pointing out that he himself is a god)?
5. **Do you not remember that, still being with you, I kept on saying these things to you?**
6. **And now you know** (have seen and are aware of) **the thing continuously holding down in a firm grasp** (detaining, restraining) **unto the [situation for] him to be uncovered** (unveiled; disclosed) **in his own fitting situation** (or: proper occasion; suitable season; fertile moment).
7. **For the secret** (hidden purpose; mystery) **of the lawlessness** (pertaining to the condition of being without law; which is this unlawfulness; having the character of being violation of the Law; from contrariness to custom; = of Zealotry; = of Sicarii) **is already continuously working within** (operating; energizing), **[yet] only until the one** (or: person; man; [note: masculine article]) **continuously holding down in a firm grasp** (detaining; restraining) **at the present moment can birth himself** (bring himself to be; = separate himself) **forth from out of the midst.**
8. **And then** (at that time) **the lawless person** (this unlawful one; the one without law; the man who violates the Law and is contrary to custom; = the Zealot) **will be uncovered** (unveiled; disclosed), **whom the Lord Jesus will take back up again** (= take away [reading αναιρεω with Nestle, Tasker & Concordant texts; Griesbach & other MSS read αναλισκω: consume, use up, expend]) **by the Spirit of** (or: the Breath-effect from) **His mouth, and will deactivate** (render inoperative and useless; make inert) **by the manifestation** (the bringing of light upon and setting in full and clear view, causing an appearance) **of his** (or: its; or: His) **presence –**
9. **whose presence is continuously existing in correspondence to** (or: in line with; in the sphere of; on the level of) **the adversary's** (opponent's; or: *satan's*) **in-working activity** (or: is constantly in accordance with the operation of the "adversary," or, *satan*), **in all power** (or: within, and in union with, all ability) **as well as signs and wonders of falsehood** (or: which are a lie),

10. **and within every deception** (delusion; seduction) **of the injustice** (wrong; thing that is not the way pointed out and which is not right) **within the folks continuously or repeatedly being lost** (or: by the folks progressively destroying themselves) **in return for which** (or: in the place of which) **they do** (or: did) **not take unto themselves and welcomely receive the love of, and from, the truth** (or: Truth's accepting Love; the Love which is Truth and Reality; or: the urge to union which is Reality), **into the [situation for] them at some point to be suddenly delivered** (restored to health and wholeness; rescued; saved; restored to the original state and condition).

11. **And so, because of this, God is continuously sending to** (or: in; with) **them an in-working** (or: operation) **of wandering** (or: from straying; which has the character of error and deception) **into the [situation for] them to believe, and to trust, the lie,**

12. **to the end that all those not being faithful to the Truth** (or: believing and trusting the reality), **but rather approving and delighting in injustice** (inequity; the thing that is not right), **may** (or: can; would) **at some point be sifted, separated and decided about** (or: judged).

13. **However we, ourselves, are presently indebted** (or: continuously owing) **to be constantly expressing gratitude to God** (or: speaking of the goodness of grace and the well-being of the favor in God) **always, concerning you: brothers** (= fellow believers) **having been loved and continuing to be unambiguously accepted by the Lord** [= Yahweh or Christ], **because God chose you for Himself, from a beginning** (or: Source), **unto deliverance,** [other MSS: God selected and took you in preference {to be} a firstfruit into a restoration to the original state and condition (or: into the midst of health and wholeness; {leading you} unto rescue and salvation)], **in a setting-apart of spirit and faith which has the character of truth** (or: in making sacred from Breath-effect and trust from reality; or: in union with Spirit's differencing and Truth's faithfulness),

14. **on into which, through our message of goodness, ease and well-being, He also called you folks** [other MSS: us] **into an encompassing** (or: forming an encirclement; establishing a perimeter; creating a surrounding, and thus a procuring) **of the glory** (or: which is the glory; from the manifestation which calls forth praise) **of our Lord, Jesus Christ** (or: [the] Anointed).

15. **Consequently, then, brothers** (= fellow believers; = family), **you continuously stand firm and stationary** (or, as an imperative: progressively make a stand; habitually stand firm) **and you continuously have** (or, imperative: progressively get) **in your strength – with a masterful grip – the things handed alongside** (transmissions; traditions) **which you were taught, whether through a word** (or: [the] *Logos*; a thought or an idea; a message) **or through our letter.**

16. **Now may our Lord, Jesus Christ Himself, even** (or: and) **our God and Father, the One loving** (accepting) **us and giving a calling alongside pertaining to the Age** (or: a performance as a Paraclete with age-lasting aid; eonian relief, encouragement, consolation and admonition) **as well as a good expectation** (or: a virtuous and excellent hope) **in grace** (or: in union with favor),

17. **at once Paraclete** (call alongside and comfort) **your hearts, and may He establish** (make to stand fast; make stable and firm) **[you] in every good** (or: excellent; virtuous) **work and word** (or: thought; idea; message) [with other MSS: in all *Logos* and in (or: by; with) virtuous action].

CHAPTER 3

1. **The remainder** (or: What is left; Finally), **brothers** (= family), **keep on praying concerning us** (surrounding us with words and thoughts having goodness and well-being), **to the end that the Word of the Lord** (or: the Lord's *Logos* and message) **would continuously run** (move quickly) **and may constantly be made glorious** (or: be characterized by a manifestation which calls forth praise; be of good reputation), **according as [it is and does] also with, and to, you,**

2. **and that we may be rescued** (dragged out) **away from the out-of-place** (or: improper; absurd; abnormal; off-base; weird; outrageous; perverse) **and misery-gushing people** (or: unprofitable, useless, unsound or evil folks), **for you see, not everyone [is] disposed to the faith**

> (or: this trust and loyalty is not associated with all people; not [yet is] the faith a source for all folks; not from all people [do we find] the faithfulness; conviction [is presently] not a possession of all people; this trust [does] not [now] pertain to everyone).

3. **But the Lord** [= Yahweh or Christ] **is** (or: exists) **continuously faithful** (loyal; full of faith), **who will progressively establish** (set you to stand fast and stable) **and keep** (guard; protect;

maintain) **you folks away from the malicious person** (or: the unsound and unprofitable; the painful labor; the malignant situation).

4. **Yet we have been persuaded and so place confidence on you folks, centered in and in union with [the] Lord** [= Christ or Yahweh], **that the things which we are repeatedly passing along as an announcement to you people, you folks both habitually do and will continue doing** (or: normally produce and will keep on producing).

5. **So may the Lord** [= Christ or Yahweh] **make fully straight, then direct and guide, your hearts into the midst of God's love and urge toward union** (the unambiguous, accepting Love which is God) **and into the relentless patient endurance which is Christ** (or: the persistent remaining under to support, which comes from the Anointed One and the Anointing)!

6. **Now we continue passing along an announcement** (or: advice) **to, and for, you, brothers** (= community members), **in the Name of our Lord, Jesus Christ, to continuously place or arrange yourselves away from** (or: avoid) **every brother** (= one who shares in the community -- Crossan) **[who is] continuously walking about disorderly** (behaving with irregular conduct; or: = in idleness), **and not according to the transmission** (transfer; thing given over and delivered alongside; tradition; commitment) **which you folks** [other MSS: they] **received** (took to your side) **from us.**

7. **For you yourselves have seen, and thus are aware of, how it continues binding and necessary to continuously imitate us, because we were not disorderly** (= idle) **among you,**

8. **neither did we eat bread as a gift from anyone, but rather [we were] in wearisome toil** (also: beating; cutting off) **and difficult travail** (or: hard labor) **continuously working night and day so as not, at any point, to be a burden upon** (put extra weight on) **any of you.**

9. **[It was] not because we continue having no right** (or: holding no authority from being), **but rather to the end that we may give ourselves to you folks [as] a pattern** (or: offer ourselves as a model and example for you) **unto the [purpose for you] to be continuously imitating us!**

10. **You see, even when we were face to face with you, we were repeatedly passing on this advice to you, that if a certain person is not continuously willing** (or: does not normally want, purpose or intend) **to habitually work, let him neither be habitually eating.** [cf Didache 12:3-4]

11. **For we continually hear [that] some among you are constantly walking about disorderly** (out of rank or not taking part in the maneuver; = living idle or with irregular conduct), **continuously working [at] nothing, but further, are constantly working in the periphery** (or: circumventing work; = living in idleness; or: = being "busybodies" and meddling).

12. **But to such people we continue passing along this announcement and paracleting** (calling alongside to encourage, admonish, and entreat [them]) **through** [other MSS: within; in union with] **our Lord, Jesus Christ, to the end that, habitually working with quietness** (or: silence), **they may continuously eat their own bread** (= food which came from their own work).

13. **Yet you yourselves, brothers** (= fellow members of the body), **while continually doing well** (performing beautifully; creating the ideal; doing finely), **you should not at any point be in a bad disposition** (or: be or do from out of what is ugly, worthless or of poor quality).

14. **But if a certain person continuously does not obey** (or: listen under and humbly pay attention to) **our word** (or: message; logos; blueprint; thought and idea) **through this letter, you folks be regularly noting this person** (or: let it be a sign to you regarding this one) **and do not constantly mix yourselves together with him or her, to the end that he or she can** (or: would) **be turned about** (or: be turned back upon himself; or: = to consider his situation and behavior).

15. **And yet you must not consider [him or her] as an enemy, but rather you must continuously admonish** (or: put [him/her] in mind), **as** (or: as being) **a brother [to him or her].**

16. **Now may the Lord of the peace** (or: the Lord Who is peace and harmony-from-joining; or: [= shalom]), **Himself, at once give the peace and joining to you folks through everything** (or: through all humanity; through all [time] and every [situation]), **within every turn** (or: in every way; [other MSS read: within every place]). **The Lord** [Christ or Yahweh] **[is] with all of you.**

17. **The greeting** (salutation) **is by my hand – Paul's – which is a sign in every letter; thus, in this way, I normally** (or: from time to time) **write.**

18. **The grace of and joyous favor from our Lord, Jesus Christ, [is] with all of you! Amen.**

[written circa A.D. 50-51 – Based on the critical analysis of John A.T. Robinson]

FIRST TIMOTHY

1. **Paul, one sent away with a commission pertaining to [the] Anointed Jesus** (or: Jesus Christ's representative and envoy), **down from** (or: in line and accord with) **an imposed arrangement from** (an injunction of; a decree and charge set upon [me] pertaining to) **God our Savior, even** (or: and) **from Christ Jesus, our Expectation** (or: concerning and belonging to the expectant Hope, which belongs to us),

2. **to Timothy, a genuine child** (a legitimate born-one) **within the midst of faith** (or: in union with trust; centered in faithfulness)**: Grace and favor, mercy and compassion [together with] peace, which is the harmony from the joining** [= shalom], **from God, our Father, even** (and; as well as) **Christ Jesus, our Lord** (Owner; Master).

3. **Just as I called you alongside – while traveling into Macedonia – to encourage you to remain focused in Ephesus, to the end that you should pass on an announcement** (could notify; would bring along a message) **to certain folks** (or: for some) **not to continue teaching different things,**

4. **nor yet to constantly hold toward** (or: heed or devote [themselves to]) **myths** (or: stories; fictions) **and unbounded** (= endless) **genealogies, which things habitually hold investigations and inquiries alongside which involve speculations and disputes, rather than God's house-administration** (management with detailed plans; stewardship) **– the one within trust, in union with faith and centered in loyalty.**

5. **Yet the purpose and goal of the notification** (the message and announcement which is brought alongside and passed on) **continues being love**

    > (the whole being's drive and movement toward reunion with another, to overcome existential separation; acceptance of the object of love without restriction, in spite of the estranged, profanized and demonized state of the object – Paul Tillich; the total giving of oneself to something or someone – Richard Rohr)

    forth from out of the midst of a clean heart and a good conscience (virtuous knowing-together; profitable impression of reality) **and of unhypocritical faith** (or: unfeigned trust; or: loyalty that is not overly critical; or: belief that lacks the qualities of being overly concerned with small details or hyper-evaluations),

6. **of which things some** (or: certain folks), **being without a mark or target** (or: deviating and swerving from the goal), **were turned aside from out of [them] into vain** (fruitless; profitless) **talking and idle disputation,**

7. **wanting to be teachers of Law and custom, [yet] by habit not mentally apprehending either what things they are saying or about what things they are constantly insisting** (thoroughly asserting and maintaining).

8. **Now we have seen and thus know that the Law** [= Torah] **is beautiful** (ideal and of good quality; useful; fine), **if ever anyone could be continuously making use in it** (employing and behaving with it, by it and to it) **lawfully** (or: legally and in accord with custom),

9. **having seen and knowing this, that a law is not continually being laid down for one in accord with the Way pointed out** (a just one; one who lives in right relationships with fair and equitable dealings; = one in new covenant standing, i.e., in Christ), **but for lawless people and for insubordinate** (non-self-subjecting; out of rank) **folks; for irreverent ones** (folks devoid of awe) **and for failures** (folks shooting off-line and missing the target; people making mistakes); **for those without regard for divine or natural laws** (impious, maligning, disloyal ones lacking loving-kindness) **and for profane folks** (people without connection to the set-apart and holy, who live in what is accessible to all); **for those who strike** (or: thrash) **fathers and for people who strike** (or: thrash) **mothers; for those murdering men;**

512

10. **for men who use prostitutes** (or: who are male prostitutes; fornicators; or: = those who "worship" in pagan temples); **for men lying in beds** (= lazy folks? [note: meaning uncertain: male sex-traffickers? *cf* LXX: Lev. 18:22; 20:13, often associated here; = those off-target?]); **for kidnappers** (those catching men by the foot; = slave dealers); **for liars; for ones who violate their oaths** (perjurers); **and whatever different thing which is continually occupying an opposite position** (lying in opposition or in replacement) **to the sound and healthful teaching,**
11. **[which is] in accord with** (or: down from; in line with and on the level of) **the good news of** (or: the message of goodness and ease pertaining to) **the glory and reputation of The Happy God, which I, myself, was persuaded to believe** (or: upon Whom I am made to trust).

12. **I continue holding** (or: having) **grace and joyous favor by and in the One enabling me** (putting ability within me; empowering me): **Christ Jesus, our Lord, because He considers me full of faith** (or: deems me loyal and faithful), **Himself placing [me] into a position of giving attending service,**
13. **– one being formerly a blasphemer** (a vilifier and slanderer; one using abusive speech and hindering the Light while bringing injury) **and a persecutor and a violent, insolent aggressor** (an overbearing, insolent, riotous and outrageous person), **but to the contrary, I was mercied** (or: given mercy), **because, being continuously ignorant** (without intimate, experiential knowledge or personal insight), **I acted** (or: did it) **within unbelief** (or: in distrust).
14. **Yet our Lord's grace and joyous favor overwhelms** (is above more than enough; is overabounding) **with faith, trust and loyalty, as well as love** (an urge moving toward reunion, with acceptance), **which are resident within** (or: centered in, and in union with) **Christ Jesus.**

15. **The Word [is] full of faith, and [is] deserving of every welcome reception of equal value, because** (or: Faithful and trustworthy, even worthy of all and complete acceptance, [is] the message and saying that) **Christ Jesus came into the ordered System** (or: the aggregate of humanity; the world of culture, religion, government and economy; or: the cosmos) **to rescue failures** (to deliver those missing the target; to save and make sinners healthy and whole; to restore outcasts to their rightful position), **of whom I myself exist being first** (or: am foremost).
16. **But nonetheless, through this I was mercied** (or: I am given mercy), **to the end that within me first** (= as the foremost case) **Jesus Christ may point out so as to publicly display every emotion which is long in arriving** (all long-suffering patience that pushes anger far away) **with a view to being an underline** (toward [being] a subtype; as facing a sketch or outline; for a pattern) **of those about to be habitually believing** (or: progressively trusting; one-after-another remaining faithful while placing faith) **upon Him, [that is,] into the midst of eonian life** (into Life which pertains to and has the qualities and characteristics of the Age [of Messiah]; into life of, and which lasts through, the ages).

17. **So, to [the] King of The Ages** (or: eons; indefinite time periods), **to [the] incorruptible** (undecayable; unspoilable), **invisible** (unseen; not-able-to be seen) **One, to [the] only God** [some MSS add: wise; so: only wise God], **[be] honor** (value; worth) **and glory** (reputation which calls forth praise), **on into the ages** (or: indefinite time periods) **of the ages. It is so** (Amen)!
     (or: Now in and by the King to Whom belongs the ages – in and by the imperishable, invisible [and] only One – in and by God [is] honor and glory, [leading] into the [most important] eons of the eons. So it is!)

18. **I am presently placing this passed-on message** (notification; announcement) **to your side, child Timothy, down from the preceding prophecies upon you** (or: in accord with the prophecies habitually leading forth upon you), **to the end that you may constantly perform military service** (or: do battle; perform warfare) **within them** (or: in union with them) – **the beautiful** (fine; ideal) **military service** (or: battle; warfare),
19. **while constantly holding** (or: having) **faith** (and: trust) **and a good conscience** (a profitable knowing-together) – **which some** (or: certain ones), **in thrusting away** (or: by pushing and driving away), **experienced shipwreck about the faith** (or: concerning [their] trust, confidence and loyalty):

20. **of whom are Hymenaeus and Alexander, whom I gave over** (or: commit; commend; transfer; handed along; deliver) **to the adversary** (or: entrust and render as a yield to be matured in and with the opponent; or: pass along to and deliver by this satan) **to the end that they would be child-trained, educated and disciplined with a view toward maturity, [so as] not to constantly blaspheme** (speak abusively; slanderously vilify, malign or defame; give a false image or misrepresent in a way that hinders the Light).

CHAPTER 2

1. **Consequently I am habitually calling you alongside to encourage, counsel and exhort you to first of all be constantly making petitions for needs, prayers** (speaking, thinking and doing toward things being well), **encounters** (or: intercessions; meetings within situations to converse or hit and obtain the objective), **[and] expressions of gratitude** (or: of the goodness of grace and favor) **over** (or: on behalf of; for) **all humans** (people; mankind) –
2. **over** (or: for) **kings and all those being folks within a position of holding control over** (or: above) **[others]** (or: being in superiority or high station), **to the end that we may continuously lead** (or: carry through) **a course of life that is still – at rest** (free from all agitation or disturbance with tranquility arising from without), **and also quiet – peaceable** (gentle, exciting no disturbance in others, with tranquility arising from within), **in all reverence** (pious and devout relations with everything) **and majestic seriousness** (dignity and gravity which inspire awe).

3. **This [is] beautiful** (fine; ideal) **and welcomingly received from the presence of, and in the sight of, God, our Deliverer** (our Savior; the One Who heals us and makes us whole, restoring us to our original state and condition, and keeps us safe),
4. **Who is constantly willing** (continuously intending and purposing) **all humans** (all humanity; all mankind) **to be saved** (delivered; rescued; made healthy and whole), **and** (or: even) **to come into a full, accurate, experiential and intimate knowledge and insight of Truth** (or: that is, to go or come into a complete realization of reality),
5. **for God [is] One, and One [is the] Mediator of God and humans** (= mankind), **a Man** (a Human), **Christ Jesus** (or: for [there is] one God, and one medium between God and humans, [the] human, Anointed Jesus [= Messiah Jesus]),
6. **the One giving Himself a correspondent ransom** (a ransom in the place of and directed toward the situation) **over [the situation of and] on behalf of** (or: for) **all** (everyone; all humanity and all things) **– the witness** [note: "the witness" is omitted by A; other MSS: the evidence of which] **[will come] in its own fitting situations** (or: the Witness for their own seasons; the Testimony to and for His own particular occasions; the evidence [appears] in its own fertile moments) –
7. **into the midst of which I, a preacher** (or: herald) **and one sent with a mission** (an envoy and representative), **was placed** (or: am set) **– I am speaking truth, I am not lying – a teacher of multitudes** (nations; the multiplied ethnic groups; non-Jews), **within faith and Truth** (or: in union with trust and reality; centered in faithfulness and a manifested appearance of essence).

8. **I am wanting and intending, then, the men** (adult males) **within every place to habitually pray** (constantly think, speak and act toward having ease, goodness and well-being), **continually lifting up loyal and dutiful hands that are pure from all crime, apart from impulse of intrinsic fervor** (or: passion and swelling desire; or: anger, indignation or wrath) **and reasonings** (debates; divisions in thinking; dialogues; computations).
9. **Likewise, women to habitually adorn and arrange themselves in an ordered and arranged system of proper behavior and descent clothing: with modesty, so as to be unseen** (or: as having downcast eyes), **and soundness of mind** (sanity and sensibility), **not in braids** (or: inter-weavings) **and in golden ornaments, or in pearls or expensive garments,**
10. **but rather – what is suitable** (proper; fitting; becoming) **in** (or: for; to) **women giving instruction on reverence for God** [note: refers to women who taught "God-fearers" in synagogues, to prepare these folks for conversion] **– through good works and virtuous actions.**

11. **A woman** (or: wife) **must be habitually learning through instruction and discovery –
within calm quietness** (without making a fuss; in peaceableness and gentleness, exciting no
disturbance in others, and with tranquility arising from within) **– in union with every humble
alignment while giving support** (or: centered within every subordinate arrangement).
12. **Now I am not turning upon a woman, so as to direct her to be habitually teaching** (or:
Yet I do not habitually turn on a wife, to regularly teach [her]) **– neither to continually act in self-
authority to use arms for murdering an adult male**

> (or: = habitually to be a self-appointed master to domineer over a man [note: this may
> have been an exhortation against Gnosticism, and a possible rendering could be: And I
> am not permitting a woman to teach that she is the originator of a man]) **– but rather to
> exist** (or: be) **within quietness** (centered in gentleness, exciting no disturbance, with tranquility
arising from within) –

13. **for you see, Adam was molded and formed first, thereafter** (or: next), **Eve.**
14. **Also, Adam was not seduced and deceived, but the woman being completely cheated
out by seduction** (or: thoroughly deluded) **has come to be and exists within deviation**
(transgression; a stepping by the side),
15. **yet she will be delivered** (rescued; saved; made whole and restored to her original state
and condition) **through the Birth** (or: birthing) **of the Child – should they dwell** (abide) **within
trust** (or: faith; faithfulness and loyalty) **and love** (acceptance) **and the results of being set-
apart** (holiness; the quality of sacred difference), **with soundness of mind** (sanity; sensibility).
The Word (*Logos*) **[is] full of faith!** (or: Trustworthy [is] this idea and message.)

CHAPTER 3

1. **If anyone is habitually stretching himself in reaching out toward a distant object upon
which the eye is fixed, he is by habit craving a beautiful deed**

> (or: If anyone continues reaching after visitation for inspection and tender guardianship,
> he fully desires a fine action; If anyone stretches out in reaching for the duties of looking
> around upon things {duties of one who watches upon, or oversees}, he completely
> desires ideal work).

2. **It is therefore binding upon** (necessary for) **the person fixing his eye upon a distant
object** (or: the one doing visitation for inspection and tender guardianship; the one watching upon
or overseeing) **to be someone not to be laid hold of** (thus: one in whom is no just cause for
blame), **a husband of one wife** (or: an adult male in relationship to one woman), **sober**
(unintoxicated; clear-headed; moderate in habits), **sound in mind** (sensible), **have his world
ordered and arranged** (or: systematic, proper, descent and decorous), **be fond of strangers**
(or: hospitable), **skillful and qualified to teach,**
3. **not addicted to wine** (or: not one who keeps wine at his side), **not quarrelsome and apt to
strike another, but rather, yielding** (lenient; gently equitable; reasonable; considerate), **not
disposed to fight nor belligerent, not fond of silver** (= money),
4. **habitually putting himself at the head of** (= lead, provide for and protect) **his own
household so as to beautifully** (ideally; finely) **stand before and lead them, having children
in the midst of, and centered in, humble alignment for support** (or: within subjection) **with all
majestic seriousness** (dignity and gravity which inspire awe) –
5. **now if anyone does not know** (has not seen and is not aware) **to put himself or herself at
the head of** (= lead, provide for and protect) **her or his own household so as to stand before
and lead them, how will she or he be thoughtful of, take an interest in, and take care of,
God's called-out community?** –
6. **not a novice** (neophyte; a newly placed member of the body), **lest, being inflated with the
fumes of conceit, she or he may fall into an effect of the adversary's judgment**

> (the result of sifting, separation and decision made in regard to someone who thrusts or
> throws something through another; or: a judgment-effect from the adversary).

7. **Yet it is also necessary and binding to continuously hold** (or: have) **a beautiful witness
and testimony** (= a fine reputation) **from those outside, so that s/he would not fall into
reproach** (lest s/he may fall into a censorious report regarding character) **and [into] a trick**
(snare; gin; device; stratagem) **belonging to or devised by the adversary** (or: whose source is

the one who, or [that spirit and attitude] which, thrusts things through folks and causes injury or division; or: which is the adversary).

8. **Attending servants and dispensers [of goods], similarly, [should be] serious** (dignified with gravity) – **not double-talking** (or: speaking with double meanings; or: divided in thought or reason), **neither [being] folks having a propensity toward much wine, nor people eager for dishonorable** (deformed or ugly; = dishonest) **gain –**
9. **continuously holding** (or: having) **the secret** (or: mystery) **of the faith** (or: faithfulness; trust; loyalty) **within** (or: in union with; centered in) **a clean conscience.**

10. **And so, let these folks also be first put through a process of examination, testing and proving. Thereafter, let them be regularly giving supporting service and dispensing [to the community], being folks that have not been called up before a judge** (or: free from accusation; unimpeachable).

11. **Women** (or: Wives) **[of the community], similarly, [should be] serious** (dignified with majestic gravity, inspiring awe), **not devils** (or: adversaries; women who thrust things through folks), **sober** (unintoxicated; clear-headed; moderate in habits), **full of faith and trust** (or: faithful; trustworthy; loyal) **in all things.**

12. **Let those giving supporting service and dispensing [goods] be adult males having a relationship with one woman** (or: husbands of one wife), **habitually placing themselves in front of their children, as well as their own households, to beautifully** (or: finely; ideally) **lead, protect and provide [for them].**
13. **You see, those giving supporting service and dispensing [goods] in a fine, beautiful, excellent and ideal manner continue in** (or: by; for; among) **themselves building around themselves a beautiful** (fine; excellent; ideal) **circular staircase** (that which enables folks to step up to a higher place) **and much freedom of speech** (confident outspokenness and boldness which is the right of citizens) **resident within faith, trust and loyalty – that which is resident within, and in union with, Christ Jesus.**

14. **I am writing these things to you, expecting to come toward you swiftly** (in quickness; or: = soon),
15. **but if ever I should be slow** (or: delay), **[I am writing this] to the end that you may see and thus know how it is necessary and binding to be twisted and turned back up again within God's household** (or: to be treated, conducted or caused to behave in God's house), **which is** (or: exists being) **a called-out community of [the] Living God** (or: whose source is a living God; which has the qualities and character of [the] living God; or: which is a living god), **a pillar and foundational seat of The Truth** (or: a base from and an effect of a settling of reality),
16. **and so confessedly** (admittedly; with common consent and sameness of speech) **great is the secret** (or: mystery) **of the reverence** (the standing in awe of goodness, with adoration; the healthful devotion and virtuous conduct of ease, in true relation to God)**:**
> **which is made visible** (manifested) **within flesh** (= a physical body),
> **is rightwised** (set in equity and right relationship in the Way pointed out; eschatologically delivered and placed in covenant) **in spirit** (in union with Breath-effect),
> **is seen by agents** (or: messengers),
> **is heralded** (preached) **within multitudes** (among nations and ethnic groups),
> **is trusted and believed within [the] world** (an ordered system; secular culture),
> **is received back in good opinion and reputation.**
> (or:
> Who [some MSS read: God; others: He] was brought to clear light within flesh (= the natural realm); was shown righteous and just (= set in covenant) within spirit and attitude; was seen by agents; was proclaimed among Gentiles {non-Jews};
> was believed within [the] world of society, religion, and government;
> was taken back up again, within glory – a manifestation which calls forth praise!)

CHAPTER 4

1. **Now the Spirit** (or: Breath-effect) **is explicitly saying that within subsequent seasons** (in fitting situations and on appropriate occasions which will be afterwards) **some of the faith** (or: certain folks belonging to this trust) **will proceed standing off and away [from the Path, or from the Community]** (or: some people will progressively withdraw from this conviction and loyalty), **habitually holding toward** (having a propensity to) **wandering and deceptive spirits** (or: straying and seducing breath-effects and attitudes) **and to teachings of demons**
> (to teachings about and pertaining to, or which are, demons [note: a Hellenistic concept and term: = animistic influences]; or: to instructions and training which come from animistic influences [= pagan religions]),
> [comment: this prophesied about the future institutionalization of the called-out community, and the introduction of pagan teachings, all of which later came to be called "orthodox"]

2. **within perverse scholarship of false words**
> (or: in association with overly critical hairsplitting of false messages; in the midst of gradually separated interpretations of false expressions; or: in union with deceptive decisions by speakers of lies), **from folks having their own consciences cauterized**
(seared; branded) **as with a hot iron,**

3. **coming from people habitually forbidding** (preventing; hindering) **[folks] to be marrying [and to be] constantly abstaining from [certain] foods – which things God creates** (or: created; reduced from a state of wildness and disorder) **into something to be shared and partaken of with thanksgiving by those full of faith** (by the faithful and loyal folks) **and by those having experienced full, intimate knowledge and realization of the Truth** (or: of Reality)!

4. **Because all God's creation** (or: every creature of God) **[is] beautiful** (fine; ideal), **and not one thing is to be thrown away – being habitually received with thanksgiving –**

5. **for it is continuously** (or: progressively) **being set-apart** (made holy; rendered sacred) **through God's Word** (or: by means of a word which is God; through a message and an idea from God) **and an encounter** (or: a meeting and falling in with someone; or: conversation; or: hitting on target within a matter to assist; thus: intercession).

6. **Placing these things under as a base or foundation, to give advice or make suggestions to and for the brothers** (= fellow believers), **you will continue being a beautiful** (fine; ideal; excellent) **supportive servant of Christ Jesus, habitually being inwardly nourished by the words of the faith** (or: in the arranged expressions, utterances and messages of trust; or: with ideas of loyalty; or: for thoughts from trust), **and of the beautiful** (fine; ideal; excellent; good quality) **teaching in which you follow alongside closely** (or: to which you nearly accompany and attend).

7. **Now you must constantly refuse and avoid** (excuse yourself from) **profane and old-womanish myths, yet habitually be training and exercising yourself, as in gymnastic discipline, toward reverence** (standing in awe of wellness, with adoration; healthful devotion and virtuous conduct of ease, in true relation to God),

8. **for gymnastic discipline for bodily exercise is beneficial toward a few things and with a view to a few people** (or: for a little while), **yet reverence** (devoutness; standing well in awe; virtuous conduct from ease with God) **is beneficial toward all things and with a view to all people, continuously holding** (having; possessing) **a promise of life – of the one now** (at the present time), **and of the impending one** (the one being about to be).

9. **The Word [is] full of faith** (or: Faithful and Trustworthy [is] the word) **and worthy of all welcomed reception,**

10. **for into this [end] are we constantly working hard unto weariness, and are continuously struggling in the contest** (contending for the prize; [other MSS: being reproached]), **because we have placed our expectation** (or: set our hope) **and thus rely upon**

a living God (or: upon [the] living God), **Who is** (exists being) **[the] Savior** (Deliverer; Rescuer; Restorer to health and wholeness) **of all human beings** (all mankind) **– especially of believers** (of folks full of faith and trust; of faithful ones)!

11. **Be constantly announcing these things to those at your side, passing them along from one to another, and keep on teaching them!**

12. **Let no one be despising** (thinking down on; having a negative opinion of) **your youth. On the contrary, continue coming to be a model** (pattern; example) **of** (or: pertaining to) **those full of faith** (of the faithful ones; for believers)**: in word, in conduct** (behavior), **in love** (centered in an accepting urge to union), **in faith** (or: trust and faithfulness), **in purity** (or: propriety).

13. **While I am coming, continue holding toward a propensity for the reading** (keep on possessing devotion in the means of knowing again), **for the calling alongside to give relief, aid, exhortation, comfort and encouragement** (in the work of a paraclete), **[and] for the teaching** (to the instruction and in the training).

14. **Do not make it a habit to neglect the care of or disregard this result of grace** (or: the effect of favor from the gratuitous, joy-producing Act) **residing within you, which was given to you through a prophecy** (a coming or manifestation of light ahead of time), **accompanied by a laying on of the hands of the body of elder folks.**

15. **Continually meditate on, give attention to and cultivate these things; be absorbed in them** (exist centered within them), **to the end that your cutting a passage forward** (your progress and advancement) **may be visibly apparent to all** (for everyone; among all folks).

16. **Habitually have a hold upon yourself and the teaching** (or: Constantly attend to yourself and to the instruction and training). **Continue abiding on and remaining in them** (or: Constantly dwell on, while settling in them; or: Be progressively and fully persisting with them), **for, in continuously doing this, you will habitually rescue** (repeatedly and progressively deliver, save and restore to health and wholeness; continue keeping safe) **both yourself and those regularly hearing you.**

CHAPTER 5

1. **You should not inflict blows upon** (or: = verbally attack; severely criticize; give reproofs to) **an older man. To the contrary, habitually call [him] alongside, as a father, to aid, give relief and assist, to encourage and exhort** (= be a paraclete to him). **[Treat] younger men as brothers,**

2. **older women as mothers, younger women as sisters, within all purity and propriety.**

3. **Be constantly honoring** (valuing; thus: = assisting and supporting) **widows – those actually being widows.**

4. **But if any widow currently has children or grandchildren** (descendants), **let these keep on learning to first show reverence with ease and virtuous devotion to goodness with pious care, for and in their own household, and to keep paying a due compensation to their parents and grandparents** (progenitors), **for this is welcomely received in God's sight.**

5. **Now the one actually being a widow, and having been left alone** (= without a dowry and destitute), **has placed expectation upon, and now relies on God, and constantly remains focused in requests regarding needs, and in prayers** (thoughts, words and deeds aimed toward having goodness and well-being) **during night and during day,**

6. **yet the woman continuously indulging herself in riotous luxury** (excessive comfort; sensual gratification), **while continuing being alive** (or: [though] living), **she is dead** (or: she has died).

7. **So keep on announcing these things along the way** (telling them to the one at your side), **to the end that they may be folks not to be laid hold of for being reprehensible** (thus: people in whom is no just cause for blame).

8. **Now if anyone is not habitually having forethought or perceiving beforehand in order to provide for those who are his or her own** (= relatives), **and especially ones of the household** (family or domestics) **she or he has contradicted and disowned** (turned her or his back on; denied; renounced; refused) **the Faith-loyalty and is worse than an unbeliever** (or: has disregarded and declined their trust and exists being worse than one without faith or loyalty).

9. **Let a widow be put on the list, and continue enrolled, who has become no younger than sixty years old, a wife of one man** (= not married a second time?),
10. **having a continuing reputation founded in beautiful acts** (ideal works; fine deeds)**: if she nourishes children** (or: reared a family), **if she is** (or: was) **hospitable to strangers and foreigners, if she washes** (or: bathed) **the feet of the set-apart folks** (the holy ones; the saints), **if she successfully wards off distress for those being constantly pressured** (or: relieves those consistently being in tribulation and affliction), **if she follows up on every good work** (attends to every virtuous deed).

11. **On the other hand, turn aside requests of** (or: refuse) **younger widows [from being on the list], for you see, whenever they may develop headstrong pride** (live strenuously or rudely) **against Christ** (or: may come down to the level of sexual impulse, be in the sphere of sensual desire, feel licentious or become wanton in relation to or in regard to the Anointed [body]) **they are continually wanting to be marrying** [note: it was a Gnostic belief that a person could gain knowledge (gnosis) by having sex with someone],
12. **habitually holding an effect of a decision: that they set-aside the first faith-loyalty** (or: continuing to possess the result of a judgment, because they displace their first trust).
13. **Yet at the same time, they also are constantly learning inactiveness** (idleness; unemployment), **wandering around the houses** (= going from home to home), **and not only [are they] inactive** (ineffective; unemployed; idle), **but further [they are] also gossips** (babblers; ones bubbling over with prattle) **and meddlers** (or: gaining knowledge by supernatural means or practicing magic), **women constantly saying unnecessary things** (or: continuously speaking the things they should not speak).

14. **I am wanting and intending, therefore, younger women to be marrying: to be bearing children; to continuously rule and manage a household; to be by habit giving not even one starting point** (base of operation; opportunity; incentive; inducement) **favoring verbal abuse** (slander; reviling) **to the person occupying an opposing position** (or: in the one lying in opposition; for the opposer or the opposing counterpart),
15. **for you see, already some** (or: certain folks) **were turned out [of the path]** (or: were turned aside [from the goal]), **behind the adversary** (= to follow after satan; or: = some were by their opponents turned out of the midst of the community to the adversarial counterpart [religion] which lay behind them).

16. **If any woman of faith** (or: faithful, trusting and believing woman) **continues having widows [in her circle of influence or in her family], let her continue warding off [disaster] for them** (or: relieving and being sufficient for them [= by paying their expenses]), **and then the called-out community [will] not be continuously burdened** (weighed down), **to the end that it may continually ward off [disaster]** (or: bring relief and be sufficient [by paying expenses]) **for those actually being widows.**

17. **Let the older men – ones having beautifully** (ideally; finely) **placed [themselves] at the head so as to stand before, to lead and to provide – be considered worthy of double value, worth and honor, especially those being continually wearied and spent with labor in [the] Word** (or: in the midst of the message) **and by teaching** (or: instruction and training),
18. **for the Scripture is saying, "You shall not muzzle a bull** (or: ox) **when it is threshing out grain,"** [Deut. 25:4] **and, "The worker [is] worthy** (of equal value) **of his wages."** [Luke 10:7]

19. **Do not normally accept** (or: receive; entertain) **[from the] outside** (= from outside the community) **an accusation down on** (or: charge against) **an older man, except "upon two or three witnesses,"** [Deut. 17:6]
20. **yet habitually put to the proof, test or expose** (or: lay bare and reprove) **the [older men] habitually missing the target or constantly being in error** (or: the [older men] repeatedly sinning; those continuously failing) **before all onlookers** (or: in the sight of all), **to the end that the rest, also, may continue holding reverence** (or: having respectful fear).

21. **I continue bearing complete and thorough witness** (or: I habitually give evidence and testimony throughout) **in the sight of God and of Christ Jesus and of the selected, picked out and chosen agents** (or: messengers; folks with the message), **to the end that you may keep watch on so as to guard these things apart from effects of fore-decisions** (prejudgment; prejudice), **continually doing nothing** (constructing not one thing) **down from** (in accord with; on the level of) **inclination** (or: a leaning toward [something]) **or bias.**
22. **In practice, place** (or: lay) **your hands quickly upon no one, neither be habitually having common existence with, partnering with, participating in or sharing in common in the failures** (errors; sins; misses of the target; deviations from the goal) **belonging to other folks. Constantly keep yourself pure** (or: Make it a habit to watch over and guard so as to preserve yourself with propriety).
23. **No longer continue being a water-drinker, but rather, habitually make use of a little wine because of your throat** (or: orifice of the stomach; neck of the bladder) **and your thick** (or: close together, firm, solid) **or frequent weaknesses** (deficiencies in strength; infirmities; sicknesses [note: this may have been a bladder ailment cause by the local water, causing frequent urination]).

24. **The failures** (shortfalls; errors; mistakes; deviations; sins) **of some people are obvious** (portrayed before the public), **continually proceeding into a separation and then a decision which leads into judging, yet also, for certain** (or: with some) **folks, they are normally following upon** (or: after; = they have not yet caught up with them; or: they are habitually accompanying [them]).
25. **Similarly, the beautiful acts** (the excellent deeds; the fine and ideal works) **are obvious** (portrayed before the public), **and yet the ones habitually holding otherwise** (having [acts or deeds] in a different way) **are not able to be continuously hidden.**

CHAPTER 6

1. **Let as many as are** (or: exist being) **slaves, joined under a yoke, constantly regard** (consider; esteem) **their own masters** (or: owners) **worthy of all honor, to the end that God's Name and the teaching may not be repeatedly blasphemed** (defamed with a false image; vilified; misrepresented in a way that hinders the Light; spoken of injuriously; slandered).
2. **Further, let not those having believing masters** (or: trusting and loyal owners who are full of faith) **be in the habit of despising** (having a condescending attitude about; be thinking down upon) **[them], because they are brothers** (= fellow believers). **But rather, let them consistently perform as slaves to a greater extent, because those being continual recipients of their good service** (receiving the well-doing in return; those being supported by the benefits) **are believers and beloved** (or: are folks full of faith and love).
Keep on teaching these things, and keep on encouraging by calling others alongside to aid and exhort them (or: continually perform as a paraclete).

3. **If anyone continues teaching something different, and is not approaching by sound words** (or: in healthful messages; with sound thoughts or ideas) **– in or by those of our Lord, Jesus Christ – even in the teaching which accords with reverence** (or: by instruction which is down from a standing in awe of wellness, with adoration, and with training that is in line with a healthful devotion to virtuous conduct for goodness, that is in true relation to God),
4. **he has smoldered and has been puffed up with the fumes of conceit, continues versed in nothing** (capable of nothing; unskilled and able to fix upon nothing; understanding nothing of

how to know), **but rather, continues being sick with a morbid craving concerning investigations** (or: seekings; questionings; inquiries) **and debates** (word fights; disputes; controversies), **forth from out of which things continually come to be** (or: are birthed) **envy, strife** (discord; contention), **blasphemies** (slanderous or abusive speeches which vilify, give a false image, defame, aver harm or hinder the Light), **bad** (labor-inducing; unprofitable; malicious; misery-gushed) **suspicions and intrigues,**

5. **altercations and mutual irritations from throughout rubbing against** (= friction with) **people being folks having been utterly spoiled, ruined, corrupted or perished in the mind** (= lost their wits), **and having been deprived from the Truth** (or: defrauded of reality), **folks continually prescribing it a customary law, inferring providing** (or: procuring; acquiring; furnishing and supplying to one's self; capital; financial gain) **to be the Reverence** (the standing in awe of wellness, with adoration; the virtuous conduct, in true relation to God; or: devoutness).

6. **Now the Reverence** (or: devoutness and standing in awe of the ease and well-being associated with God; virtuous conduct for goodness, that is in true relation to God) **is a great providing of supply** (or: means of acquiring; furnishing and supplying to one's self; or: capital) **along with a contented self-sufficiency from independent means,**

     (or: Yet is great financial gain accompanied with independent means this Reverence?)

7. **for we carried** (or: You see we brought) **nothing into the world** (the ordered system; secular society) **[and] it is evident that neither are we able to carry anything out.**

8. **So, continuously holding** (or: having) **nourishments** (foods; sustenance) **and effects of coverings** (clothing or shelter) **we will constantly be defended, made a match for, and warded off by these things** (or: we shall habitually be contentedly satisfied with and sufficed in these things).

9. **Yet those wanting and determining to be rich are continually falling in – into a trial and a trap and many senseless and hurtful strong passions** (many over-desires void of understanding and bringing weakness; disadvantageous wants and needs), **which things habitually swamp those people, sinking them to the bottom, into ruinous corruption** (or: destruction) **and loss,**

10. **for a root of all the bad things** (the worthless qualities; the injurious situations; the poor craftsmanship; the ugly personalities; the malicious desires) **is the fondness of silver** (= love of money; = covetousness) **of which some, habitually extending and stretching themselves out to reach, are caused to wander off** (or: were led astray) **away from the faith and they pierce themselves through with a rod and put themselves on a spit** (or: they run themselves through, stabbing themselves all around) **for** (or: in; to; with; by) **many pains.**

11. **However you, O human from God** (or: O person whose source and origin is God), **be constantly fleeing** (taking flight from) **these things. But continuously pursue** (or: rapidly follow, press forward and chase) **fair and equitable dealings in right relationships in the Way pointed out** (rightwisedness; justice; = loyal covenantal living), **faith** (trust; trustworthiness; loyalty), **love, persistent remaining under in patient yet relentless endurance to give support, meek and gentle sensitivity** (mildness of temper).

12. **Constantly contend** (as in the public games in the stadium or on the racecourse) **the beautiful** (ideal; fine) **struggling contest of the faith** (or: whose source and character are trust, conviction and loyalty; or: which is faithfulness). **Take hold of** (or: Get a firm grip upon) **the eonian life** (the Life that has the quality and characteristic of the Age [of the Messiah], and pertains to the eons, continuing on into the ages) **into which you were called – even [when] you agreed with** (or: confessed; said the same thing with another person) **the beautiful** (fine; ideal) **like-message of agreement in the sight and presence of many witnesses.**

13. **In the sight and presence of God – the One continuously bringing forth all things as living creatures** (the One habitually or repeatedly generating all things alive, keeping The Whole alive) **– and of Christ Jesus, the One who was testifying the beautiful like-message** (or: fine confession; making the ideal and excellent public declaration) **on [the occasion with] Pontius**

Pilate, I am announcing to you (bringing this message to your side) **and passing on this notification,**

14. **[that] you yourself keep watch on, so as to guard and preserve, the spotless, not-to-be-laid-hold-of-for-blame implanted goal** (impartation of the finished product within; inward directive; or: irreprehensible commandment), **until the shining-upon from** (or: the display in clear light of) **our Lord, Jesus Christ** (or: the manifestation pertaining to, and which is, our Owner, Jesus [the] Anointed [= Messiah]),

15. **which, in its own fitting situations** (appropriate seasons; appointed occasions; fertile moments), **will proceed to exhibit and point out The Happy and Only Able One** (only Powerful One; alone Potent One)**: The King of those reigning as kings, and Lord** (Master; Owner) **of those ruling as lords,**

16. **the Only One continuously holding and having possession of immortality** (the absence or privation of death; deathlessness), **the One continuously making inaccessible** (or: unapproachable) **light His home** (or: dwelling), **Whom not one of mankind sees, saw or perceived, nor is able or has power to see or perceive, in Whom [is] honor** (value; worth), **and eonian strength** (might having the qualities and characteristics of the Age; strength enduring through and pertaining to the eons). **It is so** (Amen)!

17. **Pass along the notice** (or: be announcing) **to those rich** (or: wealthy) **within the present age** (the current eon) **to not be habitually high-minded** (proud; arrogant; or: to ponder high things), **neither to have put expectation upon, and thus rely on, the uncertainty** (insecurity; non-evidence) **of riches** (or: wealth), **but rather, upon God, the One continuously holding all things alongside for us** (or: the One constantly offering and providing all thing to us) **richly, unto [our] enjoyment** (or: into beneficial participation; unto the obtaining of a portion to enjoy; [leading] into pleasure),

18. **to be habitually energizing goodness and working at virtue** (or: working profitably), **to continue being rich in beautiful deeds** (to continue wealthy in ideal actions and in union with fine works), **to be liberal contributors** (folks good with giving) **– folks having the qualities of community and common existence** (people who partner and are ready to share; folks who are fellow participants),

19. **constantly securing and laying away in store for themselves** (or: in themselves) **a beautiful** (fine; ideal) **foundation, into the thing being about to be** (or: unto [that which is] impending; = for the future), **to the end that they can from Being** (or: pertaining to essential existence) **receive upon themselves things pertaining to the Life** (or: so that in themselves they could lay hold upon the existing life; or: in order to lay claim to a way of being that is really life).

20. **O Timothy, guard and protect that which is placed beside [you]** (or: = the deposit laid up in trust), **constantly turning yourself out of the profane, empty voices** (vacuous sounds; fruitless discussions) **and oppositions** (or: standings against in an opposing position; disputes; antitheses; opposing technical or theoretical arguments) **of the falsely named "knowledge" or "insight"** (or: even contradictions of the lie termed "Gnosis"),

21. **which some are continuously professing and making announcements upon. They miss the mark** (or: are without a mark), **swerving** (deviating) **around The Faith and trust.**

Grace [is] with you folks! (or: The unimaginable, unpredicted and gratuitous Favor that brings joy and happiness [is] together with you people!)

[written circa A.D. 55 – Based on the critical analysis of John A.T. Robinson]

SECOND TIMOTHY

CHAPTER 1

1. **Paul, one sent off with a commission from, and pertaining to** (or: a representative of), **Christ Jesus through God's will, intent and purpose [which is] down from, in line with and with a view to [the] promise of Life – the one [which is] resident within Christ Jesus** (or: through God's design which corresponds to Life's promise, or the Promise, which is life: the one belonging to, pertaining to and from Jesus – in union with [the] Anointing),
2. **to Timothy, a beloved child** (or: brought-forth one; born one)**:**
Grace and favor, mercy and peace from the joining harmony [= shalom] **– from Father God, even Christ Jesus, our Lord** (or: from God [the] Father, and Christ Jesus, our Owner).

3. **I constantly hold grace in God** (or: I am habitually having gratitude to God, while repeatedly possess favor, by God), **in Whom** (or: to, for, by or with Whom) **I continually render sacred service – [handed down] from [the] ancestors** (or: those born earlier; forefathers) **– within a clean conscience** (or: co-knowledge; a joint-knowing from shared seeing), **as I constantly hold** (or: am presently having) **an unceasing remembrance** (or: a memory which leaves no interval) **about you within my expressions of need** (or: seekings of aid; requests), **by night and by day,**
4. **constantly and fully longing** (or: by habit yearning upon [you]) **to see you – having been reminded and being caused to be remembering your tears – so that I may be filled full of joy,**
5. **taking** [other MSS: continually getting] **a suggestion to my memory of the unhypocritical faith**
> (or: the faith that is not overly critical of matters; the trust that is not deficient in its ability to sift and decide; the reliance which is not hyper-judgmental; a loyal allegiance that is not scrutinizing and judging from an inferior position, and then becoming gradually separated) **resident within you, which first inhabited** (made its home within) **your grandmother, Lois, and then in your mother, Eunice. Now I have been persuaded and stand convinced that [it is] also within you.**

6. **For** (or: Because of; With a view to) **which cause I am periodically reminding you to habitually and progressively give life by fire again to** (or: revive the fire of; cause the live coal to blaze up for; rekindle the dormant fire into flames of; to again put a spark to) **God's** [A reads: Christ's] **effect of grace and result of favor, which has being** (is; exists) **within you through the imposition** (or: the placing or laying upon) **of my hands,**
7. **for you see, God does not give to us** (or: did not supply for us) **a spirit of cowardice** (or: a Breath-effect or attitude of timidity in us), **but rather [a spirit and attitude] of ability and of power, as well as of love** (a drive toward reunion) **and of soundness in frame of mind**
> (of wholeness in thinking; of healthiness of attitude; of sanity; of sensibility; of controlled reasonableness; of rational moderation; anatomically: of a saved diaphragm).

8. **Therefore, do not become ashamed of** (or: You should not, then, be embarrassed by) **the testimony of and from our Lord** (or: the witness pertaining to our Master; the evidence which is our Owner), **nor yet, [of; or: by] me, His bound-one** (or: His prisoner). **On the contrary, down from God's ability** (or: in the sphere of power, which is God), **experience things of bad quality** (or: worthless encounters) **together with [me] for the message of ease, goodness and well-being**
> (or: But rather, corresponding to God's power, suffer evil and hardship with the evangel; But further, accept your share in bad treatment – in accord with the ability which comes from God – in [the Way of] the Good News),
9. **pertaining to and from the One delivering and calling us** (or: which is rescuing, healing restoring, saving and calling us) **in a set-apart calling** (or: to a holy invitation; for a separated

and different sacred call); **not corresponding to our works** (or: down from our deeds; in accord with or on the level of our [ceremonial] activities), **but on the contrary, corresponding to** (down from; in accord with; on the level of) **His own prior placing** (or: previously setting-forth; thus: definite aim and purpose which He personally is bent on achieving), **even grace: that [which is] being given to us within Christ Jesus** (or: corresponding to His own predetermined purpose and the favor being given for us, [which is] belonging to and pertaining to Jesus, resident within Christ), **before times having the qualities and characteristics of the ages** (before [the] age-lasting time periods; prior to eonian times; = before [the] time segments of [the] ages [began]),

10. **and now** (at the present moment), **being set in clear light so as to become visible** (or: manifested) **through the bringing to full light** (or: the complete shining upon; the full appearance in light; the complete manifestation by light) **of our Deliverer** (Savior; Rescuer), **Christ Jesus – on the one hand, idling down death** (or: The Death) **so as to make it unproductive and useless, yet on the other hand, illuminating** (giving light to) **life and incorruptibility** (the absence of the ability to decay; un-ruinableness) **through means of the message of goodness, ease and well-being –**

11. **into which** (or: into Whom) **I am placed** (or: I was put)**: a herald** (a public announcer; a proclaimer; a preacher) **– even a person sent off with a mission** (an envoy; a representative; or: = a messenger) **– and a teacher** [other MSS add: of the ethnic multitudes (nations; Gentiles; Goyim; non-Jews)].

12. **For** (Because of; In view of) **which cause I am also continuously experiencing** (also: feeling; being affected by; suffering) **these things. But still, I am not feeling shame** (or: I am not experiencing embarrassment), **for I have seen and thus know by Whom I have believed and now put my trust** (or: in Whom I have relied and continue placing confidence), **and I have been persuaded and am continuing convinced that He is able** (He continues being powerful) **to watch over, guard and protect – on into that Day – the deposit placed alongside of me** (or: what is entrusted to my charge).

13. **Keep on holding an outline and pattern** (that which underlies and delineates the sketch or model) **of words that continue giving health, healing and a cure** (or: Habitually have a model of thoughts, ideas and messages [that] are being progressively sound and healthful) **– ones of which you heard** (or: hear) **from my side – within the midst of faith** (or: in union with trust) **and love** (self-giving acceptance)**: that [which is] resident within Christ Jesus.**

> (or: Continually be possessing the under-type – the one within [the] Anointing of Jesus –
> of healthful discourses and conversations which you heard from me, in faith and love.)

14. **Watch over, guard and protect the beautiful deposit placed alongside [you]** (or: the fine and excellent thing that is entrusted to [your] charge) **through means of [the] set-apart Breath-effect** (or: Holy Spirit) **[that is] continuously inhabiting us** (or: by a set-apart spirit: the one constantly making its home within us).

15. **You have seen, and thus know this, that all those within [the province of] Asia were turned away from me – of whom are Phygelus and Hermogenes.**

16. **May the Lord** [= Yahweh or Christ] **give mercy to the house** (or: household) **of Onesiphorus, because many times** (often; frequently) **he refreshed me** (he breathed back cool on me; he souled me up again), **and he was not ashamed of** (or: embarrassed by) **my chain** (= my imprisonment).

17. **On the contrary, on coming to be in Rome, he urgently** (quickly; diligently) **searched for** (or: seeks) **me, and found** (or: finds) **me.**

18. **May the Lord** [= Yahweh or Christ] **give to him to find mercy, beside [the] Lord** [= Yahweh or Christ], **within that Day! And how much** (or: how many things) **he gave in attending service within Ephesus, you yourself, by intimate experience, continue knowing better.**

CHAPTER 2

1. **You, then, my child** (or: one born of me), **be habitually enabled** (continuously and progressively empowered; repeatedly made powerful inside) **within the grace, and in union**

with the joyous favor (centered in the unexpected, gratuitous act that brought happiness), **[which are] within Christ Jesus** (or: [by being] in union with [the] Anointing of Jesus).
2. **And whatever you hear** (or: heard) **from my side through many witnesses, at once place** (or: set) **these things to the side for people full of faith** (or: deposit and commit these things, in trust for safekeeping, to trustworthy and loyal people; inculcate these things in reliable humans) – **whosoever will be competent** (or: adequately qualified) **to also teach others** (or: different folks).

3. **Experience things of bad quality** (or: worthless encounters) **together** (or: Accept your share of bad treatment and evil) **as a beautiful** (ideal; fine) **soldier of** (or: from) **Christ Jesus.**
4. **No one serving a tour of duty as a soldier** (currently performing military service or being at war) **habitually intertwines or entangles himself in** (or: by; with) **everyday affairs** (undertakings and activities; business performances) **of the course of life** (or: of making a living), **in order that he may please** (or: be acceptable to) **the one enlisting him in military service** (the one collecting soldiers to gather an army).
5. **So also, if anyone may be repeatedly competing in the athletic games, he is not normally being crowned with a winner's wreath if he does not compete lawfully** (according to the rules of the game).
6. **It is constantly binding** (It is of continual necessity) **for the farmer** (or: field worker) **that is habitually laboring in the field to be repeatedly first in taking a share of the fruits** (crops).
7. **[So] give constant thought to** (or: Continually put your mind to, so as to perceive and understand) **what I am now saying, for you see, the Lord** [= Yahweh or Christ] **will continue giving comprehension and understanding** (a sending and bringing things together into union) **to you** (for you; in you) **within all things and among all people.**

8. **Be habitually keeping in mind** (or: remembering) **Jesus Christ** [= the Messiah], **from out of David's seed** (or: = [Who came] from David's descendants), **being the One having been aroused and raised, and now continuing risen, forth from out of the midst of dead folks – corresponding to and in the sphere of my message of goodness, ease and well-being** (or: in line with the good news that came through me; or: to the degree and realm of my glad tidings),
9. **within** (or: centered in; in union with) **which I am continually experiencing bad situations** (suffering evil; experiencing bad treatment and conditions of poor quality) **to the point of bonds** (fetters or imprisonment) **as a worthless worker** (a criminal; one who acts badly; a worker of evil), **but by comparison, the Word of God** (God's thought, idea and message; the collected, laid-out saying, which is God) **has not been bound or imprisoned, and thus remains untied!**
10. **Because of this [fact], I continue remaining under to support all people** (humanity) **and to patiently endure all [situations], on account of** (or: for the sake of) **the selected and picked-out folks** (the chosen-out peoples; the elect groups; the choice ones), **to the end that these very same folks and groups, may also hit the target of the deliverance** (rescue; health and wholeness; salvation) **within Christ Jesus** (or: pertaining to Jesus, resident within Christ: inherent in the Anointing; in union with [Messiah] Jesus) – **together with glory** (or: an opinion; an appearance; an imagination; a manifestation which calls forth praise) **which has the qualities and characteristics of the Age [of Messiah]** (or: eonian glory; an age-lasting reputation).

11. **The Word** (or: Logos; laid-out message) **[is] full of faith.** (or: Trustworthy [is] this statement and the message:) **You see, since we died together with [Him]** (or: For if we jointly die), **we will also continue living together** (or: proceed in jointly living; constantly co-live);
12. **since we are continuously remaining under for support** (or: if we continue patiently enduring), **we will also continue reigning** (performing royal activities and influence) **together with [Him]; if we shall continue saying, "No," to** (contradicting; or: disowning; not consenting; renouncing; [other MSS: are repeatedly saying "No" and contradicting]) **[Him], That One also will continue saying, "No," to** (contradicting; or; disowning; not consenting to; renouncing) **us;**
13. **if we are habitually faithless** (or: unfaithful; untrustworthy; disloyal; without trust or faith), **That One is constantly remaining faithful**

　　　(or: if we are repeatedly disbelieving or distrustful, That One continuously remains full of
　　　faith, trust, belief and reliance – That One constantly remains loyal and reliable), **for to**

contradict or say, "No," to (or: deny; disown; renounce; not consent to) **Himself, it continues that He cannot** (He is not able; He has no power)!

(or: = You see, He cannot turn His back on Himself!)

14. **[So] keep reminding [them of]** (or: suggesting to [their] memory; causing [them] to think about) **these things, repeatedly bearing thorough witness** (giving full evidence and testimony) **in the sight and presence of God** [other MSS: {the} Lord {= Christ or Yahweh}], **not to be constantly debating** (or: fighting about words; contending over meaning of terms; entering into controversies) – **[progressing] into** [other MSS: upon] **nothing useful or profitable; [leading] on to a downturn** (or: an overturning; an upsetting; a negative turn of events [= the opposite of edifying]) **of, or for, those folks continuing to listen and hear [it].**

15. **Make haste, with earnest endeavor and diligence, to place yourself alongside as an approved and qualified workman, in and by God** (or: to hand yourself over to and for God, as a tried and approved workman), **one without cause for shame, consistently cutting a straight and direct [path** {cf Prov. 3:6 and 11:5, LXX} **in, to, or with] the Word of the Truth**

(or: habitually cutting an upright and erect [line through] the Word of Truth; continually cutting with the message of reality in a straight direction; constantly making a straight cut {or: wound} with the speech of this Reality; also: = dealing straightforwardly with the discourse of Reality; or: repeatedly dividing and marking out straight [boundaries] by the Reason which is Truth).

16. **Yet continue staying at the periphery, going out around so as to avoid the profane, empty voices** (the speeches or discussions without content which cross the threshold into the sphere of that which is not set-apart). **You see, they will cut a passage forward** (progress; advance) **upon more aspects of irreverence** (things pertaining to impiety or attitudes that lack awe),

17. **and their word** (speech; discussion; or: thoughts and ideas) **will have** (or: hold) **pasture** (or: pasturage) **for gnawing and eating away like gangrene** (or: a spreading ulcer) **– of which sort are Hymenaeus and Philetus,**   [2 Thes. 2:2]

18. **the very ones who miss the mark, deviating around the truth** (or: reality), **in repeatedly saying a** [other MSS: the] **resurrection has already occurred, and yet constantly turn back again** (or: and so overturn) **the faith, trust and loyalty of certain folks** (or: of some).

19. **Nevertheless** (or: However), **God's firm and solid deposit which is placed down** (a deposit of money; treasure; or: a foundation; basis) **stands, continuing to hold** (or: have) **this seal:**

"**[The] Lord** [= Yahweh] **knows** (or: knew) **by intimate experience those being of Him** (or: the ones that belong to Him; those having Him as their source)," [Num. 16:5; Nah. 1:7]

and:

"**Let everyone repeatedly naming the Name of [the] Lord** [= Yahweh or Christ] (or: by habit using the Lord's name) **stand away from** (withdraw from; keep away from) **injustice** (that which is unfair and inequitable, which negates relationship and does not correspond to the Way pointed out)." [Num. 16:26]

20. **Now within a great house** (or: large household), **there are not only golden and silver containers, equipment and utensils, but also wooden ones and earthenware** (ones made of baked clay). **And on the one hand some which [come] into [use for] honor** (things of value; = to be used on special occasions), **on the other hand some which [come] into [use for] dishonor** (things without value; = for everyday use).

21. **If, then, anyone should ever clean himself out from these** [aforementioned worthless, dishonorable and common] **things, he will proceed being a container** (or: utensil; piece of equipment) **[placed] into [use for] honor and things of worth, having been set aside** (dedicated and being one made sacred and holy) **for honorable and valuable use by the Owner** (Master of the house), **one having been made ready and now being prepared, [directed and now proceeding] into every good work** (or: virtuous action).

22. **So repeatedly take flight away from the youthful** (juvenile; adolescent) **over-desires** (or: rushing upon innovative things; or: full passions for revolutionary or modern wants), **yet**

constantly run after and steadily pursue justice (fair and equitable dealings, in rightwised relationships corresponding to the Way pointed out; also: = covenant participation), **faith** (trust; fidelity), **love** (an urge toward union) **[and] peace** (joining), **together with all those persistently** (repeatedly; habitually) **calling upon the Lord** [= Yahweh or Christ] **from out of a clean heart.**
23. **Yet further, consistently refuse** (avoid; request to be away from) **the stupid** (dull; silly; foolish) **and uneducated** (ignorant; crude; untrained) **questionings** (seekings through discussions or debates; controversies), **having seen and now knowing that they are repeatedly giving birth to** (or: generating) **fights** (battles; conflicts).
24. **Now it is continually binding for** (or: it is a constant necessity to) **a slave of [the] Lord** (= Yahweh's or Christ's slave) **not to be habitually fighting** (or: it is not necessary for the Lord's slave to be battling or contending), **but to the contrary [he/she] is to be gentle** (kind; mild) **toward all, qualified, skillful and able in teaching, one holding up under poor conditions** (or: having an upward focus in bad situations; holding an "up attitude" in regard to evil),
25. **in accommodating meekness and with consideration constantly educating** (training; child-disciplining; instructing; correcting) **those habitually setting themselves in complete opposition or who offer resistance. May** (Would) **not God at some time give a change of thinking to them** (or: supply in and for them a changed state of consciousness), **[directing and leading them] into a full and accurate experiential knowledge of Truth and reality?**
26. **And then they can and may sober up** (or: would come back to their proper senses) **from out of the adversary's snare** (or: forth from out of the midst of the trap of the person who thrusts something through folks or causes division) – **being folks having been [previously] captured alive under** (or: by) **him, into the will** (intent; design; purpose) **of that one** (or: that person).

CHAPTER 3

1. **Now progressively come to know this and continue realizing it, that within [the] last** (or: final) **days hard seasons** (difficult occasions and situations; irksome, perilous or fierce seasons or situations that are hard to deal with; hard appointed periods) **will progressively set themselves in** (take a stand within; put themselves in place),
2. **for the people** (the humans; mankind) **will continue being folks that are fond of themselves** (self-loving; selfish), **fond of silver** (= have affection for money or things of monetary value which makes them stingy), **empty pretenders** (impostors; ostentatious self-assumers), **haughty and arrogant** (superior-appearing), **blasphemers** (abusive slanderers; folks who defame with a false image; or: light-hinderers), **uncompliant and disobedient to parents, ungrateful** (or: unthankful), **undutiful** (disloyal; without regard for divine or natural laws; malign),
3. **without natural affection, unwilling to make a treaty** (implacable; not open to an agreement), **devils** (adversarial slanderers; folks who throw or thrust something through people to hurt or cause divisions), **without strength** (without [self-] control), **uncultivated** (wild; untamed; ferocious; fierce), **without fondness for expressions of good or aspects of goodness** (or: without affection for good people; unfriendly; averse to virtue),
4. **pre-committers** (or: ones who give-over in advance, or who abandon), **rash** (reckless), **folks having been inflated with the fumes of conceit** (or: ones being beclouded in smoke), **pleasure-lovers** (ones fond of self-gratification) **rather than friends of God** (ones fond of God),
5. **continuously holding** (having) **a form of reverence** (virtue and pious awe) **yet being folks having refused, contradicted and now denying** (saying, "No," to) **its power and ability! And so, be habitually turning your steps in a direction away from these folks and avoid them,**
6. **for you see, forth from out of the midst of these folks are the people repeatedly slipping-in, into the houses,** (or: worming their way into households) **and habitually leading into captivity little women**

> [note: this is the diminutive of "women," thus, perhaps: women of undeveloped character, ability, or inward stature. While the word for "woman" is feminine, the noun "little women" and the following participles are neuter – or neutral – so this rare word may be a figure for what was a cultural view for "feminine" aspects of all people, e.g., their feelings and emotions, or general receptive qualities]

– **those having been piled on and now being heaped up with failures** (errors; misses of the target; deviations from the goal; sins), **being constantly, or from time to time, led by** (or: in; to)

various (diverse; many-colored) **over-desires** (or: full passions; wants and wishes that are rushed upon) [A adds: and gratifications],
7. **at all times** (or: always) **folks** [note: again a neuter, or neutral, participle] **that are constantly learning, and yet not at any time being able or having consistent power to come into a full, accurate experiential and intimate knowledge of Truth** (or: which is reality).

8. **Now, in the manner which** (or: by the turn or method that) **Jannes and Jambres took a stand in opposition to** (or: resisted and opposed) **Moses, thus, also, these are continually taking a stand in opposition to** (opposing and resisting) **the Truth and reality: people** (humans) **being ones having had the mind decayed down** (ruined and spoiled down; corrupted; depraved; put into a sorry state), **folks failing to meet the test** (disqualified ones) **on all sides of** (or: about) **the faith** (or: = ones whose trust does not pass the test from any angle).
9. **But they will continue making no further progress** (not be cutting a passage forward) **upon more [folks]** (or: Nevertheless, they won't get very far), **for their mindlessness** (madness; lack of understanding; folly) **will be quite evident** (very plain; obvious; outstanding and in clear visibility) **to all, even as the [madness] of those [two, i.e., Jannes and Jambres] came to be.**
10. **Yet you, yourself, follow** (or: followed) **closely beside me: in the teaching, by the instruction and with the training; in the leading, by the guidance for conduct; in the purpose** (or: with the fore-setting or by forth-setting; to and for the proposal; [used of setting-forth of the loaves in the holy place of the Temple: Mat. 12:4; Heb. 9:2]); **in the trust, for the faith, by the conviction and with the faithful loyalty; in and by the long-waiting to be in a heat of passion** (or: with long-suffering patience while pushing anger far away); **in and with the unrestricted, accepting love which urges toward reunion and self-giving; in and by the steadfast remaining-under** (or: with persevering, patient endurance while giving support);
11. **in** (or: by) **the pursuits and with persecutions; in** and by **the effects of the experiences and with results of the sufferings – the sort of things that were birthed in me and happened to me in Antioch, in Iconium, in Lystra; the sort of pursuits and persecutions which I bear up under** (or: carried-on under) **and yet out of the midst of which the Lord** [= Yahweh or Christ] **drags** (or: snatched) **me forth from all of them.**
12. **And indeed** (or: And so) **all those habitually resolving** (intending; willing) **to be continuously living in a reverent, devout and pious manner with virtuous conduct from ease and goodness within Christ Jesus will be repeatedly pursued, persecuted and harassed.**

13. **Now people of a bad condition and of an harmful disposition** (useless and malicious humans who bring misery and hard labor), **as well as sorcerers** (folks who wail and cast spells; or: impostors and swindlers; those who juggle a situation), **will continue cutting a path forward upon the worse** (or: will be advancing and making progress from bad to worse), **repeatedly leading [folks] astray** (or: causing [folks] to wander [from the Path]) **and progressively being led astray** (or: caused to wander).
14. **Yet you, yourself, be constantly remaining within what you learned and in those things of which you were persuaded and became convinced** (became assured), **having seen, and so knowing, from whose** (what folks') **side you learned [these things],**
15. **and that from an infant** (babe) **you have seen and thus know [the] sacred Scriptures** (or: Temple writings)**: the ones being constantly able** (those continuously having power) **to give you wisdom – [that leads you] into deliverance** (wholeness, good health, rescue and salvation) **– through Jesus' faith, resident within Christ** (or: through means of the faithfulness centered in Jesus [the] Anointed [= Messiah]; by trust, which is Jesus in union with an Anointing).
16. **All Scripture [is] God-breathed** (or: God-exhaled) **and beneficial-to-furtherance toward instruction** (or: Every inspired-of-God [temple] writing [is] profitable, advantageous and augmenting, with a view to teaching or training), **toward** (with a view to) **testing unto proof** (or: exposure; laying bare), **toward full restoration to straightness** (or: straightening-up upon; = improvement), **toward child-training** (education; discipline) **of the person within the Way pointed out** (of the one in eschatologically-rightwised relationships of justice),
17. **to the end that God's [corporate] Person** (or: the person belonging to God; the human having his origin in God; humanity in relation to God) **may be exactly fitted** (can exist being

precisely prepared; would be entirely suited), **being one having been completely furnished and equipped toward every good work** (with a view to every virtuous and excellent action).

CHAPTER 4

1. **I am habitually giving thorough witness** (or: constantly testifying and showing evidence in every direction) **in the sight and presence of God – even Christ Jesus: the One now being about to be continuously and progressively evaluating, deciding about and judging living folks and dead folks down from** (in accord with; corresponding to; in the sphere of; in respect to; in line with; [other MSS: even]) **His full manifestation** (or: the shining-on from Him*) **and His reign** (or: [other MSS: and then] His added display as well as His sovereign kingdom activity). [*Acts 26:23b]

2. **Herald** (Proclaim; Preach) **the Word** (The *Logos*; the idea; the thought; the reason; the message); **stand upon [it; or: It; Him] in season or out of season** (if the situation fits favorably, if the conditions are not favorable; whether convenient or not); **test and put to the proof; show further honor** (give higher value; assess greater worth; or, negatively: respectfully charge; strongly admonish; enjoin); **within every emotion which is long in arriving** (in all long-suffering patience which pushes anger far away), **and by teaching** (or: in union with instruction and training) **give aid, relief, comfort and encouragement as you call [others] to your side** (perform as a paraclete).

3. **For you see, there will be an appointed season** (a situation; a fitting period of time) **when they will not continue holding up to themselves** (or: sustaining; holding themselves upright by; holding themselves up in; or: putting up with; tolerating) **instruction** (teaching and training) **that is being continuously healthy and sound, but rather, they, habitually having their ear gratified by rubbing, scratching or tickling** (having their hearing titillated; hearing what their ears itch to hear; or, as a middle: constantly procuring pleasurable excitement by indulging an itching) **will progressively pile and heap upon themselves** (accumulate for themselves) **teachers in line with and corresponding to their own rushing emotions** (over-desires; full passions),

4. **and then, on the one hand, they will proceed to twist the ear** (or: the hearing) **and turn away from the Truth and reality, yet on the other hand, they will be progressively turned out** (have their [steps] turned out of [the Path] into a direction) **upon the myths** (fictions; legends; speeches; rumors; stories; tales; fables; things delivered by word of mouth).

5. **Yet you – you be habitually sober** (not intoxicated [by such things]; clear-headed and steady) **within all things and among all people; experience the bad and the ugly** (or: suffer the evil and the worthless) [A adds: as an ideal (beautiful; fine; excellent) soldier of Christ Jesus]; **perform [the] act** (do [the] deed; produce the action; construct a work) **of one who brings goodness and well-being and announces ease and good news** (or: act [like] a man who has good news to tell); **be fully bent on and bring your attending service to full measure, with complete assurance and absolute certainty!**

6. **You see, I, myself, am already being progressively poured out as a drink offering, and the fitting situation** (the season; the occasion) **of my loosing up** (or: my kairos of loosening again [the tent pegs and ropes, or, the ship moorings]; or: the situation of my dissolution [as in breaking camp]) **has taken its stand upon [its appointed place] and is imminent.**

7. **I have contended the beautiful contest in the racecourse** (or: I have with agony struggled, wrestling in the ideal combat {the fine fight} in the public games); **I have finished the race** (ended the racecourse; reached the goal of my contest; I have fought to the finish); **I have kept** (observed; watched over; guarded; kept in custody) **the faith, trust, confidence and loyalty.**

8. **For the rest** (or: Finally; Henceforth) **the winner's wreath of the Course having been pointed out** (the athlete's laurel wreath consisting of the rightwised relationship in fair and equitable dealings, and pertaining to the justice of right behavior on the course; or: = the wreath from covenant inclusion and participation) **continues laid away for me** (or: is presently reserved in me), **which the Lord** [= Christ or Yahweh], **the Fair** (Equitable; Just; Rightwising; [Covenant]) **Judge** [of the games], **will proceed to pay to** (or: award in) **me within the sphere of that Day – yet not only to me! ... but further, also, to all those** (or: in everyone) **being ones having**

loved (urged toward union with; totally gave themselves to; unambiguously accepted) **His full appearance in Light** (or: the complete manifestation of Him; His fully bringing things to light; the shining upon things pertaining to Him; His full and accurate manifestation).

9. **Make haste with earnest endeavor and diligence to come to me quickly,**
10. **for you see, Demas, loving** (urging toward union with) **the present age, forsook and abandoned me and went into Thessalonica; Crescens into Galatia; Titus into Dalmatia.**
11. **Only Luke is with me. Picking up Mark, be bringing [him] with you, for he continues being very useful to me, with a view to attending service**
12. **– now I sent off Tychicus with a mission into Ephesus –**
13. **[and] in coming, be bringing the traveling cloak, which I left behind in Toras with Carpus, and the little scrolls – especially the parchment notebooks** (or: vellum [note: which is made from dressed animal skins]).

> [note: the Greek φαιλονης/φελονης, here translated "traveling cloak," literally means "bark." The Syriac version renders it "valise; book carrier." Vincent notes that the 5th century lexicographer Hesychius (of Alexandria) explained this word as a "case." He also says Phrynicus (3rd century) describes it as a receptacle for books or other things, and that this word "a wrapper of parchments" was translated figuratively in Latin by *toga* or *paenula* "a cloak." Nevertheless, Vincent and most other scholars stay with the traditional rendering, "cloak."]

14. **Alexander the coppersmith** (or: metalworker) **displayed many bad** (worthless; evil) **things [in his behavior] to me – the Lord** [= Yahweh or Christ] **will continue awarding to him** (or: giving back in him; paying back for him) **corresponding to his works** (down from his deeds and on the level of his actions)
15. **– from whom you, yourself, also be constantly guarding yourself against, for he stands** (or: stood) **in opposition to our words** (or: thoughts, ideas and messages).
16. **Within my first verbal defense no one happened to be beside me** (no one came along with me), **but rather, all forsook** (abandoned; [other MSS: were forsaking and abandoning]) **me – may it not be put to their account** (may it not be counted against them)!
17. **Yet the Lord** [= Christ or Yahweh] **took a stand beside me** (or: stood alongside in me) **– and He empowered me** (enabled me; gave me inward ability), **to the end that through me the message that is being heralded** (the contents of the public proclamation) **would** (or: may; could) **be fully carried throughout with complete assurance, to full measure, and with absolute certainty, and so [that] all the ethnic multitudes** (nations; Gentiles; Goyim; non-Jews) **would** (could; may) **hear [it] – and I was dragged** (or: drawn) **from out of the mouth of a lion!**
18. **The Lord** [= Yahweh or Christ] **will continue dragging** (or: drawing) **me away from every harmful act** (malicious or evil work) **and will continue delivering me into the midst of the imposed, heavenly reign and kingdom – the one [seated] upon the heavens** (or: into the realm of His activities and way of doing things: the one upon, and which can be compared to, the perfected atmosphere) **– which is from Him and belongs to Him, in Whom [is] the glory** (or: for Whom [is] the reputation; by Whom [is] the manifestation of that which calls forth praise; to Whom [is] the good opinion), **on into the ages of the ages** (or: into the principle ages which consummate all the ages; into the obscure time periods of the ages). **It is so!** (Amen)

19. **Embrace Prisca and Aquila and the household of Onesiphorus, as you give them my greetings.**
20. **Erastus remains in Corinth, but Trophimus, continuing weak in sickness, I left behind in Miletus.**
21. **– Make haste with earnest endeavor and diligence to come before winter** (the rainy and stormy season)! **– Eubulus, Pudens, Linus, Claudia and all the brothers** (= fellow believers) **each send hugs and good wishes.**
22. **The Lord** [= Yahweh or Christ; A reads: Jesus; others: Jesus Christ] **[is] with your spirit** ([is] in company with your breath)! **Grace and favor [are] with you folks. It is so!** (Amen.)

[written circa A.D. 58 – Based on the critical analysis of John A.T. Robinson]

TITUS

1. **Paul, God's slave** (a slave of God; one bound to, subjected under, and owned by God), **yet one sent away with a commission** (as an emissary, envoy or ambassador) **from, pertaining to and belonging to Jesus Christ** (or: a representative of Jesus [the] Anointed), **with a view to and corresponding to [the] faith of God's chosen folks** (or: in line with a trust and loyalty possessed by and characteristic of God's selected and picked-out ones) **and the full, accurate and precise intimate knowledge and experiential insight of Truth and Reality – the [truth and reality] corresponding to and in accord with reverence** (or: down from goodness which produces virtuous conduct with devoutness, and in line with ease from a true relation to God) –
2. **[based; standing] upon an expectation** (or: expectant hope) **of and from eonian life** (life having the quality and characteristics of, and its source in, the Age [of Messiah]; life for and throughout the ages) **which the non-lying God** (the God without falseness) **promised – before eonian times** (prior to the times belonging to the ages).
3. **Now He manifests** (or: brought into clear light) **His *Logos*** (His Word; the Thought from Him; the Reason, Idea, communication and expression from Him; the discourse pertaining to Him; and the message which is Him) **in Its** (or: His) **own seasons, fitting situations and fertile moments within** (or: in the midst of) **a proclamation by a herald – which I, myself, was made to trust and believe – down from, in accord with and corresponding to a full arrangement** (or: a setting-upon; a complete disposition; a precise placing in order; an injunction) **of and from God, our Savior** (Deliverer; Rescuer; Restorer to health, wholeness and our original condition).

4. **To Titus, a genuine born-one** (legitimate child [one born in wedlock]) **down from and corresponding to a common and partnered** (equally owned, shared and participated-in) **faithfulness, trust, faith, confidence and loyalty:**
Grace (or: Favor), **and peace from the joining** [= shalom; A, C2 & others: mercy; compassion], **[are; continue coming] from Father God** (or: God [the] Father) **– even Christ Jesus, our Deliverer** (or: and [the] Anointed Jesus, our Savior, Rescuer and Restorer to health, wholeness and our original condition; as well as from [the Messiah], Jesus, our Safe-keeper).

5. **From the source of, and because of, this grace and favor, I left** [other MSS: was leaving] **you off in Crete, so that you, yourself, could correct and amend – so as to be fully straight throughout the midst – the things habitually lacking, leaving defects or remaining undone, and [so] you, yourself, could thoroughly establish [the] older folks** (or: correspondingly make [the] elders to stand fast and be firm), **city by city – as I, myself, made thorough arrangements for** (or: with) **you –**
6. **provided anyone [of these] is normally not one being called up, or arraigned, before a judge** (= habitually exists being one free from reproach); **[is] a husband of one woman** (or: wife), **having trusting and believing children** (or: born-ones that are full of faith); **[is] not one in the midst of a [legal] charge** (or: an accusation; being considered in a category) **of being a person without healthful wholeness** (or: of being unwholesome; being in a desperate case without hope of safety; being prodigal; being wasteful; being on an unsaved course; being incorrigible; being dissolute and debauched) **nor [of] insubordinate [qualities]** (things not put in submission; things not placed under the arrangement; un-subjected and unruly [traits]).
7. **You see, it continues binding and necessary for the person who sets his eyes upon the distant goal, having a full-scope view, and successfully hits the target** (or: the one who surveys, inspects and watches upon; the scout; the tender guardian who oversees with attentive care) **to continue being one [that is] not normally called up, or arraigned, before a judge** (= to habitually exist being one free from reproach). **As God's house administrator** (house manager; house dispenser and distributor; estate steward), **[he should] not [be] one who pleases himself** (or: gives himself to pleasure): **not impulsive** (prone to passion, irritation or anger; not ruled by his own mental bent, disposition or propensities; not one teeming with internal

swelling or motion), **not addicted to wine** (or: beside himself with wine; = not a drunk), **not quarrelsome and apt to strike another, not one eager for dishonorable, deformed or ugly gain.**

8. **But to the contrary, [he should be] fond of strangers** (have affection for foreigners; be hospitable), **[be] fond of the good and have affection for virtue and excellence, [be] whole, healthy and liberated** (sound) **in frame of mind and disposition** ([be] sane), **[be] fair and equitable, and in rightwised relationships within the Way pointed out, [be] loyal, dutiful and pure from all crime, [produce] inner strength** ([be] self-controlled),

9. **habitually holding himself firmly to** (or: clinging face-to-face to) **the full-of-faith Word** (message; thought; idea; Logos; or: the faithful word) **– down from, corresponding to and in line with the Teaching and training – to the end that he can be powerful and able both to be constantly encouraging** (habitually performing as a paraclete; repeatedly exhorting; continually calling folks alongside to give them assistance or relief) **in the teaching that continues being sound and healthy, and to repeatedly put to the proof so as to convince by demonstration, or to refute by exposure of the test, the folks habitually speaking in opposition and contradicting.**

10. **You see, many folks, especially those from out of the Circumcision** (= the Jews), **are** (constantly exist being) **insubordinate ones** (not submitted to the arrangement; un-subjected to the order), **empty, vain and profitless talkers, even seducers of the intellect** (deceivers of the mind; people who mislead thinking),

11. **who it continues necessary to repeatedly muzzle** (gag; put something upon their mouth; or: reign them in), **who are habitually turning-back whole households** [i.e., into the Law cultus of Judaism] (or: = constantly upsetting entire families), **repeatedly teaching things which it is binding not to [teach]: a "grace" of ugly** (deformed; disgraceful) **profit, gain or advantage!**

12. **A certain one of them, their own prophet** (= poet), **said, "Cretans [are] always** (or: ever) **liars, worthless little wild animals** (little beasts of bad quality), **inactive and idle bellies** (= unemployed gluttons)." [cf Rev. 13:11-15]

13. **This witness** (or: testimony [of the poet Epimenides]) **is true** (genuine; real). **Because of which case and cause, be repeatedly cross-examining them abruptly while cutting away [at the case] and bringing the question to the proof, so as to test and decide the dispute and expose the matter – to the end that they can be sound and healthy within the midst of the Faithfulness, in union with the Trust and centered in that Loyalty,**

14. **not habitually holding to** (having [a propensity] toward; heeding and clinging in the direction toward) **Jewish myths** (or: fictions; or, possibly: oral traditions) **and to implanted goals** (impartations of a finished product within; inward directives; commands) **whose source and origin is people** (or: human commandments) **[thus] continually being twisted and turned away from the Truth** (or: reality).

15. **To the pure folks, everything [is] pure** (or: All things [are] clean for, with and in the clean ones). **Yet to** (or: for; in; with) **those having been stained and remaining defiled** (corrupted; polluted), **and to** (or: for; in; with) **faithless people** (those without trust; unbelieving ones who lack loyalty), **nothing is pure or clean – but rather, their mind, as well as the conscience, has been – and now remains – stained, defiled and corrupted.**

16. **They are repeatedly adopting the same terms of language, and habitually making confession and avowing to have perceived and now know God, yet they are constantly contradicting and denying** (repudiating; disowning; refusing) **[this] by the** (or: their) **works** (in the actions and things done), **continuing being detestable** (abominable), **incompliant** (stubborn; disobedient; unpersuasive) **and disqualified** (disapproved; rejected after trial) **with a view toward every good work** (excellent and virtuous activity).

CHAPTER 2

1. **You yourself, however, keep on speaking what things continue being fitting for, suitable in and proper to sound and healthy teaching.**

2. **Old** (or: Aged; Older) **men are to habitually be moderate and sober in the use of wine, serious** (grave; solemn; dignified; worthy of respect and honor), **sound of mind with a rational** (or: sane; sensible) **and wholesome way of thinking and attitude, being continuously sound and healthy in the Faith** (or: by trust; with loyalty; for confidence; to faithfulness), **in** (or: by; with) **the Love** (acceptance; urge toward unambiguous reunion), **in** (or: by; with) **the Remaining-under in support** (or: the persistent, patient endurance).

3. **Old** (or: Aged; Older) **women, similarly** (or: likewise), **[are to be] women in a state and resultant condition proper and fitting for being engaged in the sacred** (suitable in demeanor for serving the temple; or: = living a life appropriate [for] a person [being] a temple), **not folks who thrust-through or hurl [a weapon, or something hurtful] through [someone]** (or: not devils nor slanderous adversaries which bring division and hurt), **nor women having been enslaved by** (or: to) **much wine.**
[They are to be] teachers of beauty and of what is fine, excellent and ideal,

4. **to the end that they can** (or: may; would) **habitually bring the young women to their senses** (or: cause new [wives] to be sound-minded and with a healthy attitude) **to be habitually affectionate, friendly, loving and fond of passionately kissing their husbands [and] children,**

5. **ones sound of mind with a rational** (or: sane; sensible; clear headed) **and wholesome way of thinking and attitude, untouched so as to be undefiled and pure** (chaste), **women characterized by work at home or action from a house** (domestic; [other MSS: those with characteristics of a house-watcher/guardian]), **good** (virtuous; with qualities of excellence), **being women that are by habit supportively aligned to** (or: continue being humbly arranged for) **their own husbands, to the end that God's thought and idea** (God's Logos; God's Word; God's message) **cannot be constantly blasphemed** (abusively defamed; misrepresented; have its Light hindered).

6. **Similarly** (or: Likewise), **be repeatedly and habitually doing the work of a paraclete: calling the younger men alongside to give them relief or support, and to encourage them to be continuously sound in mind** (sane; sensible) **and to be keeping a wholesome attitude and way of thinking about everything –**

7. **[while] constantly holding yourself at [their] side, offering** (tendering; presenting; exhibiting) **yourself [as] a model** (example; pattern; an impression) **of beautiful actions** (fine deeds and ideal works), **[exhibiting] incorruptness** (absence of spoil or ruin; incapability of decay) **[and] seriousness** (gravity; dignity) [p32 & other MSS add: freedom from envy; willingness] **within the teaching** (centered in union with the instruction)**o:**

8. **[presenting] a healthful message** (a sound word; a thought or idea full of and promoting health)**: one without down-oriented knowledge and not bringing a downward experience, thus being unworthy of – and not containing any – condemnation** (or: uncensurable), **so that the person in the contrary and opposing position** (or: [acting] out of contrariness) **can** (may; would) **be turned back within himself** (or: be put to shame and be made to show reverence and regard), **continuing having nothing slight or mean** (cheap; paltry; ill; sorry; good-for-nothing; thoughtless) **to be saying about us.**

9. **[Encourage] slaves to habitually place themselves in subjection** (or: to be continually in humble alignment, supportively arranged under) **their own owners** (or: masters) **in all things – to be constantly well-pleasing and satisfying, not repeatedly speaking contrarily or refuting** (or: talking back), **nor embezzling** (secretly putting aside for oneself; pilfering),

10. **but to the contrary, habitually displaying all good faith** (every virtuous trust, faithfulness, confidence, loyalty and reliability), **so that they can progressively set** (or: arrange; order) **the teaching, which pertains to, and whose source and origin is, God, our Deliverer** (Savior; Rescuer; Restorer to health, wholeness and our original state of being; Safe-keeper), **into the System** (or: aggregate of humanity) **– in all things, within every area and among all people!**

11. **For God's saving grace**
(the salvation-imparting influence and boon of undeserved kindness, favor and goodwill whose source is God and which brings deliverance, rescue, restoration and health) **has been fully set in clear Light for all humans** (or: was fully manifested to all humanity; has been made to completely appear in all people; or: has additionally shined within all humans)

[other MSS: You see, the joyous favor of **God, a Savior for** (to; in) **all mankind,** has been fully displayed; or: So you see, the Grace, which is God, was made to suddenly appear {as} **a Savior for all humans**],

12. **progressively educating and training us so that, being people saying, "No," to** (or: refusing; renouncing; disowning; turning our backs on) **the irreverence** (lack of awe or pious fear; disrespect of and absence of duty to God) **and over-desires** (full-rushing passions) **pertaining to the System** (or: whose source is the world), **we can** (may; would) **live sensibly** (with clear-headed soundness of mind and wholesomeness of disposition and attitude) **and equitably** (fairly; justly; rightwisedly; relationally in a way which reflects the Way pointed out) **and reverently** (in devout goodness, awe and virtuous conduct, and with ease and well-being from relationship with God) **within the current age** (or: the present indefinite period of time, or eon),

13. **being folks continuously receiving with welcoming focus, and granting access and admittance to, the happy expectation – even the full manifestation** (the complete display in clear light) **of the glory of, from and which is, our great God and Deliverer** (or: Savior): **Jesus Christ,**

14. **Who gave** (or: gives) **Himself over us** (= over our situation; on our behalf), **to the end that He could loose and liberate us** (= set us free, as in releasing slaves by paying a ransom) **from all lawlessness** (or: every and all violation of law), **and then would cleanse and make pure in Himself** (for Himself; **by** Himself; **with Himself**) **a people being encircled around [Him], laid up as a super-abounding acquisition of property, zealous** (bubbling up; or: boiling hot; = extremely enthusiastic) **with regard to beautiful actions** (or: for ideal works; from fine deeds).

15. **Be constantly speaking these things, and habitually performing as a paraclete** (calling folks alongside to support, give relief and encourage them), **even be continuously putting [folks; situations] to the proof so as to convince by demonstration – or to refute by exposure of the test – with every complete disposition and full arrangement** (precise placing in aligned order; or: injunction).

Let no one surround you with his intellect, mind-set, opinion or attitude (= Don't let anyone frame your way of thinking).

CHAPTER 3

1. **Repeatedly bring folks under recollection, constantly causing them to think again and remember to be habitually placing themselves in subjection to** (or: to be supportively aligned with; be continually arranged under by) **governments** (or: rulers; sovereignties; originating headships) **– to** (or: by) **those having the right of authority – [and] to continuously comply in persuaded obedience, yielding to these authorities; to constantly be ready ones: facing and progressing toward every good work** (or: virtuous action);

2. **to be in the habit of speaking injuriously of** (blaspheming; slandering; defaming) **no one; to be folks who are non-contentious** (not disposed to fighting or quarreling), **gentle, lenient, considerate and suitably reasonable, constantly displaying all kindness and gentle tenderness while behaving agreeably toward everyone** (all mankind; all humanity).

3. **You see, we also were, ourselves, at one time people habitually being foolish, senseless and without understanding** (without perception or proper use of our minds) **– noncompliant and disobedient ones, folks being constantly caused to wander and being led astray** (or, as a middle voice: repeatedly deceiving ourselves; habitually going astray), **continuously being and performing as slaves to various** (a diversity of many kinds of) **full-rushing passions and pleasures** (enjoyments; gratifications), **habitually carrying ugly worthlessness** (bad quality or malice) **and envy** (or: jealousy) **throughout** (= leading a bad life): **detestable ones** (abhorrent folks) **continuously hating and detaching from one another.**

4. **Yet, when the beneficial usefulness in meeting needs and the affectionate friendship for mankind** (the fondness for, the liking of, and the love – as shown in kissing – for humanity) **of God** (or: from, characterizing, and which is, God), **our Deliverer** (Savior; Rescuer; Healer; Restorer), **was fully set in clear Light** (was made to completely appear; was fully manifested) –

5. **not from out of works [which arise from] within religious performance which we ourselves do** [= observances associated with the temple cultus, or codes of the old covenant]

(or: not forth from actions in union with an act of righteousness which we, ourselves, did; not in a relationship based upon our own performance; not deeds in a system of justice, equity and fairness which we, ourselves, constructed), **but to the contrary, down from and corresponding to His mercy, He delivered us** (or: He saves, rescues and restores us to the wholeness and health of our original condition) **through a bath of and from a birth-back-again** (or: [the] bathing of a regeneration; a washing which is a return-birth) **and a making back-up-new** (of a different kind and quality)**-again from a set-apart Breath-effect**

(or: of a renewal and renovation whose source is [the] Holy Spirit; or: a set-apart spirit's creating or birthing [us] back-up-new-again; a renewal which is a holy attitude) –

6. **which** (or: from which source) **He pours forth** (or: poured from out of) **upon us richly through Jesus Christ, our Deliverer** (Savior; Healer; Rescuer; Restorer; Safe-keeper),

7. **to the end that, being eschatologically delivered, rightwised, and set in right relationship in the Way of fairness and equity which has been pointed out** (or: = being set in covenant membership) **– by and in the grace and favor of That One – we can** (could; would; may) **come to be** (or: be made to exist being) **heirs** (possessors and enjoyers of the allotment), **corresponding to, in line with, and down from an expectation** (or: an expectant hope) **that comes from eonian life** (or: of life whose character, origin and realm is the Age [of the Messiah]; or: a life of unspecified duration which leads on into the ages; [the] life of and for the ages).

8. **The Idea** (The Logos; The Word; The Message; The Thought) **[is] full of faith** (or: faithful; trustworthy), **and I am continuing in intending** (determining; designing; or: wishing; wanting) **to progressively set you on thoroughly good footing** (to make you continue thoroughly stabilized and confidently insistent) **about** (or: concerning) **these things – to the end that those having put trust in God** (or: believed by God, now having faith in God and being loyal to God) **can habitually give careful thought and concern to constantly put themselves in the forefront** (or: to continually promote, maintain and stand themselves for the interests) **of beautiful deeds** (ideal works; fine actions). **These things continue being beautiful** (fine; ideal), **as well as augmenting a furtherance for humanity** (profitable to mankind; beneficial in people).

9. **Yet habitually set yourself at the periphery** (or: step around) **so as to avoid unintelligent** (stupid; foolish) **questionings** (or: seekings; investigations) **and genealogies** (studies into births or descents), **also strife** [other MSS: quarrels] **and fights** (contentions; conflicts; battles) **about Laws** (or: customs; or: = things related to the Torah), **for they are contrary to progress** (without benefit; unprofitable; regressive) **and ineffectual** (futile; vain).

10. **After one, and then a second, putting-into-the-mind** (= impartation; admonition) **of a person who chooses or promotes a sect or party** (or: of a factious person), **progressively decline yourself** (or: repeatedly excuse yourself),

11. **having seen and thus knowing that such a one has been and remains a person turned from out of the midst** (or: twisted inside-out; perverted) **and continues missing the target** (constantly fails to properly aim toward the goal; habitually errs; repeatedly makes a mistake), **being continually a person having made a decision corresponding to himself** (or: one separating himself down and out of line; or: self-condemned and sifted to his own level).

12. **Whenever I shall proceed sending Artemas or Tychicus toward you, urgently endeavor to come toward me in Nicopolis, for I have decided to spend the winter there.**

13. **With urgent endeavor and diligence, at once send on ahead Zenas, the expert in the Law** (or: the lawyer), **and Apollos, so that nothing may be lacking for them.**

14. **Now let our people** (our own folks) **be progressively learning how to habitually put themselves in the forefront** (to continually promote, maintain and stand themselves for the interests) **of beautiful actions** (fine deeds; ideal works) **[directed] into the indispensable needs** (or: wants of compressed necessity), **so that they may not exist being unfruitful ones.**

15. **All those with me continue embracing and greeting you. Greet and embrace our friends, in union with faith** (or: those who have devoted affection for us in trusting allegiance and loyalty). **Grace and favor [are] with all you folks! It is so** (Amen).

[written circa A.D. 57 – Based on the critical analysis of John A.T. Robinson]

PHILEMON

1. **Paul, a bound-one of Christ Jesus** (or: a prisoner pertaining to, because of and belonging to Christ Jesus), **and Timothy, the brother, to Philemon, the loved one, and our fellow worker,**
2. **and to Apphia, the sister, and to Archippus, our fellow soldier, and to the called-out community which corresponds to** (or: down in; = at) **your house:**

3. **Grace** (the influence and boon of undeserved favor, kindness, joy and goodwill) **and peace** (or: harmony from the joining; [= shalom]) **from God, our Father and Lord: Jesus Christ** (or: from our Father God, and [the] Owner, Jesus [the] Anointed One [= Messiah]).

4. **I always and progressively give thanks to** (or: for; with) **my God**
(or: experience gratitude in my God; express the ease of grace in my God; experience the happy fortune of abundant grace by my God; observe my God's competent and prosperous grace), **repeatedly forming a recollection of you upon my prayers**
(or: habitually making mention concerning you, upon my thinking and speaking toward having things go well, and projecting goodness, ease and well-being),
5. **constantly hearing of your love and faith** (or: of the acceptance and the loyal, trusting allegiance which is associated with you [and]) **which you are continuously holding** (or: having) **toward** [other MSS: {projected} into] **the Lord Jesus and unto all the set-apart folks,**
6. **so that the common existence, sharing, partnership, fellowship and participation of your faith, trust and loyalty can come to be inwardly operative** (may birth itself active, energized and effective) **within a full and accurate intimate and experiential knowledge and insight of every good thing** (or: of all virtue) **– of that within us** [other MSS: you] **[directed and leading] into Christ** (or: into the midst of [the] Anointing)!
7. **For you see, I have much joy and comfort** (relief; consolation; encouragement – the provision from a paraclete), **based upon your love and urge toward reunion, because the compassions** (tender affections of the very inner being; inward parts; intestines) **of the set-apart people** (the saints; the holy ones) **have been soothed and refreshed** (caused to rest again), **through you, brother** (= my fellow believer and Family member),
8. **through which** (or: on account of which), **continuing in having much boldness and freedom of speech inherent in citizenship within Christ to be repeatedly setting-on and fully arranging the thing** (or: the situation) **for you to be habitually coming back up to** (or: = to be proceeding in progressively laying out what is proper and fitting behavior for you)
9. **[and] because of this love and acceptance, I – being such a one as Paul, an old man, yet now also a bound-one** (or: prisoner) **of Christ Jesus – am rather now progressively calling [you] alongside to comfort, encourage and entreat** (or: appeal):

10. **I am now calling you to [my] side to encourage and entreat** (or: appeal to) **you about my child** (born-one), **whom I, myself, gave birth to within my bonds: Onesimus** (means: Useful),
11. **the one once useless** (unprofitable) **to and for you, yet now abundantly and easily useful and profitable to and for you as well as to and for me,**
12. **him whom I sent back again to you – this person exists being my inward parts** (tender affections and compassions; intestines; = he is a part of my very heart) **– you, yourself, reach toward, take in your arms, and receive hospitably;**
13. **[he] whom I, myself, had been intending** (or: would have liked) **to continue holding down** (to continue retaining) **to myself, so that over you** (or: on your behalf) **he could continue giving service to me, within the bonds of the message of goodness** (the ideal message of ease; the happy, beautiful and prospering tidings).
14. **Yet, apart from your opinion** (consent; the effect of your intimate, experiential knowledge), **I purposed to do nothing, to the end that your goodness** (virtue) **may and would not be as accords with necessity** (or: as along the lines of compulsion or the force of compression; thus: obligation), **but to the contrary, corresponding to what is from out of your being** (on the level of being spontaneous and voluntary).

15. **For perhaps** (possibly) **on account of this he was separated** (parted; dissociated; or, a euphemism?: = ran away?) **for an hour** (= for a brief time), **to the end that you could** (may; would) **for a lifetime** (age-lastingly; or: in the character of the Age [of the Messiah]) **fully have him** (or: continue receiving full benefits from holding him) –

16. **no longer as a slave, but in contrast, above** (over; = more than) **a slave: a dearly loved brother** (= fellow believer; = member of [His] family), **most of all** (especially) **by and to me, yet how much rather by and to you, both in [the] flesh** (= in person; or: = in the natural realm) **as well as within [the] Lord** [= in Christ or Yahweh]!

17. **Since** (or: If), **then, you continue holding** (having) **me a partner** (a fellow participant; a sharer; one equally belonging and in communion), **reach toward and receive him in your arms** (= take him as a partner), **as [you would]** (or: like) **me.**

18. **Now if he did you any wrong** (anything contrary to the Way pointed out; anything unfair or inequitable) **or continues indebted, charge this account to me.**

19. **I, Paul, write this** (= spell this out) **myself – with my own hand. I, myself, will proceed in paying it off.**

This is not to say that I am presently saying to you that you continue owing toward me even yourself!

20. **Yes, brother** (= fellow believer), **I, myself, might derive advantage** (receive benefit or profit; enjoy help, support and delight) **of you** (from you as a source) **– in [the] Lord! Soothe and refresh** (cause to rest again) **my tender affections** (inward parts; compassions; intestines) **within Christ** (in union with the Anointed One).

21. **Having confidence** (Having come to a settled persuasion) **in your submissive hearing, paying attention and obedience, I write to you – having seen and thus knowing that you will proceed in doing even above** (over; = more than) **the things which I now am saying.**

22. **Now at the same time, also proceed to prepare and set in readiness a guest quarter** (or: lodging) **for me, for I am increasingly expecting that – through the projected thoughts and words with a view to having things go well** (or: prayers) **from you folks – I will, from favor, proceed being graciously given to you people.**

23. **Epaphras, my fellow captive within Christ Jesus, continues embracing and greeting you,**

24. **[also] Mark, Aristarchus, Demas, [and] Luke, my fellow workers.**

25. **The grace** (the influence and boon of non-deserved favor, kindness, joy and goodwill) **of our Lord, Jesus Christ, [is] with the spirit of you folks. It is so**

> (or: The act producing joy and happiness, which was granted as a favor from our Owner, Jesus [the] Anointed One [= Messiah] [is] with your breath, and in accompany with your attitude. Count on it; Amen)!

[written circa A.D. 58 – Based on the critical analysis of John A.T. Robinson]

HEBREWS

1. **Long ago** (or: In the old days), **in many parts** (or: with fragments; by divided portions; = bit by bit) **and in** (or: with; by) **much-traveled ways consisting of many turns and directions, God, having spoken to** (or: in talking with; when discoursing by; making vocal utterances for) **the fathers – in** (in union with; centered in; = through; in [the words of]) **the prophets –**
2. **upon [the] last of these days spoke to** (or: speaks for and concerning; discourses in; makes conversation with) **us in a Son whom He placed** (or: sets) **[as; to be] Heir of all** (or: One who receives all humanity as an allotment; or: One who received everything as His allotted inheritance) **through Whom He also made the ages**
>   (or: forms and constructs the various designated periods of time [which compose existence, as well as God's influence and activities]; produces the life-times);
3. **Who, continuously being an effect of the radiance from**
>   (or: a result from a dawning and breaking forth of the bright light of the Day which is; a result of the outshining which is; an effulgence from; an effect of an off-shining [light]-beam belonging to; or: a result of a reflection of) **the Glory and Splendor as well as an exact impress** (or: exact likeness as from a stamp or a die; or: a carving) **of His substructure**
>   (or: of His substance [that is] standing under as a foundation; which is the underlying support of His outward form and properties; from His sub-placing; or: from His assumed groundwork of the full expression [of His idea]) **– besides continuously bearing** (or: and while progressively carrying; and then repeatedly bringing) **the whole** (all things; everything and all existence) **by the gush-effect which is His power**
>   (or: in the result of the flow from the power which is Him; or: with the saying pertaining to His ability; in the spoken declaration of, and which has the character of and its source in, His power and ability) **through and by means of Himself – in producing a cleansing of** (or: after making a ritual purification in regard to) **the failures** (the misses of the target; the mistakes and errors; or: a clearing by pruning which pertains to the sins) **He at once seated Himself within [the] right part** (or: hand; = in union with the receiving aspect, honored position and place of power) **of the Greatness centered and resident within high places.**

4. **Coming to be in a so much stronger and better** (or: Being born to a so much more excellent) **[station; position; calling; relationship] than agents** (or: messengers; or: folks who had a message), **He has come by inheritance to, and enjoys the allotment in, a so much different Name** (= designation) **which has been carried through the midst, beside them.**
5. **For you see, to a certain one of the agents He once said** (or: as an interrogative: in which one of the messengers – the folks having the message – did He once say?),
>   **"You are my son: I have given birth to you today!"** [Ps. 110:1; Acts 13:33]
And again,
>   **"I will continue being to and for him with a reference as** (or: for) **a Father, and he will continue being to and for Me with a reference as** (or: for) **a son."**
>   (or: "I will continually exist being in him, [proceeding] into a Father, and he himself will exist being in Me, [proceeding] into a son!) [2 Sam. 7:14; 1 Chron. 17:13]
6. **Now again, when He would bring** (or: But whenever He may again lead in) **the Firstborn into the civilized world that is being inhabited by housed people, He is saying,**
>   **"And so, let all God's agents** (or: people with the message) **give homage to Him** (or: worship and reverence Him; kiss toward and do obeisance to Him; = show respect and give honor to Him)." [Ps. 97:7b; note: Firstborn may = Israel, Ex. 4:22, entering Canaan]
7. **And then, on the one hand, to the agents** (messengers; folks with the message) **He is saying,**
>   **"He is the One making His agents** (messengers; folks with the message) **spirits** (or: Breath-effects), **and His public servants a flame of fire."** [Ps. 104:4]
>   [comment: this is an example of Hebrew parallelism – the second line being a restatement of the first, but in a different figure; the figure is a reference both to the

538

priests, as "public servants," and to the called-out community, figured as the lampstand in the Tabernacle in Rev. 1:20, and referencing Acts 2:3 – there being "tongues as if of fire" burning on the lamps in the one case, and upon the people in the second case; the agents speak a message of words that are "spirit," the effect of the Breath]

8. **Yet, on the other hand, to the Son**,

"God [is] Your throne, on into the age of the Age, and the scepter of straightness [is] a scepter of His kingdom and sovereign activity.
(variant rendering, with other MSS: "Your throne, O God, and the staff of uprightness, [is the] staff of Your reign, unto the chief time period of the Age.)

9. **"You love and urge toward union with** (fully give Yourself to) **fairness and equity in rightwised [covenant] relationships within the Way pointed out** (or: justice; righteousness) **and yet you hate and detach from lawlessness. Because of this, God – Your God – anointed You with olive oil of extreme joy, at the side of** (or: = more than; = rather than) **Your partners** (or: associates; fellows). [Ps. 45:6-7]

10. **And further**,

"O Lord [= Yahweh], **down from beginnings** (or: in accord with ruling [principles]; corresponding to controlling [patterns]; in line with initial starts), **You founded** (or: laid the foundations of) **the earth** (or: land), **and the works of Your hands are the heavens** (or: skies; atmospheres).

11. **"They shall progressively destroy themselves** (or: ruin, or lose, themselves) **– but You continue remaining throughout**.

12. **"And all people, as a garment, shall progressively be made** (or: grow) **old. Then like that which is thrown around [as a cloak], You will roll or wrap them up as a garment, and so they** (or: the same people) **will progressively be made another** (be altered; be changed; be transformed), **yet You are the same, and Your years will not fail."** [Ps. 102:25-28; cf Rev. 6:14]

13. **Now to a certain one** (or, as in vs. 5: Now in which one ...?) **of the agents** (or: folks with a message) **He once said**,

"Sit at (or: out of [the authority of]) **My right [hand; side] until I may place your foes** (or: hostile ones) **a footstool of your feet** (or: = turn your enemies into your footstool [= a supportive role])." [Ps. 110:1; cf Lu. 19:27; 20:17-19; Phil. 3:18; Rom. 11:28]

14. **Are not all people public-serving Breath-effects** (or: spirits; winds), **being sent forth unto attending service because of those folks being about to progressively inherit deliverance** (or: receive the allotment of salvation, health and wholeness)**?** [note: cf 1 Pet. 1:12]

CHAPTER 2

1. **Because of this, it is continuously necessary and binding for us to more earnestly** (or: exceedingly) **be continually holding to** (attending to; applying one's self to) **the things having been heard, lest we may flow** (or: glide; drift) **aside.**

2. **For you see, since the Word** (or: message) **spoken through agents** (or: messengers; folks with a message) **became firm, and every deviation** (or: side-stepping) **and imperfect hearing** (or: hearing amiss; or: disobedience) **received a fair discharge of wages,**

3. **how shall we proceed fleeing out** (or: escaping), **in not caring for** (or: neglecting) **so great a deliverance** (rescue; healing and restoration to health and wholeness), **which – after receiving a beginning** (or: a headship and place of ruling; a high estate; a principality [see Jude 6]) **to be repeatedly and progressively spoken [of] through the Lord** (or: by means of [Christ or Yahweh]) **– was made firm into us and was guaranteed as valid by those who heard,**

4. **God joining with added corroborating witness, both by signs and wonders and a full spectrum of** (or: various; multi-faceted) **powers and abilities, and by** (or: in) **divisions** (partings; distributions) **of set-apart Breath-effect** (or: of [the] Holy Spirit; from a sacred attitude), **corresponding to His willing [it] and exercising His purpose?**

5. **For, did He not align the impending habitable world – about which we continue speaking – under agents?**

(or: You see, not to messengers, or folks with a message, does He subject the habitually occupied house – the one [which is] about to be – concerning which we repeatedly speak.)

6. **Now a certain person, somewhere, made a solemn testimony** (or: gave proof through thorough evidence), **saying,**

"**What is a human, that You remember him? Or a son of man** (= the human being), **that You continually visit, inspect** (look observantly at), **help and look after him?**

7. "**You made him a brief time inferior, at the side of agents** (or: alongside folks with a message); **You crowned him with glory and honor** (or: You put a celebration and victor's wreath on him in a manifestation which called forth praise with a good reputation, and for value), **and then You set him down** (or: made him to stand; or: = appointed him) **upon the works** (or: actions) **of Your hands.**

8. "**You subjected all things** (or: You humbly align and arrange all humanity) **down under his feet, in order to support him.**" [Ps. 8:5-7]

For you see, in the [situation] to subject the whole (or: humbly align and arrange all [i.e., the entirety of creation]), **nothing is sent away not subjected** (or: supportively aligned) **by, to and in Him. Yet now we are not yet seeing or perceiving the whole** (or: everything; the all) **having been subjected in and to Him** (or: humbly aligned, placed or arranged under Him).

9. **But yet, we are continuously seeing Jesus – having been made inferior for a brief time beside agents – having been encompassed with glory** (or: crowned by a good reputation) **and with honor** (or: in value) **on account of** (or: through) **the effect of the experience of death**

(or: Now in this certain short bit of time, we keep on observing Jesus – having been made less because of the result of the suffering from, and which was, death – now having been encircled with the Victor's wreath in a manifestation which calls forth praise and with esteemed respect, at the side of the folks with the message), **so that by the grace of and from God** (or: for God's grace; in the favor which is God; [note: MSS 0243 & 1739, plus a Vulgate MS and in the works of Origen, Ambrose and Jerome and quoted by various writers down to the 11th century, the reading is: apart from God]) **He might taste of** (or: eat from) **death over [the situation and condition of] all mankind** (or: for and on behalf of everyone).

10. **You see, it was fitting for Him – on account of Whom [is] the collective whole** ([are] all things that exist) **and through Whom [is] the collective whole** ([are] all things that exist) **– in, when and by leading many sons** [note: a figure for all humanity] **into glory** (a good reputation), **to finish and perfect the Leader who first walked the Path of their deliverance**

(to bring to a complete state the Originator and Chief Agent of their rescue; to script the final scene for the Chief Conveyor of their restoration; to bring the Pioneering Bringer of their salvation to the destined goal) **through the effects of sufferings and results of experiences** [note, *paschō* means: to be affected by something - either good or bad; to feel, have sense experiences; thus, also: to suffer or undergo passion].

11. **For both the One separating and setting-apart and the ones being separated and set-apart [are] all out of One** (= spring forth from one Source). **On account of which cause** (or: motive) **He is not ashamed to be calling them brothers** (literally: from the same womb).

12. **saying,**

"**I will continue reporting Your Name** (= character and reputation) **to My brothers** (for My folks from the same womb); **in the midst** (within the middle) **of called-out communities and gathered assemblies I will sing praise songs.**" [Ps. 22:23]

13. **And again,**

"**I will continue being one having been convinced on Him.**" [Isa. 8:17, LXX]

And again [it continues],

"**Look and consider! [Here am] I, and the young children whom God** [= Yahweh] **gave** (or: gives) **to me!**" [Isa. 8:18]

14. **Since, then, the young children have participated in and commonly shared existence of blood and flesh** (= humanity), **He, nearly alongside as neighbor or lover, also partnered, took hold with, participated in, and shared theirs in common** (partook of the [ingredients] which comprise them), **in order that through means of death He might render useless** (or:

deactivate; idle-down; discard) **the one normally having the strength** (or: the person presently holding the force) **of death** (or: which is death; or: whose source is death), **that is, the adversary** (or: that which throws folks into dualism with divided thinking and perceptions; or: the one that throws something through the midst and casts division; the one who thrusts things through folks; the slanderer who accuses and deceives; or, commonly called: the "devil"),
15. **and would set them free** (or: could fully change and transform these; or: should move them away to another [situation; existence]): **as many as were through all of life held within slavery by fear of death** (or: in fear, from death: or: with fear, which is death)!
16. **For doubtless** (or: assuredly; I hardly need say) **it [i.e., fear of death] is not normally taking hold upon [the] messenger-agents** (or: folks with the message), **but even so it is repeatedly and progressively taking hold upon** (seizing) **Abraham's seed** (= descendants).
17. **Wherefore, He was indebted** (or: obliged) **to be assimilated by** (or: made like or similar to) **the brothers in accord with all things** (or: concerning everything; = in every respect; or: in correlation to all people), **so that He might become a merciful and a faithful** (or: loyal) **Chief Priest** (Leading, Ruling or Beginning Priest) **[in regard to] the things toward God, into the [situation] to be repeatedly and continuously overshadowing the failures** (mistakes; errors; misses of the target; sins) **of the People with a gentle, cleansing shelter and covering.**
18. **For you see, in what He has experienced Himself, having been tried in ordeals, He is able to run to the aid of those who cry for help – those being tried** (put through ordeals). [*cf* 13:5b-6, below; 1 Cor. 10:13; 2 Pet. 2:9]

CHAPTER 3

1. **Wherefore** (From which situation), **O set-apart and sacred brothers** (= consecrated fellow members from the same womb) **– common-holders** (partners; sharing possessors; joint-participants; associates; partaking members) **of an imposed-heavenly calling**
   (an invitation which comes from [the realm] upon the heavens; or, with *epi* as an intensifier: a calling of the complete and full heavens; or: a calling from the One [holding sway] upon the atmosphere) **– consider** (ponder; focus your thoughts down upon and think carefully about) **Jesus, the Sent-off Emissary** (or: Representative; [*cf* 1 Jn. 4:14]) **and Chief and Ruling Priest of our agreed message** (or: our like-reasoned idea; our saying of the same word; our unanimous consent and avowal; or: our binding association-agreement),
2. **[and His] continuously being faithful by and loyal to and in the One forming** (making; creating; constructing; establishing; producing; [in LXX the same word as Gen. 1:1]) **Him, even as "Moses [was loyal] within His** (or: his) **whole house."** [Num. 12:7]
3. **For this [reason] He** (or: You see, this One) **has been esteemed worthy of more glory and a greater reputation than Moses, proportionally to the degree that He who constructs** (or: prepares; fully implements) **it has more value** (honor; worth) **than the house itself.**
4. **For every house is constructed, prepared and fully implemented by someone, but the One constructing all humanity** (or: all [situations; circumstances]; = everything) **[is] God!**
5. **And so on the one hand, Moses [was] faithful and loyal in the midst of His** (or: centered in his) **whole house, as an attending therapeutic and medical care-provider** (or: trainer; cultivator; or: valet; squire; companion in arms) **– [which leads] unto a testimony** (or: witness) **of the things going to be spoken** (or: into evidence from those [future] sayings being said) **–**
6. **Yet on the other hand, Christ [is faithful and loyal] as a Son upon His house – whose** [*p*46, D* read: which] **house** (or: household) **we, ourselves, are** (or: continuously exist being)! **So if only** [Aleph, A, C, D and others add: , unto {the condition or state of} maturity (or: when to the point of completeness; until the goal is reached),] **we would fully hold in our possession, so as to retain firm and steadfast, the confident freedom of speaking and open boldness inherent in citizenship, as well as the result and effect of the boasting and exulting which [all] come from the expectation** (or: belonging to the expectant hope)!
7. **Therefore** (or: For this reason), **just as the set-apart Breath-effect continues saying** (or: On account of which, as in the same vein, the Holy Spirit is presently laying out the idea),
   "Today, if you folks could hear (or: can listen to; would pay attention to) **His voice,**
8.   **"you would not be hardening your hearts, as in the incitement to bitter feelings** (or:

the being exasperated and provoked; or: = the rebellion) **down from the day of putting to the proof by ordeals in the desert,**

9.   **"where your fathers made an attempt** (tested it), **within the putting to the proof, and yet saw My works** (actions; deeds) **[for] forty years,"**

10.   **"on account of which I was burdened by** (or: weighed down with grief for; heavy at heart with) **that generation, and said, 'They are always led astray** (caused to wander) **by** (or: in) **the heart; they do not personally or intimately know My ways.'**

11.   **"So I swore in** (in union with) **My inherent fervor** (native character; or: swelling passion and teeming desire; or: inward agitation and anger; or: disposition and impulse), **'Now since** (or: if) **they shall proceed entering into My rest** (or: the stopping down and rest which is Me, and which comes from Me) **...!'"** [Ps. 95:7-11]

12. **Exercise sight** (Be continuously observing), **brothers, [so] there shall not once be** (or: exist) **in any of you folks a bad, useless or misery-gushed heart** (a heart causing labor, sorrow or pain) **of unfaithfulness** (or: from disloyalty, disbelief or distrust; or: the source and character of which is an absence of faith and trust), **in withdrawing** (or: standing away and aloof; separating or revolting) **from the living God.**

13. **But rather, be habitually calling yourselves alongside – entreating, admonishing, encouraging, bringing relief and helping each other – daily, concerning** (or: in accord with) **each day, until** (or: as long as; during) **that which continues being called "Today"** [with A, C and other MSS: while you folks continue inviting this present Day,] **so that not any one from the midst of you folks may be hardened by a deception of failure** (or: in treachery from a miss of the target; with seduction of sin; by cunning in regard to error; by deceit relating to a mistake).

14. **For we have been born partners of the Christ** (or: we have come to be associates and participants who partake of the Anointed One and commonly hold the Anointing) **with the result that we are now in a binding partnership with Him, since surely we can fully hold in our possession – so as to retain firm and steadfast – the Origin of the substructure to the point of completion of the intended goal**

> (or: if indeed, unto [the condition or state of] maturity, we would fully hold in our possession, so as to retain firm and steadfast, the beginning [position] with regard to the substance, essential nature and basis [of the new reality] – as well as the rule of that [which was] put under, as a standing for support),

15. **in connection with it being repeatedly said,**

> **"Today, if you would hear** [active voice = hear and obey] **His voice** (or: in the thing being constantly said today, since you can listen to and obey His voice), **you would not be hardening your hearts, as in the incitement to bitter feelings** (= the rebellion)."
> [Ps. 95:7-8]

16. **For you see, certain folks, upon hearing, caused an incitement to bitter feelings** (= a rebellion). **However, in contrast, [it was] not all the folks that came forth from out of Egypt through Moses.**

17. **So now by** (or: with) **which ones was He burdened** (or: weighed down with grief; heavy at heart) **[for] forty years? [Was it] not by those sinning** (failing to hit the target; making mistakes and errors; [A reads: being without conviction, and thus, being disobedient])? **Of whom those members [of the body]** (the limbs; or: = carcasses) **fell in the desert** (or: wilderness)!

18. **Now to which folks did He swear to [that they were] not to enter into His rest, if not to the uncompliant ones** (the ones refusing to be convinced so as to obey; [p46 reads: the folks being disloyal and without faith and trust])?

19. **And so, we observe** (or: see) **that they did not have power or ability to enter because of a lack of faith and trust** (or: unfaithfulness; disloyalty; distrust).

CHAPTER 4

1. **With [the] announced promise to enter into His rest** (or; the ceasing which is Him) **continuing in being remaining left behind down on this level [for us] and fully left [open], we should, then, be at once caused to fear** (= take respectful care and be attentive), **lest at some point anyone from among you folks may be appearing** (or: seeming; or: being of the

opinion) **to have been behind** (to have come to be in the rear; or: to be deficient; or: = to have missed it)! [*cf* Greek fragment addition to Gospel of Thomas 2:4; the "reign" results in "rest"]

2. **For you see, we are people having been addressed with goodness** (or: being brought a message of ease and well-being), **even as those folks, also. But the Word** (or: message; thought; idea; Logos) **which they heard did not profit** (or: benefit) **those folks – [it] not having been mixed and blended together with faith, trust or loyalty in** (or: by; for; with) **those at that time hearing [it].**

> [with other MSS: – {they} not being folks that had been co-mingled by conviction and loyalty with those paying attention and listening.]

3. **For we, those at this point believing and trusting, are progressively entering into the rest** (or: the stopping). **Just as He has said,**

> **"As I swore in My inherent fervor** (impulse; inner agitation; anger; native disposition; or: passionate desire), **'Since** (or: If) **they shall proceed entering into My rest ...!',"**
> [Ps. 95:11]

although (or: and yet) **– with regard to the works** (actions; deeds) **– being born** (or: brought into existence; caused to happen or occur) **from [the] casting down** (laying of a foundation) **of an ordered system** (or: of [the] world; or: namely, of the works born from cosmic conception [from the usage of *katabolen* with *spermatos* in ch. 11:11]; thus: of works generated from conception of a world or of the aggregate of humanity).

4. **For He said in a certain place concerning the seventh, thus,**

> **"And God rested in the seventh day from all His works."** [Gen. 2:2]

5. **And yet in this, again,**

> **"Since** (or: If) **they shall proceed entering into My rest ...!"**

6. **Since, then, there continues being left remaining [for] some folks to enter into it, and those being formerly addressed with goodness** (or: being brought a message of ease and well-being) **did not enter because of a lack of being convinced** (or: incompliance; disobedience),

7. **again, He is determining** (or: He is again defining and setting bounds around) **a certain day, "Today!" In David He is saying, after so long a time, just as it has been said before,**

> **"Today, if you would hear His voice, you would not be hardening your hearts."**
> [Ps. 95:7-8]

8. **For you see, if Joshua caused them to rest, He would not after these things have continued speaking concerning another "Day."**

9. **Consequently, a keeping of a sabbath** (a state of rest) **is being left remaining for** (or: to; in; with) **God's people,**

10. **for the person entering into His rest also caused himself to rest from his own works** (actions; deeds), **just as God [did] from His own.**

11. **We should at once with diligence hasten, then, to enter into this rest** (or: that ceasing down [from work]; completely stopping), **so that one would not fall in the same example** (or: result of a pattern) **of incompliance** (or: stubbornness; disobedience; lack of conviction; [*p*46 reads: lack of faith and trust]).

12. **You see, the Word of God** (or: God's thought, idea and message; or: the expressed *Logos* from God; or: the Word which is God) **[is] living** (or: alive), **and active** (working; operative; energetic; at work; productive) **and more cutting above every two-mouthed sword, even passing through** (penetrating) **as far as a dividing** (or: parting; partitioning) **of soul and spirit** (or: of inner self-life/consciousness and breath-effect), **both of joints and marrows, even able to discern** (separate; judge; decide) **concerning thoughts** (ponderings; reflections; in-rushings; passions) **and intentions** (notions; purposes) **of a heart** (= core of the being).

13. **And no creature** (thing formed, framed or created) **is** (or: exists being) **out of sight** (not manifest; concealed) **in His** (or: in Its – i.e., the Word's) **presence, but all things [are] naked and have been gripped and bent back at the neck** [thus, exposing the face and throat] **to** (or: in; by) **His** (or: Its) **eyes, face to face with Whom** (or: Which) **in us** (or: to us; for us; with us) **[is] this Word** (or: with a view to Whom by us [is] the message and the account; or: toward whom, for us and among us, [comes] the Idea and the Reason).

14. **Continuously having, then, a great Chief Priest having passed through the atmospheres** (or: heavens) [note: a figure of the holy place, and the holy of holies, in the Tabernacle] – **Jesus, the Son of God** – **we can continuously be strong and lay hold of the same Word** (or: with regard to the agreement of thought, the like-reason, the same message).
15. **For you see, we do not have a chief priest who is unable or has no power to sympathize** (to have a sense-experience with; to feel a stab of sympathy or suffer together; *cf* ch. 2:10) **with our lack of strength, but One having been put to the proof – in accord with all things** (or: down with all humanity; corresponding to all people) **[and] in corresponding likeness [to us] – apart from failure** (mistake; error; sin; deviation; failing to hit the target).
16. **We should, then, be repeatedly and habitually coming to the throne of Grace** ([= mercy seat and place of Grace's authority]; or: the throne which is grace; the throne that is marked by grace and whose source is joyous favor) **with freedom in speaking and outspoken boldness as a citizen who has no fear of reprisal, so that we can at once receive and take mercy as well as grace and favor into a timely** (seasonable; well-suited) **response to a cry for help** [reading with B; or, with other MSS: receive mercy and then at once find grace and favor, unto opportune help (or: leading into help marked by a season of well-being; with a view to aid whose character is a good situation and a fertile moment of wellness)].

CHAPTER 5

1. **Now you see, every chief priest being taken forth from men, on behalf of men, is being placed down** (set and established) **in the things directed toward** (or: with a view to, pertaining to and facing) **God, so that he may be bringing both gifts and sacrifices over [situations of] and in behalf of failures** (mistakes; sins; errors; times of missing the target),
2. **constantly being able to measure feelings** (to deal gently; or: being moderate) **to habitually ignorant folks** (or: with people not normally having intimate, experiential knowledge [*gnosis*]) **and to people being constantly deceived, repeatedly led astray or habitually caused to wander, since he himself habitually environs** (has around himself) **lack of strength** (or: weakness),
3. **and so, on account of this, he is indebted** (obliged; or: he owes it) – **according as concerning the people, so also concerning himself – to offer** (bear something with a view to and directed) **concerning failures** (mistakes; sins; errors; times of shooting off-target).
4. **And no one takes the honor** (value; worth) **to himself, but rather [is] one being called** (summoned; invited) **by God, just as Aaron, also, [was].**
5. **Thus also, Christ did not glorify Himself** (give Himself a reputation; have an opinion of Himself) **to be born** (or: to come to be) **a Chief Priest, but to the contrary, [it was] the One at one point speaking to Him,**

> **"You are My Son; today I have given birth to** (or: conceived) **You** (= become Your Father)." [Ps. 2:7]

6. **Just as also in a different place He is saying,**

> **"You [are] a Priest on into the Age, down from** (or: in accord and in line with) **Melchizedek's station** (order; lineup; alignment; placement; appointment; succession)," [Ps. 110:4]

7. **Who, during the days of His flesh** (= existence as a human), **with a strong** (or: robust) **outcry and tears, offered both earnest requests** (supplications from need) **and petitions** (or: supplications; literally: olive branches carried by suppliants, which symbolized a request for help and protection) **toward the One being continually able and powerful to deliver** (rescue; save) **Him forth from out of the midst of death. And so He was being heard** (or: was being listened to), **from this discretion and precaution** (or: the disposition of taking hold well with prudent understanding; or: the receiving of goodness and well-being; or: [His] undertaking with care).
8. **Even though continuously being a Son, He learned to listen, pay attention and act on it** (or: the giving of the ear in hearing from below, and then to obey) **from the things which He experienced** (or: what happened to Him [both the good and the bad]).
9. **And being brought to the goal of [His] destiny** (being brought to maturity and completion; being finished and perfected) **He became a cause of eonian deliverance**

(or: rescue, wholeness and good health and restoration to the original state of being which pertains to and has the character of the Age; safety and healing of and for the ages) **for all** (or: in all) **those habitually listening, paying attention and acting in response** (or: the giving of the ear in hearing from below, with obedience) **to Him,**

10. **being at one time addressed and greeted in the public market place** (or: spoken toward; proclaimed) **by God** (or: under God), **"Chief Priest down from and corresponding to** (in accord with; in line with; in the succession of) **the station** (order; placement; appointment; arranging; alignment) **of Melchizedek"** – [Ps. 110:4]

11. **concerning Whom the Word [has] much to say to us – and [it is] difficult to be explained** (or: about whom the message [is] great and [is] hard to be understood [or] for us to say; or: concerning Whom, for us [there is] much to say – and [it is] hard to be understood), **since you have become sluggish** (dull) **for hearing.**

12. **For also, being indebted** (or: obligated) **to be teachers, because of the time [gone by], you again have a need of someone to be teaching you folks the elementary things** (or: fundamental principles; rudiments and rules) **of the beginning of the brief spoken words** (or: which are the principle of the short thoughts; concerning the Beginning, from the little messages) **of and from God, and so you have become folks having need of milk, and not solid food.**

13. **For everyone partaking** (sharing in) **milk [is] untried** (inexperienced) **pertaining to [the] Word of the Way pointed out** (from the message of fair and equitable dealing or an idea about rightwised relationships; also: = in regard to the idea of, and the reason derived from, covenant membership), **for he is a babe** (a non-speaking infant, or one who is still childish and unfit to bear weapons).

14. **But solid food belongs to perfected ones** (complete and mature ones; ones who are fully developed and have reached the goal of their destiny) **– those, because of habit, having organs of perception trained as in gymnastic exercise and thus being skilled, because of practice, and disciplined with a view to a discerning** (or: when facing the act of separating, making a distinction and then a decision about) **both good and evil** (both that which is excellent, ideal, of good quality, profitable and beautiful, as well as that which is of bad quality, worthless, ugly or of bad form; or: = between right and wrong),

CHAPTER 6

1. **through which [practice and exercise]** (or: On account of which), **in at some point leaving behind** (or: letting flow away) **the word from the beginning, in regard to the Christ** (or: the message pertaining to the origin of, and Beginning which is, the Christ; or: the primary thought about the Anointed One [= the Messiah]) **we can be continuously and progressively brought upon** (or: carried on [to]) **the realization of the end in view** (or: the accomplished goal of maturity; completion of the destined, finished product), **not again repeatedly conceiving** (or: laying; casting down; putting down) **a foundation which involves a change of mind with a turning away from dead works** (or: observances), **and of faith and trust upon God;**

2. **of teachings of immersions** (baptisms), **besides a placing-on of hands; and then of resurrection of dead ones – as well as of the results of an eonian decision** (or: the effects of an unspecified separation, or a judgment which pertains to and has the quality of an age)!

3. **And this we shall progressively do! – if it be that God may be permitting [it].**

4. **For you see, those once being enlightened, besides tasting** (= experiencing) **the imposed-heavenly gift** (or: the granted bounty from the One [holding sway] upon the atmosphere; the gift which has the character of the added-atmosphere) **and after being born** (or: coming to be) **common-holders** (partners; sharing possessors; joint-participants; associates; partaking members) **of set-apart spirit** (or: of a holy Breath-effect; or: of [the] Holy Spirit),

5. **and then tasting** (= experiencing) **a beautiful gush-effect of God** (or: an ideal result of the flow from God; or: God's fine speech; an excellent declaration pertaining to God; a profitable thing spoken, which is God) **– besides abilities and powers of an impending age,**

6. **and yet then falling by the side along the way, [are] powerless and unable to be repeatedly renewing again into a change of mind and state of consciousness: [they are]**

continuously suspending back up on a pole (or: crucifying) **again in, with, to, for and by themselves the Son of God, and [are] constantly exposing [Him] to public shame/disgrace.**
7. **For you see, a piece of land** (or: ground; soil; = a field; or: a territory) **which is drinking** (= soaking in) **the rain often coming upon it, and producing vegetation** (pasture; produce) **fit for and useful to them through whom it is habitually being cultivated, [is] also continuously sharing in and partaking of a blessing from God;**
8. **but when repeatedly and progressively bearing forth thorns and thistles [it is] disqualified** (worthless; unable to stand the test [for planting a new crop]) **and [is] close to** (or: near) **[the] curse** (or: a down-prayer and a corresponding wish against [the situation] is at hand), **the end** (the resultant situation) **of which [the thorns, briars, thistles and the field is] into [a time of] burning** (or: = the field ends up being burned off).

> [comment: this is a time-honored agricultural practice for preparing a field for planting a crop – the competition has been removed and the ground has been enriched by the ash]

9. **Yet we have been persuaded of more excellent things [than this] concerning you folks, beloved ones** (= dear, accepted friends) **– as well as things** (or: aspects; qualities) **normally clinging closely to** (or: holding in themselves from) **the sphere of wholeness, health, rescue, safety, deliverance and restoration – even though we keep on speaking in this way!**
10. **For the case is, God [is] not unjust** (contrary to fairness and equity shown in the Way pointed out) **to be at any point forgetful** (or: to fully escape the knowledge or be unaware; in any case to be completely neglectful, disregarding or unnoticing) **of your work and of the love** (fully giving of yourself) **which you pointed out and display into [showing forth] His Name: waiting upon and giving attending service and support of life's necessities to the set-apart** (or: sacred; holy) **folks – even continuously dispensing [goods] and habitually providing the means of living!**
11. **Now we are constantly setting our hearts and our full desires upon each of you to habitually display the same diligence** (or: earnestness; eagerness) **with a view to the bearing of the full measure of the expectation** (or: face to face with the full carrying of the expectant hope) **– until the closing act** (the goal; the end; the finished product; the completion),
12. **so that you may not be birthed** (or: come to be) **dull or lazy folks, but instead [be] imitators of those [who] through faith and long-breathing** (or: trust and long-enduring; loyalty and anger-shunned perseverance) **are normally and presently inheriting the promises** (or: one after another acquiring by lot and enjoying the added messages and announcements).
13. **For you see God – after at one point promising to Abraham – since He had, and continues to have, no greater in line with** (or: down into the sphere of; to the level of; according to; by; against) **which to swear, swore in line with** (down into; by; etc.) **Himself,**
14. **proceeding in saying,**

> **"Assuredly, continuously speaking goodness, ease and well-being** (or: blessing) **I will continuously speak goodness to** (or: bless) **you, then progressively multiplying I will progressively multiply and fill you."** [Gen. 22:17]

15. **And so, in this way enduring long** (breathing and blowing long with anger and emotion put far away) **he hit upon the target of** (= obtained) **the promises.**
16. **For you see, men are swearing by** (or: down on; according to) **the greater, and to** (or: for; with; among) **them the oath [is] an end** (limit; boundary; termination) **of all contradiction and dispute** (or: from talking-back in face-to-face opposition), **unto an established confirmation.**
17. **In [line with] which God – intending** (or: willing; purposing) **more abundantly to fully demonstrate to the heirs** (or: possessors) **of the promise the unchangeableness** (immutable position) **of His intent** (will; purpose) **– interposed** (mediated between two parties) **with an oath,**
18. **so that by two unchangeable transactions** (practice-effects) **in which [it is] impossible** (without power or ability) **[for] God to deceive** (to lie or be false), **we – those fleeing to refuge – may be constantly having** (holding; possessing) **strong consolation** (a calling alongside with relief, aid and encouragement; services of the Paraclete) **to be strong to get into one's power the prescribed and settled expectation** (or: expectant hope) **continuously lying before [us],**
19. **which we continuously have** (hold; possess) **as an anchor of and pertaining to the soul** (or: from the inner life and being), **both secure from falling and established** (firm; steadfast; =

on sure footing), **even habitually entering into the interior** (or: then progressively going fully into the inner part) **with reference to the veil** (= entering into the interior [behind] the curtain) 20. **where a Forerunner** (= spy or scout), **Jesus, entered over us** (or: on our behalf; over our [situation]), **down from** (or: in accord with; in the line of [succession of]) **the station** (order; placement) **of Melchizedek, being born** (or: coming to be) **a Chief** (or: Ranking) **Priest on into the midst of the Age** (or: [proceeding] unto the Age [of Messiah]).

CHAPTER 7

1. **For you see, this Melchizedek, a King of Salem, a Priest of the Most High God** (or: from God Most High) **– the One meeting with Abraham, [who was] returning from the cutting down** (or: smiting) **of the kings, and was speaking words of well-being to** (or: blessing) **him,** 2. **to whom also Abraham divided a tenth of all – being first, indeed, translated "King of the Way pointed out"** (King of fairness and equity; King of Justice and Righteousness; King of Rightwised Relationships; also: = King of covenant living) **and then also** (or: afterwards) **"King of Salem," which is "King of Peace and of Harmony from the Joining."** 3. **[Being] without father, without mother, without a genealogy, having neither a beginning of days nor an end of life, yet being made a likeness from** (or: being portrayed or pictured like) **the Son of God, he continuously remains a priest to the whole length** (extended or stretched into the unbroken continuance) **[of time].** 4. **Now continuously be gazing as a spectator: How eminent and distinguished [is] this one! – to Whom even the patriarch Abraham gave a tenth out of the topmost part of the heap** [= the spoils of war]. 5. **And later, on the one hand, those out of the sons of Levi, in taking the office of a priest, hold** (or: possess) **an implanted goal** (impartation of the finished product and destiny within; inward directive), **down from and in accord with the Law, to be receiving tithes from the people, that is, their brothers, even those having come out of the loins of Abraham.** 6. **Yet on the other hand, he** (or: the one the man), **being not of their genealogy, caused Abraham to pay tithes and has spoken goodness and well-being to** (or: blessed) **the one holding** (or: possessing) **the Promise.** 7. **Now without all contradiction** (or: apart from every dispute), **the inferior is being blessed by the superior** (stronger and better; = more important). 8. **And so here** (in this place), **in the one case dying-away** (rotting; withering) **men are receiving** (or: taking) **tithes; and yet there in the other case, it is being witnessed and attested that he continuously lives** (or: He constantly lives and is alive)! 9. **And thus even Levi, receiving tithes, has – if I may say it this way** (or: = as it could be said) **– been tithed** (or: = regarded as part of that tithe) **through Abraham.** 10. **For you see, he was still existing** (or: he continued yet being) **in the loins of the Father** (or: this forefather) **when Melchizedek met with him.**

11. **If indeed, then, attainment of the goal** (or: completion; perfection; maturity; the finished product and destiny) **was, and continued being, through the Levitical priesthood – for based upon it the people have been placed under Law** [= Torah] **and set in a custom – what need [is there] still [for] a different [kind or line of] priest to be raising Himself up, down from** (in accord with and in the line of succession of) **the station** (order; placement; appointment) **of Melchizedek, and not normally said to be down from** (in accord with and in the line of succession of) **the station** (order) **of Aaron?** 12. **For it follows that with the priesthood being presently place-changed** (or: progressively after-placed and transferred), **out of necessity** (or: compulsion) **even a change of law** [= Torah] **is being born** (or: also an after-placement transference of custom is coming into existence). 13. **For you see, He, of** (or: upon) **Whom these things are now being said, has chosen to take hold with and now actively share in** (or: has co-possessed and partaken of so as to have joint-participation and membership in) **a different tribe, from which no one has attended** (given heed to; held [something] toward) **to** (by; in; for) **the altar** (= participated in sacrificial duties). 14. **Now you see [it was] previously clearly visible and obvious that our Lord has risen from out of Judah, into which tribe Moses spoke nothing concerning a priesthood.**

15. **And so it is still superabundantly more clearly visible and evident if a different Priest is rising up according to** (or: down from; in the line of succession of) **Melchizedek's likeness,**
16. **Who has not been born** (brought into existence) **down in accord with a law of a fleshly implanted goal** (in line with an impartation of a finished [human] product and destiny within; or: in correspondence to a custom of a fleshly injunction; = following the pattern of a human directive), **but to the contrary, according to and on the basis of a power and ability of an indissoluble life** (a life not subject to destruction).
17. **For He is continuously witnessing** [other MSS: it continues being attested],
>   **"You [are] a Priest on into the midst of the Age, according to** (down from) **the station** (order; placement; arranging; succession) **of Melchizedek."** [Ps. 110:4]

18. **For on the one hand, a displacement** (or: setting-aside; annulment; repudiation; cancellation; abrogation) **of a preceding implanted goal** (impartation of the finished product and destiny within; inward directive) **is being born** (or: comes into existence) **because it [was] without strength and without increase** (without help, profit, benefit or gain) – [cf Rom. 8:3]
19. **you see, the Law perfects nothing** (brought nothing to its goal or destiny; finishes nothing) **– yet on the other hand [this is] a fully leading-in** (or: a bringing-in upon; an introduction; [note: according to Thayer, this was used in Josephus of the introduction of a new wife in place of one repudiated]) **of a superior** (stronger and better) **expectation** (or: expectant hope) **through which we are progressively drawing near to be at hand for, to, in, by and with, God.**
20. **Also, to the extent that [it was] not without a swearing of an oath,**
21. **for on the one hand there are indeed men that have become priests apart from a sworn oath, yet on the other hand, He [became one] with an oath sworn through, and by means of, the One saying to Him,**
>   **"The Lord [= Yahweh] swore** (or: swears) **and shall not be regretting** (having after-care), **'You are a Priest on into the Age** [other MSS add: according to and in line with the order and succession of Melchizedek]'."** [Ps. 110:4]

22. **Correspondingly, to that extent also, Jesus has become, and is, a guarantee** (pledge; surety; sponsor) **of a superior** (stronger and better) **arrangement** (or: covenant; disposition).
23. **Furthermore, indeed, many are the folks having become priests, [in succession] – because of [predecessors], one after another, being cut off** (thus: hindered) **by death from continuing in abiding near** (remaining at the side),
24. **but He, on account of His continuously remaining on into the Age** (or: unto the indefinite life-time [of the Messiah]) **constantly holds** (continuously possesses), **[as being] unable-to-be-walked-along** (or: not-going-aside; or: not transient; or: inviolate), **the priesthood.** [cf Rev. 1:18]
25. **Consequently He is also continuously able and powerful to be constantly delivering** (continuously setting-free, restoring to health and making whole) **– unto the finishing of all** (unto the completed goal of everything; into the midst of the all-perfection; unto the end of all; into the final act and destiny of all) **– those folks habitually approaching God through Him [Who is] always living to be repeatedly effecting encounters over them and to hit the internal target.**
26. **For you see, a Chief Priest such as this One was, and continues to be, fitting** (appropriate; proper) **for us: loyal and dedicated, benign** (without bad quality; harmless; without bad form; not ugly), **unstained** (undefiled), **having been parted** (severed; separated) **away from those failing to hit the target** (those deviating or making errors; the sinners), **even being birthed** (coming into existence) **higher than the atmospheres and heavens,**
27. **Who is not having daily necessity, just as the chief priests, to repeatedly offer up sacrifices over their own failures** (errors; sins) **before, and after that, those of the people. For this He performed just once and once for all [times and people], offering up Himself** [other MSS: bringing Himself toward {God, or, us} (or: **presenting Himself**); cf 9:25-28].

28. **You see, the Law** (or: custom) **is continually placing** (setting down) **people having weakness** (want of strength) **[as] chief priests. But the word pertaining to the sworn oath** (or: which was the act of taking an oath) **[which came] after the Law [appoints] a Son [Who is] One having been finished, perfected, brought to the goal, and is now complete, being made the final act, [leading] unto** (or: on into; into the midst of) **the Age [of the Messiah]!**

CHAPTER 8

1. **Now as a summary and main point, added to the things being presently said** (or: the head [topic] of the discussion)**: we continue having such a Chief and Ruling Priest, Who sat down** (or: is settled in the sphere) **at the right of the Throne of the Greatness** (or: in union with the place of power in Majesty's seat of authority) **within the midst of the atmospheres** (or: in union with and participating in the heavens; = the realm of receiving and rule over the earth) –

2. **a Public Servant** [note: this word referred to a property owner performing public service at His own expense] **of the set-apart folks** (of the holy ones; or: of the holy things; or: of the Holies; from the sacred places) – **even** (or: and) **of the true and real Tabernacle** (or: tent; = God's home among His people) **which the Lord** [= Yahweh] **pitched, not man** (or: people; humanity). [9:24, below; *cf* Rev. 21:3]

3. **Now you see, every chief priest is being placed** (or: set down; or: = appointed) **into the [situation; job] to be repeatedly offering both gifts and sacrifices. In consequence or consideration of this [it seems] necessary for this One to continue having something which He may, or can at some point, offer** (bear toward [the goal]).

4. **Indeed therefore, if He were upon earth, He would not even have been a priest, there constantly being those folks who keep on offering the gifts according to the Law** (or: in line with custom, or [Torah]),

5. **who are constantly rendering service for** (or: in) **an example** (underlying copy; the effect of something shown from under) **and by** (or: in; with) **a shadow of the fully heavenly people**
(or: of the heavenly-imposed folks; or: of the things pertaining to completely heavenly places and things; or: of things or situations from the One [resident] upon the atmosphere), **just as Moses had been managed** (or: instructed), **being about to finish**
(complete; perfect) **the Tabernacle. For He continues to bring to light by declaration,**
"Continue to observe so as to see that you make (or: construct) **all things down from and in accord with the pattern** (the type; the impress made by a strike; the mark of the wound inflicted) **shown to you** (presented to your sight) **on** (or: in; in the midst of) **the mountain."** [Ex. 25:40]

6. **But now He has hit the mark of a thoroughly carried-through public service, even by as much as He continues being a Medium** (an agency; an intervening substance; a middle state; one in a middle position; a go-between; an umpire; a Mediator) **of a superior** (stronger and better) **arrangement** (covenant; settlement; disposition) **which has been instituted** (set by custom; legally [= by/as Torah] established) **upon superior** (stronger and better) **promises!**

7. **For if that first one was being unblamable** (without ground for faultfinding; beyond criticism; satisfying), **a place of a second one would not have continued to be sought** (looked for).

8. **For continuously blaming** (finding fault and being dissatisfied with) **them, He is saying,**
"'Consider! Days are progressively coming,' says the Lord [=Yahweh], **'and I shall progressively bring an end together** (a conclusion of its destiny; or: a joint-goal) **upon the house of Israel and upon the house of Judah with a new arrangement** (a different covenant; an innovative disposition),

9. **"'not down from nor in accord with the arrangement** (covenant) **which I made with their fathers, in a day of My taking hold upon their hand to lead them out of the land of Egypt, because they did not remain** (abide; dwell) **in My arrangement** (covenant) **and, for my part, I paid no attention to and gave no care for** (or: was unconcerned about; neglected) **them,' says the Lord** [= Yahweh].

10. **"'Because this is the arrangement** (covenant; disposition) **which I shall continue arranging for the house of Israel, after those days,' says the Lord: 'progressively giving My Laws into their thought** (into that which goes through their mind; into their perception and comprehension), **and I shall progressively imprint them** (write or inscribe marks) **upon their hearts, and I shall continue being in and among them** ([in relation] to them; for them), **into** [the position of] **a God, and they shall continue being** (exist being) **in Me** ([in relation] to Me; for Me), **into** [the position of] **a people.**

11. **"'And they may by no means teach each one his fellow-citizen, and each one his brother, saying, "Know the Lord** (or: You must be intimate with [Yahweh])**," because everyone** (all) **shall progressively perceive and thus understand and be acquainted with Me, from a little one even to a large one of them,**

12. **"'because I shall continue being** (existing) **merciful with a cleansing covering for their injustices** (behaviors contrary to the Way pointed out; inequities) **and acts of lawlessness, and then I would by no means be reminded further of their mistakes and failures** (errors and falling short of the target; sins)**.'"** [Jer. 31:30-33]

13. **In thus to be saying "new: different in kind and quality," He has made the first** (or: former) **"old," and that [which is] progressively growing old** (or: obsolete) **and decrepit** (failing of age; ageing into decay), **[is] near its disappearing** (vanishing away). [cf 2 Cor. 3:7-13]

CHAPTER 9

1. **The first, indeed then, also continued having effects of rites and products of the way then pointed out** (= ordinances and regulations for the right way to do things) **in respect to worship and sacred service, besides the set-apart** (or: holy) **place pertaining to that system** (suited to that ordered arrangement),

2. **for a tabernacle was furnished** (equipped, prepared), **the first [part; compartment] – in which [was] both the lampstand and the table, even the setting forth of the breads, as well as the golden censer-altar** [reading with B: Vat. MS #1209, & Sahidic witnesses] **– which is being called set-apart** (a holy place; [the] Holy Place; a separated place).

3. **But after the second veil, a tabernacle being called the set-apart of the set-apart ones** (the Holy of Holies; the separated one of the separated ones; = the most set-apart),

4. **having the ark of the arrangement** (or: chest pertaining to the covenant), **having been covered round about by gold, in which [was] a golden pot** (or: urn) **continuously holding** (or: having) **the manna, and Aaron's rod – the one sprouting** (budding) **– and the tablets of the arrangement** (disposition; covenant),

5. **but up above her** [i.e., the ark] **[are] cherubim, which have the character and quality of and express [the] glory, continuously overshadowing the mercy seat** (the place of gentleness and graciousness), **concerning which things** (or: ones) **there is now nothing to be saying corresponding to [that] part** (or: down from, or in accord with, a part; = in detail).

6. **But of these things, having been thus prepared** (equipped; furnished; constructed), **the priests, indeed, habitually entering into the first tabernacle** [i.e., compartment], **are repeatedly completing** (ending upon; fully finishing) **the sacred service,**

7. **yet into the second one** [i.e., compartment], **the chief priest alone** (or: only), **once a year, not apart from blood – which he is offering over** (or: on behalf of) **the effects of ignorance** (things resulting from a lack of knowledge or insight) **of himself and of the people –**

8. **the set-apart Breath-effect** (or: Holy Spirit) **making this clearly visible: the Way** (Path; Road) **of the set-apart places** (or: of the separated ones; pertaining to the sacred folks; of the Holies) **[was] not yet to have been manifested** (caused to appear; brought to light) **while the first tabernacle is having a standing –**

9. **which is a parable, [pointing] unto the present season** (or: the fertile moment and situation having been placed within the midst and which is now here) **– in accord with which [parable] both gifts and sacrifices are continually being offered, [though] not being able** (or: not having power) **to perfect** (complete; bring to the goal and destiny; finish; mature), **in regard to conscience and shared consciousness, those repeatedly doing the sacred service,**

10. **[relying] only upon foods and drinks and various immersions** (baptisms; ceremonial washings), **as well as rites and products of the way then pointed out** (or: applications of fairness and equity) **pertaining to the flesh** (or: = [the] flesh's [religious] ordinances and external regulations of justice; or: = the system of human works), **continuously lying upon them** (thus: pressing upon them; = being imposed by them) **until a fitting situation** (or: season; fertile moment) **of raising-up-through** (or: thoroughly raising upright and making straight).

11. **So Christ** ([the] Anointed One; [Messiah]), **after suddenly coming to be present at [our] side [as] a Chief** (or: Ruling; Ranking) **Priest of the good things happening** (or: of virtuous people being birthed; [with other MSS: pertaining to impending excellent things]), **by means of the greater and more perfect** (more matured, complete and destined) **Tabernacle not made by hands – that is, not of this creation – and not by means of blood from he-goats and calves, but by means of and through His own blood** [cf 6:19-20; 8:2, above; 2 Cor. 4:18-5:10]

12. **entered in at once, and once for all [times and people], into the midst of the set-apart ones** (or: the holy places), **at once finding in Himself an unbinding** (a loosening for release; redemption) **proper to, belonging to and having its origin in the Age [of the Messiah]** (or: eonian, or age-lasting, liberation). [note: this passage refers to the Day of Atonement; Lev. 16]

13. **For you see, since the blood of bulls and of he-goats, as well as ashes of a heifer repeatedly sprinkling the folks having become defiled** (made common or ceremonially unclean), **is continually making [a person] set-apart** (or: making holy and sacred) **with a view to and leading toward the cleanness of the flesh** (= the physical body or human relationships),

14. **to how much greater an extent shall the blood of the Christ** (Anointed One; [Messiah]) **– Who through means of a spirit** (or: attitude; [the] Breath-effect) **pertaining to the Age offers Himself** (or: brought Himself face to face and offers Himself) **without blemish by and with God** (or: in, to and for God) **– continue cleansing and pruning your conscience and shared consciousness from works of death** (or: dead procedures and activities; deeds of dead folks) **[leading] into [the situation] to be continuously rendering sacred service, as well as habitually doing the business and duties of life, for, in, by, to and with the living, as well as true and real, God?**

15. **And now because of this, He continues being a Medium** (an Agency; an Intervening Substance; a middle state; One in a middle position; a go-between; an Umpire; a Mediator) **of and from a New and Different Arrangement** (an innovative disposition and covenant that is new in kind, quality and character) **so that, pertaining to a death occurring** (or: from a death having happened) **[which leads] into an unbinding-away of, and a release from, the steppings-to-the-side [that were] based upon the first arrangement,**

> (or: in order that by birthing Himself from death into the midst of a redeeming [of people], emancipating [them] from the deviations [that came] upon the first disposition;
> or: so that at one point coming into existence from death [and] on into the center of a liberation from transgressions [that were founded] upon the former covenant,) **the people having been called and now remaining invited can at some point take hold of** (or: may seize into possession; or: would suddenly receive) **the Promise of the inheritance pertaining to and having the qualities of the Age [of Messiah]** (or: the eonian possession and enjoyment of the allotment; or: the inheritance of, from and for, the ages). [cf Rom. 3:24-25]

16. **For you see, where [there is] an arrangement** (or: covenant; also: a will; a settlement), **a necessity to be brought [is] the death of the one arranging** (or: making the will; covenanting),

17. **for an arrangement** (a will; a covenant) **based upon dead folks [is] firm** (fixed; guaranteed as valid), **since it is never** (not once) [other MSS: not then] **strong** (or: in force) **at the time when the one making the arrangement** (or: covenant; will) **is alive** (or: continues living).

18. **Consequently, not even the first** (or: former) **has been initiated** (innovated; inaugurated; or: dedicated) **apart from blood, [signifying a death].**

19. **For every implanted goal** (impartation of the finished product within; inner destiny; inward directive) **down from the Law was spoken by** (and: under) **Moses to and for all the People, taking the blood of calves and he-goats, with water, scarlet wool and hyssop, he sprinkled both the scroll and all the People,**

20. **saying,**

> **"This is the blood of the arrangement** (covenant; disposition) **which God imparted as the goal to you** (or: directed as the end and destiny in mind, with a view to you folks; implanted as a purposed aim, face-to-face with you people)." [Ex. 24:8]

21. **Furthermore, in like manner he sprinkled the Tabernacle, and even all the vessels of the public service, with blood.**

22. **And so, down from and in accord with the Law, nearly everything is being cleansed in** (or: in union with) **blood, and apart from blood-shedding a sending-away** (or: a causing to

flow off; an abandoning or a divorce; or: forgiveness) **is not coming into existence** (is not being birthed; does not occur).

23. **Indeed, then, [it was] a necessity for the under-exhibits** (examples; copies; effects of suggestive signs) **of the things within the atmospheres and heavens to be cleansed by these [means], yet the very imposed heavenly things** (or: the things [situated] upon the atmospheres) **themselves by superior** (stronger and better) **sacrifices besides these.**

24. **For Christ did not enter into set-apart places made by hands** (= by humans) – **representations** (things formed after a pattern) **of the true and real things – but rather into the atmosphere and heaven itself, now to be manifested** (exhibited to view; caused to appear in clear light; made apparent) **by the presence of God over us** (or: in God's face and countenance [being] on our behalf).

25. **Nor yet [is it] that many times He would be repeatedly offering Himself, even as the chief priest is repeatedly entering into the set-apart** (or: holy) **places yearly in blood belonging to another,**

26. **otherwise** (or: in that case) **it was continually binding Him to experience [it]** (or: to suffer; to have sense-experiences and to feel) **many times from the founding of the organized System of [their] religion and culture** (or: the casting down of the world or universe). **Yet now** (at this time), **once, upon a conjunction** (a joined destiny; a bringing of [two] ends together ["denoting the joining of two age-times" – E.W. Bullinger]) **of the ages, He has been and remains manifested** (has been brought to light and continues visible) **into a displacement of the failure** (from the error, sin and deviation from the target) **through the sacrifice of Himself** (or: through His sacrifice; or: by means of the sacrificial altar-offering which was Himself). [*cf* Rom. 6:9-10]

27. **And now, according to as much as it continues lying-away** (or: laid away; reserved-off; stored) **in** (or: with; for; to) **mankind** (or: people) **to die-away once, but after this a process of evaluating** (a separating and making a distinction to be a judging and determining; a deciding),

28. **so also, the Christ – being once borne** (or: carried) **close into the many** (or: being offered once unto and for the many) **to carry failures** (errors; sins; mistakes; deviations; misses of the target) **back up again – will continue being made visible** (or: will be progressively seen) **forth from out of the midst of the second [place** (*cf* 9:3, 7 & 10:9; {comment: = the holy of holies})] – **apart from failure** (apart from sin; apart from a sin offering; apart from error in attempting to hit the target) **– in those** (or: by those; to those; for those) **habitually receiving** (or: progressively taking) **from out of the midst of Him, [progressing] into a deliverance** (or: [leading] into a rescue; with a view to health and wholeness; into the midst of salvation).

> [note: the Greek word translated "receiving from out of the midst of" is *apekdechomai*, which is *dechomai*, which means "to take and receive with the hands," with the preposition *apek-*, a contraction of *apo*, "from," and *ek*, "out of the midst of" added as a prefix. This verb should not be translated "looking for," or "awaiting"]

CHAPTER 10

1. **You see, the Law** (= Torah), **holding a shadow of** (having shade from) **the impending good things** (virtues; excellent, agreeable or useful qualities or results) **– not the very image of or the same reproduced likeness from those transactions** (results of executing or performing; effects of practices) **– continues not even once able** (or: still never has power) **at any point to perfect** (bring to the goal and destiny, finish, complete or mature) **those folks repeatedly coming near** (approaching) **by offering the** [other MSS: their] **same sacrifices every year, on into the whole length** (or: extended or stretched into the unbroken continuance) **[of its existence].** [Col. 2:17]

2. **Otherwise would they not cease being habitually offered? Because those constantly serving, upon having once for all been cleansed, would not still continue to have even one consciousness about sins** (or: awareness of failures, mistakes or errors).

3. **But in contrast, in these folks [there is] yearly** (or: year by year) **a remembrance of sins** (a recollection of failures and falling short of the goal).

4. **For you see, blood from bulls and from he-goats [is] without ability [and is] powerless to be periodically carrying away sins** (or: lifting failures from; taking off misses of the target).

5. **Wherefore** (or: Because of which), **repeatedly** (habitually; continually; periodically; or: presently) **coming into the System** (or: entering the cosmos and the world of religion, culture, secular society and government) **He is saying,**

> **"You did not will** (purpose; intend) **sacrifice and offering, but You completely equipped** (thoroughly adjusted down, put in order, knit together) **in and for Yourself a body for and in Me.**

6. **"And the results and effects of whole burnt offerings about sin** (concerning failure to hit the target) **You do not think well of** (or: have a good opinion about).

7. **"Then I said, 'Consider! I am arriving to do** (make; form; create; produce; perform) **Your will** (purpose; intent; resolve), **O God!' – in a little head of a scroll** (a summary of a little scroll), **it has been written concerning Me.'"** [Ps. 40:6-8]

8. **Up above, in saying that ,"You do not will** (purpose, intend), **neither think well of** (or: approve), **sacrifice and offering and the result and effect of whole burnt-offerings, even concerning sin** (failure; error) **[offerings]"** – **which things, down from and in accord with Law and custom, continue being repeatedly offered –**

9. **He then said, "Consider! I am arriving to do** (form; make; create) **Your will** (purpose; intent; resolve), **O God!"** – **He is habitually** (or: progressively; or: presently) **taking back up the first, so that He could make the second** [cf. ch. 9:28] **to stand** (or: that He may place and establish the second) –

10. **within which will** (or: in union with which intent and purpose; [note: expressed in vss.7-9, above]), **we are folks having been made set-apart ones** (sanctified folks; sacred and holy people) **through the offering of the body of Jesus Christ once for all.**

11. **And so, indeed on the one hand, every priest has stood daily, publicly serving and offering the same sacrifices many times** (or: often) – **which things not even once** (never) **are able or have power to take away sins** (failures; errors) **which surround** (which envelop) **[us].**

12. **Yet on the other hand this One, after at one point offering one sacrifice – stretched for the whole length – over [the situation of] sins** (or: on behalf of failures and errors), **sat within the right [part or side] of God** (or: at the right [hand] of God; centered in God's [place of power, honor and acceptance]) **on into the whole length** (or: extended into the unbroken continuance),

13. **continuously, one after another, taking hold with the hand to embrace and welcome from out of the rest** (the remaining and leftover) **until the hated ones that belong to Him** (His enemies; the ruiners that He has; folks who are hostile in relation to Him) **can be placed [as] a footstool of His feet** (= would be set in a humble and supportive position in relation to His body).

14. **For you see, by and in one offering He has perfected** (brought to the goal; matured; completed; finished; brought to their purposed destiny) – **on into the whole length** (or: extended or stretched into the unbroken continuance) – **those folks being one after another set-apart**

> (separated; made sacred and holy; [p46 reads: restored back up again into the original state and condition; rescued back and delivered again; made healthy and whole again]).

15. **Now the set-apart Breath-effect** (or: Holy Spirit; Sacred Attitude) **is also habitually witnessing** (or: progressively attesting; periodically testifying) **to us, for us, in us and by us, for after His having before said,**

16. **"This [is] the arrangement** (covenant; disposition) **which I will continue arranging** (covenanting; disposing) **toward them after those days," the Lord** [= Yahweh] **says, "Continuously giving My laws upon their hearts, I will even progressively write them upon their mental perception** (or: comprehension; that which passes through the mind), [Jer. 31:33]

17. **"and I will by no means still continue having called to mind** [other MSS: in no way would I at any point still be reminded of] **their failures** (sins; errors; misses of the target) **and of their lawlessnesses** (unlawful behaviors)." [Jer. 31:34]

18. **So** (or: But; Now) **where [there is] a sending away** (a release; forgiveness and a causing to flow away) **of these things, [there is] no longer an offering concerning sin** (failure)!

19. **Therefore, having freedom, openness and boldness of speech which comes from being citizens, brothers** (= fellow members), **with a view to the Entrance of the set-apart**

places (or: into the Pathway-into the midst, pertaining to the Holiest Place, which is the separated ones and which pertains to the sacred folks) – **within and in union with the blood of Jesus;**
20. **a Way** (Path; Road) **which was done anew** (or: which He innovates and makes new in species, character or mode, within and in the midst) **for us and in us, recently slain and yet living, through the veil that is His flesh** (or: which way through the veil He did anew for us – that is, His flesh (= His body): recently slain, and now living) – [cf Jn. 14:6; Rev. 5:6]
21. **along with a Great Priest [enthroned] upon God's House** (or: the house from God) –
22. **we can be continuously and progressively approaching with a true heart in union with full-assurance from the completed act of faithfulness** (or: centered within [the] full-carrying from [His] loyalty and fidelity), **the hearts having been sprinkled from a misery-gushed consciousness of what is evil or unserviceable** (or: a joint-knowledge full of annoying labor; a conscience in a bad condition), **and then the body having been bathed in and by clean water.**
23. **We can and should be continuously retaining** (holding down to have in possession) **the unwavering same Word** (or: unbent like-thought and similar message; or: unbowed, binding association-agreement) **of the expectation** (or: from the unwavering expectant-hope), **for you see, the One promising [is] Faithful, Trustworthy and Loyal!** [note: cf Ezk. 36:25-37:28]
24. **And so, let us be constantly directing [our] minds to give careful attention to** (or: keep on bearing in mind and fully considering) **one another into an incitement of love** (acceptance and self-giving) **and fine works** (or: unto a keen spurring on of unrestricted acceptance and beautiful acts; to a sharpening alongside from love's urge to overcome separation or estrangement, and from ideal deeds), [note: faith, expectation, love (vss. 22-24) – T.E. Denton]
25. **not repeatedly abandoning** (leaving down within; leaving helpless) **the leading of ourselves together upon [some person or occasion]** (or: the added gathering together of ourselves), **according to a custom for** (or: by; among) **certain folks, but rather and to the contrary, continuously calling [them] to the side for aid, relief and encouragement** (or: to receive the service of a paraclete), **even to so much greater a frequency, for, as much as you folks are presently SEEING** (continuously looking at and observing), **the Day progressively drawing near at hand!** [cf Mat. 24:15, 31, 33; 2 Thes. 2:1; Ezk. 11:17; cf 10:27, 37-38, below]
26. **For you see, [at] our deliberately** (voluntarily; willfully from one's being) **making mistakes** (entering into error; failing; shooting off-target; sinning) **as a habitual way of life, after taking hold of** (or: receiving; obtaining) **the full, experiential knowledge and insight of the Truth and Reality, there is no longer a sacrifice concerned with sins** (failures; etc.) **repeatedly** (or: continuously) **left behind** [D* reads: left around; = available for use],
    [comment: the sacrificial system of the old covenant no longer exists for a believer]
27. **but instead, [there is] a certain fearful taking** (or: receiving) **in hand from out of a separation for a decision, leading to a judging, and a zeal of Fire being about to be continuously and progressively eating** (or: consuming) **the hostile folks** (the ones under the circumstance of being in an opposing position). [comment: demise of Judaism: AD 70 – Denton]
    [comment: see ch. 6:4-8; both there and here, correction is a necessary; cf Jer. 4:5-6]
28. **Someone displacing** (setting aside; violating) **a custom of Moses** (or: Moses' Law) **is dying, apart from compassions, upon [evidence or testimony of] two or three witnesses.**
29. **By how much worse punishment** (= heavier the sentence) **do you suppose he will be thought worthy and counted deserving: the one trampling down the Son of God, and considering the blood of the arrangement** (or: covenant) **common** (= profane) – **within which he was set-apart** (made sacred and holy) – **even insulting the Breath-effect of joyous favor** (or: Spirit of Grace)**?**
30. **For we have perceived, and thus know, the One saying,**
    "Execution of right in fairness out of the Way pointed out [is] by Me (or: Maintaining justice and equity [is] in Me). **I will continue giving back** (repaying) **in its place,"**
says the Lord [= Yahweh], **and again,**
    "The Lord [= Yahweh] **will continue separating and making a decision about** (or: judging) **His people."** [Ex. 32:35-36; cf Rom. 12:19-21]
    [comment: this paragraph, and its judgments, pertains to God's people]
31. **[It is] fearful** (a fear-inspiring [experience]) **to suddenly fall-in – into hands of a continuously living God!**

32. **Yet be remembering the first** (or: former) **days in which, being enlightened** (illuminated), **you at one point remained under** (patiently endured while giving support in) **a great conflict** (contest or athletic combat) **of the effects of sense-experiences** (results of emotions, passions, sufferings and things that happened to you), [*cf* 6:4, above]

33. **partly both by reproaches and by pressures; partly being birthed** (coming to be) **folks of common being and existence** (partners; participants; sharers) **of those thus conducting themselves** (turning themselves step-by-step), **being constantly exposed and gazed upon as a public spectacle, as in a theater.** [*cf* 1 Thes. 2:13-16]

34. **For you even feel with** (experience with; sympathize with; express compassion for) **those bound or in prison** [other MSS: with me in my bonds], **and you at one point received to yourselves** (accepted) **the seizure** (plunder; confiscation) **of your possessions** (properties; things having their origin below) **with gracious joy, knowing and realizing to have for yourselves a superior** (stronger and better) **and continuously remaining** (or: dwelling; or: abiding; = permanent and lasting) **possession** (or: property) [later MSS add: within the heavens (or: atmospheres)]. [*cf* Mat. 5:10-12]

35. **Therefore may you not cast away your freedom and openness in speaking** (boldness and confidence which comes from being a citizen) **which continuously has a great discharge of wages.** [*cf* 3:6, above]

36. **For you continuously have need** (necessity of the use) **of persistent patient endurance** (steadfast remaining under for support), **so that doing** (or: performing) **the will** (intent; purpose) **of God you may carry away for yourselves – in order to provide and care for – the Promise.**

37. **For you see,**

> **"Yet a very, very little while, [and] the One repeatedly coming will by habit be arriving, and He will not be late** (or: continue delaying or taking time). [*cf* Jn. 16:16-22]

38.   **"Now My just One who is fair and equitable and in right relationship in accord with the Way pointed out** [other MSS: the rightwised person] **shall continue living from out of trust and faith** (or: from out of faith will be continuously living; [other MSS: out of My faith], **and if he should lower his sails and shrink back** (place himself under; cower), **My soul is not thinking well within him** (or: taking delight in him)**."** [Hab. 2:3-4]

39. **Yet we ourselves do not relate to or exist from a lowering of the sails and a shrinking back into a state of being lost, nor into destruction, but rather [we exist] from faith and confident trust, [leading] into an encompassing which is from [the] soul and defines soul**

> (or: unto creating a secure surrounding pertaining to life and breath; unto establishing a perimeter around [our] person; into a forming-around which originates in feelings, desires, instinct, emotions, will, expressions of life, and consciousness, which are the soul).

CHAPTER 11

1. **Now faith, or faithfulness, continuously exists being** (or: trust with loyal conviction is) **a standing-under** (a substructure; a basis; = the ground on which to build; that which underlies the apparent, and thus is the substance, essence or real nature) **of things being habitually expected and anticipated** [*p*13 reads: is a standing-away from things being presently hoped for]; **an evidence from a test which proves concerning effects of practices** (or: an evidence-based proof of the results of matters, actions or deeds) **[that are] not presently seen, normally being observed, or habitually perceived** (also = experienced; [*cf* vs. 5, below; 2 Cor. 7:8]).

> [note: Karen Armstrong, in *The Case for God*, has suggested that *pistis* not only involves trust and loyalty, but also engagement and commitment. Paul Tillich saw faith as "the state of being grasped by the Spiritual Presence and opened to the transcendent unity of unambiguous life." (*Systematic Theology*, Vol. 3, p. 131); *cf* 3:14, above]

2. **For in the midst of and in union with this the ancient ones** (or: the folks old time; the elders) **were given testimony** (or: had witness and evidence borne to them that gave them a reputation; had their record attested)**:**

3. **In faith and by confident, loyal trust, with the mind we constantly perceive** (or: with the intellect we now understand) **the ages to have been completely equipped by** (and, or: thoroughly adjusted to; knit together and put in order in) **God's gush-effect** (or: the result of that which flowed from God; or: a declaration or speech that had the source, character and qualities of

God; or: a spoken word which was God), **into the [resultant situation]: the thing continuously being seen** (being looked at and observed, or being perceived and thus experienced) **has not come into being from out of the midst of things which are normally appearing**
(or: continuously shining and exposing themselves to view; or: presently becoming visible or being given light and thus being made to appear).

4. **In faith, by trust, with loyal confidence and to express faithful allegiance, Abel offered to God much more of a sacrifice than** (or: compared to) **Cain, through which he was given witness** (a testimony) **to be one in accord with the Way pointed out, with fairness and equity in rightwised relationship** (a just one), **God's continuous witnessing [being] upon his gifts** [with other MSS: a continual testimony upon his gifts, by and in God]; **and through it [i.e., faith and God's testimony] he, being dead, is still continuously speaking.**
5. **In faith, by trust, with confidence and for loyal allegiance, Enoch was transported** (transferred; translated; changed to be in another place), **pertaining to the [situation] to not see death** (to not behold, perceive or observe a death; or: = to not experience death), **and he continued not being found, because God transported him. You see, before his transport** (transfer; change of place), **he had received testimony** (or: is attested) **to have pleased God well.**

6. **Now apart from faith, trust, confidence and loyal allegiance, [one is] powerless** (or: unable) **to please [God] well. It is necessary and binding for the person habitually approaching God to believe** (to be convinced and trust) **that He is** (or: that He exists), **and that He habitually comes to be** (or: becomes) **the One who pays back wages** (or: gives away rewards) **to, in and for those folks repeatedly** (or: constantly) **seeking Him out** (or: seeking from out of Him). [cf Rom. 14:23b]

7. **In faith, by trust, with confidence and loyal allegiance, Noah, being instructed** (or: being managed in public affairs) **concerning those things as yet not seen, acting cautiously** (or: receiving carefully; being shown [as] one who is taking hold well), **prepared** (made ready; furnished and equipped) **an ark – [leading] into a deliverance** (a rescue; a keeping safe) **of his house – through which he made a corresponding evaluation and a commensurate decision about the aggregate of humanity** (or: separated down the secular world; condemns the System; makes a judgment which falls in line with and follows the pattern of the ordered arrangement) **and came to be an heir** (an enjoyer of an allotment) **of fair and equitable dealings** (of justice and rightwised relationships in accord with the Way pointed out; also: = of covenant inclusion) **down from faith, which is in line with trust and is in the sphere of convinced loyalty.**
8. **In loyal faith, by trusting allegiance and with confident faithfulness, Abraham, while being progressively called** (or: continuously summoned), **humbly listened, submissively paid attention and then summarily obeyed to suddenly go out into the place which he was, and continued being, about to take in hand** (or: receive) **– into an inheritance** (an enjoyment of an allotment). **And so he went out, while not presently putting his thoughts on** (or: not being versed in, master of, or acquainted with) **where he was progressively going.**
9. **In faith, by trust, with confident loyal allegiance, he sojourned** (resided as an alien in a foreign country; lived alongside as a temporary inhabitant) **[settling] into the land of the Promise as not his own** (as belonging to another), **dwelling in tents with Isaac and Jacob, the joint-heirs of the same promise.** [Gal. 3:16-18, 29]
10. **For he continued taking with the hand from out of** (or: reaching in and receiving, then taking away from within) **the city continuously having the foundations – whose Craftsman** (or: Technician; Artisan) **and skilled Worker for the people** (or: Producer of a People; Architect of a public corporate entity) **[is] God.** [cf 12:22, below; Gal. 3:7-9, 13-14]
11. **In faith, by trust, with confidence and for loyal allegiance, also** (or: even), **Sarah herself – being sterile – received** (or: laid hold of) **power and ability unto a conception** (a depositing; founding; casting down) **of seed** (= offspring), **even beyond [the] fertile season of maturity** (full age and prime of life), **since a Faithful, Loyal and Believable One – the One promising – took**

the lead (led the way; presided; or, an alternate meaning of *hēgeomai* yields: since she (or: he) regarded the Promiser trustworthy and believable),

12. **on which account, also, were born from one [person/couple] – and these of one having been deadened – [people] corresponding to the stars of the heaven** (or: sky) **for fullness of multitude, and as the sand beside the lip** (shore) **of the sea: the innumerable.** [Gen. 15:5-6]

13. **Down from faith** (or: In line with confidence; Corresponding to trust; In the sphere of loyal allegiance and faithfulness) **all these folks died off, not taking hold of** (or: receiving; [other MSS: not being ones carrying off to themselves for kindly keeping]) **the promises, but still, after SEEING them forward at a distance, and drawing them to themselves and clinging to them, even speaking alike** (saying the same thing; confessing in verbal agreement) **that they are, and continue being, strangers and sojourners** (or: foreigners and alien residents living in a foreign place) **upon the land** (or: earth). [*cf* Jn. 8:56]

14. **For those** (or: people) **constantly saying such things are continuously shining within because** (or: are causing to clearly appear that) **they are habitually seeking upon** (or: in earnest seeking for) **a father-land** (a land of the Father).

15. **And if, indeed, they were still being mindful of and continued remembering that from which they came forth** (or: went out) **they would have continued having a fitting season** (situation; occasion) **to bend back up again** (or: return),

16. **yet now they are continuously stretching themselves out in order to touch a superior** (stronger and better) **one: this is one belonging to the superior-heaven** (or: that is, pertaining to the One upon the atmosphere; or: this exists being one from the added, superimposed heaven). **Wherefore God is habitually not ashamed of them, to be called upon [as] their God. You see, He prepared** (made ready) **a city for** (or: by; with; among) **them.** [12:22, below]

17. **By faith, in trust and with confidence, Abraham, being progressively tried and caused to attempt [it]** (or: Abraham, being repeatedly tested for loyal allegiance), **had brought Isaac face-to-face** (or: had presented Isaac and offered him over) **and began making an offering of the only-begotten. The one taking up and receiving the promises back again,**

18. **toward whom it was spoken that,**
> **"In Isaac a seed shall continue being called** (or: an offspring shall continue being summoned) **for** (to; in; by) **you,"** [Gen. 21:12]

19. **was logically reasoning and considering** (reckoning; figuring; counting on) **that God has power and is able to repeatedly arouse even out from among dead folks – whence also, in a parable, he took him back into keeping** (or: he recovered him). [*cf* Gen. 22:5]

20. **In faith, by trust, with confidence and for faithfulness, also, Isaac spoke well of** (or: blessed) **Jacob and Esau concerning impending things.**

21. **In faith, by trust, with confident faithfulness and for loyal allegiance, Jacob, when dying away, spoke well of** (or: blessed) **each of the sons of Joseph, and kissed his hand toward [them]** (or: worshiped; or: showed respect), **[leaning] upon the top of his staff.**

22. **In faith, by trust, with confidence and with loyalty, Joseph, finishing** (ending; completing his course; reaching the goal of his destiny), **called to mind** (was mindful) **concerning a way out** (an exodus) **of the sons of Israel, and imparted instructions for the goal** (implanted a purposed aim and destiny), **concerning his bones.**

23. **In faith, by trust, with confidence and for loyal allegiance, Moses, being born, was hidden three months by his parents** (or: fathers), **because they saw** (perceived) **the little boy [was] belonging to a city** (well-bred; well-formed, genteel), **and they were not frightened by the effect of the mandate of the king.**

24. **In faith, by trust, with confidence and for loyal allegiance, Moses, coming to be great** (= important), **refused** (said, "No," to; denies; disclaims; contradicted; rejects; disowned) **to be declared** (or: termed) **a son of Pharaoh's daughter,**

25. **choosing for himself** (taking to himself) **more** (in preference; rather) **to constantly encounter adversity and ill-treatment along with God's People, than to have a temporary** (toward a limited period of time marked by a suitableness of circumstances) **enjoyment and pleasure involved with falling short of the goal** (which are a failure; that originates with error; characteristic of missing of the target; of sin),

26. **considering the reproach associated with being the anointed one** (or: pertaining to the Christ; or: = of Israel [at that time]) **[to be] greater wealth than the treasures of Egypt, for he began, and continued, looking away and giving his attention unto the reward** (or: the discharge of wages). [cf 13:13, below; Rom. 8:18; 2 Cor. 4:17-18]

27. **In faith, by trust, with confidence and for faithfulness, he left Egypt behind, not fearing the rushing fury** (violent breathing, rage and angry passion) **of the king, for he was strong and stout as continually seeing the invisible** (or: the Unseen One).

28. **In faith, by trust, with confident loyalty and for trustworthy allegiance, he had performed** (or: has created so that it now stands as an institution) **the Passover and the pouring of the blood, so that the One presently destroying** (the Exterminator of) **the first-born of people and animals would** (or: could) **not touch or come in contact with them.**

29. **In faith, by trust, with confidence and in loyal allegiance, they walked through the Red Sea as through dry land – [whereas] the Egyptians, upon taking a trial of** (or: making an attempt at) **which, were gulped** (or: swallowed) **down.**

30. **In faith, by confidence, and with trust mixed with loyal allegiance, the wall of Jericho suddenly fell, after being encircled upon and surrounded [for] seven days.** [Josh. 6:20]

31. **In faith, by confidence, with trust and for loyal allegiance, Rahab the prostitute was not destroyed or lost with those being unpersuaded** (or: incompliant; [p46 reads: those not having faith, trust or loyalty]), **having welcomingly received and embraced the scouts** (or: spies) **with peace.** [Josh. 2:9-21]

32. **And so, what am I yet presently saying? For the time shall fail me, while progressively leading throughout and relating concerning Gideon, Barak, Samson, Jephthah, David, besides Samuel, also, and the prophets,**

33. **who through faith, trust and confident loyalty conquered** (violently struggled and fought-down) **kingdoms, worked a fair and equitable dealing** (effected justice in rightwised covenant participation in the Way pointed out; enforced deliverance), **hit right on target with regard to** (thus: experienced and obtained) **promises, fenced in** (blocked; closed up) **mouths of lions;**

34. **extinguished [the] power** (quenched [the] ability) **of fire, escaped mouths** (= edges) **of [the] sword; were empowered** (enabled), **moving away from a [state of] of weakness** (or infirmity); **were made to be** (were caused to become) **strong ones in the midst of war** (or: combat; battle); **they caused battle lines of foreigners to bend** (or: caused encampments of aliens to bow down; wheeled [the] ranks belonging to [the] armies of others);

35. **women took with the hand their dead folks from out of a resurrection** (or: wives received their dead ones out of the midst of a rising-again). **Yet others were beaten to death with rods** (or: drummed upon), **not receiving** (or: accepting; taking) **toward** (or: with a view to) **themselves** (= refusing) **the releasing-away** (liberation; setting free from bondage or prison) **so that they may hit the target of** (or: attain) **a superior** (stronger and better) **resurrection.** [1 Ki. 17:17-24; 2 Ki. 4:18-37; Acts 22:24-25; cf Phil. 3:8-15]

36. **But different ones took a trial** (or: received a test) **of mockings** (scoffings), **and of scourgings, and further, of bonds and imprisonment** (= put in chains and thrown in jail).

37. **They were stoned, they were cut in two with a saw, they were put to the proof** (tried; tested), **they passed away in a slaughter** (or: by murder) **with sword, they went around** (wandered) **in sheepskins, in goat skins, continuously being behind** (being in want; being in the rear), **being constantly pressed** (squeezed; afflicted), **habitually being held in the bad** (being maltreated; having it bad) – [cf 2 Ki. 2:13 (LXX): Elijah's mantle a sheepskin – Denton]

38. **of whom the System** (the ordered arrangement; the world of culture, secular society, religions and government) **was not worthy** (was not of equal value) – **being continually deceived** (led astray; caused to wander) **in deserts and mountains and caves and the holes of the earth** (or: ground).

39. **And yet all these folks, being given testimony** (being attested by witnesses) **through their faith, trust, confidence and loyal allegiance, did not at any point bring to themselves** (or: acquire) **God's Promise** (the promise of and from God; the Promise, which is God),

40. **He Himself foreseeing** (looking ahead of time and planning) **something superior** (stronger and better) **concerning us, so that they would not be made perfect** (brought to the destined goal; made complete; finished; made mature) **apart from us.**

1. **Consequently and for this very reason, then, we also, continuously having such a big cloud-mass** (figure for a dense throng) **of witnesses** (spectators; folks bearing testimony; people with evidence) **environing us** (lying around for us and [they] themselves surrounding and encompassing us), **after at once putting off from ourselves all bulk and encumbrance** (every weight; all that is prominent; or: getting rid of every arrow point within us) **and the easily-environing** (skillfully-surrounding; well-placed encircling) **failure** (sin; error; mistake; shooting off-target; missing of the point), **we can and should through persistent remaining-under** (or: relentless patient endurance and giving of support) **keep on running the racecourse** [Gal. 5:7] **continuously lying before us** (or: lying in the forefront within us; or: lying ahead, among us),
2. **turning [our] eyes away from other things and fixing them** (or: looking away) **into Jesus, the Inaugurator** (First Leader; Prime Author) **and Perfecter** (Finisher; the Bringer-to-maturity and fruition; He who purposes and accomplishes the destiny) **of the faith, trust, confidence and loyal allegiance, Who, instead of and in place of the joy** (or: in the position on the opposite side from the happiness) **continuously lying before Him** (or: lying in the forefront within Him; lying ahead for Him), **remained under a cross** (an execution pole for suspending a body) – **despising shame** (or: thinking nothing of [the] disgrace) – **and has sat down and now continues seated, remaining in the right [hand] of** (or: = in union with the place of receiving at; = at the place of power and honor, which is) **God's throne.** [cf Rom. 13:12; Eph. 4:22; Gal. 4:9ff]
3. **For consider attentively again** (or: logically reckon back for yourselves; gather it up in yourselves concerning) **the One having remained under while undergoing** (or: having patiently endured while giving support in) **such contradiction** (the anti-word; the message which is contrary to reason; speaking in opposition, against, or instead of) – **[which was directed] into Himself** [other MSS: {permeating} into the midst of themselves] **by those missing the mark** (the sinners; those making a mistake, committing error, missing the point) – **to the end that you may not tire with exertion** (or: labor to weariness), **being continuously dissolved** (be enfeebled and exhausted; caused to fall apart) **in your inner selves** (or: by your souls; = in your lives).

CHAPTER 12

4. **You folks do not yet resist** (or: did not as yet take a stand down against, or fully put in place opposition) **as far as blood** (= to the point of bloodshed; or, as a figure: = to the depth of your soul-life), **toward constantly struggling against** (or: repeatedly contending and fighting in opposition to) **the failure** (the sin; the error; the miss of the target; missing the point).
5. **And further, you have entirely forgotten** (or: been oblivious of) **the calling-near** (the relief, aid, comfort and encouragement) **which keeps on speaking-through** (discoursing; reasoning through and conversing; laying out the issue in every direction) **to you folks, as to sons:**
> **"My son, do not be neglecting** (giving little care to) **the Lord's discipline** (education; child-training), **neither be exhausted** (dissolved; = fall apart) **while being continually scrutinized or convicted** (exposed and put to the test; or: reproved) **by** (or: under) **Him,**
6. > **for whom the Lord** [= Yahweh] **is loving** (urging toward reunion and acceptance), **He is continuously and progressively educating** (or: disciplining; child-training), **and He is periodically scourging every son whom He is taking alongside with His hands** (accepting; receiving)." [Prov. 3:11-12; cf Job 5:17; Ps. 94:12; Phil. 1:29]
7. **[So] be constantly enduring** (or: You folks are continuing to remain supportively under) **with a view to education, discipline and child-training: as to sons is God Himself continuously bringing [it] to you. For who is a son** (or: what son is there) **whom a father is not disciplining, educating and training?** [cf Jas. 1:12; Rev. 3:19]
8. **But if you are without education, discipline and training, of which all have become partakers** (common participants; partners), **accordingly you are really illegitimates** (= rabbinic term mamzer: child of a prohibited marriage [Lev. 18], or of uncertain fatherhood) **and not sons.**
9. **Then again, we indeed used to have instructors** (educators; teachers of boys; discipliners) **– the fathers of our flesh** (= human parents) **– and we continued being repeatedly turned among [them]** (or: turned within and caused to reflect; = we listened to them and obeyed). **To a much greater extent, shall we not be continually placed under and humbly arranged and aligned by the Father of the spirits** (or: the Progenitor of breath-effects and Mentor of attitudes)? **And then we shall proceed living** (or: progressively live)! [cf Nu. 27:16; Eph. 6:2-3]

10. **You see, on the one hand, they were instructing** (educating; disciplining; child-training) **and continued thus toward a few days** (= for a little while), **according to and in line with that [which] normally was seeming [right] to them** (or: was being in line with the opinion [held] by them). **Yet on the other hand, upon this [instruction, arrangement and alignment] He is continuously bringing [things; situations] together** (progressively collecting unto profitability) **– unto this: to mutually partake of His set-apartness** (or: to take by the hands together, share and mutually receive from the holiness and sacredness which is Him).

11. **Now on the one hand, all discipline** (instruction; child-training; education) **with a view to** (or: face to face with) **what is presently at hand, does not at the time seem to be joyous or fun, but to the contrary [is] painful and full of sorrow and grief; however afterwards** (or: subsequently), **to, for, in and by those having been gymnastically trained** (exercised without clothing; = working-out while stripped of self-works) **through it, it is constantly and** [cf Jas. 3:18] **progressively yielding fruit which has the character and qualities of peace and harmony – which equates to fair and equitable dealings in rightwised relationships which are in line with the Way pointed out, and justice** (also: = from covenant inclusion and participation).

12. **Because of which [education],**

　　　　"straighten up (or: build anew and restore) **those hands hanging down helplessly, and those knees having been paralyzed or loosened at the sides,"** [Isa. 35:3]

13. **and then,**

　　　　"make straight and upraised wheel-tracks for your feet," [Prov. 4:26]

so that what is crippled in the feet (lame; limping; deprived of foot) **may not be turned or twisted out** (or: lest it be wrenched out of place or be dislocated; or: = cause one to "fall totally out of the race" – T.E. Denton), **but rather can and would be healed.** [cf Rom. 15:1; Gal. 6:2]

14. **You folks be continuously pursuing peace and joined-harmony** [= shalom] **with all mankind** (or: with everyone) **– as well as the process and resultant state of being different and set-apart** (or: sacredness; the sanctification; or: = the situation of being set aside for God's use), **apart from which not even one person will proceed in seeing** (or: continue perceiving) **the Lord** [= Yahweh or Christ] **–** [cf Mat. 5:8]

15. **while overseeing** (looking diligently and carefully watching upon and seeing to it) **[that] no one be lacking** (be falling short; be living behind or in the rear; = misses out), **[by wandering] away from God's grace and joyous favor; [that] not any "root of bitterness"** [Deut. 29:18], **progressively sprouting upward, would be crowding in to cause disturbance like the spirit of a mob, and then, through means of it, many folks may be stained** (polluted; defiled; = the whole community could be contaminated).

16. **[See to it that] no one [is] a fornicator** (one given to sexual immorality or who in some way prostitutes himself for gain; or: = an idol worshiper) **or a profane person** (one void of religious feeling; one accessible to all and who habitually treads across thresholds; unconsecrated; = the opposite of a set-apart person), **as Esau, who in place of** (or: in exchange for) **one feeding** (a meal) **gave away his own birthright** (the rights of the firstborn). [cf Jude 4]

17. **For you know that even afterwards, continuously purposing** (intending; wanting; willing) **to inherit the blessing** (to enjoy the allotment of the words of goodness and well-being), **he was disapproved and rejected, for he did not find a place of a change of mind [in the situation] – even though thoroughly seeking it out with tears.**

　　　　[comment: it was Isaac's mind that Esau was seeking to change – Gen. 27:33-41]

18. **Now you see, you folks have not approached to** (or: come toward so as to be now arrived at) **something tangible** (or: [D and later MSS read: a mountain] being habitually handled or normally touched), **and something burning** (or: having been burned by fire), **and to a thick, dark storm-cloud, and to murky, gloomy darkness** (or: the realm of nether gloom; the dark, shadowy quarter of dimness and obscurity), **and to a whirlwind** (tempest; hurricane),

19. **and to a blare of a trumpet, and to a sound of gush-effects** (or: a sound of the results of a flow; or: a voice of spoken words; a sound of declarations) **– of which those hearing [it] asked to the side that there be no word added for them** (or: of which, the folks listening refused and begged for release, to [the result that] no message be put toward them).

20. **For they were not bearing** (or: = carrying [through with]) **that [which was] being presently distinguished** (set and arranged throughout as strict orders): **"And if a little animal may touch**

(come in contact with) **the mountain it shall be repeatedly pelted with stones** (or: stoned)."
[Ex. 19:12-13]
21. **And so fearful was the thing being seen, Moses said,**
"**I am terrified** (out of myself with fear) **and trembling within.**" [Deut. 9:19]

22. **But to the contrary, you folks have approached so that you are now at Mount Zion –
even in a city of a continuously living God; in "Jerusalem upon heaven"** [cf 11:16, above]
(or: in a Jerusalem pertaining to and having the character and qualities of a superior, or
added, heaven and atmosphere; or: in Jerusalem [situated] upon, and comparable to, the
atmosphere; centered in a heavenly-imposed Jerusalem) – **also among ten-thousands**
(or: myriads) **of agents and messengers** (people with a/the message):
23. **[that is] in** (or: to) **an assembly of an entire people** (or: an assembly of all; a universal
convocation) **and in** (or: to) **a summoning forth** (or: a called-out and gathered community) **of
firstborn folks having been copied** (from-written, as from a pattern; or: enrolled; registered)
within [the; or: various] atmospheres (or: heavens), **and in** (or: to; with) **God, a Judge** (an
Evaluator and Decider) **of all mankind, even among** (or: to; with) **spirits of just folks** (or:
breath-effects from those who are fair and equitable and in right relationship within the Way
pointed out) **having been brought to the destined goal** (perfected; finished; matured; made
complete), [cf Rev. 3:12; 21:1-2; Eph. 2:6; Phil. 3:20; Rev. 14:1-5; Ex. 4:22; Gal. 3:19]
24. **and in** (or: to) **Jesus, a Medium** (or: an agency; an intervening substance; a middle state;
one in a middle position; a go-between; an Umpire; a Mediator) **of a new and fresh** (young;
recently-born) **arrangement** (covenant; settlement; a deposit which moves throughout in every
direction; a placing through the midst; a will and testament), **and to and in blood of sprinkling,
and to One continuously speaking something superior to** (or: stronger and better than) **Abel.**
[cf Mat. 17:1-5; Gal. 4:22-26; Rev. 21:1-2; 9b-22:5; Jn. 4:21; Ps. 46:4; 132:13; Isa. 28:16; 33:5]
25. **Continue looking, and see! You folks should not at any point ask to the side for
yourselves** (or: beg for release; decline; refuse; or: = turn your back on) **the One continuously
speaking** (or: the Speaker)! **For since** (or: if) **those asking aside for themselves** (begging off;
refusing; or: = turning their backs) **did not by flight escape** (or: flee out from) **the one
constantly managing** (conducting business and instructing) **upon earth** (or: [the] land), **much
more we [will not escape], that is those habitually turning ourselves away from the One
from [the] atmospheres and heavens,**
26. **Whose voice shook the land** (or: earth) **at that time. Yet now it has been promised** (or:
He has promised for Himself), **saying,**
"**Still once [more; or: for all] I am shaking not only the land** (or: earth), **but also the
heaven** (or: atmosphere; sky)." [Hag. 2:6; cf vs. 19, above; Ex. 19:18; Joel 3:16-17]
27. **Now the "Still once [more; or: for all]" constantly points to and makes clearly visible
the transposition** (transference; changeover; change of setting or place) **of the things being
repeatedly shaken, to the end that the things not being repeatedly** (or: continuously) **shaken
may remain.** [cf 2 Cor. 3:7-13]
28. **Therefore** (or: Because of which), **continuously taking to our sides** (or: progressively
receiving alongside) **an unshaken Reign** (or: Kingdom; Sovereign influence), **we are constantly
holding** (or: progressively having; [other MSS: can be now having]) **grace and joyous favor,
through which we are** [other MSS: can be] **continually serving, well-pleasingly, in God** (or:
for God; by God; to God), **with modesty** (an unseen behavior and manner) **in taking hold easily
of goodness and well-being, as well as discretion and awe as to what is proper,** [cf Jn. 1:17]
29. **for you see, "even our God [is] a continuously all-consuming Fire** (or: our God [is] also
a progressively fully-devouring fire)." [Deut. 4:24; 9:3; Isa. 33:14]

CHAPTER 13

1. **Let brotherly affection** (= friendly devotion to fellow believers) **continuously remain** (or: The
[mutual] sibling fondness [as members of the Family] must progressively dwell [with you])!
2. **Be continuously unforgetful** (or: = un-neglecting) **of fondness and affection to strangers
and foreigners** (or: Don't forget hospitality and friendliness to unexpected guests)! **For you see,**

through this, some folks were unaware (oblivious; unconscious) **of at some point receiving agents** (or: messengers) **as guests.**

3. **Be habitually reminding yourselves of those in bondage** (or: the bound ones; the prisoners), **as having been and now remaining bound together with [them]. [Take thought] of those maltreated** (or: those continually being held by the bad or in the worthless), **as being yourselves also within a body** (or: as it were even being the same – in union with [that] body).

4. **[Keep] Marriage precious** (of great value and honor) **in the midst of all folks** (or: among all peoples), **and the conjugal bed unstained and undefiled; for you see** [other MSS: yet], **God is continuously judging** (or, as a future: will be repeatedly separating and deciding about) **paramours** (or: sexual acts condemned by the Law in Lev. 18 – Nyland) **as well as adulterers.**

5. **[Have] behavior** (the turn, mode or manner of living) **[that is] without love of silver** (= money), **constantly contenting ourselves** (sufficing; warding-off for ourselves) **in and by the things being continuously present** (being at [your] side), **for He Himself has said,**
> **"I can** (or: could; would) **by no means let you go** (or: let up on you; send you back; release my grip on you), **neither by any means may** (or: could; would) **I leave you down within** (= forsake or fail you)," [Deut. 31:6; Josh. 1:5; cf Phil. 4:11]

6. **so that we, being constantly cheerfully-courageous, [are able] to be habitually saying,**
> **"The Lord** [= Yahweh] **[is] a Helper** (One who runs to the aid of those who cry for help) **for, to and with me, and I shall not continue fearing** (or: proceed to be afraid). **What shall a human proceed to do to me** (make for me; accomplish in me; perform for me)?" [Ps. 118:6; cf Gen. 2:18 (LXX); Isa. 12:2; 2 Cor. 6:10; Rom. 8:28]

7. **You folks be habitually mindful of those belonging to, and from, you folks – of those habitually leading the way: whoever has spoken or now speaks God's word** (or: the message which is God and has God's character) **to and among you – continually gazing upward upon** (or: reviewing and making close observation of) **the walking-out of [their] behavior** (or: conduct), **whose faith, trust and loyalty be constantly, progressively imitating.** [cf 1 Thes. 5:12-13; 2 Tim. 4:16-17]

8. **Jesus Christ [is] the same yesterday and today and on into the ages,**
> (or: Jesus [is and continues being] Christ [= the Messiah] – the Man Himself {or: the Very One}: yesterday as well as today, and even into the midst of the ages,) [cf 1:12b, above]

9. **[so] do not be carried aside** (or: swept away) **by various and strange** (or: with many-colored [as in tapestries], intricate and foreign) **teachings. You see, [it is] beautiful** (fine; ideal; admirably proportionate) **for the heart** (= core of our being) **to be continuously made firm with a fixed footing by Grace, whose source is joy and which comes with favor – not by** (or: in; with) **foods** (= rules and regulations pertaining to eating or what is edible), **in which those [thus] walking about** (= occupying themselves) **were not increased** (or: = which have not helped or benefited those who follow this way of life). [cf Eph. 4:14; 1 Tim. 4:1b; Rom. 14:17; Col. 2:16]

10. **We continue having an altar from out of which those who continue habitually serving in the Tabernacle** (= those involved with the whole ceremonial economy) **do not have authority** (or: right; privilege) **to eat.** [cf 1 Pet. 2:9; Jn. 6:53-58]

11. **For you see, the bodies of those animals, whose blood is still repeatedly being brought** [some MSS add: concerning sin] **into the set-apart** (or: holy) **places by means of the chief priest, are habitually being burned down outside of the Camp.** [Lev. 16:27]

12. **Wherefore Jesus also suffered** (and/or: had experiences of His bodily senses and emotions) **outside of the gate** [p46 and others: the Camp], **so that He may set-apart** (or: would make holy and sacred) **the People through His own blood.**
> [comment: this was a fulfillment of the Day of Atonement]

13. **Now then, we can keep on coming out** (or: should be progressively going out) **toward Him – outside of the Camp – habitually bearing His reproach** (= the censure and disgrace which He bore; or: the insult which pertains to Him). [cf 11:26, above; 1 Pet. 4:12-14,17]
> [comment: this was a call to participate in His sacrifice, and also to leave Judaism (or: religion), and thus to bear the same reproach and insults that He bore; it is also a call to bear away from them the mistakes and failures of others – John 20:23]

14. **For you see, we are not continuously holding** (having; possessing) **a remaining** (abiding; permanent) **city here, but rather we are progressively seeking for** (or: continuously searching upon) **the impending one** (the one that is presently about to be [here]). [cf 12:22ff, above]

15. **Through Him, then, we may and should repeatedly** (or: continuously) **offer up a sacrifice of praise in God** (by God; to God; for God; with God) **through all things** (or: through the midst of all [situations]) – **that is, a fruit of lips continuously saying the same things** (or: speaking alike) **in His Name** (by His Name; confessing to His Name; for the Name which is Him; or: = a product of speech which acknowledges His character, authority and identity). [cf 1 Pet. 2:5]

    [comment: here we see a life "in spirit and truth" referred to by Jesus in John 4:23-24]

16. **Now be not forgetful of well-doing** (performing well; producing or constructing goodness; doing good deeds of ease; creating well-being) **and of partnership** (common-being/existence; community; participation; having things in common; fellowship; sharing and contributing), **for by** (or: in) **such sacrifices God is continuously well pleased.** [cf Jas. 2:15-17; Phil. 4:10-20]

17. **Be constantly persuading yourselves by** (or: Be progressively having confidence in and continue being convinced by) **those folks normally taking the lead among you folks, and continue humbly yielding under** (or: giving way to or making way for) **[situations or people] while coming under [His] likeness, for you see, these same folks are habitually awake and vigilant** (abstaining from sleep to watch) **over** (or: on behalf of) **your souls** (your inner lives; or: the people among you folks), **as those who will constantly be rendering a word** (an account or an accounting), **so that they can** (or: would) **be habitually doing** (or: performing; producing) **this with gracious joy – and not be constantly groaning** (= complaining), **for that [would be] detrimental and unprofitable** (literally: not paying taxes or expenses) **for you!** [cf 1 Thes. 5:12]

18. **Be continuously thinking, speaking and acting toward having things go well** (or: projecting goodness and ease; praying) **concerning us, for we have been persuaded that we have a beautiful consciousness** (a fine and ideal share in knowledge; or: a sound and noble conscience), **setting our will to behave ourselves beautifully** (in a good way; ideally; soundly; honorably) **in all things and among all people.**

19. **Yet I am more exceedingly calling you alongside, urging and encouraging you to do** (or: perform) **this, to the end that I can** (or: would) **more quickly be restored** (or: returned) **to you.**

20. **Now may the God who is Peace** (or: who is the origin of and has the character and qualities of harmonious joining), **the One at one point leading our Lord** (Master; Owner) – **Jesus, the Shepherd of the sheep, the Great One – back up again out from the midst of dead folks,**

21. **at once render you folks thoroughly equipped** (fitted; adapted) **in the midst of all good and in every virtue, centered in, immersed in, and in union with, the blood of, from, and which is, a thorough arrangement** (or: a covenant; a deposit which moves throughout in every direction; a placing through the midst; or: a will and testament) **pertaining to and having the qualities of the Age** (or: an eonian – through the ages – settlement), **in order to at once do** (produce; perform) **His will** (the effect of His intent and purpose; the result of His design and pleasure) – **progressively creating** (doing; forming; producing) **within you folks and in union with you people** [other MSS: in us] **the well-pleasing and satisfying [result] in His presence and sight, through Jesus Christ, in Whom** (and: for Whom, by Whom, and to Whom) **[is] the glory** (the reputation and the manifestation which calls forth praise) **on into the ages of the ages. It is so** (Count on it; Amen)**!** [cf 9:20, above; Mat. 26:28; Mk. 14:24; Phil. 2:12-13]

22. **Yet I am calling you alongside to exhort, appeal, aid and encourage** (or: Now I am performing as a paraclete for) **you, brothers** (= fellow believers; = my family)**: progressively uphold the word of the encouraging calling-alongside for aid and exhortation** (or: the message which pertains to and is from the summons and influence of the Paraclete), **for you see, I also send** (or: even write) **[this] letter to you folks through brief [words]** (by bits).

23. **Know** (or: Take note and be personally aware) **[that] our brother Timothy, has been released, with whom, if he may more quickly be going** (or: coming), **I will see you.**

24. **Greet and embrace all the folks taking the lead among you, and all the set-apart folks** (the holy ones; the saints). **Those from Italy** (or: The Italians [here]) **are constantly embracing and greeting you folks** (or: Those [here] are now sending you greetings from Italy).

25. **Grace and joyous favor [are, and continue] with all of you! Count on it** (Amen)**!**

    [written circa A.D. 67 – Based on the critical analysis of John A.T. Robinson]

JACOB
(JAMES)

CHAPTER 1

1. **Jacob** (or: James) **a slave belonging to God and to [the] Lord, Jesus Christ** (or: a slave from and pertaining to God, even in fact, really, to [the] Lord and Owner [or, perhaps: = Yahweh], Jesus Christ), **to the twelve tribes** (or: sprouts and branches which sprang forth) **who are to be constantly rejoicing within the scattering** (or: which are within the midst of the dispersion [= the planting], "To continued joy and gladness!").

2. **O my brothers** (= fellow Israelites, or, fellow believers; or: = My family), **lead every rejoicing** (or: lead the path of all joy) **whenever you may fall into – so as to be encompassed by – various trials** (or: multi-faceted ordeals; [a tapestry of] tests and provings; or: experiments and attempts of varying hues),
3. **while habitually knowing, from intimate experience and insight, that the thing by means of which your faith, trust and confidence is tested and proved** (or: the testing and proof of your faithfulness and loyalty) **keeps on producing** (or: is progressively working down-in the results and accomplishing) **persistent patient endurance**
    > (a steadfast remaining and dwelling under some ordeal or situation; or: a holding up under sustained attacks; or: a relentless giving of sustaining support).
4. **But patient endurance** (remaining under and/or sustained support) **must habitually be having a work brought to completion** (a complete action; a perfect work; a mature production which reaches its goal) **to the intent that you may be** (or: can exist as) **perfect ones** (complete, matured and finished folks who have attained the goal), **even ones having an entire allotment** (or: whole folks having every part), **being left behind in nothing** (or: lacking not one thing).

5. **So, if any one of you is continually left behind** (or: lacking) **in regard to wisdom, he or she must keep on asking** (requesting) **from the side** (= immediate presence) **of the God [Who is] continuously giving to everyone singly** (one at a time; or: simply; or: = generously) **and is not constantly reproaching or demeaning – and it will proceed being given to him or her!**
6. **Yet he must keep on asking in faith and conviction** (or: But let her continue making [her] request in union with trust, and centered in loyalty; [based] on [His] faithfulness), **making not one hesitation from habitually distinguishing and constantly evaluating differences** (undecidedly separating throughout; discerning between uncertain points; judging dividedly to produce doubt) **within himself or herself, for the person repeatedly making undecided distinctions** (making a separation and judging dividedly unto doubt) **within himself or herself is like a surge of the sea, being constantly raised and driven, and then repeatedly tossed or hurled about, by the wind.**
7. **You see, that person must not habitually suppose** (or: normally assume) **that he or she will continue receiving** (or: taking in hand; seizing; getting) **anything from beside** (= from being in the presence of) **the Lord** [= Yahweh, or, Christ].
8. **A two-souled** (or: = divided-willed; or: = emotionally split) **adult male** (or: person) **[is] unstable** (unfixed; inconstant; turbulent; fickle; or: = indecisive) **in all his ways and paths.**

9. **Now let the low-positioned** (not rising far from the ground; or: humble; or: down-hearted or depressed) **brother** (or: fellow member/believer) **continually boast** (or: be habitually loud-mouthed) **in his high position** (or: exaltation; or: height),
10. **but the rich, in his lowness** (or: humiliation; depression), **because he will be progressively passing by as a flower of grass** (or: = a wildflower).
11. **For you see, the sun rises with scorching heat and withers the grass, and its flower falls off, and the beauty of its face** (= loveliness of its appearance) **loses itself** (finds destruction in itself). **Thus also, the rich one will proceed in being extinguished** (faded; withered) **in his goings** (journeys; business; ventures; undertakings; way of life).

12. **Happy and blessed is the adult male** (or: person; [A and other MSS: human being]) **who is continuously remaining under a proving** (a putting to the proof; or: a trial; an ordeal), **because upon being birthed approved** (or: growing and becoming proved and accepted) **he or she will continue laying hold of the circle of the life** (or: life's crown; life's encirclement; the encirclement from this living existence; or: the wreath which is the Life) **which He** [some MSS: the Lord (= Yahweh or Christ)] **Himself promised to** (or: for; in; among; with) **those continuously loving, and urging toward union with, and giving themselves to, Him.**

13. **Let no one, while being continuously probed and put to the proof, be saying "I am constantly being probed and put to the proof** (tested; tried) **in an ordeal from God," for God is One Who is not put through an ordeal, not probed, put to the proof or tried, and is [thus] without experience from not having made an attempt, in regard to things of bad quality** (or: you see, God exists un-testable, incapable of being tried and lacks experience from worthless situations or evil things or mean people), **and so He Himself is repeatedly probing no one, nor constantly putting even one person in a test, to the proof or through an ordeal.**
14. **Yet each person is repeatedly probed and put to the proof** (tested and tried in an ordeal), **being continuously dragged** (or: drawn) **out and entrapped under his own over-covering passion** (by his own longing, craving or lust; by what he sets his desires upon).
15. **Thereafter, with the over-covering passion conceiving** (seizing together so as to become pregnant), **it continuously gives birth to failure** (or: repeatedly brings forth an offspring of missing the target; progressively bears deviation and sin). **Now the failure** (error; sin; missing of the target; deviation), **being brought to full term** (being finished off; being fully formed with all its parts; being brought to its goal) **continues producing** (keeps generating; from pregnancy progressively and repeatedly bears forth) **death.**

16. **Do not be repeatedly caused to wander** (or: Be not continuously deceived), **my beloved brothers** (= family members; = fellow believers)!
17. **Every good leaving of a legacy, profitable contributing or excellent dosing, as well as all virtuous giving, and** (or: All giving [is] beneficial, and yet), **every perfect gift** (finished, complete or mature result of giving) **is from above, descending from the Father of the Lights, beside Whom there is no otherness at [His] side** (or: in the presence of Whom is no parallel otherness; [other MSS: along with Whom is not one interchange, variation, shifting or mutation]), **nor a shadow cast by turning** [other MSS: an effect caused by the passing of shadows].
18. **Being purposed** (intended; willed; resolved), **from being pregnant He gave birth to us** (brought us forth; prolifically produced us) **by a Word** (in a collected thought and blueprint; for an expressed idea; with a message; into a *Logos*) **of Truth and from Reality – into the [situation for] us to be** (or: to continuously exist being) **a specific** (or: a certain; some) **firstfruit** (first portion) **of, and from among, His created beings** (or: of the effects of His act of creating; or: from the results of the founding and creation which is Himself; [other MSS: of the Himself-creatures]).
19. **You folks have seen and are aware, so understand, perceive and know [this], my beloved brothers. So every person must continuously be quick** (swift) **into the [position or place] to listen, hear and pay attention, slow into the [readiness] to make vocal utterance, [and] slow into inherent fervor** (internal swelling of passion; teeming desire; or: agitation; anger; or: a particular mental bent).
20. **For you see, an adult male's** (or: a person's) **inherent fervor** (or: mental bent; disposition; temperament; or: swelling desire and passionate longing; or: anger and indignation) **is not working out** (producing; bringing into effect) **God's justice, or fair and equitable dealing from the eschatological deliverance**
>   (or: rightwised situation which accords to the Way pointed out, in right relationship; the quality of the thing which is right and just; also: = the covenant life from God).
21. **For this reason, putting away from yourselves all filthiness and encompassing superabundance of bad quality** (ugliness; baseness; malice; evil; qualities that ought not to be), **you folks must receive** (take with your hands) **in gentle friendliness** (absence of ego; mildness), **the implanted** (ingenerated) ***Logos*** (Word; collected thought and blueprint; idea; message), **the One being continuously able** (or: the one which is constantly powerful) **to**

deliver (rescue; keep safe; heal; make whole) **your souls** (the consciousness and being, which you folks are).

22. **So now you must continuously come to be doers and performers of [the]** *Logos* (or: creators and makers from a collected thought; builders from a blueprint; framers of an idea; producers of reason; [the] Word's doers), **and not only hearing ones** (listeners; those hearing in an auditorium), **continuously deceiving** (reckoning aside; miscalculating) **yourselves.**

> (or: So you folks must be progressively birthed to be authors of a message, and not only those in an auditorium, continuously miscalculating yourselves.)

23. **Because if someone is a hearer of [the]** *Logos* (a listener to a Word or Thought, idea or message) **and not a doer** (performer; producer; etc.), **this one is like** (resembles) **an adult male** (or: a person) **contemplating** (considering; attentively pondering) **in a mirror the face of his birth** (genesis; origin; existence; generation; lineage; or: = the face with which he was born):

24. **for he contemplated himself and has departed, and, set for ease and well-being, he immediately forgot of what sort** (which quality) **he was being** (or: the manner of place where he had been existing). [comment: for a contrast, *cf* 2 Cor. 3:18]

25. **But the one stooping down beside in order to attentively view into** (giving a penetrating look into) **the perfect** (finished and realized; matured; completed; full-grown and fully developed; purposed and destined) **law – the one which is freedom** (or: the one from, and which has the qualities of, freedom and liberty) **– and then remaining** (abiding; dwelling) **present, beside [it] – not being birthed** (or: coming to be) **a hearer of forgetfulness** (or: a forgetful listener), **but rather a performer of work** (or: but to the contrary, a producer of action – a work's "doer") **– this person will continue being happy within his performing, blessed in union with his producing, and better off, centered in his doing.**

26. **Now if someone habitually supposes [himself]** (or: thinks [herself]; presumes; or: constantly appears or seems) **to be religious** (occupied with rituals and ceremonies), **while not habitually guiding his tongue as with a bridle, but rather is repeatedly deceiving his heart, the religion** (ritual; observance of a religious system) **of this person is useless** (futile; empty).

27. **Pure** (clean) **and unstained** (undefiled) **religion, by the side of** (= in the presence of) **The God and Father, is this: to habitually visit so as to continuously look upon with the eyes in order to help** (or: oversee) **orphans and widows within the midst of their pressure** (ordeal; squeezing; distress; tribulation); **to habitually keep oneself unspotted from the controlling ordered-System** (or: away from the world of secular culture, religion, economy and government).

CHAPTER 2

1. **O my brothers** (= fellow believers, or, fellow Israelites, or, Family), **stop, or do not have the habit of, holding the faithfulness and trust of Jesus Christ, our Lord** (Master; Owner), **Who is the Glory** (the manifestation Who calls forth praise), **in respect of persons or appearances**

> (or: do not persist in possessing our Lord's [= Yahweh's or Christ's] faith and confidence in partiality or favoritism, or in the receiving of faces or personalities, thus affecting the reputation of Jesus Christ).

2. **For if a gold-ringed adult male, in a shining or radiant robe, may enter into your gathering** (or: synagogue), **but then a poor person** (one reduced to beggary; an indigent) **in a dirty or filthy robe** (or: shabby clothing) **may also enter,** [*cf* Lu. 16:19ff]

3. **and you should look upon** (or: gaze upon and regard) **the one wearing the shining robe** (= expensive, new clothes), **and you may say, "You sit here in a fine and beautiful [manner or position]** (= in a place of honor)," **and to the poor one you may say, "You stand there," or, "You sit under my footstool** (= on the floor near my feet; = a place beneath my position),"

4. **are you not thoroughly separated and disconnected within yourselves** (or: discriminating and making a distinction among yourselves) **and have birthed yourselves to become** (or: caused yourselves to be) **judges having the qualities of evil reasonings** (or: decision makers whose motives are wicked designs and harmful logistics)?

5. **Listen and hear, my beloved brothers! Did not God at one point choose** (call and speak out; pick out; select) **for Himself the poor folks in the System of the aggregate of mankind**

(or: Does not God Himself lay out and collect the beggars and those who slink and cower with wretchedness in the world of society, culture, religion and government) – **folks rich in trust, faith, loyalty and conviction, and also heirs** (those who possess by distribution of an allotment) **of the reign, sovereign activities and kingdom which He promised to and assured for those continually loving, accepting, and urging toward union with, Him?**
6. **But you folks dishonor and devalue the poor. Are not the rich people continuously exploiting** (oppressing) **you people, repeatedly exercising [their] power and abilities against you? Are they not continually dragging you into courts of law for judicial hearings?**
7. **Are they not constantly defaming** (slandering; speaking abusively of; vilifying; or: hindering the light of) **the beautiful** (fine; excellent; honorable; ideal) **Name – the one being called and invoked upon** (= put upon), **and conferred on, you folks?**

8. **Since, however** (or: If, really), **you are continuously bringing to its goal** (finishing; bringing to fruition; perfecting; ending; bringing to a close; fulfilling) **the royal law** (or: kingly custom; sovereign distribution; rule fit to guide a king), **you are performing beautifully** (doing ideally; producing excellently), **down from and in accord with the Scripture,**
> **"You will continue accepting, urging toward reunion with, giving yourself to, and loving, your neighbor** (the one near you; your associate) **as yourself."** [Lev. 19:18]
9. **Yet if you habitually show favoritism** (accept faces; behave with partiality; respond to appearances), **you are continuously working error** (deviation; a miss of the target; a failure; sin) **being ones by proof of guilt repeatedly convicted as transgressors** (folks stepping aside or across [the line]), **under the Law** (or: exposed as deviators by the custom).
10. **For you see, whoever perhaps kept** (or: may have guarded and observed) **the whole Law, yet possibly at some point stumbled in one thing, had become held** (or: caught) **within all [its aspects]** (or: = is liable for and susceptible to everything).
11. **You see, the One saying, "You should** (or: may) **not commit adultery," also said, "You should** (or: may) **not murder."** [Ex. 20:13] **Now if you are not committing adultery, yet you are now being a murderer, you have come to be** (you have been birthed) **a transgressor of** (a deviator from; [p74 and A read: one who stands away from]) **law** (or: custom).

12. **Thus keep on speaking and thus keep on doing** (performing; producing): **as those being continuously about to be separated and decided about** (evaluated; judged; made a distinction between; scrutinized) **through means of a Law** (or: custom; principle; [p74: a word; a message]) **of Freedom and from unfettered Liberty, and which is Un-restriction.** [cf Rom. 8:2]
13. **For you see, the separating, evaluating and deciding** (or: scrutinizing and judging) **is merciless in, by and with** (or: to; for) **the one not performing, exercising or producing mercy. Mercy is consistently speaking loudly, boasting and assuming superiority with regard to evaluating, deciding and separating** (or: Mercy is repeatedly bragging from making decisions; or: Mercy keeps on fully boasting in repeatedly triumphing over judging)**!**

14. **What is the advantage** (the furtherance; the increase), **my brothers** (= fellow believers; = family) **if a certain person may keep on claiming to continuously have faith** (or: may be now saying [that he is] habitually having trust, loyalty and conviction), **yet he may not normally have works** (or: keep on possessing actions and deeds)**? Is the Faithfulness** (or: faith; trust; loyalty; conviction) **not continuing able** (constantly having power) **to deliver** (rescue; save; make whole and heal; restore) **him?**

15. **Now if a brother or a sister may continuously subsist** (or: should begin now in a position under [circumstances]) **as naked ones** (= without sufficient clothing), **and may constantly be deserted** (or: wanting) **of daily food,**
16. **yet a certain person out from among you folks may be saying to them, "Be now humbly departing in peace** (or: Continue leading [your life] under [these circumstances] in union with harmony), **be continuously warming yourselves and be habitually fed and fully satisfy yourselves," but you would not give to them the body's necessities – what is the advantage or resulting benefit?**

17. **Thus also [is] The Faithfulness** (or: trust; conviction; loyalty)**: if it should not continue to have works** (include actions; possess deeds; have employment), **by itself it exists being dead** (or: is lifeless; = is unresurrected) **in correspondence to, and in the sphere of, itself.**

18. **In contrast, someone will proceed saying, "You continuously have** (hold) **faith, and I continuously have** (or: possess) **works** (actions; deeds). **You at once show me** (exhibit to my eyes) **your faith apart from the works or actions, and I, forth from out of the midst of my actions, works and deeds, will continue showing** (exhibiting to) **you the faith, trust, conviction, loyalty and The Faithfulness."**

19. **You continuously believe** (or: trust; are convinced) **that God is One** (or: that God exists being One; that One exists being God; or: that there is one God). [Deut. 6:4] **You are performing** (doing) **beautifully** (excellently; ideally) **– even the demons** (Hellenistic concept and term: = animistic influences) **continuously believe** (or: presently trust; are constantly loyal; are normally convinced [about this]), **and constantly shudder** (bristle; shiver; are ruffled).

> [comment: in this last phrase Jacob is either making an ontological statement about "demons," or he is using sarcasm, referring in a derogatory manner to the Jews who also believe this; Jesus used the term *diablos* (devil; one who thrusts-through folks) to refer to Judas in John 6:70; He used the term *satan* when speaking to Peter in Mark 8:33; this phrase could also refer to the superstitious mindsets of folks who have believed Jewish or pagan myths, or have accepted Hellenistic, animistic influences into their thinking]

20. **But are you willing to experientially and intimately know and receive insight, O empty person, that the faith, trust and loyalty, apart from the works and actions, exists being inactive** (continues unproductive; [*p*74 reads: empty; without contents; other MSS: is dead])**?**

21. **Our father Abraham was not placed within the Way pointed out** (made fair and equitable; put in right relationship; rightwised; made a just one; also: = placed in covenant) **from out of works, when offering up his son Isaac upon the altar!**

22. **Are you normally seeing that the faith, trust and loyalty continued to work together with his actions and works, and forth from out of the actions** (or: works), **faith** (trust, loyalty and conviction) **was brought to its goal** (was perfected; was matured; was finished)**?**

23. **And thus the Scripture was made full, the one saying,**

> **"Now Abraham believed** (or: put trust and confidence) **in God** (or: became persuaded by God; adhered to God), **and he was counted into the Way pointed out by Him** (or: he was considered rightwised by Him; he was reckoned fair, equitable and just in Him; alternately: so it was counted into right relation [= covenant inclusion] for him)," [Ex. 15:6]

and later, he was called "God's friend." [Isa. 41:8]

24. **Are you folks normally observing** (or: perceiving) **that humanity** (or: a person) **is normally being rightwised** (from time to time being placed in right relationship in the Way pointed out; progressively made fair and equitable; normally justified; = put in covenant) **forth from out of the midst of actions and works, and not only from out of faith and trust?**

25. **Now in this same vein, even Rahab the prostitute, taking under [her roof] and welcoming the agents** (messengers), **and then later exiting them by a different way, was not rightwised** (placed in right relationship in the Way pointed out; made fair and equitable; justified; or: shown to be righteous; also: = brought into covenant) **forth from out of works!** [Heb. 11:31]

26. **You see, just as the body apart from a breath-effect** (or: spirit) **is lifeless** (dead), **thus also the faith and trust apart from actions and works** [i.e., the living it out] **is** (exists being) **lifeless** (dead).

CHAPTER 3

1. **My brothers** (= fellow members), **do not continue to become many teachers** (or: stop becoming a bunch of instructors; or: let not many of you folks proceed to be made teachers), **seeing, and knowing, that we will continue receiving [a] greater effect from the decision**

> (or: will proceed taking more intense scrutiny and evaluation; will progressively get a stronger result from an investigation; will habitually receive heavier judgment),

2. **for you see, we all are repeatedly tripping and stumbling** (faltering; making false steps) **many times** (or: ways) **[and] are causing many to entangle their feet, lose balance, and stumble. If anyone is not continually stumbling in word** (or: collected thought; reason; or: = what he says), **this one is a mature male adult** (or: a perfect, i.e., complete and finished, person), **able also** (or: with power even) **to guide the whole body [as] with a bridle.**
3. **Now if we are thrusting the bridle bits into the horses' mouths to make them continually yield themselves to us, we also continually lead together** (or: change the course of and direct) **their whole body.**
4. **Consider also the ships, being of so great size, and being constantly driven under rough and hard winds. They are continually steered under** (or: by) **the smallest rudder, wherever the impulse of the helmsman** (pilot) **continues determining** (or: from the one set for success – by presently guiding straight, true and upright – keeps on intending).

5. **Thus also, the tongue is a little member of the body, and yet is continuously making a loud, confident declaration or a great boast** [other MSS: constantly brags about great things] – **consider how great a forest a little fire progressively sets ablaze** (or: ignites; lights up)!
6. **Well the tongue [is] a fire; [its fuel is] the System of injustice**
> (or: the ordered and decorated but dominating world of secular culture, religion, politics and government, which is unjust; or: the aggregate of humanity having the character of the absence of what is right; or: The tongue, also, [is] fire: the world of disregard for what is just).

The tongue is placed down within our members, continuously spotting (staining; = defiling) **the whole body, and repeatedly setting on fire the wheel of birth**
> (or: of coming into being; of production; from successive generation and descent; = the cycle of the origin [of life], or of generation; the wheel of *genesis*), **as well as being**

continuously set on fire by (or: under) **the garbage dump** (the depository of refuse; Greek: *Gehenna* – the Valley of Hinnom).

7. **You see, every nature** (generated essence; native condition) – **both of wild animals and of flying creatures, both of creeping animals and of those in the salt sea – is continuously being restrained** (tamed) **and has been restrained by the nature of mankind** (or: for and with the generated human essence and native condition).
8. **But the tongue – an unruly** (un-restrainable; other MSS: unfixed; unstable; restless), **worthless** (ugly; bad; malicious; unrefined; harmful; base) **[member], full of death-bearing venom – no one of humanity is able** (continues having power) **to subdue, restrain or tame.**
9. **With it we habitually speak well of** (or: speak a good word about; bless) **the Lord** [other MSS: God] **and Father, and with it we constantly curse** (pray down upon) **those people having been born "according to** (down from; corresponding to) **God's likeness."** [Gen. 1:26ff]
10. **Out of the same mouth is continuously coming forth blessing and cursing** (or: negative wishing; adversarial praying). **My brothers, there is no need** (or: it is not necessary; it ought not be) **for these things thus to be repeatedly birthed** (or: to keep on happening in this way).
11. **A spring** (or: fountain) **is not continuously bursting forth the sweet and the bitter** (or: cutting and pricking; [p74: salty]) **out of the same hole** (or: opening).
12. **My brothers, a fig tree is not able to produce olives, nor a grape-vine figs, neither brine to produce sweet water.**

13. **Who [is] wise and understanding** (adept) **among you? Let him at once exhibit** (show; present to the sight and demonstrate) **his works and actions out of beautiful behavior** (fine, ideal, excellent and appropriate conduct) **in gentleness of** (or: mild, egoless considerateness from) **wisdom.**
14. **Yet if you folks continuously have bitter rivalry** (or: jealousy) **and selfish ambition** (or: faction) **in your heart, do not habitually boast** (exult) **and lie** (speak falsely or deceitfully) **concerning the truth or reality** (or: are you not now vaunting against and falsifying the truth?).
15. **This is not the wisdom continuously coming down from above, but rather [is] fully earth-oriented** (or: earthly; earth-produced; earth-applied), **pertaining to or proceeding from the soul** (soulish; consciousness-related; = natural), **pertaining to, or affected by, or having**

the characteristics of "demons" [a Hellenistic term and concept; = influences, in that period and culture, thought of as being animistic, or as personified attitudes or orientations].

> [comment: note that the three adjectives "earthly," "natural/soulish," and "demonic" are tied together to this same context, as being of the same sphere of being – or, fruit of the same tree]

16. **For where [there is] jealousy** (rivalry) **and selfish ambition** (faction; intrigue), **in that place [is] instability** (disorder; an unsettled state) **and every ignoble** (base; vile; worthless) **practice.**
17. **But the Wisdom from above is** (constantly exists being) **indeed first** (or: primarily) **pure, thereafter peaceable** (or: peaceful; pertaining to peace and harmonious joining), **suitable** (fair; reasonably lenient; yielding; unassertive; considerate), **compliant** (easily persuaded; receptive; reasonable; willing to yield), **full of mercy** (= practical help) **and good fruits, non-separating** (not discriminatory; undivided in evaluating; unwavering; unprejudiced; impartial), **unpretending** (or: not hyper-critical; not judging from a low point of view; not focusing on tiny distinctions; not overly judgmental; not under-estimating of reality).
18. **Now the fruit of fair and equitable dealing** (or: from eschatological deliverance which brings justice and right relationship in accord with the Way pointed out; the condition of being rightwised, or turned in the right direction; also: = covenant participation) **is continuously being sown in peace and harmonious joining by and for those habitually performing** (making; doing; producing; creating; building; forming) **peace and harmonious joining.**

> [comment: this is the fruit of the Spirit, or, from the Tree of Life]

CHAPTER 4

1. **From what situation** (place; source) **[arise] battles** (or: wars; situations of combat) **and fights** (quarrels; strife; controversies) **among you folks? Are they not from this source** (or: place)**: from out of your sensual pleasures** (enjoyments and gratifications) **[which are] themselves continually performing as soldiers within** (or: waging war, centered in and in union with) **your members?**
2. **You folks are continuously strongly desiring to possess, and yet continuously you do not have; you continue murdering and are repeatedly jealous** (boil with rivalry), **and so you are perpetually unable to hit the mark** (to attain or master [something]). **You are habitually quarreling and fighting.**

> (or: You people constantly have full longing, desire and lust – and still you are not presently holding or possessing – and so you repeatedly murder. You are progressively envious, boiling with rivalry, and yet continue having no power to obtain [your goal], so you are constantly striving and having controversies – even doing combat and waging wars!)

You continue not having [your desires] because you yourself do not continue asking (or: you are not normally requesting for yourselves).
3. **You continue asking** (requesting), **and yet you continue not receiving** (taking [it] in hand; grasping [it]) **because you are asking inappropriately** (worthlessly requesting; or: = asking for a wrong purpose) **to the intent that you may spend** (= waste) **it in** (or: on) **your pleasures.**

4. **O adulterers and adulteresses** (= O people unfaithful to Christ or God as your husband)! **Have you not seen, and are you not aware, that the Domination System's friendship** (the affection whose source is this world of the controlling organization's religion, secular culture, economy and government) **is a source of enmity with God** (or: hostility and active hatred with regard to God; [Aleph reads: exists being alienation to God])**? Whoever, then, may have been made to want** (to intend; to purpose) **to be the Domination System's** (or: organization's; world's) **friend is continuing to be established** (habitually set down; progressively rendered or constituted) **[as] a hostile person, with regard to, or in relationship with, God** (or: an alienated person, or enemy, belonging to God). [cf 2 Cor. 5:18-20]
5. **Or are you supposing that the Scripture is speaking void of effect** (emptily; vainly)**? The breath-effect** (or: spirit; attitude) **which housed-down** (took up residency) **within us normally sets its desire** (longing; affection; yearning) **upon [something], with a view toward ill-will, malice, envy and jealousy!**

(or: The Spirit – which He causes to dwell in union with us – is constantly longing and progressively yearning [for us]: to the point of bubbling up zeal and enthusiasm.
or: Is the spirit and attitude which lives within us periodically longing toward envy?)

6. **Yet He is constantly and progressively giving greater** (= more abundant; more intense; larger; more frequent) **grace and joyous favor, therefore it is saying,**
> **"God continuously sets Himself in opposition to, and aligns Himself against, those that show themselves above** (the proud; the assuming), **but He habitually gives grace and favor to the low ones** (the unassuming ones; the humble ones; those of low rank)."** [Prov. 3:34]

7. **Consequently, you must be subjected by** (or: be at once placed and arranged under in; be humbly aligned with and to) **God. So stand in opposition to the [or: your] adversary** (or: take a stand [as in battle] against the person trying to thrust you through [with a weapon, or a word] or cause division), **and he or she will progressively flee** (take flight) **away from you!**

8. **Draw near in God** (or: Approach by God; Be close at hand for God; Be or stay near to God), **and He will progressively draw near in you** (or: continue being or staying near to you; habitually be close at hand for you)!
You failing folks (ones missing the target; sinners), **cleanse [your] hands** (= your actions)!
You two-souled folks (or: people with dualistic consciousness; double-minded ones; people with split affections and loyalties), **purify** (make of one substance) **[your] hearts!**
9. **You folks must endure labor and hardships, and be miserable and wretched; you must mourn, and you must cry; your laughter must be converted into mourning, and joy into dejection with [your] eyes cast down;**
10. **you folks must consequently be made low** (humbled; demoted; brought to a low station), **in the Lord's sight** (= in [Yahweh's, or Christ's] presence), **and then He will progressively lift you up** (or: continue elevating you).

11. **O brothers** (= believers in God's household), **do not be continuously** (or: stop constantly) **speaking negatively** (or: gossiping or babbling; wearing someone down by talking; talking a person down) **against one another. The one habitually speaking down against a brother** (= a fellow believer; or: = a member of God's household), **and continuously judging** (separating and making decisions about) **his brother, is continuously speaking down against law, and thus keeps on judging law** (making separations and then decisions about custom). **Now if you continue judging law, you are not being a performer** (a doer; producer) **of law** (or: a creator from Principle) **but rather, a judge** (one who makes separations, conclusions and decisions).
12. **There is one Lawgiver and Separator** (Evaluator; Decider; Judge): **the One being continuously able and powerful to deliver** (rescue; heal; save; keep safe; restore to wholeness), **as well as to cause loss** (or: bring a condition of utter ruin; or: cause [something or someone] to be lost; or: destroy). **So you, who are you, the one continuously judging the one near you** (repeatedly separating and evaluating the neighbor; or: presently making decisions about [your] associate)?

13. **Come now, those continuously saying, "Today or tomorrow we will proceed traveling into this or that city and produce** (make; perform; do [something]) **one year there, and then we can trade** (or: conduct business) **and make a profit,"**
14. **– namely, those who are not in the habit of putting their attention upon the thing of tomorrow** (or: who are not normally versed in or acquainted with the morrow; or: are not now standing upon tomorrow). **Of what sort [is] your life? You see, you folks are** (or: exist being) **a vapor** (a mist), **progressively** (or: repeatedly) **appearing for a little while** (toward a little space), **and thereupon continually** (or: repeatedly; progressively) **being made to disappear –**
15. **Instead of that, you should be saying, "If the Lord** [= Yahweh, or, Christ] **should will** (or: intend), **we also will continue living and will proceed doing** (or: producing) **this or that."**
16. **Yet now you continue speaking loudly** (boasting; gloating) **in your empty, bragging speech and displays. All such boasting is misery-gushed** (harmful; painfully laborious; miserable; bad).

17. **So for and with one** (or: in one; to a person) **having seen and thus knowing to be continually performing [the] beautiful** (doing [the] ideal; making [the] fine; producing [the] excellent), **and then not habitually performing** (doing) **[it], in him this is a failure** (for him it is error; to and with him it is sin; by him it is a missing of the target and a deviation from the goal).

CHAPTER 5

1. **Continue leading on now, you wealthy folks; burst into tears while continuously uttering cries of distress upon your repeatedly recurring hardships** (on the difficulties and wretchedness progressively coming upon you folks).
2. **Your riches have rotted; your garments have come to be moth-eaten.**
3. **Your gold and silver have been corrupted with poison** (or: corroded and covered with oxidation), **and their venom** (or: corrosion) **will proceed being unto you a witness** (or: evidence) **and will progressively eat your flesh** (= the enslaved and alienated self; = the human nature that has been molded by and conformed to the System) **as fire. You folks pile up a treasure hoard in the midst of last days** (or: [your] final days)!
4. **Consider and look to the workers' pay** (wage; hire) **– that having been withheld by you which belongs to those mowing your farms – which constantly utters** (or: shouts) **a cry, and now the outcries and shouts of those gathering in the harvest have entered into the ears of the LORD of Hosts** (= Yahweh of Sabaoth {= Armies})!
5. **You folks live a soft life in delicate luxury** (or: You self-indulge) **and take excessive comfort and live in wanton pleasure upon the land. You nourish your hearts in the midst of** (or: = fatten yourselves up for) **a day of slaughter!**
6. **You oppose fairness, equity and justice, while you degrade the way pointed out; you murder the fair and equitable person** (the Just One; the one in accord with the way pointed out; the upright person; or: the innocent); **he is not normally setting himself opposed to you** (or: is He not now aligning Himself against you, and resisting you folks?).

7. **Be patient** (long-tempered; long-passioned; slow to rush; or: Have long-term feelings and emotions, with anger pushed far away), **then, brothers, during the continuance of the Lord's** [= Yahweh's, or, Christ's] **presence and His being alongside. Consider! The worker of the land repeatedly receives** (takes out into his hands from within) **the precious fruit of the land** (or: ground), **being patient** (slow to rush and with long-term feelings; with anger far from him) **upon it, during the continuance where it can receive "an early as well as a latter** (or: late) **rain."** [Deut. 11:14]
8. **You, too, be patient** (be slow to rush while maintaining long-term feelings; putting anger far away); **establish** (place supports and make stable; firmly set) **your hearts, because the Lord's presence has come to be at hand** (has approached and now exists close to us; is accessible).

9. **O brothers, do not be groaning down against** (or: sighing in relation to; or: = complaining about or blaming) **one another, so that you may not be separated and have a decision made** (or: be put asunder, sifted, scrutinized and judged). **Consider! The Decider** (Sifter; Separator; Evaluator; Judge) **has taken a stand, and now continues standing before the doors.**

10. **Brothers, take the prophets who spoke within [the authority of], centered on, and in union with, the Name of the LORD** [= Yahweh] **as an example to be copied: of experiencing worthless responses and bad conditions while suffering from harmful treatment and evil – as well as of patience** (long-suffering; slow-rushing; long-term feelings; anger being pushed far away).
11. **Consider! We are calling happy and blessed those perseveringly remaining under** (or: patiently and humbly enduring; or: steadfast and supporting). **You heard [about] the persistent remaining under** (steadfast, patient and humble endurance) **of Job, and you saw the LORD's** [= Yahweh's] **goal** (the end attained by the LORD; the LORD's completion), **because**
>   **"the LORD** [= Yahweh] **is great of tender affections** (literally: great of internal organs; full of guts) **and is empathetically compassionate."** [Ex. 34:6]

572

12. **Now before all things** (= above all; but especially; or: before all mankind), **my brothers, do not be in the habit of promising by swearing [to, or, by] either the heaven** (or: atmosphere; sky), **nor the earth** (or: land; ground; dirt), **nor any other oath. But let your affirmation continually be, "Yes," and the negative, "No," to the intent that you may not fall under a process of judging** (or: fall by an act of sifting and separation for a decision, or by scrutinizing for evaluation, or by discriminating).

13. **Is anyone among you folks continually experiencing bad things** (misfortune; ugly situations; evil)**? Let him be habitually thinking with a view to having ease and well-being and repeatedly speak and act toward having goodness** (or: continually pray). **Is someone normally cheerful and in good spirits? Let him play a stringed or percussion instrument and make music or sing psalms.**

14. **Is anyone among you habitually experiencing weakness or normally infirm? Let him at once call to himself the older folks of the called-out community, and then let them speak well-being** (or: pray goodness) **upon him, anointing** (or: massaging) **him with olive oil in union with and in [the authority of] the Lord's** [= Yahweh's, or, Christ's] **Name,**

15. **and then faith's impartation of well-being** (or: the prayer which comes from trust; the good desire having conviction) **will progressively deliver** (restore to health; rescue; save; keep safe; make whole) **the one being continuously labored to weariness and exhaustion, and then the Lord** [= Christ, or, Yahweh] **will proceed causing him to rise, and if it may be [that] he has been making mistakes** (performing amiss; doing acts which miss the goal; deviating) **it will proceed being caused to flow away from him** (divorced and sent away for him; let go off in him; forgiven to him).

16. **Consequently, make it a habit to fully speak in accordance with and admit** (or: openly speaking out similarly about; fully acknowledge) **your failures** (errors; misses of the target; deviations; sins) **among other folks** (or: to one another), **and then be habitually speaking toward having goodness, ease and well-being over [those failures] of other folks** (or: continue praying and thinking goodness on behalf of one another), **in such a manner that you folks would be cured** (or, as an indicative: as you are instantly healed). **A binding need** (or: A petition and an entreaty out of need) **of a person within the Way pointed out** (of a fair and equitable person; of one in right relationship; of a rightwised and rightly aligned man; of a just one) **– which progressively works inwardly and itself continuously creates energy from union – constantly exerts much strength.**

17. **Elijah was a person** (a human being) **of like experiences and emotions with us, and with a thought toward having things be well he spoke toward having success** (or: prayed) **for it not to rain, and it did not rain upon the land [for] three years and six months.**

18. **And back again he spoke toward having goodness, ease and well-being** (or: offered prayer), **and the sky** (or: atmosphere; heaven) **gave rain, and then the land germinated and produced her fruit.**

19. **O my brothers** (= Dear family), **if someone among you may be led astray** (caused to wander) **away from the Truth and Reality, and someone should** (or: would) **turn him back,**

20. **continue knowing from experience and realize that this one turning back a sinner** (a failure; one deviating and missing the goal; a person living in error or under a mistake) **out of [the] straying of his way** (or: from the midst of his path of wandering), **will proceed delivering** (rescuing; saving; making healthy and whole) **a soul** (a consciousness; or: = a person) **from out of the midst of its death** [other MSS: his soul from out of the midst of Death], **and "will cover [the] fullness of [his] mistakes** (errors; failures to hit the target; deviations; sins).**" [Prov. 10:12]

[written circa A.D. 47-48 – Based on the critical analysis of John A.T. Robinson]

FIRST PETER

CHAPTER 1

1. **Peter, one sent with a mission pertaining to Jesus Christ** (or: an emissary and representative of, and from, [the] Anointed Jesus), **to selected and picked out exiles** (or: alien residents; sojourners; expatriates; strangers residing in a country not your own) **of [the] dispersion** (or: from a scattering; of [the] *Diaspora*), **temporarily living beside residents of Pontus, Galatia, Cappadocia, the province of Asia, and Bithynia,** [*cf* Rev. 2 &3]
2. **– to folks gathered, laid-out and chosen in accord with and down from Father God's foreknowledge** (or: corresponding to a previous experiential and intimate knowledge possessed by God, who is a Father), **within a setting-apart of spirit** (or: in union with the process of being set apart from common condition and use by [the] Spirit; or: in the midst of a sacred differencing which is a Breath-effect) **[leading] into an obedient hearing** (or: [focused] to being centered in a listening and paying attention with compliance) **and a sprinkling with Jesus Christ's blood** (or: a sprinkling of blood, which is Jesus Christ):
May grace (or: favor) **and peace from the joining be multiplied into fullness** (or: be brought to fullness) **in and among you folks** (or: to you folks; for you folks)!

3. **Well-spoken of** (or: Eulogized; Blessed; or: Well-gathered, laid-out with ease, and worthy of praise) **[is] the God and Father of our Lord, Jesus Christ** (or: Who is our Owner, Jesus Christ), **the One bringing us to birth again** (regenerating us; begetting us back up again; causing us to be born again) **down from, in line with and in correspondence to His abundant mercy** (or: the much-existing sympathizing and active compassion which is Him) **– through Jesus Christ's resurrection forth from out of the midst of dead folks. [We are born again]:**
       into a progressively living expectation (or: into the midst of continuously living hope);
4.   **into the midst of an incorruptible** (unspoilable; imperishable; unruinable; undecayable), **unstained** (undefiled), **and unfading** (or: unwithering) **inheritance** (or: enjoyment of and participation in an allotted portion as a possession) –
           one having been kept in view, watched-over, guarded, and which continues being maintained and kept intact within the midst of [the, or our] atmospheres (or: in union with heavens; = in realms of spirit);
– [which things were and are being birthed and entering] into the midst of you folks,
5. **the ones being continuously garrisoned within** (or: kept, maintained and guarded in the center of) **God's power, in union with an ability which is God, through [His] faithfulness,**
       into a deliverance (a rescue which brings health, wholeness and a return to your original state and condition; salvation; a [period of] rescue) **[which is now] ready to be unveiled** (revealed; disclosed) **within the midst of and in union with [this] last season** (or: resident within a final fitting situation; in a final fertile moment; on [this] last occasion),
6. **within which [season and deliverance] you folks are presently feeling constant joy and happiness and are continuing to rejoice exceedingly – though for a little while, at present, since** (or: if) **it continues being binding and necessary, being pained** (distressed; grieved; sorrowed) **within various tests** (or: different trials and ordeals) **to put you to the proof.**
[*cf* 2 Thes. 1:4-8]
7. **[This is] to the end that the examined and tested approval of your faith** (of the trust and faithfulness of you folks) **– [being] of much greater value and worth, and more precious, than of gold that constantly loses itself away** (perishes of itself) **despite being progressively tested and examined through fire – might be found [progressing] into praise** (approval; commendation) **and glory** (or: a good reputation) **and honor** (value; worth) **within an unveiling of Jesus Christ** (or: in union with a revelation whose source is, which has the character of, and which is, Jesus, [the] Anointed One; in the midst of a disclosure from [Messiah] Jesus),
8. **Whom not seeing** (or: perceiving), **you folks are continuously loving and accepting** (or: experiencing the urge for reunion); **into Whom at the present moment you folks are not constantly looking, yet are habitually believing** (or: continuously placing [your] trust and

574

loyalty). **You folks are repeatedly rejoicing and being very happy in indescribable** (or: incapable of being spoken out) **joy which also exists having been made glorious**
> (or: by unspeakable and glorified joy; in joy [that is] inexpressible and has made a notable reputation; with joy that is glorious beyond words, and which is filled with imagination and good opinion),

9. **being ones constantly bringing to, or conveying in, yourselves – as provision, attentive care and kindly keeping – the promised goal** (the finished product; the aim and result; the purpose and destiny) **of the** [other MSS: your] **faith and trust: deliverance** ([the] restoration to wholeness and health; a salvation) **of souls** (or: from inner beings and selves; or: = of people)!

10. **Concerning** (or: Round about) **which deliverance** (health and wholeness; rescue; salvation) **[the] prophets, carefully scrutinizing, sought out and then diligently searched out the [Scriptures] prophesying concerning** (or: about) **the grace and favor [directed and coming] into you folks,**
11. **constantly searching into which season or what kind of situation the Spirit of Christ** (or: Christ's spirit; or: the Breath-effect which is the Anointed One), **resident within them, was continuing to point to, making [it] evident and clearly visible, repeatedly testifying** (witnessing; giving evidence) **beforehand about the effects of the experiences and results of the sufferings [projected] into Christ, and the glories** (the manifestations which call forth praise; the good opinions and reputations; the appearances of things) **after these things,**
12. **to which folks** (or: in which ones) **it was unveiled** (revealed; disclosed) **that not to or for themselves, but to and for you people, they had been progressively dispensing and serving them – which things are now announced** (or: which tidings were brought back) **to you through those announcing** (proclaiming; bringing and communicating) **the message of well-being and goodness** (or: good news) **to you within** [or, with other MSS: by] **a set-apart Breath-effect** (or: [the] Holy Spirit; or: sacred spirit) **being sent forth from [the] atmosphere** (or: heaven) **– into which things agents** (or: messengers; folks that had the message) **are habitually and earnestly desiring** (are constantly in full passion and craving) **to stoop down beside and look** (or: peer; peek) **inside, so as to obtain a clearer and more accurate view.**

13. **On which account** (or: Wherefore), **in preparation for work or action, girding up in yourselves the clothes about the loins** (or: waist; = getting ready for action) **of your divided thoughts and the things passing through your mind** (or: mental perceptions; intellect and comprehension), **continuously being perfectly** (or: maturely) **clear-headed and sober** (unintoxicated), **direct and set** (or: being constantly sober-minded, completely direct and set) **your hope and expectation upon the grace and favor being continuously brought** (or: periodically and progressively carried) **to you within an unveiling** (or: in the midst of a disclosure) **of Jesus Christ** (or: a revelation which is Jesus [the] Anointed One; or: an uncovering which comes from and pertains to Jesus Christ).
14. **As children of** (= having the qualities of and characteristics from) **submissive, attentive hearing** (or: Like listening and obedient born-ones), **not being folks repeatedly molding, forming, fashioning or configuring yourselves to and by the former cravings** (the prior over-desires or full passions), **within your ignorance,**
15. **but rather, corresponding to** (down from; in accord with) **the One calling** (or: inviting) **you [being] set-apart** (or: holy), **you folks also let yourselves be made to be** (or: be birthed) **ones set-apart in the same way, in all behavior** (within every conduct; in all turning about or twisting up of [your] way of life),
16. **because it has been written that,**
> **"You people will continue being set-apart** (or: sacredly different and holy), **because I [am] set-apart** (or: holy; different from ordinary)." [Lev. 11:44, 45; 19:2; 20:7]

17. **And since** (or: if) **you folks are habitually calling upon a** (or: [the]) **Father – the One consistently separating and deciding** (or: judging) **impartially** (without reception of faces, persons, appearances or external circumstances) **according to** (down from; corresponding to) **each one's work or action – let the time of your sojourn** (your temporary stay, dwelling alongside as an alien resident or an exile) **be turned upward, in the fear of reverent living,**

18. **having seen, and thus knowing, that you folks were not unbound and released by a ransom of corruptible things** (things that are perishable and subject to spoiling) **– by little coins of silver or gold – from out of your fruitless behavior** (vain conduct; idle and foolish way of life) **handed down by tradition from the fathers** (= your ancestors),

19. **but rather by Christ's precious blood** (or: in valuable blood, which is [the] Anointed One; with honorable blood of anointing; by costly blood from [the Messiah]) **– as of a flawless** (unblemished) **and spotless Lamb:**

20. **being One having been foreknown** (previously known by intimate experience), **indeed, before [the] casting down**

> (as of material for a foundation: founding; as of seed in a field: sowing; as of seed of a man: conception [*cf* Heb. 11:11]; as in throwing something down: overthrowing; as in battle = slaying; in politics: abandoning [a measure]; of debts: paying down by installments;) **of [the; or: an] ordered System** (world; universe; a particular order or arrangement of things; or: = the aggregate of humanity), **yet One being set in clear light and manifested upon [the] last part** (or: final; [*p*72 and others read plural: last things, circumstances or aspects]) **of the times** (or: of the [or: these] successive chronological time periods) **because of you folks –**

21. **the ones [who] through Him [are] folks trustingly adhering unto God**

> (or: [are] believing ones, ones full of faith, and confiding ones [proceeding] [*p* 72 & other MSS read the present participle: ones habitually putting trust] into God): **the One awakening and raising Him up, forth from out of the midst of dead folks** (or: from out of union with dead people), **and giving glory to Him** (a good reputation for Him; a manifestation which calls forth praise in Him). **Consequently, your faith** (trust; confidence; loyalty) **and expectation** (or: hope) **are to continuously exist being [plugged; put; focused] into God** (or: are to be [returned] into the midst of God)!

22. **Having purified your souls** (= inner selves) **within the hearing obedience** (the humble, attentive listening and submissive hearing) **of the Truth and from Reality [which directs and leads] into unhypocritical** (non-hypercritical; non-hyper-separating so as to over-evaluate; not determined from below; non-nit-picky; or: unpretended; unfeigned; thus: genuine) **brotherly affection** (= fondness for the fellow believers), **love one another with acceptance in a stretched-out and extended way, from out of a clean** [other MSS: true; genuine] **heart,**

23. **being folks having been born again** (been regenerated; been given birth back up again), **not from out of a corruptible** (or: perishable) **seed that was sown, but rather from an incorruptible** (imperishable; undecayable) **one: through God's continually living and permanently remaining** *Logos* (or: through a message or expressed thought of [the] continuously living and constantly abiding God; or: through means of a living and dwelling Thought, Idea and Logically laid out Expression, Communication and Word, which is God),

24. **because,**

> **"All flesh [is] like grass** (or: vegetation), **and all its glory [is] like a flower of grass** (of vegetation): **the grass is caused to dry out and wither, and the flower falls off...**

25. > **"yet the gush-effect of the Lord** (result of what flowed from [Yahweh]; saying, declaration or thing spoken concerning the Lord) **is constantly abiding** (continuously remaining), **on into The Age** (or: the era [of the Messiah])." [Isa. 40:6-8]

Now this continues being "the saying" (the declaration; the gush-effect) **being announced as well-being and goodness to you folks** (or: And this is the thing, and the result of the flow, being spoken into you in the good news).

CHAPTER 2

1. **Therefore, being folks putting off** (setting away; ridding) **from yourselves all poor quality** (worthlessness; bad character; malice; what is not as it ought to be; wickedness) **and all deceitful bait** (fraud; guile) **and "answers" from perverse scholarship**

> (or: underlying decisions affecting interpretations and judgments made from opinions; or: overly critical behaviors; deficiencies in ability to sift and decide; judgments from inferior positions; legalistic pulling-apart of things for critical analysis; under-assessments) **and**

envies and all down-talks (speeches or talks which put people, issues or situations down; backbiting),
2. **as recently born infants, intensely yearn** (crave; long) **for the non-baiting** (undeceitful; guileless; honest; unadulterated) **milk belonging to the Word** (*Logos*) **which is pertaining to thought, reason and communication, and which contains the qualities and characteristics contained in the message – to the end that, within it, you folks can** (or: would; may) **grow and increase into health and wholeness** (deliverance; rescued safety; salvation; restoration),
3. **since** (or: if) **you folks,**
> **"by sipping, tasted** (= experienced) **that the Lord** [= Yahweh or Christ] **[is] good, kind and useful** (or: obliging and profitable)**!"** [Ps. 34:9]

4. **Continuously approaching toward Whom – a living Stone, on the one hand being One having been and still being thrown away** (rejected; disapproved) **by mankind** (humans; people), **as the result of a test; yet, on the other hand a Chosen One, a Precious** (Inwardly-valuable; [held]-in-honor) **One, beside God** (= side-by-side with God; = in the presence of God; = in God's view) **–**
5. **you yourselves are, as living stones, continuously being erected** (or: progressively constructed and built up) **[as; to be] a spiritual house** (a building with its source being the Spirit, with the characteristics of a Breath-effect)**: [built] into a set-apart** (or: holy; sacred; different-from-the-ordinary) **priesthood to bear up spiritual sacrifices** (or: offerings) **well** (or: most) **acceptable in God** (or: by God; to God; for God; with God), **through Jesus Christ,**
6. **so that it continues being contained** (encompassed; included) **in Scripture:**
> **"Consider** (Behold; Look)**! I am progressively setting** (placing; laying) **within Zion a chosen** (picked-out), **precious** (held in honor and value) **cornerstone lying at the extreme angle, and the one habitually trusting** (relying; believing; investing loyalty) **upon It may by no means be disgraced or brought to shame or be disappointed."** [Isa. 28:16]

7. **Therefore, in** (or: for; with) **you folks – those habitually trusting** (constantly believing and remaining convinced) **– [is] the Precious and Honorable One** (or: To you then, who continue loyal, [He is] valuable). **Yet for** (or: to; in; with) **those continuing being without faith** (or: being habitually distrustful; being constantly unbelieving or disloyal), **[He is]**
> **"A Stone which those in process of building the house reject** (or: threw away after inspecting and trying) **– this One is brought to be** (or: was birthed) **into [position of] Head and Source of [the] corner,"** [Ps. 118:22]
8. **also [He is]**
> **"A Stone that [people] strike against and that causes a stumbling-effect, even a Rock-mass which functions as a trap-spring** (designed to be a snare),**"** [Isa. 8:14]
who, continuing being unpersuaded (unconvinced and thus, uncompliant or stubborn), **are repeatedly stumbling by** (or: in) **the Word** (or: who are constantly stumbling, habitually being disobedient to the message), **into which [situation] they were placed** (= as it was planned).

9. **Yet you folks [are] "a picked-out** (selected; chosen) **offspring** (family; kin; lineage; race; species; breed) [Isa. 43:20; Deut. 7:6], **a royal** (kingly; palace) **priesthood** [Ex. 19:6; Isa. 61:6], **a set-apart** (holy; different) **multitude** (company; nation; body of people living together; swarm; association; ethnic group; caste; [Ex. 19:6; note: implies a sacred life]), **a people constructed into an encirclement** (made into a surrounding structure; set as a perimeter; made into a performance about [Him]; formed around as an acquisition; gathered into a surrounding [flock])**"** [Isa. 43:21; Ex. 19:5] **– so that you may tell forth the message of** (or: out-message; publish; declare abroad) **the excellencies and qualities of nobleness** (virtues of braveness, courage, good character, quality, self-restraint, magnificence, benevolence, reliability) **of and from the One calling you out of darkness** (gloomy dimness; the realm of shadows and obscurity) **into the midst of His wonderful** (marvelous; amazing) **light** [p72 reads: into the wonderful Light],
10. **[you] who [were] once** (or: formerly) **"not a people," but now [are] "God's people;" [formerly] being the ones having "not been given mercy," yet now [are] "folks being mercied** (being given mercy).**"** [Hos. 2:23]

11. **Folks that are loved** (Beloved ones)**: I am presently calling you alongside to encourage, aid, comfort and admonish you, as resident aliens** (exiles; sojourners; ones dwelling beside citizens in a foreign country) **and temporary residents** (expatriates; strangers) **to continually hold yourselves away from the fleshly over-desires** (passions; full-rushing upon things), **which things are constantly warring** (doing military service; battling) **down against the soul** (the inner self and being),

12. **continuously holding your beautiful behavior** (your fine and ideal turning yourselves back around) **among the multitudes** (the companies; the associations; the ethnic groups; the nations; the castes; the non-Jews, or, Gentiles), **to the end that, within what thing they are continually speaking down pertaining to you folks** (repeatedly speaking against you) **as of ones constantly doing the worthless and things of bad quality** (or: as of evildoers or criminals; as of those repeatedly creating bad situations or forming what not ought to be), **repeatedly looking upon and observing as eyewitnesses the outcome from the beautiful actions** (the fine deeds; the ideal and honorable works), **they may glorify** (or: give a good opinion of) **God, within a day of inspection and overseeing care.**

13. **Because of, and by, the Lord** [= Yahweh or Christ], **you folks are to be humbly aligned in and to every human creation and with every societal invention**

> (or: be subordinated to every human framing; let yourselves be arranged under for support of every founding or institution pertaining to mankind which brings order to a state of wildness)**: whether to** (or: by; for) **a king, as to** (or: by; for) **one being superior** (or: constantly holding over [others]; = as a prominent cultural institution),

14. **or to** (or; by; for) **governors** (government officials; rulers; leaders; guides), **as to** (or: by; for; with) **those being regularly sent** (or: dispatched) **by Him unto a maintaining of right, in regard to doers of worthlessness**

> (or: into a correction from out of the way pointed out pertaining to those creating bad situations; unto an administering of justice, fairness and equity of situations affected by evildoers) – **yet on the other hand, [sent] unto a commendation** (a praise; applause) **of those habitually doing good things** (performing with virtue; constructing excellence).

15. **Because thus is God's will** (or: For God's intent and purpose exists in this manner)**: folks habitually doing good things** (constructing excellence; performing with virtues; creating goodness) **to repeatedly muzzle** (continuously gag; thus: progressively silence) **the ignorance of senseless and thoughtless people** (humans without intellect and prudence; unreasonable folks);

16. **as free folks** (those not bound) – **and not continually holding** (or: having) **the freedom as a covering** (or: a veil) **of worthlessness** (bad quality; evil; poorness of situation) – **but still, as God's slaves.**

17. **Value everyone** (Honor all)! **Habitually love** (Keep up the urge toward union of; Repeatedly accept) **the brotherhood** (= the organism of fellow-believers)! **Practice reverence to God** (or: Habitually fear God; Be constantly respecting and revering God)! **Be continuously valuing and showing honor to the king** (or: the One Who reigns).

18. **The domestics** (house servants or slaves; members of a household), **those habitually being subordinated** (being humbly aligned and subjected for support) **by** (or: to; for) **the owners** (masters)**: [conduct yourselves] in all fear and respect – not only to the good and lenient** (reasonable, suitable; equitable; gentle; considerate) **ones, but also to the crooked folks –**

19. **for this [is] grace: if through [the] conscience, which is God,** (or: through awareness pertaining to God; or: by means of a joint-knowing with God; or: because of consciousness of God), **someone is continuing to bear and hold up under distress or pains** (griefs; sorrows; anxieties; sufferings), **continuously experiencing it wrongfully** (unjustly; contrarily, in regard to fairness and right relationship; undeservedly)!

20. **For what sort of credible report** (honorable rumor; credit; fame; praiseworthy reputation) **[is it] if, being ones habitually doing what is wrong** (failing to hit the target; sinning) **and being repeatedly beaten and struck with a fist** [*p*72 & other MSS: repeatedly lopped-off and pruned], **you folks will continue** [*p*72 & other MSS read: you are constantly] **remaining under**

and enduring [it]? But to the contrary, if while habitually practicing virtue (doing good; constructing excellence) and [at the same time] repeatedly experiencing such bad treatment (or: continually suffering) you will continue [*p72* reads: you are constantly] humbly remaining under, enduring and supporting [it], this [is] grace at the side of (or: from beside; = in the presence of) God,

21. for into this you are called (or: were invited), because Christ also experienced [this] (or: suffered) over you folks (or: for your sakes), leaving continuously below (or: behind) in you (or: with and for you) an underwriting (a writing under which you are to write or copy; hence: a pattern; a model) to the end that you could (or: would) follow-on in the footprints of Him

22.   "Who does not make a mistake (Who did not perform failure; Who does no sin; Who
           does not construct failure to hit the target), nor is (or: was) deceitful bait (fraud; guile)
           found in His mouth;" [Isa. 53:9]

23. Who, being repeatedly reviled (harshly and bitingly rebuked and insulted), was not reviling back (answering insult with insult; taking the position of harsh, biting rebuke); continuously (or: repeatedly) suffering (experiencing ill treatment), he was not threatening, but kept on giving [the situation] over to (committing [it] with; entrusting [it] in) the One at His side: the One constantly sifting, separating and deciding (or: judging) fairly (equitably; following the Path of the Way pointed out, bringing situations to a rightwised condition),

24. Who, Himself, bore back up again our failures (our mistakes; our times of falling short or to the side of the target; our sins and errors) [Isa. 53:4, 12] within His body upon the tree (the wood; the stake), to the end that, being folks suddenly coming to be parted away from the failures (mistakes; errors; sins; misses of the target), we can (or: would; may) live in (or: by; for; with) the eschatological deliverance to fairness and equity, in rightwised relationships, in the Path of the Way pointed out (or: = in covenant participation), where "you folks are (or: were) healed (or: cured) in the wound (or: by the welt; in the bruise of the blow)." [Isa. 53:5]

25. For you folks were continuing to be "like sheep, being habitually caused to wander (being led astray; or, as a middle: people constantly wandering away)," [Isa. 53:6] but now in contrast, "you are (or: were) turned around and made to return, upon" [the will of; the herding of] the Shepherd and Overseer of (Supervisor of; the One who watches over) your souls (your inner beings).

CHAPTER 3

1. Likewise (In like manner), you wives: [Be] habitually with humility aligning yourselves to your own husbands (or: women: [Be] continually arranging yourselves for support, under your own adult males), to the end that if any (or: certain ones) are habitually unpersuaded by the Word (or: uncompliant or disobedient to the message; unconvinced with the thought, reason or idea), they will continue being profited (will progressively receive advantage; or: will proceed in being acquired as gain) without a word (or: message; reason), through the behavior (or: conduct; way of life) of the wives (or: women),

2. being eyewitnesses of (or: looking upon and observing) the pure behavior (or: way of life; conduct) of you folks – which is turned upward in reverence, respect and [sacred] fear and awe –

3. whose world must not consist of the external adornment – of braiding or interweaving or struggling with [the] hair and [the] placing-around of gold ornaments, or of dressing up (putting on garments) –

4. but to the contrary, [it should consist of] the hidden person (concealed humanity; cloaked personality) of the heart, within the incorruptible and imperishable quality of the gentle (egoless; tender; mild; calm; kind; meek) and still (at ease; restful; tranquil; quiet) spirit (or: attitude; disposition; or: Breath-effect), which is (or: continually exists being) of great value and very costly in God's sight (= view, or, perspective).

5. For thus, at one time, the set-apart wives (or: the holy women) – those being in the habit of placing their expectations and hopes into God – used to normally arrange their world and adorn themselves, constantly being put in humble alignment to their own husbands (or: continuously being arranged under their own adult males, to give support),

6. **as Sarah used to humbly hear and submissively obey Abraham, habitually calling him "lord"** ("master;" "my owner"), **of which woman you were birthed children** (or: you are become her born ones [= daughters]), **women normally doing good** (performing virtue; creating excellence), **and not being repeatedly caused to fear even one dismay** (alarm; intimidation).
7. **Husbands** (or: Adult males), **likewise** (or: in like manner): **Continuously dwelling together** (cohabiting; making a joint home) **with [them] corresponding to intimate, experiential knowledge [of them]** (= with a learned insight and an intelligent recognition of the nature and aspects of a married situation), **[be] habitually assigning** (portioning-off; awarding; allotting) **honor** (value; worth) **to the female attributes** (things pertaining to a woman; or: to a feminine one) **as to a person having a disadvantaged position in her living** (or: a weaker livelihood; or: a weaker vessel, utensil, instrument, container, gear, furniture, equipment), **yet as to co-heirs of Life's grace and favor**

> (or: of [the] grace which is life; or, with other MSS: as joint-participants in an inheritance of manifold {diverse; varied; multicolored} grace – of life [p72 adds: pertaining to and having the qualities of the Age {of eonian life}]), **into the [situation where] your**

thoughts, words and actions projected toward goodness (or: prayers) **continue not to be hindered or blocked, as if by a trench being cut in their path to impede their progress.**
8. **Now [this is] the goal** (the final situation; the end of the process): **all [are to be] like-minded** (of the same frame of mind and disposition), **folks sharing and expressing the same feelings** (being sympathetic), **ones being fond of and expressing affection for the brothers** (= fellow believers; = communal members), **people tenderhearted and compassionate, folks of a humble disposition and way of thinking;**
9. **not being ones habitually giving back** (repaying; rendering; giving away) **bad in the place of bad** (or: poor quality in exchange for poor quality; evil for evil) **or abusive language in the place of abusive language** (reviling in exchange for reviling; insulting back against insults), **but just the opposite: constantly speaking things that embody wellness or give a blessing, because into this you are called** (or: were invited), **to the end that you folks may inherit a word embodying wellness** (a blessing; a message of goodness; a thought bringing ease).
10. **For you see,**

> **"the person who continues purposing** (willing; intending; wanting) **to be habitually loving** (accepting; urging toward union with; giving himself to) **life, and to see and experience good days, let his tongue at once cease from [the] worthless and poor of quality** (from [the] bad and evil) **and his lips speak no deceitful bait** (fraud; guile).

11. > **"Now let him bend to incline forth and turn out, away from [the] worthless and poor of quality** (from [what is] bad or evil), **and let him do** (practice; construct; produce) **[the] good** (or: virtue; excellence); **let him seek and try to find peace and harmony; let him also run after it and pursue it,**

12. > **"because [the] Lord's** [= Yahweh's] **eyes [are] upon** (= He looks with favor on) **[the] fair and equitable folks** (the rightwised ones; the just ones who walk in the Way pointed out), **and His ears [directed] into their request pertaining to need; yet [the] face of [the] Lord** [= Yahweh] (i.e., His countenance and posturing) **[is] upon** (= set against) **wrongdoers** (those constantly practicing worthless things, repeatedly constructing bad things or habitually doing evil)." [Ps. 34:13-17]

13. **And who [is] the person who will continue treating you badly** (causing evil to come to you) **if you folks should come to be zealots in regard to the good** (ones boiling hot from the influence of the Good; enthusiasts of virtue and excellence)?
14. **But even if you folks might continue experiencing suffering [as well as other things] because of fairness and equity** (justice; walking in the Way pointed out; a rightwised covenant positioning), **[you are] happy and blessed ones.**

> **"Yet do not fear their fear** (i.e., what they fear; or, as a subjunctive: Now you should not be afraid of the fear that has them as a source), **nor yet should you folks be shaken** (agitated; disturbed; stirred up) **[by them]."** [Isa. 8:12]

15. **Now "you folks set [the] Lord** [= Yahweh] **– the Anointed One – apart** (or: Yet, let the Lord Christ be set-apart)" [Isa. 8:13], **within your hearts!** (or: So, treat the Anointed Owner as

holy, in the core of your beings), **always ready** (ever prepared) **toward a defense to everyone – for the one repeatedly asking you for a word** (i.e., a rational explanation and a logical response) **about the expectation within you folks – but still with gentleness** (tenderness; meekness; kindness) **and deep respect** (or: serious caution; reverence; [the] fear [of the Lord]),

16. **habitually holding a good conscience** (or: having a virtuous joint-knowing, from possessing a clear joined-perception), **so that those, having a habit of spitefully abusing and harassing your good behavior** (or: conduct; way of life) **within, and in union with, Christ, may be brought to shame and disgrace relating to that within which you folks are constantly being defamed** (spoken down against).

17. **You see, [it is] a stronger [case, position or reputation] to be repeatedly experiencing harassment, abuse or suffering [while, or, because of] habitually doing good** (practicing virtue; creating goodness) **– if God's purpose** (intent; will) **may be repeatedly willing it – than [because of] constantly doing what is wrong, bad or worthless,**

18. **because even Christ** (or: considering that Messiah also) **died** [other MSS: suffered], **once for all [time, and people], concerning** (in relation to) **failures to hit the target** (about errors and mistakes; around and encompassing sins [some MSS: our failures; other MSS: your failures]) **– a Just One** (a rightwised One; One in accord with the Way pointed out; a fair and equitable individual) **over [the situation of]** (or: for the sake of) **unjust ones** (capsized folks; those out of accord with the Way pointed out; unfair and inequitable people) **– to the end that He at once may bring** (or: can lead; would conduct) **you folks** [other MSS: us] **to** (or: toward; to be face to face with) **God. [He], on the one hand, being put to death in flesh** (= a physical body), **yet on the other hand, being made alive in spirit** (or: indeed, being put to death by flesh {or: = the estranged human condition}, yet, being engendered a living one by Breath-effect {or: [the] Spirit}),

19. **at one point journeying** (going from one place to another; passing on) **within which** (or: in union with Which), **He also proclaimed** (published; preached; heralded) **the message to and for** (or: among) **the spirits in prison** (within a guardhouse):

20. **to and for those being at one time unconvinced** (unpersuaded; disobedient; noncompliant) **within [the] days of Noah, when** (or: while) **he was continuing to be receiving forth, and taking away from, out of God's state of emotional quietness** (taking a long time before rushing or being in a heat of passion; long-enduring patience; putting anger far away) **while [the] ark was progressively being prepared and equipped** (constructed to readiness) **– into which a few folks, that is, eight souls** (= people), **were brought safely through [the] water** (or: were brought safely through, by means of water),

21. **[into] which, also, an echo of correspondent form** (or: a copy; an antitype; an impress which answers back; in place of the type or pattern) **is now progressively delivering** (rescuing) **you folks** (or: repeatedly bringing you to safety)**: immersion** (submersion and envelopment which brings absorption and permeation to the point of saturation) **– not [the] putting off of [the] filth** (removal of dirt) **away from [the] flesh** (= not baptism or bathing of the physical body, or the removal of the alienated false persona), **but rather – the result of a full inquiry into the midst of God** (or: the effect of an added request unto God; or: = a further quest into "the Divine Mystery" – Paul Tillich) **made by a good conscience** (from an excellent joint-knowing; in relation to virtuous co-knowledge). **[It saves you and it is made] through means of [the] resurrection of Jesus Christ,**

22. **Who continuously exists** (or: is; has being) **within [the place of]** (or: = on or at) **God's right [side, or hand; – i.e., the place of authority and ability to exercise power; the place of receiving], going from place to place, journeying into [the] atmosphere** (or: heaven) **of those being humbly aligned by Him** (or: pertaining to those subjected, placed and arranged under in Him; which are the folks being set in order for support to Him): **of agents** (or: messengers; folks with the message), **and of authorities** (or: those who have the right and privilege from out of Being), **and of powers** (or: folks with abilities and influence).

CHAPTER 4

1. **Christ, then, having undergone experiences and suffering IN FLESH** (or: being physically and emotionally affected to the point of suffering) **over us** (or: over our [situation] and for our sakes), **you folks also arm and equip yourselves with the same mental inclination** (idea;

thought; way of thinking; frame of mind; attitude), **because the person [thus] suffering or going through physical or emotional experiences which affect him IN [the] FLESH** (or: = by [his] estranged humanity or alienated self) **has in and for himself put a stop to failures, errors and mistakes** (or: sins) [or, with other MSS: has been caused to cease from sin],
2. **[and comes] into the [condition or situation] to no longer live out the additional remaining course [of his] time within [the] FLESH** (= in the natural realm) **in the midst of** (or: in union with) **[the] full passions** (or: for [the] over-desires; to [the] rushings of emotions upon things) **of humans** (or: pertaining to or originating in mankind), **but to the contrary, in God's will** (or: for God's intent; to God's purpose).

3. **For the time** [other MSS add: of the life] **having gone by, and now being past, [is; was] sufficient** (= we have spent enough time, in [the life of] the past,) [other MSS add: for us] **to have accomplished** (to have worked down and effected) **the thing desired by** (or: the intention of) **the multitudes** (the nations; the swarms of ethnic groups living together; the non-Jews; the Gentiles), **having gone from place to place** (or: journeyed) **in indecent and licentious debaucheries** (deeds of loose conduct), **in rushing passions and over-desires, in excesses bubbling over with wine, in carousing and festive processions, in drinking parties, and in forbidden** (i.e., illegal in respect to the natural laws of reason, conscience and common decency) **idolatries** (or: being a servant to or worshiping external forms or appearances, phantoms of the mind, unsubstantial or reflected images, or conveyed impressions),
4. **within which they, repeatedly speaking abusively, slanderously, injuriously and giving a false image [about you, as well as about other folks], are constantly struck with surprise, thinking it strange and foreign that you folks are not always running together with [them], as a mob, into the same flooding** (pouring forth) **of unhealthiness and lack of safety** (or: dissoluteness of a course devoid of salvation).
5. **Such folks will continue rendering an account** (or: giving back a reason by patterned information) **to the One readily and continually judging** (repeatedly evaluating and making a decision about) [p72: prepared to judge; other MSS: constantly holding {Himself} in readiness to judge] **living folks and dead ones,**
6. **for into this [purpose], also, the message of goodness and well-being is** (or: the good news was suddenly, or at one point) **brought and announced to** (or: for; among) **dead folks, to the end that on the one hand THEY may at some point be JUDGED** (or: can be separated, evaluated and decided about) **– corresponding to humans – IN FLESH**
(or: according to humans in flesh; or: = in the sphere of people with estranged selves; or: = on the level of mankind in an alienated condition that was enslaved by the System), **yet on the other hand, that THEY can continue LIVING** (or: would be habitually and progressively living; or: but now one-after-another become alive) **– corresponding to** (down from; in line and accord with; in the sphere of) **God – IN SPIRIT** (or: by Breath-effect; with attitude; for [the] Spirit).

7. **Now the Goal** (or: the end; the final act; or: the finished Product; or: the completion of the plan) **of all people** (and: pertaining to and affecting all things) **has approached and is now near at hand and [He] is close enough to touch** (= has arrived)! **Therefore, you folks keep a healthy and sound frame of mind** (be sane and sensible) **and be sober** (be unintoxicated; i.e., be functional and with your wits about you) **into [a state, condition or realm with] views toward having goodness, ease and well-being** (or: into the midst of prayers). [*1 Cor. 13:7]
8. **Before all people** (or: = More than anything), **continue being folks constantly holding the outstretching and extending Love** (unambiguous, uniting acceptance) **unto yourselves** (i.e., into each other) **– "because Love** (the urge toward union; self-giving) **is constantly covering*** (habitually throwing a veil over; progressively concealing; [and with other MSS: will continue covering]) **a multitude of failures** (mistakes; errors; misses of the target; sins)." [Prov. 10:12]
9. **[Continue being] those [who are] stranger-loving unto one another** (= friendly, kind and hospitable to strangers, foreigners and aliens [inviting them] into the midst of each other's [homes and/or societies]), **without expressing dissatisfaction** (complaining; grumbling; murmuring),
10. **each one, according as he receives an effect of grace** (or: received a result of favor), **continuously giving supporting service and dispensing it unto yourselves** (i.e., into each other), **as beautiful** (fine; ideal) **house managers** (stewards; administrators) **of God's varied**

grace (or: of [the] diverse favor which is God; [as] of a many-colored [tapestry] of grace whose source and character are from God).

11. **If anyone is normally speaking, [let it be], as it were, God's little words** (= as inspired sayings, messages, thoughts and ideas from God; as units of patterned information about God; like little expressions of *Logos*, which are God); **if anyone is habitually providing attending service and dispensing, [let it be] as out of a strength which God is continually supplying** (furnishing; providing), **to the end that, in union with all people** (and: within all things), **God may be constantly glorified** (would habitually receive a good reputation; can continue in an assumed appearance, with imagination) **through Jesus Christ, in Whom** (by Whom; for Whom; to Whom; with Whom) **is** (or: exists) **the glory** (the manifestation of that which calls forth praise; the good reputation; the assumed appearance; the imagination; the opinion) **and the strength** (the might), **on into the ages of the ages** (or: into the indefinite time periods of the ages; into the superlative times of the eons).

12. **Beloved ones, do not repeatedly feel like strangers to the burning** (= the action of the Fire) **within and among you folks, which is habitually happening to you with a view toward your being put to the test** (or: which is presently repeatedly coming into being in the face of a proving trial for you, and is progressively birthing itself to an examination in you), **as though a strange thing or a foreign occurrence is repeatedly walking with you folks.** [*cf* Rev. 3:10]

13. **But on the contrary, keep on rejoicing and being glad to the extent or degree that you folks are continually participating with a common share and common existence in the effects of the experiences, along with the results of the sufferings, of the Christ, to the end that, while continuously exulting and celebrating exceedingly, you folks can** (or: should; would) **also rejoice within this unveiling of His glory** (or: in union with the disclosure of His reputation; or: in the midst of this praise-inducing manifestation which is Him)!

14. **Since** (or: If) **you folks are constantly being insulted and censured in** (or: [because of] union with) **the Name of Christ, [you are] happy ones** (blessed folks), **because God's spirit of glory and power** (or: the Breath-effect of the reputation and from the appearance, along with the ability of God) **is continuously "resting back upon" you folks** [*cf.* Isa. 11:2].

15. **Of course let not any one of you folks be experiencing suffering as a murderer, or a thief, or a doer of worthless or evil things, or, as a meddler** (an interferer) **in other people's affairs** (or: one who focuses on things strange, foreign or "other," or involving a place-change).

16. **Yet if as a Christian [she or he is suffering], let him or her not continue feeling shame or embarrassment, but let him or her constantly glorify** (give credit to; enhance the reputation of; bring an opinion of high status for) **God within this Name** (or: in union with this name [i.e., "Christian;" or, referring to "the Name of Christ" in vs. 14, above]),

17. **because [it is; this is; now is] the** [other MSS: a] **fitting situation and fertile moment of the appointed season for the result of this judgment** (or: the effect of the separating for evaluation and decision) **to begin** (to start) **from God's House. Now if first from US, what [will be; is] the closing act** (the final stage; the end; the consummation; the outcome; the finished product) **pertaining to those continuing unpersuaded and unconvinced by** (or: uncompliant to; disobedient to; stubborn in) **God's message of goodness and well-being** (or: good news)**?**

18. **"And if the rightwised one** (the fair and just person in right relationships in accord to the Way pointed out) **is repeatedly delivered** (rescued; brought to safety; made healthy and whole) **with difficult labor, then where will the irreverent** (the person without pious awe) **and the failure** (the one who makes mistakes and cannot hit the target; the sinner; the outcast) **proceed in making an appearance?"** [Prov. 11:31]

19. **So then, also, let those repeatedly feeling the effects of experiences and of suffering which correspond to, and [are] in the sphere of, God's will** (intent; purpose) **continuously commit their souls to a Faithful Former** (or: Loyal Founder; Trustworthy Creator), **within [the] producing of good** (in union with making of virtue; in construction of excellence; centered within the midst of performing goodness).

CHAPTER 5

1. **Therefore, I – the one [being] an older man together with [you]** (or: a fellow elder person) **and a witness of the results of the experiences and of the effects of the sufferings of the Christ, as well as the one [being] a person of common being and existence from the glory** (or: a partner of the manifestation which will call forth praise; a fellow participant who has a common share and fellowship which is the glory) **being presently about to be progressively unveiled** (revealed; or: disclosed) **– am repeatedly calling older folks among you to my side, urging, encouraging and being a paraclete:**

2. **you folks shepherd** (i.e., lead to pasture, feed, tend, protect, care for) **God's little flock [that is] among you folks, constantly watching over [them], not in a forced manner** (not by exercising compulsion or constraint; or: not unwillingly), **but to the contrary, without compulsion** (engendering volunteering; yieldingly; or: voluntarily; willingly), **in accord with** (or: in line with and corresponding to; in the sphere of) **God; neither with eagerness for dishonest gain** (greedily; for the low reason of what you can get out of it), **but rather, readily rushing toward it with passion.**

3. **Nor yet as ones constantly exercising down-oriented lordship** (acting as owners or masters, bearing down with demands) **of the members of the inheritance** (of those who are the allotments of the heritage; or: of those considered to be small objects to be used in assigning positions or portions), **but to the contrary, progressively becoming beaten models** (types made by the strike of a hammer; examples) **for the little flock,**

4. **and so, with the Chief Shepherd** (or: the Original and Ruling Shepherd) **[thus] being made visible** (being shown in clear light), **you folks will continue bringing to yourselves – with care and kindly keeping – the un-withering and unfading wreath of the glory** (or: the assumed appearance; or: the enduring recognition of achievement which comes from this good reputation).

5. **Likewise** (or: In like manner), **you younger people be humbly placed, arranged and aligned by and with** (or: subjected for support to and among) **older folks. Yet all of you folks** (or: everyone) **tie on yourselves, as an outer garment** (or: like a slave's apron), **the humble attitude** (the lowliness of thinking) **to, with, for and among one another** [other MSS add: continuously being ones that are humbly aligned to give support], **because**

> **"God habitually sets Himself in opposition, being resistant to those who try to appear conspicuously above others** (to haughty and proud ones), **yet He constantly gives grace and favor to humble** (or: lowly) **folks."** [Prov. 3:34]

6. **Let yourselves be made humble** (or: lowly), **then, under God's strong hand – so that He can** (or: would) **at some point lift you up** (or: may elevate or exalt you folks) **within a fitting situation** (or: in [the] proper appointed-season; in the center of a fertile moment) –

7. **while throwing** (or: tossing) **your entire concern** (whole worry; every anxiety) **upon Him, because He constantly cares about and takes an interest around you folks!**

8. **Be sober** (or: clear headed)! **Be awake, alert and watch! Your barrier in the Way pointed out** (your road hazard; your opponent at court; the one "in your face" opposing your fairness and equity), **one who casts or thrusts something through the midst of folks**

> (e.g., like a soldier casting a javelin or thrusting a sword through someone, or a person throwing an issue through the midst of a group, causing division; or: a slanderer), **as a constantly roaring lion, is continuously walking about, incessantly seeking to drink something or someone down** (or: searching to gulp and swallow someone down),

> [comment: this path-hazard and road barrier may have been local religions, cultural or political opposition, or a spirit of contrariness]

9. **to whom take a stand against** (withstand; set yourself in opposition), **[being] strong** (firm; compact) **ones in** (or: by) **the faith, trust and loyalty – [being] folks having seen and thus knowing about these same experiences and sufferings [that] are to repeatedly and progressively bring the goal upon** (bring perfection upon; accomplish maturity upon) **your brotherhood within the dominating arrangement of the System** (or: in the midst of the secular realm; or: in the ordered world of religion, economy, culture and government).

10. **Now the God of all grace and favor** (or: the God whose character and quality is all grace and favor; the God Who is every grace and joyous favor), **the One calling** (or: inviting) **you folks – ones experiencing a little and briefly suffering – into His eonian glory** (His glory and reputation which has the quality and characteristics pertaining to the realm of the Age and which continues on into an unseen and indefinite time) **within Christ Jesus** [with other MSS: in union with the Anointed One (= the Messiah)], **the Same One** (or: He) **will continue getting [things, or, you] down and prepare [them, or, you]** (or: repair [them; you]; fit, knit or adjust [them; you] thoroughly), **will continue setting [things; you] fast and establish [them; you], will continue imparting strength** (will make [things; you] strong), **[and] will progressively set a base upon which to ground and found [things and you]:**
11. **the strength** (or: might) **[to do these things is] in Him and by Him, on into the ages. It is so** (Count on it)! [other MSS: the glory and the strength {is} in Him, on into the superlative times of the ages (or: the ages of the ages)]

12. **Through Silvanus** (or: Silas), **the faithful and loyal brother who is full of trust, as I continue logically thinking and considering, I write through means of a few** [thoughts, lines, or, words; p72 reads: through a short {letter}], **persistently calling [you] alongside to encourage, comfort and aid [you], as well as constantly bearing a full witness and adding evidence of this continuing to be God's true** (and: real) **grace and favor, into which you folks should set yourselves to take a stand** (or, as an imperative: into which, [enter] and stand firm!).

13. **The jointly-chosen** (selected-together) **called-out community** (assembly; congregation; ecclesia) **within Babylon constantly embraces and greets you folks; also Mark, my son.**
14. **Embrace as you greet one another within love's expression of affection** (a kiss from participation in the transcendent unity of the unambiguous life, and affection which is the urge toward accepting reunion that overcomes existential separation; – a synthesis from Tillich's definitions of *agape*). **Peace** (and: joining harmony; = shalom) **[is] in** (or: [is] by; with) **you folks – all those within, in union with, and centered on, Christ** [other MSS add: Jesus]! **It is so** (Amen: Count on it)!

[written circa A.D. 65 – Based on the critical analysis of John A.T. Robinson]

SECOND PETER

1. **Simon** (other MSS: Symeon) **Peter, a slave and sent-off representative** (or: emissary) **of Jesus Christ, to** (or: for; with; among) **the folks obtaining by lot an equally valuable** (precious; honorable) **faith, conviction, trust and loyalty, along with us, within the midst of an eschatological deliverance, in union with fair and equitable treatment in rightwised relationships in the Way pointed out, and centered in covenant inclusion-and-membership, which come from and characterize our God and Savior** (Deliverer; Rescuer; Source of health and wholeness), **Jesus Christ** (or: Jesus, [the] Anointed One; = Jesus, [the] Messiah)**:**
2. **May grace and peace** (or: favor and harmony from **the Joining) be multiplied** (or: caused to increase) **to you folks** (or: by you; in you; for you) **within full** (or: accurate; complete; added) **intimate and experiential knowledge and insight of God, even Jesus, our Lord** (or: from God as well as from Jesus, Who is our Master; or: of God, and of our Owner, Jesus),
3. **just as all those things [leading] toward life and reverence** (standing in awe of goodness, with adoration; the well-being of devotion and virtuous conduct from ease, in true relation to God) **[are] being now available for us from having been freely given to us** (or: presented as a gift in us) **from His divine power and ability through the full** (accurate; complete; added) **intimate and experiential knowledge of the One calling us to His own** (or: by His own; for His own; in His own; [other MSS instead read: through; by means of]) **glory and excellence in nobleness**
    (i.e., virtues of: braveness, courage, good character, quality, self-restraint, magnificence, benevolence, reliability, moral valor).
4. **[It is] through means of which things – the precious** (valuable; honorable) **and greatest effects of the promises – [that] He has freely given** (or: [which] He Himself has presented as a gift) **to us, to the end that through these [gifts], you folks would come to be** (or: could come into existence being; should be born) **people of common-being from a divine essence and nature** (or: folks having a partnered share that is based upon a common existence from a divine born-instinct and native condition; or: fellow participants of a germination which is divine), **while fleeing from the corruption** (ruin; decay) **within the domination System** (or: that is united with the secular realm; or: centered in the ordered world of society, religion, culture, economy and government; or: in the center of the aggregate of mankind), **[which is] in the midst of passionate cravings** (rushing emotions; lusts; violent over-desires; [or, with *p*72 & Aleph: fleeing the strong desire of corruption within the world]).

5. **Yet, also, this same** (or: And yet for this very cause)**: while bringing into and alongside** (i.e., making full use of) **all diligent haste, you folks at once fully lead the chorus of** (or: completely choreograph and outfit) **the excellence and nobleness** (virtues of braveness, courage, good character, quality, self-restraint, magnificence, benevolence, reliability and valor) **[being inherent] within your faith and trust; along with the intimate, experiential knowledge and insight [being] within the excellence and nobleness** (virtues of braveness, courage, good character, quality, self-restraint, magnificence, benevolence, reliability, moral valor);
6. **also the inner strength and self-restraint [which is inherent] within the intimate, experiential knowledge, as well as the persistent remaining under in humble support** (or: steadfast, patient endurance) **[being inherently] within the inner strength and self-restraint; and then the reverence** (ease of virtuous conduct from true relation to God) **[inherent] within the persistent remaining under in humble support** (or: steadfast, patient endurance);
7. **and further, the brotherly affection** (fondness for the fellow believers) **[resident] within the reverence** (awe with goodness; well-being of devout, virtuous conduct in the ease of true relation to God); **and then finally, the love** (uniting acceptance) **within the brotherly affection.**

8. **You see, these things are constantly subsisting** (or: supportively sub-governing; humbly ruling; beginning from below) **as a possession in you folks** [or, with A and others: are continually existing alongside being present for you] **and are repeatedly being more than**

enough (abounding) – **neither [being] inactive** (or: ineffective) **nor unfruitful** (or: unproductive). **He is continually setting [these] down and causing [them] to stand in accord [in you] unto the accurate, additional** (or: full), **experiential and intimate knowledge of our Lord** (or: Owner; Master), **Jesus Christ.**

9. **You see, the person in whom these things are not continuously present exists being** (or: is) **blind, constantly blinking and closing his or her eyes** (or: progressively becoming short-sighted and nearsighted), **taking hold of forgetfulness of** (or: receiving oblivion in regard to) **the cleansing from his/her old sins** (mistakes of the past; former failure; [other MSS: from the results and effects of his/her former sins and errors]).

10. **Wherefore** (or: Because of this), **brothers** (= [my] family), **hasten to exert yourselves to a greater extent to constantly make firm** (sure-footed and steadfast) **your calling** (or: invitation) **and election** (selection; act of choosing out); **for you see, in repeatedly doing these things, you can by no means** (would under no circumstances) **stumble once** (or: at any time).

11. **For thus** (in this way) **the Path of entrance into** (or: the place and act of the Way unto) **the center or midst of the eonian reign** (or: the Kingdom pertaining to and having the character and qualities of the Age; the for-the-ages sovereign influence and actions) **of our Lord and Savior** (or: Owner and Deliverer), **Jesus Christ** [= [the] Messiah], **will continue being richly led in full chorus and further outfitted with supplies for you** (in and among you; to you; by you folks).

12. **Wherefore** (or: For this cause) **it will always continue being my intent to be constantly reminding you concerning these things – even though [you are] being folks having seen and thus knowing, and ones being set and firmly established within the truth and reality [that is] being continuously present** (existing alongside) **[with and in you].**

13. **But I am continuously considering it right, and in accord with the Way pointed out – as long as I continue existing within this tent-effect** (or: tabernacle) – **to keep on arousing and to progress in fully awakening you folks with a reminder,**

14. **having seen and now knowing that swift [in approach] is the laying aside** (or: the putting off or away) **of my tent-effect** (or: tabernacle; = body), **according as also our Lord, Jesus Christ, made clearly visible to me** (or: makes [it] evident for and in me).

15. **But I will also continue earnestly hastening** (or: quickly endeavoring) **to always have you, after my departure** (exodus; a road or path out; = death), **to continually make mention** (or: make the recollection) **of these things.**

16. **For we did** (or: You see, we do) **not experientially or intimately make known to you the power and presence** (or: ability and [the] being alongside; *parousia*) **of our Lord, Jesus Christ, by following forth in** (or: by) **wisely-made myths** (or: in being made wise by myths or fables; or: with fables modified by wisdom; or: to cleverly crafted stories), **but rather, [from] becoming** (or: being made to be; being birthed) **eyewitnesses** (onlookers; spectators) **of that One's magnificence** (or: of that greatness):

17. **for you see, from the side of** (or: [standing] beside) **Father God, [He was] receiving honor** (value; preciousness) **and glory** (or: a reputation) **from a Voice being carried to Him by the fitting greatness and majesty of glory and which came from the manifestation which called forth praise** (or: = of a Sound or Shout being swept along under the magnificent grandeur of the *Sh'khinah* Presence) **such as follows:**

> **"My Son, My Beloved One, is This One** [other MSS: This One is existing being My Son, My Beloved One] **into the midst of Whom I Myself placed delight** [other MSS: within Whom I was well pleased, and find approval; in union with Whom I have good thoughts]."

18. **And we ourselves, being together with Him within the set-apart** (or: holy; sacred) **mountain, heard this Voice being carried out of heaven** (or: swept along from the midst of [the] atmosphere and sky).

19. **And so, we continue having** (or: constantly hold) **the Idea which was spoken ahead of time in and as Light** (or: the prior-enlightened Thought and Reason; or: the Prophetic Word) **more confirmed** (validated; established; certain), **by which** (or: in which) **you folks continue doing beautifully** (performing ideally; producing finely), **while continuously holding toward** (= playing close attention to) **[it] as to a lamp continually shining within a parched place – until**

which [time or occasion] the Day may shine through and a light bearer [= a morning star] **may rise within your hearts**

> (or: constantly heeding, as to a lamp progressively making things appear in a dark, dingy or dirty place, until that Day can dawn, and a light-bringer can arise in union with your core and innermost being),

20. **constantly knowing this first, that every** (or: all) **previously enlightened information of Scripture** [p72: prophecy and Scripture] **is not coming to be unbound upon its own**

> (or: is not being born of its own unloosing; or: is not becoming its own explaining; or: is not coming into existence upon one's own releasing),

21. **for you see, previously enlightened information** (or: prophecy) **was** (or: is) **not at any time brought by** (or: in; for; with) **[the] will** (intent; resolve; purpose) **of a human, but rather being continuously carried by** (or: swept along under [the influence of]) **[the] set-apart Breath-effect** (or: Holy Spirit), **people spoke from God** [with other MSS: God's set-apart (holy) folks speak]. [cf 2 Tim. 3:16]

CHAPTER 2

1. **Yet false prophets also birthed themselves** (or: Now of themselves folks who pretended to have light ahead of time, or who had false knowledge and spoke before folks, came to be) **among the People – as also false teachers will continue existing** (or: being) **among you folks, ones who will proceed to stealthily introduce** (or: will continue bringing in alongside or smuggling in) **destructive choices** (or: destructive sects, schools or ways of thinking; sets of principles or courses of action marked by, and which pertain to, loss or destruction) **even repeatedly contradicting or denying** (disowning; disclaiming; saying, "No," of) **the Sovereign Owner** (or: Absolute Master) **having purchased them** (or: buying them at the gathering, or market, place), **continuously bringing swift loss, ruin or destruction upon themselves.**
2. **And many will progressively follow out to** (for; in; by) **their outrageous behaviors** (extravagant or licentious conducts), **on account of whom** (or: because of which ones) **the Way** [other MSS: the glory] **of the Truth and Reality will proceed being blasphemed** (vilified; defamed; misrepresented with abusive slander; or: having its light hindered),
3. **and in greed** (desire to take advantage in order to have more), **by formed** (molded; fabricated, and thus, counterfeit) **words, they will constantly exploit you** (use you for business; market you; use you in trade and travel by sea), **to whom** (or: for which folks) **the sentence** (or: the result of the evaluation; the effect of a separating process) **[coming] from long ago** (or: out of old times; forth from old) **is not continuing inactive** (is not constantly unemployed; is not remaining idle), **and their loss** (or: destruction) **is not nodding in sleep or taking a nap.**

4. **For since** (or: if) **God did** (or: does) **not spare agents** (or: folks having a, or, the message) – **but who at one point were** (or: are) **straying from the goal** (or: when failing to hit the mark; at missing the target; upon committing error) – **but rather gave** (or: gives; committed; transferred; entrusts; passes) **them over into an act of judging – of being repeatedly pruned** (cut back for correction), **while being constantly watched over, kept, maintained and protected – giving [them] the experience of Tartarus**

> [Hellenistic mythological term and concept: the subterranean world; cf LXX, Job 40:15 (the marshlands and wild areas around the Jordan River) and 41:23 (the caverns and lower parts of deep waters and the abyss)] **in dark, gloomy pits** (caves; caverns) [other MSS: in ropes (or: chains; bands; cords); = in bondage].

5. **And further, He did not spare [the] original ordered arrangement** (a beginning or ruling world of society and culture; or: [the] secular realm), **but rather spared Noah, an eighth** (idiom: = with seven others), **a proclaimer** (herald) **of eschatological deliverance** (and: justice in fair and equitable dealings that accord with the Way pointed out from covenant participation), **when bringing a deluge** (an inundation) **upon a world** (System and society; secular order) **of folks devoid of awe** (or: in bringing down a washing upon a system of irreverent and impious ones),
6. **and later He correspondingly evaluated and commensurately decided about** (or: condemns) **[the] cities of Sodom and Gomorrah, reducing [them] to ashes for twisting down** ([= for distorting the path of life]; or: by and in an overthrow; to a turning down [of activities

or of life]), **having placed** (or: set) **an example** (exhibition; a result of a specimen pointed out and set under view) **of folks habitually being about to be irreverent**
> (or: to commit sacrilege without awe) [other MSS: an example of things about to happen to (or: in; among) ones without reverential awe];

7. **and yet, He drew to Himself right-living Lot** (or: He Himself rescues Lot, a just one; or: He, for Himself, rescues Lot, an equitable person), **a person being constantly worn down under the unrestrained and unprincipled folks** (or: acts) **in the midst of [their] outrageous** (extravagant; licentious; indulgent) **conduct** (mode of living).

8. **For you see, by seeing and by hearing** (or: with a look and in listening to) **[this] from day to day, this fair and just person continuously dwelling in their midst kept on testing and distressing – as by using a touchstone – [his] just and equitable soul** (or: inner being) **by [their] lawless works** (or: actions and deeds which are apart from custom).

9. **[The] Lord** [=Yahweh], **having seen, thus knows to** (or: knows how to) **continuously drag out of danger** (or: rescue) **a reverent person** (one standing in devout goodness, in awe and in virtuous conduct with ease and well-being from relationship with God) **from out of the midst of a trial** (or: ordeal; [other MSS: trials]), **yet to constantly keep in custody, guard, watch over and maintain unjust folks** (people who live contrary to the Way pointed out; unrightwised folks) **[who are] being repeatedly pruned** (or: being progressively corrected), **[which is leading] unto a day of evaluating for making a decision [about their progress]** (or: of judging [condition]),

10. **yet especially** (or: most of all) **the people continually passing from one place to another after flesh** (= aspects of the natural realm; = expressions or experiences of the estranged self or the human nature that has been conformed to the System) **in defiling** (polluting; staining) **lust** (over-desire; full passion), **even habitually thinking disparagingly** (scorning; despising; down-thinking) **of lordship** (ownership; constituted authority). **[These are] presumptuous folks** (audacious ones), **self-pleasing people** (willfully arrogant ones), **continuously slandering** (defaming; speaking injuriously about; obscuring the light of; vilifying) **reputations,**

11. **whereas agents** (or: messengers; folks with a/the message) **[who] are being greater in strength and power** (or: ability) **[than these folks], are not normally** (or: habitually) **bringing slanderous separating** (or: defaming decision-making; injurious discriminating; or: a light-obscuring judicial process) **down on or against them before** (or: beside) **[the] Lord** [=Yahweh].

12. **But these, as irrational** (wordless; unreasoning) **living ones** (or: animals), **being creatures of instinct having been born unto capture and then corruption** (decay; ruin), **within which things – being continuously ignorant – they are constantly blaspheming** (speaking slander, insult and abusive speech; injuriously vilifying; or: hindering the Light) **within their corruption** (decay), **and they will be progressively ruined** (spoiled; caused to decay; corrupted),

13. **being folks habitually wronging themselves** (or, reading as a passive: being wronged; suffering injustice) [other MSS: will be ones getting for themselves] – **a wage of unrighteousness** (inequity; injustice; wrong; nonobservance of the Way pointed out) – **folks continuously leading or governing, while considering the luxury** (or: softness and daintiness; delicate living; effeminateness) **in daytime** (in broad daylight) **a pleasure** (enjoyment; gratification). **[They are] spots** (or: stains) **and disgraceful flaws [that] are continuously living within luxury amidst their delusions** (or: deceptions) [other MSS: love-feasts] – **folks repeatedly feasting** (or: banqueting) **together with you folks –**

14. **people always having bulging eyes very full of an adulteress** (= for nothing but adultery), **and being unceasing regarding sin and error; people by habit using bait to entrap unstable souls** (= people); **folks constantly having a heart that has been exercised** (trained in gymnastic discipline) **regarding greed** (desire for advantage and riches); **children of a cursing** (or: having the qualities and character of [the] curse).

15. **By practice leaving behind** [other MSS: at one point abandoning] **[the; a] straight path** (road; Way), **they were** (or: are) **led astray** (or: caused to wander), **following out the path** (road; way) **of Balaam of Bosor** [other MSS: Beor] **who loved** (yearned for) **[the] wage of, or from, injustice** (inequity; wrongdoing; unrighteousness; nonobservance of the Way pointed out).

16. **But he had an exposure and a rebuke leading to conviction regarding his own transgression of law: a voiceless yoke-animal – emitting a sound in a voice of a man – hindered** (or: checked) **the insanity** (madness; being beside one's thinking) **of the prophet.**

17. **These people are** (or: exist being) **springs without water and clouds** (or: mists; fogs) **being constantly driven by** (or: under) **a storm** (or: a squall), **for whom the gloom of the darkness has been maintained** (guarded; kept and watched-over) **for an indefinite period of time.**
18. **For you see, in continuously uttering over-swollen** (inflated; over-weighted; extravagant; pompous) **things pertaining to empty purposelessness** (vanity; futility; fruitless nonsense; worthless nothingness), **they are constantly using bait to trap – in the midst of cravings** (or: full passions) **of flesh** (= alienated human nature) **by outrageous** (or: licentious) **behavior – those folks scarcely** [other MSS: actually] **fleeing from** (or: barely or just now escaping from) **the people habitually twisting themselves up in deception** (or: being repeatedly turned back and forth in wandering),
19. **while constantly promising freedom** (or: liberty) **to them, they themselves continuously subsist inherently being slaves of the corruption** (the ruin; the decay) **– for you see, by whom** (or: by what) **anyone has been, and now exists being, made inferior** (or: less), **to this one** (or: by this thing) **he has** [some MSS add: also] **been enslaved, and now exists as a slave.**

20. **For if, while fleeing from the stains** (pollution; defilements) **of the ordered System** (dominant world of religion, society, culture, economy and politics; or: secular realm), **within an accurate** (or: full; added) **intimate and experiential knowledge of our Lord and Savior, Jesus Christ, but yet being interwoven** (intertwined) **back again in** (or: by; with; among) **these things, they are continuing to be inferior** (less; or: they are repeatedly worsted), **the last things** (situations; conditions) **have come to be** (or: have been birthed) **for them** (to them; in them; with them) **worse than the first ones.**
21. **For it were better for them** (or: it was existing better to and in them) **not to have known** (not to have come to an experiential full knowledge of) **the Way** (road; path) **of the fair and equitable dealing** (justice; righteousness; eschatological deliverance; or: = covenant participation) **than, fully knowing, to turn below** (or: back) **from out of** [other MSS: to bend back, into the things which are behind, from] **the set-apart implanted goal** (holy impartation of the finished product and destiny within; sacred inward directive) **– the one being given over to** (transmitted and committed in; delivered alongside among; passed along for) **them.**

22. **Now it has walked** (or: stepped) **together for them** (to them; in them) **– the true proverb** (saying; byword)**: "a dog turning about upon its own vomit," and "a sow** (or: hog), **into a rolling** (wallowing-place) **of mire, bathing itself!"**

CHAPTER 3

1. **O beloved and unambiguously accepted ones, this** [is] **already a second letter** [that] **I am writing to you, within which I am thoroughly arousing** (raising through; thoroughly awakening) **your complete thought process** (intellect, comprehension and the things going through the mind) **which has been evaluated in sunlight** (or: your sunlight-separated, sincere understanding), **in union with a putting in mind** (or: a remembrance) **[and]**
2. **to be born in mind** (or: to be called to mind), **about the flowing declarations** (or: gush-effects; results of the flow) **having been spoken beforehand by the set-apart** (or: holy; sacred) **prophets, even** (or: as well as) **the sent-forth representatives** (emissaries) **which pertained to you folks, of the implanted goal** (impartation of the finished product and destiny within; inward directive) **of, from and which is, the Lord and Savior** (Deliverer),
3. **while continuing in knowing this first, by experience, that upon** [the] **last** (or: final [phases]) **of these** (or: the) **days mockers** (scoffers) **will continue coming and going – in mocking** (scoffing; deriding), **according to their own cravings** (or: in correspondence to their personal full passions), **folks continually traveling from one place to another** (or: = people normally ordering their lives according to their personal desires) –

4. even saying, "Where is the promise of His presence? For since the fathers were put (or: lulled) to sleep, all things (or: everything) constantly remain(s) thus (in this way or manner) throughout, from [the] beginning of creation (the framing; the reduction from a state of disorder)."

5. You see, it continues unnoticed and unrecognized – [by] those folks habitually desiring this [to be the case] (or: = they deliberately ignore the fact) – that skies (or: atmospheres; heavens) and land were continuously existing from long ago (or: = from ancient times) – from out of the midst of water, and through water – being made to stand together (being placed or put together) by (or: in; with) the Word (Logos; thought and idea; reason) of God (or: which is God),
6. through which [very waters; or: directives of His Word] the ordered System (world of culture and relationships) of that time destroyed (or: lost) itself, being washed down (inundated; deluged) by water.   [comment: a reference either to Gen. 7, or to Ex. 14]

7. Yet at the present time the heavens and the earth (or: the atmospheres and skies, as well as the land), by the same Word (or: in the same Logos) – having been collected and being stored up as treasure, by (or: in; for; with) fire – continuously exist, being constantly kept (watched, guarded and maintained) with a view to a day of separating for deciding (or: with the character of evaluating for judging), as well as of loss, ruin or destruction which pertains to the irreverent humans (or: of people devoid of reverential awe toward God).
8. Yet now this one thing [p72: But in this] – let it not continue unnoticed, escape your detection, or be hidden from you – beloved ones, one day beside the Lord [is] as a thousand years, and yet a thousand years [is] as one day.   [* cf Rom. 12:2]
9. The Lord [= Yahweh] is not continually delaying the promise, as certain folks consider delay as being negligence, but rather is constantly patient (long of emotion, slow in passion, pushing anger far away, even-tempered and long before rushing heatedly; or: passionately persevering until the goal is reached) unto you, constantly not intending any folks to be lost (or: to destroy themselves), but to the contrary, [for] all people to make room, allow space, give way and progress into a change of mind, attitude and state of consciousness.*
10. So the day of the Lord [= Yahweh] will continue in arriving as a thief [i.e., suddenly and without notice], in which [day] the heavens (or: atmospheres; or: skies) will continue passing by with the noise of sudden movement, but yet rudimentary, elementary principles
         (or: basic component and parts of a system arranged in rows, or a grid; e.g., the
         elements and assumptions of a religious or intellectual system), being progressively
heated as with a burning fever, will continue being progressively loosed (unfastened; unbound; or: nullified; destroyed). And then land (or: soil; ground; earth; or: = a territory) – along with the things produced (or: actions; deeds; workmanships; accomplishments) [note: God's and/or man's] within the midst of it – will continue being found (or: discovered; found out) [p72 adds: being progressively loosed (or: destroyed); A reads: will be burned up]!
11. With all these people thus, then, being presently loosed, one after another (or: being in the process of being progressively unbound; or: with all these things being continuously dissolved in this way), in what sort of way is it continuously necessary and binding for you folks [other MSS: us; other MSS have no personal pronoun here] to constantly subsist (or: humbly rule or supportively possess)? Within set-apart (or: holy; sacred), upturned modes of behavior and [lives of] reverence (devout ease, virtuous conduct and goodness from relationship with God)!
12. – while constantly being receptive toward (or: continuing with expectation with regard to) and eagerly speeding along (or: progressively hastening after) the presence of God's Day (or: the presence, which is God's day; or: the presence of the day which has the quality and character of God and which is God; or: the Presence, from the Day of God), through which skies and atmospheres (or: heavens) – being continuously on fire – will continue being loosed (or: untied)! And so [the body of] elements (rudimentary principles and assumptions; component parts of the system), now being continuously intensely hot and burning, [are] presently being progressively melted down (or: liquefied). [cf Acts 21:24; Gal. 4:3, 9; 5:25; Col. 2:20]

591

13. **Yet we, corresponding to** (down from; in line with; in the sphere of) **the effect and result of His promise, are habitually receptive toward fresh skies and continue with expectation, face to face with atmospheres new in kind, quality and character** (or: keep an opinion with regard to different, innovative heavens) **and a land** (or: soil; ground; earth; territory) **new in kind and quality, within which [situations; conditions] a rightwising eschatological deliverance** (or: righted existence of living in covenant relationships of the fairness which accords with the Way pointed out; liberated participation in the justice and equity of the new arrangement) **is presently and permanently settled down** (is continuously dwelling and at home).

14. **Wherefore, beloved ones, while continually being receptive toward these things, be eager to be found [being] spotless folks and flawless ones in Him** (or: by Him; with Him; to Him; for Him), **in peace and centered in union with harmony from the joining** [= shalom].

>   (or: On account of which, accepted folks, in continuing with an expectation that is face to face with these [occurrences], eagerly speed along to Him unblemished and blameless folks to be found centered in peace; or: … through which loved folks are continuing expecting these [situations]. Let folks [who are] by Him absent of spot and blemish be found within the midst of peace and joining).

15. **And so, make it a habit to consider the long-suffering patience** (even-tempered pushing anger far away; long-waiting before rushing heatedly; passionate persevering unto the goal) **of our Lord** [= Yahweh, or Christ] **[to be; as] deliverance** (rescued safety; salvation; wholeness and health), **according as our beloved brother Paul also wrote to you, in accord with** (or: down from; in the sphere of) **the wisdom being given to him** (or: in him; by him),

16. **even as in all the letters, habitually speaking in them concerning these things, in which certain things are misunderstood** (or: imperceptible to the mind; hard to understand), **which the unlearned folks and unstable ones** (unfounded ones; people not set fast and firm) **repeatedly distort, as by twisting them out of place on a rack – as also the rest of the writings** (or: Scriptures) **– toward their own loss** (or: ruin; destruction).

17. **You, then, beloved and accepted ones, being ones by repeated experiences previously acquainted [with this]** (or: knowing beforehand by experiences), **be constantly on watch, guard, maintain and keep yourselves in custody, lest – at some point being carried** (or: led) **away together by the deception** (or: in straying; or: to deceit) **of the unestablished** (or: from unprincipled, inordinate or lawless) **folks – you could fall out from your own state of fixed firmness** (or: steadfastness).

18. **So be continually growing and increasing, centered within grace and in union with joyful favor, as well as [in] intimate, experiential knowledge and insight of** (or: from, and which is) **our Lord** (Owner; Master) **and Savior** (or: Deliverer; Rescuer; Restorer to health and wholeness), **Jesus Christ** (or: Anointed Jesus; = Jesus the Messiah). **By Him** (or: To Him) **[is] the glory** (or: In Him [is] the manifestation which calls forth praise; For Him [is] the reputation; With Him [comes] the imagination) **both now and on into the midst of a Day that lasts for an indefinite period of time, and which is [the] Age**

>   (or: unto a day whose character and quality is [the] Age; or: into the midst of a day whose source is [the] Age [of the Messiah]; or: to a day which belongs to [the] Age; into a Day which is an age).

It is so (or: Count on it; Amen)**!**

[written circa A.D. 61-62 – Based on the critical analysis of John A.T. Robinson]

FIRST JOHN

CHAPTER 1

1. **The One who was continuously existing from a beginning** (or: He Who was progressively being parted away from [the] Source, Headship and Rule). **The One whom we have listened to, and still hear; the One whom we have discerningly seen, and now yet perceive with our eyes** (or: in our eyes); **the One whom we contemplatively gazed upon as a public spectacle** (as an exhibit in a theater) **and our hands handled in investigation** (felt about for and touched) **– groping around the Word of the Life** [cf Lu. 24:39]

> (or: the Logos, which is the Life; the thought which pertains to life; the Information and Idea from the Life; the message with the character and qualities of the Life; the Reason which belongs to the Life; [note: I have treated *ho* as the definite article in the first four phrases here and in vs. 3; many treat it as a neuter relative and render it: That which]),

2. **and the Life was manifested** (or: is brought into the clear light and made visible)! **And so we have discerningly seen, and still perceptively observe, and are repeatedly testifying** (bearing witness; giving evidence) **and in a message are constantly reporting to you folks the Life which has the character and qualities of the Age** (or: the life of, for and pertaining to the age [of the Messiah]; eonian life) **which Certain [Life] was continuously existing [oriented and proceeding] toward** (or: was face to face with) **the Father, and was manifested** (or: is made visible; appeared) **to us, in us, by us, among us and for us.** [cf Jn. 14:26]

3. **The One whom we have seen, and still now see, and we have heard, and now continue listening to and hearing, we are also constantly reporting to you, to the end that you, too, may be continuously having common being and existence** (or: would be progressively holding partnership and participation) **with us. And yet, our common being and existence** (or: participation; fellowship; partnership; sharing) **[is] with the Father, even with His Son** (or: as well as with the Son from Him; or, in apposition: and with the Son which is Him), **Jesus Christ.**

4. **And so we ourselves are proceeding in writing these things, to the end that your joy** [other MSS: our joy] **would continually exist having been filled up and then continue full.**

5. **And this is the message** (or: And it is this message) **which we have heard – and still hear – from Him, and we are continually bringing back tidings** (or: announcing again) **to and among you people that God continuously exists being** (or: is) **Light, and within Him darkness and obscurity do not exist – not even one** (or: and so, there is absolutely no dimness or shadiness in Him).

6. **If we should up and say that we are continuously having common being** (or: constantly enjoying fellowship, participation and partnership) **with Him and yet may be habitually walking round about** (= living our lives) **within the Darkness and the dim realm of shadows** [note: a figure of ignorance, or the obscure previous way of seeing reality; the existence before the Breath-effect vibrated over us], **we are constantly lying** (speaking falsely) **and are not in the habit of doing the truth** (or: are not constructing, practicing or producing reality).

7. **Yet if we keep on walking about** (= continue living our life) **within the midst of and in union with the Light, as He exists** (or: is) **within the Light, we constantly have common being and existence** (or: hold common fellowship, participation and enjoy partnership) **with one another, and the blood of, from, and which is Jesus, His Son, keeps continually and repeatedly cleansing us** (or: is progressively rendering us pure) **from every sin** (or: from all error, failure, deviation, mistake, and from every shot that is off target [when it occurs]).

8. **If we should up and say that we have no error** (or: do not periodically possess deviation or hold sin and mistake), **we are continuously leading ourselves astray** (or: deceiving ourselves and driving ourselves off the Path), **and the Truth is not** (or: reality does not exist) **within us.**

9. **If it would be our habit to confess** (admit; avow; say the same thing as; speak in accordance with; or: would continue in agreement [about]) **our error** (our failure; our sin; our mistake), **He is constantly faithful and just** (fair; in accord with the Way pointed out and in right

relationship; rightwised), **to the end that He would at once send away for us** (or: dismiss or pardon and cause to flow away in us) **the errors** ([some MSS add: our] failures, mistakes and deviations) **and then would cleanse** [other MSS: He will cleanse] **us from all injustice**
> (all that is contrary to the Way pointed out; every unrighteousness; all unfairness, inequity and unrighteous relationships; every behavior that is turned in the wrong direction).

10. **If we would say that we have not failed to hit the target** (or: sinned; made a mistake; erred; deviated), **and exist thus, we habitually make Him a liar** (one who utters falsehood), **and His Word** (Thought; Idea; message; Logos) **does not exist among** (or: is not within) **us.**

CHAPTER 2

1. **My little children** (born ones), **I am writing these things to you** (or: for you) **to the end that you may not fail to hit the target** (deviate from the goal; sin). **And if anyone should at some point fail** (or: suddenly commit sin, make a mistake or deviate), **we constantly have One called alongside to help, give relief and guide us toward the Father** (or: we continuously possess a Paraclete, face to face with the Father)**: Jesus Christ, [the] One in accord with the Way pointed out** (or: a Just One; [the] Righteous One; [the] Fair One who is in right relationship with all; a Rightwised One; [the] right one; a Person that is turned in the right direction).

2. **And He Himself exists continually being a cleansing, sheltering cover around our mistakes and errors, sheltering us from their effects so that we can be in peaceful and rightwised relationships** (or: being the act by which our sins and failures are cleansed and made ineffective, effecting conciliation [to us]), **yet not only around those pertaining to us** (or: having their source in us), **but further, even around the whole ordered System** (secular realm and dominating world of culture, economy, religion and government; or: universe; or: aggregate of mankind)**!**

3. **And so within this [situation], if we could be continuously watchful and would habitually keep, guard, observe, and maintain His implanted purposes and internalized goals** (or: inner projections of destiny), **we [would] progressively know through experience and continue to recognize with insight, because we have come to know Him, and we now experience Him intimately with insightful knowledge.**
> (or: So in union with this [relationship] – should we constantly maintain His impartations from the finished product, and would observe His inward directives of destiny – we progressively know by experience, and recognize by insight, that we have known Him.)

4. **The person who keeps on saying, "I have come to know Him by experience," and yet is not habitually keeping** (observing) **His implanted goals** (impartations of the finished product within; inward directives), **is a liar** (exists being one who speaks falsehood) **and God's Truth** (the Reality of God; the Genuine Actuality which is God) **is not** (or: does not exist) **within this one.**

5. **Yet whoever may be habitually keeping** (attentively guarding to observe) **His Word** (Logos; Thought; Idea; message), **truly** (or: actually; in reality) **within this person God's Love has been perfected and brought to its goal** (or: the love which is God has been matured, finished and reached its purposed destiny). **In this we constantly know experientially that we continuously exist within the midst of Him, and in union with Him.**

6. **The person habitually speaking [thus, as though] to be constantly abiding** (remaining; dwelling) **within Him, is continuously under obligation himself also to go on walking about** (= behaving and conducting his life) **just as That One** (or: on the level and in the sphere as [He]) **walked** (or: walks; = lives His life).

7. **Beloved ones, I am not writing an implanted goal** (impartation of the finished product within; inward directive of purpose) **new in kind or quality to you** (or: for you), **but rather an old implanted goal** (impartation of the finished product within; inward directive of destiny) **which you folks have continually had** (or: were habitually holding) **from [the] beginning. The old implanted goal** (impartation of the finished product within; inward directed destiny) **is the Word** (Thought; Idea; message) **which you folks heard** (or: attentively hear [and thus obey])**!**

8. **Again,** (or: Once more) **I am writing to you an implanted goal** (impartation of the finished product within; inward directive) **new in kind and quality** (innovative and different in character), **which is** (exists being) **true** (actual; real; genuine) **within Him, and within you** [other MSS: us],

that the Darkness (the obscure dimness of the realm of the shadows and of lack of the light of the Day; [note: a figure of the ignorance of the prior system and realm]) **is progressively being caused to pass by, and the True Light** (or: = real knowledge and understanding; = Light of the new Day) **is already** (before now) **progressively shining and appearing.**

9. **The person who keeps on speaking [thus, as though] to be within the Light, and yet is constantly hating** (or: regarding with ill-will or detaching from) **his brother** (or: = fellow believer; or: fellow member of his society), **is a liar and continues being within the Darkness** (the obscure dimness of the realm of the shadows and lack of the light of the Day; = prior night) **until the present moment.**

10. **The person habitually loving** (seeking accepting reunion with) **his brother constantly abides** (remains; dwells; = has his home) **within and in union with the Light, and there exists no snare** (trap-spring; stick upon which bait is put; = cause for stumbling) **within him.**

11. **But the person habitually hating** (or: repeatedly having ill-will toward) **his brother** (or: = fellow believer or fellowman) **constantly exists within the Darkness** (the obscure dimness of the realm of the shadows, lacking of the light of the Day) **and so continuously walks about amidst the Darkness, and has not seen so is not aware where he is progressively departing** (or: habitually going away), **because that Darkness blinds** (or: blinded) **his eyes.**

12. **I am writing to you, little children** (or: young born ones), **that the failures** (mistakes; sins; deviations; situations of missing the goal) **have been sent away** (or: caused to flow away; put away; divorced; forgiven) **for you through His Name** (or: because of the Name which is Him)!

13. **I am writing to you, fathers** (or: parents), **that you have by experience known, and now have intimate insight of, the One [Who is] from [the] beginning** (or: the Original One). **I am writing to you, young men** (or: youths), **that you have overcome** (conquered; are victorious over) **the one bringing a gush of misery**

> (or: the useless, unprofitable situation; the wicked man; the evil one; the bad situation or sorry plight; the worthless man; the pernicious and knavish fellow; the one causing anguish and painful labor; the condition full of harassed toil and annoying perils; the base fellow) **– and this now exists as a decided victory.**

14. **I write to you, little boys and girls, or servants, who might be hit for discipline** (or: those of the age for being educated and trained), **that you have by experience known the Father; I write to you, fathers** (or: parents), **that you have by experience known, and now have insight into, the One [Who is] from [the] beginning** (or: the Original One). **I write to you, young men** (or: youths), **that you are** (or: exist being) **constantly strong, and God's Word** (Logos; Thought; Idea; Reason; message) **continuously dwells** (abides; remains) **within you and you have overcome** (conquered; are the victor over) **the one bringing a gush of misery** (see parenthetical expansion in verse 13, above).

15. **You folks should not be habitually loving** (as indicative: are not normally accepting; as imperative: Stop constantly seeking reunion with) **the world** (secular realm and the controlling ordered System of culture, religion, economy and government), **neither** (or: not even) **the things within the world** (ordered system of domination). **If anyone is in the habit of** (or: keeps on) **loving the world** (the domination System and ordered arrangement of religion, or of secular society), **the Father's** [other MSS: God's] **Love** (or: the love which the Father has; the Love which is the Father) **does not exist within him,**

16. **because everything within the world** (ordered but dominating System of the secular and the religious) **– the flesh's over-desire**

> (full passion of the alienated human nature; lust of the estranged self; earnest wants of
> the false persona that was conformed to the System), **and the eyes' over-desire, and the arrogant ostentation** (haughty, presumptuous or pretentious egoism) **pertaining to living** (= the biological and sociological life we live), **is not out of the Father as a source** (or: does not proceed from the Father), **but rather is continuously forth from out of the world** (the ordered System of society, culture and religion),

17. **and the world** (ordered System of religion, society, culture, economy and government) **is progressively** (or: constantly; repeatedly) **being caused to pass along** (pass by; pass away), **as well as its over-desire** (full passion; earnest wants; lust), **yet the person constantly doing**

(or: performing) **God's will** (intent; purpose; desire) **remains** (abides; dwells) **on into the Age** (= the time and sphere characterized by the Messiah).

18. **O undeveloped ones or folks of the age to be educated** (or: servants, little boys and little girls who might be hit in training and for discipline), **it continues being** (or: is progressively) **a last hour** (= an *eschaton* of the Day, or the closing moment [of the age]), **and according as you hear** (or: heard) **that an antichrist** (or: anti-anointing; that which is instead of, or in the place of, Christ or the Anointing) **repeatedly comes** [other MSS: the anti-anointing (or: antichrist) continuously comes], **even now many anti-anointings** (or: antichrists; many things or people taking the place of Christ or stand in opposition to the Anointing) **have been born and are here** (or: have come into existence and are at large), **from which fact** (or: whence) **we constantly know by experience that it continues being a last hour** (= a closing moment [of the age]).
19. **They came** (or: come; go; or: went) **out from us, but they were not existing out of us** (or: they were not [a part] of us), **for if they were out of us, they would have remained** (dwelt; abided) **with us; but [this was] to the end that they may be manifested** (caused to appear) **that they are not all out of us or from us.**
20. **And further, you folks continue having the effects** (or: constantly hold and progressively possess the results) **of an anointing from the set-apart One** (or: the Holy One), **and so you all have seen and are aware** (or: know; perceive; [other MSS: and you know all {those} folks]).
21. **I do not write to you because you do not know the Truth** (or: [new] Reality), **but rather because you do know it, and because every lie is not forth from the Truth** (or: even that all falsehood is not [coming] from Reality).
22. **Which one is** (exists continuously being) **the liar, if not the person habitually denying** (repeatedly disowning; constantly contradicting), **[saying] that Jesus is not the Christ** (the Anointed One [= Messiah])? **This person is** (exists being) **the anti-anointing** (or: anti-anointed person; the one taking the place of and being in the opposite position of the anointing and of Christ): **the one habitually denying** (contradicting; saying, "No," about) **the Father and the Son.**
23. **Everyone, who** (or: All mankind, which) **in continuously contradicting or denying the Son, does not even have** (or: not even is he possessing; neither holds) **the Father. The one habitually speaking like the Son** (or: the one continuously confessing and avowing the Son; the one habitually speaking in accord with or saying the same thing as the Son) **also constantly has** (possesses) **the Father.**

24. **As for you folks, let what you heard from [the] beginning be continuously remaining** (abiding; dwelling; staying) **within you. When** (or: If; If at any time) **that which you heard from [the] beginning would remain** (should abide; can dwell; may stay and make its home) **within you, you also will continue remaining** (abiding; dwelling; staying) **within the Son, even within the midst of and in union with the Father!** (or: you will dwell both in the Son and in the Father).

25. **And this is** (continues being) **the Promise which He Himself promised** (or: promises) **to us** [other MSS: to you]: **the Life of the Age**
>   (or: eonian life; life into the un-seeable future; age-lasting life; Life having the character and qualities of the Age [of Messiah]; life pertaining to the ages; Life for and on through the ages). [note: in Acts 1:4-5 the "Promise" was the Holy Spirit]
26. **I write these things** [other MSS: But I wrote these things] **to you about the folks constantly trying to lead you astray** (or: periodically causing you to wander; repeatedly deceiving you),
27. **and the effect of the anointing which you folks received** (or: receive) **from Him constantly remains** (abides; dwells; makes its home) **within you folks, and you continually have no use** (or: you are not constantly having a need) **that anyone should keep on teaching you** (or: be repeatedly giving you a course of lessons; coach you; instruct you), **but rather, just as the effect of His anointing is continuously and progressively teaching you about everything** (or: concerning all people), **and is continuously true, and real, and is not a lie, even according as it taught** (or: as He instructs) **you: you are continuously abiding** (remaining; dwelling; being at home) **within and in union with Him** (or, reading as an imperative: be constantly remaining, abiding, staying and dwelling within the midst of Him).

28. **And now** (at the present time; in this moment), **little children** (born-ones; bairns), **you are continuously** (or, reading as imperative: keep on) **dwelling** (abiding; remaining; staying) **within and in union with Him, to the end that if** (or: whenever) **He may be manifested** (or: it can be made visible, apparent and shown in clear light) **we can** (or: may; should; would) **have confident boldness** (freedom in speaking associated with citizenship; complete outspoken bluntness) **and may not feel or receive shame** (disgrace; dishonor; humiliation) **from Him, within His presence** (or: may not be shamed away from Him in the midst of His presence). [cf 1 Cor. 15:34]

29. **If you folks may have come to see** (or: perceive), **and should now know, that He is continuously One who constantly lives in accord with the Way pointed out** (is right, just, fair, rightwised and in right relationship [in covenant]), **you continue to know by experience that everyone, who** (or: all mankind, which) **in habitually making or doing fair and equitable dealing** (accomplishing that which is right and in accord with the Way pointed out; practicing justice; constructing righteousness; producing rightwised [existence]) **has been born and now exists being a born-one** (or: now stands begotten), **from out of the midst of Him** (and: with Him as the Source).

CHAPTER 3

1. **You people at once consider** (or: look and perceive) **what kind of** (what sort of; what unusual, foreign or exotic) **love** (or: acceptance) **the Father has given to** (or: in; for) **us** [other MSS: you], **which we now have as a gift, to the end that we can** (may; should; would) **be called** (or: named) **God's children** (born-ones; bairns)! **And we are! Because of this** (On account of this; Therefore) **the System** (the world; the realm of the secular and religious; the ordered arrangement of culture, religion, economy and government) **is not habitually having experiential or intimate knowledge of us** (does not know or have insight into us [other MSS: you]), **because it did not know** (or: it does not have an intimate, experiential knowledge of) **Him.**

2. **Beloved ones, now** (at the present time) **we continuously exist being God's children** (born-ones; bairns from the standpoint of origin), **and it has not yet been made visible** (or: it is not yet apparent or manifested) **what we will proceed in being. We have perceived, and thus know** (or: are aware) **that if it** (or: He) **should be** (or: whenever it {or: He} may be) **made visible, apparent and manifested, [then] folks like to Him** (like-ones to Him; ones like Him; people resembling Him) **we will be existing, because we will continue seeing and will be progressively perceiving Him just as** (according and exactly as; in the manner that) **He constantly exists** (or: He is). [cf Ps. 17:15; Col. 3:4; Rom. 8:17-18]

3. **So everyone, who** (or: all mankind, which) **in continuously having** (or: habitually holding) **this expectation** (or: expectant hope) **[placed; resting; based] upon Him is [by this] constantly** (repeatedly; progressively) **purifying himself, just as** (according as; in the way that) **That One is** (or: exists being) **pure.**

4. **Everyone, who** (or: All mankind, which) **in constantly practicing** (habitually committing; progressively producing) **the error** (or: deviation; missing of the target; sin; failure), **is also constantly practicing the lawlessness** (or: habitually commits a lawless act, or progressively does the violation of custom), **and the error** (or: the failure to hit the target; the deviation; the sin) **exists being** (or: is) **the lawlessness** (or: the violation of law or the act apart from custom is the mistake and the error). [comment: this passage contrasts the two Adams; cf 1 Cor. 15:44-49]

5. **You have also perceived, and thus know and are aware, that That One was manifested** (made visible) **to the end that He would in a point of time lift up and carry away** (or: sustain, bear and raise up) **the errors** (or: those failures to hit the target; the mistakes; those deviations; the sins; [some MSS: our sins]), **and yet error** (failure to hit the target; deviation; sins) **does not exist within Him** (or: and in Him is no sin or failure).

6. **Everyone, who** (or: All mankind, which) **in continuously remaining** (dwelling; keeping his residence; abiding; staying) **within and in union with Him, is not habitually missing the target** (practicing sin; repeatedly failing in his purpose). **Everyone, who** (All mankind, which) **in continually failing to hit the target** (habitually sinning; progressively in error), **has neither seen Him, nor come to know Him by intimate experience or insight.**

7. **Little children** (born-ones), **let no one be constantly leading you astray** (misleading or deceiving you); **the person continually doing that which is in accord with the Way pointed out** (or: repeatedly practicing rightwisedness; progressively producing the justice, fairness and equity in right [covenantal] relationships) **is** (or: exists being) **just** (or: a person in accord with the Way pointed out; righteous; fair; equitable; rightwised; someone turned in the right direction, and is in [covenant] relationships), **according as** (just as) **That One is just** (is One in accord with the Way pointed out; is righteous, fair, equitable and offers righted covenant relationships).

8. **Yet the person habitually practicing** (repeatedly doing; progressively producing) **the error** (the failure to hit the target or accomplish his purpose; or: the sin; the mistake; the deviation) **is existing from out of the adversary who thrusts something through the midst, [with a weapon, or with ill-intent], creating a wound or division** (or: = is [operating] from [the influence of] the "*devil*"), **because this adversary is habitually sinning** (or: repeatedly missing the target; continuously falling short of the goal; constantly deviating from his purpose) **from [the] beginning** (or: from [its] origin). **Into this [situation] was** (or: is) **God's Son manifested and made visible, to the end that He would unbind** (loose; untie; destroy; disintegrate) **the works and actions of the adversary who casts things through the midst of folks.** [*cf* Rom. 5:12]

9. **Everyone, who** (or: All mankind, which) **in having been given birth, and is now in the state of having been born from out of the midst of God, is not habitually practicing failure to hit the target** (repeatedly doing sin; constantly producing error; continuing in deviation), **because His Seed** (sperm) **is continuously remaining** (dwelling; abiding) **within him** (or: within, and in union with, **Him**), **and he is not able** (or: he has no power) **to constantly fail to hit the target** (repeatedly sin; continuously deviate; go on failing; continue in error), **because he has been born forth from out of God.**

10. **[Both] God's children and the adversary's children are constantly visible** (apparent; manifest) **within this [thing or situation]: everyone, who** (or: all mankind, which), **in not normally producing eschatological deliverance** (not habitually doing justice; not progressively constructing his life turned in the right direction to accord with the Way pointed out, or not being fair and equitable; not presently being in [covenant] relationships) **– as well as the one not continuously loving** (unconditionally accepting and seeking union with **his brother** (or: fellow) – **is not existing out of God** (= is not living with God being his source of life and direction),

11. **because this is the message** [other MSS: promise; or: complete announcement] **which you heard** (or: hear) **from [the] beginning, so that we are habitually** (or: to the end that we would or could progressively be) **loving** (accepting and participating in) **one another –**

12. **not [living] like** (or: not just as) **Cain. He was existing, and continued being, from out of the condition** (or: situation; or: one; thing; = influence) **causing misery and hard labor** (the unprofitable attitude; the worthless mindset; the wicked intent; the toilsome situation; the sorry plight), **and so he slaughtered** (killed by cutting his jugular vein) **his brother. And on what score** (or: for what pleasure) **did he slaughter him? Because his works** (actions) **were gushed with misery and hard labor** (were wicked or evil; were toilsome; were unprofitable and worthless), **but those of his brother [were] ones in accord with the Way pointed out** (just ones; righteous ones; fair and equitable ones; rightwised ones).

13. **Stop marveling** (Cease wondering; Quit being astonished), **brothers, if** (or: since) **the ordered System** (world of culture and religion; or: the estranged secular system of governmental control) **is constantly hating and detaching from you** (habitually regarding you with ill-will).

14. **We ourselves have seen, and thus know** (or: are aware), **that we have walked together** (or: proceeded to change, passing from) **out of the Death into the Life, because we are habitually loving the brothers** (= fellow believers; [some MSS: our brothers; {or: = our fellow human beings}]). **The person not habitually loving** [some MSS add: his brothers] **continues remaining** (dwelling; abiding; staying) **within the Death.**

15. **Everyone, who** (or: All humanity, which) **in constantly hating** (or: regarding with ill-will or detaching from) **his brother, constantly exists being a person-slayer** (a murderer), **and you have seen so as to be aware that every person-slayer does not presently have** (or: is not continuously holding) **life having its source in, or having the quality of, the Age** (or: eonian life) **presently remaining within him** (or: continuously dwelling and abiding in union with him).

16. **Within this we have come to know the Love** (acceptance which drives to overcome estrangement and achieve reunion) **by intimate experience: that That One placed** (or: places; sets; deposited) **His soul** (the consciousness which is Him) **over us. We ourselves are also constantly indebted** (obligated) **to place [our] souls** (conscious beings) **over the brothers** (folks of the same womb: fellow humans; = [God's] family).

17. **But whoever may continuously have the world's means of living** (or: may habitually hold the sustenance of the life pertaining to the secular ordered System), **and may habitually gaze upon his brother [who is] continuously having a need, and may close shut** (or: would slam and lock) **his intestines** (= his compassions) **away from him, how is God's love dwelling** (abiding; remaining; staying) **within him** (or, reading as a future: how will God's love dwell in him)**?**

18. **Little children** (little born-ones), **we should not be habitually loving in word** (by a word or thought), **nor even in** (or: by) **the tongue, but rather within action** (deed; work) **and truth** (or: reality).

19. **And within this we shall come to know by our own experience that we continuously exist** (or: are) **from out of the midst of the Truth** (Reality), **and so before Him** (in front of Him; in His very presence) **we shall progressively persuade** (prevail upon; convince; win over; reassure; set at ease; render tranquil) **our hearts,**

20. **because, even if our heart may continually condemn** (censure; know-down by experience), **God is constantly greater than our heart, and He knows all mankind,** (all people; or: everything; all things) **by intimate experience.**

21. **Beloved ones** [other MSS: Brothers], **if our heart should not be constantly condemning or censuring** (or: would not repeatedly experience negative insights or habitually have knowledge which leads [some MSS add: us] down), **we constantly have confident freedom in speaking** (boldness from our citizenship) **toward and face to face with God,**

22. **and whatever we may continuously ask** (or: habitually request), **we keep on progressively receiving from Him, because we are regularly keeping** (attentively watching over, guarding and observing) **His implanted goals** (impartations of the finished product within; inward directives of purpose and destiny) **and are constantly doing** (performing; constructing; producing) **the things [that are] pleasing and acceptable in His sight** (or: before Him).

23. **And this is His implanted goal** (impartation of the finished product within; inward directive of the end in mind)**: namely that we could, should and would be continuously believing, progressively trusting, and habitually faithful** [other MSS: would at once place faith and trust] **in and by the Name** (or: constantly loyal to and for the Name; habitually full of faith with the Name) **of His Son, Jesus Christ, and thus should be constantly** (or: habitually; progressively) **loving** (accepting; overcoming estrangement to) **one another, precisely** (or: accordingly; correspondingly) **as He gave [the] implanted goal** (or: gives an impartation of the finished product within, with an inward directive of the purposed end and destiny) **to us, for us and in us.**

24. **And the person habitually watching to attentively keep His implanted goals** (impartations of the finished product within; inward directives of destiny) **continuously remains** (dwells; abides; stays) **within and in union with Him, and He Himself within and in union with him. And within this we are constantly coming to know by intimate experience that He is continuously abiding** (dwelling; remaining; staying) **within us and in union with us: from out of the Spirit** (or: from the midst of the Breath-effect; forth from the attitude) **which He gives** (or: at one point gave) **to us** (or: in us).

CHAPTER 4

1. **Beloved ones, stop believing** (or: you must not continually believe or put trust in, be loyal or pledge allegiance to) **every spirit** (or: expression of some influence; breath-effect; attitude), **but rather, you folks must constantly examine, test and prove the spirits** (influences; attitudes) **to assay** (or: prove) **if they are existing from out of God, because many false prophets have gone** (or: come) **out into the ordered System** (world of societal culture, government, economy and religion) **and continue there.**

2. **Within this you continually come to know by experience** (or: be progressively becoming acquainted intimately with) **the Spirit of God** (God's Breath-effect, influence and attitude)**: every spirit** (breath-effect; attitude; influence) **which constantly speaks in accord with** (says the same as; speaks like; or: confesses and avows) **Jesus [the] Christ [as] having come and now continuing in flesh** (= in a physical body), **continuously exists being** (or: is) **from out of God** [other MSS: every spirit confessing Jesus Christ to have come in flesh is forth from God],

3. **and every spirit** (influence; attitude; breath) **which is not habitually speaking in accord with** (speaking like; or: avowing; confessing) **Jesus** [some MSS add: {the; as} Lord, having come in flesh] **is not out of** (does not originate in) **God. And this [spirit, expression, or speech which is not in accord with Jesus] is** (or: continuously exists being) **of the anti-anointing** (or: that which pertains to the antichrist; from something in the place of Christ) **– which you folks have heard that it is constantly** (repeatedly; habitually) **coming, and now** (or: presently) **exists within the controlling ordered System** (or: is in the world of religion, economy, government and culture; or: has being in the realms of the secular and the religious) **already** (before now).

4. **Little children** (born ones), **you continuously exist from out of God** (or: you exist with God as your source; you originate your being from God), **and you have conquered** (overcome) **and are now victorious over them, because greater is the One** (or: He) **within you than the one within the ordered System** (the person in union with the world of religion, culture, society, economy and government; or: the individual centered in either the secular or the religious).

5. **They themselves exist being from out of that ordered System** (or: they exist with the world as their source; they originate their [sense of] being from the System). **On account of this they continually speak from out of the System** (they habitually speak out of the world [as a source and perspective]), **and the ordered System** (world of ideas: culture, religion and education, as well as the control of economy and government; the arranged realm of the religious as well as the secular) **constantly listens to and hears them.**

6. **We, however, continuously exist** (or: are) **from out of the midst of God. The person habitually and progressively coming to know God by intimate experience is continually hearing us** (or: listening and paying attention to what comes from, or pertains to, us). **He who does not exist from out of God is not hearing** (or: listening to) **us. From out of this we constantly know by intimate experiences the Spirit** (or: spirit; Breath-effect; influence; Attitude) **of the Truth** (or: of reality), **and the spirit** (influence; breath-effect; attitude) **of wandering** (deception; error; straying).

7. **Beloved ones, we are** (or: can and should be) **continuously loving one another, because love** (or: the urge toward reunion and acceptance) **exists continuously** (or: is) **from out of the midst of God. And so, everyone, who** (or: all humanity, which) **in continuously loving, has been born, and exists being a born-one, from out of the midst of God, and constantly experiences intimate knowledge of God** (or: comes to know by experiences from God; gains knowledge and insight by the experience which is God).

8. **The one not habitually loving has not come to know God by intimate experience, because God continuously exists being Love** (or: for God is Love and Acceptance).

9. **Within this, God's Love is instantly manifested** (or: was at one point made visible; is made apparent and clear) **within us** (or: among us), **in that** (or: because) **God has sent** (dispatched) **His uniquely-born** (or: only-begotten) **Son as a Representative** (Envoy; Emissary) **into the ordered System** (world of society, culture, religion and government; or: the cosmos; or: = the aggregate of humanity), **to the end that we would live** (or: can experience life) **through Him.**

10. **Within this exists** (or: is) **the Love, not that we ourselves have loved** [other MSS: not that we ourselves love or accept] **God, but in contrast, that He Himself loves us and sends** (or: urged toward reunion with us and sent) **His Son as a Representative** (Emissary)**: a cleansing, sheltering covering around our sins** (failures to hit the target, errors, mistakes, deviations).

11. **Beloved ones, since thus** (or: in that manner) **God loves** (or: loved) **us, we also are constantly indebted** (or: under obligation) **to habitually love and accept one another.**

12. **No one** (or: Not even one) **has yet once** (or: ever yet) **gazed upon God as an object in a theater** (as a public spectacle). **If we are** (or: may be) **habitually loving** (urging toward reunion,

acceptance and participation in) **one another, God constantly remains** (dwells, abides) **within us, and His love** (or: the love, which is Him,) **is existing having been brought to its goal and is now matured, perfected and has reached its destiny within us, and among us.**
13. **Within this we are continually knowing by experience that we are constantly remaining** (dwelling; abiding) **within the midst of, and in union with, Him and He Himself within us, because He has given to us from out of His Breath-effect** (or: Spirit; Attitude).
14. **And we have gazed upon this public situation, and are repeatedly testifying** (giving witness and evidence) **that the Father has sent forth** (dispatched as a Representative) **the Son – [the] Savior of the world** (or: Deliverer of the ordered and controlling System of religion and secular society; Restorer of the universe; or: = the Rescuer and Healer of all humanity).

15. **Whoever may speak in accord** (confess; avow; say like words; say the same thing; agree) **that Jesus exists being God's Son** (or: is continuously the Son which is God), **God continuously dwells** (abides), **remaining in him, and he himself within God.**
16. **And we have come by intimate experience to know and have believed, trusted and are convinced of the Love which God has** (or: holds) **continuously within** (or: among) **us. God exists continually being Love** (God is Love, which is Unrestricted Acceptance), **and the person continuously remaining** (dwelling; abiding) **within, and in union with, the Love, is continuously remaining** (dwelling; abiding) **within, and in union with, God – and God constantly dwells** (remains) **within the midst of him and abides in union with him.**
17. **Within this the Love has been brought to its goal, been matured, reached its destiny and is now perfected with us, to the end that we may continuously have confident freedom of speech** (the boldness of a citizen to speak publicly without fear of punishment) **within the day of sifting and separation** (distinction, evaluation and decision; judging; judicial proceeding; or: administering of justice), **because just as That One is, we also continuously exist being: within the midst of this ordered System and within the midst of the aggregate of humanity**
> (or: because in this world of culture, religion, economy and government, even we, ourselves, progressively exist – correspondingly as, and to the according level as, That One continuously exists and is progressively being).

18. **Fear does not exist within the Love, but rather perfect love** (mature love; love having reached its goal) **repeatedly** (habitually; progressively) **throws the fear outside, because the fear constantly has and holds a pruning** (a curtailment; a checking; restraint; a lopping off – thus, a correction). **But the one habitually fearing or dreading has not been perfected within the Love** (has not been brought to the destined goal of maturity – in union with love).
19. **We ourselves are** [some MSS add: now] **habitually loving** (or, as a subjunctive: can and should be constantly loving) **because He Himself first loved** (or: urges to reunion with) **us.**
20. **If anyone may up and say, "I am constantly loving God," and yet may be habitually hating** (or: would keep on regarding with ill-will or detaching from) **his brother, he is a liar** (he exists being a false one). **For the one not habitually loving his brother** (= member of the community, or, fellow human) **– whom he has looked at and now sees – he continues being unable and has no power to be loving God, Whom he has not seen** (or: looked at).
21. **And we continuously hold** (or: have) **this implanted goal** (impartation of the finished product within; inward and purposed directive of destiny) **from Him, to the end that the person continuously loving God can, should and would also habitually love** (accept and drive toward reunion with) **his brother** (= his fellow believer, or his fellow human being).

CHAPTER 5

1. **Everyone, who** (All mankind, which) **in continuously believing, constantly being convinced and progressively trusting that Jesus is** (or: exists being) **the Christ** (the Anointed One; = the Messiah), **has been brought to birth and is now a born-one** (= is a child) **from out of God. And everyone, who** (or: all mankind, which) **in continuously loving** (urging toward reunion with) **the One bearing and giving birth** (the Parent), **should and would also love** (accept in unity) **the person having been born** (the child) **out of Him.**

2. **Whenever we are** (or: may be) **habitually loving God, and then may be habitually doing or producing His implanted goals** (impartations of the finished product within; inward, purposed directives), **in this [condition and situation] we progressively come to know by insight and intimate experiences that we are [also] normally loving God's children.**

3. **You see, that we would continuously observe His imparted and implanted goals is itself the Love of God** (or: the love which pertains to God; the Love which is God)
>   (or: For this exists being love from God so that we can progressively watch over, keep, maintain and guard His interior finished product) **– and His implanted goals** (impartations of the finished product within; inward directives) **are not heavy** (weighty, thus, burdensome) **–**

4. **because everything having been born from out of the midst of God continuously overcomes** (habitually conquers and is progressively victorious over) **the controlling System** (ordered world of religion, secular culture, economy and government). **And this is the victory** (or: conquest) **at once overcoming** (conquering; victorious over) **the controlling System** (ordered world of religion, culture, economy and government)**: our trust, confidence, faith and loyalty!**

5. **Now who is the person continuously overcoming** (or: progressively conquering) **the ordered System** (world; secular realm; religious arrangement) **if not the one continuously believing, progressively trusting and being constantly loyal to [the fact] that Jesus is** (continuously exists being) **the Son of God** (God's Son; or: the Son who is God)**?**

6. **This is the One at one point coming through water and blood and breath** (or: spirit; Breath-effect), **Jesus Christ. Not within the water alone** (or: not in only water), **but rather within the water and within the blood** (or: in union with water and in union with blood; [other MSS add: and within spirit; note: figure of a human birth, or natural lineage]), **and then there is the breath – that which is continuing to give evidence** (or: and the Spirit {Breath-effect} continuously exists being the One repeatedly testifying), **because the breath is** (or: Spirit or Breath-effect exists being) **the Truth and Reality!**
>   (or: and the spirit is the One {or: one} continuously witnessing that the Spirit is The Truth!
>   or: the breath is that which constantly gives testimony that the Breath-effect is reality...)

7. **Because there are three constantly testifying** (or: ... that three progressively give evidence; or: seeing that the normal witness-bearers exist being three)**:**

8. **the breath** (or: spirit; Breath-effect) **and the water and the blood, and these three are [coming; proceeding] into the midst of the One** (or: exist [leading] into one [reality]; are existing into the one thing; or: = are in unison; or: = are in agreement, or are for one thing).

9. **Since** (or: If) **we are habitually receiving the testimony** (the witness; the evidence) **of humans** (or: from people), **the evidence of God** (God's witness; testimony from God; or: the testimony and evidence which is God) **is** (or: exists being) **greater, because it is God's testimony** (or: the witness which is God) **that He has testified** (given as evidence; witnessed) **and it now exists available as evidence** (or: testimony), **concerning His Son** (or: round about the Son which is Him; about the Son Who originates from Him).

10. **The person continuously and progressively believing** (or: keeping confidence and habitually putting trust) **into the midst of God's Son constantly holds** (or: has; possesses) **the testimony** (witness; evidence) [*p*74 & A add: of God] **within himself; the one not believing in God** [A reads: the Son] **has made Him out to be** (or: has construed Him) **a liar, because he has not believed or put trust into the evidence** (testimony; witness) **which God has attested and affirmed concerning His Son** (or: shown as proof round about the Son from, and which is, Him).

11. **And so this is the evidence** (or: exists being the testimony, witness and attested affirmation)**: that God gives** (or: gave; grants) **Life pertaining to, and having the quality of the Age** (life whose source is the Age [of Messiah]; eonian life; Life of, for and on through the ages) **to, for and in us, and this very Life continuously exists within His Son** (or: is in union with the Son which is Him)**!**

12. **The one continually holding** (or: constantly having; progressively possessing) **the Son continuously holds** (constantly has; progressively possesses) **the Life. The person not continuously holding** (constantly having) **God's Son does not now have** (or: hold) **the Life**.
>   [comment: it seems that the Son is the Life]

13. I write these things to you folks to the end that, having seen, you may know that you are presently holding (you folks constantly and continuously have) **Life pertaining to, and having the qualities of, the Age** (life whose source is the Age [of Messiah]; or: eonian life; Life of, for and on through the ages) **– for the folks** (or: in and among the ones) **continuously believing and putting their trust, confidence and reliance into the Name of God's Son.**
14. And this is the freedom of speech with outspoken boldness inherent to citizenship which we constantly have toward, and hold face to face with, Him: that if we ourselves should keep on asking or persistently request anything in line with (or: down from; in the sphere of; that accords with) **His will** [A reads: Name], **He is continuously hearing us.**
15. And if we have seen and are thus aware that He constantly hears, and listens to, us, whatever we may keep on requesting concerning or for ourselves, we have seen and are aware that we habitually have (or: hold; possess) **the requests** (the things asked for) **which we have asked – and now stand requested – from Him.**

16. If anyone of you may happen to see his brother (= fellow believer, or, fellowman) **habitually failing to hit a target** (sinning; making mistakes), **with a failure** (error; offense; deviation) **not with a view toward** (= that would lead to) **death, he shall keep on asking** (repeatedly make a request) **and He will continue giving life to him – for those habitually failing to hit a target** (erring; sinning) **not [leading] toward death. There is a failure to hit a target** (a mistake; a deviation; sin) **[which leads or points] toward** (or: with a view to) **death** (perhaps: = bearing a death penalty, [within that culture]). **I am not saying that he should ask about** (or: concerning) **that one.**
17. All injustice (contrariness to the Way pointed out; inequity; unfairness) **is a failure to hit the target** (deviation; error; sin; a failure toward the Purpose), **and yet there is failure to hit a target [that is] not toward death** (or: deviation [that does] not [lead] to death).

18. We have seen and thus know that everyone, who (or: all mankind, which) **in having been born from out of the midst of God, is not habitually failing to hit the target** (erring; deviating; sinning; falling short of the Purpose), **but rather, the person at some point being born from out of God habitually keeps a guarded watch over himself** (or: keeps himself; [other MSS: for instead, the One born from the midst of God continuously watches over and keeps him]), **and so the fellow** (the one; the person) **that causes misery or painful labor is not habitually touching him**
> (or: the disadvantageous and worthless situation does not repeatedly lay hold of him; the base fellow is not constantly assailing him; wickedness and evil are not continuously fastening upon him; the misery-gushed [attitude] is not repeatedly affecting him).
19. We have seen and thus know that we are continuously existing from out of the midst of God, yet the whole ordered System (or: the entire realm of the religious and the secular) **is continuously lying outstretched** (lying as asleep, idle or dead; reclining) **within the gush of misery** (within the disadvantageous, laborious and worthless situation; within the sorry plight; in union with wickedness and evil; in the midst of the misery-gushed [attitude and existence]),
20. yet we have seen and thus know that God's Son has arrived and is continuously here, and He has given thorough understanding (comprehension; faculty of thought; intelligence; intellectual capacity; input throughout the mind) **to the end that we would constantly know** [other MSS: so that we do constantly know] **by experience the True One** (or: the true, the real and the genuine), **and we constantly exist within and in union with the True One** (or: in the real [situation]; in the midst of Reality): **within His Son, Jesus Christ. This One is the True** (Real; Genuine) **God, and Life pertaining to and having the qualities of the Age** (or: life having its source in the Age [of Messiah]; eonian life; Life of, for and on through, the ages).

21. Little children (born ones) **keep yourselves in custody** (or: guarded)! **– away from the idols** (the external appearances; the forms; or: = false concepts)!

[written circa A.D. 60-65 – Based on the critical analysis of John A.T. Robinson]

SECOND JOHN

1. **The old person, to a chosen-out** (selected) **Lady** (feminine form: mistress; lord, female owner or authority), **and to her children** (born-ones), **whom I love in truth and in union with reality** (or: I truly love), **and not I only, but also all those having come to know the Truth by personal experience and are now having insight of Reality,**
2. **because of the Truth and Reality [which is] continuously remaining** (abiding; dwelling; staying) **within us – and shall continue being with us on into the Age;**
3. **grace** (or: Joyous favor), **mercy [and] peace** (joining) **will continuously be with us from beside** (or: in the presence of; along with) **God the Father, and from beside** (or: in the presence of; along with) **Jesus Christ, the Father's Son, within Truth** (or: in the midst of reality) **and Love** (unambiguous acceptance and the drive toward reunion).
4. **I was made exceedingly glad and joyful** (or: was greatly graced) **because I have met with and found folks from among your children [who are] continuously walking about within Truth** (or: = living their lives in union with reality), **according as we took in hand an implanted goal** (impartation of the finished product within; inward purposed directive) **from beside the Father**.
5. **And so now I am asking you, Lady, not as writing a strange or newly different implanted goal** (impartation of the finished product within; inward directive of destiny) **to you, but one which we have had from [the] beginning** (or: one which we originally had), **to the intent that we may continuously be loving each other**.
6. **And this is Love: that we may be continuously walking about** (= go on living our lives and ordering our behavior) **according to** (or: down from; in line with; on the level of; in the sphere of; commensurate with) **His implanted goals** (impartations of the finished destiny within; inward directives). **This is the imparted and implanted goal, even as you heard from [the] beginning** (or: even which you originally heard)**: that you would** (or: could) **be continuously walking about within it** (= go on living your lives in union with it)**!**
7. **Since many wandering-astray folks** (or: many who lead astray; many deceivers) **went out into the ordered System** (world of religion, secular culture, economics and government) – **those not continuously speaking like** (saying the same thing as; confessing) **Jesus presently coming in flesh** (= a physical body; or: = in [their] inner self)**: this is the person wandering astray, even the one in opposition to Christ** (the one instead of Christ; the one in place of Christ; or: the anti-anointing) –
8. **be continuously seeing to yourselves** (looking at yourselves), **to the intent that you people would** (or: may) **not destroy** (or: lose) **what we** [other MSS: you folks] **did** (produced; worked for), **but rather may receive back full wages**.
9. **Everyone leading forward** (going ahead; leading in advance; [some MSS: transgressing]) **and yet not remaining** (abiding; dwelling; staying) **within Christ's teaching does not have God; the person remaining** (dwelling; abiding; staying) **within that teaching, this one continuously has** (or: holds; possesses) **both Father and Son** (or: the Father and the Son).
10. **If a certain person is continually coming toward you and yet is not normally carrying** (or: habitually bearing; continually bringing) **this teaching, do not repeatedly take him into a house, and do not continuously say to him, "Rejoice!"** (= giving him a greeting).
11. **You see, the person continually telling him to be rejoicing** (= greeting him as an associate) **is continually sharing in common existence with his worthless deeds**
   (having fellowship with his acts which bring a gush of misery; maintaining partnership
   with his wicked and evil works; participating in his painful, toilsome and useless actions).
12. **Having many things to write to you folks, I resolved not to – by means of paper and ink. For I am expecting** (or: hoping) **to come to y'all and to speak mouth-to-mouth, so that our** [other MSS: your] **joy can be "having been filled"** (= be completely happy)**!**
13. **The children of your chosen-out** (selected) **sister** (= female fellow believer; or: = sister community of summoned forth folks) **draw you to themselves** (= greet you).

[written circa A.D. 60-65 – Based on the critical analysis of John A.T. Robinson]

THIRD JOHN

1. **The old person, to Gaius, the beloved one, whom I myself am continuously loving in** (or: within the midst of) **truth and reality** (or: truly loving).

2. **O beloved one! I am continuously having** (or: thinking and speaking) **goodness, ease and well-being** (or: wishing and professing loudly; claiming) **concerning all things [for] you to be constantly having a prosperous journey** (or: to progressively travel a good path; to habitually be prospered unto success; to be continuously helped along the Way) **and to be constantly sound and healthy [in mind, thought and body] just as** (or: to the same degree as) **your soul** (consciousness and inner being; or: = your life) **is progressively being prospered on its journey** (helped along the Way; prospered unto success; caused to travel the Good Path).

3. **You see, I was made exceedingly glad** (or: I am caused to greatly rejoice) **at the coming of the brothers** (= fellow believers or members), **from time to time, and their bearing witness of your [being] in the Truth, according as you yourself are continually walking about within Truth**
>   (or: testifying to the reality concerning you in correspondence to the fact that you yourself are habitually living your life in union with truth and reality).

4. **I do not presently have greater joy than from these things: that I am repeatedly hearing that my own children** (born-ones) **are continuously walking about within the Truth** (= living their lives in union with reality).

5. **O beloved one! You are continually doing** (performing; constructing; forming; producing) **a faithful and loyal thing** (act of loyalty and allegiance), **whatsoever you yourself may work unto** (or: actively accomplish into the midst of) **the brothers** (= fellow believers and members of the family) **and unto** (or: into) **the strangers** (or: foreigners) –

6. **who bear witness of you for the love** (or: testified to your love) **before** (in the sight of; in the presence of) **[the] called-out community – [for] whom you will do** (or: perform; produce) **beautifully** (finely; ideally), **sending [them] forward** (or: escorting them on; = attending to their needs in their travels, giving them supplies and finances) **in a manner worthy of God** (or: = in a way equal to God's value of them),

7. **for they came out for the sake of** (or: went forth in behalf of) **the Name, continually taking** (or: receiving) **not even one thing from the nations** (the ethnic multitudes; the non-Israelites).

8. **We ourselves, then, are constantly obligated to continuously take [them] up, while placing ourselves underneath to support such people as these, to the end that we would progressively come to be folks working together** (co-workers) **in** (or: for; by; with) **the Truth** (or: reality).

9. **I wrote something to** (or: for) **the called-out community, but Diotrephes, the one constantly liking to be their leader** (to be pre-eminent among them and dominate them), **is habitually not thoroughly receiving or accepting us** (or: repeatedly not fully acknowledging us).

10. **Because of this, if I can come, I will remind him of his actions** (or: call to mind his works and bring them up [for discussion]) **which he is repeatedly doing** (or: progressively producing) **by worthless, irresponsible and abusive words – unjustified charges**
>   (or: in messages causing a gush of misery; by ideas leading to painful labor; with evil or
>   wicked verbal expressions; by laying out thoughts leading to a bad situation), **continually speaking nonsense of us or gossiping against us, and then, not being satisfied or content upon these things, neither is he himself fully receiving or accepting** (showing complete hospitality to) **the brothers** (= fellow believers; Family members; [or: = the itinerant missionaries of 5-8, above]). **And further, those continuously intending** (or: determining) **[to do so] he is habitually hindering** (or: forbidding) **– even casting [them] out of the called-out community!**

11. **O beloved one** [i.e., Gaius]! **Do not have the habit of imitating this ugly thing** (or: that which ought not to be; the base; the worthless; that which is of bad quality; the malicious; the wicked; the evil), **but rather the Good** (or: the thing of excellent quality; the virtuous)! **The person habitually doing good** (progressively producing virtue; repeatedly creating excellence) **is continuously existing from out of God; the one habitually doing what is ugly** (base; what ought not to be; worthless; evil) **has not seen or perceived God**.

12. **Demetrius has been attested** (= has received supportive testimony) **by all and by the Truth itself. Now we ourselves are also continuously bearing witness** (or: testifying), **and you have seen, and so know, that our witness** (testimony; evidence) **is** (exists being) **real and true**.

13. **I have been having** (or: holding) **many things to write to you, however, I do not normally want to be constantly writing to you by means of pen and ink!**

14. **So I am continuing in expecting** (or: hoping) **to see you immediately, and then we will speak mouth to mouth!**

15. **Peace** (or: Harmony; [= Shalom]) **to you. The friends continually greet** (pay respect to; send salutations to) **you. Be continuously greeting the friends by name** (= individually).

[written circa A.D. 60-65 – Based on the critical analysis of John A.T. Robinson]

JUDAH
(JUDE)

1. **Judah, a slave of Jesus Christ and a brother of Jacob** (= James), **to those having been, and yet being, loved** (accepted recipients of the drive for reunion; [other MSS: set-apart and made holy]) **within God [the] Father, even** (or: and) **Jesus Christ; to kept and maintained folks, to called ones**
>   (or: for the people being loved in union with and within the midst of Father God, and now being watched over, guarded and protected in and by Jesus Christ – to invited ones):

2. **May mercy, peace** (joining harmony) **and love** (unambiguous acceptance; reunion's urge) **be multiplied to the full to you** (or: be increased to fill you; be multiplied to fullness in, for and by you folks).

3. **Dearly loved and accepted ones, while progressively making all haste and performing every diligent effort to proceed in writing to you concerning our common and communal deliverance**
>   (or: the rescue, salvation, health and wholeness belonging equally to several of us, and in which we share and participate as partners; [Aleph & others add: and life]), **I possessed a compressed and constraining necessity to write to you, progressively urging and encouraging [you] to be in the habit of strenuously contending**
>   (or: to continue adding to the contest; to be repeatedly on top, in combat of the public games; to repeatedly fully participate in the race course) **by the faith, in the trust, with the loyalty and for the confidence having been once for all given over** (transferred; passed along; committed; entrusted) **to, for, in, by and among the set-apart folks** (or: sacred groups).

4. **You see, some people came in unobserved, from the side'– those having been previously written of old into this judgment** (or: people having from long ago been written into the effects and result of this decision)**: [to exist being] impious ones, people continuously changing the grace and favor of God into licentiousness, as well as repeatedly contradicting, saying, "No," to or about, disclaiming, denying and disowning our only Sovereign and Lord** (or: Supreme Ruler and Owner), **Jesus Christ** [= Messiah].

5. **Yet I am repeatedly purposing and intending to remind you** [*p*78 adds: brothers] **– you folks having once seen** (or: perceived) **and thus being aware of all [these] things – that the Lord** [= Yahweh; other MSS: Jesus (= Joshua); some MSS: God] **after delivering** (rescuing; saving) **a people out of Egypt's land, [in] the second [phase] brought to ruin and loss those folks not trusting, believing or being loyal.**
>   (or: Now I continue purposing and intending to remind you folks, ones having [already] seen, perceived and now being aware, that [Yahweh] – after once saving all [the] people out of Egypt's territory – the second [time; phase; action] brought to ruin and loss those folks not trusting, believing or being loyal!)

6. **Besides that, those agents** (or: folks having or bringing a message) **not guarding** (keeping watch over; maintaining) **the beginning of themselves** (or: the rule of themselves), **but to the contrary, after leaving away from** (= abandoning) **the personal dwelling place** (one's own abode or habitation), **He has guarded, kept watch over and maintained under gloom** (or: thick darkness) **by imperceptible** (or: in unobservable, but effecting-all) **bonds, with a view to a judging** (a sifting and a separation for evaluating; a making of a distinction and a deciding) **of a great Day** (or: pertaining to or whose source is a great day; or: which is [the] great Day).

7. **As Sodom and Gomorrah, and the cities round about them** [= Admah and Zeboyim – *cf* Deut. 29:23], **in like manner** (or: turn) **to them, being given to fornication and outlandish prostitution, and then going away after different flesh** (= unnatural vice; or: = a different expression of alienation that was formed by the existing System), **are continuously lying before [us as] – an example** (a specimen; an effect of a thing pointed out or presented to sight) **– continuing in undergoing an experience of justice** (the Way pointed out; fairness and equity; what is right) **from fire pertaining to the ages** (or: of eonian, or age-lasting, fire; of a fire of undetermined duration whose quality and character are the Age [of the Messiah]).

8. **In like manner, indeed, these dreaming ones** (folks continuing in sleep, or with imaginary experiences) **also pollute flesh** (= their or others' bodies; or: = the estranged human nature). **They are continuously setting aside lordship** (or: ownership systems) **and are repeatedly blaspheming** (speaking injuriously of and slandering; vilifying; obscuring the light of; misrepresenting) **reputations** (or: opinions; notions; glories; manifestations which call forth praise).

9. **Yet Michael** (The One Who is like God), **the ruling agent** (the first, chief, or original messenger), **when making a distinction to** (a discernment with; a thorough separation and a decision for) **the adversary** (or: the slanderer; the one who thrusts things through folks or situations, and thus causes divisions; the "devil"), **reasoned** (deliberated; spoke thoroughly; discoursed [as in using the Socratic dialectic method]) **concerning the body of Moses. He did not assume to bring a blasphemous or villainous judging upon [him]** (or: to bring in addition a judging characterized by an abusive distinction or a slanderous decision; or: bring an added evaluating which hindered the light), **but rather, He said, "The Lord** [=Yahweh] **might hold you in added honor** (or: set a value upon you; put respect upon you; award you)."

> [note: this word is from *epi*, upon, and *timao*, to hold in respect, to honor, to value, to award. It is also used in negative connotations, and thus can mean, to assess a penalty upon, to chide, to respectfully reprove or admonish. As this passage is contrasting Michael's actions to the negative actions of those who "came in unobserved," I chose the positive translation of *epitimao*. In his *Word Pictures in the New Testament*, A.T. Robertson notes that both Clement of Alexandria and Origen said that Judah here quoted the *Assumption of Moses*. (This latter is an early first century Jewish work of apocalyptic literature. Recall that Paul cites Hellenistic literature in Acts 17:28)]

10. **Yet these folks constantly blaspheme** (slander; speak injuriously of; villainize; hinder the light of) **what indeed they have neither seen nor understand** (or: know; perceive), **but what they naturally** (instinctively; by generation; by sprouting and growing) **are continuously acquainted with** (or: are versed in; became masters of), **in these things they are progressively being corrupted** (spoiled; ruined).

11. **Alas** (or: Tragic is the fate) **for them, because they pass along by the way of Cain, and they are** (or: were) **poured out to the wandering** (or: deception) **of Balaam's wages, and they lose and destroy themselves in Korah's contradiction** (opposing idea; anti-word; message in place of the Logos).

12. **These folks are sharply-cleft portions of rocks** (or: reefs; = menaces) **in your love [relationship]s** (or: love-feasts and table fellowships; movements toward acceptance with the drive for reunion), **repeatedly feasting well together, by habit fearlessly shepherding themselves. [They are] clouds without water, being swept along by winds; wasted autumnal trees – unfruitful, twice-died, uprooted**;

13. **wild waves of the sea, continuously foaming out** (or: vomiting forth) **their shames** (or: disgraces). **Wandering and deceived stars, for whom the gloom of darkness** (shadowy dimness; obscurity void of Daylight) **has been maintained** (guarded; kept and watched-over) **unto an indefinite time period** (or: into the midst of [the] Age; or: for a life-time).

14. **But Enoch also, the seventh from Adam, prophesied to, and among, these folks, saying, "Behold, the Lord** [=Yahweh] **came** (or: comes and goes) **within His set-apart myriads** (or: in union with innumerable holy multitudes, which are Him),

15. **to form a separation** (or: make a decision; construct a distinction; perform a sifting and a judging) **which corresponds to and falls in line with all people** (to the level of everyone), **and to test** (or: search thoroughly) **the irreverent folks concerning all their irreverent works** (activities; deeds) **which they irreverently did, and concerning all the hard things which irreverent outcasts** (folks in error; sinners; failures; folks who make mistakes and miss the target) **spoke against Him."**

16. **These are, and continue to be, murmurers** (or: those who speak privately and in a low voice, making a grumbling buzz of under-toned mutterings of critical and discontented comments), **complainers** (or: those who find fault with their lot; discontented ones),

continuously passing from one place to another according to their strong desires (or: lusts; full passions), **and their mouth continually uttering** (or: speaking) **over-swollen** (hyper-weighty; pompous; boastful) **things, continually admiring** (or: wondering at) **faces** (= personal presences; = individuals; = personalities) **for the sake and benefit of advantage and furtherance.**

17. **But you, dearly loved, accepted and reunited ones, remember the things spoken** (the gush-effects; the results of the flow of what was said; the flowing declarations) **by the sent-forth folks** (representatives; emissaries) **in regard to those things having been told beforehand of** (or: foretold from and concerning) **our Lord, Jesus Christ,**

18. **that they said to you, "Upon** [other MSS: Within (or: During; In union with)] **[the] last of the time folks will repeatedly be** (or: there will constantly exist) **mockers** (those acting or playing in the manner of children; sporting, using childish gestures), **continuously passing from one place to another according to** (or: in correspondence with) **their irreverent strong passions** (or: their full desires and lusts of things not having the qualities of things approved by God)."

19. **These folks are those who are separating by setting boundaries, soulish ones** (folks dominated by, or living focused on, those things which characterize the soul [= emotions; will; intellect; "feelings"] or this present, transient life) **not having [the] Spirit** (or: not habitually holding a [proper] attitude; or: not continually in possession of spirit or Breath-effect).

20. **But you, dearly loved ones, while constantly and progressively building yourselves up by your most holy trust and with you people's most sacred, convinced loyalty** (or: in y'alls' most set-apart faith), **[and] continuously thinking, speaking and acting toward having well-being and things going well** (or: praying) **within the midst of a set-apart Breath-effect** (or: in union with [the] Holy Spirit; centered in a separated and consecrated attitude and life-force),

21. **maintain** (guard; keep watch over; protect) **yourselves in God's love** (or: in union with [the] urge toward reunion and unambiguous acceptance, which is God), **being folks in the habit of welcomingly receiving, embracing and entertaining the mercy of our Lord, Jesus Christ, on into a life having the qualities and characteristics of the Age** (or: a life pertaining to the ages; eonian life; life for the ages; life whose source is the Age [of Messiah]).

22. **And so, on the one hand, you folks be repeatedly extending compassionate kindness on some folks in order to relieve their misery and affliction** [other MSS read: put to the proof; expose; convict; reprove] **while continuously discerning, sifting and thoroughly separating so as to accurately decide [about their situation]**

    (or: be continually showing mercy on some who are constantly undecided and continue
    wavering and doubting because of making divided judgment in or for themselves);

23. **yet on the other hand, be continuously delivering** (or: repeatedly rescuing and saving, restoring to health and wholeness) **others, snatching them from out of the midst of the Fire; be repeatedly extending compassionate mercy in reverent fear, while hating and radically detaching from even the garment having been stained** (or: spotted) **from the flesh** (= the alienated human nature; = the self that was formed and controlled by the System).

24. **Now in and by** (or: with; to; for) **Him being powerful and able to keep and guard you folks from stumbling** (or: tripping) **and from harm, and then to stand you flawless and blameless** (or: unblemished; without defect or stain) **in the presence of His glory** (or: down in sight of the manifestation of Him which calls forth praise and yields a good opinion and reputation; or: down in the center of a view of the assumed appearance which is Him) **in extreme joy** (in the center of a much-jumping exultation; in union with body-moving celebration).

25. **By [the] only God** (or: To and for God alone; In and with God alone), **our Deliverer** (Rescuer; Safe-keeper; Savior; Restorer) **– through Jesus Christ our Lord** (Master; Owner) **– [is] glory** (or: a manifestation of that which calls forth praise; a good reputation; opinion; imagination), **greatness, strength, honor and authority** (right and privilege from out of Being) **before all of the Age** (or: in front of the Age's entirety and all that is the Age), **both now and on into all the ages** (eons; indefinite periods of time)! **Amen** (It is so; Count on it).

[written circa A.D. 60-62 – Based on the critical analysis of John A.T. Robinson]

AN UNVEILING OF AND FROM JESUS CHRIST
(REVELATION)

CHAPTER 1

1. **An unveiling of, and which is, Jesus Christ** (or: A disclosure from Jesus [the] Anointed; A revelation which pertains to Jesus [the Messiah]) **which God gave by Him** (in Him; for Him; to Him) **to point out to His slaves that which continues necessary to come to be** (or: be birthed; happen) **in swiftness** (= speedily; or: shortly) [note: this phrase means either the manner in which events will happen, or that it is quickly going to happen]. **And sending [Him] as an emissary** (or: representative), **through means of His agent** (or: messenger) **He indicated [it] by signs** (or: symbols) **to** (or: in; for) **His slave John,**
2. **who witnessed** (or: gives testimony and evidence of) **the Word of God** (or: God's Logos; the ideas of and thoughts from God; the expressed message about God), **even the witness** (or: evidence) **pertaining to Jesus Christ** (or: the testimony from [Messiah] Jesus; the martyrdom of Jesus [the] Anointed) **– as many things as he saw** (or: as much as he perceived [of it]).

3. **Happy and blessed is the person constantly reading [it] aloud** (or: retrieving knowledge from [it in the midst of an assembly]), **and those constantly hearing** (or: listening and paying attention to; = observing and obeying) **the words of the prophecy** (or: the messages contained in the light and understanding seen ahead of time) **and habitually keeping watch over** (guarding; observing) **the things having been written within it, for the situation is close at hand** (or: for you see, the season, fertile moment and appointed occasion is near – close enough to touch).

4. **John, to the seven called-out communities** (covenant congregations; summoned forth assemblies) **within Asia: grace and peace to you** (or: favor and [the] harmony [= shalom] of the joining [are] for and among you) **folks from** [TR adds: God,] **the One continuously existing** (or: unceasingly being; Who continuously IS), **even the One Who was, and continued being, and the One Who is continuously** (or: repeatedly; habitually; progressively) **coming or going – even** (or: and; also) **from the Seven Spirits** (or: Breath-effects; Attitudes) **which [are] in front of His throne –**
5. **and from Jesus Christ, the faithful Witness** (or: reliable Evidence; loyal Martyr), **the First-born of** (or: pertaining to; from among; or: belonging to) **the dead folks: even the Ruler** (or: Prince; Leader, Beginner; Originator; One in first place) **of the kings of the earth – by** (or: in) **the One continuously loving us by loosing** [other MSS: washing] **us from** [other MSS: out of] **our failures and deviations** (or: sins; errors; situations and results of where we missed the target or fell short of the goal) **within His blood** (or: in union with the blood which is Him),
6. **and made** (formed; created; produces) **us** [other MSS: in, for, with us; of us] **[to be] a kingdom** (or: sovereign reign and actions; [other MSS: constructed of us a kingdom which brings sovereign influence]): **priests in** (or: by; for; with) **His God and Father. In Him [is] the Glory** (or: For Him [is] the good reputation; By Him [is] the manifestation of that which calls forth praise; With Him [is] the appearance which affects the opinion of the whole of human experience) **and the Strength** (or: Might), **on into the ages** (or: indefinite time periods [some MSS add: of the ages])! **It is so** (Count on it; Amen).
7. **Consider** (or: Look; Behold)! **He is continuously** (or: presently; repeatedly; habitually; progressively) **coming with the clouds, and every eye will progressively discern and perceive** (or: continue recognizing; or: repeatedly see) **Him, even whichever of you folks pierced** (or: pierce) **Him. And all the tribes** (people-groups) **of the Land** (or: territory; earth) **shall beat themselves** (strike their breasts in grief, mourning or repentance) **upon** (= because of) **Him. Yes, it is true** (amen)! [Dan. 7:13; Zech. 12:10-14; *cf* Lu. 3:6]

8. **"I am continuously** (or: repeatedly) **the Alpha and the Omega," says the Lord** [= Christ or Yahweh] **God, "the One continuously being, even the One Who was and continued being, and the One presently and continuously** (or: progressively) **coming and going, the Almighty."**
> (or: The Owner is laying out these thoughts: "I Myself exist being the Alpha and the Omega – the continuously existing God, even the One Who continued existing [as] Being, as well as the One habitually being on the go and repeatedly moving about – the All-Strong.")

9. **I, John, your brother and joint-participant** (or: sharer of common-being/partnered-existence) **within the pressure** (squeezing; affliction; tribulation; oppression) **and kingdom** (or: reign; sovereign rule and activity) **and persistent remaining-under** (steadfast, humble and supportive endurance), **in union with** (or: within; [Griesbach and other MSS: of; originating in; pertaining to]) **Jesus Christ** (= [the] Messiah),
10. **was within the island called Patmos because of God's Word** (or: the Logos of God; the message which is God; the thoughts and ideas from God) **and because of the testimony** (witness; evidence) **pertaining to and having the characteristics of Jesus Christ. I came to be** (or: birthed myself; happened to be) **within spirit** (or: in union with [the] Spirit; in the midst of a Breath-effect) **within the Day which pertains to or has the characteristics of the Lord** (the Lord's Day; = the Day of Yahweh; or, = the Day of Christ; = Christ's Day), **and I heard behind me a great voice** (or: = a loud sound), **as of a trumpet, saying** (or: = like that of a trumpet sounding a command or a message),
11. **"What you are presently observing** (or: continue seeing) **write into a scroll and send [it] to the seven called-out communities** (or: summoned-forth congregations)**: into Ephesus, and into Smyrna, and into Pergamos, and into Thyatira, and into Sardis, and into Philadelphia, and into Laodicea."**

12. **And so I turned upon the Voice, to see who spoke with me. And upon fully turning around, I saw seven golden lampstands,**
13. **and within the midst of the lampstands, One like a Son of Man** (or: a son of mankind; = [the] son of Adam; = like a human being; [or: an eschatological symbol referring to such as in Dan. 7:13 and 10:5-6]), **being clothed** (or: invested) **[with a garment] reaching to the feet; being girded about at the breasts with a golden belt.**
14. **Now His head and hairs [are] white, as white wool – as snow – and His eyes as a flame of fire,**
15. **and His feet [are] like white brass** (or: bronze; fine copper) **as having been set on fire in a furnace, and His Voice [is] as a roar** (or: sound; voice) **of many [rushing or crashing] waters.** [Ezk. 1:24; 43:2]
16. **Furthermore, [He is] constantly holding** (or: having; possessing) **seven stars centered in** (or: within the midst of; in union with; centered in) **His right hand, and a sharp two-mouthed** (= double-edged) **broadsword is continuously** (or: repeatedly) **proceeding** (issuing forth) **from out of His mouth. And His appearance** (countenance; sight) **continually shines as the sun, in its power.**
17. **And so when I saw Him, I fell toward His feet, as dead. And He placed His right hand upon me, saying, "Do not be** (or: Stop) **fearing** (Don't be terrified)**! As for Me, I am the First and the Last** (or: I Myself continuously exist being the first one as well as the Last One),
18. **"even The Living One** (or: and now, the One continuously living), **I also brought Myself to be** (or: birthed Myself) **a dead one** (or: I also came, by Myself, to be dead), **and now, Look and consider! I am living on into the ages of the ages** (or: the unspecified and indefinite time periods of the eons), **and I constantly hold the keys of, and pertaining to, the Death and of, and pertaining to, the Unseen**
>   (or: continue having the keys, which are Death and Hades [= *sheol*; perhaps: "the grave"]; habitually possess the keys from the Death and from the unseen "realm/state of the dead"; keep on holding the keys belonging to death and shadowy existence).
19. **"So then, write what things you see** (or: saw; perceived), **and then what things are presently existing** (or: what they are; what they mean or represent), **as well as which things are progressively about to occur** (or: what is now impending to be coming into existence) **after these things.**

20. **"The secret of the seven stars which you saw upon My right hand, and the seven golden lampstands: the seven stars are agents of** (or: pertaining to; belonging to; having the qualities and characteristics of; or: folks with the message from) **the seven called-out communities, and the seven lampstands are the seven covenant communities** (or: summoned-forth congregations)."**

CHAPTER 2

1. **"To the agent which is** (or: For the messenger belonging to; In the person with the message which corresponds to; For the agent of) **the called-out community within Ephesus, write:**
>   **'The One continuously holding in His strength** (or: the One being constantly strong in) **the seven stars residing within His right hand, the One continuously walking about within the midst of the seven golden lampstands, continues saying these things:**
2. >   *I have seen, and thus know, your* [note: the pronouns and verbs are singular] ***works***

(acts; deeds), **and your exhausting labor, and your remaining-under to give support** *(or: patient endurance),* **and that you are not able** *(have no power)* **to bear up** *(lift up to carry; or: put up with)* **worthless people** *(folks who are not as they ought to be; evil men; ugly situations of bad quality),* **and you put to the proof those declaring themselves to be envoys** *(representatives; "apostles")* **– and they are not – and you found them false** *(liars; deceivers);*

3.   **and you constantly have patient endurance** *(habitually hold to remaining-under),* **and you bore up** *(lifted; carried-on)* **because of My Name, and are not wearied.**

4.   **But on the other hand, I hold** *(or: have)* **[this] down against you: you** [note: still singular] **sent away** *(or: left; abandoned)* **your first love** *(urge toward reunion; unambiguous acceptance of others as being on the same ground; participating in the others; movement toward overcoming existential separation from another being – Tillich).*

5.   **You** [assembly] **must be remembering, then, whence you** [as a single entity] **have fallen, and you must change your way of thinking and feeling** *(change your frame of mind and your perceptions),* **and you** [group] **must do** *(perform; construct)* **the first works** *(deeds; actions).* **Yet if not, I am continuously** *(repeatedly; habitually)* **coming to you** [as a group]**, and I will proceed removing** *(or: moving)* **your lampstand out of its place, if ever you** [as a group] **may not change your way of thinking** *(your mind-set, paradigm and state of consciousness).*

6.   **But still, this you do have, that you are constantly hating the works** *(acts; deeds)* **of the Nicolaitans, which I also continuously hate** *(detach from; regard with ill-will).***'**

7. **"Let the person having an ear hear what the Spirit is repeatedly saying to, in and by** *(or: the Breath-effect is continuously laying out for)* **the called-out communities:**
    'In and by the one *(or: To or for the person)* **continuously overcoming** *(habitually conquering; normally victorious)* **I will continue giving by and in him** *(or: to him; for him)* **to eat from out of the substance of the tree** *(wood; log; post)* **of the Life which continuously is** *(exists being)* **within the midst of God's paradise.'** [note: same word in Gen. 2:8, LXX; Luke 23:43; a garden of fruit trees]

8. **"And in and for the agent which is** *(or: For the messenger belonging to; In the person with the message which corresponds to; For the agent of)* **the called-out community within Smyrna, write:**
    'The First and the Last, the One Who came to be *(was birthed)* **a dead one, and yet lives** *(or: lived; or: came to life),* **is presently saying these things:**

9.   **I have seen, and thus know** *(am aware of)* **your works** *(deeds; actions)* **and pressure** *(squeezing; tribulation)* **and poverty – but rather, you are rich – and the blasphemy** *(slanderous speech; hindering of light)* **of those declaring themselves to be Jews – and yet they are not – but rather [are] a gathering-together** *(a synagogue)* **of the adversary** *(Greek: of satan; or: which is satan; or: from the adversary).*

10.   **Do not be habitually fearing things which you are about to experience** *(or: to suffer; in which you are about to have sensible experience).* **Consider: the one who thrusts-through** *(the one who casts adversity through your midst; the devil)* **is about to thrust some from among you into prison** *(or: jail),* **so that you may be tried** *(put to the proof),* **and you will continue having pressure** *(squeezing; tribulation)* **[for] ten days.**
    Progressively come to be a faithful and reliable person *(or: You must be being birthed a trusting and loyal one)* **until death, and I will continue giving Life's wreath to you** *(or: for you the wreath of The Life; or: the victor's symbol, which is life in you).***'**

11. **"Let the person who has an ear listen and hear what the Spirit is presently and continually saying to the called-out communities** *(the summoned forth covenant assemblies)***:**
    'The person habitually overcoming *(or: repeatedly victorious; progressively conquering)* **may by no means be injured or harmed from the midst of the second death.'**

12. **"And in** *(or: to; for)* **the agent which is** *(or: For the messenger belonging to; In the person with the message which corresponds to; For the agent of)* **the called-out community within Pergamos, write:**

'The One constantly holding (having) **the sharp, two-mouthed broadsword is presently laying out and saying these things:**

13. *I have seen, and thus know (am aware of) where you are continually dwelling (settling down for an abode) – where satan's seat (or: the adversary's throne and place of power) [is]! – and yet you are constantly strong in (or: getting into your power) My Name, and did not deny (disown; contradict; say, 'No,' to) My faithfulness (or: trust), even in the days in which Antipas, My faithful witness who was killed alongside you folks: where satan presently dwells* (or: days of opposition from everyone against the loyal testimony about Me, and faithful witness from Me, which was killed at your side: the place the adversary continuously has an abode).

14. *But still I am holding down a few things against you: you have there those continuously strong to be retaining the teaching of Balaam, who instructed Balak to thrust a snare in the sight of the sons of Israel to eat things offered to forms* (or: sacrificed to idols), *and thus, to commit prostitution* (= idolatry).

15. *Thus, you also constantly have those being continuously strong in, and retaining, the teaching of the Nicolaitans, likewise.*

16. *You must change your mind (your way of thinking, attitude, mindset and state of consciousness), therefore! Yet if not, I am repeatedly (habitually) coming swiftly in you (to you; for you)* [again: you, singular], *and I will proceed waging war (doing battle) with them within the broadsword of My mouth.'*

17. "Let the one having an ear hear what the Spirit is now saying to the called-out community: 'By and in the one (or: To the person) **habitually overcoming** (repeatedly conquering), **by and in him** (or: to him; for him) **I will continue giving manna having been hidden, and I will proceed to give in him** (or: to or for him) **a white pebble, and upon the pebble a new** (different in character) **name having been written which no one has seen, so as to know, except the one presently receiving it.'**

18. "And to (or: in; for) the agent and message-bearer of, and which is, the called-out community in Thyatira, write:
'The Son of God, the One having His eyes as a flame of fire and His feet like burnished (or: white) **brass** (bronze; fine copper), **presently says these things:**

19. *I have seen, and thus know (am aware of) your* [singular] *acts (deeds; works), and love (urge toward reunion; participating acceptance), and faith (loyalty; reliability), and service, as well as persistent remaining-under for support (relentless, humble endurance); and your last acts (works) [are] more than the first ones,*

20. *but still, I continue holding (having) much down against you, because you are constantly letting-off (tolerating; allowing; pardoning) your wife* [other MSS: the woman] *Jezebel – she is habitually calling herself a prophetess – and she is continually teaching and deceiving (seducing) My slaves to practice prostitution (adultery; fornication) and (or: that is,) to eat things sacrificed to idols* (things offered to forms and outward appearances).

21. *And I give time to her, to the intent that she may change her mind (way of thinking), and habitually she is not intending (or: willing) to change her thinking out of her prostitution* (= attitude toward idolatry, or, association with idol temples).

22. *Consider: I am presently casting her into a bed, and those habitually committing adultery with her into great pressure (tribulation; squeezing) if ever they may not change their minds (state of consciousness) out of her works* (activities; deeds).

23. *And I will proceed killing her children within death, and all the called-out assemblies shall know that I am the One continuously searching the kidneys and hearts, and I will continue giving to each one of you down from (in accord to; in the sphere of; to the level of) your* [plural] *actions* (deeds; works).

24. *Now I am saying to you, to the rest (the remaining) within Thyatira – whoever are not holding this teaching – who do not know "the depths of satan (from the adversary),"as they are laying it out, I will be casting no other burden upon you.*

25. *Moreover, what you have (hold) you must get into your power (be strong in; lay hold*

of), ***until of which [time or situation] whenever I may arrive*** *(or, as a future: will proceed to be arriving).'*

26. "'**And [to] the one habitually conquering** (repeatedly overcoming; progressively victorious) **and keeping watch over** (guarding; maintaining observance of) **My acts** (works; deeds) **until completion** (down to a final act; as far as [the] purposed and destined goal; until an end), **I will continue giving to him authority** (right and privilege from out of Being) **upon the multitudes** (the nations; the ethnic groups; the Gentiles),

27. "'**and so he will continue shepherding** (i.e., feeding, tending and guarding) **them with a staff made of iron, as he is being continuously broken [like] pottery vessels,** [Ps. 2:8-9] **as I also have received from My Father,**

28. "'**and thus I will continue giving to him** (or: bestowing in him; granting for him; delivering up with him) **the morning star.'**

29. "**So let the person having an ear at once listen, and hear** (= pay attention and obey) **what the Spirit is now continuously saying to** (or: in; for; among) **the called-out, covenant communities!**"

CHAPTER 3

1. "**Next, to** (or: in; for) **the agent which is** (or: messenger from; person with the message of, or pertaining to) **the called-out community within Sardis, write:**
   '**The One having** (or: holding) **the seven spirits and attitudes of God – and** (or: even) **the seven stars – is presently saying these things,**
   I have seen, and thus know (am aware of) your works (actions; deeds) [and] that you have a name (= reputation) that you are living, and yet you are dead!
2. *Come to be (Be birthed) awake ones (watchful people) and establish (set fast) the remaining things which were about to die (or: rot), for I have not found your works (acts; deeds) being fulfilled (being made full) in front of and in the sight of My God (or: before God – which is Me).*
3. *Remember, then, how you have received (or: taken with the hand) and heard! Continuously keep watch (or: Guard [it]) and change your way of thinking (mindset; attitude; state of consciousness) [and turn to God]. If ever, then, you should not be watching, I will proceed arriving (or: may arrive) upon you as a thief, and under no circumstances would you know what hour I will (or: may) be arriving upon you.*
4. *But still, you have a few names in Sardis which do (or: did) not stain (soil; pollute) their garments, and they will continue walking with Me in white [garments] because they are worthy ones (folks of corresponding value).'*

5. "'**The person habitually conquering** (repeatedly or progressively overcoming) **may thus clothe himself in white garments, and under no circumstances will I proceed to erase his name from out of the scroll of The Life** (or: Life's scroll; the scroll which signifies life), **and I will continue speaking in accordance to his name** (saying the same thing as his name; confessing and avowing his name) **in front of My Father, and in front of His agents** (or: messengers; folks with the Message).'

6. "**Now let the one having an ear continuously listen, and hear what the Spirit** (or: Breath-effect; Attitude) **is normally and presently saying to the called-out, covenant communities.**

7. "**And so to the agent and message-bearer of the called-out community in Philadelphia, write:**
   '**The Set-apart One** (The Holy One; The Saint), **the True One, the One having** (continuously holding) **David's Key, the One habitually opening – and no one keeps on shutting** (or: locking) **– and He is repeatedly shutting (locking) – and no one keeps on opening –** [Isa. 22:22] **He, is presently saying these things,**
8. *I have seen, and thus know (am aware of) your* [note: pronouns & verbs are singular] *actions (works; deeds). Consider! I have given before you an open door (or: a door having been opened in your sight) which no one is able (or: has power) to shut, because you continue holding a little power (having a little ability), and you keep watch over (guarded) My Word (Idea), and you do not contradict (or: deny) My Name.*
9. *Consider! I am* [other MSS: could be] *constantly giving to those from out of the*

> *synagogue of satan (the assembly of the adversary; the congregation which is the adversary) – the ones repeatedly saying [that] they themselves are Jews, and yet they are not, but are lying – Consider! I will continue forming, constructing and making them so that they will proceed arriving, and then they will proceed worshiping in front of your feet and can know that I, Myself, love and accept you!*

10. *Because you keep watch over (observe; preserve; guard) the Word of My patient endurance (of My remaining-under), I, also, will continue keeping watch over (observing; preserving; guarding) you from out of the midst of the hour of the putting to the proof (or: trial; test) which is presently about to be progressively coming upon the whole territory where folks normally dwell (or: inhabited land; = Roman Empire), to put to the proof (to test, try and put through an ordeal) those continually dwelling down in houses upon the Land (or: inhabiting the territory).' [cf 1 Pet. 4:12]*

11. **"I am repeatedly** (habitually; constantly) **coming and going swiftly** (or: = progressively coming soon)! **You must be continuously strong in what you have** (or: you must constantly hold in your power that which you possess) **to the end that no one may take your winner's wreath** (your emblem of victory; or: your encirclement).

12. **"'The one habitually conquering** (repeatedly overcoming so as to be the victor) **– I will continue making** (forming; constructing; creating; producing) **him [to be] a pillar** (or: column) **in the Temple that is My God, and he** (or: it) **may nevermore** (by no means any more) **come** (or: go) **out** (outside), **and I will proceed to write upon him My God's Name, and the name of the City of My God: "The New and different Jerusalem" – the one habitually descending from out of the atmosphere** (or: heaven), **from God – and My Name, the one new in character and quality** [other MSS: and the new name].'

13. **"Let the person having an ear listen to and hear what the Spirit** (Breath-effect) **is repeatedly** (or: progressively) **saying to the called-out, covenant communities!**

14. **"And then, to** (or: in; for) **the agent which is** (or: messenger from; person having the message of, or with regard to) **the called-out community within Laodicea, write:**

> **'The Amen** (The It-is-so), **the Faithful** (or: Trustworthy, Reliable) **and True Witness, the Beginning of God's Creation** (or: the Prime Source of God's creation; the First Place or Chief of God's Framing; the Origin of God's act of building and founding; the Starting Point from God's act of reducing from a state of wildness and disorder) **is presently saying these things,**

15. *I have seen, and thus know (am aware of) your [singular] works (acts), that you are (continue being) neither cold nor boiling hot (or: zealous): O that you were being cold, or boiling hot (zealous)!*

16. *Thus, because you continue being lukewarm (tepid), and are neither boiling hot nor cold, I am about to vomit you out of My mouth.*

17. *Because you are habitually saying, "I am rich and have acquired wealth and continuously have need of nothing," and yet you have not seen so as to know (or: are not aware) that you continue being wretched (or: miserable; in hardship) and pitiful and poor and blind and naked,*

18. *I continue advising you [singular] to buy from Me gold having been refined (set ablaze) forth from out of fire, to the end that you may become rich; and white garments, to the end that you may clothe yourself and the shame (disgrace) of your nakedness may not be manifested (brought to light; caused to appear); and eye-salve to anoint (rub in) your eyes, to the end that you may be continuously observing (or: progressively seeing).'*

19. **"Whosoever, if I may be having affection for them** (regard them as fond friends), **I constantly put to the proof** (or: expose; reprove) **and I continuously educate** (discipline; give child-instruction). **Therefore be hot** (zealous) **and change your mind** (your way of thinking; your attitude and frame of mind; your state of consciousness)!

20. **"Consider! I have stood, and continue standing, upon** (= at) **the door** (entrance), **and I am constantly knocking; if ever anyone may** (or: can) **hear My voice** (or: sound) **and would open the door, I will proceed entering** (coming or going in) **toward him, and then I will continue eating the evening meal with him, and he with Me."**

21. "'To (or: In; For) **the person who is habitually conquering** (repeatedly overcoming; normally victorious) **I will continue giving** [the right? the ability? the honor?] **to sit** (or: be seated) **with Me within My throne, as I also conquer** (or: conquered; overcome; overcame and was victorious) **and sit** (or: sat down) **with My Father within His throne.'**

22. **"Let the one who has an ear listen to and hear what the Spirit** (Breath-effect) **is presently saying to these called-out, covenant communities."**

CHAPTER 4

1. **After these things I saw** (or: perceived) **– and now consider this! – A door** (or: gate; entrance; portal), **having been opened** (thus: standing open) **within the atmosphere** (or: heaven; sky). **And the first sound** (or: voice) **which I hear** (or: heard) **[is; was] as a war-trumpet talking with me, saying,**
> **"Come up here** (Ascend to this place), **and I will proceed showing you what things it is necessary** (binding) **to birth** (to come to be in existence) **after these things."**

2. **And then, immediately, I in myself came to exist within spirit** (or: in myself I came to be within [the] Spirit; I birthed myself in union with a Breath-effect) **– and now consider this! – A throne being laid down and lying within the atmosphere** (or: heaven; sky), **and upon the throne [was] One continuously sitting** (or: as well as [One] being permanently seated on the throne).

3. **And the One continuously sitting [was; is] for appearance** (or: to [my] vision) **like a jasper stone and a carnelian. And a rainbow, similar in appearance to an emerald, [was; is] around the throne.**

4. **Next, around** (or: encircling) **the throne, [were; are] twenty-four thrones** (or: seats; chairs), **and upon the thrones** (seats; chairs), **twenty-four elders** (or: old people) **continuously sitting, having been clothed in white garments. And upon their heads [were; are] golden wreaths** (symbols of having won in a contest, or of festal celebration).

5. **Also – forth from out of the throne – lightnings and voices** (or: sounds) **and thunders repeatedly** (or: continuously) **proceed out. Furthermore, [there were] seven shining ones** (or: lamps; lights; torches) **of fire, which are the Seven Spirits of God** (or: God's seven Breath-effects), **being continuously caused to burn before the throne.**

6. **And before the throne [is; was] a sea as of glass** (or: as a glassy sea), **like clear ice** (or: crystal). **Then, within the middle** (or: centered in the midst) **of the throne, and in a circle around the throne [were; are] four living ones** (or: living beings) **continuously being full of eyes in front and behind:**

7. **the first living one resembling a lion, the second living one resembling a calf** (or: young bullock), **the third living one has a human's face, and the fourth living one resembles a flying vulture** (or: eagle). [Ezk. 1:5-10]

8. **And the four living ones** (or: living beings), **each one of them having six wings apiece** [Isa. 6:2], **are continuously full of eyes in a circle around and internally; and day and night they continuously have no rest** (or: intermission), **constantly** (or: repeatedly) **saying,**
> **"Set-apart, Set-apart, Set-apart** (Consecrated; Holy; Sacred)! **O Lord** [= Yahweh] **God, The All-strong** (the Almighty; the Strong Holder-of-all) [Isa. 6:3; Amos 3:13; 4:13] **– the One Who was and continued being, the continuously Existing One, even the One continuously** (habitually; repeatedly; progressively) **coming or going** (= the One constantly on the move)."

9. **And whenever the living ones will repeatedly give glory and honor** (or: value; respect) **and thanks** (gratitude; good favor) **to the One continuously sitting upon the throne – to the One continuously living on into the ages** (or: indefinite time periods; most important eons) **of the ages,**

10. **the twenty-four elders** (or: older people) **will repeatedly fall before the One continuously sitting upon the throne, and will continue worshiping** (bowing; kissing toward) **the One continuously living on into the ages** (or: indefinite time periods; most important eons) **of the ages, and they will proceed casting their wreaths** (symbols of victory or celebration) **before the throne, repeatedly saying,**

11. **"You are constantly worthy** (or: of equal value), **our Lord** [= Yahweh] **and God, to receive** (or: take) **the glory** (or: the reputation; 'the opinion which is based on the whole of human experience' – Paul Tillich), **and the honor, and the power, because You create all things** (or: You brought the whole from chaos, disorder and wildness to framed and founded order), **and because of Your will, intent and purpose, they were existing, and continued being, and they are** (or:

were) **framed and created."**

CHAPTER 5

1. **Then, upon the [open] right [hand] of the One continuously sitting upon the throne, I saw a little book** (or: scroll; perhaps: codex) **having been written within and behind** (i.e., written on both sides), **having been sealed with** (or: by) **seven seals.**
2. **Next I saw a strong agent** (or: messenger; person with a message) **repeatedly proclaiming** (announcing a message openly and publicly) **in a great** (= loud) **voice,**
    "Who is worthy (of equal value) **to open the little book** (or: scroll; codex), **and to loose** (or: destroy) **its seals?"**
3. **And yet no one** (or: not one person) **within the atmosphere** (or: heaven; sky), **neither upon the land** (or: earth; ground) **nor down under the land** (earth; ground), **had power or was able to open the little book** (or: scroll; codex) **nor to see or observe it.**
4. **And so I was greatly weeping, that no one was or is found worthy** (of equal value) **to open the little book** (or: scroll; codex) **nor even to see or observe it.**

5. **Then one forth from among the elders** (or: old people) **is saying to me,**
    "Do not continue weeping! Consider! The Lion out of the tribe of Judah, the Root of (from) **David, overcame to open the little book, and to loose** (or: destroy) **its seven seals** [with other MSS: He conquers! He is presently opening the scroll, as well as its seven seals]**."**
6. **And then within the midst of the throne and of the four living ones, and within the midst of the elders, I saw a little Lamb standing, as one having been slaughtered, having seven horns and seven eyes – which are the Seven Spirits of God** (or: God's seven Breath-effects/Attitudes)**: the Ones having been and still being sent forth as envoys** (representatives) **into all the Land** (or: earth) **–**
7. **and it came** (or: went), **and it has taken** (or: received) **so that it has the scroll** (or: codex) **from out of the right [hand] of the One continuously sitting upon the throne.**

8. **Now when it took** (or: received) **the little book** (or: scroll; codex), **the four living ones and the twenty-four elders** (older folks) **fell before the little Lamb – each one constantly holding lyres** (or: harps) **and golden, shallow bowls being continuously brimming full of incenses** (things passed off in fumes), **which are the thoughts and speech toward having things going well and being at ease** (or: prayers) **of, and from, the set-apart folks** (or: holy ones; saints; sacred people).
9. **And they repeatedly sing a new song** (an ode or hymn different in character), **constantly saying,**
    "You are worthy to take (of equal value to receive) **the scroll** (or: codex; book) **and to open its seals, because You were** (or: are) **slaughtered and bought us by God** (for God; in God; with God), **within Your blood** (or: in union with the blood which is You), **from out of the midst of every tribe and tongue** (or: language) **and people and ethnic multitude** (or: nation).
10. **"And You made** (or: make; form; construct; produce) **them** [minuscule 792, the Clementia Vulgate (1592) and Primasius (6th century) read: us] **kings** [other MSS: a kingdom] **and priests in** (for; to; by) **our God, and they** [the Armenian, Clementia Vulgate (1592) and Primasiua read: we] **continue reigning** [reading with Westcott & Hort (following A); other MSS: they will continue reigning] **upon the Land** (or: the earth)**."**

11. **Next I saw and also heard a sound** (or: a voice) **of many agents forming a circle around the throne, the living ones, and the elders. And the number of them [is; was] innumerable groups of innumerable groups** (myriads of myriads), **even thousands of thousands,**
12. **repeatedly saying with a great voice,**
    "The little Lamb, the One having been slaughtered, is worthy (of value) **to take** (receive) **the power and ability, as well as wealth and riches, and wisdom and strength and honor and glory** (or: reputation) **and blessing** (a word and message of goodness, ease and well-being)**."**
13. **And then all creation** (or: every creature) **which exists within the sky** (or: atmosphere; heaven), **and on the earth, even down under the earth** (or: ground; soil), **as well as which is upon the sea – even all things** (the whole; everything) **within them – I heard repeatedly saying,**
    "The blessing (word of goodness and well-being) **and the honor and the glory** (good reputation) **and the strength** (might) **[are] in** (by; for; to; with) **the One continuously sitting**

upon the throne, and in (by; to; for; with) **the little Lamb, on into the ages of the ages."**

14. **And then the four living ones say** (or: said), **"It is so** (Amen)**!" And the elders fall** (or: the older people fell [forward]) **and worship** (or: worshiped; kissed the hand toward [the throne] and paid homage).

CHAPTER 6

1. **Then I saw when the little Lamb opened one from out of the seven seals; and I heard one from out of the midst of the four living ones repeatedly saying, as a sound** (or: voice) **of thunder,**
> **"Come** (or: Be coming; or: Go; Pass on; [TR, with Aleph, add: and see])**!"**

2. **And so I saw; now consider: A bright-white horse, and the One** (or: He) **continually sitting upon it is constantly holding a bow. And a victor's wreath was given to Him, and He came forth** (or: went out; passed on) **repeatedly overcoming** (continuously conquering), **even to the end that He may overcome** (conquer; be Victor).

3. **Next, when He opened the second seal, I heard the second living one repeatedly saying,**
> **"Come** (or: Go; [other MSS add: and see])**!"**

4. **And so another horse, fiery** (fiery-red; of the character or color of fire), **came forth** (or: went out), **and to the One continually sitting upon it, to Him it was given to take the peace out of the Land** (or: earth; territory; ground) **so that they would slaughter** (kill) **each other. And a great sword was given to Him.**

5. **Then, when He opened the third seal, I heard the third living one repeatedly saying,**
> **"Come** (or: Go; [other MSS add: and see])**!"**

And I saw; and so consider! A black horse, and the One continually sitting upon it [is] constantly holding a pair of balances (or: a balance bar) **in His hand.**

6. **And I heard a voice within the midst of the four living ones repeatedly saying,**
> **"A small measure** (a choenix: about a quart) **of wheat [for] a denarius** (a silver coin equivalent to a day's pay), **and three small measures of barley [for] a denarius; and you may not act unjustly to** (wrong; harm; violate; injure) **the olive oil and the wine."**

7. **And when He opened the fourth seal, I heard the voice of the fourth living one repeatedly saying, "Come** (or: Go; [other MSS add: and see])**!"**

8. **And I saw, and consider! A pale, yellowish-green** (pallid; ashen; colorless) **horse, and the name for Him [Who is] continually sitting upon it [is] Death, and the Unseen** (Greek: *hades*; or: = the grave) **has been following with Him. And authority** (privilege; jurisdiction; right from out of Being) **was given to** (or: by) **Him** [other MSS: them] **upon the fourth of the Land** (or: earth) **to kill within broadsword, and with famine, and within death, even by the little animals of the Land** (or: earth).

9. **Then when He opened the fifth seal, I saw, down under the altar of burnt-offering, the souls of** (inner persons of; consciousnesses which were; inner self-lives from) **the folks having been slaughtered [as in sacrifice] because of the Word of God** (or: God's message), **and because of the witness** (testimony; evidence) **which they were holding** (or: continued to have).

10. **And they uttered a cry with a great** (or: by a loud) **voice, repeatedly saying,**
> **"Until when** (How long), **O Absolute Owner** (Sovereign Lord; Master), **the Set-apart** (Holy) **and True One, are You not deciding** (separating, evaluating and judging) **and maintaining right for** (operating out of the way pointed out for; or: avenging) **our blood, out of those habitually having an abode** (dwelling) **upon the Land** (earth)**?"**

11. **And a brilliant white robe was given to each of them, and it was declared to them that they may, and should, rest themselves** (permit themselves to cease from any movement or labor in order to recover strength; [other MSS: will continue resting up]) **a little time longer** (yet a short time) **while** (or; until) **also [the number of] their fellow-slaves, even their brothers – those continually being about to be killed, even as they [were] – would be fulfilled** (made full; other MSS: can fill or fulfill [it; all]).

12. **Next I saw when He opened the sixth seal, and there came to be a great shaking. And the sun became black as sackcloth made of hair. And the whole moon became as blood.**

13. **And the stars of the sky** (or: heaven) **fell into the Land** (or: earth), **as a fig tree is casting her**

winter (i.e., unseasonable) **figs, while being continuously shaken by a great wind.**
14. **And then the sky** (or: atmosphere; heaven) **was parted away** (severed off and caused to recede, so as to disappear) **as a little scroll being progressively rolled up, and every mountain** (or: hill) **and [every] island were moved out of their places.**
15. **And the kings of the Land** (or: earth), **and the great ones, and the commanders of thousands, and the wealthy** (rich) **folks, and the strong ones, and every slave, and every free one, [all] hid themselves into the caves and into the midst of the rocks of the mountains,**
16. **repeatedly saying to the mountains and to the rocks,**
> **"Fall upon us and hide us** [Hos. 10:8] **from the Face of the One continuously sitting upon the throne, and from the inherent fervor** (natural impulse and propensity; internal swelling and teeming passion of desire; or: anger, wrath and indignation) **of the little Lamb."**
17. **Because the great Day of their** [other MSS: His] **inherent fervor** (internal swelling emotion, teeming and passionate desire; impulse; or: anger, wrath and indignation; or: natural bent) **comes** (or: came), **and who** (which one) **is continuously able** (or: continues having power) **to be made to stand** (or: to be established)**?**

CHAPTER 7

1. **After this I saw** (or: perceived) **four agents** (or: messengers; folks with the message) **standing upon the four corners of the Land** (or: earth), **continuously holding in their power** (or: restraining) **the four winds of the Land** (or: earth), **so that wind may not be blowing upon the Land** (or: earth; soil), **nor upon the sea, nor upon any tree** (or: all tree and shrub).

2. **And then I saw** (or: perceived) **another agent** (or: messenger; person with a message) **progressively ascending** (stepping up) **from [a; the] rising of the sun** [i.e., from the dawn or the east], **continually holding a seal** (or: signet ring; [Vatican MS 1160: seals]) **of the continuously-living God. And he uttered a cry with** (or: by) **a great** (= loud) **voice – to the four agents** (or: messengers), **to whom it was** (or: is) **given for them** (to them; in them; by them) **to act unjustly to** (to violate, injure, wrong or hurt) **the Land** (earth; soil) **and the sea –**
3. **repeatedly saying,**
> **"You may not act unjustly to** (hurt; injure; wrong; violate) **the Land** (earth; soil), **nor the sea, nor the trees, until we may seal** (impress with a signet ring) **the slaves of our God upon their foreheads."**

4. **Then I heard the number of the people having been sealed** (impressed; imprinted)**: one hundred forty-four thousand – folks having been sealed** (imprinted; certified; identified for ownership) **from out of every tribe of the sons of Israel.**

5. > **Out of Judah's tribe: twelve thousand sealed** (imprinted; certified; identified to the Owner)
> **Out of Reuben's tribe: twelve thousand**
> **Out of Gad's tribe: twelve thousand**
6. > **Out of Asher's tribe: twelve thousand**
> **Out of Naphtali's tribe: twelve thousand**
> **Out of Manasseh's tribe: twelve thousand**
7. > **Out of Simeon's tribe: twelve thousand**
> **Out of Levi's tribe: twelve thousand**
> **Out of Issachar's tribe: twelve thousand**
8. > **Out of Zebulon's tribe: twelve thousand**
> **Out of Joseph's tribe: twelve thousand**
> **Out of Benjamin's tribe: twelve thousand sealed** (imprinted; certified; identified to the Owner).

9. **After these things I saw** (or: perceived), **and consider! A vast crowd** (great multitude), **which no one was able to number, from out of every ethnic group** (or: nation) **– even of tribes and of peoples and of tongues** (languages) **– standing before** (in the sight of) **the throne, and before** (in the sight of) **the little Lamb, having been clothed with bright white robes** (or: equipment; uniforms), **and palm trees** (or: branches) **[are] in their hands.**

10. **And they are uttering a cry** (or: are exclaiming) **with a great** (= loud) **voice, repeatedly saying,** "**The deliverance** (Wholeness and health; The salvation) **[is] by our God** (in our God) **– by** (or: in) **the One continuously sitting upon the throne, even** (or: and) **by** (or: in) **the little Lamb!**"

11. **And all the agents** (or: messengers) **had stood and continued standing in a circle around the throne and the elders** (or: older folks) **and the four living ones. And then they fell on their faces before the throne and worshiped** (did obeisance to and kissed toward) **God, repeatedly saying,**

12. "**It is so** (Amen)! **The blessing** (or: The word of goodness), **the glory** (reputation), **the wisdom, the gratitude** (thanksgiving), **the honor** (the value; the pricing), **the power** (the ability), **and the strength [is] in** (by; for; with) **our God, on into the ages** (eons) **of the ages! So it is** (Amen)!"

13. **And one from out of the elders** (or: among the older people) **answered, saying to me,** "**These – the ones having been clothed with the bright, white robes** (or: uniforms; equipment) **– who are they and whence came they?**"

14. **And I had spoken to him,** "**O, my lord, you have seen, and thus know,**" **and so he said to me,** "**These are the ones continuously coming forth from out of the midst of the great pressure** (squeezing; ordeal; tribulation; oppression), **and they washed their robes** (uniforms; equipment) **and made them bright and white within the little Lamb's blood.**

15. "**Because of this they are constantly before** (in the sight and presence of) **God's throne, and they habitually do public service to** (in; by; for) **Him, day and night, within the midst of His Temple. And the One continuously sitting upon the throne will continue pitching a tent** (spreading a covering or tabernacle) **upon them.**

16. "**They will no longer continue hungering, neither will they continue thirsting, nor may the sun repeatedly fall upon them, nor any scorching or burning heat,** [Isa. 49:10]

17. "**because** (or: seeing that) **the little Lamb – the One back up amidst the throne** (or: the One again in the midst of the throne) **– will continue shepherding** [other MSS: is continuously shepherding] **them, and will continue guiding** [other MSS: is continuously guiding] **them upon springs of waters of life** [other MSS: living springs of water]. **And God will continue anointing** (or: wiping and smearing) **every tear shed from out of their eyes.**" [Isa. 49:10; Jer. 2:13; Ezk. 34:23; Ps. 23:1-2; Isa. 25:8]

CHAPTER 8

1. **And when He opened the seventh seal, silence was birthed** (came into existence; occurred; came to be) **within the atmosphere** (or: heaven) **for about** (or: something like; as) **half an hour.**

2. **Next I saw the seven agents** (or: messengers; or: folks with a message) **– the folks having stood and now standing before** (in the presence and sight of) **God. And seven trumpets** (or: = shofars; rams horns) **were given to them.**

3. **Then another agent** (messenger) **came and was stationed** (or: was set; is made to stand) **upon** (or: = at) **the altar, continuously holding a golden censer. And there was given to him many incenses** (or: much incense), **so that he may give [them, or, it] by the words toward having goodness** (or: would offer [it] in the prayers; that he could impart [them] to the prayers) **of the set-apart folks** (from the holy ones), **upon the golden altar which is before the throne.** [comment: this would be in the holy place of the temple, in front of the holy of holies (within which is the ark of the covenant: = the throne)]

4. **And the smoke of the incenses ascended – by and in the prayers of the set-apart folks – from out of the agent's hand, before God** (or: in God's sight and presence).

5. **Then the agent had taken the censer and filled it full out of the fire of the altar, and he threw [fire; or, the censer] into the Land** (or: earth; soil). **And thunders and sounds** (or: voices) **and lightnings and shakings birthed themselves** (or: of themselves came into being).

6. **Next the seven agents** (or: messengers) **– the folks holding the seven trumpets – prepared themselves** (made themselves ready), **so that they may sound the trumpets.**

7. **And so the first one sounded a trumpet. Then hail and fire mixed in blood was birthed** (came to be; or: hail and fire came to be mixed with blood), **and it was thrown into the Land** (earth; soil). **And**

the third of the trees was burned down, and all pale-green pasture (or: grass) **was burned down.**

8. **And then the second agent trumpeted. Then something like a great mountain, continuously being burned in fire, was thrown into the sea. And the third of the sea came to be blood.**
9. **And the third of the creatures within the sea – the ones** (or: things) **having souls – died. And the third of the ships was thoroughly ruined** (decayed; destroyed).

10. **Next the third agent sounded a trumpet. And a great star, continuously burning as a lamp** (or: a shining one), **fell out of the sky** (or: heaven), **and it fell upon the third of the rivers and upon the springs of the waters.**
11. **Now the name of the star is called Wormwood** (or: Absinth). **And so the third of the waters are being birthed** (or: are coming to be) **wormwood. Then many of the people died from out of the waters, because they were embittered** (made bitter).

12. **And the fourth agent trumpeted. So the third of the sun and the third of the moon, and the third of the stars were struck** (or: received a blow, impact or plague), **to the end that the third of them may be darkened, and the day may not shine [for] the third of it – and the night in like manner.**
13. **Next I saw and heard one vulture** (or: eagle; [Aleph with Maj. text, *Koine* proper; Maj. text, Andreas: agent; messenger]), **constantly flying within mid-heaven, repeatedly saying by a great voice,**
> **"W**oe (or: Tragic will be the fate)**! W**oe (or: Alas)**! W**oe (or: Tragedy)**! for those** (or: to or in the folks) **constantly dwelling upon the Land** (or: soil; earth), **from out of the midst of the remaining sounds** (voices) **of the trumpets of the three agents who are about to be one after another sounding a trumpet!"**

CHAPTER 9

1. **And then the fifth agent** (messenger) **sounded a trumpet, and I saw a Star – having fallen from out of the sky** (or: heaven) **into the Land** (earth) **– and the key of the well** (cistern; shaft; pit) **of The Deep was given to Him.**
> [note: the abyss, or, the Deep; that which is very deep so as to be considered bottomless; used in Gen. 1:2 (LXX), "darkness {was} up upon (or: over) the Deep, and God's Spirit was bearing (conducting) Himself over upon the water;" used of "the fountains of the Deep" in Gen. 8:2 (LXX); of "springs of the Deep" in Deut. 8:7; used in Deut. 33:13 (LXX), "And to Joseph he said, 'His land is of the blessing... from the springs of the Deep below;'" and in Ps. 104:2-6 (LXX), "Who dost robe Thyself with light as a garment.... Who covers His chambers with waters; Who makes the clouds His chariot... The Deep, as a garment, is His covering;" Ps. 107:23-26 (LXX), "They that go down to the sea.... these have seen the works of the Lord, and His wonders in The Deep;" Ps. 148:7,8, "... and all Deeps.... the things continually performing His Word;" Isa. 63:13, "He led them through the Deep, as a horse through the wilderness..."]
2. **And he opened up the well** (shaft; pit) **of The Deep and smoke ascended out of the well** (shaft), **as smoke of a great furnace** (or: kiln – for smelting, firing earthen ware or baking bread), **and the sun and the air were darkened from out of the smoke of the well** (or: shaft).
3. **Next locusts came out of the smoke [and went] into the Land** (earth). **And authority** (or: the right; permission) **was given to them – as the scorpions of the land** (or: earth) **have authority** (permission; license) **–**
4. **and yet it was declared to them that they may not be acting unjustly to** (be harming, injuring or violating) **the enclosed pasture** (or: grass) **of the Land** (earth; soil), **nor any green thing, nor any tree, except the humans** (the people)**: those not having the seal** (or: imprint) **of God upon their foreheads.**
5. **Now this was granted** (or: given) **to** (or: for) **them, not that they should be killing them, but rather so that they** [= the humans] **will be periodically examined** (or: continuously tried as metals by the touchstone; progressively distressed) **[for] five months. And their examination [is; was] as the distress** (metal testing) **of a scorpion whenever it may strike a human.**
6. **And in those days the people** (humans) **will proceed seeking** (searching for; pursuing) **death, and will continue by no means** (or: under no circumstances) **finding it. And they will continue setting their desire to die, and death will continue fleeing** (or: escaping) **from them.**

7. **Now the representation-effects** (resultant likenesses and figures) **of the locusts [were] like** (similar to) **horses having been made ready** (or: prepared) **unto battle. And upon their heads [were] something like golden wreaths, and their faces [were] as human faces,**
8. **and they were having hair as the hair of women, and their teeth were as those of lions.**
9. **And they were having breastplates – as breastplate armor made of iron – and the sound of their wings [was] as the sound of chariots of many horses continuously running into battle.**
10. **And they continue having tails like scorpions, and stings** (goads; sharp points), **and in their tails [is] their authority** (permission; license) **to act unjustly to** (to harm or injure) **the humans [for] five months.**
11. **They habitually have a King** (or One who reigns) **upon them: the Agent** (or: Messenger) **of the Deep. The name for Him in Hebrew [is] Abaddon** (Destruction; [note: see Ex. 12:23; in verb form, speaking of Yahweh, in Deut. 11:4; Ps. 5:6; Ps. 9:5; Jer. 15:7]), **and in the Greek He has the name Apollyon** (Destroyer; A Destroying One; or: One who makes folks lost; [verb form used in Lu. 17:33 and, of Yahweh, in Judah 5]).
12. **The one woe** (or: tragedy) **passed away. Consider – two woes are yet coming after these things** (or, with other MSS: Look and perceive! He {or: It} continues coming still! Two woes after these).

13. **And then the sixth agent** (or: messenger) **sounded a trumpet, and I heard one voice from out of the four horns of the golden altar [which is] before** (in the sight and presence of) **God** [note: a reference to the altar of incense which was in front of the innermost chamber in the Tabernacle],
14. **presently saying to the sixth agent,**
   "Loose the four agents: the ones having been bound upon the great river Euphrates."
15. **And the four agents were loosed – those having been made ready** (or: being prepared) **unto the hour and day and month and year – so that they may be constantly killing the third of the humans.**
16. **Now the number of the troops** (armed forces) **of the cavalry [was] two vast multitudes of innumerable groups** (or: myriads of myriads) **– I heard the number of them** (or: their number).
17. **And thus I saw the horses in the vision: and the ones sitting upon them habitually having breastplates of Fire, even resembling hyacinth** (or: amethyst) **stone, and being divine in character** (θειος: deity; divinity; divine nature or character; the fire of God; brimstone or sulphur). **And the heads of the horses [are] as heads of Lions. And Fire, Smoke and Deity** (divine nature and character) **continuously issues forth from out of their mouths.**
18. **From these three plagues** (blows; smitings) **the third of the humans were killed – from out of the Fire, and from the Smoke, and from the Deity which is constantly issuing out of their mouths,**
19. **for the authority** (the right, permission and license out of Being) **of the horses exists in their mouth and in their tails, for their tails [are] like serpents, having heads, and within them they constantly inflict injustice** (harm; injury).

20. **And yet the remaining ones** (or: the rest) **of the humans, those who were not killed in these blows** (or: wounding strikes; impacts; plagues), **did not change their mind** (change their perceptions, ways of thinking, attitudes; states of consciousness) **from out of the works** (actions; deeds) **of their hands, so that they may not worship the demons** (Hellenistic concept and term: = animistic influences) **and the idols** (forms): **the gold ones, and the wooden ones, which are able** (or: have power) **neither to see nor to hear, nor to walk about.** [Ps. 115:4-7; 135:15-17; Dan. 5:23]
21. **Also, they did not change their mind** (attitude; way of thinking; etc.) **from out of their murders, nor from out of their employment of drugs** (or: sorceries; enchantments), **nor from out of their prostitution** (fornication; [other MSS: worthless, misery-gushed {life}]), **nor from out of their thefts.**

CHAPTER 10

1. **Next I saw another Strong Agent progressively descending** (stepping down) **from out of the atmosphere** (or: sky; heaven) **– having been clothed with a cloud, and the rainbow upon His head, and His face as the sun, and His feet as pillars of fire**
2. **– and constantly holding in His hand a tiny scroll having been opened up. And He placed His right foot upon the sea, but the left upon the Land** (soil; earth).
3. **Then He uttered a cry with** (or: by) **a great Voice, even as a Lion is roaring. And when He uttered a cry** (or: cried out), **the Seven Thunders uttered their own voices.**

4. **And when the Seven Thunders spoke** (gave utterance), **I was about to be writing and I heard a Voice from out of the atmosphere** (or: heaven) **repeatedly saying, "You must seal** (or: = seal up and keep from being disclosed; place a seal on) **what the Seven Thunders uttered** (spoke)**," and "You may not write these things."**

5. **And the Agent, Whom I saw standing upon the sea and upon the land, lifted up His right hand into the atmosphere** (or: sky; heaven),
6. **and swore** (affirmed or promised with an oath) **within** (or: in union with) **the One continuously living on into the ages of the ages** (or: the Ages belonging to & pertaining to the ages; or: = the foremost of all the ages) **– Who framed** (created; founded; reduced from a state of disorder and wilderness) **the atmosphere** (or: heaven; sky), **and the things within it, and the land** (or: earth; ground), **and the things within her, and the sea, and the things within her – that a time shall not longer be**
        (or: that a period of time will not further continue being; that {a} time will not still exist; = there will be no delay; = there will be no longer a time of delay)**;**
7. **but rather, within the days of the Seventh Agent, whenever he may be about to repeatedly sound a trumpet, God's secret** (the secret, or mystery, of God or which pertains to God) **is also completed** (reached its goal and purposed destiny; finished; concluded; ended) **as proclaimed as good news to** (or: as He announced the message of goodness to) **His own slaves, the prophets** [other MSS: His own slaves, and the prophets].

8. **Then the Voice, which I heard from out of the atmosphere** (or: sky; heaven), **is speaking again with me, and is saying, "Be going** (departing), **take** (or: receive with the hand; seize) **the tiny scroll – the one having been opened up within the Agent's hand, Who has taken a stand upon the sea and upon the land."**
9. **And so I went away toward the Agent, saying to Him to give to me the tiny scroll. And He is saying to me, "Take** (or: Seize) **it and eat it down** (devour it)**: and it will proceed making your whole belly** (the hollow place; the cavity; the stomach and intestines; the innermost part; used of the womb) **bitter, but in your mouth it will continue being sweet as honey."**

10. **And then I took** (or: seized) **the tiny scroll from out of the Agent's hand, and devoured it, and it was sweet as honey within my mouth. And when I ate it, my belly** (hollow place, etc.) **was made bitter.**
11. **Then** (or: So) **He is** [other MSS: they are] **saying to me, "It presently necessitates you** (or: It is now binding [for] you) **to prophesy** (to exercise the function of a prophet) **again upon peoples and multitudes** (nations; ethnic groups) **and tongues** (languages) **and many kings."**

CHAPTER 11

1. **Next a reed like a staff** (or: rod) **was given to me, [and He was] presently saying,**
        "Rouse yourself (or: Arise; Awake) **and measure the temple of God** (God's temple, or dwelling), **and** (or: that is; namely) **the altar, and the folks continuously worshiping within it** (or: centered in Him; or: at the [altar]).
2.   **"And the court** (unroofed enclosure; [used of the sheepfold in Jn. 10:1, 16]), **the one outside the temple, you must cast outside** (throw, or expel, out of doors), **and you may not measure her because it was given to the multitudes** (ethnic groups; nations), **and they will proceed treading** (advance by setting the foot upon) **the set-apart city** (or: the Holy City) **forty-two months.**
3.   **"And I will continue giving to My two witnesses** (or: I will progressively supply for My two witnesses), **and they will proceed prophesying** (functioning as prophets) **a thousand two hundred sixty days, being clothed [in]** (or: cast around [with]) **sackcloth."**
4. **These are the two olive trees and the two lampstands** (= menorahs) **– the ones having made a stand** (or: been placed) **and are standing before** (or: in the presence of) **the Lord** [= Yahweh] **of the earth** (or: the Owner of the Land). [Jer. 11:16; Zech. 4:2-3, 11-14]
5. **And if anyone is wanting or intending to harm or injure** (or: do injustice to) **them, fire is continuously** (or: repeatedly) **issuing** (or: proceeding) **out of their mouth and is one after another devouring their enemies** (or: adversaries)**; and if anyone is intending** (wanting, willing) **to injure** (do

injustice to; harm) **them, thus** (or: in this manner) **it is necessary for him to be killed.**
6. **These continuously hold** (or: have) **authority to close** (shut, lock) **the sky** (or: atmosphere; heaven), **so that it continues that it may** (or: can) **not shower rain [during] the days of their prophesying. And further, they continue holding authority upon the waters, to continuously turn them into blood; and to strike** (beat, impact) **the Land** (or: soil; earth) **within every blow** (or: wounding strike; impact; plague) **as often as they may will – if they intend** (purpose) **to.** [1 Kings 17:1; Ex. 7:19]

7. **Now whenever they may complete** (finish; make an end of) **their witness** (or: testimony), **the little wild animal** (or: beast) **– the one repeatedly climbing up** (or: ascending) **out of the Deep** (or: the Abyss) **– will proceed making war** (or: do battle) **with them, and will progressively overcome** (or: conquer) **them, and then will proceed in killing them.**
8. **And so their fallen dead body will be upon** [other MSS: And their fall will be into] **the broad place** (street; square; plaza) **of The Great City – whatever, spiritually, is normally being called** (or: named) **"Sodom" and "Egypt" – where also their Lord was crucified** (or: where their Lord, also, was hung on a pole: suspended and executed on a torture stake).
9. **Then those out of the peoples – even from tribes and tongues and ethnic groups** (nations; multitudes; pagans; non-Jews) **– continuously see** (observe; cast a look upon) **their dead body three and one half days, and they will not proceed in releasing their dead bodies to be placed into a memorial monument or tomb** (= to be buried).
10. **And so the folks continuously having a house down upon the earth** (or: the ones normally dwelling upon the Land) **are continuously rejoicing upon them, and they will continue being gladdened** (or: made happy) **and will proceed sending presents to each other, because these, the two prophets, tested and examined** (applied the touchstone to test the purity of the metal of) **those continuously having a house down upon the earth** (or: ground).

11. **Later, after the three and a half days, a spirit of Life** (Life's breath-effect or a spirit which is life) **from out of God entered within** [other MSS: into] **them and they stood upon their feet. And so** (a) **great fear fell upon the people continuing to be spectators of** (or: watching) **them.**
12. **Then they heard a great** (or: loud) **Voice from out of the atmosphere** (or: sky; heaven), **repeatedly saying to them, "You must climb up here!** (or: Ascend at once to this place.)**" So they climbed up into the atmosphere** (or: ascended into the sky and heaven) **within** (or: in the midst of; in union with) **the cloud, and their enemies watched** (or: were spectators of) **them.**
13. **And within that hour, a great shaking** (or: earthquake) **was birthed** (or: came to be; occurred) **and the tenth of The City fell** (or: collapsed), **and seven thousand names of humans** (= people) **were killed within the shaking** (quake), **and the remaining ones** (= survivors) **came to be terrified – and so they gave glory to the God of the heaven** (or: atmosphere; sky).
14. **The second woe departed** (or: tragedy went away). **Consider! The third woe is progressively coming swiftly.**

15. **Next the seventh agent sounded a trumpet, and great** (or: loud) **voices of themselves came to be** (birthed themselves; occurred of themselves) **within the sky** (or: atmosphere; heaven), **continuously saying, "The reign of the dominating, ordered System** (of the world of religion, culture, government and economy; or: of the realm of the religious and secular; or: of the aggregate of humanity) **suddenly came to belong to our Lord** [= Yahweh or Christ] **and to the anointed of Him**
> (or: The kingdom of the arranged system of our Lord and His Christ has come into existence; The sovereign influence pertaining to the aggregate of humanity, which belongs to our Lord and His Christ, is birthed!; The rule as King, concerning the world, has come to be the possession of, and now has reference to, [Yahweh], as well as of, and to, His Anointed),

and so He will continue reigning (ruling as King) **on into the ages** (or: indefinite time periods) **of the ages** [other MSS add: So it is (Amen)]**."**
16. **Then the twenty-four elders** (or: old people) **– the people continuously sitting upon their thrones before** (or: in the presence of) **God – fell** (or: at once fall) **upon their faces and worshiped** (or: do obeisance to; began to worship in) **God,**
17. **repeatedly saying, "We are continuously grateful** (thankful) **for You** (or: we continuously give You thanks), **Lord** [= Yahweh] **God, the One of All Strength** (the Almighty, Omnipotent One), **the One continuously existing** (or: being), **even the One Who was continuously existing** (being), **because**

You have taken – so that You have in Your hand – Your great power and ability, and You reign (or: began to rule as King and began exercising sovereign influence)**."**

18. **Now the multitudes** (ethnic groups; nations) **were made angry** (became enraged; began to swell in passion; were gradually aroused and made impulsive) [Ps. 2:1]**, and Your inherent fervor** (swelling arousal; impulse; wrath; anger; indignation; natural bent) **came** (or: comes; or: went)**, and the season** (fitting situation; suitable circumstances; fertile moment) **for the dead folks to be sifted, separated, evaluated, decided about and judged, and then to give the wages** (or: reward) **to Your slaves: to the prophets and to the set-apart people, and to the ones continuously fearing Your Name – to the small** (= insignificant) **ones and to the great** (= important) **ones – and then to at once thoroughly spoil** (or: bring ruin throughout; cause decay through the midst; utterly destroy) **the folks continuously corrupting** (thoroughly spoiling, ruining, destroying and decaying) **the Land** (or: earth; soil).

19. **And then the Temple of God – the one within, or in union with, the atmosphere** (or: centered in the heaven) **– was opened** (or: was suddenly opened up)**, and the ark of the covenant** (or: arrangement) [other MSS read: ark of the covenant of the Lord; or: ark from God's covenant] **was seen** (or: is seen) **within the midst of His Temple. Next lightning and voices and thunders and a shaking** (or: an earthquake) **and great hail were birthed** (came to be; occurred).

CHAPTER 12

1. **Next a great sign was seen within the atmosphere** (or: sky; or: heaven)**: a Woman having been clothed** (cast around) **with the sun, and the moon down under her feet, and a wreath of twelve stars upon her head.**

2. **And being pregnant** (continuously having or holding within the womb)**, she is constantly crying** (or: repeatedly uttering a cry)**, travailing with birth-pangs, and being progressively tested and tried in the labor pains** (or: experiencing the touchstone) **to bring forth** (= to bear a child).

3. **Then another sign was seen within the atmosphere** (or: sky; heaven)**: and consider this! – a great fiery-colored dragon having seven heads and ten horns, and seven bands** (diadems; kingly ornaments) **upon its seven heads.**

4. **And its tail is progressively dragging the third of the stars of the sky** (or: heaven) **and casts** (or: it cast; it threw) **them into the earth** (or: onto the Land, or, ground)**. And the dragon stood** (had made a stand) **before** (or: in the presence of) **the Woman – the one being about to bring forth** (= to give birth) **– to the end that whenever she may bring forth, it may devour** (eat down; consume) **her child.**

5. **And so she brought forth a Son – an adult man** (or: male; masculine one) **Who is about to continuously shepherd** (tend and protect) **all the multitudes** (ethnic groups; nations) **in the sphere of and with relying on the use of an iron staff** (or: rod)**. Later, her child was snatched away** (seized and carried off by force) **toward God and to His throne.**

6. **Then the Woman fled** (or: takes flight) **into the wilderness** (or: desert; desolate place) **where she continues having, there, a prepared place from God** (or: a place having been made ready, from God)**, to the end that THEY may continuously nourish her there one thousand two hundred sixty days.**

7. **Next a war** (or: battle) **was birthed** (broke out; came to be; arose) **within the atmosphere** (or: sky; or: heaven)**: the One, Michael** [the One in God's likeness]**, and His agents [went] to war** (or: to battle) **with the dragon. And the dragon did battle** (or: at once battles; = fought back)**, as well as his agents,**

8. **and yet they were not strong** (or: had no strength)**, neither was their place** (or: position) **any longer found within the atmosphere** (or: heaven; [comment: a symbol of a position of authority, control and dominion])**.**

9. **And so thrown** (or: hurled; cast; tossed) **is** (or: was) **the great dragon, the serpent from the very beginning** (or: the original, or ancient, serpent) **– the one being continuously called "slanderer"**
      (one who thrusts something through [folks]; false accuser; separator; a "devil;" one who casts
         something throughout the midst [to cause division]) **and the adversary** (the opponent; the satan;
   [*p*47 and other MSS: one who stands in opposition; a counter-worker])**, the one continuously causing the whole inhabited area of the earth to wander** (or: that which causes straying; the one continually deceiving)**. It was** (or: is) **hurled** (thrown; cast; tossed) **into the earth** (or: Land)**, and its agents were**

(or: are) **thrown** (cast; tossed) **with it.**

10. **Then I heard a great** (or: loud) **voice within the atmosphere** (or: sky; or: heaven) **repeatedly saying, "At the present moment** (or: Just now) **the deliverance** (the rescue; the return to the original state and condition; the health and wholeness; the salvation), **and the power** (or: ability), **and the kingdom** (or: reign) **of our God was** (or: is) **birthed** (comes into existence; came to be), **also the authority** (privilege from Being) **of His Anointed** (or: which is His Christ; from His [Messiah]), **because our brothers' accuser** (person speaking against our members) **was cast down** (or: is hurled down) – **the one that was or is by habit repeatedly accusing** (speaking against) **them before** (or: in the sight and presence of) **our God, day and night."** [thus, the location is on earth, where there is day and night]
11. **And they at once overcame** (or: at some point conquer) **him** (or: it) **because of and through the blood of the little Lamb, and because of the word of their witness, as well as through the message from their testimony** (that reason laid-out from the evidence, which is them) – **and they love not** (or: did not participate in union with) **their soul** (soul-life; inner selfhood) **even to** (or: until; as far as) **death.**
12. **Because of this, you atmospheres** (or: heavens) – **and the folks continuously tabernacling** (or: normally living in a tent; presently encamping) **within the midst of them – must continuously make yourselves glad** (keep or develop a good frame of mind; rejoice). **Woe to** (or: Alas for; A tragedy into) **the Land** (or: earth) **and the sea, because the slanderer** (separator; opposer; "devil;" the one who thrusts-through) **is** (or: was) **cast down to you, having great anger** (violent breathing; rushing passion), **knowing that he continues having a little season** (a small suitable place; a limited circumstance; a brief fitting situation).

13. **And when** (at the time that) **the dragon suddenly saw** (or: sees; perceived; observes) **that it is thrown** (was cast, thrust) **into the earth** (or: Land), **it pursued** (pursues, presses forward, runs swiftly to catch) **and persecuted the Woman who brought forth** (= gave birth to) **the Man** (or: male).

14. **Then two wings of the Great Eagle** (or: Vulture) **were given to the Woman** (or: are given for the Woman), **to the end that she may progressively fly into the wilderness** (desert; uninhabited region) – **into her place – where** (in which place) **she is there continuously nourished a season, and seasons, and half a season** [Dan. 7:25; 12:7], **away from the serpent's face** (= its presence and ability to observe; = its influence).
15. **Next the serpent cast** (or: spews) **water, as a river** (or: stream), **from out of its mouth, behind the Woman** (at the Woman's back; after the Woman) **to the end that it may cause her to be carried away by the river** (i.e., by its current).
16. **So then the Land** (or: ground; earth) **ran to the aid of** (or: runs and helps) **the Woman, and the Land** (ground; earth) **at once opened** (or: opens) **up her mouth and swallowed** (or: swallows; gulps down) **the river which the dragon cast** (or: casts) **out of its mouth.**
17. **And so the dragon was enraged** (is angered; swells with agitation of soul) **upon the Woman and went away** (or: goes off) **to make war** (do battle) **with the remaining ones** (the rest; those left) **of her seed** (= offspring) – **those continuously keeping** (guarding; observing) **God's implanted goals** (impartations of the finished product within; inward directives) **and continuously holding the testimony of and from Jesus** (or: having the evidence about and possessing the character of Jesus).
18. [other MSS: And it was placed (set; made to stand) upon the sand of the sea.]

CHAPTER 13

18. **And I was placed** (set, made to stand) **upon the sand of the sea,**
1. **and then I saw** (or: perceived) **a little animal** (a little, wild creature or beast) **progressively climbing up** (or: repeatedly ascending) **from out of the midst of the sea, having ten horns and seven heads, and ten bands** (diadems; kingly ornaments) **upon its horns, and blasphemous names** (or, names [other MSS: a name] of slander, abusive speech and light-hindering injury) **upon its heads.**
2. **Then the little animal** (little wild creature or beast) **which I saw was and continued to exist like a leopard, and yet its feet [were] as a bear's, and its mouth as a lion's mouth.**
Next the dragon gave its ability and power, its throne, and great authority and license (or: as well as great right and privilege from out of its being) **to it** [i.e., to the little animal].
3. **And one of its heads was as having been slaughtered unto death, and yet the impact and blow**

of its death (or: its death-blow; or: the plague from its death) **was cured** (or: tended; treated), **and later the whole Land** (or: earth) **followed after the little animal with fascinated wonder and admiration.**

4. **And so people** [*p*47, 2344, *pc* read: it] **worshiped** (or: worship; do obeisance to; bow down to kiss the feet of) **the dragon because it gave** (or: gives) **authority to the little animal; and so they** (or people) **worship the little animal, saying, "Who** (or: What) **[is] like the little animal** (the little creature or beast)**? And who** (or: what) **is able** (continuously has power) **to do battle** (or: wage war) **with it?"**
5. **Then a mouth, continuously speaking great things and blasphemies** (things that obscure the light; abusive slander; harm-avering misrepresentations) **was given to it. Authority to act** (or: to make or do; to produce) **[for] forty-two months** [other MSS read: to make war 42 months; another early MS reads: to do what it wills 42 months] **was also given to it** (or: And so, a right from out of Being was allowed for it to suddenly form, construct and create [over a period of] forty-two months).

6. **So it opened** (or: at once opens) **its mouth unto blasphemies** (injurious slander) **toward God, to blaspheme** (misrepresent and hinder the light of) **His Name and His Tabernacle: those continuously tabernacling** (or: camping in tents; living in the Tabernacle) **within the atmosphere** (or: heaven).
7. **Next it was** (or: is) **given to it to wage war** (or: was allowed to do battle) **with the set-apart folks** (holy people; sacred one) **and to overcome them. And authority was given** (or: Then right and privilege from out of its being was allowed) **to it upon every tribe and people and tongue and multitude** (nation; ethnic group).

8. **And all those continually dwelling upon the earth** (or: Land) **will proceed worshiping it – concerning which folks, their name has not been written within the scroll of** (or: which is) **"The Life of** (or: pertaining to) **the little Lamb" – the One having been slaughtered from a casting-down of [the; an] ordered arrangement** (or: on account of [the] establishing of [the] world of culture, religion, government and economics; or: from [the] world's founding; or: from a disrupting, down-casting of [the] aggregate of humanity).

9.　　**"If anyone continues having an ear, let him hear.**
10.　　**"If anyone** (or: a certain one) **[is; is destined] into captivity, into captivity he is repeatedly** (continuously; presently) **departing** [Griesbach's text adds συναγει, so would read: If anyone is continuously gathering (bringing together) a captive host, into captivity he is proceeding to undergo]. **If anyone** (or: a certain one) **is continually killing with a sword, it is necessary for him to be killed with a sword. The patient and persistent endurance** (or: the steadfast, humble and supportive remaining-under) **and the reliability and faith of the set-apart ones** (or: trust and loyal confidence of the holy folks) **continually exists here."**

11. **Next I saw another little wild animal** (little creature or beast)**, progressively stepping up out of the midst of the Land** (or: earth; territory; region; soil)**, and it had two horns like a little lamb, yet it was, and continued, speaking as [the; a] dragon,** [*cf* Tit. 1:10-12]
12. **and it is continually exercising** (doing, performing, executing) **all the authority of the first little animal** (or: little wild beast) **within its presence** (before it; in its sight)**, and it repeatedly makes the Land** (or: forms the earth) **and those dwelling in her, to the end that they would** (or: may) **worship the first little animal** (little creature or wild beast) **whose death-blow was cured** (or: treated)**.
13. **And it is continually making** (doing; constructing; performing; producing) **great signs** (wonders; miracles; marks; inscriptions)**, to the end that it may** (or: that it would) **even repeatedly make (a) fire to continuously** (or: repeatedly) **descend from out of the atmosphere** (or: sky; or: heaven) **into the Land** (or: earth) **within the presence of** (in sight of) **the people** (or: humans)**.
14. **It also continually leads astray** (causes to wander; deceives) **those** [other MSS read: Mine] **who are continuously dwelling upon the Land** (or: earth)**, because of the signs which it was** (or: is) **given to it to perform** (or: allowed to do, make or construct) **in the presence of** (before; in sight of) **the [first] little animal** (little creature or wild beast)**. [It is] constantly saying – to those habitually dwelling upon the Land** (or: territory; earth) **– to make** (or: construct) **an image** (likeness; resemblance; an icon) **to** (or: for) **the little animal** (little wild beast) **which continuously has the blow of** (holds the impact, wound and plague from) **the sword, and yet lives** (or: yet sprang to life)**.
15. **And it was given to it** (or: So it was granted for her) **to give spirit** (breath; a spirit) **to the image** (or:

icon) **of the [first] little animal** (little wild beast) **so that the image** (or: icon) **of the little animal can both speak and can cause** (or: make it; arrange) **that whoever would not worship the image of the [first] little animal would** (or: should) **be killed.**

16. **And so it is continually making** (causing; forming) **all** (everyone) **– the little** (small; = insignificant) **ones and the great ones, the rich ones and the poor ones, the free ones and the slaves – to the end that they could** (would; may; [some MSS: it will]) **give to them an imprinted mark-effect** (an engraved work; emblem; result of sculpting; carve-effect [note: same root from which we get the word "character"]) **upon their right hand, or upon their foreheads,** [cf Ex. 13:16a]

17. **even to the end that a certain one would continually be unable** (or: not anyone would be continually able) **to buy or to sell if [he or she is] not the one continuously having the imprinted mark-effect** (engraving; carve-effect) **or the name of the little animal, or the number of its name.**

18. **Here is Wisdom! The one having a mind** (intellect; intelligence) **must calculate** (compute by pebbles) **the number of the little animal, for it is man's number** (or: [the] number of mankind; a number pertaining to humanity; a man's number)**: his number [is] 666** [MS C: 616].

CHAPTER 14

1. **Later I saw this – so consider! The little Lamb [is; was] standing** (or: having made a stand) **upon Mount Zion** (or: the mountain, Zion), **and with Him [are] one hundred forty-four thousand: folks continuously having His Name, and** (or: even) **His Father's Name, having been written upon their foreheads.**

2. **Then I heard a voice** (or: sound) **out of the atmosphere** (or: sky; heaven), **as a voice** (or: sound) **of many waters, and as a voice** (or: sound) **of a great thunder. And the voice** (sound) **which I heard [was] as lyre-singers, continuously playing their lyres** (or: harps).

3. **And they repeatedly sing a new** (strange) **song** (or: ode) **before the throne, and in the presence of the four living ones and the old folks** (or: elders). **And no one was able to learn the song** (or: ode) **except the one hundred forty-four thousand – those having been bought from the Land** (or: earth).

4. **These are those who were** (or: are) **not stained** (polluted, contaminated) **with women, for they are** (or: exist being) **virgins. These are the folks continuously following The little Lamb wherever He progressively leads** [other MSS: wherever He may habitually depart]. **These were** (or: are) **bought from humanity, a first-fruit in God** (by God; to God; for God), **even in** (by; with; for; to) **the little Lamb.**

5. **And falsehood was not** (or: no lie is) **found within their mouth, for they are** (or: exist being) **without blemish** (are flawless, blameless and without defect; [some MSS omit: **for**]).

6. **Next I saw an agent** (or: messenger; a person with a message [other MSS: another agent, or messenger]) **continuously flying within mid-heaven, having eonian good news** (or: a message of goodness, ease and well-being pertaining to the ages and having the character and quality of the Age [of the Messiah]), **to proclaim the good news upon those situated** (or: habitually sitting down) **upon the Land** (or: earth), **and upon every multitude** (nation; ethnic group), **tribe, tongue, and people,**

7. **repeatedly saying in a great** (loud) **voice,**

"**You people should reverence** (or: Be respecting and fearing) **God, and give glory to Him** (or: grant Him a reputation; give a good opinion in Him), **because the hour of His deciding** (judging; judicial process; making-distinction-between) **came** (or: went; comes), **and you must worship the One making** (the Maker; the One constructing and forming) **the atmosphere** (or: sky; heaven) **and the earth** (or: land; ground) **and the sea and springs of water.**"

8. **And then another, a second agent** (or: messenger), **followed, repeatedly saying,**

"**It fell** (or: It falls)**! Babylon the Great fell** (or: falls), **because it has caused all nations** (all ethnic groups and multitudes) **to drink out of the wine of the strong passion** (violent breathing) **of her prostitution** (or: = idolatry; or: sexual acts contrary to the Mosaic Law)."

9. **And another, a third agent** (or: messenger), **followed them, repeatedly saying in a great voice,**

"**If anyone keeps on worshiping the little wild animal, and its image, and is progressively receiving an imprinted mark upon his forehead or upon his hand,**

10. "**he or she will also proceed drinking out of the wine of God's rushing emotion** (strong

passion; anger) – **of the one having been mixed undiluted within the cup of His inherent fervor** (natural bent; impulse; indignation; wrath). **And he will proceed being examined** (scrutinized with the touchstone to test his "mettle") **within Fire and Deity** (or: in union with Fire, even Divine qualities) **in the presence of** (before; in the sight of) **the set-apart agents** (sacred folks with the message; holy messengers), **and in the presence of** (before) **the little Lamb."** [cf 2 Thes. 1:7-10]

11. **And so the smoke of** (or: from) **their examination and testing by the touchstone continually ascends on into ages of the ages** (or: indefinite time-periods which comprise the ages). **And those continually worshiping the little animal and its image – and if any one continually receives the imprinted mark** (carve-effect; emblem) **of its name – they, continually, are not having rest day and night** [comment: day and night are representations of time elapsing on earth; cf Heb. 4:1-16].

12. **In this place is** (or: Here exists) **the persistent and patient endurance** (the steadfast, humble remaining-under for support) **of the set-apart folks** (or: from the saints) **– the people continually keeping watch upon** (guarding, observing, having custody over) **God's implanted goals** (impartations of the finished product within; inward purposed directives and inner destiny) **and the faith of Jesus**
> (or: the trust pertaining to Jesus; the loyalty belonging to Jesus; the faith which belongs to and comes from Jesus; the conviction which is Jesus; the reliability of and from Jesus).

13. **Next I heard a voice out of the atmosphere** (or: sky; heaven), **saying,**
> **"Write: 'From the present moment** (from this time; from now; henceforth) **the dead ones [are] blessed** (happy) **folks – those continuously dying within the Lord!'" "Yes, indeed,"** the Spirit continues saying, **"to the end that they may rest themselves from out of their wearisome labor** (travail; toilsome exhaustion), **for their works** (actions; deeds) **are continually following together with them."**
> [Sinaiticus & p47 omit ναι, "yes, indeed," so an alternate rendering would be: "Happy {are} the dead ones – those continuously dying in the Lord! Henceforth, the Spirit says that they may rest, for their actions follow with them."]

14. **And then I saw, and look: a bright, white cloud. And upon the cloud One like a son of man** (= a human; or: = the eschatological Messiah figure) **continually sitting, having a golden wreath upon His head and a sharp sickle** (instrument for cutting off, cropping and harvesting) **in his hand.**

15. **Next, another agent** (or: messenger; person with a message) **came forth out of the Temple, repeatedly crying out in a great voice to the One sitting upon the cloud,**
> **"You must send Your sickle and You must reap** (gather in the harvest), **because the hour to reap comes** (or: came), **because the harvest of the Land** (or: earth) **is dried** (parched; withered; thus: = ripened)."**

16. **And so the One continuously sitting upon the cloud cast** (or: thrusts) **His sickle upon the Land** (or: earth) **– and the Land** (or: earth) **was reaped!**

17. **Next another agent came out of the Temple [which is] resident within the atmosphere** (or: within the midst of the heaven), **he, too, having a sharp sickle.**

18. **Then another agent, having authority upon the Fire, came forth out of the altar and uttered** (or: utters) **a sound by a great outcry to the one continuously holding the sharp sickle,**
> **"You must send your sharp sickle and you must gather** (pick) **the clusters of the Land's** (or: earth's) **vineyard** (grapevine), **because her grapes are in their prime** (are at the peak of ripeness)."**

19. **And so the agent cast** (or: thrusts) **his sickle into the Land** (or: earth), **and picks** (gathers) **the vineyard of the Land and he casts [it; them] into the great wine-press** (trough; tub) **of God's strong passion** (rushing emotion; or: anger).

20. **Then the wine-press** (or: trough) **was trodden** (or: is trod as a path) **outside of the City, and blood came** (or: comes; goes) **forth from out of the trough** (or: wine-press) **up to the horses' bridle – from a thousand six hundred stadia** (a fixed standard of measure; a racecourse; a stadium).

CHAPTER 15

1. **Next I saw another sign in the atmosphere** (or: sky; heaven) **– great and wonderful** (marvelous):

seven agents continuously holding the last seven plagues (blows; impacts; strikes), **because within them God's strong passion** (or: rushing emotion; or: wrath) **is** (or: was) **brought to its goal** (has been brought to its purpose; is completed; is finished; was ended; has accomplished its destined aim).

2. **And I saw as it were a glassy** (crystalline) **sea having been mixed with Fire, and the folks** (or: those) **continually overcoming** (being progressively victorious; presently conquering) – **from out of [the power and influence of] the little wild animal** (creature; beast), **and from out of [the nature of] its image, and from out of [the identity of] the number of its name – standing** (or: having made a stand) **upon the glassy** (crystalline) **sea, continuously holding God's lyres** (harps).
3. **And they repeatedly sing the song** (or: ode) **of Moses, God's slave, as well as** (or: even) **the song** (or: ode) **of the little Lamb, saying,**

> **"O Lord** [= O Yahweh], **The All-Strong** (Omnipotent, Almighty) **God, Your acts** (works) **[are] great ones, and wonderful ones** (marvelous ones)! **The King of the nations** (multitudes, ethnic groups; [Sinaiticus* & *p*45 read: King of the ages])! **Your ways** (roads, paths) **[are] just ones** (fair and equitable ones in accord with the Way pointed out) **and true** (or: real) **ones!**

4. > **"O Lord** [= O Yahweh], **who could not by all means** (or: who would not in any way; = will not really) **reverence or fearfully respect You and glorify** (bring good reputation to) **Your Name? Because [You] only** (alone; without accompaniment) **[are] appropriately pious, sanctioned, and benign** [other MSS: Set-apart (Holy)]. **Because all the multitudes** (nations: ethnic groups; [other MSS: all people]) **WILL continue arriving, and they WILL continue worshiping in Your presence** (in Your sight; before You). **Because the results of Your rightwising act and the effects of the eschatological deliverance which is You**
> > (effects of Your fairness and equity, just decrees and decisions; actions according to the Way pointed out, results of justification, actualization of justice and rightwising of relationships) **are manifested** (or: were brought to light; were made to appear)."

5. **Later, after these things, I saw, and the Temple** (Divine habitation; sanctuary), **which equates to the Tabernacle of the Witness** (or: whose source and origin was the tent of testimony and evidence), **was opened up within the midst of the atmosphere** (or: centered in, and in union with, heaven),
6. **and the seven agents – those continuously holding the seven plagues** (impacts; blows) **– came out of the Temple, being clothed with bright, clean** (unsoiled, pure) **linen** [other MSS: λιθον, stone], **and having been girded around the chests** (or: breasts) **[with] golden girdles** (belts; sashes).

7. **Then one out of the four living ones gave** (or: gives) **to the seven agents seven golden bowls** (or: shallow cups) **continuously brimming** (being full) **of the strong passion** (rushing emotion; or: fury; anger) **of the God Who is continuously living on into the ages of the ages** (or: from God, the One continuously living [and proceeding] into the [most significant] eons of [all of] the eons).
8. **And then the Temple was made full of smoke from out of God's glory, and from out of His power** (or: ability) **and no one had power** (or: was able) **to enter into the Temple until the seven plagues** (impacts; blows; smitings; strikes) **of, or from, the seven agents would** (or: can) **be brought to their purposed goal and completed.**

CHAPTER 16

1. **And I heard a great Voice out of the Temple, saying to the seven agents,**
> **You must go** (depart) **and you must pour out the seven bowls** (shallow cups; saucers) **of God's strong passion** (fury; rushing emotion; anger) **into the Land** (or: earth; region)."

2. **Then the first one went forth and poured** (or: at once pours) **out his bowl** (or: cup) **upon the Land** (or: ground; earth; territory) – **and a bad and malignant, festering wound** (or: ulcer) **came to be upon those people having the imprinted mark** (engraving; carve-effect) **of the little wild animal** (creature; beast), **even upon those continuously worshiping its image** (or: likeness).
3. **Then the second one poured** (or: at once pours) **out his bowl** (or: cup) **into the sea – and it came to be blood as of a dead person, and every living soul** (person; counsciousness) **within the sea died.**
4. **Then the third one poured** (or: at once pours) **out his bowl** (or: cup) **into the rivers** (or: streams) **and into the springs** (or: fountains) **of the waters – and they became blood.**

5. **And I heard the Agent of the Waters saying**,
> **"You are continually a Just One** (a Righteous One; One Who observes the way pointed out), **the One continuously existing** (or: being), **even the One Who was continuously existing, the appropriately pious, sanctioned, benign One, because You suddenly evaluate and judge** (or: made a decision; judged) **these,**

6. > **"because they poured** (or: pour) **out [the] blood of the set-apart folks and of the prophets, and You gave** (or: give) **them blood to drink: they are deserving [this]!"** [note: see Luke 11:50-51]

7. **Then I heard the Altar saying,**
> **"Yes indeed, O Lord** [= O Yahweh], **the All-Strong** (Omnipotent; Almighty) **God, Your decisions** (separations; judgings) **are true and real ones, and fair** (equitable; just; right) **ones."**

8. **Next the fourth one poured** (or: at once pours) **out his bowl** (or: cup; saucer) **upon the sun – and it was given to him to burn the people** (the humans; mankind) **in Fire.**

9. **And so the people** (the humans) **were burned [with] great heat, and they blasphemed** (spoke insultingly of; slandered; misrepresented; vilified; hindered the Light of) **the Name of God – the One having authority upon these plagues** (blows; impacts; strikes) **– and they did** (or: do) **not change their minds** (ways of thinking; states of consciousness) **to give Him glory** (or: credit and good repute).

10. **Next the fifth one poured** (or: at once pours) **out his bowl** (or: cup) **upon the throne of the little wild animal** (creature; beast) **– and its kingdom** (or: reign) **came to being made dark** (or: had been darkened), **and they were biting their tongues from the painful labor** (misery; travail; hard toil),

11. **and they blasphemed** (abusively slander; hindered the light of; vilify) **God with reference to the atmosphere** (or: heaven's God; the God of the atmosphere; God, Who is heaven; the God from the sky) **from out of the midst of their painful labor and from out of their festering wounds** (ulcers), **and did not** (or: do not) **change their mind** (ways of thinking; etc.) **from out of their works** (or: actions).

12. **Next the sixth one poured** (or: at once pours) **out his bowl** (or: cup) **upon the great river Euphrates, and its water was** (or: is) **dried up, to the end that the way** (road, path) **of the kings – the ones from the risings of [the] sun** (or: = the east) **– may be prepared** (made ready).

13. **And I saw – out of the mouth of the dragon, and out of the mouth of the little wild animal** (creature; beast), **and out of the mouth of the false** (lying) **prophet – three unclean spirits** (or: impure attitudes), **as frogs**

14. **– for they are spirits** (or: breath-effects; attitudes) **of, or which are, demons** (a Hellenistic concept and term: = from animistic influences), **continually doing** (making; constructing; performing) **signs – which are continuously going out** (marching forth) **upon the kings of the whole inhabited land, to assemble them** (bring them together) **into the battle** (combat, war) **of that great Day of the All-Strong** (Omnipotent) **God.**

15. > **"Consider! I continually** (or: repeatedly; or: presently) **am coming as a thief! The one continually watching** (or: in wakeful vigilance) **and keeping guard upon his garments [is; will be] blessed** (or: a happy person), **to the end that he may not be continually walking about** (or: roaming; = living his life) **naked so that they may continually see** (or: observe) **his indecency** (condition of being without proper form, shape or character; shame; ungracefulness)." [note: see 1 Thes. 5:2; Matt. 24:43; 2 Pet. 3:10; 2 Cor. 5:3]

16. **And He** [Aleph reads: they] **gathered** (or: assembles) **them together into the place being called, in the Hebrew, Armageddon** [= the hill of Megiddo; some MSS: Mageddon].

17. **Next the seventh one poured** (or: at once pours) **out his bowl** (or: cup) **upon the air – and a great voice came** (or: goes) **forth from the Temple of the atmosphere** (or: heaven) [other MSS: out of the temple from the throne; other MSS: out of the temple of God], **from the throne, repeatedly saying,**
> **"It has come to be** (or: He has been birthed; It has come into existence; It has occurred)!"

631

18. **Then lightnings and voices and thunders came to be** (occurred), **and a great shaking** (= an earthquake) **came to be** (occurred), **such as had not come to be** (or: did not happen) **since** (or: from which [time]) **the humans came to be** (or: mankind was birthed) **upon the Land** (or: ground; earth) – **a shaking** (quake) **of such magnitude, so very great!**

19. **And the Great City came to be [divided] into three parts, and the cities of the nations** (multitudes; ethnic groups) **fell, and then Babylon the Great** (or: the Great Babylon) **was called to mind** (or: is remembered) **in the presence of** (before; in the sight of) **God, to give to her the cup of the wine of the strong passion** (rushing emotion; fury; anger) **of His inherent fervor** (natural impulse; mental bent and disposition; personal emotion; indignation; wrath).

20. **Then every island fled** (took flight), **and the mountains** (or: hills) **were not** (or: are not) **found,**

21. **and hail, great** (large) **as weighing a talent** (about 70 pounds), **is continuously coming down** (descending) **out of the atmosphere** (or: sky; heaven) **upon the people** (the humans; mankind). **And the men blasphemed** (abusively slander; misrepresented and hindered the light of) **God from out of the midst of the plagues** (or: blows; impacts) **of the hail, because Her plague** (blow) **is exceeding great.**

CHAPTER 17

1. **Next one of the seven agents – the ones holding the seven bowls – came and spoke with me, saying,**

> **"Come here! I will proceed showing** (pointing out to) **you the effect of the judgment** (the result of the administering of justice; the effect of the judicial decision and equitable sentence) **of the Great Prostitute – the one continuously sitting upon the many waters,**

2. > **"with whom the kings of the Land** (or: earth) **commit** (or: committed) **prostitution** (or: fornication) – **and those continually dwelling down upon the Land** (or: earth) **[that] are** (or: were) **made drunk from out of the wine of her prostitution."** [note: see Isa. 1:21; comment: prostitution can be a symbol of idolatry]

3. **And he carried me away, in spirit** (or: within [the] Spirit; in union with a Breath-effect), **into a desert. And I saw a woman continuously sitting** (or: seated) **upon a crimson** (or: scarlet) **little wild animal** (or: beast), **[which was] continuously loaded** (freighted) **with names of blasphemy** (which hinder light; of injurious, abusive slander; or: from a misrepresented image), **having seven heads and ten horns.**

4. **The woman also had been clothed [with] purple and crimson** (scarlet). **And having been adorned** (overlaid; gilded) **with gold and precious stones and pearls, she is continuously holding in her hand a golden cup** (goblet) **[which] is continuously loaded** (freighted; brimming) **with abominations** (detestable things) **and the unclean things** (impure aspects) **of** (from) **her prostitutions.**

5. **And upon her forehead, a name having been written:**

> **A MYSTERY** (A SECRET; a matter that to gain the knowledge of which initiation is necessary) – **BABYLON the GREAT: The <u>Mother</u> of the Prostitutes and of The Abominations** (Detestable Things) **of The Land** (or: from the earth).

6. **Then I saw the woman, being continuously drunk from out of the blood of the set-apart folks and from out of the blood of the witnesses of Jesus, and seeing her I wondered** (marveled; was awestruck [with]) **a great wonder** (or: astonished perplexity; or: I wondered, "[It is] a great marvel!").

7. **And the agent said to me,**

> **"Why do** (or: did) **you wonder** (marvel)**? I will proceed declaring to you the secret of the woman and of the little wild animal [which is] continuously bearing her aloft, [and] which has the seven heads and the ten horns.**

8. > **"The little wild animal** (beast) **which you saw was existing, and does not exist** (is not), **and is about to repeatedly climb up** (or: progressively ascend) **out of the Deep, and to repeatedly lead under** (or: go away; [other MSS: then it progressively withdraws]) **into loss** (or: destruction). **And those continually dwelling down upon the Land** (earth) – **whose names have not been written upon the little Scroll of THE LIFE from [the] casting-down** (or: foundation) **of [the] world** (ordered system; or: aggregate of humanity) – **will continue wondering** (marveling), **continually observing** (beholding) **the little wild animal, that it was continuously existing** (it was), **and it does not exist** (is not), **and it will proceed being present** (exist alongside).

9.	"Here [is] The Mind (intelligence; intellect)**: the one continuously having** (holding) **Wisdom** (or: Here [is] the mind [which] has wisdom)**: The seven heads are seven mountains, where the woman continuously sits upon them,**

10.	"**and they** (or: there) **are seven kings: five fell, the one is** (exists), **the other one came not as yet, and when he may come it is necessary for him to remain** (abide) **a little while** (briefly).

11.	"**And the little wild animal which was existing, and does not exist, it is also itself [the; an] eighth, and is** (exists) **out of the seven, and progressively leads under** (or: habitually goes away) **into loss** (destruction; state of being lost).

12.	"**And the ten horns which you saw are ten kings who do not yet receive a kingdom, but they are continually receiving authority AS kings [for] one hour with the little wild animal.**

13.	"**These continually hold** (or: have) **one opinion** (or: thought; resolve)**, and they continually give their power** (or: ability) **and authority to the little wild animal.**

14.	"**These will proceed waging war** (or: do battle) **with the little Lamb, and the little Lamb will progressively overcome** (subdue; conquer) **them because He is LORD of lords and KING of kings, and the ones with Him are CALLED ONES and CHOSEN ONES and FAITHFUL ONES** (or: trusting folks; people filled with faith; loyal ones)**."

15.	**Then he is saying to me,**
	"**The waters which you saw** (or: see)**, where the Prostitute continually sits, are peoples and crowds** (mobs) **and multitudes** (nations; ethnic groups) **and tongues** (languages).

16.	"**And the ten horns which you saw** (or: see) **– even the little wild animal – these will continue hating** (detaching from) **the Prostitute, and [she] being made desolate** (having been laid waste)**, they will also proceed making her naked and will progressively eat her flesh** (= physical form) **and then they will proceed burning her down in a fire.**

17.	"**For God gave** (or: gives) **into their hearts to do** His **opinion** (thought; resolve; purpose)**, even to form** (make; do) **one opinion** (thought; resolve)**, and to give their kingdom to the little wild animal** (beast) **UNTIL God's Words** (the Words of God; the thoughts and messages from God) **shall be completed** (finished; ended; perfected; brought to their purposed and destined goal).

18.	"**And the woman, which you saw, is the Great City – the one continuously having a kingdom** (or: reigning with dominion) **upon** (over) **the kings of the Land** (region; earth)**."

CHAPTER 18

1.	**After these things I saw another Agent progressively descending out of the atmosphere** (or: sky; heaven)**, continuously having great authority** (or: privilege from out of Being)**, and the Land** (or: ground; or: earth) **was lighted** (illuminated) **by His glory** (or: His manifestation which called forth praise; or: the splendor which was Him).

2.	**Then He uttered** (or: suddenly utters) **a cry in a strong voice, repeatedly saying,**
	"**She falls** (She fell)! **Babylon the Great falls** (fell) **and becomes** (became; comes to be; is birthed) **an abode** (dwelling) **of demons** (or: animistic influences) **and a confine** (ward, prison, a place of keeping watch over) **of every impure attitude** (unclean spirit) **and a preserve** (cage; a guard-house) **of every unclean and hated** (or: rejected-from-lack-of-value) **bird and animal,**

3.	"**because all the multitudes** (nations; ethnic groups) **have drunk** [other MSS read: fallen] **from out of the wine of the strong passion of her prostitution, and the kings of the Land** (earth) **commit** (committed) **prostitution** (fornication; = idolatry) **with her, and the merchants** (those who travel by sea for trade) **of the Land** (earth) **are** (or: became) **rich from out of the power** (or: ability) **of her headstrong pride and wanton luxury** (or: reveling)**."**

4.	**Next I heard another Voice from out of the atmosphere** (sky; heaven)**, repeatedly saying,**
	"**Come out of her** (or: Go forth from out of her midst) **My people, so that you may not jointly participate with** (be a partner with; fellowship together with) **her sins** (failures; occasions of missing the mark)**, and so that you may not receive from out of her plagues** (blows; impacts),

5.	"**because her sins** (failures) **are glued together** (joined; adhered so as to be heaped, built or piled) **as far as the atmosphere** (or: sky; heaven)**. And God remembers** (called to mind) **her unjust effects** (injuries done; misdeeds; unjust acts; ill-gotten gains; things contrary to the way pointed out).

6.	"**You folks** (or: Let people) **give back and pay to her** (render for, or restore in, her) **as she also** (even as she) **paid** (or: pays; etc.), **and double to her doubles** [other MSS: double the doubles] **according to her works** (acts). **In the cup which she mixes** (blended), **mix** (blend) **double for her.**

7.   "**As much as she glorified** (or: glorifies) **herself and indulged** (lives in proud luxury), **so much give to her examination** (testing) **by the touchstone and mourning** (grief; sadness; sorrow), **because within her heart she is continually saying, 'I continually sit as a queen, and I am not a widow; I may by no means see mourning** (grief; sadness; sorrow; misery).'

8.   "**On account of this, in** (or: within; on) **one day her plagues** (blows) **will progressively arrive: death, mourning** (grief) **and famine. And she will proceed being burned down** (consumed) **within fire, because the Lord** [= Yahweh], **the God evaluating and judging her, [is] strong!**

9.   "**And the kings of the Land** (earth) – **those committing prostitution** (or: acts of fornication) **with her and indulging** (living in proud and wanton luxury) – **will proceed weeping and lamenting** (smiting or cutting themselves in wearisome labor) **upon** (over) **her when they may be observing** (or: seeing) **the smoke of her burning,**

10. "**while standing away, at a distance, on account of the fear of her examination** (testing) **by the touchstone, repeatedly saying, 'Woe, tragic is the fate of the Great City! Babylon, the strong city! Because in one hour your evaluating and judging came!'**

11. "**And the merchants** (sea traders) **of the Land** (or: earth) **[are] continually weeping and mourning upon** (over) **her, because no one continues buying their cargo** (merchandise) **any longer:**

12. "**a cargo of gold, and of silver, and of precious stones, and of pearls, and of fine cotton, and of purple, and of silk, and of scarlet** (crimson), **and every aromatic** (thyme or citron) **wood, and every ivory utensil** (or: vessel), **and every utensil** (vessel) **[made] out of precious wood** [other MSS: stone] **and of copper** (or: bronze) **and of iron and of shining marble,**

13. "**also cinnamon** [grown in Arabia & Syria] **and amomum** [fragrant white vine from India], **and incenses and essential oil** [aromatic juices from trees; used for anointing] **and frankincense** [from Mt. Lebanon and Arabia], **and wine and olive oil, and the finest flour, and grain and cattle and sheep and horses and four-wheeled chariots** (carriages; coaches), **even bodies and souls** (or: = lives) **of people.**

14. "**And the fruit season** (or: autumn; ripe fruits) **of your soul's earnest desire** (yearning) **went away** (passes away) **from you, and all the fat** (sumptuous) **things and the bright, shining things destroyed themselves** (became lost; perished) **from you, and no longer may you by any means find** [other MSS: will they continue finding] **them.**

15. "**The merchants of these things – those becoming rich from her – will proceed standing away at a distance, because of the fear of her testing** (examination) **with the touchstone, continually weeping and mourning,**

16. "**saying repeatedly, 'Woe, tragic is the fate of the Great City – the one being clothed in fine cotton and purple and crimson** (scarlet), **and being overlaid** (gilded; adorned) **in gold and precious stone and pearls – because in one hour so much wealth** (so great riches) **is** (or: was) **laid waste** (made desolate; made as a desert).'

17. "**And every navigator** (helmsman; one who steers), **and everyone repeatedly** (habitually) **sailing upon a place, and sailors** (ship men; seamen; mariners), **and as many as are continually working the sea, stand** (or: stood) **away at a distance,**

18. "**and, continuously observing the smoke of her burning, they were crying out, repeatedly saying, 'What [exists] like the Great City?'**

19. "**And they cast dust** (loose earth) **upon their heads, and were uttering cries, continually weeping and mourning, repeatedly saying, 'Woe, tragic is the fate of the Great City in which all those having ships in the sea became rich from out of her valuable merchandise** (or: preciousness; estimated worth; imputed value), **because in one hour she was laid waste** (made like a desert).'

20. "**Continue well-minded** (mentally at ease with a healthy attitude; thoughtfully considerate for good) **on her, O Atmosphere** (Heaven) – **even the** (or: that is, those) **set-apart ones, the envoys** (sent-forth folks) **and the prophets – because God decided and executed** (or: evaluates and judges; separates for distinction) **your evaluation of her** (or: the effect of a judgment pertaining to you folks and the decision-result from you folks, from out of her)."

21. **And then, one strong agent lifts** (took up; carried away) **a stone as great as a millstone, and casts** (or: cast) **[it] into the sea, saying,**

> **"Thus, by violence** (or: impetuous motion) **Babylon the Great City will be cast** (thrown) **and can by no means any longer be found** (or: be yet found).

22. **"And so, a sound** (voice) **of lyre-players/singers and of musicians and of flutists and of trumpeters may by no means be heard in YOU any more** (yet; further), **and every technician** (craftsman, artist) **of every trade** (craft; art) **may by no means be yet** (any longer) **found within YOU. And a sound of a millstone may by no means be yet found in YOU,**

23. **"and a light of a lamp may by no means any longer shine within YOU; and a voice of a bridegroom and of a bride may by no means any longer be heard in YOU, because YOUR merchants were the great ones of the Land** (or: earth) **because all the multitudes** (nations) **were** (are) **deceived** (led astray; caused to wander) **in YOUR employment of drugs** (sorcery; enchantments)."

24. **And within her was** (or: is) **found blood of prophets and of set-apart folks – even of all those having been slaughtered upon the Land** (or: earth). [comment: *cf* Mat. 23:34-38]

CHAPTER 19

1. **After these things I heard – as it were a great voice of a large crowd – folks in the atmosphere** (or: heaven; sky) **repeatedly saying,**

> **"Hallelujah** (Praise Yahweh)**!: the Deliverance** (Salvation; Rescue; Healing) **and the Glory and the Power** (or: Ability) **of, from and which is our God!**

2. **"Because His judgings** (decisions and administrations of justice; judicial processes; separations and evaluations according to the Way pointed out) **[are] true ones and fair** (equitable; just; rightwised) **ones, in that** (for) **He judged** (or: judges) **the Great Prostitute – anyone who was spoiling** (ruining; corrupting) **the Land** (or: earth) **within** (in union with) **her prostitution** (or: fornication; = idolatry) **– and He restored a rightwised situation of equity in fairness for** (or: avenges; vindicates; executes the right for) **the blood of His slaves from out of her hand."**

3. **Then a second time they have said, "Praise Yahweh** (Hallelujah)**!"**

And so the smoke from her goes on rising up on into (or: progressively ascends into the midst of) **the ages of the ages** (or: crowning time-periods of the ages; indefinite eras which comprise the ages).

4. **Then the twenty-four elders** (old people) **and the four living ones fall** (or: fell) **down and worship** (or: did obeisance, kissing toward) **the God continuously sitting upon the throne, repeatedly saying,**

> **"Amen** (Make it so; So be it). **Praise Yahweh** (Hallelujah)**!"**

5. **And a Voice from out of the throne came forth, saying,**

> **"Habitually praise our God, all His slaves – even the people continually fearing, revering and respecting Him – the small ones and the great ones."**

6. **Next I heard as a voice of a large crowd, and as a sound of many waters, even as a sound of strong thunders saying,**

> **"Praise Yahweh** (Hallelujah)**! Because the Lord** [= Yahweh] **our God, the Almighty, reigns!**

7. **"We should** (or: may) **continually rejoice** (be glad; be full of joy), **and we should continually celebrate** (exult), **and we should** [other MSS: we will continue to] **give the glory to Him, because the wedding** (marriage festival) **of the little Lamb came** (arrived and happened; or: comes) **and His Wife made** (or: makes) **herself ready** (prepares herself)."

8. **Then it was** (or: is) **granted** (or: given) **to her to the end that she may clothe herself with bright and clean fine cotton** (or: she may cast bright, pure, fine linen around her) **– for the fine cotton** (or: linen) **represents the effects of right relationship and equity in the life of the Way pointed out**

> (or: the results of being rightwised; the actualizations of justice; consequences of justice rendered from being turned in the right direction; the effects of having been eschatologically delivered and placed in the Path pointed out; or: the just acts or awards) **of the set-apart folks** (pertaining to, and on behalf of, the saints; from the sacred people; belonging to, and characterizing, the holy ones).

9. **And then he is saying to me,**
> **"Write: 'Blessed** (Happy) **ones [are] the folks having been called** (the summoned ones; those being invited) **into the wedding supper** (meal) **of the little Lamb.'"**

He also is saying to me,
> **"These are the true Words of** (or: real thoughts and messages from) **God!"**

10. **And so I fell before his feet to worship him, and he is saying to me,**
> **"See and perceive! No!** (= Don't do that!) **I am your fellow-slave and [am] from among your brothers** (or: = even belonging to [a group of] your fellow believers) **– the ones constantly holding** (having) **the witness of** (or: the testimony pertaining to, and the evidence about) **Jesus – Kiss face-to-face with** (or: do [your] obeisance to) **God! You see, the evidence of** (or: testimony pertaining to; witness about) **Jesus is the spirit of The Prophecy** (or: For the Breath-effect which is prophecy is the evidence for, and from, Jesus)."

11. **Then I saw the atmosphere** (or: sky; heaven), **having been opened – and consider! A bright, white horse. And the One continually sitting upon it being constantly called "Faithful** (Full of Faith; To Be Trusted; Trustworthy; Loyal) **and True** (or: Real)," **and He is continuously judging** (making decisions and evaluations) **and battling** (making war) **in eschatological deliverance** (within equitable dealings; in justice, fairness and righted relations which accord with the covenantal Way pointed out).
12. **And His eyes [are]** [other MSS add: as] **a flame of fire; and upon His head [are] many diadems** (kingly bands), **having a name having been written** [other MSS: having names written, and a name] **which no one knows except Himself,**
13. **and having been clothed** (or: cast around) **with a garment having been dipped in** (immersed; [other MSS: sprinkled with]) **blood** (or: dyed with blood), **and His Name is being called "The Word of God** (God's Logos; The Message from God; The Idea which is God; The Expression about God)."
14. **And the armies in the atmosphere** (or: heaven) **– ones having been clothed with** (invested with; entered within) **clean** (or: pure) **bright, white fine cotton – continued following Him upon bright, white horses.**

15. **Also, a sharp two-edged broadsword repeatedly goes out** (issues forth; proceeds) **from His mouth, to the end that in it He would bring a blow to** (or: could touch; should strike) **the multitudes** (nations; ethnic groups). **And then He will continue shepherding them with an iron staff. Furthermore He is continually treading, [as on a path],** (or: trampling) **the tub** (the wine vat) **of the wine of the strong passion of the internal swelling fervor** (natural impulse; mental bent; personal emotion; or: indignation; wrath) **of the All-Strong** (Almighty) **God.**
16. **And upon His garment and upon [His] thigh He has a Name having been written:**
> **"King of kings and Lord of lords."**

17. **Next I saw one agent** (or: person with a message) **standing in the sun. And he cried with a great voice, repeatedly saying to all the birds continuously flying in mid-heaven,**
> **"Come! Be gathered together into God's great supper** (meal taken at evening),
18. > **"so that you may eat kings' flesh and military commanders'** (commanders of 1000 men; tribunes) **flesh, even the flesh of strong ones, and the flesh of horses and of those sitting on them; both flesh of all free ones and of slaves; even of little ones and of great ones."**

19. **And then I saw the little wild animal** (creature; beast), **and the kings of the Land** (or: earth), **and their armies, having been gathered** (assembled) **to make the war** (or: do the battle) **with the One continually sitting upon the horse, and with His army.**
20. **And yet the little wild animal** (beast) **was pressed and caught** (or: is arrested), **and with him the false** (lying) **prophet – the one that did** (or: who does) **the signs in his presence** (or: before him), **in which he led astray** (or: he deceives) **the folks taking the imprinted mark** (carve-effect) **of the little wild animal, and continually worshiping its image; while living, the two were cast** (or: the two, continuing to live, are thrown) **into the midst of the lake** (or: basin; artificial pool; marshy area) **of the Fire: the one continuously burning within the midst of [the] Deity** (or: the basin of the fire being repeatedly kindled, or being constantly on fire, through union with Divine Nature). [Rom. 11:36]
21. **And the remaining ones** (the rest; the ones left) **were killed off in the broadsword coming out of the mouth of Him who is continuously sitting upon the horse. And all the birds were fed until**

satisfied from out of their flesh.

CHAPTER 20

1. **Next I saw an Agent progressively descending out of the atmosphere** (or: sky; heaven), **continually holding** (or: presently having) **the key of the Deep** (or: the abyss) **and [there was] a great chain upon His hand.**
2. **And He seizes** (or: put a power-hold on) **the dragon, the primeval** (ancient; original) **serpent, who is a false accuser and the adversary** (or: one who thrusts things through to harm or cause division, and is the opponent; a devil, even *satan*), **and He binds** (or: bound) **it** (or: him) **"a thousand years."**
3. **Then He casts** (or: threw) **it** (or: him) **into the Deep** (or: abyss) **and He closes** (or: shut; locked) **and seals** (or: stamped with a seal) **over upon it** (or: him), **to the end that it** (or: he) **can no longer** (or: would not still) **deceive** (lead astray; cause to wander) **the multitudes** (the nations; the non-Israelites; the ethnic groups), **until the thousand years may be ended** (finished, completed, perfected; brought to the destined goal; can have its purpose fulfilled). **After these [events; things], it is necessary for it to be loosed [for] a little time.**
4. **And I saw thrones** (or: seats; chairs) – **and they sit** (or: sat; are seated) **upon them, and judgment-effect** (decision-result; judicial process and verdict) **is given by them** (or: authority to judge was given to them; decisions and separations are made by them) – **and souls** (conscious beings) **of those being ones having been cut with an axe** (= beheaded) **because of the testimony** (witness; evidence) **of** (or: pertaining to and on behalf of; from; which is) **Jesus, and because of the Word of, from, and which is God – even those** (or: also the ones) **who do not** (or: did not) **worship the little wild animal** (or: beast), **nor its image, and do not** (or: did not) **take** (or: receive) **the imprinted mark** (engraving; carve-effect; result of sculpting) **upon their forehead and upon their right hand – and they live and reign** (or: lived and reigned) **with the Christ** (the Anointed One) **a thousand** [other MSS: the thousand] **years.**
5. **But the remaining** (the rest) **of the dead ones do not** (did not) **live until the thousand years may be caused to reach the purposed and destined goal** (or: would be finished, concluded or ended). **This [living and reigning with Christ is** (or: This thousand years represents)**] the first resurrection.** (or: The first rising up [is] this:)
6. **Blessed and happy and set-apart** (holy) **[is] the one holding** (or: having) **a divided part** (a piece) **within the first resurrection** (rising up) – **upon these the second death has no authority** (does not continue holding right or privilege; possesses nothing from the sphere of existing), **but rather, they will continue being priests belonging to God and to the Christ** (or: priests pertaining to God and the Anointed One; or: God's, even Christ's, priests; or: priests from God and Christ), **and they will continue reigning and exercising sovereign influence with Him the** [other MSS: a] **thousand years.**

7. **Then, when the thousand years may be caused to reach the purposed and destined goal** (or: would be finished, completed or ended) [other MSS: after the thousand years], **the adversary** (*satan*) **will proceed being loosed from out of its prison** (his place of being watched and guarded),
8. **and it** (or: he) **will continue going forth** (or: progressively come out) **to deceive** (lead astray) **those** [other MSS: all the] **nations** (multitudes; ethnic groups) **within the four corners of the Land** (or: territory; or: earth) – **"Gog and Magog"** [Ezk 38:2] – **to gather them together into the battle** (or: war)**: their number [being] as the sand of the sea.**
9. **And they ascended** (or: climb up) **upon the breadth of the Land** (or: territory; earth) **and came around the encampment** (or: surround the fortress) **of the set-apart** (holy; sacred) **folks, even the Beloved City** [other MSS: even the city of the set-apart ones]. **Then fire descends** (or: came down) **from God, out of the atmosphere** (or: sky; heaven), **and devours them** (eats them down).
10. **And so the devil** (slanderer; accuser; one who thrusts-through or causes division), **the one continuously deceiving them** (repeatedly leading them astray) **is cast** (or: was thrown) **into the lake** (or: basin; artificial pool; marshy area) **of the Fire and Deity** (or: which is Fire, even Divine Nature) **where the little wild animal and the false prophet also [are; presently exist]. And they will be examined and tested by the touchstone day and night, on into the ages of the ages**
    (or: – the place where even the small beast and the lying prophet will also experience hard situations [that lead] into the indefinite time periods of the eons).

11. **Next I saw a great bright, white throne, and the One continuously sitting upon it from Whose**

face the Land (or: ground; earth) **and the atmosphere** (or: sky; heaven) **flee** (or: at once fled). **And a place is not found for them** (or: And then no position was discovered by them or found in them).

12. **Then I saw the dead folks – the great ones and the little ones – standing before the throne. And little scrolls are** (or: were) **opened up. And then another little scroll is opened up, which is of** (or: the one pertaining to; belongs to; or: from) **The Life. And the dead ones are judged** (were evaluated) **from out of the things having been written within the little scrolls, according to their works** (down from their actions; on the level of their deeds).

13. **And the sea gives** (or: suddenly gave) **[up; back] the dead folks within it, and death and the Unseen give** (or: = the grave gave) **[up; back] the dead folks within them. And they are judged** (evaluated) **according to their works** (in correspondence with their actions; in line with their deeds).

14. **Next the Death and the Unseen** (or: = the grave) **are cast** (or: were thrown) **into the lake** (or: basin; artificial pool) **of the Fire** (or: the marshy area where there is fire). **This is the second death: the lake of the Fire** (or: the basin which is fire).

15. **So if anyone is not found** (or: was not found) **written within the scroll of** (or: which is) **The Life, he is cast** (or: was thrown) **into the lake of the Fire** (or: the artificial pool having the character and quality of the Fire; the marshy area from the Fire; the shallow basin, where there is fire).

CHAPTER 21

1. **Then I saw "a new** (new in nature; different from the usual; better than the old; superior in value and attraction; new in quality) **atmosphere** (or: sky; or: heaven) **and a new Land** (or: earth)**"** [Isa. 65:17; 66:22], **for you see, actually, the first** (former; preceding; earlier) **atmosphere** (or: heaven) **and the first** (former, preceding) **Land** (or: earth; soil; ground) **went away** (or: moved off, and passed away), **and the sea does not exist any longer.**

2. **Next I saw the set-apart** (or: holy) **city, a new Jerusalem** (or: an innovative, different Jerusalem that is new in character and quality), **progressively descending from out of the atmosphere** (or: presently stepping down out of the midst of the sky; or: steadily stepping in accord, forth from heaven), **[coming] from God, being prepared** (having been made ready) **as a bride, being arranged** (having been set in order; adorned; decorated) **for** (or: by) **her man** (husband; a male person of full age and stature).

3. **And then I heard a great voice from out of the throne** [other MSS: atmosphere; heaven] **saying, "Consider! God's tent** (the Tabernacle of God) **[is] with mankind** (the humans), **'and He will continue living in a tent** (dwell in a Tabernacle) **with them, and they will continue being** (will constantly exist being) **His peoples, and God Himself will continue being with them** [some MSS add: their God].' [Lev. 26:11-12; Isa. 7:14; 8:8, 10; Jer. 31:33; Ezk. 37:27; 2 Chr. 6:18]

4. **"And He will continue anointing** (or: progressively smear or repeatedly wipe away) **every tear from their eyes. And the Death will no longer continue existing** (or: the death shall proceed being no more) **– neither will mourning** (sadness; grief), **nor an outcry, nor hard work** (painful toil; misery) **continue existing any longer** ([they] will continue being no more), **because the FIRST THINGS went** (or: passed) **away."** [cf 2 Cor. 5:1-2, 6, 8,17]

5. **And then the One** (or: He [who is]) **continuously sitting upon the throne said, "Consider this! I am presently making all things new** (or: habitually creating everything [to be] new and fresh; progressively forming [the] whole anew; or, reading παντα as masculine: I am periodically making **all humanity** new, and progressively, one after another, producing and creating **every person** anew, while constantly constructing all people fresh and new, i.e., continuously renewing **everyone**)!" [Isa. 43:19; 65:17-25; 2 Cor. 5:17]
**Next He is saying [to me],
"Write, because these words are dependable** (or: faithful; reliable) **ones and true ones** (ones full of faith and realities)."

6. **Then He said to me,
"They have come into being** (been born; come to be) **and stand accomplished** (are produced) [Concordant Gr. Text reads, with Sinaiticus: I have become (been born)!; Griesbach reads γεγονε: It has been done; Rotherham simply says: Accomplished; Barclay, Young, Beck, NASB, NKJV,

Amplified all read w/Griesbach; Weymouth, Williams, Wuest, Robertson & Vincent read w/the Nestle-Aland & Metzger Text, γεγοναν (3rd. per. pl.)]! **I am the Alpha and the Omega: The Beginning** (Origin; Source; Headship; First Principle) **and The End** (The Goal; Consummation; The Final Act; The Finished Product; The Destiny; The Purpose).

"To him who is continuously thirsty, I, Myself, will continue giving from out of the spring of the Water of the Life, as an undeserved (free) **gift** (or: As for Me, I will freely, gratuitously, be repeatedly giving from the midst of the fountain of the water from the Life).

7. **"The one habitually being victorious** (or: progressively overcoming) **will proceed inheriting** (acquiring by lot) **these things, and I will continue being a God for him** (in him; to him) **and he will continue being a son** [Griesbach reads: the son] **for Me** (in Me; to Me; with Me; by Me).

8. **"Yet for the timid folks** (in the cowards having shrinking palpitations) **and for faithless ones** (in unbelieving or disloyal people; [TR adds: and failures/sinners]) **and for or by abominable, disgusting folks, and for or in murderers, and for or with prostitutes and for or by sorcerers** (users of, or enchanters, by drugs) **and for or by idolaters and for, in or by all the liars** (the false ones): **their portion [is] within the lake** (or: their [allotted] part [is] union with the basin; the share from them [is] in the artificial pool; the region pertaining to them [is] centered in the marshy area) **continuously burning with Fire and Deity, which is the Second Death."**

9. **And one of the seven agents – the ones holding** (having) **the seven shallow bowls: the ones being continuously full of** (or: brimming with) **the seven plagues – came and spoke with me, saying,**
    "Come here! I will proceed in showing you the Bride, the Wife of the little Lamb."

10. **Next he carried** (or: carries) **me away, in spirit** (or: in the midst of a Breath-effect), **upon a great and high mountain, and showed** (points out to) **me the set-apart** (or: holy; sacred) **city, Jerusalem, progressively** (or: habitually; or: presently) **descending out of the atmosphere** (or: heaven), **from God**

11. **– continuously having** (holding; or: = bringing with it) **the glory of God** (God's glory; God's reputation; or: God's appearance; or: the opinion from God; the manifest presence, which is God), **her illuminator** (that which gives her light; the cause of her light) **– like a most precious stone, as a jasper stone being continuously crystal-clear,**

12. **continuously having a great and high wall, having twelve gates, and upon** (or: at; or: on top of) **the gates twelve agents** (messengers), **and names** [Sinaiticus adds: of them] **having been inscribed** (engraved; imprinted) **upon [them], which are the names of the twelve tribes of the sons of Israel:**

13. **from the east** (a rising) **three gates** (or: gateways; portals; vestibules; structural entry-forecourts); **from the north three gates; from the south three gates; from the west** (a sinking) **three gates.**

14. **Also, the wall of the City continues having twelve foundations, and upon them twelve names of the twelve emissaries** (sent-forth folks; representatives) **of, and from, the little Lamb.**

15. **And he who is speaking with me was holding and continues having a measure, a golden reed, so that he may measure the City – even her gates and her walls:**

16. **And the City is lying** (or: is continually being laid) **square** (four-angled; four-cornered), **and her length [is] even as much as the width. And he measured** (or: measures) **the City with the reed upon twelve thousand race-courses** (stadiums; fixed standards of measure): **her length and width and height are equal.**

17. **And he measured her wall: one hundred forty four cubits – (a) human's measure, which is an agent's [measure].**

18. **And that which was built within her wall is jasper, and the City [is] pure** (clear; clean; cleansed) **gold like pure** (clear, clean) **crystal** (or: glass),

19. **and the foundations of the wall of the city are ones having been set in order** (made a system and are a world; or: arranged as the aggregate of humanity; or: adorned) **with every precious stone.**
    The first foundation: jasper; the second, sapphire (or: lapis lazuli); **the third, chalcedony; the fourth, emerald;**

20. **the fifth, sardonyx; the sixth, sardius** (or: carnelian); **the seventh, chrysolite** (or: topaz); **the eighth, beryl; the ninth, topaz** (or: peridot); **the tenth, chrysoprasus; the eleventh, hyacinth** (jacinth); **the twelfth, amethyst.**

21. **And the twelve gates [are] twelve pearls – each one of the several gates was [made] out of one pearl. And the broad place** (street; plaza; square) **of the City [is] pure** (clean, clear; cleansed) **gold, as a translucent crystal** (or: transparent glass).

22. **And yet I did not see an inner sanctuary** [= the holy place, or places, of the Temple] **within her, for the Lord** [=Yahweh], **Almighty** (All-Strong) **God, even** (or: also) **the little Lamb, is her inner sanctuary** (or: continuously exists being her sacred dwelling place and divine habitation).

23. **Now the City continually has no need of the sun nor of the moon, to the end that they may** (should) **continually shine for, in, or on, her, for the Glory of God** (or: the Glory which is God; the imagination from God) **illuminates** (enlightens; gives light to) **her, and her lamp [is] the little Lamb.**
24. **And so the multitudes** (nations; people groups; ethnic groups; or: non-Jews) **will continue walking about** (i.e., living their lives) **by means of her Light** (through light from her). **And the kings of the Land** (or: earth) **continually carry** (bring; bear) **their glory** [other MSS adds: and honor] **into her.** [Isa. 60:1ff]
25. **Also, her gates shall by no means be closed** (or: under no circumstances be locked) **by day, for night will not be** (or: not continue existing,) **in that place** (or: and you see, there will not be night there).
26. **And so they will continuously carry** (or: bring) **the glory** (or: reputation; notion; opinion; appearance; imagination) **and the honor** (or: value; worth; respect) **of and from** (or: which are) **the multitudes** (nations; non-Jews; ethnic groups) **into her.**
27. **And yet, under no circumstances may anything common** (or: can all profane, ceremonially unclean, contaminating or non-sacred [things]) **or the person continuously making an abomination** (or: producing a disgust-effect) **and a lie** (or: [the] false) **enter into her** [note: cf 22:14, below], **except the ones having been written** (or: those being engraved) **within the scroll of "The Life of the little Lamb"** (or: the little Lamb's scroll of "The Life").

CHAPTER 22

1. **And he showed** (points out to) **me a clean, pure river of "water of, and from, life"** (or: Life's water; or: water which is Life), **bright** (resplendent, glistening, clear, sparkling) **as crystal** (clear ice), **continuously flowing** (issuing) **forth from out of God's – even** (or: and) **the little Lamb's – throne!**
2. **Within the midst of her broad place** (plaza; square; street), **and on each side of the river, [is] a tree** (a wood; timber; a log; same word used in Gen. 2:9, LXX; figure for "the cross" in the NT) **of, and which is, life periodically producing twelve fruits, continually yielding** (or: giving away) **according to each month, and the leaves of the tree** (wood; timber) **[are given] for** (or: into) **service** (nurture, care; healing, cure or medical service; a body of household attendants) **of the multitudes** (nations; Gentiles; non-Jews; ethnic groups), [cf Ezk. 47:1-12]
3. **and every result of [something] having been placed or put down, or every effect of [something] laid down, deposited or established, will no longer exist. And God's throne – even the Little Lamb's – will continue being** (or: existing) **within Her [i.e., the City], and His slaves will continue rendering sacred service to Him,**
4. **and will constantly see His face, and His Name [is; or: will be] upon their foreheads.**
5. **And night will no longer continue existing. And so they continuously have no need of the light of a lamp, or even the light of the sun, because [the] Lord** [= Yahweh] **God will continue giving light upon** (or: will constantly illuminate) **them, and they will continue reigning** (performing as kings; having sovereign influence) **on into the ages of the ages** (or: the indefinite time periods of the eons).
6. **Then he said to me,**
    > **"These words** (messages) **are faithful ones and true ones, and the Lord** [= Yahweh], **the God of the spirits of** (or: from) **the prophets, sent** (or: sends) **off His agent** (or: the person with a message from Him) **with a commission** (as an envoy) **to show** (point out; exhibit) **to His slaves things which of necessity must** (it is binding to) **come into being** (be birthed; happen, occur) **in speed** (swiftness, quickness, – so the Lexicons; but Wuest, Williams, Barclay, Lattimore, Beck, Goodspeed, NEB, Nyland translate this phrase: soon; others give: shortly).
7. **"And consider this! I am continuously** (habitually; repeatedly) **coming quickly** (swiftly). **Blessed** (Happy) **[is] the one continuously keeping** (actively observing; watching over; preserving) **the words** (or: messages; thoughts and ideas) **of the prophecy of this scroll."**
8. **And I, John, [am] the person progressively hearing and seeing these things. And when I heard**

and saw, I fell down to do obeisance (kiss toward; worship) **in front of the feet of the agent [who] is progressively exhibiting** (pointing out) **these things to me.**

9. **And he is saying to me,**

"**See! No!** (may =: Don't!) **I am your fellow-slave, even of** (belonging to; from among) **your brothers – of** (or: belonging to and from among) **the prophets and of** (even from among) **those continuously keeping, observing and maintaining the words and messages of this scroll. Kiss face-to-face in, and with, God** (or: do [your] obeisance to God)**!**"

10. **Next he is saying to me,**

"**Do not seal the words of the prophecy of this scroll, for you see, the season** (fitting situation) **is progressively near** (or: continues existing close at hand). [Dan. 12:4, 9]

11. "**The one continuously acting unjustly** (unfairly; inequitably; contrary to the Way pointed out; also: = living out of covenant) **must yet** (or: still) **act unjustly** (unfairly; = apart from covenant); **and the filthy one must yet** (still) **be filthy; and the just one** (fair and equitable one; = the one in covenant) **must yet** (still) **do justice** (behave fairly and deal equitably in rightwised, covenant relationships); **and the set-apart** (holy) **person must yet** (or: still) **be set apart** (or: made holy)."

12. "**Consider this! I am continuously** (or: habitually; progressively; repeatedly) **coming quickly** (swiftly), **and My wage** (reward for work; compensation; recompense) **[is] with Me, to give back** (give away; render; pay) **to each one as his work** (accomplishment) **is** (= what he deserves).

13. "**I am the Alpha and the Omega, the First and the Last, the Beginning** (Origin; Source; Headship) **and the End** (Goal; Finished Product; Purposed Destiny).

14. "**Blessed** (Happy) **folks [are] the ones** (folks; people) **continually washing their garments** (equipment; [other MSS: continually doing His implanted, inner goals and directives]), **to the end that their authority** (or: right out of and from Being; privilege) **will continue being over** (or: upon) **the tree** (pole) **of The Life, and they may at any point enter into the City by the gates.**

15. "**Outside [are] the dogs and the sorcerers** (enchanters by drugs) **and the fornicators** (male prostitutes) **and the murderers and the idolaters and everyone continuously fond of** (being friendly to) **and constantly practicing** (making; doing) **falsehood** (deception; a lie).

16. "**I, Jesus, sent My agent to bear witness to, and among, you people [about] these things [coming; being applied] upon the called-out communities** (or: to testify these things to, by or in you, over [other MSS: within] the assemblies). **I Myself am** (exist being) **the Root and the Offspring of** (Family from; Race which is) **David, The light-emitting** (Shining) **Morning Star**.

17. "**And now the Spirit and the Bride are continuously saying, 'Be repeatedly coming!' Then let the one continuing to listen and hear say, 'Be continuously coming!' And so let the person constantly thirsting continuously come; let the one habitually willing at once receive Water of Life freely**"

(or: "And so the Breath-effect and the Bride are constantly laying it out: 'Be progressively going!' Also, let the person now hearing say, 'Be progressively going!" Then, let the one repeatedly being thirsty habitually come and go. The person desiring and intending must at once take the Water from, and which is, Life for a free gift [to others]").

18. **I am continuously testifying** (repeatedly witnessing and giving evidence) **to** (or: in) **everyone [who is] habitually hearing the words** (or: messages) **of the prophecy of this scroll: If ever anyone should overlay** (place upon; thus: add) **upon them, God will overlay** (impose; add) **upon him those plagues** (blows; impacts; strikes; smitings) **having been written within this scroll.**

19. **And if anyone should take away from the words of the scroll of this prophecy, God will take away his part from the tree of the Life, and out of** (or: forth from) **the set-apart City – of** (or: pertaining to) **the things being written within this scroll.**

20. **The One continuously testifying these things is saying,**

"**Yes, I am continuously** (or: habitually; repeatedly; or: presently) **coming quickly** (swiftly; promptly)**!**"

Amen (So be it; It is so; Count on it). **Be continuously coming** (or: repeatedly coming and going), **Lord Jesus!**

21. **The Grace and favor of the Lord Jesus [is] with everyone** (or: all humanity; [other MSS read: ... with all of you; ... with the set-apart ones; ... with all the set-apart folks]). **Count on it** (or: It is so; Amen).

[written circa A.D. 68-70 – Based on the critical analysis of John A.T. Robinson]

CPSIA information can be obtained
at www.ICGtesting.com
Printed in the USA
BVHW061001050821
613451BV00008B/437